Crossed Wires

Crossed Wires

The Conflicted History of US Telecommunications, from the Post Office to the Internet

DAN SCHILLER

Oxford University Press is a department of the University of Oxford. It furthers the University's objective of excellence in research, scholarship, and education by publishing worldwide. Oxford is a registered trade mark of Oxford University Press in the UK and certain other countries.

Published in the United States of America by Oxford University Press
198 Madison Avenue, New York, NY 10016, United States of America.

© Oxford University Press 2023

All rights reserved. No part of this publication may be reproduced, stored in a retrieval system, or transmitted, in any form or by any means, without the prior permission in writing of Oxford University Press, or as expressly permitted by law, by license, or under terms agreed with the appropriate reproduction rights organization. Inquiries concerning reproduction outside the scope of the above should be sent to the Rights Department, Oxford University Press, at the address above.

You must not circulate this work in any other form
and you must impose this same condition on any acquirer.

Library of Congress Cataloging-in-Publication Data
Names: Schiller, Dan, 1951- author.
Title: Crossed wires : the conflicted history of US telecommunications, from the post office to the Internet / Dan Schiller.
Description: New York, NY, United States of America. : Oxford University Press, [2023] | Includes bibliographical references and index.
Identifiers: LCCN 2022040666 (print) | LCCN 2022040667 (ebook) | ISBN 9780197639238 (hardback) | ISBN 9780197639252 (epub) | ISBN 9780197639245 | ISBN 9780197639269 (ebook)
Subjects: LCSH: Telecommunications—United States—History.
Classification: LCC TK5102.3.U6 S35 2023 (print) | LCC TK5102.3.U6 (ebook) | DDC 621.3820973—dc23/eng/20221109
LC record available at https://lccn.loc.gov/2022040666
LC ebook record available at https://lccn.loc.gov/2022040667

DOI: 10.1093/oso/9780197639238.001.0001

1 3 5 7 9 8 6 4 2

Printed by Sheridan Books, Inc., United States of America

To My Marvelous Family

Contents

Acknowledgments	ix
Introduction: A Missing History	1

PART I. ANTIMONOPOLY

1. Paths into an Imperial Republic: Posts and Telegraphs	19
2. Antimonopoly, in the Country and the City	73
3. Business Realignment, Federal Intervention, Class Confrontation	111

PART II. PUBLIC UTILITY

4. Reactivating Reform	157
5. Telegraph Workers in Depression and War	217
6. The Punishing Passage to Telephone Unionism	264
7. Consumption and Public Utility	297
8. Patents under Pressure, 1920s–1950s	344
9. Activists and Dissidents: The 1960s	388

PART III. DIGITAL CAPITALISM

10. Innovation, Dissensus, and Reaction from Above	451
11. Telecommunications and American Empire	522
Conclusion	594
Notes	611
Index	789

Acknowledgments

I am deeply grateful to the people who have helped me with the thinking and writing that have gone into this book, which I have worked on by fits and starts throughout most of my academic life.

As a complement to my PhD studies in Communications at the University of Pennsylvania, I enrolled in several graduate History seminars, out of which came a lifelong engagement with radical history. Frequent and often intense conversations with classmates, above all, with Marcus Rediker and Nancy Hewitt, were formative. Power was not unconditional: While contradictory social relations remained dominative, they were also far from one-dimensional. The views, beliefs, and actions of the dispossessed would be matters of enduring consequence for my research in communications history.

Across town at Temple University, beginning in 1979 I became one of a group of faculty members focusing on the political economy of communications. In addition to her research on "movies and money," Janet Wasko knew the realities of working for a big media corporation at first-hand. Vincent Mosco had studied broadcasting and was researching new media; he also brought a fresh experience of Washington, DC, telecommunications policymaking. Dallas Smythe's engagement with telecommunications—and radical politics—stretched back to the 1930s, and his bibliographic reach was remarkable. In this energizing milieu, I originated my first courses on telecommunications history and began to supervise talented doctoral students.

After reading a draft of my book, *Telematics and Government* (1982), Vinny urged me to undertake a full-blown revision of US telecommunications history. Our conversations about this topic were many, and fruitful. How, though, might I develop a second book about telecommunications—a subject universally written about from the top down, including by me in my earlier work—while fulfilling my goal of writing radical social history? Between visits to the National Archives I pondered this question.

In 1986–1987, Everette E. Dennis arranged for me to enjoy a year-long fellowship at Columbia's University's then Gannett Center for Media Studies. A tributary of the research I pursued there streamed into this book, from days spent in the AT&T archives—then located at 195 Broadway in New York City. The talented research assistant David Stebenne, now a senior historian and legal scholar, performed invaluable research at Columbia's libraries.

My book's next way-station was UCLA's perfumed campus. Exchanges with Chris Borgman and Elaine Svenonius in the then-Graduate School of Library and Information Science enabled me to cultivate some new thinking. The late historians Gary Nash and Alex Saxton welcomed me, and kept me close to radical social history—as did historian and librarian Cindy Shelton. Courses offered through UCLA's Communication program permitted me to continue teaching telecommunications history to undergraduate students.

In 1990 my book moved down the freeway to UCSD. My student, Meighan Maguire, produced an outstanding UCSD dissertation on telephone development in San Francisco. For an independent study class under my supervision, undergraduate Karen Frazer visited the National Archives and shared the documents she copied there on the EEOC case against AT&T. Rick Bonus and Corynne McSherry, each now advanced in illustrious careers, gave me dedicated research assistance. Departmental colleagues Ellen Seiter and Yuezhi Zhao listened, and offered questions, advice, criticism, and friendship. My doctoral students at UCSD were a constant source of inspiration. Michael Bernstein and other friends in the history and literature departments nurtured common interests and shared the burdens of our common work environment. By now I had determined through extensive archival work and teaching that the history of US telecommunications rested on dynamic and complex sociopolitical power relations: to be valid, it could not be written as a top-down exercise. The late Antonia Meltzoff helped me to see the importance of carrying the project forward, and to find a basis for doing so.

We migrated in 2001 to the University of Illinois at Urbana-Champaign. In the stacks of UIUC's Main Library, I found wonderful and unexpected friends under Dewey Decimal Number 384. Alistair Black and Bonnie Mak shared the joys and travails of historical study. Linda Smith offered helpful counsel. Bob McChesney and I enjoyed many discussions—sometimes with students—about telecommunications, media, and power. Inger Stole, John Nerone, Christian Sandvig, and Jim Barrett and the late Jenny Barrett helped lift me out of received thinking. Intellectual refreshment and reintegration came from doctoral students based in multiple departments and disciplines. Then-UIUC Chancellor Richard Herman provided resources for me to hold a conference on telecommunications history, which then-GSLIS Dean John Unsworth, an enthusiastic supporter of this project, helped me organize, under the auspices of UIUC's Center for Advanced Study. CAS Associate Director Masumi Iriye and staffer Liesel Wildhagen were key in ensuring that this event came off successfully. *Info* editor and long-time telecommunications analyst Colin Blackman both participated in the meeting and opened his journal to papers presented there. Special thanks to Jason Kozlowski and ShinJoung Yeo for imaginative and conscientious research assistance.

In 2016, we moved to Santa Fe, where I worked on this book full-time for six additional years. One portion of it was presented as lectures to Beijing University's Global Fellowship Program, under the title "Networks and the Age of Nixon." I am grateful for the invitation to offer these lectures, and to the faculty and staff at Beijing University who arranged and hosted my visit. I also cherish the memory of meal times at Beida, when I was able to meet with a number of communications graduate students and to explain my research approach. I am thankful, above all to my friend and former colleague Yuezhi Zhao, to have had opportunity to make this and other visits to China.

Andrew Calabrese and Janice Peck at the University of Colorado, Boulder have been congenial hosts for presentations based on this book; their own respective analyses of telecommunications and media are buoys for critical thought. So too Rick Maxwell, a kindred spirit who has pioneered study of the media's systemic damage to the environment. Vinny Mosco read chunks of this book in draft form and gave me numerous valuable comments and suggestions. Richard John offered detailed notes after reading a chapter; forwarded me a couple of relevant sources; and invited me to present a portion of this work at a Newberry Library seminar. Yuezhi Zhao read a long chapter draft and helpfully advised me to stick to my guns. I was fortunate to present an early version of one chapter at an annual meeting of the Organization of American Historians.

At Bolerium Books in San Francisco, I am indebted to John, Joe, and Alexander, who alerted me to literally dozens of fugitive primary sources. Caroline Nappo, who coauthored an article with me on postal and communications workers, generously permitted me to use modified excerpts from that piece in this book. ShinJoung Yeo and James Jacobs repeatedly took time from their own work to help me with thorny bibliographic issues. Jim Barrett has been a great friend to this book and its author: his vast knowledge of labor and working class history has both saved me from errors and strengthened my story. Thanks to Victor Pickard for critical readings, support, and friendship. For a semester at Annenberg/Penn, where I made a pair of presentations based on portions of this book and taught a rewarding doctoral seminar—thanks both to Barbie Zelizer and, again, to Victor. Hong Guo helped me to persevere through the final years.

The community of doctoral students with whom I have worked has been a mainstay of my life as a scholar and a teacher. Only a couple of them chose to work on telecommunications; but all became a part of this book's journey. Thanks to one and all.

I am immeasurably grateful to the archivists and librarians who helped me bear this study forward: without them this book would not exist. Special thanks to Nick Johnson, who granted me access to his exciting and underused papers at the University of Iowa Special Collections. I appreciate Alan Novak's willingness to grant me an oral history interview; and I thank Monroe Price for facilitating it.

Susan Davis has lived with this project from beginning to end, a witness to the delight of archival discovery and the agony of authorial expression. She has listened to my thoughts as they sought to form, and read and criticized long sections of this book—sometimes to my consternation, always to my benefit. No less, through the years she has greatly deepened my awareness of the historical importance of traditions of vernacular dissent and popular cultural expression. Lucy and Ethan Schiller have never been too busy to ask about "the book" and to offer advice when I requested it. My brother Zach has been a stalwart: being able to rely on him has made a material difference to my ability to complete this work.

I am grateful to Nico Pfund for keeping faith. During a virulent season my acquisitions editor, James Cook, managed to find exceptional readers for this manuscript: their learned, detailed, and critical reviews were inestimably valuable for my revision. And, always good-spiritedly, Kaya Learnard met every deadline as she read and formatted the text—a daunting and much-appreciated labor.

Modified excerpts from the following works by me have been used in *Crossed Wires*:

Networks and the Age of Nixon. Beijing: Peking University Press, 2018 (Chinese print edition).

"'Let Them Move the Mail with Transistors Instead of Brains': Labour Convergence in Posts and Telecommunications, 1972–3" (coauthored with Caroline Nappo), *Work Organisation, Labour and Globalisation* 4, 2 (2010). https://www.scienceopen.com/hosted-document?doi=10.13169/workorgalaboglob.4.2.0010 License at: https://creativecommons.org/licenses/by/4.0/.

"The Hidden History of U.S. Public Service Telecommunications, 1919–1956," *Info* Vol. 9 Nos. 2/3, March 2007: 17–28. Emerald.

"Social Movement in U.S. Telecommunications: Rethinking the Rise of the Public Service Principle, 1894–1919," *Telecommunications Policy* 22 (4), 1998. Emerald.

Introduction

A Missing History

The infamous Chicago Democratic convention of 1968 nearly didn't happen, because of a telephone strike.

Illinois Bell Telephone Company was to wire up Chicago's International Amphitheater, the city's major hotels, and other downtown locations with extra telephone lines and a variety of specialized circuits. News agencies, national newspapers, and regional and network TV broadcasters would flood into Chicago for the media-rich confab, which was scheduled to begin on August 26th. The complex wiring process would require five weeks to be completed, before the convention could begin.

Nearly 12,000 members of the International Brotherhood of Electrical Workers (IBEW) walked out at Illinois Bell on May 8, seeking wage gains to make up for high inflation. (1968 saw the greatest strike wave since 1959, and most of the strikes were significantly motivated by economic factors.) By early summer, as the strike grew prolonged, Democratic officials began to worry. Rumors circulated that Miami was being considered as an alternative site. On July 15, the *New York Times* reported that an IBEW leader hoped "to avoid the embarrassment of Chicago losing the convention because of our dispute."[1]

At the last minute—July 23—an extraordinary fix was arranged by Democratic Mayor Richard Daley, the Chicago Federation of Labor, and IBEW officials. Albeit with some reported "dissension," the city's own labor movement authorized 300 IBEW members to install much of the needed wiring on a "voluntary basis"—that is, to undercut the strike. Labor leaders vowed to step up their support for the continuing IBEW walkout in other ways, and restrictions were imposed on the volunteers: no work would be supervised by Bell managers; and no circuits would be installed outside the Amphitheater. The convention could proceed, and Democrats breathed sighs of relief.[2]

This did not end the matter. Descending on Chicago to greet the official gathering were thousands of anti-Vietnam War demonstrators. They were met by 12,000 Chicago police in riot gear, and an additional 15,000 Army and National Guard troops. As the convention got underway, demonstrators and journalists were tear-gassed and clubbed; many demonstrators were dragged off to jail amid a bloody police riot.[3]

Crossed Wires. Dan Schiller, Oxford University Press. © Oxford University Press 2023.
DOI: 10.1093/oso/9780197639238.003.0001

Yet breaking news of the protest and its repression did not reach the convention floor. CBS News anchor Walter Cronkite recalled, that "delegates had no idea what was happening." The reason? IBEW volunteers had not installed microwave circuits needed to broadcast live TV outside the Amphitheater, so that videotape needed to be hand-delivered from Lincoln and Grant parks, where much of the violence was occurring, to the Amphitheater miles away. There, it was processed and broadcast. This arrangement caused delays of an hour or more. When the video was belatedly aired, so that both delegates and tens of millions of other Americans witnessed the events taking place on the streets, uproar ensued. On live television, Connecticut Senator Abraham Ribicoff called out Mayor Daley's "Gestapo tactics" to his face. The existing division between pro- and antiwar factions of the Democratic Party widened into a chasm in real time. The convention, a scholar writes, "suffered a political crisis of epic proportions."[4]

The IBEW walkout continued until September 21, so that it lasted 137 days all told. Many union members found other jobs as the economic pressures of being without work became acute. Though IBEW officials urged members to reject Bell's final contract offer, in the end they voted to return to work by a nearly two-to-one margin.[5]

This story reveals that telecommunications may claim an unexpected significance on the historical stage. It also shows that decisions about networking—in this case, about providing microwave circuits for live coverage—may be a function not of engineering but of power relations and political horse-trading. *Crossed Wires* unearths many such stories. They illuminate a history that has evolved through contention and struggle. If we would understand these moments of conflict and change, we need to connect them to prevailing social and political power relations. Thus, the approach adopted here is not to appeal to an overarching economic theory, a managerial vision, a legal concept, a technological necessity, or a civic consensus. My aims are two: to restore the contour lines left by a divided and dominative society upon network development; and to emphasize how recurrent struggles by workers, consumers, and political radicals have also shaped them. The narrative arc of this book is formed by the marks made on telecommunications, again and again, not only by social and political pressures, but by counter-pressures from below and from the sides—as with the Chicago Convention of 1968.

*

How may we open the study of telecommunications in this way, across the span of US history? I have adhered to two chief guidelines in developing my arguments. First, my account places networks within a broad historical sweep, and therefore I have needed to consult an extensive secondary scholarship.

Recent revisions to historical understanding offer vital aid to the student of American telecommunications. The territorial conquests on which the US republic was based, and which indigenous peoples experienced and resisted, were essential to the buildouts of postal and telegraph networks. How diversely exploited workers and small farmers came to labor in the shadow of corporate "monopolies" had everything to do with the swelling late nineteenth century movement to reform privately owned telegraphs and telephones. During the late 1960s and early 1970s, struggles to overcome racist and sexist employment discrimination were essential to a rejuvenation of a public utility conception of telecommunications. In short, because historians have enlarged and often upended received thinking, it has become possible to plot the course of telecommunications differently.

However, to get close to the ideas and priorities held by the people who built and operated telecommunications systems, and who clamored to have use of them, a second pathway to knowledge is also needed. This dimension of historical recovery has necessitated research in numerous specialized libraries and archives and antiquarian bookstores. Consulting these source collections has been an indispensable counterpart of scouring the secondary scholarship that is reorienting the American past. It has allowed me entrée to flyers, pamphlets, underground periodicals, letters, memoranda, and ephemera that circulated below and behind official records of events. As a result I have often been able to learn more about how postal clerks, letter carriers, telegraphers, telephone operators, and other members of a changing network labor force thought about how these networks were organized. Their ideas and actions of course foregrounded, but also went beyond, the terms of their own employment. Workers notably pressed for more inclusive service provision and for alterations to ownership and control; some even pushed for changes to US patent law. Their mostly disremembered efforts are recognized in this book.

In light of these two methodological priorities, I have undertaken a far-reaching revision. Each chapter crystallizes a particular era, aspect, or noteworthy episode; cumulatively, my eleven chapters remap more than two centuries of US telecommunications history, from the Post Office to the internet.

*

After decades of neglect, historians have recaptured for the US Post Office some of its former stature. As Richard R. John demonstrates, this longtime government department both interacted with major political and cultural movements of the early-to-mid nineteenth century and provided institutional foundations for state-building and industrialization. This recognition, vital in itself, does not complete the task of revaluation.

We will see in Chapter 1 that the government Post Office and, subsequently, the corporate telegraph shared two shaping features. First and foremost, both served a voracious territorial imperialism. Posts and telegraphs were parts of the process of military conquest and settlement, to the west and to the south of North America. Imperialism was, from the outset, a defining historical feature of the US political economy—and telecommunications networks were bound up in it. Second, these two networks catered for business users; telegraph service in particular placed the communicative needs of the general population distinctly second.

There were also divergences. Entangled in party politics, during the second half of the 19th century the Post Office provided an increasingly cheap, efficient, and universal service. For many contemporaries, therefore, it came to exemplify the best side of the postbellum state. The telegraph, by contrast, was a paragon of modern corporate corruption, the center of a web of monopoly predation, financial machinations, and political influence-mongering. The government Post Office and the corporate telegraph thus presented contemporary Americans—who tended to take for granted, even to naturalize, their common imperial role—with a sharply polarized model of network system development.

There was no question as to which system enjoyed greater esteem, as Chapter 2 emphasizes. Uniting under a credo of "antimonopoly," reform movements aimed to "postalize" the country's now swiftly evolving telecommunications in their entirety. Negatively, antimonopolists sought to eliminate powerful corporate monopolies, including those of the Western Union Telegraph Company and, slightly later, the American Telephone & Telegraph Company (AT&T). Positively, they hoped to expand access to telegraphs and telephones; to rationalize rates; and, for some of the workers who campaigned under their banner, to improve labor conditions. This movement carried forward for several decades and it increasingly targeted the wondrous third network system that was being established around the telephone.

Not surprisingly, the postalization scheme and its proponents drew obdurate opposition. AT&T was surpassing Western Union, and AT&T's executives attempted energetically to disarm the antimonopolists. Municipal, state, and federal authorities were all drawn in, and played disparate roles. Episodically, and through moments freighted with contingency, Chapter 3 shows, during the first two decades of the twentieth century the postalization movement splintered. Key groups of participants—big business users of networks and independent suppliers of telephone service, thousands of which had rushed in to provide telephone service—unevenly reached a separate peace with the giant telephone company. Many telecommunications workers nevertheless continued to struggle for postalization, out of a conviction that the state would be a less onerous employer than a private corporation.

As testimony shows, many wage workers wanted "industrial democracy"; many citizens wanted to curtail corporate power over the polity; many residents wanted telephone access at home. For a period of years culminating in and immediately after World War I, workers pressed ahead with what proved to be a final drive for postalization. They then endured a bitter lesson at the hands of the Post Office, as the Department actually took over the operation of telegraphs, telephones and cables on grounds of the war emergency. For a one year interval, advised by top executives from AT&T and Western Union, the Post Office ran the nation's networks. After women telephone operators exhibited sustained and disciplined militancy in resisting the Post Office's high-handed management—which was concurrently damaged in middle-class public opinion for other reasons—the administration of President Woodrow Wilson decided to reprivatize the wires. This double exercise of state power not only cut out the ground under telegraph and telephone workers, but also finally shattered the popular network imaginary centered on postalization. Already partially hollowed out by defections, a decades-long effort to restructure telecommunications now collapsed.

Chapter 4 shows, however, that a disparate reform movement commenced virtually at the same moment. New administrative agencies had been established by dozens of states during the late nineteenth and early twentieth centuries—public utility commissions (PUCs)—and these had helped broker more stable relations between carriers and big business users. After World War I, some PUCs unexpectedly began to form a locus of substantive change. A scatter of state commissioners chafed at the restraints on effective regulation that stemmed from what was sometimes termed a "foreign corporation": AT&T. This vertically and horizontally integrated company was now the country's largest unit of capital. Its rate structure was beyond their reach; its financial practices remained mysterious. In the absence of an effective federal regulator to act as a counterweight, AT&T's power posed what some intrepid state regulators identified as intractable problems of oversight and accountability.

Initially, their challenges to AT&T were often rhetorical, and lacked political punch. However, in New York City and, above all, Chicago, persistent municipal rate fights attained expanding importance as political opportunities opened after the onset of the Great Depression. The economic collapse caused many subscribers to give up their telephones, and AT&T responded by cutting hundreds of thousands of telephone jobs, notably those of women operators, without cutting its generous dividends to investors. These actions by the telephone monopoly instilled a bottomless antipathy among workers, and created growing support for telecommunications reform. So, paradoxically, did ruinous competition in telegraph service—between Western Union, the market leader, Postal Telegraph, its beleaguered rival, and a handful of new radio-telegraph companies. While these competitors battered one another, and as Western and Postal supplicated their corporate customers with discounts and rebates, already straitened telegraph workers began to protest their pitiful wages and miserable working conditions.

The experimental genius of the Roosevelt government was to establish what was, for a few years, an unusually robust and interventionist Federal Communications Commission (FCC). The FCC investigated and rescued the telecommunications system from what it identified as twin evils: monopoly in a telephone industry dominated by AT&T, and competition in a telegraph industry spinning out of control around multiple suppliers. The New Deal also renovated and modernized the Post Office.

The centerpiece of its stabilization program was a freshly creative conception of public utility. Rather than continuing merely to anchor legal doctrines for negotiating the terms of trade via state commissions and courts, in the New Deal years the public utility framework was rejuvenated, opened to far-reaching reform initiatives. It became a domain of political ferment; and an unfinished vessel, to be filled in ways not yet wholly evident.

At its outset, the FCC gained authority to undertake an unprecedented critical investigation of the nation's telephone industry. Drawing on a special congressional appropriation, the inquiry combed through AT&T's corporate records and compiled documentary findings that proved essential to antitrust prosecutions of the giant company over the succeeding forty years. In the immediate context, nevertheless, AT&T managed to neuter the FCC's most radical policy prescriptions.

As big business's credibility had been badly wounded by the Depression, organized labor began to make its own inroads in claiming a public mandate. Chapters 5 and 6 detail how telegraph and telephone workers established industrial unions and how these organizations in turn intervened in telecommunications policymaking—at some points working closely with members and staff at the FCC.

Independent telegraph unions made their voices heard from the start of President Franklin Roosevelt's New Deal, and their critique of the industry's problems differed sharply from that offered by telegraph company management. Amid an upswell of radical militancy in the working class, an upstart union of left-wing radio telegraphers renamed itself the American Communications Association (ACA). The ACA emerged just as a great new industrial labor federation—the Congress of Industrial Organizations—was rapidly organizing US heavy industry and pushing forward an often-radical social unionism. The CIO awarded ACA a charter which conferred upon the small union jurisdiction to organize the entire electrical and electronic telecommunications services industry. (Telecommunications equipment manufacturing was reserved by a far larger, also Communist-led, CIO affiliate, the United Electrical Workers.) The ACA threw itself into industrial and political action. From its base in a failing rival of Western Union—Postal Telegraph—ACA attempted to enlarge its membership at other carriers. Above all, however, it struggled to stave off a merger between Postal and Western Union. Wall Street had aimed for such a combination since the early years of the Depression, and it was expected to result in widespread layoffs—especially among the ACA members who worked disproportionately at Postal Telegraph. With its allies in the CIO and the New Deal administration, ACA's militant social unionism succeeded in forestalling a merger until the middle of World War II.

Again backed by the CIO, ACA organizers also spread out across the far-flung telephone subsidiaries of AT&T. Here they made more limited progress. Their difficulties were initially a function of AT&T's strength as a bastion of "employee representation plans"—company unions—and an unrelenting foe of the CIO's social unionism. As the war period continued, however, ACA's lackluster success in AT&T reflected a different development: self-organization by telephone workers. Telephone workers were haltingly transforming dozens of AT&T company unions into independent unions and beginning to unite these organizations, separate from either the CIO or the AFL. Composed nearly entirely of white women and men, and fragmented by gender, craft and region, this vast employee group had deemed itself as privileged. However, spurred by lagging pay and the nationwide unionization movement, AT&T employees undertook an uphill climb to establish a genuine industrial organization of their own. After two strikes—one an epic triumph, the next a near-catastrophic rout—telephone workers united in 1947 within a new international union, the Communications Workers of America.

This arduous process reflected not only internal workplace factors but also convulsions in US politics and foreign policy. As World War II ended, business leaders and right-wing politicians mobilized in a bid to arrest the process of domestic New Deal reform, and to contain the reach and power of unions—above all, CIO unions. A great international initiative fed into and strengthened this domestic reversal, as US leaders seized the leadership of global capitalism while, simultaneously, they moved to combat Soviet socialism and to coopt and canalize the revolutionary nationalism that was erupting in the colonial world. The Democratic coalition around Harry Truman (who fell into the presidency at the death of Franklin Roosevelt in April 1945) threw itself into this fraught and complex mission; and the US lurched into a global cold war. Facing intense pressure from within and without, the CIO responded by realigning itself to comport with this cold war policy. This wrenching transition left claw-marks across US society, including on telephone unionism. The CIO stripped the Communist-led ACA of its jurisdiction and pushed it aside, in order to bring an initially fragile and lastingly mainstream CWA into the federation as an affiliate union. Throughout the 1950s and 1960s, CWA won successive wage and benefits gains for its increasing membership while becoming one of the nation's largest industrial unions.

Chapter 7 switches perspective to focus on the sharply changing domain of consumption. The three major services followed distinct paths here. Despite the Western Union-Postal Telegraph merger, telegraph service was still used by only a small fraction of Americans and continued to cater to business users; starting in the late 1950s it became additionally marginalized by a new product-substitute: computer communications. Despite management rescue schemes, throughout the next decades it became moribund. By contrast, the Post Office lost none of its general popularity. It did, however, become more commercial. It had acted as a formal channel for the marketing and distribution of commodities since the late nineteenth century, and these functions were massively expanded during the decades after World War II. Commercial mailings, circulars, and catalogs flooded the mails. Likewise, the telephone network was substantially repurposed to accelerate commodity circulation. Telephone instruments had previously been both beautifully designed and built to last—but on a standard pattern. In the 1960s a widening array of models and styles were introduced, as handsets were turned into objects of consumer desire. Meanwhile, new services, notably outward and inward wide-area telecommunications (800 numbers), breached the defenses of household castles, which again became sites of commercial invasion.

Throughout the first two postwar decades, therefore, the public utility framework itself was modified. On one side, completing a process that had originated decades earlier in urban movements for cheap telephone access, a multifarious regulatory program for lowering residential rates at last succeeded, and household telephone service became relatively universal. However, this tremendous achievement was far from an unmixed blessing. It contributed to making endless private commodity consumption, and all that followed from it, a necessity for economic growth. Simultaneously, as Chapter 8 demonstrates, a second mutation also perverted the public utility conception. During the first postwar decade policymakers used this model to inject an urgent priority to US corporate-military technological innovation in and around networking.

Throughout prior decades AT&T had built up the world's preeminent corporate research and development facilities. During the 1930s and 1940s, the patent policies that AT&T affixed to its process of corporate invention drew intense critical scrutiny. Chicago Federation of Labor representative Edward Nockels and a variety of New Deal officials charged that AT&T's patents constituted an economic affliction, that the company's patent monopoly collided with the government efforts to kickstart the economy and reduce mass unemployment. Labor and government reformers alike demanded forceful intervention. An investigation by the Justice Department commenced during World War II, as responses to my Freedom of Information Act requests reveal. This became a formal antitrust prosecution in 1949, which aimed to break up AT&T so as to lower local telephone rates and thereby to stimulate demand for telephone service. Culminating in the sharply different context of the Cold War, however—when regulators were successfully widening household access to telephone service through other means—the agreement reached between AT&T and the Justice Department in 1956 possessed a quite different basis. This consent decree left AT&T's integrated structure intact, while it formally limited AT&T's commercial services to the regulated telecommunications market as demarcated by the FCC (with the state PUCs). In these ways it ratified the *status quo*. However, the decree also compelled AT&T to share its unrivaled trove of patents on easy terms with outside companies, while permitting AT&T itself to operate free of restriction as a military contractor. Thus it bespoke a militarization of public utility.

At the time, these provisions were generally seen as a slap on the wrist; ultimately, however, they placed AT&T in a vice. Across every industry, from oil to agribusiness, from banking to aerospace, and from chain retailing to auto manufacturing, big businesses were already beginning to integrate innovations in network systems and applications. AT&T, however, was not permitted to supply corporate users with these specialized offerings, which fell outside the realm of regulated telecommunications. Emerging equipment vendors, notably based in the computing industry, sprang up in hopes of catering for this proliferating corporate demand. Might the two be reconciled within the public utility conception? On what terms? Conflicts over these questions roiled telecommunications policy throughout the late 1960s and early 1970s.

Chapter 9 examines this moment of transition in light of both rank-and-file insurgencies springing up among postal and the telephone workers and social movement activism churning through American society.

It was a charged era. Both before and after the election of 1968, notably, there were huge demonstrations against the US war on Vietnam. The incoming Nixon administration, however, also faced a gathering international financial crisis and initiated a profound re-gearing of geopolitics and US foreign policy. Nevertheless, the status of the US Post Office was a far from inconsequential item on the presidential agenda. Like his Democratic predecessor, Nixon wanted to transform this longtime government department into a government corporation, with an independent board of governors and a mandate for efficiency—defined principally in terms of introducing computer technology and catering more fully for corporate bulk mailers.

Most of the politically powerful postal unions rejected such a reorganization, and it remained boxed up in a congressional committee. In March 1970, however, tens of thousands of miserably paid postal workers, federal employees who were not legally allowed to strike, staged an unauthorized walkout: a wildcat. The strike started in New York City and spread outward from there, across the country and across the different postal crafts. While calling out the National Guard to restore mail service—a largely symbolic move—the President began to negotiate behind the scenes, through his trusted aide Charles Colson. Colson importuned James Rademacher, the president of the National Association of Letter Carriers, who had backed Nixon in 1968. Working closely with Rademacher, and offering pay raises and government recognition of collective bargaining rights for the postal unions—though not a right to strike—the administration induced the wildcatters to return to work and gained the unions' acquiescence to postal reform. Nixon's postal reorganization plan thereupon sailed through Congress, with bipartisan support: the United States Postal Service was established. This profound institutional alteration was brokered through compromise with the postal labor force—opposed by many rank-and-file postal workers—whose labor rights were strengthened in the process.

In telephony, meanwhile, the late 1960s and early 1970s again saw a labor upsurge. Groups of militant CWA telephone workers—mainly but not only in heavily unionized New York—demonstrated both antagonism toward their employer and hardening unwillingness to abide by edicts issued by their own union officials. Their actions portended that business-as-usual within a bureaucratic union, content to operate within the state's canalized labor relations machinery, could no longer be taken for granted. A national CWA strike in 1971 became an occasion for dissenting rank-and-file telephone workers to exhibit considerable strength and staying power. Some of them displayed a new social unionism, one that opposed CWA's official alignment with US foreign policy as well as AT&T's racist and sexist employment policies.

Social movement activists—some working within AT&T and others outside it—were concurrently allying with sympathetic lawyers and a maverick member of the FCC to use the telecommunications industry's legal status as a public utility to try to force an end to employment discrimination. Black, Mexican American, and women workers all contributed. Gay rights activists also demonstrated for employment rights at the telephone company, slightly later. During the Nixon years, their joint endeavors succeeded. The nation's largest corporate employer was compelled, through a consent decree signed with the Justice Department, to institute affirmative action programs. These spelled out dramatic change even beyond AT&T. They established a template for curtailing employment discrimination across the face of corporate America. Revived by workers' movements to mesh labor and civil rights, and brought home by federal intervention, public utility principles became a springboard to greater social justice and seemed about to open outward on even greater possibilities.

Where might such disruptions to the *status quo* end? How might they be arrested and, if possible, reversed? Business and political elites persuaded themselves that the political and social problems of the early 1970s lay in too much "entitlement," too much democracy. The initiatives being undertaken by contemporary rank-and-file workers and activists, many if not most of them women and minorities, did not attest the existence of a unitary movement, indeed, their varied movements betrayed substantial centrifugal force. However disparate, they nevertheless reinforced a conviction among elites that too much power had been amassed—was being exercised—from below. In the view from above, it was the whole messy combination of dissident rank-and-file insurgency, social movement activism, and organized labor's institutional strength that needed to be contained and countered.

The Nixon Administration engaged this critical problem by redirecting the course of electronic telecommunications through regressive policy interventions. As with postal reorganization, Nixon's entry point was already established: an Executive Branch proceeding on communication policy conducted by the Democratic administration of Lyndon Johnson during its final tumultuous year. Chapter 10 unravels the hidden backstory of this proceeding, which was supervised by Undersecretary of State Eugene Rostow, exposing sharp internecine conflicts within the undertaking as it progressed. The Rostow Report endorsed the introduction of competition into a limited set of advanced telecommunications services, but expressly *retained* the public utility framework. The President, however, handed off the unpublished Report to his successor's transition team, with no recommendation.

During the first postwar decades, right-wing businessmen had sponsored a recrudescence of free-market economic ideas and policies as an antidote to what they deemed intolerable government regulation. Liberals, by contrast, were becoming persuaded that government had lost an effective purchase on the regulated industries: that regulators had been coopted by the interests they were supposed to oversee. The result was an increasing convergence in mainstream political opinion. While Democrats endorsed limited competition to restrain a hidebound telephone monopoly, Republicans demanded to pare back regulation on new network industries and markets. It was the Nixon Administration that brought this advancing synthesis to bear upon telecommunications.

Nixon's men published the Rostow Report, after determining that it could be used to justify their own much more radical policy program. Nixon's point-man, a young MIT PhD named Clay T. Whitehead, worked directly with some of the incoming President's closest advisors, including especially Peter M. Flanigan, an investment banker serving as a top economic aide. Together they set in motion a great lurch in policymaking for advanced networks, initiating an era of digital capitalism.

Nixon plucked Dean Burch, a seasoned Republican political operative, to head the FCC. Henceforward, Burch collaborated closely behind the scenes with Whitehead and other Nixon officials. Their aims were to open networking to a frontier process of computerization on behalf of big business users, who were demanding access on privileged terms to specialized new equipment and services; and to support new and, though this was never mentioned, antiunion suppliers of such equipment and services.

The early part of what became a protracted transition was conditioned by the hands-off stance adopted by the Communications Workers of America. Rejecting direct political participation in an increasingly bipartisan process of policy liberalization, CWA nevertheless attempted to set up a bulwark against a renewal of corporate power. Early in the 1970s, CWA president Joseph A Beirne initiated merger talks with the two biggest postal unions. CWA's express goal was to strengthen organized labor by establishing an overarching "American Communications Union"; Beirne glimpsed clearly that CWA needed to prepare itself for contests with capital at a moment when capital was reconfiguring around new networking technologies. However, this attempt to unite networking labor faltered and, in 1973, it failed—establishing a partial parallel with the 1940s passage to telephone unionism, in which internal fractures and divisions had figured centrally. The top-down movement to policy liberalization thus proceeded without being conditioned by a concomitantly strengthened labor organization.

Incremental, and camouflaged by a specious rhetoric of competition, liberalization ultimately engulfed US telecommunications. As a growing variety of local and wide area data networks proliferated, and as wireless and satellite systems began to be installed, more and more of the infrastructure big companies used to process and exchange information was stripped out of the casement of public utility. While regulators—Republicans in the Nixon years and Democrats under President Carter—proved complaisant, unions possessed declining leverage—and foreshortened jurisdiction—outside the shrinking sphere of regulated telecommunications. In a trend that rapidly widened through the 1970s and 1980s, corporate employers buttressed their proprietary network operations by embracing union-avoidance strategies. Pivoting sharply at the outset of the Reagan administration (1981), the federal government offered them sanction. Attempts to reenergize public utility languished decisively in the face of a booming neoliberalism, and its credo that unalloyed corporate decision-making freedom should drive network modernization—both domestically and internationally.

In Chapter 11, I return to the formative links which were forged, at the outset, between networking and US empire. Throughout the republic's first century the Post Office and, subsequently, the telegraph, were stitched into a process of territorial seizure and occupation. US imperialism proving both durable and dynamic, telecommunications continued to be vital throughout its subsequent figurations.

US imperialism was always an extracontinental force, however, during the 1890s this quality became systematic with annexations of Hawaii and, by way of the Spanish-American War, of Puerto Rico, the Philippines, and other Pacific territories. Hawaii's strategic location as a cable landing-point was a factor in its takeover. By this time, however, established and emergent capitalist powers had already colonized much of the world, so further opportunities for US territorial occupation were limited. US leaders began to experiment with strategies for securing US investment and profitmaking outside national boundaries through informal empire. An "American system of international communications" became a cornerstone of this undertaking.

During the interwar period US interests built up several international telecommunications networks, skirmishing with Britain which possessed what was by far the world's largest territorial empire, backed by its own still-unmatched submarine cable system and unrivaled navy.[6] During World War II, often relying on bases in other countries, the US built out a global network of cables and radio circuits to support the logistics needed to fight the war. With peace, this Allied communications system crumbled.

Global capitalism was then reconstructed. In the face of revolutionary nationalist movements, debilitated colonial powers, and a Soviet Union that not only survived the Nazis but quickly restored its industrial base, the US erected a new-model empire anchored in its own huge economy. This redesigned system of dominance was built atop multiple pilings. After World War II the US exercised preponderant power over freshly organized multilateral organizations, including the International Monetary Fund, the World Bank, the General Agreement on Trade and Tariffs, and the United Nations system. US industrial and financial might faced few significant postwar capitalist constraints; and, piggybacking on this strength, US foreign direct investment—previously constrained by preclusive colonial blocs—surged across borders. Hundreds of strategically sited US military outposts, negotiated both with allies and vanquished enemies, now ringed the world. High technology research and development bore the stamp of US military-industrial dominance.

Also constitutive of this informal US empire was an emerging system of US-managed international communications. Now based on satellite technology, its chief beneficiaries were US multinational corporations and US military command and control structures. An International Telecommunications Satellite (Intelsat) consortium, was set up in the 1960s. It was anchored, crucially, by states, which were represented through the government ministries that operated existing telecommunications services: posts, telegraphs and telephones. The US possessed no such ministry; but it took care to organize Intelsat so that the US signatory, the private satellite company Comsat, possessed a majority ownership share—and majority voting rights—in the system.

Resented by other signatories, this arrangement was agreeable for the US side. However, fissures deepened as Intelsat moved toward definitive treaty arrangements. Meanwhile, a fresh wave of antiimperialism grew throughout the countries of what was often called the Third World; while European and Japanese capitalist rivals posed mounting threats to US economic dominance—notably, in the strategic field of networking and information technology. Once again it was during the Nixon years that US policy for networks began to be redesigned with an eye to meeting these international challenges.

In keeping with its concurrent efforts to extricate domestic telecommunications from the public utility framework, the Nixon administration first formulated policies designed to narrow the power of (other) states over international network services, and to augment the role of corporate capital in their stead. This policy program broadened subsequently. During the 1980s and 1990s, the US maneuvered to privatize telecommunications networks worldwide. Dozens of domestic telecommunications operators—previously prized as national flag carriers—were supplanted in any orgy of mostly foreign corporate network investment. At the same time, network functionality was modernized and rearranged to support data transmission between and among computers. As in the United States itself, computer communications was at this stage principally a service for and within corporations and military agencies. It was also disparately configured. There were local as well as wide area networks, most built around proprietary and non-interoperable technical standards. US commercial and nonprofit data networks alike were implemented across political jurisdictions; while European and Japanese policymakers sought, somewhat desultorily, to erect protective bulwarks against US networking dominance.

This was the context in which, through an opaque and involuted process, one mode of data transport—the one we call the internet—gained over its rivals, shunting state-based competitors into the margins. Its triumph came just after the collapse of Soviet socialism and the embrace of the capitalist market by China, India and other countries throughout the Global South. The US trumpeted the internet's ascendancy as a redemption of human rights, and a huge gain for the wretched of the earth. In fact, however, the global internet had been engineered and managed by US-based organizations, and its leading services and applications were dominated by US companies—and well-insulated from (other) states. It was by far the most universal and multifunctional cross-border telecommunications system ever devised: a network fit for a full-fledged US empire of capital, built around wage labor in what was now a genuinely world market.

Only in 2013 did it become generally known that the global internet was being systematically exploited by interlocking US intelligence agencies and globally commanding US tech companies. After this, some of the same centrifugal forces that had hit earlier against the Intelsat system again showed themselves with respect to the internet. Economic competitors, above all China, seized internet markets for non-US equipment and service suppliers, while geopolitical rivals—China again in the lead—began to chip away at US organizational dominance.

From the Post Office of the early republic to the internet of the present day, networks figured throughout US imperialism as the American empire itself was resisted and reorganized. *Crossed Wires* concludes by sketching how the long and jagged line of political conflict and social struggle likewise continued to mark US telecommunications during the 21st century.

PART I
ANTIMONOPOLY

1
Paths into an Imperial Republic
Posts and Telegraphs

During the first century of the republic, two modes of communication at a distance—telecommunications—were etched into lands inhabited by Native Americans; contested by rival European powers; and occupied by the United States. Both telecommunications systems supported this expanding US territorial empire but, despite this overarching commonality, they branched apart in other ways. One network was owned by the state and the other by capital, and the two branches of the telecommunications system developed disparate rate structures, patterns of access, and social and institutional relationships. During the decades after the Civil War their divergence became politically charged. Would one model prevail over the other? Going forward, would it be the government Post Office or the corporate telegraph that set the terms of telecommunications development?

The Post Office was the nation's originating system for communication at a distance. Both before and long after it was elevated to a cabinet department in 1829, furthermore, the Post Office was by far the largest unit of the central state. In 1831, the nation's 8,700 postmasters comprised three-quarters of federal civilian employment; half a century later (excluding temporary postal employees and ordinary and railway mail clerks and letter carriers), some 50,000 postmasters accounted for perhaps one-third of all civilian employees in the executive branch. Though its relative weight as a government employer diminished after this, its workforce continued to swell. During the last two antebellum decades, meanwhile, an emergent technology—the electrical telegraph—was passed quickly from the federal government to private capital. The two systems' institutional identities immediately began to contrast in other ways.[1]

Both networks were bound to the project of expanding what, in the mid-1840s, Illinois Democratic Congressman Stephen Douglas hoped would be "an ocean-bound republic." Both aided in "unleashing the energies of colonizing settlers, land speculators, and slaveholders" for purposes of Western annexation, Indian removal, and great-power rivalry. Despite these common functions, however, one system was superior—and believed to be superior—in meeting popular needs. Though enmeshed in partisan politics and honeycombed by corrupt contractors, the Post Office nevertheless provided an effective, locally accessible, and technologically progressive service. Upon the telegraph, by contrast, speculative investors, commercial business users, corporate managers, and legislators and officials founded a special-purpose service, nominally open to the general population but dominated to an extent unique among the developed capitalist economies by the property-owning class. The big telegraph companies which emerged during the 1850s were investor-driven vehicles driven by shaky finance, service discrimination, and political chicanery.[2]

As Western Union consolidated its power over the telegraph nationwide after the Civil War, a broad stratum of Americans came to resent and even fear the new system. Business users bridled at high and often arbitrary rates, inadequate service, and discriminatory practices. Many others perceived a deeper structural threat to US democracy and society. Investors repeatedly launched competitive telegraph companies—sometimes casting themselves as principled reformers—while doing their utmost to exploit political connections, newspaper publicity, and the freshly burgeoning institutions of corporate finance to enrich themselves. Western Union responded in kind, implementing tactics that would amply justify the "robber baron" label that contemporary critics affixed to several of its board members. The victims included not only telegraph workers but the public at large. Diverse Americans in turn threw themselves into a struggle to reform this nexus of corporate predation. Better, they believed, to place Western Union in the government Post Office.[3]

Yet corporate telegraphy persisted nonetheless, decade upon decade, even as its diverse adversaries carried forward attempts to institute a "postal principle" throughout the length and breadth of US telecommunications. In this chapter I lay historical foundations for a more detailed account in the next two chapters of how this contest reached its denouement—as a new telecommunications medium arose and both state and society altered.

The Early US Post Office

Duly impressed by how the mails operated to "enlarge the common life" a mid-twentieth century historian also asserts that, in the early republic, "[n]o necessity . . . existed" for using the postal system "to advance the country's economic interests in foreign lands." This second claim is fundamentally mistaken. During the early years of US nationhood foreign lands lay just west of the Appalachians. This territory was inhabited and organized by native peoples "as nations, tribes, confederacies, and other durable polities."[4]

Even before the formation of the United States, indeed, from the beginning of settlement, colonists were invading others' lands and, thereafter, pushing west beyond hazy legal boundaries. During the Republic's first decades, furthermore, political elites' "carefully drawn plans... for the orderly surveying and settlement of the West were simply overwhelmed by the massive and chaotic movement of people": in just one generation, Americans occupied more territory than they had taken over during the entire 150-year-span of the colonial era. Historian Steven Hahn specifies that, from the outset, "power in the Pacific had been central to the continental ambitions of American leaders and policy makers." The west coast offered both a launch-point for ventures seeking economic riches in east and south Asia, and a line of opposition against the designs of competing powers active in different parts of North America: Britain, France, Spain, Russia, and Mexico (after it won independence in 1821). Thomas Jefferson, who as president engineered the Louisiana Purchase from France in 1803, wanted ports on the Gulf of Mexico for an "empire of liberty" which, he hoped, would ultimately also encompass Florida, Cuba, Mexico, and Canada. The year before he actually sent out Lewis and Clark in 1804, Jefferson already planned "an ostensibly scientific but also a covert military and commercial expedition into the Spanish-held trans-Mississippi West"—whose real destination was the Pacific coast. Between 1801 and 1817 Jefferson and his successor as president, James Madison, overlaid a veneer of comity on the killing or displacement of tens of thousands of Indians by negotiating fifty-three treaties of cession with Native American groups. Jefferson's powerful Treasury Secretary, Albert Gallatin, insisted that only "by opening speedy and easy communication through all its parts" could "the inconveniences, complaints, and perhaps dangers" of so "vast [an] extent of territory be radically removed or prevented." Virtually every successive administration asserted this same dictum; and the settlers themselves wanted river access and roads, to help them market some of what they produced. The Post Office figured as an essential component in this program, a vital participant in "a violently expansive empire of settlers, feeding on land and displacing everything in its path." Wars to dispossess and expel Native Americans, settler occupation, and westward postal expansion were intertwined features of a century-long process.[5]

Even before 1800, American merchants and manufacturers were reaching into regional markets; their need to exchange bills, checks, receipts, bank notes, credit reports, specie, and commodity price information increased with every rise in shipments of cotton, iron, grain, lumber, and consumer goods. To facilitate these information flows among dispersed and typically small units of capital, a postal infrastructure linking city centers with distant markets was successively extended, sometimes even in advance of any direct commercial imperative. Thus the Post Office functioned as a two-stroke engine, firing on behalf of both territorial conquest and market intensification. "(N)o inconsiderable amount of the active capital of the country, in some form or other, passes through the mail," reported the capable Postmaster General John McLean in 1828—as much as $100 million annually by 1855, in one estimate, or nearly twice the total federal budget. Not by accident did Congress provide for the death penalty in instances of mail robbery, which remained a capital crime until 1872. The young nation's postal telecommunications provided an indispensable platform for the circulation of capital; and business and commercial users delimited its primary functions. Looking back from the vantage point of 1866, Postmaster General Alexander Randall boasted with considerable justification that the Post Office "has done more to aid in developing the resources of the country than anything else except the cultivation of the soil."[6]

Political considerations also were bound up in this. With the election of president Andrew Jackson in 1828, the benefits that the robustly expanding postal establishment stood to confer proved irresistible. New post offices, mail contracts for postriders, stagecoach, steamship, and subsequently railroad companies, not to mention an expanded and improved postal service, were all but guaranteed to enhance the popularity of legislators who, assembled in Congress, held the power to authorize new postal routes. During and after the 1820s, postmasterships became a primary site of political patronage by the governing party. A franking privilege, finally, enabled incumbent legislators to enjoy a direct, publicly-sponsored, link to prospective voters. By the early 1840s, in one estimate, members of Congress would bestow their franks on 300,000 letters and 4.3 million documents per year.[7]

Its political charter positioned the Post Office to pursue a program of prodigious expansion. An enabling Act of 1792 recreated the primitive US mail service that had been established by the British. Mostly but not entirely supplanting less comprehensive systems of informal and private carriage, the Post Office became the principal means of written message exchange in the young United States. "Though in 1789 postal operations barely scratched the eastern seaboard, by 1800 service was provided to the farthest reaches of the western and southern frontiers," writes Richard John. The postal mechanism operated through what historian Cameron Blevins terms an "agency model," in which as they established a local community, settlers would write and sign petitions for new mail service to Washington. Congress would then "rubberstamp" as many as some thousands of new mail routes annually, and pass them on to the Post Office Department—which likewise "rarely rejected" such requests. In addition, there existed scant administrative oversight of this increasingly expansive territorial system. If, however, as Blevins argues, "the periphery, rather than the center, drove the western postal network's growth and managed its on-the-ground operations," then both the periphery and the center were committed to the overall project of territorial occupation.[8]

Relying on this agency model and the private contractors and political patronage which honeycombed it, within a few decades the United States brought forward a more far-flung national postal service than existed either in Britain or in France—and, "the envy of Europe," as a historian calls it, the Post Office only continued to grow. By 1861, a few years after the status of this government service was reaffirmed by Congress, there were 28,586 operating post offices staffed by 30,000-odd postmasters, carriers, and clerks, the nation's largest single workforce. Not even the rapidly growing railroads yet approached the Post Office in its operational scope. Postal expenditures, which had accounted for a scant 1.1 percent of federal outlays in 1792, totaled nearly one-fourth of the national government's spending by 1860. Over these years, the number of letters transmitted annually increased from 300,000 into the hundreds of millions.[9]

Until 1845–1850, however, licit use of the mails was confined to a fraction of the population. Business messages accounted for the lion's share of correspondence; businessmen are said to have produced an average of between 100 and 1,000 letters per year. More widespread social access was restricted, in an era when the average one-page letter cost 14.5 cents to send through the mail, meaning that—as the New York *Tribune* and other newspapers exclaimed in the 1840s—it cost more to send a one-page letter down the Hudson River from Troy to New York City than to ship a 200-pound barrel of flour over the same route. High letter rates sustained a policy of network expansion and provided subsidies, both to specific categories of mail and—not least—to the private contractors who transported them.[10]

Networks accrue value in proportion to the quantity and quality of connections that they enable between users; and increasing the number of such connections generally requires substantial capital investment and clear-eyed strategy. High letter rates paid by New England and Mid-Atlantic merchants—between six and twenty-five cents, depending on distance sent—not only enabled the Post Office to extend to the South and the West but also underpinned a growing distribution of public rather than only private information. During the Republic's first several decades, newspapers, reprints of congressional speeches, and government reports and documents accounted for a significant fraction of the country's overall publication and a large portion of its mail.[11]

The newspaper press generated by far the largest class of material sent through the mails. In this pretelegraphic era, as participants in a "culture of reprinting," editors relied on exchanges of newspapers from other towns and cities for the bulk of their nonlocal reports. By the 1840s, indeed, "every newspaper published in the United States received free of charge an average of 4,300 different exchange newspapers every year." They also utilized the posts to send newspapers to subscribers. During the 1830s, the newspaper press was institutionally redefined, as the elite sixpenny journals of the nation's early decades began to be supplanted by penny newspapers aimed at urban tradespeople, and newspaper circulation began to soar. By 1845, in turn, nine-tenths of the mail by weight was composed of printed materials—paying "about one-ninth of the expense," in the words of the Postmaster General. Acting in concert, the newspaper and the Post Office embodied a workaday system for circulating public information throughout an otherwise fragmented republic. By underwriting these postal news flows, however, these great subsidies satisfied an emerging third purpose, beyond commercial expansion and a (highly restricted) democratic franchise. By the 1820s and 1830s, newspaper subsidies also functioned as incentives to lure the nation's editorial corps into the service of whichever of the two major political parties happened to be in office. In this way they sustained postaldom's potent patronage function, welding the mails to the administration of political power.[12]

High letter rates, though subsidizing both network growth and public information, were far from popular. Indeed, dissatisfaction with price levels was channeled into political and market support for Post Office competitors. The result was to destabilize the foremost agency of the state.

Conflict over Postal Rates and the Quest for Territorial Empire

During the 1820s and 1830s, while Northern merchants as a group profited disproportionately from the expanding postal network, individual businessmen nevertheless often were pointedly dissatisfied with Post Office practice. Seeking to penetrate into the hinterlands, merchants were on the watch for information concerning distant markets and trading conditions; fortunes could be made by knowing before others did when to buy cheap and to sell dear. Some businessmen turned, accordingly, to emerging "private express" companies, which employed horses, steamships, and, later, railroads, along heavily trafficked commercial routes to race ahead of the general mails. Owing to the speculative profits that might be obtained, especially as the cotton trade ascended, businessmen in Northern cities developed keen incentives to circumvent the Post Office in favor of these interurban expresses. Business users of these expresses could steal a march on rivals by gaining private information advantages; prominent among these users, however, were also newspaper enterprises keen to publish this news ahead of competitors.[13]

Beginning around the same time, local "letter expresses" also proliferated. Postal services relied upon central collection and pick-up offices; users had to visit these sites to send and receive mail. Taking advantage of a legislative loophole that allowed private operators into this field, in growing conurbations commercial pick-up and delivery services carried mail between central city Post Offices and merchant-class businesses and households. Established in New York, Philadelphia, Cleveland, San Francisco, New Orleans, and Chicago, city delivery firms also emerged in some smaller towns—Easton, Pennsylvania, for example.

"During their heyday, in the three decades before the Civil War, these firms introduced many of the innovations associated with the modern postal system, including mailboxes and postage stamps," writes Richard John. All of this entrepreneurial initiative rested on Congress's refusal, from 1792 all the way to 1845, to make private mail carriage flatly illegal—as Great Britain and France had done.[14]

Both kinds of expresses charged rates substantially lower than those of the Post Office and, therefore, these rivals soon handled what one observer called "the greatest portion" of the nation's correspondence. The chairman of the Senate Committee on Post Offices and Post Roads declared in 1844 that "not more than, if as much as one-half the correspondence of the country passes through the mails." Low rates were feasible because the private expresses were neither compelled nor disposed to adopt the Post Office's mission: pursuing encompassing system development while also carrying political information on behalf of the citizenry.[15]

In interurban markets, private expresses attacked the Post Office at its most vulnerable points, those created by its subsidies. They transported letters, parcels, specie, gold, and light freight, leaving to the Post Office unprofitable mail such as newspapers, franked matter, and periodicals. In addition, they also competed principally on "the great and profitable thoroughfares," so that, as one Postmaster General conceded in the 1840s, "between New York and Boston, between Philadelphia and Baltimore, between New York and Buffalo, individual enterprise might supply the wants of the community in the rapid and cheap transportation of letters and packets." But, he added, "Will the same enterprise penetrate the savannas and swamps of the South, or the wilds of the West, and daily or weekly convey to the door of the planter and the husbandman the letter of business or friendship, the intelligence of commerce and politics?" The Post Office did; and so, by 1840, it was transferring to postal operations in the South Atlantic, the Northwest, and the Southwest 12 cents of each dollar in revenue generated in New England—and nearly half of each dollar coming from the Mid-Atlantic states.[16]

Although, during the early republic's first several decades, the Post Office was required to be self-supporting, policymakers rejected the tenet that each individual postal route should recover its full financial costs. "By withdrawing mail communication from all unproductive regions," explained Postmaster General John McLean in 1828, "and substituting a horse for a stage transportation on many others, a very large surplus of funds would accumulate, but the public convenience would be greatly lessened. To connect important places by frequent lines of intercourse, combine speed with all the security possible and to extend the mail wherever it may be wanted constitute the objects which have influenced our policy." Here surfaced two essential precepts, combining the properties of networks with the social mandate given to the government posts. To spearhead and to sustain continuing rapid expansion of the imperial republic, rates had to be set to support the overall network rather than discrete individual routes. I will further clarify this approach to rate-making shortly.[17]

For the moment, the essential point is that, as long as letter rates seriously inhibited access by those of modest means, the Postmaster General could not look for popular support to cohere behind his policy. Efforts to ward off the threat of competition by private expresses thus were stymied because the benefits of postal service were too narrowly enjoyed. Stoking additional disaffection were the notoriety of partisanship in postal appointments and percolating corruption in commercial contracting practices.[18]

Nevertheless, popular antimonopolism was a blade that cut two ways. Advocates of *private* information advantage via freedom to enter postal service markets also had to contend with it. Adherents of what historians call an "equal rights" political tradition, including both farmers and city-based artisans, decried undue concentrations ("monopolies") of property, power, and—for our purposes most salient—knowledge. Private expresses and, prior to the mid-1830s, prohibitively expensive newspapers *together* acted to prevent these "producers," productive laborers as opposed to "parasites," from claiming what they deemed their rightful republican inheritance. These special-purpose systems prevented commercial and political information from circulating outside a narrow entourage of speculative merchants, bankers, and lawyers: parasites. Political support for the Post Office's efforts to ward off private competitors initially sprang from the commodity-producing regions. Should buyers be permitted to use advance knowledge of markets to take advantage of sellers' ignorance? Should the government intervene to equalize the nation's informational condition—to neutralize one class's capacity to create systemic informational advantages for its members—by extending its role in telecommunications provision? A North Carolina newspaper in 1825 urged that *postal* expresses be adopted in order "to put a stop to the system of speculation which has lately been so extensively practiced by individuals of one commercial town on those of another who were not possessed of the same means of information." Two Senators from western states testified a few years later that the "whole Western country" actively supported such a postal express route from New York to New Orleans, "without which they might be exposed to the dangers of sacrificing the products of their labor without obtaining a fair equivalent." Southern and Western interests joined with Northeastern antimonopolist artisans, in efforts to check the systematic discrimination that piggybacked upon private expresses. Here, in a forerunner of later developments, the threat was posed not by the state but by unaccountable private actors. In the 1820s, the capable Postmaster General McLean responded by vigorously asserting federal power.[19]

Following the lines laid down by McLean, during the next decade a nationwide *postal* express service was indeed established on strategic routes. This comprised a deliberate attempt to target what two Senate allies of President Andrew Jackson termed "that advantage which those acting with a knowledge of the state of the market in other parts of the world always have over those who do not possess similar information." In a strategic concession to one institutional user postal expresses were even authorized to carry newspaper dispatches for free. The hope was that cooperation between public post riders and private publishers keen to proffer readers the latest market news would curtail speculative profiteering and private information systems, by encouraging timely publication of what was deemed should be public information—and, perhaps, to diminish the sway of anti-Jacksonian Eastern newspapers in the hinterlands.[20]

Postal expresses, however, proved insufficient to quell the competition because rates remained high and were still pegged to the distance that a letter traveled. Between 1839 and 1845, both local mail delivery companies and interurban express companies flourished. A campaign to supplant the Post Office with for-profit business gained ideological legitimacy and political traction.[21]

Pointing to unassailable evidence of financial mismanagement and corruption, the influential editor William Leggett and the Speaker of the House John Bell of Tennessee were among those who, during the 1830s, urged that the Post Office function be privatized. "[W]e might easily imagine [the post office] to be carried on by a private association, without its changing in any degree its essential character," agreed the German-born political economist Francis Lieber in 1841. A year or so later, Henry Wells, a pioneering expressman who would go on to head a major bank, reportedly proposed to take over the agency. In 1843 the Postmaster General himself acknowledged that the view "that the Post Office system is an odious monopoly, and ought to be abolished" had become a threat to the agency's existence—even if, he suggested, this view was chiefly "sustained by the influence of those whose interests are involved." Would this admixture of political purpose, ideological alignment, and commercial self-interest overwhelm the institution?[22]

During the mid-1840s, the issue came to a boil. Of hundreds of petitions on postal topics conveyed to Congress at the peak of the privatization drive, Richard John finds that "*none* called for the outright abolition of the Post Office Department. . . . Postal improvements, in short, were popular, while private mail delivery was not." In keeping with this sentiment was Congress's move to strengthen the Post Office's prerogative.[23]

Although they still permitted private carriers in adjacent and some overlapping services, legislative reforms of 1845 granted the Post Office exclusive responsibility for carrying letters and packets. Hereby the Department gained what would prove an enduring federally sanctioned monopoly over first-class mail. At the same time, Congress initiated a series of laws which progressively reduced postage rates while concurrently eliminating distance as a factor in rate-setting. These rate measures culminated in 1863, explains Cameron Blevins, "when Congress instituted a universal postage rate of three cents for all letters, regardless of their origin or destination." Declining rates threw open the mails to huge increases in popular usage, as the Postmaster General had predicted in 1844. In 1851, the Post Office was granted a right to declare city streets as well as interurban routes post roads under its aegis. And, crucially, the straitjacketing policy of "requiring the department to sustain its own expenses," as Postmaster General Cave Johnson phrased it in 1844—self-support through full cost-recovery—was finally jettisoned. Post Office historians have termed this new mandate "service first." Section 7 of the Act of March 3, 1851 decreed that "No post office now in existence shall be discontinued, nor shall the mail service on any mail route in any of the states and territories, be discontinued or diminished in consequence of any diminution of the revenues that may result from this Act." As a matter of political decision, when the postal system could not cover its costs, henceforward an appropriation was to be made by the Treasury Department. Richard John underscores the profound significance of this change, adding that "the presumption that the postal system should not be obliged to 'pay for itself' ... would remain a pillar of postal policy from 1851 until 1970."[24]

Why, confronted by repeated and seemingly successful demonstrations of entrepreneurial initiative, did Congress enact these far-reaching countermeasures? Why, within an avowedly capitalist economy, was it the Post Office and not its commercial rivals that triumphed? Did the rejection of privatization signify a commitment to renew democratic ideals?

It would be tempting to believe so. A racially defined democratic current indeed had strengthened throughout the late 1820s and 1830s. Reviewing postal practices in 1835, a Senate Committee related how the agency had responded when the sixpenny New York *Journal of Commerce* had established an express between Philadelphia and New York to obtain news ahead of the mail, thereby gaining a beat on the paper's competitors. "As was to be expected, this produced dissatisfaction, that a private individual could obtain intelligence for himself and patrons before the Government furnished it to the citizens generally," the Committee explained, adding that the Postmaster General had "deemed it his duty" to respond by instituting a postal express to beat back the private competitor. The Committee was emphatic that "It should not be permitted that an individual should establish a mode of communication and continue it by which intelligence should be received and acted upon by him before the community at large can have the benefit of it through the medium of the Government mails." Its reasoning bears emphasis: "If such a measure on the part of an individual cannot be corrected by law, then Government should not hesitate to adopt means, although of an expensive character, to place the community generally in possession of the same intelligence . . . It should defeat the efforts of individuals to exercise functions and powers belonging exclusively to itself; especially where such efforts are attended with the effect of giving them advantages over the rest of the community."[25]

This critique of the advantages derived from privileged network access resonated within an antebellum political reform coalition. With roots stretching back to the eighteenth century, it would emerge as a more full-fledged ideology of antimonopolism after the Civil War when, as we will see, it figured in wide-ranging struggles to reorganize the structure and policy of telecommunications. Antimonopoly arguments therefore were, and have remained, a staple justification for policy reforms, and they often permeated postal rhetoric. Nevertheless, a bulked-up commitment to democratic norms does not adequately explains Congress's decision in 1845 to reentrench the government Post Office. Arguably more important to this outcome were quite other factors.[26]

One of these pertained to the disparate structure of postal demand. In an early expression of what would be a persistent trend, the reduction of letter rates constituted a capitulation to heavy users of postal and private express services. James W. Hale, who had established a news express for Boston newspapers which ultimately became the prominent Adams Express firm, was lionized by a writer in 1851 as a "pioneer . . . whose name must for ever stand identified with the cause of cheap postage, and quick and reliable conveyance." Although, he continued, Hale "was overwhelmed with prosecutions, instituted by the post office department, the sympathies of the business community were with him," and this had set the stage for the Post Office decision to lower letter prices. When he declared that "public opinion seems to demand a reduction in the rates of letter postage," Postmaster General Johnson himself specified that this judgment reflected the sentiments "of the very intelligent and highly respectable Chamber of Commerce of the city of New York, as expressed in their letter to the department." This admission spoke to the already-existing, though often obscured, power of business users to shape US telecommunications policy. We will find throughout this book that, though typically unrecognized, business users have often constituted the pivot of US telecommunications system development. Indeed, during the late 1840s they mobilized again, to demand that the US government pursue a postal treaty with Britain in order both to reduce the cost of posting letters and to cut the rates for newspapers, periodicals, and pamphlets; such a treaty was signed in December, 1848 and ratified the following January. As historian Peter A. Shulman details, however, the larger project of which this formed a part—"a global network of postal communication powered by steam and at least partially under American control"—continued to "frustrate[] and tantalize[] Americans" throughout this period. Transoceanic programs for US imperial telecommunications would be realized, we will see, only in the following century.[27]

The Postmaster General himself, meanwhile, strained to cast the 1845 reforms as falling within the equal rights tradition, by asserting that "The reduction of the letter postage . . . was but an act of justice to that class of our citizens who had been so long and so oppressively taxed for the benefit of others." He likewise made much of the federal government's obligation, as one writer expressed it in 1850, to "put all men on equal footing" in the "transmission of intelligence" by making it "as free, as quick, as sure and as cheap as the light of day." Improved information circulation would amplify and expand the public good. If lowered letter rates lessened the "tax" on heavy commercial users, then this would redound to the benefit of the wider community: "Postage is a tax not only on the business of the country," wrote Johnson in 1847, "but upon the intelligence, knowledge, and the exercise of the friendly and social feelings; and . . . should be reduced to the lowest point which would enable the department to sustain itself." The Postmaster General formulated the issue in 1848 in inclusive, but vaultingly abstract, terms: "a well digested cheap mail system affords . . . a rapid interchange of ideas between different sections of the country, and the consequent increase in knowledge; its influence upon society, but little, if any, less than that of printing; its importance to every interest, social, commercial, and political." Beneath this highflown rhetoric, reducing the burdens on heavy commercial users and opening postal service to general use certainly do help to explain the refoundation of the Post Office monopoly in 1845.[28]

Most important of all for this outcome, however, was a recurrent and, by around 1840, an "explicit national political objective": to expand the jurisdiction of the United States to continental scope. This trend already had been decades in the making. Purchase of the Louisiana Territory from France in 1803 doubled the size of the United States; the Onis-Adams Treaty of 1819 with the Spanish Empire then gained East and West Florida. During the 1840s, the US completed the process with the annexation of Texas, the Oregon Treaty with Britain, and the invasion of Mexico—followed by the seizure of land stretching all the way to California and the coveted Pacific coast. On the ground, these spasms of territorial acquisition could only be accomplished through continuous deployments of military force against indigenous peoples. On every side, the birth of the Republic was both accompanied and followed by wars with Indian nations. In 1830, President Andrew Jackson induced a divided Congress to pass legislation to compel all Native American groups east of the Mississippi River to abandon their lands in exchange for territory located farther west. To hold the continent for white settlers and official purposes, by the mid-nineteenth century the US operated sixty major forts west of the Mississippi River alongside 138 smaller posts.[29]

Ever since the 1792 Act, the Post Office had been bound up in this process of westward and southward expropriation; and it possessed an irreplaceable importance in the Republic's sustained program of territorial imperialism. A study heralding postal progress from the vantage of the 1920s simply took it for granted that "Postal communication was a vital necessity for without it the great West could never be held within a nation administered from Washington." Nineteenth-century defenders of a government-run mail service were prone to tie their support expressly to the agency's function as the spearhead of settlement for, in truth, no other organization of sufficient scale was available. Were the Post Office to be jettisoned, its operations left to the whims of smaller market agents, then a foundation-stone of settler-colonialism stood to be relinquished. "How are we to develop, cherish, and protect our immense interests and possessions on the Pacific, with a vast wilderness fifteen hundred miles in breadth, filled with hostile savages, and cutting off all direct communication?" asked Senator Stephen Douglas in 1854. All the way down to the present, we will see, US leaders have remained determined to fold telecommunications into the projection of imperial power beyond existing borders.[30]

In 1825, attempting to tie in frontier settlements as quickly as possible to governmental authority, Congress had permitted the Postmaster General, in advance of legislative authorization, to establish a post road to the courthouse of any newly established county seat. Two decades later, President James K. Polk—an ardent annexationist—underlined the role of the Post Office by telling Congress how the "extension of the mail service . . . will be demanded by the rapid extension and increase of population on our western frontier." Mail facilities, Polk insisted in another message to Congress the following year, "should be afforded to our citizens west of the Rocky Mountains." Throughout the antebellum period, congressional hearings and debates are chockablock with discussions of postal services and mail subsidies.[31]

Promoted for fifteen years prior to the Civil War, the transcontinental rail network that was completed in 1869 likewise depended on huge government subsidies to railroads, mostly in the form of hundreds of millions of acres' worth of land grants. It is not sufficiently appreciated, however, that these subsidies were based upon Congress's postal power. Members of both leading parties argued for federal support of a transcontinental railroad because it would comingle military and postal functions. Southern slaveholders were determined, though, to ensure that *their* United States of America would become a coast-to-coast empire built on unfree labor and, concomitantly, that both a transcontinental mail service and a transcontinental railroad therefore would be established along a far southern route.[32]

Northerners would have none of it. The transcontinental railroad proved a lightning rod for political conflict between free labor and slave states so that, before the Civil War, Congress never approved it. However, as Kevin Waite details, in the run-up to the war Postmaster General Aaron V. Brown, earlier a Tennessee governor and US congressman and a law partner of former President James Polk, did manage to transform the Post Office into "a southern-oriented, continental system." His administration underwrote a costly new mail service between St. Louis and Memphis in the east and San Francisco in the West—which traversed Little Rock, Arkansas, El Paso, Southern New Mexico, Yuma, and Los Angeles en route. This service was expressly intended to lay the basis for a railroad and to provide a highway for troops; and, as operated by the contractor—the Butterfield Overland Mail—to make post offices double as fortresses "manned by four to five soldiers equipped with Sharps rifles and Colt revolvers." Between 1858 and 1861, Waite shows, the Overland attested that "western infrastructure and American imperialism fit hand-in-glove."[33]

This linkage between infrastructure and empire, however, was more expansive than the designs harbored by the Slave South. California and the Oregon Territory also were joined to the burgeoning postal network and, moreover, during the 1840s postal service figured "in drawing into the American orbit the islands that would become the nation's possessions and protectorates by 1898": Cuba and Hawaii. Supporters of postal expansion could be remarkably forthright. Hoping to secure the Post Office's role in a regular overland mail route from the Mississippi Valley to his own state, in the mid-1850s California Senator Weller expressed the relationship like this:

> I believe, by the establishment of a mail route with little posts every ten miles you will have in fact military posts all along that road. In this way you will give protection to your emigrants. That is what I am after . . . This I regard as vastly important to the future interest of your possession on the Pacific.

He was correct; and military involvement with postal operations was an engraved feature. Six of the twelve US Postmasters General who served between 1789 and 1845 had been high-ranking military officers and, according to John, early postal service was organized on a "military model." Once so designated by Congress, early post roads—notably, the Natchez Trace (Nashville to Natchez) and the Federal Road (Georgia to New Orleans)—actually were constructed by soldiers. Postal officials might negotiate with indigenous peoples, but they relied on military force to secure service along new routes that traversed Indian nations; the first US mail ever carried overland from the Pacific to the Atlantic coast was borne, in 1848, by Kit Carson as a military operation. Around the same time, steamers controlled or subsidized by the War Department and the Navy transmitted mail on selected international lines—New Orleans to Vera Cruz, and Havana to Chagres [Panama] for example. Postal service remained a governmental function, therefore, above all because it lodged networking within this young nation's militarily enforced project of settler-colonization. It functioned, in Headrick's term, as an irreplaceable "tool of empire." By contrast, as one steam mail promoter declared in an 1858 letter to the chairman of the Committee on Post Offices and Post Roads, "Private enterprise cannot be depended on for providing such communication."[34]

Postal Network Economics and Politics in the Antebellum Era

As post offices proliferated and postal routes spread, new means of transport also were integrated. Navigable waterways were declared to be post roads in 1823, railroads in 1838. These actions made additional room for profit-making contractors. In 1848, the Pacific Mail Steamship Company was incorporated, on the strength of a Post Office promise of $199,000 in annual compensation to carry a monthly mail from Panama to Oregon; a decade later, the Post Office recorded an annual loss of nearly $2 million to service the Pacific Coast via no less than six different contracted mails. Some 700 mail contractors transported mail in 1828; by 1850, 5,544 contractors plied the country's postal routes, and expenditures for mail transport totaled more than twice the cost of the second largest Post Office outlay: nearly $1.8 million in compensation for postmasters. Given to unscrupulous and dishonest practices, private contractors also were essential to the agency's capacity to expand rapidly and flexibly to the west. During and after the Civil War, the Post Office's dependence on contractors resulted in pervasive and heavily publicized, corruption.[35]

As it enriched private transport operators through its policy of territorial expansion, the Post Office simultaneously assumed a principal institutional role within the US party-state. Not only did incumbent legislators make heavy use of their congressional franking privileges. Beginning in the 1830s and 1840s, the Post Office also became a well-oiled engine of patronage jobs for whichever political party was in office, and it continued to cook up much of the political glue with which the party system was stuck together. The agency held in its gift more patronage jobs than remainder of the executive, judicial, and legislative branches all told; the same Polk Administration (1845–1848) which, in 1000 days, wrested the continent for the United States, doled out 13,500 postmasterships. Whigs, and later Republicans, joined Democrats in "a six-decade contest over the spoils of electoral victory." In turn, reformers of different stripes often derided postaldom's "patronage army," for "post offices gave the ruling party a ready-made campaign office in every precinct in the country from which postmasters could distribute campaign literature, mobilize voters, hand out election ballots," and so on. Patronage has sometimes been overemphasized in the reentrenchment of the government postal monopoly in 1845, but there can be no doubt that it gave "all but the most marginal of politicians a vested interest in its continued operation under government control."[36]

If, during the 1840s, would-be privatizers were tethered and the US Post Office was reentrenched, these reforms were also packaged as adhering to the best practice model of the day: that of the British Post Office, which had been reorganized around a cheap post in 1839. "The radical change in the rates of postage on letters, recently adopted in Great Britain," reported US Postmaster General Amos Kendall that same year, "has attracted much attention in the United States." He and his successor needed to contemplate how they might institute a comparable policy for the much larger, and still mightily expanding, jurisdiction of the United States. I have already underlined that the outcome was to reconsecrate the postal monopoly and to begin to lower rates and to increase popular access to the network. How were these massive changes accommodated by network economics and redesigned postal rates?[37]

Realizing the goal of establishing "a well digested cheap mail system," Postmaster General Cave Johnson publicly elaborated in 1848, "requires a careful examination." Government control remained essential: had postal operations "been left to private enterprise, the more wealthy and populous portions of the community would no doubt have been amply provided for; but others, less favored, would have been left destitute of the means of diffusing intelligence among the people." Financial support for enlarged postal operations could only be gained, the Postmaster underlined, via some kind of "tax on the people." Johnson's reasoning went like this: "A large number of the people have little or no connexion with the mail system. To subject that class to share the burden of its support by a direct tax, or by imposts levied upon the necessaries of life, would meet, it is believed, the approbation of but few disinterested citizens." A tax on postal users would be the fairest solution: "every letter or package conveyed in the mails should pay a just and fair proportion of its cost of transportation, and other expenses attending the delivery. There should be no exception." And yet, this too posed a problem because, like his predecessors, Johnson understood that "It is difficult, if not impossible, to ascertain with any degree of accuracy the actual cost of each letter or package conveyed in the mails." US topography and settlement patterns were too varied, its transportation systems too different, indeed the very need of mail service too disparate from area to area, for letter costs to be calculated individually:

> In no two sections of the country—probably on no two mail routes—would the cost of transportation be the same. . . . the cost of each letter or package must depend in some degree upon the amount paid the contractors. The contract

changes every four years, and the price paid for the service depends upon considerations connected with travel over the route, the chances of competition, the cost of supplies, &c., as well as upon the distance.

"The expense of receiving, forwarding, and delivery," added the Postmaster, also needed to be factored in. This imponderable complexity signified to him, as it had to Postmaster Maclean two decades earlier, that "The best and only practicable criterion will be the expense of the whole system, compared with the revenue, and the adoption of such a rate as experience shows to be enough to make the one meet the other, approaching as nearly as possible the cost."[38]

If it was impossible to calculate cost-based rates route-by-route, let alone letter-by-letter, then rates needed to be set so as to sustain the network in its entirety. The numerator in the relatively simple formula proposed by Johnson was overall expenses; the denominator was—roughly—mail volume, adjusted to take account of the subsidies which helped to underwrite differentially priced classes of correspondence (notably franked government mail and newspapers). This was indeed a potent rate-making formula, and one that would carry over, with adjustments, far into the future. Indeed, it also would be adopted by telephone rate-makers many decades later.

It turned out, however, that this breakthrough was not sufficient to ensure placid postal development. The Post Office, which was, alongside the US Army, the leading incarnation of central-state authority, instead became bound up in the struggle that pitted advocates of slavery against abolitionists, northern free traders, and some settler colonist adherents of federally sponsored "internal improvements." The policy of "service first" embroiled the agency in the deepening struggle over Black slavery.

For a full quarter-century beginning in the mid-1830s, the Post Office effectively barred mailings of abolitionist literature to the slave states, establishing an "intellectual blockade," or *cordon sanitaire*, as historian Clement Eaton long ago underlined. This was of course discriminatory, and in flagrant contravention of postal statutes. Nonetheless it stoked rather than diminished the spiraling conflict between free and slave states. The Post Office ceded to southern postmasters, as Elizabeth Hewitt explains, "*de facto* authority to determine what mail material they would or would not allow to be delivered, even though federal law positively refused to legalize this censorship"—and abolitionists were not slow to point out that free speech in regard to the most profound political issue facing the nation in turn was routinely denied. The American Anti-Slavery Society argued that, by restricting the circulation of its literature, southern despotism infringed the liberties of all Americans. The skewed cost structure of the postal network added fuel to the fire. Abolitionists dissected the Post Office's published financial statistics to claim that the slave states' censorship was additionally illegitimate, because their post offices did not pay their own way. (Such a proclaimed deviation from sound market principles would have been intended to inflame Northern opinion in its own right.) The censorship practiced by southern postmasters prompted some northerners to underline "the implicit links between the tyranny of the postmaster and the tyranny of the slave-master."[39]

All the while, however, rates declined and became less dependent on distance so that the North's general literary culture penetrated throughout the South. Propagandists of slavery were outraged. "Our postage laws are admirably contrived, and were no doubt intended," declared George Fitzhugh—a "fire-eater," that is, an extremist defender of slavery (and an acute critic of the northern states' wages system)—"to rob the South.... The iniquity of our postage laws ... affects injuriously all Southern interests." Fitzhugh was incensed at the flood of "vile, useless, and noxious" cheap literature that traveled from north to south, and angered that southerners "import their books, their thoughts, their very fashions from abroad," learning from books "to admire and ape what is English or Northern, and to despise what is Southern." He targeted precisely the economic policies—free trade and cheap postage—through which this result was contrived. "The New-York merchants send out catalogues of their complete assortment of books and other merchandise to all quarters of the Union; and the man who wants a book, being charged no more for postage for writing to a house in New-York than to one in his own neighborhood, is sure to send to New-York for it, because his neighboring bookseller may not have it, or, if he has, the iniquitous post-office laws charge him as much for remitting the book twenty miles as they charge the New-York merchant for sending it three thousand miles." Postal network economics—service first—sustained a veritable cultural invasion.[40]

The Civil War reconstituted the United States, making it no longer a "Union" of states but a true nation-state which, as it formed, also "reconfigured the character of its empire, first in the South and the trans-Mississippi West before reaching overseas." The Post Office formed a part of this bloody transformation. It may be a little overstated to say, with Richard Bentsel, that between the outbreak of the War and the end of Reconstruction in 1877 "the American state and the Republican party were essentially the same thing." However it is fair to assert that this Republican-dominated US state acted as "the vehicle of common interests in economic development associated with northern finance, industry, and free soil agriculture." Folded into this program was a new crop of postal extensions and enhancements, from city home delivery to a money-order option—initiated to serve Union Army soldiers desiring to send home some of their pay. During the Civil War as well came the first recorded stirrings—local and short-lived—of trade union organization by urban postal workers. We will find that both service expansion and collective self-organization carried forward, as the Department loomed larger in American life.[41]

The Corporate Telegraph and the Civil War

In the meantime, a quite different vector of change was radically altering the general telecommunications system. The policy changes made in the 1840s to sustain a burgeoning continental mail did not curtail the growth of interurban expresses, some of which stepped into existing service gaps as contractors. Along thriving routes west of Salt Lake City, during the 1850s a historian tells us that the government awarded contracts "to just about anyone daring enough to try and turn a profit"; however, in 1860, Wells, Fargo took over many of these contracts and "soon became Nevada's prime mover of U.S. mail." Wells was joined by American Express and Adams Express in charging what the traffic would bear to convey packages, bullion, specie, even correspondence (so long as it was not designated first-class) from and to the booming gold and silver fields in California and Nevada. They also pyramided into banking and financial services. Most well-known was the storied Pony Express, which operated between Missouri and Sacramento for a scant eighteen months beginning in the spring of 1860, thence becoming fodder for a century's-worth of reveries. The Pony Express originated as a publicity stunt intended to help secure a large government mail contract to compete against the South's Butterfield Overland Mail. Before the Civil War, some of these private expresses already were substantial enterprises; by 1910, half a dozen of them were collecting annual revenues of between 10 and 30 million dollars, making them major corporations.[42]

Around the emerging medium of electrical telegraphy, however, corporate capital introduced a more far-reaching disruption. Early commentators might wonder at the sublime speed at which telegraphed messages traveled, but the fledgling telegraph's institutional basis excited political controversy. After an initial $30,000 appropriation in 1842, for an experimental electrical telegraph line to connect Baltimore and Washington, Congress refused any extension of its ownership role in 1845. This bifurcation of US telecommunications proved enduring and its ramifications profound. Beginning from the moment that the telegraph was privatized, ownership and control of the awe-inspiring medium sparked debate.[43]

The telegraph's US inventor, Samuel Morse, urged Congress to take control of the new technology and, early on, much of the press "agreed with Morse that the telegraph should not be left to the exploitation of individuals." Not least because they sensed a potential encroachment on the news market, prominent editors, including William Swain of the *Philadelphia Public Ledger* and James Gordon Bennett of the *New York Herald*, editorialized in favor of a government telegraph. (An early adopter of the telegraph, the *Herald* nevertheless remained a leading critic of corporate telegraphy throughout the following decades.) Reacting to the threat posed by private expresses, during the

1830s, Postmasters General had fumed over how far government would "allow individuals to divide with it the business of transmitting intelligence." This sentiment carried forward. Smaller and less-well-situated merchants often shared the opinion voiced by Postmaster General Cave Johnson in 1845: "In the hands of individuals or associations, the telegraph may become the most potent instrument the world ever knew to effect sudden and large speculations—to rob the many of their just advantages, and concentrate them upon the few." Some leading politicians concurred, notably, Whig presidential hopeful Henry Clay, who backed vigorous use of federal power to expand the capitalist political economy.[44]

Despite critics and dissenters, during the 1840s prospectors successfully exploited telegraph technology as a profit-making domain, while attempts to prevent the medium from falling into self-interested hands foundered. "(P)owerful opportunists"—notably F. O. J. Smith, then chairman of the House Commerce Committee—"quickly recognized the commercial possibilities and fought for private control." The fledgling telegraph system was depostalized in 1845 and almost at once began to divert "an appreciable amount" of correspondence from the mails. Capital's incursion would rebalance institutional relations: "Never again could the central government presume to outspeed private enterprise in the transmission of market information," observes a historian.[45]

This, however, did not signify that entrepreneurs were better at providing service or at implementing a modern network infrastructure. For decades, akin to the railroads, system development took second place to speculative investment as a motivating priority. Scarcely a decade after the telegraph's denationalization in 1844, consolidation reached a new height: the entire territory of the expanding United States was divvied up among six regionally dominant carriers. By this time, the new medium had already played a key part in wiring news of the US invasion of Mexico to newspaper readers in the eastern seaboard cities. Fixing his attention thereafter on the indigenous inhabitants of North America, in 1854 Senator Stephen Douglas admonished that "The Indian barrier must be removed. . . . We must therefore have Rail Roads and Telegraphs from the Atlantic to the Pacific, through our own territory." The telegraph thus functioned almost from the very start in the wider process of US empire-making. By the early 1850s commercial telegraph lines were being built scattershot across the trans-Mississippi west; by October 1861, months before secession and the outbreak of the Civil war, a federally supported Transcontinental Telegraph organized principally by one of these systems, Western Union, offered a regular, and profitable, service. During the Civil War, James Schwoch shows, the Transcontinental Telegraph expanded not only across the western plains but also up the Pacific Coast to Alaska. In telegraphy as more generally, Lloyd Gardner sums up, "it became harder and harder to draw a distinction between the American rush to occupy the continent ... and U.S. attitudes about the rest of the world." In their mind's eye it seemed theirs for the taking.[46]

The actual inhabitants possessed other ideas. Incursions by settlers, surveyors, roadbuilders, and railroads were unwelcome and sometimes resisted. Although a historian explains that Indians "produced few written manifestos," they understood the strategic significance of telegraphic communications. After Colorado's infamous Sand Creek massacre in late November 1864, James Schwoch relates, indigenous warriors mounted "the first sustained ... attack against the means of electronic communication wielded by an occupying power on the North American frontier." By cutting telegraph wires and burning telegraph poles across the plains—where trees were scarce—Lakotas, Cheyennes, and Arapahos "paralyzed overland traffic" along the Platte Road segment of the Oregon Trail for six weeks, disrupting electrical communications with the West and its market-moving gold and silver mines; the stage line shut down service so that mail to and from California had to travel via Panama. Flush with victory in the immediate aftermath of the Civil War, the imperial leadership of the United States was now bent on fully occupying the continent and bending it to its purposes. It responded to the Native Americans' campaigns with savage reprisals, war maneuvers—and, by 1867–1868, peace negotiations. Though the Indian wars continued, treaties struck in 1868 between the United States and several Sioux nations "recognized Lakota sovereignty and established a nation-to-nation relationship between the Lakota nation and the United States"—and provided that these Native Americans would withdraw opposition to construction of railroads, military posts, and roads.[47]

A pool of entrepreneurial talent had already led the telegraph industry westward into what was, for speculators, uncharted terrain. As Alfred M. Lee long ago observed, the various express services had "developed practices and trained men ... afterwards enlisted in organizing the utilization of the magnetic telegraph." As "the drumbeat for improved communication with the West" grew louder, a decade of profligately wasteful promotion, and rapid unplanned growth, resulted in "a rudimentary telegraphic grid"—first in the Northeast and the Midwest and then beyond. System development was characterized by contradictory impulses. An omnipresent need for funds with which to build out these capital-intensive networks was accompanied by feverish competitive rivalries typified by ratecutting, rival patent claims, bans on interconnection, and speculative investment. Paradoxically, however, these same practices, alongside first-move advantages and corporate combinations that were financed through "stock watering"—issuing new stock shares whose value bore little relation to corporate assets—strengthened a concurrent tendency to consolidation. Also contributing to this merger trend was the fact that patchwork systems, and the rekeying of long-distance messages that they necessitated, hindered the accuracy and coordination of long-distance telegraph traffic flows: telegraph service exhibited strong "network effects." Joshua Cohen has demonstrated that, again like the transcontinental railroads, the process which culminated in a nationwide corporate telegraph monopoly in 1866 was driven as much by the financial machinations of speculative investors and capitalists as by efficiency considerations or system development needs.[48]

The Civil War shook the ground beneath the nation's telecommunications, and literally sundered connections. On one hand, the Confederate Post Office deviated sharply from the US Post Office's service first policy in that it pursued a strict mandate to achieve fiscal self-sufficiency; a historian has found that, "in conjunction with a multitude of war-related privations," this requirement eventually led the Confederacy's state-capitalist postal system to virtual collapse. On the other hand, at the outset of the conflict companies whose telegraphs spanned both Union and Confederate states sometimes found their lines cut, and Northern companies turned their systems in the South over to Confederate war managers. The Union then established a United States Military Telegraph Corps (USMT) to direct a strategic effort in telecommunications. Union Secretaries of War Simon Cameron and his replacement, Edwin M. Stanton (who formerly had been a director of a telegraph corporation), embraced the wireline medium as an essential aid "in coordinating complex military operations on a continental scale." During the Mexican American War some fifteen years earlier, the military had relied on wagon trains and horseback couriers. By contrast, in the Civil War the telegraph was incorporated to aid in transporting soldiers and supplies across the burgeoning rail systems—likewise newly assimilated into military strategy— of both North and South. Telegraphy had a dramatic impact, both during the war and afterward, as railroads adopted it for coordinating train movements as well as for routine business.[49]

Rather than taking possession of the Union's telegraphs and placing them under military control, as Congress had authorized, the USMT worked closely with commercial telegraph companies—principally, the American Telegraph Company and the Western Union—and USMT managers were designated officers in the Quartermaster Corps even as they served concurrently as managers of the commercial carriers. The director of the USMT was Western Union's general manager, Anson Stager; likewise, the president of the Southern Telegraph Company headed the Confederate military lines. The North's carriers granted military and government messages priority over their commercial service, which continued; the South's apparently did not. However, the Union's wartime telegraph system "blurred the boundaries between public and private interests until they were almost indistinguishable," Cohen relates, as the government became "the client, protector, and builder of the private telegraph companies."[50]

This situation was of course advantageous to the two major Union carriers and their investors. During the conflict, stock prices and dividends increased: the carriers gathered "enormous wartime profits."[51] This did not exhaust governmental largess, partial precedent for which had already been set. The US government had passed a "Pacific Telegraph Act" in 1860, to grant subsidies to the first transcontinental telegraph line (completed years in advance of a transcontinental railroad, in 1861). Now central-state support rocketed. By the war's end, Union telegraph system buildouts had erected some 15,000 miles of lines, both in the North and, as Union armies advanced, in the South, costing $2.5 million (the South, by contrast, built out around 1,000 miles' worth of lines). Although few records survive to detail the manifestly corrupt disposals that followed immediately after the War, the US government released the lines, including those built at public expense, to the private carriers.[52]

Within months, Western Union, which also had acquired two of its surviving rivals during the conflict, merged with its major remaining competitor, American Telegraph—and moved its headquarters from Rochester to Broadway in New York City. Midway through 1866, it emerged as one of the first two nationwide US corporate monopolies. This single, sprawling corporation controlled four-fifths of the nation's wireline telecommunications. This was a destabilizing and, for many Americans, frightening.[53]

Antimonopoly sentiment flared, finding its way into the murky corridors of the Republican party-state. Herein, rank opportunism and financial self-interest intermingled with and, ultimately, overpowered, diversely rooted political efforts to reconstruct the United States around more egalitarian principles. After considerable lobbying, there crystalized the nation's first federal regulatory legislation for electrical telecommunications: the National Telegraph Act of 1866. From the moment of its own corporate formation and periodically throughout the half century that followed—in part, owing to the Telegraph Act—Western Union was compelled to wrestle with threats from the political arena.[54]

Western Union as a Reference Model

The Civil War—the War of the Rebellion, as Steven Hahn enjoins us to remember it—wrought an epic transformation. The most profound change was the abolition of slavery and the recasting of citizenship in national terms; but the war also catalyzed and consolidated related and far-reaching shifts. Capitalist social relations expanded rapidly, as manufacturing grew and nationwide distribution channels were built: a self-confident industrial-financial capitalist class now increasingly confronted a working class populated less by independent tradespeople and farmers than by permanent wage-earners. Now swift to solidify as well was a powerful central state, overlooking a continental nation and enmeshed, as it had been since the formation of the Republic but now in ever-more potent ways, beyond this vast jurisdiction. An expansionary national political economy permeated by the wage relation and overseen by a cohesive federal government, however, brought little stability.[55]

A financial panic, triggered by a collapse of railroad securities in 1873, engendered a major depression, and this was followed by two other downturns throughout the following two decades—notably, the excruciating depression of 1893; meanwhile, a chronic deflation persisted until late in the 1890s, the longest such stretch in US history. Throughout these pinched years, many Americans reacted angrily to great aggregations of capital and hardening forms of exploitation and inequality. Calls for structural change multiplied. Hahn writes that this "cascading crisis ignited more than two decades of political struggle, threatening social upheaval and calling into question many of the basic ways in which the political economy worked." Differing and overlapping by turns, the experiences of farmers and city-dwellers, men and women, white and Black and Spanish-speaking workers, channeled into varied forms of collective self-organization and political movement. Grangers and Populists, freedpeople and feminists, temperance reformers, anarchists, socialists, craft- and industrial unionists, threw themselves into debate and purposive action in hopes of regenerating the political economy. No shared or uniform agenda resulted: different groups possessed aims and that were disparate and sometimes at cross-purposes. Nevertheless, commitments to far-reaching reforms focused often on the great capital-intensive industries of the era. They traced a fifty-year arc in US telecommunications, between the Civil War and World War I. Their twin reference points were the Post Office and Western Union.[56]

Western Union exercised awesome power; however, paradoxically, during the decades after the Civil War the giant corporation itself was continually made a hostage. One set of financial predators—the Vanderbilts—was ousted from Western Union's board of directors, only to be replaced by another, this one led by Jay Gould, and including Collis P. Huntington, Cyrus Field, and J. P. Morgan. Such men targeted the telegraph monopoly to line their pockets. Cohen shows how throughout these years Western Union was a creature of railroad investors and, more generally, of speculative finance, "the manipulation of Western Union stock for the enrichment of its large shareholders" becoming its trademark feature. As it stumbled along, Western Union thus incarnated the finance capitalism that was sweeping through the greater political economy. Expansionary, efficient network development was sacrificed in favor of returns to investors, exacted both from Western Union's employees and its customers. For contemporaries, therefore—and crucially—"monopoly" did not merely denote a highly concentrated industry of supply capable of controlling prices, but also implicated a subterranean spider-web of practices introduced by corporate and finance capital. Disfiguring the commonweal, government "subsidies, influence over government policies, and insider information" became a staple of capitalists' endeavors, and "tipped the playing field in their favor." They also degraded the structure and policy of telegraph service.[57]

Throughout its early decades, telegraph innovation fell within the machine-shop tradition that was generating technological changes in a variety of emerging industries. Patent rights to inventions quickly acquired strategic significance. Throughout the first postbellum years, Western Union not only kept a vigilant eye out for potentially relevant patented inventions but actually purchased and implemented some of them, to invade adjacent markets while defending its own, to increase message speed and line capacity, and to reduce labor costs. These innovations notably included stock tickers, early automatic telegraphs to send and receive messages without relying on skilled operators, acoustic telegraphy (adjacent to telephony), and multiplexing technology. Under its able President William Orton (1867–1878) Western Union likewise moved to formalize a commitment to research and development: Increasingly, innovation occurred within carefully administered R&D facilities, both inhouse and via independent contractors (notably Thomas Edison). After the late 1870s, however, as the telegraph monopoly became enmired in the schemes of predators focusing rigidly on short-term profits, its priorities altered and Western Union managers presided over what historian Paul Israel deems a "decline of innovation." Hereafter the carrier lagged consistently in network modernization projects, a tack that its executives tried to justify as appropriate for a "mature" service. The actual extent of the vulnerability caused by this failure was revealed only by the ascent of an overlapping and far more technologically progressive telephone industry.[58]

This is not to say that the corporate telegraph ceased to grow. Western Union's offices indeed increased from under 4,000 to over 19,000 between 1870 and 1890; and its 21,000 operators and managers serviced four-fifths of the country's telegraph traffic and garnered for the carrier nine-tenths of total industry revenue. An expansive and far-sighted modernization program was eschewed, however, in favor of monopoly control and short-term profits. Throughout this deflationary era, Western Union's profit rate, on a vastly inflated nominal capitalization and *exclusive* of huge dividends to shareholders, hovered between 3 and 6 percent.[59]

The defects of this system were glaring. The carrier's rate schedules were impenetrable and confusing, even irrational. Railroads, collectively among the heaviest users of telegraph service, were irked by their dependence on Western Union's lines for internal communications, which eventuated in inadequate service, sometimes compromising the safety of trains and passengers. The roads found themselves bonded to Western Union's self-interested strategy: "Instead of expanding telegraph services to keep pace with growing traffic demands," explains a historian of railroad telegraphy, Western Union's "restrictions forced managers on poorly capitalized railroads to limit access to it." Western Union's short-term profit orientation worked all too effectively to "hinder[] meaningful technological and operational reforms," which might have aided its big customers and expanded its own business.[60]

During these decades when, furthermore, US corporate, military, and political elites were maneuvering to carve out a growing global role, Western Union placed its own corporate self-interested ahead of a coherent transoceanic projection of US power. The huge capital investment needed to lay a trans-Atlantic submarine cable created an irresistible incentive for spreading the risk of such a venture. For this reason, and also as an adjunct of a coeval burst of European imperialism, a definite preference developed among mainly European submarine cable carriers for cartelized markets, exclusive concessions, and extravagant government subsidies. While not welcomed, upstart rivals might be admitted into a cartel if they could grant something of value to it in return. In Daniel Headrick's pithy phrase, again and again (albeit, sometimes covertly) the cartel's operated as a "conspiracy against the customers."[61]

Western Union fitted itself into this pattern from the moment that it became a *de facto* monopoly. What proved to be the first working trans-Atlantic cable was laid, by an Anglo-American consortium, in 1866—with Western Union as its US correspondent. The company's control over North American feeder lines enabled it to gain solid leverage in negotiating with Europe-based cable operators. Artificially high rates and spurious or nonexistent competition were the results, in the North Atlantic international communications market as elsewhere. As a later US expert acerbically noted, such cozy arrangements "do not of necessity benefit the fellow citizen of the one who obtains such exclusive concessions." Access to submarine cables granted to aspiring transnational enterprises (especially banks and news agencies), to diplomats and to military departments an ever-widening theater of operation, therefore, but at an exorbitant price. Rather than moving boldly to help form an independent US submarine cable industry, Western Union opportunistically annexed itself to the global system that was dominated by imperialist Britain. We will see that the result was very different when, four decades later, Western Union attempted this again.[62]

Meanwhile, during the 1870s and 1880s, Western Union's relations with its most important single customer—the Associated Press news agency—raised additional anger against it. Here, the impacts reached beyond news reports, as the combined interests of telegraph company and news agency became engraved in the nation's politics and public-opinion formation.

Cooperation between six leading New York City newspapers in procuring Mexican War news in 1846 created an incubus for a more permanent telegraphic news distribution service for diffusing information more swiftly to the country's press. A cooperative effort to cheapen the gathering and transmitting of timely dispatches by sharing the costs among its members, the Associated Press at once also betrayed an exclusionary impulse. Symptomatically, the cooperative rejected "desperate attempts" by one journal—the New York *True Sun*—to be accepted as a member. The *True Sun* had originated as a strike newspaper; its treatment at the hands of the AP foreshadowed the news agency's enduring ideological antagonism to organized labor. The *True Sun* was compelled to pay five dollars for the same quantity of news that cost the agency's New York associates forty cents. This was why the *True Sun* dubbed the news agency the "associated press of this city"—an antimonopoly epithet. Prefiguring Western Union itself, the Associated Press was in fact "the first private-sector monopoly to operate on a national scale in the United States."[63]

To preempt would-be competitors, the AP proceeded to forge exclusive agreements with Western Union for the transmission of telegraphic news. This was congenial to Western Union. The telegraph giant would later enter the market for distributing stock and commodity quotations itself but, overall, it abided by its agreements because the AP, the largest single user of telegraph service, was a customer that Western Union could ill afford to lose. For its own part, the AP, headquartered in New York City, furnished to members nationwide "a consolidated report, steadily increasing in scope." A Chicago Associated Press franchise in 1879 was valued at $100,000; the worth of such a franchise sometimes exceeded the assets of the newspaper that enjoyed it.[64]

The exclusive link between Western Union and the AP became much-reviled for accommodating practices of news management. Newspapers sympathetic to labor unions for example, might experience a threat of withdrawal of their AP franchise and its transfer to a local competitor. Franchisees likewise might experience repercussions if they spoke out against the Associated Press itself, or if they assailed one of the Republican politicians favored by the news agency's executives. The ramifications of the AP–Western Union alliance could factor directly into electoral politics, for example, when mass meetings by Democrats targeting voting fraud in the Midwest went unreported. The AP, it was alleged, colluded with Western Union to hold back election returns during the 1884 presidential contest, a charge that proved incendiary enough to bring thousands of protestors into the streets of New York City (though this charge was probably fallacious, it was accepted as fact for decades to come). In the run-up to the election of 1876, a contest whose outcome was to curtail Reconstruction and to enable Jim Crow laws and racist terrorism to flourish in the states of the old Confederacy, ushering in an era of white supremacy that would persist for the next three-quarters of a century, the AP's role in managing the flow of election information and promoting its insidious result has been documented.[65]

Reviled above all was that the corporate telegraph was systematically discriminatory. Two categories of discrimination need to be distinguished. First, like the railroads, the telegraph monopoly did not hesitate to charge different rates to different users and on different routes. Businesses that paid to gain timely access to the network could compete more formidably on the basis of better information. Between 1880 and 1900, symptomatically, nearly all stockbrokers came to lease from Western Union both private circuits and printing telegraphs, called tickers. A different competitive advantage arose around the single-track railroads that were prevalent throughout the later nineteenth century: here, integrating telegraph service could substitute for the much greater investment of capital that was required to lay a second track. Again, using the telegraph could help enable once-local industries to expand their market territory, as in fresh produce and meat-packing. Specific units of capital therefore benefited by enhancing their communications; put differently, telegraph-related market development engendered highly unequal gains.[66]

However, the benefits derived from access to the telegraph not only favored some individual economic agents over others but, simultaneously, contributed to the remaking of social relations overall. This went beyond the fact that farmers were pinched, as railroads and telegraphs overcame barriers to the flow of goods and people so that what economists called intermarket commodity price differentials for commodities such as wheat and flour diminished. For telegraph service discriminated wholesale against the laboring class. In some capitalist countries, the telegraph was being assimilated into national postal systems and was offering "a vital social link joining families and friends in joy and disaster . . . . [and] transferring knowledge, instructions, and human feelings from city, country, suburbs, capital cities, and back again." In the United States, by contrast, such "social uses" of telegraphy were retarded and suppressed by exclusionary rates. Du Boff credits no less than 90 percent of early US telegraph demand to business and press interests; and, throughout the century, business telegrams constituted a similar proportion of the world's undersea cable traffic. Despite declines throughout postbellum years, rates remained prohibitive for workers and family farmers, let alone sharecroppers and renters. Looking back on his childhood at the turn of the century, the writer Gene Fowler related how "A telegram was a great event in anyone's life, and a fearful one as well. No one other than capitalists . . . ever sent or received telegrams unless there was illness or death in a family." The telegraph, in short, was and remained a discriminatory service catering for the business class.[67]

It was simultaneously a material party to the advantages that were pyramiding around capital, as institutionalized inequality in access to telegraphy became a facet of a more enveloping reconstruction of the political economy. Even by 1870, less than one-tenth of the country's economically active population "can be listed as non-agricultural employers, corporate officials, and self-employed producers or professionals." When agricultural occupations are added, then employers together with the self-employed accounted for an estimated one-third of the total. For the first time in US history, wage workers—formerly, chattel slaves in the South and, elsewhere, independent commodity producers of different kinds—comprised the largest group; and the wage relation not only widened its hold but also became increasingly a permanent experience. A statistical report from Massachusetts, where manufacturing had developed precociously, underlined that wage labor was becoming "universal, 'a system more widely diffused than any form of religion, or of government, or indeed, of any language.'" While freedpeople and farmers and local crafts workers transformed into participants in a wage-earning working class, those who commanded the great new enterprises reciprocally reconstituted themselves as a New York City-based national capitalist class. A synthesis of recent scholarship explains that "the Civil War that seemed to ensure the triumph of a free-labor society—of small individual producers bound together by contract freedom—was really a rather large step in the demise of that society." A social chasm was cutting through the United States.[68]

This fissure was emblematized by corporate telegraphy. Its beneficiaries—first and foremost, railroads', banks', and Western Union's own executives and investors—were the much-hated adversaries of those who lacked access to the telegraph. Those who labored to produce telegraph service in particular faced wage declines and worsening working conditions. "Critics of the great monopoly frequently charged that to maintain dividends on watered stock it made up the difference by cutting employees' wages and overcharging the public," writes Gabler, who explains that "[s]hady corporate practices may well have been conducted at the operators' expense in the form of speedups and pay reductions." Western Union's maltreatment of employees provoked bitter and unsuccessful strikes in 1870 and, notably, in 1883; the strikes' failure added to a perception that the corporate telegraph was a primary agent of an encompassing and malevolent disequilibration.[69]

Many workers and radicals understood this takeover of the US political economy by nationwide ("foreign") corporations as an expression of class injustice. Yet, however much they rebelled at the wage relation (the foremost labor union of the 1880s, the Knights of Labor, expressly hoped to eliminate it), they apprehended the circumstances they faced overwhelmingly through a conception of monopoly. In this formulation, the great nodes of reorganization—railroads, banks, and telegraphs—became the foremost targets of antimonopoly reform movements. Antimonopolism in turn functioned both as a strong political current—"the most significant political movement of the Gilded Age," states Richard White—and "a language of resistance to the growing concentration of economic and political power." Drawn upon by both Democrats and Republicans, by some merchants and—above all—by farmers and labor activists, it was a composite. Antimonopolism faced off against the triumphant political-economic liberalism that dominated the era, insisting that a different direction, a different future, was urgent. Workers adopted antimonopolism to their own purposes, above all in the great social upheaval around the railroads in 1877 and the eight-hour day protests of 1886; because workers targeted "wage slavery" for elimination, the line between antimonopolism and anticapitalism could be thin. However, antimonopolism neither originated in nor militated toward a politics of social class, and this accounted for much of its appeal. This is not to suggest that antimonopolism made room for everyone. Though there were Black antimonopolists in the South and desultory interracial initiatives elsewhere, overall, antimonopolism was saturated with racism: in the North as in the South it often targeted African Americans while, moving eastward from California and Denver, antimonopolism likewise carried a vicious anti-Chinese racism.[70]

Within this complex discourse the corporate telegraph appeared as a "uniquely dangerous" emergent feature, threatening both political democracy and economic opportunity. Western Union seemed an all-powerful predator, able to bring down any prey that came in its sights. Indeed, during the later decades of the nineteenth century, Western Union's corporate telegraph crystalized into a widely shared negative reference model for thinking about telecommunications. Recent historians have established that previously ignored federal legislation—the Telegraph Act of 1866—acted as a brake on Western Union's owners' and managers' freedom of action. This law, however, was not sufficient to check, let alone to reverse, the destabilizing shifts to which Western Union itself was a party. A reconstructed liberalism, ascendant but not yet dominant, did not inhibit a wide spectrum of Americans from perceiving the corporate telegraph as a scourge. Western Union's rates barred ordinary people from using it for social purposes, while even those businesses that were advantaged by it complained that its rates were arbitrary and its service inadequate. Its tactics and structure inflicted harm upon the polity, subverting both independent journalism and independent producers: its labor and employment policies were infamous, its financial practices tainted. Millions of Americans demanded that corporate domination of the telegraph be redressed.[71]

Radical Thinking about Postalization

Despite its manifest flaws, the government Post Office offered a strong positive contrast with the corporate telegraph. Alarmed and angered, reformers looked to the Post Office—to the principles that had enabled the nation's unrivaled postal network to expand service and lower rates—as a guarantor of a brightening future.

Antimonopolists could identify and take heart from the Department's recently more-impressive record. US letter rates had been reduced in 1845 and again in 1851; the postal network thus became more accessible to those of modest means. A letter that had cost a minimum of six cents, prepaid, to mail in 1845 (a much greater sum if it traveled more than a few hundred miles), cost a standard three cents a decade later, and two cents by 1885; penny postcards were initiated in 1872 and began at once to circulate in the tens of millions. As well, a work force of thirty thousand-odd paid postal officials in 1861 swelled to 136,192 by 1901, and 70,000 additional staff members had joined the force by 1910. Over this half-century, the number of Post Offices more than doubled, to 76,945, an all-time high. The network had grown tremendously as the imperial republic had been filled in.[72]

Perhaps most impressive, the agency became increasingly infused with ideals of efficiency and technological progress after it introduced a trial railway mail during the Civil War (1864), and a permanent Railway Mail Service soon after (1869). This crucial development introduced mobile mail sorting by highly skilled clerks aboard special-purpose (and perilous) cars, and rapidly increased the Department's reliance on railroads: the percentage of postal mileage traveled by railroad shot up from one-tenth to one-half during the decade from 1860 to 1870. The Railway Mail not only brought the Department directly and permanently into overseeing mail transport—"the role of private firms in the postal system would decline inexorably"—but also established direct linkages between officials based in Washington and tens of thousands of rural postmasters; by 1890 this burgeoning of administrative coordination allowed the Postmaster General to term the railway mail "the spinal column of the service." At this time the Post Office, with 95,000 employees, remained by far the largest branch of the federal government—more than twice the size of the armed forces.[73]

Nor did all this exhaust the Department's record of achievement. Citywide home mail delivery, previously a province of letter express companies, was implemented by the Post Office in 1863; farmers thereupon protested against this inequality of provision and began to press for legislation to establish rural free delivery (RFD). RFD was introduced first (in 1887) as an experiment, for towns of at least 10,000; in 1896 the experiment was broadened to permit delivery to isolated farms and cottages. Thereafter RFD was institutionalized. Between 1902 and 1905, the number of rural postal routes increased fourfold, from 8,298 to over 32,000; the zenith came in 1926, when there were 45,315 rural mail routes. Early in the twentieth century, a capillary network was functioning throughout rural America, bringing postal access to big-city dwellers and remote farmsteads alike. The mails now enabled nearly universal communicative exchanges.[74]

It bears emphasis that this was a general-purpose network on which *all* postal users perforce relied; doubtless more than any other existing organization, the Post Office encompassed disparate uses and users. Subsidized rates and special services for business users were facets of this. If, however, around 1890 mail pickups in New York City's financial and business district occurred every ten minutes, then this preferential treatment did not curtail a mounting general enthusiasm for postal service. Although problems persisted—during the 1880s several companies took out insurance policies against lost mail—penny postcards, Railway Mail, and free home delivery in the cities rendered postaldom increasingly popular. Early in the twentieth century, as organizational reforms and the Railway Mail diminished the department's consistent yearly deficit (it ran a surplus in 1911 for the first time since 1883), the Post Office possessed an overarching public reputation for efficiency.[75]

Both business and political elites continued to find reason for embracing the agency's mission. The Mail Classification Act of 1879, for instance, refined the category of second-class postage with the intent of separating informative periodicals, which Congress judged meriting of preferential subsidy, from advertising matter—which now would fall into a less-favored new category of third-class mail. The low second-class rates, not surprisingly, "tantalized publishers and advertisers looking for a way to reach the reader-consumer," so that soon they began to flood the country with the national magazines that became beacons of urban mass culture. The commodities advertised in these often colorful journals followed close behind: reforms of 1896 and 1912 brought direct access to farmsteads via the postal network for merchandise sold by mail order businesses such as Sears, Roebuck, and Montgomery Ward (itself a byproduct of the Granger movement). The drive to enlarge the capitalist political economy to continental proportions, and to circulate capital efficiently throughout this vast territory, meant that many business leaders threw support to postal expansion and improvement.[76]

Adding new functions to the Post Office also conformed to international "best practice." During the late nineteenth and early twentieth centuries, major European trading partners of the United States utilized their state powers to create multifaceted Post Office administrations, with responsibility for both posts and telegraphs. France declared its far-flung optical telegraphs a government monopoly in 1837, before electrical telegraphic systems had even been invented—giving rise to Stendhal's novelistic depiction of this telegraph as a workhorse of corrupt political operatives. Britain, having instituted a penny post for inland service in 1839, authorized a government takeover of its domestic telegraph industry in 1868. Following Italy, which consolidated posts and telegraphs during its national unification in 1870, the just-established German state also brought the telegraph into its Post Office in 1876. Nor did the telegraph supply the sole example of extended agency responsibilities. Both parcel posts and postal savings banks were designed by Maejima Hisoka, during the first years of Japan's Meiji Restoration (1868), so that "state and postal modernization occurred more or less simultaneously, thus enabling the postal network to assume a wide range of tasks relating to state expansion and consolidation." A General Postal Union (renamed the Universal Postal Union four years later) was established in Bern in 1874, by treaty among twenty-two cooperating states, to harmonize efficient mail exchanges across political jurisdictions between their postal administrations.[77]

This state-centered development of national Post Offices, however, was not a reflex of a globally shared antimonopolism. The large number of continental European states, and the recurring threat of land war that they faced throughout the nineteenth century, made unification of wire telegraphy under centralized governmental command a pressing consideration for elites. Long-standing traditions of centralized state administration, notably but not only in France, encouraged government ownership as a compromise in the aggravated commercial contest that set press and telegraph interests against each other in a battle for control over a lucrative and politically sensitive commodity—news. A postal telegraph also might enable political adjustments to the terms of trade between the government supplier and business users, who often welcomed this reform. Although international networks remained preponderantly in private hands throughout the nineteenth century, both imperialist administration of colonies and international rivalries encouraged intimate ties between state and capital in telecommunications. Meiji Japan used its growing Post Office network to negotiate withdrawal, in 1879, of the British post offices that had been compromising its state sovereignty in Japanese treaty ports; this lesson learned, Japan went on to integrate its own postal service into its imperial conquests of Taiwan, Korea, and north China.[78]

Yet another propellant of state control sometimes came from elites' attempts to combat rebellious working classes. One legislator argued, in the context of the French government's declaration of a monopoly over telegraphy in the 1830s: "Governments have always kept to themselves the exclusive use of things which, if fallen into bad hands, could threaten public and private safety: poisons and explosives are given out only under state authority, and certainly the telegraph, in bad hands, could become the most dangerous weapon. Just imagine what could have happened if the passing success of the Lyon silk workers' insurrection had been known in all corners of the nation at once."[79]

A comparable complexity was present in the United States which, early in the 1880s, saw a burst of opposition to the privately owned component of the US telecommunications complex. This industrial segment was very large and complex, and about to experience tremendous additional growth. It included not just the telegraph and the long-distance express companies which, leaving letter correspondence to the Post Office, specialized in the conveyance of parcels, money, and light freight. Also privately owned were international submarine cable companies, whose investors often remained behind opaque screens of ownership and which were of critical importance to big business users venturing into foreign markets. Last but far from least were the fledgling local telephone systems, licensed by the Bell patent interest beginning in the late 1870s, soon to transform the greater industry.

With—and against—the government Post Office, these corporate-owned systems constituted a bipolar forcefield. The clash between their competing principles of organization and service—public expansion, represented by the Post Office, versus the restrictive and often corrupt monopolism that pervaded the practices of the express companies, the corporate telegraph, the submarine cable companies and, perhaps, the emerging telephone industry—set the terms of reference for a searing political contest over ownership and control of telecommunications.

Assuredly, the Post Office was no paragon of virtue. As a component of the party system, an agency of the state's ideological power, a repressive employer, and a complicit party to corrupt contracting practices, it shortcomings were on widespread display. An abiding source of partisan spoilsmanship, the Post Office was frequently disparaged: in the 1880s a trade unionist scornfully called it "the province of rum-shop politicians." To boot, fraud and corruption in mail contracting reached such a level that they prompted Congressional investigations during the 1860s and, a decade later, a court trial with a flood of newspaper publicity. Its use as an ideological weapon had been forcefully demonstrated against Abolitionists in the long run-up to the Civil War; it was freshly evidenced in Congress's passage, "at the urging of cultural-purifier Anthony Comstock," of an 1873 Act that granted the Post Office Department (and Comstock himself) "near-absolute power to regulate material sent through the mails." Singling out vice and "obscenity" but leaving their meaning conveniently vague—it could encompass everything from birth control to blasphemy—the Comstock Act created an elastic category with which postmasters could "shape the practical and imaginative universe of Americans." The Post Office, as Daniel Carpenter argues, thus became "perhaps the central player" in the period's "moral reform" movement, through which the campaigners mobilized the machinery of the state to effect class- and gender-coded attacks on practices and people they deemed offensive. The institution also participated in Jim Crow segregation, by deploying a "colored window" for service to Blacks and, in the West, to Chinese patrons. Through the 1930s, postmasters sometimes abused their authority to fend off the infections of trade unionism and political radicalism, including among postal workers. Collective self-organization grew among clerks and letter carriers nevertheless, and, around the turn of the twentieth century postal managers responded with a campaign of ideological and political repression.[80]

Despite all this, by comparison to the damages engendered by the corporate telegraph the postal model indisputably retained growing allure. Why? The attraction held by the Post Office for antimonopoly movements may seem especially bewildering today, when the Post Office may be viewed as necessary but, also, as inefficient and technically backward ("snail mail")—even as a site of irrationality ("going postal" connoting acts of senseless violence). Working back to the actuality of the late nineteenth century thus requires that we pierce a screen of anachronism. It also necessitates that we move beyond the anodyne orthodoxy of postal uplift, already beginning to be codified in 1885 by, among others, Postmaster General William F. Vilas: "It is obvious that the postal service is of a general public value, of vast importance, quite distinct from that value which is only the combined sum of its usefulness to particular persons whose errands it performs. The chief feature of this general kind is the common good which arises from the dissemination of intelligence, the spread of intercourse, and the increase of facilities for procuring the small things which bestow the comforts of life, resulting in the diffusion of a greater happiness among all the people." Contemporary officials and elite figures and officials were quick to exalt communication as an abstract conceit. Drawn from a poem by Harvard University President Charles W. Eliot, the agency's motto—"enlarger of the common life"—would be carved into the granite face of the Washington, DC Post Office at the instruction of US President Woodrow Wilson. Striving to implant an ameliorative program adhering to an "ideal of classless social harmony," middle-class reformers cast the Post Office as a vehicle for universalizing the benefits of communication by wrenching away rhetorically from the riven and politically fractious United States that actually existed.[81]

Social division and political conflict, however, were not so easily papered over. Dissenters and critics were many, and they cherished great hopes for the state's largest department in providing a multifaceted public service. Postaldom played host to radical visions, and seemed to many contemporaries to offer a workaday basis for regeneration. Once more, neither the institution's enlistment as a tool in partisan political infighting nor its complicity in fraudulent contracting practices nor the repressive practices of some local postmasters and federal postal officials condemned it from playing this role.

Utopian projectors had taken the Post Office for a touchstone from its inception in seventeenth-century England: the institution had flashed through the radical imagination during the 1640s, for example, in the Digger-revolutionary Gerrard Winstanley's program for common provision of education and invention. Through its immeasurably more farflung, inclusive, and technologically advanced network, by the late nineteenth and early twentieth century the US

Post Office not only enabled movements for regenerating the political economy to circulate news and opinion, but also supplied their theorists with a practical foundation. Postal extensions and enhancements, despite catering for business users, were not enjoyed solely by capital.[82]

Throughout the late nineteenth century, the same second-class mail privileges that opened fresh the national market to magazine publishers and national advertisers also granted opportunities to important antimonopoly groups. The publications of the Populists—journals which, among other things, campaigned for a nondiscriminatory and accessible system of intercommunication by telegraph—thus circulated freely across much of rural America. The Paiute Indian Wovoka's message—that white settlers would vanish from the West if his followers (who came from several nations) practiced the Ghost Dance—was spread in part through the use of the mails. Broadening the institutional reach of the general-purpose Post Office in turn elicited widespread and disparately rooted political support. The Knights of Labor and then the Farmers' Alliance demanded to curtail the corporate telegraph via postalization. Nearing their height of influence, in their Omaha platform of 1892 the Populists declared that "the powers of government—in other words, of the people—should be expanded (as in the case of the postal service) as rapidly and as far as the good sense of an intelligent people and the teachings of experience shall justify, to the end that oppression, injustice, and poverty shall eventually cease in the land." Historian Sheldon Stromquist writes that "members of the producing classes" thus "began to conceive of a state that might acquire and operate railroads, telephones and telegraphs, coal mines, and even manufacturing monopolies, or that might construct and finance a vast network of cooperative warehouses and granaries." Perhaps the foremost trade unionist and socialist of the turn of the century era, Eugene V. Debs, was unequivocal that "Some monopolies must be taken over by the people. . . . What is true of the telegraph is true of the telephone. It is true of railroads. The people should own them, or they will own the government."[83]

Many—not least, many postal workers—understood that the Post Office itself required internal democratization. This included, but spanned beyond, a painfully slow embrace of civil service reform. Passed into law in 1883 following years of effort, the Pendleton Act purported to supplant spoilsmanship with merit-based appointments and prohibitions on political contributions by office holders. However, its scope of operation was limited and successive administrations found ways to evade it—particularly in the all-important postal patronage machine. Writing privately to the Democratic Grover Cleveland administration two years after civil service reforms had been legislated, former party leader Samuel Tilden underlined that "the importance of the little postmasters is very great. In many of the purely rural districts, there is one to every hundred voters. They are centres of political activity. They act as agents and canvassers for the newspapers of their party, and as local organizers." In 1890, by one estimate, between one-third and three-quarters of each Congressman's time was consumed by the need to make postmaster recommendations. Though early twentieth century reforms meant that the lion's share of federal employees, including postal employees, fell under civil service classification by 1913, the Post Office's importance for party patronage did not fully drop away until the New Deal.[84]

Nevertheless, writers and intellectuals whose affinities lay with oppositional movements still often placed the Post Office in the center of their reform schemes. Writing in 1884, the Danish émigré and state socialist Laurence Gronlund averred that the department was "already essentially a Socialist institution." Still, he insisted, two additional changes were needed "to make it so fully"—and in this view, Gronlund was representative of many contemporary radicals who sought to restructure the state. First, Gronlund underlined, the agency's salary schedules required far-reaching revision; "In the Cooperative Commonwealth, the Postmaster General will not receive $10,000 while letter carriers must be satisfied with $800." Second, appointments to jobs within the Post Office "will be made from below": "the letter-carriers will elect their immediate superiors; these, we will say, the postmasters and these in turn the Postmaster General." Presaging a subsequent syndicalism, these proposals were often drawn into working-class arguments for postal reform for the next thirty-five years.[85]

Gronlund's book sold 100,000 copies in the United States, and offered a vision of postal reorganization that was congruent with those who, after the Civil War, came to believe that US society had divided into warring classes of producers and parasites. Other political reformers promulgated overlapping rationales. Edward Bellamy, whose writing galvanized a substantial movement during the early 1890s, cast the Post Office unqualifiedly—shorn of Gronlund's radical proposals—simply as "the prototype" of a variant of state socialism that he called "Nationalism." The program elaborated by Henry George, a printer and journalist who possessed first-hand knowledge of the abuses perpetrated by the Associated Press and Western Union, agitated continually for a government takeover of the telegraph. He became the country's leading antimonopolist after publication in 1879 of his bestselling book, *Progress and Poverty*—which sold a reputed two million copies over the next quarter-century. His labor-union backed campaign for the mayoralty of New York failed in 1886, but only because terrified capitalists and Tammany politicians took extreme measures to prevent his victory: George's memorial in 1897 was attended by 100,000 New Yorkers. Gronlund, meanwhile, sought to "clinch" an argument for enlarging postal functions in the United States by asking, in 1884: "suppose a proposition was submitted to the people to relegate our mail-service back to private corporations, can any sane man doubt, that it would be overwhelmingly defeated?" This comparison remained potent into the 1910s, the more so as the Post Office added RFD and other amenities and service extensions.[86]

Bellamy, George and Gronlund staked out positions that placed them within a more multifarious and far-reaching radical discourse. As historian Daniel Rogers has influentially argued, many reform proposals circulated across the Atlantic Ocean and washed up on US shores. In strategizing about how the working class might conquer political power, European socialists found frequent occasion to consider the post office. In the *Communist Manifesto*, first published in 1848, Marx and Engels had proposed "Centralisation of the means of communication and transport in the hands of the State" as a "pretty generally applicable" goal "in most advanced countries." Through subsequent decades, radicals of varied stripes tried continually to clarify how working-class movements and coalitions should engage and transform the state. Fissures opened as anarchists and syndicalists, evolutionary socialists, Fabians, and Marxist social democrats debated. Should the working class aim to abolish the state, or to bulk up its functions?[87]

In England, the journalist and ethical socialist campaigner Robert Blatchford asserted that economic competition between firms resulted not in the most effective production and distribution "but in the effort to undersell and overreach with each other." Blatchford thus placed his faith instead in "cooperation." "And fortunately," he declared in a book that sold a million copies during the 1890s on both sides of the Atlantic Ocean, "we have one actual example of this existing in the postal and telegraphic departments of the State. For it is a fact which no one attempts to deny that the post office manages this branch of the national business a great deal better than it ever was or ever could be managed by a number of small firms in competition with each other." A decade later, Blatchford specified that "Socialism is only a method of extending State management as in the Post Office and Municipal management, until State and Municipal management become universal throughout the kingdom."[88]

Marx distanced his thought from such mild doctrines. Taking note of the defeat of the Paris Commune in 1871, Marx amended his earlier ideas about centralization in the state, declaring that "the working class cannot simply lay hold of the ready-made state machinery, and wield it for its own purposes." Stressing a need for a revolutionary transformation that swept up both state and society, he carried over this formulation in an explicit revision to the 1872 edition of the *Manifesto*. By 1892, after numerous countries had nationalized their telegraph systems, the German Social Democratic politician Karl Kautsky—then one of Marx's leading exponents—specified that, of itself, the growth of the state's economic functions did not guarantee essential changes. "If the modern state nationalizes certain industries," Kautsky specified, it does not do so for the purpose of restricting capitalist exploitation, but for the purpose of protecting the capitalist system and establishing it upon a firmer basis, or for the purpose of itself taking a hand in the exploitation of labor, increasing its own revenues, and thereby reducing the contributions for its own support which it would otherwise have to impose upon the capitalist class.

His conclusion was blunt: "The state has never carried on the nationalizing of industries further than the interests of the ruling classes demanded, nor will it ever go further than that."[89]

For such Marxists as these, postalization was insufficient to restructure the power of the capitalist state. For some, postalization was indeed even caught between incompatible strategic aims. On the eve of World War I, a Social Democratic member of the Belgian government warned against confusing socialism with "statism"—"to see in the progress of statization so many partial victories of collectivism, to imagine that to assure the future of socialism it will suffice to push to their final consequences the development of ... State monopolies." For Marxists, Emile Vandervelde declared in a book written in 1914, socialism and statism actually constituted opposites: the ultimate objective was and should be, after all, "not the omnipotence of the State"—which was fundamental to domination over society by the capitalist class—"but on the contrary its *abolition*." Rather than demanding that public services be provided by the state, therefore, the working-class movement had best "attack[] those which exist and which constitute so many obstacles in the way of proletarian organization and action." "The more industries the bourgeois State concentrates, the more individuals it binds to itself and interests in its preservation."[90]

Even among Marxists, this was an extreme view. More common was the belief that, rather than forming an end in itself, the enlargement of state functions in the post office should be a springpad to a more ambitious transformation. Kautsky, for example, had held that "[t]he economic activity of the modern state is the natural starting point of the development that leads to the Co-Operative Commonwealth." A quarter-of-a-century later, in Russia, Vladimir Lenin picked up this theme, asserting that although "At present the postal service is a business organized on the lines of a state-*capitalist* monopoly. ... the mechanism of social management is here already to hand":

> To organize the *whole* national economy on the lines of the postal service, so that the technicians, foremen, bookkeepers, as well as *all* officials, shall receive salaries no higher than "a workman's wage," all under the control and leadership of the armed proletariat—this is our immediate aim. It is such a state, standing on such an economic foundation, that we need.

Socialism in one department—the Post Office—thus might become the germ of a wider revolutionary reconstruction.[91]

More fully fledged, and perhaps more inviting to some of the many Irish American telephone operators of that day, was a critique of nationalized industry published in 1899 by the Irish socialist James Connolly, who would go on to help lead (and to be executed for his part in) the Irish Rising of 1916. Connolly again categorically distinguished government ownership and operation from "co-operative control by the workers of the machinery of production." Without true workers' control, he insisted, "we would still have in our state industries, as in the Post Office to-day, the same unfair classification of salaries, and the same despotic rule of an irresponsible head. Those who worked most and hardest would still get the least remuneration, and the rank and file would still be deprived of all voice in the ordering of their industry, just the same as in all private enterprises." Connolly alleged that "an immense gulf separates the 'nationalising' proposals of the middle class from the 'socialising' demands of the revolutionary working class. The first proposes to endow a Class State—repository of the political power of the Capitalist Class—with certain powers and functions to be administered in the common interest of the possessing class; the second proposes to subvert the Class State and replace it with the Socialist State, representing organized society—the Socialist Republic. To the cry of the middle class reformers, 'make this or that the property of the government,' we reply, 'yes, in proportion as the workers are ready to make the government their property.'" Connolly's disparagement of proposals for nationalization as "middle class" was too reductive—but his clear-eyed understanding that of itself, nationalization was insufficient to produce social justice was prophetic.[92]

Political Mobilization Breaks Through

One did not need to be a socialist—or a theorist—however, to embrace the US movement for a multifaceted postalization. Inflected by rural agrarians and urban immigrants, as well as middle-class reformers, hopeful and clamorous struggles to extend and generalize the US Post Office model gained ground. Proponents wished to use the Post Office specifically against what one called, in 1898, "[t]he gold ring, the monopolies, and trusts" which had come to "control the avenues and agencies of rapid communication and intelligence." Their goals were constructive as well as defensive: many participants aimed for nothing less than to render citizenship more robust—more fully fledged—in the dramatically changed context of industrial capitalism and permanent wage labor. As Chicago settlement house reformer Jane Addams framed this in 1892, they meant "to make the entire social organism democratic, to extend democracy beyond its political expression." Acting from a diversity of motives, evincing more varied political and conceptual affinities, and exhibiting considerable porousness as they fitfully advanced, political coalitions variously emerged from farm organizations, trade unions, reform-oriented local and national political parties, women's civic and suffrage and community groups, as well as some business leaders and postal officials themselves. They found a common cause around an enlargement of Post Office functions.[93]

Their most significant affinity was to a creed of antimonopoly, which, as Richard White emphasizes, became "the largest and broadest" of the reform themes during the later nineteenth century. A contemporary Anti-Monopoly Party declared in its 1884 platform that "[t]he great instruments by which [interstate] commerce is carried on are transportation, money, and the transmission of intelligence. They are now mercilessly controlled by giant monopolies, to the impoverishment of labor, and the crushing out of healthful competition, and the destruction of business security. We hold it, therefore, to be the imperative and immediate duty of Congress to pass all needful laws for the control and regulation of those great agents of commerce." However, many different reform groups embraced these goals, and helped in actually augmenting postal functions so as to make them impinge on each of these three great "instruments." RFD, parcel post, and postal savings were notable expressions.[94]

Consider first "money," that is, banking. "In post-Civil War politics, finance was at the center of debates over economic change," writes one specialist; and several political parties arose in pursuit of "an agenda of financial reform," specifically, "financial antimonopolism as an alternative to the rise of corporate liberalism." Both to put their savings to work within local communities and to prevent them from flowing away to Wall Street predators, farmers and trade unionists sought, over decades, to eliminate private banks and to replace them with government-owned postal savings banks. Two historians relate that the eventual achievement of a US postal savings system demonstrates

> the influence of peripheral societal forces in shaping the modern state. Agrarian and small-business representatives, not corporate capitalists, kept the idea alive until a capitulating, ambivalent Administration and conservative congressional leadership faced the political music.... Although enactment of the postal savings system in 1910 represented ... a diluted version of the original agrarian vision, it demonstrated that old-line Republicans and capitalists opposed to governmental regulation were fighting a defensive battle against greater state involvement in controlling the vicissitudes of the economy.[95]

Postal savings institutions, declared a contemporary academic analyst in justification, had been introduced by "most of the other great nations of the world."

Many of these proved enduring. England established a national postal savings bank in 1861; by 1946, the largest savings institution in Britain, its branches served 24 million active deposit accounts. Canada authorized postal savings in 1867, Italy and France in 1875, Sweden in 1884, and Russia in 1889. Germany's postal savings system, initiated some years later, became the embryo of an institution that, in 1986, boasted 20.9 million accounts in a country of 61 million. Japan's postal savings system dates to 1875; used by 83 percent of households by 1997, it then held $2.44 trillion in deposits, helping to make the Japanese Post Office the world's largest financial institution. India, then a British colony, inaugurated a system in 1882 and boasted over a million accounts by 1910; Taiwan opened its system in 1906, but Republican China established postal savings only in 1919 (by 1922 there were 334 offices scattered throughout major cities and serving a small scattering of government employees, teachers, students, merchants, farmers, and postal workers). By the turn of the twentieth century postal savings banks had been established in thirty countries, including both formidable industrial nations and colonized territories.[96]

The US Post Office established a money order service in 1864, which proved popular at once, above all for Union Army soldiers looking to send their wages back to their families safely and cheaply. This postal money order system was and remained limited—only available at post offices that generated sufficient revenue to make it self-sustaining or profitable. It transmitted small sums, at first less than fifty dollars. It allowed patrons to send money to other people; and, increasingly, to companies selling commodities into the hinterlands. Scarcely three decades after it had been established, as Cameron Blevins explains, "a system that had originated as a personal remittance service for Union soldiers had increasingly turned into a channel for commercial transactions." It had proved a smashing success—23 million postal money orders passed through the US mail in 1895, worth $169 million—and it had been dramatically enlarged in 1892, as a part of Postmaster General John Wanamaker's modernization program. Why not move beyond this?[97]

"For fifty years before its establishment," Representative Clyde Kelly recognized in 1931, "there was a wide-spread public demand for a postal savings bank." Beginning in 1873, as postal money orders had already proven their popularity, dozens of bills proposing such a system were entertained by Congress. Eight Postmasters General and four presidents supported postal savings. The very idea of direct contact between a government financial institution and individual savers predictably "enraged the banking community," however, and eastern bankers continually staved off this incursion. They charged that postal savings would fall prey to partisan political pressures; but the overriding self-interest of bank adversaries became plain when they conceded that postal savings would instantly acquire great popularity, a consequence of their "undue advantage" over private institutions "because of the great confidence in the Government held by working people." "[T]he democratic atmosphere which pervades most Post Offices," added an academic analyst in 1917, stood in marked contrast with "the aristocratic one that pervades most banks."[98]

By dramatically undermining public confidence in the private banking system, the "panic," or recession, of 1907 and the financial scandals that were publicized throughout the same period brought the controversy to a head. Within two years, deposit guaranty laws had been passed in some old strongholds of Western Populism: Oklahoma, Kansas, Nebraska, South Dakota, and Texas. Responding to this pressure, while asserting that "habits of thrift" should be more widely inculcated among those citizens possessed of modest means, the major parties agreed that some kind of postal savings be established. The question then became what kind of a postal savings system would be created—and prodded by President Taft, in 1910 a divided Congress passed a conservative bill. The measure arranged for strict limitations on deposits, withdrawals, and interest rates paid, so as to circumvent criticism that the new system would compete directly with private banks. Indeed, at a time when the United States tended toward higher interest rates than most European nations, the postal savings rate mandated by Congress—2 percent—was the lowest in the world (Japan paid 4.2 percent; Austria 3 percent; even Britain paid 2.5 percent). Far from coincidentally, in addition, the legislation permitted an overwhelming proportion (upwards of 90 percent) of postal savings deposits, "hoards" which hitherto had escaped the machinery of the banking system, to be funneled to "qualified" private-sector financial institutions. Many banks, not all of them local, perversely acquired an additional source of cheap funds.[99]

Nonetheless, postal savings trespassed "upon the previously hallowed ground of private enterprise." Building on the department's now-ingrained capacity to process money orders, the postal savings system that was launched early in 1911 could be accessed at 12,151 Post Offices by the end of 1913. Over the next few years, this number was cut by about a third by Postmaster Albert Burleson, of whom we shall hear more in the next chapter. By 1916, though, the system was yielding the government a tidy profit. Postal savings accounts speedily gathered nearly half a million depositors, the majority of whom were immigrants including, especially, recent arrivals from Russia and Italy who had been familiar with postal savings in their countries of origin. Comparatively heavy use of the new system was made by immigrant communities in small mining and industrial towns in the far west, and by new residents of New York City. A Cleveland banker fumed at the prospect of postal savings, inveighing that "what we need . . . is to Americanize our immigrants, not to Italianize our Post-Office Department." During the 1920s a few trade unions (mostly in the railway and clothing industries) introduced labor banking programs under their own auspices, but these did not survive the Great Depression. By contrast, postal savings banks attained an unexpected importance after the 1929 crash—when, in preference to depositing money in one of the scores of failing private banks, millions turned to accounts which offered a guarantee of full indemnity against loss, and whose unvarying interest rate of 2 percent, in a condition of protracted economic slump, seemed suddenly inviting. Usage of the Post Savings System reached its peak in 1947, when over 4 million depositors had accounts totaling $3.4 billion; the System was discontinued, after a protracted decline, in 1966—at the threshold of financial deregulation.[100]

Postal savings built institutional momentum, and this powered fresh efforts to augment postal functions. A second key reform pertained to transportation. Carrying everything from gold to fresh oysters, big express companies moved their trade more than twice as fast as regular railroad freight, and enjoyed a lucrative business carrying perishables from farm to city markets. By the early twentieth century, six express companies—Adams, American, Pacific, United States, Wells, Fargo & Co., and Southern—were tightly interlocked with the giant railroad systems and controlled 93 percent of the traffic in parcels weighing over four pounds (the weight limit on mail carried by the Post Office). Their powerful "monopoly" earned them what a historian terms "almost universal hatred." Express companies were scored for refusing to serve unprofitable rural areas, for furnishing a mediocre service that required visits to inconvenient depots to pick-up orders—in shabby contrast with the Post Office's home delivery—and for charging exhorbitant rates which bore "no relation to the economic rules of transportation, such as mileage, amount or kind of traffic, frequency of traffic, volume, care required, hazard, or any other known element or combination of elements." Maryland Democratic Congressman David J. Lewis, who led the legislative movement for a parcel post, disparaged the private express companies as "economic parasites . . . squatters on the postal function."[101]

The establishment of RFD became a key stepping-stone: Why should not rural households also use the postal network to send and to receive packages as well as correspondence and catalogs? Demands for RFD had surfaced as far back as the 1870s, after the Post Office began to experiment with residential mail delivery in large cities in 1863. By 1890 about 450 cities were enjoying door-to-door deliveries by letters carriers. A movement of farmers called the Order of the Patrons of Husbandry—the National Grange, with strongholds in the Middle West and the West—folded RFD into its program. During the late 1880s and early 1890s, a more explicitly political agrarian movement, the Populists—turned it into a high-profile campaign issue. An 1892 report from the House Committee on the Post Office and Post Roads recognized this by observing that "rural free delivery will aid materially in stopping much of the growing discontent that now seems to exist among the farming population."[102]

However, as Blevins argues, the doubling of railway mileage between 1880 and 1900; Congress's 1884 transfer of administrative authority over the country's mail routes from the legislative branch to the Post Office; and the emphatic support for RFD and other modernizations offered by Postmaster General John Wanamaker also must be factored into the new initiative. Cultivating agrarian support, Wanamaker instituted a small-scale experimental program in 1891–1892; this was expanded in 1896 under Postmaster General William L. Wilson. In a call-and-response pattern, a newly appointed superintendent of RFD, August Machen, publicly requested that groups of farmers who hoped to gain such service should petition Congress. They did so by the thousands. This "deluge of agrarian sentiment," Carpenter explains, "was orchestrated by the bureaucracy" of the Post Office Department. In 1899, when it seemed that the Senate might curtail its experimental appropriation of funds for the program, the officers of the National Grange raised a petition of 75,000 names in opposition. Farmers also involved themselves directly in the actualization of RFD, planning their own routes, drawing sketches of them, and plotting them on maps for postal officers—though routes were finally determined by postal officials. These successful tactics engendered formal Congressional approval in 1902. By 1910, there existed more than 40,000 RFD routes connecting households across much of the nation's countryside. We must qualify somewhat Carpenter's conclusion: that RFD "was no mere extension but an overhaul of the entire national delivery network," in that it allowed the Post Office to institute centralized control over its far-flung operations, at the expense of star route carriers and, especially, of fourth-class rural postmasters and post offices, whose numbers declined by 20,000 and 17,000, respectively, between 1900 and 1913. This is because, as Blevins shows, before 1904 a mere 3 percent of the 24,556 RFD routes then in existence were operating west of the Kansas/Colorado border. It would take additional years for RFD to help make the Post Office Department "an integrated projection of the American state."[103]

In the meantime, private express companies, wholesalers, and small-town merchants anxious about new competitors vociferously objected to yet a further extension, a parcel post; farmers, however, drew support from mass retailers and catalog sellers such as Montgomery Ward and Sears, Roebuck, and from political reformers like Maryland Congressman David Lewis, a former miner who would emerge as a leader of the concurrent attempt to nationalize telephones and telegraphs (of which more below). Joining the Grange in the struggle for a parcel post were some less-obvious adherents, including the National American Woman's Suffrage Association, the Equal Suffrage Association of the District of Columbia, and the Pennsylvania Federation of Labor. Congressional backers asserted that a parcel post would help to abolish the economic disequilibrium that they identified between farm and city and between production and consumption. By eliminating parasitic middlemen whose ability to set monopoly prices resulted in a vast inflation of the cost of living, a parcel post would putatively restore a nationwide economic balance. The rhetoric may have been overblown but, in 1912, the struggle for a parcel post succeeded: "The parcels post system," a later writer crowed, "is the greatest extension of postal facilities to be found in postal history." This claim was not overblown: Historian Richard Kielbowicz explains that parcel post "marked a dramatic departure in public-sector initiatives: it put the federal government in the transportation business to compete with well-established private firms." Although eschewing more radical proposals to nationalize the delivery of packages by invoking its constitutional postal power, the "phenomenal success" achieved by the government parcel post dealt an immediate blow to the highly profitable express companies. The volume of packages conveyed by the Post Office rocketed up—within two years it was projected at 100 million each month—producing the first postal surplus in decades, while Sears, Roebuck "nearly collapsed" under a five-fold increase in mail orders in 1913 alone. Subsequently, press reviews listed "the inauguration of the parcel post as the top story of that year of political change."[104]

The establishment of a US parcel post, as Leonard Laborie shows, "did not just emerge from domestic factors. . . . Internal demand and pressure arose simultaneously with or even after international pressure to exchange parcel post with countries which had themselves experienced a boom in their parcel post traffic." Germany's domestic system, set on improved foundations in 1873 within the wider context of German national unification, became an influential model, as also was England's, established in 1883. From Argentina to Australia and from China to Egypt, domestic Post Office shipments of packages became a fixture among US trade partners. "One of the most powerful arguments for the adoption of a parcel post in the United States," an analyst declared in 1914, "was the uniformly successful operation of foreign systems." In this period of growing cross-border labor flows and transnational corporate expansion, demand quickly intensified for international package mailings. In 1880, "a cosmopolitan community of postal officers" succeeded in harmonizing low rates and uniform services within the organizational context of the Universal Postal Union, spectacularly easing shipments of packages from one country to another. Although the US did not sign the convention, by the end of the decade this postalized system of international parcel exchange was impinging on its domestic political economy as it did in numerous other countries. Through dozens of bilateral agreements, rather than through formal adherence to the UPU's multilateral convention, a US Post Office foreign parcel service was incrementally introduced. Initially interconnecting with Britain's colonies in the West Indies and some Central American nations, by 1910 the US foreign parcel post had grown to include exchange arrangements with forty foreign nations and colonies. Though not expropriated, the entrenched domestic system that was controlled by private express companies was restructured as a government-owned and operated competitor swiftly took pride of place.[105]

And, finally, a quick peek at electrical telecommunications—"intelligence," as it was called—which will be extensively studied in the next chapter. The corporate telegraph was undoubtedly the foremost object of postal reformers. Historians have noted that Congress considered dozens of bills designed to restructure telegraphy between 1866 and 1900, which began by contemplating a "postal telegraph"—a government chartered and subsidized private competitor to Western Union—and ended by trying to set up a full-fledged national telegraph system owned and operated by the government Post Office. Many remained wary that such a transposition might widen and entrench existing evils, that is, that a government telegraph system would be incorporated into the sprawling networks of patronage and political preferment that were controlled by Post Office administrators. "Why this post office department is so lauded is something I could never understand," declared a trade unionist in 1894, in a discussion of the merits of a government takeover of telegraphs and telephones: "Control by the government is not control by the people and never can be for the government is the natural enemy of the people." His reasoning, which still resonates today, we have already seen led to questions about the aims and organizational practice of the state itself: "We know that to-day in the Post Office, which is held up as a shining light of socialism, we know that no one but a Democrat or a Republican can get a position therein, and to do so we know he has to chase some of the politicians to get there. We know very well that no Populist in the East could obtain a government position, we know very well that any man with radical opinions is shut out of government office. Therefore I am opposed to any legislation which will tend to increase governmental power." Working from such perceptions, some working-class reformers preferred to pursue "democratization" and workers' control in their proposals for telegraph industry reform.[106]

Plans to vest operating control of an independent telegraph system in an appropriate trade union followed from such thinking. "One of my principal objects in joining" the Brotherhood of Telegraphers, recounted H. W. Orr—one of the union's seven-member executive committee during the Brotherhood's 1883 "Great Strike" against Western Union—"was to bring about co-operative telegraphing among the operators themselves." While, Orr conceded, most union members enlisted simply for "protection against their employers," his own ambition was grander: to join in building and operating an independent telegraph system. Telegrapher and trade unionist John C. McClelland favored "a line built by those engaged in the business of telegraphy, without the intervention of any middlemen or third parties . . . the line-men now in the employ of the telegraph companies could construct the line, and the operators and the managers now in the employ of the telegraph companies could operate it."[107]

The experience of two nationwide telegraph strikes, in 1870 and again in 1883, entered into such appraisals. Neither strike had checked corporate power: Western Union had only persisted on its course of wage cuts, longer hours, speedups, and loyalty oaths. Despite hopes that John Mackay's carefully named Postal Telegraph company (in the creation of which union telegraphers played a part, as their 1883 strike began to falter) would catalyze a revival of competition and the more favorable work environment that competition might enable, grinding conditions at Western Union did not abate. Their economic power revealed as insufficient, some telegraphers turned to a political strategy. These working-class reformers were not daunted by the prospect of a Post Office takeover of telegraphy for the practice and theory of American government.[108]

"I do not recognize the necessity of our telegraphic industry . . . being a capital stock concern," declared McClelland, testifying before a Senate committee in mid-August 1883. Abuses perpetrated by the corporate telegraph were familiar in the late 19th-century labor movement, and prompted hundreds of thousands of workers to press for an enlarged state role. "The United States Government should own and work telegraph wires for public use as an adjunct of the postal system," testified Gideon Tucker, a contemporary journalist. Tucker reflected meaningfully on his own political passage: "I began life as a State-rights Democrat, fearing governmental interference and centralization, and especially the Federal Government. But this is as different a world from that into which I was born as though it were another planet." Specifically, he charged,

> There is now no way to protect the people from the monopolies of almost demoniac power which they have created but by and through the action of Government. If you say this is unconstitutional . . . the reply is that constitutions can be amended, and that they must be made to conform from time to time to new popular wants.

A postal preemption of Western Union's operations in turn comprised a key locus of what Frank Parsons, an academic economist of the 1890s, called "the great case" of "The People v. Monopoly."[109]

This postal telegraph movement, historian David Hochfelder agrees, "was a major episode in American politics," and seemingly demonstrated "remarkable continuity over its fifty-year life" between 1865 and World War I. Senators and Representatives, Postmaster Generals, even (quietly) the occasional President, joined academics, labor leaders and "a host of other eminent men in every walk of life" in championing postal telegraphy as "the cause of the people." Major newspapers, "representing every phase of political opinion"—the *New York Herald, Boston Globe, Philadelphia Times, Chicago Tribune, Albany Express, Washington Gazette, Omaha Bee, Denver Republican, San Francisco Post, New Orleans Times-Democrat*, and a host of other journals, many of which have faded into obscurity—again supported postalization. National magazines, such as the *Arena*, devoted substantial space to the subject, while scholars supplied learned argument and documentation. The telegraph joined the railroad as fuel for controversies in which academic economists played prominent early parts. In 1890, furthermore, the Postmaster General—again, John Wanamaker, a Philadelphia department store magnate—made pointed reference to the support shown for a postal telegraph by major business users of telegraph services. Memorials in favor of a postalized system had been received, he wrote, "without any effort on my own part," from the National Board of Trade, and from some two dozen local boards of trade and chambers of commerce, representing commercial users in, among other places, Baltimore, Boston, Chicago, Cincinnati, Detroit, Indianapolis, Milwaukee, Minneapolis, New York, Philadelphia, and San Francisco. This view of Western Union as a "grasping monopolist" was also shared by many state legislatures and city councils. "That man must be willfully blind who does not see the vast and rising tide of public sentiment against monopoly," declared Wanamaker, in proposing yet another version of a postal telegraph, in his 1890 *Annual Report*.[110]

It is worth underlining that, between the 1890s and the 1910s, postal telegraph proponents could and did cite efficiency concerns. That government enterprise evinced an inherent tendency to *in*efficiency was already an ingrained precept. In 1873, for example, the liberal economist David Wells argued with some cause that the US government's operation of the Post Office was "dilatory, expensive and vexatious"; its "utterly inadequate" discharge of its "business responsibilities," he declared, made it unthinkable that the nation's telegraph system should be placed in Federal hands. However, two decades later, as the commercial contracting scandals that had afflicted the postbellum Post Office receded and the Railway Mail and new services were brought forward, anticorporate reformers could successfully deflect attempts to disparage the agency on efficiency grounds. Indeed, reformers often charged that the costs entailed by operating the telegraph as a freestanding business were needlessly duplicative and wasteful. To put an end to separate plant and facilities for each of the two systems of communication, Parsons asserted that telegraph administration and operations should be folded into the existing Post Office network. The cost-economies he and other reformers hoped to realize in this way were substantial and, they reasoned, these could be distributed to the population at large in the form of lower rates, thereby enlarging access. Such arguments held rising attraction, both for individual consumers and business users.[111]

Apart from a "small but powerful group of politicians and conservatives," Parsons reckoned, active support for the status quo, that is, for Western Union dominance, "has come from a single source—the group of capitalists who claim the exclusive right to send the English language along an electric wire"

> The line of battle is clearly drawn. On the one side the farmers, merchants, mechanics, and working classes—the whole body of the people—with the philosophers, statesmen, philanthropists, and reformers; on the other the Western Union, the politicians, and a few individuals who have not recovered from the soporific doses of the ancient political economy of bestillity, and letaloneativeness injected into their thought in their college days and who are not yet sufficiently awake to know that the days of laissez-faire are done.

As we have seen, some early twentieth century radicals disparaged "Post Office socialism" for being middle-class—insufficiently proletarian; and ameliorative, that is, for offering what one disparaged as "a thin gruel of government-owned industries." A recent historian offers some support for this view, holding that the postal telegraph movement did not succeed because "support for a postal telegraph was broad but not deep." This is true enough, in the sense that the alliance behind postalization was both encompassing and heterogenous: it was not—yet—a working-class led movement. The movement for postal telecommunications was defeated, however, neither because its adherents were middle class nor because they were insufficiently ardent. It was, rather, because the multifarious cross-class alliance that propelled postalization proved unstable and increasingly vulnerable to defections. During the first decades of the twentieth century, antimonopoly began to give way as a doctrine capable of animating broad political mobilization. However, we will see that a push for postalization persisted. As some key participants in the political coalition were peeled away, workers—above all, telecommunications workers—were left to carry the burden of additional reform. They would face relentless opposition from their employer: the US government.[112]

Postal Work

A working day lengthened by unpaid overtime accompanied the Post Office Department's nearly continuous growth. The work-places where postal clerks and letter carriers labored were often foul, the pace of work exhausting, and risk of injury or even death real—most of all for clerks in the antiquated wooden cars operated by the Railway Mail. To this extent, we may say that the consumption of postal communications posed an escalating contradiction with their production, as reformers succeeded in layering additional services onto the far-flung and now-inclusive Post Office infrastructure.

Starry-eyed visions came down to earth quickly for those who experienced the hard realities of Post Office management. Since 1868, eight hours had been the legislated workday for "laborers, workmen and mechanics" employed by the federal government. Though subverted by executive departments and the courts, this apparent early success (an initiative of Radical Republicans) demonstrated that a victory won within the state might be a lever to induce pyramiding change throughout society. By 1886, a mass movement of workers had made the eight-hour day a foremost demand.[113]

When letter carriers petitioned for the eight-hour day during the 1880s, withal, the Post Office rejected their request and ruled that this law did not apply to them. In 1888, pressured by local assemblies of the Knights of Labor organized by letter carriers in New York, Chicago, Omaha, and Buffalo, Congress enacted an eight-hour law for urban letter carriers. The Post Office Department responded by choosing to interpret this statute as denoting a fifty-six-hour week, comprising seven eight-hour days, and continued to impose crushing work-days on letter carriers; postal clerks, meanwhile, remained outside the scope of the law to limit the working day.[114]

Postal workers were subjected to other onerous restrictions. As servants of a republican state, historian Sterling Spero long ago explained, they faced "a peculiar duty of obedience different and distinct from the obligations of ordinary wage-earners to their employers." Post Office employees thus possessed neither a right to strike nor a true mechanism of collective bargaining. The federal government therefore imposed extraordinary measures to restrain and canalize self-organization among its employees. These, thought Samuel Gompers—who led the American Federation of Labor from before it supplanted the Knights of Labor as the preeminent representative of trade unionism, all the way to 1924—meant that the option of government ownership of other utilities should be rejected: workers "were better off dealing with private employers." Gompers was not the last unionist to arrive at this conclusion, however, he expended considerable energy in an attempt to gain collective bargaining rights and improve conditions for postal workers. Solidarity also could be expressed from the bottom up. In what may have been the country's foremost union town in 1900, local buildings trade workers managed to give a lesson in collective bargaining rights to the state's paramount leader. President William McKinley, a historian has documented, "was practically compelled to join the bricklayers' union, as an honorary member, before laying the cornerstone of Chicago's new post office building."[115]

The letter carriers and the postal clerks and railway mail clerks established separate national trade unions, beginning around 1890. The original clerks' organizations fell sufficiently short of independence to be categorized as company unions, however, and the first letters carriers' union proved abidingly conservative. These groups looked instead to Congress, with its statutory authority, to improve pay and working conditions. More assertive independent unions also emerged, however. The most important was the National Federation of Post Office Clerks, which grew nationally after 1900 from its initial base in Chicago; but railway mail clerks also organized an insurgent organization in the first decade of the new century. Highly skilled railway mail clerks faced acute peril. Their workplace—again, a wooden mail car—was typically sandwiched between the engine and a steel car behind it: in any collision "the wooden mail car was invariably crushed." In addition, because light was provided by oil lamps, wrecks frequently engendered fires. The railway clerks' union sought for decades to require that cars made of steel be substituted, as one worker put it in 1904, for the existing "clattering charnel house of postal car."[116]

The Post Office responded by greatly expanding its corps of inspectors, whose responsibilities extended to monitoring the behavior of postal workers, and attempting to dissolve the union. As well, beginning in the 1890s, a series of US presidents issued ever-stronger executive orders, forbidding government employees—here in a measure promulgated in 1902 by President Theodore Roosevelt—"either directly or indirectly, individually or through associations," from remonstrating before legislators to increase their pay "or to influence or attempt to influence in their own interest any other legislation whatever . . . in any way save through the heads of the Departments in or under which they serve, on penalty of dismissal." Through these diktats—they were widely known as "gag orders"—Roosevelt and his successor, William H. Taft (1909), stripped postal workers of what had been their sole authorized means of bargaining. They simultaneously subverted postal workers' First Amendment rights. Throughout the twentieth century's first decade, the clerks and carriers fought back against these gag orders, which consumed much of their energy. A clear victory came in 1912, in the form of the Lloyd-LaFollette Act. This Act not only offered protection to workers against arbitrary firing, but also granted that (Stat. 555 5 U.S.C. 7211) "the right of employees . . . to furnish information to either House of Congress, or to a committee or Member thereof, may not be interfered with or denied." Lloyd-LaFollette also freed postal unions to affiliate with independent organizations, meaning with the American Federation of Labor. Notwithstanding this gain, the law still expressly prevented postal unions from striking.[117]

This did not exhaust the use of executive power around postaldom, which was deployed against not only postal employees but also workers more generally and, not for the last time, in the name of protecting the public. In June 1894, George Pullman, a Chicago-based manufacturer of special railroad sleeping cars, cut his employees' pay and hours; he refused, however, to lower rents for those of his workers who resided in his eponymous company town. Twenty-four railroad corporations possessed terminals in Chicago, where they employed 220,000 people. What was called the Pullman strike—one of the great collective working-class actions in US history—began as members of the year-old American Railway Union, who operated these roads, decided to boycott trains equipped with Pullman cars—and walked out in solidarity. Not only in Chicago, but across much of the western United States, the boycott led on to shutdowns of rail traffic. Railroad executives, intent on curtailing this militant industrial union in favor of the more conservative existing railroad brotherhoods, both organized among themselves and requested aid from the Grover Cleveland administration. Attorney General Richard Olney, "a laissez-faire liberal who had made his money as a railroad attorney for subsidized railroads," acted as the chief agent of state repression. Olney averred that, were the strike to succeed, it "would seriously impair the stability of our institutions and the entire organization of society as now constituted." Not surprisingly, George Pullman and the railroad capitalists wholeheartedly agreed. Compressing a complicated history in order to pinpoint this essential feature, the US government threw the US Army at the strikers—on the grounds that they threatened the movement of the mails. Obstructing the mails was a legal device—a pretext, for there was scant evidence of any direct threat to the mail—whose use against labor had been built up "step by step" by courts, beginning in the great railroad strike of 1877, and which "laid the legal foundations for the blanket injunction that in 1894 would prohibit any interference with the operation of any railroad carrying the mail or interstate commerce." Historians have noted that some contemporaries floated proposals that the federal government require strikers to permit daily passage of one mail train on each line and, alternatively, that railroads simply remove Pullman cars from their trains. The managers of the railroads refused such prospective measures point-blank, insisting instead that the central state should intervene more aggressively on the side of railroad capital. At the strike's height, on July 6, amid renewed calls by Populist senators for government ownership of railroads, telegraphs, and telephones, Democratic President Grover Cleveland indeed chose to throw Washington's support to capital, trumpeting that "if it takes the entire army and navy of the United States to deliver a postal card in Chicago, that card will be delivered." This was decisive. Despite initial support by the public for the workers who had walked out and, most unusual, declared opposition to federal intervention by Illinois Governor John Peter Altgeld, federal troops crushed the now-violent strike.[118]

In such an episodically charged historical context, what would prove to be the fates of the postal and telegraph models? And how, furthermore, would the telephone—a wonderful new medium, now quickly coming into its own—insert itself into this distinctly polarized forcefield: Would it be attracted toward the

Post Office, or toward the telegraph? To contemporaries it seemed that these were indeed the possibilities.

To engage these questions we must scrutinize the further progression of capitalist development in telecommunications, the episodes of social and political struggle against it, and the changing role of the state in response to both—as the institutions of communication at a distance lurched and shivered to accommodate all three systems. While the telephone indeed incorporated features drawn from each of its precursors, it was not subsumed by either of them and instead took its own distinctive course. Now predicated on an imperial republic of continental sweep, between its innovation and the end of World War I the telephone system's build-out cast a brilliant bitter light on the workings of the American power structure.

2
Antimonopoly, in the Country and the City

> It is love and war and money; it is the fighting and the tears, the work and want,
> Death and laughter of men and women passing through me, carrier of your speech...
> A copper wire.
> —Carl Sandburg, "Under a Telephone Pole"

Carl Sandburg's poem, "Under A Telephone Pole," bespeaks more than the sheer novelty of voices traversing a wire, for it engages the telephone's *own* conflicted history, scored by social division and resistance to corporate and state power. "Pine and cedar tree trunks sunk into city streets," a historian tells us, "embedded ... the telephone into both physical spaces and local political milieus."
Thus they also were planted within decades-long movements to reform electrical telecommunications. During the 1910s these attempts reached their apogee.[1]

We have long understood that this was a momentous juncture. Through a protracted process of conflict and redefinition, large businesses and state agencies recommitted the nation to capitalist ownership of telecommunications. If, therefore, as Robert MacDougall declares, "the history of the wire and the incorporation of North America were inextricably intertwined," then this change emerged from complex, contested, and fluid historical circumstances. At the center of this saga was a new entrant on the telecommunications scene: the American Telephone and Telegraph Company, or AT&T. As its grip over system development strengthened, AT&T quickly became even mightier than Western Union.[2]

For decades afterward, scholars tended to portray this transition as a simple supply side drama. Act One saw the ascendance of AT&T toward nationwide monopoly based on its control over the telephone patents of Alexander Graham Bell, followed by a sudden spike of competition in telephone service provision once AT&T's (also known as Bell's) ruthlessly defended seventeen-year legal patent monopoly lapsed in 1893. So-called "independent" telephone providers quickly grew numerous. By 1907, the highpoint of the competitive era, AT&T retained only half the market and "dual service"—provision of local telephone service by two or more suppliers over entirely separate and typically unconnected networks—prevailed in nearly one-half of US cities. In some Midwest states, such as Iowa and Indiana, independents served a majority of telephone subscribers.[3]

Analysts then lowered the curtain, and quickly raised it again. In Act Two, fresh from the great merger movement at the nineteenth century's end, a bank-led corporate reorganization in 1907 placed Theodore N. Vail—who had cut his teeth as a manager at the railway mail and then gone on to become a top executive at Bell itself from the late 1870s until the late 1880s—in command of AT&T and furnished him with capital sufficient to pursue aggressive expansion. Buyouts of key independent telephone companies followed, and these carriers were quickly interconnected with AT&T's increasingly crucial long-distance network. In this older account, vertical and horizontal integration were not sufficient in themselves to guarantee AT&T's reascendancy. The company's triumph occurred only because AT&T also coopted the state public utility commissions, which had recently been vested with jurisdiction over telephone service (forty PUCs had been established by 1913). Vail's prescient acquiescence to regulation by administrative commission was cast as a cardinal factor in AT&T's stanching of competition and its rationalization of the industry. Passage of the Mann-Elkins Act, which in 1910 expanded the oversight of the Interstate Commerce Commission to encompass telephony, did not give need to qualify this judgment, as the ICC was said to have remained all but inert. Ceaselessly publicizing Vail's strategic slogan—"One System—One Policy—Universal Service," AT&T thus regained its monopolistic stewardship of the industry and, during the decades that followed, exercised the pricing and service prerogatives that commonly characterize monopolies. Indeed, both the telephone company's market power and its political influence could not be matched by any other US corporation.

Drawing on fresh archival sources, and asking some different questions, recent historians have enriched and qualified this account. Richard John opened the process of system development more fully to politics than the older interpretation had permitted. He and others show, as well, that it actually took thirty fractious years for the sprawling local telephone operating companies that licensed the Bell patents in the late 1870s and early 1880s to cohere into a centrally administered "Bell System." Throughout the first decades of US telephone development, these subsidiary operating companies demonstrated greater independence than AT&T executives preferred. Revisionist historians have explained that, relatedly, rather than constituting an essential feature of AT&T's strategy from the outset, long-distance service attained critical importance in unifying the "Bell System" only during the 1900s and after. Robert MacDougall, meanwhile, shows that initiatives aiming to unseat the monopoly exercised by American Bell commenced within just a few years of the telephone's innovation.

An impetus to independent (again, non-Bell) telephony, for example, actually antedated the expiration of Bell's patent monopoly, as some municipal authorities sought to franchise rivals; only Bell's aggressive prosecution of its patent claims contained this centrifugal impulse. In 1894, however, Bell lost a decisive patent case brought all the way to the Supreme Court by an aggrieved independent telephone equipment manufacturer. "With the end of Bell's patent monopolies," MacDougall concludes, "battles boiled over that had been simmering for years" as thousands of independent service providers mushroomed—above all, throughout the Midwest. John, and especially MacDougall, have also made plain that contests between system operators and business users over the terms of trade in telephone service were also a vital feature. System development thus was no mere supply side affair. AT&T had to grapple not only with independent telephone companies but also with powerful business user groups. A final recent revision has been to emphasize that historical contingency imbued both politics and market structure throughout the process of telephone system development. On one hand, as they pursued their profit strategies, telephone executives elicited variable responses from differently situated independent rivals and from state managers who ranged from city councilpersons to cabinet members. On the other hand, no inexorable logic—no intrinsic "natural monopoly"—compelled AT&T's restoration as a national operator of US telecommunications.[4]

Today's revisionist historians have gone far to clarify the political-economic dynamics through which telecommunications system development progressed during the fraught years around the turn of the twentieth century. In keeping with the earlier historical interpretation, however, they continue to write as if political-economic changes unfolded simply "from above," stripped of their relationships with the environing society. The telecommunications infrastructure evolves, they appear to believe, overwhelmingly from the suites of corporate executives and the offices of government administrators. Richard John camouflages this tendentious approach by reviving the notion that a sweeping societal consensus cohered around the idea of "progress." He imagines that an overriding "civic ideal" or "civic mandate" incarnated this shared understanding. Robert MacDougall is more open-minded, when he expressly declares that debates over the control and social purpose of the telephone were "never contained" by AT&T: "Which understandings of telephony won ... was not to be determined by the Bell companies alone, but also by telephone users, competing firms, city councils, state legislatures, and federal courts." Yet, for all its virtues, even MacDougall's approach remains narrow and unbalanced; the individuals whom he quite validly insists "left their mark on the development of the industry" include, in addition to Alexander Graham Bell and Theodore Vail, only independent telephone entrepreneurs, business users, and government officials. Kept at a remove from the story are workers—notably, telecommunications

76 ANTIMONOPOLY

workers. In fact, working people repeatedly claimed significant roles in the telephone controversy. And the debate over ownership and control of the wondrous new medium itself raised fundamental questions about the US power structure.[5]

The historical record gives evidence aplenty, as this chapter and the next relate, of popular social agency throughout the entire period from the emergence of telephony to the end of World War I. In outline, my own argument runs as follows:

Opposition to corporate control of US telecommunications expanded to encompass telephony within just a few years of the filing of the originating Bell patents in 1876. Disparate antimonopoly reformers labored to freight the telecommunications industry with overarching societal responsibilities, many of which did not harmonize with the preferences of the Bell group or its investors. In an initial reform thrust, this broad antimonopoly coalition threw its support to independent telephone suppliers. By the 1880s, in addition, farmers and workers inclined to more direct intervention, notably including public ownership. During the 1910s, at the peak of the Progressive era, urban workers joined and sometimes led political campaigns for municipal ownership of local telephone systems. Before, during, and immediately after World War I, finally, workers found themselves increasingly on their own as they renewed an attempt to postalize both the telegraph and telephone systems.

Intermittently throughout this entire period, workers helped to establish a ring of political pressure within which the schemes and strategies of telecommunications companies were repeatedly improvised. Those who could not demonstrate a property interest in telecommunications were nevertheless mostly excluded from the new order that consolidated after the end of World War I. The concerns that corporate and state leaders deemed legitimate continued to comprise only a shadow of more sweeping demands for accountability and "industrial democracy" in the telecommunications workplace. Foregrounded instead were the needs and preferences of corporate capital in telecommunications supply, on one side, and the business users who collectively dominated telecommunications demand, on the other. The expressed concerns of telecommunications company employees continued, by contrast, to be consigned largely to the realm of private contracts; while localized campaigns to restructure the dominant social purposes of telecommunications were evaded or overpowered.

The 1910s witnessed the first great reconstruction of US telecommunications, nevertheless. Along with commercial independent telephone companies and business telephone users, and alongside AT&T executives and government officials, women's groups and civic reform associations and working-class trade unionists were prime actors in this drama: Their energies contributed, directly and indirectly, to a fundamental political-economic realignment. Although, in their own terms, telecommunications workers failed to democratize the industry for which they labored, they and their sometime allies nevertheless catalyzed a decisive response by the central state. This response went far to set the terms of development going forward—and sealed the fate of nineteenth century antimonopolism.

This dramatic history can be explained best by underlining that, as it proceeded, the reform effort underwent a process of social redefinition. Those who had made common cause against "monopoly" during its early decades found that, by the 1910s, their divergent interests pulled in different directions. The phrase gained fresh prominence after the turn of the twentieth century yet, ironically, as a lodestone of reform "The People" lost coherence and began to be hollowed out. Within telecommunicatons specifically, private settlements reached with AT&T by, respectively, core business users and smaller service suppliers went far to unravel the antimonopoly coalition which had fired reform effort. Because these settlements did not touch the interests of telecommunications workers, however, labor continued to press ahead. The results were, for them, savagely unexpected. For more than one year during and after World War I, the federal government took over the telegraph and telephone wires—deployed its power directly against the largest segment of the industry's fractionated workforce. A bitter revelation to employees, the World War I experience also brought telecommunications executives into an intimately close relation with the central state. US telecommunications was restabilized, therefore, not in the early 1890s as a recent telegraph historian has implied; and not between 1907 and 1913, when independent telephony declined, state regulation proliferated, and federal antitrust pressure induced AT&T to offer some concessions—but six years later. It was the Post Office's brief stint as operator of the nation's wireline systems which both ended half-a-century's antimonopoly effort and opened fresh avenues toward reform.[6]

Postalization Apprehends Both Telephone and Telegraph

During the later nineteenth century, resistance to corporate control of telecommunications entered at multiple points into the process of historical eventuation. The first nationwide labor organization in the US—the National Labor Union— had "excoriated" the alliance between the Associated Press and Western Union late in the 1860s, and called for the postalization of the telegraph. "[P]ostal telegraphs and telephones," declared the representative of New York's Central Labor Union fifteen years later, would not only curtail Western Union's "great monopoly," but "would give the people the advantage of telegraphic communication between all parts of the country, instead of confining it, as it is confined now, to the lines between the points which pay." Antimonopolism streamed against the structure and practice of the corporate telegraph, widening during the 1880s to include the corporate telephone. The Post Office, a historian writes, "grabbed the Populist imagination," so that in 1893—as a hardy independent telephone manufacturer was carrying to the Supreme Court a legal fight to break the Bell patent monopoly, which would succeed in 1894—the Populist newspaper, the *Alliance,* discerned an overriding need: "The Populists will not be satisfied until the people collectively get all the benefit there is in the telephone by the government owning all the telephones and running them in connection with the postoffice. The telephone is not only a luxury any more; it has become a business and social necessity and must be run as a social institution. Its accommodations and profits must be socialized; it must not continue to be the property of private parties. Its functions are public; it therefore must be owned and operated by the public in the interests of the public." Trade unions of the 1890s continued to lend support: in 1892, delegates to the American Federation of Labor's annual convention endorsed government ownership of telegraph and telephone networks and, after a two-year battle about whether and how to engage in politics, most of the AFL's affiliate unions approved a political program that called for nationalization of "the means of communication." This included the United Mine Workers, the iron- and steelworkers, tailors, painters, brewery workers, street-railway workers, shoe workers, textile workers, machinists, and mule spinners.[7]

The two wires crisscrossed in reformers' imaginations for good reason. AT&T itself—formed in 1885 as a long-distance subsidiary of its then parent, American Bell, but transformed fifteen years later into the parent holding company for the Bell interests—sported in its name not one "T" but two. The monopoly's original patent foretold this overlap: Patent Number 174,465, granted to Alexander Graham Bell on March 7, 1876, was for "Improvements in Telegraphy." Western Union, furthermore, entered the telephone field alongside Bell and, in an 1879 cartel agreement reached by the two companies to end their competition, Western Union gave Bell its telephone patents in exchange for 20 percent of the gross earnings on all telephones leased in the United States—a license that had transferred around $7 million to Western Union by the time the patents expired in 1893–1894. Western Union likewise retained valuable stakes in individual Bell operating companies: the telegraph monopoly was a large stockholder in New York Telephone, New York and New Jersey Telephone and, until almost the turn of the century, the Southern Bell Telephone Company. On the other hand, Bell began to furnish private-line telegraph facilities for business users in 1887.[8]

Engraved corporate connections between the two systems went beyond even this. Claude Mackay's Postal Telegraph Company, which emerged in the 1880s to compete with Western Union, held the single largest block of AT&T shares in 1909—when AT&T purchased a controlling interest in Western Union, thereby compelling Mackay to dispose of his stock holdings in AT&T. During the volatile years that followed, until December 1913—when, as we'll see, AT&T's control of Western Union was dissolved as a result of action by the US Department of Justice—any prospective system restructuring necessarily encompassed both telephone and telegraphs. After 1913, moreover, AT&T's involvement in the telegraph business continued to grow. Not only did AT&T lease circuits on a dedicated, or private-line, basis to business users, but it also carried forward its long-standing practice of "interchanging facilities" with Western Union itself, by leasing circuits to the technologically backward telegraph company. AT&T in 1930 acquired the Teletype Corporation, a specialized manufacturer of telegraph equipment; the following year, AT&T introduced its switched teletypewriter exchange service—which cut deeply into the telegraph industry's core market. It is indeed fair to claim that AT&T continued to boost its share of the domestic telegraph business all the way through the first half of the twentieth century.[9]

Between 1909 and 1913, when AT&T held a controlling interest in Western Union, the two carriers converged toward a common system of decision-making, as they would do again during the period of postal operation in World War I. The notion that they functioned as the Scylla and Charybdis of US telecommunications gave way correspondingly, to a widespread perception that they constituted a tightly synchronized corporate unit. A competitor notified the US Attorney General in mid-1915 that common bankers (Kuhn, Loeb) and common facilities still allowed AT&T to control Western Union. The "Wire Trust" still existed in 1915, agreed "the Telegraphers of New York Jewish Boys" in their telegraph to President Wilson: "The [AT&T-owned] Western Electric Company makes automatic machines and these auto machines are placed in the Western Union Offices these machines are being conducted by girls and boys they are paid six dollars a week would you please this coming session of congress investigate this merger and it is the wishes of all the telegraphers all over the country that they favor the bill known as the lewis bill government control of the telegraph and place the telegraph with the post office dept so telegrapher [sic] can support their families and get a decent wage to live on." The following year, "A Telegrapher Of NY" expropriated the wires to share his thoughts with G. Carroll Todd of the US Department of Justice:

> I THOUGHT YOU WOULD BE INTERESTED WITH THE SO-CALLED TELEPHONE AND TELEGRAPH TRUST. THE AMERICAN BEEL [sic] STILL CONTROLS THE WESTERN UNION AND THE SHERMAN LAW TO [AT&T President] VAIL IS A JOKE.... ITS A SHAM THESE MEN CAN WIN OUT IN THE U.S. COURTS JUST BECAUSE THEY HAVE MONEY A POOR MAN STEALS A PIECE OF BREAD IS SENT TO THE PRISON WHILE RICH MEN CAN DO WHAT THEY PLEASE. THE WESTERN UNION IS IN THE HANDS OF THE AMN BELL CO VAIL IS REALLY THE PREST. MR CARLETON IS THE PRSESIDENT [sic] AND CAME HERE FROM THE WESTERN ELECTRIC CO WHICH IS ALSO CONTROLLED

BY THE AMN BELL CO.... THE W U HIRES YOUNG GIRLS IN THE DAY TIME AND BOYS AT NIGHT TIME TO TRANSMIT THESE MESSAGES AND GIVES THEM A SALARY OF 8 OR 9 DOLLARS A WEEK. YOU SHOULD INVESTIGATE THESE BIG TRUST AND PUT THEM BEHIND THE PRISON BARS WHERE THEY BELONG VAIL IS NO SAINT HE KNOWS HE BREAKS THE LAW AND SHOULD BE PUNISHED FOR IT I WOULD BE AFRAID TO SIGN MY NAME AS I WOULD GET FIRED AND HOPE YOU WILL BREAK THIS UP.

These communications offer a foretaste of conflicts and struggles discussed in this section. For now it is enough to underline that the sustained linkages between the two wireline media found expression in a popular critique that was both tenacious and widespread. Opposition to the dominant order in telecommunications broke through first in the movement for independent telephony.[10]

Independent Telephony: A Political and Business Movement

"There is no fight, unless perhaps a bank fight, which is a harder fight than a telephone fight."

Robert MacDougall has shown that "independent telephony was a quasi-municipal movement constructed by the franchise-granting power of local governments," often in response to a demand by local business elites; it was especially significant throughout the Midwest. Efforts to establish non-Bell, or "independent," local suppliers originated during the mid-1880s, but Bell's waged no less than 600 patent-infringement prosecutions to preempt them. Those who demanded an independent alternative to AT&T fought back. AT&T's patent monopoly was broken in 1894; despite its best efforts, it could win from the courts no extension of full-scale proprietary control of telephone technology. At this point the company enjoyed the distinction of having become, over less than two decades, one of the country's most hated corporations. Denouncing it for being a grasping monopoly when it announced a shift from flat- to measured-service rates, in 1886, well-off telephone subscribers in Rochester actually conducted an eighteen-month boycott of the Bell affiliate there—a "telephone strike" in which they hung up their instruments—until Bell capitulated and restored the prior flat-rate offering.[11]

The core of this antipathy was Bell's exclusionary dominance of telephone service which, replicating the despised practice of Western Union, enabled it to severely restrict system development. Subscriber access was limited to a small part of the demand that existed, as Bell exercised its prerogative as a monopolist: the price of its service was very high and its quality, at best, indifferent.

Between 1879 and 1894, the company was "able to control the rate of expansion of the telephone industry . . . as well as the charges for rendering telephone service"; Bell's annual profit margin is estimated to have averaged a mind-boggling 46 percent. The increase that occurred in the number of telephones (to around 291,000 by 1894) was, in the understated language of a later government report, "very gradual"; growing at a compound annual rate of about 6 percent between 1885-1894, telephone service afforded a mere 4.1 conversations per thousand persons in the population. Importantly, telephony also constituted, nearly exclusively, a business service. In 1894, an estimated 85 percent of phones were placed in business establishments, while about 2 percent of households were so equipped. Residential service was unmistakably a luxury, confined to the upper classes. In New York City, phone service cost $20 a month in 1896, when the average worker's monthly income was $38.50. San Francisco's 21,324 telephones in 1900—representing one instrument for every sixteen inhabitants—gave it the highest penetration level of any large US city; Boston was second with one telephone for every twenty-four residents, and Chicago, with one telephone per sixty-one inhabitants, was thirteenth.[12]

At the turn of the twentieth century, AT&T engineers and statisticians segmented local markets to estimate demand for telephones. They declared that a maximum of half of "second class" households would have means to purchase service, and just 5 percent of households within the lowest segment. In 1915, other AT&T planners stipulated in an internal report that families with annual incomes under $1100 were not likely to subscribe. It was no secret, however, that AT&T corporate policy also raised barriers to access that went beyond pricing. A book published in 1915 acknowledged that AT&T restricted system development on other grounds: satisfaction of "requirements" in "an average American city, in which practically everyone is white," this work asserted, mandated "at least one telephone for every eight inhabitants": "Where a large portion of the population belongs to the negro race, or a considerable portion of the population is made up of very poor workers in factories, the requirements will be less. In some cities one telephone to fifteen inhabitants is all that can be expected." A 1911 Bell report on telephone conditions in St. Joseph, Missouri, counted 102 subscribers to the rival independent telephone system there as "undesirable" on account of their being "colored." Later I will discuss more carefully the political fallout resulting from what even a Bell System executive would concede were policies that "essentially ignored the service needs of small business men and residence users"—let alone the needs of minorities and workers.[13]

As already mentioned, what Bell deemed "pirate" telephone systems are known to have existed throughout parts of the Midwest even during the 1880s. As soon as the Bell patents entered the public domain—in 1894—literally thousands of fledgling telephone systems sprang up. When authorized "competition" did finally arrive, however, it was far from a purely economic reflex. The emergence of "independent telephony" was more a social movement than a hidden hand.[14]

"[E]nterprising manufacturers and promoters casting about for business possibilities in the stagnant early nineties," an AT&T in-house historian later suggested, "kept a watchful eye on the comparatively prosperous telephone industry and fed the anti-Bell sentiment that existed." "Promoters believed that profitable opportunities were available in undeveloped markets as well as those that Bell was already serving," observes an economic historian. True enough; the scent of cash is sufficient to explain the start-up of many of these small telephone systems. Promoters often were drawn from among local business elites, whose members sought profits from new investments as well as lower telephone prices and improved service. From its beginnings, the independent movement dressed up entrepreneurialism in antimonopoly finery. The Iowa Telephone Association, formed in 1896 "for the mutual protection and development" of the state independents, provides an example:

> No tyranny is so galling as that of concentrated wealth of the many unrighteous combinations that have been drawing for a quarter of a century the life blood from the individual business life of the United States. The American Bell Telephone Company stands easily the first. Opposition to that company is the bounden duty of all who believe in the right, revere justice and love their fellow men.

But independent telephony was no mere reflex of entrepreneurial initiative, and market forces exhausted neither its social sources nor its political significance. In cities large and small, only the stability afforded by a municipal franchise could provide the collateral demanded by anxious capital markets—that is, by investors. Not only did formal politics thus impinge broadly on telephone issues, but more broadly popular political mobilizations also often resulted. Measured by its success in obtaining municipal franchises, indeed, the momentum of the independent telephone movement was little short of astonishing; as Stone observes, except for a few of the very largest US cities, independents were authorized to operate "in virtually every community in which they sought such rights." No less than 5670 exchanges were run by independents in 1902, and these could rely on plant and equipment produced by some 100 independent manufacturers. Five years later, 451 out of the top 1002 cities in the country had authorized (though not necessarily realized) "dual telephone service," whereby at least one independent operator was permitted to compete against the local Bell affiliate in expanding the area's subscriber base: New York, Philadelphia, Pittsburgh, Chicago, Detroit, Minneapolis-St. Paul, Kansas City, Cleveland, Atlanta, New Orleans, Dallas, Houston, Los Angeles, San Diego, San Francisco, and Seattle. By no means did all of these cities actually see independent competition, as AT&T exploited every available tactic to prevent, forestall, or degrade it. More than a hundred smaller cities, however, were served *only* by independents.[15]

In rural America—where over half of the US population lived at the turn of the century—the argument for treating the telephone as what Fischer calls "a grassroots 'social movement'" is even stronger. Entrepreneurs sought to profit from telephony here, too; however, in one belt of states reaching from Minnesota down to Oklahoma and Texas, and another across the Great Lakes states and, to a markedly lesser degree, also in the South, the nature of "competition" to AT&T contravenes any abstract economistic interpretation. While in the cities and towns, independent telephone companies had to be, or to become, substantial capitalist enterprises, "competitors" in rural areas were more often cooperatives and mutual systems, totally or partly bypassing market imperatives. Such systems were mostly small, joining as few as five to twenty-five households; but frequently they came to connect "to a commercial, or larger mutual, company's switchboard in town, and through that, to the wider world."[16]

Paralleling the near-concurrent rural free delivery mail routes, literally thousands of these rural cooperative telephone systems sprang up: 21,335 nationwide by 1907; 30,317 by 1912; 51,034 by 1917. The telephone giant rarely condescended to serve thinly populated areas; if farmers wanted telephone service, they would have to provide it themselves. As a result, in 1902, only a very small proportion of farms had phones, as against perhaps 14 percent of nonfarm households; but in 1920, 39 percent of farms and just 34 percent of nonfarm households possessed them. These national averages conceal considerable regional variation: in 1920 in the prosperous Great Plains states over 80 percent of farm households kept up telephones while, in the impoverished Black belt in the South, the comparable figure was less than 5 percent. Many of these systems took a tenacious hold. A study undertaken in 1936 found that, of a sample of some 1600 cooperative telephone systems operating in that Depression year, two-thirds of which claimed fewer than fifty subscriber-members, the lion's share had been formed in the periods 1900 to 1909 (49.5 percent) and 1910 to 1919 (38 percent); the entire sample evinced an average reported age of twenty-six years.[17]

As MacDougall shows, independent telephony was "animated" by the rhetoric of Populism, "with demands on behalf of 'the people' for locally controlled networks of cheap and accessible telephones." One independent telephony booster in 1906 called this "the 'uprising of the people,' speaking telephonically." Extending a practice that had been used by gas companies in New York City early in the 1880s, some of the mutuals and commercial independents chose names that mildly emphasized their connection to political reform: "Mutual Telephone Company" (Erie, PA); "Citizens' Telephone Company" (Grand Rapids, MI); "Home Telephone Company" (Louisville, Los Angeles, and several other places); "Peoples' Telephone Company" (Superior, WI); "People's Mutual Telephone Company" (San Francisco); even "Chautauqua Telephone and Telegraph Company" (Kennedy, NY). Moreover, despite the differences between coops and mutuals, and commercial telephone companies, the independent telephone movement remained broadly united, until about 1907, around the practical goal of shattering AT&T's corporate domination of US telephony.[18]

As early as 1884, Charles H. Haskins, an executive at Wisconsin Telephone (a Bell affiliate), worried that if rates were not lowered, any would-be competitor would be "greeted gladly," and pointed out that in Wisconsin—a strong Granger state—activists would be able to create difficulties for Bell in the state legislature. Looking back from the perspective of 1913, an independent telephone manufacturer concurred that it had been Bell's "oppression"—in the form of high rates and underhanded business methods—that had acted as "the cause of the springing up of Independent telephone companies . . . and the people in every village throughout the United States are personally conversant with this matter . . . The Independent telephone exchanges have been born of sheer necessity and disgust by the common people." During the intervening years, the independents initiated a sustained political campaign against the Bell. The president of the Eastern States Independent Telephone Association, writing to President Theodore Roosevelt on behalf of the 500,000 stockholders who, he claimed, held interests in independent telephone securities, declared in 1908 that in some of the Western and Midwestern states, "the telephone question has already figured as a political issue in local elections, with the telephone trust fighting on one side and the Independents on the other. In every case the Independents have triumphed in these contests because they have naturally and properly had the people with them"—as well they might, he confided, when the telephone trust was one far more odious and all-embracing than that of Standard Oil. Robert La Follette—who went on a decade later to lead the effort, as Governor of Wisconsin, to establish that state's pattern-setting Railroad Commission, and who then participated, as Senator, in extending Interstate Commerce Commission authority to telecommunications—already by 1895 had joined the ranks of independent telephone company entrepreneurs.[19]

Explanations of independent telephony that associate it strictly with "competition," as if market forces existed in pristine separation from politics, are thus historically invalid. "Competition" was not a one-dimensional product of *homo economicus*; a majority of rural independents, recall, were not even profit-seeking enterprises, and some mutual systems recoiled at the idea of allowing commercial telephone companies access to their subscribers, via interconnection to their lines. Some leaders of commercial independents, furthermore, continued to espouse anti-Bell positions on policy issues, even after their own self-interest might have been better served by reaching an accommodation. Finally, and decisively, political struggles aimed at local control and against the "foreign" AT&T actually succeeded in embedding substantive regulative controls in "competition" itself—that is, in the municipal telephone franchises that independents needed to operate. Here, price limits and subscriber levels were explicitly specified; there, municipal ownership clauses were inserted, to be activated if the newly authorized independent system sought to sell out to Bell; and provisions for the employment of union labor and the eight-hour day were also sometimes made. Local competition enabled local communities, including local workers, to enhance their prospects of shaping telephone service provision.[20]

In terms of quality of local, or exchange, service, urban independents were not always mismatched against Bell. On one hand, they often wrestled with funding shortfalls, as they learned that big-city service was an exceptionally capital-intensive undertaking. Inadequate provision for depreciation was a particular problem. Independents found to their chagrin that, with the addition of subscribers, costs actually rose rather than declined—as in other more familiar industries. Their low rates, locked in by the terms of their franchises, did not generate sufficient revenue for them to pursue profitable system development. On the other hand, they actually led in innovating switching technology, as they spearheaded the introduction of dial, or automatic, telephone service. As early as 1902, there were fifty-four automatic offices nationwide, fifty-three of which were operated by independents; by the end of World War I, two out of three of large US cities with independent service used only dial system technology. Dial technology, which by automating the process of local telephone calling produced a major and early self-service industry, took jobs from telephone operators. During the 1920s, after what we will see was a bitterly intense confrontation with its workforce, AT&T cut the ground out from its thousands of telephone operators by introducing automatic systems on a nationwide scale. According to historian Paul Miranti, Jr., the number of telephones served by automatic exchanges soared, from several hundred thousand in 1920 to 3.5 million—27 percent of the total—in 1929.[21]

AT&T responded to the independents through a multifarious new strategy, as we will see later. To understand both AT&T's counteroffensive and the political responses that it in turn impelled, however, we will need to take account—as contemporaries did—of a marked divergence in the social pattern of telephone subscribership and use. This pattern, engraved as independent telephony entrenched itself, anchored dual-service not only in market competition but also in social-class relations.

Class Divergence in Telephone Subscribership and Use

Between 1894 and 1920, the uses and users of the telephone increased and diversified. If, as we saw, during the years of Bell's patent monopoly telephony had followed in the path of telegraphy by operating what was essentially a business service, then during the quarter-century that followed, telephony expanded toward residential service. Several more decades would pass before telephones became a household fixture, but the idea that the instrument should remain a business-class luxury was forgotten.

Between 1894 and 1920 the number of telephones in use in the United States increased from 291,000 to 13,329,000, nearly a forty-six-fold increase. This remarkable growth came, first, as a result of the independents' achievements; beginning around 1900, selectively rather than comprehensively, it also resulted from innovations made by a few Bell operating company managers. Already in 1907, some urban working-class households subscribed to telephone service; ten years after this, Leon Trotsky would remember that the apartment he had rented "in a workers' district" of New York for $18 a month, came "equipped with all sorts of conveniences that we Europeans were quite unused to: electric lights, gas cooking-range, bath, telephone. . . . we had not had this mysterious instrument either in Vienna or Paris." Trotsky's memory was sound: Gotham was the largest of the world's twelve largest telephone exchanges in 1910, and with some 361,000 telephones it possessed nearly five times as many as did Paris, which then occupied seventh place. A decade later, the situation remained the same: the number of telephones in New York had increased to almost 846,000, while Paris now boasted 155,000 instruments. According to AT&T estimates, the contrast was more general: some 8.8 percent of the US population had telephones in 1912, compared with only 0.7 percent of Europeans.[22]

Some revisionist historians would later claim that women played a formative role in this expansion, by reorienting residential telephone use toward "social" as opposed to business purposes. Though this view has been challenged, women were by any account vital in the *production* of telephone service: by the 1910s, tens of thousands of wage-earning women telephone operators comprised the mainstay of the urban service workforce, while farm women often acted as unpaid switchboard operators, effectively managing countless rural telephone systems. And there is little doubt that AT&T did resist the turn toward "social" calling, especially before around 1900. Claude Fischer pictured AT&T as it "battled" with residential customers "over social conversations, labeling such calls 'frivolous' and 'unnecessary,'" and as it employed advertising to attack the use of the telephone for gossip and transmission of music. Considered as telephone users, though, as MacDougall suggests, "Our portrait of talkative women as the inventors of telephone sociability has been overdrawn, both by hostile

Bell executives in the 1880s and 1890s, and by sympathetic historians a century later." The more fundamental spur to sociability, he shows, was flat-rate pricing plans: "When flat rates were available, as they were on most independent systems, both men and women made heavy use of the telephone for nonbusiness purposes." Where measured-service was the only option—as the Bell operating companies, serving mostly big cities, preferred—telephone sociability was concomitantly suppressed.[23]

However, the dichotomy between independents and AT&T ran deeper than this. In the cities, dual-service telephony became differentiated, albeit with some blurriness, along social-class lines. Explicating a rare AT&T inventory, which broke down telephone subscribers in Louisville, Kentucky in 1910 into several social and occupational categories, Mueller detects a "marked preference" for the Home Telephone Company among businesses patronized by workers, such as bowling alleys, billiard halls, and saloons. Other small-scale businesses, including bakers, barber shops, tailors, grocery stores, druggists, coal-dealers, butchers, and plumbers, likewise preferred the independent to Bell. Such establishments, especially druggists and grocery stores, might offer telephone service to their customers for free, as a means of keeping their business or drawing them to purchase other products. On the other hand, law firms, banks, railroads, hotels, express companies, laundries, and insurance companies often opted either to dispense with a subscription to the Home Telephone service, or to complement it by paying for access to the Bell system as well. They justified this added expense in part because of AT&T's increasingly expansive long-distance network. "If there are two systems, neither of them serving all," generalized AT&T president Vail in 1907, "important users must be connected with both systems."[24]

A study of telephone subscribership in Los Angeles in 1910—when it was a dual-service city—allows us both to substantiate and to flesh out Mueller's findings. Consider the data in Table 2.1.

A random sample of 534 subscribers to the independent Los Angeles Home Telephone Company in January 1910, when referenced against the manuscript census for that year, shows that of the 279 residential subscribers who could be

Table 2.1 Telephone Subscribership in Los Angeles, 1910

	Home Tel. n=534	Pacific T& T n=453
Business Subs	131	139
Residential Subs	279	211
Unknown	124	103

traced, 153 or 55 percent (with forty-eight not specifying their type of occupancy) were homeowners. Moreover, just under one-quarter (24.5 percent) of all Home subscribers were business as opposed to only residential customers. A second random sample, of 453 subscribers in January 1911 to the AT&T affiliate, the Pacific Telephone and Telegraph Company, when matched with the manuscript census for 1910 revealed a substantially higher fraction of homeowners—73.5 percent, or 183 out of 249 (with 7 unaccounted for). Similarly, business users made up a greater proportion of Bell subscribers (30.7 percent). If the subscriber base of both telephone companies overrepresented the well-off, then the Bell affiliate catered to a wealthier, and more business-oriented, stratum.[25]

The two sets of subscribers were also differentiated in social terms. In Los Angeles around 1910 a small minority of private residences subscribed to both telephone services; sixty-nine out of 582 (11.9 percent) across the two samples did so. Higher proportions of business subscribers, however, connected with both systems: Over half (69 out of 131, or 52.7 percent) of the sample of business subscribers to the Home Telephone Company also took service from Bell's Pacific Telephone and Telegraph Company. For the sample of businesses subscribing to PT&T, on the other hand, the pattern of dual-subscriptionship was even more blatant: 89 out of 139, or 64 percent, did paid twice for telephone service. On the other hand, subscribers to the Home Telephone service who *did not* subscribe to service from PT&T comprised, in socioeconomic terms, a distinctly more modest and locally rooted group. These fifty-two subscribers included a scattering of real estate brokers, engineers, and lawyers; but less well-heeled, less cosmopolitan, occupations preponderated: a horseshoer, two dentists, a tailor, a men's outfitter, three grocers, a watchmaker, a benevolent society, a bar, two rooming houses, a junk and bottle store, and a rubber stamp company. Bell's affiliate, by contrast, served as an exclusive conduit for banks and investment firms, insurance companies, railroads, and steamship lines, the Singer Sewing Machine Store, even the US Navy Recruiting Office. PT&T's residential customers, moreover, included four "managers," two "owners," one bank president, one university president, two manufacturing company presidents and four vice presidents, as well as four foremen and one "investor"; scarcely any of these job titles appears in the Home Telephone subscriber sample.

AT&T's Pacific Telephone and Telegraph subsidiary was thus unmistakably the preferred provider, both for members of the business class and businesses that were tied in with the emerging nationwide corporate economy. AT&T's President Vail acknowledged as much in 1909, when he specified that, "[i]f it is universal in its connections and intercommunication"—as AT&T's system aspired to be—then a telephone network would be "indispensable to all those whose social or business relations are more than purely local," that is to say, "[t]hose of large and extended social or business connections."[26]

This partial bifurcation of subscribers found parallels in divergent patterns of telephone use. Telephony's first use, local calling, remained overwhelmingly dominant among residential subscribers. Long-distance telephone calls comprised a scant 2.5 percent of total daily conversations in 1900, 2.4 percent of total daily conversations in 1910, and 3.1 percent of total daily conversations in 1920, during an era when the number of daily conversations overall rose more than sixfold—from less than 8 million to nearly 52 million. While most long-distance calls were made to adjacent communities, only a very small proportion of telephone users regularly made long-distance calls of any kind. As late as 1933, leading social scientists portrayed the telephone as augmenting and strengthening local, as opposed to extra local, ties. We will see, however, that this generalized account washed out crucial social-class distinctions.[27]

Reliance on toll calling, a service dominated by AT&T, exhibited further stratification. Indeed, the pattern of toll calling was even more sharply differentiated than was dual-service subscribership or, indeed, residential telephone subscribership overall. David F. Weiman uncovered an inhouse corporate study, this one focusing on uses and users of the fledgling AT&T network in upstate New York, during one month in 1901. It revealed that just one-third of residential customers, as opposed to two-thirds of business subscribers, made long-distance calls. The skew was actually much greater than this: one-tenth of business subscribers accounted for nearly 60 percent of business toll calls, and over half of all toll calls; business users overall accounted for nearly 90 percent of long-distance calling. Most urban residential users, by contrast, "called within their immediate vicinity, and except for occasional calls to or from the central business district, rarely contacted subscribers in other neighborhoods." Mueller too detects this tendency, which he characterizes as a "high degree of self-contained communication" within the different neighborhoods of each city. Mueller explains that the preponderance of local calling carried a significant implication: that "[t]he lack of interconnection between the two systems was less of an impediment to the telephone users of 1910 than it would be now."[28]

We will see that AT&T's executives and public relations personnel developed and drew on their knowledge of this sharply differentiated pattern of use as they poured increasing resources into their long-distance subsidiary. Theodore Vail is renowned for pronouncements concerning his company's commitment to a "universal wire system"; he had envisaged telephone system development in an integrated way, even beyond US borders, when he had served as General Manager of American Bell. In 1885, the certificate of incorporation of AT&T— created as American Bell's long-distance subsidiary—declared that its circuits would connect every city, town, and place in New York State "with one or more points in each and every other city, town or place in said state, and in each and every other of the United States, and in Canada and Mexico ... and also by cable and other appropriate means with the rest of the known world, as may hereafter become necessary or desirable in conducting the business of this association."

After rejoining AT&T as its president in 1907, Vail's commitment to this principle remained unshaken: "It is impossible to define the territorial limitations of a telephone system because," he declared in 1910, "from every exchange center communication is wanted up to the talking limits in every direction."[29]

However, to consider Vail's idea of a territorially unlimited "universal" service only as an admirably consistent corporate purpose is insufficient. The meanings of universal service were different in 1885 from what they would be beginning in 1907–1908, when Vail turned the idea of "universal service" into an AT&T totem. During the early years of corporate patent monopoly, when competition was not a substantial threat and long-distance service was only beginning, Vail offered the grandiose vision of a system-builder intent on carving out a sweeping franchise. Vail's consecration of the concept, after his return to AT&T in 1907—"One System—One Policy—Universal Service"—performed quite different work, however, because now the political-economic context had altered fundamentally. As Milton Mueller pointed out decades ago, in 1907 Vail's "universal service" functioned as a rationale for his attempt to destroy dual service by elevating AT&T's increasingly integrated network above the patchwork systems of his thousands of rivals.[30]

This meaning of universal service found many adherents among government officials. Attorney General Wickersham, in January 1913, argued that "the value of a telephone service depends largely upon the facility of connecting every individual telephone user with any point upon any telephone line in the United States." In 1918, the California Railroad Commission, acknowledging that subscribers "almost unanimously demand a consolidation into one system," charged that "there should be one universal service as this will enable complete interchange of communications between all telephone users in the community." Postmaster General Burleson emphasized in 1919 that "It is generally true and should be universally the case that every telephone user should be able to reach any other telephone user in any place in the country." And by this time, though its network did not yet approach Burleson's vision, AT&T was indeed capable of transmitting human speech by wire from one end of the country to the other.[31]

Vail's mighty ambition was evident as well in a second sense of his use of "universal service," which comprehended extensions of AT&T ownership and control to what Vail conceived as "complementary" media—notably, the telegraph and, later, radio. "The idea of operating the telephone and the telegraph in accord, each supplementing the other, is not a new or untried one, but has been ineffective because of the lack of common influence in the control of the operations," wrote Vail in 1909, after acquiring a controlling interest for AT&T in Western Union. What he went on to term "inter-operations" between the two systems would result not only in greater convenience to the public—by extending the reach of the telegraph—but, also, Vail expected, overall cost savings and other efficiencies through joint operation and management. To rationalize this turf-grab, Vail had actually coopted the antimonopolists' argument for folding the telegraph into the Post Office on grounds of economic efficiency. By 1912, he forthrightly contemplated "a universal wire system for the electrical transmission of intelligence [written or personal communication]."[32]

It is worth repeating that AT&T's certificate of incorporation had given notice a quarter-century earlier that its wireline system should not be delimited by US territorial boundaries. AT&T's purchase of a dominant interest in Western Union gave it stakes in several transatlantic telegraph cables, however, these remained under British control. Vail continued to hold that "There should be some unification of both the intra-national and international electrical communication system. They should be brought together." His predominant focus, however, remained on the North American market, as in his assertion that this "universal wire system" should ideally stretch "from every one in every place to every one in every other place, a system as universal and as extensive as the highway system of the country which extends from every man's door to every other man's door."[33]

Though it quickly became common sense among elites, vitally, Vail's impressively ambitious conception of universal service made scant room for working-class households. Vail himself remained tellingly indeterminate about just when AT&T might be expected to place a telephone in every home within its service area. In fact, AT&T emphatically had *not* committed itself to extending service into the tenement apartments of big US cities: decades would pass before household telephone access approached inclusiveness. MacDougall reports that, after he returned to head AT&T in 1907, Theodore Vail "opposed" Bell operating company executives' innovations that aimed to expand service to urban residents, notably "nickel-in-the-slot" phones and party lines. Perhaps more important, these innovations did not put the nation at the verge of a comprehensive and effective household telephone service. A US Senate Report tacitly acknowledged as much in 1914, in averring only that the telephone had become "a means of social intercourse to which all classes properly aspire." Nickel-in-the-slot phones, moreover, did not answer the problem of effective access. "Would you kindly have Inspectors investigate our Bell Telephone System," wrote "A Working Woman" from St. Louis in 1920: "For several times in a week I dropped nickel in slot + did not get my number or did not get my nickel back—<u>I am only one person</u> to have this happen in a week + I am a working woman at that Every nickel counts with me please investigate I have complained to Southwestern Bell Telephone Co. before + still drop in nickels with <u>no results and no nickel back</u>." The most Vail would concede in this era (and in a passive voice) was that "It is believed that some sort of a connection with the telephone system should be within reach of all."[34]

Even near the onset of the Great Depression (1929), only two-fifths of the nation's households possessed telephones. Among a Houston-based sample of workers for whom the telephone was a "business asset," such as electricians and longshoremen—whose location of work varied and who needed to transport their tools and to be in touch with hiring halls—only half possessed their own telephones in 1935. For them, as for much of the urban working class, telephone service constituted a site of much-needed mutual support and reciprocity rather than individual consumption. Claude Fischer underlines that, throughout the interwar years, Bell executives still did not ordinarily assume "that the telephone would reach the near universality in American homes of, say, electricity or the radio." However, Bell did continue to prioritize business subscribers. During the 1920s, Bell installed the private branch exchanges (PBXs) that directed calls within large organizations in large offices, hotels, and factories, and these accounted for 19 percent of total telephones and 17 percent of local telephone volume.[35]

AT&T's lack of enthusiasm for enlarging residential access, let alone on terms suitable for working-class budgets, functioned as a significant sociopolitical irritant. Many workers sought an immediate and rapid expansion of telephone access vertically through the urban class structure. "We will make it possible for the working man to have a phone in 'his' house when the workers capture Los Angeles, this fall," wrote a hopeful Socialist in August 1911—a couple of months before James and John McNamara, on trial for bombing the *Los Angeles Times* building the previous year, changed their pleas to "guilty" and thereby helped wreck the chances of the Socialist candidate, Job Harriman—who led the field until then. Though the Socialists' platform of municipalizing public utilities likewise lost, this political sentiment persisted. Rates should be reduced, proclaimed another resident five years later, so that "the humblest home in the city may have its phone." In Chicago, we will see, trade unions and affiliated reformers likewise made universal access a cornerstone demand. But how might the blockages that restricted household telephone access be overcome?[36]

For most working-class families, it needs to be underlined, this question was essentially about local telephone service. Long-distance usage patterns remained heavily skewed at least until the arrival of mobile phones at the end of the twentieth century; the telegraph sufficed for announcements of births, deaths, and illnesses; and the Post Office provided an efficient and cheap nationwide service for longer messages. Only US entry into World War I precipitated even an infrequent take-up of long-distance services by workers, and this only after AFL President Gompers successfully petitioned the Wilson Administration in 1918 to institute a low long-distance telephone and telegraph rate to all training camps, so as to "keep us in closer touch with our loved ones." Before this, suggestively, it was not a manual laborer but a traveling salesman "who would like to phone to his wife occasionally," who wrote to ask President Wilson in 1913 to "compell [sic] the Bell Phone Company to restore their old night rates" so that he might again have means enough to do so. Workers may not have been totally uninterested in long-distance telephony but, by contrast, their concern for local service was keen indeed.[37]

Throughout the twentieth century's early decades, this was all but taken for granted. S. J. Small, former president of the Commercial Telegraphers' Union, declared to a newspaper in 1919 that, unlike the telegraph, the telephone constituted nothing less than "a local institution." Nearly fifteen years later (1933), the American Federation of Labor resolved at its annual convention that "a large portion" of local telephone service customers "never have, never will and never desire to use . . . long distance service."[38]

After AT&T's monopoly had been reconstructed, it was often said that independent telephony, or "competition," had flown in the face of an irresistible centralizing trend—that, confronted by a "natural monopoly," competition between rival systems was foredoomed to fail. Later still, as the theory of natural monopoly itself came under attack, a newer theory stressing "network effects" again engendered the same result as had its "natural monopoly" precursor. To enable communication between all subscribers to the telephone wherever they lived, the theory of network effects held, one telephone system must inexorably supplant rival services. In the face of such weighty theories, support for dual-service seemed to have been founded on either naivete or delusion. Only sheer ignorance of economic-technological realities could explain opposition to a unified nationwide telephone system. On the other hand, it was Vail's canny foreknowledge of necessity (be it predicated on natural monopoly or network effects) that enabled him to prevail, by accepting regulation in exchange for a now-legitimate AT&T monopoly over universal service. There was no other way. "Under Theodore Vail," according to one textbook, "the Bell Telephone companies sought . . . to ensure virtually universal service to all American households." A more critical commentator confides that the "real history" of "'[u]niversal service in telecommunications" reveals "a sweetheart deal cut with private industry. The deal was: In exchange for providing universal access, telephone companies like AT&T . . . were assured a cozy rate of return on their investment" as regulated monopolies.[39]

Revisionist historians—Milton Mueller, Richard John, and Robert MacDougall—have gone far to discredit this interpretation. In neglecting how AT&T itself was also caught up in wider relations of capital and class, however, they have left the job unfinished. Local versus long-distance telephone service figured as a class-coded distinction *and* these divergent patterns of subscribership and use factored into the political economy of telephone system development.[40]

Throughout the 1900s and 1910s, a chasm separated the demand for a widened and improved mode of local telephone service provision from the existing forms of supply. This gap provided a prime opportunity for politicizing the telephone issue, beyond the AT&T executive suite and, indeed, beyond the independent telephone movement. For competition by independent operators established only a first means for addressing local demands by subscribers and would-be subscribers. Urban workers, especially workers organized into trade unions, were embracing political as well as what AFL President Gompers called "pure and simple trade union"-based remedies to social problems. "Municipal politics in a number of cities around the turn of the century," writes historian Shelton Stromquist, "was restructured by the pulse of class warfare that realigned the field of social polarities." Telephone service figured—sometimes centrally— in this metamorphosizing struggle.[41]

Beyond Actually Existing Telecommunications: The City for the People

Independent telephony had increased the number of telephones and lowered rates and, around 1900, at least some of the local Bell companies were reducing their rates in response. Access to the telephone in turn was diffusing widely throughout middle-class households and began to reach working-class residences. Notably in San Francisco and Chicago, where workers who had organized into trade unions also constituted a political force, canny Bell executives responded with innovations to enlarge access in working-class communities: "nickel-in-the-slot" coin telephones located mainly in drugstores, saloons, and many apartment buildings; measured-service rates; and multiparty lines. Yet it was because most laboring families did not possess a household instrument that telephone service became joined to the circuits of working-class reciprocity. Lack of household access along with other experienced deficits prompted members of the organized urban working-class to launch, or to join, a political alternative to the options preferred by business users, independent operators, and AT&T: municipalized telephone systems.[42]

The reconstructive movement, as it took hold in big cities between the 1880s and the 1910s, was complex. Distinct interests and varied actors played parts: craft unionists were prominent, but campaigns for municipal ownership—of telephones as of other, earlier utilities—brought together into local coalitions intellectuals, newspapers, women's groups, professional reformers, and some businessmen. Political frictions sprang up, between zealous "good government" reformers aiming to root out boss rule and trade unionists who focused on wages, working conditions and the availability of services in working-class neighborhoods. Some radicals might not support municipalization, as it would not eliminate capitalism root-and-branch. Nevertheless, often demanding "home rule" and deploying the initiative and the referendum (the same new political tools which were also sometimes used by the Independent telephone movement), proponents sought to curtail corrupt and predatory corporate monopolies over "public utilities" by more fully actualizing the self-owned city. During the late nineteenth century, they developed a powerful and multifaceted critique—analytical, political, and sometimes moralizing—of privately owned utilities. Sporadic attempts to bring about municipal ownership and control of telephone systems fell within this context. "Municipal ownership of telephone operating companies remained on the political agenda in many cities," Richard John observes, "from the 1890s until the First World War." Why, then, have telephone historians all but dismissed the municipalization movement? Mostly, no doubt, because it did not succeed in establishing city-owned telephone systems; indeed, municipalized telephony vanished from the reform picture by around 1917. Does this provide a sufficient reason to neglect it?[43]

In a word, no. It is anachronistic to minimize agitations for municipal telephony on the grounds that they were not consummated; to do so is to forsake how a power-laden conflict ramified throughout system development. Energized by cross-class alliances of labor unions and middle-class reformers, attempts to engender local government takeovers of utilities including the telephone became a locus of acute political struggle. Nor, moreover, did the defeat of attempts to municipalize telephone service diminish this movement's formative importance for telephone system development going forward.[44]

Reformers could look to a series of adjacent successes, both in the United States and, as Daniel Rodgers underlines, in Europe, where cities such as Glasgow and Berlin had been spurred to action during the nineteenth century and now were cited as models of municipal supply of local utilities. Between 1896 and 1906, the number of US city-owned electric plants increased substantially, and among large cities Cleveland, Seattle and Los Angeles instituted public power. The 1890s also saw the ownership of local waterworks shift from private capital to municipalities. Four big cities came to own or operate their transit lines: Detroit, San Francisco, Seattle, and New York; and municipal gasworks came into being in three others. Municipally supplied telephone service came no closer, however, than Trondheim (Norway) and half a dozen cities in Scotland, Wales, and England, notably, in Hull—which operated an independent municipal service for the next century.[45]

The sharpest point of conflict was the requisite legal franchise. The franchising process was shot-through by corruption, as suppliers offered kickbacks to avaricious city council members in exchange for their votes. The services that this venality engendered were characteristically insufficient and overpriced and, in the case of street cars, also unsafe. Wages and working conditions posed problems not only for consumers but, first and foremost, for employees. Ownership and control of gas, electrical power, and street railways figured as local political issues during the 1880s, as New York City and Chicago became equipped with these amenities. By the end of the next decade, sometimes caught up in a great merger movement backed by finance capital, for-profit providers of water, power, local transport, and telecommunications consolidated into hugely lucrative corporate monopolies. Within many industrial cities, municipalization movements to lower rates, reduce political corruption, enhance service, and improve working conditions, strengthened reciprocally. A comprehensive volume on the subject, edited by the reform economist Edward Bemis, appeared in 1899; in 1901, the economist and lawyer Frank Parsons, who had contributed a chapter on the telephone to Bemis's earlier book, once more positioned telephones squarely among the utilities crying out for municipal ownership in his own book, "The City For the People."[46]

By the mid-1880s, following the discovery of nearby reserves, Toledo, Ohio "became the scene of an important experiment with municipally supplied natural gas," which split the city's citizens as it squared off against the giant Standard Oil Company. While much of the business community rejected the proposal that Toledo take over provision of natural gas, the Central Trade Union endorsed it. That the Toledo campaign for municipal "free gas" was aimed, in part, as an inducement for manufacturing industries to relocate may have motivated some workers to see it more as a boondoggle than as a step toward the cooperative commonwealth. However, nearly fifteen years later, having elected a crusading reformer as their mayor in 1899, Toledo-based trade unions then supported Samuel M. Jones in his campaign for Ohio's governorship on a more ambitious municipalization platform that singled out "The extension of the principle now operating in the public ownership of the Post Office, to the operation of Mines, Highways, Steam and Electric Railroads, Telegraphs, Telephones and Water and Lighting Plants." Cleveland, under Mayor Tom Johnson, hosted a similar municipalization attempt a couple of years later.[47]

Among the most prominent instances of this diversely rooted project cropped up in New York City. Municipal provision was first contemplated in a desultory fashion, as the local populace encountered private street railways and commercial gas and electric companies during the 1880s. However, according to Joseph Sullivan, both because the new utility services were not yet widely used and because the economic and political power of competing corporate suppliers was "still limited," utility reform did not figure as a major political issue. Only during the 1890s, as more people became reliant on rapid transit, gas, and electricity, and as monopolistic control patterns deepened, did reform gain political legs. Enlisting well-recognized figures including the novelist Hamlin Garland, the soon-to-be mayor of Cleveland Tom Johnson, and Louis F. Post, the future publisher of the *Public* magazine, the radical Henry George made public ownership and operation of utilities an issue in New York's mayoral campaign of 1897. Persistent corruption and price-gouging broadened political support for this objective in the aftermath, following George's untimely death just before the election. Aiming to impose heavy taxes on existing franchise-holders and to cease granting franchises in the future, the Franchise Tax and Municipal Ownership League formed in 1900; another pro-municipalization group, the Civic Council, consisted of representatives of sixty-seven labor unions and more than thirty reform associations. The issue continued to simmer in the Empire City. Pulling in a reform-minded judge as its leader in 1904, the Municipal Ownership League included the Central Federation of Labor as one of its founding members. Drawing on his experience in Chicago, where his two daily papers had provided a fulcrum for a municipal ownership campaign, newspaper magnate William Randolph Hearst now turned to harness his outsized political ambitions to the reform hopes of workers in New York. Hearst, a historian explains, only promoted municipal ownership "when it coincided with his personal interests"; however, his New York *American* became "practically the official organ of the Municipal Ownership League." Hearst presented himself as what another historian calls "a national spokesman for the labor movement." He published strike news, supported the eight-hour day, agitated to establish a parcel post, postal savings and a postal telegraph and, before becoming disenchanted with the conservative labor leader, he even offered AFL President Samuel Gompers a staff position on his New York *American*.[48]

The immigrant working-class constituted much of Hearst's political base. Unions of teamsters, printers, meat-cutters, starch workers, bricklayers, electrical workers, and commercial telegraphers were among those that endorsed Hearst's candidacies for, first, mayor of New York City (1905) and then governor of New York State (1906). So did New York City's Central Labor Union, and its Central Federated Labor Union, as well as the New York Women's Trade Union League. Hearst's platforms in these contests called for municipalization and effective antitrust action against corporate monopolies. Though he did not win either election, he gained a majority in many working-class urban districts—and the project of municipalizing utilities attained greater prominence. Soon afterward, Hearst's newspapers shed their vibrantly opportunistic two-way connection to organized labor's political agenda; however, as late as 1925, AT&T still attended carefully to the Hearst chain's penchant for municipal ownership.[49]

New York's was merely an especially visible attempt to wrest for city-dwellers a greater say in deciding whether and to whom to allot local franchises, so as to eliminate citizens' "bondage" to corrupt alliances between "shrewd capitalists" and "politicians." In numerous cities, battles for municipal ownership were becoming a primary venue for a rising "local labor-oriented politics." A near-contemporary historian of Seattle concluded that "Municipal ownership has always been one of the cardinal principles of the local laboring class and their constant agitation for it has no doubt been an important cause of its adoption." The historian Philip Foner asserts that, during the turn-of-the-century period, "an analysis of organized labor's participation in municipal politics is essential." Urban conflicts over local telephone service developed in this context, notably during the final phase of the municipalization campaign.[50]

In Los Angeles, where the local union of electrical workers had been "largely responsible for the establishment of municipal power and light," a ballot initiative created a Municipal Board of Public Utilities in 1910; another in 1915 found the vast majority of voters in favor of compulsory interconnection between the two telephone systems then operating—Bell, whose service dated to 1880, and the independent Home Telephone Company, which had introduced automatic or dial service in 1904, under a franchise that was not slated to expire until 1948. This proving intractably difficult, in 1916, a third initiative to municipalize the city's telephone systems, sponsored by the Socialist Party, was defeated by a mere 3–2 margin. The Bell company and its rival then sought to merge. Such a merger, though, itself required electoral approval. That approval was forthcoming, but only after voters successfully insisted—in flat opposition to Bell's entrenched policy of manual-only measured service—that they be afforded a choice between manual and automatic service. A historian of telephone development in Los Angeles calls the merger, consummated in 1918, "the single most important event that forced Bell into large city dial service," largely because the newly created California Public Utilities Commission then agreed that Bell should expand the city's established dial system to conform to subscriber preferences.[51]

During the 1910s, Buffalo, Chicago, Indianapolis, Denver, Cleveland, San Francisco, Seattle, and many smaller cities saw the formation of political coalitions around a perceived need to reorganize local telephone service provision. Further research is needed to unearth the history of these restructuring efforts. Though they did not succeed, these campaigns not only established a substantial policy alternative but also introduced a potent centrifugal force into telephone system development—and at the very time that many members of the business class were deciding to throw their support behind AT&T's interconnected local- and long-distance telephone network. Mobilizations for municipal telephony also imparted an additional lesson: that the independent telephone movement did not stretch far enough to respond to working-class needs. The Chicago fight illustrates this.[52]

"In cities like Detroit, Cleveland, and Chicago, and on the state level in California, Illinois, and Massachusetts," writes Julie Greene, a "working-class agenda focused on issues like municipal ownership and tax reform." The Chicago Teachers Union took an especially significant role in that city's campaign. Simultaneously the center of independent telephone manufacturing, the headquarters of the Independent Telephone Association of America, and the major site of AT&T's own sprawling Western Electric manufacturing operations, Chicago—home to tens of thousands of telephone and telegraph workers—saw an especially well-articulated attempt to municipalize the telephone.[53]

AT&T's Chicago Telephone Company affiliate held a franchise that was due to expire in 1909, and which came up for a twenty-year renewal in 1907. The Bell company's most privileged subscribers, the city's business elite, had been battling through the Illinois Manufacturers Association since the 1890s to gain more favorable terms of trade with Bell's Chicago Telephone Company. After likely paying handsome bribes to Chicago aldermen, an independent rival—Illinois Telephone and Telegraph—was chartered to construct an underground conduit for its wires in 1898; its initial investors included important independent telephone equipment manufacturers and the St. Louis beer-magnate Adolphus Busch. These backers then sold their franchise to a speculative investor consortium, which leads one historian to assert that this independent was the product not of "visionary promoters but venal speculators backed by a notoriously corrupt city official." All this conceded, however, Illinois T&T nevertheless went on to occupy an important place both in Chicago's labor history and in the city's telephone system development.[54]

Illinois T&T subscribers never surpassed 20,000, and thus the company did not mount a credible challenge to Bell in any direct way. During the protracted negotiations that led the city council (after 100 meetings) to renew the Bell affiliate's franchise in the depression year of 1907, Richard John shows, no fewer than twenty-eight business groups led by the Chicago Board of Trade insisted on additional concessions. AT&T countered by lavishing half a million dollars on publicity and promotion to support its bid, and Chicago Telephone Company operators shepherded the circulation of a petition urging the city council to refranchise the Bell company: no fewer than 250,000 city-dwellers had signed it. The result was a compromise between the city, the Chicago Telephone Company, and big business users. Flat-rate service for heavy business users was retained even though, a 1910 engineering study showed, this service paid for only half its cost of provision. Small subscribers joined in the settlement to the extent that they would enjoy an actual rate reduction—to no more than five cents—for calls within the greatly expanded territory of the city. Bell retained its franchise; and no new rival was authorized. After garnering large kickbacks, the city's aldermen nevertheless reserved the right under the new franchise to set telephone rates and to purchase the company at a price to be negotiated.[55]

The renewal of Chicago Telephone's franchise, Richard John holds, "signaled the demise of antimonopoly in the telephone business as a civic ideal." It did not, nevertheless, spell the end of the local campaign for a municipal telephone service. Nor did it exhaust the historical significance of this movement for system development.[56]

The origins of Chicago's telephone fight go back to earlier contests over a different utility service: During the 1890s, franchises for street railways were flashpoints of conflict in the Second City. Chicago's trade unions were swelling with members and, after the turn of the century, its union movement was becoming both more inclusive and more politically focused and engaged. A resurgent initiative to municipalize street railways placed the Chicago Federation of Labor, the city's central labor body, in the center of the fray. Throughout the 1890s and early 1900s, both the corrupted franchise process and the inferior, unsafe, and overpriced service provided by three noncompeting streetcar companies, drew increasing outrage from Chicago's workers. Many local middle-class reformers sympathized. In 1902, voters overwhelmingly opposed franchise extensions for the streetcar companies; general public support for streetcar workers when they struck the traction companies the next year made the municipal ownership movement "a major political force in the city."[57]

When news circulated of an imminent vote on streetcar franchise extensions by the city council, in November, 1903, the Chicago Federation of Labor called for citizens to attend the meeting "in a body," in order to "demand municipal ownership." Thousands did so, and the city council curtailed its deliberations. Pressure from labor only mounted thereafter. In the mayoral election of 1905 the victorious Democrat, Edward Dunne, was labor's candidate. Backed by Hearst's two Chicago dailies, his platform centered on municipalizing the street cars. The CFL, meanwhile, in 1905 petitioned the Illinois Legislature for an enabling act, to permit Chicagoans to draft a new charter, which would mandate both an eight-hour day for government employees and public ownership of utilities—now including telephones. By this means, the central labor council targeted the city's independent telephone company, Illinois Telegraph and Telephone.[58]

From the perspective of local trade unionists in 1905, the Illinois Telephone and Telegraph Company had turned in a dismal performance. In 1898, the city council had conferred on it a right to construct tunnels beneath the streets, ostensibly to build its telephone network. But, for the new company, as we have already seen, telephones were not uppermost in mind. "Publicly claiming to lay telephone cables, the Illinois Telegraph and Telephone Company (sic), in fact, constructed railway tunnels accommodating three thousand steel cars and one hundred electric locomotives." Its sixty-two miles of tunnels under the Chicago Loop enabled freight deliveries to proceed without facing the congested city streets. During the bitter teamsters' strike of 1905, Illinois Telephone and Telegraph made this network available to downtown department stores, in order that they might receive merchandise below ground—subverting the teamsters' violent but effective shutdown of freight traffic on the streets above. Prior to this strike, the CFL had learned of the freight tunnels, and filed a complaint with the city demanding a public investigation, to no avail. The investor consortium behind Illinois T&T instead allowed it to "participat[e] in underground warfare against the teamsters."[59]

The teamsters' strike escalated, as a result of a concerted employer counter-offensive against the city's most powerful union. When the strike was finally broken, the unions were weakened and organized labor's public political role diminished, as erstwhile allies deserted. Mayor Dunne, notably, lost his earlier appetite for municipalization. And patrician and middle-class reformers had been frightened and put off by the episodes of violent class conflict that had marked the strike. In consequence, though the CFL's commitment to municipal ownership did not ebb—in 1907, the federation appointed a committee to cooperate with the City Council's own Municipal Ownership Central Committee—this movement proceeded with attenuated public support. Now perceiving the structural remedy of municipal ownership as too radical, businesses, mainstream politicians, and middle-class progressives eschewed it in favor of an enhanced regulatory scheme. As Leidenberger sums up, this highpoint in the attempt to enact municipal ownership in Chicago was "defeated by undermining the movement's social basis."[60]

This experience underlay Chicagoans' engagement with independent telephony. Around 1906, Illinois T&T apparently tried to sell out to Bell. This was too much even for the city council to countenance, and it intervened: the independent company was told to extend service to at least 20,000 Chicagoans before June 1, 1911, upon penalty of forfeiting its franchise, plant, and equipment to the city or its chosen licensee. This at last spurred Illinois T&T to action, to comply with its franchise. The company adopted the well-regarded automatic system of telephone switching, and the labor needed to construct its network was performed under a closed-shop agreement with the International Brotherhood of Electrical Workers. The Bell System with which Chicago Telephone was affiliated, in contrast, was intransigently antiunion. Illinois T&T's belated "active competit[ion]" with Bell, therefore, at this point signified something beyond mere competition in service provision: an advance for trade unionism.[61]

It was evident that the fight was unfinished, and that serious obstacles lay ahead. A union activist suggested darkly that "the Bell hand" had been apparent when Illinois T&T "began going down hill, until today, it is questionable whether they have one-half the required number of subscribers." In 1913, he continued, "the Bell merger engineers appeared on the job and together with the attorneys for the Automatic interests came before the city council and asked permission that the Automatic be allowed to sell out to the Bell." Many IBEW members, he went on, "saw in this a clever move to beat the city out of a telephone plant which no doubt stands forfeited under the terms of the franchise, and also take from the electrical workers a closed-shop and force upon us Bell wages and working conditions. From here on," Ben A. Tatzlaff summed up, "the fight was earnest and bitter. We organized the Penny Phone League.... We demanded that the city seize the Automatic plant for violation of its franchise to operate it as a municipal institution."[62]

Labor unionists and Socialists established the Penny Phone League (PPL) in 1914. The trigger for forming the PPL was the Bell attempt to merge its local affiliate, Chicago Telephone Co., with Illinois T and T. The independent had entered receivership in 1909 and, reorganized, John avers that "it limped along until 1913, when Bell quietly bought it out." However, the story was not so simple. The acquisition required the approval of the Chicago city council and, as John allows, this was not forthcoming. The three years that followed, before the city council finally authorized the Bell takeover, were the period when Chicago's Penny Phone League and its allies agitated for a municipal takeover. During these three years, the campaign for municipal telephony helped stave off the curtailment of telephone competition in Chicago. The reformers also intervened repeatedly to try to influence the terms of the settlement, especially on issues having to do with the valuation of the property and, therefore, of the rate-base on which Bell, after its absorption of its rival's plant, might legally charge for service under the terms of its franchise.[63]

Morton L. Johnson, PPL president, was, like the new organization's secretary and treasurer, a member of the International Brotherhood of Electrical Workers. With the IBEW as its organizing base, according to Treasurer Ben A. Tetzlaff, the fledgling group then "enlisted in our cause The Chicago Federation of Labor and many other labor, civic, and political bodies." The CFL cooperated, organizing a "Public Ownership League" in 1915, and the labor council continued to declare its support for government-owned telephony through 1918.[64]

The PPL should be seen, however, as something more than a transparent attempt "merely" to protect union jobs. Throughout the decades after the Civil War, the objects of working-class struggles for justice had both expanded and altered. As wage labor became permanent, and drew in most of the labor force, artisan-inspired campaigns against "wage slavery" and corporate "monopoly" gave way to industrial workers' battles for a democratic polity and a "living wage." By this, Lawrence Glickman writes, they meant wages sufficient to sustain a historically malleable "American standard" of living, encompassing elements of both work and consumption. Escalating dominative race and gender relations, struggles for a living wage also linked up with AFL union affiliates' typically exclusionary practices. The Chicago Federation of Labor's attempts on behalf of reform proposals thus often advanced white working-men's needs and aspirations first and foremost. Within these often-severe constraints, through the PPL and kindred mobilizations, local telephony was folded into labor's campaign for a living wage and a just polity.[65]

The PPL, the IBEW, the CFL, and the Socialist party collaborated and—though middle-class reformers' support for labor projects no longer could be taken for granted after 1907—so did women's civic and reform organizations. Women reformers were guided, according to Maureen A. Flanagan, by a broad vision of "municipal housekeeping" in which the telephone figured explicitly. Members of Chicago's Women's City Club, in opposition to the men of their own class, thus sought to cooperate with the Chicago Federation of Labor, the Chicago Federation of Teachers, the Women's Trade Union League, the Woman's party, and the Socialist party of Illinois in sponsoring a talk in Chicago by Congressman David L. Lewis—of whom there will be more to say—"advocating government ownership of the telephones." "Women's Civic and Political Bodies," again including the Women's Party of Cook County and the Women's Civic League, concurrently joined other reformers in a demand for municipal ownership of telephony. As union militancy and political radicalism surged—even after the US had entered World War I—in the city where its national office resided Chicago's Socialist party polled 34 percent of the popular vote in the municipal elections of November 1917.[66]

The PPL's aims folded bread-and-butter issues into a political agenda that sought to bridge between workers as laborers and as consumers: "Improved Telephone Service at Reduced Rates; Telephone in Every Home at One Penny a Call; Telephone Operated for the Benefit of the People." Small Chicago users, the PPL declared, were subsidizing large ones, allowing the Bell operating company to pay out fat dividends to stockholders and license contract fees to AT&T for management and technical services. The PPL may have taken characteristically inadequate account of the fact that network costs increased with subscriber growth; but even if so, this misperception did not undercut the group's demand for municipal ownership. For the PPL, municipal ownership addressed complaints issuing not only from consumers and would-be consumers of local telephone service, but also of producers. "The motive of the telephone business is wrong, works a hardship on the people in telephone service at high rates, and on the employees in poor wages and working conditions." The president of the Chicago Federation of Labor, which had specifically "opposed . . . the private ownership of the telephone" by 1907, now likewise chipped in that municipal ownership would obtain "for the community better politics and business." Local telephony became an issue around which organized labor claimed to represent not only employees but the public at large.[67]

The Penny Phone League and the CFL did not succeed in bringing local telephone service inside an expanded municipalization project—"the city for the people." The highpoint of Chicagoans' efforts to municipalize utilities had already passed, during the traction fight between 1902 and 1907; throughout the 1910s, organized labor became more politically isolated. The municipal telephony campaign, however, not only demonstrated that workers took an important role in the campaign to alter the character of local telephone service provision, but also provoked significant responses—both in the economy and the polity.

AT&T sought to outflank the threats posed by independent telephone systems and municipalization campaigns through business initiatives and political and ideological counter-moves. The giant carrier crafted a response that was strategically directed at the pattern of telephone subscribership and use.

Though too often neglected by historians, businesses, and, especially, large businesses have always constituted a primary axis of telecommunications system development. In many cities, business users had been a decisive force in motivating the initial entry by independent telephone providers. Often corporations themselves, business users thereafter began to lobby collectively in many cities, to win more favorable rates and service policies from service suppliers. By the 1900s and 1910s, however, business users were pushing for something beyond a mere rebalancing in their terms of trade. They were swinging back in favor of a monopoly system—if they could impose some key structural alterations on the industry.

Developing what they call "a modified version of the predation hypothesis to explain how competition was effectively eliminated in the territory of the Southern Bell Telephone Company," David F. Weiman and Richard C. Levin show that core business users sided with Bell's "campaign to oust independent exchanges in large cities." In Birmingham, Savannah, Jacksonville, Norfolk, Raleigh and other southern cities, between 1904 and 1912 "Boards of Trade, Chambers of Commerce, and Retail Merchants Associations—all representing core users—petitioned municipal authorities to revoke the franchises of independents, thereby compelling their consolidation into the SBT network." Their acquiescence to monopoly, however—and crucially—hinged on obtaining guarantees that they would have a voice in rate-setting and other policies.[68]

This impulse had been influentially established already within the heartland of finance capital. An AT&T vice president estimated in 1904 that Manhattan provided a fifth of all Bell operating company profits. Business users in this vital market were split on whether to press to establish an independent competitor to Bell's New York Telephone Company. When one business organization backed an investigation of telephone conditions by the State of New York, to suggest that competition was needed, the Bell affiliate quickly made strategic concessions to the other. In 1905, New York Telephone acquiesced to a review of its rates and an examination of its books by the Merchants' Association of New York and, after this appraisal was complete, the company also acquiesced to a substantial rate reduction. The Merchants Association then reciprocated. This powerful group declared that no State investigation of New York Telephone was needed; it blocked an attempt by an independent company to enter the New York City market; and it published an influential report on its nationwide survey of businessmen—which found growing dissatisfaction with the expense and duplication of dual service. A similar pattern was becoming widespread. In Chicago, the national center of the independent telephone movement, in 1906 Mayor Dunne issued a public statement favoring a single citywide telephone system. By around 1910, in both first- and second-rank cities such as Milwaukee, business users were concluding that competition had achieved its purpose; they were now ready to reach for a deal with AT&T. Vail declared that "there is no question but that the public are tired of dual telephone exchange systems, and that so fast as confidence in protection against the real or imaginary evils of monopoly increases, opposition against mergers will decrease." Weiman and Levin explain a *quid pro quo* was essential to this swing in sentiment by the telephone suppliers' most important customers: to gain the support of major business users for an end to dual service, "Bell companies agreed to various forms of rate regulation and thereby made credible commitments to restrict the use of monopoly power."[69]

This pattern of accommodation between AT&T and local groups of core business users placed counterpressure on the reform movement, and helped set in place a foundation-stone on which Theodore Vail attempted to reconstruct AT&T's corporate monopoly. Vail's codified rhetoric of "system" and of "universal service" bespoke a toughminded awareness of the market realities that constrained his project of expanding and integrating a nationwide telephone network under AT&T's control. The foremost object of "universal service," in the new context, was to underline the carrier's unique capacity to enable long-distance and local communication for business users and among middle-class households. The slogan supplied ideological glue for a series of linked AT&T efforts: to extend its long-distance lines so as to encompass the maximum possible territory; to buy out leading "opposition" companies; as MacDougall persuasively shows, to centralize AT&T's management control over its own operating companies; to license interconnection with small noncompeting independents while withholding it from direct rivals, thereby effectively splitting the movement; and to neutralize the threat of municipalization. AT&T, writes MacDougall, had to reconstruct its dominance "city by city"; "universal service" functioned as a sign that, throughout these contests, AT&T was willing to grant a real measure of deference to politically influential and economically powerful business users. Throughout the remainder of this watershed period and beyond, big capital—including both AT&T and its large business customers—united loosely around the imperative of establishing a unitary interstate network.[70]

AT&T concurrently pursued predatory tactics against the independents. With easy access to financing from big banks, AT&T cut its telephone rates by as much as two-thirds in selected markets, and soon was in a position to buy out some of its bigger rivals; it attacked other competitors both through lawsuits and by curtailing their access to the capital markets, sometimes by extralegal methods. During the first decade of the twentieth century, AT&T precluded the independents from developing a rival long-distance, network; imposed burdens on their capacity to keep up the quality of their service; and often drove down their market value. Correspondence from an independent telephone equipment manufacturer and internal memoranda drafted for two Attorneys General of the United States corroborate MacDougall's finding that AT&T, backed by J. P. Morgan, pushed hard to buy out strategically placed independent rivals at tempting prices where this was deemed necessary. Between 1907 and 1913, some big commercial telephone companies swung onto the AT&T axis.[71]

Local business groups sometimes "brokered negotiations with city governments, the Bell affiliates, and their independent rivals. . . . and a consensus among business users for some kind of regulated monopoly emerged." Independent telephone interests, business users, and Bell operating companies responded to the municipalization threat by helping to revive what Daniel Rodgers has acerbically called—with respect to workers and residential customers—"a policy device of proven impotence": the state regulatory commission. "The most important effect of the municipal ownership furor," Rodgers explains, "was to resuscitate the regulatory commission device and shove it into the political breach." As dozens of state governments placed intrastate telephone service within the jurisdiction of recently established or newly expanded public utility commissions in the years after 1907, "they were reacting to this new consensus." We will see later that the PUCs gained additional momentum after World War I.[72]

With the courts, the PUC served to bring the evolving telecommunications system into a formal legal relation with principles of public utility and common carriage. For, as Alan Stone writes, the creation of many of the telephone industry's legal obligations antedated the instrument's widespread adoption. Mostly as a result of insistent agrarian protest over railroad rates and discriminatory service, administrative regulatory procedures and common carrier precepts had already grown more systematized. During the 1880s, legal authorities began to agree that telephone firms too should be classed as "public service companies." Henceforward, commissions and courts operated in light of four primary obligations: to serve all who applied for service "and who are willing to abide by the reasonable regulations of the firm"; to furnish adequate service; to provide impartial, nondiscriminatory service; and to charge reasonable rates.[73]

This enlarged regulatory commitment established a vital entry point for future reformers. The "duty to serve" which had entered late-nineteenth-century American jurisprudence presented opportunities to impose social accountability obligations on private capital; as a result, capital's freedom could be substantially qualified and constrained. The carryover of this public service conception into telecommunications, however, was not an outgrowth of a presumed liberal consensus—an overriding "civic ideal." Only during the interwar years did it become more firmly established. By removing decision-making from local authorities, often to sites remote from big-city centers and working-class politics, like Sacramento, California, and Springfield, Illinois, public utility commissions made it difficult for urban workers to translate their demands into effective political action. So did the sharply circumscribed powers of the commissions, alongside the fact that commissioners were political appointees rather than popularly elected officials. So, finally, did the PUCs' reliance on obtuse and exclusionary administrative procedure, including doctrines of "standing" that barred those lacking a direct property interest from participation.[74]

For these reasons, however, the state commissions triggered not relief but animadversion, even contempt. Many critics, among them advocates of city home rule, responded to the commissions with a potent rhetoric (which academics subsequently reinvented as a theory of "regulatory capture"), which stood service in the rough-and-tumble of contemporary politics. That state regulators were subservient to the industries they oversaw found a specific counterpoint in the municipalization drive.[75]

In the 1890s, the reform economist Frank Parsons cast a critical eye on state regulation of public utilities; continued abuses by the transcontinental railroads also soured Greenbackers and then Populists on the efficacy of utility commissions. Dismissing competition out of hand, both because "it forfeits the benefits of monopoly" and because it simply could not be sustained in what he took to be natural monopoly industries, Parsons provided an equally incisive appraisal of the newly emerging administrative commissions. "Though of decided use," he allowed, the PUCs offered no ultimate solution because "Private ownership of monopoly means antagonism to public interest, and it also means power." Even were they stoutly determined to do so, the commissions were simply not strong enough to stand up to such power.[76]

For the duration of the municipalization project, regulation by state commissions was routinely apprehended as a utility-company plot to subvert a revitalization of democracy in the cities. A journalist who aligned his self-interest with the commercial independent telephone companies wrote to tell President Wilson how he had "exposed the Bell Company's conspiracy in creating the state laws and the state commissions for its control of the telephone situation throughout this country"—and to propose that "proper action" by the Interstate Commerce Commission might offer a more effective remedy for these "despotic conditions." The Milwaukee Socialist Daniel W. Hoan, city attorney and soon-to-be-mayor, denounced regulation in 1914 as "a failure and a fraud," which never could succeed in creating an effective "peace between the public and the corporations." Some academically trained analysts recognized that "the popular prestige of public service commissions is waning," and "a great many are coming to fear that the commissions as organs of government are primarily organs of the public utility interests to protect themselves from the mosquito-bites of rampant democracy." As a result, observed Delos Wilcox—one of the country's foremost public utility experts—"there is a noticeable revival in the movement for municipal ownership and a strengthening of local resistance to the practical abrogation of municipal home rule as it relates to public utilities." As late as 1918, perhaps sensing an encroachment on his jurisdiction after the Ohio Supreme Court upheld the power of the state agency to regulate telephone rates, a judge heaped scorn on "'the state commission plan,'" for being "pure, practical autocracy" and, plainly, an "undemocratic, un-American, unconstitutional doctrine.'"[77]

Far from comprising a sober academic clarification after the fact, then, the rhetoric of 'regulatory capture' was first of all a weapon used by contemporaries who strived to make telephone utilities democratically accountable. State regulatory commissions, agreed the Penny Phone League's Morton Johnson in a 1914 letter to the US Attorney General, were blatantly in league with Bell. Johnson expatiated on his critique in a trade union journal. Openly rejecting competition as "a failure," Johnson declared that the Bell "monopoly" was using every trick in the book to induce rivals to acquiesce to mergers, interconnection agreements, and equipment purchases that "would eventually" give it "complete control" of both network operation and manufacturing. These assertions were largely accurate; and, again aptly, Johnson also charged that AT&T was attempting to win intellectual leadership over the telephone question, by "moulding public opinion in favor of one system on the theory that the business is a natural monopoly and that monopoly it the Bell." A veritable avalanche of corporate publicity was pouring forth: "this work is being done on the press of the country, through advertisements and articles tending to prove the correctness of the Bell position and the fallacy of Government Ownership." Though a breakaway section of the independent movement was organizing, "for the purpose of carrying on a more aggressive warfare against the Bell Co.," the telephone giant, supported by the big business users that disproportionately relied on it, was breaking the unity of the independents. The independent telephone movement was splitting into assimilationist and anti-Bell wings.[78]

Meanwhile, some cities actually fended off state regulation—for example, in California. While the Bell interests were in the forefront of the campaign for state regulation there, they were thwarted for several years by what the President of Pacific Telephone in 1912 castigated as "one-sided, elastic provisions in connection with the retention and surrender of certain powers by municipalities." Notably, Los Angeles created its municipal Public Utilities Commission in 1910; it took five more years for the California Railroad Commission to wrest away its powers. Even after this, localities managed to constrain the freedom enjoyed by state commissions, as cities vied against state authorities in the courts. It was not until the 1930s, writes David Nord about the nationwide contestation between local and state regulators, "that the state commissions were finally able to take over the regulatory function completely." James W. Sichter was correct to hold that, into the 1920s and beyond, cities "continued to play an advocacy role in state regulatory proceedings," especially in the arcane but important matter of telephone industry "separations" (allocations of telephone company network investments for jurisdictional and rate-setting purposes).[79]

The battle to municipalize utilities including local telephone service demonstrates, finally, that the historical push to "regulation" is invalidly narrowed and diminished if it is equated merely with administrative commissions. An initial attempt to regulate the Bell monopoly emerged, as we have seen, in the independent telephone movement; concurrently, it emerged again in a politically charged demand to municipalize city utilities. In 1914, an academic authority cast the imperative to regulation in an even more sweeping and open-ended way:

> All now seem to assent to the proposition that municipal utilities must be regulated. The point of difference is as to the method and extent of regulation. Methods of regulation may be roughly classed as [1] regulation by governmental authorities under private ownership of public utilities, and [2] governmental operation and ownership of such utilities.

The following year, Nathaniel T. Guernsey, AT&T General Counsel, concurred that neither regulation's form nor its substantive aims had yet been fixed. "Regulation, in the sense in which the term is used with reference to public utilities," he averred, meant "to subject to rules, restrictions or governing principles." But rules, restrictions, and principles of what kind? And exercised by whom? Guernsey strongly favored both "general" rules rather than impositions on "the details of management," and state administrative commissions over municipal controls. Yet, Guernsey conceded, "[t]he matter of the regulation of municipal utilities is still in the development stage . . . both as to the law and as to the practice and procedure." Serious uncertainties persisted into, and even after, the altered conditions produced by US entry into World War I. A consistent and encompassing conception of public utility regulation had not yet gained a definite political-economic anchor.[80]

Throughout the early decades of the twentieth century, AT&T gingerly acquiesced to state regulation by administrative commission, preferring it over other forms of oversight, particularly municipal. For, though it did grant relief to Bell from the municipalization's threat of fragmentation and decentralized control, state regulation via public utility commissions was not always a shell game orchestrated by Bell. Richard Kielblowicz has explicated the multifaceted scope and intellectual sophistication of AT&T's needful attempt to mould public discourse in favor of its continued corporate operation of the telephone system; and AT&T executives had to scramble in what Delos Wilcox in 1914 aptly called "the play for advantages in the regulatory system now being established." Six years earlier, as regulation by state commission first became significant, Vail reported to AT&T shareholders, "we have had many questions before the courts, state commissions and other public bodies." Although the results "have been on the whole satisfactory," he emphasized that "during these discussions the anxiety of the officials of our companies has been keen." By the 1910s AT&T was already spending considerable sums to meet the requirements of federal and state regulation. The scope of its attempts to "play for advantages" via lobbying and press agentry quickly became legendary: recall that the company's affiliate in Chicago spent $500,000 (about $12.5 million in 2021 dollars) on PR during the months before the city council vote on its franchise renewal. Nevertheless, AT&T's domination of state regulatory proceedings was not as reliable as its executives would have preferred.[81]

As administrative regulation by state commissions provoked renewed debate, the defeat of successive movements for municipal telephony did not curtail reform efforts. Advocates of structural change did not meekly retire, nor did they agree to confine their efforts to the obtuse procedures instituted by remote public utility commissions. Proponents of market competition and adherents of democratic accountability and social justice instead broke free of local moorings. Federal officials throughout all three branches of the central state played key roles in the ensuing struggles.

3
Business Realignment, Federal Intervention, Class Confrontation

Sometimes on behalf of employees, often in support of customers, antimonopoly reformers looked for redress not only from cities and states but also from the federal government. After the turn of the century, in particular, pressure mounted in Congress. A year after the Panic of 1907, Progressive Wisconsin Senator Robert La Follette introduced a bill to disallow free telegraph or telephone franking for public officials, and to prevent discrimination in interstate telephone and telegraph rates. The Interstate Commerce Commission (ICC) had been established in 1887; severely restricted by Supreme Court decisions of the 1890s, its powers were revived by the Hepburn Act of 1906. In 1910, passage of the Mann-Elkins Act then granted the ICC ratemaking power over interstate telegraph and telephone companies.[1]

Mann-Elkins gained support both from some independent telephone companies and organized labor, which was renewing its campaign for federal intervention. In 1906, the AFL had resolved to support the International Brotherhood of Electrical Workers, after this affiliate union reported that it was "in difficulty" with AT&T in no less than twenty-five states "in defense of the right to form and maintain an organization." Not only did the labor federation empower its officers to impose a levy on affiliated unions to aid the IBEW in its campaign to end "persistent discrimination" by AT&T, it also resolved, through its Legislative Committee, to support the IBEW's endeavor "to have the Telephone and Telegraph Companies declared common carriers and brought under the provisions of the Interstate Commerce Law." During the run-up to Mann-Elkins, another AFL affiliate, the Commercial Telegraphers Union, followed suit. These hopeful efforts made by sections of the organized working class added to the momentum to institute federal regulation over telecommunications. AT&T quietly acquiesced to ICC jurisdiction: no company representatives testified on the measure before Congress.[2]

The campaign to bring telecommunications to account did not rest with the strengthening of the ICC and the extension of its jurisdiction. One further highpoint came when the Justice Department compelled AT&T to make significant structural changes and to alter some key business practices. A second arrived when the ICC went on to conduct a far-reaching inquiry into the relationship that powered the industry: that between carriers and business users. A third pinnacle—the most important one—was reached when, during and just after World War I, the federal government actually assumed operating control over the nation's telegraphs, telephones, and cables. These interventions by the central state comprised a complex and extended moment of political struggle, involving both a recrystallization of institutional relations and of social class dynamics. This fraught historical drama shattered fifty years of struggle to postalize US telecommunications across the board. In consequence, those who sought to align networks with the needs of workers and would-be residential customers would be compelled to seek fresh paths to reform, as the discourse of antimonopolism lost its social basis and its visionary political purchase.

The Kingsbury Commitment

Vail's aggressive attempts to eliminate or acquire independent companies and, above all, his 1909 purchase of a controlling interest in Western Union, galvanized the anti-Bell faction of the independent telephone movement—both service providers and equipment makers—to turn for relief to state and federal antitrust law. Between 1908 and 1913, first under Republican President Taft and then under Democratic President Wilson, the US Department of Justice turned a sympathetic ear. As against the "home rule" proponents discussed above, these advocates of independent telephony hoped that the Executive Branch would offset the burgeoning state public utility commissions, whose pro-Bell orientation they deemed notorious. From Gallipolis, Ohio, for example, a booster of commercial independents, the journalist N. G. Warth, wrote in 1913 to President Woodrow Wilson, to complain of "the Bell Company's conspiracy in creating the state laws and the state commissions for its control of the telephone situation throughout this country." His remedy was, in the first instance, "proper action of the Interstate Commerce Commission"—which indeed had commenced its own investigation of the telephone industry earlier that year. The assistant to President Taft's Attorney General offered a different formulation in a letter to businessman Harold McGraw in 1911: "Personally, since the installation of telephones has been so widely extended, I am not sure but what Government ownership of telegraphs and telephones would be preferable, but in the meantime I think that the only way whereby a strong Company like the Bell can be successfully regulated is by competition."[3]

By 1913, AT&T faced mounting federal pressure along three fronts: an antitrust case brought against the Bell in July by the US Justice Department in Oregon (and resolved by a consent decree in March 1914); a potentially wide-ranging investigation of AT&T's practices by the ICC, concomitantly initiated in late July; and most worrisome to Bell managers, a renewed postalization campaign, flourishing in the House of Representatives but also reaching into the Executive Branch, during November and December of 1913.[4]

In a November 1913 letter to President Vail, AT&T's comptroller confided his fears about the deteriorating situation. He comprehended that the drive to regulation was neither strictly judicial nor administrative (as later scholars often would assume), but broadly social; this was why, despite the ongoing spread of regulatory commissions, the movement to restructure the nation's wireline system was stronger than ever:

> The people generally are convinced that the telephone is a natural monopoly, but I do not see that there is a general disposition to depend on the Commissions to properly regulate monopolies. Consequently we are getting regulation or attempts at regulation from many different sources—legislatures, municipalities, court proceedings and departments of justice. From all this there is likely to result even worse confusion than we now have, and this confusion means for one thing the utmost difficulty in financing.

This put Bell in a bind because, with its gigantic reliance on debt, "[i]f we do not continue to meet the demands for extensions and improvements of the service, the general sentiment against private monopoly will naturally increase." "To many," he declared, "it will seem that the only way out of this labyrinth must be directly toward government ownership." Reports of federal officials' support for a government takeover also circulated.[5]

A confidential Post Office memo written during a critical interval in early December reported on a conversation with "one of the higher officials of the Bell Company," and reaffirmed that considerable uncertainty over the company's future existed within AT&T's executive ranks. This correspondent (of the undersecretary of the Post Office) declared that he had been led "to believe that in certain quarters this great corporation would not be displeased" by the prospect of a government takeover—presumably because the terms of such a buyout could be made highly favorable to investors. His informant at Bell, he related, "spoke of trouble, trouble, trouble, at many points, coming from state commissions—crowding the Bell Companies. The people, through their state commissions and city commissions, are closing in on the Bell Companies, and before their attorneys are through with a hearing at 'A' they are rushed to 'B' to attend another hearing."[6]

A week later, on December 16, AT&T stock suddenly declined by five points; over the course of the year it had lost thirty. The *New York Times* reported that "Much talk of a reduction of the dividend was heard not because of earnings but because it was thought that the Directors would want to conserve resources until they knew definitely what the Administration had decided about the telephone business." Vail put up a good front when, the next day, he declared the usual quarterly dividend ahead of schedule, to "set at rest rumors" of federal intervention: "If it were not for the feeling of uncertainty among our stockholders because of talk of Government ownership, I would not be at all concerned over the possibility of such a development." He went on to insist that, in the event the Government did move to acquire the nation's wirelines, its formal appraisal of AT&T property would be highly favorable to stockholders. On the December 18, the *Times* took note that nationalization was being promoted by the Postmaster General, in a just-released annual report, and that a takeover bill had been drafted by Representative David Lewis of Maryland. However, the Times reassured its readers, "no such legislation would be enacted at the present session of Congress"; and, it portended, for the moment at least, Lewis would not even introduce his bill.[7]

Did the paper have foreknowledge of what was soon called the Kingsbury Commitment, which was formalized three days later in a letter on December 19? Backed by a congratulatory message from President Wilson, the agreement arrived just in time to upstage Congressman Lewis, who in fact had decided only the previous day that he would indeed introduce a resolution requesting that a House committee investigate "postalization of the telephone networks of the United States." "Telephone Trust To Be Dissolved" was the page-one headline with which the *New York Times* greeted the news of the Kingsbury Commitment; "Federal Ownership Halts" read a second, less conspicuous, headline the next day.[8]

Nathan Kingsbury committed AT&T to a program of change worked out with Attorney General James C. McReynolds who, according to the preeminent historian of the Wilson administrations, was "at heart an extreme conservative with a narrow view of the proper role that government should play in economic affairs." McReynolds, who Wilson would appoint to the Supreme Court in 1914, did harbor an "undoubted antagonism to monopoly," historian Arthur S. Link explains, in keeping with most contemporary conservatives' strong belief in competition as "the perfect governor of economic activity." The pact McReynolds reached with Kingsbury required that AT&T sell off its interest in Western Union; that it adhere to explicit policies to enable independents to interconnect with its long-distance network (though these policies remained favorable to AT&T); and that henceforth it restrict its acquisition of competing independent telephone companies. Progressive Republican Senator Joseph L. Bristow of Kansas, whose extensive knowledge of Post Office operations rendered his sharp criticisms of postalization more effective, had caustic words about the Kingsbury settlement. "Judging from the effects on the stocks," the senator observed, "this is apparently a more satisfactory dissolution to those dissolved than the one of the American Tobacco Company, or that of the Standard Oil Company. . . . this mutual agreement on the dissolution seems to have been a pretty good thing for the owners of stock in the American Telephone and Telegraph." AT&T's stock had gained back five and a half points—$19 million—on news of the agreement.[9]

A top manager of the Holtzer-Cabot Electric Company, a rival of Western Electric in telephone equipment manufacturing, also minced few words in casting the agreement as a "sop" in a letter to the Attorney General. Declaring that a federal takeover "should have been done fifteen years ago," he called for the government "to purchase at a fair appraised value . . . the complete telephone system of the United States, both Bell and Independent: also both telegraph systems of the United States, and have them operated by our Government as they should be, and as they will be absolutely, eventually." Because it momentarily took the wind out of the sails of the postalization campaign, the Kingsbury Commitment has been often seen as a capitulation to AT&T, both by some contemporaries and later observers.[10]

In its own terms, nonetheless, the pact required AT&T to make significant structural alterations. The Commercial Telegraphers Union announced that the agreement of December 1913 "will long be remembered by the W.U.-Bell trust as one of the most painful months it ever experienced." "The trust," declared the union's journal, "was slammed good and plenty all along the line and then it capped the climax by surrendering to the government unconditionally on December 19 and promising to be good." Also in January, *The Transmitter*, an independent telephone journal published since the 1890s in Fort Worth, congratulated the Attorney General and the President for "bringing the telephone trust to its knees." The Bell monopoly, the journal underscored, had been "forced into the agreement"; although still warily concerned to ensure that the "promise" of the Kingsbury Commitment was duly matched by actual "performance," *The Transmitter* conceded that "it seems that a great victory has been won." "Events of the past few days," it crowed, had "completely changed the telephone situation of the country." Years later, Harry B. MacMeal, an authority on independent telephony, agreed that the agreement had been forced on AT&T. "In the face of the Attorney General's warning that A.T.&T. would either have to accept terms of surrender or else face dissolution proceedings," Woodrow Wilson's biographer affirmed, "the company's directors accepted" the need to capitulate.[11]

Largely unrecognized to this day, however, was the genius of the agreement. Well known to scholars is that Kingsbury granted AT&T a mandate to dominate US telephony, at the price of backing away from its overt contemporary attempt to become the exclusive or "universal" system of multimodal electrical intercommunication dear to its then-president. Less well acknowledged is that the pact's reestablishment of Western Union as an independent company would carry enduring consequences. No less important and least understood, Kingsbury stabilized both AT&T *and* key members of the independent telecommunications industry. That is, it forged a compromise through which the main body of capitalist enterprise in telecommunications began to shelter under one roof. This brought about a far-reaching shift in the political economy of system development, whereby AT&T became the *de facto* network manager, as Alan Stone dubs it, of a sprawling patchwork of systems across the entire nation, including not only its own gargantuan network but also those of thousands of interconnected independents.[12]

In 1909, there existed forty commercial independent telephone companies, each of whose outstanding stocks and bonds were worth at least $1 million, and another thirty-five whose properties were valued at between $500,000 and $1 million. On the other hand, there were also tens of thousands of smaller commercial independents and mutual and cooperative systems. Not surprisingly, disparately situated "independents" responded variously to the Kingsbury compromise. Profit-seeking companies harbored inclinations distinct from cooperatives and mutual networks aimed at breaking even and community service. The agreement thus "drove a permanent wedge between independent companies on the issue of their associations with Bell companies." For nearly a two-year interval, beginning eleven months before the Kingsbury announcement, the National Independent Telephone Association broke into two opposing factions, one led by those hoping to reach an accommodation with Bell, and the other by stalwarts who refused in principle to accept links of any kind with the "octopus."[13]

Kingsbury helped fashion an institutional framework that benefited AT&T as well as leading commercial independents. By formalizing relations between these carriers and Bell, it expedited the development of a relatively stable capitalist class interest in telecommunications. By imposing strictures against untrammeled Bell acquisitions of competing independent companies (as well as through the Western Union divestiture), Kingsbury compelled Bell to accept the coexistence of independent capital—both service providers and manufacturers. As Woodrow Wilson, whose early political career had made a touchstone of antitrust action, wrote about AT&T in a tactfully phrased and heavily publicized message accompanying the Kingsbury Commitment, "It is very gratifying that the company should thus volunteer to adjust its business to the conditions of competition."[14]

Because of the agreement, the US Department of Justice became a significant federal regulator, gaining what one high-ranking official termed "direct control over the telephone situation." Far from rubberstamping AT&T's preferences, the Assistant Attorney General purported several years afterward, "under the commitment the Department can have something to say about any transaction, no matter how trivial, whereas under the law it would probably wait for an accumulation of offenses before it would feel justified in taking action looking to the institution of legal proceedings." What use did the Justice Department make of its newfound regulatory power?[15]

In the three years following the agreement (1914–1916), AT&T was authorized by the Department of Justice to buy and sell telephone stations, resulting in a total net gain to the Bell system of 56,279 telephones; during the next three years, which embraced the war and immediate postwar period, AT&T netted nearly twice as many stations, 100,974. This record seems to validate the charge that Kingsbury was merely a ploy by AT&T executives: between the announcement of the agreement and November 1919, the Department of Justice passed upon more than 100 telephone transactions involving AT&T and, by the agency's own admission, all but one such request was approved.[16]

However, the procedures leading to these results again lend support to a different interpretation. Mueller shows that Bell now promoted local consolidations only after ensuring that they had the tacit consent of business telephone users. Before sending a request for approval of a telephone transaction to the Justice Department, furthermore, AT&T also submitted it informally to the now-reunified US Independent Telephone Association (USITA). On this basis, the Department of Justice then once more consulted with the USITA to confirm its approval. Not surprisingly, the Independent Association "has not objected to the consummation of probably 95 percent of the transactions submitted to the Department by the Bell System." Indeed, recounted Roger Shales, the Assistant to the Attorney General, USITA's president told him in 1919 that the Kingsbury Commitment was working quite well:

> the transactions consummated have not resulted in increasing the monopoly of the Bell System; and ... through the exchange of properties the particular weak spots in Independent telephony have been eliminated and the Independent situation as a whole is stronger physically and financially than ever before.

No longer outrage directed at a rapacious corporate predator, this was an expression of comfortable good fellowship, if not between equals then among kindred capitalists. The train of events that was capped by the Kingsbury Commitment thus provides an example of how, in keeping with an argument made by Martin Sklar, large corporations were working at this time to "align[] strategic sectors of the small and middle-range bourgeoisie . . . with large-scale corporate enterprise."[17]

Realignment and rapprochement led on to a relatively stable structure. Even during the one-year disruption of 1918–1919 (of which more momentarily), when the nation's telephone and telegraph systems were taken over by the Post Office—helping to administer service provision throughout this period was a four-member "Wire Operating Board" on which AT&T vice president U. N. Bethell rubbed elbows with a representative of the independent telephone companies.[18]

Another flurry of industry consolidation followed World War I. Passage of the Willis-Graham Act in 1921 thereafter exempted telephone mergers from antitrust review once they had been approved by state public utility commissions and by the ICC—whose existing functions were expanded as it inherited the Justice Department's regulatory role. By the 1930s, there were fifty-two independent telephone companies that reached at least 10,000 subscribers; one, a holding company known as the Gary Group, held ownership interests in 200 telephone operating and manufacturing units not only in the United States but also worldwide. The domestic market served by independents, which itself underwent economic concentration as the decades progressed, was very large when seen in a comparative perspective. In 1932, the independent companies of sufficient size to be legally bound to report their revenues to the FCC serviced a user base of 1.7 million telephones—down substantially from their historical height in 1907, but still enough taken together to be outranked by just two nations: Germany (with 2.96 million phones) and Britain (2.15 million). In 1966, US independents operated 17,100,000 telephones: nearly as many as those in use in Britain and France combined.[19]

By brokering a political deal to strengthen that fraction of the independent telephone movement which limited its concerns to securing the rewards of entrepreneurship Kingsbury simultaneously weakened the more radical wing of this formation. This in turn established a second limit, as the number of allies pressing to restructure dwindled in number and political influence. After December 1913, those who hoped to deepen corporate accountability in telecommunications would campaign in an environment where a strategic accommodation with Bell was becoming both viable and attractive not only to core business users, but—under federal auspices—to the foremost commercial independents as well.[20]

Even so, the compromise did not curtail the campaign for a federal takeover of the nation's wires. In the wake of both administrative regulation by state and federal agencies and the Justice Department's settlement with AT&T, popular political struggle to achieve more comprehensive social justice persisted. Meantime, a much less well-known initiative, carrying far-reaching implications, was undertaken by an independent congressional agency: the ICC.

The Interstate Commerce Commission Investigates Private-Wire Contracts

If in the Kingsbury Commitment AT&T confronted a federal effort to sustain the interests of independent capital in telecommunications, then in a 1917–1918 inquiry conducted by the ICC, AT&T and Western Union together confronted a federal attempt to support the needs of big business users. The purpose of the ICC's inquiry was to scrutinize the lawfulness of specialized services provided by the carriers to corporate customers—services that had been introduced after the Civil War. "Private wires," or "leased lines," offered exclusive and uninterrupted use to a single customer of a telegraph circuit between two fixed locations, for a prespecified period: a full day, or a part of a day, each day over the term of the (monthly) lease. This so-called Morse private wire service might be set up between corporate headquarters and a branch plant; or between brokers' offices in two cities; or, by means of "drops" at intermediate locations, between several sites of one company; or between locations of two or more lessees. Customers did not actually rent a specific wire, but contracted to gain access to one (or more) of a carrier's available commercial circuits "for the transmission of messages between the points . . . named during the hours specified." These corporate customers hired their own telegraph operators.[21]

Private-wire contracts proliferated in tandem with the expansion of big businesses. This was not mere happenstance: private lines helped enable enterprises to administer and coordinate their activities at regional and, increasingly, at national scale. Located disproportionately across a belt of northern states, private-wire systems stretched from the Atlantic coast far to the west; some larger systems crossed the border to link locations in the United States and Canada. Major users ran the gamut. Railroads were large customers, often developing explicit sharing arrangements with Western Union to aid in their movement of freight from one road to another. The Associated Press adopted a similar course and, indeed, the AP was the heaviest collective user of leased lines. In 1914, exclusive of railroads, the lion's share of telegraph private-wire leases (perhaps as much as four-fifths of the total) went to bankers and brokers, some of whom built up rented systems "covering the entire country"; and an additional 9 percent by meat-packing, iron, and steel companies (a newspaper reported that all of U.S. Steel's plants and subsidiaries "are connected by private telegraph wire"). Standard Oil was accounted to be a very large user, and G. F. Swift, by then the nation's largest meat-packer, spent $200,000 annually on telegraphic communications during the 1890s. "Practically all of the industrial lessees of Morse service," the ICC underlined, "are among the larger and more powerful in their respective lines." The ICC found it expedient to confine its investigation to contracts between the carriers and financial and industrial concerns, thereby excluding railroad common carriers and press interests (which had entered no complaint).[22]

In turn, private wires quickly became an important market segment for the carriers. In 1878, one carrier catering to banks and brokerages rented 300 private lines with 1,200 miles of wire in and around New York City. AT&T's Morse service, which dated from when the company started (and was distinct from its four-year controlling interest in Western Union), accounted for 22 percent of AT&T's total network mileage in 1915. Provision of this specialized class of service was lucrative, indeed, by the early twentieth century it had become "the greatest source of revenue of the telegraph companies," as the *Wall Street Journal* reported in 1909. By one account, 31 percent of Western Union's net income derived from "sources other than toll messages" in 1896; but the proportion ranged upward of 60 percent by 1906–1908. A Western Union official stated to a Congressional panel in 1909 "that this business was so much more profitable than handling messages that the company had considered a suggestion that it cease to handle messages entirely and turn its entire attention to leased-wire business." AT&T did exactly this in the telegraph service market, as it used its capacious telephone circuits to implement leased-line telegraph offerings on top of its newer private line telephone or voice service. The ICC professed that this so-called talking service was not used extensively; but it listed thirty-two leases for full talking service, thirty-eight for half talking service, and "more frequent" contracts for short-period service (down to a daily period of just fifteen minutes)—as opposed to 183 contracts for Morse service.[23]

AT&T's leased-line telegraph business was worth $1.2 million in 1905; by comparison, Western Union's leased-line business was then worth $3 million and Postal Telegraph's $940,000. AT&T's acquisition of a controlling interest in Western Union in 1909 therefore would grant it an unassailable dominance over this remunerative market. Whereas, around 1904, AT&T garnered 28 percent of the industry's private-wire revenue, by 1914 its share had doubled, to 56 percent. Moreover, although as we saw the Kingsbury Commitment compelled AT&T to dispose of its interest in Western Union, this decree did not bar the giant carrier from the private-wire telegraph market—indeed, it permitted AT&T to retain access to Western Union's railroad rights-of-way and to keep for itself Western Union's important printing telegraph patents. As a result, AT&T and Western Union switched places, respectively claiming $2.8 million and $1.1 million in private-wire revenues by 1917; Postal's share continued its decline, to a little over half a million dollars.[24]

It was in this context that the Grain Dealers' National Association lodged what the ICC characterized as "an informal complaint" about some prevalent features of the private-wire business; the Grain Receivers' Association of

Chicago became the formal complainant. Other private-wire lessees participated in the proceeding that ensued, including brokers, magazine publishers, and meat packers: a generalized business user interest thus acted as the core source of the investigation. "Extensive" hearings were held in Chicago and New York City, in support of the Commission's inquiry. Of specific importance in the originating complaint, and the study that followed, was that "under the terms of the private-wire contracts of the Western Union Telegraph Company use is made of its public wires at less than the published tariff rates and that persons other than parties to the contracts frequently use the private wires of lessees the transmission of private messages free of charge, in violation of the act to regulate commerce." The ICC's investigation, however—taken on its own motion—encompassed a wider field of issues. It set about studying "contracts for private telegraph and telephone wires, and the rates, rules, and regulations therefor and the practices thereunder," and ordered that all three carriers be respondents. Private-wire contracts for both Morse and "talking" service were studied, and AT&T and Western Union, stated the Commission, "bore the burden of defending the practices under investigation." By contrast, the Postal Telegraph-Cable Company ("Postal") concurred with the grain shippers in requesting a radical alteration to policy and practice. "In effect," the ICC explained, "we are asked to abolish the private wire services."[25]

Facing this frontal challenge to the lawfulness of a crucial "class" of service, the Commission was at pains to underline that it had happened onto unfamiliar territory. The legislation that had expanded its jurisdiction to include telecommunications made no provision for private wires: "Had the Congress desired either to recognize the propriety of such contracts, or to forbid them, it could have expressed this intent. . . . This was not done." However, the ICC apprehended that the issues raised by the complaint fell within the heartland of its enlarged responsibilities, in that they charged the carriers with practicing discrimination. This discrimination was, the inquiry revealed, both systematic and multifarious. First and foremost, the ICC laboriously calculated, the carriers provided corporate users with leased lines at a steeply discounted price as compared to their charges for using the public networks on which households and smaller businesses were compelled to depend. "The record warrants the conclusion that in rendering Morse private wire service and the public message service at their present rates," the ICC summarized, the carriers "are furnishing the more valuable service at a relatively lower charge, contrary to recognized principles of classification." Price discrimination, the Commission found, was coupled to other forms of favoritism.[26]

If, for some reason, a customer found that private line service had been interrupted, they were contractually permitted to make use of the public message service at half the ordinary commercial rate. Furthermore, such messages were accorded pride of place over "ordinary" telegrams as the carriers instituted a hierarchical policy for transmission. Lessees had, in addition, been "subletting" private wires to others, sometimes even permitting unaffiliated users to send messages of their own. No one knew how widespread this practice was. Also, lessees sometimes shared use of their private wires with outside companies, not parties to their contract but involved in the conduct of their business. Again, the extent of this sharing was not known. Both practices—"resale," and "sharing," as they came to be called decades later—diverted trade which, otherwise, would have had to pay full freight in order to traverse a public message network. Finally, Bell's "talking service" contracts for "full," or all-day, service, permitted users to terminate "their" circuit in the carrier's central office; this enabled such customers both "to call for any telephone number within the local area ... and, at his option, allowing any telephone subscriber within the local exchange area to call for connection with the full talking circuit." These features again found some parallel with service options of the 1960s and afterward (foreign office and 800 numbers).[27]

Far from being walled off from the public networks and thus engendering only isolated effects, therefore, these discriminatory practices bore down on the general system of networking. In declaring to the ICC the "position that this Commission ought to put a stop to the leasing of wires to those lessees who can in turn sublet it or do sublet it to others," Postal and the grain traders threw a grenade into policymaking. If the ICC heeded their complaint, it faced three options. It might abolish private-wire contracts; or, it might rule that charges for private wires needed to be raised, to make them equivalent or comparable to charges for ordinary public network messages; or, it might hold that charges for public network messages must be reduced. No matter which of these alternatives the ICC might choose—as a Western Union attorney acknowledged sixteen years later—it was beyond doubt that private wires indeed incarnated "an unjust discrimination against the sender of the ordinary message, as a service furnished at a rate inherently too low."[28]

Caught between Western Union and AT&T and the diverse large businesses that predominated as lessors of private wires, the ICC found itself on a very hot seat. Though discrimination was unmistakable, an authoritative finding of discrimination would have grave repercussions. The agency would need to reconcile its finding with its statutory responsibilities, which—in line with antimonopolism—prohibited discriminatory practices by common carriers. That is, it would actually have to produce a remedy. Lowering rates for use of the public network would set off a firestorm of objections from the carriers; but the elimination of private wires would be even more explosive. Leased lines were not only a highly lucrative slice of the carriers' business, but their withdrawal would also induce a chaotic disruption into the operations of the carriers' largest customers. If business users the likes of Swift were made to relinquish their preferred status, could they rebuild their existing regional and national operations? If the ICC raised the rates for leased lines, finally, business users would be apoplectic: their dissatisfaction had prompted the inquiry in the first place. No matter what its course, the ICC could be nearly certain that a phalanx of corporations operating in many states would respond to its transgressions by appealing to the agency's legislative overseers, that is, to Congress. No doubt to its chagrin, the ICC had brought to the surface a submerged foundation-stone of US networking, and one whose problematic significance would only continue to increase for the remainder of the twentieth century. How could the Commission maneuver out of its dilemma?

The ICC's ruling came encrusted in indirection. Finding that the prime source of discrimination—the existence of private telegraph wires—actually was not a violation, and that private lines constituted a distinct and legitimate class of service, the agency went on to hold that some lesser abuses merited elimination. A Morse service provider would be "justified" in removing from its contracts the provision that if the private wires were interrupted, the public wires could be used at half the regular rate. A carrier also would be "justified" in inserting into its contracts a clause restricting the use of private wires to the business of the lessees "and providing that messages shall not be transmitted for other persons or firms." The ICC "can not prescribe a minimum rate" for use of private wires, nor, because "the charges for messages other than by private wire are not in issue," did it find that the rates for ordinary commercial telegrams should be reduced. It proposed only that carriers "should consider whether or not their rates for Morse private-wire service should be revised." Finally, because the record showed "no essential differences" between private-wire talking service and the toll service of the Bell company, "we are of the opinion that the classification of messages into private-wire talking service is not a just and reasonable classification." The ICC elaborated that, "in maintaining this talking service the Bell Company unduly prefers messages sent by private wire and the lessees of such wires and subjects to undue prejudice messages sent at the toll rates and the senders thereof." However, Postal was incorrect to assert later that "the Interstate Commerce Commission found that leased-line telephone service was discriminatory against the small user and in favor of the large user and should be discontinued." In all respects, the ICC delivered not a bold, authoritative judgment but only a meek opinion. It fully recognized, but only very selectively challenged, a practice of wholesale discrimination which had already become engraved. The ICC had compiled facts demonstrating that US telecommunications revolved around something beyond carrier monopolies, and large business users of specialized private wires would continue to shape the structure and policy of US telecommunications going forward. Indeed, ultimately—in the era of the Internet—they would transform the very foundations of networking.[29]

Withal, in 1918, the ICC found means of sidestepping even its own timorous opinion. "By virtue of the President's proclamation," the Commission declared in the final paragraph of its ruling—which, purportedly, was "decided" just three days after a government takeover went into effect—the nation's telegraph and telephone systems "are now under federal control." Because the classification and charges for all services now had passed into the hands of government authorities, the agency professed, "the entry of an order would serve no useful purpose." Nevertheless, it concluded, "since this statement of facts may be beneficial . . . we have deemed it expedient to promulgate this report." It thereupon passed into obscurity.[30]

What did it signify, that the President had ordered a takeover of the country's wireline systems? Did it herald an end to the systemic discrimination that elevated big carriers and big corporate users over the general public? Did it come as a vindication of the antimonopoly movement?

The Run-Up to Postalization

Trade unions are not static or fixed, but mutable and evolving organizations. A given union may be, or become, exclusionary or inclusive; democratic, or brittle and bureaucratic in its procedures; outward-looking and sociopolitically engaged with the aim of transforming the wider society, or focused narrowly on bread-and-butter objectives to strengthen and enhance the work-lives of its existing members. In 1907, in behalf of the Commercial Telegraphers Union (which had just lost a three-month strike against Western Union), the American Federation of Labor resolved to petition Congress to establish a commission to inquire into conditions in the telegraph industry and to develop "such remedial legislation as may bring about Government ownership of all telephone and telegraph lines with the least possible delay." Although under its president Samuel Gompers the AFL had often eschewed party politics, the federation went on to support government ownership consistently throughout and immediately after World War I. The perils of private ownership had been repeatedly identified during the preceding half century, and broad union support for a Post Office takeover carried forward. In early 1914, a Chicago stalwart recollected for the Postmaster General that, since the 1870s, the Knights of Labor had demanded that "hereafter no charter or license be issued to any corporation for construction or operation of any means of transporting intelligence, freight, passengers, or power." "When congress and the administration reach the conclusion that the time is ripe for taking over the wire service of the country," boasted a committee of union printers—a powerful grouping within the AFL—"the International Typographical Union can justly claim to be the one labor organization that has consistently and persistently advocated this step for the past quarter of a century."[31]

It is revealing, in this context, that AT&T's 1913 Annual Report to shareholders—the very one that devoted a trifle over four pages to consideration of the Kingsbury Commitment—directly followed this brief discussion with thirty-four pages of material attacking "Government Ownership and Operation." Numerous newspapers and periodicals endorsed this proposal—and not only those run by radicals, such as *The Appeal to Reason* (circulation of about 750,000). AT&T would acknowledge a few years later that "[h]undreds of dailies, headed by the Hearst organs, and a larger number of weeklies, including many labor organs, have continually printed newspaper stories in behalf of government ownership." Both the comparatively large number of independent commercial papers in this era predating chain dominance, and the ability of oppositional groups to foot the bill for establishing their own journals, enabled this trend.[32]

Nationalization of telegraphs and telephones or, simply, "means of communication," was a plank in at least one third-party platform in every presidential election between 1884 and 1924, and until the 1910s this reform goal enjoyed an expansive social reach. Greenbackers and Populists had propelled it into the last years of the nineteenth century and, by an AT&T manager's admission, as late as 1917 "[a]gricultural organizations, such as the National Grange, the Farmers Union, the Farmers Equity Society, and the Farmers Educational and Co-operation Union, carrying on their traditional policy of radicalism in matters affecting public utility corporations, [were] favorably disposed toward all government ownership measures." Rural interests were important because they could and in this case did translate into a disproportionate measure of congressional support. An AT&T manager privately estimated that, at the close of 1916, twenty senators and forty-four representatives were on record as supporting telegraph and telephone ownership by the government.[33]

Maryland Democratic Representative David J. Lewis became the leading legislative voice for postalization. Lewis possessed a background markedly at variance from that of most of his peers in Congress. A fulltime miner in the coal pits of Pennsylvania at age nine, then an organizer for the Knights of Labor and, during the 1890s, a Populist, Lewis had learned the law through study after completing his ten-hour shift in the mines. This arduous self-education led him into state and then federal politics. Lewis was not entirely isolated in Washington. Fifteen trade unionists served as members of Congress in 1912; and the incoming cabinet secretary of the just-established Department of Labor, William B. Wilson, was another former miner, Knights of Labor leader, and official of the United Mine Workers. He and Lewis were good friends, and Lewis took over from Wilson as the chair of the House Labor Committee, following him as labor's "chief spokesman . . . within the federal government." AFL President Samuel Gompers stumped for Lewis in his 1914 campaign, as did Secretary of Labor Wilson and, less predictably, Postmaster General Burleson and President Woodrow Wilson. Considered the father of parcel post—which, alongside postal savings, continued to be hailed by Democrats as a key expression of their party's record of success during the campaign of 1916—as well as a top congressional expert on Post Office economics, one of Lewis's repeated challenges to Vail was that AT&T was obstructing popular access to telephone service.[34]

In a speech to Congress in 1913 Lewis interpreted Vail's own commentary, delivered in an AT&T report: "We are virtually told that of the three great agencies of postal communication only one, the letter post, may be used by the people, and that the other two, the phone and the telegraph, are conveniences or luxuries, not popular necessities, and for that reason should be at the cost of the few, i.e., of the rich, to which class largely the present rates confine the service." An admittedly self-serving journalistic campaigner in behalf of commercial independents picked up Lewis's theme. Competition and postalization, he held, were both preferable to AT&T monopoly: "should the people not get proper relief through" administrative regulation by the ICC, "the ultimate remedy would lie in the ownership and operation of the telephone utility by the Government. That remedy will no doubt eventually be necessary and is desirable because the telephone is everybody's common means of communication, wherein, more so than with written communication, all tongues, all thought and expressions can be conveyed or transmitted by the persons interested, direct, without resort to writing and really by personal conversation."[35]

Postmaster General Albert S. Burleson was joined by at least five other members of President Wilson's cabinet, including Navy Secretary Josephus Daniels, and the President's secretary—whose duties "were political rather than clerical"—Joseph P. Tumulty, in supporting the principle of government ownership. Prominent economists and reformers concurred. In August 1915, the controversial Final Report of the Commission On Industrial Relations called for purchase, after proper valuation, of telegraph and telephone facilities and plant by the Federal Government—for whom, in deference to the postal model, was "specifically reserved" by the Constitution "the transmission of intelligence." President Woodrow Wilson himself had written privately to Postmaster General Burleson soon after taking office in 1913 that he had long believed that "the government ought to own the telegraph lines of the country and combine the telegraph with the post office."[36]

The claim survives that the decision to keep US telecommunications in private hands "was taken as a matter of course, without significant debate or serious consideration of alternatives." This assertion is mistaken. Throughout the run-up to US entry into World War I in 1917 (after Lewis's defeat as a Maryland senatorial candidate) postalization possessed quite general political legitimacy. The US Post Office was, as we have seen, at the height of its popularity. That government operation of telecommunications had become a general international norm also was referenced widely—notably, by Frank Parsons in 1899 and Arthur Holcombe in 1911. In Germany, for example, the telephone had been superimposed on an existing postal-telegraph ministry. In France the telephone industry was nationalized in 1889, in Britain only quite recently—in 1911. Closer to home, the western Canadian provinces of Manitoba, Alberta and Saskatchewan bought out their Bell-owned telephone systems between 1907 and 1909. As the conservative Democratic Postmaster General Burleson put it later, "The fact that nearly every other progressive country treats the telephone and telegraph as a governmental monopoly and operates them as parts of their postal systems banishes the suggestion that in doing likewise we should do anything partaking of the startling, radical or revolutionary." The political coalition behind postalization possessed both a broad base and a high reach. At the time of the second Wilson inauguration in March 1917, when the President was seemingly allied with the AFL and with a far-flung community of "progressives, labor militants, and radicals who advocated the democratization of industry," the momentum behind postalization appeared to be well-nigh unstoppable.[37]

Concern was rife within AT&T's executive ranks. Top AT&T managers, including Vice Presidents Thayer and Kingsbury and, especially during the vulnerable months surrounding the Kingsbury pact, President Vail himself, made it their business to track carefully the fortunes of the postalization movement. A "Public Ownership Bureau" operating out of the office of the Commercial Engineer, C. F. Barnard, submitted monthly reports on the campaign for public ownership in cities across the nation. The company's Public Relations Bureau was formally established in 1912, and expressly aimed to deflect proponents of a government takeover. In October 1914, in response to an inquiry from AT&T vice president Thayer, Barnard tallied US opinion concerning government ownership of utilities—by federal, state, and municipal officials, by newspapers, by industrial, labor, farmer, and other organizations, and by prominent individuals. This was not casual surveillance; the company marshaled considerable resources, beginning in 1912, to generate intermittent but detailed files on virtually every social interest involved in the government ownership agitation.[38]

Though a robustly popular "network imaginary" pivoted around postalization, its concrete political content still varied. Mainstream proponents of nationalization stressed economic efficiency and extension of access. In particular, the argument that massive cost reductions would follow from folding the nation's wireline systems into its network of post offices carried considerable weight. The assumption by the Post Office of "the function of electrical communication," Postmaster Burleson repeated in early 1918, "would permit of substantial savings and economies through the coordination of these two, now diversely organized and operated, services of communication." Because they duplicated established Post Office activities, Burleson held, such functions as telephone and telegraph "revenue accounting, revenue collecting, collection expense, salaries of general officers, and their clerks" might be substantially reduced. Other expenses borne by the private-wire carriers—"advertising, canvassing, promotion"—would be "susceptible of complete elimination." Echoing Congressman Lewis—who quietly coordinated the extensive research on which he depended—Burleson also sounded a second note when he underlined that social access to electrical communication systems stood to be enlarged under Post Office control. "Communication," Burleson declared, "is a means primal to the gratification of all human requirements. It should therefore be made accessible to all persons, whatever their fortunes may be, as considerations of public economy will allow." Charged by the Constitution with this function, the federal government should make available "ample facilities" for providing service at reasonable cost—"in fact at as low cost as efficient service permits, so that the largest number possible may use it." He sharply contrasted the nation's postal and telephone systems:

> The postal system has so realized these great objects, so formulated its rates, that the poorest self-sustaining human being can afford to use any service it performs. The only postal limitation on his communicating from end to end of the Republic is the cost of a two cent stamp. On the other hand the use of these great facilities of communicating by electricity is woefully restricted among the masses of the people by the necessities of the interest of private persons who own and manage them. . . . They represent failures, grave failures in modern communication, but they are failures judged by postal standards, not by the standards of private enterprise.

Contemporary radicals and trade unionists often continued to think in their own different terms. While many embraced the efficiency and, especially, the expanded access cited by Burleson, they grounded their support for postalization in other aims and concerns. Referring to evidence taken by the Industrial Commission, the AFL considered a resolution of the Commercial Telegraphers' Union of America at its 1915 Convention, this one in support of the Lewis bill—"providing for the Government ownership of the telegraph, and advocates and will support any similar measure introduced in the next Congress . . . with a provision included, granting to the employees of the Government engaged in such service the right to organize." Collective self-organization—trade unionism—was the intended axis.[39]

Leaders of the National Public Ownership League, formed in 1916 and headquartered in Chicago, included the Socialist Carl D. Thompson and Morton

L. Johnson of the Penny Phone League. The National Public Ownership League sought "democratic control of public utilities" through a government takeover of the telephone. Democratic control again encompassed, first and foremost, a right to working-class self-organization. "[T]he only way to overcome the monopoly of the Bell Company," Morton Johnson declared, was through the International Brotherhood of Electrical Workers' organization of the nation's 200,000-odd telephone employees. IBEW locals, he argued, could look to move forward with this project by approving two linked resolutions and forwarding the vote results to Congress and to Postmaster General Burleson:

> Resolved: That we heartily approve of the immediate postalization of all telephone lines....
> Resolved: That we will appreciate your active efforts to bring about the speedy enactment of the proper legislation to consummate this object.

In early 1917, the Chicago Federation of Labor resolved unanimously in favor of a more modest bill introduced as a steppingstone to a more comprehensive postalization by Representative Lewis—the Telephone Postalization Experiment—to take over the telephone system of the Chesapeake and Potomac company (a Bell affiliate) within the District of Columbia. Other letters supporting this second Lewis bill streamed in from central labor councils and AFL affiliates in, among other places, South Bend, Indiana; Mahoning County, Ohio; Aurora Illinois; Baltimore, Maryland; Globe, Arizona; Waterbury, Connecticut; Petaluma, California; Kenosha, Wisconsin; Reno, Nevada; Rochester, New York; Phoenix, Arizona; Erie, Pennsylvania; Lansing, Michigan; Portland, Oregon; Milwaukee, San Francisco and Detroit.[40]

Postalization, many unionists hoped, would presage union representation and collective bargaining rights. In 1917, we will see, proponents began to emphasize military necessity in a time of national emergency; even in this increasingly fraught context, however, organized labor never stopped pressing for changes that lay well beyond efficiency and service extension. The 1918 Convention of the AFL again resolved, in accord with resolutions brought in by the CFL and by the Railroad Telegraphers, in favor of an "immediate[]" government takeover "for the period of the war and"—significantly—"as long thereafter as may be deemed advisable." In what proved a prescient warning, however, one AFL delegate backhandedly underlined an urgent need to prioritize the right to organize.

Postmaster Burleson was infamous for repressing postal unions, despite the fact that these unions had been sanctioned by the Lloyd-LaFollette Act in August, 1912: legislation that came into force on the very day that Burleson became Postmaster. Postal workers thus faced both draconian Post Office managers and an absolute ban on strikes by federal employees. This AFL member "urged the delegates to consider very carefully the proposition to have the government take over the telegraph systems unless accompanied by a guarantee that the workers would have the right to organize and to petition Congress in their own behalf. He referred to the experience of the post office clerks and the efforts that [had] been made to prevent them from organizing and becoming affiliated with the American labor movement." The ensuing resolution picked up his suggestion. Still demanding postalization, it insisted that the right to organize should not be ceded. It went on to flay the management of Western Union and Postal Telegraph for "arrogantly flouting public opinion, and in other ways abusing the powers and privileges that the people have conferred upon them." Battling Burleson would be an uphill fight, no doubt, but the alternative—the status quo, dominated by private capital and aggressively supportive courts—seemed worse. Moreover, circumstances had been generally more propitious for organized labor during the first Wilson administration. Thus, among telecommunications workers, the long-standing critique of private monopoly's negative ramifications began to fuse with hopes that postalization would enable concrete advances. Divergences persisted; and so did solidarity.[41]

Political radicals continued to play a lively part. In 1912 the American Socialist Party enjoyed greater legitimacy than ever before, with over 115,000 members; as many as three million Americans read avowedly socialist newspapers. In the 1912 election, Socialists were elected to public office in 340 municipalities scattered across twenty-four states. In Milwaukee, Victor Berger had won the mayoralty with his state socialist approach, very nearly taking for granted that the sheer fact of government ownership could be counted on to engender the cooperative purpose around which society should be reconstructed:

> Whenever the nation, state, or community has undertaken to manage and own any large industry, railroad, mine, factory, telegraph, telephone, mill, canal, etc., this invariably redounded to the benefit of the commonwealth. Business will be carried on under Socialism for use and not for profit.
>
> This is the case now in the post-office, public school, waterworks, etc.— wherever owned and managed by the people.

Echoing the Marx of the Communist Manifesto, Socialist Party leader Morris Hillquit could agree that "the inherently national" functions of telegraph and telephone lines qualified it for a government takeover. However, by contrast to Victor Berger, but akin to Marx in *The Civil War in France* (1871), James Connolly in 1899, and Lenin in 1917, Hillquit insisted that postalization per se would not be sufficient. His explication is noteworthy for its clarity. "Socialists," declared Hillquit, "entertain no illusions as to the benefits of governmentally owned industries under the present regime." Nationalization often occurred, he stated, not as democratic measure but merely to furnish revenue to the government or to support its military operations. In these instances government ownership might "strengthen rather than loosen the grip of capitalist governments on the people and its effect may be decidedly reactionary." At the same time, nationalization was often supported by middle-class parties of reform, mainly in order to decrease the taxes paid by property owners and reduce the rates of freight, transportation, and communication for small business. By contrast, Hillquit continued,

> The Socialists advocate government ownership primarily for the purpose of eliminating private profits from the operation of public utilities, and conferring the benefits of such industries on the employees and consumers. Their demand for national or municipal ownership of industries is always qualified by a provision for the democratic administration of such industries and for the application of the profits to the increase of the employee's wages and the improvement of the service... In other words, what the Socialists advocate is not government ownership under purely capitalist administration, but collective ownership under a government controlled, or at least strongly influenced, by political representatives of the working class.

Socialists, therefore—as often—were not of one mind; the Belgian Emile VanderVelde rejected government ownership out of hand, remember, on grounds that workers needed to abolish the capitalist state rather than to expand it. What needs to be stressed again is that these were not mere musings by sequestered theorists. At the turn of the century, rather, workers both at European PTTs and in the United States were often prone to agree that government ownership was a necessary starting-point.[42]

English postal workers used the twenty years after 1897 to gain bargaining clout by merging what had been dozens of small unions; World War I engendered a struggle to establish that form of workers' control known as "guild socialism" and, by 1921, the Union of Post Office Workers claimed 100,000 members, the Post Office Engineering Union represented "technical" employees in the telegraph and telephone services, and the two were attempting to coordinate their efforts. In France, a 1909 strike by postal, telephone, and telegraph employees did not succeed; they then moved to affiliate with the Confederation Generale du Travail, the radical syndicalist union of industrial workers within which they soon became a powerful voice. Suffering from inflation and goaded by autocratic state managers, German postal workers were concurrently establishing themselves as a militant faction within the encompassing Federation of Civil Servants. As Lenin turned to assess postal organization, he had before him the example of a union of Russian postal and telegraph workers, which became "especially active" under the provisional government that existed in 1917, before the October Revolution: rank-and-file employees of the Post and Telegraph Ministry demanded an eight hour day and cost-of-living wage increases in the face of raging inflation. Union members likewise insisted on "democratization," Daniel Orlovsky explains, "by which they meant an all-out attack on the workplace hierarchy." Letter carriers and telegraphers wanted elections of their own managers and unit chiefs; their workplace committees demanded a transfer of authority within the Ministry to elected collectives and "pressed their union to assume full administrative authority while transforming power relations within the ministry." Probably of most immediate relevance to the Irish American women who made up many of the telephone operators in Boston and New York City were actions in Ireland. The Post Office was the largest employer in Ireland, with 17,000 workers operating postal, telegraph, and telephone services and, in 1916, Dublin's just completed General Post Office became the core of the Easter Rising. As what Dublin newspapers disparaged for being "a nest of Sinn Feiners," the General Post Office now is considered by some historians to be "the birthplace ... of an independent Ireland."[43]

Of course, neither the mostly male telegraphers nor the disproportionately Irish American women telephone operators of the Northeastern states were direct participants in these far-flung and diverse national experiences—but, to carry forward a theme of the previous chapter, in this age of "transatlantic crossings" they were not remote. Those who were even indirectly familiar with the top-down administrative practices of European post and telecommunications ministries would have had more than an inkling that, without democratic representation in workplace decision-making, workers might have something to fear from postalization. For many US telegraphers and telephone operators postalization galvanized hopes of a fresh start in the struggle to improve wages and working conditions through self-organization and collective bargaining. As real wages were hit by ravaging inflation, and working conditions remained harsh—for railway mail clerks, often deadly—hard reasoning inclined them "to gamble," as Christopher May puts it, that the Government would prove a less-intolerable employer than the private companies.[44]

Though some historians have purported to discern an overarching "anticompetitive consensus," once more, business-minded proponents of economic efficiency operated with disparate premises, and were likely to draw different conclusions, than male trade unionists intent on attaining collective bargaining rights and women telegraph operators resisting sexism in the workplace—to say nothing of radicals harboring visions of revolution. However, one year into US participation in World War I, telephone and telegraph operators' hopes for postalization seemed realizable. In April of 1918 President Wilson issued labor policies for private employees, to be implemented by the War Labor Board;

these accorded a right to organize and to bargain collectively, and mandated that "employers should not discharge workers for membership in trade unions." "[I]t was natural, therefore," recollected Julia O'Connor, the militant president of the Telephone Operators Department of the IBEW, "that the telephone workers looked to Government control as a way out of their difficulties." O'Connor (Figure 3.1) went on to underline that, among the operators, a federal takeover had been "heralded as a hope and possibility for the democratization of the telephone industry."[45]

Figure 3.1 Julia O'Connor. President of Boston Local 1A of the IBEW's Telephone Operators' Department, in 1919 O'Connor led New England's telephone operators in a successful strike against the Post-Office-run telephone service. Courtesy of The International Brotherhood of Electrical Workers.

In this "fertile and fluid" moment, "industrial democracy" was a term to conjure with. At one pole, some executives, journalists, academics, and jurists—Louis Brandeis was the most influential—invoked it to signify a joint effort by capital and labor: to manage disputes between workers and businesses in a way that would avert strikes and violence. They felt that principles of democratic participation and accountability might be broadened beyond political citizenship so that, for many of them, the goal became to place the economy on a stable and productive basis under the aegis of paternalistic corporations. By contrast, for Samuel Gompers and many other AFLers, the essence of the program was to compel corporate acquiescence to workers' collective bargaining rights, absent which labor could not win tangible benefits. Still again, for socialists industrial democracy gestured in grander ways toward control of the means of production. Radical members of the Industrial Workers of the World used "economic democracy" to signify a need for collective power exerted by workers over individual plants and factories: syndicalism. Engaging these often-conflicting aspirations, Joseph A. McCartin contends, industrial democracy "possessed an electric appeal precisely because it promised to harness contending interests to what seemed to be shared goals: a more powerful state, a more democratic workplace."[46]

A self-described proponent recollected a few years later that the prewar union movement "was exceedingly wary of the extension of governmental ownership unaccompanied by labor control of government or by labor participation in management." To improve wages and enhance job security and working conditions, telephone and telegraph workers insisted on their rights to union representation and collective bargaining. These they deemed elemental and concrete criteria for realizing industrial democracy.[47]

As their struggle fed into a resurgent campaign for postalization, the operators' experience placed them in key ways at the forward edge of efforts to remake state and society. Akin to other women wage workers, telephone operators faced gender-based pressures and constraints that ranged beyond inadequate pay and benefits and onerous working conditions; some were sensitized to gender-based employment discrimination and sexual harassment on the job. In daring to demand independent collective bargaining rights alongside male wage workers, however, they met with discrimination not only from their employers but also from fellow trade unionists. The operators' jobs were also suffused with racist practices of employment discrimination, as Venus Green shows; and these women operators came to personify an exclusionary "white lady" identity. In an era marked by Jim Crow segregation, the labor force in telecommunications tended to share, rather than challenge, the nation's commitment to white supremacy. When, upon assuming office, President Woodrow Wilson "brought a kind of de facto segregation to the federal government," separating black and white postal workers in the workplace and instituting a photograph as a mandatory requirement for Post Office job applicants in order exclude Blacks, he gained support among the white working class, including among federal workers.[48]

Within the glaring limits on solidarity imposed by "living wage" sexism and flaring racism, telecommunications workers hopefully pressed their case. During these years individual workers spoke out for radical changes. The telecommunications industry's "duty to serve"—acclaimed by later liberal scholars—thus was not in thralldom to legalistic doctrines and administrative regulation. Instead, admittedly fragmentary testimonies demonstrate, a movement to alter the social uses of telecommunications in the United States remained grounded in a multifaceted critique of corporate capitalism. "The truth is we have been shamefully underpaid," an IBEW telephone operator told the Seattle Central Labor Council in November 1917, "and that we have been forced to fight for everything we ever got from the Seattle Telephone Company." Other telecommunications workers gave eloquent and extended testimony to their experience and independent thinking.[49]

Here is Andrew Plecher, from Florinda Florida, who wrote to the First Assistant Postmaster General in 1915 to propose "U.S. Tel's. + Tel's. so that our newspapers become free ... from infernal bondage and enormous puplic [sic] lies be eliminated." His complaint—that private monopoly in telecommunications had corrupted the news media—was congruent with that of the International Typographical Union (ITU). The ITU spent a reported $100,000, and fielded committees in Washington for over twenty years, "to labor for the nationalization of the telegraph systems" on the grounds that whenever "there was trouble in any particular part of the country between organized labor and those in opposition to it the facts were distorted" and the minds of the people "poisoned for a great many years by these unfair reports that have been sent broadcast by the press monopolies that are in control of the great newspapers of America"—the Associated Press and the United Press.[50]

Rank-and-file support for a substantive transformation of the social purposes of telecommunications broke through in letters written to agencies of the executive branch and, in particular, to the Postmaster General. Persistent intervention by advocates of government ownership, after the ascent of regulation by state commissions and after the promulgation of the Kingsbury Commitment, testifies that the campaign for social justice and democratic accountability was spilling over the channels that these measures sought to establish.

Here is William Brown, a telephone installer employed by AT&T's manufacturing subsidiary Western Electric. Brown wrote in August 1914 to tell the Justice Department that he wished to transfer to a job with New York Telephone, where he believed he "would have a better opportunity to get ahead." At a moment when workforce turnover had surfaced as a critical cost issue for corporate managers—the quit rate in electrical and machine-building plants increased 329 percent between 1913 and 1918—the Bell System placed restrictions on the movement of employees between its affiliates. Brown related how, accordingly, he had been told "that the Western Electric Co. has an agreement with the Bell Companies throughout the country, not to employ or consider employing men in the employ of the Western Electric Co." "Isn't this agreement a violation of the law or at any rate a violation of the spirit of fair play and could you do anything to stop this practice?" Brown asked. In a second letter, two weeks later, Brown clarified a key detail. At Western Electric where he worked, he asserted, "wages are lower and hours higher and work harder than in the Bell Cos." The agreement between Western Electric and the Bell companies, to his way of thinking, "prevent[ed] a man from selling his services freely"; did it not therefore "constitute a combination in restraint of trade"? G. Carroll Todd, the Assistant to the Attorney General, casually dismissed Brown's complaint in a response to this second entreaty: "By long established tradition and practice," he wrote Brown, "it is not permissible for the Attorney General to express opinions upon questions at law except at the request of the President and the heads of the Executive Departments." If, however, Brown could provide evidence to support his statement that there existed a discriminatory hiring agreement between the Bell companies and Western Electric, then "the Department [would] take appropriate action in the event that a violation of any Federal law [was] disclosed."[51]

Here is Archie E. Rainey, who wrote the Postmaster General in 1918 to argue, portentously, that the telegraph should be turned into "a public utility" through government ownership. A telegrapher who had been dismissed from his job, he claimed, for membership in the Commercial Telegraphers Union of America, Rainey's conception of "public utility" lay at odds with existing administrative and legal usages. He believed that with government ownership it would be possible to "discontinue the leasing of thousands of miles of wire at present in use in every city big + small in the country in gambling resorts;—gambling in stocks + grain options etc." Such a project, which resonated through the years from Laurence Gronlund to the Prohibitionist Party in 1916, struck directly at an economy reliant on finance capital and on the specialized telecommunications-based institutions, such as commodity and stock exchanges, that animated it. It merits brief explication.[52]

David Hochfelder shows that, after 1877, the availability of telegraph stock tickers rapidly popularized speculation through the new institution of "bucket shops"—"betting parlors in which patrons wagered small sums on the price movements of stocks and commodities." Unlike speculation conducted via brokerages, however, wagers placed at bucket shops had no influence on stock prices because these were private transactions in which the house always took the bet against a patron. During the 1880s, in an attempt to regulate the bucket shops and to drive more of the speculation back into "legitimate" brokerages, "most states banned stock and commodity transactions in which delivery was not contemplated"; but a legal loophole permitted the bucket shops not only to survive but to thrive. Telegraph service was essential to their operation—and Western Union thus became a complicit party to them, just as it also was for legitimate stock exchanges and brokerages. A "widespread public confusion about the difference between speculation and gambling" not surprisingly also persisted. Additional counter-measures against the bucket shops ultimately led to their demise, by 1913 or so. It is not certain whether Rainey was singling out the bucket shops, but from both his language and the date of his missive (May 1918) it seems likely that he was targeting legitimate brokerages. "There are between five + ten thousand of the most expert operators now in the brokerage business, receiving the highest compensation averaging $150 a month," Rainey declared: "Place these telegraphers in the government service + I am convinced the country will develop one of the greatest + most successful telegraph systems in the world." In considering his proto-syndicalist plan, Rainey asked the Postmaster General to "bear in mind I am only a telegrapher, who, after thirty years service + accounted one of the countrys most expert operators received a wage of four dollars a day + was dismissed without a moments notice. I am out on the street, hoping that while my son, Archie E. Rainey is on his way to France to fight for our country, that the government will not permit the telegraph trusts to starve his father in this country."[53]

And here, finally, is Miss. L. L. Laundine (?), of Mobile, Alabama, whose criticism of the abuses engendered by corporate telegraphy came through in her 1918 letter to the Postmaster General. "I am a lady of most unquestionable character + enjoy the confidence + respect of the best people along this coast from Mobile to New Orleans, + am prepared to prove every statement I make," she declared. She listed a litany of "abuses" observed during "many years" of service at both major US telegraph companies. First, "I notice the enormous extravagances, waste, + unnecessary expenses, that would be saved if one had Govt. Control + even if telegraph + telephone tolls were reduced, in order to remove such a burden from the people—it would soon amount to enough to pay for the property taken over." Examples of such waste, she declared—in another instance of radical interpretation—included certain forms of advertising, "spies and spotters," and overpaid salaried officials:

> Federal Control would be hailed with joy by the army of men + women, slaving year by year on a mental strain, mistreated + under paid, and nearly all of them nervous wrecks before they reach middle life.
> Our country is fighting for world freedom + Democracy + yet the Autocrats of its Telegraph Lines, are enslaving over 50000 people in our midsts in body

+ soul—It is more that an operator dares, to resist this tyranny or oppose their unjust demands or sympathize with a Union that seeks to better their condition or strikes off—their shackles—or they are blacklisted + discharged.

Ms. Lauundine went on to link private ownership and control of telegraph specifically to sexual harassment which, she charged, had poisoned her work environment. For her, the idea of industrial democracy might have required reforms that often exceeded those sought by male telegraphers. She concluded that she would "watch with interest all legislation favoring Govt ownership, + freedom to the slaves of the telegraph world."[54]

Trade unionists and radical reformers urged changes that went demonstrably beyond legal formalisms. The testimony of William Brown and L. L. Lauundine and Archie Rainey likewise refutes interpretations of telecommunications development that rest on any form of consensus, and shows that the quest to improve employment conditions was bound up with workers' proposals to transform the very structure and purpose of telecommunications. Clashes over these issues reached their apogee during 1918–1919, when the Post Office actually took over and operated the nation's wire networks. At this point, in keeping with Joseph A. McCartin's thesis, "the struggle to determine what vision of industrial democracy would prevail in the wartime workplace" became "a battle to influence the state itself."[55]

"Mr. Burleson's Adventure"

Commencing with independent telephony and the emergence of dual service in major cities, and continuing on through the municipalization drive and the Kingsbury Commitment, at the verge of US entry into World War I, the movement to reform telecommunications had repeatedly coalesced and regrouped. In 1916, an internal AT&T memorandum declared—no doubt, to the relief of executives—that "agitations for municipal ownership of telephones" were becoming "less frequent." The reform campaign to postalize telecommunications, however, had gained fresh momentum. Both this movement and the intensifying conflict that it provoked reached their peak during 1918 and 1919.[56]

Throughout earlier decades, initiatives to reform telecommunications had been broad-based, allying businessmen, government officials, women's groups, radicals, and rank-and-file trade unionists. During the 1900s and early 1910s, however, its enabling conditions came into flux, as changes gripped the political economy of telecommunications. First, as we saw, core business users in large cities—beginning in New York in 1905—began to fashion their own separate *modus vivendi* with Bell. Next to settle with the telephone monopoly, beginning around 1908 and definitively after the Kingsbury Commitment, was a substantial fraction of independent telephone capital. It was in this substantially altered structural context that two other developments now also came to impinge. First, following the election of 1912 the drive to postalize the wires gained newfound political strength and ideological legitimacy, as Progressive reform seemingly claimed the White House. Second, akin to their peers in other industries, restive telegraph and telephone workers pressed their demands for industrial democracy with hopeful urgency.

In April 1917, as the US entered World War I, blanket legislation was passed authorizing the president to proclaim a federal takeover of both railroad and telecommunication systems. In late December 1917, Wilson did indeed assume operating control over the nation's railroads (apart from street railways) and water transportation systems. The railroad telegraphers were covered by this action; it thereby drove a wedge between their experience and that of commercial telegraphers and telephone operators—each of whom continued, for the moment, to work for corporate carriers. Only eight months later (on July 16, 1918), did the President obtain Congress's authority to declare the necessity of federal operation and control of telegraphs and telephones; postalization commenced two weeks later. The US by this time had been at war for over fifteen months. "Why there was this delay . . . is not known," confessed a well-informed critical expert on the US telephone industry twenty years later.[57]

In the moment, however, it was common knowledge that postalization was in fact "precipitated by a labor crisis"; more recent historians have clarified this claim. What motivated the Administration to assume control over the wires was an impending nationwide telegraph strike.

Between 1898 and 1914 living costs in nonagricultural areas had increased by nearly 40 percent; the war period brought an additional increase of 40 percent for food, clothing, and fuel and, within months of the November 1918 Armistice, consumer prices spiked again.[58] Steep inflation was ravaging real wages. By the end of 1917, food costs were up 85 percent over what they had averaged in 1913, clothing costs 106 percent, and medicines 130 percent. Commercial telegraph workers suffered more than any other group of public utility workers from spiraling living costs. And, while telephone workers' wages stagnated between 1902 and 1914, limited wages increases in 1915 and 1916 were summarily "swept away" during the next few years—so that by 1920 they were earning 7 percent less than they had in 1902. Postal workers likewise "lost ground" early in the twentieth century—in 1914, they could purchase 9 percent less with their wages than they had been able to during the 1890s—and the rise in prices during World War I knocked down their already reduced real earnings by an additional 22 percent just during 1916 and 1917; the next year this drop worsened.[59]

Partly in response, trade union membership rocketed and strikes multiplied. The Commercial Telegraphers Union of America (CTUA), routed by Western Union in a 1907 strike, renewed its attempts by staging a fresh organization drive. Managed by a principled opponent of independent trade unions and a onetime AT&T protégé of Theodore N. Vail, Newcomb Carlton, Western Union responded by summarily firing 800 trade unionists. In the face of this lock-out, the CTUA in turn threatened to walk out, and it appealed to President Wilson's just-formed National War Labor Board. In April 1918 the NWLB intervened, engendering its first fundamental test. Both NWLB co-chairs—former president William Howard Taft, by no means friendly to organized labor, and Frank Walsh, the AFL unions' most influential supporter in wartime Washington—together demanded that Western Union reinstate the employees and recognize their right to join a union. Carlton remained recalcitrant; Taft and Walsh thereupon appealed to President Wilson. While a railroad telegrapher wrote to the NWLB's Frank Walsh that "The Courts are jailing men who are not as dangerous as Mr. Carlton is to the military success of the United States," President Wilson appealed to both Carlton and his counterpart at Postal Telegraph, Clarence MacKay, to acquiesce on patriotic grounds in the Labor Board's decision; to defer to Carlton, Wilson knew, would cripple the NWLB just as it was getting started, leaving his administration's overall labor policy in shambles. McKay agreed, however, Carlton stonewalled President Wilson's request. Alongside other union officials, B. J. Konenkamp, the president of the Commercial Telegraphers then warned that his members would strike in 400 cities, and predicted that "the refusal of the Western Union to accept the mediatory efforts of the National War Labor Board would lead within a few weeks to the taking over of the company by the Government."[60]

Konenkamp proved correct. With the nation at war, Postmaster General Burleson declared that a nationwide telegraph strike would engender "the paralysis of a large part of the system of electrical communication . . . with possible consequences prejudicial to our military preparations and other public activities that might prove serious or disastrous." Burleson urged passage of a resolution offered by Louisiana Democratic Congressman James B. Aswell, to authorize a government takeover on open-ended terms: government operation would be permitted not explicitly as a wartime necessity and not necessarily for a period limited by the duration of the war. Representatives and Senators openly voiced doubts: even as they voted to authorize Executive branch operation under the Constitution's war power, they asserted that this action seemed a mere pretext for a permanent nationalization. This was anything but a secret. The two cabinet members who pressed hardest for a federal takeover—Josephus Daniels, the Bryan Democrat who was now Secretary of the Navy, and Albert S. Burleson, the Postmaster General—each declared before a congressional committee that, once undertaken, a nationalization of the country's wire systems would never result in a resumption of private control. Political support for public ownership being "enormous," however, Congress voted for it by lopsided margins: 222–4 in the House; 46–16 in the Senate. Postalization thus arrived as a response to a stand-off between capital and labor in telegraphy, which jeopardized even any wider labor peace.[61]

In addition to redressing problems long identified by proponents of postalization, CTUA members nevertheless hoped that a government takeover would result in wage increases and collective bargaining rights. Postalization, however, had arrived not in recognition of a need for industrial democracy but as a top-down response to workers' militancy. The nation's wireline systems were also to be overseen by what turned out to be a singularly recalcitrant unit of the executive branch.[62]

The President inaugurated federal control of the nation's wire networks as of August 1, 1918, and remanded this responsibility to the Post Office. His proclamation specified that Postmaster General Albert Burleson would discharge his new duties "through the owners, managers, board of directors, receivers, officers, and employees of the telegraph and telephone systems" who, unless otherwise ordered by Burleson, "shall continue the operations in the usual and ordinary course of the business of said systems."[63]

The Postmaster thereupon established a "Wire Control Board," consisting of two high Post Office administrators and former Maryland Democratic Congressman David J. Lewis. (After losing a race for a Senate seat for Maryland in 1916, Lewis had been appointed a member of the US Tariff Commission by President Wilson, so he remained at the center of things in Washington.) Lewis was very likely the reigning government expert on telecommunications, and, as we saw, his affinities lay unmistakably with labor. Throughout the one-year period of government control that ensued, nevertheless, the Wire Control Board was shaped more by Burleson, Vail, and Carlton than by Lewis. Not only was Vail appointed special advisor to the Wire Control Board, but AT&T garnered a contractually specified right "to inspect the books and accounts kept by the Postmaster General relating to the property of the Bell System or to the operation thereof." Formalizing this arrangement, a separate "Wire Operating Board" was appointed in December 1918; also known as the "United States Telegraph and Telephone Administration," its members were two executives at AT&T, one at Western Union and—significantly—one representative of the independent telephone companies. (Additional AT&T managers were appointed to this body a few months later.)[64]

Descended from a founder of the former Republic of Texas, and fathered by a Confederate officer, Postmaster General Albert Sidney Burleson had learned the ropes of Congress during his service as an eight-term Democratic member of the

House of Representatives. He won his cabinet position not only because he was championed by his close friend and fellow Texan Colonel Edward House—the president's closest advisor—but, in the words of historian Arthur S. Link, "more importantly, because the conservative Democratic leaders in the House knew that Burleson would protect their patronage interests and insisted that Wilson appoint him." And Burleson did protect them. "I am going to make 56,000 appointments," he declared to the president, insisting that spoils should be doled out according to the conventional method of adhering to recommendations made by legislators—legislators who were frequently hostile to any program of Progressive reform. President Wilson acquiesced in this result. Because this signified that the President was committed to working through the Democratic Party rather than attempting to forge a genuine Progressive coalition, a leading chronicler of the Wilson Administration calls this choice "one of the decisive turning points in Wilson's presidential career." It ensured that the reform agenda, even as it burgeoned, would be weighed down by entrenched political and commercial interests.[65]

Burleson, in any case, had already demonstrated an intense hostility to working-class self-organization, one that was exceptional in Wilson's executive branch. An early historian of labor relations in the Post Office observed that for this very reason Burleson ironically "did a great deal to make the growth of organization militancy inevitable." He had blocked wage increases even as prices continued to soar, cutting harshly into postal workers' purchasing power. He had attempted to "work the force longer and without increasing costs." He had demanded that Congress repeal the law permitting postal workers to unionize. In short, Sterling Spero found, Burleson "gave the postal service what the workers called a 'sweatshop reputation.'"[66]

Despite these inauspicious portents, the American Federation of Labor threw its support behind the government takeover. Often well to the left of the national body its affiliate, the Chicago Federation of Labor, unanimously resolved in favor of postalization as the authorizing measure moved through Congress. The CFL's resolution declared that government operation likely would ensure "a fair and equitable adjustment of the existing labor difficulties," and thereby prevent "a widespread and disastrous strike involving three great labor organizations of over 100,000 members . . . which if not averted, will tie up the entire electrical means of communication of the country and paralyze not only the commercial industries but the military affairs of the nation." A successful effort to unify and coordinate the telegraph and telephone lines with the postal system, the CFL (Figure 3.2) ventured to hope, would release "thousands of skilled workers and great quantities of material used in duplication which is needed now in connection with the conduct of the war."[67]

Figure 3.2 Labor Leaders in Chicago, 1907. Edward N. Nockels is second from right; American Federation of Labor President Samuel Gompers is at left. Secretary of the Chicago Federation of Labor from 1903 until his death in 1937, Nockels worked tirelessly to transform telecommunications and later, radio broadcasting, to serve the needs of the US working class. Credit: DN-0005317, Chicago Daily News collection, Chicago History Museum.

Burleson, however, responded true to form as the Wire Boards commenced to merge the nation's two wireline systems into the Post Office. This process of organizational rationalization made no effort to inaugurate a shopfloor democracy and proceeded by way of management edicts from above. As the operators' leader Julia O'Connor would recall, Burleson seemed deliberately to want "to disabuse the workers' minds of all such fallacies" as that the "democratization" of the industry for which she herself struggled could occur through the simple expedient of nationalization. Penned in 1921, her summary of the debacle of government control claimed that "Never was the oppressive, anti-union policy of the telephone company so freely exercised as during this period. Unions undertaking to strike against the tyranny and autocracy of their conditions found themselves fighting not only the powerful gigantic corporations, but the prestige, the wealth and the strength of the government of the United States itself." She went on to specify:

Repudiated agreements, to one of which the Government itself was a party, the breaking of contracts, interruption of friendly relations, destruction of long established relations for collective bargaining, persecution and hostility for membership in a union—this was the unpleasant history of government control of the industry. Methods of discrimination, unparalled [sic] under private control, were practised by telephone company officials upon employees who joined or remained members of a union.

Over a span of months, in short, the "faith of the telephone operators" in the postal administration was "completely dissipated." James Connolly's deep skepticism about nationalization unaccompanied by worker control was borne out.[68]

The contrast with the experience of the railroad telegraphers was pointed. In the face of a strike threat by the powerful railroad brotherhoods, both the railway lines and the telegraph systems that coordinated their traffic had been taken over late in 1917, under the jurisdiction of a new Railroad Administration. Its Director-General William Gibbs McAdoo (President Wilson's son-in-law) then accorded serious attention "to establishing harmonious labor relations." Indeed, the rail unions' leadership gained official standing in the Railroad Administration. For the affected telegraphers, the results were little short of spectacular. With union recognition by the Railroad Administration, membership increased, wage gains secured, working conditions improved, and the eight hour day put in place. "There is perhaps no railroad organization which derived more substantial permanent gains from federal control than did the Order of Railroad Telegraphers," concluded a historian. The Railroad Telegraphers' experience of government operation probably helped sharpen other unionists' enthusiasm for postalizing the nation's wireline systems. It soon became clear, however, that the Commercial Telegraphers working for Western Union and Postal Telegraph, and the International Brotherhood of Electrical Workers-affiliated telephone operators faced overwhelming antagonism from the Burleson regime.[69]

Finding himself in principled opposition to the labor policies of his former collaborator on the postalization project, David J. Lewis resigned from the Wire Control Board on March 8, 1919. This was an important sign that the antimonopoly alliance had broken beyond repair. In his chronicle of the telephone operators' experience of government control during 1918–1919, Steven Norwood underscores the militant response that government control brought out from these mainly youthful women workers. Barely staving off strike action during the war, in the face of the Postmaster General's "reign of terror," as O'Connor called it, operators—who had previously constituted themselves as a collective bargaining unit only in the Boston area—staged a massive walkout five months after the war had ended. Throughout the New England states, despite the ban on strikes by federal employees thousands of operators walked off their jobs, shutting down telephone service regionally for five full weekdays during mid-April 1919 and demonstrating the extent to which business users had come to depend on their labor. "The issue," as Burleson tried to capture it in a missive to President Wilson on April 19, was "whether a labor organization can defy [the government's] authority and put into effect their will regardless of the rights of others and the public interest." Burleson sympathized, he wrote the President, with the fear expressed by "many owners," that any wage increase won by the New England operators, if it set a new national standard, would "seriously impair the value of the properties." The US Telephone and Telegraph Administration, in momentarily keen contrast with the Railroad Administration, saw itself as engaged in a fierce combat against the wireline workers.

Burleson found himself savaged in the court of public opinion. Newspapers inveighed against his heavy handedness; the governors of the five affected states cabled to President Wilson in France to urge him to take matters into his own hands; the Providence *News* relayed to the President an appeal by local and state union officials that Burleson's intransigence was threatening "to produce a general strike in all industries"; and Governor Coolidge wired the Postmaster directly, to propose acerbically that Massachusetts assume responsibility for telephone service in the Boston area "for the duration of the disability of the U.S. Government."[70]

After five days the strikers had battled Burleson and the telephone executives to a standstill and, in a resounding victory, they won wage increases and the right to bargain collectively. This was a great triumph—too great to be tolerated for, we are about to see, it helped to precipitate a fundamental policy reversal. A politically intense class struggle, the operators' strike catalyzed the Wilson Administration's decision to denationalize telecommunications, albeit in the context of additional factors: threats to civil liberties, special-interest maneuvering, and maladroit administration.[71]

Burleson's rough-handed censorship had given cause for sporadic protest since the US entry into the war but, in the wake of the operators' strike, this repressive practice was more widely publicized. Allegations, widely circulated in the press, were conveyed by Samuel Gompers directly to President Wilson: the Postmaster General would not distribute the house organ of the Postal Telegraph Cable Company—which was critical of his administration—among the firm's own employees, as they now technically worked for him. The *coup de grace*, however, stemmed from commercial press interests. It came about when Burleson denied telegraphic transmission to an article that Joseph Pulitzer's New York *World*, a pro-administration newspaper, planned to syndicate. Gompers wrote President Wilson that the article depicted Burleson as a "snoop, trouble maker, disorganizer, autocrat, and arch-politician." Post Office employees were being told that "they must not criticize any act of Burleson or in any way express their opinion of Burleson's control." Wireline surveillance and self-interested news suppression thus were cast publicly as standard features of the Postmaster's policy.[72]

The outcry against postal control grew louder still, as Burleson imposed steep telephone- and telegraph rate hikes. The Postmaster, recall, had deployed reformers' long-standing argument—that federal control would lower costs and reduce rates, thereby widening access—to legitimize postalization. Within months of taking over the wireline systems, however, his administration instead instituted a series of rate increases. In January, 1919, long-distance telephone charges were raised 18–20 percent; in April, the charge for a telegram increased by 20 percent. Even after the decision to denationalize the wires, Burleson continued to approve telephone rate increases. While Burleson cut back both Rural Free Delivery and Postal Savings, he allowed $42 million in telephone rate hikes.[73]

Despite the inflation that characterized the era, Burleson's rate increases were generally denounced. Public anger focused not only on their size, but also on their autocratic character: they were introduced without taking any account of the state regulatory commissions which purportedly possessed jurisdiction over intrastate services. On April 27, barely one week after the strike settlement, front page news stories recounted that a federal court had cleared the way to contest the Postmaster General's attempt to fix intrastate telegraph rates. No fewer than thirty states were cooperating to lodge an appeal at the Supreme Court, hoping to gain back for their states the right to regulate rates for utilities operating within their borders. "You can have no idea of the intensity of the people in these matters," President Wilson's secretary wired his boss a few weeks later. Burleson, though, remained impervious. The very day after the strike settlement was announced, he declared that the only way to meet the pay increases won by the operators would be through additional telephone rate hikes. When it was learned that the rate increases traced back to consultations with "the directors of the telegraph and telephone companies," Tumulty related to Wilson, the outrage only intensified. These executives, Tumulty went on to suggest, had deliberately proposed the rate hikes "with the idea that . . . our administration will have to bear the blame." David Lewis—the only likely dissenter—was now gone from the Wire Control Board.[74]

Two rate increases added the fuel of special interest to this fire. Clarence H. Mackay's Postal Telegraph Company was a secondary player in the markets for domestic telegraph service and submarine cable service; but Mackay believed that he had been cavalierly treated, and he seized the moment—late April, 1919, in the wake of the operators' strike—to announce that, if the wire and cable systems were given back to their private owners, he would immediately reduce rates by 20 percent—obviating the rate increase which Burleson had instituted. Private enterprise, he boasted, was more efficient.[75]

A different rate increase, for a class of mail service dear to the hearts of the print media, generated a more damaging attack on the Postmaster. In late April the Publishers Advisory Board, representing some 300 national periodicals, and the American Newspaper Publishers Association collectively denounced Burleson's regime. Assailing the second-class mail rate increases which the Postmaster had instigated, publishers' representative Clarence J. Post impugned not only Burleson's policies but also his personal reputation. The affair became nasty when Post repeated the New York World's charge of April 23: that the Postmaster General had whipped convict laborers on his Texas plantation. Burleson, in turn, grew certain that he was the object of an "organized propaganda" by publishers.[76]

Amid this affray, a fresh source of labor strife also loomed. On April 7, the Commercial Telegraphers had authorized their own strike vote. Even before the telephone walkout ended, reports had circulated that the telegraphers were likely to join the operators in a second illegal walkout against Burleson's labor policies. "Some of the telegraphers," reported the New York Times on April 20, "said that nothing short of the removal of Mr. Burleson would prevent one of the greatest strikes in the history of the country."[77]

From the perspective of business and political leaders, a walkout by the telegraphers posed serious risks. The obvious danger was a disruption of service. Transcontinental telephony, initiated in 1915, was prohibitively costly, while commercial airmail had not yet arrived; for big businesses, the long-distance telegraph remained essential. A strike indeed might shake the national economy and its transnational linkages. At the same time, President Wilson was in the middle of what would prove to be an eight-month stay in Paris, negotiating the peace settlement that followed World War I. Throughout this interval, he was engaged in what one historian has called "government by cable." The telegraphers' ability to curtail access to these international circuits jeopardized not only US diplomacy but also the president's ability to keep up with developments at home. Finally, framing all of this, a prospective telegraphers' strike fed US elites' spiking political fears. Beginning with a general strike in Seattle early in the year, 1919 was an epic year of walkouts and unauthorized wildcats, engulfing railroads, coal, and steel. With headlines screaming Bolshevik bedlam in Russia and Germany and many pronouncements about revolutionary unrest in nearby Mexico, US political and business leaders worried that the strike wave might presage a revolutionary uprising. When the railroad brotherhoods issued an ultimatum—that they would embark on a nationwide general strike unless the Administration moved to make permanent its operation of the railroads—Joseph Tumulty advised President Wilson that the unions were actually giving "the first appearance of the soviet in this country." In this fearsome atmosphere, both AT&T and

Western Union helped organize US big business around a demand to denationalize the nation's wireline systems: capital closed ranks.[78]

In the aftermath of the telephone strike, "the situation, condition and feeling have not been materially changed" affirmed Samuel Gompers in his April 23 cable to President Wilson: "All through the country the same feeling of unrest among the employes [sic] and their sympathizers is manifest, and the immediate future is not at all reassuring." The strikers' victory, that is, had added fuel to the fire. Gompers went on to relay the views of one of his correspondents, a Mr. Minnis, the Detroit manager of the Postal Telegraph Company, who underlined that the Commercial Telegraphers' Union "has two and one half million pamphlets ready for distribution throughout the country when the strike vote is recorded," which "will give an account of the treatment accorded telegraph employes by Mr. Burleson's administration." Gompers cautioned the President that,

> in his opinion, both organized and unorganized men from messengers up to superintendents will walk out in the event that a strike is called . . . .A strike vote is now being taken. Viewing the whole situation, it is the opinion of this superintendent that in the event of a strike 'they (the companies) won't be able to turn a wheel.' He further says 'The newspapers will be paralyzed and as people are so disgusted with the Burleson administration, what injury will it do the Democratic Party when all the newspapers in the country get after the administration'

The reference to the Democrats was calculated to touch a sensitive nerve, and it probably did. The spiraling partisanship that suffused the campaign against Burleson seems to have been the straw that broke the camel's back.[79]

Burleson grudgingly gave way. Four days after capitulating to the women operators' chief demands, on April 24, the Postmaster General sent a cable to President Wilson offering a big concession. He proposed a limited denationalization, offering the re-privatize the submarine cables in an attempt to save his domestic postalization program. The President's secretary Joseph Tumulty, however, was unsympathetic to Burleson's policies and fearful of the political fallout that he felt would be caused by Burleson's attempts to handle another strike. Further, the Democrats now controlled a lame-duck session of Congress, and the Republicans who had prevailed in the 1918 election were about to assume control over key committees. Already during the telephone workers' strike, the president of the Massachusetts Democratic Club had cabled Wilson that Burleson was "wrecking the party" and, observes John Blum, "This opinion, shared by many leading Democrats, fortified Tumulty's growing conviction that the Postmaster General had become a political liability and should be dismissed from office." On April 25, Tumulty interceded, requesting that Wilson, "not reply to message from Burleson re cables until I can cable you further." Later that day, with his customary candor, he transmitted to the President an extended assessment of the politics of telecommunications in this highly charged moment. "In connection with the suggestion of the early return of the cables," Tumulty began, in an extraordinary political appraisal, "there is no present source of irritation and popular discontent affecting all classes of the people comparable with that growing out of the continuance of control of cables, telegraph and telephone lines by the Postmaster General." He went on to underline that "there is no reason apparent to the public why this control should be continued." Tumulty then turned to the party politics of the moment:

> I am inclined to think that it would be very desirable to return the cables at any early date but that a failure to return the telegraph and telephone lines or to take steps by public announcement looking towards their return at the same time would be construed as an evidence of an intention on the part of the Administration to retain the telegraph and telephone lines indefinitely. The Republican leaders openly announce that one of the first things they intend to do when the take hold is to pass a resolution providing for the immediate return of these instrumentalities. This would be very good politics from their standpoint and give our opponents a tremendous advantage over us.

He elaborated in order, perhaps, to offer Wilson a justification for acting in what Tumulty deemed the most politically expedient way. "I am satisfied," wrote Tumulty,

> that public opinion is not ready for government control of railroads, telegraph or telephone lines or cables, and that the wise, constructive thing for you to do is to announce immediately . . . that you have definitely determined to return all of these instrumentalities to private control but that you will insist on the immediate enactment by the Congress of appropriate legislation to protect the rights of the security-holders in that connection. It is evident that this is the practical politics of the situation. . . . The release under proper conditions by the Government of the control of these agencies will do more to hearten American business and clarify the air than anything you can do. Our failure to do so will give our enemies their great opportunity. I would suggest that in reply to the Postmaster General you diplomatically inquire if the time is not opportune to release government control over the telegraph and telephone lines.

On April 28 Wilson cabled Burleson firmly to this effect. The President insisted that, subject to congressional authorization, the Postmaster announce that both the cables and the nation's wireline systems would be returned swiftly to their corporate owners. The class interest of "American business" had intersected to resounding effect with the party politics of the day.[80]

What the *New York Times* called "Mr. Burleson's adventure" was at an end. Now the only question was, what form would be given to the congressional authorization to denationalize the wireline systems. Even as he announced the forthcoming denationalization of the wirelines systems, Burleson's conviction remained unshaken that postalization was sound policy, still on grounds of cost efficiency.[81]

He was correct; but now this characteristic Progressive-era appeal to economic efficiency had been significantly discredited. Norwood writes that the management of New England Telephone—a Bell system affiliate—"was not altogether displeased with the strike because it believed the strike could serve to discredit permanent government ownership of the telephone system." In late 1916, the Merchants' Association of New York—the same organization that, a decade earlier, had successfully interposed its members' interests against AT&T's to gain regulatory power over the carrier—had resolved that it was "opposed to government ownership and operation of railroads, telephones, telegraphs, and other public utilities, believing that such utilities are far more effectively operated under private ownership, subject to public regulation . . . and that it would be a national calamity to subject these instruments, indispensable to the welfare of the whole country, to the hampering, inefficient and wasteful methods inseparable from governmental undertakings." Like much of the nation's commercial press, The *New York Times* adhered to the business leaders' credo in proclaiming that government operation had been an abject failure. In an editorial on April 20—the day the operators' strike was settled—the *Times* echoed Representative Aswell, who had introduced the bill authorizing the takeover, but who had since gone on to apologize publicly for his share in the "misadventure," declaring that "the death knell of Government operation" had been sounded. "The telephone strikers say that Government operation is not responsible," declared the Times: "They charge it all to Mr. Burleson." But the editors disputed them, and called instead for an end "forever" to "all talk of Government operation as a means of providing public utility services 'at cost.'" In a second editorial ten days later, taking account of the denationalization announcement, the *Times* tightened the noose:

> The minds of men have been much upset by the disturbance of war, and many of them have dreamed dreams and seen visions of a new order in the social, business, and political relations of men. But for this venture in Government control and operation of railroad and wire communication there would have been a flood of talk about the blessings of State socialism. We have had our experience,

it was short and sharp, our demonstration, which is all-sufficient. The people have rendered their verdict of practically unanimous condemnation.

This set down orthodox opinion on the subject for the following century.[82]

In actuality, though—through the strike and beyond, as the *Times* itself reported, telecommunications workers and union leaders continued to press for Burleson's dismissal rather than for an end to government control. Just prior to Burleson's announcement that the wireline systems would revert to their private owners, the Commercial Telegraphers posed the question of how to make a permanent government takeover an issue in the upcoming 1920 presidential campaign. Notwithstanding many workers' sentiment, notwithstanding the women operators' epic victory over Burleson, denationalization became effective August 1, 1919. Though demands for a government-run system continued to surface, and though nationalization of utilities remained a plank in the platforms of radical political parties throughout the early 1920s, the movement had been not only defeated but, for many Americans, discredited. The renewed bifurcation of the telecommunications system came about as a consequence of the exertion of class power over the state—and not merely because of the designs of the AT&T monopoly.

In contrast to the railroad brotherhoods, members of which continued to push for a permanent government takeover of the railroads even after denationalization of the roads in March 1920, on the basis of their own recent experience many telecommunications workers came to harbor ambivalent, sometimes downright hostile, feelings toward government ownership. Under Burleson, the Post Office had subjected both postal and telecommunications employees to fierce repression. Julia O'Connor conceded two years after the operators' strike, in the reactionary years that quickly followed, that "the brief and sorry experiment in government directorship . . . accomplished nothing for the telephone workers." Indeed it "served to handicap them in the normal exercise of their economic power." Its most significant defect, O'Connor specified, was to "enormously aggravate[]" the "utter lack of democracy in labor relations" that prevailed in the telephone industry. Telephone workers therefore had been left with a positive "distaste for Government operation of the wires." O'Connor herself was palpably bitter: "Better the evils of private than of public autocracy. They are at least less damaging to our patriotic ideals." In a subsequent study of the telephone operators' counterparts in Britain—who labored in that nation's Post Office Department—O'Connor went even further: "But however one's intelligence may accept the logic of public ownership of the telephone, the actual workings of the system can produce little affection for it from the point of view of the employees and their right to democratic participation. There is indisputably a psychological reaction which produces in the mind of the public servant a peculiar theory of his relationship to his job, a relation which is stultifying in its effect upon democratic organization." Lurking behind these lines, we may conjecture, loomed the malevolent Burleson.[83]

O'Connor's pioneering international women's union, whose achievement was to forge a women's-led department in the International Brotherhood of Electrical Workers in the face of intense sexism and class prejudice, albeit a racially exclusionary one, henceforth had to confront a fresh obstacle before it could reignite a reform movement: its own members' cynicism. Postalization schemes no longer could count on hopeful support by a substantial segment of the American working class. We will find later that telephone historian John Brooks overstates things when he claims that, "for a decade to come, the view that the private communications companies could best serve the public interest with little or no government interference would prevail in all but the wilder of radical circles." Nevertheless, the animating ideal that reformers had held out for half a century now rang hollow as the antimonopoly alliance that had powered their efforts faltered and failed.[84]

On May 2, 1919, submarine cables were returned to their corporate owners; and, at the end of July 1919, the domestic wireline systems likewise reverted. Just as Tumulty had feared, public cynicism and anger indeed did target the Wilson Administration. From the vantage of late 1919, a confidential report on the just-ended period of federal control to the directors of AT&T acknowledged that "the Postmaster General, by virtue of his position, has received the principal share of the burden of public criticism" inflamed by government operation. Burleson tried to deflect these attacks, declaring that "[t]he recent temporary control afforded no more of a test of the virtues of government ownership than could be had through a temporary receivership in a court proceeding." But neither he nor his successors would gain a second chance.

Mere weeks after legislation to denationalize the wires sailed through Congress, in mid-June AT&T President Theodore N. Vail retired. His labors had helped to ensure that the executives who succeeded him would enjoy a freer hand. As AT&T belatedly introduced automatic "dial" technology; like Western Union, helped inaugurate big US companies' attempts to introduce pliable "Employee Representation Plans"—company unions; and pioneered other forms of worker control, the womens' independent operators' union and the larger prospect of collective self-organization were set back for a generation.[85]

The accommodations that had been reached, serially, between AT&T, leading independent telephone companies, and business users, coalesced in a seemingly secure institutional casement. This trio of propertied interests now scrambled for advantage among themselves, attempting to manipulate rates and services within an emergent system of administrative regulation constituted by state public utility commissions, a now-lackadaisical Interstate Commerce Commission, and the courts. This elevation of corporate privilege, we have seen, was predicated on a profound historical reversal. Carriers and business users had been freed to operate largely over the heads of once forceful actors—noncommercial independent service providers, frustrated would-be telephone users and, above all, network workers—because they had succeeded in repulsing these actors' struggles. US telecommunications workers carried into the postwar period a much-constricted capacity for mutual endeavor, splintered as they were into gender-subordinated, and segregated or exclusionary craft unions and, in the case of most telegraph and telephone employees, channeled into company unions. No less important, their radical "network imaginary" had been shredded, following the break-up of the antimonopoly coalition—their activating visions of a telecommunications system repurposed to enable democracy at work reduced to hopeful flickers. Capital then turned to expand and modernize what was already the world's most advanced and far-reaching network infrastructure, as if these radical visions had been inconsequential all along.

This is not to say that antimonopolism left no palpable trace. Far from it! Antimonopoly precepts became institutionalized, as we will find throughout this book, in specialized legislation and new government agencies, as well as in attendant discourses of jurisprudence and economics. The Sherman Antitrust Act, the Clayton Antitrust Act, the Interstate Commerce Commission, the Federal Trade Commission, forty-odd state public utilities commissions, the Justice Department's Antitrust Division, and specific Senate and Congressional committees and investigations still carry an opaque impress of this late nineteenth to early twentieth century movement to remake the American political economy. As worries about specific corporate abuses continued to arise during the decades after World War I, they funneled into this formidable governmental apparatus. In turn, the rough-and-tumble popular politics of antimonopoly was mostly supplanted by formalized procedural initiatives, which, furthermore, were canalized to reform particular industries and individual corporations: antimonopoly was no longer an attempt to remake the entire political economy.

Symptomatically, in 1920 the Ohio Republican presidential candidate Warren G. Harding campaigned successfully by promising a "return to normalcy." Postalization had no part of his—or his successors'—agenda. That it had been permanently stymied, however, neither obviated the alterations that had been made to the prewar terms of trade in telecommunications nor, more important, forestalled additional reform movements. Already during the decade following World War I, in fact, a renewed campaign for reform commenced. However, now it occupied a somewhat different ground. Reformers again singled out harms engendered by an unaccountable corporate power—AT&T—and aimed to introduce positive changes, notably widened household telephone access, but the foundation of their actions lay in a vitalizing conception of "public utility." It was characteristic that, by 1924, a sober academic analyst could liken the Post Office itself to "a public utility, performing a service indispensible [sic] to the economic and social life of the community." To take stock of this fresh cycle of system development and reform effort, which would soon come to pivot around workers as well as consumers, constitutes the purpose of Part Two.[86]

PART II
PUBLIC UTILITY

4
Reactivating Reform

For decades following the growth of the telegraph, antimonopolists had tied their hopes to the Post Office as a superior alternative to networks built and operated by corporate capital. In 1919, however, weakened by desertions and facing management attacks, what remained of the postalization movement had the ground cut from under its feet through President Wilson's depostalization of the wires. Attempts to engender greater social justice in telecommunications now commenced from a different side.

This renewed effort to reconstruct the political economy of networks was stemmed from an unlikely source: the doctrine of public utility, which had actually taken institutional form within the antimonopoly movement. In 1869, Massachusetts became the first state to establish a permanent regulatory commission charged with overseeing railroads: its powers were restricted chiefly to publicizing abuses. A scattering of other states followed during the next three decades, as did many others after the turn of the twentieth century. What were typically called state public utility commission (PUCs) gained jurisdiction over the intrastate operations of, variously, railroads, and electric, telegraph, and telephone companies; often, their responsibilities became progressively augmented. Crucially, and unexpectedly, given the judiciary's knee-jerk tendency during these decades to recoil against "takings" of private property without just compensation, the Supreme Court in 1876 upheld public utility regulation as constitutional. When regulated entities were "affected with a public interest," the Court declared—"when private property is devoted to a public use"- it "is subject to public regulation." As clarified in a later Supreme Court ruling (which implied an efficacy that was far from guaranteed): "At the dawn of modern utility regulation, in order to offset monopoly power and ensure affordable, stable public access to a utility's goods or services. . . . legislatures established specialized administrative agencies . . . to set and regulate rates." Thereby antimonopoly was carried over as a legal touchstone, though public utilities did not have to be monopolies to fall under regulators' purview. Defending its judgments by tapping into the professional expertise of economists, engineers, and lawyers, and inserted within a judicial system that was bound by many threads to capital rather than labor, after the Armistice these administrative commissions nevertheless proved capable of a desultory—yet occasionally surprising—independence. As we will see, for example, they responded robustly to what they deemed an arbitrary federal preemption at the end of World War I. During the fifteen years that followed, as well, influential PUC officials asserted themselves again by protesting that a second blockage obstructed them from pursuing their mandate: AT&T's corporate power. The ultimate result was to enlarge the very substance of the public utility conception.[1]

The years between the Armistice and the election of Franklin Roosevelt in 1932 were marked, therefore, not by quiescence but by discontent; and this discontent reached far into the domain of telecommunications. Criticism of AT&T's often mysterious role flared up in commission proceedings, court cases, and investigations undertaken by the nation's great cities. Less tangible, but at least as important, antagonism to AT&T surged through public opinion. Out of these sources—thus, not as a reflex only of legal and juridical doctrines—some of the lineaments of a renascent reform agenda came into view. This agenda remained a work in progress, a patchwork. Operating as both cause and effect were challenges to high telephone rates mounted variously by business users, consumer groups, the occasional trade unionist and political radical, reform-minded academics, and some state regulators. Charged with overseeing the giant carrier, the state commissions in particular found their own efforts repeatedly beaten back, diverted, and evaded. Operating at a distance from organized labor—which was forced onto a defensive footing during these "lean years"—reformers nonetheless persevered in attempts to school a nationwide, integrated, and politically potent monopoly carrier in the tenets of democratic accountability. Their difficulties brought hard-won lessons, which they carried forward when, suddenly, it became feasible to propose a more effective regulatory mechanism with the 1932 election of Franklin Roosevelt to the presidency.[2]

A profound crisis—the Great Depression—granted this fresh room for maneuver. Precipitated by the industry's economic travails, by abuses perpetrated by AT&T, by an increasingly angry working class, and by new political openings, civilian federal authority over telecommunications then was strengthened. A campaign to generate and impose norms of accountability became an intense and, for several fraught years, an open-ended and hopeful social struggle. Telecommunications indeed became a bearer of the "extraordinary era of innovation" noted by William J. Novak, during which a growing corpus of public utilities law was transformed into "a vibrant and expansive arena for experimenting with unprecedented government control over business, industry, and the market." This public utility imaginary gained even more expansive horizons. The agenda was reformist, not revolutionary; but it was also open-ended. Competent, assertive regulation hit AT&T as a bitterly unwelcome imposition. It also opened up a real prospect of far-reaching alterations to telecommunications system development. How far-reaching became the central site of political struggle.[3]

It needs emphasis that central state authority had long been evident in this realm. We have seen how, throughout the nineteenth century, the Post Office acted as the, then a, policymaker; and how, earlier in the twentieth century, the Department of Justice had intervened to bolster independent capital in telecommunications. In addition, during World War I, as the US bid more forcefully for overseas empire the Navy had worked closely with AT&T to stimulate innovation of high-technology radio, and the Army Signal Corps likewise united with AT&T to bring forward networks for the use of the American Expeditionary Force in Europe. A military-industrial complex was already being erected, and AT&T was one of its charter members. Nor did this exhaust the federal government's prior role in policymaking. The Interstate Commerce Commission had been vested with responsibility for telegraph and telephone systems as we have begun to see. Throughout the late 1910s and 1920s, finally, most notably under Secretary Herbert Hoover, the Commerce Department supplemented these interventions by systematizing and promoting business opportunities in telecommunications both domestically and internationally. The Depression years are not, therefore, to be characterized as marking an epic departure: substantial federal involvement in telecommunications was already an accomplished fact. Rather, the Depression energized an unprecedented effort to expand the central state's power to bring private capital in networking to account, now around an invigorated conception of public utility.

New Deal reforms transformed what had been a fragmented, incomplete regulatory system based on state regulation into a working interjurisdictional policy mechanism. As this procedural shift unfolded, New Deal advocates of public utility tried to reshape the big carriers' profit strategies, structural features, and service models. Carefully planned and insistent federal action ultimately did induce substantial change in system development and service provision. This, however, transpired only by way of a climactic struggle. A previously unimaginable federal intervention to bring the nation's largest corporation to heel was partly checked, as AT&T fought back to limit the range and tame the spirit of the New Dealers' program for public utility telecommunications.[4]

To chart how frustration led on to breakthrough, we return to 1919, so that we may reexamine the denationalization of wireline systems from this fresh vantage point.

The Impasse, 1919–1934

During early May, 1919, as the nation's wireline systems were handed back to AT&T, Western Union, and Postal Telegraph, the Postmaster General reflected on the federal role in telecommunications. Unchastened, Albert Burleson suggested in a cable to President Wilson that "efficient service to the public cannot be maintained if the complex, contradictory and overlapping control of states and municipalities over rates and operating conditions is to continue." "We cannot simply release the wires," he declared, "and go back to the old conditions of private management, wasteful attempts at competition and multiform regulation by state and federal authorities." His hopes for permanent Post Office control over telecommunications had been blasted away, yet Burleson still was convinced that governmental "regulation and control" of telecommunications had become "a necessity." He counseled Wilson that the nation now should seek "an intermediate course of modified private control under a more unified and affirmative public regulation."[5]

Two weeks later, in a letter to the House Committee on Post Offices and Post Roads, which was evaluating how to denationalize the wireline networks, Burleson clarified his thinking about this needed regulatory agency. He declared that "it is impossible to secure any uniformity of rates or to maintain adequate revenue for the service" when there exist so many independent regulatory commissions—and when "the intrastate and interstate activities are so interdependent that what affects one affects the other and the character of this traffic has so changed through development that the interstate features have become the dominant and controlling factor."

> Hence it is believed that the law should be so amended as to empower the Interstate Commerce Commission to fix rates for telegraph and telephone companies subject to the provision of the act, and that any telegraph or telephone company whose lines are located entirely within a State but which transacts direct interstate business through switching or other arrangements with other lines should be made subject to the act.

Burleson overstated the importance of interstate networking at this time, but his proposal took valid account of an increasingly severe regulatory gap engendered by the mismatch between US federalism and the structure of AT&T and Western Union.[6]

Principally aimed at the railroads, the Mann-Elkins Act of June 1910 had vested oversight of interstate communications by wire and wireless in the Interstate Commerce Commission. Nearly from its establishment in 1887, however, the ICC itself had recognized a basic limit placed on its jurisdiction. As early as 1889, its first chairman, constitutional scholar Thomas M. Cooley, had unsuccessfully asked congress to grant his agency jurisdiction over intra- as well as interstate railroads. Now, thirty years later, Burleson hoped to augment the ICC's oversight responsibilities, to match those that he and a coterie of telecommunications executives had tried to impose during the period of Post Office administration. He aimed specifically to rebalance the nation's federal system, by greatly extending the power exercised by central-state regulators. A precedent for expanding the ICC's authority in just this way had been supplied by a Supreme Court ruling in 1914. In the so-called *Shreveport Rate Cases*, the Court had granted the ICC the right to alter intrastate railroad rates in cases where these rates had been found to discriminate against interstate rates. In May 1918, the nation's wartime Railroad Administration had gone on to order a 25 percent increase in all rail rates, intrastate and interstate. Congruent proposals were aired to extend federal authority over emerging wireless radio technology, not only domestically but—to support the US's now quickly rising global power—internationally.[7]

Hoping to rationalize domestic telecommunications ratemaking in keeping with these precedents, Burleson had imposed two successive telephone rate increases during the period of government operation of the wires. These measures, however, provoked fierce opposition and prolonged conflicts. These constitute an essential starting-point for evaluating the interwar history of telecommunications reform.

The inspiration behind the Postmaster's new rates was complex. Confronted by the rampant inflation of the World War I years, concerned that wireline service efficiency not deteriorate in the emergency, looking to the Railroad Administration for precedent, and prodded by AT&T executives, during the first months of his stewardship Burleson also himself believed that rationalizing telephone and telegraph rates was a crucial step, especially if they were to remain postalized services. AT&T President Vail confided to Burleson that the general public had greeted the Government's wireline takeover in August 1918 with the "impression . . . that there would be a general reduction in rates." On December 13, 1918, however, Burleson ordered increases in telephone toll rates; and on March 19, 1919, he went on to promulgate "a comprehensive scheme of changes in the local-exchange rates for the properties of the various operating companies of the Bell System." As a result of these two orders, rates increased by $42 million annually or, as AT&T figured with respect to its own network, "approximately 12%."[8]

To many contemporaries, these rate hikes appeared flagrantly inimical to the spirit of the Post Office and rendered Burleson himself a mere catspaw of AT&T. Certainly, both the increases and the Post Office's intervention to set all rates, intra- as well as interstate, did coincide with the preferences of AT&T's Theodore Vail. In October 1918, Vail told the presidents of the Bell operating companies that any ratemaking conflicts with the PUCs should be referred to the Postmaster General, "not conceding jurisdiction to any local authority." Danielian later showed that telephone company officials had "bent their efforts toward securing rate increases with the approval of the Postmaster General." A letter of February

1919, prepared and sent by Vice President Thayer in the name of President Vail to the heads of all of AT&T's subsidiary operating companies, asserted—as against the belief that continuing Federal control of the nation's wires would lead to full-scale Government ownership—that "my views are exactly to the contrary." The nation's telephone properties, this letter projected, ultimately would be returned to their prior owners. However, Thayer and Vail boldly insisted that

> There has not been in the past and there probably will not be for a generation in the future, a time as favorable as the present for a sound adjustment of the relation between the Government, the public and the utilities, and we should address ourselves to it with all of our energies.
>
> There is a much better prospect of getting the necessary consideration and action now than after the properties are turned back. Now it is a concrete question. Then it will be an abstract question.

All this indeed made it look as if the rate increases expressed a stark fusion of corporate and state power, contrived under pretense of military emergency to fleece the public.

This portrayal is not so much wrong, as one-dimensional. The gap between state and federal regulation certainly lent itself to abuses by carriers; but AT&T officials pushed for rate hikes from vulnerability as well as from strength. AT&T had responded to the threat posed by municipalization by acquiescing to regulation by state public utility commissions. By now, however, the sheer proliferation of these agencies—as well as the contingencies that state regulation introduced—had resulted in a destabilizing centrifugal force. In private correspondence, AT&T executives expressed wariness throughout the period of Post Office operation about their uncertain prospects before the PUCs. In language that anticipated Burleson's statements several months later (quoted above), Vail wrote in an internal memo that "[a]s it stands, we have diverse and conflicting control and regulation of the National Government and forty-eight sovereign states, neither coordinated or co-related with each other or with the operation of the utility." Soon after the second rate increase, Vail wrote Charles Francis Adams, an early and influential proponent of state regulation, concerning "the fallacy of undertaking to regulate a utility system by a multiplicity of bodies, particularly where no one body has authority over the whole system or over the completed service of any system." As we will see, AT&T was concerned in particular that the PUCs might jeopardize its plans for a Herculean nationwide network build-out after the War.[9]

AT&T and the Postmaster agreed on ratemaking policy; and Burleson was not a mere corporate mouthpiece. The Postmaster General understood that only by lowering telephone rates would "the largest number possible" of prospective users be able to gain access to telephone service. Notwithstanding this clarity of insight, he raised rates. Burleson's motive was chiefly not to add to AT&T's coffers but to introduce what, in contemporary business discourse, was being called "system" into the telephone industry's bewilderingly complex and disorderly rate structure. "A wide variety of schedules were in effect in the various states prior to 1919," he explained; even methods for calculating route-distance varied. These disparities, creating a hodgepodge reminiscent of the nineteenth century telegraph monopoly and the early twentieth-century express companies, barred the establishment of a coherent nationwide telephone system. They needed to be supplanted. To erect a more rational system, Burleson planned to institute a pricing structure based on the principle of "rate averaging." This entailed, as Burleson's Committee on Telephone Rate Standardization proclaimed in 1918, that "the best results to the public will be obtained . . . [by] establishing for such standard service standard rates which will be uniform for the same distance in any part of the country." Here, Burleson drew on a deep fund of Post Office experience. The mandatory use of stamps had permitted postal rates to be conveniently averaged in just this way for many decades; and rate averaging had thereafter been adopted as a tool of system development in some pockets of the prewar telephone industry. Decades afterward, when Burleson's "reign of terror" had faded from memory, federal and state regulators would credit him for trying to establish a more uniform nationwide rate schedule, both for state and interstate toll services and local calling.[10]

Owing to Burleson's ham-fisted approach, however, his quest for "system" cut little ice. Days after assuming control of the country's wireline systems, the Postmaster brusquely notified members of several state public utility commissions "that he proposed to make all rates and would expect the State Commissions to cooperate." Through subsequent orders, Burleson conveyed the same message: that he would brook no challenge to his executive authority. Despite a general penchant for cooperation with Washington, state regulators reacted defensively to this bid to centralize federal power at their expense. What role was the Postmaster leaving for them to perform?[11]

State regulators instantly mobilized to challenge the Post Office's scheduled rate increases. They charged that he was concurrently enacting both a corporate boondoggle and a jurisdictional encroachment. A historian later recalled that they "created a furor throughout the country, in and out of Congress, among both Republicans and Democrats, seldom equaled in intensity and bitterness." The impact spilled over, not only into the election of 1920 but into the subsequent history of US telecommunications.[12]

Burleson's attempt to rationalize the nation's telephone rate structure set into motion a subtle and contingent historical sequence. No sooner had he announced the new toll rates than challenges began to issue, from Florida to

Nebraska. Opposition only escalated, after he instituted the second series of rate increases for local-exchange service. A letter from AT&T General Counsel Nathaniel Guernsey to W. H. Lamar, Post Office Solicitor, opined five days prior to the Postmaster's March 1919 announcement of these local rate increases that "I think we may anticipate that efforts will be made to enjoin these rates, just as efforts were made to enjoin the toll rates." Two weeks later, by Guernsey's tally, suits in the courts of ten states seemed guaranteed—while additional legal challenges were "probable, but less certain," in twelve others. A month later, an internal AT&T document warned that the Chairman of the National Association of Railroad and Utility Commissioners (NARUC), Charles E. Elmquist, had telegraphed a call for a meeting to representatives from each state commission so that they might "consider attitude commissions will take with regard to intrastate rates promulgated by Postmaster General." Attempts to coordinate policy for telephone issues among the state commissions brought them together as never before. These attempts stemmed as much from their mutual concern to defend their agencies from federal preemption as from a view that, as NARUC's rate committee reported in 1919, "Some of the charges . . . appear to be exorbitant, or at least without reference to actual cost." NARUC's suggestion that "investigations are likely to become very general," not only signaled that the organization was digging in for a fight but also galvanized a movement toward interstate cooperation.[13]

Proponents of enlarged federal authority then escalated a reciprocal campaign. Men who performed double duty, both as AT&T executives and Post Office officials, "took the leadership," Danielian would write, "in formulating a test case before the Supreme Court" to dispose of the injunctions against rate increases that the state commissions had secured in lower courts. A South Dakota injunction prohibiting Burleson from instituting his toll rates and affirmed by that state's Supreme Court was duly appealed to the US Supreme Court by AT&T, the Postmaster General and the US Attorney General together; and, on June 2, 1919 (Brandeis dissenting) the nation's highest court overturned the judgment, affirming the Postmaster's ratemaking authority on the basis of Congress's delegation of it under the war power. The Court held that the President had the "right . . . to take complete possession and control to enable the full operation of the lines embraced in his authority"—including the right to set telephone rates "for business done wholly within the State." "Legally the 'success' belonged to the United States Government," Danielian acerbically commented in 1939; "practically it was a success for the Bell System." No less important was that, in this era of Jim Crow segregation, quite apart from its substance the judgment fueled resentment over federal usurpation of states' rights.[14]

After the Supreme Court's verdict, the battleground shifted to the question of the terms on which AT&T's wireline network would be handed back to the giant carrier. President Vail sought to render Burleson's rate schedules immune to legal challenge by conferring on them a congressional stamp of approval. Therefore he requested that legislation to denationalize the wires should fix the new rates for at least one year. In this, Vail did not succeed. As enacted, the law authorized the Postmaster's toll and exchange rates "for a period not to exceed four months after this act takes effect, unless sooner modified or changed by the public authorities—State, municipal, or otherwise—having control or jurisdiction of tolls, charges, and rates or by contract or by voluntary reduction."[15]

Freshly concerted action by state public utility commissions underlay this reversal. During the period when Congress was deliberating on the bill, NARUC President Elmquist petitioned legislators to make the Postmaster's rates effective for just 60–90 days. Some commissions pushed for even more severe restrictions. Oklahoma's Corporation Commission "do not approve of placing any time limit during which present rates shall be continued." The Illinois Commission refused to commit to a one-year period of upholding Burleson's rates, and an AT&T executive reported that "We were unable to persuade Ohio Commission to make any recommendation with respect to the pending legislation in congress or commit themselves as to future action regarding P.M.G. rates, beyond statement they would deal fairly with the companies." New Mexico's Commission objected on principle to "centralized regulation" and said only that it would continue to regulate "as heretofore." Montana's Commission acquiesced to the continuation of the Postmaster's rates "until such time as state commissions have had an opportunity to make investigations and pass upon the reasonableness of present rates." Charles B. Hill, chairman of the New York commission, presented a detailed rebuttal of AT&T's, and the Postmaster's, case. "We beg to suggest that the telephone companies are asking Congress to legalize the very action which gave rise to the great public protest which is evidenced by the litigation now pending in many of our states," he began. Protesting that legalizing the Postmaster's rates "would place the burden of proof upon the public," he stated:

> We feel that the state commissions are able to deal justly with the wire companies in the future as they have in the past, and that there is no excuse whatever for the course of action proposed by the officials of the companies and endorsed by the Postmaster General.
>
> . . .
>
> In view of the facts stated, the commission feels that the wires should be returned . . . without any legalization of the rates put into effect by the Postmaster General.

Both the full-court press mounted by AT&T and the Postmaster and the denationalization process served to ratchet up anxieties among state regulators as well as city officials. Their concerns arose from what they perceived as the fusion of two centralizing tendencies. On one hand was the federal government's preemption of state authority; on the other, AT&T's massive corporate power, both across and within state jurisdictions. During the decade that followed, it would become clearer that AT&T's aim was in part to lay foundations for a prolonged and hugely costly build-out of an integrated nationwide network. In October 1919, however, in the face of a new centralization of corporate and federal decision-making, NARUC itself also demanded that "the regulatory powers of the states as now existing be vigilantly safe-guarded."[16]

This argument was deployed in various contexts, including state regulators' passive-aggressive challenge to the Interstate Commerce Commission's role in postwar telecommunications. Although that agency's regulatory responsibilities suffered from real limitations, the *Shreveport Rate Cases* had validated its role in intrastate ratemaking. An authoritative study published in 1931 thus could hold that "the Commission is endowed with broad powers over telephone, telegraph, and cable companies." Did it employ this power? The common answer has been that the ICC was already too busy to do so—"overloaded and worked almost to death" overseeing railroads, as Senator Clarence Dill put it in 1926—and so found little energy for regulating telecommunications. This portrayal of an agency overwhelmed by its responsibilities is only partly valid, because it neglects the state regulatory agencies.[17]

We saw before that, in fact, the ICC did foray meaningfully into telecommunications between 1914 and 1918, though its activities cannot be fully documented owing to the loss of the agency's records in these years. We do not know if the ICC's attenuated role after the war came in part because, once burned, after its multiyear inquiry into private lines was deflected the agency became twice-shy. We may, however, be confident that the ICC's quietude as regards postwar telecommunications reflected something beyond understaffing and indifference. Within the context of their larger effort to "stall the centralization of regulatory power," the state commissions' stout defense of their prerogatives over intrastate telephony contributed to the ICC's hands-off stance. In 1930, as a representative of the independent telephone companies put it, the states had "rushed in and made State laws and practically took control away from the Interstate Commerce Commission, due to the fact that the bulk of the business is intrastate." Throughout this period, the ICC looked into a mere four complaints over interstate telephone rates, although rate issues as we'll see momentarily, were generating controversy nationwide. In hearings on the Communications At of 1934, though, perhaps trying to requite itself, the ICC testified in favor of a more comprehensive federal regulatory role.[18]

The prolonged lethargy of federal regulators, in any case, seemed to many to be yet another boon to AT&T. And the giant company indeed was still trying to shape regulatory dynamics. Throughout the 1920s and early 1930s—albeit unevenly, and owing much to prodding by aggrieved municipalities—some intrepid state regulators sought to enlarge government authority over the nation's telephone system. AT&T, now definitively the centerpiece of this system, resisted any augmentation of the federal role and loudly proclaimed the virtues of the state commissions—even as, simultaneously, the carrier resisted those state regulators who actually did try to impose tougher controls. The result was a nationwide plunge down a rabbit hole of rulemakings and court appeals. For fifteen years after denationalization in 1919, PUC advocates of enlarged public accountability and expanded service provision were locked in an intractable standoff: an impasse. To members of this group—certainly a minority among the state commissions—the latter had proved both ineffectual and, at times, pliant in regulating telephone rates while, paradoxically, they often seemed happy to acquiesce to an inert federal presence. Regulation was and, in these circumstances, also appeared to be, a palpable failure. Scholars in turn have tended to portray telecommunications regulation during the post–World War I period as complaisant or simply inactive.

This record merits additional consideration. Overall, what a historian has called "struggles for justice" bridged between the World War I era and the Great Depression. Between 1919 and the emergence of the New Deal in 1933, indeed, political activism traced a nearly unbroken line, and among its objects was to restructure telecommunications. Initially defensive, a series of campaigns instigated at the municipal level found scattered support both from NARUC and specific public utility commissions and maverick commissioners. These, it turned out, prepared the way for the central state's subsequent forceful intervention, as it sought to formulate a New Deal for telecommunications. The overall movement was, procedurally speaking, toward more cooperation between federal and state authorities; but this "federalism in transition" did not cohere into a straight-line consensus. Nor was it strictly a procedural contest over the respective jurisdictions of states versus national authorities. Instead, substantive policy conflicts pitted an expansion-minded AT&T against some of the nation's cities; and these conflicts were both aggravated and extended by the patchwork jurisdictions of state and federal regulators.[19]

Little-remembered, these contests between 1919 and Roosevelt's New Deal built toward a threefold achievement. First, as cities and PUCs experienced AT&T's corporate power at close hand, some regulators recognized a need to take the measure of how AT&T's structure intertwined with its profit strategy to engender public harm. Second, struggles to effect specific reforms gained firmer legal and political foundations. Third, a new rank of battle-tested cadres emerged—officials, economists, lawyers, and the occasional trade unionist—people whose knowledge of the prevailing system was only exceeded by their frustration at its limits.

AT&T and the Problem of Integrated Corporate Power

Essential tenets of public utility obtained legal expression alongside the proliferation of PUCs and the court cases that frequently followed PUC decisions. On offer by 1928 was a one-thousand-page compendium on "public utility service and discrimination" that brought together a vast array of case law concerning telephones, railroads, electricity, and gas, and other utilities. In so elevating "discrimination," the text credited a related concept—"common carriage"—a long-standing yet somewhat circular legal doctrine, signifying that when an enterprise undertakes activities of a quasi-public nature—above all, when it solicits business from the public—it assumes a special burden of care: Regulation aiming to ensure nondiscrimination may be imposed on carriers found to be affected with a public character.[20]

During this era, however, between legal principle and real-world practice lay a chasm. Throughout the 1920s, state commissions adumbrated the public utility conception to include standards of service, nondiscrimination, and extension of access, and the enigmas of valuation, depreciation, and ratemaking theory; and yet—still—telephone rates remained high enough to keep service out of reach for more than half of the population. Ratepayers actual and prospective were goaded to respond, in cities across the nation. Thus the seemingly mundane task of rate regulation led on ineluctably to deeper waters. In particular, it led some—regulators and members of the public—to consider AT&T's corporate structure and, more urgently, the unaccountable power that this structure somehow afforded to AT&T's executives and managers. Time after time, telephone rate hike requests brought activists to press beyond this seemingly tightly defined matter, as the search for democratic accountability translated into a demand that AT&T's opaque profit strategies be fully—finally—clarified.

At the same time, AT&T's own corporate strategy was freighted with great new ambition. During the mid-1920s, the company, which had been precocious in venturing into foreign markets, exited from nearly all of them (Canada was the exception) in order to focus on its domestic US network. Greatly expanding its use of open-wires and, more important, incorporating capacious new transmission media such as cables and carrier systems while also making changes to the labor process involved in handling nonlocal calls, the Bell System prioritized long-distance services. In sum, the company reengineered and modernized its nationwide network.

Its operative principle was that a minimum number of switches would be most efficient in enabling calls between any two points in the country. On this foundation, it established a nationwide network hierarchy: at the top, eight major regional switching centers were interconnected directly with high-capacity circuits; about 147 "primary outlets" were each connected directly to at least one of these regional centers; and, finally, each of the remaining 2,576 toll offices was to be connected to at least one of the higher-level switch points. Between 1923 and 1928, very long haul calling led the way: while nonlocal or toll calling as a whole increased by a dramatic 67 percent, New York to Chicago calling grew by 194 percent and transcontinental business—New York or Chicago to San Francisco or Los Angeles—rocketed by 430 percent. AT&T's extraordinary network upgrade consumed staggering quantities of capital; and it engendered a 14 percent decline in the number of person-hours needed per unit of output between 1920 and 1929—though to handle just the long-distance business in New York City required 1275 switchboard positions in 1930.[21]

AT&T could only actualize this strategy by gaining regular approvals for rate increases—and these approvals were not foreordained. Danielian recounts how, after denationalization, "the Bell companies fought not only to retain the rates established during Federal control but to raise them. These attempts had the aspect of a national campaign, with all the resources of the Bell System mobilized under the leadership of A.T.&T." Not only did AT&T expand its pioneering public relations unit; it also deliberately enlarged the geographic and social range of its shareholder base. As with almost anything pertaining to the giant carrier, the scale of its endeavors was impressive all by itself: during just the three years prior to October 1922, the Bell companies were parties to 205 rate cases nationwide.[22]

Notwithstanding AT&T's endeavors to win over public opinion, as Alan Stone observes, its proposed rate increases—and its efforts to defend existing rates—provoked a reaction as ubiquitous as it was intense: "numerous interests, including cities, chambers of commerce, users, and so-called public advocates," Stone explains, "frequently appeared at rate proceedings." Haltingly, unevenly, these proceedings accentuated what, for some state regulators, was a politically unpalatable insight: that effective rate regulation was quite impossible absent oversight, analysis, and ratemaking power over the entire Bell System rather than just one or another of its two dozen local subsidiaries. In the moment, states-rights proponents found themselves at a loss: how was a state—let alone those cities as still were intent on achieving "home rule"—to win accountability over the *nation's* network manager? The AT&T behemoth evaded or, where it deemed it necessary, defied local authorities, arguing by turns that its interstate network and specific units of its vertically integrated company lay outside the jurisdiction of regulators who were legally confined to matters within each state.[23]

Cities and states that managed against the odds to exert some measure of control over local rates might yet trigger perverse results, as AT&T responded by imposing higher charges elsewhere, or by reducing its in-state network investment, or simply by maintaining exorbitant rates for interstate long-distance calls. "Between the jurisdictional confusion and vacuum of control at the national level," one analyst concludes, "AT&T in effect was able to pull revenue out of the local operating companies into the parent company. All through the 1920s AT&T was profitable and paid consistently high dividends, while the financial situation of the local operating companies was far less rosy."[24]

Over time regulators began to recognize that, if they were to take seriously their responsibilities for intrastate and local ratemaking, they would need to plumb the depths of AT&T's forbidding operations overall. Awareness perversely increased that the barriers to effective oversight were structural, as obscure and torturous legal battles pitted units of Bell's vertically and horizontally integrated corporation against municipalities and state regulators. As the obstacles before regulators were traced back repeatedly to AT&T's impenetrable system, these contests turned, almost imperceptibly, into touchstones for an audacious reform program.

Drawing on its unique structure as part holding company and part operating company, AT&T possessed multiple advantages over its ostensible overseers. Because regulation increased the risk to the telephone company of what one early writer termed "the problems of compulsory publicity," AT&T introduced a battery of tactics to deal with this threat: public relations, legal proceedings and appeals, administrative, and lobbying activities. A precocious advocate of corporate public relations, as we saw, by 1915, Theodore Vail chafed that regulation not only diverted management from addressing other matters, but also compelled large expenditures: "Many detailed reports are called for, and prepared at great expense." Attempting to outflank federal and state regulatory initiatives indeed was costly. By the 1930s, however, AT&T's far-flung and diverse efforts to manage publicity had succeeded in touching discourse nationwide.[25]

Broad informational requirements imposed by state and federal regulators were more easily borne by the immense AT&T than by its numerous small-fry rivals. As a result, AT&T was simultaneously able to cultivate a new kind of competitive advantage by manipulating the regulatory process. Resources that AT&T could draw on to overawe unusually intrepid or principled regulators were diverse, ranging from high-priced legal talent and access to the labyrinth of appellate courts, to revolving door jobs for ambitious regulatory personnel. The obtuse field of ratemaking theory thus became heavily influenced by telephone company accountants, lawyers, and economists. Through such initiatives, AT&T attempted with considerable success to concretize its own self-interested interpretation of the obligations and responsibilities of service providers. By contrast, the state regulatory commissions were chronically understaffed and undernourished. In the 1930s an investigation found that "with the exception of a few states, the commissions generally are not provided with sufficient funds to carry on the multiplicity of tasks that is imposed upon them in the regulation of various utilities within their respective jurisdictions."[26]

AT&T played on this weakness by threatening to tie up significant rate cases in litigation; regulators faced the politically problematic prospect of being engulfed. Adding to their vulnerability, AT&T could count on the fact that, through the 1920s, federal courts seemed inclined to "strangle" any propensity toward independence shown by state regulators; the "low esteem" in which the courts tended to hold state regulation was reflected in their willingness to retry cases de novo, presuming that their expertise rivaled that of the regulators'. Adding to this problem, again, was that regulation by the federal Interstate Commerce Commission had become cursory. Preoccupied with railroad regulation, lacking what it now deemed to be an authoritative congressional mandate in the telecommunications field, presented with but few actionable complaints, and—as I have already suggested—confronted by state PUCs jealous to ward off federal attacks on their jurisdiction, after World War I the ICC's only real achievement was to adopt a Uniform System of Accounts—one that conformed to AT&T's accounting preferences. Telephone companies (meaning AT&T) remained, in the anodyne language of a later Department of Justice document, "free from ICC regulation in determining their rates, return on investment and service obligations."[27]

In addition to all of this, an emergent problem loomed increasingly large before regulators. Both fractionated and incomplete, regulators' jurisdictional authority rendered them largely incapable of taking an active role with respect to the hugely expensive makeover of nationwide networking plant and facilities that AT&T had determined to undertake. This difficulty was deeply rooted. Years before Theodore Vail returned to the giant carrier, an AT&T counsel already had notified subsidiary Pacific Telephone Company officials (in 1900) that "the liability of regulation of states through legislative action is . . . much lessened by extending the area of operation in a single Company over several states and the increased interstate character of the business. It is much more difficult to regulate a portion than the whole. The jurisdiction of the Federal Courts is also secured to a much larger extent, which I consider a great advantage, particularly in the event of being obliged to contest excessive taxation of rates fixed unreasonably low by some regulatory body." Again, in 1901, as its rivalry with independent telephone providers escalated, a lawyer for AT&T argued in a letter to company president Frederick P. Fish "that it is extremely important that we should control the whole toll-line system of intercommunication throughout the country. This system is destined, in my opinion, to be very much more important in the future than it has been in the past. Such lines may be regarded as the nerves of our whole system. We need not fear the opposition in a single place, provided we control the means of communication with other places." Increasingly during and after the 1910s, moreover, AT&T had taken pains to consolidate and strengthen its control over its far-flung affiliates. The parent AT&T's ownership shares in its local operating companies were boosted, independent carriers were merged and assimilated, and administrative controls were strengthened. Between 1900 and 1922, an early historian reported, AT&T's total assets increased by an extraordinary one billion dollars, the greatest portion of which—nearly $780 million—came about "by way of increased holdings of the expanding operating companies." Now, however, the giant carrier planned to undertake an even more ambitious and costly modernization, to upgrade plant and equipment across its nationwide network.[28]

For ratepayers, AT&T's integrated structure engendered a form of exploitation that was both multifarious and obscure. Regulators might apprehend the general forms that this exploitation took; but the limits on their jurisdiction barred them from gaining specific knowledge as to its consequences for rates in their community or state, let alone from making restitutive changes.

A flagrant instance concerned the "license contract," whereby Bell service companies handed off a proportion of their gross annual revenues to AT&T for a range of management services. This transfer of resources had originated in the earliest years, when individual licensees were charged by Bell for the lease and use of instruments covered by the Bell patents; formalized in 1902, as a charge of 4.5 percent of the total gross operating income of each Bell operating company, during the postwar era it drew mounting criticism. "Of all the Bell policies," wrote a scholar in 1925, "the one that receives the greatest condemnation is the so-called four-and-one-half-per-cent charge." A few years before, AT&T President Thayer had devoted a significant portion of his speech before the annual gathering of the National Association of Railroad and Utilities Commissioners to defend the license contract as "absolutely essential to a national telephone system" because it afforded the central corporate coordination without which local telephone providers would be unable to provide a "national universal service." Although the amount called for by the license contract declined to 2 percent after 1927 and 1.5 percent by 1930, as AT&T came under increased pressure, even at this reduced level it signified a transfer of many millions. A contemporary expert related that "The payment is stated as a charge for the rental of the transmitters and receivers used by the operating companies and for certain services of a professional character. These services seem to be nowhere described by contract. Their exact nature appears to be more or less indefinite." The license contract had evolved into a device for extracting payments from ratepayers, in exchange for the parent company's financial advice and assistance, research and development work, legal support, and operating and engineering advice to its operating companies. Were ratepayers getting their money's worth? "These service charges," wrote two eminent public utility analysts in 1932, "have aroused much public criticism and have been a thorn in the company's flesh in its relations with public service commissions." The holding company appeared to enjoy an "almost complete freedom from control" that "seriously threatens the effectiveness of public utility regulation."[29]

As state regulators looked on, revenue streamed into the AT&T holding company from its local-exchange service subsidiaries. During the patent monopoly period ending in 1894, license fees may have contributed more than half of the parent company's total revenue of $44.5 million. Reductions during the competitive early years of independent telephony (1894–1899) nevertheless continued to permit millions to be extracted each year, and license fee transfers increased again after the turn of the twentieth century—from an estimated $2.5 million in 1900 (23–25 percent of total AT&T revenues) to an absolute high of more than $34 million in 1927 (13 percent of total revenues). Put differently, license contract payments received by AT&T between 1900 and 1927 totaled $356 million. Reductions in the license fee in the late 1920s, followed by the economic contraction of the Depression, brought the sums received by the parent company to a low of $13 million in 1934, about 6 percent of total revenues. But the onerous charge persisted as a concrete sign of local exploitation by a "foreign" corporate parent. And local regulators were largely powerless to curtail AT&T's commitment to redistribution upward, as money paid into the system by millions of residential subscribers in the form of rates was taken out of it by hundreds of thousands of AT&T shareholders in the form of dividends. Before World War I, moreover, a government investigation had shown that monopoly companies were routinely overcapitalized, and that "redundant securities established streams of investment income that corporations pointed to as fixed costs, precluding lower prices or higher wages." A decade later, AT&T President Thayer put the best face he could on the matter, conceding before NARUC that the carrier's "plant has been built out of the savings of the people."[30]

AT&T's ability to exploit the license contract to influence intrastate rates stemmed ultimately from its integrated corporate structure. Interstate long distance, or toll telephone calling, opened a second window onto this conditioning feature. Though long-distance calls continued to constitute a tiny percentage of overall calling volume and made up a mere fraction of Bell System revenue, during the 1920s AT&T's program of network modernization turned the arcane question of how the carrier priced telephone services into another highly charged issue.

Again, the issues went back decades. From Bell's formation of AT&T as its separate long-distance subsidiary in 1885, the importance of this functional unit gradually ascended, as the company began to lavish resources and strategic attention on its "toll," or interexchange, long-distance service. After the Bell patents lapsed, as we saw, long-distance gained crucial strategic value for AT&T as an incentive for business users to prefer it to independent carriers. By 1916, mostly at the expense of telegraph service, long-distance voice circuits carried about half of the country's rapid intercity traffic. Bell engineers, meanwhile, were bringing forward new networking technologies, beginning with the recently devised three-element vacuum tube that permitted New York and San Francisco to speak to each other for the first time, again in 1915. As, after World War I, AT&T's ability to bind its local telephone systems into an integrated transcontinental network became a top priority, long-distance experiments and technical advances increased. Bell engineers embraced long-distance transmission as a research focus and, as new technologies were integrated into the system, their breakthroughs in signal amplification and multiplexing (encompassing radiotelephony, carrier systems, coaxial cables, and eventually microwave radio) began to translate into decreasing costs, improved efficiency and increased capacity in long-distance carriage.[31]

All well and good; but how did the changing status of long-distance networking affect the price of service? This opaque issue introduced growing vexation. To comprehend it, we must briefly evaluate how AT&T priced telephone service; and how, during the 1920s, its extraordinary network modernization program impacted on its existing rates.

Mueller explains that, "[t]o increase the utility of the system"—which, hitherto, had been physically divided into largely discrete local- and long-distance networks that shared in common only subscribers' handsets—beginning by 1889, "Bell decided to integrate local and long-distance telephony by upgrading local exchanges to the transmission standards of the long-distance system." This change took decades to accomplish because additional technical innovations were concurrently assimilated. In the perspective afforded by 1951, regulators agreed that, "In general, improvement and development in exchange facilities have accompanied those in toll facilities."[32]

AT&T's policy of upgrading local plant to support an increasingly integrated nationwide system impressively enhanced its operating performance. In 1920, the average elapsed time from the placing of a toll call until connection was established was about fourteen minutes; by 1940, the average had dropped to 1.4 minutes. Unsurpassed capital investment programs were required for AT&T to erect its integrated nationwide network upon these continually modernized technological foundations. However, these changes to networking technology engendered a parallel qualitative shift in network economics. Specifically, "[t]he furnishing of state and interstate toll services, involves the joint use of a large part of telephone equipment, plant and operating personnel." A single network that enabled both local and long-distance calls, in other words, turned telephone service into what economists call a "joint-cost" commodity.[33]

By 1925, a mere 200,000—or 1 percent—of US telephones did not interconnect in some fashion with AT&T's sprawling network. AT&T's simultaneous control of an interstate monopoly over long-distance service and of local service monopolies covering four-fifths of US telephone subscribers, enabled it to manipulate joint-cost telephone service in fractionalized rate-setting proceedings. Its tremendous network modernization project brought home to regulators as never before, that the joint-cost status of an integrated telephone service possessed major ramifications for telephone rates.[34]

Under AT&T's long-standing pricing system, local ratepayers had paid disproportionately for the carrier's cumulating investment in long-distance plant and equipment. Long-distance users, that is, did not pay local-exchange operators for the joint cost of furnishing long-distance service. This policy, writes Horwitz, was "dear to AT&T"—for a compelling reason.[35]

That local ratepayers were on the hook for much of the expense of continually modernizing AT&T's long-distance system, notably including the retrofitting of local telephone plant during the 1920s, meant that AT&T captured a greater portion of the charges for long-distance calls as profit. The Commission would estimate that, notwithstanding voluntary long-distance rate reductions, between 1913 and 1936 AT&T's average revenue per toll message had grown from 20 to 33 cents; and long-distance traffic carried by AT&T's Long Lines subsidiary rather than shorter toll calls carried by its local operating companies accounted for a disproportionate share of this increase. In 1930, correspondingly, merely 1.5 percent of telephone message traffic crossed state lines—but these calls accounted for nearly 10 percent of Bell System revenues.[36]

When AT&T ramped up network modernization outlays after World War I, it assumed that this pattern would continue, despite, or because of, the fact that telephone use remained overwhelmingly local. Lacking legal jurisdiction beyond their state's borders, regulators were essentially powerless to do anything: AT&T's monopoly over the nation's interstate long-distance network enabled it to steer around the patchwork of existing regulation. "[P]otential evasion of regulation," the FCC would charge in 1938, "is inherent in the Bell System organization and the management policies applied thereto by the centralized control vested in the American Co. executives." Specifically, "The failure to enact Federal regulatory legislation earlier and the apparent lack of active interest in the level of interstate telephone rates," the FCC would conclude, "has permitted the development of the existing toll-rate structure and the expansion of interstate toll-line facilities virtually without effective regulatory control."[37]

AT&T possessed still another means of manipulating its joint-cost telephone service. Again, this could be traced back to its integrated corporate structure and, specifically, to a constitutive vertical feature. AT&T's Western Electric manufacturing subsidiary granted AT&T a legion of opportunities to render its cost structure and system development strategy impervious to would-be regulators, while deploying transfer pricing to boost its profits. Western Electric's sales to the Bell System between 1913 and 1931 accounted for an estimated 60 percent of Bell's gross costs for plant and equipment and 30 percent of the total costs which (via an authorized rate-of-return on an allowed rate base) served as the basis for fixing telephone service charges. This gave the question of Western's prices and underlying costs a "direct pertinency," as a New Deal rate expert put it, "in any consideration of operating company rate bases." But Western, perversely, was "perhaps the only large manufacturer which keeps no record of true costs of any of its products, keeps no direct record of the cost of sales, and maintains such a voluminous, intricate, and unreliable mass of records and estimates as a substitute for a cost accounting system that the determination of true and actual costs therefrom is an impossibility. In the absence of knowledge of Western's manufacturing costs State commission regulation breaks down in the face of costs built up from prices fixed arbitrarily by the Western Electric Co. under American Co. direction." Indeed, on the basis of a detailed study, the FCC eventually estimated Western's manufacturing costs (in 1936) to be 27 percent above justifiable manufacturing costs; in the agency's eyes, limiting Western Electric's costs to those of comparable manufacturers and restricting its profits to 6 percent, would produce price reductions of fully one-third for Bell system telephone apparatus.[38]

It would become an article of faith for New Deal regulators that the state-centered regulatory regime had suffered from irremediable structural deficiencies when it came to AT&T. "[T]he Bell System's corporate organization," concluded a top FCC staffer in 1938, "has at all times made it impossible for the local regulatory authorities to examine and properly to rule upon the ultimate facts, as a result of their inability to reach the parent company and its operations by direct process." Though they may not have understood how the corporate magic was worked, by the 1920s, state regulators were well-aware that AT&T's corporate structure functioned to prevent them from exercising effective oversight. In 1924, for example, the Maryland PUC characterized its difficulties in obtaining needed information with undisguised bitterness:

> No information bearing on this matter [intercorporate relationships within the Bell System] that the company or companies could prevent this Commission from obtaining was secured. The commission was met with a positive refusal of any information relating to the American Telephone & Telegraph Company affairs that was not a matter of public record, or which could not be found in the records of the Chesapeake & Potomac Telephone Company of Baltimore City.

The fact that most of the important books and records of the local company are kept outside the state made the securing of information [more difficult].

Contemporary academic specialists also pointed to this deficit as a primary reason to improve the regulatory apparatus. J. Warren Stehman concluded in 1925, in an especially important and well-used study, that "efficient regulation" constituted "a national matter":

It is impossible for local authority to regulate properly the long-lines service, which covers the entire country. . . . Thus it is at once apparent that the authorities who would accurately regulate this service must have control over any part of the system which helps make the connection. This means at once that the control must be more extended than is possible with any authority short of national. It seems clear that this must be true whether one considers regulations concerning the quality of service, the need for orders compelling additional and more extended service, or the rates charged.

"The need for strong federal regulation of the telephone industry was obvious to most state regulators by 1930," a later historian agreed.[39]

With this recognition came efforts to tame the giant carrier. AT&T reported in 1929 that bills to "give or extend" the right of government ownership and operation of the telephone had been presented to eight state legislatures, mostly in the Midwest and Great Plains. Bills seeking to resurrect this old goal—either by postalizing the telephone system entirely, or through a government takeover of interstate telephony—were also introduced into the House of Representatives in every Congress between 1923 and 1928. More significant, and certainly more portentous, was that members of Congress repeatedly entertained resolutions calling for investigations of telephone industry practices—above all, rate-setting and service—between 1923 and 1931. Within NARUC, there were concurrent efforts to institute what historians label a "cooperative federalism" in telecommunications regulation. Still sensitive about central-state incursions, the felt need was nevertheless to forge new machinery so that state and federal agencies might partner to quell AT&T's evasion and manipulation of the regulatory process.[40]

Hearings on early versions of what would eventually become legislation to establish a federal communications commission flagged many of the shortcomings described above. Members of the Senate Interstate Commerce Committee in late 1929 and early 1930 subjected AT&T's structure and behavior to searching (but at some points also tellingly ignorant) questions. AT&T's President Walter S. Gifford was interrogated for a full day as to the carrier's excess profits, holding company structure, rate overcharges, transfer payments to Western Electric, patent control and associated license fees extracted from operating companies, depreciation practices, and inadequate accountability to state and federal regulatory bodies. Scrutiny was accorded to the causes and character of the Interstate Commerce Commission's apparent ineffectuality. Mandated by Congress, a major follow-up study justified its call for a regulatory overhaul by repeating that "At the present time there is little, if any, Federal regulation of the rates, practices, and charges of the several branches of the communications industry."[41]

By and large, the 1920s' discontent and reform activism around telephony have faded from memory. In a much later filing, the US Department of Justice would accurately recollect, however, that "During the 1920's and early 1930's members of Congress repeatedly expressed their concern about the status and conditions prevailing in the telephone industry." By Roosevelt's first term in office (1933–1937), a contemporary FCC investigation agreed, "public dissatisfaction with the policies prevalent in the telephone industry, and in the Bell System in particular, together with its manner of conducting business, had been growing articulate for more than a decade." Of particular note, the agency underlined, "a movement had developed looking toward more positive federal occupation of this field." States and cities were at the forefront of this agitation.[42]

Agitation for a Public Utility Service

AT&T's immunity to genuine public accountability made some state regulators and legislators determined to address the insufficiencies of the existing oversight mechanism. In 1922, the Hon. Clyde M. Reed, Chairman of the Public Utilities Commission of Kansas, mounted a head-on challenge to AT&T President H. B. Thayer, who was also participating in this same gathering of the National Association of Regulatory Utility Commissioners. Mr. Thayer, declared Reed, "is the head of the nearest approach to a complete monopoly in any important service or manufacturing process that exists in this country." Not Standard Oil, nor US Steel, nor any of the great meat-packing companies, nor any railroad approached the market dominance possessed by AT&T. "It would probably be a shock to the public mind and perhaps a surprise to many members of this Association to realize the extent to which the telephone service of the country has passed into the control of a single interest." Reed's proclaimed that it was the responsibility of state regulators to publicize the current "threat to public service":

> there is no service which the state commissions can render to the public greater than that of acquainting it with the telephone situation as it exists. To my mind the rapid pace at which we are traveling toward a complete telephone monopoly in the country is a threat to public service and will impose a burden of hundreds

of millions of dollars upon the users of telephone service, both local and long distance.

AT&T's studied indifference to the opposition its rate hike requests generated itself fed into initiatives seeking to strengthen the nation's regulatory capacities. Virtually from June 1919, when the legality of Postmaster Burleson's toll rates was affirmed by the Supreme Court, opposition to Bell System petitions snowballed.[43]

Between 1900 and 1922, during which time population increased by 45 percent and railroad plant and equipment investment increased by 135 percent, AT&T enlarged its investment in telephone plant by 960 percent. Whereas the annual investment in fixed capital made by most industrial corporations was ordinarily exceeded by their gross revenues, for telephone companies (like other public utilities) plant investments averaged between four to six times gross revenues. And, far from diminishing, during the postwar years AT&T's capital spending continued to rocket.[44]

Now focused on installing automatic switching for self-service (dial calling), AT&T was bent on integrating its nationwide long-distance network more fully with local exchanges. President Gifford would recall in 1930 that "right after the war," the telephone business "had an enormous program of construction to go forward with"; investment accelerated to the point that "more than half of the telephone plant in this country . . . has been built within the last five years"; and the business still "requires hundreds of millions of dollars of new money each year if we are going to go forward." Although, Gifford implied, the great carrier was making selfless efforts to lower ratepayers' costs by conducting systematic research and development, he argued that upward pressure on rates was still inescapable owing to the company's need to complete this far-reaching network modernization.[45]

AT&T's financial requirements during the nine years 1923–1931 amounted to over $3 billion; of this, $2.5 billion represented net additions to telephone plant, nearly all of which went to its affiliated local operating companies. Only about a quarter of this colossal sum was met through AT&T's internal sources: depreciation reserves and undistributed profits. The FCC later calculated that AT&T thus needed to raise some $2 billion from outside sources, and it did so by selling bonds and, above all, through stock issues. AT&T's continual requests for rate hikes thus were the outcome of its need to guarantee returns to the investors who supplied the capital it used to upgrade its nationwide network. This financial arrangement appeared to engrave even more deeply than before the social disparity that had long divided local- and long-distance callers. Long-distance users, remember, were preponderantly businesses and middle-class households; working-class ratepayers made almost exclusively local calls. Consciously or not, when the American Federation of Labor resolved in 1933 that "a large portion of the local service customers never have, never will and never desire to use ... long distance service," it was speaking to the injustice of how AT&T's mammoth financing needs for long distance bore on local rates.[46]

During the 1920s and early 1930s, in four large and politically influential states—California, New York, Illinois and Wisconsin—the Bell System's rate requests provoked fierce and protracted controversies. These debates, which necessarily took a legal form, were rooted in social division and conflict. They became crucial inputs to the diverse reformers who, seeking to ease the crisis of the Great Depression, subsequently redrew the boundaries of power in US telecommunications in line with a dramatically changed national policy for network system development. On one side, these controversies went far to reveal the disabling limits of the existing system, which combined ignorance about what the Bell system encompassed and how its component parts interacted, with tightly constrained jurisdictional oversight. On the other, they began to generate the nationwide political momentum that was required for substantive reform of this flawed system.

San Francisco

Investigations of long distance and local-exchange rates became frequent in California after 1911, when the California Railroad Commission (CRC) gained jurisdiction over telephones. Already before the US entry into the Great War, the Railroad Commission understood that it needed to scrutinize Pacific Telephone & Telegraph Company with respect to its corporate structure, its contractual relations with its parent AT&T and with Western Electric, its depreciation practices, and its division of revenues between toll systems and exchange accounts. But the telephone company was only one of the Commission's adversaries. After Postmaster General Burleson's rate increases—which the CRC unsuccessfully attempted to forbid in-state telephone companies from implementing—and the return of intrastate jurisdiction to state authorities, the Commission instituted proceedings to determine the reasonableness of the new rates.[47]

Opposition persisted. San Francisco, according to telephone historian Meighan Maguire, "home to the earliest, largest, and most technically sophisticated Bell exchange in the West," constituted both a key node in AT&T's nationwide network and an active site of ratemaking conflict. The relation between telephone rates and the size of the community or, more precisely, the number of customers served, was assessed during 1924 by the new California Rate Commission's Telephone and Telegraph Division. Studying the records generated by telephone utilities serving 950,000 exchange stations scattered throughout the state, the Commission found that, unlike other utilities and, indeed, most other businesses, "The greater the number of subscribers or telephone served within one exchange area, the greater the cost per telephone station. . . . As a telephone system grows larger, the cost of equipment per telephone and the expense of operation and maintenance per telephone increase. . . . As subscribers increase, each telephone user can talk to an ever widening circle of friends and business associates. Operating costs per telephone grow as more frequent talks are held. Subscribers' lines begin to run farther and ever farther from the exchange until a big percentage of them are . . . expensive to build and increasingly expensive to maintain. . . . For this reason the larger cities, not only in California but elsewhere, will have higher rates than smaller cities. Also, as a city grows in size the rates for service will increase."[48]

As would also prove true elsewhere, however, the rationality of local rates remained both mysterious and controversial, because it intertwined not only with the changing economics of networks but also with AT&T's corporate power. What portion of local rates in a given city's case should be attributed to escalating costs? What part should be traced, instead, to the profit-maximization strategies that were uniquely available to a vertically integrated interstate telephone company? Regulators could not be sure. Thus they could not be confident of just how badly their constituents were being gouged. However, ironically, of one thing they could be certain: Their inability to discern the character and extent of the investment on which rates needed to be calculated—the rate base, as they called it—was a function of AT&T's structure.

Typical was the experience of the California Railroad Commission when, in 1924, Southern California Telephone—another Bell affiliate—refused to submit any evidence relative to the costs to its parent AT&T of rendering service within the state, "contending that such information was not relevant and that as the American Co. was not a public utility in California, this commission could not require such information to be presented." As a consequence of this refusal, the City of Los Angeles, and the League of California Municipalities Special Committee on Telephone Regulation, ultimately lodged protests before a US Congressional committee. Representing these two bodies, as he had represented the city and county of San Francisco before the California Rate Commission, was the chairman of the legislative committee of "The Telephone Investigation League of America," attorney Dion R. Holm. This League, Holm stated, "is made up of the cities of Seattle, Spokane, Portland, Oregon City, Oakland, Tacoma, San Francisco, Fresno, and Los Angeles." Appearing alongside Holm before Congress was Seattle's city attorney, Charles L. Smith. The two men were treated respectfully by the Senate Committee, as they underlined the insufficiency of the existing system of state-centered regulation in its dealings with the Bell System.

Concurrent proceedings in New York State escalated this issue to national prominence.[49]

New York

"In 1919 and 1920 the New York Telephone Company filed ... new schedules of rates which greatly increased the existing rates throughout the entire state," an official history of the Empire state's rate proceedings would begin: "Practically all of the cities, towns and villages questioned the propriety of these increases and a large number of these municipalities filed formal complaints" with the PUC in 1931. "Extended public hearings" followed, initiating a legal cut-and-thrust over telephone rates that would continue for over a decade.[50]

Opposition pyramided, motivated by a belief that New York Telephone was engaging in "profiteering." In New York City, in 1920, the Bell company's proposed 33 percent rate increase threatened to provoke "an avalanche of protests, chiefly from small telephone users" before the Public Service Commission, which (the *New York Times* held) portended a repeat "of scenes which characterized the telephone investigation conducted about a year ago, when witnesses protesting any grant of higher rates to the telephone company sometimes became more than emphatic in their complaints." John F. Hylan, New York City's mayor at the outset of this conflict, complained to the state regulator that Bell's generous dividends to shareholders rendered the proposed rate increases "unwarranted and unjustified." After telephone rates were increased anyway, 1921–1922 witnessed what the *New York Times* called "protests, amounting virtually to a revolt among telephone users in up-State communities" such as Buffalo.[51]

Successive municipal administrations, both in New York City and elsewhere, led the campaign against Bell. But other social actors joined the struggle. In 1925, organized labor throughout New York State pressed the fight after Bell announced a plan to impose another new surcharge; both the City's Central Trades and Labor Council, representing 700,000 workers, and the State Federation of Labor called on "all public agencies charged with defending popular rights to join in an effective opposition." When, after further skirmishing, the Bell affiliate removed a rate hike request from the jurisdiction of the Public Service Commission to the Federal Court, legal advisors to cities across the state unanimously resolved to request the state's Attorney General, Carl Sherman, to represent them "in all litigation affecting the telephone company's move."[52]

A second aspect of the New York rate case became evident as Bell again encountered nationwide opposition. In 1926, city authorities in Boston, Los Angeles, Indianapolis, Youngstown, and New York City, joined by the Ohio State Utilities Commission, threatened to cooperate with one another to launch a "concerted attack before the Interstate Commerce Commission against the American Telephone and Telegraph Company, charging that it exists as a monopoly in violation of the Clayton act." The complaint, initiated by Boston but also "made many times by the Corporation Counsel of the City of New York before the Public Service Commission," was that high telephone rates were a consequence "of the alleged illegal control" by AT&T of its in-house manufacturing subsidiaries, preeminently, Western Electric. "This combination of companies" not only rendered "subscribers . . . unable to obtain reasonable rates," but also— charged the originating complaint—"hindered and obstructed a full investigation and appraisal of the assets of the Bell telephone system by any regulatory body." In 1930, a plea of the same kind came from the "Public Utility Rate League"—a business group based in Atlanta—to Governor Franklin D. Roosevelt of New York; the League requested "complete information" about the New York controversy over telephone rates, because "we are preparing to institute proceedings in this and other Southern States looking to general reduction on charges for telephone services." Roosevelt's standard response to the numerous letters he received on this issue from businesses as well as individual subscribers offered a portent: "the case shows the necessity of a complete restudy of the relationship between the State and public service utility companies, which companies are in theory and in fact creatures of the State, operating under licenses known as charters granted to them by the State itself."[53]

By 1928, the New York case had seen 355 court day hearings, during which over one thousand witnesses produced 31,000 pages of testimony; meanwhile, the Republican-led New York Legislature, receptive to the lobbying and legislative tactics of the private utility companies, forestalled meaningful legislative intervention. Twisting and turning through the judicial system, the case thus continued to wend its way from venue to venue. After New York Telephone appealed the case to Federal Court, and the Court in turn appointed a special master—who thereupon found in favor of New York Telephone's proposed increases—Governor Roosevelt himself publicly intervened.[54]

Roosevelt possessed extensive knowledge of public utility issues, pertaining, in particular, to electrical power (he wrote to an uncle in 1929 that he had "read literally hundreds of papers and documents on the whole subject"), and he coupled this expertise to an adroit sense of their political value. This was a governor who made the abuses of private utilities a touchstone of his political career. He was hardly alone. During the decade after World War I, private power utilities became objects of major congressional scrutiny, and a political initiative commenced to develop publicly owned water power at Muscle Shoals, Alabama. This was momentarily stymied. However, it was followed in the late 1920s by hugely publicized scandals which engulfed the nation's leading power companies, companies whose opaque finances and ownership structures, as they collapsed, soon would be credited with having helped tumble the nation into the Depression. Roosevelt made the debacle a campaign issue, first in his successful bid for the governorship of New York State and then for a higher office. Among FDR's many notable achievements upon ascending to the presidency, indeed, was a multifaceted intervention to set the private power industry on different foundations: not only through the government-owned Tennessee Valley Authority and the Rural Electrification Administration, but also through legislation, bitterly opposed and resented by owners and investors, to rein in some of the most egregious features of public utility holding companies themselves.[55]

The telephone industry and the electric power business bore many parallels (and some points of convergence, as we will see in a later chapter), and regulatory ideas—and regulators themselves—moved from one to the other. As Governor, Roosevelt held that for redress to come from the existing chief instrument of rational regulation—New York's public service commission—the agency's powers had to be both expanded and refocused. His timing was impeccable: during late 1929 and early 1930, telephone rates and ratemaking jurisdiction were hot-button political issues. With "protests against the new rates being voiced from all parts of the state," fifty-eight cities in New York formed "a coalition for presenting a solid front in the fight against the telephone rate increases."[56]

Roosevelt now insisted that the Commission had to act as agent of the public, upon its own initiative as well as upon petition, to investigate the acts of public utilities with respect both to service and rates as well as to enforce adequate service and reasonable rates. The Commission, whose Republican chairman had resigned and been replaced by a Roosevelt appointee, agreed that its legal counsel should relinquish an exclusively advisory function in order to actively represent the scores of cities arrayed as plaintiffs against higher telephone rates. "His new role," the *New York Times* suggested darkly, "makes him to a large extent a public utility prosecutor." Over protestations made by Bell's New York Telephone, the Commission went on to lower residential rates, to reduce New York Telephone's valuation and revenue, and to request that New York State amend its statutes "to give the commission broader jurisdiction over holding companies." But Roosevelt urged that still more was needed: "The people of the State, paraphrasing an old expression, will probably say 'For this much, some thanks' "; he requested that the Public Service Commission initiate "a searching inquiry" into rates. Roosevelt also announced that recent events had "brought to the fore in a striking way the whole question of interference by the United States courts with the regulatory power of our Public Service Commission." Masterfully, Roosevelt castigated actions by telephone companies as well as other utilities to shift forums from state to federal authorities:

Time and again we have seen utility companies rush into the Federal courts to obtain injunctions against state commissions....

The people of our state are more and more resentful of the assumption and retention of jurisdiction by Federal judges. We have had many examples in electricity, gas, telephone and subway cases. It means that hearings and trials which rightfully should be held before our Public Service Commission or before State courts are, by a scratch of the pen, transferred to a special master appointed by the Federal court. The state regulatory body, set up by our law to inquire into matters of valuation, depreciation, operating expenses and other factors entering into rate-making, its laughed at by the utility . . . The special master becomes the rate-maker; the Public Service Commission becomes a mere legal fantasy.

We have already seen how sensitive the question of federal preemption of state jurisdiction could be. Roosevelt now proclaimed "the necessity of immediate steps to deprive federal courts of power to interfere with the actions of state regulatory bodies."; and he worked with New York City Mayor Fiorello LaGuardia and New York Senator Robert Wagner on behalf of legislation to "abrogate this power." The Governor likewise continued to hammer on the theme. In a campaign speech broadcast the following autumn (1930) from the Bronx, his rhetoric sharpened: "And now we come, on this battle front, to two great regiments, recruited from all over the state, on the farms and in the cities,—regiments composed of men and women who are fighting to end the excessive and exorbitant rates for electricity in the homes, for telephones, and for other utilities,—people who are fighting for a great principle in behalf of this generation, and all the generations to come. (applause—prolonged)."[57]

The Governor thus staked a claim in the raging debate over utility regulation. Harvard Law Professor Felix Frankfurter advised his friend Franklin Roosevelt that his speeches on the issue had made him "the most powerful single influence in bringing the serious public interest behind present tendencies in utility management before the public. And there is no better issue on which to stake a popular fight."[58]

The New York rate case not only allowed Roosevelt to inject himself into telecommunications policy, but also contributed both substantively and procedurally to the impulse to reform. It injected new dynamism into the old tactic of using public exposures of abuses to generate pressure on private utilities—a tactic that would be employed again after Roosevelt was elected President and established a new Federal Communications Commission. New York's Public Service Commission also concluded that there was a need to investigate holding company structure, and to systematize and, where necessary, to contest the arcane data that went into ratemaking. Another policy tenet likewise later came to be embraced by the New Deal. The New York Commission reasoned that reductions should be made to residential—rather than to business—rates, on the grounds that "extensive use of residence telephones" resulted in "making the telephone almost invaluable to the general business subscriber." "The ordinary business subscriber does not give due consideration to this fact," the Commission suggested. "As is natural, he considers his telephone from the viewpoint of his outgoing calls, and tends to forget the tremendous number of incoming calls which he receives without additional charge. These incoming calls measure, for practically all business subscribers, the greatest value to them of telephone service, since under modern conditions the telephone is used as a means of ordering and selling merchandise." In sum, "the value of the telephone to business subscribers . . . varies in almost direct proportion with the number of residence telephones"—and business users therefore should pay proportionately more. This ratemaking principle became known as value-of-service.[59]

Another richly destabilizing vector of reform converged, as a result of a protracted struggle over telephone system development policy in the nation's second city.

Chicago

The proceeding that is known as the Chicago Rate Case was formally initiated in 1921 by Illinois state regulators, as part of a prolonged conflict over the terms on which local telephone service was provided and in a context where sentiment in favor of "home rule" remained strong. An especially far-ranging investigation of Bell's Chicago Telephone Company's rates and service had been undertaken fully one decade earlier, by the reform-minded economist Edward W. Bemis for the Chicago City Council Committee on Gas, Oil and Electricity. Bemis's findings were credited by a contemporary as reflecting "the most extensive investigation of telephone rates ever made in this country." His survey posed questions and concerns that would carry over for decades to come, in attempts to establish effective public utility regulation in telephony.[60]

Bemis already comprehended in 1912 that "the relations of local Bell companies to the American Telephone and Telegraph Company . . . are so close that it is difficult to study local conditions without the help of the National government as to the facts with regard to the parent company, whose business is nationwide. Fortunately, the power to secure this information has just been granted to the Interstate Commerce Commission, but it will take time to secure results from this source." Bemis's optimism regarding the ICC would prove to be misplaced; but his assessment of the issues was prescient.[61]

Chicago possessed more telephones in 1912, over 251,000, than any other city beside New York—more than London, Paris, or Berlin. An additional 85,000-odd phones operated in suburbs ranging for 100 miles along Lake Michigan and from 30 to 60 miles back from the city's shoreline. All this was the domain of Bell's Chicago Telephone Company (CTC), whose operations spanned 128 local exchanges, only 33 in Chicago proper, and located in eight Illinois counties and two Indiana counties, with toll lines extending to Kenosha and Lake Geneva, Wisconsin. Bemis's appraisal, which concluded with a call for lowered rates, analyzed CTC's earnings, investment, depreciation, and expenses; it specifically questioned "the yearly payment by the local company, in common with every other Bell company, of 4 1/2% of its gross receipts from telephones to the A.T.&T. Co.,—a company, it must be remembered, which, by its ownership of the majority of the stock of these various companies, stands at both ends of the bargain."

> The more, however, that the right hand—the A.T.&T. Co.—decides that the left hand—the Chicago Telephone Company—shall pay, in the form of a percentage of the gross receipts, the higher must be the charges against the subscriber, to pay this disguised dividend. The payment made by the Chicago Telephone Company in 1911, of $537,585.12, amounted to $1.69 for each of the 318,135 telephones . . . in use.

In exchange for relaying this license fee, Chicago Telephone garnered "three advantages"—equipment rentals and repairs; patents; and legal, accounting, and engineering assistance from AT&T. All were scrutinized by Bemis.[62]

Half a dozen years later, Illinois was at the forefront of the protest that greeted Postmaster General Burleson's edict setting new intrastate toll rates. In his 1919 bid for renomination, in fact, Mayor William Thompson cited his effort to "protect the interests of the people in the pending revision of telephone rates so that the existing rates may be lowered and the present poor service improved." What became the Chicago Rate Case impinged again on electoral politics during the 1924 gubernatorial contest, and it remained alive municipally throughout the entire decade, by way of a home rule referendum and negotiations over renewal of what was now called Illinois Bell's local franchise.[63]

After the Postmaster's rate-setting power was affirmed in 1919 by the Supreme Court, city authorities remained ready, the *Chicago Daily Tribune* reported, "to lock legal horns" with Illinois Bell "over the new upward revision of telephone rates." Mayor Thompson, grandstanding, transmitted a telegram to Chicago's congressional delegates, to urge that "The public has a right to be heard on a question of this magnitude, the decision of which means millions of dollars to our people. Previous efforts of the telephone company to raise rates have been considered by our citizens as brazen attempts to rob the people of Chicago." The political stars were so aligned that the City Council concurred. After denationalization and an appeal by Illinois Bell to the Illinois Commerce Commission lifted the issue out of local hands, the City initiated legal action.[64]

In September 1921—on its own motion—the Illinois Commerce Commission ordered Illinois Bell to show cause why Chicago and adjacent area telephone rates should not be reduced. In the guise of an almost incomprehensibly arcane argument, the ICC had delivered a bomb. It sought to lower the amount of Bell's investment that qualified for inclusion in its Chicago-area operating company's intrastate rate base, insisting that Illinois Bell's parent company, AT&T, was not "properly reimbursing the Illinois Company, the Chicago local-exchange plant, and other facilities" for the joint costs that were incurred in providing long-distance service. This appeal to joint-costs was audacious—even incendiary—as AT&T insisted that there were none. That is, AT&T held that, for rate-making purposes, long-distance and local-exchange services were entirely separate and discrete, even though they increasingly made use of the same equipment. Because AT&T was not compensating its Chicago affiliate for a portion of the costs it bore to supply long-distance service, in short, local-exchange rates were higher than they would have been otherwise. Left unstated was that business-class users again were being subsidized by workers.

Following literally dozens of additional legal moves and countermoves, in August 1923 the Illinois Commerce Commission ordered Bell to reduce rates applicable to four classes of coin-box telephones in Chicago homes and businesses, in the amount of $1.7 million annually; about 385,000 of the city's 450,000 subscribers were affected, the lion's share of them (309,403) four-party coin-box subscribers. As Richard John emphasizes, coin-box telephones—called "nickel-in-the-slots"—had been introduced by Chicago Telephone Company beginning around 1900 in order to extend service; they worked to simplify payment methods by permitting a connection to be established with an operator only after deposit of a fee. Coin-box units were not strictly public telephones, but instruments installed in apartments and boardinghouses, principally throughout working-class neighborhoods. Bell, arguing that the existing rates already produced "less than a fair return on the fair value of our property," held that the ICC's order was "confiscatory of the company's property"; and it appealed to the US District Court. This court ordered a temporary injunction against the rate decreases, and this temporary injunction was affirmed after an appeal to the US Supreme Court. The case then proceeded and, in January 1930, the Court for the Northern District of Illinois held that the Illinois Commission's rate increase indeed was confiscatory, and made the injunction permanent. The Illinois Commerce Commission, joined by the City of Chicago, then appealed this ruling to the US Supreme Court.[65]

On December 1, 1930 the Supreme Court remanded this labyrinthine case to the lower court for additional findings and evidence. The Court's rationale, however, in itself marked a sea-change with respect to existing practice. It held both that AT&T charges to Illinois Bell had to be justified by reference to AT&T's own costs for providing specific services to its affiliate; and that long-distance services would henceforward have to underwrite some portion of the joint-costs of the local-exchange. "The proper regulation of rates can be had only by maintaining the limits of state and federal jurisdiction," the Supreme Court opined, "and this cannot be accomplished unless there are findings of fact underlying the conclusions reached with respect to the exercise of each authority." In other words, "the validity of the order of the state commission can be suitably tested only by an appropriate determination of the value of the property employed in the intrastate business and of the compensation receivable for the intrastate service under the rates prescribed."[66]

The bomb delivered by the Illinois Commerce Commission had now detonated. The *Smith* decision did not in itself resolve the issue of how to allocate the joint-costs of providing long-distance telephone service between a local-exchange company and AT&T's long-distance unit. AT&T stalled, warding off alterations to its preferred rate-setting procedure. On the substantive question of Illinois Bell's rates in Chicago, however, it turned out that the Supreme Court had more to say. After remand, the District Court again found for Bell (on April 29, 1933), whereupon the Commission and the City of Chicago appealed a second time to the nation's highest court. On April 30, 1934 the Supreme Court reversed and again remanded the case—this time with instructions to dissolve the injunction, institute reduced rates, and refund to subscribers the amounts collected for telephone service in excess of the rates prescribed by the ICC in its 1923 order. After a tortuous eleven-year saga, Chicagoans and the ICC had gained victory.[67]

Illinois Bell needed to assemble a special workforce of 2,000 employees, "to carry on the necessary work involved in making refunds." This AT&T affiliate was compelled to remit to a specific class of Chicago telephone subscribers the substantial sum of $16,998,00—at an administrative cost to Illinois Bell of $2,759,000. In all, this distribution process required over 1,189,000 separate refunds. This yielded an average refund of less than seventeen dollars which, spread over eleven years (beginning with 1923), translated into an average per subscriber of around $1.50 annually.[68]

The case's outcome reverberated, engendering something more than a measure of justice for subscribers of modest means. Coming as a Supreme Court decision, it destabilized the entire nation's system of rate-setting and the regulatory complex in which it was encased. *Smith v. Illinois* portended that some defensible scheme had to be crafted, to allocate a portion of local-exchange costs to the interstate rate base, on the grounds that local telephone plant bore some part of the expense of providing long-distance service, as a joint cost. In the radically altered context of the Depression and the New Deal, this finding helped to engender pyramiding policy changes which I consider below.

For now, I will underline that the case constituted not only a legal proceeding but also a social drama. Considerable effort was required to mount the Chicago Rate Case, and to keep it alive for eleven years. "Only after a vigorous and costly fight did the city get the telephone-rate case before the Supreme Court," was the understated opinion of one commentator in 1935, looking back. In June of 1920 the City had appropriated upward of one hundred thousand dollars to gird itself for a court fight which, some already anticipated, might lead all the way to the US Supreme Court.[69]

Though turning as a practical matter upon rates, the case touched an array of related issues. By December, 1921, Illinois regulators had ordered Illinois Bell to produce a "complete list of all contracts in effect. . . . This will include copies of all contracts with the Western Electric Company . . . and will also include all contracts with the American Telephone and Telegraph Company." Specifically included as well was to be a "complete statement of materials, labor, services and benefits received by the company in consideration of the amounts paid to the American Telephone and Telegraph Company and included in the account 'License Revenue.'" By 1923 the Illinois Commission was contending that "profits of the three organizations"—Western Electric, AT&T, and Illinois Bell Telephone Company—"are so closely affiliated they should be considered in determining a fair rate for the Illinois Bell Telephone Company." Of specific concern in this regard were Bell's allegedly inflated depreciation fund and overall valuation; and, following through, the license contract which, by siphoning off 4.5 percent of Illinois Bell's gross revenues each year to its parent company, annually cost local ratepayers a $1.5 million. Closely related to this concern was that, through the license contract, "the American Telephone and Telegraph Company obtains funds from its subsidiary companies for radio research, yet makes no return to the companies when royalties are received." This was not an inconsequential matter. Between 1923 and 1931 AT&T charged the entire cost of radio R&D, more than $9 million, to its subsidiary operating companies, one of which was Illinois Bell, and garnered royalties from this work in the amount of $5,229,141. What became the pivotal grievance was also evident at the beginning. "One of the major contentions" of the City's lawyers "was that the American company uses free of charge in its own long distance service the Chicago local-exchange plant, representing in 1923 $50,000,000 book cost."[70]

The telephone company later grudgingly conceded in an internal document that "It was inevitable that sooner or later there would be a public demand for lower telephone rates and that this demand would be supported by some politicians and organizations." The Chicago rate case carried forward, meeting all of the obstacles the telephone company threw up to its progress, because it garnered strong, continuing support from the local populace.[71]

"Industrial and civic leaders from a half-score of towns and villages which encircle the outer rim of Chicago" persistently attacked high telephone rates; in 1927, as the Chicago case dragged on, they launched "a determined move to bring about a cut in telephone rates between their homes and offices and the city"—from ten cents per call, to five. Evanston, Oak Park, Berwyn, Cicero and Chicago Heights, represented by officials as well as Lions, Rotary, and Kiwanis clubs, and the Optimists, Bankers' and Realtors' associations, organized a mass meeting on the issue in response to a request by the Chamber of Commerce of Berwyn. Another conflict over rates broke out in 1929 between the Chicago Hotel Men's Association and Illinois Bell, over the sharing of revenues from nickel booth phones located in hotels. But rate reform was an issue that, once the Depression struck, touched a larger share of the city's inhabitants.[72]

At the close of 1929, Illinois Bell operated 987,891 telephones in Chicago. During 1930, as the Depression set in, a bare 130 new telephone stations were added throughout the city. During 1931, however, subscribership began to plummet, with a net loss of 56,541 telephone stations; during 1932, the difficulty snowballed, as 174,676 stations were disconnected; during 1933, there was yet another net decrease, of 52,130 subscribers. 1934 turned out to be the first year since 1929 in which an appreciable increase in subscribership occurred. Rates typically spelled the difference between retaining a telephone and giving up service. Local pressure to reduce rates intensified sharply through these years of dearth, funneled in part through a "Utility Consumer and Investor's League." This was the context in which the Supreme Court issued its pair of rulings. The Supreme Court's decision at the end of April 1934, as Illinois Bell's internal corporate history would later concede, in fact constituted "the breaking point in the Company's effort to maintain 1929 rates."[73]

The status of the telephone, as we saw in Part One, had been a significant issue for the Chicago Federation of Labor from 1907 through 1918. Although I have found no evidence that the CFL took a direct role in the Chicago Rate Case, there is little doubt that telephone policy in general, and high local rates in particular, continued to simmer as a political issue, eliciting involvement by at least some union leaders—as indeed they did elsewhere. Members of both the Chicago Federation of Labor and the International Brotherhood of Electrical Workers in 1933 signposted the social and political inequity of the nation's system of telecommunications provision before the annual conference of the American Federation of Labor in Washington, DC; their resolution was passed unanimously. The following year, the indefatigable Edward N. Nockels, who had spent much of the past decade struggling to bring radio broadcasting into the service of the city's working class, carried forward this remarkable resolution (discussed further below) into Congress's hearings on communications. Nockels and organized labor, in other words, attempted with some success to raise the national visibility of telephone issues. In his testimony, Nockels cited the still-pending Chicago Rate Case to make the argument that AT&T's high and unaccountable local rates required federal regulatory intervention.[74]

Influential state regulators elsewhere concurred. Soon after the Supreme Court's decision in *Smith v. Illinois*, the state's northern neighbor ventured an important step farther down the road to public accountability. During 1931, a rejuvenating Public Service Commission of Wisconsin undertook on its own motion an investigation "of the rates, rules, services, practices and activities of the Wisconsin Telephone Company"—Bell's subsidiary. After listening to a parade of economists drawn from across the country, among them Wisconsin's venerable John R. Commons, the Commission found "that an emergency . . . exists and that this emergency injures the 'business and interests of the people.'" The chief practical consequence of this voluminous, twenty-three-month proceeding, after legal appeals by Wisconsin Telephone had been exhausted, was to institute a 12.5 percent reduction of local rates. The judgment, and the proceeding that underlay it, pivoted not on whether, but by how much, local ratepayers were subsidizing long-distance services. Even the *New York Times* accepted matter-of-factly in July 1932 that "the Bell System's long-distance business has been somewhat of a parasite on the local exchange system."[75]

Unexpectedly, one of the factors used by Wisconsin's Commission to justify its rate decrease played an important role in stimulating federal intervention. The issue concerned the same joint costs that I have already discussed. What the Wisconsin Commission termed "toll use of exchange property"—the fact that the same telephone handset and network plant were used to make both local and long-distance ("toll") calls—had not been reflected in long-distance rates. Local telephone subscribers, as the *New York Times* article cited above underlined, were paying a premium for potential access to the long-distance network, even though most of them rarely, if ever, made long-distance calls. The Wisconsin Commission found that "the amount of property classified by the Company as exchange which should be excluded from the local-exchange rate base because of the use of exchange plant in the transmission of toll messages" constituted 9.46 percent of the exchange property carried on the Company's books in 1931 and 8.04 percent in 1932.[76]

The point echoed in Illinois in the wake of the Supreme Court's 1934 ruling, when the Illinois Commerce Commission initiated a further investigation of Illinois Bell rates (June 13, 1934), and ordered the Company on July 10 to show cause why its intrastate rates should not be reduced state-wide.[77] Most important, Wisconsin's initiative also carried forward to Washington, DC, where several staffers from the Wisconsin Commission inquiry were soon employed in a bold attempt to extend federal authority. Among the lawyers who succeeded in winning the dramatic refund for Chicago's working-class telephone customers, on a contingency-fee basis, was David Lilienthal. Lilienthal had come to Wisconsin's Public Service Commission from the Chicago rate case. After the Wisconsin Telephone Company, a unit of the Bell System, "led a movement to get rid of him" in 1933, Lilienthal went on to play a leading role in shaping and administering the New Deal's preeminent initiative in public power, the Tennessee Valley Authority. Lilienthal's central conviction was that "*A public utility enterprise is a public business.*"[78]

A political judgment motivated local rate reduction attempts: As part of the effort to impose principles of public service responsibility in a context of severe economic distress, ratemaking policy required modification so that long-distance callers paid more, and local subscribers less; regulators also needed to monitor AT&T's earnings from long-distance more stringently. Though traveling in obtuse and cumbersome legal vehicles, during the worst years of the Depression, this dramatic policy departure attempted to address the telephone service needs of the American people, including its large working class. Before it could precipitate rate reductions, however, the policy first required a comprehensive tally of the size and distribution of costs across the entire nation's network rate base. That is, it necessitated an accounting appraisal of the investments in plant and equipment by telephone companies which qualified for fair compensation through rates. First and foremost, this daunting task had to find—or to establish—a legal basis for targeting AT&T's horizontally and vertically integrated interstate and intrastate business operations.

The reform campaign was not manifested only at these four locales or limited to these specific legal and rhetorical manifestations. A public utility conception of telecommunications was being actively imagined and promoted. Its aims remained experimental, both open-ended and contested. Notably, as we will find later, it was already beginning to encompass struggles to expand the tenet of nondiscrimination so as to include equal employment opportunity for African Americans. In the suddenly altered circumstances of the Great Depression, the public utility conception became poised to expand and diversify. In particular, the political demand for a "telephone investigation" which had been voiced by municipal authorities, state regulators, and courts now carried forward with a sudden urgency onto the national stage.

The Impasse Overcome? The Communications Act and the Activist FCC

In 1932, the different participants in the wireline telecommunications industry confronted difficulties of greater or lesser severity. With Postal Telegraph struggling for its very survival, its investors' capital was at risk.

Faring only less poorly, Postal's larger competitor Western Union was unwell and its investors were unhappy with its performance. Telephone subscribers and, above all, telegraph and telephone workers faced not asset depletion but actual distress. As in Chicago, all around the country legions of telephone subscribers found it too burdensome to keep their phones. During 1931, around 250,000 telephones were abandoned nationwide, a figure which rocketed to 1,745,000 the next year; by spring 1933, subscribers had dropped an estimated 15 percent of the telephones in the United States. Local service revenues likewise declined, notably at the independent companies but also at the Bell units—by nearly 15 percent between 1929 and 1932—while more price-elastic long-distance revenues plummeted by 41 percent. As hard-pressed households abandoned service, AT&T laid off thousands of employees and its mammoth decade-long network build-out ground to a halt. All the while, by contrast, AT&T made a point of paying out shareholder dividends at their pre-Depression level. The causes of this crisis in telecommunications were both disparate and intertwined.[79]

From the vantage of the telegraph industry, the culprit was palpable: too much competition amid declining demand. Telegraphy was what a CIO unionist would later characterize as "a dying industry." The prosperity of the 1920s had masked deep-seated problems, afflicting both Western Union and its smaller rival, Postal Telegraph—which was acquired in 1928 by the giant International Telephone and Telegraph conglomerate. Whereas, in 1916, the telegraph industry had garnered half of overall electrical telecommunications revenue, by 1930 its share had dwindled to under 30 percent. The number of messages transmitted by telegraph companies grew to nearly 230 million by 1927; but, in short order—even before the Depression struck—this total dropped, to 209.5 million in 1929. Partly responsible were incursions by two disparate modes of rapid interurban communications. Air-mail service via the Post Office, introduced in 1918, competed effectively with a telegraph service known as "deferred," which had allowed users to pay a lower rate for sending their telegrams overnight. The new radiotelegraph carriers led by RCA operated in a dozen or so big cities and charged lower rates than the wireline carriers, chiefly in order to feed their own international networks with messages bound to foreign countries. Diverting additional traffic from Western Union and Postal Telegraph, the US military also now ran its own telegraph services; these military telegraphs were, in addition, available for use by some other Federal departments.[80]

The most severe competitive threat stemmed, though, from AT&T. The woes of the telegraph industry became apparent as far back as 1913 when, in the aftermath of the Kingsbury Commitment, AT&T agreed to divest its controlling interest in Western Union but not—as it turned out—actually to curtail President Theodore Vail's program of integrating the two wireline systems. Bell

System telephone booths displayed signs directing customers to "say Western Union" into the receiver so as to send a telegram—leading Western Union, as late as 1926, to advertise that "virtually every coin-box telephone is a telegraph station." AT&T, however, exacted its pound of flesh by imposing a commission on telegrams sent this way. The messages could be paid for directly, by dropping coins into properly equipped phone boxes, or it could be charged on the next regular telephone bill. During the early 1930s, Bell outstripped Postal Telegraph, Western Union's smaller rival, by taking an 18 percent share of the total domestic telegraph revenues, as compared with Postal's 15 percent and Western Union's 64 percent. But the skew between AT&T and, on the other side, Western Union and Postal Telegraph, went beyond this.[81]

AT&T's increasing competitive superiority was the corollary of its research-based long-distance network modernization program, centering by the late 1920s on a technology called "carrier current" and on a strategy of integrating the nation's cities and towns into its capacious network. Had the telegraph carriers devoted themselves during the 1920s to aggressive campaigns of engineering research leading on to heavy investments in independent network building, it is possible—barely—that things might have turned out differently. Instead, the dependence of both major telegraph carriers on AT&T became coupled to an equally damaging trend toward product substitution. "Whereas in 1915 the telegraph industry received approximately 50 percent of consumer expenditures for rapid intercity communication services, by 1930 its share had declined to less than 30 percent, and it was to fall steadily thereafter." Instead of full-rate telegrams, business customers—who continued to make up most of the market, just as they always had—came to rely on alternatives including, most damagingly, a trio of services offered by AT&T: leased telegraph wires (or private line service), teletypewriter exchange service (TWX), and intercity (or toll) telephone service.[82]

Leased wires, we have seen, had been integrated on a widening scale by banks, shippers, and manufacturers during the final three decades of the nineteenth century. In the 1920s businesses renewed their efforts to reorganize operations around networks and, owing to the AT&T's tremendously expanding capital investments, this redounded disproportionately to the benefit of the giant carrier. Between 1922 and 1927, indeed, AT&T's telegraph business grew at a higher rate than that of Western Union or Postal Telegraph. In 1930, AT&T operated private telegraph circuits totaling over two million kilometers, one-third of which were used by press associations and newspapers; and the carrier managed 300 private telegraph lines between New York and Chicago. By 1933 (during the worst of the Depression) AT&T was gathering annual revenues from leased telegraph circuits that were nine times as large as Western Union's $2 million. Postal's share of the leased-line market had shrunk to a negligible $121,000. AT&T's leased wire customers thus diverted from the telegraph companies what a Postal executive termed "a staggering volume of the most profitable telegraph business."[83]

AT&T was indeed leasing circuits both to Western Union and Postal Telegraph—permitting these straitened carriers to indulge the fantasy that they could "defer new construction on their own lines." Because they did not invest in modernizing their own facilities, the major portion of the telegraph carriers' traffic now traversed lines that they themselves rented. During the interwar period, half of Western Union's total wireline plant, accounting for a still higher proportion of its message traffic, was leased from Bell.[84]

An additional skew reinforced this disparity, as AT&T attorneys related, as "the scope of the private wire service" was "widened" after teletypewriters began to be connected with them (in 1915); by 1931 the Bell System was furnishing big customers with more than 10,000 teletypewriter machines and, in the process, "utilizing approximately one-half of its private leased wire mileage in their service." For heavy organizational users, teletypewriter service was more convenient than public telegraphs in that it enabled them to locate the machines directly on their own premises. A related innovation also arrived in 1931, when AT&T introduced TWX ("timed wire exchange") service, providing business subscribers the option of near-simultaneous two-way written message service. TWX dramatically enlarged the range of subscribers' interaction by allowing them to exchange messages via an AT&T switchboard. Organizational users hired their own operators to transmit at speed during a fixed three-minute billing period. Longer messages were charged for in one-minute increments.[85]

A decade after TWX had been introduced, FCC Chairman James Lawrence Fly would declare that "For large users, the teletypewriter exchange or TWX service is very nearly an ideal arrangement." Unlike ordinary telegraph customers, a TWX subscriber "has a teletypewriter in his own offices. A direct circuit can be established between his machine and that of any of the 15,000 other Bell System teletypewriter subscribers in the country in about the time it takes to complete a long-distance telephone call. The message tapped out in the office of one subscriber is simultaneously printed in the office of the ultimate recipient. And the cost per word is considerably lower. . . . It is hardly surprising that large users have turned from the telegraphs to Bell System TWX and leased-line service, so that today the Bell System revenues from such services exceed the total revenues of Postal Telegraph from all sources." Bell's low-priced, convenient, proprietary services for business users, Fly went on, undercut the telegraph industry's overall cost structure. Western Union and Postal had felt pressure to respond with "special rates"—discounts and rebates—in an attempt to keep their largest customers from deserting them.[86]

Four-fifths of telegraph industry business derived from a phalanx of large corporate customers and, as the Depression struck, these discriminatory practices became rampant. A Postal executive explained "that competition becomes keenest to secure and hold the business of large customers and that such customers have it in their hands to secure special advantages from either telegraph company always under the implied threat that otherwise their business will be taken to the competitor." Western Union's exclusive contracts with nearly every major railroad—which economist Clair Wilcox saw as the source of its preeminence—were of long standing, but their lawfulness was now seriously questioned. Adding further to this fratricidal rivalry was a scramble to gain exclusivity with hotels, terminals, and baseball parks. Negotiable prices and free or discounted services for business users were other symptoms of this pervasive crisis of competition. Between 1930 and 1943, Postal Telegraph faced annual losses of $2–$3 million; the company went into voluntary reorganization in 1935 and emerged from it in 1940, still losing money. During 1930–1940, its larger adversary Western Union brought in an average of $6.6 million in net operating income, for an annual return of 2.5 percent—but, after sixty-eight years without failing to dole out an annual cash dividend to investors, in 1933 the company began to miss dividend payments. Employees bore the brunt: tens of thousands of workers were laid off, long-stagnant wages declined further, and the industry's reliance on child labor worsened as working conditions also deteriorated.[87]

During the Depression decade, the telegraph industry fell victim to yet another telephone industry-induced affliction, which one analyst called "the outstanding development in American intercity communications": "the tremendous expansion both in over-all toll business, and particularly in long distance toll." Between 1926 and 1949, long-distance call volume increased by 627 percent, to 226 million calls. This product substitution slowed during the Depression, but by then it was already a scourge. Again reflecting AT&T's network modernization programs, the growth of long-distance telephony accelerated anew, with the "large-scale dispersions of civilian and military population" brought about by World War II. It then redoubled after the War.[88]

That AT&T set the terms on which an ostensibly separate telegraph service now was provided was predictably resented by the two domestic telegraph carriers; and Postal Telegraph executives appealed repeatedly to the federal government for a solution. (Four-fifths of the telegraph business was interstate long distance, meaning that the state public utility commissions were powerless to come to the carriers' aid.) Most industry executives and bankers, however, preferred a private solution. Sosthenes Behn, the president of IT&T, suggested such a course in congressional hearings as early as 1929, where he presented it as a strategic competitive response to Britain's recently formed Cable & Wireless combination. The plunge into depression radically increased this pressure to consolidate, both to shore up profits and to right the industry. The *New York Times* reported in May 1931 that "There are many men in Wall Street who believe that if all telegraph and radio communications were merged and sold to the American Telephone and Telegraph Company, the ideal solution would be found"—but questioned whether AT&T "would welcome any adoption of the telegraph business." A year later Newcomb Carleton, still the president of Western Union, told stockholders that he was contemplating a merger with Postal Telegraph that would confer joint control on Postal's parent, IT&T; the two carriers' 1931 launch of a joint nationwide interconnected printer system to compete with AT&T's TWX may have been a harbinger.[89]

Congressional authorization was required for such an anticompetitive change. The Transportation Act of 1920 had been amended to allow mergers of interstate telephone companies, subject to ICC approval—but no comparable waiver of antitrust statutes had been granted to interstate telegraph carriers. To the consternation of Postal Telegraph executives, the Hoover Administration offered no concession. After his election, President Roosevelt was reported to be pondering a merger authorization in late 1933, on the theory "that it might be well to encourage monopolies and bring them under strict government supervision"; but he deferred, considering the problem "extremely involved." Symptomatic of this political complexity, FDR's Railroad Relief Bill of 1933 was passed only after Congress insisted on eliminating an amendment that would have authorized telegraph mergers following approval by the Interstate Commerce Commission; and the Communications Act of 1934 expressly retained the existing ban. Action to stabilize the telegraph industry thus remained in limbo during the early New Deal; during the late New Deal and into World War II, as we will see in the next chapter, a telegraph merger was staved off by industrial union activism.[90]

The telephone industry's difficulties, by contrast, stemmed from starkly different causes. AT&T constituted a classic example of a holding company: its massive vertical and horizontal integration, alongside the accommodation it had contrived with independent telephone capital, made it both the US telephone system's *de facto* network manager and the world's largest corporation. Layoffs, price-gouging, low and now-declining household access, and often mysterious evasions of public accountability were the chief hallmarks. Here, the scourge was not competition but, equally certainly, monopoly.

How could strong and secure foundations be built for what two experts called the "necessity of regulation"? Any successful reform of the nation's telecommunications provision had somehow to engage the seemingly incommensurable problems cropping up at the ends of this bifurcated industry. This, crucially, was not a new problem: it had been endemic in the context of late nineteenth century railroad regulation. No had it disappeared, indeed, in the depressed 1930s, telecommunications comprised a bellwether: similarly flexible and capacious policies were needed, many believed, to address the damaging dual syndrome that afflicted much of the overall US economy. Political concern persisted into the war period. In a message to Congress during his third term, President Roosevelt himself framed what had congealed into the New Deal's common wisdom, declaring that American business should enjoy the right "to trade in an atmosphere of freedom from unfair competition and domination by monopolies." How then was this legerdemain to be worked? How was it possible to craft effective policy for an industry that was beset simultaneously by too much competition and too much monopoly power?[91]

Historian Ellis Hawley emphasized years ago that New Deal economic policy was not of one piece; that it unfolded through disjointed and contending—sometimes clashing—initiatives. Proponents of government-backed industry cartels as the means by which to rationalize troubled market structures vied both with advocates of antitrust action to restore competition and adherents of centralized government planning and aggressively interventionist regulation. Compounding the resulting ambivalence and vacillation, economic policy was not made by an expressly dedicated agency; and reformers based in one department sometimes conceded defeat only to transpose their struggle to a different unit, sometimes even to a different branch of government.[92]

The movement to subject telecommunications to federal authority strengthened sharply with the onset of economic crisis, and New Deal telecommunications policy successively encompassed all three alternatives: cartelization, strengthened regulation, and antitrust. We will see later that, in the telegraph industry, cartelization was recurrently sought and continually staved off, as antimonopoly strictures found a new purchase among mobilized telegraph workers. When industry consolidation was finally achieved, furthermore, telegraphy was on the verge of superannuation at the hands of new data communications technologies. By contrast, in the telephone industry cartelization was not a rational option: a vertically and horizontally integrated Bell System already functioned as network manager interconnecting thousands of small local telephone service providers and, for its many detractors, this concentrated economic power itself constituted the leading source of the industry's travails.

During the 1940s, we will see, antitrust initiatives moved to the forefront of policy-making for telephony as cartelization finally proceeded in telegraphy. In the interim, for several crucial years beginning in 1933, newly established central-state authority to regulate the industry constituted a fundamental new policy basis for both telegraphs and telephones. This made it a compelling exemplar of the argument made by historian William J. Novak, who writes that between the Progressive era and the New Deal "the public utility idea" proffered to many proponents "a more comprehensive conception of the 'social control of American capitalism.'" As applied to telecommunications, the core of the public utility idea was constituted by a newly chartered Federal Communications Commission. How came the Commission to be established?[93]

To begin with, in response to the effects of the Depression. Facing a drastic decline in living standards and the Bell System's stout defense of its rates, consumers once again began to organize to gain cheaper telephone access. In Muskogee, Oklahoma, more than 3,100 telephone users—perhaps three-fifths of the city's subscribers—demanded that the State Corporation Commission lower rates for Southwestern Bell's business and residential services, threatening "wholesale discontinuance of telephone service" unless monthly charges for residential phones were slashed from $3 to $1.50, and for business services from $5 to $3. Throughout Illinois, New York, California, Alabama, Washington, DC, Nebraska, Pennsylvania, Minnesota, Georgia, and other states as well, telephone rates became a renewed object of protest. An internal memo by a Southwestern Bell official conceded with dismay that "The depression in business has been so severe and so prolonged that considerable discussion and agitation is taking place involving prices of all kinds and utility rates in particular. The telephone business has not escaped this agitation and in the State of Texas the question of telephone rates has been raised in numerous places." A contemporary researcher matter-of-factly suggested that these controversies were not only visible, but also increasingly effective: "Consumers' groups all over the country are organizing to fight for lower rates. Legislatures are making investigations and directing the state commissions to issue reduction orders."[94]

"Probably the most radical reductions have been urged by citizen groups." In California, a petition to the commission was filed by "the Telephone Rate Reduction Association," arguing that Southern California Telephone Company rates should be slashed by at least 25 percent and demanding a refund to all subscribers of 25 percent of the rates paid during the past two years. Meanwhile, "The Public Utilities Consumers' League of New Jersey is circulating a petition for the legislature to abolish the Utility Commission unless it lowered utility rates." This antipathy was becoming endemic: "At present," wrote an analyst, "the public is against its utilities. It is for government ownership, for taxes, lower rates, or anything which will give the utilities trouble." All the way through the 1930s, sentiment flared up again against private ownership in telecommunications. A public opinion survey commissioned by *Fortune* magazine in 1939 found that 29.5 percent of those asked believed that "the government should own and operate all or some" of the nation's telephone and telegraph systems. An insider's account later recalled that, throughout the interwar period, AT&T's fear of a government takeover exercised a significant influence over its strategy. By contrast to the turn of the twentieth century, however, there no longer existed a politically significant movement for nationalization.[95]

"Despite all these efforts," McMillen concluded in 1933, "there were very few rate reductions in telephone service. There has been no general reduction during the depression." Consumers in turn joined other social groups to elevate the prolonged interwar policy impasse into a priority for national politics.[96]

Telephone industry unemployment contributed further impetus to federal intervention. AT&T investment in new telephone plant, which despite the stock market crash slowed but minimally in 1930, was slashed during 1931; during 1932, wrote one contemporary analyst, "not only was there no addition to plant, but replacements were cut down to the extent that there was an actual reduction in plant after depreciation had been deducted." Operating expenses were savagely reduced, as AT&T laid off nearly 100,000 workers (exclusive of Western Electric and Bell Laboratories employees) between 1930 and 1932—27 percent of its 1929 total. The company likewise imposed mandatory time-off for continuing employees, without which additional layoffs would have proceeded. A harsh irony surfaced when, in 1931, President Hoover appointed Walter Gifford, AT&T's chief executive, to direct the President's Organization on Unemployment Relief: A leading instigator of hard-times was now ostensibly to lend comfort to the afflicted.[97]

AT&T's responsibility for deepening the severity of the Depression unleashed public anger, as the Bell System's mass layoffs were linked to its new network technology. During the 1920s, AT&T, perfecting a switching system that had been introduced by the independent telephone movement, commenced upon a vigorous program of conversion to automatic, or dial, telephone technology— in some part, historian Venus Green has shown, expressly to free itself from dependence on unruly operators. During the 1930s, this transition toward a uniform nationwide network technology operated by means of a self-service procedure continued, as layoffs were presented as cost-saving measures. But although the installation of "machine switching" reduced the expense to Bell of operating each subscriber's telephone, "this decrease is offset . . . by the tremendous increase in investment in plant necessary to give this machine-switching service," as the New York Commission confirmed in 1930; thus, intertwining with the build-out of AT&T's long-distance network, machine switching perversely contributed to rate hikes as well as layoffs.[98]

That AT&T was substituting network technology for workers during a catastrophic Depression could well seem not only unjust but intolerable. "Contrary to popular opinion," an academic text protested weakly in 1936, "the dial system does not dispense with operators altogether, since a considerable number are required to handle toll and other special calls." (But Bell was even then also planning to minimize these exceptions through further cycles of automation.) Finally, amid this carnage, AT&T never lowered its nine-dollar dividend to shareholders. This came as a pointed reminder that workers and consumers— not executives and investors—were bearing the brunt of the Depression. It also supplied tinder for arguments in favor of assertive intervention by would-be federal regulators.[99]

At least some leaders of the postwar generation of state public utility commissioners, battle-scarred from their legal campaigns to rein in AT&T, astute in reckoning the weaknesses of the existing regulatory system, and sympathetic to the concerns of residential telephone ratepayers and, sometimes, to unemployed workers, were prepared by all this to support a thoroughgoing redesign of the nation's reeling system of provision.

In casting about for solutions, they looked to their own experience and, limited though these had been, to their achievements. In 1930, as we saw, the Supreme Court had held that the telephone industry was based in some part on joint-cost investments; and, specifically, that local plant, whose use the Court held was necessarily shared by local (exchange) *and* long-distance (interexchange) services, occasioned costs that had to be separated for ratemaking purposes between federal and state regulatory jurisdictions. This in turn mandated "the extension of federal regulation into what was formerly an area solely under state authority," and necessitated establishment of some kind of procedure for cooperative ratemaking by state and federal officials. Which agency might represent the interstate interest in such a mechanism; and what principles would guide its endeavor?[100]

The answer again drew on prior experience. As the US economy cratered during the Hoover presidency, a congressional investigation of the telephone industry was authorized. Published only after his successor, Franklin Roosevelt, entered office, the deliberations engendered a 4,000-page report supervised by Dr. Walter Splawn, economist, president of the University of Texas, and then special counsel to the House Committee on Interstate Commerce. Splawn also had just completed an investigation of the nation's private power utilities. "The importance of the industry, and the magnitude of its operations call for actual and not nominal regulation," declared Splawn, in a report recommending enactment of legislation to codify existing federal law in communications, centralize still-splintered federal jurisdiction in this field within a single, adequately funded commission, and provide for further study of communications holding companies (read AT&T)—which "has been found as a result of this investigation to be as prolific of abuses in the field of communications as in other utilities already studied." The Splawn Report urged that "the first step ... [toward] effective regulation" should involve "a thorough and detailed study" by a proposed Federal Communications Commission of the large communications companies and their subsidiaries, including their accounts, operating expenses and rates.[101]

From within the Executive Branch, support for a prospective FCC came from an Interdepartmental Committee on Communications created by President Roosevelt, chaired by the Secretary of Commerce, Daniel C. Roper (who had been First Assistant Postmaster under his friend and fellow plantation owner Postmaster Albert S. Burleson) and again advised by Dr. Splawn. The Interdepartmental Committee's report, issued early in 1934, took for granted that corporate-commercial ownership of telecommunications should continue; critics would disparage it for refusing to sanction a government takeover of telecommunications, and thus for abetting the abuses perpetrated by the nation's powerfully integrated corporate telephone monopoly. The Roper report also, however, echoed the charge that the ICC had not exercised significant authority over the rates and practices of telecommunications companies, in the face of "many complaints" about the quality and expense of AT&T's service. The telegraph posed disparate but again glaring difficulties. Roper and, in turn, President Roosevelt agreed that a new regulatory agency should be established with jurisdiction over the entire field. Contributing to the momentum behind an FCC, we will find later, was Roosevelt's frustrated attempt to address the industry's ills through his National Recovery Administration—an initiative that drew effective opposition from both AT&T and Western Union. The President now cast about for fresh means of combating the economic calamity that was devastating this key industry, in a politically advantageous way.[102]

The origins of the FCC, however, do not lie only in the top-down maneuvers of a reform-oriented Executive Branch. In addition to the consumer movements already mentioned, on the West Coast a number of cities had joined together by 1930 to push for a telephone investigation. In 1933, moreover, the American Federation of Labor had gone on record with a similar proposal. In 1934, the CFL's energetic Edward Nockels relayed this demand by organized labor directly to the Senate Interstate Commerce Committee, which was deliberating on the need for legislation that would establish a new Federal Communications Commission:

> *Resolved*, That it is the consensus of opinion of the American Federation of Labor that the American Telephone & Telegraph Co. and associated companies be subjected to the closest public scrutiny by means of a congressional investigation of inclusive scope, and the necessary congressional legislation be enacted to prevent the abuses and impositions on the public by the operations of the American Telephone & Telegraph Co.; and be it further
> *Resolved*, That the securing of such investigation by Congress and the passage of such legislation be made part of the major legislative programs of the American Federation of Labor.

Committee Chairman Clarence Dill's response to Nockels may have been posturing; but it was not dismissive: "[AT&T CEO] Mr. Gifford's strenuous opposition to some of the provisions of this bill has resulted in so much information being given me in the last few days as to what the subsidiaries are doing and as to the way the funds of the American Telephone & Telegraph Co. have been used that I am preparing a resolution to provide for an investigation of the American Telephone & Telegraph Co., either by this committee or a subcommittee. I am inclined to think that it will be a good thing for this country to have the full facts about this organization."[103]

For Nockels himself, by contrast, the need for a telephone investigation was a matter of political principle. Testifying before Congress in early 1930 about the assignment of radio licenses, he clarified the fundamental issues at stake. "What is the 'public interest, necessity, and convenience' which the law fixes as the sole test for granting radio licenses" (and which the Communications Act of 1934 would enshrine as its governing principle), Nockels expounded:

> it is the same as the "public welfare." That which contributes to the health, comfort, and happiness of the people is in the public interest. That which provides wholesome entertainment, increases knowledge, arouses individual thinking, inspires noble impulses, strengthens human ties, breaks down hatreds, encourages respect for law is in the public interest. That which aids employment, improves the standard of living, and adds to the peace and content of mankind is in the public interest.
>
> ...
>
> The public interest, necessity, and convenience is nation-wide. It is age long. It has to do with the physical, mental, moral, social and economic welfare of all of the people.... It is not enhanced by the granting of special favors to a few individuals or corporations, however rich and powerful they may be.

Through Nockels, the broad radical demand to reorganize the system of telecommunications that had endured for half a century before it was rebuffed by Burleson and Vail, once more carried forward: the public interest in telecommunications had not, and was not now, to be rigidly circumscribed by mere legalisms. Rather, Nockels provided an up-to-date, open-ended, robustly social conception, in which private gain was to be expressly subordinated to the wants and desires of the working population. The hallmark of the New Deal era in telecommunications was to grant Nockels' expansive conception legitimacy within official discourse and, albeit for a limited time and to a limited extent, in actual policymaking.[104]

After literally thirty years of engaged struggle to remake telecommunications across its expanding range, from telegraphy and telephony to broadcast radio, Nockels died in 1937. His old comrade, the poet Carl Sandburg, memorialized him in an unpublished sacrament: "The only praise Nockels cared for was that of the rank and file of the labor movement ... There were hundreds of men who loved Ed Nockels not merely with affection, with enjoyment of his lighted face, with appreciation of his loyalty to Labor first of all, which they knew was absolute. They loved him with the kind of feeling that would send them out ready for suffering, for sacrifice. He was a Great Captain and there will be writers of Labor History who will give the details. For the moment it is not easy for those who worked close to him to think that Ed Nockels is gone." Subsequent writers of labor history have, in fact, provided some of the details—but, though both sustained and diverse, Nockels' exceptional contributions to the struggle for justice in telecommunications (as opposed to radio broadcasting) remain mostly unexplored.[105]

For a prolonged moment, however—as the central-state activism that erupted in the charged political context of Roosevelt's presidency seemed to draw most everything else in its wake—Nockels' vision for telecommunications seemed open to fulfillment. It was during this moment that FDR called for Congress to pass legislation that would unify federal jurisdiction over all communications facilities in a new regulatory commission, and specifically charged that this new agency should be accorded "full power to investigate and study" existing communications companies, and to make its recommendations for additional legislation to Congress. Clarence Dill, the bill's Senate sponsor, explained that the agency was to have a tripartite divisional structure—radio, telephone, and telegraph. Each division would possess an independent jurisdiction, and full commission power of decision, with the FCC chair serving on all three units to lend coherence. The divisional structure was intended to guarantee "that a certain number of members of the commission would give their entire time to a study of the telephone and telegraph question, which has never been studied, and because of which there has never been any effective regulation." "The danger," Dill declared, "is that the full commission will become a body giving all its time or the major part of its time to radio only, and the regulation, study, and investigation of telephones and telegraphs will not receive the full time and attention that is believed necessary." AT&T was the elephant in this room.[106]

Title II of the Communications Act carried over and codified the new commission's responsibilities with respect to telecommunications common carriers. Not less important, as mentioned, the Act empowered the new Federal Communications Commission to undertake a comprehensive investigation of telephone industry structure. Still chary of centralized federal power, the executive committee of the National Association of Railroad and Utilities Commissioners (NARUC) nonetheless resolved unanimously in favor of the statute's requirement of "a full, thorough and complete investigation of the relations and business dealings of the American Telephone and Telegraph Company, its subsidiaries, affiliates and associated companies with all its operating telephone utilities, to determine the reasonableness of payments made by such operating utilities for equipment, supplies and services." NARUC even "pledge(d) to said Federal Communications Commission the co-operative aid of this Association in all practicable ways in the making of said investigation." In fact, leading NARUC officials—Kit Clardy from Michigan's Commission, and Oklahoma's Paul Walker—had already begun to cooperate with the Roosevelt Administration by the end of 1933, to develop this enabling legislation.[107]

Increasing the Communications bill's chances of passage was that the carriers were split over the fact that the legislation would unify federal regulatory authority over broadcast, wireline, and cable communications. Western Union, and a recently formed radio telegraph company, RCA, were supportive; ITT, active in international telecommunications, was skeptical; and Walter S. Gifford, president of AT&T—supposing "that there can be such a thing as too much regulation to permit management to function efficiently"—assailed "[t]he injection of a commission with a veto power" over any of AT&T management's accustomed prerogatives. Boasting that there were six times as many telephones in the United States as in Europe (proportionate to population), Gifford demanded that the new Commission should not be granted any additional authority beyond that which was already available to the Interstate Commerce Commission. He specifically targeted Section 215 of the proposed legislation. When the bill was introduced, the new FCC was to be awarded broad control over "interservice contracts" governing relationships between the parent AT&T and its many subsidiaries. Gifford's objection to what the bill's sponsor termed this "entirely new power"—Senator Clarence Dill related that Gifford had been "insistent that it would wreck the telephone company's business"—resulted in the substitution of a weaker provision. As passed, the Communications Act directed the new FCC to "examine into transactions entered into by any common carrier which relate to the furnishing of equipment, supplies, research, services, finances, credit, or personnel to such carrier," to report its findings back to Congress, and to recommend to Congress whether there should be legislation controlling the contracts between AT&T and its affiliated companies.[108]

Prior to the revisionary account offered by historian Robert W. McChesney in 1995, the broadcasting provisions of the 1934 Communications Act were typically viewed as an unexceptionable outcome of an overarching political consensus. "The Radio Act of 1927 was incorporated, with very minor changes, in the Communications Act of 1934," claimed Rupert Maclaurin in 1949, skipping over the intervening years and setting the tone for future researchers: "The new Federal Communications Commission was established to extend communications regulation to telegraph and telephone services and to centralize all such regulation in one government body." In a meticulously documented study, however, McChesney elaborated on a point made earlier by Erik Barnouw to demonstrate that, between 1927 and 1934, debate over ownership and control of radio was actually both widespread and intense. The broadcasting provisions of the law functioned predominantly to the benefit of ascending media corporations; patently, they did not express the general will.[109]

In regard to telecommunications a comparable prevailing opinion remains unrevised. This is that the New Deal legislation that established the FCC was but a secondary administrative measure. Morton Keller breezily asserts that the need for federal regulation of telecommunications was accepted "with relatively little fuss." "With respect to common carrier regulation," two other historians declare even more sweepingly, "very few major controversies emerged prior to 1960." Even a onetime member of the Commission, Glen O. Robinson, concurs, claiming that the FCC "is only nominally a New Deal product," and that its creation in 1934 "was incidental to the waterfall of social and economic legislation that transformed American government in this period": "the Communications Act did not inaugurate a new regulatory scheme. . . . [and] did not prompt intense controversy." Scholars have purported that the Act ushered in a long interval of "regulatory normalcy," whose acceptance of monopoly in telecommunications had, as its chief practical consequence, FCC complicity in "the institutional structures of the industries it was charged with overseeing," specifically including "the regulatory protection of AT&T."[110]

The historical record simply does not substantiate these views. On one side, as we just saw, AT&T CEO Walter Gifford sharply objected to the telecommunications provisions of the Communications Act in congressional testimony. Early in its life as a federal agency (1938), on the other hand, the Federal Communications Commission declared that "With the enactment of the Communications Act of 1934 . . . the regulatory situation was radically altered." Claims that "the FCC has consistently been unable . . . to implement effectively its statutory telecommunications authority" are of a later vintage, and cannot be relied upon to assess the Commission's early years. Specifically, they ignore a brief, but profoundly consequential, moment of New Deal activism—competent and assertive—collapsing it from both sides, as it were, into a prior interval of frustration over a crippling regulatory impasse and a subsequent era when the winds of reform again were stilled. More accurate is AT&T's own, admittedly self-interested assertion, that regulatory policies "were not infrequently forced upon unwilling carriers." Throughout the first several years of its existence, the Federal Communications Commission generated intense pressure on AT&T; and the Commission remained hospitable to what the *New Republic* called "New Deal ways of thinking" into the war period—after most other government agencies had relinquished them.[111]

The activism in telecommunications policymaking incarnated by the early Federal Communications Commission may be traced back in part to specific appointments. Independent regulatory commissionerships frequently involve horse-trading and the repayment of political favors, however, throughout the first two Roosevelt administrations, such patronage did not preclude the selection of commissioners who possessed both a deep fund of experience and commitments to reform in utilities regulation.

An important pool of expertise that streamed into the new Federal Communications Commission had been created through the regulation of electrical power. Thad Brown, who joined the FCC from the antecedent Federal Radio Commission, also had been chief counsel for the Federal Power Commission (FPC) during 1929. Frank McNinch, appointed to chair the FCC in 1937, arrived fresh from the FPC; he had been a member since 1930 and chair since 1933. McNinch's successor as FCC Chairman, the impressive James L. Fly, came to the FCC in 1939; Fly had been general solicitor and head of the legal department of the Tennessee Valley Authority, FDR's huge public power operation. As general counsel of the TVA in 1937 he had proceeded to "win[] its two major cases in the Supreme Court." While these commissioners possessed varying administrative capabilities and had to contend with increasingly hostile Republican adversaries at the Commission, they shared a loose political affinity to the New Deal's program for public utilities.[112]

Joining them was the FCC's pivotal figure in telecommunications, Paul A. Walker. Commissioner Walker served on the FCC from its 1934 launch, chairing the new agency's telephone division, and eventually (in 1952) ascending to chair of the Commission. Prior to this, Walker had amassed a wealth of experience in the regulation of public utilities. He had worked for eighteen years, and assumed escalating levels of responsibility, at the State Corporation Commission of Oklahoma, concluding his stint there as chairman. Walker, very significantly, also had chaired the Committee on Cooperation between Federal and State Commissions of the National Association of Railroad and Utilities Commissioners (1925–1934). In his person, the frustrations, convictions, and contacts of a leading state regulatory activist were embodied within a federal agency which, by the same token, gained added legitimacy with the state commissions.

If the need was to forge a more effective jurisdictional arrangement—a more cooperative federalism—between federal and state regulators, then Walker was an ideal choice. By the early 1920s, he had become certain that an assertive federal regulator was needed and that coordination across state and federal regulatory domains needed fundamental improvement. "[C]o-operation between Federal and State Commissions," he wrote in 1928, "should be further encouraged and whatever legislation may be needed to guarantee its success should be secured." Months before passage of the Communications Act, Walker was consulting with the White House and specifically with Commerce Secretary Roper about its prospects; so did members and key staffers of the activist Wisconsin Public Service Commission. Weeks before he testified before the Interstate and Foreign

Commerce Committee, Walker wrote Senator Clarence Dill that he was "not unmindful of the argument which will probably be made against the establishment of an interstate communications agency on the ground of interference with states's rights. A bill can be so drawn as to protect the states in the regulation which is essentially intrastate, and at the same time give to the federal government the power of regulation over those matters which are purely interstate." Walker then offered pungent testimony on this subject during the congressional hearings on what became the Communications Act of 1934. Here, Walker first underlined that, "At the present time there is little or no regulation of telephones so far as rates and services are concerned." His own Oklahoma's Corporation Commission was representative of other state PUCs, he averred, in that "from the standpoint of matching dollars, so to speak, and all that goes with it . . . it is an impossibility for the State of Oklahoma to do the work in any reasonable time necessary to make anything like the same kind of a showing that the telephone company makes. Now, in a situation of that sort, of course the public does not get its day in court, as I see it." Walker then outlined his substantive concerns:

> even if the State had the money, the interstate feature of the matter, the ramifications of the holding companies, the complications brought about by the manufacturing companies which sell to the telephone companies, makes it an impossibility for the State commissions to get anywhere so far as results are concerned in a telephone-rate investigation.
>
> If there is to be effective regulation at all of the telephone business, it must be brought about through the Federal Commission.

Walker and his staff would attempt to establish—if given a chance, to impose—a new, nationwide political settlement. Their bold initiative began to be realized from the moment of the FCC's establishment.[113]

In one of its earliest proceedings, the FCC used Section 212 of the new Communications Act to signal that AT&T's top executives could no longer expect things to proceed as they had. Section 212, on "Interlocking Directorates," required that an individual could serve as an "officer or director" of more than one carrier subject to the Act only "upon due showing in form and manner prescribed by the Commission, that neither public nor private interests will be adversely affected thereby." The FCC held that AT&T CEO Walter Gifford, along with nine other top-ranked executives, would no longer be permitted to remain directors both of AT&T and of one or another of its twenty-one principal operating companies. This broadside against AT&T's holding company structure closely paralleled the strictures set into place by President Roosevelt's Public Utility Holding Company Act of 1935, itself a high-water mark in the administration's attempts to tame corporate power. Herewith, the young FCC inaugurated a policy of unparalleled regulatory activism. Throughout its first five years, although infighting and illness cut into its effectiveness (two successive chairman departed, in 1936 and 1939), the FCC's Telephone Division moved loosely in accord with and, indeed, helped set the pace for, the New Deal's left-liberal program.[114]

By no means an attack on capitalism, despite pounding right-wing rhetoric to the contrary, this New Deal program provided an ideologically flexible, experimental effort to stimulate both consumption and employment. It sometimes became incoherent, owing to internal political disagreement and business resistance. Commencing with industry-wide planning and government spending, the New Deal later foregrounded regulatory and antitrust initiatives. However, the general diagnosis of the economy's ills became more widely shared as the Depression wore on into the later 1930s. Alan Brinkley explains that many analysts were persuaded that the nation's major industries had reached a "mature" stage, and were nearing "the limits of their capacity to grow." This signified that "the current economic crisis was not a temporary aberration, but part of a fundamental transformation." In turn "an economic climate in which private industry was incapable of creating dynamic growth," many now came to believe, "would place nearly unbearable pressures on capitalists to avoid risks, to collude in raising (or 'administering') prices, and hence to produce further stagnation. Only a strong regulatory state could combat this danger."[115]

The Telephone Division, made up of three members of the new Federal Communications Commission including its Chairman, acted as a fulcrum for levering this insight into the nation's telecommunications system. The early FCC's regulatory activism stands out most clearly in its unprecedented "Telephone Investigation." Prescribed by the agency's enabling legislation, this investigation commenced during the FCC's first months of existence. In November, 1934, Walker, joined by Commissioner Thad Brown and FCC Chairman Anning Prall, announced that the Telephone Division would undertake a substantial inquiry into Western Electric's contracts with AT&T and the Bell Operating Companies. When, four months later, the seventy-fourth Congress passed Public Resolution No. 8—a joint initiative of both Houses of Congress, and formally ratified by President Roosevelt on March 15, 1935 as his administration began to move to the left—the FCC's inquiry was elevated into an overarching governmental responsibility: to use a special appropriation (initially, a substantial $750,000) to draw up a comprehensive report on the telephone industry and to recommend to Congress in light of its findings whatever amendments to the Communications Act might be required. Walker announced to the press in June 1935 that the AT&T inquiry was underway "full blast."[116]

The investigation both borrowed from and contributed to the conviction that, under the prior patchwork regulatory system, corporate actors had proved unwilling to produce—or incapable of producing—beneficial societal results. This view, which circulated freely throughout New Deal thinking, was bitterly chastised by business leaders. The larger New Deal economic policy of stimulating consumption and employment required that it impose "social discipline" on capital, in Robert Griffith's useful phrase. The ethos of this program was captured by Wyoming Senator Joseph C. O'Mahoney, the chairman of the exceptional Temporary National Economic Committee (TNEC) that President Roosevelt convened in 1938, to ascertain the underlying causes of the Depression. In a combative draft of a speech intended for a meeting of the National Association of Manufacturers at New York's Waldorf-Astoria Hotel O'Mahoney declared: "When, therefore, it is suggested that business should be permitted to regulate itself without what is called 'government interference,' it is merely proposed that one element of society should be permitted to draw rules which will affect all others." During the second half of the 1930s, O'Mahoney's stance placed him squarely within Roosevelt's left-liberal alliance. In keeping with his 1936 election campaign theme of fighting to tame "economic royalists," President Roosevelt used his 1938 request to Congress to call for a study of the concentration of power in American industry: this was the origin of TNEC, often called the "Monopoly Committee." The President himself declared that "the liberty of a democracy is not safe if the people tolerate the growth of private power to a point where it becomes stronger than their democratic state itself. . . . Concentration of economic power . . . and the resulting unemployment of labor and capital are inescapable problems for a modern 'private enterprise' democracy." Monopoly's multifarious ability to "administer" pricing—to lift the pricing mechanism above the workings of the free market, ostensibly contributing to and prolonging the Depression—was the major target.[117]

Within this political moment, efforts to build up adequate central-state regulation of public utility industries were freighted with surpassing significance. Leland Olds, an Amherst-trained economist whose expertise and reform passions were directed at the private power industry, but who also had played a role during 1929–1930 in New York's telephone rate wars, helped frame the New Deal's approach to utilities. Then-Governor Roosevelt had appointed Olds in 1929 to be executive secretary of the New York Power Authority; in 1939, after first thinking to place him on the FCC, President Roosevelt appointed him instead to the Federal Power Commission. In 1935, Wilbur Cross, editor of the *Yale Review*, solicited from Olds an article on public utilities with the comment that "I am taking it for granted that in the treatment of the subject you will feel that the centre of discussion has moved back from the long debated issue of rate regulation to the more fundamental issue of the nature and control of company structure in this industry." That Cross could issue such a direct statement of his editorial intention spoke eloquently to the political distance that had been traversed. Efforts at ratemaking had led on already to increasingly searching concerns about the links between corporate structure and corporate power.[118]

The FCC's "Telephone Investigation," which commenced in this same year—1935—pivoted exactly on these links. At its height, the investigation drew upon 250 FCC staffers and a supplemental budget allocation amounting to a considerable fraction of the agency's regular annual funding. "[T]he administration strongly desires to obtain a more complete picture of the ramifications of the communications industry," observed the *New York Times*, although "[w]hether the broad investigation will result in further legislation beyond the supervisory authority already held by the commission will be determined by the investigation." For AT&T's resentful executives, who fought it tooth and nail, the investigation comprised a dangerous and unwarranted infringement of the rights of property. The FCC's studies of the company's history, structure, strategy, and routine practice provided fodder for cascading revelations, not only with regard to rates, but also to finance, intercorporate relations, patents, public relations, forward, and backward linkages to other communications and media industries, and a gamut of other issues.[119]

The inquiry had been stamped at its outset with a presidential imprimatur. During the spring and summer of 1936, moreover, it was reported that Walker asked for Roosevelt's "advice"—as well as his help in obtaining an additional Congressional appropriation—"because the inquiry might be considered to reflect general administration policies." That appropriation duly made, and the inquiry completed, its special counsel, Samuel Becker, resigned and returned to Wisconsin—where he had been an advisor to Governor LaFollette. FDR accepted Becker's resignation, again underlining the importance of the investigation in the laudatory letter that he released to the press: "It is a hard job at which you and your associates have been so devotedly working—digging quietly and patiently into the intricate transactions of great businesses to piece together the facts which affect the public's interest. But it is a job which must be done with increasing thoroughness if government is to be truly intelligent."[120]

The extraordinary documentary record compiled by the FCC was not written up and released for another year. Eventually, it had far-reaching ramifications, as the FCC's findings underpinned two subsequent prosecutions of AT&T under federal antitrust law. The first, between 1949 and 1956, as we will see, ended with a consent decree that threw open Bell's trove of patents to mandatory free licensing and barred AT&T from unregulated businesses including commercial data processing, thereby denying it entry until the 1980s into what was becoming a decisively important market. The second suit, between 1974–1982, broke up the telephone company. In the immediate moment, however, the FCC's telephone investigation met a far less auspicious reception.

Walker's report constituted a ringing call for structural change. Released in April 1938, it declared that "The field of effective state action is dependent largely upon the aid which may be rendered by the Federal Communications Commission in those matters which, due to the Nationwide structure of the Bell System, cannot be reached by local authority. . . . Such information should be compiled continuously and made available or the use of State commissions." The Report then laid out an argument for a "broad national policy":

> If regulation is to be successful, it is axiomatic that jurisdiction be coextensive with the subject to be regulated. . . . The jurisdiction of the Federal Communications Commission, as presently constituted, is not sufficiently comprehensive to regulate effectively the quality and cost of telephone service. These circumstances suggest the necessity for the promulgation of a long-range national wire communications policy which will achieve a balance between the public interest, which requires efficient service at minimum cost, and the utility company's interest, which requires a reasonable return on invested capital. It is submitted that this balance can be achieved through the adoption and intelligent administration of the following broad national policy with respect to national wire communications service: *Development of a progressively increasing volume and constantly improving quality of national wire communication service at a progressively decreasing unit cost.*[121]

In keeping with this dramatic statement of prospective national policy, Walker's Proposed Report urged congressional legislation to redress the power imbalances that characterized the existing system of telecommunications provision. It singled out a need for a direct FCC role in approving or disapproving "all Bell System policies and practices promulgated by the central management group of the American Co."—and for regulating Western Electric as a public utility, with direct oversight of its prices and costs for telephone apparatus and equipment. It also sought congressional authority to review and approve or disapprove all intercompany contracts and financing. No less noteworthy, Walker's Proposed Report requested congressional authority "to limit the scope of Bell System activities to the communications field."[122]

This last plank in the Telephone Division's platform for legislative change requires brief explication, in view of its subsequent role. The FCC's telephone rate counsel, Carl I. Wheat, brought home the importance of restricting AT&T to its monopoly telephone business: "the very concentration of interstate telephone business in the Bell System" signified, Wheat declared, that "the opportunity for effective federal regulation seems greatly simplified"—if only "efficient machinery for the continuous scrutiny of interstate telephone operations" could be put in place. Economist Clair Wilcox added flesh to the bones of this thesis two years later, before the Temporary National Economic Committee: "There are but a few areas in which it is clear that the public interest can be better served by monopoly than by competition," Wilcox asserted, holding that "in the telephone business, the nature of the function performed is such as to demand coordinated development under common control." In this and a small number of kindred instances, he continued,

> The advantages of monopoly, in general, are the converse of the disadvantages of competition. Monopoly can avoid wasteful duplication of productive facilities. It can simply standardize its products. It can minimize expenditure on advertising and salesmanship. It can command essential information and cut the cost of bargaining and negotiation. It need not shroud its technology in secrecy; it can apply the discoveries resulting from research to the entire output of a trade. The monopolist is under no competitive pressure to give short measure or to adulterate his goods. He is not driven to depress the standards of labor. If he wishes, he can so conduct his business as to serve the common interest. But, in the absence of effective public regulation, he is under no compulsion to do so.

Wilcox, Wheat, and other New Dealers agreed not only that, in telecommunications, the doctrines of economic competition held little promise. The parlous condition of the telegraph industry demonstrated all too clearly, as we'll see, the afflictions that competition visited on this field. More salient and, perhaps, more surprising, was the hope they shared about the prospects of taming the gargantuan AT&T monopoly. Monopoly, they agreed, could constitute a tool of the public interest—if it could be made accountable to a scrupulously principled, knowledgeable, and adequately empowered regulator. Today, these doctrines lie forgotten. During the 1930s and 1940s they were the hard-won results of two decades of struggle to bring about effective means of state and federal oversight.[123]

The Proposed Report's release was deemed sufficiently newsworthy to be the lead story in that day's *New York Times*, where it appeared under the headline "25% Cut In Phone Rates Feasible." AT&T's response was visceral. Supplemented by internal dissension at the FCC amid a "war against the New Deal" following the 1938 by-election, it proved sufficient to stall the agency's reform program in its tracks. Upon release, the Telephone Division's report was attacked by Federal Communications Commissioner T. A. M. Craven; and procedural and substantive reservations were circulated by one of the inquiry's own staff members, John Bickley. Its status as an official document was undercut: the Telephone Division's publication appeared as a "proposed report" because it required approval and adoption by the full Federal Communications Commission prior to its submission to Congress. When it was finally transmitted, more than one full year later, the FCC's Report reprinted the text of its precursor but concluded—contrary to the Proposed Report—that no new statutory authority was needed in order for the agency to carry out effectively its "highly technical" oversight responsibilities. Thereafter, the FCC proved willing to lend its name to a dismal fiction: that regulation as presently constituted was sufficient to discharge the responsibilities tendered to the agency by the 1934 Communications Act. This hollow claim would come back to haunt the agency and the telecommunications system over which it purported to preside in the wake of the defeat of its erstwhile activist program.[124]

The Walker Report's call for legislation to engender both massive structural alterations to AT&T and much-heightened regulatory powers for the FCC had been left by the wayside. The Telephone Division's hope of obtaining additional funding from Congress with which to support research on telephone rates on a continuing basis did squeak through. Turned back, however, were its proposals to force public utility status upon Western Electric and to gain managerial oversight of AT&T's interservice relations. The FCC's regulation of telephony was of course profoundly set back by this debacle. Eschewing bold activism, its record after the late 1930s testifies to more than the ebb and flow of individual commissioners' reform impulses, or their cooptation by AT&T's corporate power. The New Deal's effort to institute effective oversight and control of US telecommunications became hedged in with restraints. Throughout its first four years, by contrast, internal bickering and outside opposition notwithstanding, the FCC Telephone Division made a home for principled reform activists and functioned as a seedbed of New Deal thinking and experiment.[125]

The FCC's subsequent lackluster record turned the agency into a target. The House of Representatives' Antitrust Subcommittee chastised the FCC, declaring in 1959 that "the Commission has neglected in the 24 years of its existence to establish fundamental principles or standards by which to judge the reasonableness of the Bell System's interstate telephone rates." In fact the agency did not initiate a full-blown investigation of AT&T's interstate rate structure, inclusive of Western Electric's pricing policies and their impact on the cost of telephone service, until 1965. Sixteen years later, the Justice Department charged that the FCC "has not been able to develop the means of systematically assuring the validity of the data upon which carrier initiated tariff filings are based." Yet these later appraisals ignored, or forgot, that the Commission once had tried—hard—to do better. Its early activism was a casualty of vilification and lobbying by AT&T, as well as of political infighting and bureaucratic reorganization. Both anachronistic and caricatured is the idea that a "captive" FCC acted as AT&T's creature from the moment of its establishment.[126]

Even taking account of the defeat of its telephone investigation, the New Deal FCC must be credited with enacting substantive changes in the political economy of telecommunications. A confidential report to members of the Temporary National Economic Committee stated that, "The powers vested in the Federal Communications Commission by the Act of 1934 and the information brought to light by the ensuing telephone investigation have been effectively used to implement and strengthen both State and Federal regulation." On this basis the FCC would succeed, as state and city reformers long had hoped, in establishing an expansionary nationwide conception of residential network access. Less creditably, because it was compelled to do so, we will see that the Commission also eventually widened its conception of public service responsibility in telecommunications.[127]

It was far from coincidental, however, that struggles over how to augment and direct this new governmental machinery broke out during the same historical moment that working-class self-organization was surging through basic industries, including telecommunications.

5
Telegraph Workers in Depression and War

Franklin Roosevelt was borne to the presidency amid what was, after the Civil War, "the most traumatic experience in the history of the United States." Following the stock market collapse in autumn 1929, the Great Depression mired wage-earners and struggling farmers into unremitting distress. Home foreclosures skyrocketed and construction nearly ceased. Joblessness cascaded: 9 percent of the nation's labor force was unemployed in 1930, 16 percent in 1931, and nearly 24 percent by the 1932 presidential election. In some cities, however, half or more of the laboring population was without work. "Unemployment," a historian summarizes, "was the overriding fact of life." At the nadir, October 1932 to March 1933, between twelve and seventeen million people were unemployed—nearly one-third of the labor force—and an additional thirteen to seventeen million could find only part-time jobs. Workers began to insist on improvements to a desperate *status quo*. The Hoover administration rebuffed them (indeed, it mounted an actual attack on the World War I veterans who thronged to the capital to demand that their promised pensions be released early). Protest against want and rejection of indignity fused into righteous anger. The two years between 1931 and early 1933 saw hunger marches, rent riots, demonstrations by the unemployed, blocked evictions, and strikes, notably, by toilers in agriculture, textiles, coal mining, and rubber manufacturing. Bursting into political society, the grievances and anger, the hopes and demands of the working class began to swing the social-political balance. The Roosevelt Administration swept into office cognizant that an economic rescue was all-important—in vital part, to placate workers. Bold experiments in policymaking, it understood, were urgent.[1]

Roosevelt's "New Deal," however, did not curtail but instead triggered cascading working class industrial and political action. Members of the upper class recoiled in horror in 1934 as citywide walkouts—general strikes—in Minneapolis and San Francisco seemed to them to verge on insurrection. In a lengthening list of industries workers thronged to establish unions; several existing unions called for decisive changes in organizational and political strategy. The American Federation of Labor's ingrained craft unionism, and its generally racist practices, rendered it unwilling to countenance a more inclusive industrial unionism. Seizing the moment, in 1935 the Mine Workers and a few other AFL affiliates formed the Committee (later, Congress) of Industrial Organizations and, following their expulsion by the AFL the next year, they embarked on an expansive program of industrial unionization. The response was little short of explosive. Millions of workers signed on. Trade union membership had declined by 1933 to 2.7 million; by 1937 it had more than doubled, to 7 million. The AFL also drew additional members, but the CIO was the driver.[2]

The CIO itself was a mixed bag. Despite his prior anti-Communism as the head of the Mine Workers' union and his later "mini-purge" of Communists in the CIO in 1939-1940, the federation's formidable leader, John L. Lewis, relied on Communists during the CIO's first years to help lead organizing drives of rank-and-file workers. He also appointed leftists including Lee Pressman (General Counsel) and Len DeCaux (director of publicity) to top CIO staff positions. Communist, or left-led, affiliates of the CIO included the Fur and Leather Workers, the National Maritime Union, the United Cannery, Agricultural, Packing and Allied Workers of America, the International Longshore and Warehouse Union, the United Electrical, Radio and Machine Workers, the Farm Equipment Workers and the Transport Workers Union. Striving to represent workers both skilled and unskilled, early on the CIO broke through the color line. Its Communist and sometimes African American organizers fanned out "to recruit black workers for the new unions and soon challenged the hegemony of the racially exclusionary... AFL in each major manufacturing group." The result was astonishing: from the beginning of the Depression to the end of World War II, African American union members increased from perhaps 60,000 to around one million. "Ecumenical in makeup," and breaking up "encrusted barriers of skill, religion, ethnicity, gender, and even race," by organizing the previously unorganized the CIO built "inclusive unions and a living sense of social solidarity": it was not merely an organization, but a social movement. The impetus, vitally, "came from the bottom, where discontent of volcanic proportions existed." This had been building since the first years of the Depression; and, by 1936 and 1937, sit-down strikes in Akron rubber plants and Flint auto factories left the CIO scrambling to stay abreast of the rank-and-file, both on the shop floor and in communities of industrial workers. Despite this, some CIO officials tolerated and even encouraged racist practices, including Philip Murray, Van Bittner, Adolph Germer, and Franz Daniel; while Murray, who succeeded Lewis as President, and another top leader, Sidney Hillman, hewed to the overriding goal of allying with the New Deal Democratic Party, and by the late 1930s began to work to rein in the CIO's Communists.[3]

In the meantime, though, the CIO tapped into and expanded workers' social agency, transforming organized labor into an engine of social, political, and cultural reconstruction. It shifted power across society, opening possibilities for local, national and, prospectively, international reform. In consequence, Alan Dawley observes, "the political initiative shifted from elites to masses," and this forced "redistributive ideas onto the political agenda." Redistribution was not revolution but, to most of the capitalist class, the reforms it required spelled out heresy, in that they lifted power out of the hands of business owners and brought it into the realm of political negotiation. The US President at first acquiesced in this sea-change only gingerly, but as union workers became vital to his electoral coalition he went on to include "freedom from want" as an overarching priority and, ultimately, to enumerate an expansive "economic bill of rights." Until after World War II, despite its varying political strength, its ever-changing institutional structure, and the hard opposition it drew from political conservatives and employers, the New Deal both legitimized institutional efforts to elevate the social wage and pointed up a need for additional reforms. As a demand to improve workers' living standards gained political traction, for many New Dealers a project that some called "economic citizenship" appeared hopefully open-ended.[4]

The contrast with the immediate past was intense. In 1929, the president of the National Association of Manufacturers had declared that "the interests of labor and capital also of management and public are inseparable and practically indistinguishable." However, as Ahmed White explains, CIO unionists began to "counter employer resistance armed with the argument that it was they who now represented legal right and an official vision of the commonweal." After 1936, workers fastened expressly on the goal of representing the general public, often citing the palpable need to stimulate mass purchasing power as a basis for aligning "the interests of the worker with those of the rest of society." Their success was not inconsiderable.[5]

Myron C. Taylor—the chairman of the US Steel Corporation, and a longtime foe of the closed shop—justified his 1937 decision to recognize an independent steelworkers' union by conceding that "The lines of interest of the Corporation considered as a whole and of the public considered as a whole must run parallel—for the Corporation cannot exist except as it serves the public." In 1940, the *Republican* nominee for president, Wendell Wilkie, quoted Abraham Lincoln approvingly before a ball-park crowd in Pittsburgh: "Labor is ... the superior of capital and demands much higher consideration." Deemed responsible for wrecking the economy, and confronted by snowballing working-class self-organization, business leaders could no longer conjure up belief in their claim that capital's interests equated with those of society at large. Amid what a historian calls "a true crisis of confidence and authority," the CIO unions stepped into the breach.[6]

With the presidency of the shrewdly experimental Progressive, Franklin Roosevelt, the federal government adapted and moved to reset the course of events—first by trying to coopt, and ultimately by sanctioning what the propertied classes deemed a dangerously unbridled labor movement: A "complex and intricate dynamic ensued between political leaders and the aroused populace with whom they now had to contend." The Roosevelt administration's first initiatives aimed to rescue and rationalize the collapsed economy by opening opportunities for businesses to cooperate as long as they acceded to government oversight and to ambiguous official support for trade unionism. The National Industrial Recovery Act of 1933 was an originating New Deal initiative which, by enabling scores of industry groups to establish "codes of fair competition," sought to protect prices, curtail ruinous competition, and thereby hasten a return to profitability and decreased unemployment. To the anger and bafflement of many employers, however, for the first time in the nation's history, NIRA also granted to workers (apart from farm laborers and domestic workers) a right to join unions. Although employers moved quickly to interpose their own preferences by holding that NIRA allowed company unions—indeed, they established hundreds of these "employee representation plans" immediately after the bill became law—the NIRA opened space for independent self-organization. Before this, the federal role in labor relations had been overwhelmingly repressive. Judicial injunctions and, in some cases, military force were routinely used to quell working-class actions. By contrast, under NIRA some company unions faced pressure to assume a more assertive role in representing their members while, in many industries, workers pushed to establish genuinely independent local and national unions.[7]

Many business owners deemed even NIRA's limited legitimation of collective self-organization inimical, if not actually damnable: they were jubilant when NIRA was adjudged unconstitutional by the Supreme Court in May 1935. In the meantime, however, surging rank-and-file action combined with the results of the 1934 by-election—which gave President Roosevelt an overwhelming Democratic majority in Congress—to tip the political balance further toward reform. Over the course of the next two or three years, in the face of what has been termed "one of the largest working-class insurgencies in American history," the CIO came to represent several million unionists. Dumbfounded and angry, newspaper moguls, auto manufacturers, and California fruit growers turned to repressive counter-measures; but federal support of labor rights only strengthened. With passage of the National Labor Relations Act, also in 1935—upheld by the Supreme Court in 1937—the Roosevelt administration "was unequivocally protecting industrial workers' right to organize and to demand higher wages and better conditions from their employers." NIRA's corporation-friendly provisions had permitted both company- and independent unions; NLRA eliminated this ambiguity, by outlawing overt management control of labor organizations. NLRA also created machinery for federal intervention in labor-management conflicts via a new National Labor Relations Board; and how the NLRB would interpret the many unknowns engendered by its enabling legislation became a fresh storm-center. Concurrently, a US Senate Committee on "violations of free speech and the rights of labor" began to investigate and to catalogue, in unprecedented scope and exhaustive detail, how big companies continued to rely on industrial espionage, private police, munitions, and strike-breaking services to obstruct and, if possible, to neuter, the collective bargaining rights that the Wagner Act had enshrined. The CIO had an inside track, both with the NLRB and the Senate's LaFollette Committee.[8]

The breathtaking advance of working-class organization, and its own bold legal maneuvers, enabled the CIO to throw real political weight so that, as employers abandoned the New Deal, Roosevelt made a calculated turn to the left in the 1936 election. The president won a huge reelection victory by attacking "economic royalists," even as a CIO strike wave pulsed through "heavy" or "basic" industry. The New Deal's commitment to labor rights remained far from comprehensive; and it was fundamentally compromised with respect to workers of color and women. Nevertheless, the years after 1933 and, especially, between 1935 and 1939, witnessed what historian Stanley Vittoz calls "intense interactions between the agencies of the state, on one hand, and society's principal antagonists during the Depression era—labor and capital—on the other." Through the fraught interactions that ensued, Vittoz goes on, "industrial relations in the United States during the 1930s were upset, rearranged, and at least in some respects 'rationalized' with unprecedented ferocity." If employers' antagonism and repression underlined the CIO's conviction that state support was an essential prerequisite for genuine collective bargaining then, as Christopher Tomlins points out, some unionists understood "that in seeking the state's aid they were of necessity making themselves hostage to a power over which they had historically enjoyed little control." Labor union growth encompassed industrial action, political organization, and ideological combat as it interacted with the new legal and administrative framework created by the National Labor Relations Act and modified over ensuing years by other state agencies.[9]

While local and left-led radical initiatives branched out into the culture of working-class communities, after 1937 the CIO's national leaders aligned their movement with the New Deal coalition. As it advanced, therefore, industrial unionism also altered. Sometimes uncomfortably, labor leaders rubbed elbows with legislators, managers, and staffers of federal agencies, Ivy League social scientists and reformers, prominent lawyers and jurists, and corporate leaders. Although it was rare for top-level politicians to make public commitments to the CIO, many government departments now contained ardent liberals and diverse radicals whose sympathies with it meant that "government policy had the potential to be shaped in a way favorable" to CIO goals. By the late 1930s, Steve Fraser recounts, "the strategic leadership of the CIO was connected by a thousand threads to a newly emergent managerial and political elite, an elite which in collaboration with the CIO would foster a permanent political change not only in the national political economy but in the internal political chemistry of the Democratic Party." Industrial unionism was changing but, in consequence of the measured support offered by the second Roosevelt administration, "the social momentum of the CIO seemed practically irresistible." The combination of a suddenly responsive regulatory state and an activist, organized citizenry generated both tantalizing possibilities and buoyant over-confidence. For employers and political conservatives, by contrast, this ongoing reconstruction of US society was both frightening and loathsome.[10]

Those who operated the nation's telecommunications were caught up in this force-field as they tried to improve wages and working conditions and—though markedly less ambitiously than during the Progressive Era—to alter the priorities guiding network system development. As federal employees, Post Office workers continued to face a legal ban on strikes, one that Roosevelt showed no interest in abrogating. Stronger momentum for change was evident in electrical telecommunications. In telegraphy, a pair of AFL affiliates—the Commercial Telegraphers Union and the International Brotherhood of Electrical Workers—languished, in the face of company unions and depression-induced layoffs; the IBEW in particular pursued a strategy of conciliation with employers while fending off rival unions. However, the National Labor Relations Act granted a government sanction to collective bargaining, and this enabled the formation of new unions—in telegraphy and telephony as in the more well-known case of manufacturing. As vectors of workers' self-organization grew, they also crisscrossed. In 1937, a group of marine telegraphers gained a sweeping union charter from the young CIO for their American Communications Association (ACA). As they moved to organize in and across telecommunications, they also intervened politically to help shape the restructuring of the telegraph industry. Telephone workers, meanwhile, turned AT&T's company unions into their own National Federation of Telephone Workers, which arduously transformed into an independent national union. As they decided whether to affiliate with either the AFL or the CIO, telephone workers made over the NFTW into the Communications Workers of America (CWA)—and jostled against the left-led ACA. In Western Electric's equipment manufacturing plants, CWA faced off against the United Electrical Workers (UE). In the late 1940s, these jurisdictional contests moved toward resolution. Internally divided and dependent on a government whose tolerance of social unionism was narrowing, telecommunications workers did not elaborate a bold public agenda for networks within organized labor's postwar reconstruction plan: their efforts to equate their interests as workers with those of the general public were rebuffed. Nevertheless, the CWA planted itself in the nation's voice network, and it made successive collective bargaining gains for its members even as it also joined the postwar liberal reform coalition.[11]

In this chapter I engage the extraordinary efforts to renew their industry made by CIO-affiliated telegraph workers—who then joined the struggle to unionize the telephone industry, examined in the following chapter.

The Telegraph Crisis

After the World War I era, writes David Montgomery, "Less than a decade ensued before the economy collapsed, and a resurgence of worker militancy reopened the irrepressible question" of how workers might establish industrial as well as political democracy. Activism in telecommunications resurfaced first among restive telegraph employees, workers who demanded in 1934 "that conditions which prevent increased wages and increased employment should be eliminated." Some advanced a tough-minded critique of the structures and practices that constituted the industry and inhibited their collective self-organization. This critique broke through in the adverse setting of President Roosevelt's first attempt to stabilize the cratering economy: the National Recovery Administration (NRA).[12]

Between 1933 and 1935, the NRA aimed to alleviate the Depression by enabling businesses and trade associations to reorder their respective industries. Because it accorded labor to only modest representation, and because each of its deliberations resulted in a government sanctioned code of fair competition, the NRA may be viewed as an employer-friendly corporatism.

A code for the telegraph industry proved elusive. The carriers submitted their proposal for one in September 1933—only to have it be rejected by the NRA, principally because of its inadequate provisions for labor. Hearings conducted by the NRA officials showcased the parlous condition into which this once-mighty industry had fallen. Postal Telegraph executives, testifying for the weakest of the carriers, revealed a dismal reality. "There is no industry in this country that needs a code of fair competition more than the telegraph industry, first, to protect it from the invasion of the Bell System, and, secondly, to save it from its own abuses and follies," exclaimed Colonel A. H. Griswold, executive vice president of Postal Telegraph. Not only, charged Howard L. Kern, another executive at Postal, did AT&T's telegraph services (discussed in the previous chapter) attest an "unfair encroachment of the telephone company," they also amounted to abusive discrimination, because "Naturally the customers solicited by the telephone company . . . were the large users of the telegraph service, as they were the users who would yield the telephone company the largest revenue with the least expense. . . . The profitable business of the telegraph companies is the business of these same large users." AT&T's telegraph services therefore ramified, as Western Union and Postal Telegraph were compelled to vie with one another as well as with the much larger AT&T to secure leased-line contracts with the business customers who dominated the demand function. The telegraph companies' intensifying rivalry was, Postal charged, actually an outgrowth of AT&T's improper and discriminatory occupation of what was, for AT&T, a mere "byproduct" market. A ruinous competitive syndrome had taken hold, with exclusive contracts, discriminatory free services and special rates "not available to the general public." This syndrome threatened not only the industry, but service to the public and employment as well. "There is," Postal shamelessly declared to the NRA examiners, "no justification for the Government's permitting the continuance of a situation which forces the telegraph companies to carry on discriminatory services and wasteful practices, in order to meet similar discriminatory services rendered by AT&T."[13]

Postal's executives alleged that the disabling features that riddled the telegraph system were actually illegal. Griswold based this assertion on the findings of the Interstate Commerce Commission during its prior investigation of private wire contracts. Seeking to revive the ICC's conclusions, Postal denied that its purpose was to persuade the Government simply to abolish leased telegraph circuits: "It is doubtful if it would be a wise policy to have leased wire telegraph service entirely eliminated. It has been in existence for a good many years and there probably exists in the minds of the users a real need for the service." Rather, Postal argued, two destructive practices had grown up around private wires, and required governmental action. First, leased circuits had become "heavily loaded with the large volume of traffic of many users"—brokers for example—and this undue sharing discriminated against the users of the regular telegraph wires. Second, the broad take-up of printer exchange telegraph services, notably, AT&T's TWX, had established a form of competition with leased-line telegraph service that was directly analogous to the private-line telephone service which the war-period ICC had deemed discriminatory. Both abuses needed to be corrected for the telegraph industry to gain stable footing.[14]

Attacking these two practices amounted to a direct strike against the relationship that powered US telecommunications: the nexus between big business users and the carriers. Perhaps sensitive to this, Griswold understated his case, suggesting delicately that "a certain few large users should not be permitted to obtain such service—leased line—at wholesale rates." In addition, he sought to trace the debacle to an ostensible outside force: AT&T. "Why," he insisted, "should the Bell System in its own selfish interest and by the uses of by-product facilities obtained under a telephone monopoly, be allowed to destroy the telegraph industry?" Thereby, Postal executives conflated AT&T's predatory monopoly of supply with the much wider vested interest that had been built up around private wires offered to many large business users by both Western Union and AT&T. Postal's complaints were, nevertheless, well-founded: what Kern labeled "special benefits... at the expense of the general users of telegraph service"—themselves still a small minority of the overall US population—lay at the center of telegraph industry travails. Redress was urgent. "We ask that the N.R.A. use its authority to obtain the cooperation of the other units of the industry to bring about the improvement in conditions which will benefit all members of the industry."[15]

Postal could levy these charges because it was much the weaker of the two landline telegraph carriers and possessed only a tiny share of the leased-line market. Both Western Union and AT&T—which proclaimed that all its operations, including leased telegraph lines, would be better served by instituting a separate code for the telephone industry—responded to NRA's proposed telegraph code. Western Union declared that, because it was already regulated by the Interstate Commerce Commission, the NRA possessed no authority over it. RCA, a radio-telegraph carrier, then launched its own salvo against Postal. And, finally, as *Time* reported, "telegraph and radio companies and their big customers" appeared "to protest against what may soon be the first code imposed by Executive order.... Hotfoot to Washington went fruit growers and commission merchants, fearing higher rates on the mass of facts & figures which they flash by wire daily. Brokers feared for their leased wire systems; railroads, for their ancient and exclusive contracts with Western Union; newspapers and news services, for their favorable press rates." *Time* averred that Western Union had appealed to its business customers seeking to cultivate a more formidable opposition to NRA: "A Western Union vice president dismissed as gross exaggerations reports that his company had sent out 10,000 telegrams, suggesting protest."[16]

The NRA Code Authority could do little to address the telegraph crisis when—unlike in most other industries—only a few suppliers existed, the most important of which, making common cause with their largest users, wanted nothing to do with any code. FDR joined the fight in late December 1934, the *New York Times* reported, "to bring under a code of fair competition the largest uncoded industry at the request of the National Industrial Relations (sic) Board." The President served an apparent ultimatum on the two major telegraph companies—either accept the NRA's code or come up with an acceptable alternative—but executives remained disinclined. Meanwhile, political pressure built against the NRA in its entirety until, months later, the Supreme Court judged the NRA unconstitutional.[17]

Meanwhile, other federal officials signaled that they were persuaded that telegraph carrier rivalries indeed constituted an instance of what was widely termed "destructive competition." An influential Executive Branch committee, whose recommendations led to the establishment of the Federal Communications Commission in 1934, claimed that "It is in the field of two-way telegraphy that existing problems are most acute," and identified the "waste and strife of unrestrained competition" as its debilitating symptom. The evidence obtained by the NRA hearings added to this appraisal: "The effort spent by the companies in competing with one another as they have," observed a doctoral dissertation in economics in 1935, "has not been of any benefit to the public. It has been seen that it has resulted in wasteful and uneconomic practices which will eventually weaken the entire communications system of the United States." Echoing the Interdepartmental Committee convened by President Roosevelt, this student found that the country's "disintegrated system" might be placed on a sounder foundation only through a massive and concerted policy intervention. The Federal Communications Commission's telegraph inquiry laid the industry's troubles at the door of destructive competition. Its conclusion bears strong emphasis: "It has long been recognized that in many fields, competition normally provides assurance for the best service at the lowest possible cost to the public," the FCC began. However, the history of the domestic telegraph industry testified to a very different outcome. In this field, competition had engendered "useless paralleling of facilities, duplication of operations, and wasteful expenditures of resources and manpower." It was indeed largely "responsible for the unsatisfactory financial condition in which both Postal and Western Union have found themselves during the course of the last decade or more." The agency found, finally, that a profound corollary for policymaking could and should be drawn from the nation's dismal experience with competition in telegraph service:

> telegraph service appears to fall within the field of 'natural monopolies,' such as the telephone, power and gas distribution utilities, where it has usually been found by experience that one company adequately regulated can be expected to render a superior service at lower cost than that provided by competing companies.

While business users voiced reservations about a combination's impact on the international service market, and military officials sought to ensure that it would not destabilize their special relationship with AT&T, for the FCC, therefore, a telegraph merger remained on the cards.[18]

Two groups dissented from this formulation, and in strong and unyielding terms: political radicals and militantly defensive trade unionists. Notwithstanding their frequent mutual antagonism, both pressed to avert a telegraph merger, the outcome to which the leading contemporary critique of destructive competition in telegraphy seemed destined to lead. During 1934–1935, affiliates of the Communist Party and officers of the AFL's Commercial Telegraphers Union of America both argued that, even though "ruinous competition" had unmistakably engulfed the industry, measures to restore the field to health should *not* include merger between Western Union and Postal Telegraph. They grounded their argument in a bedrock of mistrust for the companies' management, formed by decades of experience, and in intransigent opposition to additional job-cutting. As speed-ups, lay-offs, and mechanization each persisted through the depressed 1930s, so did this perspective. As a result, consolidation of domestic wire telegraph companies, which was bruited by executives and bankers as early as 1929–1933, was repeatedly staved off. To be sure, this outcome expressed more than intervention by telegraph unions and Communists. But telegraph workers, including, in particular, those who became CIO unionists, substantially succeeded for nearly a decade in reframing the telegraph merger debate around the rights of labor rather than the prerogatives of property-owning capital.[19]

During the 1920s, the aspiring writer Henry Miller worked at Western Union's New York employment bureau. From this perch he contemplated the job of telegraph messenger boy as "the lowest job in the world." Across his field of vision also passed what he deemed another parade of human wreckage: telegraph operators. Miller hired and fired ceaselessly, he recounted, even recklessly, in an endless attempt to keep up with a churn of workers dissatisfied, sick, drunk, crazy, rampaging, or just self-seeking: one-fifth of the workforce, he claimed, was "steady," while the remainder he called mere "driftwood." Hired to spy on the company's behalf, he preferred to underline that "The whole system was so rotten, so inhuman, so lousy, so hopelessly corrupt and complicated, that it would have taken a genius to put any sense or order into it, to say nothing of human kindness or consideration." When Miller somehow succeeded in stanching the turnover, the "Cosmodemonic Telegraph Company" responded by informing him that its notoriously low wages must actually be too high—and cutting them. Service predictably suffered: "Nobody was satisfied, especially not the public." The same conditions, he said, were evident during the 1930s.[20]

Despite Miller's disparagements, telegraph workers actually were generating a potent critique of prevailing industry practice and helping to set the terms for policymaking so that employee protections and public responsibilities moved closer to the forefront. The NRA constituted the initial forum at which telegraphers asserted their interests as workers and in public. Their analysis of the industry's travails and how to overcome them was starkly at odds with that offered by the carriers' executives. A critique anchored on the notion of "ruinous competition" took profitable operation for its desideratum; but the telegraph crisis presented quite a different face when scrutinized by those who were intimately knowledgeable of industry practices and yet entirely unpersuaded that profits should come first.

By the 1930s, telegraph workers had tried to win collective bargaining rights for more than half a century, an unbroken uphill climb. Trade unions did emerge, but they remained fragmented and weak. The Order of Railway Telegraphers was organized during the mid-1880s, and did not advance notably until the nationalization of the railroads during World War I. Boasting an impressive 78,000 members out of a possible 80,000 at the height of its strength in 1920, the Order was thereupon overpowered by a deep recession, by the loss of a less-than-hostile government, and by the denationalization of the railroads. It remained alive—in 1929, it had 63,000 members—but members of the Order still stood apart from their peers. In part an offshoot of the ORT, the Commercial Telegraphers Union of America was an AFL affiliate formed in 1903. The CTUA had, we saw, engaged in sometimes fierce conflict with management before and during World War I; as with the ORT, it became supine afterward. Antiunion on principle, like AT&T, in 1918 Western Union formed a company union: the Association of Western Union Employees (WEA). Early in the Depression the CTUA possessed only a few thousand members, mostly at Postal Telegraph. The WEA was, by contrast, a going concern.[21]

To enroll in the WEA—and managers expected employees to join—a telegrapher was compelled to sign a "yellow-dog" contract, forswearing membership in any organization that sanctioned use of the strike. Western Union instituted other practices typical of company unions, which were organized and sustained by management rather than through worker self-support: an official paper, *The Telegraph World* (established 1919); and mostly trivial or cosmetic agreements on wages and the conduct of work life. The WEA both played upon and accentuated the conservatism of many telegraphers, and it retarded the growth of independent working-class organization. Indeed, the WEA grew by 1930 to its all-time high, of 38,600, a very large proportion of those eligible for membership. An early historian was not wrong to conclude, in reference to the onset of the WEA, "The CTUA had never shown any ability to make headway in Western Union, and the task would be even more difficult now." Postal Telegraph proved more congenial, but only somewhat: from World War I until the mid-1930s, the CTUA gained toeholds there. Meanwhile, as their own freight traffic collapsed and the railways' income and investment plummeted, the railroad telegraphers faced different employers and work practices, and divergent industry dynamics. Amid the universal devastation wrought by the Depression, however, despite internecine divisions many telegraphers embraced skeptical—often, indeed, deeply antagonistic—views of their companies' practices and financial health.[22]

As the repercussions of the financial panic of 1929 deepened, Postal Telegraph plunged into full-scale crisis; and Western Union was brought low. Demand for telegraph service, heavily skewed toward business users, was very elastic. At the Depression's nadir in 1932, the number of messages transmitted by telegraph carriers had sunk by two-fifths. While Western Union, barely breaking even, still mostly kept up its shareholder dividends, Postal Telegraph claimed a loss each year beginning in 1930, and in 1935 the company entered bankruptcy—from which it would emerge as a free-standing entity in 1940, and then only because the Reconstruction Finance Corporation stepped in with $13.5 million in loans.

In the face of all this, though industry-wide worker solidarity remained a distant goal, diversely situated telegraphers launched a ferocious common critique of industry practice.[23]

By December 1930, CTUA reported that 15 percent of its members were unemployed. By 1932, the two carriers had laid off around 30 percent of the workers they had employed in 1929; Western Union's ranks dropped from 69,409 to 48,338 over these four years. Western Union and Postal Telegraph also cut wages and sped up the pace of work. Would a telegraph industry merger, contrived as a top-down affair amid cataclysmic unemployment, actually serve workers' needs?[24]

It is remarkable that, at the 1934 NRA hearings, telegraph workers took for granted that industry consolidation should be a political issue rather than merely a business decision. As the president of the Association of Western Union Employees parroted the company line—that no NRA code was needed—internal dissension increased both within the WEA and independent trade unions, which clamored for and gained a hearing before the NRA. So did the AFL-affiliated Commercial Telegraphers Union. These union telegraphers were immovable in their testimony that telegraph industry woes were of its own executives' making. Pointing up the discriminatory contrast between the companies' dismissals of employees and their payments of dividends to shareholders, interest to bondholders, and high salaries to themselves, unionists viewed the attempt to combine the carriers as just another scheme to further enrich these groups—at labor's expense. This appraisal laced through their sharply pointed structural critique of industry practices.[25]

Frank B. Powers, president of the CTU, emphasized that Western Union had enjoyed "a considerable increase in revenue" between 1933 and 1934, and that "the employees should have gotten a much larger percentage of that increase." Any assertion by the company that its costs had concurrently climbed, he declared, "should not be considered as based on fact." Powers illuminated a foundational issue: whether big business users should continue to be accorded volume discounts, even though these discounts had contributed substantially to the carriers' straits: "Telegrams cannot be handled in bulk form. They must be handled one by one. I do not believe that there is a justification for a less rate for the large volume users of the telegraph."[26]

"Private line" or "leased wire" services, a Postal Telegraph executive conceded at this same NRA hearing, were, "in reality, misnomers. There is no actual leasing in the sense that particular physical property (except for terminal equipment) is set aside for the use of the so-called leases. Terminal facilities on the premises of one customer and terminal facilities on the premises of the same or a corresponding customer, perhaps in a distant city, are set up. These facilities are interconnected by the communication company during a certain fixed rate per month, the rate being based on a charge for the connecting circuit at so much per mile, plus a charge for certain terminal facilities. The customer (or customers) furnishes his own operators and has full control of the circuit during the period available and can send as many messages over the circuit as the capacity of the circuit will permit. What is granted by the so-called leased wire or private wire contracts is the right to unlimited service over one or more channels of communication between certain points during certain times." Seen in this light, Powers' critique of current practice was a devastating indictment of discrimination, of favoritism toward big business customers. K. M. Whitten, General Organizer for the CTU, provided additional details of how the carriers' routine discrimination in favor of their largest business customers was grounded in the labor process of telegraph operators.[27]

W. J. Shinnick, General Chairman of the CTU, went so far as to cast doubt on the commonplace that capital investment constituted a wholesome objective. His argument, and his expression of his argument, merit extended quotation. Was it justifiable for Postal Telegraph to have spent about $11 million for plant equipment during 1930? Dr. A. J. Hettinger, Jr., of the NRA's Legal Division, Shinnick recounted, had supported these outlays with the argument "that those particular expenditures helped to maintain the percentage of employed personnel at that particular period":

> The doctor evidently attempts to justify this particular expenditure on the theory that [Postal Telegraph] very patriotically and with every consideration for the welfare of their employees had evidently attempted to maintain the employment level of the year previous.... Knowing intimately the altruistic methods of modern business practice, the honorable doctor would have us believe that this expenditure of $11,000,000, which, incidentally, was about one and a half million more than the Western Union expended during that year for the same item, was made to maintain employment at a high level.
>
> We maintain that this expenditure was unwarranted and unjustified.... I believe that the expenditure was atrocious, when wage cuts and part-time employment were becoming so prevalent in this company...
>
> Labor has been bearing the burden of the competitive folly so clearly demonstrated by officials of both companies.... we insist that the N.R.A.'s previous codes have seen fit and have been able to eliminate some of these unfair practices in other industries, and we see no reason why, if labor is to be given a decent and living wage, that these practices cannot be eliminated. They must be....
>
> The entire problem, as we see it, boils down to just one thing, that most companies are selling service below cost, that this practice must be eliminated in order to pay decent salaries to the employees of the telegraph industry.... salaries

must be restored to some sort of decent condition, and employees must be served along the lines of employees first and stockholders next.

Returning to the supreme importance of employment at a decent wage, CTU General Organizer Whitten in his turn declared that a wholesale redistribution of the carriers' net income should be the policy solution:

> President Roosevelt is quoted in the newspapers as having said, and I assume that he is quoted correctly, that an industry that cannot pay decent wages has no right to exist. I would assume from that that if the telegraph company cannot pay decent wages without taking the entire net receipts, I would say, Yes, that we have the entire net receipts, and after the testimony here today showing the fact that the net receipts have been so greatly reduced by the mismanagement and the follies of management, I would like to ask Dr. Hettinger if he does not think that we are entitled to pretty nearly all of the net receipts.

The United Telegraphers of America (UTA) characterized itself as a "fighting independent rank and file controlled union," consisting of Postal and Western Union workers (also see Figure 5.1). Probably formed in 1934, it approached the NRA that summer about its members' grievances at Postal—but gained no redress. Asked to testify before the NRA panel, Harold L. Bates, vice-president of the UTA (which he now described as "an independent organization of communications employees") extended the argument made by CTU officers. "It is time that communications are placed in the proper category among the things civilization cannot do without and proper recognition be given to the employees thereof." Bates then offered his own tally of the carriers' abusive profit strategies, and spoke about why Western Union had not agreed with Postal that the money-losing services they both used to wrest big business users away from one another should be abolished. His supposition, he said, was that "The Western Union, financially stronger, desirous of either merging with or eliminating its competitor, the Postal, was perfectly willing in order to further its desires to suffer these great losses, requiring the Postal to do likewise." He attacked I.T.&T., Postal's parent conglomerate, for being "too severe in charging maintenance to its adopted children"; he contended that AT&T, which "has the telegraph companies coming and going," "should come under the telegraph code or go out of the telegraph business"; and he lashed out against the Association of Western Union Employees, the company union. "If I was to give a personal opinion," Bates concluded before the NRA Administrator, "I would suggest that all the companies be sunk into the Atlantic Ocean, and the Government institute new companies."[28]

During these years-long double-digit unemployment and radicalism's revival, the existence of such strong sentiments—the last a carryover from what were

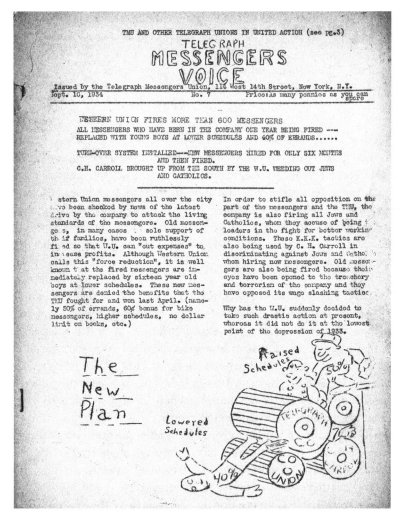

Figure 5.1 *Telegraph Messengers Voice.* During the early years of the Great Depression, rank-and-file telegraphers established several independent unions in collective efforts to overcome their miserable pay and working conditions. The *Voice* was the organ of the Telegraph Messengers Union. Author's Collection.

now the old days of the World War I era—is not surprising; what is remarkable is that they were expressed, unvarnished, at a public federal government venue. Here sounded the voices of flesh-and-blood telegraphers, reflecting on their experience as employees of a besieged industry and demanding concrete radical changes that would place their needs as workers foremost, before those of investors and managers.

Bates posed a rhetorical question: how should an NRA telegraph code of fair competition be framed? His members demanded seniority recognition in discharging and promotion; no employment of persons under sixteen; a minimum wage not less than $15 per week in any city of over 500,000—prorated down for smaller cities; a thirty hour work week; and the elimination of so-called training schools for telegraphers—which, as Downey shows, Western Union operated to legitimize its practice of continually pumping fresh streams of devalued child labor into the industry. "Experience and investigations have disclosed," observed Bates, that, contrary to the Andrew Carnegie legend (and Henry Miller's observations) "those unfortunates who become telegraphers usually die telegraphers." By the late 1930s, 75 percent of the carriers' nonmessenger employees had worked there for at least ten years, and one-third had served twenty years or more. Western Union's high proportion of older workers was a documented fact.[29]

A Communist Party pamphlet appearing in 1935 assimilated some of these arguments and reworked them into a searing antimonopoly indictment. During recent years, this text charged, Western Union and Postal Telegraph—anticipating and trying to accelerate their merger—had systematically colluded, in the process generating office closures, extortion of customers, and a deterioration of working conditions via understaffing, speed-ups, and technologically induced layoffs. One result had been to damage the extent and quality of telegraph service: a slowdown of telegraphic communication had been accompanied by selective withdrawals or curtailments of service. Another consequence had been overt discrimination in favor of big business customers over others, a major theme of the NRA Code hearings. In the pamphlet, however, unlike in the testimony of telegraph unionists, the full import of this disparity actually remained obscure. An adequate account of discrimination would have revealed the limits of the antimonopoly credo. The CP publication was content to state that monopoly carriers were contravening the terms of the 1934 Communications Act: "There are . . . companies who get special service over and above what the general public gets." Lost in the shuffle was that discrimination attested the systemic power of big capital at large, inclusive of carriers *and* large corporate users, rather than merely the abuses perpetrated by a pair of monopolies. The culprit, in turn, was not monopoly but monopoly capitalism. The pamphlet's relentless focus on the profit-hunger of the big carriers resonated, however, with the sentiments of AFL telegraphers.[30]

In 1934, three independent rank-and-file telegraph unions existed: the United Telegraphers of America, which embraced all telegraph workers apart from messengers; the Telegraph Messengers Union, based in New York City; and the American Radio Telegraphists Association, formed by marine radio-telegraph operators in 1929, "with branches in every important coastwise city." That same year, moreover, these three unions established what they hoped might become "a permanent committee for close cooperation and joint action of all telegraph unions." This particular initiative subsided; yet radical analysis and organization to meet the telegraph crisis carried on beyond the NRA, as the New Deal evolved in light of organized labor's strengthening political purchase. Though never free from challenge, telegraph workers' voices began to be heard—to command attention—in the arena of policymaking. One of the new industrial telegraph unions was key to this development.[31]

The American Communications Association, the CIO, and the Communist Party

The fraternal bonds of the American Radio Telegraphists Association, which had originated in marine radio, lay with West Coast maritime workers and the left-led unions that they went on to create, or recreate, between 1934 and 1937. In 1935, alongside half a dozen other maritime unions, ARTA responded to a call issued by the foremost western waterfront labor leader, longshoreman Harry Bridges, to join together in a federation. ARTA's president Mervyn Rathborne, a college-educated English Communist, became secretary of the resulting CIO's Maritime Committee. Also in 1935, radio operators conducted a sympathy strike with the AFL-affiliated Seaman's Union and, late in 1936, ARTA was one of the unions that walked out in a test of strength against West Coast shipowners and allied businesses; this ninety-nine-day strike shut down the waterfront. The unions' victory produced significant changes, not only pertaining to wages and working conditions but also collective self-organization: Bridges converted what had been a district union into a new International Longshoremen's and Warehouseman's Union, which received a CIO charter in August 1937. ARTA retained these ties, joining the National Maritime Union, Bridges' ILWU and four other CIO affiliates as members of the industrial federation's Maritime Committee in 1938; and it continued to urge solidarity among CIO maritime workers as late as 1946. If its feet were planted in two distinct industries, though, the telegraph union's energies were always directed toward organizing communications workers.[32]

Committed to industrial unionism by 1935–1936, ARTA had tried to affiliate with the AFL through the Commercial Telegraphers Union. Rebuffed, in the weeks that followed the 1936 strike ARTA concluded that "such an affiliation is unquestionably impossible, due to the attitude and position taken by the international president of the C.T.U., Mr. Frank B. Powers." Like a dozen-odd other dissatisfied AFL unions, ARTA then applied for membership to the new Committee for Industrial Organization, exactly as this breakaway federation was placing its prospects in the hands of sit-down strikers in Flint and other industrial cities and gathering in members each month by the tens of thousands.[33]

Yet another new union, much larger and claiming an adjacent jurisdiction, presented an immediate issue for ARTA. The United Electrical and Radio Workers of America was formed in March 1936, and its membership so increased at GE, Westinghouse and RCA factories throughout the following year that, after joining the CIO late in 1936, it became the federation's third-largest affiliate. UE leaders were reluctant to grant ARTA a CIO charter. In March 1937, the UE's twenty-six-year-old president, James B. Carey, received a letter from an ARTA local official assuring him that ARTA would not compete with the UE, and that the two groups shared a common goal: thoroughly organizing the greater communications industry. Roy A Pyle, secretary of ARTA Local 3, confided to Carey that "communications is a basic industry," providing "the nerves which directly control the flow" of "our present economic and social system." However, he went on,

> The conditions under which the workers in the communications industry are at present working are intolerable, and considering the fact that the majority of these workers are semi-skilled, their wage scales are miserably low. The average work week in this industry is forty-eight hours or more. The average pay is less than $100 per month. We believe this condition to be incompatible with the president's desire to establish a forty-hour week at a living wage.

Improvement was urgent. Pyle told Carey that "the only possible remedy to this situation is for the C.I.O. group to take hold of the situation and do something about it." He elaborated:

> Since the victory of the C.I.O. over the steel and auto industries, it is my firm belief that the communications industry is the remaining national stronghold for company unions. In addition to this fact, new company unions are being established. It is my opinion that the C.I.O. Organizing Committee probably underestimates the economic and political strength of this more than a quarter-million unorganized workers.

Because the organizations representing communications workers, aside from company unions and, of course, the nascent ARTA, were AFL affiliates—ORT, CTU, and IBEW—and because "the strength, influence, and future possibilities of the I.B.E.W. and the C.T.U. are negligible in the communications industry," Pyle forecast, the ARTA "can form the base of an industrial organization in this industry which would give the present C.I.O. affiliates tremendously increased strength on the political and economic front." "The C.T.U. and the I.B.E.W. could be pushed off the battlefront, if such is the desire of the C.I.O. Organizing Committee." He concluded with an appeal to UE leaders to support ARTA's affiliation with the CIO.[34]

Pyle's letter is noteworthy for what it suggested about travails still to come. Not the least of the barriers thrown up both by Western Union and AT&T against organizing independent industrial unions, as Pyle related, were their "employee representation plans"—company unions. How could this entrenched institution be eliminated? A second question concerned the strategic importance of communications which, Pyle insisted, should be seen as a "basic industry" and, therefore, within the heartland of the CIO's mission. This meant, as he also stated, that the CIO's ability to mount effective political and industrial actions was in fact contingent on the federation's success in organizing communications. What he did not say also would have been plain: should industrial unionism in communications fail, or even be delayed, then a critical vulnerability might overtake the CIO itself. Finally, Pyle cast the existing AFL union affiliates as all but inert; we may surmise that it would be music to UE President Carey's ears to hear that his own union's major rival, the IBEW, could be given a thrashing. Again, however, a threat lurked just beneath this surface; for what if the AFL could not be banished so easily?

The following month—April 1937, amid cascading successes (and before its June reverse in "Little Steel")—the CIO awarded a charter to ARTA. Federation President John L. Lewis extended greetings to the federation's new affiliate by way of a front-page article in ARTA's "Communications Journal": "By the establishment of this union, embracing all workers in the industry, you are meeting effectively widespread demand for organization in your field."

> The communications industry, which stretches like a vast network across this continent, has remained until now practically untouched by organization. The only union in the field, the AF of L Commercial Telegraphers Union, has always been small and impotent. The powerful company-fostered Western Union Employees Association has stood in the way of other attempts at unionization....
>
> the greatest impetus in this drive for a bargaining power which will increase your pay and improve the hours and conditions of your employment must come from you. The Committee for Industrial Organization stands ready to give you every assistance in its power, but in the end, the success of this campaign must depend upon the workers of this industry themselves.

As Pyle had hoped, at a stroke the jurisdiction of what had originated as a tiny band of marine radio telegraphers became hugely enlarged. It now encompassed employees of all the landline and cable telegraph companies, workers in the radio-telegraph companies, and employees of radio broadcast stations including NBC and CBS. ARTA took care to observe a limit on its jurisdiction placed by the United Electrical & Radio Workers, which explicitly claimed the right to represent both Western Electric and Bell Laboratories employees and those in other AT&T subsidiaries—"except those directly engaged on wire services," who were to be covered by ARTA. "A close cooperation shall exist at all times between the U.E. & R.W.A. and the A.R.T.A.," underlined the leaders of the two unions in a formal document co-signed by John Brophy, first national Director of the Committee for Industrial Organization. Thus was agreed "the structure of organization that will lead to a complete unionization of the workers engaged in the various branches of the communications industry."[35]

Almost at once, the question of jurisdiction over telephone workers arose. In May 1937, Brophy wrote to ARTA President Rathborne and, under separate cover, to UE President Carey: "To avoid any mistake, I wish to get a statement from you and Mr. Carey as to the disposition to be made of inquiries from employees of telephone companies engaged in the central switchboard, etc." Rathborne responded, on CIO letterhead and with a copy to Carey. Portending clashes with both the International Brotherhood of Electrical Workers (AFL) and AT&T's numerous company unions, Rathborne stated, "It is my understanding of our agreement with the UE&RW that the ARTA was to have jurisdiction over all telephone company employees who are actually engaged in operating of telephone equipment. This would include switchboard operators, testers, and other persons employed in operating and maintaining telephone equipment. The jurisdiction of UE&RW includes all persons who are engaged in the design, manufacture, installation or repair of telephone equipment." With this proviso, as a historian has observed, ARTA's jurisdiction "was enlarged to cover the entire communications field on land and sea, with a potential membership of some 360,000 workers." In prospect, ARTA activists hoped, was an industrial union that would transcend the anachronistic division between the telephone and telegraph industries at the level of working-class self-organization, and actualize what McKercher and Mosco call "labor convergence." At its convention that summer, to consecrate this vital shift, ARTA became the American Communications Association (ACA). Unbroken use of the term "association," rather than "union," may have tacitly gestured to the grip held over many telecommunications workers by the Western Union Employee Association and by AT&T's many company unions. Like the UE, the ACA nevertheless shared in the CIO's foundational effort to organize industrial rather than craft unions. For the first time, along with operators and technicians, contingent, dreadfully paid telegraph messengers united around the objective of attaining collective bargaining rights. Meanwhile, in a different segment of the electronic communications industry, the ACA undertook organizing drives among radio broadcast technicians.[36]

Like nine other CIO unions, ARTA/ACA and UE were led by Communists. Initially, CIO leaders were not troubled by this, indeed, they welcomed the dedication of Communist organizers. After 1938, however, when Congress authorized Texas Democratic Congressman Martin Dies to undertake a well-publicized investigation of "un-American activities," a fissure opened in the federation. Two competing blocs called themselves the "Leftwing" and "Rightwing" factions. Both, as historian Steven Ashby explains, "were led by unionists with a similar social-democratic ideology . . . who supported New Deal social reforms, but who disagreed on domestic strategies, the role of the Communist Party in labor and, in 1940–1941 and after 1947, over foreign policy." Congress repeated reauthorizations of Dies' Red hunting subcommittee, and the coalescence around it of a network of professional anti-Communists, added to the centrifugal force within the CIO. UE president James Carey—voted out of office by UE members in 1941, but thereafter installed as Secretary-Treasurer of the CIO—became a vocal adversary of the CIO's Communists. In varying degree, much of the CIO leadership shared his aversion. Beginning sporadically in 1939–1940, and hardening into a consistent policy in the years after World War II, the federation abandoned its even-handedness.[37]

In light of how these issues became fixed in the amber of historical memory, it is essential to clarify what contemporary US Communism meant and did not mean. A meaningful entry-point for this appraisal is ACA President Joseph P. Selly's 1951 testimony before Nevada Democrat Pat McCarran's Senate Internal Security Subcommittee. McCarran assailed Selly and the ACA as primary agents of "subversion in the telegraph industry." Selly responded to a battery of questions by repeatedly asserting his Fifth Amendment right, that is, by refusing to testify against himself. Had he been a member of the International Labor Defense? Of the Action Committee to Free Spain? The American Council for Democratic Greece? The American-Jewish Labor Commission? The National Committee for American-Soviet Friendship? Had he participated in the National Emergency Conference for Civil Rights? Had he been a sponsor of the Committee for a Democratic Foreign Policy? Of the National Conference on American Policy on China and the Far East? Had he been a member of the People's Radio Foundation? For McCarran's Subcommittee such affiliations attested subversion. And Communists indeed were active in organizations that targeted US domestic and foreign policies, groups which, taken together, formed what historian Michael Denning has called a "cultural front." This cultural front, as Denning shows, was powered less by the Communist Party than by a wider spectrum of radicals and reformers, including many New Dealers and, for present purposes most important, many social unions and unionists. Some were Communists, some were not. Selly was one of many engaged participants in a multifaceted American radicalism, rejuvenated by the era's agonizing social and political crisis.[38]

The US Communist Party's ideological orientation and public standing were conditioned by its allegiance to the Soviet Union and the Moscow-based Communist International (Comintern). Menaced by England as well as by Nazi Germany, in August 1939 the USSR announced a far-reaching nonaggression pact with Hitler in defense of its state interests, which threw "the entire international Communist movement . . . into unprecedented disarray." Prior to the pact Communist-led organizations had been resolute opponents of fascism; after it was announced, they—the ACA among them—responded by calling for a halt to US war preparations. Suddenly, Communists now pronounced, to want to fight Hitler was to reveal oneself as a war-mongering imperialist. This stance rendered left-led CIO unions like ACA damagingly susceptible to accusations that they were mere instruments of the Comintern. Officials' charges of subversion began to hit at CIO unions and some cultural front organizations. When, in June 1941, Germany invaded the Soviet Union, the US Communist Party line—and ACA's—veered back to antifascism and an alliance with the USSR. This reversal, and the Communists' ensuing general antagonism to wildcats and shop-floor actions that interrupted production, both impeding the US military effort and disrupting supplies bound for the USSR, added to many workers' mistrust. Communists' support for Soviet state interests often outweighed rank-and-file attempts to resist management at the point of production.[39]

ACA's commitment to Soviet policies did not always fit this pattern. Atypically for a left-led union, ACA did not restrain its members' militancy, even to the point of permitting a strike vote, after the Nazis abrogated the Hitler-Stalin Pact. Late in September 1941, three months after Operation Barbarossa brought Nazi armies far into the Soviet Union, Joseph Selly, now ACA's president, notified the Roosevelt administration that the union was calling a referendum authorizing "any economic action which may become necessary" against RCA Communications, hoping for wage increases and a closed shop there. "Because of our appreciation of the integral part the RCA Communications system is in the national defense effort to defeat Hitlerism," Selly explained, "we have taken every step possible to avoid any dispute which might result in the disruption of this vital service." "Unfortunately," he continued, "we are faced with the cold reality of a company which seeks to impose its backward social philosophy upon workers who have no intention of surrendering those gains for which they have long and bitterly fought." The union took care to forward notice of its planned strike vote and of its letter to President Roosevelt to CIO Director of Organization Allen S. Haywood, who replied cautiously: "These are organization problems and I trust that your efforts will bring results."[40]

US Communism, moreover, was also a more capacious, diverse, and multifaceted movement than is often allowed. Following its formation in 1919 the CPUSA assumed the mantle of an indigenous US radicalism, recruiting across the spectrum of radical organizations, and from all sections of the country. In keeping with the multifarious engagements and affinities of the world's Communist trade unions, political parties, and front groups, and with the Comintern's sometime inability to control all of these, US Communists played a central role in building the mass movements of the 1930s, "mobilizing the unemployed, students, farmers, the elderly/retirees, immigrants, and ethnic groups and, above all, leading the fight for racial equality and the right of African-Americans." At the city level—Chicago has been carefully scrutinized—and with respect to affiliated organizations during the period of the Popular Front (after 1935), CP initiatives continually interacted with local needs and conditions. "The Party clearly aimed to put its mark on its Popular Front organizations and the reform movements it sought to lead," notes James Barrett, "but there was always the danger that the opposite would occur: that Communist activists . . . would come to see their trade union, or antifascist, or electoral work as their prime focus and the Party . . . as an impediment to success in these crucial efforts." Communist-led unions threw themselves into numerous struggles to combat inequality, exploitation, and white supremacy; and they were among the most democratically run unions. As Nelson Lichtenstein explains, the left-led CIO affiliates thus spanned beyond militant trade unionism in striving for "the defense of civil liberties, protofeminism, and above all, the movement for the liberation of African-Americans."[41]

The Communist Party regarded ACA—one of the CIO's eighteen original affiliates—as "particularly important"; and, from its beginning, ACA carried forward the Communists' general endeavor to target racism, both as a nationwide scourge and within its ranks. White supremacy had long permeated telegraph unionism. As recently as 1925 the updated Constitution of the Commercial Telegraphers Union-AFL expressly specified that only "white persons" were eligible for membership. Its progenitor, the Order of Railway Telegraphers, like the National Association of Railway Mail Clerks, and the Brotherhood of Electrical Workers among others, excluded all but white men from membership. ACA, by contrast, explicitly confronted Jim Crow during its early days, when its leaders attempted to open their union to nonwhites. This proposal outraged some members; and when crafting its constitution the nascent union underwent "endless and bitter wrangles and floor fights." One member of the losing faction was Karl Baarslag, who went on to claim a role as what he called a "real hard-core anti" (-Communist), in an increasingly powerful network of peers. Then a marine telegrapher, Baarslag thereafter worked as a postal clerk and an AFL unionist, a member of the antisubversive unit of the Office of Naval Intelligence, a "research specialist" at the American Legion, and a staff member for Joseph

McCarthy's Subcommittee on Investigations. In 1951 he got back at his old adversaries, by testifying that ACA's policy of equality during its formative years had resulted from Soviet machinations: "Up until this time the ... seagoing radio profession, had been exclusively Caucasian white, and the last woman operator had folded her bag and gone ashore about 1920 or thereabouts. ... Therefore, most radiomen wanted to limit the craft, the membership, to white Caucasian males." Union leaders, Baarslag recollected, "argued about this interminably all that summer, in meeting after meeting.... it was the first inkling that we had that these people were extremely broad and liberal, and that they wanted to go against the will of probably 95 percent of the membership for what seemed to us mainly dogmatic or doctrinaire purposes." Baarslag must have exaggerated this disproportionality; however, he was certainly correct that Communists, ACA's among them, were committed to battling against white supremacy. Racism, Communist unionists believed, hindered working-class solidarity and social agency, and the ACA's leaders were tenacious in opposing it. They did not foreground antiracism (or antisexism) sufficiently; for, as Trotter explains, they tended "to reduce all facets of the 'race problem' to issues of class inequity." Nevertheless, their fights against white supremacy won them many African American supporters.[42]

US Communism's adherence to Soviet edicts and the state interests that generated them were superimposed on this many-sided domestic radicalism. Party discipline was certainly a conditioning factor: through the Party's system of "democratic centralism" decisions were taken in light of Comintern instructions, and Party members were expected to conform to them. However this internalization of Soviet policies reflected something beyond Party discipline. For comrades worldwide, working-class solidarity in the cause of socialism knew no boundaries. It was axiomatic that they should spring to defend the existence— the survival—of the homeland of international socialism. For, were the Soviet Union to collapse in the face of a foreign military assault, the prospect of socialism everywhere would be profoundly set back. "For those who believed in the necessity of defending the world's only socialist nation from outside attack, the CP's policy changes had eminent justification," sums up historian Roger Keeran. "Unfortunately for the Communists," Keeran continues, "few Americans shared this assumption." Whatever the respective importance of their Party discipline and their commitment to international class solidarity, "At best, Communists found themselves without much support on foreign policy; at worst, their opponents called them fools, traitors, and puppets of Moscow."[43]

After World War II an existing or prior affiliation of any kind with US Communism would be cast as a link to an "immense conspiracy," whose singular malignant purpose was to infiltrate and destroy American institutions. In the hands of commercial news magnates, Democratic and Republican politicians, corporate employers, the network of professional anti-Communists, the Association of Catholic Trade Unionists and many other union officials, the charge of "Communism" now was directed much more widely than just at the CP and its supporters. It became an effective tool used to combat the liberalism of the New Deal state; to discredit the campaigns and ambitions of the cultural front; and, perhaps above all, to split and enfeeble the CIO's earlier far-ranging social unionism.

All this provided the context for ACA's endeavors in telecommunications. After winning its CIO charter in 1937, ACA's energized members and officials set out on the work that lay ahead. "Due to limited finances and forces we have been concentrating our efforts in the radio and telegraph fields and have made no effort to organize telephone employees," wrote Rathborne to Brophy in the heady days of May 1937. "Inasmuch as there are approximately 260,000 telephone workers in the United States we believe that a drive to organize this industry should be jointly planned, financed, and conducted by the CIO, UE&RW and ARTA. At some future date when the CIO's organizing campaign in the basic industries has progressed to a point where there are forces and money available for telephone organizing work, I suggest that Mr. Lewis and yourself meet with a joint committee from UE&RW and ARTA to discuss a National CIO campaign to organize the telephone industry." That time arrived a few years later, during World War II.[44]

In the meantime, the CIO was already funneling substantial resources to its new affiliate. The CIO appointed and bore the cost of twenty full-time organizers for ACA, including two who went on to become president and secretary-treasurer of the union; over the next four years, the CIO ran up a deficit of $80,000 in financial assistance to ACA. Between 1938 and 1942, ACA duly expanded its organizing and intensified its political interventions. The hopefulness, the sense of possibility, of this period was expressed in ACA President Mervyn Rathborne's September, 1939 directive to three other ACA leaders—Joseph Selly, Daniel Driesen, and Joseph Kehoe: "When in doubt, take the offensive." As the union embraced the strategy and tactics of the CIO, ACA simultaneously staged sit-down strikes, mounted audacious legal appeals, and fielded political lobbyists. In one 1938 initiative, which gained CIO backing, ACA President Rathborne wrote to FCC Chair Frank McNinch requesting that he try "to have a WPA project established for unemployed communications workers": the proposal intended not only to provide work but also to aid the FCC in collecting data about labor conditions in the communications industry. A second initiative, unveiled at the ACA's annual convention in 1938, was also bold—the union called for direct labor representation on the Federal Communications Commission. Neither plan bore fruit but, amid the buoyant hopefulness of the early CIO, they testified to the ACA-CIO's audacious and improvisional tactics. Its social unionism repeatedly spilled over the formal channels of NLRB-sanctioned collective bargaining.[45]

These tactics were complements to organizing and industrial action. Within months of gaining its CIO charter ACA signed a limited contract—ousting the CTUA-AFL—with the smaller and weaker of the two telegraph carriers, Postal Telegraph; two years later, in 1939, Postal acquiesced to a full-fledged national contract with ACA. Accessing the machinery of the new National Labor Relations Board, ACA also won representation elections in Globe Radio and in RCA Communications. In 1937 it possessed a mere 4,204 members, working in marine radio, wireless, and telegraph jobs within 30-odd broadcast companies and 65 steamship lines; by June, 1938, its membership had tripled, to 13,108. Was ACA about to undergo a great membership surge, such as those which had lately transformed the electrical workers, the steelworkers, and the autoworkers into mighty working-class organizations? Could ACA force its crusading social unionism upon one of capital's remaining citadels: the nation's electronic communications system?[46]

These were heady days. ACA contemplated and actually undertook actions in multiple venues, in light of their organizing potential. At the same time, it participated actively in CIO unions' efforts to develop and enrich the role of organized labor as the guardian of a wider public interest.

ACA for Labor and Accountable Public Service

Between 1938 and 1942, ACA continued to insist than a new and far-reaching investigation of the telegraph industry should precede any combination between Western Union and Postal Telegraph, both to open public discourse to labor's needs and to ensure that a merger addressed them. ACA's stance signaled its commitment as a CIO union to an expansive public policy agenda for telecommunications, one that extended far beyond the danger of monopoly pricing to encompass employment, service provision, and democratic accountability.[47]

Rank-and-file telegraphers backed their union leaders' call for a telegraph investigation and for legislative provisions to protect labor and the public interest in the event that a combination was authorized. Asked to undertake letter-writing campaigns to Congressional representatives, ACA-ers responded impressively. As 1939 gave way to 1940, an astonishing 34,000 communications from ACA telegraphers were received by the office of Senator Burton K. Wheeler, who chaired the Interstate Commerce Committee. ACA officials also appealed to Commerce Secretary and Roosevelt confidant Harry Hopkins, while they continued to lobby the Senate Interstate Commerce Committee, the FCC, and the Department of Justice, whose assistant attorney general was the trust-busting maverick Thurman Arnold. Between 1938 and 1940, ACA also undertook a flurry of political initiatives. Senator Wheeler managed to push through a resolution authorizing his Interstate Commerce Committee (rather than, interestingly, the FCC) to undertake a telegraph investigation; however, its $5000 budget cut short any inquiry and itself offered testimony, ACA asserted, to interference by employer lobbyists.[48]

ACA also pushed hard at the FCC. In the aftermath of its stymied telephone inquiry, the FCC remained on a defensive footing. Doubtless aware of this, ACA nevertheless insisted that the agency do more than merely "bail out the telegraph companies." A day after the FCC published a report again recommending legislative authorization for a merger, an ACA release to the evening papers charged that the it was "acting as the 'hatchet-man' in a scheme concocted by communications moguls to throw thousands of employees out of their jobs and to undermine the public interest in an adequate communications service." Senator Wheeler's committee, President Rathborne exclaimed, might best "probe the FCC," in light of the "outstanding fact revealed" by its report: "its admitted abysmal ignorance of conditions in the industry which are common knowledge to the average messenger boy." The agency's lack of knowledge of working conditions was itself, Rathborne underlined, a damning and all-too-typical sign:

> In its report the Commission states that, among other things, it is ignorant of the speed of service being furnished the public, it does not have the necessary facts to determine whether the workers in the industry are subjected to speed-up which results in decreased efficiency, it has no knowledge of the effects of mechanization on employment and service, and it has no reliable information on real wages. These factors are precisely those which must determine the conditions of merger legislation if the interest of the public is to be safeguarded.

Wheeler, who proclaimed himself unfriendly to monopoly in any form, continued to hold up merger legislation. One reason for this probably had to do with the fast-approaching 1940 presidential campaign. Wheeler harbored presidential ambitions; and these were staked to his isolationist rejection of US participation in a European war. ACA played to Wheeler, going on record "as withdrawing its support from President Roosevelt for re-election." This was 1940 when, as German troops overran western Europe, the Communist Party line condemned any US involvement; but ACA claimed, not entirely unpersuasively, that its decision to abandon FDR had a different rationale: The president had thrown his support to legislation that would loosen protections for unionized railroad workers—railroad telegraphers among them—who were faced with industrial consolidation.[49]

It is worth explicating ACA's charge, that New Deal regulators had not scrupled to understand the telegraphers' work, and its suggestion, that the union stood ready to remedy their ignorance. FCC Chairman Fly, a seasoned

New Dealer, conceded publicly that labor did constitute a blind-spot: "I am sorry to say that the Federal Communications Commission has never been sufficiently staffed or equipped to undertake painstaking, continuous, scientific analyses of the problems of labor economics in the communications industry," Fly told the Senate Interstate Commerce Committee. When ACA President Selly (Figure 5.2) testified a week later, he bored into Fly's admission: "the source of his information on all vital questions affecting the public interest and labor in this industry is invariably statistics prepared and presented by the companies.

Figure 5.2 American Communications Association President Joseph P. Selly. Beginning his tenure as president in 1940, Selly led this CIO affiliate through major organizing drives in the telegraph and telephone industries, and a grinding but ultimately unsuccessful lobbying campaign to prevent regulators and legislators from authorizing a "mass-layoff" telegraph industry merger. American Communications Association, Local 10, New York, NY, records, 1931–1971, Call number: PH Mss 321, Wisconsin Historical Society.

The record does not indicate that the companies are a reliable source of information relating to the vital factors of speed of service to the public, speed-up of the workers in the industry, and so forth." The FCC, although it continually made "recommendations concerning the disposition of jobs of workers" in the telegraph industry labor, had never taken independent initiative to learn about these workers' circumstances. "The Commission, since its establishment, has done nothing whatever in the way of actual field investigation of the type of work performed by employees in the industry and their wages, health, and other conditions of work. It has maintained no staff with the remotest knowledge of the problems involved. . . . The Commission has not even bothered to seek the aid of other Government agencies such as the Department of Labor or the United States Public Health Service." Was this apparent call-and-response merely coincidence—or might Chairman Fly, himself no shrinking violet, have opened the door for ACA President Selly to walk through?[50]

Either way, as Fly acknowledged, its lack of knowledge about labor conditions in the communications industry was indeed a categorical defect of the agency. Even its mammoth telephone investigation had not attended methodically to work and employment issues. ACA succeeded in inspiring federal legislators and regulators to recognize this deficit. But the union pressed for more, and continued to demand an investigation of the telegraph industry that would foreground labor conditions. Possibly in response, in 1943 the FCC hired as its chief economist Dallas Smythe, who had previously worked on telegraph labor and who had strong and long-standing connections to ACA representatives Driesen and Kehoe. ACA in turn kept the agency's feet to the fire by underscoring the specific links between labor conditions and public service standards:

> Certainly everyone will agree that one of the most important factors affecting the public interest in connection with the telegraph industry is speed of service. There is no evidence in Mr. Fly's testimony that the F.C.C. has studied this problem under the existing set-up.

Had the agency only chosen to investigate, Selly proclaimed (again echoing prior NRA testimony), it would have found that employee speed-ups, mechanization, and lay-offs were organically related to the declining efficiency with which telegrams were handled. These charges did more than portray the FCC as remiss in discharging its duties under the Communications Act; they held up ACA-CIO as the guarantor of the public interest.[51]

ACA's campaign also threw its weight to a related and hotly contested reform. Prior to 1935, historian Jerold Auerbach relates, "employers could oppose organization of their workers by almost any means they chose. Employees had no legal recourse against anti-union tactics; they did not, in fact, even have the legal right to organize a union." Passed by Congress and signed into law in 1935, partly in response to rank-and-file militancy, the National Labor Relations Act broke through this impasse by granting workers a right to form independent trade unions as legal bargaining agents, free of coercion by employers. Without unions, the Wagner Act reasoned, individual workers' negotiations with giant corporations remained lopsidedly unequal. The result of this inequality of condition was to constrict mass purchasing power and, thereby, to contribute to the Depression. In turn, as Auerbach goes on to explain, a result of making unionization "the cornerstone of national labor policy" and of fostering "labor organization as a recovery measure" was also to heighten "sensitivity to civil liberties in labor relations": Trade union growth hinged on effective use of First Amendment freedoms: meetings, speeches, unencumbered conversation, picketing, pamphleteering, and news publishing. In turn, "the need to protect labor's right to organize thrust the federal government into the civil liberties domain."[52]

A federal effort to guarantee this positive speech freedom was spearheaded by a subcommittee of the Senate Committee on Education and Labor, the so-called Civil Liberties Committee, led by Wisconsin's Robert La Follette, Jr. Between 1936 and 1940, the La Follette Committee employed a strategy of spotlight publicity, both to aid the young National Labor Relations Board and to coordinate with the CIO's organizing campaigns in steel, auto manufacturing, and mining beginning even before the Wagner Act was upheld by the Supreme Court in April 1937. By detailing the tactics and practices of specific employers—strikebreakers and detective agencies, private police, stockpiled munitions and corporate espionage—the La Follette Committee showcased systematic violations of the rights of workers seeking to unionize. It enabled industrial unions to expand their institutional role, by acting as safe-keepers both of their members' economic- and First-Amendment rights. The cornerstone of this endeavor was a belief that "the right of workmen to organize themselves into unions has become an important civil liberty" in itself.[53]

In broad form, organized labor had long aspired to such a broadly protective role. During the late nineteenth century, craft unions had operated in the belief that their House of Labor was the chief defender of (white and male) workers' rights and that their unionism was a prerequisite of a just state. After 1936, top CIO staffers carried forward this conviction, holding that "It was only through labor organizations that employees could truly exercise" their constitutionally protected First Amendment rights. Industrial unions, CIO officials and New Dealers such as Senator La Follette believed, constituted the public's bulwark against abuses of the commonweal: "guardians of democracy," in the short-hand of historian Jerold S. Auerbach.[54]

The ACA's engagements with the FCC with respect to labor and public service carried this conviction into telecommunications. So did its tenacious maneuvering to forestall regulators and legislators from enacting a merger between Western Union and Postal Telegraph; and to ensure that, if it did come about, such a combination would protect both employees and public telegraph service.

ACA and the Telegraph Merger

More forceful and effective federal regulation was one aim of the New Deal's zig-zag program, and the Federal Communications Act signed into law in June of 1934 reflected this. The 1934 by-elections thereafter augmented President Roosevelt's existing congressional majority; while political pressure from the left became more insistent. Roosevelt, writes one of his biographers, responded by moving "cautiously from a program dependent upon the cooperation of the business community to one aimed primarily at bettering the lot of the dispossessed." The NRA Code hearings had seen charges flying back and forth about carrier abuses and, as Senator Clarence Dill explained, his Interstate Commerce Committee "not knowing the facts, felt that this was something the commission should investigate." The FCC quickly initiated attempts to stabilize the telegraph industry.[55]

The FCC had quickly decided that the culprit was "ruinous competition" per se. After conducting hearings, in January 1935—as its Telephone Investigation was just getting underway—the FCC duly recommended to Congress amendments to the recent Communications Act. These aimed to establish a procedure for the Commission to rescue the industry, by authorizing a merger between the two straitened wireline telegraph companies. However, the agency declared also that, absent mandatory safeguards, the merger "will not inure to the benefit of the public and of the employees of the telegraph companies as well as of the investors in telegraph securities." Here the young FCC demonstrated its absorption—or, at least, awareness—of at least some of what telegraph unionists had told the NRA. The Commission declared that it would make substantial efforts on labor's behalf in determining whether any forthcoming merger proposal actually served the public interest. "Employees," the FCC stipulated, "may be retired or dismissed as a direct or indirect result of the consolidation only upon the payment to them of retirement annuities or dismissal compensation to be determined by the Federal Communications Commission or some other administrative agency as may be designated by the President." Other FCC injunctions applied to wages, seniority, and transfers of employment, and portended additional protections for telegraph workers. This was still pie in the sky until Congress followed through by enacting legislation; but that the FCC publicly advocated protections for telegraph workers was extraordinary in its own right.[56]

The FCC also tied its prospective authorization of a merger to new service requirements. The combined company would have to "agree that (1) it will extend service to or improve the service at any place, and will open a cable or radio circuit to any place . . . which the Commission . . . shall find to be desirable . . . ; and that (2) it will not abandon or diminish the service at any place or over any cable or radio circuit without the prior consent of the Commission." The reasoning here was that because consolidation was expected to result in the elimination of duplicate facilities, it should also be made to demonstrate "lower rates with better service." Expansion was imperative: telegraphy, the FCC charged, "has never been a really national service." Under its proposed policy, however, "A consolidated telegraph system would have the obligation to provide a national service." Specifically, the commission sought a grant of "the power to compel action if the management should be reluctant to extend telegraph service to smaller communities."[57]

These were the priorities of the early, activist FCC—the same FCC that was investigating AT&T and seeking wholesale reform of US telecommunications. By 1938–1939, this FCC's crusading reformism had been blunted, though there remained a couple of ardent New Deal commissioners, including its incoming Chairman Lawrence Fly. In addition, however, political support for merging Postal with Western Union faced fierce but divided counterpressure from organized labor.

From before its CIO charter award until the middle of World War II, the twists and turns of a telegraph merger bulked large in ACA's calculations. This question was highly complex. In engaging it, ACA was obliged to attach priority to Western Union including, most urgently, the Western Union Employees Association. If ACA could demonstrate legally that WUEA (also called WEA) was actually a company union, then the machinery that had been set up by the Wagner Act and the Fair Labor Standards Act could be used to dis-establish it. Such a decertification would open the Western Union door for ACA organizers. For reasons about to be explained, for ACA this was an overriding strategic necessity for ACA.

Mere months after the Supreme Court's upheld the Wagner Act, Western Union refused to recognize the ACA to represent its employees, insisting instead that it would bargain only with WUEA. The ACA thereupon turned to the NLRB. The outcome marked a telling contrast with the preceding generation's experience. Theodore Vail had argued in AT&T's 1915 Annual Report that federal regulators should intervene on *management's* side against the company's employees, to guarantee lower wage rates and labor stability, and we saw earlier how the one-year period of Post Office operation only accentuated management's power over workers (Figure 5.3). Twenty-five years later, the shoe was on the other foot. Western Union's company union was decertified by the

THIS IS NOT 1918!

WESTERN UNION HAS OVERPLAYED ITS HAND IN PUSHING THE NEW "INDEPENDENT" TO IMMEDIATELY START IN WHERE THE AWUE LEFT OFF. THE POLICY BEHIND THE NEW COMPANY UNION SET-UP, WHICH IS LED BY SUCH AWUE STALWARTS AS VITUCCI, MANNEY, MILLER, TASCHNER AND DOWLING IS "BE READY TO TAKE OVER AS SOON AS THE COURT DECISION THROWS OUT THE AWUE".

THIS DEVELOPMENT IS NOT UNEXPECTED. THE ACA HAS LONG PREDICTED THAT THE COMPANY WOULD TRY TO TETTER EMPLOYEES WITH ANOTHER AWUE. AS A MATTER OF FACT THE BIG INDUSTRIALISTS, ORGANIZED IN THE NATIONAL ASSOCIATION OF MANUFACTURERS, ARE TRYING TO INVENT A NEW FORM OF COMPANY-DOMINATED UNION-THE "INDEPENDENT"-SINCE OUTRIGHT COMPANY UNIONS HAVE BEEN DISCREDITED.

IN WESTERN UNION IT IS VERY CLEAR THAT THE COMPANY IS SEEKING TO PUT ACROSS A "LEGAL" AWUE ON ORDERS FROM THE 22ND FLOOR OF 60 HUDSON ST. WILLEVER FIGURES: "IT WORKED IN 1918, IT'LL WORK IN 1940". HE THINKS YOU CAN FOOL ALL OF THE PEOPLE ALL OF THE TIME.

THIS MOVE IS AIMED AT ISOLATING WESTERN UNION EMPLOYEES AND DEPRIVING MUNICATIONS WORKERS IN THE ACA. THE ACA HAS PROVEN ITS ABILITY TO PRODUCE PRACTICAL GAINS AND BENEFITS FOR COMMUNICATIONS EMPLOYEES. "INDEPENDENT UNIONS" HAVE ALWAYS FAILED, JUST AS THE AWUE FAILED, BECAUSE THEY ARE DOMINATED BY THE COMPANY. THEY FAIL BECAUSE THEY ISOLATE THE EMPLOYEES OF ONE COMPANYFROM THE ENTIRE LABOR FIELD. THEY FAIL BECAUSE THE LEADERSHIP CAN BE EASILY "BOUGHT OFF" AND INTIMIDATED BY THE COMPANY.

EMPLOYERS ARE TRYING TO GO EVEN FURTHER. THEY WOULD LIKE TO BREAK THE WAGNER ACT AND KEEP THEIR EMPLOYEES FROM ORGANIZING IN UNIONS OF THEIR OWN CHOOSING. THEY WOULD LIKE TO DESTROY THE WAGE-HOUR LAW SO THAT THEY MAY LOWER WAGES AND LENGTHEN HOURS OF WORK. THE COMPANIES AND BIG INDUSTRIALISTS UNITE SO THAT THEY ARE MORE POWERFUL INACCOMPLISHING THESE ENDS.

THE EMPLOYEES ARE LEARNING THE SAME LESSON. THEY ARE JOINING THE ACA AND UNITING WITH OTHER COMMUNICATIONS WORKERS SO THAT THEIR STRENGTH AND RESOURCES ARE MULTIPLIED. THERE IS NO MIDDLE ROAD. THE COMPANIES WANT UNIONS WHICH THEY CAN CONTROL AND RUN. EMPLOYEES NEED AND WANT A BONAFIDE UNION RUN BY THE MEMBERS THEMSELVES FOR THEIR OWN GAINS.

THE TIME HAS COME TO WIN JOB SECURITY IN THE FACE OF MECHANIZATION AND MERGER. TO SHORTEN THE WORK WEEK, ELIMINATE PART TIME AND SPEED UP AND INCREASE WAGES. THESE CONDITIONS CAN BE ACHIEVED ONLY THROUGH THE A.C.A. PROGRAM.

JOIN THE A.C.A. TODAY

AMERICAN COMMUNICATIONS ASSOCIATION

WESTERN UNION LOCAL NO.36B

10 BRIDGE ST. N. Y. C.

Figure 5.3 This Is NOT 1918! New Deal versus Open Shop—the contrast between 1940 and the bitter historical memory of the aftermath of World War I. After the National Labor Relations Board decertified Western Union's AWEA for being a company union in 1940, ACA was quick to seize on any hint that Western Union might try to reinstate this practice—which the carrier had initiated in the reactionary era that followed the Great War. Author's Collection.

NLRB following an appeal to the Circuit Court which, in August 1940, upheld the NLRB's ruling.[58]

It proved easier to disqualify the WEA on legal grounds than to dispel the conservatism of its members. "Telegraph operators have for the most part always regarded themselves as belonging in the professional category," the onetime telegrapher and later historian, Vidkunn Ulrikkson, recollected in 1953 (though his characterization did not take account of telegraph workers' militancy during the 1880s or the World War I years):

> theirs was ... a highly skilled craft, described frequently as a 'genteel' one, an appellation which they took rather seriously .... For that reason, it was always difficult for the telegrapher to identify himself with ordinary workers who felt the need for organization. His was a typical middle class, 'white-collar' psychology, and hence, there was little feeling of solidarity among the 'Knights of the Key.' To the contrary, there was a strong feeling of competition among them which the employers encouraged from the very beginnings of the industry.

At its 5th National Convention, held in Chicago in April 1940, ACA continued to elevate the goal of organizing Western Union. That carrier, then ACA President Mervyn Rathborne asserted in a memo to CIO President John L. Lewis, "is one of the largest anti-labor and open-shop corporations ... The International Officers of ACA believe that the organization of Western Union is a subject of major importance not only to ACA but to the CIO as a whole." Rathborne was duty-bound to relate that Western Union was doing "everything within its power to keep the AWUE intact."[59]

ACA faced a third obstacle, in addition to Western Union's cautious employees and its intransigent management: the American Federation of Labor and its affiliate, the Commercial Telegraphers Union. After ACA-CIO had done the work of clearing out the company union, Rathborne related, the CTU chose to take a "direct interest" in organizing Western Union itself. Rathborne asked that CIO grant financial assistance for ACA's competing organizing drive, and the CIO provided it.[60]

Both ACA and CIO leaders understood that the struggle with the CTU-AFL laid bare the ultimate stakes in any merger between Western Union and Postal Telegraph. In question were the jobs of Postal's 16,000 or so employees which, now that ACA had won a national contract at the carrier, constituted the CIO's largest base in telecommunications. However, a new corporate telegraph monopoly would reshuffle the deck. Would the combination grant the CIO a springboard to industrial unionism throughout the nation's telecommunications—or would the AFL defeat it, and aid Western Union in laying off Postal's ACA workers? This question spun through the complicated maneuvering that wove through the merger movement.

CTU opposed a merger. It did not trust that a merger was needed to restore the industry to financial health; it believed that the resulting telegraph monopoly would throw now-gratuitous employees on the street; and, not least, it knew that a combination might grant opportunity for ACA—and the CIO—to enlarge their hold at CTU's and the AFL's expense. ACA, by contrast, was ambivalent. A merger might open the door to successful organizing and rapid ACA expansion; however, instead it might accelerate the telegraph industry's mechanization drive and in turn, as CTU believed, engender job losses. Who, most fundamentally, would determine how many and which employees were retained by a merged company, and the benefits provided to terminated workers? ACA had already pitted itself against the creation of "an unregulated monopoly," insisting that legislation was needed to protect the jobs—and, though it did not say so, the ACA membership—of Postal's employees. Here was the bitter nub of the issue between the rival unions: Were Western Union to combine with Postal, was it not likely that rank-and-file ACA-ers would become management's first targets?[61]

Ambiguity and uncertainty, as well as overlaps in the two competing unions' thinking, ensured that the journey to a merger would be fraught. So did the moribund status of the telegraph industry. "[T]he telegraph portion of communications is becoming more and more a restricted field—is tending to become a dying industry," Willard Bliss, executive vice president of the ACA, had declared in 1938. Should a revival of competition fail, Bliss told a Senate subcommittee, "there can be only one way out for the industry, and that is for the Government to take over the entire operation of the telegraph industry, coordinating it with their postal service." Bliss's proposal circulated within the union as the nation prepared for World War II—and as the ACA and the CTU squared off.[62]

The ACA had established a beachhead at Western Union's New York City hub. The decertification of Western Union's company union threw open the way for ACA to organize telegraphers carrier-wide. The CTU responded by vilifying the ACA as a Communist front. Such charges became a staple. During 1941 hearings before Congress, the CTU's secretary-treasurer, W. L. Allen, warned that "The Communist Party of America has for many years tried to capture the communications industry of the United States. We in the Commercial Telegraphers' Union are continually fighting to prevent the Communist Party from achieving its objective. We believe the communications industry . . . can be best protected from subversive influences if there is no merger." Allen responded to Senator C. Wayland Brooks' request that he "amplify" his statement in regard to "how a merger would encourage any subversive influences," by insinuating that "in event of any merger, where all employees would be more or less thrown together, some Communist Party members might be in a position to circulate more freely among the employees, and perhaps gain more converts." The CTU's red-baiting campaign may have persuaded some telegraphers to distance themselves from ACA, and it set the mold for later developments. For the moment, however, anti-Communism did not become a full-blown crusade, and rank-and-filers supported ACA's left leadership. Many Western Union workers, on the other hand, chose not to cast their lot with either ACA or CTU. Small independent unions emerged from the ashes of the Western Union Employees Association, a pattern that would find a parallel in the telephone industry; and they garnered considerable rank-and-file support.

ACA had introduced its political strategy in the depressed conditions of February, 1938. At an evening meeting for members of its New York locals at Postal and Western Union, Rathborne revived the NRA-era unionists' criticisms: Western Union and Postal "want a merger . . . to protect the investment of the owners of stocks and bonds of both companies." Western Union's financial condition, Rathborne suggested, was indeed precarious. Nevertheless, establishing a telegraph monopoly would "make possible closing down of telegraph offices," and result in "lay off of thousands of employees" so that the merged companies could "realize a return on their investment." The two carriers were already "illegally cooperating to create a monopoly" through mutually coordinated lay-offs and closures of branch offices, but "if we bring this sharply enough to the attention of the people who have jurisdiction in these matters, the Department of Justice, FCC and Congressmen and Senators, we can stop the companies." Political intervention was therefore imperative, and Rathborne introduced Danny Driesen, ACA's Washington-based legislative representative.[63]

Driesen invoked before ACA members the straitened railroad industry, and the "fact that merger was withheld for many years because of solid organization of railroad employees. When merger was effected workers had voice in determining various protective clauses because of their organized strength. No reason why communications people cannot do the same." Driesen's notes for this talk suggest that ACA was already working behind the scenes to resist the combination: "Because of vigilance of union and widespread interest by employees we have made such moves impossible and have laid plans to forestall any merger unless under our conditions." And he echoed the ACA's Willard Bliss

> To statements that telegraph industry is dying and needs merger we point out that it is still a 48-hour week industry, employees' hours should be cut down to 30 hours per week, speed-up cut out, wages increased; and if the companies are not in a position to do this then the US Government can do it. If the companies refuse to give decent working conditions we will seek that remedy and inform the Congress and the Senate and the FCC that in the best interests of the public

and employees in communications, that the Government should take over the telegraph industry.

Speakers representing various locals chimed in. Many telegraphers' mistrust of their employers remained as visceral in 1938 as it had been during the NRA hearings five long years earlier. W. V. Wheaton, a Postal employee based in New Mexico, was among those who sent a standard telegram, in this case to ask that Senator Carl Hatch "give us the very best possible consideration when the matter is being handled in your branch of congress": An inquiry into the financial affairs of the two carriers, he declared, "would, beyond doubt disclose that such difficulties, if they really do exist are due solely to overcapitalization and bad management. Certainly none of it could be due to wages since they have hardly paid a subsistence wage in all these years."[64]

As the nation's entry into World War II became more certain, what the feisty union deemed a "mass layoff merger" likewise began to seem more likely. During this tense moment, the ACA continued to pursue legal appeals, employee organizing drives, and collective bargaining, looking to augment its leverage when and if a merger was authorized. For CIO telegraphers it became especially urgent "to organize Western Union and protect our job security through our organized strength."[65]

The ACA's campaign required that it coordinate with top CIO policymakers— a delicate and sometimes combustible negotiation. During one attempt to crystallize merger legislation in 1939, the union decided to slam the FCC and its new Chairman, James Lawrence Fly, in its journal, *ACA News*, for their ostensibly inadequate response to telegraphers' needs. Informed of the editorial in advance by ACA legislative representative Dan Driesen, CIO legal counsel Lee Pressman "threw up his hands and told me to get out and that we was through, etc. He said that we should not blast the FCC before first going to Fly and stating our position and pointing out to him that we would blast them if they did not pay some heed." ACA complied; it "changed the tone of the editorial, pointing out the anti-labor record of the FCC and asking the question as to what the new chairman was going to do." This shift was justified, Driesen confided to ACA's president, because "the support of the CIO will be one of the greatest, if not the greatest, single factor in the success of our fight on the merger"—and the CIO was tying itself increasingly closely to the Roosevelt Administration. ACA sought, however, to educate CIO officials, as it concurrently schooled the FCC, about conditions in the telegraph industry:

> Pressman is in agreement . . . although he still doesn't understand our position in that he thinks we should carry the ball for compulsory merger, when

actually... we want the Administration to carry the ball for compulsory merger *with* safeguards for labor.

Over the two years that followed, the CIO seems to have accepted that ACA's strategy was a good one: At its convention in September 1941, the CIO unanimously adopted a resolution expressing support for ACA and opposition to the merger. The union's political strategy thus exhibited missteps, as befit a work-in-progress.[66]

ACA also kept vigilant watch on the CTU-AFL. A 1939 confidential memo between ACA leaders related that "certain sources at the FCC which it would not be well for us to put on the spot" had provided an account of a meeting between CTU President Frank Powers and FCC Chairman Fly. Powers had stated that the CTU and the AFL "thought Government ownership was the ideal solution," but—also like ACA—they were "willing to agree that the merger was the only way out." Confirming ACA's fears, however,

> Powers said he did not see why the jobs of the workers in Postal should be preserved and that the best solution was some form of severance pay.... The Government officials present definitely got the impression that the CTU and the AFL were asking that fifteen thousand Postal workers be dumped out in the street in order to prevent the CIO from getting a foothold in Western Union. It was further the impression of these officials that the CTU and the AFL were only interested in preserving their own organization at the expense of the workers in the industry.

By 1940, as the administration readied for war, the ACA understood that the merger issue was again heating up. "One new factor needs to be emphasized," the union observed (this was during the period of the Hitler-Stalin pact): "The FCC and the companies have a powerful potential ally in the newly-created Defense Communications Board which is heavily weighted with company officials, representatives of the FCC and of the Army and the Navy. An attempt will be made by the companies to utilize the present war hysteria to put across their monopoly program under the guise of national defense. The public and the workers in the industry know that national defense does not mean defense of monopoly profits. True national defense is defense of the American people, their civil rights, institutions, security and living standards." Again noteworthy was the identification of "the public" with "the workers in the industry"; also, the implicit comparison to the World War I mobilization, in which Americans' "civil rights" and "living standards" had been invidiously transgressed.[67]

During World War II, unions underwent far-reaching institutional change. "Maintenance of membership" agreements for government contract work, ruled the National War Labor Board, provided that in union-represented workplaces union members needed to sustain their membership—and pay their union dues automatically, a practice known as the check-off—for the duration of the contract. This greatly bolstered both labor federations: the CIO's membership more than doubled between 1939 and 1944. It also added to the legitimacy of unions; indeed, Zieger relates, it increased "the likelihood of the CIO joining the constellation of power brokers dominating the American political economy" and helping to shape a postwar settlement. However, both the AFL and the CIO also had agreed to a No Strike Pledge so as to ensure uninterrupted production; acquiesced to government arbitration of union disputes with management; and ceded to government and, by extension, to government contractors, control over jobs and materials. Unions as an institutional force were strengthened, paradoxically, as their power at the point of production was canalized. Capital was not slow to use these changes to gain back some of the shop-floor prerogatives it had lost during the CIO's formative years.

ACA's concerns about the Defense Communications Board (DCB) established on September 24, 1940, emanated from the union's forebodings that war mobilization portended antidemocratic incursions such as those experienced during the Great War. In the run-up to World War II, ACA employed what resources it could draw on to resist such attacks. CIO President Phillip Murray wrote FCC Chairman Fly to support ACA's demand that labor be adequately represented on the Defense Communications Board; ACA President Joseph P. Selly was Murray's nominee for the DCB's Labor Advisory Committee. After Fly complied, Selly quickly conveyed his worry about the DCB's direction in a public report to ACA members in March 1941. He stated that the record of the Defense Communications Board, led by FCC Chairman Fly, had been "not very re-assuring to labor. While continuing to deny labor adequate representation on the vital industry committees and attempting to maneuver to isolate and undermine the CIO representative on the Labor Advisory Committee, the [DCB] industry committees have gone ahead in their consideration of problems vitally affecting communications workers." Following publication of this report, Selly received enthusiastic letters of support from twenty rank-and-file union members, men and women affiliated with ACA's Chicago, Indianapolis, and New York-area locals. "To permit a merger without consideration of the employees would place a stigma upon a government agency that years of effort of such agency could not lift.... Keep up the good work," wrote Natalie Brennecke. "You have taken the right stand in regards [to] the DCB," stated Marie Michalski: "It looks very much like colusion (sic) between a government agency (The FCC) and the telegraph Companies. We are a democratic institution in a democratic country and we dont go for that."[68]

Repeatedly, as movement toward consolidation waxed stronger, ACA members traveled to Washington to represent their union before Congress, *en masse*. The broad authority of the DCB was reaffirmed in 1943, when it became the Board of War Communications; and though it did not try to bypass the legislature in order to ram through a merger from the top down, as ACA feared it might do, it did help narrow and restrict the CIO's hitherto more expansive social unionism. What historian Paul Koistinen finds, overall, was also true here: "Throughout the defense and war years, union influence was largely confined to the areas of labor supply and labor relations." Although unionists attained representation not only on the Board's Labor Advisory Committee, but also on several others, ACA and CIO representatives competed with other labor members plucked from the AFL and, after 1944, from an unaffiliated union that was emerging out of AT&T's company unions, the National Federation of Telephone Workers. In every case except that of the Labor Advisory Committee union representatives were outnumbered by government and corporate officials. Although union membership increased by an impressive 4.5 million during the war, and unions now claimed a seat at the table of government policymaking, they remained divided among themselves and, even taken together, they constituted what Koistinen calls "a distinctly secondary power group in a system increasingly dominated by industry and the military."[69]

During 1942, a merger bill was approved by the Senate Interstate Commerce Committee (S. 2598). Prior to introducing it, Senator Ernest W. MacFarland, one of its sponsors, asked ACA leaders to discuss it with him—another acknowledgment of ACA's political legitimacy. Selly and Driesen "reiterated that the law should be based upon the needs of the nation in relation to the war effort, not upon the narrow economic interests of the owners, and that both labor and the general public must be protected." In consequence of disparate factors—Japan's surprise attack on the US fleet at Honolulu, Hitler's invasion of the Soviet Union and the ensuing demise of the Nazi-Soviet pact, ACA's own clear-eyed assessment of the ways in which war mobilization was enhancing the power of capital over labor—the union now at last relinquished its public opposition to the merger. ACA notified Senator MacFarland, as well as members of the Senate Interstate Commerce Committee, FCC Chairman Fly, and Secretary of Commerce Jesse Jones, that "the entry of our country into the war" had set a new context for enacting policy. However, the concrete content of the ACA policy recommendation was unchanged:

> All discussions of merger prior to Pearl Harbor revolved around permissive legislation designed to solve the financial problems of the carriers. If the Congress should determine, upon advice of the Army, the Navy, the Federal Communications Commission and other competent witnesses that immediate

merger was vital to the national war effort, we will advocate mandatory legislation with specific and proper safeguards for the public and labor. It should not be left to the discretion of the companies to consummate a merger immediately essential to the war effort in their own time and on their own terms.

Elbows out against the CTU-AFL, ACA concurrently proposed that "mandatory legislation" should protect the continued operation of the plant of Postal Telegraph. The union presented its demand as a war measure: "The cessation of service by Postal Telegraph would be disastrous in this emergency. The Postal facilities and personnel cannot be permitted to deteriorate but on the contrary stand in need of much improvement."[70]

ACA had gone public with what had, for at least a couple of years, been its underlying position. In 1940, the union's Executive Board and membership had approved the following statement: that, although the merger was a solution offered by the companies "to extricate themselves from a dilemma which they have created," nevertheless, "All available evidence indicates that a monopoly, either through merger or liquidation . . . is inevitable." What mattered were "the conditions under which any merger may take place"; and in this regard ACA insisted, characteristically, that it should both support the public interest as regards service standards and contain express guarantees against lay-offs and speed-ups as well as mandate a shorter work-week, collective bargaining rights, and higher wages. The continued introduction of new machines, though pushed by corporate executives in order to reduce their wage bill, "can contribute to the general social welfare" *if* workers "share in the benefits possible under mechanization, in the form of shorter hours, higher wages, and job security." Obstructing such a positive resolution, ACA believed, were not only the carriers but also the FCC, which had continued to hold the benighted view that a merger should be expedited, with labor's concerns taken care of "afterward." This, ACA insisted, was not a satisfactory solution.[71]

Yet there was reason for hope. By 1941, FCC Chairman Larry Fly was publicly endorsing a position congruent with ACA's. A pair of issues was paramount, Fly told Congress, and the first was national defense. "You cannot let a major telegraph company just close up shop," he declared, agreeing with ACA that Postal Telegraph and, by implication, ACA's stronghold there, should be preserved: "A hit-and-miss abandonment of any of our present communications routes or services would be very likely to weaken the Nation's ability to withstand emergency stresses." The second issue, he stated, was the status of telegraph workers: "An equally important reason why we cannot let any major telegraph company be forced to abandon service is the effect on labor." A previous FCC report had recommended "that the establishment of labor safeguards be left to the Commission." Fly, however, once more acceding to ACA's demand, proposed "to go beyond the Commission's earlier views and to recommend that specific minimal labor safeguards be written into the merger legislation itself." The need, Fly proclaimed, was to work out "means to insure that a merger shall be carried out without injury to the workers in the telegraph industry." To his credit, Fly did not duck the argument that telegraph workers were doomed to a future of mechanization-induced job losses. He himself raised "the question of what action society might properly take on a broad scale to counteract or to control the effects of the machine age upon employment opportunities," in order to underline "the more limited theory that we must, not only as practical people but also as responsible public officials, be concerned at this time with protecting the jobs of real people who today derive their livelihood from this industry, and who tomorrow may find themselves in jeopardy unless we are vigilant in guarding their interests." Policy should be governed not by an abstract deference to so-called technological progress, but by a nitty-gritty concern to protect present-day employees. A world removed from the proclamations of policymakers throughout later decades, Fly was emphasizing that government policy needed to be framed in terms of what historian David Noble later called "present-tense technology."[72]

Fly's testimony expressed not only personal conviction but organized labor's stature within the New Deal state. When they appeared before Congress, even telegraph industry executives stressed their purported concern for their employees. But high-flown affirmations and political grandstanding offered scant protection. While Fly testified, ACA kept up the pressure by rejecting merger proposals that "would mean monopoly profits for the few people who own the industry, and mass layoffs, worse conditions and reduced salaries for the thousands of workers who keep the industry going." During the summer and fall of 1942, as merger legislation continued its halting progress, the CIO-backed union lobbied against its insufficiencies and advanced its own five-point conversion program for placing the telegraph industry on a war footing. Its proposals again bonded government support for telegraph workers to strengthened public service standards of provision. And, aided by the radical New York Congressman Vito Marcantonio, ACA once more succeeded in staving off passage. However, fresh legislation, without the safeguards ACA wanted, was again drafted and, finally, it passed through Congress early in 1943. Despite members' efforts to move FDR to veto the bill, ACA now tried to induce the FCC to make the merger authorization contingent on explicit provisions for employees. Withal, on 8 October 1943 Postal Telegraph was taken over by Western Union, as Ulrikkson relates, "leaving a host of details as to seniority, differences in ACA and CTU contracts, bargaining units, and many others to be solved." In the end, the union had failed to persuade the administration, as Driesen phrased it, "to carry the ball for compulsory merger *with* safeguards for labor."[73]

Nevertheless, with CIO support, ACA had helped postpone the long-delayed merger for a period of years. Further, ACA to help wage this defensive struggle ACA had mounted a sustained campaign to demonstrate that its members' needs were fundamentally congruent, indeed, mutually intertwined, with those of the general public. In these and other ways, such as proposing that there be a labor representative on the FCC, as a part of its wider social unionism ACA had forged key elements of an independent union program for telecommunications throughout these years of struggle.

ACA at once pressed its case for arbitration by the National Labor Relations Board and the War Labor Board, attempting to institute protections for telegraph workers against top-down technological change. The CIO union now also renewed its efforts to organize Western Union. Having won its appeal to the NLRB, in 1940, that the Association of Western Union Employees was a company union and that, therefore, it must be disestablished, in the wake of the telegraph merger ACA had to strive to represent the employees of the now-combined company. Otherwise, it stood to lose jobs to its AFL rival.[74]

In 1944, the National Labor Relations Board ordered elections to be held in Western Union. The US Labor Department deemed the carrier's employees to be nearly evenly divided at the time, as between AFL and CIO union affiliates: 18,353 for ACA, 20,000 for CTU. Likely more than 20,000 additional employees either were members of the AFL affiliates IBEW or the Federal Labor Unions that had emerged out of Western Union's company unions—or else they had not joined any union. ACA stated flatly to organizers that "The majority of the Western Union employees are not in either union." Going into the election ACA appeared to be holding its own, with a commanding majority of members in Detroit, Duluth, Salt Lake City, some Midwest districts and—critically important—in Western Union's controlling hub in New York City, where it had won bargaining rights for 8,000 workers in 1942. Individual CIO unions and the parent confederation together spent over $75,000 on this campaign, and loaned organizers to the ACA to conduct it (Figure 5.4). ACA's guide for field organizers commenced with the statement that "The CIO has declared that the organization of the 60,000 employees of the Western Union Telegraph Company into ACA-CIO is the Number One organizational concentration for the CIO in 1944." The union understood that this endeavor would be as difficult as it would be vital. The stakes hardly could have been higher for the union. "This is a showdown contest between the American Communications Association, CIO and the American Federation of Labor to determine whether CIO or AFL shall represent these employees." The carrier, according to ACA, "naturally supports the AFL in an effort to restore company unionism among the employees, under an AFL label." For its part, the AFL recirculated a 1940 Dies Committee report on ACA's president Joseph Selly, which had ludicrously branded him in the words of a later historian as "one of the most dangerous individuals in the country."[75]

TELEGRAPH WORKERS IN DEPRESSION AND WAR 261

Figure 5.4 THE NO. 1 CIO ORGANIZING JOB THIS YEAR. In 1944, the CIO devoted substantial resources to its ACA affiliate's organizing campaign at Western Union, in the run-up to a contentious union election between ACA and the AFL-backed Commercial Telegraphers of America. Author's Collection.

The election handed CTU-AFL a decisive victory, with wins in six of Western Union's seven national divisions. ACA held only its existing stronghold: Western Union's New York metropolitan area headquarters. Despite this grave setback, ACA persisted in its social unionism and its other organizing drives.

Figure 5.5 Western Union Workers Are On Strike. Occurring within the massive nationwide strike wave in 1946, this thirty-three-day strike in New York City resulted in a significant wage increase for ACA members. American Communications Association, Local 10, New York, NY, records, 1931–1971, Call number: PH Mss 321, Wisconsin Historical Society.

A nationwide strike wave burst out during the two years that followed World War II, and in this context an ACA walkout for higher wages against Western Union in New York, in January 1946, drew more than 7,000 participants. Demonstrating strong solidarity, the workers' action lasted for thirty-three days and resulted in a victory for ACA (Figures 5.5 and 5.6). ACA tied ambitious bargaining goals to modest rhetoric: a 1946 flyer announced that "Western Union workers are on strike for a living wage." The union also progressed on its organizing drives in international communications. By 1947, the ACA held contracts with Western Union, Mackay Radio and Telegraph Company, RCA Communications, Commercial Cables, All America Cables, Commercial Pacific Cables, Press Wireless, Globe Wireless, Heintz and Kaufman, French Cables, Pan American Airways, over thirty broadcasting companies, and more

Figure 5.6 Bee-Line Bus Strikers TWU-CIO Support WU Strikers ACA-CIO. Worker solidarity in 1946 New York City—a union town. American Communications Association, Local 10, New York, NY, records, 1931–1971, Call number: PH Mss 321, Wisconsin Historical Society.

than sixty-five American steamship companies. With the CIO behind it, furthermore, ACA now trained its attention on the heartland of its jurisdictional grant. "Recently," wrote a historian in 1947, "the union, in competition with other labor organizations, has been making noteworthy progress in organizing the employees of various telephone companies."[76]

6
The Punishing Passage to Telephone Unionism

Most wage workers in the telephone industry labored for a uniquely entrenched unit of capital. AT&T was not only the nation's biggest corporation, but also its largest private employer. It also was an intransigent adversary of trade unionism. CIO President Phillip Murray captured this powerfully in 1949, *after* genuine telephone unionism had been achieved: "aside from the vast influence of such a financial giant on the economic lives of the people of the United States," AT&T "was also the last big citadel of anti-unionists left in the United States." "What made telephone management an especially forbidding antagonist," according to historian John N. Schacht, "was the antiunion leverage it derived from the structural and technological features of the industry, the social and job attributes of the work force, and elaborate personnel measures."[1]

Serving three-quarters of the nation's population, as local monopolies AT&T's operating companies exercised enormous leverage against their employees. It was all but impossible (as it had not been during the turn-of-the-twentieth-century era of independent telephony) for an employee to seek work with a competitor. "Workers, once they had been dismissed for union activity, would have to move from their home area to have any chance of regaining telephone employment." In addition, Bell operated as a veritable "caste system," remembered Joseph A. Beirne, who had been a Western Electric sales employee before becoming the first president of the Communication Workers of America. Interactions among workers were marked by "suspicion and distrust" across regional and gender lines, and these divisions were reinforced by the company's divisional organization into plant, traffic, accounting, and commercial departments, each with distinct skill requirements and hiring practices. The country's largest private employer of women, Beirne recollected that (male) Bell System managers "hate women, detest them." Employment discrimination in favor of native-born whites also was ingrained: in 1940 blacks comprised 10 percent of the US population and 0.7 percent of telephone workers. Often content that this racist employment discrimination lifted them above factory operatives, white telephone workers were far from averse to management's exclusion of Blacks.[2]

There were still other challenges to an effective industrial unionism. Mechanization around dial technology, begun in 1920 in reaction to the earlier cycle of employee self-organization, and half-complete by 1935, hampered union power: by foisting self-service work on telephone users the immediate impact of strikes was reduced. Pioneers of the open shop movement, after World War I AT&T executives also had responded to telephone operator militancy by instituting an unusually comprehensive program of paternalistic company unionism: an adroitly designed and elaborately implemented mode of labor control. After the Wagner Act made company unions illegal, AT&T reorganized its existing "employee representation plans" into more than 180 new labor organizations, whose independence from management remained ambiguous and whose very fragmentation inhibited mutualism and solidarity. After employees began to recreate these organizations as independent trade unions, the company still much preferred working with them than with unions affiliated with the AFL or, especially, the CIO.[3]

The number of wage-earners in the Bell System plummeted as the Depression worsened. Between 1929 and 1935, AT&T cut its labor force by nearly 40 percent, to 270,000 from 455,00; no less than 77,000 women telephone operators were fired. Other cost reductions were concurrently pursued, using methods that were familiar to telegraphers: shorter hours and part-time work, mechanization, and speed-up. Despite these travails, and despite the fact that, into the 1920s, their wages had lagged those of postal, utility, and manufacturing workers, in the aftermath of the Wagner Act telephone employees were better off than their brethren in the telegraph industry. AT&T's non–Western Electric employees' earnings placed them twenty-second on a Bureau of Labor Statistics' list of workers in 123 different industry groups. Both telephone- and telegraph workers recognized this disparity. Indeed, awareness of it helped motivate telephone workers to ally with their employer in resisting legislation to transfer AT&T's TWX and private-line telegraph wires to a merged Western Union/Postal Telegraph. In congressional testimony a telephone unionist in 1941 declared that "We have listened carefully to representatives of the American Communications Association describe conditions now existing in the telegraph industry, and, to put it mildly, they are subnormal in comparison with those in existence in the Bell companies. No good could come . . . through a transfer of our members to another company." Across this industrial chasm, a shared sense of working-class agency would not come easily.[4]

Many Bell System employees felt themselves to be generally set apart, and possessed little awareness of common purpose with other workers; interracial class solidarity in particular was far-removed. In keeping with Bell workers' distance from the larger labor movement, which took years to overcome, the story of telephone unionism has been told as if it were an internal metamorphosis: from company unions; to disjointed semi-independent unions representing a minority of employees and loosely connected through the National Federation of

Telephone Workers (NFTW); to the full-fledged Communications Workers of America (CWA), an industrial union that emerged in 1947 and affiliated with the CIO in 1949. This inward-looking account, however, does not fully explain the arduous passage to telephone unionism, which involved something other than the self-actualization of the CWA. The growth and strengthening of the NFTW and its metamorphosis into the CWA, instead were scored by struggles to fend off the left-led ACA's CIO grant of jurisdiction, until biting political and ideological changes persuaded CWA's leaders that an affiliation with one of the labor federations had become both needful and congenial. As Venus Green observes, telephone unionism therefore was marked by coalescing after both the early, hopeful surge of working-class self-organization and the peak political strength of the New Deal reform coalition.[5]

In 1938, Mary Heaton Vorse offered an impassioned account of "the growth of a people's power" through the emergence, over just three years, of industrial unions in rubber, steel, auto, mining, and other industries. "An incalculable force" she declared, had been unleashed with the formation of the Congress of Industrial Organizations. The new pathways of labor's collective agency seemed, at that moment, earth-shaking in their import. The CIO's program, wrote Vorse, "was the organizing of all labor into industrial unions, at the same time making the workers conscious of their political power." In actuality, the CIO experienced setbacks in 1938; more relevant here, Vorse hardly noticed the renewed stirrings of organization in telephony, undoubtedly because telephone workers were only just commencing on their struggle for an independent union. A hawk-eyed analyst of AT&T specified in 1939 that "Labor organization does not present any immediate problem to the Bell System," adding that "Although the International Brotherhood of Electrical Workers and lately the C.I.O. have tried to organize telephone employees, they have made little progress. The management of A.T.&T. has no immediate fear of limitation of its absolute power from this quarter." Eight years later, nevertheless, AT&T confronted a nationwide telephone union claiming 200,000 members; and, during postwar decades, this organization grew to be one of the largest and strongest US industrial unions.[6]

The rhythm and character of telephone unionism grew out of the industry's prior history. In the manufacturing, or "plant," segment of AT&T's sprawling operations an independent union had managed to subsist—the International Brotherhood of Electrical Workers, established in 1891—but, throughout the interwar period, the IBEW embodied the strategically defensive, often politically conservative, orientation of the American Federation of Labor. Evincing scant concern for the women telephone operators who made up the majority of the Bell System workforce, some of whom in turn had abandoned IBEW and their second-rank status within it, during the Depression years IBEW accorded a low priority to telephone organizing. After the Supreme Court upheld the legality of the Wagner Act—and during the great labor upsurge that powered the CIO's growth during 1937—Bell System workers began to transform their company unions into genuine worker-led organizations. This process was desultory, incomplete, and sometimes not genuine. Workers who had been appointed to preside over AT&T's "ten cent," or company, unions sometimes carried forward as leaders of the partially repurposed organizations that succeeded them. As some self-proclaimed "independent" associations formed, these organizations joined together to form a disjointed umbrella group: the National Federation of Telephone Workers. First organized in 1937-1938, NFTW lacked a fulltime president until 1941, and its members granted it no right to call strikes or to bargain collectively on their behalf. Power lay with its many autonomous, often noncooperating, union affiliates, who collected dues separately from one another; until 1946, NFTW officers' attempts "at some sort of a coordinating job," recalled Joseph Beirne, who became president of the NFTW in 1943, were largely confined to "exhortation"—writing letters and making telephone calls admonishing members to "stick together."[7]

Some NFTW affiliates also carried over company-union practices, like allowing supervisors to attend meetings and to jawbone about elections, and accepting management subsidies for office equipment and clerical work. Perhaps more important, they embodied the results of AT&T management's tactics, whose result President Beirne termed "the *separation* of people." Unwilling to cooperate "in anything but limited kinds of action," these differentiated groups found it all but impossible to present a united front to their employer. "Many members of these organizations," writes Venus Green, indeed "abhorred strikes and looked to the organization merely as a means to share information and possibly develop strategies around common issues such as pensions." The inheritance of company unionism also lingered, in "local self-sufficiency, distrust of militancy, grudging acceptance of worker status, and an ingrained sense of inferiority in dealing with management." For many who worked for Bell, even the NFTW was a bridge too far. The proportion of union-eligible Bell workers represented by NFTW unions rose above one-in-three only in 1945. Long and difficult was the transition, as the union later recalled, from a "loosely-knit federation of autonomous independent unions to a closely integrated international union"—and, thereafter, to a formal affiliation with the wider US labor movement.[8]

Whether it was the American Communications Association and the United Electrical Workers, both CIO affiliates, or the IBEW-AFL, outside unions found that the telephone industry presented a dauntingly inhospitable field. A faction within the NFTW did discern a need for a unified industrial union with nationwide reach; however, these activists also insisted that this prospective union still should be independent. In November 1943, the NFTW's monthly journal acknowledged that both the AFL and the CIO were "casting covetous eyes on the members of the Unions in the Telephone Industry, and that both of these organizations are embarking on ambitious raiding programs." NFTW candidly rejected the AFL, for being "top-heavy with a lot of old men who have outlived their usefulness." By contrast, NFTW acknowledged, "the social outlook of the C.I.O. is healthier than that of the A.F.L. and its entire program is more dynamic. But even with this organization, we can see little to be gained through affiliation." Subsequently, *The Telephone Worker* spelled out the CIO's chief defect, charging that ACA and UE were led by "party-liners" whose unions "are actually being used mainly as pipelines to infiltrate ideologies and forms of government, concocted, inspired and ordered in a foreign land."[9]

Opinion among members of the mutually mistrustful organizations which emerged from the chrysalis of AT&T's employee representation plans swung toward strengthening the NFTW, in order to counter AT&T's corporate power by channeling telephone employees' grievances and demands into the labor relations machinery now operated by the federal government. Confusing conflicts ensued. NFTW affiliates, small independent telephone unions, the IBEW, the ACA, and the UE—and, behind them, the AFL and the CIO—scrambled for representation rights over segments of the telephone workforce. AFL as well as CIO unions condescendingly, and mistakenly, called out NFTW affiliates for being company unions. Collective organization became a protracted process, scored by recrimination and contingency; it climaxed only as the New Deal project unraveled in the face of gathering attacks. For ten years, in the words of a leading participant, telephone unionism in turn seemed to proceed "isolated" from the main body of the labor movement.[10]

Going into 1944, IBEW staged raids on NFTW affiliates in Ohio, Connecticut and Louisiana. June McDonald recollected that AT&T preferred the IBEW over CIO-affiliated unions, and she testified that NFTW shared in its antagonism toward ACA and UE: ACA, she remembered more than twenty years later, "was a Commie outfit . . . Worked like dogs, those Commies. Don't put them down. They're workers, they're dedicated. . . . There is only one way to deal with a Commie—I learned that. You don't argue. You just get some wood workers or big steel workers and beat the hell out of them." NFTW's *Telephone Worker* was content to assail ACA rhetorically.[11]

In the industrial Midwest, especially Michigan and Ohio, some telephone workers sensed that they were not matching the progress made by the CIO unions: "Many of these people," Ruth Wiencek recalled, "had relatives among Auto Workers, Steel Workers, and they felt they wanted to be part of the labor movement." However, the CIO's intrusions also brought anger and acrimony. Beginning in 1940 the UE attempted to raid an NFTW affiliate, the Western Electric Employees Association, which was established in 1937 and affiliated with NFTW in 1939, at a big manufacturing plant in Kearny, New Jersey.

Unsuccessful, in 1942 the UE then charged before the NLRB that WEEA was dominated by Bell—that it was a company union. This invalid claim infuriated the NFTW, not only because refuting it required the fragile union to expend precious money and energy, but also because "the company domination charges against the Kearny union and against other affiliates of the NFTW are a planned campaign to use the NLRB as a tool for organizing" by the CIO. Thus they presented a "danger for all telephone workers." NFTW's attorney reported that the case was "kicked back and forth . . . from April 1942 to September of 1944," at which point the NLRB preliminarily upheld the UE's claim. As NFTW and WEEA contested this finding, the case seemed to constitute "the testing ground by the National Labor Relations Board with respect to Bell System labor unions, and it would be well for Bell System workers to keep a weather eye on this branch of the Government." NFTW had actually already been involved with the federal government through another years-long struggle to gain direct representation for telephone workers before the National War Labor Board. The problem it faced here was that, as a small unaffiliated union it lacked the weight of the AFL and the CIO—each of which possessed standing at the War Labor Board. In January 1942, in protest, NFTW union presidents refused to endorse the wartime no-strike pledge which had been signed by AFL and CIO leaders and left-led unions such as UE and ACA. In the aftermath of a strike by NFTW telephone operators in Dayton, Ohio, which threatened to spiral into a more general walkout, at the end of 1944 the NFTW succeeded in placing a couple of its affiliates' officials on WLB committees. These struggles not only enhanced the NFTW's prestige among telephone workers but also strengthened the union as a repository of expertise in the details of labor relations.[12]

On the West Coast, ACA built a regional base when the Order of Repeatermen and Toll Testboardmen affiliated with it in 1942. ACA President Selly was encouraged: "We have recently heard from telephone workers in San Francisco and New York raising the possibility of affiliation with ACA and we are trying to work something out along these lines." Selly waxed optimistic about ACA's prospects for organizing the telephone industry, in that "a trend seems to be developing nationally among affiliates of the National Federation of Telephone Workers toward a legitimate national affiliation with the CIO through our organization, the American Communications Association, which has jurisdiction in the field of communications." By 1943 ACA "had made inroads in some NFTW groups," while AT&T's Long Lines Telephone Workers union "pondered CIO affiliation." At a January 1943 meeting the federation's organizing director, Allan Haywood, eschewed the piecemeal efforts being made by ACA and UE: he had already determined that it would be best for the telephone organizations to enter the CIO as a single industrial union. Evidently, he was not certain that this should be ACA, as he informed the Long Lines union representatives "that he did not think it would be mandatory that the ACA have jurisdiction over all communications workers." ACA's Selly thereupon complained about this threatened transgression on ACA's jurisdiction directly to CIO President Philip Murray; but Haywood's reservations about ACA and UE efforts turned out to be a presentiment.[13]

Meanwhile, NFTW's difficulties were also compounding. Turnover in the Bell System—especially, in the Traffic department where telephone operators labored—was becoming unmanageable; the FCC's chief economist, Dallas Smythe told the NFTW affiliate in Pennsylvania that more than 187,000 workers in the telephone industry would leave their jobs in 1944—out of a total of 500,000 (425,000 of whom worked for Bell). Telephone workers chafed at management's arbitrary power, at regimentation, at inadequate pension provisions, at speed-ups engendered by the wartime spike in long-distance calling volume, and at their increasing deprivations as telephony lurched "from a high-wage to a low-wage industry." In Chicago, for example, telephone operators' weekly wages in October 1943 seriously lagged weekly living expenses. NFTW President Beirne asked: "What is wrong with a form of society in which a telephone girl's minimum expenses total $25.74 a week and her average wage rate is approximately $21.00 per week? The kindergarten class in sociology should be asked to answer that question." An NFTW operator, however, recollected that it was not only the "the lousy money," but above all working conditions that inspired her workmates to organize and to act: "if you rang a wrong number you got sent home, docked a day. You had to wear your hair a certain way, you had to wear hose instead of socks . . . We had on—what you called 'on-call days.' That is, they would schedule you to work four days a week and the fifth day you had to stay home and wait. If they needed you, they would call you. If they didn't need you, they didn't let you get paid for it. Oversupervision, we got treated like dirt."[14]

Strikes were rare, but walkouts did occur—notably, in Ohio and Illinois during 1942 and 1943. The November 1944 strike over wages by Dayton telephone operators spread to include 10,000 telephone workers, from Ohio to Detroit to Washington, DC, portending a nationwide shutdown. Only intervention by the War Labor Board prevented a paralysis of the nation's communications; and the event provoked threats of a government takeover. The Ohio union won not only new wage schedules but the establishment of a National Telephone Panel at the War Labor Board—which ultimately elevated two NFTW leaders as its permanent labor members and heard many dispute cases prior to its termination after the war's end. This was a breakthrough, as it granted the NFTW both legitimacy and formal standing. In a dozen-odd NFTW unions, meanwhile, militancy was spreading; among women telephone operators in the Traffic department it was kindled by thousands of poorly paid young newcomers. Even as NFTW's role grew, a conviction took hold that it needed to become more cohesively organized and assertive.[15]

ACA made some inroads and tried to parry competition from the NFTW. In February 1945, as the war in Europe neared its end and just weeks after its lackluster showing in the Western Union election, ACA's executive board received a report from Oakland telephone members of Locals 101 and 111. Kay Dmytryk, secretary of ACA Local 111, recounted that they had held a conference "to discuss our perspectives of conducting an organizing campaign in the traffic department of the Pacific Telephone & Telegraph Company." Immediately, she added, "It was generally agreed that because of the results of the Western Union election, the telephone staff will have to be conducted without the large sum of money and the large staff of organizers that we might have had if we had won in Western Union. The telephone campaign will have to be conducted from the inside by the workers themselves, with the help of Local 101 and the International." The conferees drew up a bare-bones budget, and soberly conceded that the obstacles to success went beyond Bell's opposition. Because "the National Federation of Telephone Workers is attempting not only to take over the existing telephone organization but to establish bargaining rights, it will be necessary for us to conduct a campaign and wage a struggle against the National Federation of Telephone Workers." These activists underlined an awareness that "the beginnings of ACA in telephone is (sic) in this Northern California area . . . We feel sure that the Executive Board know that the future of our organization in telephone, as well as the future of ACA, is at stake in this campaign."[16]

> A report by ACA Local 103's 350 telephone workers signaled still greater urgency, declaring that "the time has come for an all out drive to organize the half million workers of the Bell System"—beginning with AT&T's Pacific Telephone and Telegraph subsidiary and its 10,000 Plant and Traffic Department workers in the Los Angeles Metropolitan Area.
>
> We respectfully urge that the Congress of Industrial Organizations and the American Communications Association start the telephone organizing drive at once, for it is our belief that if the initiative is lost in 1945 as it was in 1919, the NFTW will "represent" the telephone workers in the same manner as the "Plan of Employees Representation" did in the past, and another generation of telephone workers will be denied the benefits of genuine collective bargaining.

Regional ACA offices indeed were established in San Francisco and Los Angeles. During a continuing wave of strikes throughout much of US industry in 1946, the union claimed an important victory when a commanding majority of eligible members of the Northern California- and Nevada-based Telephone Traffic Employees Organization voted by secret referendum to withdraw from NFTW in order to affiliate with ACA. At this stage, the ACA effort in telephony seemed to gather momentum. Chiefly because of its record in winning wage gains, the ACA was making "rapid headway in raiding the now restless membership of the NFTW unions"—not only on the West Coast, but also in Michigan and in Midwest units of AT&T's Long Lines Department. NFTW, however, harbored its own hopes of bringing all the West coast telephone organizations "into one big union," and it countered by establishing a Telephone Workers Industrial Union for this purpose. ACA charged that AT&T's Pacific Telephone and Telegraph Company had "encouraged and assisted" NFTW's effort, so that "at the present time practically all of the union-busting efforts of the Company are centered in TWIU." The TWIU did not succeed; and the ACA continued to hold to the invalid belief that the NFTW was not an independent formation of unions.[17]

As the war in the Pacific came to its apocalyptic end, US business leaders maintained a hard-and-fast opposition to wage increases and demanded that the government abolish its Office of Price Administration, which had exercised significant control over prices. Employees, on the other hand, faced both inflation-engendered reductions in real wages and a serious erosion of their gains in shop-floor working conditions and union grievance procedures. (There had been thousands of short, unauthorized wildcat strikes over employers' reassertion of control over the shop floor during the years of the "no strike pledge," especially in 1944.) Almost at once after the war ended, thus, labor-management conflict intensified and, during the autumn, it erupted. In the year beginning August 1945, more than 4,600 work stoppages took place, drawing in nearly five million workers and resulting in a loss of almost 120 million work days: 1.62 percent of all work-time during this interval. Underway, in fact, was "the most massive sustained strike episode in American history," according to historian Robert Zeiger. Starting with the auto workers, and rolling on into other heavy industries, already by February 1 one-quarter of the CIO's membership had walked out: electrical workers, meatpackers, and steel workers, followed by miners and railroad workers. Meanwhile, outraged at President Truman's attempt to use them to "squash radical nationalist movements" in China, the Philippines and beyond, tens of thousands of workers in uniform—often CIO members—were protesting at US military bases early in 1946, demanding immediate demobilization. Working-class power was, it seemed, poised for renewal.[18]

Telephone workers participated in this upsurge, above all through their unaffiliated NFTW unions. In November 1945, Illinois Traffic went on strike and picketed for six days. In December, an attorney for the NFTW unions, Henry Mayer, wrote to White House Assistant Labor Secretary John Steelman (who headed the Conciliation Service), "The telephone situation is still seething." There existed, he warned, "explosive potentialities": Mayer hoped "that we both can find some way to avert what would be in the nature of a public catastrophe"—a nationwide strike. Three different NFTW affiliates undertook strikes in January, 1946 and seventeen NFTW unions voted to strike together on March 7. This would amount to a nationwide shutdown of service. In keeping with its quarter-century of experience in managing employee relations, overconfident AT&T executives had made scant preparation. They were caught out by worker militancy, by the Labor Department's efforts to help reach a settlement, and above all by the unexpected unity displayed by the National Federation of Telephone Workers. Had AT&T not capitulated, the federal government probably would have intervened, as it did when it broke strikes by railroad workers and miners. Assistant Secretary of Labor John Gibson remembered that "In 1946, I had cleared seizure orders and was carrying them in my pocket for that purpose."[19]

However, minutes prior to the strike deadline that had been called by the Long Lines affiliate of NFTW, AT&T agreed to a wage increase—averting a nationwide walkout. For NFTW, this amounted to an epic victory. Not only did their pay gains, averaging 18 percent, rival those garnered around this time by the most powerful CIO unions (though the UAW and other CIO unions had demanded 30 percent increases), but the terms of the settlement were guaranteed by AT&T's top negotiator, Cleo Craig, to apply to workers across the length and breadth of the Bell System. This was huge, because it implicitly confirmed what AT&T had always been at pains to deny: that labor policies across its scattered operating companies and equipment plants were coordinated by AT&T executives at 195 Broadway in New York City. AT&T's concession demonstrated incontrovertibly that telephone workers would benefit from a strong union representing every nook and cranny of the gigantic system. The result also encouraged a belief among members of NFTW's fragile and often-riven affiliate unions that they had achieved what contemporary big business deemed an anathema: nationally coordinated bargaining rights. This in the face of the telephone company, a bastion of capital's strength.[20]

The sudden solidarity evinced by NFTW affiliates shocked not only AT&T but the AFL and the CIO. What was the character of this disjointed union? How cohesively had the spirit of unionism taken root among telephone workers? At the same time, the success of their 1946 near-strike instilled in many NFTW members a misplaced confidence and buoyancy. Telephone operators in the Detroit area "overturned the trucks," according to Ruth Wiencek, and "were probably as militant as any Auto Workers on strike": "the regimentation so typical of the telephone companies caused workers to finally kick off the control of Ma Bell over their personal lives ... sort of kicking over the traces." Indeed, Bell's informal policy of hiring as operators young women who lived at home with their parents in order to use this "family subsidy" as a rationale to pay low wages, now "kicked the telephone company right in the teeth because the gals who lived at home obviously could hold out longer and their families carried them along."[21]

Hoping to lift their wages in the face of unremitting inflation, in 1947 a majority of NFTW members pressed for a new round of industrial action against AT&T. Their leaders—and a significant minority of fellow-unionists—advised caution. Though none of the major strikes of the previous year had been defeated by employers, President Truman had broken the rail strike in May 1946—and unorganized workers, white-collar employees, farmers, and small business owners keyed into the propaganda being circulated by the National Association of Manufacturers and the commercial media and lost sympathy for unions. In the immediate postwar context of inflation, shortages of meat, housing, and other necessities, and a looming fear that a new Depression might soon engulf the nation, sentiment grew that union workers' wage gains were boosting prices and that their strikes were disrupting a return to normalcy. Thus the strikes and the limited wage gains they engendered came at a steep price. Not only were radical initiatives repulsed, such as a UAW proposal that General Motors should open its books so that the public could determine whether the auto company could indeed afford a wage increase with no comparable increase in the prices it charged for its cars. Above all, President Truman's decision to break the rail strike in May 1946, and the environing mobilization against labor by big companies, many politicians, and the commercial media, heralded a sharp move away from the New Deal settlement. Looking ahead, NFTW President Beirne was wary of calling a strike until after the federation's constitutional convention, scheduled for June 1947; Beirne foresaw that the convention would vote to replace the fragmented NFTW with a nationally coordinated organizational structure. Thus bolstered, Beirne hoped, even amid increasingly inauspicious circumstances NFTW might gain victory in a second confrontation with the telephone company.[22]

Beirne's background and thinking would play a long-standing role in telephone unionism. From an Irish Catholic family, Beirne's father had been a trade unionist and a railroad worker; Beirne himself became a salesman for Western Electric and, in the late 1930s, he abandoned night-school training for a prospective career as a lawyer and threw himself into the cause of telephone unionism. Beirne later held that the mission of "the working men and women of the nation" had been to "restore" pluralism to a society that had forsaken it. Between the end of the Civil War and the Great Depression, he believed, the "artificial creature, the single-minded corporation" had come to dominate US society. "For nearly 70 years there had been no force in America to counteract or even to contain the power of the corporations." However, as industrial unions established themselves in the late 1930s and 1940s, a "counter-force against the narrower goals of business enterprise" at last coalesced. A large industrial union could face even the largest corporation as "a tightly-organized, single-minded opponent and not a disorganized, idealistic crusade." Indeed the labor movement then turned itself into the "one substantial private institution... whose primary dedication is to the best interests of all the American people. It is the organization whose resources, manpower and money are used in the interests of all our people." Thus the "assertion of independence by labor," in Beirne's conception, "proved that pluralism was truly re-established." By "pluralism," he denoted a constructive "balance-of-forces, both economic and political, in our social structure." The labor movement had to bend its efforts ceaselessly to learn how "to be as close to the center of power as it can possibly get"; however, the existence of a "strong, permanent, on-going labor movement" allowed Beirne to persuade himself that an "electoral triumph for a conservative candidate will never again bring a return to the old ways." Beirne, in sum, held that organized labor was the key to establishing and maintaining a responsible democratic capitalism.[23]

In the moment, though, Beirne and a band of other NFTW officials were swept along by rank-and-file militancy. The result, in April 1947—two months before the union convention—was a strike in which telephone workers' primary goals were a large wage increase and permanent system-wide (national as opposed to local) collective bargaining with AT&T. It quickly became apparent that AT&T's spine had stiffened; a historian observes that, for the telephone company, "the crux of the dispute was recognition." In fact, as John N. Schacht explains, "The overriding issue in the 1947 strike was whether an ambitious union movement—one bent on acquiring large and continuing influence over the conditions of telephone labor—could survive management's attempt to destroy it." The fledgling NFTW suddenly found itself in a fight for survival.[24]

On the eve of the walkout, the Twentieth Century Fund assessed the state of collective organization in the industry, reporting that the NFTW included "39 autonomous but cooperating unions," joined by an additional 38 independent unions not affiliated with NFTW; furthermore, "about 15,000 workers are represented by seven AF of L unions and four CIO unions which are not parties to this dispute." The leading AFL participant was the IBEW; its CIO counterpart was the ACA. Militancy among telephone workers was not in question. In Chicago, the operators in the Traffic department "were one hundred percent," remembered one of them; and they were angry. Strikers' violence was met by overzealous policing, according to June McDonald, resulting in 1001 picket-line arrests; "one was a man. The rest were women." Helen W. Berthelot, who had started as an operator in 1923 and who would go on to become the CWA's Legislative Representative, recalled that "daring" women strikers "threw out marbles" when mounted police appeared. But would militancy be enough, in the face of a determined and massive corporate adversary, a still-fragmented union organization—and a federal government that had become, at best, indifferent? Both AFL and CIO leaders understood the portentousness of the telephone strike, not only for NFTW but for the labor movement in its entirety.[25]

The strike was a watershed. Schacht sums up its import: "It was the first nationwide telephone strike, the largest strike of 1947, a strike that reached into more communities than any strike in American history, and—since nearly two-thirds of the participants were females—the biggest walkout in the history of American women." Actually, unlike the World War I debacle, women and men participated together in this industrial action. Outside unions also contributed, not only through donations but also by lending support in the streets. In Detroit, teamsters told telephone operators where they could buy rotten eggs; seafarers came in one day "with their white hats, and they were great"; and in nearby Midland, "where all the mine workers were," Berthelot remembered, "I really had to talk fast to keep them from blowing in the door of the telephone building." NFTW-ers improvised disabling tactics in light of their knowledge of telephone labor processes: "we asked everybody... instead of boycotting the telephone, to use it to the greatest extent. They would make all kinds of long distance calls and person-to-person calls to crazy places and fictitious names and so forth... We wore them down."[26]

Perhaps above all, however, the 1947 telephone strike concurrently fed into a gathering process of political reaction. This counter-movement was constituted by interlocking domestic and international initiatives. The former took shape as the nation's business leaders and political conservatives seized the moment to try to "to rid the country of the New Deal," as the CEO of General Motors put it. The telephone strike had the misfortune to occur exactly within this moment of fraught political and ideological reversal.[27]

Some members of Congress denounced any interruption of telephone service. New Jersey Representative Hand proclaimed that the "Nation-wide telephone strike... is merely the latest of a long series of events which establish to my mind the absolute necessity for prohibiting strikes of such character." A few days prior to the walkout, Michigan Representative Hoffman posed to the House "the all-important question of what the Congress intends to do about strikes which injuriously affect public health, safety, and welfare, which is emphasized at the present time by the threatened industry-wide strike of telephone employees." New York Representative Reed luridly invited his peers to "Take the telephone strike now impending. We saw in the paper this morning the picture of a couple of babies that were saved because they were able to get the necessary drugs and get them quickly. Suppose there were no telephone facilities by which they could reach the right doctor, the right surgeon, or the right institution in order to save life? It could carry itself to a point where this would be anything but a free country when people are deprived of their life as well as their liberty as the result of a group tying up the country in such a way that it might almost be called murder of the innocent."[28]

The idea that in some key industries, walkouts were tantamount to a national emergency had been used, since the great railroad strikes of the late nineteenth century, to legitimate the use of governmental force against labor. Federal troops had crushed the 1894 Pullman Strike. Government had also instituted preemptive action, as when railroads, telegraphs, and telephones had been taken over by central state agencies during World War I; and again, during World War II, the federal government had repeatedly seized productive property to ensure uninterrupted operation. Extraordinarily, however, as the nation transited into the Cold War, plant seizures persisted. For nearly a decade beginning in 1945, the government took over assets in meat-packing, harbor tugboats, railroads, and bituminous coal—even though, according to a constitutional scholar, these measures "proved ineffective to prevent a stoppage on numerous occasions." Legal machinery to enable such government takeovers during peacetime was forged in 1947, in immediate proximity to the telephone strike.[29]

One week prior to the walkout, Representative Fred A. Hartley, Jr., Republican chairman of the House Labor Committee, introduced a bill to authorize the federal government to halt strikes by injunction in transport, utilities, and communications. This measure was distinct from the encompassing, and better-known, initiative that Hartley was concurrently pressing Congress to pass with his Republican colleague, Ohio Senator Robert A. Taft. The latter—the Taft-Hartley bill, which Hartley intended to report before the end of April—included provisions for dealing with "national emergency disputes"; these were in keeping with its broader aim of reining in the legal rights of working-class self-organization that the Wagner Act had granted twelve years earlier. Meanwhile, the Governor of New Jersey declared that, in the event of a strike, his state would seize the New Jersey Bell Telephone Company and, advised by his special counsel—who was a director of New Jersey Bell—he "pushed through the state legislature an anti-strike bill inflicting $10,000 daily fines against the striking unions and $250 to $500 penalties against individual strikers." In Virginia, Indiana, Massachusetts, Texas, and seven other states, legal restrictions were placed on strikes in public utilities. By April 7, the day the strike was to commence, a majority of Taft's Senate Labor Committee also informally agreed on and publicly released a specially added provision to the omnibus bill that was to become the Taft-Hartley Act, "to put down by Government injunction great strikes, such as that now silencing many telephones, where national health or safety was deemed imperiled." The threatened telephone walkout thus became a factor in a widening campaign of politically organized labor repression. As well, this time AT&T had prepared scrupulously; overconfidence characterized not executives but telephone workers.[30]

Urgency flooded the White House. Three days prior to the strike, Democratic President Truman announced that he had asked Attorney

General Tom C. Clark to clarify his legal authority to take over the telephone system; Clark responded the next day that the President did indeed possess that power. A "Telecommunications Coordinating Committee" was convened. Its composition closely tracked that of the War Communications Board (representatives were plucked from the FCC, and State, Treasury, Navy, War and Commerce Departments), offering a foretaste of the more encompassing Cold War machinery that was being established. The new group's "emergency committee," the FCC's Denny promised, would obtain "minute by minute information on the areas affected by the strike." It would organize a pool of government leased telephone facilities and emergency radio facilities "so that urgent government telephone traffic may be handled." And it would prepare an Executive Order "so that the President may be in a position immediately to take over the operations of the telephone industry if, in his opinion, the welfare of the country requires." Denny had, he added, already coordinated with Attorney General Clark to ensure that an Executive Order could be issued swiftly. Perhaps especially in New England, where telephone unionism had put down its deepest roots, some workers would have recalled—or recalled hearing about—Postmaster General Burleson's fearsome nationalizations during World War One. In any case, access to President Truman by NFTW officials was denied.[31]

During the strike's first two weeks, FCC Chairman Denny sent Truman advisor Clark Clifford memos discussing emergent developments, attached to which were colored maps detailing the strike's effects nationwide, as of 9 a.m. on April 7, April 8, and April 21. Denny's first memo already hinted that the strike was having a limited impact: there had been no interruptions to commercial and governmental leased line service; no interruptions to service on the broadcast industry's wire networks; and the Bell System's 20 million (out of 26 million US) dial telephones were purportedly unaffected. However, in one respect—critical to businesses and government agencies alike—the telephone strike *was* registering: long-distance service was crippled, as between two-thirds and three-quarters of the long-distance operators had walked out. Confirming this collapse in business service was a 40 percent spike in Western Union's telegraph traffic, as long-distance telephone users turned to this partial product substitute.[32]

Despite their suspicions about NFTW, ACA telegraphers added to the strike's effectiveness. In testimony before a Senate committee a few years later, J.L. Wilcox, a Western Union executive, attacked the ACA for having used the 1947 telephone strike to subvert management's power, by acting to support the striking long-distance telephone operators. Because, he stated, on the first day of the walkout the striking telephone workers caused "a little trouble" for long-distance service, Western Union's "business increased rapidly":

At such occasions as that, it is common practice for the company to indicate to employees that we might need them overtime, so that they can make necessary arrangements at home . . . So a notice was placed on the board that supervisors and operators would be held overtime that night. There is no obligation for the company to meet with the union to declare a state of emergency. We feel that is in our hands . . . But contrary to that, the union took the stand that it was necessary for the company to bargain with respect to a state of emergency.

Evidently reading from copies of handbills that had been posted by ACA members, Wilcox relayed that ACA had declared that "'we will determine our policy in regard to the so-called state of emergency'"; the next day, he continued, ACA had posted a sign on the union bulletin board stating "'No compulsory overtime. All ACA members must attend important meeting tonight. Optional to work overtime before the meeting.'"[33]

Western Union's capacity to furnish a product substitute for long-distance telephone service was thus obstructed. Of course, Western Union would wish to curtail this incursion simply on financial grounds; but it also made common cause with AT&T in combating worker solidarity in the face of ACA unionists' shop-floor power. ACA members' solidarity with the telephone workers occurred notwithstanding ACA's attempts to brand the NFTW a "phony" union with an ingrained deference to AT&T management. In addition, although NFTW was not affiliated with either federation, both CIO and AFL unions provided funds and other support to the telephone strikers. CIO rank-and-filers nevertheless did not exhibit uniform support for the NFTW walkout. Four days into the strike, complaints reached CIO president Phillip Murray that ACA members were acting to "disgrace all of organized [labor] by refusing to honor . . . picket lines" set up around Pacific Telephone and Telegraph properties in San Diego by the NFTW-affiliated United Brotherhood of Telephone Workers. The walkout in turn threatened to widen.[34]

At the moment of the 1947 strikes, sensations of hopeful optimism remained widespread about the prospective content and scope of organized labor's role within the postwar United States. Radical social unionism persisted in many unions and numerous individual rank-and-file workers. As Venus Green points out about the system's employees, Bell's behavior had "led many to question whether its employment and economic policies conformed to the standards expected of a public utility." Some telephone workers were nothing short of outraged. Vivian E. Pierson, Vice Chair of the Pasadena Local of the Federation of Women Telephone Workers of Southern California (an independent union), mentioned the Taft-Hartley law in a letter to President Truman in which she insisted that he must act to restore fairness and justice to the industry. "As one of many Telephone Operators, who though not on strike are observing the picket line," Pierson began, "I am appealing to you to intervene ... so that both sides will be forced to get together and arbitrate." Almost "all of our girls," she went on, "feel justified" in supporting the union's demand for higher wages "as most of us are supporting not only ourselves but one or more members of our family and find it very difficult on the present wage scale with prices so high." She went on to elaborate a bare-bone political rationale:

> A pay day to pay day living is not a decent living wage and if illness or accident or death strikes our families we are forced into the hole so deep that we are in debt the rest of our lives.
>
> The present Anti-Labor law is also most unjust, unless it can also control monopalistic (sic) management control, which is the real reason back of most strikes.
>
> We do not want to control management nor do we want to be controlled by them but we do request fair play + we do feel you can and should help us.

During the recent war against fascism, in addition, the industry's public utility status acquired additional interpretations, and these prompted further, and portentous, political demands. On the eve of the Second World War, an African American organization based in Cleveland, the Future Outlook League, printed and dumped thousands of handbills from downtown office windows that read: "DO YOU KNOW? that the Ohio Bell Telephone Company, a public utility and a monopoly, refuses to employ negroes solely because of their race; that this vicious discriminatory policy is the same thing that America is preparing to go to war with Hitler for; that this is a direct insult to American womanhood; that thousands of Negroes are being drafted into the armed forces of the nation to help protect the business in our city?" Possibly the Bell System's first black operator was hired in New Jersey, in 1943; black installers were employed in Chicago for the first time in 1942. African American employees were increasing in number; and in Detroit, at least, white women operators showed sufficient solidarity with black janitors, cafeteria workers, and cashiers that, Ruth Wiencek recollected, "not one black ... crossed the picket line" during the 1947 strike. Not for the first or the last time, the concrete responsibilities of a "public utility" were a live issue.[35]

Actually, however, only a year after the tumultuous strikes of 1946 both the politics of labor and the direction of public opinion had changed markedly. One week into the strike, following rejections of his proposals for a settlement by both AT&T and the NFTW, Secretary of Labor Schwellenbach discussed the walkout in an address carried to listeners (over AT&T lines) by the American Broadcasting System. The country's telephone system had been "severely crippled," thundered Schwellenbach. "The public has borne the brunt of this strike," he proclaimed, in a formulation that distanced the strikers from the wider community. By no means the most conservative member of Truman's cabinet, the Labor Secretary, who had thrown some support to NFTW earlier on, now picked up the rhetoric being used by right-wing legislators. He emphasized the pathos caused by this industrial action—rather than, for example, dramatizing the human vulnerabilities made by the declining real wages of telephone workers: "During this last week I have lived in mortal fear that as a result of this strike some child will be deprived of medical care; some women will be prevented from going to the hospital; some aged mother or father will suffer after being stricken—all because the telephone was not available." His recommendations for a settlement attempted, he said, "to reach a middle ground between the positions of the parties"; in turn, "The fact that both sides rejected my proposal indicates to me that it was a fair proposal— so fair that neither side wanted it." Keying in to reactionary laws under consideration by Congress, and others already passed by several states, Schwellenbach insisted that "What the parties to this dispute forget is that they are in a public utility industry. The health and the safety and the welfare off the people of the United States depends upon the constant maintenance of that industry." In conclusion, the Labor Secretary announced to his radio audience, "I am asking you who want telephone service, and who pay the telephone bills, to demand of each side that they accept the proposal which I made."[36]

Leaving aside that residential telephone ratepayers still accounted for only about half of all households, Labor Secretary Schwellenbach positioned a public caught between AT&T and its employees. Though this was in keeping with statements by other national leaders during this watershed moment, it marked a stark contrast with CIO rhetoric during the labor insurgency of the 1930s and war period, when CIO unions, ACA in particular, had purported to constitute the *guardians* of the public interest. This marked another rhetorical struggle. The president of the United Electrical Workers insisted before a Senate Committee early in 1946 that his union's near-concurrent nationwide strike was "in the interest of the entire American people." The rejoinder by his adversary, General Electric President Charles E. Wilson, demonstrated that the purported linkage between organized labor and the public was newly open to challenge: Wilson, who would go on to serve as a top Cold War official for President Truman, and as Secretary of Defense for Republican President Eisenhower, declared that labor was merely "one small segment of the public," a formulation that was congruent with Schwellenbach's. During and after the postwar strike wave, their characterizations rooted a still-fragile nascent common sense. By 1950 a Senate Report could specify that "It must never be forgotten that transcending the rights of the Bell System and transcending the rights of the unions is the paramount right of the public to have this great system of telephone communication, upon which our domestic economy is so dependent, operated without serious interruption." Far from accepting radical social unions as the public's spearhead, as ACA/CIO had hoped, in mainstream discourse labor and the public were diverging. Many un-unionized workers, white collar and professional workers, and farmers were weary of the disruptions to daily life caused by strikes during an already arduous process of reconversion to peacetime; they acceded without complaint to the idea that labor was a special interest. This in turn rendered even conventional unionists defensive, CWA President Joseph A. Beirne among them. In his union's newspaper, Beirne observed a couple of months after the strike that big business propagandists and right-wing politicians had "persuaded a lot of people, including some of our own members, that organized labor and particularly the leaders of unions, had no regard for the American public. That unions were almost anti-American, being run by either racketeers or Communists." His rebuttal, like that of CIO Legislative Director Irving Richter in May of 1947, did little to alter the perception.[37]

Contravening GE's President Wilson and Labor Secretary Schwellenbach—and also the growing unhappiness over strikes expressed by many Americans—a Gallup poll conducted coast-to-coast between April 11 and 21 found that twice as many people were in sympathy with the workers as with the company (though a "substantial number" expressed no opinion). "Even among those in homes with telephones," a news account related, "the weight of sentiment is more on the side of the workers than on the side of the company." Tellingly, among people in nontelephone homes—as so many households still were—"sentiment is about 3 to 1 with the workers." However, by 1947 most of the public were pleased for government to intercede, to reduce further disruption in the face of meat shortages and other problems of reconversion. The poll revealed "wide public support for the contention that the issues should be arbitrated and the workers return to their jobs. The majority of voters believe the Government should require the workers to go back to work while the strike is being settled." (It is worth noting that the poll found that "that feeling is especially strong among those in homes with telephones.")[38]

War mobilization, notably, the formation of the Board of War Communications and of the National Telephone Commission of the War Labor Board, had already narrowed attempts to vest public utility industries with greater responsibility for social justice. The 1946 elections, in which workers repulsed by Truman's antiunion actions and bellicose foreign policy threw support to Republicans, produced Republican majorities in both houses of congress for the next two years (for the first time since before FDR's election). This in turn injected further momentum into the nation's rightward shift. Even prior to their 1946 strike threat, "reservations about the propriety or feasibility of striking a public utility" had been expressed by some NFTW members. In 1947, meanwhile, AT&T showed no signs of backing down. After more than two weeks on the picket lines, the NFTW strikers began to lose confidence. AT&T then went on the offensive, seeking to destroy NFTW's fragile unity by offering what it termed "reasonable" wage increases to affiliated unions which agreed to abandon NFTW's coordinated bargaining program. Some affiliates held out, but others buckled; in a piecemeal process, the strike collapsed after about a month. "We're telling the company we're not part of the switchboard anymore," a telephone worker had proclaimed hopefully near the start of the walkout—but it did not work out this way. Just a few years later a novelist conjured up a telephone operator's "strained, white face, as if the black leech of the earphones had already drawn too much blood."[39]

Having just barely survived its strike against a resurgent AT&T, NFTW unions convened in June 1947 to establish a genuine industrial union: the Communication Workers of America. Weary and dispirited, they elected a slate of officers, including Joseph A. Beirne as their first president, and set about rekindling their members' spirits and rebuilding their union. They faced urgent unfinished business.

Into 1947, ACA's regional presence on the West Coast gave it hope that it might spring-board to system-wide predominance and thus begin to occupy in practice the jurisdiction granted by its CIO charter. By ACA's estimate, in the autumn of 1946 West Coast telephone unionists numbered about 45,000, divided into four areas and thirteen different unions. ACA claimed around 13,000 of these; NFTW around 16,000, and other unions around 16,000. The single largest bargaining unit, representing 12,000 workers, belonged to ACA: Local 120, which had been the Telephone Traffic Employees Organization. However, the context of telephone unionism was not only divided but also altering precipitously, as the CIO reframed its role and NFTW coalesced into an independent industrial union. Responsible were two intertwined changes: the emergence of CWA as paradoxically vigorous and vulnerable; and the rightward lurch of US politics. The final moves toward telephone unionism would be measured in four beats as these changes progressed.[40]

The first came in May 1947, as the CIO initiated a major new organizing campaign through its newly formed Telephone Workers Organizing Committee. TWOC was modeled on the CIO's temporary organizations for unionizing industries such as steel, paper, and textiles late in the 1930s, but now in the dramatically altered circumstance of postwar. Some successes followed. The CWA, in a lowball estimate, stated in 1948 that TWOC affiliated unions represented "about 35,000 members"; a year later, the now CWA raised this. The CIO's own figures, in contrast, purported that TWOC possessed 85,000 members. Some strategically important units of NFTW certainly were encompassed, whatever the correct figures, and TWOC included unions representing every field of telephone employment: plant, long lines, traffic, commercial, and accounting,

Western Electric manufacturing. The long lines workers (and the often IBEW-represented installers) held particular strategic value, as they alone among AT&T employees possessed a summary ability to shut down telephone service nationwide. As some NFTW unions and telephone workers threw in their lot with the CIO, the CWA faced a prospective threat to its independence. Internecine struggle followed.[41]

The CWA's newspaper cast TWOC as "a pressure instrument to push CWA into joining the CIO"—and a contemporary historian, Jack Barbash, agreed that TWOC was mainly intended as "a bargaining device to get CWA to look more sympathetically at CIO affiliation." CWA unionists had but barely forged an industrial organization; still very vulnerable two months after its formation, CWA protested that "launching of TWOC when phone workers were just coming out of their first nation-wide phone strike" amounted to an unconscionable "raid." TWOC, however, also threatened ACA. The CIO's decision to establish TWOC markedly altered the course of telephone unionism.[42]

From the perspective of CIO leaders, telephone workers had become a dangerous wild card. With the stimulus of World War II mobilization and the snowballing success of governmental network expansion projects, the industry's work force had doubled: no fewer than one out of every 70 nonagricultural and nongovernmental US employees was a telephone worker. The union that had emerged to represent these workers, however, was weak, incomplete, and unaffiliated with either labor federation. In the wake of the strike, CWA thus posed a real threat both to organized labor's economic gains and its increasingly uncertain political clout. "The movement cannot sit idly by and permit these workers to be kicked around and to endanger by their weakness the whole national wage structure," tensely explained the CIO's vice president and director of organization Allan S. Haywood, as he justified TWOC. Research conducted by the CIO showed that, with average hourly earnings of over 80 cents, "the telephone workers were 18.3 cents better off per hour in 1939 than the average worker in manufacturing." But by 1947, even after their gains in 1946, telephone workers' hourly wages now lagged those in manufacturing by 2 cents; while, computed on a weekly basis, the differential was greater. Telephone employees' wages had dropped below those even of telegraph workers.[43]

Also alert to these developments, the rival AFL likewise exhibited definite interest in CWA; indeed, negotiations to bring the CWA into the AFL became serious in the aftermath of the 1947 strike. Owing to the strength within the AFL of the 400,000-strong International Brotherhood of Electrical Workers, however, the AFL refused to offer CWA independent status as an international affiliate, but only a subordinate position within the IBEW. The AFL had acted comparably before, with respect to the United Electrical Workers in 1935–1936 and, more directly, to what had become IBEW's Telephone Operators Department during the

1910s. AFL-IBEW attempted to portray its offer to CWA in a spirit of egalitarian unionism, purporting that "The women members in the branches have equal rights in every way with the male members, locally and nationally." However, rather than preserving CWA's hard-won and still-fragile identity, the AFL-IBEW would have dispersed CWA members into both existing and fresh IBEW units. It is worth pondering how IBEW's proposal would have resonated among CWA telephone operators in 1947, some of whom held memories of IBEW's earlier demeaning treatment of their own, or their mothers' or sisters' or aunts', militant trade unionism.[44]

Forced into a defensive crouch by the nation's largest corporate employer, and now faced with the AFL's insulting proposal, CWA leaders for their part were painfully aware of the risks to their union. Within CWA, elements of support for the CIO were present. As Schacht relates, "strong movements for TWOC affiliation were underway" in several NFTW/CWA unions and, as mentioned, a few of these groups actually resigned in order to join the TWOC. Ruth Wiencek recollected President Beirne's statement—"I've appointed a pro-CIO committee"—as he convened a group to study issues of affiliation. Nevertheless, both CWA officers and many, perhaps most, CWA members harbored reservations about the CIO's continued opposition to US foreign policy and, specifically, toward ACA, whose "reputation as a left-wing union was always a barrier to its organizing telephone workers."[45]

In this context, the CIO's decision to establish TWOC in order to bring telephone unionization directly within the federation's control constituted more than a revamped organizing strategy: more than a pragmatic improvisation in light of the fact that CWA's membership outstripped that of ACA by an order of magnitude. Keying into a highly charged moment in national politics, the CIO's creation of TWOC also enabled anti-Communism to permeate further into the labor movement, even helping to reshape the labor federation's overall stance on Communism. The crucial factor was an interrelated second dimension of the US swing to the right: CIO leaders' embrace of an aggressive Cold War foreign policy.[46]

Elements of a "cold war in the working class" had long been present; AFL unions, led in this case by IBEW, had been red-baiting CIO rivals since the 1930s and continued to do so. As early as 1940, Steven Fraser writes, "anticommunism was bidding fair to become the new civil religion of American politics, a black box of all the fears and resentments about what the New Deal had done and might still do to a mythologized American republic; an obsession that despite the putative object of its wrath, had precious little to do with the Soviet Union." Yet this "civil religion" remained contained until mid-1947. Anti-Communism was checked by the wartime alliance between the US and the USSR, by the persistent hopes of much of the working class for postwar cooperation through the United

Nations and by its widespread anti-imperialism, and finally by the CIO's own unwillingness to break ranks with its leftists. In the Spring of 1947 all this changed definitively. In turn, not only the New Deal state's domestic welfarist policies but also the CIO's "outspoken opposition to colonialism, interventionism, and anti-Sovietism" became targets.[47]

The US embarked on a program of Cold War containment not because its political and military leaders feared attack from the war-damaged Soviet Union but, as historian Melvyn P. Leffler emphasizes, because they were committed to preempting Soviet power internationally. A dramatic escalation and, indeed, an institutionalization of anti-Communism was essential to this purpose for, as Steven Ashby has demonstrated, early in 1947 Americans—notably, CIO members—were not persuaded that US foreign policy should be, or become, anti-Soviet and imperialist. In the run-up to the 1946 presidential election, the New Deal coalition had come unglued, as many workers turned their backs on the Truman Democrats' strike-breaking and anti–price control policies—with high inflation, shortages were hitting everything from meat to housing. Despite CIO leaders attempts to rouse workers to vote for the party, the Democrats were routed. Truman and his advisors decided in the aftermath of the by-election to pursue an aggressive political counter-initiative. To bring the American people to acquiesce to permanent peacetime military forces stationed at bases across the world (and, he hoped, to bring them to support his bid for reelection in 1948) Truman determined to frighten them, by declaring that it had become urgent to embrace a bellicose anti-Sovietism.

First came his executive order mandating loyalty oaths for government employees; Secretary of Labor Lewis B. Schwellenbach pushed to legally outlaw the Communist party. The Truman Doctrine, announced with massive publicity in March 1947, spelled military aid to Greece (where Britain could no longer afford to fight) and Turkey, and portended comparable campaigns against radical insurgencies elsewhere. This heavy-handed militarism was, however, widely unpopular: many workers, as Ashby argues, preferred for US foreign policy to be anchored in Roosevelt's UN-based international cooperation. The tide of popular sentiment began to turn only after Truman purported to endorse economic aid over military action. Three months later, the Administration announced a rollout of the Marshall Plan. Commonly named after General George Marshall, now Truman's Secretary of State, this Economic Recovery Program stressed that a massive US economic aid program would elevate living standards in a shattered Western Europe, preventing popular unrest and the threat of Communism—and administering a big boost to the US's own economy: thus, the Marshall Plan was sold as serving US workers' class interest. This was a turning-point.[48]

Political discourse narrowed vertiginously. As the president took over from Britain the role of repressing democratic self-determination in Greece and initiated Marshall Plan aid to Europe, employers, commercial news media outlets, politicians, and congressional committees coordinated, circulated, and amplified the message of anti-Communism. The war against the New Deal thereupon converged with a foreign policy that sought to ring the world with permanent US military forces stationed at hundreds of bases. What historians call the "second Red scare" escalated. Willing to wield it in internecine struggle, CIO Rightwingers—notably the socialist Walter Reuther of the United Auto Workers and the social democrat James B. Carey of the United Electrical Workers—found that their liberal social-democratic affinities were a poor match against the fearsome political reaction that had ensued.[49]

One institutional actor that sought to cultivate anti-Communist sensibilities among workers, notably telephone workers, drew on bonds of religion. Trade unionists overall were disproportionately Catholic and, during the 1940s, some well-connected church leaders organized conferences, labor schools and a specialized organization to expunge Communism from organized labor: the Association of Catholic Trade Unionists (ACTU). CIO unions, particularly left-led ones, faced ACTU opposition caucuses within their ranks, as groups formed to disrupt their programs and to discredit their leaders. Both the United Electrical Workers and the American Communications Association were targeted. By contrast, Joseph Beirne of the NFTW/CWA was an active ACTU supporter. Less than one year after TWOC's formation, an official of a CWA-affiliated telephone equipment workers union wrote to Beirne, expressing hope that "Joe" would accept his invitation to address an ACTU-hosted breakfast "since it will give you a chance to tell our story to a diversified group of Unionists who I'm sure will evince more than a passing interest in what you say." Beirne accepted, confiding to "Jimmy" that he would "do everything possible to make the other three speakers look like amateurs."[50]

Anti-Communism was by no means confined to the ACTU. "The onslaught against the unions whose members and leaders were in or close to the CP came from all sides," writes historian Ellen Schrecker. Corporations, news media, voluntary associations: "all joined forces to drive Communists out of the labor movement. But it was the federal government that guaranteed the success of the endeavor." The Taft-Hartley Act was one key benchmark. After much politicking to contain and constrict trade union power, in June 1947, a Republican Congress passed the act over Truman's veto. Taft-Hartley supplanted pro-labor provisions of the 1935 Wagner Act with onerous restrictions on union organization and tactics, and confined unions to working within a narrowed legal and administrative mechanism for collective bargaining. Formally titled the Labor-Management Relations Act of 1947, it was the "culmination of an anti-labor drive which had begun during World War II"; and the Act was fueled not only "by the spectacle of the steel, auto, and electrical unions simultaneously on strike in 1946" but, as we have seen, also by the concurrent telephone strike. Among its other impositions, Taft-Hartley required that in order to gain NLRB jurisdiction a union's leaders must sign a non-Communist affidavit. This provision hit against all the left-led unions, including ACA and UE, and became a rallying point for ACTU-inspired opposition to leaders who refused, on principle, to compromise their union's independence. At stake was far more than the existence of Communists in unions. Taft-Hartley, writes historian Steven Ashby, "was designed to 'contain' the labor movement, hamper further union organizing, force the union leadership to police their own rank and file, and limit strikes." He explains that the legislation "banned all the tactics used by militant rank and file unionists to build the CIO and to expand the AFL in the 1930s. . . . What was at issue . . . was the whole future strategy of the labor movement: would labor fight the business offensive and the red scare with the militant tactics of the 1930s, or 'cooperate' with business?" Beyond even this, Taft-Hartley also struck at CIO members' assertive participation in the wide-ranging radical-reform organizations of the cultural front, which had characterized the late 1930s and the war period.[51]

Elevating a particular interpretation of how "to protect the rights of the public in connection with labor disputes," Taft-Hartley stipulated that "employees and labor organizations" could be penalized for engaging "in acts or practices which jeopardize the public health, safety, or interest." It also empowered individual states to pass "right-to-work" legislation "that stripped unions of powers that the NRLA had conferred on them." That Taft-Hartley did not eliminate collective bargaining per se, despite pressure to repeal the Wagner Act altogether brought by right-wingers such as newspaper magnate Frank E. Gannett, hardly diminished the force of its sanctions. Above and beyond the specific restrictions and conditions that it imposed on unions, the law's import lay in signaling "that the social and political 'revolution' of the New Deal years" was being "burnt out"—that business was regaining its power. Taft-Hartley—"a slave-labor law," in the view of contemporary labor leaders, not all of them leftists—was what historian Nelson Lichtenstein characterizes as "a fulcrum upon which the entire New Deal order teetered."[52]

Taft-Hartley was one among several converging developments that convulsed and reshaped the US polity. The 1948 election confirmed the reversal. Attempting to keep alive a New Deal domestic program and a United Nations-centered foreign policy, Henry Wallace—who in 1945–1946 had been seen by many CIO members and likeminded others as Roosevelt's heir-apparent—barnstormed to large crowds in 1947. He then undertook a somewhat reluctant bid as a third-party candidate in the upcoming presidential election. His Progressive Party championed a renewal of New Deal priorities, and a policy of cooperation with the Soviet Union in international relations. Castigated by the commercial media and mainstream Democrats for being a stooge of the Communist Party, and damaged by the CIO's rejection and its belated decision to support Truman, Wallace confronted working class voters who were increasingly skeptical if not simply indifferent. He went down to crushing defeat. The Dixiecrats, another new party led by South Carolina's arch-segregationist Strom Thurmond, fared better, winning four Southern states. Truman managed to eke out an upset victory over his Republican challenger Thomas Dewey; and the Democrats regained control of Congress. Within this altered forcefield the ACA and other left-led unions, which had rejected CIO federation policy and supported Wallace, now became pariahs; by contrast, the CIO's Rightwingers decisively advanced. Backed by a solid majority of members, and hoping for a revival of government support, they threw themselves behind Truman's Cold War program.[53]

In 1942, then-president of NFTW Paul Griffith wrote to request a message of greeting from President Roosevelt, to welcome NFTW's national convention in Baltimore; the Labor Department intervened, stating that the Labor Secretary would send a message, and recommending that FDR not do so—on grounds that "This is a company union." Two years later, by contrast, the Administration responded amicably to the ACA—still a CIO affiliate—and supplied a greeting from the Labor Department on behalf of the President to the left-led union's Kansas City convention. Finally, as the 1948 presidential election neared, the CWA granted a forum for the hard-pressed President to address its members. The next question for the telephone workers was whether to affiliate with the CIO. At this moment, the CIO was reluctantly announcing its endorsement of Truman as it became determined to preserve its affiliation to the Democratic Party, even above intra-federation solidarity if that became necessary.[54]

The NFTW and then the CWA had dropped hints that the CIO might win their affiliation if it would turn its back on the ACA. *The Telephone Worker* had castigated ACA throughout the war; a September 1945 article headlined "The CIO Should Clean House" charged that "an extreme radical fringe" controlled NFTW's rival. The American Communications Association, declared the report, "has as much chance of taking over the telephone industry as the Communist Party has." Two months later, the NFTW organ offered an extended editorial comment, in which it stressed jurisdictional infighting over the proper course of telephone unionism *within* the CIO and portrayed this—validly—as part of a larger battle "between the Communists and what might be called the less radical group." The CWA hammered away at the issue, underlining its leaders' ideological alignment during this historic moment of transition: "If the Telephone Workers Organizing Committee is to allow itself to be infiltrated with Communists," charged the CWA early in 1948, "telephone workers have a right to know it." The formation of TWOC in itself proved insufficient, therefore, to induce the CWA to affiliate with the CIO. CWA wanted additional guarantees.[55]

The CIO's TWOC had been created as a response both to external pressure and internal division. From the moment of the federation's own formation there had been "multiple and intersecting lines of fracture" within the CIO and, over time, collisions intensified as CIO leaders chose to pursue their political affiliation with the Democratic party over other commitments. The CWA's nasty comment about TWOC's relation to ACA at the end of 1947—that "the CIO realists have little stomach for pouring more money down a rathole"—captured this. TWOC's shifting character constituted a second beat, as the CIO began to muscle ACA aside.[56]

Intended as "an interim organization that was to enlist members and eventually be converted into a full-fledged telephone workers' union," TWOC established for other telephone unions "an avenue of affiliation that did not require joining the ACA or UE." When considered in light of the fact that, like ACA's CIO charter, CWA's constitution laid claim to the whole field of communications work, the CIO's formation of TWOC therefore potentially portended a mortal threat to its left-led telecommunications union. Were CWA and TWOC to join, the result would be more than a jurisdictional rival to ACA. It would establish with CIO backing a full-scale replacement—a successor. Yet there was little that ACA could do. In September 1947, three months after TWOC's establishment, President Selly reported on ACA's recent record to Allan S. Haywood, CIO vice president for organizing and a leading member of the federation's ascending anti-Communist wing. Appointed point-man for TWOC, Haywood tallied up ACA's NLRB- and direct election victories in around twenty cases, in the shipping, airline, radio, submarine cable, and broadcast industries—while Selly pleaded that "Telephone has been the major concentration of the union in the past year."[57]

Haywood now "viewed with grave concern the multiplicity of independent unions attempting to operate in the telephone industry and the ineffectiveness of such a confusing structure in obtaining for the telephone workers the wages and working conditions that their services justify. The denial to these workers of full participation in the councils of labor, thereby has enabled the telephone companies to capitalize on such isolation to the detriment of the workers involved and the labor movement as a whole." The 1947 telephone strike, "in spite of unprecedented support and public approval," had "failed in its main objectives." During what the federation now allowed had been the "pioneering period" prior to the 1947 strike, ACA had made a "splendid effort . . . at the cost of many sacrifices"—as a result of which "the message of the C.I.O. has been brought" to many telephone workers, especially on the Pacific Coast. Initially, the CIO still hoped to unite in TWOC groups of telephone workers who were represented through ACA with others, whose membership came through TWOC itself. In December 1947, the CIO declared that "they should and must be brought together in order to eliminate any possibility of confusion and to bring added strength to all of them." Quickly, perhaps predictably, this arrangement proved unstable, as TWOC hovered between two stools: representing ACA and attempting to draw in CWA.[58]

A member of Beirne's committee to explore affiliation with either the AFL or the CIO recounted that "finally at one of our meetings we were told that the CIO would tell the American Communications Association that they would prefer that the ACA would release the ... CIO from the jurisdiction which they held." A small union, nowhere near on a par with the Steelworkers, the Autoworkers, or the Electrical Workers, once the CIO determined to create TWOC, ACA had little choice but to cede its domain in telephony to the new organization; in return, according to ACA President Selly, early in 1948, CIO President Philip Murray reassured him that the CIO would "assist us financially to maintain and expand our organization." In private, Murray told Selly, "I want to take this opportunity of commending you for your unselfish and splendid cooperation in bringing about agreement and understanding on the question of the transferring of your telephone workers' local unions into the Telephone Workers Organizing Committee. I know that you and your associates and your members have put in much effort, not to mention the cost of organizing these workers into your organization." The matter of its jurisdictional charter now resolved, ACA was actually being pushed out of the telephone field. TWOC had subsumed ACA's jurisdiction over telephony, in a nominally genteel step toward what turned into an openly vituperative end-game.[59]

Beginning in Fall, 1948 and continuing in the run-up to the CWA's third annual convention in 1949 came a third beat in the final movement to telephone unionism. This one commenced in the margins, as CIO leaders contemplated how to respond to a raid against ACA by another CIO affiliate, the "American Radio Association." The context was ACA's effort to gain a union contract covering 900 members at the Mackay Radio & Telegraph Company, an international carrier owned by I.T.&T. The crux of the problem between ACA and the American Radio Association lay in the Taft-Hartley Act's requirement that union officers sign non-Communist affidavits to qualify for representation before the National Labor Relations Board. ACA leaders had refused to do this, on grounds that this provision of the act comprised an infringement of constitutional rights; and they had joined a legal challenge to Taft-Hartley by the United Steelworkers, which was moving to the Supreme Court. While ARA's leader, who was asked to clarify the situation by CIO officials, concurred with other mainstream labor leaders that "opposition to the signing of the non-communist affidavits is commendable," he went on to charge that this stance betrayed the interests of the Mackay workers merely to sustain the Communist Party's current line: "let the officials of ACA sign the non-communist affidavits and demonstrate that they will fight for the interest of the workers and the ARA will withdraw with the consent of those workers." In this charged context, with rank-and-file communications workers as well as ACA officials writing CIO leaders to express shock and indignation at the federation's acquiescence to strike-breakers, dismissals, and incursions by the ARA, CIO leaders reversed their prior vote in support of ACA in favor of ostensible neutrality as between ACA and ARA.[60]

This ugly skirmish possessed national import. The CIO's General Counsel Arthur Goldberg telephoned ACA President Selly to urge that ACA join the Steelworkers in requesting that their Supreme Court challenge to Taft-Hartley be postponed. He asserted, Selly recounted, that CIO leaders believed that argument on this issue before the Court, "and consequent publicity on non-Communist affidavit," would "jeopardize the legislative situation in regard to repeal." Selly convened ACA's Executive Board to consider Goldberg's recommendation. Although members of the Board proved "extremely reluctant" to postpone the Supreme Court test, they did so at Selly's urging. Uncomprehending that the CIO "had failed to stop this raid" by ARA, the Board specifically requested that Selly convey their sentiments to Murray:[61]

> "We have written you on several occasions in the past month, asking that you take action to restrain the ARA from continuing its raiding activities, and we have not to date been favored with a response from you. Under the present circumstances, where we have given up an important weapon in our fight by agreeing to your request for postponement of the Supreme Court case, the Board feels that the least we can expect from you is immediate action to prevent the ARA from continuing its unconscionable raid against our union."[62]

The CIO's response was perfunctory. The federation's Assistant Organizational Director, R.J. Thomas, wrote ARA to state: "In my judgment the ARA should respect the jurisdiction of the ACA and cooperate in every way to bring about the greatest protection for these workers within the union they originally belong" (*sic*). But raids against ACA persisted, within a wider context of union raiding. A raid against ACA initiated in 1950 brought into CWA its first nontelephone unit; one member of this group was Morton Bahr, who rose within CWA officialdom to become its president in 1983.[63]

The CIO's actions to preempt ACA succeeded in enticing a months-old CWA to join the federation. The CIO's victories in unionizing some of the nation's most resistant employers in steel, auto, electrical, rubber, and other industries; and the confidence of federation leaders that "they are capable of dealing with the largest of all Corporations—The American Telephone and Telegraph Company," was of course a major motivation. CIO's political standing at the National Labor Relations Board, its members' joint strength as affiliates of a six-million-member federation, and its "no-strings attached" promise of autonomous international status and industry-wide jurisdiction portended that "the job of dealing with AT&T, the real owners of the major part of the telephone industry, will become easier." CWA President Joseph A. Beirne notified AFL-IBEW executives that "The structure of the corporate control in the industry, namely, A.T.& T., makes it imperative that telephone workers be together in one union and with a set of rules that will permit them to act as a unified group." Though CWA constituted the largest labor organization in the telephone industry, by one account representing 42 percent of the Bell System's nonsupervisory workers, it still spoke for a minority. (TWOC represented an additional 15 percent, the AFL's IBEW about 4 percent, and nonaffiliated independent unions fully 35 percent of AT&T's workers.)[64]

After formal letters were exchanged between CIO and CWA in February 1949, CWA members then voted two-to-one to accept their Executive Board's recommendation to affiliate with the CIO; the machinery needed to merge the CIO's TWOC unions into CWA was immediately crafted. Chartered as CWA Divisions were eleven TWOC affiliates, representing employees at AT&T Long Lines, Western Electric's Installation Division, four Bell Operating Companies and two independent telephone companies. If CWA thus began to centralize its organizational structure, however, then this process remained incomplete. Affiliate unions continued to collect their members' dues, forwarding a per-capita sum upward to the international "when they got around to it," as Joseph Beirne later recollected. As against other big industrial unions, CWA had not yet attained a "two-level" structure, with local unions chartered and overseen by the international. Only in 1950 would CWA members approve a second restructuring, instituting the two-level framework in which members sent their dues directly to the international, which in turn sent a proportion of them back down to the locals.[65]

On May 9, 1949, the CIO formally presented a charter to the CWA, bringing into its ranks the largest single group of workers—though probably fewer than the claimed 350,000—since the affiliations of the CIO's founding unions. CIO Vice President Allan S. Haywood hailed this as "the most significant development in the history of collective bargaining in the telephone industry." AT&T's bargaining power, derived from the isolation and disunity of its workers, now could be challenged by a nationwide CIO union. Telephone workers "will begin to achieve the industrial democracy which has already become an accepted fact among other organized workers." As a result, Haywood promised, pensions, wage rates, grievance procedures and conditions of employment "will begin to overtake those enjoyed by other CIO members." For Haywood, CWA's affiliation also portended greater political empowerment for labor. Not only would CWA generate for the CIO "an opportunity to bring its message, through these workers, to millions of citizens in small-town and rural areas who have heretofore been isolated from CIO members," and thereby strengthen and extend "labor's political arm." Because CWA constituted "the largest single white collar workers' union," as well, "these new CIO members will inspire and lead all other white collar workers into the field of organized labor." TWOC unions were amalgamated into CWA two months later. Backed by $350,000 in national CIO and individual CIO union fund pledges, CWA thereupon launched an organizing drive to bring more telephone workers into its ranks. ACA could only look on.[66]

Philip Murray's 1949 address to CWA's convention recognized that "the greatest profits in history [had been] made last year at the expense of the buying public," and charged "that big business is actually conducting a 'cold war' against the people of the United States" by trying "to destroy the trade union movement." Following these accurate but also self-serving remarks, Murray welcomed CWA members into the CIO by proclaiming his federation's embrace of the Cold War: "I am going to recommend to the CIO Convention, which opens October 31 in Cleveland, that a constitutional amendment be adopted to bar any organization from representation in the CIO Board or in the CIO Councils which fails to live up to the decisions of our convention or to the Constitution. The CIO is no place for those who place loyalty to the Communist Party above loyalty to the Government, the CIO and the labor movement." And then, if additional reassurance were needed, he concluded: "Thank God both CWA and TWOC are free, clean organizations with no taint of Communism."[67]

The fourth beat hit with the CIO's expulsion of ACA and ten other unions, representing nearly one million members, on charges of "Communist domination." Initiated during the Spring of 1949 after Truman's reelection, and ratified the next autumn at the 11th CIO Convention, the burnt offering was actually made in June 1950 at the verge of the Korean War. Amid all the other changes it wrought, the US mobilization for this war also sped intensive militarization of electronics and networking: the first step in a series of changes that would ultimately reconstitute the telecommunications infrastructure. ACA, meanwhile, persisted in its social unionism, defending itself against repression while still episodically seeking greater justice in telecommunications and beyond through the 1950s and into the 1960s.[68]

Conclusion

In retrospect, the obstacles to telephone unionism appear even more daunting than they did in the moment. A workforce that was scattered across the country; fragmented by craft, fractured by gender, and marked by a systematic racist discrimination; schooled in the practice of company unionism by one of the country's most formidable units of capital; and caught up in labor's own internecine political struggles: in these inauspicious circumstances telecommunications workers' achievement of a bona-fide union was a miraculous triumph—and a last hurrah of New Deal–era collective self-organization. We have seen, though, that this victory exacted a steep price. CWA's emergence both attested and contributed to deep splits in the working class, which damaged and severely restricted the uninhibited social unionism that had flourished throughout depression and war. This would give US policymakers a freer hand in their imperial foreign policy and inhibit class solidarity across racial and gender differences for decades to come. It would also diminish the likelihood that the dominant union in telecommunications would prepare and pursue an independent working-class agenda for network equipment and services.

CWA's formation and affiliation with the CIO did, however, help organized labor on its way to becoming a key participant in the Democratic party coalition and a junior partner in the US state. In fact, the federation had already taken steps to align itself with US foreign policy and, in 1947, the European Recovery Program (the Marshall Plan) had "revived the CIO's hopes for an international role"—which it got. When asked what the CIO obtained from CWA's affiliation a CWA leader thus forthrightly responded: "A good right-wing union with intelligent union members who exercise their brains for the benefit of all." To be sure, the young CWA harbored an ambitious domestic reform program. In 1945, its journal, *The Telephone Worker,* espoused "some measure of centralized control over the economy" to alleviate capitalism's propensity to crisis, even declaring that "There is nothing undemocratic about such controls; rather they are the essence of the democratic process." In keeping with the ACTU and the CIO Right, CWA harbored a socially conservative but essentially social-democratic political and economic agenda. In the run-up to the 1948 election, CWA's platform thus embraced guaranteed full employment, lower prices accomplished through reduction and/or redistribution of corporate profits, equal pay legislation to end exploitation of women workers, an "adequate housing program, reduction in personal income taxes, Federal aid to education, extension of social security" and lowering "excessive" telephone rates. After AT&T, pressured by the Fair Employment Practices Committee, began to make at least some hires of African Americans, in 1946–1947 CWA finally abandoned NFTW unions' exclusion of blacks from membership and even placed an antidiscrimination clause in its constitution.[69]

Not only were many of these early hopes neutered or slowed by Cold War splits, splits of which CWA's own formation was a testimony. In addition, the

CWA's 1948 platform evinced no sign, beyond reducing telephone rates, of an independent program for network system development—something akin to the one workers had developed decades before, under the rubric of antimonopoly. This absence would carry punishing ramifications, as fresh policy challenges began to gather during postwar decades.

7
Consumption and Public Utility

During the decades around the turn of the twentieth century, the US political economy grew a new carapace. Observers high and low struggled to understand this metamorphosis of consumption, both of itself and in relation to the mighty changes that were concurrently transforming production.[1]

Historians have also scrutinized this transition. One rolling change began in the late nineteenth century: a successful struggle for an eight hour workday by a fraction of the US working class. How was increased working-class leisure configured? Numerous analysts have detailed how commercial amusements and private commodity consumption expanded to fill many workers' new leisure time. Corporate marketing, and individual purchases, of branded goods—endlessly reified, as if severed from the labor of production—cumulated by the 1920s in a "land of desire," and, by the late 1940s, in a "consumers' republic." Corporate selling became a zone of omnipresent experiment, tapping into workers' struggles to elevate their standard of living. This, though, was an uneven and multifarious shift, for the swelling consumption of commodities ranging from dishwashing soap to roller-coaster tickets, national magazines to radios, was far from uniform. Members of a diversified working-class and of a burgeoning middle-class crisscrossed in their purchasing, sometimes destabilizing their social distance and rendering consumption itself a fraught issue. Scholars also have plumbed the perplexed and sometimes angry controversies that erupted over the quality of the emergent commercial culture.[2]

The reworking of consumption, however, must not be equated merely with the demand for or the supply of a mounting pile of private commodities; for it was not so confined. When American Federation of Labor President Samuel Gompers famously demanded that white and male working-class unionists should have "more," as Roseanne Currarino explains, he gestured at more than a single objective. As important as material goods and personal possessions were cultural pursuits and common opportunities: playgrounds, education, music, self-improvement, happiness. The issues adhering to consumption were multifarious and they induced widening societal adjustments.[3]

After World War I, weakened by resurgent business- and state attacks and the sharp recession of 1920–1921, organized labor adopted a defensive crouch. Although workers were not well-positioned to push for wage gains, let alone for larger social and political goals, rising real wages and a moderation in the business cycle in the wake of the recession imparted a vital new feature to the question of consumption. In 1925, the department store magnate Edward Filene was one of a diverse group who asserted that the country's massively expanding "surplus-producing ability" signified nothing less than "that we shall have to readjust completely our whole plan of national life." Filene forecast that "the business man of the future, whether manufacturer or merchant, will make more money by reducing prices than the business man of the past has ever made by raising prices"—that, in short, "Mass production requires a great body of consumers." Throughout the 1920s, Commerce Secretary Herbert Hoover's circle of influential academics, officials, business executives and craft unionists, held that "means of achieving high-level consumption and so prosperity" were essential for balancing out the effects of what now seemed a boundlessly productive industrial economy.[4]

Which social actor or agency might become a fulcrum for entrenching and, when necessary, enforcing mass-purchasing power? Hoover dismissed as inimical both trade unions and a coercive state. Affirming that capital and labor shared a common interest in economic growth and increased consumption, he sought to ensure these outcomes through nothing more than deliberation and investigation by attentive government agencies, perhaps working with corporate trade associations. Throughout the unevenly shared but real prosperity of the 1920s "New Era," the Hoover pipedream prevailed. Some AFL researchers demurred from the common wisdom, that production and consumption were in balance; some even dared hope for "a more reliable and effective foundation for the labor movement"—that is, an expanded role for trade unions within politics and society. Sidney Hillman, president of the Amalgamated Clothing Workers, spoke for many workers when he declared that "a high standard of living" sufficient "to create a consumers' demand for almost unlimited output" would serve "our system of mass production" *and* "justice." Racially exclusionary and gender-segregated though most of them were, AFL unions thus began to purport that, in spearheading the quest for mass-purchasing power, they represented the general public. Late in the 1920s, indeed, AFL researchers forecast that economic output had grown so much that bold measures to expand purchasing power were urgent, to avert a syndrome of overproduction leading on to collapse. Present were neither the labor reforms nor the consumer purchasing power nor the racial and gender justice that might have shored up the prospect of such an economic balance.[5]

Beginning in 1929, the AFL researchers' prediction was born out. The financial crash halved the national income, wiped away 80 percent of the stock market's value, triggered a punishing deflation, and led on to unemployment and destitution on an unprecedented scale. Amid this misery, the Great Depression vaulted the economic role of consumption—its alignment with production—into the mainstream of political discourse.[6]

The question of mass-purchasing power quickly attained legitimate political heft. Even prior to Roosevelt's election in 1932, economists such as William Leiserson were asserting with new force that recovery depended on "a prior revival of purchasing power and consumer demand." With the political opening created by the New Deal, and the surge of working-class protest and self-organization into it, "labor's high wage, high consumption arguments gained currency as economists, politicians, and commentators came to see the twin problems of low wages and under-consumption ... as crucial to ending the Great Depression." Senator Robert Wagner, whose National Labor Relations Act sanctioned collective bargaining in 1935, forthrightly declared that "The function of unions ... is to maintain purchasing power at a high enough level to absorb the products of business competition." Among workers this tenet became ingrained common sense. Looking back from the other end of the tunnel of economic collapse (followed by wartime price controls), in 1949 a union bulletin flatly informed telephone workers that the Depression had come about because "purchasing power was not equal to carrying the production load."[7]

The interim years engendered dramatic institutional changes. Throughout the Depression and World War II, economic policy see-sawed, as business and labor vied to answer the question of "how state powers should be conceived of and deployed."[8]

Many business leaders insisted at the outset of the New Deal that, through cartelization and related forms of self-organization, they could "buttress and enhance the purchasing power of the working citizenry, with the expectation that that alone would go a long way toward restoring the nation and American business to economic good health, thus obviating the need for any deeper adjustment of the basic institutional structures of society." By contrast, Hillman and other trade unionists asserted that the stricken economy could be rescued only by instituting strong collective bargaining rights, as a guarantee of higher wage rates and increased purchasing power. As the Depression worsened, and political and ideological fluidity increased, government economic policies gyrated. The Roosevelt administration first borrowed from prior attempts to rewire the nation's institutional circuitry during the World War I mobilization, and from further revisions to thinking during the "New Era." In the 1920s Filene had proclaimed that "The way to success will lie through increasing the efficiency of labour by better management, through reducing overhead expense and other production costs by greater standardization of products and by mass output, and finally through reducing the price to the consumer, taking a smaller profit per article, and working for mass sales." Because of persistent catastrophic unemployment, however, building purchasing power on the scale that was needed required alterations that not even large companies (during the 1920s Ford had been a much-cited example) could institute by themselves. Macroeconomic innovations were necessary. One was deficit spending by the federal government, still an anathema to businessmen and, indeed, uncomfortable for President Roosevelt; federal support for independent labor unions was another. Those who chastised the President for favoring redistribution—those to whom stewardship came not only as an entitlement but, they deemed, a responsibility—in any case, a habit—grew as frustrated as they were fearful and antagonistic.[9]

A crisis of legitimacy gathered. The goal of expanding consumption became bound up, as Hillman had hoped, with a more general and open-ended reconfiguration of social and political power. If the floodgates were opened by the Wagner Act, legalizing collective bargaining and establishing federal legal machinery to support it, then millions of workers thronging into the CIO were the collective agent of change. From a now-discredited capitalist class industrial unionists and their adherents began to wrest a right to speak for the wider public.[10]

The New Deal remained a directing force, continually lobbing ideas and launching experimental programs, yet economic rights—rights now being demanded by millions of workers—occupied center-stage in its endeavor. Roosevelt bruited a concept of economic rights in his initial 1932 presidential campaign and, conditioned by a suddenly radical and militant labor movement, New Dealers embraced them increasingly forthrightly. By 1936, the history professor and consumer advocate Caroline F. Ware (with her husband, Gardiner C. Means) specified that "economic security" was a crucial precondition for an effective political economy. In 1940, Ware explicated this idea in testimony before the Temporary National Economic Committee. Here she outlined a requirement for what she called "economic citizenship," explaining that "the problem of effective economic citizenship is a twofold problem of effective participation, as a producer and as a consumer." To institute reasonable living standards demanded a triad of reforms: higher wages, backed by a vigorous labor movement; fair labor practices, overseen by the federal government; and careful oversight of prices, product quality, and consumer information, again the province of the state. This was redistribution—not revolution—but, to many business leaders, its programmatic content seemed dangerously radical. At the eve of US entry into World War II, and in his 1944 election campaign, President Roosevelt himself memorialized "freedom from want" and an expansive "economic bill of rights." So acclaimed, economic rights both legitimized the improved social wage for which workers were battling and pointed up a need for additional reforms.[11]

Crucially, the New Deal platform for boosting mass-purchasing power spanned beyond individual wage packets and private purchases, into the realm of common provision of basic services. Municipal, regional, and national infrastructures formed the essential underpinnings for expanded household consumption. Without electricity, refrigerators and radios could find no place in the home; the absence of gas for heating and cooking likewise limited household commodity consumption, as did the restricted availability of hot and cold piped water. Stimulating demand for these services required immense investments, and carefully planned and -engineered infrastructures—even, perhaps above all, where private owners of infrastructure preferred not to make such investments. Controversies over systems needed to furnish homes with water, gas, electrical power and telecommunications, however, have often been short-changed; as far back as the turn of the twentieth century some contemporary radicals disparaged what they called "sewer socialism" for offering what they took to be an attenuated reform program. Nevertheless, building out these infrastructures now once again came to constitute a crucial dimension of political-economic reform. Nascent during the 1920s, flowering during the New Deal, and bearing fruit throughout the early postwar decades, were new programs to expand and enhance infrastructure-reliant household services, and to extricate them from blatantly insufficient and in some cases corrupt control-structures.

What historian William J. Novak calls "the public utility idea" seemed to many Americans to offer an "innovative, capacious, and extraordinarily efficacious" fulcrum for effecting this transformation. For a vital historical instant—the moment of the CIO's formation and of the New Deal coalition's peak strength—rescuing and rebuilding the political economy pivoted in part on expanding common use. Public utilities were the vehicle for this. How might public utility services be extended and enlarged? (Such were the times that proposals were offered—and quickly dispatched by big publishers—to turn newspapers into public utilities.) Whose social stamp would be given to public utility institutions—would they be made more democratic and less discriminatory? During the 1930s and 1940s these questions entered both public opinion and public policy.[12]

In 1930, barely half of American homes cooked with gas; by 1940, more than three-quarters of them had been electrified. Between 1940 and 1960, the proportion of US homes lacking a flush toilet dropped from above one-in-three to just one-in-ten. In 1940, nearly half of US households did not have complete indoor plumbing, defined as hot and cold piped water and a bath-tub or a shower; by 1970 this figure had declined to 7 percent. If these statistics suppress gaping urban-to-rural and social class and racial disparities, still, they point up the trend. The process of change involved something beyond mere access, however; and it was not consensus-driven but hotly contested. Public utilities burned into the New Deal's political agenda; and the New Deal era itself became a hinge-point in the provision of public utility services.[13]

This point is basic to understanding the contemporary reworking of the tripartite US telecommunications system. Telecommunications utilities contributed in complex ways—negative as well as positive—to a rolling transition. In spite of attempts to rescue it, one of the nation's premier network infrastructures grew moribund, while both of the other two systems were revamped, in substantial part to bulwark consumption. Let us consider telegraph, postal, and telephone services in this fresh light: in what degree and in which ways did these three networks enable and exemplify a reorganization of US consumption around mass-purchasing power? And how were they themselves reshaped in this metamorphosis?

Telegraphy

During the later nineteenth century the telegraph had comprised a negative reference model in part because, focusing on the business market, its corporate owners effectively suppressed access to telegraph service by the working-class public. Their poor treatment of their employees was another factor. After AT&T joined Western Union and Postal Telegraph in the market for business telegraph services, neither of these conditions changed. Their numbers and meager wages declining, their working conditions notorious, during the 1930s some telegraphers tried to renew independent trade unionism. Joined by a scattering of federal officials, they sought to revive the old idea that widening access might rescue commercial telegraph service and, with it, the fortunes of those who labored to provide it.

We have seen that, for a period of nearly a decade, the American Communications Association helped stave off a merger between Western Union and Postal Telegraph. Still controversial, after extensive public hearings a merger was approved by a divided FCC in 1943. By this point the FCC had sought for years that Western Union "modernize its facilities as rapidly as possible"; now, projections of greater access (alongside cost-savings) became an argument for combination. Officials thus "anticipated that among the long-run benefits" of merger "should be an extension of telegraph service coverage and improvement in the speed and quality of service." The FCC strived to stimulate demand; in 1938, for example, the agency denied Western Union a rate increase on the grounds that, by inducing greater numbers of consumers to use airmail as a cheaper substitute, increased telegraph rates would compound the industry's problems. In 1941 a congressional committee forecast that "this will remain a 'sick' industry until it has reduced costs through mechanization [such] that it can attract volume business through 'postalization' of rates and other improvements." During World War II President Roosevelt (through Commerce Secretary Jesse Jones) even resurrected the idea that a merged telegraph company could achieve cost-economies by relocating "hundreds, if not thousands" of its offices to the nation's recently refurbished Post Offices—"where it would be an economy to the Government and to the patron of the service, as well as a convenience to the public." The idea was opposed by the AFL's Commercial Telegraphers Union, on the grounds that turning postmasters into telegraph agents would enable Western Union to contract out work. No action was taken on FDR's proposal.[14]

Extension of service nevertheless remained a primary goal of the telegraph unions and, after the merger, they were belatedly joined in this objective by Western Union's executives. Entering the postwar period, it appeared to one expert FCC staffer that "Both the FCC and Western Union are interested in price changes that would increase the demand for telegraph service." Absent forceful government intervention, though, both the carrier's long-standing orientation to business service and stiffened intermodal competition rendered realization of this aim highly uncertain. "A major question to be determined" wrote an FCC staffer in 1947, "is the nature of the cost curve" for Western Union's telegraph service:

> If over a significant area, unit costs decrease with an increase in traffic, a vigorous expansionary program may be in order. Such a program would involve slashing rates, extending and improving service, and launching an aggressive advertising campaign.

By 1947, however, the increasing popularity of substitute services—the "intensely competitive nature of the communications industry"—lessened the probability that such an expansion could be contemplated:

> The next few years should witness extension, improvement, and perhaps some reduction in rates for toll telephone and TWX service. Air mail will certainly make giant strides in the direction of speedier, more reliable, more extensive, and cheaper service. Radiotelegraph carriers may perhaps seek to re-enter the domestic field and compete for the more profitable business.

Undeniably, a rescue of the industry might be arranged through structural intervention: federal subsidy, merger of telephone and telegraph, government ownership. Policymakers, however, first of all would have to face tough questions: "What function does, or can, telegraph serve? Is it akin in public need to the mail service? Shall the policy of thirty-five years' standing of competition in the domestic communications field, especially between telephone and telegraph, be continued?" Depending on the answers, perhaps policymakers should instead decide to *shrink* the telegraph service, and encourage Western Union "to restrict service to the more populous and profitable urban centers."[15]

In the event, regulators mapped out no concerted strategy. To expand access and diversify service offerings, after World War II Western Union pursued small-scale experiments and some outright schemes. Traversing Baltimore in the late 1940s, for example, were a couple of "telecars"—automobiles specially equipped by Western Union to relay telegrams via mobile radio. (It occurred to rival RCA to employ a radio-relay of television-facsimile transmission so that "tons of mail could be beamed through the air cost-to-coast to be received and reproduced as exact duplicates of the original letters.") In the business market, between 1944 and 1948, Western Union built two microwave radio networks using terminal sites located in five states, thereby becoming the first US common carrier to implement this historically vital new telecommunications technology. Western Union, however, concurrently increased its reliance on AT&T's network, so that during the 1950s it depended on its rival for 60–70 percent of its circuit capacity; a renewal of the telegraph company's fortunes, of necessity, would have to be predicated on eliminating this dependence. As well, the once-mighty telegraph carrier gave little sign of expanding its consumer commercial service.[16]

Western Union simultaneously confronted still another problem: its wages bill. When, after the war, the telegraph unions succeeded through appeals to the government in gaining substantial wage increases for their poorly paid members, Western Union responded by petitioning for—and obtaining—rate hikes, rather than the price decreases for which the FCC had recently hoped. Passing along its higher costs to consumers again hastened the decline of the carrier's public telegram business. Only deepening its woes was Western Union's belated postwar mechanization program, and the drastic reduction in employment that this brought. Fixated on solvency rather than independence and expansion, Western Union plied the FCC with requests to curtail or decrease public telegram service, requests that the FCC generally approved (albeit with reservations). During the late 1940s and early 1950s, Western Union petitioned the FCC to close 4,000 offices and continued to lay off employees; 52,235 people worked at Western Union in 1941, prior to being joined by Postal Telegraph's 14,000 workers—but, confirming the ACA's fears of mass lay-offs, a mere 43,047 were employed by the combined company in 1950.[17]

Weakened by internecine strife and, in the case of ACA, by state repression, telegraph unions did not succeed in halting the contraction of public message service. Smaller communities especially faced shorter operating hours, fewer telegraph offices, and a reduced and less efficient workforce. The public message business creaked and groaned; between the end of World War II and 1959 the number of telegrams sent by Western Union decreased to 110 million from 180 million. There was little outcry against this wasting, perhaps, ironically, because so few Americans had enjoyed regular access to commercial telegraph service in the past. We will see later how a new mode of product substitution within the robustly expanding market for private-line service put the final nail in the coffin of the telegraph industry as, during the 1950s, specialized business communication system began to be innovated around the computer. Far from regenerating itself as a popular service the telegraph instead became increasingly moribund. Yet is passing was slow. In 1969, after President Nixon delivered a nationwide TV address asking that "the great silent majority of my fellow Americans" support his war-making on Vietnam fifty thousand mostly supportive telegrams flooded into the White House—"the largest number of wired messages any presidential address had ever drawn." Western Union sent its last telegram a recently as 2006. Western Union lives on, its long-standing money-transfer service still active, also as a trademark and a memory.[18]

The Post Office

Sharply different from the declining telegraph, during the early decades of the twentieth century the Post Office had become "one of the country's basic industries"; in a striking instance of this concept's historical elasticity, in 1924 this analyst also specified that the Post Office constituted "a public utility performing a service indispensable to the economic and social life of the community." Befitting this status, the Post Office now commenced on an encompassing modernization. This process, though, was two-sided. If, by the mid-1960s, the agency still could be cast as an "enlarger of the common life," then its democratic features were being badly damaged by its function as a channel for commercial commodity consumption.[19]

Throughout the first third of the century, the Post Office integrated adjacent technological improvements into its system of message-transport. Akin to the railway mail half a century earlier, air mail was one principal innovation. Air mail not only sustained an acceleration of Post Office service for those who could pay, but supplied a crucial boost to the aviation industry. During the 1920s, alongside the railroads, corporate air carriers were showered with contracts to transport mail; the Air Mail Service—and the subsidies that underlay it—declared Congressman Clyde Kelly, who fathered the legislation that authorized both, constituted nothing less than "the foundation of commercial aviation" for young and fragile US airlines. Unionized postal clerks agreed, though they disparaged these subsidies for coming at the expense of postal workers' wages, as they had hit out earlier against railway mail for its often fatally dangerous working conditions. Domestic airmail expanded rapidly, though it still commanded only a slight share of the intercity communications market and was used disproportionately by businesses and well-off households: from 3 million ton-miles in 1931 to 41 million in 1949, as coverage expanded from a few dozen cities to 596 locations. Electric jazz guitarist Charlie Christian enthused over the service in the song "Air Mail Special," performing with Benny Goodman's popular sextet in 1940–1941.[20]

Other enhancements also commenced. Late in the 1920s, Congress appropriated funds for repairs and fresh construction: in 1931, a fifty-acre, twelve-story monument. implanted in downtown Chicago and fitted out with the latest in delivery-, conveyor-, sorting-, and canceling technology, was hailed for being the largest post office in the world and a model for the rest of the country. During the Depression, postal modernization was showcase for sometimes-inspiring revisions to what had been a spare public aesthetic. Congress authorized New Deal public works programs to spend a quarter of a billion dollars to erect 1525 new Post Office buildings; during the course of the 1930s, three times as many post offices were erected than had been built over the past half-century. The murals painted by Works Projects Administration-supported artists to adorn many of these (and other) government buildings established a vibrant form of public art, in which—sometimes to the chagrin of both local and federal authorities—the contributions of laboring people to the American past were celebrated. And the benefits and efficiencies of the institution continued to be hailed. In 1938, when the Post Office garnered annual revenues of around $730 million ($13.2 billion in 2021 dollars) and employed over a quarter of a million people, Postmaster General and Democratic presidential hopeful James Farley bragged, it was "one of the most efficient publicly owned business organizations in the world, and the service it renders is seldom eclipsed, or even matched, by private industrial organizations comparable in extent." Farley elaborated:

> The cost of mailing a letter is down just about to a minimum, deliveries are regular and prompt, and the department performs its functions with a minimum of friction and with very little criticism, public or private.

This embodiment of civic function, though hyperbolic, was not merely a promotional concoction. Born in 1934, Ralph Nader remembered the Post Office of his boyhood this way:

> When I was growing up in New England during the 1940's, the symbol for reliability, punctuality and efficiency was the United States Post Office. People could almost tell the time of day by the postman's rounds (twice a day delivery) and the frequent pickups at corner collection boxes throughout the neighborhoods.

Use of the Post Office had spread to the point of genuine inclusiveness; this network's immeasurable value for persons came from its ability to link any and all. Multiple daily mail deliveries were instituted at many locations, without significant increases in the price of stamps.[21]

Universality and efficiency notwithstanding, the inside workings of the Post Office were far from democratic. Working conditions, notably within modernized facilities such as the gigantic Chicago plant, were unpleasant and sometimes even insufferable. Richard Wright's novel, *Lawd Today*, featuring the Black workers who, around 1930, accounted for more than a quarter of employees at the main Chicago branch, depicted both racism and a deadly mechanization. And Farley's praise might not have sparked much enthusiasm among postal workers; he conceded a forty-hour work-week only at President Roosevelt's insistence. More generally, throughout the interwar years the federal government was far from responsive to postal workers' demands to improve wages and benefits.[22]

Referring to the policy of reducing postal rates, one facet of what he termed the "Service First" model of provision that had taken hold during the mid-nineteenth century, Pennsylvania Republican Congressman Clyde Kelly in 1931 portrayed the Post Office as the innovator of the "quantity production idea, which is the basic principle underlying the second great industrial revolution." He purported that only subsequently had the much-ballyhooed automobile industry adhered to the Post Office precept, that "quantity production is not a method but an idea and back of it is the law that the greater the volume of a standard product or service, the lower the unit cost." Had Kelly been a theorist of Fordism, he might have emphasized the role of the Post Office in building and sustaining commercial private consumption. The Post Office had subsidized the nationwide circulation of magazine advertisements and mass merchandisers' catalogs beginning in the late nineteenth century; of parcel post delivery early in the twentieth century; and of direct mail advertising after World War II. Postal money orders were purchased in the millions, offering means of payment at a relatively nominal charge. The functions of the Post Office were closely tied to US society's dominant institution—for-profit business—and as business's needs and demands changed, the Post Office also altered.[23]

After World War II, the agency's "Service First" character became tinged by an increasingly pervasive commercialization. As its infrastructure was overhauled to extend and accelerate the circulation of commodities, and to saturate households with marketing propaganda, the Post Office experienced protracted stress. Post Office costs in particular faced pronounced upward pressure. In part these resulted from changes carried within the postwar boom. A population shift to newly built suburbs, alongside the rise of truck-based transport, strained postal transmission and disrupted the agency's delivery system: postal routes proliferated even as the number of mail trains decreased, leaving only a fourth of US post offices in cities that provided rail service. Second- and third-class class mail volume spectacularly outpaced the capacity of existing processing facilities. Rapidly growing consumer magazine publishers pressed to take advantage of low second-class rates, while catalog merchants and direct-mail advertisers exploited the newer (1928) third-class rate option, all of which pumped an unprecedented quantity of commercial mail into the consumer economy.

Overall mail volume doubled, from 35 billion pieces in 1946 to around 70 billion pieces in 1963; a perceptive analyst observed that the Post Office's growth rate between 1950 and 1960 "was unequaled by any business of comparable size in the private sector." Bulk mailers and magazine publishers did not pay anything approaching the true cost of processing their voluminous mailings of publications, advertisements, promotions, and catalogs; and they demanded specialized facilities to speed mail processing. How was this specialized—and discriminatory—program of expansion accommodated?[24]

To answer this question we must train attention on the Post Office labor force. The number of part-time postal workers, which had rocketed from 87,000 to 158,000 during World War II, remained high—135,000 in 1956, 154,000 in 1960 and, following a major service failure (discussed later), 193,000 in 1969. Reliance on part-time labor grew in part from a 1950 congressional measure to reduce the number of permanent new government employees. However, regular fulltime Post Office employment also shot upward, from 278,000 in 1945 to 374,000 in 1956 to 546,000 in 1969. The government's largest nonmilitary workforce, the Post Office therefore responded to altered and enlarged demand for mail services with a sustained labor-intensive strategy.[25]

Vern Baxter underlines that, prior to its 1970 reorganization, the Post Office "was prohibited from acting like a corporate employer, attempting to mechanize and consequently reassign, radically change, or eliminate jobs." In 1959, the postal labor force was represented by thirteen unions, six of which were affiliates of the AFL-CIO, boasting a combined strength of 406,000 members and accounting for over 80 percent of the Post Office Department's employees. In other federal agencies the unionization rate was far lower—one historian suggests 21 percent. The two largest postal unions, each of which dated back to the late nineteenth century, the National Association of Letter Carriers and the United Federation of Postal Clerks, campaigned for pay raises repeatedly, and often effectively, within the institution's politically denominated framework. John T. Tierney explains that all important decisions concerning postal employees, including wage schedules, classification of positions, job security, and work assignments

> were determined by Congress (the House Post Office and Civil Service Committee in particular) through prolonged tripartite bargaining with the Post Office Department and the postal unions. In order to get the most out of these political negotiations, the postal unions over time became expert at lobbying Congress.

There was a corollary: With ingrained skepticism concerning technological changes to mail handling that arrived bereft of worker safeguards and controls, postal unions tended to resist additional mechanization. Throughout the first postwar decades, their refusal was both sustained and successful. The Department instead obtained from Congress a succession of emergency appropriations with which to add workers to process and deliver the mail; the result was to increase labor-intensivity. By the mid-1960s, net assets per employee at the Post Office were a mere one-twenty-fifth as great as those of AT&T, while personnel costs—wages and benefits—comprised four-fifths of its total budget. As the President's Commission on Postal Organization accurately declared in its 1968 Report, "manpower considerations dominate postal economics."[26]

An increasingly severe stand-off over postal policy ensued. Between 1939 and 1953, as mail volume began to rocket, according to Deputy Postmaster General Maurice Stans (who became President Eisenhower's Budget Director and, subsequently, President Nixon's Commerce Secretary), capital expenditures for postal plant "had been almost nil." At the onset of the Eisenhower Administration, Stans asserted, "Mail service to the public had not only failed to keep pace with improvements in other living conditions, but in some respects had been allowed to deteriorate, although the rate of deterioration was sufficiently slow so that its impact on the public had not yet accumulated to the point of general dissatisfaction." A 1954 report by political conservatives characterized the Post Office as having suffered "from years of neglect."[27]

This, though, was a misstatement. The problem was how to absorb and handle huge spikes in the volume of heavily subsidized categories of mail. Should the publishers of *Life*, *Zane Grey's Comics*, and *Better Homes & Gardens* be allowed to pay so little for swamping the postal network with their mailings? Early in 1949, then-Postmaster General Jesse M. Donaldson requested that they be made to pay more, when he asked that Congress curtail subsidies for magazine and newspaper publishers by upping second-class mail charges. Indeed, he also requested that any publication containing more than 75 percent advertising matter more than half the time lose its second-class mail status. For good measure, Donaldson added that Congress should increase the rates for third- and fourth-class mailers (advertisers and nonprofits respectively) by 100 percent. He encountered bitter resistance; in this post-New Deal period, only much smaller rate increases were levied on corporate mailers. Lawrence F. O'Brien, who served as Postmaster General in the Johnson Administration between 1965 and 1968, omitted the question of second-class publications but still recollected the underlying issue: "Here you are, with a volume of mail equal the volume of the entire rest of the world, growing constantly, [and] a rate structure that was ridiculous—third and fourth-class mail users are being subsidized."[28]

As a public issue the question of the postal rate structure was suffused in deceit. Newspaper publishers rejected the use of the word "subsidy" to describe the benefits they received from the Post Office, demanding that Congress institute a different cost-accounting system to show that the Department actually profited from circulating their products. Only somewhat more abashed, the Magazine Publishers Association exclaimed that subsidized second-class rates contributed "to the free and unrestricted flow of information, education and enlightenment of the people"—even though both newspapers and magazines were highly self-interested businesses whose primary commitments included catering to advertisers. The publishers even argued that the Post Office should remain "a public service to the people of the United States and not a public utility which is expected to exact from users of the mails revenues to balance expenses." Rejecting the idea that the Post Office ought to be placed on a self-supporting basis, the publishers asserted—disingenuously—that the success of the Post Office had come because it had been "wisely designed to stimulate the dissemination of knowledge rather than the accumulation of profits." In this tortured logic, because first-class mail claimed "primacy and priority" within the postal system, it should continue to be assigned "the major part of the burden of postal costs." Second- and third-class categories should continue to enjoy lowered rates, with the resulting deficits made good by congressional appropriations. The politically connected publishers preferred that rate-making "must remain an exclusive function of the Congress"; proposals for an independent and impartial rate-making commission constituted "a bold attempt to kidnap from the representatives of the people powers rightly exercised by them."[29]

Should commercial mailers pay the full freight for the junk flyers and catalogs that they directed into urban homes with increasing precision, as a result of innovations around mailing lists? It is not well-appreciated that direct mail volume doubled from $918 million to $2.1 billion during the decade to 1961, making direct mail the nation's second-ranking advertising medium (behind newspapers). By now, catalogs were old news, a means by which merchandisers such as Sears, Roebuck and Montgomery Ward sold to farm families. As these giant rural retailers now moved into cities and suburbs, both they and big urban department stores again relied on the Post Office (alongside what was called "telephone catalog service" to enable customers to place orders). Noteworthy was the scale of change: advertisers were the largest clients of the nation's 30,000 commercial printers in 1960, and catalogs and other advertising material accounted for more than twice the revenue flowing to printers from either books or magazines. Postal workers met the torrent of subsidized mailings by petitioning Congress for additional help, in the form of new full- and part-time postal employees. Were they somehow more self-interested that the bulk mailers?[30]

What the Magazine Publishers Association in 1956 referred to as "a rate struggle already too long continued" plunged Post Office into a quagmire. The agency might have been extricated at any time, if only Post Office finances had been accorded a regular federal budget appropriation. Such an appropriate would signify that the venerable Post Office possessed legitimacy on a par with, say, the Defense Department. This mandate was, however, withheld; instead, a sword was permitted to hang over the agency's head. One might encapsulate the character of postwar political discourse in the fact that, unlike the vastly greater funding accorded to the Cold War military, the annual $1 billion to $5 billion that would have been needed to balance the Post Office's books was increasingly singled out as intolerable.[31]

The Post Office Department was stretched on Procrustes' bed. Rather than being accorded a stable foundation as a technologically modernized, adequately supported public service, during the vaunted golden age of postwar prosperity its much-publicized "deficits" offered a pretext for rate increases, service reductions, management reorganizations and, soon enough, catastrophic breakdowns. All of this fanned perceptions of beleaguerment and even illegitimacy. The Post Office was presented as the supreme incarnation of a wearisomely publicized tenet: that government services were inherently inefficient and wasteful, incapable of competing with the so-called "private sector" except as a result of political fiat. But this result testified both to sustained battles over Post Office structure and function, and to an insistent ideological campaign to discredit the institution.

Post Office travails began to escalate when the department was subjected to the ministrations of two high level commissions, the first reporting in the late 1940s and the second in 1955. Modernization and accounting changes were recommended by a Commission on the Reorganization of the Executive Branch of Government, led by the rehabilitated but unreconstructed political conservative, former President Herbert Hoover. "What the new Hoover group has proposed," the *Wall Street Journal* stated with unusual candor, "amounts to a revolution in Washington's way of governing—or it might be called a counter-revolution against the changes wrought by the New Deal and its successors." As a staff of "business-experienced executives" was hired in, "to bring about efficiency and modern practices," Maurice Stans projected what was "perhaps the largest reorganization that has ever taken place in one sweep in any business in or out of government, anywhere." His hopes were not born out, but his use of the noun "business" to characterize the Post Office was a harbinger. Ideologically loaded, it was congruent with the terminology of the Hoover Commission—which vied with the publishers by holding that "the principal policy nettle" was "whether the Post Office is a business or a subsidized public service." The fanciful notion that "Public Ownership Can't Compete With Private Management," now again gained favor within the investor class. It was portentous that, instead of imposing meaningful rate increases on commercial mailers between 1950 and 1952—and over the noteworthy opposition of the Association of Letter Carriers AFL—the spiraling revenue needs of the Post Office were met by cutting residential mail deliveries throughout the nation's cities from twice to once daily, and by increasing the price of a postcard—a staple at one penny since the 1870s—by 100 percent. The historical contrast with the Progressive Era hardly could be more stark. Now, instead of being absorbed into the popular and expansionary government Post Office, the corporate telecommunications industry became the model on which the Post Office itself was judged—and found wanting. Private services commenced and grew in some big cities, with deliveries and pickups on behalf of corporate users such as banks. In New York City, the Santulli Mail Service, founded in 1946 and handling some 3000 bags of mail each day, was the largest by 1968.[32]

The Post Office was ringed in. Powerful and self-interested corporate producers of bulk mail were intent on modernizing postal facilities while externalizing their costs. Rank-and-file employees and their politically wired unions stoutly defended their labor-intensive service model. Constituents pressed their congressional representatives not to use their budget authority to cut back popular postal services. These disparate ingredients mixed, fueling what proved to be explosive pressure. As its altering social function played havoc with postal finance, efficiency, employment policies and working conditions, nevertheless, and crucially, households continued to rely on the Post Office as an essential service.[33]

Between 1945 and 1963, the average number of pieces of third-class mail received annually per household more than doubled, from forty-one to ninety-nine. Correspondence between individuals were outweighed—literally, and vastly—by business-to-household transactions including bills, promotional advertising, and catalog sales. Yet, over this same span, letters received (1st class and airmail) likewise increased—from 166 to 199 per capita. Although the agency was being remade into an advertising channel and a sales infrastructure, for innumerable families and individuals personal correspondence remained foremost. The profile of demand morphed but, for a quarter-century after 1933, the first-class letter rate remained politically untouchable at a price of three cents. This was so despite that, by the mid-1970s, greeting cards and personal letters together accounted for less than one-fifth of first-class mail; and households sent 17.5 percent of all mail but received 60.9 percent of it. The Post Office likewise continued to incarnate quite disparate, because noncommercial, principles and practices. Through its network streamed, at heavy subsidy, government documents as well as educational materials; as recently as 1928 a new "library rate" had been instituted. During the great postwar boom, this public function came into its own. Not only libraries, schools, and universities, but—following Congress's decision in 1949–1950 to grant them a special rate for mass mailings—nonprofit organizations came to rely on the US mail to circulate their religious and educational materials, humanitarian and political critiques, topical appraisals, and fundraising appeals. The major organizations of the Civil Rights movement, from SCLC and CORE to SNCC, all "depended on the postal system for financial support."[34]

In essence, then, the Post Office was riven by a largely unspoken social contradiction. On one side, it continued to serve as an essential medium for personal correspondence, binding together individuals, families, and friends across town and country; and it performed vital communicative functions for government agencies and a swelling number and variety of nonprofit organizations. On the other side, in a process that began in the late nineteenth century and that accelerated with great force after World War II, the Post Office was transformed into a sales channel and a marketing tool on which modern big business relied to an ever-growing extent. Unreconciled, this was the contradiction with which the institution found itself trying to cope.

What, finally, of the telephone system, poised to undergo a fresh cycle of modernization? After World War II regulators at last found means of ensuring that the voice network would be made available to nearly the entire US population.

Telephony

While Western Union's expenditures for network modernization between 1946 and 1950 totaled $40 million (over and above its normal plant outlays of $34 million), during these five years the Bell System spent $5 billion improving its plant. Its spectacular investment persisted throughout the 1950s and 1960s, encapsulating what economic historians have sometimes labeled a "golden age" of prosperity. Put differently, at the end of World War II fewer than half of US households possessed telephones but, by 1970, only 13 percent lacked for them.[35]

If a growing, better-paid US labor force possessed growing discretionary income, however, then this alone did not account for the expansion of residential telephone access. The key lay in the public utility framework that encased telephone, giving new purpose to its now-mammoth network investment. Through an opaque and intricate process which took years to complete, government regulators universalized telephone service, enabling almost all US households to enjoy its benefits.

Throughout the first decades of telephone system development, up to and including the so-called "competitive" era (1893–1910), as we saw, the Bell System service monopoly demonstrated a consistent preference for business- and relatively wealthy residential users. It possessed little need to market telephone service, or the instruments that it rented to subscribers. The 1920s produced an upsurge, which the Depression then curtailed. Durable, though hardly conflict-free, cooperation between federal and state regulators was the procedural innovation required to widen household access; and it began to be actualized during and after the New Deal. This inter-jurisdictional mechanism became a primary means—alongside the threat of antitrust action—through which the price of local telephone service was finally lowered. Voice communication in turn became an omnibus service for everyday use by the population at large. Like the postal service, by the 1950s the telephone system also was becoming an essential scaffold for private commodity consumption.

This great change drew on policies devised nearly simultaneously in the adjacent industry of electrical power. Similarities and overlaps between the two fields of enterprise abounded. In its capital structure, its status as a network industry on which depended much of the nation's economic and cultural life, its many mutual corporate and executive interconnections, its reliance on electricity, and in the experience and outlook of the New Deal regulators who oversaw it, telecommunications both borrowed from and contributed to the power industry. With this linkage in mind, it is helpful to situate telephony within the Roosevelt Administrations' ramifying program for what historian Ronald Tobey calls "the electrical modernization of the American home." As the freshly created Home Owners Loan Corporation, Federal Housing Administration and, soon afterward, the Veterans Administration, worked to insure millions of long-term mortgages issued by private banks, thereby bringing homeownership within the reach of tens of millions of (disproportionately white) families, Tobey shows that the New Deal also expanded household use of electricity and thus activated a burgeoning residential market for electrical products.[36]

Prior to the changed political context of the 1930s, household wiring had been typically inadequate, often nonexistent; electrical appliances such as refrigerators, cooking ranges, and water heaters were restricted to upper-income segments, and major power companies marketed service mainly to the same favored enclaves—and above all to commercial and industrial users. During the 1920s, however, a growing fraction of the capitalist class sought to build profits by developing new consumption-oriented industries. This helped invigorate debate over how to reform recalcitrant power companies, which rejected more-inclusive residential access to electricity.[37]

Pressed from below by rank-and-file militancy and the social unionism of the CIO, and hit from above by many business leaders' demands to resurrect a shattered capitalism on their terms, FDR's New Deal looked to build out these new industries. Key changes were made to the structure of provision, so that residential access to electricity and electrical products expanded. Through the

Tennessee Valley Authority and allied public power facilities, some of which had already long been in the sights of Progressive reformers, New Dealers invalidated what had conventionally passed for wisdom: cheaper prices for household electricity *did* translate into dramatically enlarged residential use. Tobey argues that radio broadcasting's surge during the late 1920s precipitated the insight that household demand for electricity was not inelastic, as adherents of private power had claimed, and that demand stimulation around residential electricity might be profitable. We take this knowledge for granted today but, until the 1930s, it was a fiercely contested tenet.[38]

New Deal political interventions created federal home loan programs, upgraded housing codes, and liberalized consumer credit, establishing an expanded class of (disproportionately white and male) homeowners. Ensuring these homes' access to electricity necessitated still other initiatives. It is noteworthy that policy was not entrusted to a single regulatory agency charged with broadening residential markets for electricity and electrical products. Loosely congruent federal initiatives unfolded across a series of agencies and initiatives. Political setbacks suffered in one context thus might be overcome or neutralized by shifting to a different theater of government action.

Tobey asserts that the telephone was *not* a part of this multifaceted New Deal program—perhaps because his evidence, drawn from a sample of Riverside, California households, overstates the extent of residential telephone penetration. Riverside's nearly 50 percent in 1922 was high; nationwide, residential telephone access by 1920 had reached just over one out of every three households (35 percent). Much as the power companies had restricted residential access to electricity, the Bell System had been lackluster in promoting the telephone habit among working-class households. As Richard John shows, in big cities such as Chicago and San Francisco, innovations of measured service and nickel-in-the-slot telephones by Bell affiliates beginning early in the twentieth century had stimulated use among residents of modest means. However, both in the city and in the countryside, AT&T remained indifferent to a deliberate program for inclusive service. Chronically inhibiting network use were high rates, coupled with lack of investment in immigrant, black, and rural farm communities.[39]

In the aftermath of World War I, we have seen, reformers viewed AT&T's practice of limiting household access as an unconscionable fetter. "The telephone is a luxury," imperturbably declared one Bell company executive before the Kansas public utility commission in the early 1920s; the Chairman of the Kansas Commission responded by chastising Bell for rates and other behaviors "contrary to what we believe to be sound public policy." Notwithstanding, in the impasse that characterized that era, Bell's local rates continued as barriers to popular use. Fischer concludes that "the gap in telephone subscription by income stayed constant or widened between 1900 and 1940." While the urban working class began to win greater residential access to telephony during the 1940s, government-sponsored "subsistence budgets" did not include money for telephone calls for another generation; and it would take until the 1960s, Fischer adds, "to complete the spread of the telephone down the class hierarchy." The fulcrum for this change was created during the years following the establishment of the FCC in 1934.[40]

The idea that demand for telephone service had not been fully tapped was widely on offer by the Depression years. A 1935 finding by the Louisiana Public Service Commission held that "It is generally recognized that substantial rate reductions have the effect of . . . inducing an increased volume of business." Within AT&T as well, there were pockets of awareness that market opportunities remained unfulfilled and that, by expanding residential demand for long-distance service, the company's profit might be increased. AT&T investigators concluded in a study of Peoria, Illinois in 1930 that, "Unquestionably a field of great possibilities in toll development will be found to exist in at least the upper half (economically speaking) of the residence markets, and further analysis and experiments are much needed." The same analysts recommended that "Toll selling methods which would apply more forcefully to the lower rent-paying families may and should be developed."[41]

The Depression demonstrated conclusively that demand for telephone service actually was elastic: as incomes dropped and unemployment increased, we saw, the number of telephone subscribers plummeted. Might it not follow that demand—and, in turn, telephone industry investment and employment—would grow, if only telephone rates could be reduced? Advocates of purchasing power looked to government action to alter the ingrained pattern of constricted household telephone service consumption. The seeds of a strikingly different regulatory consensus were planted so that, even by 1941, an analyst at the League for Industrial Democracy could be forthright in declaring that "Due to the elasticity of telephone demand, lower rates would result in wider telephone use." A decade later, with memories of depression and wartime privation receding, a joint committee representing the FCC and the National Association of Regulatory and Utility Commissioners offered as settled opinion that the "fundamental objectives" of the toll rate structure were to meet public service requirements; produce adequate and stable income; and "encourage use of service."[42]

Regulators at the new Federal Communications Commission were poised, from the start, to engage these policy questions by way of administrative innovations. The first sentence of Section 1 of the New Deal statute that created the FCC consecrated a genuinely inclusive concept of universal service: "For the purpose or regulating interstate and foreign commerce in communication by wire and radio so as to make available, so far as possible, to all the people of the United States a rapid, efficient, Nation-wide, and world-wide wire and radio communication service with adequate facilities at reasonable charges . . . there is hereby created a commission to be known as the 'Federal Communications Commission.' " The FCC repeatedly reaffirmed the dictum that, as in this 1937 formulation, "a wider use of telephone service can be attained by proper rate adjustments and that the efficiency and growth of American telephone systems will be enhanced thereby." Broadened household access to the telephone had been an abiding popular goal; at last, with the FCC, it became an official priority of public utility regulation. Though clearly stated, this objective, which harmonized with the New Deal's more general project of kick-starting and sustaining effective demand, would not be simple to realize.[43]

Because the Commission's authority was confined to the interstate jurisdiction, it had to restrict its direct intervention in rate-setting accordingly. The bottleneck caused by AT&T's rates for interstate long distance was considerable in itself: "Experience indicates that telephone toll business, and in particular the interstate toll business, has in no sense 'struck its level,'" asserted the FCC's telephone rate counsel in 1938:

> Indeed, the ultimate potentialities of long distance telephone service in this country seem hardly to have been touched. And wherever possible such stimulating effects should be fostered in the interest of the telephone-using public.

The movement toward inclusive residential service was powered by the FCC and the wider political coalition that drove the New Deal. This objective in turn hinged on both territorial extension and household rate reductions. To attain these, regulators instituted a series of complex and detailed policies; although often couched in a numbingly opaque jargon, these interventions were deliberate, sustained—and successful.[44]

"Telephone-rate reductions effected during fiscal year 1937 . . . are of far-reaching importance to the public," declared the Commission in its Third Annual Report. The agency boasted about its achievements as far as interstate toll services and rates, because any hint that it sought to make policy at the level of local exchange- and intrastate toll services stood to embroil it in jurisdictional conflicts with state regulators. It was not merely that public utility commission regulators and staff might recollect Postmaster Burleson's transgressions. Throughout an entire region—the South—the PUCs operated cheek-by-jowl with white-supremacist Democrats who exploited the cry of "states' rights" to limit and channel the New Deal program. Committed to stimulating intrastate as well as interstate telephone use, the FCC nonetheless looked for means of working with state regulators across the nation: Local, or exchange, calling accounted for a commanding proportion of the country's telephone service and any program of demand stimulation had to assign it priority were it to substantially expand purchasing power.[45]

From early on, the FCC tried to go out of its way to include state commissions in its rate-setting reforms. The agency portrayed the information compiled through its mammoth Telephone Inquiry as having use "to State regulatory agencies as basic material in the effective regulation of the industry," and it distributed copies of dozens of staff reports to all the PUCs. After its Telephone Inquiry had been repulsed, in an important interstate rate case occurring between 1939 and 1941 the FCC took an additional step, by directly inviting state regulatory authorities based in California, Washington, Oregon, Idaho and Nevada to cooperate. "We have availed ourselves of their advice in considering the proper disposition of the proceeding and they concur in the views herein expressed, and in the result," the FCC carefully underlined in reporting its decision. Virtually from the moment of its establishment, the FCC—whose Telephone Division, recall, was led by the erstwhile Oklahoma utility commission chair Paul Walker—was mindful that it needed to accommodate state commissions "where matters of mutual concern were involved." And the agency crowed after it managed to get AT&T to accede to interstate rate reductions in 1937 that these "in some instances have influenced or been reflected in intrastate reductions."[46]

The substantive goal of expanding telephone-service demand was tied to an intractable procedural precedent: the Supreme Court's decision in the Chicago Rate Case. *Smith v. Illinois*, we saw, held that an important category of local telephone plant used for making long-distance telephone calls (specifically, the connection between the local exchange or switchboard and the individual subscriber, inclusive of outside plant, inside wiring, and handset) required some kind of separation of costs as between these two functions. That is, the Court determined that a portion of local telephone plant costs should be seen as common to intra- and interstate calling, and that for rate-making purposes these costs required allocation as between intrastate and interstate jurisdictions. This, however, mandated a division of common investment and operating expenses between the two services; it did not address, let alone resolve, the question of what ratio should be used. Nor did it provide a guide for establishing some sort of inter-jurisdictional rate-setting mechanism. Summing up the situation, FCC Commissioner Paul Walker recounted that, between 1925 and 1934, "It had become an accepted fact . . . that the best regulation . . . could not be achieved with Federal and state commissions acting independently." Walker himself stewarded "a permanent plan of procedure" to enable the federal and state governments together to supervise Bell's increasingly integrated network. Established was a Joint Board, comprised of FCC and PUC officials—provision for which had been incorporated earlier, in Section 410 of the FCC's enabling legislation. Regulators used this mechanism to try to ensure that long-distance service—dominated by business users—would no longer be granted a free ride at the expense of local, mostly residential, ratepayers.[47]

This federal-state endeavor was far from monolithic, and it faced recurrent challenges. Some politically appointed regulators were loath to confront AT&T in rate proceedings, especially as AT&T's single-minded pursuit of its corporate self-interest continued to render such opposition both intellectually arduous and politically costly. Outflanked and under-resourced, the state commissions' reluctance to regulate AT&T effectively was nearly as notorious as AT&T's own carefully honed talent for gaming this system. After its rebuff in the Telephone Inquiry, moreover, the FCC itself retreated: the agency's searching public scrutiny of AT&T's investments and expenses during 1935–1938 was not followed up by another formal study for another thirty years. Caution and compromise in turn characterized the Joint Board's innovations in rate regulation.

Nevertheless, these innovations did engender essential change. As the interjurisdictional rate-setting mechanism of the Joint Board was institutionalized during the postwar years, local telephone rates dropped to more affordable levels. And the vast Bell System found reason to participate with regulators in developing tools for enlarging service provision.

Attempts to restrict AT&T to the voice telephone market date back at least to the 1920s. Even prior to this, a federal antitrust initiative had placed significant limits on AT&T's market ambitions: the Kingsbury Commitment of 1913 had abridged and contained Theodore Vail's strategy for a universal electrical communication service. During the decades after World War I, the company's maneuvers in the rapidly growing and multifaceted field of high-technology electronics prompted renewed antitrust action. In consequence, AT&T had exited tempting markets in radio broadcasting, film, and sound recording. Nevertheless, in 1934 AT&T still flagrantly exceeded the boundaries of the voice telephone market. First and foremost was its ownership of a huge captive supplier of electrical and electronic components, Western Electric. Second, AT&T remained a power in telegraphy. Third, based on its Bell Laboratories' unexcelled programs of science and engineering research, AT&T continued to pioneer adjacent fields.

A prerequisite for rate-making innovations to promote network access was for the central state to demarcate definitively a domain of regulated telecommunications. On one side, from the 1930s to the 1956 culmination of a subsequent antitrust case against AT&T (covered in the following chapter), regulatory authorities attempted "to limit the scope of Bell system activities to the communications field." As an outcome of its Telephone Inquiry, the FCC sought a carefully qualified authority from Congress "to prohibit any common carrier subject to the Commission's jurisdiction from devoting its assets and energies to commercial exploitation of noncommunications fields when it appears that such activities may be detrimental to the public interest." The FCC turgidly unambiguous expression to its intent: "Consistent with the development of a national communications service contemplating a progressively increasing volume and constantly improving quality at progressively decreasing unit cost, is the necessity of protecting Bell System financial resources against the risk inherent in participation in the competitive exploitation of noncommunications enterprises." Regulation to promote enlarged network access, the agency believed, had best be coextensive with the operations of the service supplier.[48]

The other side of this coin was the erection and enforcement of entry controls over telecommunications markets. Soon after its establishment in 1927, the Federal Radio Commission had reported "a constantly increasing number of applications for the use of these frequencies has flooded the commission, covering a wide variety of services and experiments." This agency, the FCC's predecessor, initiated a proceeding to take up the applications of the spectrum made by disparate claimants, ranging from oil corporations and retailers to film companies. The opening of this docket in itself signified a conviction that national administrative regulation already reached beyond broadcasting; and the FRC decided in 1928 in favor of many of these business users' specific demands. However, it also granted a deliberate and well-reasoned pride of place to the carriers. "Those applicants proposing to engage in the communication business serving the entire public or a particular class of the entire public, and assuming the duties, obligations and responsibilities of common carriers are deemed to be in a better position to meet the standard of public interest than any of the other applicants," went the Commission's thinking in a precedent-setting 1929 judgment. In a different proceeding, the Radio Commission also underlined "that applications would not be granted for service which would duplicate that already furnished by land-line companies." The reasoning behind this decision strikingly clarified the public interest in controls over market entry:

> It may be that the commission owes the wire telegraph companies no duty to protect them from competition by radio services. But there is a much broader consideration than this. The commission, while encouraging the development of radio, should . . . take into consideration the possibility of a radio company competing unfairly with a wire service to such an extent that the general public may suffer.

The Federal Radio Commission elaborated, employing much the same logic that Post Office officials had employed during the 1840s to justify their monopoly before Congress. There being no "constant relationship" between the investment, labor, and operating expenses for a wire circuit and its volume of traffic, the cost of that circuit between small communities could not always be justified by the income it generated. Yet, the Radio Commission, continued, "the offices in small communities must be maintained to preserve the utility of the entire service to all the people of the Nation." In turn, the rates for message traffic coursing over the more profitable circuits between large population centers "must include some charge for the maintenance of the less profitable circuits." Only thus would the wire companies' readiness to serve be equitable.

From this reasoning followed a clear policy choice: the Commission "cannot, from the standpoint of national welfare, encourage the establishment of radio communication systems based solely upon the selection of the most profitable points of communication." To do so would be to accede to radio companies taking "the 'cream' of the business at reduced rates," which might "impair the utility and economic structure of the wire companies." Nor, the agency specified, would it sanction "discriminatory arrangements" for big business users:

> Upon the same considerations, the commission must not lend itself to the establishment of radio circuits which will rely upon the handling at reduced rates of the bulk traffic of individual large corporations between their various offices, to the practical exclusion of the less profitable occasional traffic of the general public, especially under circumstances where the wire communication companies are prevented by law or regulation from making such preferential and discriminatory arrangements.

Though these precepts could not have contrasted more sharply with the philosophy of federal regulation that animated the final three decades of the twentieth century, these Hoover era tenets directly foreshadowed those that were pursued by the New Deal Federal Communications Commission.[49]

The FCC not only carried over but supplemented the Radio Commission's conception. On one side, the agency attempted to restrict AT&T exclusively to the market for regulated telecommunications; on the other side, potential market entrants were compelled to accept FCC-PUC jurisdiction. End-to-end jurisdiction was the *sine qua non*.[50]

A mid-1940s Supreme Court judgment resoundingly affirmed this FCC policy. The agency had been legally challenged for enjoining hotels from continuing to collect surcharges on interstate and foreign telephone toll calls. Tariffs filed before the FCC, the Court held, provided no room for such middlemen: "message toll telephone service is furnished to hotels, apartment houses, and clubs upon the condition that use of the service by guests, tenants, members, or others shall not be made subject to any charge . . . in addition to the message toll charges of the telephone company." This verdict signified that the only beneficiary of long-distance revenues would be AT&T; hardly a judgment likely to displease the telephone company. Its larger purpose, though, was to ratify the regulators' end-to-end mandate.[51]

From here, regulators experimented with plans to widen network access. They did so out of conviction that telephone service both would achieve its greatest utility and contribute most substantially to macroeconomic health, when the number of pathways it allowed between subscribers increased toward its maximum. Several policies were implemented. Some came as revisions rather than full-scale departures; all attempted to expand household telephone access. Although these sometimes highly technical rate-making doctrines remained susceptible to manipulation by Bell System managers, as they brought telephone rate-making under the aegis of the emerging inter-jurisdictional procedure, New Dealers rolled back more or less long-standing social and territorial limits on access. Pressured by New Dealers to serve households of modest means—"renters"—AT&T for its part learned that the new arrangements stood to be highly profitable.

One locus for this broadening of network access formed around so-called "jurisdictional cost-separations": the arcane name of the tool used for assigning network costs unambiguously to local, intrastate toll and interstate jurisdictions. At the height of its reform activism, in 1938 the Commission identified this as a topmost priority. Its objective was progressively to increase the volume of toll business, with steadily improving quality and progressively decreasing costs—by means of "charges which make such services attractive to the public."

The toll rate structure therefore should be revised at frequent intervals to provide the most satisfactory and economical toll service to the public consistent with a fair rate of return. Such revisions should give consideration to the adequacy of the payments to the Associated and connecting companies for originating and terminating long lines toll business.

In turn this necessitated that the Commission should develop "simplified methods of separation, and direct the telephone companies to report currently the property used, associated expenses and the revenues derived from exchange, interstate toll and intrastate toll operations respectively."[52]

It was necessary to determine the investment- and operating costs of a telephone network—expenditures for switches, local loops, handsets, and trunk lines, as well as outlays for different categories of labor—because these costs supplied the basis for setting telephone rates. The greater the investment costs assigned to local service, for example, the higher local telephone rates need to be set in order to recoup these outlays. The problem was that calculating the investment and operating costs for, say, local exchange and intrastate long-distance services was—and is—intrinsically problematic. On one side, functions such as line repair and, beginning in the 1920s and 1930s, operator services, were used to enable both offerings concurrently. On the other side, as AT&T lavished resources on modernizing its network, a substantial and increasing portion of telephone plant was shared by both local and long-distance calling: notably, a subscriber's telephone handset, the pair of wires connecting her telephone to the local switching office, and the switching equipment itself, which collectively accounted for most of the cost of network plant overall.

"To the extent that the costs of these jointly-used facilities vary with their use in interstate and intrastate service," the Department of Justice later explained, "the costs may be assigned for rate-making purposes to one jurisdiction or the other on that basis." However, assigning costs according to proportional use introduced its own complications. First, usage-based cost apportionment took no note that, as the Justice Department later stated, "a large part of the costs of these facilities do not vary with usage—as in the case of the telephone instrument and the subscriber's access line, the initial costs and service life of both of which are almost totally unaffected by the relative extent of their use for intrastate versus interstate calling."[53]

Second, these so-called "non-traffic sensitive costs" were escalating quickly between 1920 and 1940, as AT&T invested to reconfigure its network around toll services. How could jurisdictional separations be used to address this fundamentally indeterminate ratio?

Though wrangling proved persistent, down through the decades experts agreed on the essential arbitrariness of the principles employed in the valuation of network access—specifically including the principles of cost-allocation of nontraffic-sensitive plant among distinct classes of service (local exchange versus intra- and interstate long distance), and as between different user categories (rural and urban, business and residential). No self-evident axiom could be consulted to settle policy. AT&T itself eventually conceded this, though only after its corporate interest gave it reason: "because the costs involved are true joint and common costs, there is no rational economic basis of allocation, and any allocation formula must inherently be based upon social or other non-economic considerations."[54]

The New Deal FCC's great achievement was to wrest away control over allocative principles from AT&T, and to subject them instead to explicit *political* determination as a core element of the agency's own program to stimulate mass consumption of telephone service.

This achievement did not come easily. Surmounting the received wisdom—and AT&T's opposition—required the FCC to extricate rate-making from a near-bottomless pit. For decades prior to the 1930s, an obscure but essential doctrine had simultaneously privileged business users and wealthy residential callers *and* generated lucrative earnings for AT&T. The so-called "board-to-board" theory had assigned *de facto* priority to the long-distance function. First, it purported to establish the cost-basis for long-distance rates in such a way as to include *only* interexchange plant and operating expenses. Although, from early on, local service was needed both to initiate and to complete each long-distance toll call, the plant used to provide it arbitrarily "was assumed to have nothing to do with the provision of interexchange service." Through fees accorded on a per-message basis, AT&T putatively provided full compensation to its affiliated operating companies, as well as to interconnected but independent providers of exchange service. But this arrangement *excluded* payment for "the exchange service facilities required to establish connection between the exchange station" (i.e., the subscriber), "and the toll-terminal plant." For years, too, AT&T had repulsed regulators' occasional proposals to supplant the board-to-board framework for setting long-distance rates. Because the network became an integral system, local and toll rates were ever more deeply interrelated; but the board-to-board doctrine crippled PUCs' attempts to identify, let alone to properly administer, their relationship.[55]

The problem was rendered all the more intrusive as a result of AT&T's imposition of high toll rates, consistent with its general policy of charging what it deemed the market could bear. As early as 1922, influential state regulators were singling out long-distance rates as "an economic scandal." After this, technical innovations and improvements generated continual cost-efficiency gains in long-distance service provision, aggravating the "scandal." But regulators were nearly powerless to address this disparity. Limits on their jurisdiction combined with the board-to-board doctrine, to deny the escalating investment in local telephone plant a role in long-distance rate-making. Prior to 1930, investment in nontraffic-sensitive plant was allocated entirely to intrastate rates; and interstate rate-making costs were contrived so as to include only the expense and investment associated with toll lines terminating in local switchboards. In other words, local subscribers made massive, sustained rate contributions to building up AT&T's long-distance system, even as AT&T also concurrently gouged the large business users which disproportionately employed its toll network. The effect, in each case, was to suppress access and retard use.[56]

If a greater share of cost allocations could be transferred from the local exchange to the interstate jurisdiction, then local telephone rates might be reduced. Benefits then would flow both to the greater populace and to the economy at large. Indeed the system's center of gravity would shift, in light of the New Dealers' precept that, as Commissioner John O'Hara of the Michigan PSC expressed it in 1940, "telephone rate structures should be designed to promote the maximum practicable development and use of the service—exchange and toll." Pressure to lower telephone rates in turn intensified, as proceedings of the National Association of Regulatory Utility Commissioners show; in 1942, amid wartime price controls, Commissioner Richard J. Beamish of the Pennsylvania Public Utility Commission underlined that the collaboration between the FCC and NARUC "is making and breaking new ground in regulatory history in the United States. I am one of those who believe that telephone rates in America are too high. Telephone service at the present time is a luxury. Communication by the human voice is a method of transmission which should be open to persons of modest means."[57]

This expansion of household telephone use through rate reductions was unlikely to harm AT&T financially, as long-distance transmission technology was improving and enabling additional efficiencies. And New Deal regulators were mindful—indeed, some were highly agitated—that, as matters stood, even such rate reductions as they might compel AT&T to accept would merely bring the carrier's outsized profits into line with those of other corporations. Transfer pricing on equipment purchased by its operating companies from its captive supplier, Western Electric, was—as the FCC had learned through its Telephone Inquiry—hugely inflating AT&T's supposed costs. Other accounting techniques enabled AT&T to wring additional profits from ratepayers. There was no question that AT&T would be able to absorb increased interstate cost allocations without hiking long-distance rates in compensation.[58]

The FCC's statutory mandate allowed the agency to find that specific interstate tariffs should be altered. As the nation had plunged into depression, toll telephone messages transiting the Bell System had declined sharply—from 1.027 billion in 1929, to 669 million in 1933; toll revenues decreased in step. In response, at the moment of the FCC's maximum leverage during its Telephone Inquiry, informal FCC negotiations with AT&T resulted in substantial reductions in interstate rates. Lowered rates were a boon to the business users that dominated demand for long-distance services, and, in line with the New Deal's economic platform, a stimulus to demand. The FCC jawboned AT&T to lower interstate long-distance rates no less than ten times during the years between 1935 and 1946. The effect, amplified by the mobilization for World War II and then by postwar prosperity, was to induce repeated spikes in toll calling. Intra- and interstate long-distance calls had declined from 756 million in 1929 to 538 million in 1933, but then increased to 805 million in 1940 before rocketing to 1.4 billion in 1945, and to nearly 2 billion in 1949. Toll revenues (again inclusive of both inter- and intrastate long-distance) saw comparable changes: from $319 million in 1929, to $213 million in 1933, to $315 million in 1940, to $765 million in 1945, to nearly $1.1 billion in 1950. "The unusual gains in toll telephone revenues during the war," an authoritative study declared, "reflect the large-scale dispersion of civilians and military personnel throughout the nation and the greater need for long-distance communications in the coordination of wartime production." But the war's spur to telephone demand was temporary: it could not be relied upon to propel continual enlargement of household access during peacetime.[59]

The inter-jurisdictional mechanism was key to the FCC's changing rate policies. NARUC's 1943 attendees heard testimony that "The Federal Communications Commission has dealt with more matters of importance under the cooperative procedure during the past year than in any prior year of its history." In keeping with New Deal purchasing-power theories, the FCC wrestled with AT&T to alter its cost-allocation scheme. The agency hoped to substitute for the board-to-board scheme an equally opaque but, for adherents of purchasing power, more productive doctrine: the so-called station-to-station conception. This pivoted on the idea that local and interexchange calling possessed joint-cost features and that the Joint Board should allocate costs in light of the perceived need to expand use of the network. In 1943, after decades of resistance, AT&T not only acceded to the station-to-state doctrine, but also accepted a further $50 million interstate toll rate decrease.[60]

AT&T predictably learned to exploit loopholes and weaknesses in the emerging inter-jurisdictional mechanism. For the New Deal rate strategy to succeed, it was incumbent on each state commission to institute reduced intrastate rates. And yet, such reductions as did occur totaled a mere fraction of the amount that could—and, according to the FCC and NARUC's own committee on cooperation with the FCC, that should—have been made. AT&T was all-too-evidently still able to have its way with many states.[61]

The FCC responded in its turn. Its long-distance rate decreases accentuated disparities between interstate and intrastate toll calls over comparable distances. That is, on many routes and in many regions, intrastate toll calls now cost more to make than interstate calls over similar distances. Such imbalances were used to generate political pressure on state PUCs, to induce them to lower intrastate charges, so as to make them conform with FCC interstate long-distance rates. Just this course was attempted by PUCs in Louisiana, Georgia, Pennsylvania, Michigan, Utah and other states. Local Bell System companies tried to outflank them, however, by petitioning often-complaisant or ignorant regulators to institute proportionate intrastate rate *raises*. As PUCs tended to acquiesce to Bell and to subvert the FCC, the FCC stuck to its groundbreaking effort to enlarge network use.

Some state regulators, though, were keen adherents of the FCC's program. "Unless the state commissions are both diligent and effective in securing rate reductions of value to intrastate toll users or exchange subscribers in the respective states," NARUC's committee warned sternly in 1944, "we should anticipate that the Federal Communications Commission will promptly move to investigate the interstate rates and earnings of the Bell System companies and endeavor to effect further savings to consumers." With another massive network upgrade following the World War II, subscribership rocketed and pressure to increase local rates correspondingly intensified; in the postwar period through May, 1948, Bell

System companies applied for increases totaling $242 million in intrastate rates in forty-three states and the District of Columbia, and 60 percent of this total was granted by state regulators. By this time, however, by way of repeated informal negotiations with AT&T, the FCC had also managed to lower annual interstate charges by a total of $110 million. The resulting disparity between state message toll schedules and the interstate schedule was estimated for 1950 at $125 million a year. A greater number of state regulators demanded to eliminate these skews—which made them look inept, or worse, as telephone users compared rates for inter- and intrastate services—and insisted that a greater share of the increases in joint costs stemming from the postwar program of network expansion be borne by interstate long-distance services. During the years that followed, the Joint Board met this demand by altering separations procedures.[62]

Progress therefore occasioned significant inter-jurisdictional conflict; nonetheless, real progress was made. In 1943 AT&T had acquiesced to the principle of reapportioning network cost allocations within the context of the Joint Board and, over time, the result was that a greater proportion of revenue recovery requirements was allocated to the interstate jurisdiction. During the postwar period these cost separations became one of the bases of an uneven but fundamental shift toward socially inclusive telephone access. This transformation was also enabled by new innovations in long-haul telecommunications technology.

Whereas toll and exchange services had been performed largely as discrete operations in the early telephone system, now they were fusing into an integral self-service dial network. This reengineering afforded distinct service categories—local and long distance—at joint cost, and at a moment when technical change was swiftly rendering the provision of one type of service (toll, or long distance) more cheaply. "The development of jurisdictional separations since 1943," wrote Sichter, "has reflected the attempt not to subdivide the indivisible, but, contrary to the implications of the word 'separations,' to treat the telephone system as an economic whole. Briefly put," he continued, "separations have been utilized to share the benefits of the economies of scale realized in the provision of toll services with the local exchange services (where no comparable economies of scale were available). As the earnings of the interstate services would become excessive, it became common practice not only to reduce toll rates but also to revise separations procedures to allocate more and more local exchange costs to the interstate jurisdiction. However, the economic environment of the toll services was not static, and the growth of the toll services (partly due to the stimulation of demand caused by reduced toll rates), combined with increasing economies of scale, would again produce excessive interstate earnings, reinitiating the cycle of reduced toll rates and changes in separations procedures."[63]

Beginning in 1951, nearly twenty years after *Smith v. Illinois*, revisions to regulators' cost-allocation methodology resulted in increasingly preferential rates for local telephone users. From the point of view of residents and local exchange access, this program proved an unexcelled success. As we will see, however, almost from the moment that the FCC and the states instituted this cooperative mechanism for shifting joint costs to the interstate jurisdiction, business users began to lobby the FCC for specialized, low-cost long-distance services whose effect was to place destabilizing pressure on this same settlement. Throughout the ensuing policy debates the Joint Board's reductions to local rates were typically characterized as a "cross-subsidy"; however (as also was true for the Post Office) this was a misleading label, a red herring used by detractors to impugn public utility regulation.

The cross-subsidy argument rests on the proposition that the rates Bell was charging for local service were insufficient to pay back the costs of providing that service; toll service charges, in this view, were increased to make up the shortfall between costs and revenues for local service. This proposition was specious, on two counts. First, it mistakenly assumes that the costs of providing local service can be straightforwardly separated from the costs of toll service. Second, it ignores the prior history of the network and its cost structure. For half a century before separations began to shift the industry's cost structure to emphasize inclusive household access, AT&T had implemented its own cost-allocations principles to serve its strategy of building a profitable, unregulated long-distance network. This despite the fact that, from World War I onward, changes in the technology of network development increasingly intermixed local and toll (both intra- and interstate) functions.

Let us also recall that the structure of demand was far from uniform: long-distance users were not spread evenly throughout the population. Long-distance telephone calling remained for many decades a luxury service—a mere 3.1 percent of total daily conversations in 1920. In one account, early in the century business users overall accounted for almost 90 percent of long-distance calling, while one-tenth of business subscribers accounted for nearly 60 percent of business toll calls and over half of all toll calls. In the early 1920s, a study of one state jurisdiction (Nebraska) found, "a minority" of local telephone customers originated toll calls, and a mere 5 percent of subscribers accounted for more than 95 percent of the toll charges. "Since the volume of intrastate toll calls business is about twice that of interstate traffic," added another analyst, "it can be surmised that an even smaller proportion of exchange ratepayers generated interstate message toll business." An AT&T study of the market for toll calling in Peoria during the late 1920s found that just seventy business subscribers—grain distributors, stock yards, flour mills, large distilleries and manufacturers of agricultural machinery and accessories—originated around one-quarter of that city's toll business.[64]

The New Deal recipe for growth altered this arrangement, and it won impressive results. In 1952, the average subscriber used her telephone about 3 percent of the time for interstate calls, and 97 percent of the time for intrastate and local calls; the allocation of common investment costs was in rough accord with this pattern of use. (By one reckoning, in 1940 fully 84 percent of toll calls traveled less than 42 miles.) But successive increases then were mandated in the percentage allocation of subscriber plant costs to interstate rate-making; between 1952 and 1970, the principles were amended six times, so that an ever-greater share of the joint costs of telephone company plant were allotted to the interstate jurisdiction. By the late 1970s, in consequence, about 22 percent of the Bell System's common use plant was allocated to interstate long-distance service, even though only 7 percent of the minutes of usage of an average phone were for interstate messages. Under 1982 FCC rules, the share of joint costs designated as interstate long distance increased again, and totaled $7 billion. Below, I will introduce evidence of what this sustained policy preference meant for residential rates; for now, I will simply underline Weinhaus and Oettinger's conclusion that it "helped to keep local rates lower than they would have been without such a shift":

> The high cost of the local loop and its crucial position in the network make subscriber plant the focus of the industry and of its regulators. Payment of the costs solely through local rates has historically been unacceptable in an environment where regulators believe basic local rates must remain relatively low to encourage the broadest possible distribution of service.

AT&T itself allowed that "the straightforward purpose of separations is to remove cost burdens from intrastate ratepayers and impose those burdens upon interstate ratepayers in order to hold down local rates." The real issue was not "cross-subsidy," but the social purpose of the telecommunications infrastructure. Under the evolving terms of the New Deal political settlement (which endured only until the early 1970s in telecommunications) household consumption— or residential use—was enormously enlarged through lowered local telephone rates.[65]

This change in social function, crucially, did not come at the expense of AT&T. AT&T's nationwide integration, together with its ability to influence regulatory proceedings, meant that telephone rates generally incarnated *both* New Deal measures to ensure universal local service *and* monopoly profits for the telephone company. Two disparate revenue channels—one benefiting US residential telephone users, the other granting super-profits to AT&T—coursed through the bewildering pathways of the rate structure. The two were often not distinguishable. First, state and federal regulators sidestepped a need for accurate cost data by deliberately adhering to rate-averaging policies. Second, transfer pricing between different operating units within AT&T increased or decreased apparent costs, to benefit the corporate parent's bottom line. Additional routine business practices added to the murk. Debt financing could be employed to subsidize particular services by taking out loans as bonds or (as the telephone company had long preferred) by selling stock, backed by the promise of stable, regulated rates of return, and payments strung out over decades. Western Electric's monopoly over Bell System equipment enabled depreciation schedules for capital recovery and replacement to conceal profits. The rate of return authorized by regulators could be haggled over and, to an extent, manipulated. Whether a given service was priced reasonably thus was a function of contestable assumptions about costs, meaning that pricing decisions were almost infinitely controversial. AT&T even may have managed to continue to earn super-profits from exchange service, as former FCC chief economist William Melody would insist. Overall, then, there is no doubt that AT&T benefited from revamping its practices to conform to the New Deal's mass-consumption-oriented political settlement.[66]

In his campaign for the governorship of New York in 1930, Franklin Roosevelt had declared that "public utility corporations must never be our masters but our servants—well paid as all good servants should be, but our servants still." That New Deal regulators did not check AT&T's monopoly profits did not mean that they failed in a more important objective: to widen household access to local telephone service—to create a mass market—by rectifying the prior system of cost-allocations, which had systematically discriminated in favor of the interstate jurisdiction and its wealthy users. Regulators decreased local rates and kept them low, as compared both with toll charges and the general cost of living. Correspondingly, they delivered to the nation a qualitative expansion of residential access.[67]

Rate-setting policy was altered in another way, to support a second basic New Deal aim: a territorial extension of the network to provide rural telephone service. As AT&T put it later, regulators' goal was to "structur[e] the carriers' rates so that basic residential exchange service and long-distance service to high-cost areas would be supported by revenues from other parts of the business." Among the means employed was so-called *value of service* pricing—signifying that business subscribers were charged higher rates than household users for service, irrespective of the relative costs of furnishing the two types of service, because businesses derived additional value from the enlarged residential use of telephones that followed when household users paid a lower rate.

This linkage had originated during telephony's early decades. "Any attempt to make rates proportionate to cost would result in residence charges so high that few householders would use the telephone at all and this would result in greatly impairing its value to the business user," declared the Oregon Public Service Commission in 1919. Value of service pricing also reflected AT&T's own early rate preferences. The Justice Department later would concede that "the value of service pricing concept was well established" by AT&T "before the onset of regulation"; and "Bell developed, applied and pressed for application of the value of service . . . pricing concept[] to serve Bell's own business purposes." However, regulators "expanded and modified" the value-of-service tenet to make it more consistent with New Deal cost-allocation revisions, in other words, "to mean pricing on the basis of non-cost factors to pursue social goals." Value-based pricing policies also underpinned graduated rates, as the size of the local exchange—and the number of subscribers who could be reached on the local network—increased from small town to large urban center.[68]

A related regulatory initiative was rate averaging within local exchanges, among exchanges within a state and, nationwide, across intra- and interstate toll routes. Rate-averaging for the purpose of "area coverage" became a key determinant of enlarged rural telephone access; rate-averaging likewise underlay the postwar trend toward "extended area" exchange service, introduced to facilitate easy routine intercommunication between increasingly dispersed inhabitants of far-flung cities and suburbs. By systematically suppressing cost variations attributable to such factors as subscribers' distances from the local exchange, differences in terrain, varying population densities, types of existing exchange equipment, and service usage characteristics, rate averaging worked both to standardize pricing and to extend network access.

Regulators again had articulated this policy rationale early on. In the New Deal period, the Pennsylvania Public Service Commission linked rate-averaging to the goal of inclusive service provision by resurrecting its own Progressive-era finding:

> If we are to have a comprehensive telephone service in the commonwealth, it is advantageous that such service should be rendered by companies under one control, and that such companies should receive the benefits of being treated as to revenue and expenses from a statewide and not from a segregated or local standpoint. If the segregated theory is to be adopted, there will necessarily result a constriction of telephone development in the state by reason of the companies refusing to develop the unprofitable places. In order to provide for a comprehensive development it seems necessary to have the companies' operations as to service and rates considered from the standpoint of their revenue and expenses as a whole, and if they are found to be reasonable, then an equitable distribution of the burden of the charges can be made between the various communities.

Here was an argument that lodged effective regulatory oversight of a monopoly provider in network economics. The reform-era FCC committed itself to rate averaging precepts for the same reason. In 1937, Carl I. Wheat, the Commission's telephone rate counsel, declared:

> It has also been universally recognized that telephone toll rates cannot successfully be based upon the particular costs involved in transmitting messages of particular routes . . . An averaging process is therefore essential, charges over any particular route and distance being ordinarily the same as for messages over similar distances on any of the other routes served, regardless of the particular costs involved in each individual message or over each individual route. The availability of "long distance" service to patrons on little-used routes is thus vastly broadened, without unduly burdening any particular group or class of potential consumers.

The US Department of Justice later contended that "Regulators were not intent on manipulating an intricate system of subsidies for selected services because the value of service and rate averaging pricing approaches eliminated the generation of cost data that would be essential to regulators' identification of what services were being subsidized and to what extent." But did regulators' use of rate-averaging merely mimic AT&T's corporate preferences, as detractors later charged, or was it instead "largely due to their desire to avoid more cumbersome rate regulation processes which were administratively impracticable"? The FCC disinclination to cost-out individual services along each and every route certainly possessed a rationale beyond the machinations of a conniving monopolist; it expressed regulators' preference no less than practical exigency: "The possibility of attaining . . . nation-wide interstate telephone rate uniformity," forecast the FCC's general counsel in 1939, actually would "eliminat[e] the necessity for the expensive separation studies which must otherwise be undertaken." New Deal regulators *preferred* not to gather specific cost data, because rate averaging itself could be substituted, as a mindful policy, to broaden the scope of standard telephone service. By 1952, the FCC crowed proudly that its goal of nationwide rate uniformity in interstate message toll rates had been attained: "In the years since the creation of the Commission in 1934, there has been a steady movement toward uniform interstate message toll telephone rates throughout the United States."[69]

Other forthright government policies to extend telephone service throughout rural America piggybacked upon the Rural Electrification Act passed in 1936; and demands were vocal that government should supply access to underserved areas of the country on the eve of US entry into World War II. The percentage of farms reached by the telephone network—which, as Fischer shows, declined dramatically between 1920 and 1940—was estimated at 31.8 percent in 1945; however, across the southern states where many Black farm families subsisted (North and South Carolina, Georgia, Alabama, Mississippi, Louisiana, Arkansas) less than 10 percent of farms enjoyed telephone service in 1945. A substantial minority of farms that did possess telephones, moreover, suffered from inferior service owing to inadequate and outmoded facilities.[70]

Congress addressed this disparity somewhat, by amending the Rural Electrification Act to authorize long-term, low-interest loans for telephone organizations that wished to improve and extend service throughout rural America. This federal loan program, as the Justice Department later underlined, "brought about the substantial improvement in farm telephone service." Notably, both Bell and many for-profit independent telephone companies opposed the measure. In rebuke, the House Committee on Agriculture charged that their arguments ("Just let the private telephone industry alone. We're doing the job as fast as it can be done.") echoed those used by the power companies against enactment of Rural Electrification in 1936. While less than 11 percent of the Nation's farms possessed electricity in 1936, fully 70 percent had gained access to electrical lines by 1949. Thus, the Committee declared, "[t]he method of aiding the telephone industry proposed here is one which the Nation knows will work. It has been in operation for more than 13 years for rural-electrification purposes and the tremendous achievement it has stimulated in that field is so well known and universally approved that it needs no commendation here."[71]

For self-serving reasons, AT&T later marshaled evidence that early state and federal regulators' had made impressive legal efforts on behalf of "service extensions" to remote users. Cases from New Jersey in 1913 and Missouri in 1912 were among those cited by AT&T in an effort to claim partial credit for reforms whose realization actually awaited concerted political intervention. From the very beginnings of state utility commission regulation during the Progressive Era, the company declared, the nation had given diligent support to the principle that "A public service corporation may be required to make reasonable extensions of its service even though such extensions do not yield the cost of the service. The losses thus brought about are to be recovered from the business of the company in its entirety." Before the New Deal, though, such support remained desultory and inconsistent, never approaching a true national commitment. Not only did AT&T oppose rural telephony in its own right. According to FCC Commissioner Clifford J. Durr in late 1944, when his friend Senator Lister Hill was drafting a bill with the objective "of getting rural telephone service to the farmers," the Bell companies had put "pressure on the telephone industry periodicals," and many commercial independents were "under the Bell influence."[72]

For this initiative to succeed took additional years. In pushing for enactment of the Rural Telephone bill in 1949, the House Committee on Agriculture recognized the limitations of the piecemeal policy that had prevailed, and sought to refocus on overall system development policy:

> The key to adequate rural telephone service is area coverage. This means planning, financing, and constructing a rural telephone system so that service will be available to all the subscribers within the company's area who want it, whether the installation and operation of their particular telephone will be profitable or not. In other words, it means planning and building the entire area system as a unit rather than following the prevailing practice of telephone companies of building lines where business is most profitable, establishing a rate structure on that profitable business, and then either refusing to extend lines into unprofitable areas or requiring the consumer to bear the expense of such lines.

"When they build a new rural line," the Committee explained, the majority of contemporary telephone companies "count the subscribers who will be served by that line and assure themselves that it will be profitable to operate before it is undertaken":

> This is the exact opposite of area service. Although they claimed to favor the area service type of development, witnesses for the telephone industry, both independents and Bell system operators, almost unanimously refused to commit themselves to provide area service in the areas in which they operate and over which they have in most cases a monopoly. There is every indication that unless they are forced to take such action, they will continue their policy of 'skimming the cream' of the telephone business, running their lines down the highways into the most profitable areas and relegating farmers in the less profitable service areas perpetually to a nontelephone hinterland.

Some 330,000 farm families—three times the increase in any previous year—were hooked up in 1946–1947, and similar increments were added in the two years that followed. This postwar surge in telephone service extension—"the very fact that it is now expanding into many of the more easily reached and highly profitable rural areas"—paradoxically rendered enactment of the Rural Telephone bill "a matter of urgency":

> New lines are being built and new customers added on a selective basis—where the business is most profitable. This type of expansion, with a rate structure and amortization schedule based on these high-profit areas, makes it all the more difficult to add at a later time lines which will be less profitable or even operate

at a unit loss, and all the more certain that farmers in the remote, less profitable areas, will be forever without telephone service.

The clarity of purpose behind the Rural Telephone Act underlay its success. Within a decade of passage of this legislation, over 400,000 rural subscribers had obtained telephone service. By 1968, 80 percent of US farms, some two million rural subscribers, enjoyed telephone service—modern, dial telephone service—and by 1977, the countryside had achieved a rare parity with the city, as fully 94 percent of US farms possessed telephones. Building up rural telephone access originated as another key component of the New Deal's redevelopment of the network as a public utility. Thereby it conveyed into US telephone service a commitment that had been actualized in the nation's Post Office a century before.[73]

*

A congressional report quoted approvingly in 1951 by a joint telephone rate committee of the FCC and the National Association of Railroad and Utility Commissioners sought to enumerate the factors that underlay the huge postwar network buildout. "Due to the depression," it began, the number of newly occupied housing units lagged its normal growth, real family income declined, while the price of telephone service declined less than that of many other consumer goods and services. By contrast, in the immediate postwar years, "these influences were sharply reversed."

> There was a high rate of family formation and a large excess of business births over business deaths. Business and consumer buying power increased sharply above the prewar levels and telephone rates lagged behind the general increase in prices.

This formulation ignored that telephone access was not merely a byproduct of family formation and increased buying power: working-class households *desired* telephone service after World War II, just as they had done since the 1910s. Now, finally—owing to New Deal rate policies—many more of them could satisfy this want. Startled by the surge in telephone service, in 1948 *Nation's Business* cast revealing light on this change:

> Tremendous demands for phones have come from households which the phone people formerly classified as 'can't affords.' Recently a phone installer arrived at an address in a tenement district, looked around, and quickly called the business office. 'This can't be the right place,' he said. 'Why, eight people are living

in one room here.' But when the records were checked the phone went in. Since the end of the war a Georgia cotton mill town has climbed from 1,950 phones to 4,800, an Alabama mining community from 773 to 2,055 . . .

Higher wages, boom times and relatively cheap telephone rates are believed to be the biggest factors in telephone expansion.

A key ingredient, cheap telephone rates were a political achievement. Although the rate of growth of telephones in use was higher during the 1920s than during the late 1940s (4–5 percent versus 3+ percent), during the former period household access was far more limited and smaller increments translated into a higher growth rate. The number of telephones added *each year* between 1945 and 1950 reached 1.3 million, as opposed to three-quarters of a million during the 1920s. At the end of 1950, the 43 million US telephones marked an increase of 96 percent over those in use as of 1940—and three-quarters of this increase had occurred after the War. By the end of 1950, of the nation's 227 largest exchange areas, sporting a collective population of about 64 million, only eleven exchange areas showed a household telephone penetration rate of less than 50 percent; in sixty-nine of them, fully four-fifths or more of all households possessed a telephone. Although many analysts have used the idea of a "golden age" to overstate the extent to which workers—even white, male, unionized workers—actually enjoyed secure prosperity, telephone access was indeed approaching inclusivity.[74]

Once more, this did not happen only because (contrary to many forecasts) a great economic boom was underway; more people having money in their pockets was necessary but, in itself, not sufficient. Household tele-density increased because, in addition to postwar prosperity, New Deal precepts enabled household telephone access to begin to meet demand. In 1946, an academic assessment of the performance of state public utility regulation in depression and war still could declare that, if the commissions "work actively to persuade utilities to adopt rates contrived to explore the lower levels of consumer demand in search of . . . the maximum service consistent with the required earnings, we are in the presence of regulation at is current best—and its rarest." Thereafter, however, this best practice became general. AT&T data suggest that, between 1947 and 1978, Bell system prices overall rose at an annual rate less than half that of the general price level in the economy. Between 1960 and 1973, while average consumer disposable income increased by 122 percent, and the Consumer Price Index increased by 50 percent, the rates for basic residential telephone service increased by 14 percent. Between 1973 and 1978, the CPI increased by nearly 47 percent but residential telephone rate hikes were held to 14 percent. Meanwhile, the redistribution of benefits stemming from increased telephone worker productivity ensured that even long-distance rate hikes were very modest; in 1978, in the aggregate, they were only 9 percent higher than they had been in 1950 while, on some routes, they had declined.[75]

AT&T brought forward these data to serve its corporate interest; but they attest the success of the political drive to broaden network access through public utility regulation. A US Department of Commerce study for the years 1960–1971 demonstrated that the average American needed to work less than twenty-six hours per year to pay for basic telephone service, the lowest total among fifteen nations studied. By contrast, in France one year of basic telephone service cost 179 hours of labor. Local household telephone rates declined in real terms throughout the period; and throngs of new subscribers redeemed the New Deal promise that reallocating costs would stimulate network access. Indeed, between 1950 and 1980, the price of residential local telephone service fell in real dollar terms. Local service revenues reported to the FCC doubled just between 1945 and 1951 as the carriers belatedly learned that exploring the "lower levels of demand" was indeed highly profitable. Still heavily skewed toward business users, long-distance service nevertheless became more affordable—Chuck Berry sang out "Long distance information, get me Memphis, Tennessee."[76]

The New Deal's substantial reconstruction of public utility telephone service brought additional benefits. The FCC oversaw, and ultimately codified, service standards relating to customer waiting times for installation. By mid-1948, two-thirds of Bell telephones were dial technology instruments; a job-killer for operators, dial systems nevertheless translated into efficiency gains. Between 1950 and 1973, the time required to establish a domestic long-distance telephone call dropped from three minutes, on average, to less than forty seconds.[77]

Three additional features of the telephone system's modernization—a program undertaken by AT&T within the public utility framework—merit emphasis. First, it quickly led to the appearance, for the first time, of something approximating comprehensive residential telephone service. By 1956, an estimated 95 percent of households in Boston had telephones. So did 90 percent of households in Los Angeles, 82 percent of households in New York City, 87 percent of households in Pittsburgh, 88 percent of households in San Francisco, 90 percent of households in Washington, D.C., 83 percent of households in Denver, 94 percent of households in Lincoln, Nebraska, and 84 percent of households in Detroit. A swath of southern and southwestern states continued to lag. In three regions—the South Atlantic, East South Central and West South Central states—five out of six farms lacked telephone service in 1948. By 1956, telephone density had improved only somewhat. City household telephone penetration in these regions was estimated at 62 percent in Augusta, GA, 56 percent in Charleston, SC, 62 percent in El Paso, 63 percent in Fort Lauderdale, 54 percent in Huntsville, Alabama, 42 percent in Laredo, Texas. African Americans and Mexican Americans were still palpably underserved and neglected. Despite these persisting inequalities residential access overall continued to expand, so that upward of 90 percent of all US households enjoyed telephone service by the 1970s. Summed up differently, between 1945 and 1968, the number of telephones in the United States quadrupled; and, while the overall cost of living rose by 140 percent between 1940 and 1968, total telephone rates [local and interstate] increased by just 10 percent.[78]

Second, this swelling residential market altered the telephone industry's structural center of gravity. Even as all categories of telephone service expanded, the proportion of business to residential telephones declined. In 1944, this ratio had stood at 57 percent; by 1955, it had dwindled to 43.3 percent; and it continued to drop until, for around a decade between 1965–1975, it stabilized at about 36–37 percent. This did not owe to a decline in business telephone use—to the contrary, corporations were intensifying their use of networks. It occurred, rather, because residential telephone demand was even greater. As something approaching universal residential telephone service at last came into its own, the industry itself relied increasingly on household provision. Through a coherent national system of public utility regulation aimed toward universal service, that is, AT&T's corporate fortunes were now welded more strongly to the residential market.[79]

The telephone was a fixture within the everyday experience of nearly 200 million individual lives by 1968. However, this huge network expansion had been matched by an altered social purpose. New Deal attempts to rebuild telecommunications as an encompassing public utility coexisted and intertwined with the enlistment of the telephone, paralleling the Post Office, into the sales effort. The social functions of telephone service were in part redirected, as policymakers and corporate executives bent their efforts to strengthening the telephone network's capacity to help circulate and absorb privately produced commodities.

*

In 1928, the Illinois Bell Telephone Company published a slim volume on "Planning For Home-Telephone Conveniences." Depictions of homes were graded, from lavish mansions to modest middle-class residences. Neither renters nor the urban or rural poor were accorded representation. "With the growing appreciation on the part of telephone subscribers of the conveniences to be obtained from adequate telephone service," the booklet observed, "a greater number of telephones is being installed in homes. The telephone company," it continued, "will be glad to consult with architects, builders and home owners concerning the location of telephones and the variety of services which are available to meet differing household communication requirements." The Bell affiliate offered additional telephone lines, as well as additional bells, switches for intercommunication between telephones, portable telephones for plugging into jacks at "appropriate" places, "and many other related convenience facilities."[80]

While gesturing toward convenience and plenitude, the volume limited its marketing effort to privileged social strata. Other telephone company practices likewise bespoke a comparably constricted approach. Inclusive residential consumption of telephone service was still remote—blocked.

During the growth era of the 1920s, withal, AT&T began to marry its engineering concerns for network efficiency and service quality to consumer preferences concerning telephone aesthetics, style, and convenience. Over ensuing decades this approach became concretized in the telephone receivers it provided for "access to the network." Its 500-type telephone, introduced in 1949, was trumpeted as a triumph of engineering research and development, "utilizing new circuit principles, new materials, and new knowledge of the human factors in telephone usage." The set was produced "so efficiently by the Western Electric Company," boasted a later Bell Telephone Laboratories publication, "that its price to the Bell companies was well below that of any other telephone set available in the entire world."[81]

AT&T had not embraced the auto industry's ballyhooed annual model changes, which showcased minor stylistic alterations to increase sales. Continuing to furnish subscribers with a basic black telephone, AT&T's paramount goals instead remained performance, reliability, durability, and cost: its telephones aimed, first and foremost, to reproduce and convey speech with fidelity and to manage signals efficiently. It would be a mistake, nevertheless, to think that at midcentury AT&T's telephones embodied only an artless utilitarianism.[82]

Redesigned to attain higher levels of engineering performance during the interwar years, AT&T's handsets also began to model—indeed, they helped to pioneer and popularize—a modernist aesthetic. For this, AT&T turned to a leading industrial designer, Henry Dreyfuss. Dreyfuss worked with Bell Laboratories for three decades beginning in 1930 (the company he founded continuing in this relationship thereafter), and produced breakthrough handset designs, notably, the 302 (1937) and the model 500 desk set—of which a stunning 93,412,000 units were produced between 1950 and 1982. Michael Sorkin aptly underscores the significance: "the phone is unique among examples of mass design for consumer use in that for much of its history it has been sheltered from the vagaries of taste and the manipulations of the marketplace."[83]

This was a remarkable achievement. Western Electric's telephones encapsulated design as a collective aesthetic rather than a marketing tool. They were sheltered from the compulsion of incessant model changes by public utility regulation of AT&T's monopoly.

Although they had been available on a marginal (because very expensive) basis for some decades, color options came into widespread use only beginning in the mid-1950s. And Bell exacted from early adopters of color an additional installation fee, a premium averaging a substantial $6 as late as 1964. This surcharge acted as a disincentive so that, of the 71 million AT&T telephones in service in 1964, more than 40 million were black. Even in 1978, after the emergence of competition in US telecommunications and with pushbutton phones now in the majority and decorator and special feature instruments abundant, over one-third of all US telephone set production—6.3 million units—still was devoted to manufacturing standard rotary dial telephones. Standard sets including the 500 series, the Princess and the Trimline accounted for 97 percent of phones installed that year.[84]

AT&T's corporate power and the public utility regime together continued to infuse telephone design. Habituated to a particular handset numbering scheme, to the placement of the dialing mechanism, and to the familiar pitch of the instrument's ring, subscribers could not be arbitrarily ordered to accept capriciously designed new models. A *Life* Magazine article of 1949 extolled how "exhaustive research produces new shape and controlled ring" and crowed over how "change-overs from one model to the next are a costly and gradual process." Participation in this public good aesthetic proved both enduring and widespread.[85]

That AT&T's telephones could not be purchased but only rented also needs to be set in this context. Originating in AT&T's insistence that it should control all network elements, ostensibly to ensure the service quality and safety of the system, for decades the handset-rental policy also bulwarked the company's monopoly. In the altered context of New Deal regulation, however, AT&T's rental policy was vested with additional significance: it encouraged a dependability that was atypical among consumer industries. Handsets were built to last—for decades; and their long depreciation schedules guaranteed not only steady profits for AT&T but also lower rates for residential subscribers. Service plans were correspondingly limited, and consumer marketing undeveloped. Once more, this did not signify a monopolistic stasis, but that the telephone utility should incarnate public good attributes.[86]

"Information" likewise was bundled into the package of basic residential telephone service. "Information" offered hints of how expansively the labor of telephone operators was etched into the nation's everyday life. With the postwar growth of household telephone service, subscriber requests for information from Bell System operators soared. In 1960, there were 350 million such calls; by 1970, the number had risen to nearly 500 million. In this period, some 3 percent of all telephone calls were "information" requests, and the Bell System employed 40,000 Information operators. For decades, members of the public made staggeringly multifarious requests. Travel information, baseball scores, recipes: "'They even ask us to recommend doctors,' says Anna Mae Wise, a New York Telephone

Co. information operator for the past 17 years." When this cultural habit surfaced in news accounts, as in this 1969 story, it was treated as an odd-ball curiosity, and subjected to sexist condescension. Incontestably, however, decades before the World Wide Web, throughout the quotidian US telephone users urged a broadened function upon the public utility telephone system—and the operators often did their best to oblige. Dorothy de Phillis, a New York City information operator, "tells of a little old lady who used to call often throughout the day 'to find out if it is two o'clock so I can take my medicine.'" Into the late 1960s, and despite AT&T management opposition, "In actual practice, many operators help out if they can. If someone asks for travel directions, for instance, the operator will provide the number of a railroad or an airline. Some operators say they have given out the names of doctors—and even recommended a method for cooking spareribs." This is not to suggest that relationships between operators and subscribers were uniformly mutualistic or cordial. Venus Green shows that, during the early 1970s, as AT&T belatedly hired African American women into the ranks of its operator work force, often "subscribers mercilessly abused" them with racist and sexist epithets. I am arguing, rather, that "Information" betrayed a complex and sometimes-resistant relation with the trend toward consumerism in telecommunications.[87]

The popularity of "Information" was, however, increasingly at odds with AT&T management strategy. Company executives began to try "to reduce information calls to the barest minimum" and mandated that their previously expansive nature be canalized to the provision of telephone listings for subscribers. It would be but a small step to automated and, eventually, online self-service. This suppression of "Information" as a cultural habit occurred within a more sweeping campaign to set the telecommunications industry on an altered political-economic foundation. First, the telephone company studied the issue, and learned that, supposedly, only a small fraction of subscribers accounted for the vast majority of calls for information. On the basis of this finding, second, AT&T subsidiaries began to institute substantial charges for what was now a more limited service, relabeled "Directory Assistance." Early in 1974, Cincinnati Bell instituted a 20-cent charge for each such call and, *Business Week* chortled, "the results have been spectacular. In a month, directory assistance calls dropped by 80% from residences and 75% from businesses." Cost savings followed: Cincinnati Bell, for example, reduced its operator force by 24 percent to 237. People protested this curtailment, for example, in California, where in 1976 it was attacked by the Campaign Against Utility Service Exploitation—for contributing to higher unemployment. But, seemingly inexorably, the trend went national. By 1988, only Tennessee among the fifty states had imposed no fees at all for Information calls, though some other states continued not to charge residential subscribers. Automation of operators' jobs, a continuing management fixation, completed the task of Information's impoverishment even as it decimated the occupation whose function was to provide it.[88]

Inroads against the common attributes of the telephone as a public utility came as AT&T gave increasing thought to catering for consumers. AT&T's design strategy in turn became circumscribed increasingly by marketing considerations, as the telephone company unveiled new handset models with specialized features aimed at specific target groups (women), and paid more attention to segmented markets (teenagers). Color options were more widely marketed. As scarcity belatedly gave way to abundance, Bell looked for revenue growth by marketing extension phones; and the number of lines per residence increased.[89]

Akin to the Post Office, the telephone network was significantly reoriented, to enhance its functions as a tool for marketing and circulating *other* commodities. Yellow Pages advertising helped set the trend. Originating late in the nineteenth-century as brief sheets of local business listings, by the postwar period a portion of the telephone directory was already an established means of selling advertising to businesses, still mostly local. But national advertisers were beginning to fasten on this medium also. In 1950, a print ad in the *Wall Street Journal* admonished readers to "See Your Local Ford Dealer Conveniently Listed In The Yellow Pages Of The Telephone Directory." In 1960, it became possible to place advertising in as many of the nation's 4,000-odd directories as desired, through a single centralized office—and with commissions to advertising agencies, who now fitted this arrow into their quiver of media-marketing tools. The profile attained by the Yellow Pages was elevated to the point that it provoked an international incident: Amid China's Cultural Revolution, the giant US commercial publisher, Reuben H. Donnelly, received an angry response from Chinese officials after it listed Taiwan as the Republic of China in its International Yellow Pages directory.[90]

Still operating under public utility strictures, telephone companies needed authorization from state regulators for their Yellow Pages charges, especially when they requested rate increases. By 1975, when AT&T's operating companies alone provided 2,200 separate directories, national advertising agencies such as Doyle, Dane, Bernbach were instituting specialized telephone marketing-services divisions. Seven years later, when AT&T announced its break-up as a result of a Justice Department antitrust suit, its Yellow Pages publishing unit constituted a two billion dollar advertising channel—in the vicinity of advertiser expenditures for broadcast radio and print magazines.[91]

A second milestone in the partial repurposing of the telephone system arrived in 1967. Inward WATS (wide area telephone, or toll, service)—toll-free numbers, the first batch of which used the long-distance prefix 800—harnessed the residential telephone to the cause of corporate marketing. WATS was an instant success. Customers, who had previously been encouraged to make "collect" calls in order to connect with nationwide corporate sales and marketing departments, had not embraced this option: it seemed cumbersome, confusing, and perhaps even prone to result in an erroneous charge on the residential subscriber's bill. When AT&T rolled out toll-free 800 numbers, by contrast, callers no longer had to make such calculations. Client companies' payments for this service in turn rocketed: By 1972 National Data Corporation, headquartered in Atlanta, spent $200,000 each month for 170 WATS lines, over which traveled 100,000 daily calls; the system was used chiefly to verify charges for 200 million gasoline credit cards. Leading applications of Inward WATS were motel reservations, credit card verification, and customer calls to ascertain where an advertised product was available for purchase.[92]

By the early 1970s, corporate sales campaigns routinely listed toll-free numbers in broadcast and print advertising (including the Yellow Pages). A US Army recruiting drive during the Vietnam War showcased an 800 number in a thirteen-week, $10.6 million broadcast advertising effort, to provide information about where to find local recruiting offices. The corporate take-up of toll-free lines, however, was the fulcrum; by 1972, five years after they were introduced, 10,600 businesses had signed up as customers. The consumer response resulted in an impressive volume of calls, and AT&T staffed a dedicated 800-number in East St. Louis to handle this specialized category of Information or, as it preferred, "Directory Assistance." For AT&T, Inward WATS and Outward WATS—a service permitting corporations and other high-volume customers to make outgoing calls at discounted rates—together reaped about $315 million in 1967, rising to $1.9 billion in 1976 and then tripling to $6.1 billion in 1982, the year of the AT&T break-up. Toll-free calls, exclaimed an AT&T spokesman in 1972, had already "almost created a new industry." With the telephone-tree automation that followed, again it would be but a short step to the self-service that later would engulf us with the World Wide Web.[93]

*

The New Deal's premier achievement was to reconstruct the telephone network as an inclusive public utility for use by the nation at large. Households and individuals were enabled to put the network to a plethora of uses, involving family and friends, community activities, voluntary associations, governments—and commodity consumption. For, throughout the early postwar decades the telephone system joined the Post Office as a vital business channel for marketing and circulating commodities. Mounting commercialization was accompanied by a second profound alteration to public utility telecommunications as, during the decade after World War II, the federal government intervened to ensure that the unmatched technological resources of AT&T would better serve US imperial and Cold War interests.

8
Patents under Pressure, 1920s–1950s

A government grant, a patent constitutes what courts and lawyers once forthrightly called a "privilege." The content and form of this privilege have varied. The US Constitution declares that, in order to stimulate innovation and, thereby, to promote social well-being, publicly accessible patents on inventions may be deeded to individuals for a limited term. When this period expires, a patent reverts to a common fund of open knowledge. Within this framework the range of things patentable, the term and transferability of the patent monopoly, the privileges accorded to patent-holders, and thus the overall orientation of the patent prerogative have been mutable. Historians have discovered that this opaque realm has witnessed recurrent contestation and change.[1]

This chapter begins by reviewing a well-known episode of telecommunications technology development during the early decades of the twentieth century. Between the 1910s and the early 1930s, some of the very largest US corporations collectively endeavored to erect a proprietary patent monopoly over the fledgling radio industry. They were soon met by substantial, but only somewhat successful, counter-pressures. During the Depression that followed, though, these companies' efforts to exert proprietary patent control widened into a major political issue—one that gained renewed relevance during and after World War II. Marshaling fresh evidence I showcase the pivotal role of patents in a Justice Department antitrust action originating in 1943, formally lodged against AT&T in 1949, and settled in 1956. This case, brought in order to break up the giant company—but settled virtually without reference to that motivating objective—has, for this reason and others, often been viewed as a sell-out to Bell. However, its outcome is best seen in a quite different light. The prosecution itself helped ensure that the foundational technology of digital capitalism—microelectronics—would not be ensnared in a proprietary web of AT&T patents. The settlement went further, by securing AT&T's unrivaled research and development facilities overall as a patent utility for the US corporate-military establishment, rather than what they had been: a more purely private enterprise.

The Nineteenth Century Patent System Bends for Monopoly Capital

During the late nineteenth century corporate research laboratories burgeoned into a primary feature of big capital in high-tech industries including chemicals, telecommunications, and electrical power. As they increased and formalized their reliance on R&D, large enterprises turned to the patent system, which vested patent-holders with exclusive proprietary control: a state-sanctioned monopoly that was unique among the nation's trading partners. The importance of these corporate "idea factories" burgeoned, for business profit strategies, for the engineers and scientists who worked for these high-tech corporations and who were contractually obligated to turn over rights to their inventions as a condition of employment, and for the political economy at large.[2]

Patents were a volatile matrix of policy and practice. High-tech corporations sought, in the first instance, to control new inventions solely in their own right. This, however, often proved impossible and, sometimes, undesirable. In such cases they tried to extend exclusive proprietary arrangements by instituting patent-licensing schemes, so as to divide up—that is, to cartelize—a market among a small group of companies, simultaneously defending against incursions by outside units of capital. If such a pooling agreement could not be satisfactorily concluded, companies' rival or overlapping patent claims might thwart their overarching mutual drive for profitable market development. Under these circumstances, government-mandated patent licensing could supply an emergency solution; and this solution indeed was applied to strategic industries during World War I. In 1917, for example, one government-brokered program signified "that the American aviation industry would operate without major patents": members of the Manufacturers Aircraft Association would share among themselves the necessary ideas and techniques so that "the combined knowledge of everybody concerned is brought out."[3]

Testimony offered later on by Bell Laboratories President Frank B. Jewett clarified a second crucial benefit afforded big companies by patent-sharing schemes: "I think that not only for the telephone company, but for a great many industries, some form of cross-licensing arrangement is of prime necessity.... the only way to do a physical thing which is of very great advantage . . . is to bring it to a common picture in some way, the necessary parts which are covered by patents held adversely." Their imperative for unfettered creative technology design joined their interest in arranging mutually profitable market divisions as the underpinning for high-tech corporations' agreements to pool knowledge.[4]

Patents continued to function as the coin of the realm in an emerging cycle of high-tech capitalist development; but the mints were corporate research laboratories operating on multimillion dollar budgets and employing hundreds, even thousands, of scientists and engineers both on problems of basic science and on the cutting edges of practical innovation. As Aitken states, the power of these corporate titans of high-technology lay not only in "the arsenal of patents" they commanded, "but in the fact that General Electric, Western Electric, and Westinghouse were the leading centers of industrial research in electronics." It was their ability to exploit science and engineering that endowed these companies with leverage in deploying patents as strategic leverage to ensure that they could retain freedom of design in their research and development of new technologies.[5]

There were many Americans, however, who believed that monopoly capital's proprietary cross-licensing schemes disserved both polity and society: that the patent privilege had been usurped. During the early decades of the twentieth century those who thought this way included inventor-entrepreneurs, small businesses, labor union leaders and working Americans.

Perhaps the leading magnet of conflict over patent issues was the nation's preeminent corporate research and engineering power: the facilities, already operated by a technical staff of perhaps two thousand early in the 1920s, that became AT&T's Bell Telephone Laboratories in 1925. Debate over AT&T's peerless scientific and engineering resources twisted through the decades, before veering toward resolution in the 1950s.[6]

*

In the run-up to World War I, versatile new forms of radio technology were at the threshold as the electromagnetic spectrum began to be harnessed to transmit telegraph and telephone signals. The result was paradoxical: As in aerospace and auto manufacturing, a thicket of patent claims and counter-claims obstructed both system development and market mastery. "Development of the radio industry, both in the manufacture of radio apparatus and in the operation of reliable commercial transoceanic systems," recalled a 1924 account, "was retarded while the numerous broad and fundamental radio patents were owned and controlled by opposing interests." This outcome threatened to paralyze radio's effective exploitation during the World War. Assistant Secretary of the Navy Franklin D. Roosevelt interceded, indemnifying manufacturers of radio apparatus against rival patent interference claims. A viable patent pool was established, enabling fulfillment of large and profitable military orders. Radio technology was freed to participate in the murderous business of World War I, where it was deployed principally to make wireless telegraph apparatus. What, though, would be the fate of this lucrative and effective patent-sharing arrangement once peace came?[7]

A few Navy officers, intent on developing a US-based system of international telecommunications, appealed on grounds of patriotic duty to Owen D. Young, corporate chairman of General Electric, which possessed some of the vital patent rights to radio. Perhaps more important, they also offered Young a tempting ready-made market in the form of naval procurements. Young thereupon established the Radio Corporation of America, bidding to rationalize corporate control of radio technology on a wider basis by forging intricate intercompany patent agreements with a few other large high-tech companies. With his success, the prewar frustration over radio technology gave way—Young would hold—to a rational arrangement that was beneficial to the public:

> I was confronted with the problems of trying to get, with all these scattered patents, a functioning radio system. . . . It was utterly impossible for anybody to do anything in radio, any one person or group or company at that time. The Westinghouse Co., the American Telephone & Telegraph Co., the United Fruit Co., and the General Electric Co. all had patents, but nobody had patents enough to make a system. And so there was a complete stalemate. Radio could not go ahead at all, and the patent mobilization was not for the purpose of creating a monopoly, but it was to relieve the restraints upon the art, so that somebody could create and develop radio.

RCA became the centerpiece of Young's bold profit strategy. It would function as the hub of an evolving corporate cartel, or "trust," whose member companies' initially controlled around two thousand patents, including some tossed in by the US Navy. Subsequent historians have agreed that, in total, these encompassed "practically all the patents of importance in the radio science of that day." These were pooled on an exclusive basis, permitting the corporate cartel members to divide among themselves the overall market for radio equipment and wireless-telegraph services. Monopoly capital thus seemed to be presiding over a decisive historical expansion of the nineteenth century patent model, based on unabridged proprietorship and excludability.[8]

RCA's establishment fitted a larger historical contour. During the turn of the century decades, US leaders committed the country to policies of global expansionism and, very often, imperial expansionism. This program drew in political-economic, financial, cultural, and military projections. All of these in turn interacted with, and increasingly relied upon, telecommunications. RCA was established, with US Government participation (two Naval officers were appointed to its corporate board), to constitute a "chosen instrument" of US policy—by anchoring a transoceanic system of wireless telegraph communications with the United States as its command center. Initially, RCA seemed to incarnate a veritable fusion of corporate and state power.

This story, and the unanticipated emergence of radio broadcasting that altered it, has been told many times. But neither the depth of the opposition generated by the high-tech cartel nor the long-lasting ramifications of its blatant exercise of corporate patent power have been adequately clarified. As the members of the cartel fell out among themselves over broadcasting, the trust's patent practices—AT&T's perhaps above all—became intensely controversial. Some government agencies began to investigate and attempt to check such abuses. These attempts turned out to be early salvos in a little-known process of transforming AT&T's proprietary patent model, which concluded only in the mid-twentieth century.[9]

High-tech capital's version of patent policy was far from universally agreeable. This was, first of all, because of its stunning ambitions. Territorially, the radio cartel's reach carried far beyond the domestic industry. From the outset—late in 1919, when it still encompassed only GE and RCA—its objectives were demonstrably international. The originating US companies began by instituting both patent interchanges and traffic agreements with the existing global leader in radiotelegraph service, British Marconi. A testament to the changing postwar balance of power, British Marconi not only bowed out of the US market by selling its subsidiary, American Marconi, to RCA, but also acquiesced to market-sharing arrangements with the US-based company. Thereafter, even as AT&T, United Fruit, and Westinghouse came in with GE's radio consortium, a pair of additional European companies joined up at their end; detailed market-divisions were instituted on a worldwide basis. During the Fall of 1921, the so-called "AEFG consortium," historian Hugh Aitken relates, was "hammered out by Young in a series of difficult negotiations" with representatives of the dominant radio companies based in England, France and Germany. Slated to endure until 1930, in the case of AT&T, and until 1945 for the other signatories, these agreements granted to each cooperating company "the exclusive right to the use of the other company's patents within its respective territories, as well as for 'mutual traffic arrangements wherever possible throughout the world." This international market arrangement clashed increasingly with RCA's concurrent role as a chosen instrument of US foreign policy.[10]

A second and less-familiar vector of intended scope added another vast industry to their venture. "Under the agreements made among the five companies," opponents charged, "they have apportioned, not only the entire field of radio but . . . the entire field of electrical development." That the attempt was to cartelize not just communications, but "the huge field of electricity," aptly observed a spokesman for independent radio equipment manufacturers, was palpable in the very definitions set forth in 1920 by GE and AT&T in the legal instrument by which they jointly agreed to distinguish their respective markets in communications and power. For Oswald F. Schuette, these definitions revealed the grotesque immensity of the corporate collaborators' aims. For example,

'Wire telephony' is the art of communicating or reproducing sound waves (created, directly or indirectly, by the voice or by musical instruments) by means of electricity, magnetism or electromagnetic waves, variations, or impulses conveyed or guided by wires, and includes all generating, measuring, switching, signaling, and other means or methods incidental to or involved in such communication.

And:

'Power purposes' are defined as including all prime movers and their accessories and all generation, use, measurement, control, and application of electricity for light, heat, and power, but does not include any communication purposes.

Grating dissatisfaction followed in the train of this corporate enclosure, provoking a 1924 report by the Federal Trade Commission. Not least, this was because by this time radio broadcasting had suddenly and unexpectedly overtaken wireless telegraphy as the technology's most explosively expansive application. Opportunities were opening rapidly for competing suppliers; as early as late 1922 there were perhaps two hundred independent manufacturers. "This movement was so overwhelmingly strong that the original conception of GE and Westinghouse of supplying almost all the radio-set demand was impossible of execution," writes Maclaurin: "The new capitalists who entered the industry, in such companies as Philco, Zenith and Emerson, were hard-hitting and aggressive." Nor was monopoly control over broadcasting service immune to the interlopers.[11]

AT&T was pursuing a broad program of research and innovation in radio technology, notably to complement its existing wireline network. AT&T also decided, in 1922, to push off on its own behalf by establishing a network, or "chain," of affiliated radio broadcast stations, led by its WEAF in New York City—and refused to extend wire connections to competing broadcasters, either for networking of their stations or coverage of special events via its network connections. The response to AT&T's action may be seen as a precursor of the campaign for "network neutrality" in our own time. Marcus Loew, part-owner of Ridgewood, New York radio station WHN, responded in a front-page news story after AT&T brought suit in 1924 against his unlicensed (by AT&T) station: "The issue between the American Telephone and Telegraph Company and the radio public is not a narrow question of patent infringement.... The broad issue is whether the American Telephone and Telegraph may own and control to its own aggrandizement the most important source of public information of the future.... If that corporation, a quasi public service corporation, be given the right to control this vitally important source of public information, there is no restraint upon its distortion of public opinion to its own ends. What is to prevent the attempt to influence public opinion to support unreasonable telephone and telegraph rates! . . . We do not believe that the patent laws were intended to grant to any one such despotic power as the plaintiffs claim, but if they do, it is essential that those laws be changed at once." AT&T's actions likewise generated conflict *within* the cartel, whose other members were no less intent on moving into broadcast markets and who also claimed the right to do so under the suddenly ambiguous cross-licensing agreements. AT&T's "drive for licensing," as Maclaurin stresses, thus "caused great opposition": "The broadcasters feared that the Telephone company would attempt to obtain a monopoly of entertainment broadcasting, after an initial experimental period, as it had done in telephone communications."[12]

In response, a newly christened Radio Group (RCA, GE and Westinghouse) attempted to leverage its own patent position and to compel users to lease or purchase its equipment; its members demanded royalties from outside manufacturers trying to break into the market by making and selling vacuum tubes and radio sets of their own. RCA would grant patent licenses—at a 7.5 percent royalty rate—only to large ($100,000) customers and, significantly, required that licensees give RCA an option to acquire any of their radio-related patents. In what Maclaurin in 1949 termed "an interesting story of the use of patents to dominate an industry," GE, Westinghouse and RCA "did succeed, after a lengthy struggle in the 1920's, in substantially reducing the number of manufacturers during these years and requiring those remaining in business to take a license from them." As a result, according to Howeth, "for over half an important decade, the development of radio had been slowed by the patent policy of the largest manufacturers."[13]

All this corporate infighting, and especially that by the members of the cartel, left a deep political impress. By the early 1920s, backed by a congressional resolution, the Federal Trade Commission was investigating RCA and its corporate affiliates for potential antitrust violations. The cartel's efforts to monopolize vacuum tube technology comprised the central concern. "Patent racketeering," a critic volunteered, best characterized the Trust's use of patents to intimidate would-be market entrants. "The Radio Protective Association," a trade group comprised of smaller companies mushrooming up in manufacturing centers nationwide, carried out an active campaign in Washington against the Radio Corporation of America and its affiliates companies. A prominent member of the Executive Branch also reacted. Historian Leonard Reich declares that "Secretary of Commerce Herbert Hoover was clearly referring to Bell when he wrote in 1924, 'I can state emphatically that it would be most unfortunate for the people of this country to whom broadcasting has become an important incident of life if its control should come into the hands of any single corporation, individual or combination. It would be in principle the same as though the entire press of the country were so controlled. The effect would be identical whether this control arose under a patent monopoly or under any form of combination.' "[14]

Critics brought disparate ideals and concerns to the debate, but they shared a conviction that the patent provision of the US Constitution was being perverted. Rather than being used to lay claim temporarily to a discrete invention, the patent prerogative was being held in thralldom to wall off an ever-expanding territory of profit on a permanent basis. Onerous conditions and restrictions also were being routinely imposed on prospective market entrants. Patents, that is, were being employed in restraint of trade. Adversaries bent their efforts to limit the reach of these corporations' patent privileges.[15]

A significant legal basis for some sort of reform seemed to have been built. One of RCA's attorneys conceded to Congress in 1928 that "there is extreme disagreement between many as to the rights patents confer." However, as domestic broadcast markets boomed, the members of the Radio Group settled their internal rivalries profitably through a new market restructuring; moreover, during the mid-1920s, AT&T withdrew from a direct role in broadcasting. This did nothing to allay anger at patent abuses, as independent capital flooded into radio where it still confronted the Radio Group. Political efforts to restrict and undercut exclusionary market-development strategies persisted. Although RCA had momentarily succeeded in establishing "an almost complete patent monopoly on all phases of radio broadcast receivers," therefore, by the late 1920s it had been forced onto the defensive. Not least, the cartel's patent practices had entered popular consciousness—and, subsequently, collective memory—as a widely available negative reference model, and thereby helped carry forward the debate over patent policy into subsequent decades.[16]

The 1920s produced two further political counter-initiatives: a Department of Justice antitrust proceeding beginning in 1928, and the antimonopoly provisions of the Radio Act, passed in 1927. Competing and would-be competing capitals inspired much of this political effort; but the sites and sources of opposition to RCA were disparate.

The Radio Act expressly targeted monopoly control. Section 13 directed the Federal Radio Commission to refuse the award of a station license to anyone found guilty in federal court of attempting to monopolize radio communications "directly or indirectly, through the control of the manufacture or sale of radio apparatus, through exclusive traffic agreements, or by any other means or to have been using unfair methods of competition." Section 15—expressly reversing the previous Harding Administration's promise of antitrust immunity to the patent-based cartel—provided that US laws relating to unlawful restraints and monopolies and to combinations, contracts, or agreements in restraint of trade "are hereby declared to be applicable to the manufacture and sale of and to trade in radio apparatus and devices entering into or affecting interstate or foreign commerce and to interstate or foreign radio communications." Section 17 prohibited cross-ownership of radio systems by submarine cable or wireline telegraph or telephone system owners.[17]

The incorporation into the enabling legislation of these antimonopoly provisions was exceptional; experts attributed it to the cartel's systematic pursuit of patent excludability. The Radio Law committee of the American Bar Association reported in 1929 that "in part at least, it is to the ... cross-licensing agreements and to the endeavors of the owners and licensees to enforce their patents that we owe the drastic antitrust provisions of the Radio Act of 1927." "That the provisions were aimed primarily at the Radio Corporation of America, the General Electric Company, the Westinghouse Electric & Manufacturing Company, and others included in what has frequently been referred to as the 'radio trust,'" the ABA committee summed up, "is not open to doubt."[18]

These strictures carried prospectively dire consequences for the Trust. The American Bar Association explained that Section 17 "forbids combination of practically any sort between persons engaged in wire communication and persons engaged in wireless communication." Thus was an early attempt at corporate convergence in communications halted in its tracks. The ABA underlined as well a second essential feature of the provision: "The licensing authority is given no discretion whatever; it must refuse a license to any person convicted of an unfair method of competition, no matter how trivial the offense may have been and without regard to its effect (or lack thereof) on radio communication."[19]

It did nothing to help the Radio Trust when it was revealed that its profit strategy had been predicated on patents claims that were widely taken to have been corrupt. The US Alien Property Custodian had seized a trove of 106 German radio patents during World War I; on February 6, 1919, the Navy then secured these patents for its own use by purchase. Very likely, Navy Secretary Josephus Daniels, who was pressing for a thoroughgoing and permanent Navy takeover of radio, planned to use them in his bid; in any case, they went into the wartime patent pool. The denationalization of US telecommunications following the War left open the fate of these patents, some of them important. Because the Navy was just then helping to establish RCA as a "chosen instrument" of US foreign policy, they were quietly added to the company's patent portfolio.[20]

Looking back ten years later, Senator Clarence Dill diplomatically suggested that, "owing to the creation of the Radio Corporation of America, at the suggestion of naval officers, the policy of the Navy Department has been not to fight the Radio Corporation of America about its patents." Other analysts were less forgiving. Collusion between the radio cartel and military agencies, a representative of the independent radio interests charged, had persisted: the Navy had refused to intercede, even when smaller market rivals pressed the question of a crucial patent's provenance through a pair of US lawsuits: This key patent, they asserted, should not have been made available solely to RCA. The patents controlled by the Radio Cartel nonetheless acquired legal priority. Lieutenant Colonel Joseph I. McMullen, Judge Advocate of the US Army, in 1928 testified that the issue "has all been ironed out," affirming that "with regard to some things you have got to build up monopolies in order to get good public service."[21]

In fact the question of RCA's patent monopoly remained anything but settled. It erupted again during congressional hearings the next year, over the establishment of a prospective Federal Communications Commission. Attention focused once more on purported machinations over the German patents between the Radio Trust and Executive Branch agencies. Led by Captain Stanford C. Hooper, Director of Naval Communications and previously a principal in the formation of RCA, a succession of representatives from the War Department and the Navy testified, with evident discomfort, as to what had transpired. A Navy officer, Harold Dodd, refuted the claim by Oswald Schuette of the independent radio manufacturers, that the Navy had forbidden the cross-licensing of its patent holdings to small radio equipment manufacturers. But no witness rebutted Schuette's assertion that the Navy had refused to test its patent rights in court against those of the Radio Group. Senator Robert B. Howell excoriated this as mutual back-scratching: "the Navy Department has not been insisting upon its prior rights to the tuned frequency patent, but has allowed the Radio Corporation of America to go on and sell the apparatus and compel manufacturers to pay them a royalty, amounting to millions of dollars; so that we might say that was as a sort of recompense for their organizing this Radio Corporation?" RCA's drumbeat claim, that it had been established as a matter of high national purpose, now looked more like tawdry self-promotion: the company's backers had draped it in the flag merely to deflect attention from an illegitimate union of military and corporate power.[22]

Peter Irons observes that "the industrial elite was unpleasantly surprised by the vigorous antitrust policies of the . . . Hoover administration." Certainly, this was true for the radio side of telecommunications. In May 1930, President Herbert Hoover's Department of Justice brought forward an extraordinary antitrust suit charging Sherman Act violations against the radio cartel. In 1931, Attorney General William Mitchell sent out a release suggesting that the case might be settled by instituting "an open patent pool into which all patents important in the radio field might be brought and their use made open to the public on terms fair and reasonable to patent owners on one side and the industry on the other and the industry be largely relieved of interminable and expensive disputes over patent rights." The Justice Department, claimed his announcement, "has kept in close touch with the representatives of the independents in the radio industry and the creation of such a patent pool is one of the proposals advanced by them as a possible solution." However, the Attorney General's hopes were not at once born out: "We have postponed bringing it on for trial month after month in the hope that some adjustment, through the creation of a patent pool, could be made which would eliminate much of the Government's complaint," Mitchell wrote in a reply to a request for an opinion by President Hoover in June 1932—"but nothing was ever accomplished." He was not deterred from bringing the case to trial, and a court date was set for October 10, 1932; results followed quickly. Resolution came in the form of a Consent Decree on November 21, 1932 (after Hoover's defeat in the presidential election that year), meaning that the defendants conceded no guilt but that they committed themselves to cease certain objectionable practices.[23]

This prospective prosecution, Hugh Aitken relates, placed RCA in genuine danger. The attitude that might be taken toward the suit by the incoming Roosevelt Administration remained unknown. Should the case come to trial, it was possible that RCA would be found guilty of acting as a monopolist in restraint of trade which, under the terms of the Radio Act of 1927, would require that it be stripped summarily of the many lucrative radio licenses that provided its core market and revenues. Better to settle out of court, by admitting no guilt and consenting to concessions—specific, legally binding alterations in corporate structure and behavior—stipulated by the Justice Department. These did not require the formation of a comprehensive open-access regime, in which all radio patents were flung open for anyone to use; but they did destabilize the existing arrangements.[24]

For its part, AT&T had canceled its revised 1926 patent license agreement with GE late in 1931; to make ironclad its assurances of patent non-exclusivity, in July 1932 AT&T submitted a modified contract to the Justice Department. Approving this altered contract, and dismissing the suit in regard to AT&T as it did so, the 1932 consent decree also voided the exclusivity clauses of the past decade's several agreements binding RCA to GE, AT&T, Westinghouse, and United Fruit; it compelled GE and Westinghouse to dispose of their stockholdings and management control of RCA; and it rendered RCA's foreign traffic and licensing contracts non-exclusive. The cartel's patent licenses could no longer function such that "the company owning rights to a particular patent could not itself use them in market areas designated for others." Because it broke up these intercorporate ties and market divisions, Aitken rightly states, the radio decree "is commonly regarded as one of the great achievements of the Sherman Act, comparable to the meat-packing decree of 1920 and the dissolution of Standard Oil in 1911." It showed that it was politically viable to target legal excludability and to insist that pro-competition precepts should apply to corporate science and engineering.[25]

This outcome was resisted by General Electric's Owen Young and RCA's President J.G. Harbord. Although it explicitly intruded upon their preferred profit strategies, however, of course it did not foreclose the radio field to capital; on the contrary, the suit was intended to open radio to more extensive exploitation. Nor, even, did it vanquish big capital from its pivotal role. On one side, it granted David Sarnoff, an executive intent on reconstituting RCA under his own administrative control, the foundation he sought to separate from GE and Westinghouse and to set out for RCA a newly independent profit strategy. Two days after the decree was announced came news reports that Wall Street deemed that RCA had been strengthened by it. On the other side the decree rendered legal the past behavior of the other corporate signatories, thereby neutralizing any threat from the Radio Act: It left untouched, apart from severing their ties to RCA, the entrenched positions in radio already acquired by GE, Westinghouse, and AT&T.[26]

The claims ventured by independent capital in and around radio likewise continued to proliferate; several important product innovations, notably, smaller and cheaper home receivers and car radios, were introduced by new entrants such as Emerson and Galvin (later Motorola); others, including Sylvania, Philco, Zenith, and Raytheon, also took an increasing share of the market for radios during the 1930s. Their efforts to pursue their own profit strategies helped keep up the political pressure against monopoly in fledgling electronics markets as Hoover gave way to Roosevelt. For all its shortcomings, therefore, the consent decree of 1932 must be counted as both a step toward further reform and an indicator of continued instability. Akin to the concurrent ratemaking initiatives of select state regulatory commissions, the antimonopoly provisions of the Radio Act of 1927, and a landmark court decision—Smith v. Illinois—and, soon thereafter, of the FCC's Telephone Inquiry, the decree constituted a legal restraint: it limited the legal reach of patents held by some of the largest US corporations in their efforts to develop markets for electrical power and communication under proprietary auspices. The controversy over corporate patent practices would become still more charged as the Depression struck and the voices of labor rang out in national political discourse.[27]

Patent Power in Depression and War

Struggles against US corporations' exploitation of patents, both to monopolize markets and to launch new industries—around electricity, chemicals, communications—are coeval with the emergence of national capital during the final decades of the nineteenth century. This was when the seventeen-year monopoly over telephone service conferred by the Bell patents provoked biting resentment: as rival telephone companies organized to provide network access, AT&T's progenitor, the American Bell Telephone Company, shut them down with patent infringement suits—over 600 of them, between 1877 and 1893. An in-house attorney confided to Bell's president in 1891 that "The Bell Company has had a monopoly more profitable and more controlling—and more generally hated—than any ever given by any patent."[28]

Animus against AT&T became an ideological current for the next century. During the first half of the twentieth century, opposition to AT&T's patent policies specifically targeted the so-called license contract. Promising continued technical support from AT&T in exchange for an annual payment of a percentage of the gross revenue of each operating company that licensed its telephone patents, from early in the twentieth century the license contract functioned to extract revenue from local ratepayers and transfer it to the parent company and its investors. Though the notoriety of the license contract has lately been submerged (a recent business historian does not mention it), during the 1930s the FCC acknowledged that payments to AT&T via the license contract had been a "perennial" complaint, "the subject of controversy . . . almost from the beginning of attempts to regulate Bell System operating companies." This antagonism persisted into the early postwar era, when it resurfaced in a major Justice Department antitrust prosecution in 1949 (discussed below).[29]

If corporate power over patents was a recurrent target of struggles to shape telecommunications system development, then the dispensation of patents in and around radio technology constituted a crucial flash-point in this longer history. The 1924 FTC Report divulged that Article II of the GE-AT&T pact stipulated "that the license granted under this agreement includes not only all existing patent rights but all patents hereafter issued." "This paragraph," a critic asserted a few years later, "is highly important in considering the question of how far the patents pooled by this agreement are competing patents and therefore pooled illegally for the purpose of restraining commerce and creating an unlawful monopoly. . . . there can be no question that the future patents of these great laboratories would include inventions that are directly competitive, and that there this agreement, is, on its face, a violation of the antitrust laws." Aiming to seize both existing and prospective markets, what came to be called the Radio Trust bid fair to renew an exclusionary patent strategy under the auspices not of a single company but of a monopoly cartel.[30]

The radio patents controversy spilled out beyond the complaints of aggrieved small capitalists and vying giant companies. Testimony heard by a Senate Committee in the late 1920s underlined this and, indeed, demonstrated that some analysts deemed current corporate practices to be fundamentally illegitimate. The indefatigable Edward Nockels, representing the Chicago Federation of Labor, declared that the Constitution's patent clause (Article One, Section 8) possessed two purposes, both of which the radio trust flouted:

One was to reward workers for great intellectual effort and inventive genius. The other object was to secure to society, through holding out rewards for such genius, the promotion of science and the useful arts.

Nockels went on to specify that "The rewards to bankers and lawyers in the minds of the writers of the Constitution would have been considered incidental and not the great and primary purpose." He declared that "a great combination of capital such as the radio trust" clearly "defeats both of the constitutional purposes of the patent section." It rendered the inventor "helpless," because he "has only one customer."

> As a representative of the organized workers of the United States, I urge upon this committee that the use of great combinations of patents for the purpose of monopolizing the radio art and industry is an evil that can not be too strongly condemned. That it is a perversion of the fundamental purpose of the patent system seems too palpable for discussion.

"I am among those," the Mineworkers' President John L. Lewis had written a few years earlier, "who do not believe that God ever put an idea in the mind of an inventor for the sole advantage of an employer." Agreeing wholeheartedly, Nockels specified tougher sanctions than those given by the 1927 Radio Act. Legislation, he diplomatically averred, "does not go quite far enough to protect the interests of the workers in the allied industries represented by the Radio Corporation of America." In Nockels' view, two practices particularly required correction. "The placing of limitations upon the use of patented articles by manufacturers with the intent of securing control over collateral field [sic] of commerce should suffer some penalty which would stop the practice."[31] Corporate patent rights, furthermore—a demand that would grow louder during the Depression— should be forfeited when they were not actively used to innovate products. Nockels, interestingly, did not recommend that nonexcludability be abrogated; his was essentially a demand that workers' interests be defended by maximizing employment.

Far from dissipating, after the 1932 Consent Decree antipathy to the corporate patent regime intensified. During this catastrophic depression decade, antagonism to corporate patent power attained both a wide societal basis and a measure of real urgency. Attempts to restructure the patent policies of specific firms and industries overlapped with more sweeping reform initiatives.

In 1935, the controversy over radio patents still fresh and US workers moving toward the greatest cycle of self-organization and political intervention in the nation's history, a House committee summoned corporate leaders and independent inventors to testify on their experiences of patent pooling;

a trio of executives from different AT&T units was grilled about the provenance and deployment of the company's 9,170 patents (as of the end of 1934). The object of concern was no longer broadcasting; but the flagrantly self-interested use of radio patents by giant companies carried forward. Indeed, now it became joined to an overarching policy concern: how to alleviate the Depression. For example, Dr. Frank B. Jewett, President of Bell Telephone Laboratories, was challenged by Committee Chair, New York Congressman William I. Sirovich, "Do you think anything could be done through the medium of the cross-licensing or pooling of patents agreements that have been going on that would make it possible . . . for New York users of the telephone to pay less than 5 cents for a telephone message?" This sentiment was hardly surprising, in a decade when hundreds of thousands of households abandoned telephone service. Highly placed officials found it expedient to voice agreement with the conclusion offered by a major law-review article of 1938, "that in the past decades the patent has emerged as the greatest single monopolistic vice."[32]

Revisions to the nation's patent policies moved higher up on the New Deal's agenda. Between 1935 and 1938, much of the action was legislative, as the House Committee on Patents brought in bills to mandate compulsory licensing, on the theory that reducing the excludability conferred by patents might diminish big business's ability to suppress new inventions in order to perpetuate its domination of existing markets. Massachusetts Representative Lawrence J. Connery asked a patent attorney representing Eastman Kodak about "the ordinary rumor . . . that the Radio Corporation of America and Bell Laboratories, and all these scientific outfits are withholding television due to the fact that they want to be able properly to commercialize it and are withholding it from the public as a result." "Most of it is pure gossip without any substance or foundation," pronounced the attorney. Yet awareness of this practice evidently had congealed into a widespread common sense. "We believe that patents are suppressed, and that in the course of two or three years they ought to be thrown open to the public," Edward Nockels had declared matter-of-factly in 1928. Might a requirement that corporations work their patents ameliorate a situation where people were out of work in their millions?[33]

As unemployment spiked during the recession of 1937, and as the CIO detonated changes in both politics and society, this concern became more pointed. "It is possible to plan a program of patenting which would consider public interest to a larger extent in directions where such interest needs protection," suggested the President of the Carnegie Institute, John C. Merriam, in an official and well-publicized report of the National Resources Committee. The Chairman of the House Patents Committee raised the issue more sharply in 1938: "Many members of Congress who have come before this committee feel that if we could develop 10 new industries in this country through the use of patents we could absorb the army of unemployed."[34]

Reform-minded legislators, however, faced a disconcerting practical problem. Opposition to a general program of compulsory licensing stemmed not only from big business, but also—they were to learn—from many small businesses and independent inventors, who New Deal legislators had hoped would support their contemplated patent reforms. Small capitalists and inventors were nearly of one mind, indeed, that compulsory licensing would not restore their economic well-being. Rather, they protested vociferously, it would strip them of any vestige of bargaining power with their larger rivals, companies that already enjoyed immense advantages owing to their economies of scale in production and their massive research and development facilities. Alluding to practices which were, as we saw, already apparent during the 1920s, one witness explained that "The large companies could in most instances simply sandwich in under a license agreement practically all of the smaller outfits": "compulsory licensing would increase monopoly for the large well-financed companies because they are the only ones who could afford to take the risks of development." If the purpose of the prospective legislation was "to discourage and destroy the activities of production," another witness acerbically declared—unemployment stood at perhaps 18 percent—then legislators were headed in the right direction.[35]

Less unexpected was the opposition to the legislation that was expressed by big research-oriented corporations. The bill would have preserved their term of exclusive patent protection for a scant three years. For this special interest group, profits were predicated on extended product development, production, and marketing schedules; and costly and capital-intensive manufacturing processes. "No concern would be willing to venture its capital on any new product, the successful exploitation of which in any event is hazardous, in the knowledge that even before that patent had become self-sustaining, the patent owner would be forced to share it with others," declared a representative of the Rubber Manufacturers Association.[36]

This remarkable legislative endeavor to mandate compulsory patent licensing was turned back. Reformers, however, also had thrown themselves into sector-specific initiatives, aimed at reforming patent practices to reduce particular companies' capacity to exclude others from their proprietary knowledge, and thereby to spur production and employment.

A significant move in this direction came as part of the young Federal Communications Commission's Telephone Inquiry. The agency's preliminary report of its findings devoted an entire chapter to patents and a second to the closely related license contract, declaring that "[o]ne of the principal devices" by which the Bell System had achieved its primary strategic objective—"a full and complete occupation of the public service telephone communications field within the United States"—"is, and has been, the ownership and control of patents relating to the telephone field and to adjacent fields which hold the threat of encroachment upon telephony." But, the FCC charged, the harm did not stop there. AT&T's policies had "retarded" system development and "delayed introduction of improvements," at a cost to the System and its subscribers of "hundreds of millions of dollars." A related staff report declared that Bell had not worked fully 3,400 unused patents—the better to forestall competition. The FCC verdict against AT&T was uncompromising: "The Bell System has at all times suppressed competition in wire telephony or telegraphy through patents. It has always withheld licenses to competitors in wire telephony and telegraphy under its telephone and telephonic appliance patents, and this exclusion is extended to patents covering any type of construction. Moreover, the Bell System has added to its . . . patents any patent that might be of value to its competitors. This policy resulted in the acquisition of a large number of patents covering alternative devices and methods for which the Bell System has no need."[37]

This finding was well-publicized. Picked up by the National Resources Committee in 1937, two years later it figured prominently in N.B. Danielian's classic study of AT&T's "industrial conquest." Incorporating the FCC's findings for a general readership, Danielian devoted three chapters to how AT&T had incorporated science to "occupy the field" of voice telephony; to colonize and partition adjacent new media industries, notably, sound film and radio; and to continue its takeover of the public-utility service of telegraphy. AT&T's objective, he stated, had been "to absorb as much industrial territory as possible." AT&T, on one side, and the Radio Group allied around RCA, on the other, had been consistent—indeed, relentless—in pursuing this goal: "Like the Rome-Berlin axis," Danielian suggested, in his fearsome simile of 1939, "they have their differences, but also many common aims."[38]

In connection with its request, authorized by the legislation that enabled the Telephone Inquiry, that Congress authorize it to require AT&T to divest its Western Electric manufacturing unit, the FCC also asked for legislative backing to pursue a vital double reform. First, the Commission desired "to compel AT&T to license others upon reasonable terms under any patents obtained in connection with communications." Reciprocally, the agency wished to grant the Bell System "the right to use patents, owned by others, which may be essential to the rendition of its communications service to the public." These alterations, the FCC believed, would not only remove an economic chokepoint but also render federal regulation more effective, because they would function to help restrict AT&T to telephone service provision alone. As we found in a previous chapter, the Telephone Inquiry was stymied—but the first of these intended reforms would be find new traction during the 1950s.[39]

The New Deal continued, meanwhile, to offer gathering political opportunities. After the election of 1936, Roosevelt swung left to acknowledge his political debt to the CIO and an aroused working class. Then, unemployment increased sharply again during the recession of 1937. Not only a scattering of legislators, but also high officials of the other two governmental branches—Supreme Court Justice William Douglas, Secretary of Agriculture Henry Wallace, Assistant Attorney General Thurman W. Arnold and, during Spring 1938, President Franklin Roosevelt himself—called to reform the patent system. In a message to Congress, Roosevelt assailed the "concentration of private power without equal in history"; patents, some New Dealers charged, had undergone an "antisocial adaptation" as corporations amassed private property in invention.[40]

Many members of the New Deal coalition deemed two features of science-based business's patent policies dangerous. First, their reading of the development of radio during the 1920s showed that patent pools—cross-licensing between allied big businesses—might be used to exert predatory pressures against smaller enterprises seeking market entry. In consequence, member companies were able to accrue virtually unassailable "first-mover" advantages. Second, in line with Nockels' prior assertion, corporate control over patents tended toward self-interested suppression; in order to extend the life of its existing markets, a corporation might deploy its patents to throttle competing technologies in their infancy, or to impose restrictive licensing provisions on others' use.

This biting critique of patent monopoly kept up pressure on AT&T. Indeed, the lessons offered by the world's largest company seemed paradigmatic: that corporate control over inventions jeopardized not only a working market system, but also US democracy. In introducing automatic switching to cut its operating staff, refusing to work patents that might generate new industries, cartelizing new industries so that entrepreneurs and small businesses could not participate fully in their development, and deploying its massive public relations apparatus to miseducate the public about the true nature of these self-serving arrangements, AT&T seemed to have turned its back on the nation's founding ideals. Its corporate power perverted the process of innovation, both by developing socially harmful but privately lucrative applications, and suppressing or canalizing genuinely useful inventions to retard or distort the shape of new industries. Its attempts to legitimize this behavior compounded the problem, by poisoning public opinion with self-aggrandizing publicity that undercut principles of self-government. AT&T's patent practices therefore appeared to symptomatize a calamitous dual tendency in which, seeking to augment and centralize its own power, the nation's single largest unit of capital curbed employment and deepened economic stagnation while it also subverted democracy.[41]

Although Congress did not approve the FCC's Telephone Inquiry reform proposals, similar recommendations were soon introduced in other venues, notably, the Justice Department. In 1938, at the highwater mark of its activism, the FCC criticized the agreements brokered by former President Hoover's Justice Department in 1932 for not embodying "the inherent characteristics of true cross-licensing; that is, there was not accomplished a free interchange of rights to use the patents in all fields." Almost immediately thereafter, spokesmen for the Justice Department testified in favor of compulsory patent licensing in a second, more encompassing campaign for reform by the Temporary National Economic Committee.[42]

The TNEC was an exceptional collaboration between the Legislative and Executive branches, convened late in 1938 and continuing for about two-and-one-half years. It compiled a fact-filled multivolume portrait, drawing on "state of the art" research, "on the actual condition of the American economy." One index of the political significance of TNEC was that the Government Printing Office circulated fully 230,000 copies of TNEC's dozens of hearings and monographs. Commencing its labors with a searching probe of the patent system headed by the activist assistant attorney general for antitrust, Thurman Arnold, TNEC concluded that the "patent monopoly" indeed had been "shamefully abused," by being utilized "as a device to control whole industries, to suppress competition, to restrict output, to enhance prices, to suppress inventions, and to discourage inventiveness." Some characteristic practices used to promote corporate monopoly included:

> The patentee who licenses other firms to operate under his patent rights may include in his contract provisions which are designed to preserve, strengthen, and extend his monopoly. He may prescribe the quantity that his licensees may produce, the territories in which they may sell, the customers with whom they may deal, and the prices which they must charge, thereby limiting their freedom to compete. He may insist that they buy exclusively from him, thereby restricting the market available to his competitors. He may require them to buy unpatented materials from him, thereby extending his control into fields where his patent does not apply. His power to refuse or withdraw licenses may thus be employed as a weapon whereby varying degrees of power over the markets for various products may be acquired.

TNEC identified AT&T as an egregious offender. The Bell System had originated in a continually contested patent monopoly, and its recent behavior gave little indication that its instinct for predation had dissipated. Grilled by the TNEC in 1939, the President of Bell Telephone Laboratories, Frank Jewett, offered testimony which did nothing to vitiate the "ample evidence" collected by the panel "that the patent system as it has developed has fostered an unfortunate variety of practices antagonistic to the purpose which guided the framers of the

Constitution": to promote science and the useful arts. "By 1934," asserted a radical analysis of US industry's tendency to monopoly that drew both on TNEC hearings and on the published report of the FCC's Telephone Inquiry, "American Telephone & Telegraph had 9,255 patents of which 1,307 had never been put to use. Some nine improvements were found by the Federal Communications Commission which had been deliberately withheld by A.T.&T. for from nine to over 30 years."[43]

Despite repeated attempts to legislate compulsory patent licensing, however, opposition by small businesses and big corporations alike helped block passage of each successive reform bill. High-tech companies like AT&T allied with conservative and already influential science policy entrepreneurs, notably Vannevar Bush, who would go on to become a member of AT&T's corporate board. Corporate capital wished to be free to pursue cross-licensing initiatives as a reflex of proprietary profit strategies, as and when it preferred and undiluted by government interlopers. Entry by the United States into World War II afforded new opportunities for big business to repulse patent reformers even as, paradoxically, it created acute needs for patent sharing.

"The conduct of the war, so it was argued, called for a carefully planned, highly controlled, and well-coordinated economy," explains historian Ellis Hawley: "Accordingly, as this new system was established, the center of influence shifted from the antimonopolists to the business-oriented directors of the new defense agencies." Critics of corporate patent practices in this context found it harder to gain political traction; though proponents of antitrust action argued that GE, Alcoa, Dow and other big companies' anticompetitive practices were hindering the war effort, sometimes, indeed, by collaborating with their corporate peers in the Axis countries, they found themselves on the defensive. Immediately after entering World War II, Roosevelt convened a high-level National Patent Planning Commission, "to conduct a comprehensive survey and study of the American patent system, and consider whether the system now provides the maximum service in stimulating the inventive genius of our people in evolving inventions and in furthering their prompt utilization for the public good." With Owen D. Young of General Electric and other highly placed businessmen among its five members, the Patent Commission recommended mandatory licensing of patents for national defense programs during the emergency, but affirmed that the US patent system as it existed "is the best in the world... the foundation of American enterprise."[44]

The war period saw renewed conflict over government patent policy, and its aftermath witnessed fierce infighting over science and technology policy per se. As a Justice Department investigation and inventory of practices at different agencies would reveal, opportunities for reform remained alive. High-profile judgments in a series of antitrust cases began to normalize compulsory licensing as a legal remedy, while some federal agencies favored a more open patent regime. One was the Department of Agriculture, which, at the verge of World War II, remained the Government's lead agency in generating scientific and technical information; another was the Tennessee Valley Authority, whose phosphate patents helped establish a new fertilizer industry. The military departments—Navy and War—advanced an antagonistic program, in which state-funded innovation by corporate contractors occurred behind a wall of secrecy.[45]

However, and strikingly, during the war exclusionary corporate patent proprietorships were increasingly checkmated *within* this zone of militarized innovation. Mobilization for World War II engendered what Riordan and Hoddeson have characterized—they refer to the specific context of transistor development but the point possesses wider relevance—as "a remarkably open sharing of information among the expanding network of scientists and engineers working ... under the dark umbrella of military secrecy." At the same time, "the war brought a great many new companies into the electronics industry for the manufacture of such important war products as radar." Some of these were small, entrepreneurial outfits; others, such as Sperry and Bendix, were well-established. However paradoxical, this wartime institutionalization of openness wrapped in secrecy proved a harbinger.[46]

Beyond this burgeoning military domain of information sharing, more expansively open science and technology policies claimed influential adherents throughout the war—as former vice president and then Secretary of Agriculture Henry Wallace, Texas Democratic Representative Maury Maverick, West Virginia Democratic Senator Harley Kilgore and other New Dealers fought to redefine and redirect Government-funded research and development. Their aim was to move from an industrial machine for waging war to a strengthened and restructured peacetime economy: government should use its power to direct science and technology toward seeding new industries and small businesses, in order to generate full employment. This project was not a scheme of independent state managers, but a program for political-economic reorganization that stood in a loose congruence with the CIO's "Peoples' Program" of 1944. The president himself sometimes seemed congenial. By Executive Order, during the war President Roosevelt authorized the seizure of foreign-owned patents and foreign interests in patents, and thereby made more widely available to American industries (though the biggest corporations came out best) manufacturing processes for the production of synthetic rubber, magnesium, pharmaceutical products, "and many other products of vital importance to the war effort." Scientific and technological information, in this vision, needed to be set on markedly different institutional foundations to guarantee widespread prosperity rather than merely to inflate corporate profit margins.[47]

Importantly for this see-sawing struggle over the ends of science, the US Department of Justice brought numerous antitrust suits against specific corporate offenders. The wartime Justice Department initially carried forward its vigilance in pursuing monopoly "bottlenecks," under the direction of Thurman W. Arnold, who had been appointed as Assistant Attorney General for Antitrust in March 1938. Arnold, as Alan Brinkley observes, "promoted an anti-monopoly ideal largely stripped of its populist and democratic content" and, despite his ardor, his achievement was mixed: "Case after case was vetoed by the planning and defense authorities" during World War II for, "while the Standard Oils, DuPonts, GEs, and Alcoas were guilty of heinous conduct, these companies were also absolutely vital to the US war effort, and many of their executives were now leaders in the planning and production effort." In January 1943, Arnold was removed as the nation's chief antitrust officer by President Roosevelt; after the war, nevertheless, his successors as Assistant Attorney General for Antitrust selectively revived his program. The Nebraskan Wendell Berge, who had worked in the antitrust division since 1930, rose to become Arnold's chief deputy before himself assuming the post of Assistant Attorney General for Antitrust. Berge warned in 1944 that in many areas of the economy "vast monopolies" now exercised "a dominating influence over research": "it is the abuse and misuse of patents by such concentrated groups wielding tremendous economic power which have brought patents into conflict with the fundamental purpose of the patent law and the Sherman Act."[48]

Although it did "severely weaken" the Antitrust Division's prosecutorial energies, World War II did not fully neutralize them. Nor did it curtail the complex blend of antimonopoly economics and democratic political sentiment with which hardy New Dealers sought to reorient science policy. Vociferously opposed by business, during the war years legislators tried repeatedly to pass reforms that would prohibit corporate licensing pacts that would restrict sale price or output. Soon after his removal, Thurman W. Arnold nevertheless drafted testimony on a Senate bill to reorganize the country's science and technology infrastructure, in which he charged that "Cartels have not tried to suppress experimentation. They have tried to corner it. They have kept the savings of new technique for themselves instead of passing them on the consumers." Thereby, an injurious "industrial bottleneck" had been created. "The evidence is overwhelming," Arnold underlined, "that practically all our shortages in basic materials and in chemicals, the very things that are necessary to give us strength in war and wealth in peace, are due to the control of research and invention by domestic and international cartels. . . . the production and distribution of such vital elements as magnesium, zinc, rubber, aviation gasoline, beryllium . . . electrical equipment, plastics, dyestuffs, machine tools, fuels, communications, and a variety of other products necessary for both our war effort and our industrial progress have been impeded and delayed, and in some cases totally blocked, because private groups dominated industrial research." The remedy was, he asserted, for government to take actions sufficient to help "spread knowledge of modern experimentation" to allow "the free use of the results of that experimentation to every competing industry." This bill (S. 702) failed, but efforts to pass positive legislation continued; and they fed into a battle to establish a National Science Foundation for the purpose of supporting a robust civilian economy. Meanwhile, the Justice Department undertook detailed planning for antitrust prosecutions, in hopes of eliminating "bottlenecks"—specific corporate chokepoints over the economy that it deemed to be intolerable.[49]

The 1949 Antitrust Case against AT&T

A paramount instance came with its action against AT&T, formally initiated in January 1949. The suit's originating purpose was to sharply reduce AT&T's corporate power: the same objective that had motivated reformers all the way from the Progressive era through the New Deal Federal Communications Commission. On one hand, AT&T's far-flung corporate monopoly all but eliminated price competition, and—during the 1940s—continued to enable the company to manipulate telephone rates. The vertically and horizontally integrated behemoth thereby still obstructed the realization of universal household telephone service. The Justice Department thus chose to focus its case on a chief reform objective of FCC's Telephone Inquiry a decade earlier: to cut AT&T's Western Electric manufacturing unit free of the encompassing Bell System. Justice's aim was to decouple supply and demand in telephone equipment markets and, by doing so, to lower rates: antitrust lawyers expected that, by compelling the Bell operating companies and AT&T Long Lines to purchase networking gear from unaffiliated companies at competitively set prices, the cost of telephone service would decline. There was a closely related second motivation. Again carrying forward a goal of the FCC's Telephone Inquiry, the Justice Department believed that an AT&T divestiture of Western Electric would enable regulation itself to become more comprehensive and robust. This was because, after the spinoff, no part of the company that remained would fall outside regulators' jurisdiction. If at last they could confine AT&T entirely to the provision of telephone service, then regulators could gain a much more effective purchase over the telephone company. There was also, however, a third motive behind the government prosecution, one possessing a lower profile but harboring common social and political objectives. If AT&T's proprietary patent practices could be pried open, then the monopoly's massive science and engineering resources might be redirected, to some extent, toward New Deal priorities: employment and consumption.

Neither the suit's character nor, as it happens, its outcome have been adequately assessed. Chiefly this is because they have been framed narrowly in terms of AT&T's organizational status and incentives, rather than of the encompassing political economy, within which even the world's greatest unit of capital was compelled to maneuver. New evidence now allows us to clear the way to interpreting what in fact occurred.

Researched and then postponed for years beginning in 1943, the case was brought to court only after Democrat Harry Truman's narrow election victory in 1948. This timing itself is anomalous: The government was threatening to break up one of the nation's preeminent military contractors just as the newly initiated US policy of global cold war was heightening the administration's dependence on it. The anomaly increased with the US decision to undertake the Korean War in June 1950, which saw a mammoth enlargement of US military production—and which also saw the Justice Department throw itself into the case with renewed prosecutorial vigor in late summer 1951. Following the 1952 election of Republican Dwight D. Eisenhower, moreover, the Justice Department bargained with AT&T for four additional years. Justice resolved the case through a consent decree, finally, rather than by simply dismissing it as AT&T's lobbyists continually demanded. What accounts for the anomalous timing, tenacity, and mode of resolution?[50]

From the moment of its settlement in 1956, those who have considered the 1949 antitrust case have concentrated on the improprieties that marred and, some assert, explained its outcome. There is indeed considerable justification for disparaging the 1956 consent decree, as a result connived at by AT&T, the Defense Department, the Justice Department, and the Federal Communications Commission. The original complaint, as mentioned, attempted to divest Western Electric from AT&T, in order to engender a long-sought structural remedy against rate gouging and to enable more effective FCC regulation. Yet the actual 1956 settlement not only preserved Western Electric intact within a still-integrated Bell System but also granted this gigantic company a newfound and much-coveted legality; a status that seemed to guarantee unbroken monopoly profits while affording AT&T immunity from further antitrust prosecution. Unearthing numerous procedural irregularities, critics pilloried the government for having let off AT&T with a token penalty. Typical was the bitter insight that the decree "would give legal sanction to the AT&T-Western Electric relationship—an umbrella to shield their marriage from court action if a later Attorney General proved more interested in trust-busting." That two Justice Department lawyers working on the case refused to sign the decree was taken to be compelling evidence of betrayal.[51]

The seeming irrelevance of the relief obtained to the goals sought, and the institutional corruption and individual dishonesty that tainted the proceeding, have distracted analysts from pursuing deeper questions. What interests did the suit advance? What structural logic did its outcome express? Did AT&T acquiesce to a government-mandated truncation of its profit strategy, or not? What did the case and its consequences signify for the ongoing reorganization of the political economy? Research has pierced the meaning neither of the prosecution nor the consent decree that resolved it.

Indeed, few scholars have touched on this incongruous history. These few are united in asserting that the suit stemmed from a late burst of New Deal activism, carried over from the FCC to the Justice Department by independent-minded staff members. Recently unearthed documents do demonstrate conclusively that the suit's origins should be traced back to the New Deal, but this finding does not dispel a significant historical conundrum. After Henry Wallace's resignation as Secretary of Commerce in September 1946, a historian explains, "there were no New Dealers left in the cabinet and few in the Congress"; and the 1948 election result sealed this sea-change. How, then, did a high-profile "New Deal" project *gain* political traction sufficient to proceed in January 1949? How indeed did it carry forward for seven additional years, almost all the way through the first (Republican) Eisenhower administration?[52]

My interpretation, which is based in part on documents brought to light by Freedom of Information Act requests, supports three findings. First, the Justice Department suit constituted a renewed attempt to restrict AT&T to providing regulated telecommunications service and, despite the company's successful retention of Western Electric, this provision of the settlement attained a real measure of success. Second, the prosecution carried another overarching objective: opening up high-tech know-how for expedited and enlarged corporate-military development. From its onset during World War II to its conclusion in 1956, the effect of the investigation and of the litigation itself was to pressure AT&T to loosen its proprietary stranglehold over patents and to license its unexcelled research in communications and electronics to outside companies. Abstract economic theory possessed little relevance here. Rather, to build out a capacious and dynamic infrastructure for imperial interventions and a global Cold War required that AT&T abandon its exclusionary patent strategies. On the other hand, third, it also required that AT&T itself be reoriented, to enable it to participate fully in the redesigned circuits of war-making. Although the pyramiding importance of these provisions settlement could not yet be discerned at the time, the bright legal line that it drew around AT&T's regulated telephone business turned into an increasingly severe constraint—in no small part, ironically, because of the hot-house innovation that was fostered by the same settlement's patent-sharing provisions. The settlement therefore carried profound consequences for the telecommunications industry and for AT&T itself.

The case's roots go back to World War II, for which AT&T officials had begun to prepare by the late 1930s, in close contact with Navy and Army brass. Reviving their role during World War I, AT&T executives embraced an interventionist war stance and succeeded in making their company an irreplaceable military adviser and supplier. Bell Laboratories began working on radar in 1938, atomic energy by 1939. More than eight months before Pearl Harbor, Bell System vice-presidents were ordered by senior AT&T executives to reduce sales efforts aimed at stimulating orders for new telephone station apparatus, outside plant, or central office equipment, because the magnesium, aluminum, nickel, zinc, and copper used to provide telephone service were "essential to the national defense program." AT&T wished to strengthen its already close ties to Army, Navy and other military agencies, and indeed it garnered literally thousands of war contracts. In January, 1941, government work accounted for an estimated 10 percent of Bell Labs' expense, climbing to 80 percent in 1942 and 1943. Western Electric's Kearny New Jersey plant garnered prime contracts during the war worth $1.4 billion for radar and radio equipment, and its Chicago plant an additional $1 billion. Historian James W. Spurlock details how its Bell Telephone Laboratories engineers and scientists labored on a staggering range of more or less urgent war projects, including (analog vacuum-tube) computerized fire control, chemical weapons, submarine detection systems, and pioneering forms of encrypted digital speech transmission.[53]

This was not the moment to pursue high-profile antitrust actions in sensitive fields. A postponement of ongoing trials deemed inimical to prosecuting the war was still in force. Moreover, Thurman Arnold, the aggressive Assistant Attorney General for Antitrust, had been reassigned to the federal bench. Nevertheless, in September 1943 the US Justice Department quietly originated a fresh inquiry, with an eye to prosecutions across the electrical industry.[54]

In the communications equipment segment, the Antitrust Division was studying whether grounds existed for it to try to break up cartels in everything from printing telegraphs and submarine cables to radio equipment. An internal memo relates that Western Electric's relationship to its parent, AT&T, comprised a central focus and, indeed, that "The desirability of divorcing Western Electric from American Telephone & Telegraph Corporation constitutes one of the most important phases of the entire electrical investigation." The axial lesson of the 1920s and 1930s had been retained and was being freshly interpreted: that electronic communications constituted a unitary technology and a massive industry that was riddled by corporate predators acting in restraint of trade. There can be little doubt that the Justice Department proceeding against AT&T was motivated by this conviction, and that its foremost aim stemmed from the New Deal's depression-era agenda: to establish leverage for lowering telephone rates and thereby to stimulate demand for service and, thereby, employment. Bonded to these goals was a conviction that an antitrust prosecution could confine AT&T to providing regulated telephone service—once more, an engraved reform ambition. With this, the inquiry reached directly into the question of patents.[55]

In 1945, Sigmund Timberg, one of the two special assistants working on the prospective suit against AT&T, sent comments to the other, Holmes A. Baldridge, who had led the FCC's Telephone Inquiry and who, earlier still, had worked for the Oklahoma Public Service Commission. In keeping with long-standing criticisms of AT&T's patent policies, Timberg underlined that "the prayer for relief asks that the whole Bell System technology, including patents, be made available to outsiders." For the FCC in the late 1930s and, as we saw, for the FTC, TNEC, the Justice Department, and the earlier congressional investigations, restraining AT&T's ability to use patents to project proprietary control over market development had been a recurrent concern. From the perspective of New Dealers, AT&T's track record only underscored its tenacious instinct to predation: first and foremost, it deployed patents to "occupy the field"—not only of telephony but, prospectively, also radio, telegraphy, musical recording, sound film, and other new industries.[56]

The lawyers who crafted the government's case worried, however, that they might make their case vulnerable by assigning patents high prominence. The "patent story," fretted Timberg in this May 1945 memo, presented a prosecutorial dilemma: on one hand, "all except one of the major contracts on which this case rests have as their basis the disposition and control of patents and patent rights claimed by or against the Bell System"; on the other, it would be difficult for Justice "to show that AT&T and Western have made improper use of their patents and related technology" because AT&T and Western would defend themselves by stressing "that they were merely making a proper, business-like exercise of powers and privileges validly conferred upon them by their patents." Timberg confided to Baldridge that, "While I favor any approach that will minimize the patent features of this case, I am afraid that it will prove extremely difficult, if not impossible, to keep them from bobbing up." Although a "re-examination" of the Bell System's patent practices in the light of recent Supreme Court decisions might, he hoped, provide means of skirting this problem, for tactical reasons the Justice Department tried to de-emphasize patent issues.[57]

By March 1946, a draft complaint was circulating. It called for divestiture of Western from the Bell System "on the general theory that Western Electric has attained by illegal means a monopoly of the manufacture and sale of telephones and telephone equipment," as well as "various monopolies, attempted monopolies and trade restraints . . . in non-telephonic fields." Though the "probable imminence" of the complaint seemed evident, however, the suit was not lodged in court for nearly three additional years. In a revised draft of June 1948 the charge resurfaced that AT&T's monopoly had been built around its "control of patents"; but still, patents were downplayed. One article of relief (ninth out of ten desired changes) pertained: "AT&T, Western and Bell Telephone Laboratories are required to make all their patents or patent rights available to all applicants on a reasonable royalty basis." In accord with the concurrent FCC emphasis on rate policy as a prerequisite of system expansion; and with passage by Congress of rural telephony legislation, the case had become connected to letters of complaint during 1947 sent by representatives of public utility commissions from Tennessee and Minnesota about their powerlessness to control Western Electric prices, and it continued to be presented as an attempt to lower telephone rates for subscribers. AT&T attorneys, however, would certainly have been attentive to the article that sought to mandate patent licensing.[58]

Charging extensive violations of the Sherman Antitrust Act beginning as far back as the 1880s, and relying almost entirely on documentation collected by the FCC in its Telephone Inquiry, the suit sought that AT&T divest its wholly owned manufacturing subsidiary, Western Electric; that Western transfer its 50 percent ownership share in Bell Telephone Laboratories so as to leave AT&T the sole owner; that the Bell System purchase telephone equipment through a process of competitive bidding; and that AT&T and Western Electric license their patents to all applicants on a nondiscriminatory and reasonable royalty basis, as well as "to furnish such applicants with technical assistance and know-how in connection with the use of such patents." The then-US Attorney General had been a participant in the invigorated antitrust milieu in which this prosecution had germinated as the war drew to a close. The Texan Tom C. Clark had worked under Thurman Arnold and served as Assistant Attorney General for a short period during the war, before he was named Attorney General by President Truman in 1945. Clark issued an accompanying statement which highlighted that the suit was being brought to court because the lack of competition in telephone equipment manufacturing "has tended to defeat effective public regulation of rates," and that a government victory in the case was expected to "lower the cost of such equipment and create a situation under which state and Federal regulatory commissions will be afforded an opportunity to reduce telephone rates to subscribers."[59]

Clark's public rationale was not disingenuous. A private memo by Holmes A. Baldridge, who later stated that he had done the preparatory work on all areas of the suit except patents (Timberg's specialty), reaffirmed that the suit's purpose was "to reduce costs of equipment, which, in turn, will permit State and Federal regulatory bodies to reduce telephone rates to subscribers." Baldridge explicated the theory of the case, conceding that there existed significant political contingencies. "The whole point of the case," Baldridge began, "lies in the fact that it is only because A.T.&T. has a monopoly on buying telephone equipment that it can monopolize the selling of such equipment through Western Electric." For this reason, he conceded, it would have been logical for the Justice Department to seek to divest not only Western Electric but also all the operating companies, leaving AT&T only with its Long Lines service. "Thus, we would have broken up both the buying and the selling monopolies." The suit had not sought a break-up of "the buying monopoly," however, because the operating companies were regulated by state and federal agencies; because such a prosecution was simply too ambitious "and the courts would be unwilling to go along"; and because "the company would put on a great public campaign of condemnation based upon the groundless charge that we were attempting to wreck the best telephone system in the world."

> Since Western is not subject directly to regulation by State and Federal commissions (operating companies may be required to justify costs and expenses in certain categories) such a charge could not be effective with respect to a suit to dissolve Western. Hence, the suit is confined to a break-up of the selling monopoly only. Since the buying monopoly will remain intact, we have insisted upon competitive bidding in purchases made by operating companies as well as a requirement that A.T.&T. make available to all telephone manufacturers on a non-discriminatory reasonable royalty basis, all of their patents, specifications, and know-how.

The suit therefore aimed to create new leverage with which to pursue the abiding New Deal objective of effectively regulating AT&T's telephone monopoly with the aim of reducing rates and expanding access to service—in part, by mandating that AT&T license its patents and "know-how" to outside electronics manufacturers.[60]

However, patent issues also bore other—and vital—freight. To fight the war, US policymakers devoted unprecedented resources to weapons research and development, above all, around military radar and the atom bomb. These huge programs not only birthed fearsome weapons, but also entrenched distinctive institutional norms and practices. The unparalleled mobilization of scientific and engineering talent was predicated on equally unprecedented levels of collaboration. Garry Wills recounts how J. Robert Oppenheimer, the physicist-administrator who directed the Manhattan Project's scientific work at the mountain outpost of Los Alamos in New Mexico, persuaded the overall head of the program, General Leslie Groves, "that a total isolation of the working team from the outside world would meet the security requirements while allowing the free play of ideas within the compound." There was an imperative need not only for design, but also for production information-sharing by and among military contractors. Margaret Graham keys in on this paradox, with the observation that "electronics was a different kind of research field after World War II, one that no single company could hope to dominate and one that also needed major infusions of new knowledge." The boundaries of existing knowledge were being rapidly pushed back and many new research-oriented companies had entered the field:

> Philco, for instance, having enjoyed free wartime access to patents that it previously would have had to license, was not willing to leave research to RCA after the war. GE and Westinghouse both became more heavily involved in electronics R&D, and several smaller organizations merged to form larger units with adequate resources to support continued activity. Public criticism focused on RCA's patent position as having inhibited radio-related research during the prewar period by depriving other members of the industry of the incentive to do research. The government responded by deliberately encouraging more competition in research.

Behind a wall of state-secrecy, throughout the war government-appointed coordinating committees in fact actively compelled scores of corporate contractors to share high-technology know-how. Although AT&T's Western Electric unit was the largest corporate beneficiary of the radar effort, for example, there were more than 70 other prime contractors, fourteen of whom produced radar equipment valued at $20 million or more. General Electric, Philco, Raytheon, Westinghouse, RCA, Hazeltine, Sperry, Zenith, Admiral, and Bendix were among these. Thus were forged some of the constitutive technical information-sharing practices that sustained what—a few years after the war—was to become a permanent garrison state.[61]

These moves against excludability in corporate knowledge impinged in a fundamental way on the Justice Department's intended remedy for AT&T's antitrust abuses. By 1945, almost certainly aware of the Justice Department's ongoing investigation, AT&T was readying a response. Its rejoinder showcased what the company hoped would be a preemptive public defense: its vast program of wartime cooperation including, in particular, its indispensable research into "the development of new tools of war." AT&T declared that it had generated knowledge "which was made freely available to all properly concerned," above all, in the strategic and economically promising field of radar. Additional efforts at public persuasion were quickly forthcoming; during 1948 and 1949, AT&T took pains to emphasize its concern to ensure that "our new knowledge is made available to society." Just as the Justice Department determined to bring forward its case, the company boasted that it was formalizing a policy of "mak[ing] available upon reasonable terms to all who desire them non-exclusive licenses under its patents for any use."[62]

AT&T's rhetoric did not assuage concern about this essential point. Memories of how the company had recurrently seized turf by using its patents during the interwar years were being rekindled, owing to sensitivities about a fundamental, and still nascent, breakthrough in electronics. Coming out of the World War II development of radar, Bell Telephone Laboratories scientists and engineers were investigating and, by the late 1940s, beginning to file for patents on a groundbreaking new technology. Fears circulated widely that, akin to some other large high-tech companies such as RCA, the huge corporation might stage a return to the disabling excludability that had stained its patent practices in the past. A 1947 essay on radar published in the influential *Harvard Business Review* stressed that "the value of industry-wide accessibility to patents was indicated during the war when licenses were granted freely under existing patents," and linked AT&T to its erstwhile corporate partners in predation: "With the return of peace the problem of patent strength soon became acute. Of the 1,500 or so important new radar patents, about 500 are owned by the government, while most of the rest are controlled by Western Electric, General Electric, RCA, and Westinghouse."

The article proceeded to recommend "widespread licensing of patents at moderate royalty rates" as being "in the long-run national interest."

> To avoid expensive litigation and crippling restrictions on the use of radar patents, the industry has been moving toward the establishment of a patent pool to include all patents important to radar design and production. While this move may produce a satisfactory condition in the industry, governmental observance and possibly action seem necessary to prevent the patent pool from being used for the oppression of small firms and the monopolization of radar knowledge and production.
>
> It is to be hoped that the radio industry will demonstrate the fundamental strength of free enterprise by continuing to push forward the technological advances stimulated by the war. Most of the wartime compulsions have been removed; it would be pleasant to think that the aim of serving the American national interest is almost as effective.

Similarly, Rupert Maclaurin concluded his groundbreaking study of the radio industry by underlining in 1949 that

> The role of patents in stimulating or retarding technical progress is a special problem of monopoly. Recent public discussion has been focused on the abuses of the patent system which tend to impede technological change. Many people believe that these weaknesses are sufficiently deep-seated to warrant abolishing the patent monopoly altogether, or drastically reducing patent life.

The Justice Department move against AT&T must be set in this context. It transpired, most fundamentally, exactly as the US ascent to leadership of the world capitalist political economy tinged these same issues with a fearsome significance. Sustained by government contracts, a great high-tech industry of war production would devise armaments with which to combat international socialism and to repress or contain nationalist insurgencies throughout the global South.[63]

Machinations ensued to deflect, postpone and, if possible, to dispose of the case. Congressional hearings later would reveal how corporate-state interlocks operated to support AT&T's integrated structure: the military demanded continuing access to all of its elements, including both Bell Labs' research and Western Electric's closely related production expertise. In 1952, Secretary of Defense Robert A. Lovett formally requested that the Attorney General defer the antitrust suit; then, incorporating points made in a memo drafted and submitted to him by an AT&T executive, in a subsequent intervention following the 1952 election Lovett wrote the incoming Eisenhower Administration that it should "postpone" the case for the duration of the Korean "emergency." Lovett's successor as Secretary of Defense, Charles E. Wilson, followed up in July 1953 with yet another letter importuning the Attorney General—a letter which, with two small revisions, again turned out to be identical to one previously drafted and submitted to him by AT&T. In 1954, after publicly announcing that he was reviewing Justice Department litigation to decide which cases should go forward and which dismissed, Eisenhower's Attorney General Herbert Brownell suggested to an AT&T executive that "a way ought to be found to get rid of the case" and invited the company to look for "things we [AT&T] are doing which were once considered entirely legal, but might now be in violation of the antitrust laws or questionable in that respect." (AT&T followed up with a request that the case be dismissed.)[64]

Belatedly brought to light were other glaring infractions. The Defense Department had conveyed to AT&T copies of its own official interagency correspondence about the case with the Justice Department. A responsible Justice Department official had conferred about the proceeding at a private dinner at his home with AT&T's ranking attorney. Replying to a Justice Department inquiry, the Chairman of the Federal Communications Commission—who had previously worked as an executive for New York Telephone—had echoed the specious claim made by the sanitized 1939 Final Report in the FCC's Telephone Inquiry: that state and federal agencies already possessed regulatory authority sufficient to oversee Western Electric. Pointing to this assertion, the Justice Department sought to justify its abandonment of divestiture from its prayer for relief. Capping off these improprieties, at one point the Justice Department claimed a right under executive privilege to refuse access by a congressional committee to its documentary record of the case.[65]

This scandalous history ignited a new and, as it proved, an enduring round of antimonopoly sentiment against AT&T; for us, however, it must prompt a further question: Why was the case not simply dismissed? Given the power of the interests working against it, what accounts for the suit's persistence?

It is possible, even likely (congressional testimony is ambiguous) that as the denouement approached, AT&T *preferred* a consent decree to an outright dismissal. Such a decree could be—and in fact was—molded to grant legal sanction to AT&T's long-controversial integrated corporate structure: with this, AT&T's ownership of Western Electric presumably would escape further antitrust action. Perhaps, on the other side, Eisenhower's Justice Department had arrived at the view that it could neither win the case nor find a persuasive rationale—and a propitious political moment—for abandoning it. As it was, when it was announced the settlement brought a storm of. "A slap on the wrist," declared *Business Week*; but some thought the settlement worse than this: a sham, a sell-out, even a shake-down. Congressional hearings into the case followed.[66]

In hindsight, nevertheless, the provisions of the consent decree do not bear out such cavalier dismissals. The settlement limited AT&T to a pair of markets—regulated common carrier telecommunications, and projects contracted for by the Federal Government. Additional provisions bound AT&T to license its 8,600 pre-Judgment patents royalty-free to any domestic applicant, and to license subsequent patents on reasonable and nondiscriminatory terms. AT&T presented these as severe penalties—fundamental concessions—and, reciprocally, the Justice Department crowed over its purported achievement. Though posturing was certainly abundant on both sides, both sets of claims also possessed validity.[67]

What AT&T tersely identified afterward as "the major objective" of its patent policy was "the freedom to design and manufacture the best possible equipment." Not surprisingly skipping over its prior record of monopolistic practices, AT&T's legal counsel specified the importance of this curious proprietary freedom—taking care to equate his company's profit strategy with the public interest: "when you are talking in terms of patents that we need in our business, you are not talking just about a patent on a telephone or some device which is only useful in telephony." Rather, he went on, "You are talking about patents which have much broader use in the whole electronics art."

> There are many patents which have great, if not primary use outside the communications business, and as to those patents we might have some and they might have some. Where we have cross licenses largely they are with companies which are not ... in the telephone or communications manufacturing business.

They are in quite different types of business, and we have something which has been developed in our research looking toward the improvements in the communications art which reads on their equipments. They similarly have something which reads on our equipments, so if we do, we are in a position to keep them from excluding us from going forward with the best possible developments in the communications art by saying to them, 'If you are going to exclude us, we will exclude you, but we do not want to exclude you. All we want to do is to be sure that we can give the public the best, most up-to-date equipments, and if we need your patent, we want you to give it to us in return for our giving you a license under our patent.'

That is basic to this whole situation.

High-tech corporations greatly preferred to be unencumbered as they pursued research and development, and patent-licensing compacts were by now an established means of accomplishing this. Western Electric, a front-rank manufacturer of electrical and electronic gear, worked with no less than 6,000 subcontractors and suppliers on military projects in 1951—many thousands more in total. An AT&T executive reiterated a few years after the 1956 decree that the company had long followed "a general policy of licensing its patents to anyone who had patents in which Western Electric was interested, if he would license Western Electric under his patents. Western Electric was thus using its patent position for the purpose of gaining access to the technology of others rather than as a means of excluding others from its technology." As news of the settlement flashed into business discourse an AT&T spokesperson sought to sooth investors' anxieties, with reassurances that all that had been accomplished was "to make compulsory a practice we've followed for years."[68]

These assertions were disingenuous, however. First, in a given case AT&T might decide that it was in its interest to cross-license patents—or not: the difference between this voluntary action and a compulsory mandate remained decisive. Second, its account sidestepped the inconvenient fact that pressure stemming from the protracted antitrust case—alongside increased military contracting—engendered its increased willingness to cross-license. In 1936, 100 companies had been granted licenses to AT&T's patents; and, in keeping with mandated wartime information sharing, by 1944 there were 400 licensees. But in 1953, four years after the suit was launched but three years *prior* to the Consent Decree, there were 800 such licensees. These agreements were by no means necessarily inimical to AT&T's corporate self-interest.[69]

As I have underlined, the antitrust case subjected AT&T to stubborn pressure for six years before it was lodged and seven additional years until it was settled. During this protracted period, despite the vagaries of the case, the company's enormous and sustained contributions to technology development remained generally susceptible to political pressure. This is not to claim that the federal government operated with one mind: We have seen that the Defense Department attempted to inveigle the Justice Department to postpone or dismiss the case and, indeed, congressional testimony hints that the National Security Council also may have conveyed a verbal (and therefore unrecorded) injunction against divestiture to the Justice Department. Nor is it to suggest that the government possessed unique foresight. It is, however, to assert that the antitrust division's intensifying focus on patents altered the pattern of interaction between the nation's foremost corporate center for science and engineering and the wider political economy.[70]

This is evident, first, because similar issues entangled companies beside AT&T. Culminating an investigation that had commenced seven years earlier, in 1952 the Justice Department launched a major antitrust action against IBM, among other things for predatory patent-licensing practices; and it initiated a third prosecution against RCA in 1954, charging RCA with monopolizing patent licensing in radio apparatus. Stanley N. Barnes, now chief of the Department's Antitrust Division, freely boasted—the day after the AT&T settlement was reached in 1956—that all three cases were "part of one program to open up the electronics field."[71]

The provisions of the AT&T settlement were remarkable in that they mandated an institutional change that rippled and ramified outward. First, the government imposed compulsory royalty-free licensing on *all* existing AT&T patents, including those unrelated to telephone equipment. Second, AT&T also was enjoined to license on generous terms all *future* patents. Finally, the decree required Bell also to make available to licensees technical information, drawings, and specifications. AT&T was being directed to help outside companies absorb what they wanted from its vast and actively expanding reservoir of technical knowledge; two years afterward, the then-ranking antitrust official at the Justice Department repeated in the face of skeptics that the judgment's patent provisions were, in fact, exceptionally "stringent." Its effect was to withdraw corporate patent excludability across a vast realm. What was now the world's paramount capitalist country had imposed a paradoxical policy of mandating a public utility for high-tech—above all, for military—R&D.[72]

Contemporary critics perceived one overarching beneficiary: AT&T. They had some cause. Not only did Western Electric remain a part of AT&T, but the settlement granted a formal sanction to AT&T's monopoly over the enormous regulated common carrier telecommunications market. The telephone company attempted, moreover, to manipulate the "regulated telecommunications" boundary, so as to enter other markets—such as private networks for major corporate and other organizational users.[73]

In the government market, the other realm left to AT&T by the consent decree, the results were equally beneficial to the company. Indeed they were spectacular. The years of prosecution spanned the onset of the Cold War; Bell Labs' President Kelly volunteered to a congressional committee that "this emergency was a way of life." But crisis spells opportunity, as it is said, and in practical terms the long-standing interpenetration of AT&T—a charter member of the nation's military-industrial complex—and the US Department of Defense proved a continual boon. Nearly seamless ties meant that it was indeed sometimes difficult to tell where one organization ended and the other began, as AT&T was endowed by the Department of Defense with quasi-official functions. This arrangement also bequeathed great prizes for the holding company. First was the growing revenue stream AT&T derived from Cold War military contracts: on the eve of the Korean War buildup, in 1950 Western Electric garnered around $99 million from the federal government, accounting for about 13 percent of its overall sales; in 1956, its "mainly" military contracts from the US government amounted to $724 million, or over 30 percent of total sales of $2.374 billion. For purposes of comparison, the 1956 Fortune 500 tally shows total revenues of $564 million for IBM, $629 million for Honeywell, $688 million for Sperry, and $1.1 billion for RCA: well above these, at number 12 on the Fortune list, was Western Electric—and its military revenues alone were greater than the overall revenues garnered by each of these other tech companies apart from RCA. Only because the parent company dwarfed its Western Electric unit—AT&T's revenues for 1956 came in at nearly $6 billion—did it look as if its government work was of secondary economic importance. Second was that, as an adjunct of its activities as a top war contractor (some of which are itemized below), AT&T remained at the forefront of technology development across a nearly unrivaled range. Third was that AT&T derived great public relations benefits from its national "defense" role. Continued ownership and control of Western Electric, finally, sustained AT&T's opaque transfer-pricing power (though fresh pressure was building for government regulators to address this long-standing irritant).[74]

Each of the two market domains left to AT&T by the decree was huge and, during the 1950s, growing frenziedly as residential telephone service rocketed while the Cold War and US combat against revolutionary insurgencies became permanent global phenomena. By contrast, because the settlement inflicted no harm to AT&T in either of these outsized realms, its restrictive patent provisions could appear as inconsequential. As we will see, though—they were not.

Almost from the moment that it was lodged, AT&T's unexcelled status in corporate America seemed to loom over the suit. Both a contemporary legislative committee and a later historian have clarified how, early on, an unexpected new interlock between AT&T and the US nuclear weapons-making complex shaped the proceeding. Bell Labs had been working for years in nuclear science, and Oliver Buckley, then head of Bell Labs, had accepted an appointment by President Truman to the Atomic Energy Commission's General Advisory Committee effective August 1, 1948, for a six-year term. The next year, Truman requested that AT&T take over management of Sandia National Laboratories. Sandia was then a branch of the more famous nearby lab, Los Alamos; both facilities were operated for the Atomic Energy Commission by the University of California. In 1949, however, the University prudently declared that it wished to be relieved of its responsibility for Sandia: Where Los Alamos specialized in the underlying nuclear physics, chemistry, and metallurgy, all of which could be considered in an academic guise, Sandia was a production-oriented engineering and bomb assembly unit: it was where warheads were actually built—work that might jeopardize academic respectability. Was there a organizational substitute to take over Sandia?[75]

During 1949 the Atomic Energy Commission decided that AT&T was singularly well-suited to fill this role and, in May, as historian James Spurlock explains, President Truman wrote to Buckley and, separately, to AT&T president Leroy Wilson requesting that it take over operations at Sandia. The company did not at once accept; indeed, AT&T president Wilson held that he would not accept such an arrangement unless something could be done about the antitrust suit. In July, Wilson wrote to AEC Chairman David Lilienthal that he was "concerned" about Attorney General Clark's prosecution: the Justice Department, Wilson clarified, was using the pending litigation to "terminate the very same Western Electric-Bell Laboratories-Bell System relationship which gives our organization the unique qualifications" that the AEC wished to exploit at Sandia. He asked that Lilienthal "acquaint the President with the situation." Because AT&T's prospective responsibilities at Sandia would encompass the same "combination of design and production elements criticized by the [Justice Department] suit," a second account of these events suggests, Wilson, requested an assurance from Attorney General Tom Clark that there would be no adverse effect. Though these dealings remain opaque, it seems evident that a resolution awaited a decision by a higher authority than the Attorney General. Unearthed by James Spurlock, a confidential memo written by Wilson for his own files in mid-August, as AT&T was in the thick of negotiations to take over Sandia, clarifies that Lilienthal indeed had "spent considerable time with President Truman . . . going over the Sandia problem" and that Truman offered reassurances that "we . . . should have no concern": Lilienthal "indicated in an indirect way that there is no program by the Department of Justice to press the Western suit. . . . [and] that the Bell System could carry on just as we were without further attack." Corroboration comes from a memo by the Assistant Secretary of Defense, divulged years later to a legislative oversight committee, that "the anti-trust suit was called to the attention of the President" before mid-1949.[76]

Spurlock shows that contingency intervened to enable President Truman to finesse the "Sandia problem." Supreme Court Justice Frank Murphy had died on July 19, and on August 2 Attorney General Tom Clark, following Senate confirmation, was elevated to the nation's highest judicial tribunal. Therefore, as Spurlock puts it, "the Department of Justice was in flux": the new Attorney General, J. Howard McGrath, was not appointed until August 24, 1949—nine days after AT&T and the AEC seem to have reached an understanding. Western Electric (with Bell Laboratories) took over the contract to operate Sandia, effective November 1, and continued in this role for the next forty-four years. As President Truman decided in favor of developing the hydrogen bomb (over the objections of the illustrious members of the General Advisory Committee to the Atomic Energy Commission, including Bell Labs' Oliver Buckley) for a couple of years the antitrust litigation remained apparently in abeyance.[77]

Truman's regard for AT&T was affirmed in 1950 when, after his retirement as Chairman of the Board of AT&T, Walter S. Gifford was anointed by the President as Ambassador to England. AT&T's public service role in defending the nation was multifaceted and though sometimes little-heralded: "it seemed a given that presidents and vice presidents of Bell Labs would contribute their time and opinions to the government's cold war intelligence endeavors"—including to the super-secret signals intelligence programs of the young National Security Agency. By 1953, Sandia Corporation's staff consisted of 5600 people, of whom 1000 were scientists and engineers: "There is no major weaponry program that is in a superior state of readiness or that is closer to the forefronts of science," boasted AT&T.[78]

Subsequent exposures showed that AT&T apparently continued to be successful in deflecting the antitrust prosecution. Referred to in congressional testimony but long classified, a memo written in 1953 by the President of Bell Laboratories attempted to spur the then Assistant Attorney General for Antitrust, Stanley N. Barnes, to drop the litigation, by underlining that a fully integrated Bell System was key to national security. Fleshing out subsequent scholarship, the memo traced the threads that bound AT&T to the US military and carried on the refrain that "the Bell System's form of organization and method of operation, which are of vital importance to the success of the nationwide telephone system, have proved also to have unique value to the national defense." Proclaiming the benefits of integration of Western Electric and Bell Laboratories, the text underlined that "The organization and methods of operation that Laboratories-Western have evolved through the years to meet the Bell System's requirements are uniquely suited, almost without change, for rendering a corresponding service to the military departments in the creation of new weapons and communications systems and the modernization of old ones."[79]

AT&T had billed the government $2.1 billion for military projects carried out during World War II. It had produced more than half of all US radars used during the conflict, together with a great range of related electronics; developed and manufactured what it described in 1953 as "the first large sized electrical digital computer for solving ballistic and aerodynamic problems"; created new electronically guided torpedo systems; worked successfully on rocketry and on specialized microwave and other communications systems. After the War, as the public utility framework sustained surging domestic telephone demand, AT&T Laboratories reduced its defense work "to the extent of about one-fourth of its activities for the Bell System"—still a very considerable amount. The Korean war, however, "brought a new policy," and AT&T rapidly re-accelerated its military contracting: at Bell Labs from $15 million in 1950 to $55 million in 1953; and at Western Electric from $110 million in 1951 to $450 million in 1953, "with a backlog in excess of a billion dollars." This resulted in a web of interdependence: "[T]he normal pattern is for the contractor to design and produce in quantity a specific item of equipment to meet predetermined military specifications." In contrast, "[t]he Bell System's work has in great part originated either with its own suggestions to the military, based on conceptions resulting from its telephonic research, or with a request by the military either that it create a complete new communications or weapons system or that it study such an existing system and make recommendations for improving its entire operation."[80]

Guided missiles, notably successive generations of the Nike missile, constituted a central initiative from 1945 to 1953, and on this AT&T cooperated with Douglas Aircraft; research and development work also proceeded under contract for radar detection and fire control systems—with a general emphasis on supporting computers and communications and specific attention to submarines, missiles, and aircraft. In association with MIT's Lincoln Laboratory, AT&T commenced in 1952 to develop a "radar fence stretching from Hawaii across the Aleutians, Alaska, the extreme northern part of this continent, Greenland, Iceland, and to the United Kingdom." "Following the presentation of this study to the National Security Council"—a salient point, because this event occurred only weeks before Secretary of Defense Lovett interceded on AT&T's behalf with the incoming Eisenhower Administration—Lovett wrote to the President of AT&T: "it is my judgment that the nation must depend on the Bell System to bear the responsibility for this project." AT&T also was pivotal to the Air Defense Command, which by 1953 employed over 70,000 people. If, as Leffler documents, US Cold War policy sought to establish a preponderance of power over the world's industrial infrastructure, skilled labor, raw materials, and forward bases, then it was likewise essential to US purposes to secure dominance over science and high-technology, including but not restricted to telecommunications.[81]

Notwithstanding the numerous, lucrative, and enduring collaborations between AT&T and military and intelligence agencies, however, the settlement exemplified and ultimately triggered additional far-reaching changes to the political-economy of networking specifically. The government's intervention reoriented AT&T, subjecting it to different determinations. A structural alteration to AT&T's profit strategy came via the patent-sharing provisions of the Consent Decree, which helped guarantee that the US's "permanent war economy" could continue to be based on all-out development of high-technology. Critics who dismiss or belittle the patent-sharing strictures have missed this: government-mandated non-excludability constituted a bedrock feature, not just of the consent decree but of the state's mobilization of military industry. And this, coupled with the settlement's restriction of AT&T to regulated telecommunications, subjected AT&T's existing system of networking to pressure that intensified to the point that ultimately it became irresistible.[82]

We may clarify this by turning to an AT&T engineering discovery which immediately gained an unrivaled place among its pantheon of achievements. AT&T's memo emphasized this: "the Laboratories continuously evaluates the new knowledge arising from its Bell System research and development programs for its worth in military applications . . . One example, of major importance, is the transistor":

> The transistor was invented by the Laboratories in 1949. It has revolutionary significance, both in communications and in electronic weaponry. Before announcing the invention the Laboratories disclosed it to the military and indicated its significance. From that time responsible military people cooperated with the Laboratories in determining policy as to publication. The Laboratories also cooperated with the military in an educational program on transistors and their circuits for the laboratories of military establishments and their industrial contractors. Although use of the transistor in Bell System communications will be important, priority has been given to the development of military applications of this device.

The settlement impinged on—actually, infused—a quickly widening technological transition, in which electronics, data processing, aerospace, communications—and, ultimately, business at large—were rebuilt around successive variants of solid-state digital microelectronics. And, crucially, the Justice Department was demanding, as Riordan and Hoddeson have shown, that this strategic technology remain free of the exclusionary corporate proprietorships and legal infighting that had encumbered radio throughout the 1920s and early 1930s.[83]

During World War II, the importance of solid-state microelectronics was already apparent to Mervin Kelly, the leader of this unit of Bell Laboratories and the executive who would come to head Bell Laboratories itself throughout most of the antitrust case. Kelly initially hoped to retain proprietary control over the transistor because he "wanted Bell to have an exclusive opportunity to learn how the solid-state amplifier might be employed in ordinary electrical devices, especially those used for radios, television, and telephones." Protestations to the contrary notwithstanding, AT&T thus exercised close control over the manufacturing art actually needed to fabricate transistors. Prior to filing for transistor patents, further, the company had imposed strict secrecy over its researchers' discoveries.[84]

This narrow corporate self-interest persisted. A 1955 report prepared by AT&T again cast the importance of microelectronics in narrowly telephonic terms:

> Since the close of World War II, the research programs of Bell Telephone Laboratories have made available a family of new electronic devices that give promise of a sweeping revolution in the technical character of Bell System equipment and telephone service in the decades ahead.

Despite this carefully circumscribed reference, however, Bell Labs' Mervin Kelly himself had foreseen back in 1943 that solid-state microelectronics "will come into large-scale use in the Bell System only gradually. Other fields of application—military electronics systems, home entertainment, special services—may well have the larger initial uses." As the potential applications of transistors began to be apprehended, other principals in the antitrust case quickly came to glimpse the new technology's promise. Judge Barnes, who negotiated the consent decree for the Eisenhower administration, claimed in congressional testimony two months after the settlement that "licensing under future patents of the defendants is compulsory, and at reasonable and nondiscriminatory royalty rates . . . The importance of these provisions, extending beyond the telephone field, is difficult to exaggerate. Consider, for example, the transistor inventions owned by defendants—now available royalty-free." Barnes underlined military applications: "the transistor patents are vital to production of defense items like guided missiles and electronic range-finders."[85]

Even by 1952, Riordan and Hoddeson conclude, the prosecution had impelled AT&T to "make a concerted effort to reveal everything it knew about making transistors." Throughout the 1950s the major beneficiaries of this change were other, sometimes allied, military contractors and subcontractors, working on military projects. To ensure what Thomas J. Misa calls "a war-ready industrial base," military officers and strategists in the Department of Defense made concerted efforts to diffuse knowledge of microelectronics and to refine this technology. The Army and, in particular, the Signal Corps, actually underwrote the construction costs of manufacturing plants needed to produce transistors, not only by AT&T's Western Electric, but also by GE, RCA, Raytheon, and Sylvania. "By sponsoring applications studies, organizing bureaus for production development, and disseminating the new technology to industry, the military assumed responsibility for presiding over the process of technological development."[86]

Within this crucial field of military industry, therefore, the decree ensured that innovators both within and outside of AT&T might participate in what, it was becoming evident, would be a technological sea-change. A telling contrast in institutional practice appeared within the fledgling microelectronics industry itself. On one side were companies which divulged their innovations only if and when this suited their profit strategies; some even "purposely avoided military funding for their research so that the basic technology was privately owned." This would lead to a situation whereby, by the 1970s, "Intel scientists did not give talks that could benefit competitors. They did not publish technical papers," writes a biographer of Intel's leader, Robert Noyce. On the other side, the giant in this field as in others—AT&T—now was prevented from embracing a comparable course. All the way through the prosecution, as well as after the settlement, AT&T's behavior remained subject to overriding constraint. The "ongoing antitrust suit," declares Misa, "persuaded Bell to release its technology to industry quickly in order to avoid appearing to monopolize the transistor field."[87]

Existing and new businesses therefore could make unencumbered use of otherwise proprietary information in developing a vast array of high-tech aerospace, electronics, and computing equipment and services. The settlement made a prominent contribution to guaranteeing that norms of openness would prevail, paradoxically, within what Edwards aptly terms the "closed world" of military high-technology development, and again in conformity with what AT&T identified as "the major objective" of its patent policy: "the freedom to design and manufacture the best possible equipment."[88]

The case's resolution denoted an overarching commitment by corporations and military agencies to advancing high technology in the service of "national defense." New military technologies followed in steady succession; and, though it ran Sandia under a nonprofit contract, AT&T itself was a primary beneficiary of military largess. In the medium-term at least, this and the decree's patent-sharing provisions worked to ensure AT&T's own unbroken centrality to a militarized political economy. In a longer-term context, however, AT&T ironically succeeded too well. It fused itself so fully to the US military-corporate industrial base that it left itself open to dangerously centrifugal appropriations of its patents by corporate interlopers. In 1956, however, this possibility probably did not seem to be an inordinate concession to AT&T executives.

The stakes were, however, much higher than this. That policymakers had at last prevailed against AT&T's proprietary patent strategy bespoke a hollow triumph for the New Deal's erstwhile crusade against corporate chokepoints. The democratic political priorities that had gained political traction throughout the 1930s and that had retained influence during the 1940s had been exchanged for policies that centered on mobilization for endless war. The US fight against any additional expansion of global socialism, and its combat against revolutionary nationalism throughout Asia, Africa, Latin America and the Middle East, triggered a structural transformation of the US's own political economy. One part of this wider metamorphosis was to make AT&T a patent utility for military agencies and corporate-military contractors. Through this means, AT&T guaranteed its position at the apex of a US war economy.

Over a longer span, however, AT&T's seemingly stable new status opened a mortal wound. The result of the settlement was to generate and sustain a stream of innovations that were not and—because of the decree—*could* not be monopolized by the telephone company. The settlement thus helped catalyze a structural mutation, by both accelerating and greatly widening the development of digital systems and services. Within a decade, this change would build toward an irresistible challenge to the AT&T-centered telecommunications system, as it launched a spiraling confrontation between AT&T and its largest customers. In the 1980s a consultant to the Justice Department captured this irony: "a Consent Decree that was intended to cement AT&T's pyramid in place ... for a thousand years" instead "absolutely guaranteed that the pyramid would be dismantled piece by piece."[89]

The bitter verdict of many contemporaries—that the 1956 decree was a sellout to AT&T—actually turned out to be doubly flawed. The sellout was not to a single corporation but to a more complex corporate-military redevelopment of the US political economy, including US high-technology networking. Far from being a mere reflex of the telephone company's self-interest, moreover, the decree ultimately imposed punishing restraints not only on AT&T's profit strategy but also the public utility framework on which it had come to be based. The outcome of the case therefore cast a long shadow.

The public utility model originated in attempts to tame corporate power in essential industries, telecommunications among them. During the first half of the twentieth century, as workers and consumers fought to improve standards of employment and to gain inclusive residential service, it was stretched and widened in the same general direction. As the US took the reins of global capitalism after World War II, however, the public utility model was afflicted with two counteracting structural alterations: both intensifying commercialization and a half-hidden but far-reaching militarization of the US network infrastructure. Paradoxically, moreover, the very consent decree that sealed AT&T's military role also unleashed a technological modernization that helped to enable AT&T's largest customers and their allies to subvert the public utility conception itself.

9
Activists and Dissidents: The 1960s

Even as the structures of consumerism and militarization held and, indeed, became further enlarged, during the 1960s and the early 1970s the United States entered another deeply conflicted conjuncture. On one side, oppositional energies flared, as the Black freedom struggle intersected with protest against the US war on Vietnam, in turn boosting other social justice and counter-cultural movements. On the other, while political conservatives batted against the resultant liberalization of politics and society, big companies hit out against restive workers and their unions. No sooner did the boundaries of the New Deal settlement begin to stretch and enlarge, that is, than did a massing political and economic reaction set in. Social struggles and political collisions reached such intensity that a historian has summed up this period as "the shattering."[1]

This chapter explicates one aspect of this polarization, by detailing how rank-and-file labor and social justice activism erupted in and around telecommunications. Succeeding chapters delineate the processes of reaction.

Telecommunications provision had become heavily unionized. During the late 1960s, however, many restive postal and telephone workers came to believe that their unions were led by self-satisfied bureaucrats, indifferent to or incapable of addressing rank-and-file concerns. Might their conditions be improved, their unions democratized? Discontent widened, because wages lagged behind inflation while work itself bore management's imposing hand. As well, grievances proliferated against corporate employment and labor policies among those who had been marginalized, once again, by the New Deal. Workforces were recomposing, as increasing numbers of Blacks and Latinos were hired into manufacturing and service jobs; and many postal employees and some telephone workers joined larger struggles against racism and gender discrimination. Legal and political campaigns demanding equal employment rights for women, Black, Latino, and gay workers made telecommunications a bellwether—because the public utility framework within which this industry operated granted reformers room for struggle that was much-reduced in other sectors. Around as well as within the postal and telephone unions insurgencies sprang up. Aaron Brenner argues that the labor upsurge of the 1960s and early 1970s constituted a "rank-and-file rebellion," in which postal and telephone workers mobilized impressively against both capital and the state.[2]

Outbreaks of rank-and-file activism saw sick-outs, demonstrations, and strikes. Campaigns for workplace justice drew on civil rights and antidiscrimination struggles waged by African Americans, Mexican Americans, and Puerto Ricans; anti-Vietnam war protests; and what Dorothy Sue Cobble calls "the other women's movement"—a long-haul push for women's workplace justice for women. Although these contentious energies did not converge on an overarching common purpose, they did result in "opening the American workplace" and thereby realizing a more comprehensive economic citizenship: a signal victory.[3]

Postal Workers and Unions in the 1960s

Apart from the brief period of postalization in 1918–1919 Post Office and telephone workers had always been institutionally separated, and in the combustible 1960s they continued to trace mostly separate trajectories. Each group staged important strikes: postal workers in the momentous Spring of 1970 and telephone workers in Summer 1971. The postal workers who conducted and led their walkout wanted wage and benefit gains in a context of high inflation. A significant number of them also intended to uproot racism as a hindrance to postal unionism and to replace their splintered, top-down union structures with more democratic and inclusive organizations.

In the 1960s, there were nine significant Post Office unions. Some of the biggest had been formed during the Jim Crow era, and when the clerks, carriers, and handlers worked in isolation from one another. Support for industrial unionism, though—for one union to embrace all postal workers—had long been present. A Joint Council of Affiliated Postal Organizations representing AFL-affiliated unions to further interunion cooperation had been established back in the 1920s. The goal of establishing an industrial union to represent the entire nonmanagerial postal workforce thereafter surfaced repeatedly.

However, divisions by AFL-CIO affiliation, around gender, craft-structured institutions, and racist discrimination had proved intractable. As recently as 1958–1960, radical members of the National Federation of Postal Clerks had split that union, leaving two separate organizations: the rump membership became the United Federation of Postal Clerks, while the departing workers established an integrated National Postal Union. The National Alliance of Postal Employees, with 2,500 members by the late 1920s when African Americans made up 9 percent of the postal labor force, expressly attempted to promote Black workers' civil rights and labor rights. As historian Philip Rubio recounts, by World War II African American workers' battles with white supremacy targeted not only Post Office managers and federal policies, but also culpable union leaders and many white rank-and-filers. By 1949, the National Alliance represented 25,000 Black postal workers, some of whom were victimized by President Truman's loyalty boards. The union survived and continued to be powered by its ideals during the 1960s. Meanwhile, the National Postal Union was even more "militant, industrial, antiracist." Neither was an affiliate of the AFL-CIO. Blacks accounted for about one-fifth of the overall postal workforce during the 1960s; while African Americans made up a majority of workers in several big-city Post Offices (Chicago, Los Angeles, New Orleans, and Washington, DC), and close to half of the total in Philadelphia, Detroit, Houston, Cleveland, Cincinnati, Memphis and Atlanta. Less significant numerically in the New York City Post Office, African Americans helped make Gotham perhaps the most militant city in postal-dom during the mid-1960s. Women had worked for the agency, mostly as clerks, since the Civil War era; in 1965, overall, they numbered nearly 50,000 (around 8 percent of its 600,000 employees), and their number would double within the next four years. These employment patterns contributed to placing the Post Office at the forefront of both of public sector unionism and of the movement to overcome racial and gender discrimination in the workplace. Nevertheless, at the conservative end of the postal union spectrum lay big, politically connected AFL-CIO affiliates: the National Association of Letter Carriers and the United Federation of Postal Clerks. Their Jim Crow locals were not entirely eliminated even following presidential executive orders in 1961–1962, which sought to curtail racial discrimination in federal employment. (Seeking to moderate an increasingly militant Civil Rights movement while also countering socialist influence throughout the Third World, Kennedy's people purported that the Post Office was a "showcase for gender as well as racial equality.")[4]

Despite these entrenched divisions, there was an evident tendency to rank-and-file solidarity, as the postal crafts converged around shared complaints. The Post Office was a pot of simmering resentments. Above all, employees were severely underpaid, especially as inflation cranked up in conjunction with Vietnam War deficit spending, and especially in the high-priced cities of the Northeast. By one estimate, 7 percent of postal workers collected welfare checks. Letter carriers in the Empire City earned maximum annual pay of $8442, at a time when, according to government estimates, "a family of four needs $11,236 to maintain a moderate standard of living in New York City." They faced working conditions that ranged from indifferent to "horrible." Post Office management was arbitrary and authoritarian while, unlike their unionized peers working elsewhere throughout corporate America, employees enjoyed no rights to collective bargaining on economic issues and—above all—no right to strike. Adding fuel to the fire was that postal union bureaucrats' chief function was to lobby Congress for pay and benefits—and that they had become demonstrably unable to deliver. Turnover at the Post Office was high. By 1966, finally, three-quarters of all postal workers were veterans, increasingly, veterans of the escalating US war on Vietnam, where, by the late 1960s, soldiers were often likely to disobey their officers' commands. This, then, especially at the network's big-city nodes, was far from a docile labor force.[5]

Clerks often called the huge processing facilities built to decorate such cities as New York and Chicago "letter factories." This was apt. The nation's largest single industrial workforce moved the mail through a relatively small set of centralized hubs: giant urban or, now sometimes suburban, processing centers. The basis for opposition at these nodes lay in collective organization: the astonishingly high unionization rate in the Post Office—estimated at 84 percent overall in 1963, with the letter carriers joining their union, the National Association of Letter Carriers, at a 90 percent rate—found no parallel anywhere else in US industry or in the US Government. (The US unionization rate in private industry had declined to 25 percent in 1970, from its 1954 peak of 33 percent; government workers were 43 percent unionized in 1968.) By 1968–1969, postal worker militancy had markedly intensified. Slowdowns, mass absenteeism, solidarity between union locals, and a couple of local strike actions were signals that, for the rank-and-file, the *status quo* had grown intolerable. Two or three national postal unions even passed resolutions to examine the possibility of striking their federal employer, probably attempting to cool down their members. In 1970 Frederick Kappel, erstwhile chairman of AT&T and a protagonist in an emerging postal "reform" campaign, would diagnose the agency's top problem as "widespread disquiet among postal employees." By the time he issued this pronouncement, however, postal workers' unhappiness was on display for all to see.[6]

Leveraging Crisis in Chicago

The nation's letter factories were breaking down. An especially dramatic instance developed at a vital mail-processing node in Chicago. On September 26, 1966, "as sack after sack of mail was backing up in the cavernous work rooms," Henry W. McGee was sworn in to head Chicago's Post Office, one of the nation's largest. McGee was the first African American to hold this position; this was also the first time that an employee (McGee began to work at the Chicago Post Office in 1929) had risen from the ranks to lead a big metropolitan post office. His appointment followed protests against Chicago Post Office employment discrimination the previous Spring: African Americans made up 61 percent of the organization's 28,000 employees, but just 15 percent of supervisors, charged a local activist, Robert Lucas, mail-handler and chairman of the Chicago chapter of the Congress of Racial Equality. Chicago had been a significant, and continually growing, site of Black postal employment since the beginning of the Great

Migration; McGee himself had long been a member, and a local leader, of the National Alliance of Postal Employees—the African American–led industrial postal union committed both to civil rights and labor rights. At once, McGee found himself beset by a full-on crisis. Over the course of two weeks between late September and mid-October 1966, the mechanism for processing mail in the nation' second city ground to a halt; an estimated ten million items failed to reach their intended destinations.[7]

The crash reflected both immediate contingencies and longer-term trends. It occurred during the weeks leading to Christmas, when the system typically absorbed the heaviest mail flows. The downtown Post Office had been built to take deliveries by railroad cars rather than trucks. Now it was also hit not only by snowstorms but also by a labor shortage attributed to a Presidential order cutting overtime work for Government employees. As well, it choked on a huge and unanticipated stream of advertisements and circulars. The outage radiated outward because Chicago acted as the nation's premier intercity mail processing facility. Postmaster General Lawrence F. O'Brien recollected it as "the most serious situation I faced while I was in the job—very, very difficult. It was on the edge of complete debacle for days . . . it was the major crisis of my time."[8]

McGee, disputing activists' contention that the breakdown possessed what the *Times* called "racial overtones," turned to combat the emergency. Persuading 1,000 employees to shift their schedules in an attempt to relieve the backlog, McGee gradually reintroduced order to Chicago's mail processing, hiring 10,000 temporary workers, undertaking repairs, cracking down on "loafing and unexcused absenteeism," accelerating mechanization, and mandating that Chicago's 6,500 bulk mailers comply with regulations requiring presorting and zip-coding. Embarrassment as well as injury had been heaped on the Chicago operation: two sacks of mail had been dumped in Lake Michigan in August— before the crash—and afterward, in December, three other sacks fell off a truck, their contents scattered irretrievably.[9]

McGee was quoted in support of the findings of an internal Post Office investigation, which claimed that the breakdown had stemmed not only from the unexpected spike in mail volume, but also from an out-of-service loading dock, a tight labor market, and "abnormal absenteeism among employees." This was code for action taken by rank-and-file employees; and Postmaster General O'Brien recalled two decades later that "problems with the unions" indeed had figured: "you were in a slowdown, you were in disruption." Chicago's unemployment rate was pegged at only 2.6 percent, while entering local postal employees received $1.64 an hour at a time when minimum wage was $1.25. Not surprisingly, therefore, employee turnover and absenteeism were high among the Black and women workers who preponderated at the Chicago post office, many of whom moonlighted at nearby factories to augment their earnings.[10]

Postmaster General Lawrence O'Brien eventually acknowledged that, along with rank-and-file action, bulk mailers had been pivotal in the network outage. Without first notifying the Post Office, direct mail companies had summarily diverted a huge quantity of mailings from New York City—which had imposed a tax on printing—to Chicago. After attempting to reassure the nation that the Post Office would succeed in processing the avalanche of Christmas mail (nationwide volume in December was up to almost 9 billion pieces, or nearly 9 percent over the same month in 1965) O'Brien reversed course. A Democrat, O'Brien warned a House committee in February 1967 that "at present your Post Office Department is in a race with catastrophe." "Our postal system serves 6 percent of the world population, yet it sags under the weight of half the world's mail," O'Brien would declaim. Overall US mail volume was, moreover, increasing by an increment of three billion pieces annually, and so threatened to overwhelm the "inadequate, badly located, and aging" physical facilities through which it flowed. The Chicago pile-up would not prove to be an isolated incident, he warned. In Milwaukee, San Francisco, Washington, D.C., New York—"a logjam could happen in any post office, and will happen in any or all, unless we are given the tools to move ahead rapidly." The Postmaster demanded rate increases and support for Zone Improvement Plan (ZIP) Code based computerization. In April 1967, he went further, proposing that the Post Office be turned into a private corporation. O'Brien's plan to privatize the Post Office, however, actually had been hatched soon after his appointment, in the period around the 1966 Chicago outage.[11]

Similar conditions existed in many cities, as the Post Office network became "trapped between proliferating skyscrapers that multiply the mail volume, and the gelatinized auto traffic that clogs collections." Manhattan's sixty-two Post Offices by 1967 handled around 34 million pieces each day, about the daily total for all of France. The Empire State Building, requiring between 21 and 26 carriers to complete two deliveries each day, was the world's busiest mail route. An additional outpouring of commercial mail disrupted this already overburdened system. During the week following Christmas 1966, Chicago was expected to process 94 million pieces of advertising of one kind or another, compared to just 43 million during the comparable week in 1965. Mail processing was suffering from concurrent changes in land use, transport, and demand; and postal employees were resisting or, more often, simply absenting themselves, from working conditions they deemed insufferable.[12]

In the wake of the Chicago meltdown, postal administrators immediately advanced claims that only basic structural changes would rescue the Post Office from such fiascos. Rapid mechanization and partial corporatization (with the possibility of subsequent full-on privatization), they exclaimed, would put paid to the institution's otherwise intractable problems. These proposals quickly captivated the political establishment. Early in April, 1967, speaking to the Magazine Publishers Association and the American Society of Magazine Editors, Postmaster General O'Brien publicized a recommendation that he had offered to President Lyndon Johnson: that his cabinet department be replaced by a non-profit Government corporation. O'Brien fumed that Congress would not fully fund the rate increases required for his top-down modernization scheme, while he also faced a need to continue Government subsidies of around 70 percent for second-class (magazines and newspapers) and 40 percent for third-class (direct mail advertising) shipments. O'Brien explained later that, in light of its "intolerable" low rate of capital investment and its ageing plant—2500 "major facilities" had been built prior to 1940—modernizing the Post Office would require an additional one billion dollars a year for five years to fund new post offices, computers, and mail-processing equipment. He also tried to shift blame, arguing that some of the Department's service failures should be laid at the door of the nation's railroads, even though as its reliance on trucks increased, the number of rail cars used to transport the mail had declined—from 10,000 to fewer than 900 over the previous thirty years. Rates needed to be increased at once, while reorganization was needed to engender essential capital investments over the long term.[13]

In a message to Congress days after O'Brien's speech, President Lyndon Johnson declared that the postal service—"the key link of the nation's commerce"—"must be responsive to the needs of the public and the needs of the business community." To propel postal efficiency, the President called for rate increases for all classes of correspondence. A progressive feature was evident: proportionally greater increases were to be borne by second- and especially third-class mailers. The President followed up by convening a ten-person commission, to determine "whether the high quality postal service which Americans have come to expect can better be performed by a Cabinet department, a Government corporation or some other form of organization." With such a charge, the commission's conclusion was preprogrammed—especially as, to head the group, Johnson chose retired AT&T board chairman Frederick Kappel. Kappel was flanked by other business leaders, alongside one representative of organized labor, George Meany, president of the AFL-CIO. (After the reorganization that would follow, Kappel went on to chair the Postal Service's oversight body, the Board of Governors, again with other corporate executives.)[14]

President Johnson requested that the commission inquire specifically into the views of Congress, major mail users, the general public, and unionized Post Office employees. Postal unions proved skeptical, as did some members of Congress and government officials. It was inconvenient, for example, that J. Edward Day, who had served as President Kennedy's Postmaster General, should respond that the Department's problems were caused by a "penny-pinching Congress." Flatly opposed to reorganization, Day insisted that "The Post Office Department needs more prestige, rather than less." The commercial news media, by contrast, proved strongly inclined. *The New York Times* backed O'Brien's plea for what it hailed as "a fundamental change" in the "department's relationship to the Federal Government." Citing the Chicago debacle as Exhibit A, the *Times* recapped the trends which, it purported, had doomed the status quo. Obsolete and poorly located, the capital plant of the Post Office was geared to handle only half of the mail volume it faced. And, vitally, because Congress "makes the key budgetary, wage and rate decisions," the Department remained starved of capital and enmeshed in politics and patronage, preventing it from managing operations efficiently. The *Times* also placed blame on postal workers. Because "the current mail explosion has taken place in a period of high employment," the paper editorialized, it had become "difficult to recruit and retain a permanent, high-quality work force." Seemingly weighing the matter judiciously on a pluralist balance, the nation's most important news organ declared that "a major contributory cause to the present plight of the postal service is that powerful vested interests, notably the postal unions and associations of specialized mail users, have successfully and repeatedly imposed their will upon the system." This was a spurious rhetorical equivalence: postal workers were placed continually on the defensive, as the system strained to channel the cataract of items generated by big corporate mailers.[15]

The *Times* headlined a major story to show that the proposal to replace the Post Office Department with a nonprofit corporation had "the enthusiastic endorsement" of officials at the unruly Chicago operation (including Henry W. McGee). Assailing the existing system of postal subsidies, the *Times* editorialized in favor both of an immediate rate hike and a "basic study" to begin to correct inequities and to reverse the "financial malnutrition" that had forestalled capital investment and reorganization. Lacing its coverage was an evergreen *non sequitur* the *Times* placed in the mouth of McGee: that the agency's re-establishment as a nonprofit corporation would "enable the post office to obtain the best management skills from industry."[16]

After fifteen months of deliberation, and flush with reports supplied by blue-chip consultancies such as Arthur D. Little, the president's special commission reported its findings in June of 1968—not three months after Lyndon Johnson's presidency fell a casualty to the Vietnam War. It commenced with a declaration that the Post Office was in a state of crisis and devoted extensive scrutiny to postal labor relations. In its June 1968 Report, *Towards Postal Excellence*, the Kappel Commission recommended that the Post Office should be converted into a nonprofit government corporation, supplied with professional management, and operated like a business.[17]

"Authoritative sources" duly conveyed to the *Times* that the time for "piecemeal improvements" had passed: "Only a basic change in direction can prevent further deterioration of this essential public service." Misleadingly, because its mandate was not to function as a for-profit corporation, the paper's coverage of the Report merely echoed its claim that the "Post Office has failed as a business because it is run as a political institution." The Department's historical mandate had been reaffirmed as recently as the Postal Policy Act of 1958, which had stated that its operations should be paid for not out of postal revenue but through a Treasury appropriation, because it "clearly is not a business enterprise conducted for profit or for raising general funds." Scarcely a decade later, business and political leaders had chosen to forego—to forget—this engraved responsibility.[18]

The *Times* lent its pages to an enveloping discourse of system failure and malfeasance. In Newark, readers learned, July of 1967 saw 100,000 pieces of mail diverted and mail delivery halted, as a result of that summer's urban insurrection. The scope of postal inadequacy was, it now seemed, universal. Australia's mail service had been "paralyzed" by a strike, the *Times* related in January 1968; deliveries to and from South Vietnam had been suspended for five days, the paper reported in February; the US House of Representatives "refused today to eliminate most Saturday mail services," the *Times* sourly conveyed in April. "It is hard to resist the impression that any change in the management of the United States Post Office would be an improvement," the *Times* charged midway through 1969, "since the trend in mail service has slowly but steadily been approaching the public service standards of nineteenth-century Bulgaria."[19]

The *Times* even deigned to showcase left-liberal criticisms of the Post Office. For example, in 1969, *New York Times* columnist Russell Baker offered the thought that "Traditionally, every time the price of mailing a letter goes up a penny, the Post Office devises a new scheme for making its service even worse than it was before." Baker cited Archibald David, "father of the ZIP code," to the effect that "since the day of the three-cent stamp the department, with each successive increase, has curtailed deliveries, shut down post offices, eliminated collections, placed aggravating new restrictions on letter sizes and shapes and, in order to discourage use of the mail, ordered its collection trucks to double-park in clogged thoroughfares and hounded people to remember long sequences of digits before going to the mailbox." Enumerating plausible reasons for the erratic circulation of what he called "snail mail," Baker concluded that the most recent rate increase had motivated "Pessimists in the department [to] believe there is very little to be done short of dumping the mail-bags on scows for burial at sea."[20]

In a feature for the *New York Times Magazine* in 1968, similarly, Robert Sherrill offered a lurid depiction of postal workers run amok and supervisors afraid for their lives. Displacing altogether rank-and-file struggles to improve wages and working conditions, Sherrill still shed some bright light on governing priorities.

For "a fraction of the cost of a month's fighting in Vietnam," he wrote—without mention of employee protections—the Post Office could be outfitted with much of the modern equipment it needed to improve service. His incisive conclusion was that "Although the postal service is the only part of the Federal Government that benefits the daily lives of most people, it is also, strangely enough, the only major Government service whose cost is looked upon as an unnecessary drain." While billions of dollars in the budget of the Defense Department "are acknowledged to be no more than subsidies for defense industrialists," and additional billions were paid to farmers in crop subsidies, "it is only the postal subsidy of $1-billion a year . . . that bothers the Kappel group."[21]

By the 1968 election, therefore, portraits of a damaged organization were engraved. Postal officials attempted to absorb an ever-increasing mail volume by means of patchwork improvements and limited overhauls. Supplanting Chicago's once-much-praised 1.9 million square foot facility as the largest Post Office in the world, and replacing structures erected in 1910–1913, plans for a new $100 million complex in Manhattan were released in 1968, with completion expected in 1974. The complex would boast 2.5 million square feet and twenty-five-foot ceilings, to accommodate fifteen-ton letter sorting devices and other modern equipment. From Thanksgiving to Christmas of 1968, outgoing Postmaster General W. Marvin Watson boasted, the Post Office would need to move an unprecedented ten billion pieces of mail. Watson declared that he had established a "command post" to "pinpoint problem areas and order solutions," and he decided to use fewer seasonal employees and to pay overtime to experienced workers instead. In 1969, the Department put up an automated mail processing facility in San Francisco, for speeding the 15,000–20,000 letters then being "misdelivered" each day to various destinations in Vietnam (all told, around 100,000 items of mail flowed each day into the war zone).[22]

Wildcat

Against this backdrop, and further "enraged" after President Nixon postponed their scheduled July 1 pay hike until January 1971, and also stated that he would veto any new pay raise legislation that did not mandate reorganization of the post office as a corporation—a rank-and-file insurgency blew up on March 18, 1970. After starting in New York it moved quickly outward to other East Coast, Midwest, and far West cities—key processing hubs—just as it also spread from the letter carriers to other postal crafts. Shutting down mail service across the country, the largest wildcat (unauthorized) strike in US labor history altered the course of postal development (Figures 9.1 and 9.2). More than 200,000 postal workers, out of a labor force of 739,000, walked out of 671 post offices in dozens

Figure 9.1 Letter carriers shout as they picket the General Post Office in New York City, March 18, 1970—the first day of the wildcat strike. AP Photo/Anthony Camerano.

Figure 9.2 Picketers' signs contrast recent pay increases for the President and members of Congress with those sought by striking postal workers. March 21, 1970. Joe Petrella/New York Daily News.

of cities and towns. "It was the first truly national federal strike," wrote Murray B. Nesbitt in 1976, "and its ramifications will be felt for years by the entire federal establishment." Postal workers not only defied the ban against striking their federal employer, but also rejected some of their existing union leaders. Through their week-long rebellion, rank-and-filers catalyzed fundamental change in both institutions: their own unions and the Post Office itself.[23]

Both the power and the vulnerability of wildcats stems from their volatile, bottom-up, character. They overrun established institutional channels but, if they do not quickly generate organization and direction, they may fall prey to a better-prepared counterforce. The Administration already knew what it wanted for postal-dom, and deployed state power not only to combat the walkout but to channel it in a predetermined direction. President Nixon, Aaron Brenner has shown, demanded tough action; Nixon's chief of staff H. R. Haldeman noted that a meeting between the President and his advisors on March 20 resolved that "if people can be fired fire them[.] if troops can be moved move them . . . all out attack . . . it's the principle." Nixon thereupon called out the National Guard to run mail processing in New York City, the strike's center. The Guardsmen did not possess the skills needed to move the mails, but their presence dramatized the federal government's intervention. Polls bespoke public approbation for the strikers but, paradoxically, they also showed support for Nixon's aggressive action. Meanwhile, the Administration was locked in negotiations with the largest postal union, the National Association of Letter Carriers. NALC President James Rademacher, alongside New York Local 36 President Gus Johnson, announced an attractive agreement, including a substantial pay rise retroactive to October 1969. This turned out to be false but, having won what seemed like a victory and facing a court injunction that imposed large fines if they stayed out past March 25, the strikers went back to work. Keeping this sketch in mind, we may turn our attention to the revealing details of the drama that was unfolding behind the scenes (Figure 9.3).[24]

An initial emphasis must be that passage of legislation for postal reorganization, inherited from the previous Democratic administration, was incoming President Nixon's priority all along. "I have been working with the postal employees groups on both the postal pay raise issue and, more importantly, the postal reform issue," wrote Special Counsel Charles Colson to Nixon's chief of staff, H. R. Haldeman, in December 1969. In early February 1970, Colson emphasized that "We have been working closely with the National Association of Letter Carriers. Their support has been critical to the progress we have made on Postal Reform." James Rademacher, NALC president, backed Nixon's plan. A bill, H.R. 4, had been formulated in 1969 to reorganize the Post Office under a new executive council, and to allow it to raise funds through bond sales and, significantly, the bill had made no mention of collective bargaining

Figure 9.3 Chicago Postmaster Henry McGee, with Fred P. Metzen and workers picketing at the Main Post Office, March 20, 1970. Chicago History Museum, st14002786_0009

between the executive council and postal unions. Strongly opposed by the postal unions, H.R. 4 was languishing in the House Post Office Committee after a tie vote of 13–13. Colson related shortly before the wildcat that he had interceded, in a bid to rescue the bill, because Nixon's Postmaster General Winton "Red" Blount had summarily rejected any negotiation with the NALC. "The real problem was that the Postal Unions were at swords points with the PMG," Colson explained. "This resulted in the Unions turning a number of members of Congress against us. Had Red established any kind of relationship with the Union, the bill would have passed the House. Because I've known Jim Rademacher . . . for a long time I volunteered to try to make a deal with Jim. Red resisted my doing this, claiming that we couldn't possibly ever trust any Union leader." Requesting that Nixon telephone Rademacher on March 12— less than a week before the wildcat broke out—Colson vouchsafed that the previous December Rademacher had committed to aid the President in passing postal reform:

> Rademacher is President of the largest postal union. He had to fight all of the other postal unions who are opposed to compromise but he stayed with us all the way. Without his sticking to his agreement and without his very effective lobbying, the Bill could not have been reported out of Committee.

TALKING POINTS: Thank him, congratulate him, and urge him to work hard on the Senate.

Colson did not choose to mention that not only other postal union leaders but also thousands of rank-and-file postal workers had resisted proposals to transform the Post Office into a private corporation from the moment the suggestion was publicized, by Democratic Postmaster General O'Brien, to its reiteration by the Kappel Commission. Nor did Colson tell Haldeman that these unionists insisted that a pay hike be legislated without reference to postal reform.[25]

One day after the wildcat broke out, it leapt across all postal unions apart from the rural letter carriers and began to extend throughout the country, remaining weak only in the South. The Administration sprang to make "the balance of power shift[] back to the bargaining table between union and government leaders." President Nixon involved himself directly, endeavoring not just to end the strike, but to canalize and co-opt it.[26]

The Post Office, it bears emphasis, remained a vital telecommunications mode. Big corporate retailers, such as Woolworth, and large magazine publishers led by Time-Life and McGraw Hill, telegraphed the President that the strike constituted an immediate and dire threat to operations. Credited the day after it began with being "100% effective in halting deliveries in the city," the strike "prevented banks, insurance companies and Government offices from sending out bills or receiving payments." The New York Stock Exchange, *Time* reported afterward, had experienced its lowest turnover of the year and, indeed, as the action carried into a second day it was said to be considering a shutdown "if the strike continued much longer." Between Friday March 20 and Tuesday March 24, administration records show that the postal wildcat was an urgent issue in the Executive Office; Nixon himself remained personally involved in settlement discussions all the way through the first four days of April 1970.[27]

The previous autumn, President Nixon had publicly declared that he would "veto any pay bill not coupled with reform." However, wildcatting workers now appeared to be winning on this crucial issue. The *New York Times* reported hints on March 24 that the Administration "might accept Congressional action on a pay increase for postal workers without insisting that the increase be tied to postal reform." The following day, as postal employees returned to work in large numbers, Postmaster General Blount expressly stated that "there has been no effort, no statement, on the part of the administration that pay is hostage for reform"; and AFL-CIO President George Meany underlined that the postal unions "will refuse to combine any sort of postal reform measure with a pay raise bill," and that this position "has the full support of the AFL-CIO." Throughout a period lasting a week or ten days, the status of postal reorganization remained ambiguous and, seemingly, secondary. As late as April 1, *The New York Times* reported that, in the negotiations that followed the strikers' return to work, the Administration was "no longer insisting that the postal workers support its plan for reorganizing the Post Office Department before agreeing to the increase." Nixon and Blount then sweetened the pot, offering a two-step 14 percent pay increase for postal workers and compressing the time needed to reach the top pay grade for most jobs from twenty-one years to eight. In the immediate aftermath of this new offer came a dramatic reversal: by April 2, 1970, all of the AFL-CIO postal unions had agreed "to link pay raises to postal reorganization." In his diary entry for April 7, Nixon's chief of staff H. R. Haldeman trumpeted this outcome. If, he chortled, Congress had run the negotiations then postal workers likely would have gained a higher wage increase, but the administration had held the line "and got reorganization."[28]

Reorganization remained an uncertain outcome until April, however, not only because of opposition by postal workers but also because of infighting within the Nixon administration. In particular, Postmaster General "Red" Blount—a wealthy Alabama businessman, whose hostility to the postal unions was implacable—had to be finessed. Several days into the strike, complexities abounded and Haldeman noted that Blount in particular was problematic (using "P" to denote President Nixon and also mentioning Labor Secretary George Shultz):

> P. leans to start neg. <u>now</u>...
> 1 Blount can<u>not</u> negotiate
> 2 " " will never let Shultz negotiate
> 3 P. will have to negotiate
> Maybe worthwhile talk to Meany
> certainly believe mtg 7 unions is worthwhile
> since P has committed his prestige he must handle this...
> can't drop Rademacher

As clashes between Blount and Rademacher persisted, moreover, Colson worried that Blount was deprecating him before the President's powerful Assistant for Domestic Affairs, John Erlichman. Colson therefore sent the president's other top advisor, Chief of Staff John Haldeman, a remarkable hand-written memo, enumerating key episodes in the battle that was underway in order to justify his own role. This self-serving document, written toward the end of the wildcat, began by recalling that "When I got into the act in December, Postal reform was dead. Blount and Rademacher despised each other with a passion." Colson then stated that, with Blount's agreement, "I romanced Rademacher and won him over to <u>our</u> package." He specified that "The package was negotiated by me but with Blount—Erlichman—Harlow & Presidential approval." In January, however, Blount had evidently "backtracked" on the employee benefits that had been agreed. "I warned Blount that we could not get away with less—the strike has shown that to be correct," declared Colson. "It took some long arduous sessions with Erlichman, Harlow et al to keep Blount under control." In the meantime, Colson said, "I kept Rademacher in line."[29]

Then, during the weeks preceding the House vote, Blount and Rademacher had "worked together intimately—Rademacher was constantly in Blount's office cooperating Totally." The House voted 17–6 for "our bill." The earlier vote was 13–13 in October and the bill was defeated, Colson reminded Haldeman: "The only difference was Rademacher's support." However, immediately after the vote, "Blount would have nothing to do with Rademacher. I had to step in + keep romancing Jim." The President had called Rademacher to thank him; Blount had not.

This all related, Colson turned to the Administration's efforts to tame the wildcat. On March 19, he wrote, Rademacher called "to tell me the strike was out of control, he couldn't hold his members and that only an agreement on our part to meet with the unions could forestall a disaster." Colson had passed this news to Erlichman, who had convened Shultz and Blount. Blount had called Colson before the meeting "to tell me that under no circumstances would he sit down with the unions. He refused to take Rademacher's calls." Rademacher thereupon "called me in a state of desperation. He said he had been voted down by his executive council and been ordered to call a National strike." Colson phoned Erlichman who was meeting with Shultz and Blount, and Shultz in turn phoned Rademacher and persuaded him that there would be negotiations. "This call was 5 minutes before Rademacher's press conference. Rademacher 'bit the bullet,' went on TV and asked the strikers to return to work." Throughout the weekend that followed, Colson stayed with Rademacher, "coached him and kept him under control." His "defense of us and repeated pleas to the strikers, I believe, averted a disaster."

> I know you think Rademacher was only trying to save his own neck. Had he wanted to do that he would have followed his own executive council and called the strike. He has lost his union because of his commitment to me and the President.

Colson's narrative attests how far the rank-and-file upsurge had borne down on the Administration's strategy, how fluid the situation had grown.[30]

Even as the walkout ended, with worker militancy still widespread, especially in New York City, Colson counseled that the administration should remain solicitous toward Rademacher. In a March 25 memo to Erlichman, Colson again stressed the extent of the historical contingency. Colson divulged that

Rademacher's wife had been hospitalized with a serious ailment; that the NALC president himself "passed out once this week from fatigue and required medical attention"; that Rademacher's daughter had recently undergone an operation for cancer; and that his closest uncle had died the previous Sunday: "I think, therefore, that Rademacher could blow with the slightest provocation. This could be, of course, disastrous to the negotiations and to the possibility of a new strike." Colson summed up: "During the past seven days I have literally been a nursemaid to Rademacher inquiring about his wife's health daily, coaching him on what to say to support our position, urging him to help us get the strikers back and finally being a release valve for his pressure cooker. I believe that was an important activity because I think that his defense of us was politically helpful. I also believe that had he gone the other way, the entire Post Office would be on strike still.... Also, we might need him again." For indeed, until Congress passed Nixon's postal reform legislation, labor relations did remain volatile.[31]

The wildcat strike therefore was exploited by the leadership of the Executive Branch, allied with a strategically placed union leader, to drive through postal reform legislation. AFL-CIO President Meany backtracked and, ultimately, supported this outcome, on the grounds that it authorized collective bargaining by those postal unions covered by the pact, and tacked on a larger pay increase than the Administration had initially proposed. However, Meany's endorsement was not universally shared. An official of New York's NALC Branch 36— the initial core of the wildcat, and a site of persistent militancy among letter carriers—declared to a congressional committee weeks after the settlement, "I'm very unhappy with it. The postal authority wasn't supposed to be tied to the pay bill but it is." For its part, the antiracist National Postal Union explained what it foresaw had been sacrificed, in its testimony that the reform legislation would "destroy ... the possibility of ever achieving one industrial union of all postal employees." NPU also continued to hold that the postal service "is and should be and must remain a government service, and should be supported at least in part from general taxation, if that is necessary to ensure postal workers a fair share of the national product."[32]

As union solidarity cracked, bipartisan political support cohered. Former Democratic Postmaster General Lawrence F. O'Brien was enlisted by Republican President Nixon to help sell the idea of postal reorganization. O'Brien co-chaired a "Citizens Committee for Postal Reform, Inc.," established by Postmaster General Blount, bankrolled by big mail users, and including half a dozen members of the Kappel Commission. With this formidable lobby behind it, Nixon's reorganization bill sailed through Congress with resounding majorities: 359–24 in the House and 76–10 in the Senate. The Postal Reorganization Act that was signed by President Nixon on August 12, 1970 established a United States Postal Service whose operation commenced the next year. No longer a government department, the USPS was administered as an independent establishment within the Executive Branch by an appointed Board of Governors; and the Postmaster General was removed from the cabinet. This was the largest restructuring of a government agency in US history.[33]

Its consequences were complex. The postal mandate to provide a universal service carried forward; however, now it was to accomplish this cut free of Congressional control and operating without government subsidies. Creation of the USPS in turn elevated a new "market imperative," historian Richard R. John concludes, and thus—as the business users who had lobbied for the enabling legislation had preferred—"the relative position of mass mailers, advertisers, and package carriers" was "improved." In 1977, the proportion of first-class mail volume consisting of nonhousehold-to-household mail was 39 percent; by 1991 it had increased to 44 percent. The composition of the postal revenue stream was shifting further away from personal correspondence and toward commercial mail. The venerable institution's communicative function was altering, its once-popular public service basis narrowed and constrained so that it might be reconstituted as a platform for sales and marketing.[34]

Considered in terms of labor and employment relations, however, the strike and the reorganization that followed exhibited a sharply polarized pattern. On one side, "postal workers won many of their demands and set a precedent for strike action," as historian Philip Rubio emphasizes, including substantial pay increases and—above all—full collective bargaining rights for AFL-CIO-affiliated postal unions. The strike's success also "encouraged democratic militant tendencies in the participating unions that challenged and in some cases overturned their respective entrenched leaderships." On the eve of reorganization, postal workers constituted the largest unionized workforce in the country, and one that tended to regard management's plans for reorganization with skepticism; the reorganization quickly substantiated their fears. Incoming USPS management insisted on productivity gains, and the postal unions had to fight continually to preserve bargaining rights in the face of technological change, outsourcing, understaffing, and growing reliance on noncareer employees.[35]

Democratic President Kennedy's Postmaster General Lawrence F. O'Brien still fumed, years later, as he remembered the strength that the postal unions possessed during the mid-1960s: "The role of the unions in the Post Office Department exceeded the role of any other federal union by far . . . The inability of the postal service to progress in terms of mechanization, facilities, and the rest because of budgetary restrictions, had brought about a totally unacceptable situation." Postal reorganization only began the process of rectifying what O'Brien termed a flatly "unacceptable situation." Postal employees had won substantial wage increases, a no lay-offs clause, and a guarantee of binding third party arbitration.[36]

Some unions responded to reorganization by renewing calls for industrial unionization across the postal crafts. During the strike, many rank-and-file members of different postal unions had refused to cross picket lines; this accentuated a sense of shared purpose and common destiny. Meanwhile, the new mandate—to bargain not with Congress but with USPS management—instilled a felt need among many unionists to bulk up. While granting collective bargaining rights to seven AFL-CIO affiliated postal unions, however, postal "reform" denied them to the two most Civil Rights–conscious, industrial, and unaffiliated unions, on grounds that these organizations did not represent a sufficient proportion of eligible workers. One responded by building on the cross-craft, interracial cooperation that had been demonstrated by the wildcat: in May, 1971, after the USPS had been established, members of the militant National Postal Union joined members of four other postal unions in voting overwhelmingly to merge into a new American Postal Workers Union (APWU). By contrast, having been excluded from the new structure of collective bargaining, the National Alliance of Postal and Federal Employees refocused its efforts around equal employment opportunity advocacy. Hereafter the APWU and the NALC constituted the two largest postal unions.[37]

APWU President Francis Filbey wanted to go further, out of a conviction that "in One Big Union we can meet One Big Management on something near an equal footing." Filbey, whose American Postal Workers Union now represented 320,000 workers, "expressed the hope that the remaining postal unions, including the National Association of Letter Carriers, will be inspired to join the merger ranks" and thus soon "make One Big Union a reality in 1971." In August 1971, after the formation of APWU was complete, new merger talks were held with the NALC. APWU General Executive Vice President David Silvergleid reported hopefully that "recent meetings between the APWU and NALC merger committees have indicated mutual realization of the need for one postal union." In November 1971, however, the NALC Executive Council released a list of conditions for merger, which included a stipulation that the APWU would serve as a "federation of Postal Service labor organisations" and that "each division shall operate under its own Constitution and By-Laws." As NALC officials remained more than skittish about a full-on consolidation, David Silvergleid had little choice but to concede that "we are resigned to the fact that merger cannot take place under the conditions outlined above . . . we regret that the inevitable and essential One Postal Union will be delayed."[38]

Merger talks continued, nevertheless. In May 1972, NALC President James Rademacher stated that he was optimistic about merger prospects, acknowledging that it was what "everybody wants." At this same juncture, we will see later, APWU leaders also began to explore a separate merger proposal floated by the Communications Workers of America. For now it is most vital to underline that the reorganization that established the USPS in 1970 also generated an additional impetus to solidarity among postal workers. These employees also gained with respect to some immediate issues: pay, benefits, and—above all—collective bargaining rights, which continued to be denied to other federal workers. Over the ensuing decade, furthermore, militants from the wildcat were returned by rank-and-file workers' votes as the leaders of some of their transformed and partly merged unions. The process of creating this USPS took several years to accomplish, as rank-and-file workers, postal management, corporate bulk mailers, and the Executive and Legislative branches of government vied to shape it. Proponents prioritized the demands of bulk mailers, through additional automation and associated changes in the postal labor process. They draped these objectives behind the much-publicized goals of efficiency and self-sufficiency. Many postal workers understood that these initiatives would come at their expense. As a result of their collective self-organization they possessed new weapons with which to fight back.

The Telephone System: Liberal Business Unionism and Bottom-Up Insurgency

Industrial unionists had faced a difficult climb in telephony but, by 1960, they had succeeded in establishing a strong union in the Communications Workers of America. Late in the 1960s, however, many telephone workers grew increasingly dissatisfied. Lagging wages, stifling AT&T management, and union leaders' indifference to rank-and-file members' concerns were nagging complaints. As with the Post Office, workers' growing anger prompted action that spilled out beyond institutional channels when, during 1971, the telephone industry erupted.

Other scholars have scrutinized the postwar telephone industry's labor and employment policies; its race and gender relations; and its workers' restiveness, and I draw extensively on this body of research. However, my motivating questions cut in a somewhat different direction: Did the complex struggles for labor rights and economic gains that marked electronic telecommunications during the 1960s and early 1970s trigger substantive policy changes, as they did at the Post Office? Was the existing settlement to provide telephone service reshaped in light of organized labor's collective actions? In particular, did mobilization by rank-and-file telephone workers lead to a rejuvenation and enlargement of the public utility model of provision? To engage these questions requires a bit of backtracking.

No sooner had CWA established itself than AT&T mounted a years-long counter-offensive against it. Despite its painfully won CIO affiliation, after its near-catastrophic 1947 industrial action the young CWA was both under-financed and "strike-shy." In 1950, Sylvia B. Gottlieb, director of CWA's Research and Education Department, declared that her union "has been fighting a battle for organizational survival ever since its inception." The CWA's legislative representative, Helen W. Berthelot, continued the story as she remembered that, with the onset of the Republican Eisenhower Administration in 1953, "people from the labor organizations were persona non grata": labor unions "just weren't welcome." Trade unionists "survived the eight Eisenhower years," CWA President Joseph A. Beirne recollected, "in ideological foxholes and storm-cellars." Nevertheless, CWA began to forge a record of wage gains and improved benefits for a nationwide work force, and to carve out a place for itself within the institutions of collective bargaining.[39]

By the late 1960s, in consequence, telephone workers were represented by a powerful industrial trade union whose leaders concentrated their efforts—with broad success—on bread-and-butter issues, while largely abdicating any independent role in policymaking for telecommunications system development. Above all, CWA officials chose not to challenge the federal government's decision to liberalize and deregulate telecommunications at the point when this choice was still emergent and provisional. Meanwhile, struggles commenced to overturn job discrimination, by Blacks, Latinos, women, and gays, all of whom attempted to combat AT&T's long-standing racist and sexist employment policies. The Bell System in turn became a strategic staging-ground for efforts to eliminate discrimination in the American workplace. Below I trace these developments.

*

During the twenty-five years after its formation, the Communications Workers of America plunged into mainstream politics, encouraged extensive community service engagement by its members, and pursued organizing drives and industrial action. This third prong of CWA's strategy remained urgent, as the purge of the left-led unions from the CIO and CWA's CIO affiliation had not diminished the telephone company's antagonism. President Beirne later characterized some of AT&T's managers during the era between 1947 and the late 1950s as "Neanderthals," and indeed CWA's adversary remained implacable. AT&T undertook "a decade-long struggle," Schact relates, and sought at various times "to decertify the union in most of its bargaining units, to withhold the union dues that Bell deducted from workers' paychecks, to change wages and working conditions without prior bargaining, and to impose no-strike contract clauses and agreements whereby unionists refusing to cross picket lines could be disciplined by management." Early in the 1950s, especially, the signs of this posture were abundant. AT&T's Pacific Telephone unit reprinted for its employees a speech by a free-enterprise ideologue, who charged that the US had assimilated the program of Karl Marx and that to remedy this "the law should never mention a race, or a color . . . or a labor organization," and that "no person may force another person to pay a certain wage." In Weirton, West Virginia, in 1950 AT&T's Chesapeake & Potomac subsidiary ignored the National Labor Relations Act by intimidating and harassing workers (the company tapped the home telephone of one organizer) to deter them from joining the CWA.[40]

Attempting to defend itself, during these difficult years the CWA also used its CIO affiliation as a springboard to political intervention. This strategy bore fruit when the union succeeded in 1950 in inducing the US Senate Labor Committee to investigate labor-management relations in the telephone industry. The Committee recommended national bargaining between the Bell System and CWA; though this required twenty more years, it was ultimately accomplished. Throughout its first decade, meanwhile, both wildcat strikes and CWA-initiated walkouts by bargaining units occurred across the country and at different AT&T operating companies, Western Electric, and independent telephone companies. The union's biggest strike action to that date, commencing April 7, 1952, saw 70,000 workers join picket lines and tens of thousands of other telephone workers honor those picket lines, in New Jersey, Northern California, Michigan and Ohio, before it broadened to the entire country. "Faced with an increased traffic load, management was unable to cope," wrote *CWA News*: "When picket lines were placed before Chicago exchanges, for example, it was virtually impossible to place a call out of the city." The solidarity shown during this strike was a major achievement, as the union was quick to publicize; and it was additionally noteworthy that this solidarity had extended to an estimated 10,000 CWA operators and other CWA members, who observed picket lines set up by an independent telephone union—the Telephone Workers Union of New Jersey—in a two-day strike beginning March 26. In a grueling seventy-two-day walkout during the Spring of 1955, 50,000 workers struck Southern Bell across 600 communities located in nine southern states—eight of which had passed "right-to-work" laws. AT&T was still trying to break the union; however, it did not succeed. Even at Southern Bell, CWA won a contractual right to respect picket lines, wage increases and provisions for arbitration. "Out of this developed a new momentum," a historian concludes "that placed the weight of the organized telephone worker against that of a corporate giant." It was in the aftermath of the Southern Bell strike that AT&T grudgingly acquiesced to the union's existence.[41]

Organizing was a nearly continuous feature of CWA strategy from the union's formation: it had to be. Between 1938 and 1946, when many members of affiliates of the decentralized National Federation of Telephone Workers suspected that a centralized union would jeopardize their independence, organizing had been urgent. The subsequent conflict between CWA and TWOC then triggered desertions, motivating fresh efforts to augment CWA's membership. During the

1950s, raids by the IBEW stimulated new rounds of organizing; and the Southern Bell strike of 1955 resulted in a membership decline in the region, compelling CWA to undertake a rebuilding effort in the southern states. AT&T's "divide-and-conquer" tactics added to the pressure. Even in 1960, when CWA boasted 256,000 dues-paying members and a 75 percent representation rate among workers employed at existing bargaining units, it included only a minority of AT&T employees overall. Its hard slog against AT&T inched forward. Thus it was business as usual in 1969, when a veteran CWA District Representative insisted that the union's "number one" task was "the need to organize the unorganized."[42]

A limited form of system-wide pattern bargaining was instituted in 1959, prompting historian John Schacht to conclude that AT&T management "had clearly decided that the CWA was a union it would have to live with and that agreements were better than showdowns." CWA gained representation rights over a growing proportion of eligible workers, notably in 1961, when it won 24,000 New York Bell plant workers—the largest single group to join since its initial years. Substantial numbers of telephone workers nonetheless remained outside the union's ranks. CWA vowed to broaden its base through "internal" organizing and, urged on by President Beirne, delegates to the 1965 CWA Convention stepped up this initiative. In consequence, by the end of the 1960s, with 422,000 members CWA had become the fourteenth largest union in the United States. Nearly three-fifths (58.4 percent) of all telephone workers (disproportionately craftsmen and operators, the industry's largest occupations) now were union members. This was a tremendous achievement, for this level of representation was nearly double that of the nation's unionization rate.[43]

The telephone workforce continued to expand. Between 1950 and 1980, the overwhelmingly male craft workers who installed and repaired telephones and network equipment at AT&T more than doubled in number, from 124,000 to 280,000. By contrast, the number of AT&T's women telephone operators declined sharply, from about 185,000 during the early 1950s to 100,000 in 1980. Black employment increased slightly during the 1950s, mostly in the large cities outside the South—to 2.5 percent of the telephone workforce by 1960; but then it accelerated, to 9.8 percent of Bell System employees by 1970. As Venus Green explains, this welcome quantitative change took place only as the quality of work as a telephone operator was degraded. Those operators who were not replaced, as AT&T substituted automation and customer self-service for paid labor, were as intensively monitored and supervised as factory operatives.[44]

The sheer survival of the union was a testimony to working-class self-organization; after 1949, CWA's political and community engagement and its organizing drives and industrial action recurrently enhanced telephone workers' wage and benefit packages. Beginning around 1952, issues of *CWA News* testify to incremental improvements in the standard of living of telephone workers.

Better pay and pensions, compressed schedules for advancement, fringe benefits including longer vacations and more extensive employer-based medical insurance were among the gains from CWA's contract bargaining. President Beirne forecast in 1959 that a settlement reached with AT&T's Wisconsin Bell unit would become a nationwide pattern, and "will ultimately cover, at least from the vacation and pension standpoint, the almost 800,000 employees in the Bell System, union-represented and management alike. Further the wage settlement, with minor variations, will, no doubt, be extended to all CWA-represented people in the industry." Despite Beirne's forecast, the union still was unable to conduct genuinely national bargaining with AT&T—a prerequisite for attaining uniform contract terms across wages and benefits across the length and breadth of the giant Bell system. In the wake of an eighteen-day walkout in 1968—the first nationwide strike since 1947—CWA achieved increases in wages and medical benefits amounting to 20 percent over the life of the three-year contract. Moreover, for the first time, "the overall terms of all the Bell system contracts were worked out nationally between representatives of the union and representatives of AT&T." Even so, Southern Bell and several other Bell companies settled "in a piecemeal fashion" with CWA.[45]

The CWA still struggled with the sprawling Bell System over this critical issue. The union repeatedly faced bargaining with each of the twenty-one Bell affiliates, a process that lent itself to energy-consuming negotiations and, especially early on, threats to union cohesion. From the outset, CWA believed that it should only have to negotiate with one entity—AT&T—because AT&T management constituted the actual policymaker and bargaining force for the nationwide Bell System. In January of 1974, CWA at last announced that it had won an agreement to bargain nationally with the centralized AT&T.[46]

A sketch of CWA leader Joseph Beirne's mature worldview adds to our sense of the union at this stage. During these final years of his long-standing presidency, Beirne continued to demonstrate that he was not bound by a philosophy of "pure and simple" unionism whose ambition was solely to augment his own members' wages and benefits. "There is very little historical reason for workers to trust either the good faith or the omniscience of management," Beirne declared. Indeed, "the first point that must be recognized in any discussion of unions and technology," wrote this workforce leader after a quarter-century of service as CWA President, "is that management, left to its own devices, simply doesn't give a damn what happens to people." A second point, equally basic, was again forthright: "sheer efficiency, by any name—technological progress, automation, cost analysis and all the rest—is not an end in itself except to pure technocrats. The purpose of any society . . . is the well-being of its members." Beirne concluded from this that only sweeping changes in social policy might neutralize the threats posed by new technology. As altered instruments of production were interposed into "more and more aspects of economic and social life," Beirne called to actualize a program that had been entombed in the unsuccessful Employment Act of 1946: to universalize "economic security." To this end, the federal government should be made an employer of last resort; to actualize a full employment policy, unbroken economic growth would demand aggressive fiscal and monetary policy; and "we ought to insist that every person is entitled to a free education all the way ... Free through graduate school and free right up to the doctorate." Also needed were a battery of allied measures—to grant a minimum income to those who could not work, to end racial discrimination, to improve access to medical care and hospitalization, and to assure that adequate housing was available. To increase the likelihood of realizing this agenda and, in any case, to guarantee that working people's interests were adequately expressed, Beirne insisted that "the labor movement must retain force as a weapon." By this, he meant the right to strike: "the right to strike is as important to democratic pluralism as the right to vote."[47]

Beirne, therefore, expounded New Dealers' precepts of economic citizenship, asserting alongside other white liberals that now they needed to be expanded and universalized. He did so, however, out of conviction that organized labor had won for itself a secure place in the nation's decision-making structure (Figure 9.4). Trade union strength, he asserted, provided the "balance"—the "counterforce"—that was needed to ensure the "perpetuation of democracy itself." By contrast to the narrowly self-serving ambitions of the National Association of Manufacturers and right-to-work laws, the labor movement constituted "the one substantial private organization in the United States whose primary dedication is to the widest and best interests of *all* the American people." The CWA President continued to worry that "businessman, large and small, still remain the one substantial force in America which does not accept what I call pluralism." He was sanguine, nevertheless, as to the role of the federal government, even imagining that incoming President Nixon "cannot threaten the basic institutions and premises of the labor movement." Posterity has shown that, though he disparaged radicals for holding romantic notions, Beirne's was the more credulous assessment. We will see in the next chapter that, even as the CWA president was formulating these ideas, the central state was laying out the ground for a sustained attack on the structure and policy of existing network system development—and on the workforce that made it possible.[48]

For all Beirne's liberal social unionism and for all CWA's achievements, between 1968 and 1974, many workers felt goaded into insurgency. Perhaps the key precipitant was that their wage gains eroded faster than they were won. Surges of Vietnam War–era inflation devalued their earnings, especially in high-cost cities. Between 1965 and 1968 purchasing power was chipped away by more than 3 percent each year; this increased to around 5 percent annually between 1968 and

Figure 9.4 CWA President Joseph A. Beirne with President John F. Kennedy at the White House, February 14, 1962. Beirne believed that his union's strategy should be to fight "to be as close to the center of power as it can possibly get." AR7042-B. Abbie Rowe. White House Photographs. John F. Kennedy Presidential Library and Museum, Boston.

1971, and to 7 percent a year between 1971 and 1974. Under strain were working-class expectations that living standards would continue to rise, a view formed by the experience of the first two postwar decades. Joseph Beirne conveyed in an oral history interview in 1969 that about 10–12 percent of CWA members were actively engaged in the union's efforts. Outside this circle of activists, disparate grievances coursed through the ranks; the resurgence of militancy during the late 1960s and early 1970s attested both keen dissatisfaction with wages, anger at a lack of union democracy, and widening opposition to the nation's social and political priorities. Beirne's leadership proved unable to contain these centrifugal forces. The pivot of protest was again New York City: the Bell System's preeminent networking hub and, as postal workers had demonstrated the previous year, a site of militancy in the nation's working class.[49]

Following earlier job actions by telephone operators and other employees, 1500 craftsmen belonging to New York City CWA Local 1101 walked out on January 11, 1971, initiating a two-week strike. Marked by what one rank-and-file group called "unprecedented militancy," the strike and the ensuing arbitration to which it led amounted "to a standoff between the Bell System and the CWA in the first skirmish of the 1971 contract battles." Brenner's account emphasizes that, because the CWA hierarchy took a dim view of the strike, the way was opened for rank-and-file activists to lead it. Their insurgency fed into what became a protracted contest during a contract-year; the issues at stake extended beyond wages, and beyond New York City.[50]

In response to the service outage of 1969–1970 and, as Brenner details, also in order to prepare for what they feared would become heightened market competition, AT&T executives mounted a drive to achieve sustained productivity gains. CWA had had to confront the giant company's programs for technological change since its inception and indeed, union leaders had already begun to target emerging networking technologies as key to CWA's growth. Envisioning "a membership potential of two million communications workers by 1970," delegates to CWA's 1960 annual convention in St. Louis had been told that their union's prospective domain was rapidly widening: "The field of communications which includes telephone, radio, television, PBX, answering service, manufacturers of electrical and electronic equipment, and other industries within the jurisdiction of CWA are growing at a fantastic rate." In 1960, the diversification of telecommunications gave cause for optimism among CWA leaders: if its horizons were expanded and diversified then the union could increase its membership and thus its strength. "For many years we have confined our thinking to our own particular group," declared Gus Cramer, assistant to CWA vice president Hackney, "but we are a communications workers union and we do not have any restriction jurisdictionally in the field of communications." This rosy forecast, we will see, could not have been more mistaken.[51]

In 1971, automatic or dial telephone conversion was essentially complete and, at massive cost, AT&T was unrolling a nationwide program of electronic switches. CWA President Beirne captured what this meant: "The $30 billion computer they call the Bell Telephone System is just about the most spectacular achievement in the whole world of automation—but without the skill of our members who repair it and keep it running, that computer will eventually become an enormous pile of junk." At the heart of US banking and finance, AT&T's local subsidiary, New York Telephone, was increasing its network investment, introducing advanced technology, employing thousands of new workers, and attempting to extend its control over their wages and work processes. In this context of automation and speedup New York Telephone imported at least one thousand craft workers from other Bell System subsidiaries to take up six-month tours in New York City—with the inducement of twelve to sixteen hours of guaranteed weekly overtime. For a vocal fraction of Bell workers in New York City, however, CWA's earlier gains in collective bargaining rights, contract enforcement and workplace organization seemed inadequate to the task of combating Bell's technological initiative. Brenner explains that "the union's long-term inability to mount sufficient opposition to management's offensive sparked the emergence of local rank-and-file groups seeking to organize their own job actions and to challenge the union leadership." As was also true for other contemporary US industrial employers, as corporate executives pushed to accelerate productivity and institute controls on the shop-floor, "workers introduced a new weapon of resistance: the rank-and-file organization." It remained to be seen whether this was a sign of strengthening creative resistance, however, or merely an action by those whom Beirne disparaged as "hard boys"—those who allowed frustration to overwhelm good judgment. Yet it is beyond argument that the New York City insurgents, alongside their less-documented counterparts in the San Francisco Bay Area, Los Angeles and elsewhere, carried multifarious ideas, not only about how to extract higher wages and benefits, but also how to reorganize telephone industry employment and labor relations, how to reform their union, and how to transform their society.[52]

AT&T's reliance on reassigned outside workers reduced New York Local 1101 members' ability to log overtime, which they needed more because their wages were worth less. This pitted workers against one another, as AT&T "wanted to start us fighting among ourselves for the overtime on which we all depend." New York Telephone craftsmen bridled at AT&T's use of out-of-town workers drawn from other Bell units, therefore, but also charged that their work as "scabs" lent them a charged strategic importance beyond helping the company catch up with unfilled telephone service orders. "What really is at stake here," declared a flyer written by insurgents, "is preparation for the upcoming national telephone strike in the spring or summer." The broadside then offered another portent: "Bell Telephone knows that N.Y. Telephone is the weakest part of the whole system, and that if we can stop N.Y. Telephone from functioning, they will have to settle on our terms. They have brought in all those out-of-state workers to get everything in working order so that they will be able to hold out longer and we will have to stay out longer—all of us." Some rank-and-file New York workers repeatedly forged this link: "Management knows that only a nation-wide strike against Bell can win real gains in our new contract and they are preparing to defeat that strike by keeping service up for as long as possible. N.Y. Tel is the first place where service will collapse during a strike. A failure of service in New York would force them to settle on our terms, and, brothers and sisters, they don't want that to happen."[53]

A walkout against "scabs" spread throughout New York State, incurring judicially imposed fines. After thirteen days out, and following negotiations between CWA President Beirne, District One Vice President Morton Bahr, and Local 1101 union leaders, the New York Telephone employees returned to work pending arbitration. The panel's deliberation produced a draw. AT&T remained free to use outside workers, but local Bell employees also had to be guaranteed equal opportunity to work sixteen hours of overtime per week throughout this temporary period. This outcome not only left unresolved the friction between CWA leaders and local New York City telephone workers, but—as Brenner puts it—"energized the rank-and-file groups and their supporters." Protest literature began to circulate through the telephone work force, both in and far away from New York (Figure 9.5).[54]

In May and early June, CWA conducted a mail ballot and its members authorized their leaders to call a nationwide strike in July, with the proviso that the members themselves would vote to authorize any decision to end their strike. After contracts covering 400,000 CWA unionists expired July 1, although AT&T and the union were within one percentage point of each other on wage increases, disagreements persisted over the union's demand to reduce pay disparities regionally and between male and female employees. Rank-and-file militancy was ratcheting up. United Action stated late in June that there was a good chance that the July 14th strike deadline would pass with "no strike and no acceptable settlement." Were this to occur, one of its now-nearly regular newspapers declared, "we believe that much as the N.Y. local of the Postal workers took matters into their own hands last year, the N.Y. local of Western Electric, backed up by 1101, must act without the support of the International."[55]

Disparities appeared between the demands made by United Action and those being negotiated with AT&T by CWA officials. By April 1971, to "catch up with the 17% inflation which has cut so hard into our purchasing power over the last three years," United Action asserted that "our first fight in the battle for a decent contract will be with the international, not the company." Because 1101 was the largest local in the CWA, "we can effect (sic) the course of national bargaining." After its petition drive succeeded, and Local 1101's elected leaders began to accede to some of the Bell Workers Action Committee and United Action objectives, the insurgents' efforts "to unify New York Telephone workers around a fighting program for the upcoming contract strike" divulged priorities sharply distinct from those being pursued by CWA executives. The Local, said United Action, should insist on several demands: a short, one-year contract; a 50 percent wage increase with a full cost-of-living clause for all telephone workers; abolition of all craft and departmental wage differentials so that a single wage scale was instituted for all employees; abolition of management prerogatives in dealing with worker absence and lateness; a pension based on "30 and out at full pay"; the elimination of the contract's no-strike clause; and "the opening of all craft jobs to all telephone workers reguardless (sic) of department, sex, or race." Eight proposals put forward by the Bell Workers Action Committee and United Action came as formal resolutions, passed by vote of the membership of Local

Figure 9.5 Wildcat telephone strikers picketing at New York Telephone Building in Brooklyn. January 16, 1971. Tom Middlemiss/New York Daily News.

1101—notably, a demand for a 50 percent wage increase; a demand that eighteen workers fired during the January strike be reinstated; and a commitment not only to organize telephone operators into 1101 but to honor job actions by operators who were *not* members of the Local. These rank-and-file telephone workers were pushing beyond the horizons of CWA officialdom.[56]

Commencing nationwide on Bastille Day—following a day of wildcats in Washington, Florida, Virginia, Ohio, California and South Dakota—an authorized strike lasted for one week. In San Francisco Bay locals, rank-and-file anger ran ahead of official union structures from the beginning. "On Tuesday, July 13, we walked out early to avoid being sold out by Joe Bierne's (sic) boys in the CWA national" wrote one striker. In the Berkeley Tribe, an underground newspaper which claimed to donate half its subscriptions free to prisoners, this anonymous Bell worker asked readers to help striking employees by following one or more of a variety of detailed instructions for burdening the telephone system.

> If you know anyone at a military base overseas, place a call to their address using a false name. Call Thailand: Udorn AFB. Give a 4 digit number and say the person you're calling is in radar or field maintenance.
>
> All calls to ships at sea are bummers. Ask for a friend at sea (its (sic) an emergency). Ships that never answer their phones are the SS Monterey and the SS Mariposa. Ask the operator to try calling every hour.

The contract agreement reached between CWA and AT&T spelled an apparent victory for the union. The national settlement granted employees a 33.5 percent wage gain over the life of the contract (less than half of this increase was slated for the contract's first year); and CWA leaders crowed that the contract "exceeds the gains in any other basic industry" and "features many new items including a cost-of-living adjustment and strong union security clause." Nevertheless, telephone workers were far from agreed over the result. In high-cost cities including, above all, New York, the seemingly hefty wage increase did not even make up for the previous three years of inflation. The pact did raise wages for female craft employees—from 62 percent to 65 percent of wages paid to men in the same jobs. Some women workers deemed this nominal decline in the gender disparity downright insulting. Many AT&T workers chafed that President Beirne had called them back to work without the required membership vote on an agreement.[57]

In the wake of the announced national settlement, as many as 90,000 workers scattered across several states—New York, New Jersey, Pennsylvania, Connecticut, California and Arizona—refused to cross the picket lines that were still being staffed by independent unions attempting to reach their own agreements with different Bell Companies. "Reject The Sellout" was the headline of the next issue of United Action; and twenty-three CWA local unions across New York State actually did so. Those in New York City remained on strike, in fact, for an additional seven months, into 1972. They held out for better vacations, pensions, overtime pay and medical coverage, a big-city living allowance and a union shop. They also continued to demand a much bigger immediate wage increase. "The 500,000 men and women whose daily labors make AT&T the richest corporation in the world know that for a living wage something closer to a 50% settlement is in order," United Action had declared before the strike, as activists focused their discontent on union officials. Angry that CWA had curtailed the strike from above, stung by the national contract's shortcomings—with regard to immediate wage increases, employment discrimination, and local control—and bridling at union leaders' red-baiting, the insurgents in United Action, Strike Back, and Bell Workers Action Committee insisted that union democracy was now paramount. For their part, CWA officials believed they had good reason to end the strike in summary fashion.[58]

H. I. Romness, the CEO of AT&T, tried to telephone President Nixon in Washington, DC early in the afternoon on Bastille Day, presumably, to brief him on AT&T's ability to handle the nationwide strike that had commenced. Romness did not get through: his call was taken by a Nixon assistant. Having removed to the western White House in California, the president had shut himself off from all but the urgent business he had at hand. Nixon was meeting with National Security Advisor Henry A. Kissinger, who had just returned from a top-secret trip to Beijing, where he and Chinese Premier Zhou Enlai had worked to prepare the way for a presidential visit to China early in 1972. The next day, July 15, Nixon would go on network television to herald an earth-shaking geopolitical change: the opening to China.[59]

Nixon only initiated a four-minute telephone call to AT&T Chairman Romness on July 21—after Beirne had notified CWA members to curtail their strike. The substance of the contract settlement and its timing combined, however, to pose a significant political challenge. The Administration had imposed a ninety-day wage-and-price freeze, effective August 15, in a bid to arrest inflation by attacking workers' living standards, and a 34 percent wage and benefit hike flouted this scheme, especially as CWA members' vote on whether to accept the contract settlement was to be conducted as a postal ballot whose result might not be known until after the directive went into effect. It turned out that mere hours before the wage freeze came into force, CWA announced the tally: the membership had voted in favor of the contract, by a claimed margin of two-to-one nationwide. Beirne had averted a direct clash with the Nixon administration.[60]

In New York, however, many rank-and-file telephone workers were unimpressed. "The government estimates that to live decently, a NYC telephone worker would need about $12,000," stated United Action, adding that "For the average member of Local 1101 to reach that figure a base wage increase of 50% would be required." CWA's New York Local 1101 demanded that the strike continue unless and until telephone workers could vote to end it. United Action, whose members included people laboring in all three segments of the industry—Plant, Traffic, and Commercial departments—rejected the agreement as "a rotten contract," and "a miserable settlement," and hoped "to force Beirne to renegotiate." Calling the settlement a "sellout deal," arrived at "over the heads of the bargaining team and the local presidents," United Action insisted that "THE STRIKE CAN BE WON!" (Figures 9.6, 9.7, and 9.8).[61]

Because CWA officials already had called for a return to work, this declaration might seem benighted. After all, in addition to their own union hierarchy, they faced another obstacle: Alongside fellow-militants belonging to the Bell Workers Action Committee, United Action had to counter "a news blackout about the strike across the country," an effect of which had been to suppress knowledge that telephone workers had initially remained on strike not only throughout New York State, but also in Ohio, Washington D.C., New Jersey, Connecticut, Philadelphia, Pittsburgh and the San Francisco Bay area. Dissecting the apparently generous wage package, and showing that it was skewed to favor the most senior craft workers and, at best, granted less than a 15 percent raise the first year, angry New York City rank-and-filers again demanded a 50 percent across-the-board wage increase for all telephone workers, with a full cost-of-living clause, a much-improved pension plan, the elimination of a reviled practice known as the "Absence Control Plan" which allowed managers to mete out arbitrary punishments, and a contractual right to strike. Equally prominent was a demand that AT&T agree in writing to pull out the hundreds of out-of-town craftsmen and foremen it had transferred into New York from other units. "There are out of state foremen from at least nine CWA bargaining units working here" United Action charged.[62]

The insurgency spilled over into a larger fight-back against Nixon's wage controls, and beyond. By late September 1971, the eleventh week of the strike, United Action was holding its own against not only AT&T and New York Telephone, but also the Nixon Administration, CWA's national leaders, and some officers of Local 1101 "who want to divide us." These militants trumpeted that "Despite all these opposing forces, we have stayed out and, in the last two weeks, rebuilt the strike." United Action's members, "together with others in the postal, taxi, health, and communications industries," called a demonstration to insist on "unconditional opposition to all forms of wage-price controls" at New York City's Central Labor Council Meeting on October 21, 1971.[63]

Leaflets, broadsides, and other contemporary publications open a window onto the dissenting consciousness of these New York telephone workers (Figure 9.9). While primary objectives were to raise wages and to reconstruct the CWA

Figure 9.6 After rallying outside Governor Nelson Rockefeller's midtown office, about 3,500 telephone strikers move through Manhattan. January 13, 1972. New York Daily News.

Figure 9.7 CWA strikers march up Third Avenue, as some get out of the way of a mounted policeman at 37th Street. January 13, 1972. Paul DeMaria/New York Daily News.

Figure 9.8 Rank-and-file telephone workers rally at New York Telephone Company headquarters at Broadway and Fulton Streets, February 5, 1972. Charles Frattini/New York Daily News.

CO. MAKES KILLING FROM WAR

There is a full scale war going on in IndoChina, that the majority of the American people are against, yet the U.S. government as well as the major corporations make sure it continues. As operators the war is close to home. We handle all the calls between this country and IndoChina. Daily we speak with wives of soldiers, who don't have enough money to feed their families, and who wonder if their husbands will come home. Our husbands, boyfriends and brothers are also there, fighting an unjust war that only the rich are benefiting from.

We surely gain nothing from this war and more importantly the land and the people of IndoChina are being destroyed! But the company we work for, which we have to contend with daily gains much from this war—profit. AT&T is the largest American corporation of any kind in the world. It has assets of 40 billion dollars, larger than any other 50 U.S. corporations combined. Its net income is 1/3 larger that 50 of the U.S. largest commercial banks put together. AT&T is directly involved with the defense industry, which needs a war economy to thrive on. Since World War II, Western Electric which is owned by AT&T has been developing and designing atomic weapons at the Atomic Energy Commisions laboratory in Albequerque, New Mexico.

Figure 9.9 Operating Underground. This leaflet, like other counter-cultural and antiwar publications of the 1960s and early 1970s, opposed US imperial foreign policy—and linked it directly to the Bell System. Author's Collection.

as a democratic union, rank-and-file militants also attacked AT&T for its service to an imperial US foreign policy. United Action, the Bell Workers Action Committee, and a third rank-and-file organization called Strike Back, indeed tied their struggles against AT&T *and* CWA into the ongoing movement to end the US war on Indochina. Calling for a contingent of telephone workers to join an upcoming March for Peace, United Action charged that "It was corporations like AT&T that got us into the war." "It's clear that the inflation is largely caused by war spending," the group asserted; in turn, the CWA leaders' official support for "Nixon's policy of prolonging the war . . . is wrong." And again, "while the government has wasted billions of dollars in the Southeast Asian war, money to build schools, homes, and hospitals has dried up."[64]

"Operating Underground," a pamphlet issued in late June 1971 by operators belonging to CWA Local 9415 in Oakland, sharpened this social critique. "As operators the war is close to home. We handle all the calls between this country and IndoChina. Daily we speak with wives of soldiers. . . . Our husbands, boyfriends, and brothers are also there, fighting an unjust war that only the rich are benefiting from." The article stated that "the company we work for, which we have to contend with daily gains much from this war. . . . AT&T is directly involved with the defense industry," observing that its Western Electric subsidiary acted as a major weapons contractor. CWA, the pamphlet underlined, was complicit, in that the union had passed a resolution at its 1971 convention offering official support for the war. "The strike coming up," the article finished, "is a way for us to hurt this company where it counts—in its pocket. We need a strike, for an increase in our wages, and a change in our working conditions. If we get our offices together . . . it can mean a change for us as well as a blow against a corporation which profits from this war!"[65]

On the residential consumer side, a complementary antiwar initiative also targeted AT&T. A campaign to refuse payment of a 10 percent telephone excise tax, restored specifically to help finance the Vietnam war, got started in 1966. Together with a 1 percent increase in the automobile excise tax, the Committee for Nonviolent Action estimated, the tax would raise $1.2 billion in fiscal 1967, a sufficient amount to "pay for about twenty days of killing in Vietnam." Coalitions supportive of war tax resistance formed; flyers, circulars, and newspapers spread the word (Figure 9.10). By 1973, the movement claimed forty "Alternative Funds" across the country, where war tax resisters were pooling the money they had refused to send to the government. In turn these funds were distributed to such groups as the Catholic Workers, the War Resisters League, the United Farmworkers, and the American Civil Liberties Union. Albeit on a modest scale, seeds of antiimperialism were sprouting in and around AT&T, both in the workplace and in residential telephone service.[66]

Another aim of the New York strikers was to reshape telephone industry employment and service practices. United Action demanded "to fight racist hiring and promotion policies." The CWA, this group of Local 1101 unionists asserted, "must commit itself to aggressively attack the Bell System's policy of discrimination against Blacks, Women and Latins in Hiring, Job classification and Upgrades." United Action also specified that "CWA should oppose rate increases on residential service. If the Bell System needs more money, let it raise rates on

Figure 9.10 Our Telephone Taxes Pay for War! An effort by the National War Tax Resistance Coordinating Committee within the larger context of the anti-Vietnam War movement, this was a campaign to refuse to pay a telephone excise tax that helped fund the war. Author's Collection.

business." Whether or not these local unionists recognized it, this position pitted them directly against the Nixon Administration's emerging policy framework for network system development—which, we will see in the next chapter, was working to privilege business users with lower rates and specialized network services.[67]

As the insurgents circulated these proposals, Nixon's wage freeze supplied Bell affiliate New York Telephone with a state-sanctioned bargaining advantage: that, in order to conform to the Presidential guidelines, after August 15 the company was barred legally from offering an improved contract. The New York locals ignored the Administration's plea for them to return to work. Later it would be revealed that their action had caused the backlog of phone installation orders to mushroom, to 200,000—up more than threefold from the average backlog of 60,000. Following federal mediation, however, in January 1972, members of these holdout CWA locals at last went back. They had made few material gains beyond those offered in the national contract the previous July. However, they did win a full union shop, in which workers had to become union members within a specified interval after they were hired; and, the long strike by rebellious rank-and-filers generated pressure on CWA's national leaders. A few years earlier, before this challenge became so forceful, CWA President Beirne had conceded that "we in the labor movement should be more flattered than annoyed by the critics who charge that the AFL-CIO is moribund. It isn't. But the charge itself is evidence that the American people, including the young generation, expects a great deal from the labor movement. And they should. They expect labor to lead the forces of social progress, and are bitterly disappointed when it seems to be less militant or purposeful than they would like." No such attempt at common spirit-edness issued from CWA's president now.[68]

Insurgents drew their own conclusions from the debacle of 1971. In the San Francisco Bay area, *The Bell Wringer*, which billed itself "a voice for rank & file phone workers," looked back on "the sellout national strike" charging that it had left members of area locals "demoralized." Bowing to Nixon's imposition of wage-and-price controls, the dissidents explained, Beirne had flouted the wishes of the rank and file—CWA members had voted 3 to 1 to reject AT&T's final contract offer—and instructed local union presidents "to tell their membership to return to work before voting on the new contract." Resentful at this top-down exercise, many members had not bothered to vote; Beirne thereupon surprised them again, by counting unreturned ballots as 'yes' votes. "Most CWA members disliked the new contract offer and there were scattered walk-outs all over the country, but the big New York bargaining unit was the only one that rejected the sell-out contract." That they had won "very little," the flyer asserted, was because the International denied them strike sanction "and kept them isolated from the rest of the country." CWA leaders, the two-sided flyer asserted, were simply "afraid of the militancy of the rank and file." *The Bell Wringer* underlined that the biggest beneficiary of these actions was AT&T. Confirming this were recent events in Oakland, where AT&T's Pacific Telephone affiliate had fired a just-hired Black operator, suspended nineteen workmates who had walked out in protest and, as the stand-off escalated, gone on to fire the president of the local union and suspend the other members of the local's executive board. The dissidents assailed management's acts as "AN ATTACK ON THE WHOLE UNION" and stressed that, no matter how deficient CWA leaders had proved themselves to be, "We must prevent the company from wrecking our union." Critical would be the 1974 contract negotiations, upcoming the next year. *The Bell Wringer* demanded that CWA commit to a nationwide strike with "rank and file control over strike demands." Its own checklist of priorities centered not only on wages and benefits, but also on women workers and minorities: "union controlled . . . 24 hour child care paid for out of company profits, with no rate increase or loss in wages"; at least twelve paid sick days a year; and a shorter work-week with no loss in pay ("30 for 40"), to increase employment and thus to "unite black, white, male, female and other minority workers together by creating jobs for all." Dissidents in CWA Local 9490 in Oakland also cited the removal by CWA "higher-ups" of a job steward for being "unable to get along with the union officials" as a symptom of the union's undemocratic practice of appointing—rather than electing—stewards. Two other shop stewards who attempted to go around the higher-level union bureaucracy by calling for a meeting directly with Bell managers were removed nearly at the same time. "When you are an appointed job steward, you do what the tops want or you are out. When you are elected, you do what the rank and file want or you are out. You cannot have it both ways." These mutinous unionists added that "It's a good idea to form caucuses around whatever bugs you—Black caucuses, women's caucuses, rank-and-file caucuses. That is the only way to force reluctant union leaders into representation of what you really want."[69]

New York City's United Action also drew sober lessons from what it called a "largely unsuccessful" strike. First of all, it acknowledged, Local 1101 had not put in place a plan "for getting the operators to join the strike." This signified a crucial lapse. "No matter how well organized the plant dept is, without the operators, we can't quickly hurt the company." The need to close ranks between craftsmen and women operators and clerks thus was a primary strategic objective. Other lessons, however, also needed to be absorbed—and quickly. Local 1101 had largely neglected to contact other big-city locals across the country "to put pressure on the International, and to explain why this strike was important for all CWAers." Unless the Local "is prepared to really organize an open rebellion against Bierne (sic) among all the bigger, city-based locals across the country, we're going to go on getting the shaft." Top CWA leaders had turned on the 1101, attacking it for employing an illegal tactic when the Local's leaders had acquiesced to activists' demands and sent picketers to Newark, Washington, New Haven and Detroit, all increasingly African American cities—where their picket lines were honored by local union members. Finally, United Action conceded, the New York City picketing had been "totally disorganized" and often ineffective.[70]

The remedy, the insurgents specified, was to reconstruct the union "*at the bottom*, [emphasis in the original] building by building"—by holding meetings open to all nonmanagement employees, electing stewards and chief stewards, and insisting that they be directly accountable to the rank-and-file. United Action began to contemplate a petition drive within Local 1101, to compel its officials to call a union meeting and thereby "to continue the process of remaking our local into a fighting instrument." Dispirited telephone workers, United Action agreed with *The Bell Wringer* in the Bay Area, should not quit CWA but instead should transform it. The CWA, United Action charged, indeed was "a union that is poorly organized and whose leadership is short on guts. But it's the largest of all the unions which represent phone workers and it's the only one which is a national union. We must stay in it, work to build it, and most importantly, fight to change it."[71]

The next round of bargaining, in 1974, was not punctuated by a strike and once more resulted in contractual improvements to workers' living standards. The union won national wage and benefit raises amounting to nearly 36 percent, carrying a total value of $3.1 billion; this meant that, over the course of the previous decade, nominal wages in the industry had doubled—though Vietnam war-induced inflation continued to ravage their gains. After a quarter of a century of effort, moreover, CWA also finally compelled AT&T to relinquish the fiction that its subsidiary operating companies were independent entities, by bringing the parent company to bargain centrally on a national basis on issues having broad application. The union also succeeded in gaining an agency shop, in which existing telephone workers were permitted to stay out of the union but still had to pay a fee to help cover the costs of the collective bargaining from which they benefited. Rank-and-file workers nonetheless continued to clash with CWA officials as well as Bell executives over workplace issues: automation-induced job downgrades, the lack of a no-layoff clause in their contract, forced overtime. In September 1980 another dissident sheet based in New York City, *The Bell Buster*, warned Beirne's successor as CWA President: "Put Glenn Watts and his cronies on notice that their time of running the union for Ma Bell's benefit is running out."[72]

This admonishment may be seen as a kind of final testament to the militant spirit of the rank-and-file between the mid-1960s and the mid-1970s. During these same years, however, the telephone work force also was recomposing and, as we will now see, dogged attempts to open the telephone occupations to minorities and women at last succeeded—so that AT&T was compelled to alter its employment practices. These changes imparted additional fluidity to this already turbulent moment of transition in US telecommunications.

Struggles against Discrimination in Public Utility Employment and Service

Historically, the telephone industry workforce exhibited two sharp demographic differences from the occupational profile of the Post Office. In 1953, women telephone operators accounted for about 41 percent of telephone industry employees (702,000); if women clerical workers are added then the proportion of women workers made them a majority (though their share of total telephone employment was declining). By contrast, women workers then comprised a much smaller proportion of the postal labor force. Second, Blacks and Latinos together accounted for a tiny percentage of telephone workers until after the 1964 Civil Rights Act and, just as women workers were largely confined to clerical and operator positions and precluded from advancing either into management or so-called "skilled" blue-collar jobs, the Blacks and Latinos who managed to find work in the telephone industry during the 1960s were segregated into low-paid, low-status occupations. During these decades, by contrast, the Post Office depended increasingly on Black labor. Indeed, the Post Office's 132,000 black employees in 1970 made the agency the nation's largest employer of African Americans.[73]

At its origin, the CWA had echoed the War Labor Board's call for equal employment for women and, pressed by labor-feminist activists such as Helen Berthelot, during the decades after World War II the union continued to advocate for women workers. Yet the glass ceiling women workers faced at AT&T was compounded by their second-class status in their union. Indeed, as Dorothy Sue Cobble explains, partly for this reason several independent telephone traffic unions stayed out of the CWA for years after its formation. Throughout the 1950s, moreover, when automation and self-service dialing hit against the jobs of telephone operators, CWA officials did not elevate technological change into a bargaining priority. The union likewise underrepresented women in its own leadership. CWA thereby not only helped reinscribe a profound gender division among telephone workers, but also weakened itself for future struggles as automation extruded into other segments of the transforming industry's occupational structure. Only during the 1970s, facing a reinvigorated working-class women's movement, did CWA leaders more actively promote equality within the union.[74]

As Venus Green has shown, a racial fault-line ran still deeper. AT&T, with the backing of its white union workers, adhered to a long-standing policy of race discrimination in hiring and employment. Its few Black employees were removed from providing telephone service to subscribers. African Americans could work as janitors, kitchen staffers, lounge attendants and elevator operators. Far into the post–World War II era, the Bell companies often staved off integration, among other restrictions, by adhering to a so-called "moral" stricture, which could be invoked to bar Blacks from employment: Southern Bell expressly refused to hire women with "illegitimate" children. In southern states especially, AT&T was faced scant compulsion from regulators; through 2015, Mississippi had never appointed an African American to its public utilities commission, while Georgia did so for the first time in 2000. As was true of corporations and state agencies generally, however, AT&T's employment discrimination was not merely regional.[75]

African Americans initiated protests against Bell employment practices during the depths of the Jim Crow era. Blacks began an episodic struggle as far back as the 1910s; the contest proceeded both locally and nationally, as activists improvised both theoretically and tactically. As far back as 1919, *The Messenger*, a radical African American monthly coedited by a young A. Philip Randolph, singled out "The Negro in Public Utilities" and declared that "equality of opportunity" must be the "measure and test of democracy." As Venus Green details, protests against discrimination by AT&T came to include "boycotts, all-night vigils, mass bill pay-ins (sometimes in pennies), mass phone-ins to tie up the equipment, protest stickers attached to phone bills, demonstrations, and legal complaints to various government agencies." During the late 1920s and early 1930s, Blacks targeted AT&T in a widening campaign for equal employment. The locus of this tactic was activists' argument that the telephone industry's status as a public utility should forbid it from practicing race-based job discrimination. Among the "denials of civil rights" flagged by Randolph at the establishment of the National Negro Congress in 1936 was "access to public utilities." Public utilities also were among the racist industries targeted in New York City soon after World War II.[76]

During the Depression and the war itself, activists who combined antiracist and working-class commitments pressed demands for equal treatment in employment and work. African Americans, Mexican Americans and other nonwhite workers mobilized to surmount their second-rate status. The Roosevelt administration sought to placate them with tepid promises. The most famous response came when, as war loomed, A. Philip Randolph—by now "the most visible black activist in the United States"—called for African Americans to join a March on Washington Movement, to protest discrimination in federal contracts and open defense industry jobs to blacks. Roosevelt capitulated, mandating nondiscrimination provisions for all defense contracts and establishing a Fair Employment Practices Committee (in Executive Order 8802 in 1941, extended in 1943 under Executive Order 9346).[77]

In this wider context, the Black freedom struggle sometimes singled out the local telephone industry. "The year 1941 will be remembered by Clevelanders," wrote a leader of a local African American political group in 1947, because the

Ohio Bell Telephone Company was finally forced to begin hiring Blacks into at least some white-collar jobs. "For many years, this company had complacently ignored the pleas of more conservative organizations that the company liberalize its employment policies with regard to Negroes." "At regular intervals, the conservative Negro civic organizations would call politely on Ohio Bell officials and ask, 'Why can't the company give our Negro girls a chance to become switchboard operators, clerks, and receptionists? Why are our Negro men refused jobs as collectors and operators and linemen?'" "The company," in this account, "met these recurrent delegations with great courtesy and smoothly ambiguous answers. Favorite retreat for the Ohio Bell bigwigs was the excuse that 'the union won't permit it.'" Then the Future Outlook League stepped into action. The Future Outlook League, formed in the mid-1930s, turned to street demonstrations and other organized actions to press its agenda of economic equality. Through a campaign of agitation and confrontation, the FOL involved Cleveland's Black community in the struggle. "DO YOU KNOW?" read one of its handbills, dumped by the thousands from office windows onto downtown streets, "that the Ohio Bell Telephone Company, a public utility and a monopoly, refuses to employ negroes solely because of their race; that this vicious discriminatory policy is the same thing that America is preparing to go to war with Hitler for; that this is a direct insult to American womanhood; that thousands of Negroes are being drafted into the armed forces of the nation to help protect the business in our city?" The strategy achieved modest success. Agreement was reached that Ohio Bell would employ fifteen black women—as elevator operators—and several men. Five years later, there were ninety-seven black women employees in seventeen different occupations in the downtown exchange, while African American men were employed as truck drivers, mailing room helpers, and service inspectors. The company had even hired its first black lineman and outside repairman. In this one city, however, palpable limits remained on genuinely equal employment. "Cleveland has yet to see a Negro woman employed as an exchange operator," reprimanded the Future Outlook League in 1947. Protests broke out as well in other cities, as racist exclusion and discrimination persisted in workplaces nationwide. From Chicago, the African American rights activist and CIO union leader Willard S. Townsend declared in a 1944 essay that "fundamental shifts in the base of economic control of our national resources and services" were warranted. One of these changes, Townsend specified, should be the nationalization of public utilities—"with decentralized community controls." These actions did not arrest, let alone reverse, AT&T's wholesale job segregation. However, they did signal that momentum was gathering in the fight against employment discrimination.[78]

It is worth repeating that employment discrimination itself attested more than only a racist management practice. Commitments to racism and gender preference were recurrently expressed by members of the white working class, and were ingrained in many unions, especially AFL-affiliates—nineteen of which still excluded Black members in the early 1950s. Far from joining the fight against white supremacy, Bell System workers, men and women, repeatedly conducted racist initiatives. Emblematic was white workers' protest against integrated work crews, late in 1943, and their demand that management segregate restrooms at Western Electric's Point Breeze facility—a manufacturer of radio and radar equipment—near Baltimore. This call was expressed through the Point Breeze Employees Association, which was eventually disbanded for being a company union; when the War Labor Board turned back the demand for separate restrooms, white workers staged one of the most significant of the wartime "hate strikes." The War Department ended the walkout only by seizing the plant for six months.[79]

When the American Communications Association-CIO turned to telephone organizing in the early 1940s, therefore, many telephone workers may have seen its antiracism as a liability. "At a time when the CIO made racial unity a cornerstone of its organizing drives, the overwhelming majority of unions affiliated with the NFTW omitted antidiscrimination clauses from their constitutions, and some explicitly excluded black members," explains historian Venus Green. There were exceptions; and, by the time CWA established its constitution in 1947, it contained an antidiscrimination clause. As the CIO's postwar drive to organize unions in the "right-to-work" southern states sputtered, and the federation's commitment to job equality flagged, however, CWA's establishment of "a major trade union beachhead, covering nine states with 126 locals reaching into more than 600 southern communities," did not translate into a principled and effective antiracism.[80]

Not rhetorical adherence to egalitarianism but concrete struggles engendered inroads. In 1930, there were 4000 Black workers in a telephone labor force of 579,000, including just 331 Black women among the nation's 235,259 telephone operators. Two decades later, in 1950, there were 7920 Black workers out of a total of 594,000. Although Black workers made some gains during the 1950s, what progress they achieved was concentrated chiefly in states that had passed equal employment legislation, notably, New York, Pennsylvania, Michigan and California. As the Black freedom struggle gained fresh momentum, union jobs began to open: in New York City, in a 1958 account, "communications companies" were placing "help wanted) ads in "Jewish, Chinese, and Negro papers, as well as in the general press" (*sic*). In 1957, just the same, only sixteen of the country's twenty major telephone companies employed Blacks and other minority groups in their technical services and as operators—a record, according to this avowedly pro-union account, "the Communications Workers of America points to with pride." Racist resentment simmered away among many white telephone workers, and CWA officials did little to counter it. This persisted after passage of the 1964 Civil Rights Act, as AT&T began to hire minority women into some hitherto excluded occupations. In 1968, an internal poll by CWA showed that 39 percent of its members expressed support for the candidacy of the racist George Wallace during that year's presidential campaign, though "only" 11 percent admitted to voting for him (nationwide, 13.5 percent of voters cast their ballots for Wallace).[81]

Protests against discrimination at work encompassed other groups as well (Figure 9.11). During the war period, meanwhile, the Department of Labor's Women's Bureau began to coordinate with activists to press for legislation to address the unequal status of women at work. Historian Dorothy Sue Cobble shows that women trade unionists and their supporters in federal agencies pushed for antijob discrimination measures between the 1940s and the 1970s, via diverse forms of "labor feminism." The telephone industry was once more at the forefront of this movement for redress. Not only was it was the largest private employer of women, but it was also a service industry—where labor feminists had made few inroads during the 1940s and 1950s, and to which, as they began to succeed in heavy industry, they trained their attention (Figure 9.12).[82]

Activists outside and inside the telephone industry had pressed for years to open telephone jobs to Blacks and Latinos and to break the glass ceiling that prevented women from moving up out of the ranks of telephone operators. I have stressed that protests directed specifically against employment discrimination in telephony possessed a longer history—in 1940s New Mexico, where Latinos made up a majority of the population, "a number of citizens' groups" enjoined Democratic Senator Dennis Chavez to pressure the Bell affiliate to hire Latinos. Gay activists began to attack employment discrimination concertedly during the second half of the 1960s; what the Gay Alliance characterized as a "major demonstration" against AT&T's Pacific Telephone took place in San Francisco in October 1971. Individual workers turned to the federal government's Equal Employment Opportunity Commission, established in 1965 following a twenty-five-years-long campaign, to launch antidiscrimination lawsuits against units of the Bell System. In 1970 the dam began to crack open, as rank-and-file workers filed more than one thousand separate charges of discrimination against AT&T subsidiaries. These complaints against AT&T made up 7 percent of the EEOC's annual total, though AT&T then accounted for 1 percent of national employment. The EEOC grouped the cases together, hoping to muster a compelling documentary record and legal foundation. Activists' initiatives thereby built a basis for an audacious legal challenge to discriminatory corporate employment practices.[83]

At its establishment, Republican and Southern Democratic Senators had sought to enfeeble the Equal Employment Opportunity Commission by placing

ACTIVISTS AND DISSIDENTS 435

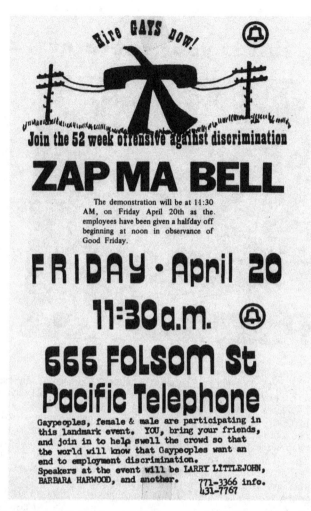

Figure 9.11 Zap Ma Bell. During the 1960s and early 1970s, social justice activists pressed forcefully to end employment discrimination at AT&T—the nation's largest corporation and public utility company. Author's Collection.

restrictive amendments on its enabling legislation (Title VII of the Civil Rights Act, passed in July 1964). Prevented, prior to further reforms, from filing suit on its own behalf in the nation's courts, the EEOC was compelled to appeal to other agencies to gain a legal footing. To meet this procedural requirement in pursuing its case against AT&T, in December 1970 the EEOC petitioned the Federal Communications Communication to reject a long-distance rate increase sought by AT&T.[84]

Figure 9.12 This Is Your Operator. Bay Area Women's Liberation, Tooth and Nail. Vol. 1. No. 4 (January 1970): 2.

The EEOC reasoned that the FCC should disapprove AT&T's rate increase request, on grounds that it was both unconstitutional and contrary to the public interest—because AT&T "had engaged and continued to engage in extensive violations of Federal, State and constitutional prohibitions against job discrimination." "The entire Bell system," charged the EEOC, "is permeated with violations of the Civil Rights Act":

> At every stage of the employment process, women, blacks and Spanish-surnamed Americans face an unbelievable myriad of discriminatory policies. Most of these policies are the result of nationwide institutional practices indigenous to the Bell system. The nation's largest private employer is also one of the nation's worst and most blatant discriminators.

The FCC did not accept that employment discrimination constituted grounds for denying AT&T's rate increase—but, extraordinarily, it did accord the EEOC formal status within its own separate rule-making on employment discrimination.[85]

The agency's incoming chairman, Nixon Republican Dean Burch, was unsympathetic; but the EEOC's appeal was compatible with the FCC's own regulations and the agency had a couple of liberal commissioners and faced strong pressure from Civil Rights activists and allied groups: the National Association for the Advancement of Colored People, the Mexican American Legal Defense and Education Fund, the American GI Forum, the National Organization for Women, and the American Civil Liberties Union. These organizations, and many determined individuals within and around them, insisted hopefully that the time was right to attack race and sex discrimination head-on through a challenge to the nation's largest corporate employer. They undertook interlocking initiatives, both on the shop-floor and, as the documentary record compiled by the EEOC for this FCC proceeding attests, through legal action. Their endeavor must be grasped, therefore, not as a narrow legalistic undertaking but a robust sociolegal construction. For such litigation to succeed, historian Nancy MacLean specifies, there needed to be dedicated and courageous plaintiffs, and "committed and well-trained attorneys to translate their grievances and the movement's demands into language that could sway judges and juries." In the case against AT&T—there were.[86]

The FCC ordered public hearings to examine the employment practices of AT&T and its subsidiaries, thereby providing "a quasi-judicial forum" that drew on representation from around the country.[87]

Some of the testimonies brought forward in this proceeding have been documented and assessed before. Lorena Weeks was an African American who in 1965 had worked at Southern Bell as an operator; but her job had been phased out. In her testimony to the EEOC, Weeks recounted how her performance review had been switched from "excellent" to "unsatisfactory" in the course of six days, after she had bid for the (male) job of switchman. She had received no support from her local union president, who "told me I didn't get the job and when

I asked him why he said because is a job for men. I said why is that and he said it was because the man is the breadwinner in the family and women just don't need this type of job." Weeks testified that abusive discrimination along lines of sex *and* race or ethnicity honeycombed Bell System employment. She proceeded to bring suit against an AT&T subsidiary.[88]

Helen J. Roig had entered employment with Southern Bell in 1940 as an operator, and had spent her entire working life at the phone company. A personification of the labor feminism analyzed by Dorothy Sue Cobble, Roig brought suit against her employer and, though years belated, this action eventually garnered her a better job at Southern Bell as a test deskman—a job classified as men's work. "What gave you the courage to wait so long and fight your lawsuit so many years to get this job . . . ?" she was asked. "I guess many things," answered Roig: "I would think really it would go back to my background, the way I was raised. I was raised on a farm. I was a sharecropper's daughter. It did not make any difference whether you were a man or a woman. You worked in the field and you were paid the same thing. It just depended on how much cotton you could pick in a day. We were raised to a very hard life. In my young life, I never did realize I was a second-class citizen. I decided that things were not going to change for me until the status of all women would be changed and upgraded in society." Roig was an activist: not only a shop steward but also head of a special committee in her union local. Roig's committee, she said, was "involved with women's activities. That would include all women's activities . . . There would be a number of things referred to me but if we have any females in our local that does not have possible rights under the grievance procedure, then these grievances would be referred to me." Roig further explained that, where she now worked in New Orleans, "We have a group of women who started trying to break these jobs open for women in the telephone company, quite a few of us." Roig's lawsuit against a Bell subsidiary became grist for the swelling protest.[89]

Allying with lawyers and other social movement activists, women and minority workers waged a successful fight against employment discrimination. They did so by turning to the public utility conception, harking back to African American struggles of the 1920s and 1930s. The idea was that, because the telephone company was a public utility and therefore subject to laws and regulations prohibiting discrimination, these rules had to be observed throughout *all* aspects of AT&T's operations including its employment practices. This tenet gained an unprecedented formal status at the federal level, in the EEOC's petition to the FCC. In the introduction to this filing, the EEOC declared that, because AT&T's unmatched size "enables it to affect the public to an uncommon extent," AT&T likewise faced "an uncommon obligation to consider the public interest." "But, even more significantly," the EEOC continued, "AT&T is a government-licensed monopoly, a 'public' utility, and is guaranteed a market and fair return on its investment." The EEOC anchored this claim in recent sources, including a months-old judgment by the FCC itself and an academic analysis, *The Negro in the Public Utilities Industry*. In this book, Bernard E. Anderson reinforced the EEOC's own claim by specifying that "the public interest extends beyond mere concern for equitable rates; it also includes concern for protecting the environment and practicing equal opportunity in its employment."[90]

The EEOC charged that AT&T's discriminatory employment practices violated Section 202 (a) of the Federal Communications Act, which held that "It shall be unlawful for any common carrier to make unjust or unreasonable discrimination in charges, practices, classification, regulations, facilities, or services for or in connection with like communication service ... or to make or give any undue preference or advantage to any particular person, class of persons, or locality, or to subject any particular person, class of persons, or locality to any undue or unreasonable prejudice or disadvantage." Bringing to bear Supreme Court decisions originating in disparate contexts, the EEOC demanded that the FCC's enabling statute be interpreted broadly, rather than merely to protect users of telephone service from monopolistic predation by carriers: "The plain language of [Section] 202 (a) bars any unjust discriminatory practice of a communications common carrier."[91]

The EEOC went further. It declared that "the relationship between AT&T and the Federal Communications Commission is so substantial as to subject AT&T to the strictures of the Fifth Amendment." A government-licensed monopoly, properly facing "extensive regulation by a federal agency," AT&T "operates in the public interest" and must carry "constitutional obligations." "It has long been held that when the state permits private parties to conduct essentially governmental functions," asserted the EEOC, "the private parties must conform their actions to the requirements of the constitution. AT&T clearly performs an essentially governmental function: it provides a vital service to virtually every home in the nation: it is a public utility." As a "public trustee," AT&T was linked by the EEOC to a recent judicial ruling, in which the FCC's complicity with another regulated industry had been exposed and discredited.[92]

The EEOC was quoting an Appeals Court decision. A high-water mark in the effort both to reform the nation's communication system and to make it a steppingstone to wider reforms, this—the so-called WLBT case—constituted a dramatic legal victory for the Civil Rights movement. As Robert B. Horwitz shows, this drawn-out proceeding was grounded indomitable activism. Complaints about the racist broadcasting that permeated much of the South had long circulated. The Reverend Everett C. Parker, who directed the Office of Communications of the United Church of Christ, determined to try "to establish a process to challenge broadcast licensee power and build in accountability to the public." This required petitioning the Federal Communications

Commission, which assigned spectrum licenses to broadcasters. Working with the President of the Mississippi NAACP, Aaron Henry, and Henry's colleague in the Mississippi Freedom Democratic Party, Robert L.T. Smith, as well as with sympathetic attorneys, Parker deliberately selected for a target an important corporate owned radio station, whose racist outpourings had long outraged many inhabitants of Jackson, Mississippi. (WLBT was owned by media group Lamar Life Broadcasting.) The FCC responded to the petition by dithering, finding pretext after pretext for not revoking the station's license, though its performance flagrantly violated FCC standards for licensees. Activists then turned the FCC itself into a target: Parker took the case to the US Court of Appeals for the District of Columbia.

On its face, this appeared to be an even more inclement venue. Presiding over the court was a well-known conservative, Judge Warren Burger, soon to be appointed by President Nixon as chief justice of the Supreme Court. The chances of succeeding were rendered still more remote, because Parker's case rested on an untested and, it seemed, inauspicious bid to establish legal standing before the Court.

The legal idea of standing as it was then interpreted vested the public interest in regulatory agencies themselves: thus it was the FCC, rather than claimants, that embodied and expressed the public's role. Moreover, even the right to be heard before regulatory agencies and to bring actions to court—legal standing— was commonly restricted to those able to demonstrate an economic interest. In broadcasting, only economic injury and electronic interference typically constituted grounds for participation in an administrative proceeding. Parker and his colleagues were attempting to win legal standing as a representative of the public interest when the FCC *itself* was accredited as the latter's legal incarnation in communications and, additionally, when they could evidently demonstrate no economic interest.[93]

Unexpectedly—extraordinarily—the Appeals Court ruled, not once but twice, for Parker. In 1966, Chief Judge Burger "issued a powerful opinion that not only cast doubt on the FCC's actions and reasoning, but served to open standing to parties without property interest." The defense of the public interest in this field of communications, Burger held, would be served by allowing the participation of "legitimate listener representatives fulfilling the role of private attorneys general." The Appeals Court, Horwitz tells us, "essentially elevated citizen groups to the level of private attorneys general who could bring actions before regulatory agencies and courts." This constituted a defining watershed in legal revisionism. It was not evident at the time that its importance for reactionaries would ultimately outweigh its significance for social justice movements.[94]

Burger ordered the FCC to conduct hearings on the station's performance and its discharge of its public responsibilities. After duly convening a field hearing in Jackson, at which the biases—actually, the defiance—of the local Hearing Examiner were placed on blatant display, the FCC proceeded nevertheless blithely to approve by 5–2 the Hearing Examiner's findings and to renew WLBT's license. The United Church of Christ's Parker thereupon appealed the FCC's ruling to the Burger Court in Washington, D.C. Once more the result went beyond reformers' hopes. "In a blistering opinion, the Court of Appeals reversed and remanded the Commission's decision on the license renewal" and, as Horwitz puts it, "excoriated" not only the Hearing Examiner but the FCC majority. The Burger Court then went beyond precedent by preempting the FCC as the legal agent for the station's license renewal process, and invited would-be broadcasters to apply to use this electromagnetic frequency.[95]

The EEOC's filing against AT&T employment discrimination arrived at the FCC the year after this unprecedented Appeals Court ruling, on the shoulders of the Civil Rights movement's success in routing the FCC majority. In this new case, however, the now-democratized doctrine of standing was used not to challenge racist broadcast owners, but to combat employment discrimination in the telephone industry. "AT&T," EEOC went on, "has grown to be the world's largest utility because of federal government sufferance. This sufferance is more than passive: the government guarantees AT&T's profits and insures that it operates in the 'public convenience and necessity.'"[96]

The EEOC underscored that "the Courts have repeatedly made it clear that they will not hesitate to reverse a Commission determination when the Commission lags behind in adjusting to changing concepts of the public interest. No clearer example exists," the EEOC took pains to specify, "than the protracted litigation involving the Federal Communications Commission and the United Church of Christ." EEOC rested its case by insisting that the FCC had no choice but to declare AT&T's proposed rate increase unlawful. "Failure of the Commission to take such action would be an abdication of its responsibility matched only by AT&T's callous indifference to the Equal Employment laws." The implication was starkly clear: if the FCC did not act to rein in AT&T then, just as in the WLBT case, regulators would show themselves to be captive—not just to corporate power but to a racist system of white supremacy.[97]

The filing succeeded: a chastened FCC accepted that equal employment would be an issue in the rate case. Far more important was that, following two years of hearings, the EEOC, the Justice Department, and the Department of Labor undertook negotiations with AT&T. These parties announced on January 18, 1973 that they had signed an agreement spelling out far-reaching changes to Bell System employment practices. This consent decree—which called both for payments to victims of past discrimination and implementation of "far-reaching programs for increasing employment and promotional opportunities for males and females, both minority and non-minority, in job classifications and locations where they [had] been underutilized"—comprised "the largest and most comprehensive civil rights settlement ever reached in the United States."[98]

Some restitution, at least, was offered to thirteen thousand female and two thousand minority male workers who had been victims of AT&T employment discrimination; and the company agreed to a wholesale transformation of its personnel policies going forward. This outcome carried repercussions economy-wide, because the high price it exacted from AT&T constituted "dramatic evidence to companies and unions that continued discrimination would be at the risk of significant financial liability." Two additional consent decrees were needed to bring the telephone company into full compliance but, by the mid-1970s, the results at AT&T were reverberating widely and affirmative action policies were becoming commonplace at big companies.[99]

At AT&T itself, the curtailment of ingrained discrimination was offset by new forms of job degradation, as a concomitant productivity drive by AT&T bore down on the content of telephone labor processes. Historians have shown that the carrier's reassertion of control around the introduction of new technology substantiated Civil Rights activists' fears, expressed as early as 1961–1963, that accelerating automation would punish African American workers disproportionately. Though profoundly important in its own right, AT&T's grudging and belated capitulation to equal employment therefore proved opportunistic. As many of the nation's cities came to be inhabited disproportionately by Blacks and Latinos, AT&T's productivity-oriented profit strategy gave it an incentive to open its increasingly automated urban plant to non-white Traffic workers. In 1969—before the impact of the Justice Department/EEOC suit—African Americans already accounted for nine out of ten new operators hired in New York City. Now AT&T could boast of its supposed commitment to job equality.[100]

Nevertheless, the process of reaching the consent decree possessed surpassing importance. First and foremost, the judgment constituted a milestone in "opening the American workplace" to what had long been subordinate and excluded fractions of the working class. Although, as Bayard Rustin anticipated in 1963, "when a racial disparity in unemployment has been firmly established in the course of a century, the change-over to 'equal opportunities' . . . does not wipe out the cumulative handicaps," nevertheless, by gaining legal rights in the workplace minorities and women won a resource that invited further action toward social justice. Second, during the process of pushing forward the AT&T case some workers also made clear that service provision itself also suffered from severe discriminatory practices.[101]

Workers' words reveal that telephone employees and their legal representatives identified a gaping deficit in existing telephone service provision and, in this way, their movement for remedy stretched the public utility model beyond equal employment. Poignant as well as telling was the account offered by Paula

V. Jimenez, from East Los Angeles. Upon her high school graduation Jimenez took a fulltime job with the telephone company. Her work unit, she observed to an FCC hearing examiner, was disproportionately staffed with Blacks and Mexican Americans. While white workers moved into supervisory positions garnering higher wages, she saw minority workers languishing in the lower job grades without promotions or pay raises. Offered pats on the back for her own performance, but discouraged by supervisors from seeking a role in management, Jimenez resisted: "after being there awhile, and I just was not getting anywhere ... we started organizing within the union" (the CWA). By 1968 she was, she said, "pretty fed up with the system around here. I don't want any part of it, and I said I am getting out." Jimenez declared: "I quit on March 7, 1968, liberation day." She found work instead at American Express, where she was quickly promoted into management.[102]

Jimenez linked the occupational discrimination she had faced to a second stark inequality in telephone service. A survey taken by college students in April 1972 showed that "if a Spanish-speaking person is in need of immediate help, because of an attack, fire, etc., in most cases the delay before help would arrive will be increased by five to ten minutes and in some cases, no help will arrive for lack of bilingual operators." Jimenez provided examples, drawn from her own experience, of how telephone service shorted Spanish speakers. Her mother, she recounted, "is a monolingual" and, "When we first got our telephone installed ... I had to stay home from school to interpret, because they had nobody to relate to her in Spanish." Then Jimenez's cousin had visited from Mexico. Attempting first to telephone Jimenez and then, on other occasions, to telephone her own family in Mexico, the cousin had found that "there was no operator that could assist her." "She stood on the phone an hour and a half, and there was no one that could assist her, and she turned around and told me I will never come back to this country."

> You go to Mexico. Whatever language you speak, somebody will speak to you, and you talk about the system and the telephone being bad ... This is the most horrible country you can find as a tourist. You can't communicate with people, because no one can help you in your own language.

In "the Chicano community," Jimenez continued, the reputation of the telephone company was, simply, "terrible."[103]

Jimenez's personal experience was amplified by California Rural Legal Assistance and the Mexican American Legal Defense Fund. These organizations directly supported the EEOC petition before the FCC, emphasizing that they represented 300,000 long-distance subscribers in California. To a considerable extent, they wrote, these Spanish-speakers "are presently without local, long distant (sic) and international telephone service and are totally dependent upon individuals who speak English to place calls for them or private local services which charge rates that are four times higher than those charged by the AT&T's operating companies." To further validate these claims they demanded that the FCC conduct a field hearing in or near San Francisco in order to gather testimony about AT&T's systematic discrimination, from Mexican Americans who, otherwise, would be unable to provide it because of "the economic realities of life." Their reasoning harked back to the WLBT victory. In this they demonstrated how immediate and resounding had been the movement's assimilation of the WLBT judgment's enlargement of legal standing: "Without such hearing, CRLA and MALDF will not be able to share in the arduous responsibility of regulating a public phone system": they would be unable "to assure that the FCC does not permit its regulated industries to engage in employment discrimination in violation of its regulations, the Constitution, and National Policy." Belatedly introduced, Spanish-language Information would join other forms of "Directory Assistance" to become monetized service rather than a bundled free-of-charge part of "Information."[104]

A different service deficit was revealed in 1968, when four homophile groups requested that Pacific Telephone publish a separate category heading in its San Francisco Yellow Pages directory under the listing "homophile organizations." The Bell subsidiary denied their request, whereafter the organizations obtained a hearing before the California Public Utilities Commission. After three days of hearings, their lawyer stated to the hearing officer: "The homosexual must have full and ready access to every method and avenue of communication. The telephone must be in truth a public utility which can be fully utilized by the homosexual . . . in the same manner and to the same degree as it is made available to and utilized by the heterosexual." Within a few more years, organizations which now referred to themselves as gay were listing together in San Francisco's and New York's "People's" Yellow Pages.[105]

Answered not by Bell but by noncommercial community groups were other, often freshly evident, needs. Volunteer-staffed hotlines were established for a range of would-be users, from depressed or isolated teenagers to drug users to stressed-out veterans. "Tell-A-Woman" was a local news sheet and feminist calendar set up in Philadelphia by the Women's Switchboard. The People's Yellow Pages in New York City grew from a conviction that "information is essential if people are to make choices, change their lives, find alternatives." Committed to "the necessity of our creating new counter-institutions, ones that do not simply replace the established, profit-making methods but institutions that will provide us with new form," it provided "a directory of non-rip-off services, but localized to New York communities." A People's Yellow Pages serving San Francisco and the Bay Area was produced by a collective of women to be a "directory of alternatives." Listings were for goods and services "that seem to affirm the dignity of the individual and disavow exploitation." "Perhaps, some time," the collective wrote in the 1972 second edition, "these qualities will no longer represent 'alternative' life styles, but will be embodied in the mainstream of our society. That time seems far away, however, and so we continue to call ourselves the 'counter-culture.'"[106]

The late 1960s and early 1970s thus constituted a historic moment of conflict, change, and, it seemed, hopeful possibility. Some of the diverse oppositional energies that were flourishing concentrated around the public utility conception. Black, Mexican American, and white women workers fought to make the public utility status of the telephone industry into a lever with which to pry open equal work opportunities at the nation's largest private employer: they made it necessary for a sometimes-reluctant government at last to compel AT&T to institute antidiscrimination programs. This giant corporation's occupational structure was then grudgingly reorganized.

Bland legalism could carry the force of a grenade: as legal standing was expanded, so in turn was the substance of the public utility model enlarged. The EEOC declared forthrightly before the FCC that, in a rate-making proceeding, the FCC "must consider not only economic factors but *all* factors which touch the public interest." EEOC cited another just-concluded Supreme Court judgment to underline that this portended a sweepingly extensive recalibration: The public interest, the agency declared, may reflect "aesthetic, conservational and recreational as well as economic values." In the past the primary criteria regulators had used to determine the public interest had been narrowly economic; however, "it seems reasonably clear that problems of consumer protection, environment and civil rights will become increasingly important in the administration of regulatory statutes. These problems are of major national significance and cannot legitimately be ignored by the Federal Communications Commission." A battle to expand and enrich the public utility model was underway.[107]

Complementary legal rulings powered by allied social justice struggles had placed public utility and the public interest (the regulatory standard used for broadcasting) at the core of what seemed might bid fair to become a far-reaching reconstruction of the nation's electronic communications. The consent decree with AT&T was one of numerous proceedings that appeared to unlock the status quo and to move communications toward greater accountability and equity. Like the equal employment consent decree signed by AT&T, the Supreme Court's Red Lion decision in 1969 marked this trend, by holding that factors beyond commercial property interests were fundamental and could no longer be marginalized. In the Red Lion case, indeed, the public interest was judged "paramount," that is, superior to the property interests of the broadcasters, to whom the right to use the airwaves had been merely delegated. In both telecommunications and broadcasting, therefore, upswells of social justice organizing were bearing fruit and upsetting the established order. Springing up as well was a crop of citizens' groups intent on imposing political oversight on both the regulatory agencies and the industries they purported to oversee.[108]

*

CWA President Joseph Beirne declared in 1969 that his union's strategy was to fight "to be as close to the center of power as it can possibly get." Although militant rank-and-file unionists assailed the wisdom of this approach, by then—during the presidency of Richard M. Nixon—many business executives and conservative politicians deemed that Beirne's strategy had succeeded all too well. Greatly compounding their agitation were the actions and initiatives being pursued by contemporary rank-and-file workers, women, African Americans, Mexican Americans, and gay Americans. These did not attest the existence of a unitary movement, indeed, their different activisms betrayed substantial centrifugal force. However disparate they were, however, movements for social justice nevertheless reinforced a conviction among the elite that too much power had been amassed—and was being exercised—from below. In the perspective of the boardroom, it was the whole messy combination of organized labor's institutional strength, dissident rank-and-file insurgency, and social movement activism that needed to be countered, co-opted, and contained. Labor Secretary George Shultz cautioned the NALC's James Rademacher at the outset of the postal workers' unauthorized 1970 walkout: "There's only one thing worse than a wildcat strike—a wildcat strike that succeeds." How might the authorities regain the initiative, the better to address capital's increasingly urgent need to revive lagging profits and the state its sociopolitical control?[109]

This was a critical historical moment; and the Nixon Administration engaged it by seeking to halt disruptive movements from below while redirecting the course of telecommunications through regressive policy interventions from above. Rank-and-file workers and social justice movements, in other words, helped catalyze a Thermidorian reorganization of US network system development.

With respect to postal-dom the administration's response was direct, as it quickly established the US Postal Service, and pragmatic, in that it conceded full collective bargaining rights—though not the right to strike—to the seven AFL-CIO affiliated postal unions: The two Black-led postal unions were not included. With respect to electronic telecommunications, the Nixon government set in motion foundational policy changes. However, because these dramatic alterations to the structure of networking were both piecemeal and opaque, and because their prime beneficiaries were hidden in shadow, their meaning remained largely impenetrable. If minority and women worker-activists were effortfully regenerating the public utility conception, then—as the administration's

ACTIVISTS AND DISSIDENTS   447

policy changes cumulated—big businesses moved to eviscerate it, just as they concurrently participated in an alliance to discredit regulation itself. Corporate users of networks had become intent on capturing for themselves the organizational benefits and alluring profit-potentials of emerging computer communications technologies.

This counter-movement came at the expense of AT&T's regulated monopoly—and of the highly unionized telecommunications industry. As this politically contrived reaction gained ground, Joe William Trotter, Jr. explains, there followed "a relentless long-term process of deindustrialization and resistance to the democratization of American society [which] unraveled the socioeconomic and political foundation of the new equal-opportunity regime." It also placed activists and insurgents on the defensive for decades to come. Radiating from government's repeated authorizations of proprietary and mostly unregulated computer networks for corporate users, there arose a vibrantly regressive digital capitalism.[110]

PART III
DIGITAL CAPITALISM

10
Innovation, Dissensus, and Reaction from Above

Under the administration of Dwight D. Eisenhower (1953–1961), the public utility model in telecommunications seemed to have stabilized in light of a Cold War consensus. Restricted by the 1956 antitrust decree to regulated telecommunications and government markets, AT&T was nevertheless hugely profitable. Cooperation between federal and state regulators was reducing local rates, bringing unprecedentedly inclusive residential telephone access and nurturing a mass consumer economy. The Communications Workers of America was entrenching itself as a bureaucratic industrial union, continually improving telephone workers' wages and benefits. AT&T's unrivaled research laboratories and vast manufacturing facilities pumped out weapons systems and patented discoveries for US military industry, helping to sustain the United States as the ultimate guarantor of world capitalism. Against the hard shell of this regime critics of AT&T's integrated power complex made few dents. By metrics of access, performance, and extent, as its defenders claimed, the US boasted the best telephone system in the world.

Nevertheless, this settlement was coming under pressure. Though remote from the everyday experience of most Americans, changes at the margins of the networking infrastructure were etching new directional trends. Vexing questions accompanied the assimilation of computer networks by big corporations and military agencies. On what terms—technical, industrial, and political—would computer communications be made available? Would AT&T shepherd data networking into the US business system? Would the public utility conception be renewed and extended to guide this new technology into the national network infrastructure? Or, might some other arrangement—and some other standard than public utility—govern? The structure and policy of telecommunications faced gathering uncertainty; and ideological dissensus soon broke into the open. By the mid-1960s, calls to revisit policy made their way onto the agenda of top decisionmakers.

Computerization

To supply armaments and materiel for World War II, US authorities not only awarded military supply contracts to an enormous array of businesses, but also financed construction and operation of thousands of defense plants and related facilities. As the government built up manufacturing capacity in basic industry, historian Mark R. Wilson details, it also moved into producing military high-technology, ranging from army ordnance and naval ships to next-generation fighter planes and atomic bombs. At the war's end, government-owned factories were worth about $15 billion (1945 dollars), accounting for about one-fifth of the nation's industrial capacity. This vast, taxpayer-funded capital plant, United Auto Workers' leader Walter Reuther proposed, should be permanently nationalized under a new Tennessee Valley Authority-type agency under a mandate to ensure full employment. Recoiling against this possibility of extending "New Deal-style schemes of state enterprise," business leaders and conservative politicians instead demanded that reconversion to a peacetime economy pivot on privatization. As the political tides shifted, they prevailed. The ensuing disposal of government-owned facilities—"the largest set of state-owned assets outside the Soviet Union," as Wilson puts it—also "represented the largest privatization of public property in American history since the land sales of the nineteenth century." Under the ministrations of a rehabilitated Herbert Hoover and Oliver Buckley, director of AT&T's Bell Laboratories, most of this huge stock of war plant was sold off at a steep discount to corporations, providing what may be "the largest one-time capitalization of private industry in American history." Nuclear weapons development remained under direct federal control; however, the privatization drive encompassed government facilities in other dynamic high-tech fields, including radar, sonar, computing, and aerospace engineering. In this way, between 1945 and 1960 the political economy's productive base was structurally reoriented. Set within this privatization trend, and the Cold War reactionary politics that enveloped it, innovation in these key areas was all but foreordained to move in a direction contrary to public accountability.[1]

It was exactly during these years that the early development of digital electronics began to open breath-taking vistas. Historians have amply studied the supply side of this trend.

Pressure to improve information processing capabilities had amped up through the twentieth century; David Mindell shows how a focus on feedback, leading on to cybernetics, became a preoccupation in high-tech corporations and military agencies. Engineers concentrated on how to mechanize technologies of information storage, retrieval, processing, and exchange. Electromechanical computers and vacuum-tube technology supplemented the work of human computers, mostly women.[2]

World War II lent overarching urgency to additional innovation. Near-instantaneous calculation based on recurrent feedback was essential for mobile artillery installations on ships and airplanes; nuclear weapons could be manufactured only by performing a huge number of intricate calculations; wartime intelligence agencies—a historian has called these "knowledge factories"—required expedited throughput of information converging from operational theaters scattered across the world. The complexity of procurement and logistics needed to support armies and fighters across Asia, North Africa, and Europe also placed a premium on efficient information handling. The volume, diversity, and urgency of wartime data processing posed an acute problem. Crash programs to develop radar and television as well as computing enriched theoretical understanding and quickly led on to practical breakthroughs.[3]

This impetus carried over into postwar research and development, with an especially crucial contribution arriving with the invention of the transistor at AT&T in 1949. Between 1940 and 1950, the number of vacuum tubes produced in the US increased more than threefold, to 382 million. With the transistor, this growth became exponential: merely between 1954 and 1957, the number of transistors produced rocketed, from 1.3 million to 28.7 million, amid a tremendous burst of innovation around electronic instruments, sensors, control systems, calculators, probes, computers, and telephone switches.[4]

Existing manufacturers of vacuum tubes, some quite large, threw themselves into the promotion of digital information processing under military auspices: General Electric, Raytheon, Motorola, RCA, Sylvania, Philco, and Westinghouse and, of course, AT&T. Jumping into the same arena were makers of specialized gear for radar, such as Varian Associates and Eitel and McCollough; and semiconductor producers such as Hewlett-Packard, Fairchild Semiconductor, Texas Instruments and Hughes Semiconductor.

Institutions were built, and others rearranged, to channel and speed innovations in information processing into the for-profit political economy and to defend the interests of the companies that took up residence in the sector. A crop of trade associations constituted one component. With backing from an important military-connected electronics company (RCA), the Armed Forces Communications and Electronics Association was established in 1946, with the purpose of systematizing exchanges between government and industry. Venture capital also began to carve out a place: "A number of private companies, public companies, and investment banks had begun to accumulate funds from wealthy individuals, corporations, pension funds, and endowments to invest in start-up companies pursuing technologies connected with the military." Law firms specializing in microelectronics industry issues also sprang up around Silicon Valley.[5]

Between 1955 and 1963, military procurement of electronic systems and components more than doubled, and weapons systems began to be based on microelectronics technology—which was more reliable, smaller, less likely to fail, and used less energy. Starting in 1956, "the Air Force championed the digitalization of avionics equipment," insisting that corporate contractors "employ silicon transistors as much as possible." Seven years later, the entire Defense Department was urged by its Director for Research and Engineering to do likewise. By 1967, eighteen of the top fifty industrial contractors for the Defense Department were based in electronics and communications; and the emerging tech industry sold "well over 60% of its output" to the government. Military contracts continued to power the market for transistors, integrated circuits, and ultimately, microprocessors. Companies headquartered in Silicon Valley (a term introduced by a journalist in 1971) rode this war-making wave to global market supremacy, and never relinquished it. What one scholar called "the permanent war economy" thus cradled digital capitalism in its infancy and succored it into adulthood.[6]

Even as the Justice Department brought a new antitrust suit against AT&T in 1949, the transistor's civilian spinoffs were also being heralded. *Consumer Reports*, which had begun the 1940s by agitating for lower telephone rates and which had trained attention on the suit's prospective impact on phone rates earlier in 1949, underlined that the antitrust suit was motivating Bell to make its patents more widely available and projected "numerous consumer benefits": new kinds of temperature controls, elevators, and electronic computers. By the time of the 1956 decree, the transformative potentials of microelectronics were actually being demonstrated across a great industrial expanse. Henck and Strassburg recollect that "The prize among Bell research for a host of manufacturers of electronic products was the transistor.... The transistor was widely licensed by the Bell organization, and it opened the door to a whole new electronics industry." Small manufacturers, they recount, credited Bell's now-easy licensing program "with reducing the selling price of transistors in four years by as much as vacuum tube costs had been trimmed after thirty years." As transistor sales shot skyward, a dozen start-ups had emerged by 1957, and joined established firms such as Motorola and Hughes Aircraft, to sell to the US military and its contractors. Four years later, electronics stocks were sizzling, with between 150 and 200 semiconductor company participants. The promise of digital information processing engendered a cataract of innovations but, as Gerald Brock writes, "the most significant beneficiary of the progress in semiconductors was the computer industry."[7]

During the early 1950s dozens of companies invested in computer manufacturing, notably, IBM, but also Honeywell and Burroughs and NCR and Control Data and Sperry Gyroscope and, soon after, the venture capital-backed

DEC; in 1955, there were twelve major US producers. Philco delivered the first general-purpose transistorized computer under contract to the National Security Agency, and turned it into a commercial product in 1958. Redesigned as versatile, general-purpose data-processing machines rather than mere calculators, computers fueled a great new industry; by 1960, manufacturers "had delivered about 5,000 computers in the United States and another thousand or two in the rest of the world," with applications in every major sector. Business users and computer vendors worked closely with one another; and, between 1963 and 1968, US business- and government agency outlays on computer hardware tripled, from $1.5 billion to $4.5 billion. As the 1960s ended, a historian relates, "electronic computers and their associated peripherals formed the basis of a $20 billion industry ... growing at an average rate of more than 27 percent annually." These years saw as well a boom in commercial software. Seeking to develop software as an isolable component despite mighty IBM's strategy of bundling it with its leased mainframe computers, independent software and service suppliers multiplied, adding to the industry's scope and dynamism. In 1961 about forty of the larger software and computer services companies formed a trade group: the Association of Data Processing Service Organizations. By 1966, perhaps 700 software and services companies were generating half a billion dollars in annual revenue; just two years later (1968), this total had doubled.[8]

This roaring industrial engine was built, serviced, and marketed by a labor force which, in sharp contrast to its precursor in analog electronics, was essentially unorganized. Beginning early in the twentieth century, AT&T and General Electric and Westinghouse had found themselves contending with AFL affiliates; but, by the mid-1930s, GE and Westinghouse found themselves compelled to deal with one of the CIO's strongest and most assertive left-led unions—the United Electrical Workers. For its part, AT&T managed to hold off the Communications Workers–CIO until World War II. From the start, by contrast, the companies that pioneered the digital transition were union-free from the outset and, as some of them grew into giant units of capital this intolerance became ingrained and industry-wide. Corporate heads in semiconductors and computing, including at Intel and IBM, were hostile to unions in principle, and worked actively to discourage them. Digital systems and services developed far-removed from the collective bargaining that characterized labor relations at AT&T's now-heavily unionized national network.

And these would-be rivals also developed, ironically, with sustained nourishment from AT&T. Bell Telephone Laboratories collected patents, ultimately, at a rate of one each day; between 1956 and its break-up in 1982 it gathered nearly 20,000. Having signed the 1956 consent decree, AT&T now had to license any and all of these on easy terms. "Some of these licenses," a government report would observe, "have spawned entire new industries." As Endlich writes,

AT&T's decision in the 1956 settlement to retain its Western Electric unit and to accept in return a domain limited to regulated telecommunications and military contracts "seemed a minor concession; in the end, it may have been the most costly business decision in history." This has inspired a related, and misleading, observation—criticized in passing in a previous chapter:

> Had AT&T seized the technological advantages that were already within its grasp ... it might now be the leader in any number of high-tech industries. Bell Labs' mind-boggling list of innovations included the transistor, laser, optical amplification, cellular transmission, frame relay packet switching, UNIX operating system, and the computer language C. All were commercialized by other companies, among them Sony, Ciena, Nortel, Cascade, Sun Microsystems, Hewlett-Packard, and Microsoft.

The implication is that a gross managerial miscalculation was symptomatic of AT&T as a corporate dinosaur, a slow-moving bureaucracy incapable of exploiting the wondrous inventions of its own engineers and scientists. However, that AT&T did not pursue a hard-driving profit strategy around solid-state microelectronics was—we saw—a result of the vise in which it had been placed by the Justice Department in 1956: on one side, mandatory patent licensing; on the other, an express prohibition against AT&T entry into these noncommon carrier industries. Still fresh at that time were memories of how, during the 1920s and early 1930s, AT&T had muscled into electrical acoustics: "the symbiotic relation between electrical recording, sound film, radio broadcasting, and mass public-address systems." The Justice Department settlement with AT&T had compensated for curtailing this potential for predation, by legitimizing AT&T's lucrative role as a high-tech military supplier.[9]

This government action was taken, however, exactly as stand-alone computers were being endowed with communicative capabilities. The military's ambitious project SAGE, a command and control system that garnered huge contracts for IBM and AT&T, got going in 1952. SAGE engendered a wealth of early knowledge about networking. A decade later, the Pentagon established an Information Processing Techniques Office within its new Defense Advanced Research Projects Agency, to improve the performance of military systems; by strengthening this critical area of military industry, IPTO itself was "elevated ... from a small DOD office to a player on the world stage of computing development." Cycles of experimental innovation and upheaval followed one another, as mainframe computers were connected to remote access terminals via different kinds of telecommunications circuits. The digital computer industry dominated by IBM thrived, historians have shown, by working closely not only with military agencies but, soon, also with large corporate customers including railroads, airlines, and insurance companies. Computer system vendors threw themselves into exploring "time-sharing," the first systematic response to the burgeoning corporate demand for data communications. Time-sharing networks provided seemingly simultaneous access by multiple users, via terminals, to centralized information processing and data storage facilities located in giant mainframe computer facilities. Undertaken in 1964, MIT's Multi-Access Computing [Project MAC], sponsored by DARPA, supplies a conventional benchmark. Erecting networks around successive generations of mainframe computers, corporations joined military agencies in experimenting with specially engineered telecommunications circuits to enable access to remote computational facilities at multiple locations. According to one forecast, "Communications and computer companies hesitate to estimate how big IDP will become—but they are sure it will be very big."[10]

Was time-sharing to be diffused to industrial users via specialized, purpose-built "integrated data processing"—systems decoupled from the public telecommunications network? Or, would time-sharing recapitulate the tendency that had long characterized telegraphy and telephony, meaning that the economies of scale deriving from large capital investments in mainframe computers would militate toward highly centralized provision?

Western Union, by now becoming moribund, made a last-ditch attempt to pursue both courses in a bid to resurrect itself around time-sharing.

Still leasing circuits from AT&T, on one side, Western Union built private wire networks (as it had for US Steel in the 1930s and for a variety of banks and other companies at the turn of the century) for big corporations and government agencies: E. F. Hutton, General Electric, and the new (1950) Bank Wire system that linked 188 banks in 54 cities by 1959. The US Government contracted for a Western Union system connecting over 200 Air Force bases. The carrier established another substantial network for Sylvania Corporation, "whereby sixty-three plants transmit payroll information, billing, and other information to a computer in Camillus, New York, for quick analysis and evaluation." This private network strategy later underlay Western Union's attempt to be the first company to launch and operate a domestic satellite in 1974.[11]

On the other side, Western Union also began moves to construct a centralized "computer utility," or "information utility," in which it would provide an expanding range of applications and services. As the core of the US telecommunications system, the obvious candidate for such a role was AT&T—but AT&T was barred from assuming it by the 1956 consent decree, which had outlawed its entry into commercial services beyond regulated telecommunications. The language of its projected redesign presaged what we have come to equate with services available via the internet—information pertaining to travel, news, corporate inventories, library resource sharing, law, and medicine were highlighted. In an internal corporate memo, Western Union outlined the scope of its projected information utility:

> What is now developing, very rapidly, is a critical need—as yet not fully perceived—for a new national information utility which can gather, store, process, program, retrieve and distribute on the broadest possible scale, to industry; to the press; to military and civilian government; to the professions; to department stores, banks, transportation companies and retailers; to educational institutions, hospitals and other organizations in the fields of public health, welfare and safety; and to the general public; virtually all of the collected useful intelligence available, through locally-, regionally- and nationally-linked systems of computers. Just as an electrical energy system distributes power, this new information utility will enable subscribers to obtain, economically, efficiently, immediately, the required information flow to facilitate the conduct of business, personal and other affairs.

Dramatically distinct from later vendors of cloud computing services, Western Union placed its proposed business squarely within the public utility framework. It emphasized that there existed no insurmountable technical obstacles to reinventing itself as a nationwide information utility, even in respect to "storage and retrieval techniques"—as the founders of Google more than three decades later might have been surprised to learn. Owing to experience gained by providing for the Department of Defense "the largest and by far the most sophisticated data system in the world," and through its ability to leverage an existing network of thousands of telegraph stations, Western Union proposed to ally with independent local telephone companies to establish "Department Stores of Service." This metaphor too is striking testimony to what we have seen was a swelling consumerism within public utility telecommunications: Western Union was bidding to market a miscellany of for-profit services to consumers within its "information utility." Familiar economies of scale would, it suggested, exert a primordial force: "The cardinal economic principle at issue here is that an information utility serving a large number of users can provide service to each more economically than he can provide it for himself, just as a power system can provide energy to its customers at lower cost than they, individually, can generate it for themselves." The carrier fantasize that, in consequence, Western Union, the "data company," might someday come to rival AT&T the "voice company."[12]

This outline placed Western Union within a ferment of contemporary thinking about computer networks and information utilities. Indeed, for a few years during the 1960s such conceptions helped organize more general terms of debate over telecommunications system development. This largely forgotten episode offers lessons about the ascent of business users within the concurrent process of computerization.[13]

Some agreed with Western Union that the computer utility would emerge as a centralized service; but just how encompassing might its scope become? Under whose auspices, and according to which principles, would it operate? Might the supply of computers, terminals, and software alike be vested in subsidiary units of a vertically integrated information utility—a model based on AT&T's (and Western Union's projected plan)? As Martin Greenberger wrote in 1964, "interesting uncertainty" was being raised about how "the dream of large utilities built around the service of computing systems . . . will materialize." "Perhaps the most important question of all," he underlined, "concerns the legal matter of government regulation. Will the information utility be a public utility, or will it be privately owned and operated? Will some large companies have their own information utilities, just as some companies today have their own generating plants?"[14]

While some thought that the information utility market might be contoured around suppliers based in the computer- and telecommunications industries, Greenberger, a professor at MIT, perceived that market entry might be thrown open on both the supply and demand sides: "Whichever way the balance tips, it is clear that information utilities will be enterprises of considerable size . . . Logical candidates among existing companies include not only the large communication and computer enterprises, but also the big computer users." He enumerated, with considerable prescience, some of the applications that might take hold in this emerging sphere of profitmaking, recognizing that the development of an information utility meant that "an increasing percentage of the day-to-day functioning of man, the economy, and society will become documented and mechanically recorded in easily accessible form," and that in turn this would allow "data studies" of innumerable sorts to be fed back into "decision mechanisms that regulate the economy and the activity of companies." This portent of what two later writers would call a "cybernetic capitalism" in turn became a steppingstone to a fantasy of administrative control proffered by an emergent post-industrial theory: "With the information utility keeping a vastly expanded and mechanized Federal Reserve type of scrutiny and control over the flow of credit and the operation of markets, the United States could be within an arm's length of stabilizing the behavior of its economy, an elusive goal that is almost as old as the economy itself."[15]

Greenberger's thinking situated him within a wider management and engineering discourse, where virtually all commentators agreed that there were two chief issues. Was the computer utility to be incarnated as a single gigantic supplier; or—as a 1966 report by the American Management Association discerned—was it instead a "generic term which describes a whole spectrum of computer-oriented facilities which offer various services appropriate to a variety of dissimilar user requirements"? "In addition to the general-purpose public form," another analyst agreed, "there are countless other possible shapes that a computer utility might take," involving special- and multiple-purpose applications. Was the "ultimate environment of computer utility services" to evolve, then, "as a regulated or a competitive industry"?[16]

Exactly where it intersected with concepts of market competition, meanwhile, the information utility idea became tied both to corporate networks and to reviving precepts of antimonopoly. "The traditional lines separating data processing and communications have been softened by the emergence of a new industry which, for lack of precise description, is known as the data, computer or information utility," wrote the economist Manley R. Irwin in 1967:

> Within the decade, electronic data centers will provide computational power to the general public in a way somewhat analogous to today's distribution of electricity. Computer systems will blanket the United States, establishing an informational grid to permit the mass storage, processing, and consumption of a variety of data services: computer-aided instruction, medical information, marketing research, stock market information, airline and hotel reservations, banking by phone—to mention only a few. Many of these services already exist in embryonic form; and their growth prospects have received enormous impetus from recent developments in computer technology known as time-sharing or multiple access computer systems.

Irwin aptly asserted that "The growth of data processing has subjected both the restrictive practices and the technology of the communications industry to pressures that literally have no precedent." He concluded his scrutiny of policy options by hinting that "a government data processing network may cease to be an unthinkable alternative."[17]

That an expert could mention government ownership as a possibility in 1967 shows how much openness—or delusion—then existed. By 1966, suppliers of specialized data-processing services, led by banks, which were often built on IBM computers, numbered between 800 and 900. As *Fortune* magazine added computer companies to its annual list of the 500 largest US industrial corporations, demand grew among corporate computer customers to modify telephone and telegraph circuits so as to enable software programs to be shared—in part, to relieve shortages of skilled programmers. Networking issues in turn came to constitute common ground for a rapidly widening class of business as well as government computer users. The technical standards, interconnection capabilities, performance features, and costs of networks were becoming primary problems not only for specialized and secret military systems, that is, but for corporate telecommunications users. As this transpired, policymakers were advised to take note.[18]

To grasp these issues more fully, we may turn to the demand side of the emergent digital networking industry. Recall that the beneficiaries of the 1956 government restraints on AT&T spanned beyond other emerging network equipment vendors—beyond the computer industry. Networking gripped the political economy of US capitalism overall, not solely the supply side. Historians have devoted less scrutiny to the metamorphosis occurring on the demand side, as networks were enhanced or freshly built out by corporations and government agencies anchored in retailing, finance, manufacturing, aerospace, and oil and gas.

Large companies actually had long since begun to integrate prior modes of telecommunications into business processes, as we have seen in previous chapters. During the late 1920s, industry groups drawn from a great variety of large businesses, from movie studios and newspapers to department stores and forest products companies, had successfully pressed the newly founded Federal Radio Commission to allocate radio frequencies for a raft of specialized industrial uses. Infrastructural industries in transportation and energy were especially important nodes of reorganization. Commercial airline service was predicated, for example, on entailments by two federal agencies. Funding and planning by Secretary Herbert Hoover's Department of Commerce during the 1920s sustained the innovation of radio-based means for coordinating communications, navigation, and weather data on behalf of aspiring commercial airlines. Then, in 1929, developing directly out of a proposal by the Aeronautical Chamber of Commerce, a body named Aeronautical Radio, Inc. [ARINC] was established as a private company, to manage radio frequencies assigned for aviation communications by the Federal Radio Commission—which likewise lent support to this endeavor.[19]

The pan-industrial assimilation of radio slowed with the economic collapse of the 1930s; however, after World War II, it came rushing back. Federal authorities proved willing to vest responsibilities for specialized radio spectrum management in trade associations. In 1948–1949, the American Petroleum Institute and a sister organization, the United Telecom Council, were empowered to act as national representatives on communications matters for different wings of the energy industry; the radio spectrum placed at the disposal of API members by the FCC allowed them to pioneer a deployment of newly innovated industrial microwave facilities. Telegraphy and Telephony with Railroad Applications, a volume consisting of 465 pages and 35 chapters, had been published in 1924; in the decades after this, radio technology was integrated into railroading under the aegis of another trade group, the Association of American Railroads. Financial and insurance companies had been extensive users of electromechanical information processing machines going back to the nineteenth century; throughout the postwar years their investments in ICTs increased prodigiously. Still little-noticed in this context is the American Bankers Association, whose lobbying would help reshape telecommunications policy during the 1960s and 1970s.[20]

As these and other businesses expanded and modernized during the "golden age" that followed World War II; as they became far-flung multiunit enterprises taking advantage of specialized production, distribution and sales efficiencies nationwide; and as they integrated forward and backward into related product markets—their reliance on networks expanded and altered. As I documented in earlier research, major users of telecommunications, from Exxon to Citicorp to Sears, and from the Insurance Company of North America to General Motors, worked with specialized suppliers to introduce digital systems across a plethora of industrial settings. James Cortada has detailed these demand-side manifestations, tracing their uneven diffusion and concluding that digital systems "became a highly visible technology apparent in all major sectors of the American economy." Payroll and benefits, inventory, R&D, transaction, administration, and many other functions were supported increasingly by specialized computer networks. Rather than satiating the need, the trend to smaller, decentralized units of computing power, which grew sharply after Digital Equipment introduced a line of minicomputers in the early 1960s and again after desktops appeared in the 1980s, heightened corporate demand for such networks—to effectuate what began to be called "distributed data processing." Both in coordinating dispersed corporate operations and generating a welter of applications to cut costs and/or develop profitable new markets, digital network systems became an essential business infrastructure starting in the 1950s and 1960s. Corporate telecommunications users, barred from attaching computers to the public network operated by AT&T, often relied on privately leased telecommunications systems; now they began to demand access to something more expansive, beyond the voice-oriented public network—on which they still also depended. As a need for networking tools became generalized, how were they to be supplied?[21]

For its part, AT&T was obliged to operate solely within the lucrative and hugely growing realm of regulated telecommunications. To modernize and expand its telephone plant, AT&T spent nearly $5.5 billion in the first five postwar years, and through much of the 1950s it spent upward of $2 billion each year. Forecasting a "big future" for a new data offering within this context, the giant carrier publicized its "Dataphone service" in its annual report for 1957. The Dataphone would transmit data over ordinary telephone lines by converting it into analog tones; and it was pitched to commercial customers as advantageous for its tenfold speed advantage over teletypewriter service. However, although "future growth is expected to be explosive" according to a government report of 1964, data service still accounted for a mere 1 percent of telephone industry operating revenues. The next year AT&T's "Data Communications Planning Section" published a college textbook on the subject. "Because of the growing use" of data communications, this text explained, "many of the nation's business concerns are training their people in this field." AT&T was by no means oblivious; but it was making out exceptionally well serving the regulated voice market, and data communications revenue remained a tiny fraction of its swelling total. AT&T thus endeavored to integrate data transmission as an evolutionary adjunct of its encompassing, technologically advanced voice network.[22]

Disagreements began to pile up over the uses to which AT&T's public network might be put, over how—and how fast—it might be technically upgraded for data transmission, and over whether a single supplier of general-purpose data networking capabilities would be optimal. Related controversies broke out over would bear the cost of this far-reaching modernization project; how to implement the special-purpose equipment and services that business users were demanding; and at what price data services would be provided. Consensus over system development policy became increasingly elusive and, by the mid-1960s, it was under intensifying strain. We will see that a spiral of policy conflicts ensued, in which AT&T was pitted against both its biggest customers and their allies, purveyors of new digital systems and services.[23]

Businesses generated the lion's share of the carriers' long-distance revenues, and a small group of the largest users accounted for most of this total. As late as 1980, 25 percent of residential customers used no interstate toll, while another 50 percent made only one to three such calls each month. Nearly 40 percent of all residence customers generated interstate toll billings of less than one dollar per month. On the other hand, 10 percent of business customers generated 90 percent of all business long distance revenues, inclusive of outward (WATS) and inward 800 service. A mere 1 percent of business customers generated 60 percent of business long distance (again inclusive of WATS/800 service) revenues. This skewed concentration of demand lent weight to the preferences of business users; their policymaking power was augmented, as they organized into a pressure group. The International Communications Association had formed in 1948, to advance the interests of several hundreds of the largest business users and the American Petroleum Institute had created a "Central Committee on Radio Facilities." Other business user advocacy groups also were established. For AT&T not to foreground the preferences of this elite group of customers, it would seem, would be tantamount to indulging a death-wish.

However, from the later 1950s on, big business users began to insist on changes that were no longer feasible to accommodate within AT&T's integrated network. Their opposition to the *status quo* was becoming elemental; for the first time, it began to place them in a zero-sum game with the existing system. As one corporate trade group put it in 1957, its members wanted "the same latitude in the use and implementation of our communications facilities that we enjoy in the use and implementation of the many thousands of other tools, facilities and services necessary to the conduct of our business." This candor was rash, in that AT&T could not oblige such a demand without tearing into the foundations of the public telecommunications infrastructure. Why should it do so, when its existing market was hugely profitable and the immeasurably valuable and popular service it provided to households continued to be built up under government protection? A protracted collision ensued, as big business customers acted to translate into policy their goals of instituting purpose-built networks and preferential treatment. Amid this structural conflict over system development, deepening cracks appeared in the ideological consensus that had sustained the public utility framework.[24]

Ideological Dissensus

AT&T had lobbied legislators to halt the New Deal FCC's Telephone Investigation, and they had pressured the agency to drop it. This was because the FCC's assertive regulation confirmed for many legislators that the central state was all too likely to transgress on ingrained power prerogatives—for Republicans, those enjoyed by business interests and, of outstanding concern for Southern Democrats, those of white supremacists. The investigation once terminated, the New Deal's commitment to stimulating mass consumption turned out to be spectacularly lucrative for the telephone company, as AT&T adapted to the new interjurisdictional ratemaking process. During the 1950s, the workaday practices of public utility regulation expanded residential access each year, while the FCC's moment of bold activism turned into a fading memory.

Exposure of the FCC's participation in the shenanigans that attended the 1949 antitrust suit against AT&T thereupon undercut the agency's probity. Congressional oversight of antitrust issues and corporate mergers had been regularly exercised since 1955, under the watchful eye of House Judiciary Committee Chairman Emanuel Celler. The Brooklyn Democrat convened hearings in 1958 which focused on the AT&T-Justice Department consent decree. These brought AT&T's relationships with its supposed regulators into glaring relief. Just thirty-two fulltime FCC employees oversaw a multibillion dollar telephone industry—a herculean task. However, Celler's hearings revealed that the agency had been not merely resource-poor but also complicit in its presettlement dealings with the telephone company. Chairing the FCC between 1954 and 1957 was Republican George McConnaughey, a "telephone man," who had come to the agency from

Ohio Bell. Under his watch, entirely inappropriately, FCC officials had met with AT&T representatives to discuss the antitrust case, and in doing so, they had tarnished not only their own independence but the judgment's face validity. As Congressman Celler acerbically phrased things, the Justice Department and the FCC together counted as AT&T's "ace in the hole and . . . trump suit up the sleeve."[25]

As these improprieties surfaced, public utility regulation faced new waves of skepticism at both poles. That is, both AT&T's monopoly power and the apparent futility of vesting authority in the Federal Communications Commission drew fire. One highly cited research article of 1962 theorized that regulation itself engendered incentives for regulated monopolies to overinvest in order to increase their profits. Others became enamored of policies with which to tame AT&T's corporate power by questioning the engraved idea that telecommunications constituted a "natural monopoly." They wondered whether it might be feasible to introduce competition into some telecommunications markets. The focus was shifting, in short, toward how to reform a public utility model that continued to permit one corporation to dominate existing and—of increasingly pressing concern—future US telecommunications. To trace the winding course of postwar system development requires that we examine how these responses arose and where they led.[26]

The charge that state regulatory commissions were actually catspaws of the Bell telephone interests had arisen in the early twentieth century alongside administrative regulation itself—chiefly, we saw, as a goad used by reformers to mobilize support for postalization. That Bell indeed was adroit at manipulating state regulation helped prompt the New Deal reforms which encouraged, for a few years, a robustly independent FCC—and which appeared to show that a more assertive and successful mode of regulation indeed was feasible. It was not long, however, before the same forces which had preempted effective local and state regulation made themselves felt at the federal level. Lee Pressman, who had worked for the Agricultural Assistance Administration and who would go on to become the CIO's general counsel, was much impressed by the English Marxist John Strachey's assessment of the early New Deal and, especially, by Strachey's argument that "it would be captured by the forces that it intended to control." Scarcely had the FCC backed off from its 1930s activism, when a well-reasoned critique of regulation's failings achieved renown within the specialized discourse of economics. For the next generation its author, Horace M. Gray, a professor at the University of Illinois, remained a bastion of what might be termed the New Deal conscience in telecommunications. As the postwar decades wore on, however, it became evident that analysis of regulation was being regeared. Now grounded in academic research into the behavior of federal and state regulatory agencies, the critique of regulation had slipped away from the needs and demands of workers and unions. It made no room for the nineteenth and early twentieth century reform movements' overarching concern to end exploitative social class relations and class control over the state. Instead it foregrounded monopoly power over pliable state agencies and, through this means, over citizens.[27]

Frustration over the 1956 AT&T consent decree again sharpened the question of effective regulation and—significantly—it remained a political issue. Among liberal Democrats, even as residential service was becoming nearly inclusive, many now thought that public utility regulation had accomplished too little, too late; even, that it had been taken captive by the industry it purported to oversee. "[S]ome eight million low income households ... remain without local telephone service," charged the economist Richard Gabel in 1967; "in this segment of the economy, price is apparently a principal deterrent to exchange service development." That this was to some extent a racialized and ethnic divide, and that the finding appeared while the civil rights movement was at its peak, raised the issue of discrimination in residential telephone service provision. In January 1968, *The New York Times* ran an article recapping a report in the *Southern Courier*, a Civil Rights publication based in Montgomery. The story concerned a rural Alabama community populated overwhelmingly by Black residents, who were said to be "unhappy" that Southern Bell offered them no telephone service. The company countered that economic considerations alone were responsible, but that eventually telephone service could be counted on to reach the 210-odd residents of the town, Bogue Chitto. Mrs. Willie I. Pugh retorted that she had pursued a ten-year effort to get a phone, and that "Right down the road here ... there's a lady between two white folks' houses. They both got phones, and we can't even get a phone." *The Times*' reporter also quoted Charles Pettis, a small business owner: "The TV comes on and talks about getting different phones in each room, different colors and all that. We can't even get one in our community." Such testimonies stoked some white liberal Democrats' resolve to improve the public utility framework and the role of regulation within it.[28]

Liberals' concerns about regulation and their burgeoning unhappiness with the public utility model itself meshed with sentiments that were being seeded on the Republican right. Recent scholars have done much to reveal how, funded by wealthy backers, during the late 1940s and 1950s political and economic doctrines that had been discredited during the Depression resurged. This campaign was initiated and carried forward by an unlikely bloc of multimillionaires and corporate executives, politicians, think-tank staffers, press magnates, white suburbanites, free-market economists, individualist ideologues, and hangers-on. Its ingredients were disparate: Anticommunism, religion-fueled rearticulations of "traditional" racial and gender inequality, white supremacist fury at the civil rights movement, reassertions of self-interested corporate power, and sheer social class entitlement. One ingredient of this mélange was an economic theory whose conceit was to unmask the flaws and delusions of the Keynesianism on which New Deal economic policy came to be based. Though it possessed earlier intellectual roots, this theory came to be totemically associated with the prolific writings of Milton Friedman of the University of Chicago, a politically engaged fighter for market supremacy whose book, *Capitalism and Freedom*, appeared in 1962. Throughout succeeding decades, supported by and supportive of right-wing politicians and business leaders, Friedman's thinking ascended to international stature. The movement for telecommunications liberalization would come to draw on his market fundamentalism, which expressly targeted both the Post Office and government regulation of the telephone monopoly. Ideological dissatisfactions with public utility regulation in turn also possessed bivalent political sources.[29]

However, during the mid-1960s—the years of the Lyndon Johnson presidency—it was liberal Democrats rather than either stand-pat or free-market Republicans who led in the adoption of these ideas. Battling against regulatory capture from within and from outside official Washington, some of these activists—FCC Commissioner Nicholas Johnson was one vital figure—allied with the integrationist civil rights movement, which we saw was concurrently striving to rejuvenate the public utility model itself. The result was a composite, combining concrete struggles for social justice across the broad reach of US communications, notably through equal employment opportunity, with efforts to reduce AT&T's power by introducing limited economic competition into specific telecommunications markets.[30]

In 1968, the Democratic political coalition that had uncomfortably housed this endeavor fell apart. His hopes of building a "Great Society" devastated by his war on Vietnam, Democratic President Johnson announced that he would not seek re-election in March. The civil rights movement, riven by the departure of its Black Power advocates from its integrationist wing, lost considerable support from white voters—as a furious political reaction to Black equality built around the overtly racist Alabama Democrat George Wallace and the always-opportunistic Republican, Richard Nixon. Even prior to the Nixon victory, the public utility framework began to strain. Both monopoly *and* regulation became targets.

On one side, many liberal Democrats were committing themselves to building new agencies to oversee public utility regulators themselves. "The government's cure may unwittingly be worse than the disease, as is characteristic of so many New Deal and present regulatory measures," argued a well-informed analyst of AT&T in *The Monopoly Makers*, a 1973 Nader Report on regulation and competition whose title itself was emblematic. "The independent regulatory commissions," wrote economist Walter Adams in a venue set up by Nader, "have proved to be [a] near-disaster." On the other side, at least some Republicans concurred. Andrew Hacker, who in 1973 had the strength of principle to confess before a Nader group that he was a registered Republican "who has voted for Richard Milhous Nixon four times," agreed with these critics of corporate power that "[r]egulatory bureaus ... have seen themselves as handmaidens of private industry."[31]

This overlap did not testify to a unity of purpose. Nader evinced a principled opposition to the buildup of corporate power. He followed in the tradition of antitrust law that Thurman Arnold had engraved at the Justice Department during the late 1930s and early 1940s and that big businesses had fought from then on. Yet Nader's charge that regulation contributed substantially to corporate malfeasance and monopoly power, was now helping to effect a political convergence with Republican thinking, which had never been comfortable with government regulatory oversight of the corporate marketplace.

Even before the reigning Keynesianism caved in during the economic crisis of 1974, the project of attacking the public utility model was drawing bipartisan support. Many conferees at a meeting of economist and lawyers convened by the Brookings Institution in 1971 noted "the strong, persistent criticism of regulation during the past fifteen years." Soon afterward, the institutional economist Harry Trebing elaborated: "in the years since World War II, regulation has lost much of its legitimacy. Criticism has come from a number of sources, including political scientists, practitioners, popular reformers, consumer advocates, administrative lawyers, former regulators, and economists. Regulation is accused of being a captive of the regulated, of having a perverse effect on efficiency, of failing to protect the consumer ... From the standpoint of its critics, regulation now has become the villain, and the regulated firm often appears as simply a passive participant reacting to faulty signals." This two-flanked attack found a pivot in an economic discourse that was animated not only by right-wingers such as Milton Friedman, but also by liberals like Alfred Kahn, whom the American Antitrust Institute later celebrated for acting as Democratic President Jimmy Carter's "field general for deregulation." The discrediting of public utility regulation quickly became one site in a wider elite effort to curb the "excesses of democracy"—as a proponent put it a few years later.[32]

Economists were making careers by charging that the incentives incarnated in regulatory practice engendered distortions in the regulated companies' behavior, and that this in turn induced inefficient outcomes. Thus germinated a curious and potent hybrid. Its bywords were "competition" and "deregulation"; and these were not synonyms. Reformers targeted something in addition to AT&T's market monopoly, something, indeed, beyond any market structure: namely, the political settlement within which telecommunications service provision was encased. During the years of the first Nixon administration (1969–1973) they came to cast regulation as a core problem; and they aimed to erode and, if possible, to topple, *both* the corporate monopoly provider and its public utility casement. When compared to the radical and wide-ranging social and political criticisms associated with the term "monopoly" by late nineteenth century reformers, the public utility conception of the mid-twentieth century was, admittedly, insufficient. It paid far too little attention to the systemic interlocks between telecommunications and the military; telecommunications and consumerism; telecommunications and racism; telecommunications and social needs beyond those of business—above all, those of telecommunications workers. However, and this was crucial, the public utility framework remained historically elastic. This was the reason that, during the late 1960s and early 1970s, mobilized social justice activists had been able to make room within it for equal employment opportunity. What space would remain open in official Washington in which to cultivate a relatively independent politics of network development, when liberal-left reformers were jostling elbows with free-market Republicans?

*

Serious and heavily publicized service failures were, at this juncture, afflicting the nation's electronic telecommunications, and these factored into the changing ideological milieu. A benchmark came when a power blackout in November 1965 left 25 million people spread across nine Northeastern US states and two Canadian provinces without electricity: this outage did *not* cause telephone service to fail, despite that calling volumes peaked in the nation's largest urban telephone market at this same moment. The exemplary performance of the Bell System affiliate, New York Telephone, was publicly hailed.[33]

Just four years later, by contrast, telephone service failures confronted the Bell System with what a historian called "its worst operational crisis since . . . the beginning of the century." The 1969–1970 breakdown was both sudden and stubbornly persistent. In the AT&T network's foremost node, New York City, lengthening waits for dial tones, false busy signals and rings, dead circuits, call failures, cross talk, and incorrect bills all "became common." In July 1969, a Brooklyn customer received forty-six telephone calls, dialed from all over the nation, that were intended for an Army base. After a local walkout by unionized telephone workers compounded the difficulty, *The New York Times* editorialized that the city's telephone service "is getting to resemble that of prewar Paris." "Week in and week out," recalled a chagrined AT&T executive, "the nation listened to New York's telephone troubles as recounted by network news broadcasters. More telling were the jibes at telephone service—and telephone people—by radio and TV entertainers. In a few short months what had been one of the nation's most admired institutions became a laughing stock."[34]

"The situation came to a dramatic climax in July 1969," Brooks relates—six months after Nixon's inauguration—"with the almost total failure of PLaza 8, a key exchange in the heart of the city's commercial district." The crisis then at last receded, after the Bell System threw unprecedented resources—both capital and labor—into repairs: between 1969 and 1972 "the physical plant in New York City was virtually rebuilt." Meanwhile, however, comparable service problems overtook other major cities: Atlanta, Boston, Chicago, Denver, Houston, Los Angeles, Miami, and Washington. The Public Service Commission of New Jersey served notice that it might revoke the franchise of New Jersey Telephone, a non-Bell system carrier, if it did not improve things within six months.[35]

The service problems reflected a range of factors. During this era of mounting Vietnam-war era inflation company pressure for rate increases intensified, and state regulators sometimes turned back these requests. An organized opposition emerged against Bell's rate increase requests; opponents linked overcharges to Bell's monopoly control over network equipment supply. AT&T in turn responded that its mammoth capital spending and -network maintenance projects were not being funded adequately. Employees, protesting corporate negligence, charged that New York Telephone had "deliberately maintained an under-manning program," and that their overtime requests were being denied while calling volumes grew. The turnover rate for operators at New York Telephone hit an astonishing 59 percent per year, while more than one-third of the company's craft workers possessed less than five years of experience in 1969. Contrary to telephone company forecasts, there was also a sudden spike in demand for telephone service. During 1969, New York Telephone installed 19,000 telephones each month, compared to 15,000 each month during the previous year. Disparate factors contributed to this surge. After welfare authorities determined in 1968 that the cost of local telephone service could be added to welfare payments, requests for telephone installations multiplied, and there were concomitant increases in calling volumes: to 48 million per day in 1969, up more than 20 percent (or 10 million calls daily) from the average in 1967. Calls placed between subscribers in two poor neighborhoods, Brooklyn's Bedford-Stuyvesant district and Manhattan's East Harlem, sometimes could not be completed owing to blocked lines, and these were then automatically rerouted through other offices—adding stress. During the same year, as Wall Street concluded that back-office processing problems could benefit from further computerization, trading volume on the New York Stock Exchange rocketed: "Since each trade almost certainly involved at least one telephone call and some involved many, the effect on demand for service in the Wall Street district was enormous." A New York Telephone spokesman stated that calling volume was growing five times faster in the financial district than anywhere else in New York City. AT&T's longtime boast—that the United States enjoyed the world's best telephone network—now rang hollow.[36]

It did not help that the company's image was being wrested away from its enormous public relations unit and reappropriated. In the San Francisco Bay area, "The People's Yellow Pages Collective," a group of five women, issued their first "directory of alternatives" in 1971 and, responding to "tremendous interest," published a second issue the next year. Their "People's Yellow Pages" selected for inclusion goods and services "that seem to affirm the dignity of the individual and disavow exploitation." Alongside more innocuous and everyday entries, many coming out of the era's counterculture, its table of contents carried listings for "Abortion," "Black Liberation," "Food Stamps," "Gay Liberation," "Labor," "Libraries," "Native Americans," "Pre-Natal Care," "Political Action," "Senior Citizens," "Tax Resistance," "Unemployment Insurance," and "Unwed Mothers."[37]

Other rearticulations surfaced in high-profile commercial culture. In the 1967 film "The President's Analyst," written and directed by Theodore J. Flicker, actor James Coburn was caught up in a comic conspiracy that wound back not to a meddlesome "Federal Bureau of Regulation," a "Central Enquiries Agency," and "The Telephone Company"—an organization by turns ludicrous and insidious, whose goal was to garner presidential support for a "Cerebrum Communicator" that would require every human being to be equipped with a number and a prenatal implant. (Today this may seem less like science fiction than prescience.) On network television, Lily Tomlin's brilliant caricature of a telephone operator named "Ernestine" for Rowan and Martin's "Laugh-In," came amid the New York City service problems. Commencing in February 1970 and continuing through half a dozen episodes, Tomlin drew on popular antipathy to AT&T and, more specifically, on a stand-up sketch introduced by Elaine May and Mike Nichols a decade earlier. But if Ernestine seethed with a nastily bureaucratic corporate indifference, she also displaced both the human sympathies carried by actual telephone operators and the unruly rank-and-file protests against their employer in which many operators were participating. The Bell System became, in the person of Ernestine, by turns implacable and impervious. Worst of all, from AT&T's standpoint, it was reduced to being the butt of jokes.

By the end of the 1960s, in other words, an ideological tissue extending from formal criticisms in economics and regulation to antagonistic figurations in popular culture wrapped around the public utility model in telecommunications—and AT&T in particular. How then did structural change and ideological dissensus come to bear on practical politics, especially when, from the point of view of most residential telephone users, public utility provision had been a ringing (if belated) success?[38]

Early Policy Changes and the President's Task Force on Communications Policy

Revisions to regulatory policy commenced as far back as 1956–1959 when, pressured by the Justice Department, the FCC roused itself to authorize industrial microwave radio systems. Though it carefully limited the deployment of these new systems, the FCC granted to big businesses access to a capacious new transmission technology. Hereafter, big companies spread across virtually all economic sectors could—and did—purchase specialized equipment to set up their own point-to-point proprietary microwave networks, which the FCC grouped within its "Industrial Radio Services." Moreover, the FCC intended that its ruling should contribute as well to the growth of an independent (non-Bell) industry of equipment supply. Finally, after AT&T tried to counter the microwave threat by introducing a heavily discounted private-line offering called TELPAK—which aimed to divert high-volume customers from building their own private microwave systems—the FCC criticized TELPAK for being priced at less than a compensatory rate of return, and eventually ruled that TELPAK itself was discriminatory. By 1965, it was already feasible for an academic specialist in the economics of networks to conclude that "a reading of recent decisions reveals that the Commission has attempted somewhat cautiously to sponsor more diversity in long-distance communication."[39]

The existing structure of telecommunications was being altered, at AT&T's expense and, now, under Democratic auspices. Perhaps the foremost example was an initiative originating in negotiations between Congress and the Executive Branch: the Communications Satellite Act of 1962. This legislation aimed to shepherd into existence not only a domestic but an international satellite communications service. The bill sparked a bruising battle in Congress. Liberals and radicals, supported by Assistant Attorney General Lee Loevinger, demanded to place the nascent satellite service in the federal government—to nationalize it. Representative Lester R. Johnson (a Wisconsin Democrat) charged on the floor of the House that "turning over the government developed space communication system to any private corporation would represent an unprecedented giveaway; every private scheme which has been proposed would lead to domination by A.T. and T. an industrial monopoly anyway." This proposal was batted aside, as the Kennedy Administration ordained that the system should be privately owned. AT&T and three other international carriers thereupon partially co-opted the venture, acquiring a joint 50 percent ownership stake in the new organization, known as Comsat, in order to prevent the formation of a full-on satellite competitor against their existing wire-line and submarine cable systems. Critics attributed the carriers' 50 percent ownership role to a toxic exercise of corporate and military power over the state.[40]

Nevertheless, the strength of the opposition to a flat-out takeover of satellite technology by AT&T and lesser private carriers had caused Comsat to be created as a government corporation, with a couple of presidentially appointed board members and a close relation to military and intelligence agencies. AT&T's executives were chagrined that, despite having pioneered the technology via their Telstar satellite, which had transmitted its first voice phone call in 1962, AT&T was denied the opportunity to implement satellite services on an exclusive basis—and was restricted to a minority ownership role in the venture. Thus, a second hole was torn in AT&T's monopoly, in addition to the one that had opened around private microwave systems. "The establishment of the Communications Satellite Corporation," an internal Western Union management memo recognized in 1965, "is the most recent and effective evidence of the deep concern felt by government generally as to the dangers inherent in further and enlarged expansions of the functions and powers of the Bell System:

> There can be no question from the Telstar experience that AT&T had the technical capabilities to do the job, from the ground station up. But, nevertheless, there was a quite well-understood, and frequently voiced general apprehension as to placing one more large sector of the nation's economy and future in the hands of the world's largest corporation.

Still another regulatory hedge against AT&T was laid around a different transmission technology, this one adapted for long distance telephone signal carriage and for the residential television market: coaxial cable. The predominant view, as Ralph Lee Smith explained in 1970, and David Miller detailed in 1976, has been that, for some decades after the innovation of "community antenna television" in the late 1940s—later simply called "cable" or CATV television—FCC policy was shaped by its concern to protect over-the-air commercial broadcasters. Out of deference to powerful broadcast networks and station groups, this argument goes, the FCC deliberately inhibited the growth of cable-based television program distribution in major urban markets. A majority on the Commission held in 1966, in one characterization, "that unless it could be assured that cable would not compete with broadcast television, it would strictly control CATV to prevent any harm to the broadcasting service."[41]

Though the FCC's solicitousness toward the broadcast industry is not in question, it should not be taken as a desideratum. The agency's rulemaking on telephone companies incursions into cable television were at least as telling, for the FCC intervened expressly to prevent AT&T from dominating the fledgling cable television market. Miller goes as far as to claim that "the FCC has been the protector of cable television": "Were it not for the FCC, cable television now would probably be owned by the telephone companies." Although AT&T

had developed coaxial cable technology for its long distance network, the 1956 Consent decree barred AT&T from the market for television distribution to consumers, and prohibited what were still mostly small local cable systems from making use of its telephone poles, conduits, and easements. AT&T had evaded this stipulation, however, by offering to install, service, and lease turnkey systems to would-be cable TV system operators. Though cable companies protested that the financial terms AT&T was offering were "prohibitive," by mid-1965, Bell System companies had filed tariffs to furnish CATV service in twenty-six states. A veteran CATV operator declared that same year, "This telephone company activity is the most serious threat that has arisen to CATV."[42]

With support from staffers, Federal Communications Commissioner Lee Loevinger (who as head of the Justice Department's antitrust division had participated in the fight over Comsat) sought in late 1965 and 1966 to restrain AT&T in cable television markets. The Commission preempted state PUC jurisdiction over interstate telephone companies' proposed leaseback cable television systems; and then issued a cease-and-desist order to bar telephone company-originated television system-building. Additional restrictions followed. To protect independent cable television systems, the agency escalated its contest with the telephone company in an array of proceedings between 1966 and 1970.[43]

The private microwave, cable, and satellite sagas make clear that, by the mid-1960s, Democratic administrations were restricting expansion of the AT&T monopoly into new telecommunications technologies and markets, just as the 1956 consent decree had ordained. As well, there were striking indications of a new regulatory assertiveness. In October 1965, the FCC announced a major investigation of AT&T's interstate rates and integrated structure, the first since the Telephone Investigation. The next year, the agency commenced on a proceeding that carried potentially earthshaking consequences for AT&T's monopoly: "the most important one the Commission has ever embarked upon," declared the chief of its Common Carrier Bureau. Setting out to study the "interdependence" of computers and communications and, in particular, whether unregulated computer services might be provided by independent (non-AT&T), organizations, the FCC was signaling its "affirmative duty to insure a full measure of responsiveness by the common carrier industry to the communications needs of . . . the computer industry and its customers." A second proceeding of 1966 underlined the same point. The FCC began to deliberate on whether it should authorize the attachment of independently furnished customer equipment, notably, computers, to AT&T's network. Such an authorization would constitute a historic policy departure: regulators had continued to authorize AT&T's possession of comprehensive end-to-end control over its network for decades, meaning that only AT&T-supplied equipment could be used. Finally, also in 1966, President Lyndon Johnson nominated and the Senate confirmed the independent-minded Nicholas Johnson as a Democratic Commissioner to the FCC.[44]

The most ambitious and comprehensive Democratic attempt to revamp public utility telecommunications came not from the FCC, however, but through a high-profile Executive Branch undertaking. At the undernourished Federal Communications Commission, regulatory policy was pursued piecemeal, by political appointees and within the constraints of administrative law. The Task Force, by contrast, was wide-angled, drew on a national pool of top-level expertise, and was backed by presidential sanction. Why was it established?[45]

By the mid-1960s, specialized suppliers of new technologies—microwave radio, satellites and, above all, computers—were emerging in symbiosis with surging corporate demand for their products. Banks, oil companies, manufacturers, aerospace and electronics companies, media conglomerates, and chain retailers alike wanted to take greater control over their increasingly diverse and far-flung internal and external communications, and to augment and extend further their uses of networks.

This placed both actual and would-be vendors and corporate network users on a collision course with AT&T. AT&T supplied 80 percent of the country's telephone service, and it was advancing its own claims to all of the new technologies that these industrial allies were clamoring to develop. Corporate users and independent equipment and service suppliers asserted that AT&T stood in the way of a far-reaching demand-side modernization of business operations, one that also would enable them to cultivate new profit centers. They organized to open— that is, to liberalize entry into—what, under the public utility model, had been tightly and often carefully restricted investment, equipment, service, and pricing options in telecommunications.

Political engagement was a necessary corollary, because only through such intervention could the thick web of formal legal rules and restrictions that structured telecommunications markets be pierced. The Democratic FCC had begun to deliberate about liberalizing telecommunications in specific proceedings; but the audacious inquiries it had initiated in 1966 were moving like molasses and, by 1967, it had evidently become plain to top policymakers that the FCC itself was part of the problem. Vastly outmatched by a strongly resistant telephone company, the agency's own make-up and administrative procedures in any case rendered it an unlikely vehicle for a general program of policy change. Commissioners were political appointees mostly lacking expertise and subject to fierce lobbying pressures. Proceedings were discrete and issue-driven; arguably not since the New Deal years had they unfolded as parts of an encompassing strategy. Something had to be done, and the President's Task Force was convened to do it.

Such was the sensitivity of the matter, though, that considerable diplomacy was needed. President Lyndon Johnson's "Special Message to the Congress on Communications Policy" in August 1967 singled out three far-ranging problems: the uses of the electromagnetic spectrum; the organization of the federal government for communications policymaking; and how best to assimilate satellite technology, both internationally and domestically. Though the President accented "our entire international communications posture," he also stated that he was "setting in motion the necessary studies for a better understanding of policy needs in domestic and international communications." Summoning up a Presidential Task Force on Communications Policy, he granted to it authority to "establish working groups of government and non-government experts to study various technical, economic and social questions." This sweeping and open-ended mandate was well-publicized. *The New York Times* reported that the Task Force had been charged with making "a broad study of both domestic and foreign aspects of U.S. communication policy."[46]

Given its intended scope, LBJ's pick to chair the group was well-chosen. Dean of Yale Law School before joining the administration in 1967, Eugene V. Rostow occupied the State Department's number-three post as Undersecretary of State for Political Affairs. An ardent proponent of US world power, Rostow would be preparing himself to overcome opposition to the US-dominated International Telecommunications Satellite (Intelsat) consortium in upcoming negotiations. However, his qualifications in the domestic policymaking sphere were also substantial.

Though he had not focused on telecommunications, Rostow's research had expressed a definite preference for deploying the antitrust laws to induce greater market competition in the organization of US industry, and on grounds that went beyond economic efficiency. In keeping with many New Dealers during and immediately after World War II, Rostow declared in 1948 that "The degree of competition in the organization of industry will have a good deal to do with determining whether we remain a community long capable of social and political democracy." This academic background factored into his selection as chair. He would recall that, when he had been approached by presidential advisors to lead the task force, he had "raised the question whether a State Department official should be Chairman, since it would obviously be necessary to go pretty far into domestic communications policy in order to deal seriously with the questions raised by the document." "The answer," he continued, "was that I had been given the assignment not only as an Undersecretary of State, but in my personal capacity, because of my background as a student of industrial organization. The message, I was told at the time, called for the most fundamental and broad gauged study of communications policy in forty years": "all aspects of the 1934 Communications Act and the 1962 Communications Satellite Act."[47]

Such a charter meant that it would be politic for the Task Force to be broadly representative of the administration. Members were indeed drawn from the upper reaches of fifteen Executive Branch departments and agencies. There was, however, one extraordinary exception: the Post Office Department was excluded. It is remarkable—and indicative of the agency's deepening embroilment—that the government's constitutionally mandated telecommunications operator was accorded no role in what were intended to be fundamental deliberations over the future of the nation's network infrastructure.

The group's otherwise inclusive composition increased the likelihood of contention; it did not guarantee that all voices would be equal. The Defense Department could be expected to throw disproportionate weight, both because of its unmatched budget and its primary role in maintaining US global dominance. The Vice-Chairman of the Task Force, General James D. O'Connell, had led the Army Signal Corps before becoming Director of the recently established Office of Telecommunications Management, which operated the National Communications System used by the Federal Government. Both the Defense Department and the Office of Telecommunications Management were advocates for AT&T.[48]

Backing for liberalization, on the other hand, came both from without and within. In addition to Rostow himself, the Electronics Industries Association flatly told the Task Force that "there is a need for high level Federal Government leadership to open the door for private initiative to explore new adventures in telecommunications." Key Task Force staff members agreed. One was Executive Director Alan R. Novak, from Yale Law School, whose most recent post had been chief of staff for Senator Ted Kennedy; another was an intense graduate of Harvard Law, the FTC and the Justice Department, who would become a famously influential appellate judge—Richard Posner, the Task Force's General Counsel; and, finally, Director of Research Leland Johnson, a prominent telecommunications economist working at the RAND Corporation. Several other individuals who would become important proponents of market liberalization, acted as consultants to the Task Force, notably including William F. Baxter—a Stanford Law Professor who, as Assistant Attorney General in the Reagan Administration fifteen years later, oversaw the break-up of AT&T.[49]

Well aware of the risks of doing so, Rostow permitted the group to consider "emerging policy problems in the field of carrier regulation and television." Inescapably, this brought AT&T into the center of its deliberations. Bearing this in mind, let us turn to consider the hitherto-hidden involvement in the Task Force by a leading communications reformer of the period: FCC Commissioner Nicholas Johnson. Archival records reveal that, through Johnson, the social movement insurgencies of the 1960s actually touched this well-insulated body.

Nicholas Johnson (unrelated to President Lyndon Johnson) assumed his duties at the FCC near the high-water mark of the liberal Democratic coalition, in July of 1966. Unlike most of his peers at the agency, he was youthful, articulate, tenacious, and independent-minded—indeed, critical of engraved power relations. He was already on cordial terms with Eugene Rostow when Rostow arrived in Washington; and the two men lunched together days after the Task Force was formed. Nicholas Johnson confided to Rostow that it was "a relief to know that you will be taking the leadership in pulling us out of the communications morass," and he pledged to cooperate with the incoming Executive Director of the Task Force, Alan R. Novak, "to put together materials" for Rostow. Commissioner Johnson did more, however, than furnish bibliographic support. Early on, he ghost-wrote documents circulated to the Task Force over Rostow's signature; and, throughout the proceeding, he prodded the group from behind-the-scenes.[50]

Commissioner Johnson's views contrasted starkly with those of the then-Chairman of the Federal Communications Commission, Rosel H. Hyde—an *ex officio* member of the Task Force. Indeed, FCC Chair Hyde continually clashed in contests with his junior colleague; and Hyde had sometimes lost. Beginning in 1966, Johnson had fought against the conglomerate ITT's attempt to take over the television network ABC, on grounds that such a cross-media combination would have antidemocratic results. This put him crosswise with Chairman Hyde who, because he had worked at the FCC in different posts ever since its formation in 1934, was closely identified with the agency; and who journalist James Ridgeway called "the voice of ITT" for signing off on its plan to combine with ABC. Ultimately this merger was defeated. The antagonism between Hyde and Johnson sharpened in the broadcast proceeding, already discussed, in which civil rights activists sought formal legal standing before the FCC on behalf of mostly African American radio listeners in Jackson Mississippi so that they could try to strip a racist commercial station of its FCC license to broadcast. Hyde was opposed, Johnson in support. Overturning the FCC's do-nothing decision, in a historic judgment an Appeals court opened communications regulation to general public participation. More generally, the veteran Hyde, put out by Johnson's public charges that the FCC was a hidebound captive to the companies that it purported to regulate, was loath to join Johnson's call to alter the *structure and purpose* of the communications system as a necessary precondition for renewing American democracy. "What are the forces regulating the development and rate of introduction of the new technology?" he asked: "Are they effective in serving interests beyond private economic gain?" Hyde would have flinched at these radical questions, which did not name but nevertheless indicted both AT&T's monopoly and the FCC.[51]

Johnson sounded the alarm that "communications crises" blocked attempts to redress the nation's spiraling social and political problems and, weaving through these, its unbalanced economic relations. To clarify these linkages, Johnson used his FCC commissionership as a platform. Not only in his often dissenting FCC opinions, but also through numerous speeches, articles, news stories, books, and interviews (the most famous appeared in *Rolling Stone* in 1971), Johnson did his best to educate Americans to the problems caused by unaccountable corporate power over communications. This criticism possessed deep historical roots. During the late 1960s, it resurged as a new wave of consolidation crested in the communications industry. Chunks of the recording, film, broadcasting, and newspaper businesses were reassembled into chains and early multimedia conglomerates, while AT&T and other tech companies vied to take over emerging markets in networking. In this context, Commissioner Johnson sounded a tocsin that "communications crises" were endangering American democracy.[52]

He did so by tapping the energies of the Black freedom struggle; of nascent campaigns for media reform; and of Ralph Nader's consumer advocacy: his papers are chockablock with correspondence that attests direct and sustained contacts with each of these sociopolitical movements. As he interacted with diverse activists, Commissioner Johnson drew on their knowledge and experience, as well as his own—and attempted to cut new channels into the official thinking of the Task Force.[53]

Two weeks after the Task Force had been established, Commissioner Johnson sent notes to Rostow, to underline that the group's "purposes-goals-assumptions" should be encompassing: "All social needs/programs (e.g., race relations, poverty, education, transportation, urban planning—also free expression, privacy)" were "interrelated with communications system/uses/policies; [and/or] substantially altered by communications technology revolution." It was, Johnson declared, the "responsibility" of the Task Force "to comprehend implications, [and to] make [sure that these were] publicly understood." Between the group's formation and early 1968, Johnson ghost-wrote a letter for Rostow and criticized draft texts sent to him by Novak: "there is very little emphasis placed on major issues I call "media structure" and "media responsibility." Johnson explained that "By these terms I refer to the problem of who owns the media . . . and how that media is used": "These are issues I think really extremely important—really the basis of a democratic society—and deserve at least some recognition from the Task Force." He continued by saying that "In the enclosed notebook you asked for I have tabbed the ABC-ITT opinions and the speech on racial communications as illustrative of these concerns."[54]

While, channeling civil rights and other social movements, Nicholas Johnson challenged the group to engage the nation's "communications crises," there is no evidence in the archival record that the members of the Task Force truly considered, let alone responded to, his urgings. Clinging to the raft of the executive branch nonetheless did not safeguard them from the rip-tide of 1967-1968. For, exactly as the Task Force was deliberating, the liberal reform coalition that had powered LBJ's initiatives in civil rights, health care, immigration policy, education and environmental protection, was splintering. During 1965-1966 an "increasingly conservative Lyndon Johnson" was opting for guns rather than butter, as he pushed the US to wade ever deeper into the Big Muddy—that is, into the Indochina war. With war-induced inflation eating at incomes and racism tearing at US society, Black Power militants split away from the integrationist wing of the civil rights movement and assailed the administration for its laggardly stance toward racism and poverty. College students were exchanging teach-ins and demonstrations for nonviolent direct action to stop the war. Some major union officials, notably at the United Auto Workers, broke with the Johnson administration over Vietnam. In 1967-1968, Martin Luther King, Jr., spoke movingly in public against the Indochina war, and pressed for a far-reaching domestic social and economic reconstruction. While "mainstream liberalism and movements to its left . . . [had] penetrated one another" within the Democratic coalition, in 1968 this political formation shattered.[55]

Events now moved quickly. In late February 1968, Lyndon Johnson named James H. Rowe, Jr., for thirty years a Washington wire-puller and the manager of LBJ's own 1960 presidential campaign, to head a "Citizens Committee for Johnson and Humphrey" for the upcoming 1968 campaign. Meanwhile, the Tet Offensive had been underway in Vietnam; though it did not succeed militarily, this nationwide uprising exerted a sharp political effect on the churning US scene. Demonstrating that the war probably could not be won, Tet both undercut US elites' support for it and split asunder the Democratic Party. In the early presidential primaries of 1968, antiwar Democratic presidential candidate Eugene McCarthy and, a month later, Robert Kennedy demonstrated that the sitting president's vulnerability was acute. The Alabama segregationist George Wallace, running as an independent, was winning substantial support from both southern whites and northern industrial workers—promising to take votes from whomever became the Democratic candidate. On the last day of March, conceding that "there is division in the American house," the President announced that he would neither "seek nor accept" the Democratic nomination. Martin Luther King, Jr., was assassinated on April 4, and marches, memorials, and rebellions followed in more than one hundred cities. Historians assert that LBJ's presidency "collapsed," and that, by mid-1968, the "formulas of postwar liberalism" had lost their purchase.[56]

Did this profoundly altered political situation impact on the Task Force? Circulated as the end of July, 1968, Richard Posner's draft chapter on the domestic telecommunications industry certainly lit a fuse. The text urged not only competitive market entry into specialized private-line services and terminal equipment and the deregulation of computer communications services, but also divestment by AT&T of its Western Electric manufacturing unit. Reformers had unsuccessfully pressed for such a divestiture for decades; and the proposal remained incendiary. "The same day Posner circulated his paper," Staff Director Alan Novak recollects, "the President of AT&T called the President and he went ballistic."[57]

I was not able to substantiate that this conversation took place; but pressure indeed was applied at the highest level. More than a month before Posner's chapter circulated, in a June 1968 letter that LBJ placed in his confidential file, none other than James Rowe told the President that the Task Force Report "is going to cause a lot of problems a) if the rumors about the report are true and b) if the members of the Task Force follow the recommendations of the staff." Rowe acidly commented that "I am not at all convinced that Yale law professors are the most helpful persons to make policy in this area." In an attached memo he warned that LBJ was likely to face opposition not only from members of Congress, but also from AT&T. "[B]ased on a purely theoretical approach," Rowe finished, "the Staff indicates it is considering recommending a radical restructuring not only of international but also of domestic communications. For example," he wrote, cutting to the chase, "it is reviewing the matter of whether it is appropriate for a common carrier to own a manufacturing organization, a question which clearly addresses itself to the antitrust laws and the Justice Department. It appears that the Staff recommendations would involve proposals for fragmentation of the communications industry which have been carefully studied and rejected in the past."[58]

The President, however, did not bend; he neither quashed nor truncated the Task Force inquiry. By going on in his letter to question whether its mandate actually had extended to the domestic communications industry, Rowe offered the President an expedient way out. Several weeks later, this suggestion resurfaced. Task Force Chair Rostow recollected to LBJ that "We proceeded on . . . track until the late summer of 1968, when, you will recall, the Secretary of Commerce [C.R. Smith] raised with you the question whether the Message of August 14, 1967, authorized the Task Force to go into domestic policy questions at all." The precipitant this time was that the issue of divestiture had burst into public view. At an August 16 White House press briefing, a reporter asked whether the Task Force indeed would propose "that AT&T be required to sell Western Electric"; and the Newark *Star-Ledger* immediately reported that the Task Force's "draft report to the president" contained "recommendations to break up the giant American Telephone & Telegraph Co." The *Star-Ledger* also stated that these proposals had drawn "strong opposition": "a communications union has been the most vocal leader." The story added that CWA President Joseph Beirne "had become aware of the plans six weeks ago" and, "concerned at the effect on his members' jobs," Beirne had thereupon "protested vigorously to various members of the task force and is now planning to take his case to the public."[59]

Perhaps, back in June, Beirne had leaked word of the divestiture "recommendation" to James Rowe. In any case, in CWA files, the *Star-Ledger* story is attached to a reassuring letter from Task Force Chair Eugene Rostow to Beirne, dated the very day of the press conference—August 16, 1968. Also attached, Beirne's own statement held that the news account was "grossly erroneous in substance, in tenor and in detail"; that "there is in being no draft Task Force report as yet"; and that "the alleged 'recommendations'" described in the *Star Ledger* story "patently misrepresent the ideas contained in the Staff papers being considered by the Task Force." Beirne's attempt at damage control is accompanied by a letter *to* Beirne dated one week later, from CWA District 3 Vice President Robert Ben Porch. Porch's purpose was to brief Beirne about a meeting he had held earlier that week with South Central Bell President Cecil Bauer. Bauer, he related, "was extremely complementary of your actions" with respect to the Task Force, "and voiced what he described as his personal opinion that your actions would have a much greater impact on the ultimate outcome than anything the Bell System might do." "Knowing Cecil," Porch added, "I am of the opinion that he was voicing the thinking of the System rather than the comment only being a personal opinion." Beirne, still stoutly supporting Johnson's war policy in Indochina, was evidently trying to call in his chips on behalf of his members; without making promises, Rostow was attempting to placate the president of a major union within the Democratic coalition.[60]

Returning to the President's conversation with Rowe, we saw that the President *had* authorized the Task Force to study and recommend on domestic policy and that suggestions that it had not were deceitful. LBJ's withdrawal from the presidential campaign had altered the political calculus, but he had neither disbanded the Task Force nor narrowed its purview. W. DeVier Pierson, the President's special counsel, summed up the course of events as the group's Final Report was being readied, telling LBJ that "There was intense disagreement within the task force membership as to whether some issues—specifically, those dealing with domestic common carrier industry and opportunities for television—were appropriate subjects for study.... The task force did not resolve these issues and, in fact did not meet during the final months of its deliberation." In consequence, Pierson related, its Final Report "is largely the report of the Chairman and the staff—not of the entire task force." Individual members did not sign the document; two filed partial dissents.[61]

As the liberal Democratic coalition collapsed, the Final Report reveals a public utility framework straining to accommodate contending purposes and demands. On one side, the Task Force responded positively to business users and independent suppliers by elevating what were actually concrete demands to an abstract standing under the rubric of "economic competition." Economic competition, the chairman and some staffers agreed, indeed should be permitted in these instances. These were, however, selective departures: this was far from a full-blooded embrace of market competition. Accompanying these concessions, moreover, were new liberal welfarist measures. The group's politically engaged staff converged, therefore, on the thesis that *both* competition *and* regulation should be strengthened and housed *within* the existing public utility framework.

The Final Report recommended "widespread applications of telecommunications to the problems of disadvantaged minority groups," and declared that such programs "will be realized only with the initiative or support of government." It found it feasible to reconcile this proposal with its endorsement of limited competition in private-line service, and more generally with its prescription that telecommunications policy "should seek to develop an environment always sensitive to consumer needs." Recalling the Depression-era debates, indeed, it insisted on "strengthening regulatory capabilities to prevent destructive competition," and held that "integrated control" of public telephone service "remains vital": "the case for private monopoly regulated by public authority is convincing." Going even further, it was unequivocal that "Among the most pervasive of our findings ... is the need to strengthen governmental capabilities, both in the FCC and in the Executive Branch." It pronounced on a need "to protect society against the risks of concentrated power, in the hands either of government or of the communication companies." While suggesting that "integrated provision" of domestic public message telephone service should be preserved, on the other hand, Rostow's Report expressly recommended that the FCC endorse "the removal of unnecessary restraints to promote innovation and to encourage greater responsiveness to consumer needs" in the case of "services which supplement those of the basic public message telephone network." The Report artfully labeled "teleprocessing" such a "supplemental" service, for which "the removal of tariff restrictions on the sharing of communications lines, on splitting or resale of channels, and on message switching, seems compatible with maintaining the integrity of the basic communications network." This language accorded with how the FCC was, concurrently, drawing upon its own earlier decisions to continue liberalizing market access to the public switched network. Rostow was attempting to use executive branch power to reinforce and generalize this policy agenda.[62]

The Report thus also supported liberalized "foreign attachment" rules, meaning that a greatly widened range of network equipment—preeminently, computers—could be used in concert with AT&T's telecommunications facilities. This recommendation comported with the FCC's recent, precedent-shattering,

Carterfone decision of June 1968—by far the most important liberalizing measure the agency had taken. In this proceeding, opened ten months before the Task Force was convened, the FCC opened the market for terminal equipment to non-AT&T suppliers; hence, AT&T opposed it bitterly and was contesting it in the courts when the Task Force was concluding its deliberations (and long afterward). FCC Chairman Hyde recruited his adversary to write up this groundbreaking judgment ("It is beyond me why I was permitted to write the majority opinion in *Carterfone*," Johnson would recollect). The decision bespoke great gains for market liberalization and, reciprocally—for Johnson no doubt at least as important, a weakening of AT&T's corporate power.[63]

The Task Force recommended a third policy change which again would harmonize with a soon-to-be-delivered FCC decision. The Report asserted that the FCC should approve licenses for prospective carriers such as MCI, whose petition for authority to compete with AT&T in specialized business markets was then under review by the FCC. In August 1969, seven months into the Nixon presidency, the Federal Communications Commission approved—four Democrats against three Republicans—an application by MCI to supply specialized microwave service to business customers between Chicago and St. Louis. Recalling AT&T's recent service deterioration in New York City, Democratic FCC Commissioner Nicholas Johnson charged that "AT&T's managers have adopted policies that simultaneously produce higher prices and worse service for the public" and suggested that "200 million Americans can think of a lot more things to do with a communication network than one corporation can think up for them—particularly if it's not thinking."[64]

In sum, therefore, the Rostow Report proposed to synthesize an agenda for what Rostow hoped would be a substantial modernization and enhancement of the public utility framework. Rejecting Richard Posner's frontal attack on AT&T, the Task Force nevertheless recommended *both* dramatic measures in support of demands by business users and independent suppliers, *and* strengthened and improved government regulation along with welfarist measures. We cannot know if this emboldened public utility framework would have succeeded in balancing such an internally conflicted agenda. The contest pitting AT&T against big business network users and network suppliers had already generated serious political-economic instability. Might it have been feasible to stabilize? Might this have been accompanied by the growth of collective bargaining rights in the realm of digital networking? Equal employment opportunity rights for women and minorities? Privacy requirements and general accountability strictures such as those accruing to the Post Office and AT&T? Might computer communications have been brought within the Communication Act's Title II requirements, so that public utility regulation came to cover data networks? Might the ratemaking policies that had finally expedited a universal telephone service have been augmented, in support of a program of inclusive access to state-of-the-art data services? Might these ultimately have come to include applications such as search engines and social media? Posing such questions is vital, merely in order to delineate what was at stake—but, beyond this, speculation is pointless.

As it actually worked out in 1968, with a lame-duck president and beset by powerful and mutually antagonistic industrial forces amid an intensely charged sociopolitical field, the Task Force was stymied. Days before submitting its Report, Rostow attempted to persuade President Johnson that it should be accorded extensive circulation and publicity:

> It takes a long time to get a Task Force of this kind established and into motion. The opportunity should not be wasted. In my view, the line of policy laid out . . . is moderate, balanced, and right, and its articulation in a Task Force Report could help to influence the pattern of decisions by the F.C.C., by industry, and by Congress in a constructive way for a long time to come. Our efforts and the discussion of the draft chapters have already had a marked effect both on the F.C.C. and on A.T.&T. policy.

The President proved disinclined to accept and publish the Report. However, Alan Novak recollects, Rostow's plea persuaded LBJ not to pull the plug and shut it down. Whether or not his decision owed to Rostow's urging, this proved a fateful choice.[65]

Behind-the-scenes controversies between August and December 1968 about how to handle the Task Force Report had not been settled. W. DeVier Pierson, the President's special counsel, wrote to LBJ the day after its Report had been submitted to the President, that the group "has completed its work in a curious fashion. There was intense disagreement within the task force membership as to whether some issues—specifically, those dealing with domestic common carrier industry and opportunities for television—were appropriate subjects for study. . . . The task force did not resolve these issues and, in fact did not meet during the final months of its deliberation." In consequence, Pierson told the President, the final Report "is largely the report of the Chairman and the staff—not of the entire task force." Individual members of the group did not sign the completed document, reflecting pronounced and unresolved disagreement, to which DeVier Pierson himself had been a party. Pierson also told the President that, because the deliberations had broken down, "I am afraid the report will be of very limited value as a public document. The communications industry, the Congress, and the FCC hold highly divergent views on these issues. If a task force composed of the executive branch cannot reach agreement, I see no practical benefit form (sic) the publication of its findings." The president's assistant counseled him that it would be "desirable to give the new Administration an opportunity to evaluate the proposals of the report and reach its own conclusions as to their feasibility," by making the material available to President-elect Richard Nixon's transition team.[66]

The day he actually transmitted the Report to the President, Eugene Rostow explained in an accompanying memo that the Task Force's pursuit of "emerging policy problems in the field of carrier regulation and television" had "proceeded . . . until the late summer of 1968, when, you will recall, the Secretary of Commerce raised with you the question whether the Message of August 14, 1967, authorized the Task Force to go into domestic policy questions at all." Commerce Secretary C. R. Smith "argues that Chapters 6 and 7 would 'poison the well,' by stirring up so much controversy as to imperil the possibility of gaining support for the rest of the program proposed in the Report." However, after subsequent conversations in October 1968 "at a meeting of the members of the Task Force chiefly concerned with this controversy," Pierson told Rostow that he had "'a green, or at least an amber light' to proceed on the basis of the work program which the Task Force had approved, and to see how much of a consensus could be reached on the full Draft Report, including the two chapters in dispute." Rostow had discussed these issues in separate conversations with Task Force members and, despite their unresolved disagreements, he remained convinced that the full report made "a useful contribution."[67]

Nine days after Rostow submitted the Report to him, in an extraordinary telephone conversation, the President spoke to his old advisor and sometime friend, James Rowe. A recording he made of this exchange reveals the guileful Johnson telling Rowe that he had "hoped" that the Task Force "wouldn't even get into this thing" (domestic communications); and that he didn't want them to file a report but that—as if Rostow, or he himself, had been helpless in the face of it—"their staff had forced it." LBJ then fed back to Rowe an exaggerated version of the very point that Rowe had conveyed to him in his June letter: that Rostow "had some boys, I think from Yale, and they just went berserk, it looked like to me." The President imparted the political takeaway as a seeming afterthought: that he would probably pass the Report along to the incoming administration without a recommendation. Rowe would have understood instantly.[68]

President Johnson had decided that the issues engaged by the Task Force still required executive action. Throughout all the internal disagreement and outside pressure, he had kept the Task Force in action. Through Pierson, his legal counsel, he had signaled as late as October 1968 that Rostow had "a green, or at least an amber light" to press on with the most controversial chapters. Despite his lame-duck status; despite that the Democrats had now lost the presidency, the issues that the Task Force had been convened to engage remained unresolved—and pressing. Early in January 1969, outgoing President Lyndon Baines Johnson chose not to release either the Report or the Staff Papers. Instead he handed them off to the Nixon administration with no recommendation.[69]

In mid-November 1968, weeks before the final act of this drama, *Business Week* reported that "Taken in its entirety, the proposed reshuffling of the communications industry is so sweeping the report might have been treated as a hot potato by the Administration that set it in motion. And a Republican Administration might be expected to be even more reticent." Yet, the story continued, "the problems that led to formation of the task force are so acute that any Administration will have to try to solve them" and it predicted that "the chances are good that the report . . . will carry weight with Nixon decisionmakers." This proved accurate on both counts. Yet if Johnson neither disbanded the Task Force nor suppressed its Report, then his successor found means of using them to rip away at the foundations of the public utility framework.[70]

The Hand-Off to Nixon

It has long been appreciated that, by establishing an Office of Telecommunications Policy midway through 1970, Nixon's Executive Office wrested greater control over communications policymaking. It is less well-known that planning for this change began immediately as the incoming president set up his administration. Nor that the Task Force Report served as a catalyst for transformative policy change in and around networks.[71]

Handed off to Nixon's transition team, the Task Force Report circulated for deliberation within a tight circle of advisors. At the center of these deliberations was Clay T. Whitehead—a thirty-year-old management and operations research PhD from MIT, who had gone on to RAND and the Nixon campaign. Whitehead reported to Peter M. Flanigan, an executive at the investment bank Dillon, Read who had worked with Nixon since 1959, serving as Nixon's deputy campaign manager in 1968 and as a "talent scout" who helped recruit staff-people both for Nixon's transition team and his administration. The President named Flanigan himself to be his principal aide for business and financial issues, and he remained a key presidential assistant until 1972, when he was appointed director of the Council of International Economic Policy (successor to Peter G. Peterson, who became Secretary of Commerce). He departed the administration mere weeks before Nixon resigned as a result of the Watergate scandal, to which Flanigan was not linked. Too little-remembered, Flanigan was one of the President's "most trusted, influential, and well-connected aides": "Administration officials compared his influence on business issues to Henry A. Kissinger's on foreign affairs"; a different view came from Ralph Nader, who called him a "mini-president" and the "most evil" man in Washington. Alongside Nixon advisors

Peter G. Peterson, another investment banker, and George Shultz, previously dean of the business school at the University of Chicago, Flanigan's brief was to devise recipes for US economic rejuvenation and to head off financial and economic crisis.[72]

"Advanced technology" bulked large in these schemes; as Peterson spelled out in 1971, it had become "indispensable" to "bring technology increasingly to bear upon the process of enhancing both the quality and quantity of our production." This was not a passive process of acceding to an ineffable technological pressure, but an active—indeed, a boldly insistent—political program. Peterson continued that the need was "to take the offensive against the defects in the present international system, and in our own economy." To be sure, the administration included cabinet officials with disparate visions of how—and even whether—to pursue this "offensive." Nevertheless, from the very outset a crucial plank in the evolving platform for "advanced technology" pertained to networks.[73]

Within two weeks of the inauguration, indeed, some of the highest-ranking members of Nixon's administration allied to make the Rostow Report serve a revamped telecommunications policy. Nixon himself requested the establishment of "a small review committee to assess this report, and to prepare whatever legislative proposals may be needed" in light of its "far-reaching recommendations on telecommunications." The group was convened by Robert Ellsworth, special assistant to the president, and on his way to becoming US Ambassador to NATO and Assistant Secretary of Defense for International Security Affairs. It was, as this suggests, a high-level body. In addition to science advisor Lee A. DuBridge, its members included National Security Advisor Henry Kissinger, Budget Bureau Director Robert Mayo, and Chairman of the Council of Economic Advisors Paul McCracken. Ellsworth's own delegated representative was Clay T. Whitehead. This group was charged with making recommendations to the President. Nixon wrote to allay concerns expressed by another longtime advisor, Commerce Secretary Maurice Stans, whose department harbored a small unit charged with spectrum allotment responsibilities for federal government users. "I have requested a detailed assessment of the Task Force Report on Communications Policy," wrote Nixon to Stans portentously, "taking into consideration the recently completed study of the Federal Communications Organization, with a view toward preparation of legislative proposals or reorganization plans for the management and administration of communications matters within the Executive Branch."[74]

Though it carries on its cover the date at which it was transmitted to LBJ—December 7, 1968—the actual publication of the Rostow Report actually came months later, in May or June of 1969, when Whitehead wrote to the Government Printing Office to underline the "great urgency in getting the Report of the Task Force on Telecommunications (sic) . . . printed as expeditiously as possible," and requested that GPO produce an additional 300 copies for use by the White House and another 1000 for the Office of Emergency Preparedness. The postponed release of the Report made time in which to reconfigure the Executive's power and objectives in this area. The Director of the Task Force, Alan Novak, remembers that Whitehead "took all our staff studies and used them," but the appearance of bipartisanship and continuity was contrived. Although in some fields Nixon carried over Great Society programs, his agenda for networks ripped away from the moorings that had anchored federal policymaking since the 1930s.

The point-man for radical changes was Whitehead. Whitehead threw himself into this work even before legislation established a formal basis for his activities. Already by May 1969, he possessed sufficient authority under Flanigan and Ellsworth to request that FCC Chairman Rosel Hyde supply him with "an informal, short statement of what our national communications policy is . . . This should particularly include the authority for the various key elements of our policy; to the extent possible, the rationale; and also any important gaps." In a separate memo to National Communications Agency Director, General James O'Connell, Whitehead repeated these lines, explaining that "I propose to use this . . . also as a basis for a substantive look at our communications policy"; he asked that O'Connell specifically clarify what authority was conferred on the President by the Communications Satellite Act of 1962 in regard to the "the characteristics of a domestic satellite system."[75]

Scarcely one month later, and still eight months before a new Office of Telecommunications Policy was created as an Executive Branch agency, Whitehead sent a memo to Peter M. Flanigan, strategizing about how to revamp the FCC—whose enabling legislation had established it as an independent agency reporting to Congress. An incoming administration held a customary right to select a new FCC chair. Whitehead underlined that this individual needed to be especially capable, "to permit him to quickly become the leading spokesman for the future of communications." In existing circumstances, this meant that "He should have the where-with-all to tackle Nick Johnson on intellectual grounds, while at the same time having the ability to work with . . . the White House to get constructive agreement on new policies." Drawing Flanigan's attention to the fact that several Commissionerships were slated to fall open within the following year, Whitehead suggested "that we should give serious attention to the makeup we would like to see for the Commission and consider these four appointments as a package. If you agree, I will try to put down some thoughts about how we could proceed." A blueprint was being sketched both for alterations to FCC policy and transforming the Executive Branch into its coordinating force.[76]

These developments quickly became legible to AT&T's top management. AT&T Chairman H. I. Romnes and Vice Chairman John deButts asked to meet with President Nixon, a request that was relayed to chief of staff H. R. Haldeman on May 14, 1969. Haldeman rebuffed them; no meeting took place.[77]

Meanwhile the administration undertook a more encompassing review of federal operations. Nixon established a President's Advisory Council on Executive Organization and, on April 5, 1969, appointed as its members Chairman Roy L. Ash of Litton Industries; ex-governor of Texas and Nixon's own future Treasury Secretary John B. Connally; Richard M. Paget, a well-placed management consultant with ties to the Navy; former Dean of the Harvard Business School George Baker; and the ubiquitous ex-AT&T chairman, Frederick R. Kappel. President Nixon also added to this group his then special counsel, Walter N. Thayer, chairman of Whitney Communications Company—which held interests in television, radio, magazines, and newspapers. The Ash Commission thereupon submitted a series of reports, covering not only Executive Branch departments but also the independent regulatory agencies. Its July 1970 report on these commissions laid groundwork for the sweeping project of regulatory "reform" and dramatically centralized Executive Branch decision-making through its recommendation to establish a new Office of Management and Budget. (Roy Ash himself became the first director of the newly elevated OMB.)

In this way a Republican-led but often bipartisan program for attacking regulation was prepared. The Ash Commission concluded that delays in decision-making, a lack of clear policy guidelines and of effective coordination between different agencies, and an overemphasis on legal procedure as opposed to economic and engineering evidence, all contributed to reducing the efficacy of regulation and, in the anodyne formulation of Roger Noll, "that greater presidential authority . . . would increase the sensitivity of regulatory agencies to the general public interest in regulation." The Ash Commission report on independent regulatory agencies ushered in an increasingly extreme discourse, pivoting on the point that the edifice of regulation by administrative commissions was deeply flawed. A Brookings Institution "conference of experts" convened to evaluate its proposals underlined that the Ash Commission had helpfully publicized "the virtually unanimous opinion of informed observers that reform of regulation is necessary." Participants underscored "the excessive sensitivity of regulatory agencies to the welfare of the industries they regulate." Noll reported that "a substantial majority of the participants" were convinced that "the primary purpose of regulation should be to contribute to economic efficiency—promoting competition, keeping prices in line with costs, permitting cost-reducing or service-augmenting technological change, and perfecting consumer knowledge of product quality." Carefully excluding the social and political purposes that had inhered in the public utility conception, and that were concurrently in prospect of rejuvenation by social justice activists, the Nixon administration worked to cultivate a reactionary discourse of "regulatory reform."[78]

Several of the Report's chapters expressed ideas and proposals on which Whitehead could, and did, capitalize. Chapter Five urged that an "experimental" domestic satellite service be authorized free of AT&T control. Having excised Posner's suggestion that AT&T be separated from its captive manufacturing unit, Western Electric, Chapter Six retained proposals to permit competition in high-growth markets "adjacent" to the public network. Chapter Seven on television suggested that policymakers widen opportunities for cable television to expand into the nation's major cities. Chapter Nine, on government reorganization, held that the Executive Branch's planning function for networks should be strengthened, to complement the work of the FCC. Whitehead's foremost early effort to reorient US telecommunications centered on a drive to induce open markets for domestic satellite services.

He was already pushing forward a review and reform of national policy in this area by May 1969; and, throughout the months that followed deliberations over satellite policy ascended to a higher administrative plane. On July 1, Peter M. Flanigan gave notice to FCC Chairman Rosel Hyde that "Federal policy toward applications of communications satellite technology is a most important issue for which the President and the Federal Communications Commission both have responsibilities." Flanigan added that he was convening a "small group from appropriate agencies," and invited Hyde to join it. Taking care to underline that "the purpose" guiding this initiative was not to judge the merit of particular "applications and filings before the FCC," Flanigan's initiative nonetheless preempted the FCC by assuming a primary role in framing "appropriate national policies." The group's charter was already largely written. Flanigan told Hyde that, "In our review of Federal policies relating to the communications industry, it has become clear that prompt action is desirable. It is also important that our initial policies encourage full exploration of the potential of this new technology." Two days later Whitehead began to circulate three "talking papers for a conference between executive branch people and the FCC on the domestic satellite policy." By early August, he was notifying top members of the Administration that:

We intend to present, by October 1, Administration recommendations to the FCC on guidelines for the use of satellites for domestic communications by commercial organizations. Our objectives in formulating these guidelines should be to:

- assure full benefit to the public of the economic and service potential of satellite technology.

. . .

- minimize unnecessary regulatory impediments to technological and market development by the private sector

- encourage more vigorous innovation generally among communications entities to develop new telecommunication services and markets.

Herein—more than half a year before the formal establishment of a new Office of Telecommunications Policy within the Executive Office of the President—was expressed not only the language, but also the substance, of a reoriented telecommunications policy. This was formulated not by the FCC but the Executive Branch.[79]

The reasoning and ambitious purpose animating these proposals for domestic satellite policy was conveyed in a pair of exceptional memos. The first was sent on July 1 to Peter Flanigan. Whitehead here underlined that "this is probably the only major decision for some time that gives us the leverage necessary to promote a re-examination of the need for extensive common carrier regulation of all U.S. communications by the FCC and to stimulate a more vigorous and innovative competition in the communications industry." He emphasized that "Our objectives would be to . . . use this approach as a wedge to encourage a more vigorous and innovative competition among communications organizations." The radically expansive program that lay behind Whitehead's preferred policy option for domestic satellite services ("open skies") merits lengthy quotation:

> It is important to recognize that this is probably our last foreseeable opportunity to use a specific decision as a device for challenging the need for regulation as arbitrary and extensive as evolved by the FCC. This particular case is appealing because it goes to the basic principles of regulation and to the heart of the industry structure fostered by the FCC, yet it is not such a large economic issue that existing interests are severely threatened. Finally, there is a very good chance our approach would receive acceptance: the FCC is in a very awkward (and weak) position; we can offer a significant change from the status quo that is not patently adverse to AT&T, Comsat, and other major interests; and there is so much uncertainty in the FCC and the industry that a strong Administration proposal would in all likelihood dominate public discussion. Finally, even if we are not able to sell a significantly improved approach, we can go on record in favor of clearly desirable end objectives.

Whitehead sent a second memo several months later to three other Executive Branch officials as well as, once more, to Flanigan: Science Advisor DuBridge, the head of the Council of Economic Advisors, Paul McCracken, and General George A. Lincoln at the Office of Emergency Preparedness. Here he provided a skillful general assessment while stressing "the desirability of competitive forces" and the accompanying need to pry further changes from regulators. "The telecommunications industry is in transition," he wrote, "from a relatively small and self-contained industry dominated by the provision of switched public message (telephone) service on a monopoly basis to a large, rapidly changing industry providing a wide range of economically and socially important services." Both regulatory policies and industry structure "are heavily oriented toward centrally planned, often monopolistic, operations." Whitehead allowed that "There can be no argument that the past performance has on the whole been superb."

> However the rapid technological, social, and economic change surrounding the industry is causing problems. There are increasing numbers of specialized service demands and of potential suppliers eager to meet those demands. It is very difficult, however, for the FCC in spite of its fine staff to keep track of and be responsive to such rapid change within the past framework.

Whitehead's momentum carried forward, because the objectives that fueled it found support in the top echelon of the Nixon Administration, particularly from Peter Flanigan. In a January 1970 memo, Flanigan tutored the President's assistant for domestic affairs, John Erlichman, on satellite policy. The issues, he stated, had been "unresolved since 1965. The Federal Communications Commission has been unable to deal with this problem primarily because of the complexity of competing economic interests, which can in part be traced to the Commission's own past regulatory policies." Lock, stock, and barrel, Flanigan had accepted Whitehead's argument—that the satellite proceeding offered a strategic entry point for a comprehensive policy reorientation; and Flanigan now reiterated this to the president's top aide for domestic policy, John Erlichman:

> The primary reason for executive branch intervention in this regulatory policy area is that the introduction of satellite technology into the U.S. domestic communications industry offers a convenient lever to move regulatory policy out of a deepening rut of unnecessary regulation and compromise.

Asserting that an open skies policy would prove politically feasible ("We expect no strong opposition from the Hill.... The two major communications companies ... AT&T and COMSAT will have mixed feelings, but I expect neither to offer serious opposition") Flanigan requested that Erlichman approve the transmission of a memo to the FCC—"and that a press release identifying the President with the free enterprise objectives of the position be issued along with the public release of the memorandum itself." This was a calculated bid to align the FCC with the Administration's changing policy priorities.[80]

Erlichman, meanwhile, received a second memo that same day from his deputy, thirty-two-year-old Kenneth Cole. Cole, who had worked for H. R. Haldeman at J. Walter Thompson, joined the Nixon campaign in 1968 and entered the Administration in 1969. Reassuring Erlichman that a consensus had cohered around the altered satellite policy, Cole further clarified the process through which it had been reached: "In developing the policy, a very broad group including the Commerce Department, Department of Transportation, OEP, CEA, OS&T, and the FCC was involved in the investigation of this subject and the subsequent recommended policy proposal." Cole added that the Justice Department, the Post Office and, not least, newly appointed FCC Chairman Dean Burch also had approved the plan. Finally, he specified that although General Lincoln, Director of the Office of Emergency Preparedness, "agrees," his own Director of Technical Management at OEP "is in disagreement because they are in favor of more government regulation and monopolistic domination—a basic economic philosophical difference (I believe we should go with Lincoln)."[81]

President Nixon announced these policy recommendations the following day; and Flanigan wrote Dean Burch at the FCC, formally recommending a policy of "open entry" into domestic satellite communications. Flanigan thereupon crafted a new memo, to brief the President for an upcoming meeting with all seven FCC Commissioners on February 3, 1970. Flanigan asserted that the first order of business at this meeting was for Nixon to "urge prompt FCC adoption" of the Administration's domestic satellite policy, which called "for relatively more reliance on competition than past FCC policies"; and he armed the President with intelligence that "Every Commissioner except Johnson supported the policy statement."[82]

Convergent initiatives consolidated the Nixon Administration's liberalization and "deregulation" drive. One was to strengthen Executive Branch power over networks, by carrying through with the establishment of an Office of Telecommunications Policy. Efforts to craft the needed legislation culminated as 1969 gave way to 1970. Peter Flanigan wrote John Erlichman that both the Budget Bureau and the President's Advisory Committee on Executive Organization (the Ash Commission) had "assisted in the preparation of this recommendation," and asked for comments from Erlichman so that a "final recommendation" might be transmitted to Nixon. Flanigan provided justifying documentation to Erlichman, some of which prefigured the legislative language used to establish OTP. "The Administration," he wrote, "is largely unable to exert leadership or take initiatives in spite of vulnerability to criticism for FCC policies." This was aggravated by the "rapidly growing importance of telecommunications." Declaring that "there is a serious lack of effective machinery for dealing expeditiously with domestic telecommunications issues," Flanigan enumerated several of the FCC proceedings, some still ongoing, through which the liberalization drive was unfolding—"with only limited success."

There is a current tendency to resolve such issues by past precedents and by compromises between the FCC and various agencies in the executive branch, but the increasingly rapid rate of technological change and introduction of new services makes policy-by-precedent increasingly less relevant, more restrictive, or counterproductive.

The document, almost certainly prepared for Flanigan by Whitehead, explained that "There is now no office in the executive branch with the responsibility or the capability to review the whole range of national telecommunications policies as expressed in legislation and in FCC policies." Neither the Justice Department's Antitrust Division, nor the Commerce Department, nor the Council of Economic Advisors, nor the Office of Science and Technology "are equipped to address the fundamental economic and institutional problems of the communications industry and its regulation by the FCC, or the problems of the government's own telecommunications." Reviews by the Ash Commission and the Budget Bureau made plain "[1] that stronger coordination from the top is required in establishing Government policy for its own telecommunications requirements, and [2] that the Federal government should take a stronger role in the evolution of national telecommunications to deal with the increasingly rapid rate of technological change and industry growth. There is also agreement that a much stronger analytic capability within the executive branch is needed to achieve these goals."[83]

An accompanying memo outlined the responsibilities to be entrusted to the new OTP. The agency's director "develops the executive branch position on national telecommunications policy," and "serves as the President's principal advisor on telecommunications policy." His mandate expressly extended beyond the Government's own telecommunications systems, to encompass the length and breadth of the commercial industry including satellites, and not only to formulate but also to publicly assert "the Executive branch position" on "The organization, practices, and regulation of the U.S. domestic and international communications industry":

> The Director assures that the executive branch position on telecommunications policy issues is effectively presented to the Congress and to the Federal Communications Commission in the form of legislative proposals, recommendations, and testimony as required . . . " [and] carries out the responsibilities conferred on the President by the Communications Satellite Act.

This gave to the OTP Director an expansive and robust institutional foundation. Whitehead was appointed to be Director midway through 1970—at thirty-one, he was the youngest director of any agency in the Executive Office. Flanigan wrote another memo for the President to underscore the political importance of OTP: "While this is not an area that should require your personal attention, in order for Whitehead to pull together the competing bureaucratic interests and keep agency conflicts to a minimum, Presidential identification with this new office will be an important consideration."[84]

As Director of OTP, Whitehead proved a hard-driving proponent of liberalization and the deregulatory displacement of the public utility conception. His assistants were carefully selected to aid in this project. Dr. George F. Mansur had been formerly director of microwave and space systems at Collins Radio Company; and Stephen Doyle had worked at both the FCC and the State Department as a specialist in international organizations for satellite communications. As economist Thomas Hazlett put it in a memorial following Whitehead's death in 2008, "Well before there was phone competition, cellular, cable TV entry to challenge broadcasters—when natural monopoly was the operative assumption everywhere in the sector—and particularly so in the high fixed cost satellite industry—Tom Whitehead developed, pushed, and won FCC adoption of rules to permit multiple firms to offer satellite communications. That was huge. It created the means for cable TV program network distribution; competition was soon unleashed to broadcasting. Voice and data services were next." The refashioning of satellite, cable television, and ultimately telecommunications more generally was styled by OTP—in tandem with the FCC chairman.[85]

Coordinating with senior figures in the White House, Whitehead was the architect, but the prime movers and leading beneficiaries were the corporate users and -suppliers of emerging networking technologies. Both had long demanded that they be allowed to introduce data communications systems and services, and to add, subtract, and combine functionality in line with their proprietary profit strategies. In the Nixon years, their collaboration as an organized political force became decisive and the state's response concerted.

Whitehead's use of OTP to reorient US telecommunications already hinted at even more radical objectives. Soon after his appointment as Director, he wrote an antitrust official at the Justice Department to ask "three questions of varying legal content":

> First, I hear a lot about due process and would like to know what this means in terms of constraints on the FCC's actions and to what extent OTP is bound by such considerations. Secondly, I would like to know what the courts have said about competition vs. regulation in regulated industries and, in particular, to what extent a regulatory agency is free to regulate by simply 'not regulating' but merely monitoring. Finally, I would like to know what the interactions between antitrust law and regulatory law are and how they are handled. Is

the responsibility for conforming to the antitrust statutes in the hands of the Commission or is it in Justice?

Finally, could you please send me a good primer on antitrust policy and practice?

Here, he was probing how far he might extend his own executive power; how far he might try to push the FCC to restrict its own; and how he might best activate a new antitrust prosecution against AT&T. Three years later, Whitehead's OTP published a report on "anticompetitive practices of the Bell System"; and Bruce Owen, who worked at OTP under Whitehead, went on to the Justice Department where he helped prepare the antitrust case that undertook to break up the company in 1974–1975.[86]

Whitehead was undertaking a sweeping policy offensive which fed into decision-making by the Federal Communications Commission. A 1971 memo for John Erlichman by Whitehead offers a sense of the process, and hints at additional intrigues around the FCC's upcoming decision to allow a new class of specialized common carriers to serve large business users:

> You inquired about our plans regarding the pending FCC docket in the area of competition in the specialized communications carrier field (e.g., Datran).
>
> A decision by the FCC is expected next week. Dean Burch anticipates that the outcome will be pro-competition, as do we, but we cannot be sure how decisively so....
>
> This particular pending docket is only a partial resolution of the problem. If the FCC action is favorable as expected, we will pursue the other aspects—such as interconnection policies, restrictions on existing common carriers, and tariff structures. Because of continuing discussions, I must be careful to preserve our credibility with AT&T and Western Union on these matters. If the FCC hedges on this docket, we will aggressively pursue the whole matter.

A ramifying process of radical policy change was loosely steered from the apex of the Nixon Administration.[87]

A watershed came with the appointment of Dean Burch as the new Chair of the Federal Communications Commission. Burch, who was recommended to the President for the post by Nixon's Treasurer of the United States, Dorothy Andrews Elston, took over in October 1969 from the old-school Eisenhower Republican, Rosel H. Hyde. Burch possessed entirely different qualities. As a member of the "Arizona mafia," he had been an advisor to Senator Barry Goldwater before rising to deputy head of the Goldwater presidential campaign of 1964 and, a year later, to the chairmanship of the Republican National Committee. Burch was politically in-sync with the strident free-market doctrine embraced by a changing Republican Party; his appointment to be FCC Chair in turn signaled more than a routine personnel change.[88]

With Burch in place, the Administration became able to redirect telecommunications policy and to in large measure to coordinate its preferred policies with the FCC—while giving an appearance of independence. "The potential danger of OTP using the prestige and influence of the White House to overwhelm the FCC" was pointed out in May 1970 by a legal assistant to FCC Commissioner H. Rex Lee, Edwin B. Spievack—who charged that the OTP threatened "improper political encroachment upon the independence of the regulatory agencies." Even earlier, in hearings on the establishment of OTP, reports circulated of Congress's suspicions that OTP "would muscle in illegally on commission adjudicatory proceeding"; that OTP "would acquire sufficient research capability to 'overwhelm' the FCC"; and that OTP "would impose its own philosophy of spectrum usage on the Commission." With Chairman Burch in place, however, he could testify in behalf of his agency "that the OTP would be a help rather than a hindrance to the commission." Burch was well-versed: "I am sure I speak for the entire commission when I saw the commission does not intend to relinquish any of its powers because of this new office." This nominal expression was sufficient to placate Congress. For the duration of his tenure at the agency, Burch liasoned not only with Whitehead but also with some of the President's heavy-weight advisors, including Haldeman, Erlichman, Colson, Haig, Klein, and Flanigan.[89]

The Nixon Administration grew infamous for harassing and intimidating the US news media, on grounds of "liberal bias." Although OTP was the locus of a persistent attack against "liberal" broadcasters and "ideological bias" in commercial network news," its political importance lay above all in its "centralization within the White House of decision-making control over the future development of American communication"—in particular, in telecommunications. Working together with the hard-charging Whitehead, FCC Chair Dean Burch propelled the adoption of market-liberalizing, antiaccountability tenets no matter if these collided with AT&T's preferences. This was not a onetime change, but an ongoing evolution—episodic but concerted. And, though Democrats inveighed and fulminated against Burch's attacks on the liberal broadcast media, many of them at least acquiesced in his liberalization agenda for telecommunications. FCC Commissioners and staffers tended to agree that liberalization constituted a desirable policy path. Only a strong measure of cynicism with respect to the public utility conception can explain this result. Democratic reformers looked to exploit any crack in the system, any foothold, to push back against AT&T's corporate power. Ignorant of, or oblivious to, the damage wrought earlier in the century to telegraph industry labor and service standards under competition, 1970s liberals again helped raise the banner of competition as if it offered a real solution. At the same time, because liberals inclined to perceive regulation as structurally complicit with corporate power, they found little basis for opposing a rollback of the public utility model.[90]

Liberalization carried over at the Commission with the appointment of Republican Richard E. Wiley as General Counsel in Fall, 1970—and with his elevation the next year to FCC Commissioner and, eventually, to Chairman of the agency. Wiley's appointment as commissioner, by his own account, owed to a member of Nixon's inner circle. In a personal letter to Charles Colson, Wiley stated:

> Dear Chuck:
> I am writing to express my profound appreciation for your very generous support in connection with my nomination to the Federal Communications Commission. In light of the particular complexities of the matter, I am fully aware that my impending appointment would not have been possible without your personal involvement and support. It goes without saying that I am deeply grateful and will expend every effort to justify the confidence which you have exhibited in me. Sincerely yours, Dick

Wiley had been director of state organizations in the Nixon campaign and, recounted *Broadcasting*, "Nixon talent scouts referred his name to Chairman Burch, who was under White House pressure to find a Republican replacement for Mr. [Henry] Geller, a Democrat." The trade journal hinted that "Wiley brings his own approach to key FCC post," and "approaches proposals for new government regulation with some wariness." This was understated. Wiley worked steadfastly to implement additional liberalizing measures and to ensure that new networks would be exempted from public utility responsibilities.[91]

Wiley's shift from general counsel to commissioner indeed did carry the "particular complexities" that he mentioned to Colson. He was appointed in January 1972, to replace the Kansas Republican commissioner, ex-broadcaster Robert Wells. Wells, FCC Chairman Burch relayed in an "eyes only" memorandum for White House presidential advisors, had been appointed by Nixon in 1969 "in fulfillment of the President's commitment to the N.A.B. that one of their own would be appointed to the Commission." However, Burch continued, Wells "is a 'favorite son' of the entire industry—not only broadcasters but common carriers as well"; Burch preferred that the President nominate Wiley for this reason, that is, because, unlike Wells, he could be expected to promote the interests of business users in telecommunications. While Wiley's appointment, he was careful to point out, "will be greeted with favor" by the broadcast industry, Wiley was "a strong free enterpriser," and Burch believed that his arrival at the FCC would help to entrench this philosophy at the agency. Wiley indeed did sustain the liberalization program, especially after he became FCC chair upon Burch's departure in 1974.[92]

In light of a perceived "paucity" of "serious policy research" in this increasingly vital area, President Johnson's Task Force had urged "governmental, foundation, and business support for increased inter-disciplinary research and training in telecommunications policy." Whitehead followed up, but narrowed the agenda to cultivating research that could be used to legitimate the shove toward "competition" and "deregulation." Telecommunications economics and economics-grounded policy especially were elevated and institutionalized as a policymaking resources. Under Whitehead's direction, OTP's chief economist, Bruce Owen, used his base at the agency to inaugurate (in 1972) what was to become an annual conference on telecommunications policy research. His purpose, Owen later recounted, was to forge a "channel" through which "policy-relevant" research could reach—that is, could provide ideological cover—for regulators bent on dethroning the public utility framework. Researchers working at or with think tanks, such as the RAND Corporation, the Aspen Institute, SRI and the Brookings Institution gained prominence, along with academics funded by government grants. Growing loud were advocates of technological and marketplace "efficiency." By contrast the thoughts and preferences of workers and residential customers no longer tended even to be ventriloquated, within the hotel conference rooms in which conference papers were delivered and debates staged.[93]

Telecommunications liberalization and deregulation developed not as a straight-line movement, under the sign of market competition, but as fraught discontinuity. Through 1968, Democrats had sought to a limited liberalization process within the public utility framework; with the onset of the Nixon administration in 1969, a more comprehensive liberalization program was accompanied by a sharp turn to deregulation. Eugene Rostow himself addressed this abrupt directional change soon after it had taken hold. "The early FCC decisions released dynamic forces which have proved to be extremely powerful. As a result, the Commission has lost control of its experiment," he testified to Congress in 1975: "the FCC has become a prisoner of the process it started.... It has allowed the quest for competition as an end in itself to become the controlling theme of its decisions ... at the expense of ... the unity of the integrated national telephone network." Rostow did not mince words: "The Commission has now adopted rules which violate the most fundamental policy of the Communications Act of 1934."[94]

However, by this time, a serious oppositional challenge by the Democrats was unlikely. After losing the election in 1968, the Democrats remained divided; and they were routed in 1972 and remained out of power until 1976. Meanwhile, influential Democrats all but abandoned attempts to reconstruct communications within the public utility framework. The first Democratic Chair of the FCC since the Johnson years was President Jimmy Carter's appointee, Charles D. Ferris

(1977–1981)—a staunch proponent of extending the agency's now-thriving program of liberalization.

*

The Republicans had been the party of big business since the Civil War. With respect to telecommunications, however, during the 1960s and 1970s, big business was divided. On one side stood the planet's largest single unit of capital; on the other, gigantic oligopolies based in every other sector of the economy, and their allies—the suppliers and would-be suppliers of emerging network technologies. This was a lopsided contest. In 1974, the Nixon White House announced that it would no longer sanction AT&T's monopoly, and later that year it initiated yet an antitrust investigation of the company; a legal scholar has called this "the largest and perhaps most consequential case in the entire history of the competition laws." Under Attorney General William B. Saxbe, who continued in his position after Gerald Ford replaced a now-disgraced Nixon as President, the Justice Department brought suit. Eight years later, this victorious prosecution split asunder AT&T. Under Nixon, the Republicans began to hail entrepreneurs and new industries, playing to the demands of a newly crucial electoral constituency. Cultivating network-intensive military and tech businesses in the politically important Sunbelt was closely intertwined with Nixon's "Southern strategy" of capturing the votes of white Democrats for Republicans. Whitehead himself walked through the revolving door that he had helped to frame, by becoming an executive in the now burgeoning private satellite industry; this was emblematic of the administration's commitment to making corporate-commercial exploitation of networks the tent-pole of the nation's political economy.[95]

To see this project in such terms is, however, incomplete. It was not only about gaining partisan advantage or, indeed, about granting favors to business users and independent suppliers by transforming the terms of trade in the telecommunications industry. It was, finally, a reactionary class project. A cavernous gap between words and things concealed this. "Competition" and "deregulation" were talismans, and many true believers ardently believed that they were working to reinstate the one and engender the other in order to propel the political economy back into something approaching its natural state. In actuality, however, elevating already-powerful corporate users while dislodging the already-weakened accountability controls that had been built into the public utility model virtually ensured that workers and consumers would be placed at a structural disadvantage in the period to follow. Backed by a strong state, business users and a rapidly growing independent industry of suppliers were set to alter policies in light of one desideratum: freedom to develop private corporate networks and equipment as they themselves preferred. An explosively dynamic proprietary networking sector was thereby cut free of the historical costs, regulatory responsibilities, and unionized workforce that had gone into building and operating the nation's unexcelled public network infrastructure. Additional code words once more operated to disguise this dislodgement: private data networks carrying "supplementary," or "enhanced" services were rendered seemingly marginal to—even separate from—the public telecommunications network. They were not. Established to carve out a privileged status for big business network users, these increasingly distended systems actually were cut free of the public utility framework.

Labor Disarmed

What were the conditions of possibility for his historic policy transformation, away from public utility and into digital capitalism? In truth, they showcased determined state managers and politically assertive corporate users and suppliers; but they also involved a potentially antagonistic force. This was the collective agency of US workers including, specifically, telecommunications workers. How did the people who built and operated telecommunications take part in this momentous transition? Were they well-prepared to engage? Did they try to influence the principles that would govern the deployment of a digital network infrastructure? What role did the telecommunications unions take within the sequence of liberalization and deregulation?

This final part of Chapter 10 explicates the complex ways in which labor's capacity to engage the transforming politics of telecommunications came to be limited and constrained.

*

Unionism in the United States had reached a peak during the mid-1950s, at which time unions represented around a third of all wage and salary workers; in 1968, this share totaled a still-substantial 28 percent. The telecommunications sector was, by contrast, exceptionally well-organized. The extent of Post Office unionism was actually astonishing; estimates put the unionization rate at 84 percent overall in 1963, and the letter carriers joined their organization, NALC, at a 90 percent rate. Meanwhile, with several hundred thousand members, by the late 1960s the Communications Workers of America had become the nation's fourteenth-largest union. Nearly three-fifths (58.4 percent) of all telephone workers (disproportionately craftsmen and operators, the industry's largest occupations) had joined either CWA or one of the lesser telephone unions. Though lagging that of the Post Office, the union representation rate in the telephone industry was double that of the nation.[96]

After 1965, struggles in and around the workplace intensified. On one side, many big corporations were determined to raise profit rates, as they faced both rising overcapacity and growing competition from European and Japanese rivals. Executives in turn took a tougher line in bargaining negotiations, and in resisting organizing drives; and companies became freshly determined to modify labor processes, introduce new technology and speed up production. Movements from below erupted in response: a "rank-and-file rebellion" brought sick-outs, slowdowns, and wildcat strikes, often introducing difficulties for bureaucratic union leaders. Meanwhile, civil rights- and antidiscrimination struggles waged by African Americans, Mexican Americans, and Puerto Ricans were targeting the workplace, while what Dorothy Sue Cobble calls "the other women's movement" battled to improve labor rights for women. As activists pressed to open the American workplace, the existing social settlement—covering both corporate- and many union bureaucracies—faced mounting strain. With increasing numbers of African American and women employees, both AT&T and the Post Office became theaters of rumbustious contestation.[97]

Did rank-and-file postal and telephone workers step forward at this juncture, attempting to shape subsequent system development? Or, were they disinclined, or indifferent? In a word, workers in both industries were preoccupied by their overarching needs to defend against their employers and to democratize their unions. I have not identified evidence, in their news-sheets and strike bulletins or anywhere else, that they felt they possessed a stake in the ongoing liberalization and deregulation trend—or even that they understood that this trend existed. Though cognizant of this threat, on the other hand, their union leaders were habitually indisposed toward mobilizing rank-and-file workers to take political action, as the ACA had done in the late 1930s and 1940s. This not to say, though, that the CWA's leaders were inert. During the late 1960s and early 1970s, rather, they devoted themselves to bulking up as part of an industrial strategy. Building up their dues-paying membership through a great combination of unions would be a milestone in itself, in that it would occur at a historical hinge-point in the political economy of networking.

*

CWA President Joseph A. Beirne accepted the state's well-oiled machinery for collective bargaining, backed up by the occasional strike. This was the basis for organized labor's elevation of living standards, Beirne was convinced, which in turn would propel ameliorative reforms for the population as a whole. Among the objectives that Beirne advanced during the 1960s were full employment; better housing; and free public education from kindergarten to PhD.[98]

Two essential assumptions underlay Beirne's assessment. One was that, going forward from the mid-1960s, productivity advances would sustain corporate profits and that, mostly as a result of union action, a continuing share of these profits would be redistributed to workers. The other was that the federal government would anchor workers' collective bargaining rights. Like most of his peers at the top of the labor movement, Beirne had persuaded himself that organized labor had built a permanent home for itself within a relatively stable economy and a pluralist polity. Akin to other AFL-CIO leaders, he worked to cement the unions' place within this system by supporting and jockeying for influence within the Democratic Party and cooperating in US foreign policy. Rank-and-file concerns over life on the shop-floor he displaced, akin to most other union leaders, preoccupied with gaining, and holding, a seat at the table of policymaking. As well, executives at most big unions were predisposed against attempts by their members, and by workers in general, to challenge—let alone to disrupt—the capitalist structure and imperialist orientation of the US political economy.

Following in the footsteps of the AFL and then of the CIO, Beirne welded CWA into the institutional circuits of US foreign policy. His personal anti-Communism had been put on public display during the early 1950s, and Beirne's CWA soon began to take active part in the international Cold War. For example, he supported "Cuban Telephone Workers in Exile," an anti-Castro group based in Miami; and he worked to keep the Postal Telegraph & Telephone International federation with which CWA had affiliated—and of which Beirne became president—"steadfastly in the democratic camp," that is, in an anti-Communist stance. This involved strenuous effort, rather than just acquiescence. In 1961, Beirne proposed to the AFL-CIO Executive Council "that we take the lead in establishing a program to assist and encourage free trade unions in Latin America"; the next year this initiative became the American Institute for Free Labor Development which, under Beirne's aegis as secretary-treasurer, both solicited and obtained "active participation, personal and financial" from the Agency for International Development and big business—and, though Beirne neglected to mention it, likewise from the CIA (usually via dummy foundations. By 1967, overall, the CIA was pouring $100 million annually into labor unions). AIFLD staff were involved in the coup against Chile's President Salvador Allende though, as Angela Vergara points out, it is less clear that the AFL-CIO exercised real influence on Chilean labor unions in this polarized period. Some top US union leaders, including stalwart anti-Communists, belatedly chose differently; Walter Reuther, the president of the United Auto Workers, broke publicly with the AFL-CIO over its support for US Cold War foreign policy. By contrast, Beirne's CWA sustained a formal tie to US government international labor programs and Beirne himself offered continued public support for the US war in Southeast Asia. Indeed the day after President Nixon announced his invasion of Cambodia in 1970, Beirne "declared that the war actually helped workers economically." Only in 1972, swallowing whatever reservations he may have held in order to preserve his union's ties to the Democrats, did Beirne allow CWA to endorse the antiwar Democratic Presidential candidate George McGovern.[99]

The CWA had long experience of the technological trends pressed by AT&T executives into US telecommunications. Technological change struck at telephone workers, to take the foremost example, through mechanized self-service calling based on increasingly powerful telephone switches: as call-volumes skyrocketed, the ranks of telephone operators were culled. This menace had been apparent even prior to the formation of the NFTW, CWA's precursor, during the 1920s and 1930s. Because NFTW had retained residual company-union qualities, and because this wave of technological change hit at an occupation dominated by women, the NFTW leadership did not make it a priority. Indeed a historian has found that mechanization "in its initial stages (when it only affected women), had been welcomed by the national leadership" of CWA. As newer technologies came to threaten the jobs of skilled male workers, however, mechanization (as it was generally termed early on) belatedly gripped CWA leaders' attention. A portent arrived in 1949, when the CWA's monthly journal declared that "The real meaning of mechanization in the telephone industry was made clear with sledgehammer blows last month . . . No section of the industry seems likely to escape the Bell drive to cut working forces. Manufacturing, installation, telephone plant forces, traffic workers and clerical workers already have been hit in different degrees."[100]

Much of the postwar labor movement wrestled with what, beginning around 1950, began to be called "automation." In 1954 CIO President Walter Reuther stated that unions should have "supervision of the way in which mechanical brains and muscles are introduced, and above all, some method to keep men at work." Many of Reuther's peers participated alongside him in struggles for a direct say in how technology was implemented, in order to preserve (or ensure new) jobs and improve wages and benefits. However, they mostly accepted that new technologies were management's prerogative, and indeed were key to the productivity advances that they took to be the bedrock foundation for gains in workers' living standards. Beirne shared this view. Throughout his long postwar tenure as CWA president, his union strove to clarify the impact of "automation" on telephone work and workers, and to influence public policy in light of this knowledge. Beirne testified before Congress in 1955 and again in 1960; and he gave prominent attention to "radical technological change" in a book published in 1962. In 1964 CWA also initiated its reliance on management consultancies by engaging the Diebold Group—one of the foremost proponents of the ideology of automation—to report to the union on its ramifying consequences for telecommunications work.[101]

Accepting automation as "inevitable" in 1969, Beirne's CWA often managed to bargain successfully for "higher wages, better jobs, longer vacations, shorter hours." The union's acceptance had carried disproportionately dire consequences for union telephone operators and clerks, however, 80,000 of whom had been technologically displaced by 1965. Withal, Beirne believed that technological change could be tamed through pluralism: "the highest form of pluralism, the complete and complementary efforts of all elements in American society, must be enlisted if a solution is to be found." In 1969 Beirne might have deemed this approach realistic rather than chimerical: the Task Force on Communication Policy had only just recommended that "the Executive should have the capability to determine (with the Department of Labor) the nature and extent of any employment effects which might result from the organizational and technological changes flowing from this report, and develop appropriate employment and adjustment assistance measures to meet any potential problems." Indeed, Rostow's group had gone as far as to recommend that "the government should develop measures for protection against possible adverse effects due to technological change." Though he recognized that US society had reached a "plateau," and that it now faced its "most serious challenge" in thirty-five years, Beirne still could wax optimistic about the current prospect: "an application of intelligence, goodwill and dollars" would be sufficient to "move us safely through this technological revolution."[102]

Once again, pluralism did not obviate the union's need for the occasional strike. CWA's president recognized that automation "moderated" the "direct impact of its strike weapon"; however, Beirne also knew that the strike remained "highly effective in securing economic benefits for our members." Nevertheless, he argued that the CWA had best adopt a threefold strategy, which pivoted around community service and political activism as well as industrial action. By political activism he meant tightly bounded activity, directed—or contracted for—by the union's top leaders. Rank-and-file direct action was not part of the script.[103]

After 1965, accelerating introduction of new technology into the workplace was a major feature of a more enveloping syndrome. US corporations now faced both increased overcapacity and intensifying competition from European and Japanese rivals; executives' predictable efforts to raise profit rates in response revolved around far-reaching strategies. Many companies diversified their lines of business, embracing conglomeration and/or vertical- and horizontal integration. They relocated production in search of cheaper labor. They poured effort into modifying labor processes, by introducing ostensibly efficiency-enhancing technology and by reorganizing production. Despite struggles to equalize job opportunities, corporations maneuvered to lower their labor costs as they brought forward and modernized long-embedded strategies of segmenting work and dividing workers. US employers concomitantly stepped up their resistance to union organizing. Retaining the ingrained antagonism that was common to most members of their class, by the 1970s corporate executives were increasingly pressing to evade, subvert, and sometimes directly challenge the nation's industrial relations machinery. (This was one of the ways in which telecommunications liberalization advantaged employers as, in the newly proprietary data networking field, leading companies—both suppliers such as MCI and IBM and big corporate users—were alike determined to preempt collective bargaining.) Robert Brenner explains that union militancy in this period "represented less the flexing of muscles of an increasingly powerful labor movement . . . than a defensive struggle for survival provoked by the assaults of an increasingly well-organized and aggressive class of capitalist manufacturing employers and catalyzed by an angry rank and file." As the working class recomposed, Lane Windham shows, women, Blacks, Latinos and immigrants pressed with undiminished ardor to join and to build unions. That unions had tied themselves to the state during the New Deal, however, now increased their members' vulnerability as the government sanction for collective bargaining began to wane.[104]

Though a sustained attack against organized labor was commencing, until his tenure as CWA President ended in 1974 Joseph Beirne remained trapped within a partly self-constructed pluralist cage. While committed to, and benefiting from, the Democratic coalition of Lyndon Johnson, CWA's leaders were constrained by their union's history from mounting a political challenge to the state's network-liberalization drive even after the Democrats fell out of power. Beirne was not, however, unwilling to act: industrial action remained an option.

Beirne had already escalated CWA's membership drive into a top priority. By becoming a bigger organization representing hundreds of thousands of additional members, he believed, CWA could push ever-closer toward the center of decision-making. CWA therefore pursued internal and external organizing campaigns, beginning at the union's 1965 Annual Convention. Beirne indeed announced a drive to triple CWA's membership—which then stood at some 400,000—within just one decade. The union soon added tens of thousands of members to its rolls and, in 1969, it contracted with Arthur D. Little, Inc., a blue-chip consultancy, to make strategic recommendations for additional growth. CWA's selection of ADL was not happenstantial. In contrast to the 1930s "leather-jacket concept," Beirne declared, "today's national union leader, if he is to be even moderately successful at his job, must be surrounded by economists, lawyers, public relations men, statisticians, accountants, social security and insurance specialists, teachers, recreation directors and geriatrists." ADL's recommendations would come coated with a welcome patina of legitimacy.[105]

CWA convened a special meeting in March 1971 to evaluate the consultancy's recommendations. Arthur D. Little advised CWA not only to sustain its attempt to augment its membership but also—significantly—to diversify the types of workplaces it represented. In January 1972, Beirne reaffirmed CWA's priority: to more than double the union's size (to 1.25 million members) by 1975. As Beirne saw it, "If CWA is to continue to be successful at the bargaining table, it must enjoy the growth necessary to equip it for battle against highly organized, giant conglomerates with diversified holdings which make them highly defensible in dispute situations." The union regularly reported recruitment victories—400 electronics workers in Oregon, 300 independent telephone company workers in Iowa, another 2,500 in Alabama, a group of cable television employees in Texas and another in New York. Though these were modest increments, the variety of industries in which the union recruits worked suggested that the CWA had taken up ADL's recommendation and was indeed beginning to diversify—that it intended to be something more than a telephone union. Public employees, manufacturing workers, construction workers, cable television and interconnect company employees: CWA established beachheads among each of these groups. Beirne reported the next year that, between 1965 and 1973, the union had gained 158,592 members, so that CWA now boasted about 560,000 members; this, however, was far shy of the 1.25 million he had previously hoped to represent by 1975. How might CWA make up this deficit?[106]

Beirne now also embraced a second strategy: consolidation with other unions. At its 1972 meeting CWA approved a resolution which the union characterized as "perhaps the most important action taken at the 34th Annual CWA Convention." It authorized the formation of a committee empowered to proceed with merger talks with the two largest postal workers' unions, APWU and NALC.[107]

Why did Beirne target these organizations? As sitting president of a global telecommunications union federation—Postal, Telegraph, and Telephone International—he may have been impressed by the power that a combined union could wield, as evidenced by the organizations of workers toiling in the different departments of the government telecommunications ministries that then prevailed worldwide. However, he also would have known that solidarity could not be taken for granted across the divisions of these ministries of posts, telephones, and telegraphs. PTTI had supported Britain's postal strike of 1971—the first nationwide postal strike in British history—but the seven-week walkout had been hampered by some telephone workers' willingness to provide a partial-substitute service: voice telephone calls. For Beirne, recent changes to the status quo in US telecommunications were probably more important. To comprehend these requires a backward glance.[108]

Congressional hearings on the establishment of a US communications satellite system had been held in 1962, three years before CWA commenced on its "Growth" strategy. It was a mark of the stature CWA had achieved that Joseph Beirne was invited to testify. Beirne took the opportunity not only to reject a government takeover of satellites—one option under consideration—but to sing the praise of private ownership. Indeed he called to restrict ownership of satellite facilities specifically to existing telecommunications carriers: "This nation's . . . industrial evolution is [] based on private enterprise. We believe the private sector of our economy, having developed the greatest communications system the world has known, and having demonstrated its ability to provide for the extension of the existing system by means of a communications satellite system, should be permitted to go ahead now." This stance placed him alongside UAW (and onetime CIO) President Walter Reuther, a longtime champion of "free enterprise" conducted "to serve the public interest." Beirne's testimony therefore revealed no hint of engagement with the burgeoning trend to public-sector unionism that followed President Kennedy's 1962 executive order permitting federal employees to join unions and to bargain collectively with their government employer over some of their working conditions. Nor, more important, did it demonstrate a concern about the ramifications of permitting corporate capital to mass around new networking technologies. His posture was inward-looking, defensive; and all but oblivious of any need for an independent union-led policy and strategy for telecommunications.[109]

Beirne might have disparaged such considerations, in his turn, for being pie-in-the-sky. His dismissal of nationalization was grounded in a stubborn protectiveness—he might have called this realism—toward his union. Federal employees possessed few-to-no collective bargaining rights: CWA would not be able to organize or bargain forcefully on behalf of workers laboring for a government-owned network. Only if public-sector workers could gain comparable status with their peers working for private corporations might CWA represent them effectively. In 1962, then, the decisive factor for Beirne was almost certainly that a privately owned system would lend itself better to union organization. (Best of all for CWA would be for AT&T to own and operate the prospective satellite service, as CWA's membership base was at AT&T—but this was not how it worked out). Beirne sought to defend union jobs by gaining for CWA a reasonable chance to organize the workers who would operate the new telecommunications service.

In light of this, the outcome of the 1970 Post Office strike presented CWA with what Beirne probably saw as a prime opportunity. The Postal Reorganization Act signed by President Nixon on August 12, 1970 established a US Postal Service (USPS) as an independent government corporation to be administered by an appointed Board of Governors (first led by former AT&T executive Frederick Kappel). Concurrently, however, postal workers had gained a right to bargain collectively—though not the right to strike. Not less important, "the success of the strike encouraged democratic militant tendencies in the participating unions that challenged and in some cases overturned their respective entrenched leaderships." A massive workforce regarded management's plans to prioritize productivity gains with skepticism and suspicion. Some postal union leaders, especially those brought to power by the votes of rank-and-file workers who had been impressed by their militancy during the strike, called to establish an industrial union covering all postal workers, to strengthen workers' collective agency. Building on the cross-craft, interracial cooperation that had been demonstrated during the wildcat, after postal reform one militant union (the NPU) merged with four of the other organizations, creating the 320,000-strong American Postal Workers Union (APWU) in May 1971.[110]

APWU President Francis Filbey wanted to establish an overarching industrial postal union: "in One Big Union we can meet One Big Management on something near an equal footing," he stated. Filbey hoped that the other postal unions, notably, the large National Association of Letter Carriers, "will be inspired to join the merger ranks" and thus soon "make One Big Union a reality in 1971." NALC held out but, in May 1972, NALC President James Rademacher conceded that a merger was desirable. In their newly authorized right to collective bargaining, public-sector postal workers were converging on the status possessed by their peers in private industry. Could they overcome their historical separation in light of common threats, and unite the postal workforce? Now that the APWU and NALC had gained collective bargaining rights, furthermore, might they be open to merging with CWA? Beirne was keen to pursue a combination. So was his counterpart at the APWU.[111]

In 1972, the Communication Workers of America proposed a merger with the American Postal Workers Union; the National Association of Letter Carriers soon joined this attempt. A three-way amalgamation would have constituted a new testimony to working-class self-organization in the United States. Unconsciously recalling the American Communications Association of the 1930s and 1940s, its name was to be the "American Communications Union." The prospective combination also matched the ACA's ambition of organizing a far-flung industrial communications union: it would have brought together around one million members. APWU President Filbey told his members that the merger "in response to the imperatives of swiftly-changing technology in the whole field of communications would create one of the biggest and most powerful unions on earth." By ending the bifurcation of the telecommunications labor force, the American Communications Union would have spelled out a form of what McKercher and Mosco call "labor convergence." And it would have done so relatively in step with the state-channeled trend to privileging big business users and their suppliers.[112]

This attempt was rife with potential, and fraught with difficulty. APWU President Francis Filbey, who attended the CWA Annual Convention in June 1972, two months before his own union's founding convention, declared that "the day must come when all workers, in all aspects of the communications industry, must be unified for the protection of all. No longer can postal employees say they have nothing in common with their fellow citizens in other communications fields . . . we must get together to protect one another." Mechanization was rapidly spreading beyond dial telephone-based self-service, to a more multifarious computerization of postal and telephone work processes; as well, in the early 1970s a product-substitute that would be called email was being introduced in a limited-purpose system called Arpanet. How would these jurisdiction-bending innovations be assimilated? Erecting defenses was urgent.[113]

Telling APWU members that "a merger in response to the imperatives of swiftly-changing technology in the whole field of communications would create one of the biggest and most powerful unions on earth," Filbey placed a resolution to pursue merger with the CWA and the NALC before the APWU convention. A voice vote on the convention floor was sufficient to pass the resolution only "despite a loud minority chorus of nays." Beirne then reached out to the National Association of Letter Carriers. In a letter to NALC President (the same James Rademacher whom Charles Colson had importuned on behalf of the Nixon Administration), Beirne wrote, "The essence of the resolution we are looking at is the acceptance of the idea that there should be one great union in the entire postal and communications field." Talks commenced at the NALC's biennial convention in 1972, and its merger committee recommended "that we accept the invitation of the Communications Workers of America—AFL-CIO—and conduct meetings with that group to study the possibility of merger." In keeping with APWU and CWA, NALC affirmed that organized labor needed to respond to the challenge posed by consolidating corporate power: "the three unions involved in the merger talks are concerned about the trend toward industrial conglomerates and want to be prepared and able to display and utilize their combined strength to maximize effectiveness."[114]

Before summer's end, the CWA, the APWU, and the NALC were in the thick of negotiations. A merger between these three would have created the largest single union in the AFL-CIO. The confederation itself had encouraged mergers since 1955, when its own formation had resulted from a merger between the two once bitterly rivalrous federations. In blessing the proposed combination, AFL-CIO President George Meany recounted this logic at a gala dinner in honor of Francis Filbey held in November 1972: "I hope they succeed because, the way things have developed in America in the last ten or fifteen years, we need not a lot of small unions, we need stronger unions, where the combined assets, and the combined talents, and the combined energies can be put to work for all in an industry or a calling that is related."[115]

Beirne, Filbey, and Rademacher and merger committees from their respective unions began to meet in October 1972. A significant portion of this day-long event involved discussion of each union's current organizational structure, and of how it might fit into a consolidated postal and telecommunications union. Subcommittees were formed, their members tasked with drafting reports on national and local structures for each union. In December, Beirne reported hopefully in his monthly column to members, that the subcommittees' findings confirmed that "there is a common basis for the merger." He pointed out that CWA members would not need to increase their dues in a restructuring but, ominously, that APWU and NALC members indeed would face "a substantial increase." The reason, he wrote, was that scantily supported APWU and NALC locals would need to bulk up to reach a comparable level with their CWA counterparts.[116]

In January 1973, the three unions thrashed out an agreement on a provisional draft of a constitution for an American Communications Union. The merger committees established by each union then met independently, to review the draft and to make any needed changes. Filbey told his members that he hoped that, soon, "a proposal will be ready for submission through referendum procedures to the membership." Beirne's December 1972 column to CWA members confirmed that "We . . . anticipate that all of the necessary legal work can be done during the year 1973 so that we can be prepared for the operation of a merged organization in 1974." An unprecedented organization of telecommunications workers seemed on the verge of realization.[117]

The draft-constitution of the American Communications Union was an extraordinary document. Bearing in mind the diverse racial and gender composition of the would-be combination, its text sung out "that all communications workers and all members of labor have the right to economic, political and social justice." More concrete was its proposal that the new union should establish "bargaining councils," not only for the nation's telephone and postal workers but also for both nonpostal public employees and—crucial above all—for "non-Voice" workers laboring in computer communications. That is, the prospective ACU pointed up an imperative for collective organization in the now explosively developing field of digital networking. To extend union jurisdiction into digital networking therefore was, unequivocally, a primary motivation for merger.[118]

The CWA's separate draft version of this constitution elaborated: "Technology tells us to merge," stated the document—repeatedly edited and refined—explaining that existing "differences in methods of transmitting, handling and receiving messages" "will soon be a thing of the past." Further, "the technological improvements in hardware and modern techniques of transmission have reduced the differences between voice and the handling of written communications . . . exclusive work in the communications media is no longer reserved to a particular corporate structure or agency." In an arresting formulation, CWA's call for merger held that the respective unions' "leadership . . . must seize upon the opportunity to ensure that we do not become pawns in what others might call progress." Specifically, it discerned, "the recent move to de-federalize the American postal system, and the trend toward industrial conglomerates both warn us that we must be prepared and able to display and utilize our strength to its maximum effectiveness. We know that those whom we confront at the bargaining tables have already developed their corporate strength to the maximum degree." The unions sought to re-entrench a governing tenet of New Deal-era industrial unionism: that escalating corporate concentration left individual workers relatively powerless to bargain with their employers, engendering not only private suffering but also an overarching public harm—a reduction of the nation's purchasing power.[119]

From these texts it can be seen that, under CWA intellectual leadership, the prospective American Communications Union held a clear-eyed purpose and strategy. Nevertheless, disparate factors undermined the unions' attempt to consolidate their power across postal, telephone, and data services: financial vulnerabilities, organizational and political tensions, and sexism. The NALC possessed a substantial treasury by the early 1970s, and its leaders were reluctant to be absorbed into another union without retaining authority over allocation of their members' money. The APWU, on the other hand, found itself nearly overwhelmed by the costs of running a large union, as well as the difficulties of managing the merger of the five unions from which it had been formed. Two months after the APWU was established, Francis Filbey bluntly admitted, "With the final costs of the merger referendum, the final cost of negotiations, the cost of programs we have going ... yes, we're going to have troubles." CWA members, for their part, paid higher dues than did postal workers. The NALC's concern that the merger would be financially unbalanced—seems justified. Rademacher's union was also squabbling with the APWU over jurisdiction: the APWU charged NALC with raids on its membership. Sexist condescension also tore against solidarity. NALC's membership was 95 percent male, and its leaders voiced suspicions that CWA's 53 percent female membership might up-end its hierarchy within the prospective American Communications Union. In January 1973, the NALC actually was contemplating merger offers both from CWA/APWU and the International Brotherhood of Teamsters. The NALC's Midwest coordinator Henry Zych characterized the choice before his union in telling language: "a merger with the Teamsters would be a more logical move and would do us more good than the communications workers representing telephone operators."[120]

Merger became a steep uphill climb, as the APWU struggled to rally sufficient support among its ranks for a CWA merger without the NALC, whose leaders rejected it in March 1973. First, they did not want to sanction what would likely have been a 50 percent increase in member dues for financially strapped letter carriers. Second, NALC's executive board could not bring itself to establish an organization whose leaders were certain to be drawn disproportionately from the CWA. With NALC's pull-out, the APWU's own fervor cooled. A round of APWU bargaining negotiations with USPS managers was set to begin in April, and these claimed urgent priority. Stating that they would recommence after the APWU had completed bargaining, in fact, the merger talks were suspended indefinitely. Each of the three big unions fell back on its separate resources.[121]

Fighting cancer, midway through 1974 Beirne resigned from the presidency of the union he had led for thirty years; he died on Labor Day. Before stepping down, Beirne announced that CWA's members—now totaling 600,000—had won a historic victory over their largest employer: at long last, AT&T had agreed to national collective bargaining. This achievement actually belonged to rank-and-file workers at New York Telephone, whose protracted wildcat strike in 1971–1972 had finally convinced AT&T that national bargaining would be in its corporate self-interest. An American Communications Union, nevertheless remained a pipe-dream. Not external repression but their ingrained traditions, internecine frictions and prejudices, and financial inequalities doomed the endeavor.[122]

If organized labor's limitations helped condition the Nixon administration's capacity to intervene in telecommunications beginning in 1969, then capital's growing strength and assertiveness went on to help engender a new era of vulnerability for labor. The state's successful efforts to elevate the interests of business users indeed set working-class communities directly on digital capitalism's destructive path.

*

Corporate employers were pushing harder against unionization, demanding givebacks and concessions; during the 1970s, even as restive workers continued to protest, living standards began to drop and workplace rights suffered. Less than a decade later, President Ronald Reagan conducted a mass-firing of 11,000 striking air-traffic controllers, signaling to corporate executives that the government would abide their use of scab labor. They were not slow to read this signal and, as the strike-tactic began a long-term decline, the 1980s turned into a "decade of crisis" for organized labor. At the expense of US working-class communities, private data networks were one of a few "permissive technologies" that allowed profit-maximizing corporations to relocate manufacturing operations on a national and transnational scale. The trend carried forward through Democratic as well as Republican administrations, and the unionized segment of the US workforce dwindled as union power waned. In stark contrast to the leading industry of the first half of the twentieth century—automobile manufacturing—the dynamic segment of the economy that built up around networks toward the century's end was constructed as a "union-free" zone.

Freshly created jobs seldom brought collective bargaining rights. In this multiply divided society, those possessing power and resources took and those lacking them yielded.[123]

During this extended historical moment, recomposing class solidarities synched with state- and corporate attacks on unions to diminish labor's collective power. Givebacks proliferated; economic inequality deepened; racism renewed its hold. Amid this regression, unaccountable data networking flourished ceaselessly.

*

In 1972, as merger negotiations proceeded, the policy liberalization that was the indispensable predicate of private corporate networks and the digital capitalism that built upon them remained incomplete—still malleable. Might bold actions by a union boasting one million members have qualified or arrested the trend to liberalization and deregulation? This counterfactual question needs to be posed for, otherwise, the process may seem inexorable.

It was not. Its juggernaut power stemmed from assertive capital, an activist state, and what had become a fractured and politically dependent unionism. Both before and in the wake of the failed merger, it is striking that CWA—the strongest of the three unions—took virtually no autonomous political action with respect to the liberalization/deregulation trend. Joseph Beirne worked assiduously to expand CWA's membership base in the new network industries, hoping that his union's strength and its ties to the Democratic Party might carry it forward until the political climate improved. This defensive approach failed to engage the scale of the threat posed by the Nixon administration's radical liberalization measures and its accompanying attacks on the public utility model. Nor, of course, could it anticipate the political changes that followed in the wake of Nixon's resignation and Beirne's death in 1974.

CWA's leaders had not prepared the union to resist business users' up-ending of telecommunications policy. *CWA News* had published virtually no stories about the prior FCC proceedings that would come to be synonymous with the early trend toward liberalization. Nor had the journal granted more than nominal attention to LBJ's Task Force. Nor, according to the official *FCC Record*, did the union actually participate in any of the agency's groundbreaking rulemakings, either before or after the transition from LBJ to Nixon. Perhaps the first instance of direct union involvement is telling in itself. A couple of years after the collapsed attempt to create an American Communications Union—in 1975–1976—AT&T was lobbying Congress to pass legislation to reinstate the unreformed public utility system. Beirne's successor as CWA President, Glenn Watts, thereupon allied his union with AT&T, as Beirne had done before, in a broader coalition aiming to pass this "Consumer Communication Reform Act."

Flanked by a top Republican lobbyist and the head of a leading independent telephone company, AT&T Vice Chairman William Ellinghaus was able to gain a meeting with President Gerald R. Ford. Though CWA was not represented directly at this meeting, Ford's records of the event include a statement from CWA's executive board urging a restoration of the old order, including a declaration that "Congress should reaffirm its long-standing policy of network unity, with the network providing all needed services within its capabilities." AT&T threw everything it had into this campaign, with CWA in a support role. The attempt failed.[124]

In fairness to the union, the times had become suddenly inauspicious with the election of Richard Nixon. The liberal Democratic coalition had been sundered, and with Nixon the heady years of fraternal access to the Democratic administrations of Kennedy and Johnson came to an abrupt end. Remote from his rank-and-file members and, with the bottom-up turbulence around the 1971 strike, mistrustful as well, Beirne was now denied his preferred mode of "political activism": working from near the center of power in Washington. After Nixon's resignation, the interregnum of the Gerald Ford presidency was also a time of transition at CWA as, in 1974, Glenn E. Watts replaced Beirne. Thereafter, the ideological tide turned within the Democratic Party, as it became tinged with greater faith in "competition." Uncomfortable with unions, after the 1976 election the incoming Democratic engineer-president Jimmy Carter wrote his newly appointed FCC Chair Charles D. Ferris that he supported actions "to promote competition in all areas of communications." Because Carter quickly lost political capital, and because AT&T remained obdurate, the result was an impasse; but legislative trench warfare did not checkmate piecemeal liberalization at the FCC. Nor did it throttle the Justice Department's ongoing antitrust case against AT&T. In Congress, during the early 1980s Tim Worth, Gary Hart and Al Gore were among the so-called "Atari Democrats" who supported competition and investment in high-technology as a road to economic renewal. After the late 1960s, in turn, CWA did not find the narrow "political activism" that so contained its leaders' efforts to be a very effective strategy.[125]

Historian Nelson Lichtenstein explained late in the 1980s that "labor's postwar abdication from any sustained struggle over the structure of the political economy has it its own debilitating consequences," chief among them being to deprive unions "of any effective voice in the contemporary debate over the reorganization of work technology or the reindustrialization of the economy." Data communications systems exemplified this. Built out amid the unions' unwillingness to forge an independent political program, in light of their leaders' benighted pluralism, data networking during its formative years was stamped by organized labor's diminishment. A second conclusion must also be contemplated: "The profound defeat of the U.S. labour movement over the past three to four decades is usually measured by the loss of things that workers once took for granted like decent wages and benefits. A less quantifiable but ultimately more decisive indicator is the retreat from possibilities."[126]

Perhaps the decisive loss for CWA pertained to the issue of union jurisdiction. Beirne undeniably understood that it was imperative to extend his union's base into computer communications. But he and his allies and successors in CWA did not craft an independent union strategy for halting, or at least qualifying, the movement of network "intelligence" out of AT&T's centralized hubs and into the premises of major business users. As policies were liberalized, oil companies, banks, manufacturers, big retailers, aerospace and electronics corporations were working closely with specialized equipment and service suppliers to implement proprietary computer networks. How could CWA reach into these demand-side workplaces, so that the jurisdiction-bending innovations cropping up within and around them continued to be vested with adequate job protections? In bidding to establish bargaining councils in "non-voice communications," the leaders of the prospective American Communications Union understood that this constituted a fundamental problem: that the workers who built and operated data networks had to be organized if the transformation of telecommunications was not to come at the expense of their members.[127]

After the failure of the merger, CWA seems to have relinquished this already-articulated need to extend its jurisdiction to the scattered corporate "IT" workplaces that constituted the key sites of computer network-building. Organizing and uniting in concert small groups of workers within hundreds of giant hostile corporations were probably unattainable goals. Nevertheless, had an American Communications Union been realized, and had it shown sufficient militancy to threaten a nationwide shutdown of telecommunications, inclusive of mail and voice services, it is possible that it might have altered the terms on which demand-side data networking was proceeding. Possible—*if*, in lieu of being shut out of the inner circles of power, the union now developed and activated a genuinely independent political program. Generating the resources needed so that the membership might educate themselves, their families, their communities and other workers to oppose policies privileging business users and independent suppliers and to mount a mass-action political campaign was, however, completely out of step with CWA's history. In consequence—as demonstrated by CWA's own history after the failed merger—its members were left largely blind-sided and disarmed. Organized labor's ingrained unwillingness to wage intense and, if necessary, sustained struggles over the general direction of the political economy came to a sharp point exactly here.

The unions' political weakness did not, however, signify a general powerlessness or a hesitation to put this power to a purpose. CWA remained a forceful presence even through the Reagan inclemency. In August 1983, during a three-week strike by 675,000 telecommunications workers, AT&T's huge (300,000-strong) supervisory workforce and its now extensively mechanized self-service operations, combined to reduce the strike' impact on call-completion rates among both households and big corporate users. Even so, the strikers had real impact. New installations and repairs slowed while, after three weeks, many big corporate users thought that the walkout portended a cascading deterioration of service. Owing to its dependence on corporate demand, AT&T agreed to settle the strike on relatively favorable terms for telephone workers: the carrier had gone into the contest seeking givebacks, but emerged from it offering pay increases, improved job security, and better pension- and health benefits. In 1989, after AT&T had been broken up, a four-month strike mounted in New York and New England by units of CWA together with those of the International Brotherhood of Electrical Workers succeeded in holding the line against a former Bell unit's demands for medical plan givebacks. The two unions staged "a coordinated campaign of membership education and mobilization, in hundreds of workplaces in six states" and began to foster "a culture of militancy and union solidarity" that changed their character significantly during the next thirty years.[128]

It is also important to note that the elevation of business users did not signify that public opinion favored the reshaping of telecommunications. An AT&T-commissioned poll in 1979 indicated only scant demand to open markets to competition (of course people were not given a choice: as a Bell executive ruefully noted a few years later, "there has been no . . . referendum"). Five years after the break-up of the Bell System, the *New York Times* reported that, for the majority of residential telephone users who did not place many long distance calls, the most prevalent results were "confusion and higher rates." A bottom-up union political mobilization might have gained traction.[129]

In the event, though, organized labor's political marginalization was patent. This was evident in the resolution of the government's antitrust case against AT&T in 1982. According to soon-to-be CWA president, Morton Bahr, "At no time during the entire process" of breaking up the world's largest corporation, "did any party to the antitrust suit address the concerns and futures of the employees who built the system." Bahr stated that "the labor movement had no role in the consent decree. We didn't have any involvement in the process of divestiture until after the agreement was reached and all the major decisions had already been made." Bahr's admission revealed both bafflement and subordination: The union's commitment to "private enterprise," as Beirne had called it, had combined with its deference to the federal government to leave CWA entirely sidelined. Ingrained practices and assumptions about how the government would and would not act were being overturned: the late 1940s' CIO decision to cast out its radical social unions had come home to roost. Though CWA remained comparatively strong and, indeed, throughout the past decades it successfully diversified both across the greater communications industry and beyond, this legacy proved difficult to abandon. As late as 1998, its then-president—a long-time union veteran who had moved into CWA early in the 1950s from the American Communications Association—still offered up the standard line: "the changes brought about by . . . technological development . . . we knew to be inevitable."[130]

The ravaging of public utility principles was no less consequential for postal-dom. Postal Service executives were bent on accelerating computerization, again chiefly to meet the commercial-mailing demands voiced by their largest business customers. Relying on this infrastructure, in 1978 USPS administrators inaugurated what they deemed a highly promising electronic product-substitute, in the form of a hybrid email service. This offering ran into immediate implacable opposition from would-be corporate rival suppliers, including AT&T, ITT, Graphnet and IBM. Political pressure was applied; and the USPS was forced out of the provision of email service, not only domestically but also internationally. Might an alert and mobilized "American Communications Union" have staved off this privatization, so that email service would remain a postal prerogative and the union retain its jurisdiction over the work required to operate it? In any case, as Ryan Ellis shows, the withdrawal of Postal Service email carried a punishing ramification for personal privacy, and one that possessed an enduring effect. E-COM, as it was termed, incorporated the privacy protections that had been affixed to first-class mail since the establishment of the Post Office. With the order to abandon the Postal Service's email offering, Fourth Amendment defenses against unreasonable search and seizure were rendered porous and contestable. We continue to live in that shadow of that giveaway.[131]

The public utility model, then, was not exhausted but attacked and subverted. In its stead, during the Reagan ascendancy, policymakers embraced a full-fledged market fundamentalism: the idea that the public interest equated solely with what passed for free-market efficiency. This radical truncation of policy would shape the ensuing decades; in 1997, a scholar acknowledged that "it has become extremely difficult to assert a non-market-based conception of the public interest in today's communication world." First to be withdrawn from public utility oversight were purveyors of equipment for computer communications systems and specialized networks, both inhouse company services and commercial carriers. Regulators also chose to place cellular telephone networks, when they emerged, beyond reach of the robust authority they possessed under Title II of the Communications Act; cable TV- and wireless-internet access were again exempted. The logic was uniformly that, as market conditions became characterized as competitive, public utility regulation could be phased out and "collaborative industry-led initiatives" entrusted with self-regulation. Meanwhile, for all the shrill hullaballoo about the urgency of "deregulation," in actuality, as Nicholas Johnson protested, executive power over civilian communications was strengthened. The state acted both as a prod to liberalization and a buttress against democratizing pressures. Through proceeding after proceeding, accountability to the commonweal was pared down and market openings enlarged, as ownership and control of network technologies were lifted out of the web of responsibilities that had encased public utility telecommunications— amid spurious claims to be enhancing the public function. During the 1970s and 1980s, this trend passed from the periphery of the public switched network to its core, as AT&T executives and state managers progressively extricated the giant company from its public utility responsibilities. The coup de grace came when the federal antitrust suit that began in 1974 broke up AT&T in 1982. Curtailing end-to-end service provision, the divestiture constituted an implosion of the industrial structure that had dominated US telecommunications and of the public utility framework that had been built to encase it.[132]

The result was to replace a single corporate monopoly with a monopoly large enough to profit the better part of the capitalist class. Meanwhile, even critics of networking policy sustained a knee-jerk focus on how to rein in the power of mammoth, centralized service suppliers—which, in truth, did remain hugely powerful in the market for residential and individual services. However, the political-economic power that had gathered at the demand side of corporate capitalism was now unprecedented, and both critical analysts and organized labor remained disengaged from it. Unless and until this deficit could be corrected, no adequate program for democratic reconstruction around networks could be imagined, let alone actualized.

The consequences remain with us. The number of US employees in IT occupations has undergone decades-long growth—a tenfold increase between 1970 and 2014, to 4.6 million people. Labor was set to work imagining, designing, manufacturing, operating, and repairing digital systems in every sector of US industry. Just as capitalist industrialization reorganized most major sites of profitmaking beginning in the late eighteenth century, albeit raggedly unevenly, so digital systems and services began to be bolted to virtually all significant segments of the political economy. Between 2005 and 2015, on the other hand, while the number of telecom workers declined by 19 percent (to 883,000), the number of union members in the industry fell by half, to 188,000. In 2016 the telecommunications unionization rate stood at 14.6 percent, while workers in computing and mathematical occupations showed a mere 3.9 percent unionization rate. Just between 2006 and 2012, meanwhile, the USPS cut its career workforce by nearly one-quarter and each of the big postal unions reported corresponding drops in membership; membership in USPS labor unions fell from 632,000 in 2000 to 458,000 in 2012. By 2020 the USPS employed 496,000 "career-"and

148,000 "non-career" workers, though it then pumped up its workforce substantially during the Covid-19 epidemic.[133]

The last decades of the twentieth century were, finally, when internet technology germinated and began to spread. Domestically, the internet became a rare cause of celebration within what was for most Americans a general experience of deteriorating public services, mounting inequality, and diverging and diminished solidarities. To take adequate account of this extraordinary moment, however, we must also train our attention outward. For the internet was only the latest incarnation of an abiding program to establish an "American communications system" for the wider world.

11
Telecommunications and American Empire

To a restive working-class, strengthening social justice movements, disorder in the international financial system, and resurgent intercapitalist competition, US elites were compelled to respond. Winding through their responses were networking systems and services. Profitable investment was renewed by energizing new industries and reorganizing existing ones, both of which relied heavily on computer-communications. Policymakers had helped to spur this awakening business demand by recasting the foundations of US network system development, forthrightly, in the case of the Post Office, and more opaquely in electronic telecommunications. In the Post Office, the wildcat strike from below precipitated a direct restructuring of provision, leading on to an agonizing dialectic of attrition and resistance. In electronic telecommunications, workers' protests fed into a complex and ramifying process of politically induced reorganization. The dispensation of the public utility framework formed the locus of struggle. While Blacks, Latinos, women, and gays strived to broaden it, demanding equality in employment and service provision, business users worked to subvert it to expand their own specialized advantages in networking. In electronic networking and perhaps to a lesser extent, in postal service, regressive modernization elevated executives, investors, and business users and undermined the power of workers and their unions.[1]

Amid the ruins of the public utility foundation, between the 1980s and the 2000s an initially obscure variant of data networking ultimately raced ahead of all its rivals. To fully grasp the phenomenon that became the global internet we must return to where this book began: the role of networks in US empire. For the story of American telecommunications becomes fully legible only by tracing elites' outward-looking imperial project from the nineteenth century capture of a continent into our own era. After a few words about imperialism itself, I will sketch how networks and imperialism coevolved throughout subsequent US history. Then it will be time to set the internet into this framework.

*

Initially haphazard, obstructed, and sometimes reversible, modern imperialism is rooted in "the expansive drive of each advanced capitalist nation to operate on a world scale" in competition with other capitalist powers. Crown-sponsored voyages of discovery and plunder, privateers, companies of merchant adventurers, royally chartered trading companies and, eventually, multinational corporations and powerful capitalist states successively "transformed, adapted, and manipulated ... the economies and societies of the conquered or dominated areas" to serve "the imperatives of capital accumulation at the center." Aided by local collaborators, at every step imperialists incited opposition and resistance. Initiated in coastal enclaves and commercial entrepots, over decades and centuries the imperialists' spheres of operation grew.[2]

During the fifteenth century Iberian imperialism launched as a seaborne force. Europeans enslaved Africans to work as household servants, urban laborers, farmers, and herders in Portugal and Spain; developed or inserted themselves into commercial trade routes in Africa and the Indian Ocean; and plundered silver from Latin America. As the demand for slaves shifted out of the household toward other forms of labor, the slave-based plantation in Brazil, the Caribbean and North America fed raw materials into Europe's commercial economy. By the second half of the seventeenth century, the Dutch Republic, England, and France "possessed their own steadily expanding and increasingly lucrative overseas empires, often carved from the margins of the Iberian empires." Soon thereafter, especially in the case of England and its colonies, "industry and empire" became a regenerative circuit: formal colonialism expanded in in support of manufacturing. As Europe's swelling productive output necessitated greater supplies of raw materials and labor, previously unconnected trading networks were tied together into extended commodity chains. Colonialism helped answer capital's burgeoning need to lock in export markets as Europe's leading states worked to bind up "their" colonies in Asia, Africa, the Middle East and the Americas into separate and exclusive economic blocs—while penetrating the defenses of other colonial empires. As top-dog Britain and the now-lesser European powers "occupied, controlled or laid claim" to four-fifths of the land surface of the world, the years around 1900 also saw "the territorial division of the globe and the first global struggle for redivision" as a new group of technologically advanced capitalist countries—Germany, Japan, and the United States—threw themselves into the "unremitting inter-state competition" for empire.[3]

The bearers and the character of imperialism thus have recurrently altered. Imperialism has been reconfigured not only in light of the twists and turns of a rivalrous process of capitalist development but also through resistance to it. The narrative arc of this final chapter traces how telecommunications coiled through what ultimately became the dominant capitalist imperialism: that of the United States.

Territorial Empire

"A nation without borders," as historian Steven Hahn titles it, the United States was constructed through territorial land-grabs: empire commenced long before nation-hood, as US settler colonialism expanded across the North American continent and beyond. Telecommunications constituted a cornerstone of empire-building: The government-run Post Office helped sustain the seizure and occupation of indigenous lands, as we saw in Chapter 1, and the agency drew on its legislative charter to build out its system of communicative exchanges ever-westward, even in advance of white settlement. Within just a few decades, in consequence, the fledgling US Post Office eclipsed the scope of the postal systems operated by Europe's major powers. Several decades later, the privately owned corporate telegraph was fitted-out for the same role. During the 1840s, a rudimentary telegraph network was patched together to carry news of the US war on Mexico to New York and Washington. In the 1860s Western Union established a "Russian extension" to push telegraph lines up the Pacific coast into Canada and on to Alaska. During the 1870s and 1880s, US military officers—"prairie imperialists," as a historian calls them—coordinated their attacks on "Indian country" through both posts and telegraphs. Meanwhile, as US railroads tracked toward the southwestern frontier, New York financiers invested in telegraph companies to reach into Mexico and beyond, as far south as Lima, Peru. Such efforts laid foundations for a capitalist market of unrivaled size. Correctly viewing posts and telegraphs as incursions, we saw, Native Americans staged raids against both systems, with momentary success during the 1860s in Colorado and the Great Plains.[4]

The question of how US telecommunications might expand beyond continental borders, where networks would have to interact with their foreign counterparts, intersected with the construction of a US "domestic" infrastructure. A portent of US ambitions arrived in the form of a project to build a prospective 16,000-mile extension of Western Union's network, via British Columbia, Russian America [Alaska], and the Bering Sea, on to Russia and, finally, to Europe. This project was abandoned, in 1866, after the US submarine cable capitalist Cyrus Field succeeded in laying a rival, and operational, trans-Atlantic cable. However, both initiatives demonstrated that US telecommunications was already freighted with untrammeled supranational objectives. In 1869, in a memo sent to 23 foreign governments, Secretary of State Hamilton Fish signaled US aspirations, as he pressed to gain for the US a "central position in the communication of the world." In 1870, Vice-Admiral David D. Potter wrote to Cyrus Field in favor of a Pacific cable, routed through the Sandwich Islands (Hawaii)— which, he held, would ultimately become "a part of the United States," adding that "it can easily be seen what an advantage this freedom of communication would be to our people in the great race for supremacy in China." During the early 1890s, sugar plantation owners brought in US troops to overthrow Hawaii's queen and, in 1898, the US annexed the islands. US president McKinley calculated that Hawaii would serve as an indispensable staging-ground for the US military as it moved to seize the Philippines during the Spanish-Cuban-American War. Nearly simultaneously (1899–1900) Secretary of State John Hay confirmed the larger purpose of this imperial strategy when he formulated the Open Door policy for trade relations with China.[5]

This expansionism triggered a major public and political movement of opposition to US imperialism. It drew hundreds of thousands of supporters from across the political spectrum, up to and including Democratic President Grover Cleveland (1893–1897) and his successor as Democratic Presidential candidate, William Jennings Bryan—who made antiimperialism a central issue in the election of 1900. Despite fierce and persistent opposition, the annexed US territories were neither relinquished nor transformed into US states. Amid this debate, President McKinley expressly underlined the importance of communications for US conquest to the US Congress: "The United States will come into possession of the Philippine Islands on the farther shore of the Pacific. The Hawaiian Islands and Guam becoming US territory, and forming convenient landing places on the way across the sea, the necessity for cable communications between the United States and all these Pacific Islands has become imperative. Such communication should be established in such a way as to be wholly under the control of the United States whether in time of peace of in war." He might also have mentioned the new US territory of Puerto Rico, as well as Cuba where the US planted a permanent base at Guantanamo. An early mode of radio technology controlled by the US Navy thereafter helped the US to consolidate its strategic interests both in the Caribbean and the Pacific. US telecommunications therefore was enfolded into what appeared to be an expanding territorial imperialism congruent with the European colonial model.[6]

As US big businesses and military agencies looked beyond continental strategies, the question of erecting a great international communications network with a US command-center moved to the forefront of policy. This goal, which would anchor US policy in international communications for the next century and beyond, both grew out of and inflamed geopolitical-economic conflict. During the last three decades of the nineteenth century, amply supported by its home state, British capital dominated international communications. By about 1900 submarine cables interconnected the far-flung territories of the British Empire—from Australia to Hong Kong to India to Egypt to South Africa to Canada. Led by the largest multinational corporation in the world, the Eastern and Associated Telegraph Company, Britain controlled three-fifths of the world's cables in 1898, and possessed a disproportionate lead in technology development and operational support: Britain operated 28 cable ships, compared to France's five and the US's two. At its apex, before World War I, no less than 49 discrete cable cuttings would have been needed to isolate the island of Britain. To a great extent, in turn, before 1900 the entire world depended heavily on Britain for constructing, laying, and repairing undersea cables—anywhere. Not coincidentally, much of the globe's commercial, military, and diplomatic intelligence passed before British eyes. US leaders paid close attention to this during and after World War I, when Britain cut and rerouted Germany's undersea cables; circulated jingoistic and self-serving news accounts to the US press; and decrypted—and in one famous instance, the Zimmerman telegraph, publicized—ostensibly secret telegrams transiting British networks.[7]

This lesson was absorbed. Britain's preponderance in international communications motivated and shaped US policy. Its takeover of Hawaii had already allowed the US to preempt a British-operated Pacific cable from landing there. It became common knowledge early in the twentieth century that Britain's unrivaled global cable system "came in conflict with interests claimed by the United States in two strategic areas, Latin America and the Far East"; and that the US had responded by "intervening in many places"—above all, in South America—"to check the growth of Britain's communications power."[8]

US decisions and policies in communications became a serious concern for Britain and other rivals. During the decades around the turn of the twentieth century, the continental United States of itself constituted the largest and most dynamic market for telecommunications service. "To create a long-distance telegraph service to all parts of the world without the means of collecting and distributing messages in America," wrote the managing director of British Marconi in 1913, "would be like playing *Hamlet* without the Prince of Denmark." The terms on which US commercial and state authorities authorized interconnection to foreign networks became correspondingly contentious. Even more so were US efforts to project control over international networking.[9]

The US's objective of erecting an expansive cross-border network managed by and catering for US businesses and military and diplomatic agencies was not, however, exceptional. Japan wove telegraphs and cables into its growing territorial empire in East Asia. Though sometimes having to rely on British cables, France did likewise in Indochina, the West Indies, and West Africa. Germany's belated efforts to reach the Middle East, the Western Pacific and South America reflected its latecomer-status as a colonialist. Plans to control international telecommunications, we may say, constituted a typifying general feature of nineteenth and twentieth century capitalist colonialism, which shared the goal of imposing practices of cost containment, profit-maximization, and labor control beyond a given home-state jurisdiction. US leaders maneuvered especially against the global hegemon, Britain; and we will see that it only succeeded when, later, it became entangled in a reconfiguration of US imperialism itself. In the meantime, corporate infighting and intercapitalist rivalry predominated in international telecommunications.[10]

Beyond Continental Borders after World War I

"Understanding the rise of the United States in the twentieth century," writes historian Jonathan Winkler, "requires tracing how this nation passed from periphery to the center of world communications." This was the work of decades. The process began as US capital called upon the state to extend multifarious forms of aid to the carriers and, behind the carriers, to their customer-base: large corporations—as build-outs of US undersea cables and radio-telegraph systems confronted a competitively charged international environment.[11]

Scholars have long understood that the US institutionalization of radio comprised a watershed; and that giant corporations and military agencies predominated throughout this process. Organized in 1919 by General Electric (GE), at the behest of middle-ranking US Navy officials, the Radio Corporation of America (RCA) intended to become the "sales agent and operating company" for GE. A deeper purpose was also evident: to forge a chosen instrument of the US Government, in order to establish an international system of "American owned and operated radio communications," as RCA put it. Britain had quickly assumed international control of the first generation of radio technology, through the Marconi company. By 1912, "Marconi was on the verge of total domination of global radio communications." During and immediately after World War I, however, US corporate and Naval officials maneuvered successfully to seize the lead with respect to a second, and more capacious and versatile, generation of radio. By 1924, RCA management claimed that it had met its charge: "the United States is now foremost among the nations of the world in international radio telegraphy, marine radio service, as well as radio broadcasting and the development of radio apparatus." As it instituted service along high-traffic trans-Atlantic routes, RCA also forced substantial rate reductions on Britain's cable operators.[12]

RCA's service radiated beyond the Atlantic. Japan, Hawaii, Indochina, the East Indies, the Philippines, Hong Kong, Shanghai, Fiji and Australia each interconnected into RCA's radiotelegraph network by 1930. In Latin America and the Caribbean, RCA then furnished service to Argentina, Brazil, Colombia, Venezuela, Chile, Panama, Costa Rica, Cuba, Puerto Rico and the Dominican Republic.[13]

In thralldom to its own profit imperatives, however, RCA turned to make common cause with its major international competitors: not only French and German but also British radio interests. Indeed, RCA helped establish what a historian has called "an international cartel, held together by the cross-licensing of patents and by traffic agreements." Antagonistic commercial ambitions and contending geopolitical designs persisted and, in some regions and some product markets—South America and East Asia; wire service news and radio communications equipment—struggles between RCA and its allies were fierce. However, the existence of the cartel also went far to truncate US political leaders' ambitions.[14]

So too, paradoxically, did the increasingly capacious and versatile character of radio technology, as it evolved from arcs and alternators to vacuum tubes. Within just three years of RCA's formation in 1919, an unanticipated application of wireless exploded on the scene: commercial radio broadcasting. RCA scrambled to revamp its strategy. As the company refocused around the suddenly very profitable markets for domestic radio broadcasting receiver equipment and, soon after this, for advertising on the new radio networks like its own NBC, it de-emphasized its international telegraph operations. Meanwhile, Britain leapfrogged ahead in this field by innovating a third generation of wireless technology—short-wave radio, or "beam" transmissions to directional antennas—which greatly improved point-to-point transoceanic communication.[15]

Short-wave service did advance US commercial and military purposes throughout Latin America and parts of the Pacific and East Asia; but this did not amount to a frontal challenge to Britain's resurgent "international preeminence" in wireless. By the mid-1920s, RCA's much-heralded promise of an "American system of international communications" had been blunted. Though RCA lost few opportunities to drape itself in the flag, it had become not a chosen instrument but a "conventional, profit-oriented company attuned increasingly to the provision of entertainment to the American public." In 1930, RCA actually tried—unsuccessfully—to hive off its international operations.[16]

The company RCA hoped would buy its international radiotelegraph unit—also a newcomer—made a second bid to expand a US-managed system. The International Telephone and Telegraph Corporation (ITT) was formed in 1920, "to control and direct the development of local or national telephone companies throughout Central and South America and the West Indies" by establishing subsidiaries or affiliated companies. Initially, ITT was a secondary player, with subsidiaries in Puerto Rico and, via a joint-venture with AT&T, in Cuba. Within just a few years, however, ITT established itself as a formidable power not only throughout South America and the Caribbean, but also in Europe and the Pacific.[17]

ITT benefited from a limited trend toward denationalization, wherein several countries moved to adopt the US model of corporate-commercial ownership of their wireline networks. In 1922, ITT anticipated expansion in South America and Europe as a result of this switch to private ownership. By the end of

1924, ITT had assumed control of Spain's telephone system; a French telephone manufacturing company; and the Mexican Telephone and Telegraph Company. (Overall, however, privately owned and operated national telecommunications systems remained much in the minority.)[18]

Most significant for ITT's growth was a transaction undertaken during the summer and early autumn of 1925. Following months of behind-the-scenes bargaining, on September 30, 1925 ITT completed its purchase of almost all of AT&T's international telephone manufacturing subsidiaries. These were unmatched. The sale conferred on ITT a newly renamed "International Standard Electric" subsidiary, possessing wholly owned telephone manufacturing plants in England, Belgium, France, Spain, Italy and the Netherlands; a controlling interest in factories located in Japan and China; and wholly owned distributors of telecommunications equipment in Norway, Australia, Argentina, and elsewhere. "Aside from being one of the largest industrial deals between American companies doing an extensive foreign business," reported *The New York Times*, "the effect will be to give the International Telephone and Telegraph company business affiliations in practically every part of the world an opportunity to extend its telephone service in those countries by competing with the domestic monopolies in the production and sale of equipment." With support from its bankers, ITT quickly added to this massive manufacturing complex two operating telegraph cable systems: All America Cables, and the Mackay System. This granted it a nationwide US presence, in competition with Western Union, and bequeathed to it long-distance circuits stretching to the West Indies, Central and South America, Canada, Mexico, and a number of points in Europe and East Asia. Finally, ITT also obtained telephone service concessions in Uruguay, Chile, Brazil, Argentina, Peru and Colombia.[19]

It was this deal with AT&T that turned ITT into a global power. AT&T's International Western Electric unit, which had subsumed AT&T's overseas telephone equipment manufacturing enterprises into a single subsidiary in 1918, had been built up over thirty prior years, making AT&T one of the leading US-based transnational corporations. Why did AT&T part with its foreign properties? What caused AT&T to swim against the tide of contemporary transnational corporate expansion by US companies, especially as AT&T had been precocious in establishing successful overseas operations? Why, ultimately, was it not AT&T that became the US chosen instrument in international telecommunications? Answering these questions helps explain the difficulties that confounded a US-managed system of international communications between the two world wars—some of which would prove persistent.

During the summer of 1923, AT&T had performed a confidential analysis of "The Foreign Business of the Western Electric Company." This study revealed that AT&T's subsidiaries had amassed an impressive share of world telephone apparatus sales. AT&T companies claimed 19 percent of telephone equipment sales in Australasia; 36 percent in Europe, exclusive of both Germany and Russia; 66 percent in Asia; 73 percent in Canada; and 77 percent in Latin America. In the supply of submarine cables, where Britain continued to lead, AT&T's business was less rosy. All told, nevertheless, AT&T's International Western Electric had generated an average profit of about 11 percent annually during the five years through 1922. This made it, unquestionably, a going proposition.[20]

ITT's offer to pay AT&T about $33 million to acquire its foreign manufacturing business (apart from its Canadian subsidiary, which AT&T retained) reflected this. Because AT&T had already recouped its entire $15 million original investment, it stood to gain a nominal profit of $17 million. This made the transaction far more than a fire-sale; so why should AT&T have accepted ITT's offer? AT&T had been expanding its international units profitably since 1882; and its foreign subsidiaries might have contributed to a differently configured "American system of international communications." Why, during the early 1920s, should AT&T have chosen instead to divest its foreign operations?[21]

Both domestic and international factors played into its decision. A top AT&T executive intimated that, by demonstrating the company's willingness "to confine the financial interests of the System to the United States and Canada," the transaction would allow AT&T to concentrate on the tumultuous US scene. We saw in a previous chapter how the giant holding company vied to manage a vexatious system of state and federal regulation; and to undertake the gigantic capital investment programs which, as we also saw, were needed to expand its "domestic" (indicating that this embraced Canadian properties as well) long-distance network. In themselves, these considerations furnished incentives for executives to turn inward, to focus their energies on North America.[22]

However, another element also entered into the equation. AT&T's endeavor to administer operations and strategies throughout a score of foreign countries necessitated "such a variety of treatment and so much intricacy of detail that our best efforts so far leave it far below our ideal." The politics of telecommunications seemed to be becoming far less stable and, therefore, more likely to cramp AT&T's maneuvering room. "From the standpoint of sales and profits," Charles DuBois confided in his report to AT&T top management, "our position is not yet firmly and permanently established." Where the principal purchasers of cable and telephone apparatus were states—as in Europe, where Ministries of Posts, Telegraphs and Telephones operated 90 percent of the continent's telephones—DuBois explained that for "political reasons," the authorities were unwilling to depend on a single source of supply. Instead, "they deliberately cultivate competition in telephone manufacturing" and this competition pivoted on something beyond strict market considerations. AT&T's rivals, wrote DuBois, had developed "political relationships" and were emphasizing "their ownership by nationals of the country where they operate as against our complete or partial American ownership." "We have much yet to do," he warned in euphemistic language in 1923, "in attracting local financial interests into cooperation with us and in building up our personal acquaintance and relationships with the higher governmental authorities."[23]

AT&T's uncertainties in foreign markets were, its executives surmised, likely to compound. The company was preparing to initiate transoceanic radiotelephone service and, to do so, it required cooperation from foreign network operators—typically, the same operators with whom it was already negotiating to supply politically sensitive equipment. In a handwritten note to AT&T's incoming CEO Walter Gifford, the just-retired President of AT&T, H.B. Thayer, offering counsel on the prospective sale to ITT, underlining a concern about the future profitability of AT&T's overseas manufacturing operations: "With the terms stated don't see but what you will have to come through if (ITT CEO Sosthenes) Behn accepts. Doubt however whether he can make it profitable but that isn't our lookout. 'Caveat Emptor.'" Once the sale had occurred, AT&T was free to collaborate with the big European PTTs—above all, with the British Post Office—to furnish trans-Atlantic radio telephone service; the elite and cozy club that resulted from this pact would continue for decades to decide on planning and investment for cross-continental telephony, first by radio and, beginning in the 1950s, via voice-grade submarine cables.[24]

Also looming were threats to AT&T within its home market, around the new technology of radio. Would AT&T be able to carry over its monopoly in domestic two-way telephony? Or, might a rival US company—RCA, or GE, or Westinghouse perhaps—deploy radio to provide a competitive form of telephone service, domestically and/or internationally? Concurrent negotiations between AT&T, GE, RCA and the other members of the domestic radio cartel underscored the depth of AT&T executives' anxiety about radio. In the same letter to AT&T President Walter S. Gifford, past president Thayer cited a contract revision then under review by the corporate members of the domestic Radio Group—a revision that "seems to give us pretty close to a free field in two-way telephony and that is worth more than money."[25]

Yet these complex international and domestic considerations still did not exhaust the contingency of the ongoing transition, which encompassed technical, geopolitical, and market factors. Would radio be assimilated both as a broadcasting medium and as a competitor of wireline networks? Would it be integrated into established companies and government PTT ministries, or would it be allowed to carve out an independent business identity? How might radio alter the respective spheres of influence in electrical communications possessed by Great Britain, which emerged from World War I heavily indebted, and the United States, which held Britain's debt? What procedures would govern allocation of the radio spectrum, upon which all wireless communication depended? What policies would apply to interconnection, tariffs, and operating agreements between different national networks, both wireline and wireless? Which international forums would engage and, perhaps, settle these complex but urgent political and market issues—or would they be negotiated bilaterally? The communications industry was, suddenly, undergoing wholesale international redefinition.

The result was that the dominant US network operator, AT&T, dramatically cut back its transnational telephone interests. European markets accounted for the largest share of AT&T's foreign investment, but—probably judiciously— AT&T concluded that, going forward, its foreign business was jeopardized by strengthening political counter-pressures and the unpredictability that ensued from them. Because the cumulative value of AT&T's foreign properties paled by comparison to its huge, and now hugely growing, investment in the US wire network, the latter had to be defended at all costs. Especially was this so when the prospective dangers that attended radio's domestic institutionalization remained opaque. Executives turned to focus on wireline system development within the US.

ITT was the foremost corporate beneficiary of AT&T's decision; however, this did not guarantee that ITT would succeed in anchoring an "American System of international communications." In 1927, a British policymaker endeavoring to harness wireless wrote that a combination of British-run cables and the new "beam," or short-wave, wireless organizations would be vital in counteracting the threat to the Empire posted by "the activities of (ITT CEO) Col. Behn and American bankers who are striving to set up a world monopoly in telephones." By establishing the globe-spanning Cable & Wireless company, Britain maneuvered successfully to outflank both RCA and ITT. "We have made great strides in this country in international communication," declared a Commerce Department official in 1930, "and the British feared that lead which the United States was taking." Their formation of Cable & Wireless in 1928, he warned, "was aimed directly at the United States."[26]

ITT and RCA had separately made inroads into British domination: in light of Cable & Wireless, should they unite their efforts? RCA positioned its support for such a consolidation in the national interest. Major General Harbord, RCA's president and former Chief of Staff of the American Expeditionary Force in World War I put things this way in 1929: "Sitting between the hind legs of the British lion with the tail of that noble beast wrapped around his neck will be a poor perch for the American eagle from which to recover lost leadership in world communications.... This new combined British communications interest will affect American relationships in every part of the world. There will hardly be a port or a principal city on the planet which will not be reached by British communications. American trade in every quarter of the globe cannot but be profoundly affected. The national defence of the United States must reckon with the planetary domination of communications by the British." Harbord's fellow-executive, RCA chairman Owen D. Young, boasted that RCA had taken "a foremost place in radio communication throughout the world." "The question," he emphasized, "is whether we can hold that place." In Young's appraisal, the rapid reorganizations of communications by major trade partners had rendered the US freshly vulnerable: "Whether we look east or west we find cables and radio united in all the great nations of the world as a protection to their national interests." In the field of international communications, Britain had compelled a unification, as had France, Italy, and Japan; Germany was in the process of doing so. "How can our competitive companies in America, three of them or more, meet, from the standpoint of national interest, these consolidated units of other countries?"

> Any one of our three companies may be obliged, to save itself from ruin in the international field, to accept such terms as the unified interests may dictate to us. This may affect not only rates of service, but character of service. It may affect quality of service. The communication services of the United States, which are essential to the development and extension of our business in times of peace and always essential to the national defense, should not be put in a position where others may dictate to us here and we are powerless to protect ourselves.

Young envisioned a comprehensive consolidation of US overseas communications operators, embracing RCA, ITT and Western Union. If legislators could not be moved to permit unification of these separate carriers within a new private company, he went on, "I beg of you, in the national interest, to unify them under government ownership." Telecommunications workers might have learned to fear state control, but at least one flexible-minded capitalist was open to the possibility. His preference, though, was for corporate-commercial control and, to expedite matters, Young already had helped arrange a transfer of RCA's international radio telegraph service and facilities to ITT. For this transfer to be finalized, however, the US Congress would have to delete or alter "antimonopoly provisions" of the recently passed 1927 Radio Act, which as we saw specifically prohibited the elimination of competition between wireline and wireless systems. Young cast the issue in stark terms: "If Congress does not pass the necessary enabling acts it must take the responsibility of weakening, perhaps irretrievably, the position of the United States in the field of international communications. Parity is important to the United States in more fields than war ships; in none more so than communications."[27]

During legislative hearings, Young's views were endorsed by Sosthenes Behn, the CEO of ITT; but they were resisted by the president of the third big international carrier, Western Union. Government opposition to the merger was also considerable. Legislation to allow consolidation did not pass and, in 1931, the RCA-ITT merger agreement was terminated; no company akin to Britain's Cable & Wireless was formed in the United States. Nor did the US government assume comprehensive and direct control over international telecommunications. Within a short time, moreover, the heavily debt-financed recent ITT expansion fell prey to the depression. Not until 1943, Peter Hugill relates, did the US government shed its dependence by gaining access to a transatlantic cable that did not transit through Britain. When it arrived, however, World War II became the pivot of ramifying general change—both for telecommunications and empire. Actualized during and after the conflict was a different and far more expansive US imperialism, operating within a multiply divided and resistant world.[28]

Recasting Empire: World War II and After

The Nazis overran continental Europe in 1940, and the German air force battered Britain throughout late summer and autumn. British Prime Minister, the arch-imperialist Winston Churchill, pleaded for ships and munitions and entreated the United States to enter the war. The US formally enrolled in combat against the Axis, however, only after Japan bombed US bases in the Pacific in December 1941. The Allies counted among themselves the United States, Britain, the Soviet Union, and two dozen other nations. Grand rhetoric suffused the antifascist cause of these "United Nations," but their sonorous speeches concealed calculated ambiguities, and these reflected cleavages over the war's purposes and the shape of the world that should follow their victory. Hoping for a restoration, Churchill resisted any diminishment of Britain's empire. Roosevelt intended, however, to breach the old colonial order to accommodate unrestricted US investment and trade—to make the United States the command center of the postwar order. Stalin's urgent aim was to motivate Britain and the US to open a second front in Europe, which would require Hitler to move troops away from the hellish eastern front; for the USSR the overriding question was survival. Finally, major anticolonial movements throughout Asia and Africa were bringing often-longstanding struggles for national self-determination into high gear. Both divergences and direct clashes were present.[29]

The war itself was remapping the global political economy, including in international networking. The US's unrivaled manufacturing base became a gigantic armamentarium: by 1943 the US was supplying its own military and those of its Allies with more tanks, ships, guns, and munitions than Germany and Japan could destroy. This, as historian Daniel Immerwahr explains, necessitated the formation of a tremendous logistics network. To provision the Allies, during the war the US established 2000 military bases around the world, linked variously by ships and aircraft and railroads—and by cable- and radio circuits. This unprecedented ad hoc logistics system constituted the first iteration of a genuinely global US-managed network.[30]

In its entirety, the US military communications network built to fight World War II cost three times as much as the existing international plant owned by the US commercial carriers. At the war's end, this Army Command and Administrative Network (ACAN) constituted "a world-girdling wire and radio communications system such as had theretofore been wistfully conceived only in rather imaginative plans." Operated by the Signal Corps, which we saw played a forward role in nineteenth-century US western expansion, and leasing plant from the commercial carriers as well as erecting its own facilities, ACAN "gave visual and concrete evidence of what a single, well integrated, closely coordinated and effectively directed international communications enterprise could accomplish."[31]

Some insiders sought to make ACAN's system, heavily reliant on radio, the foundation for an encompassing "peacetime American owned and operated international communications system." There was also considerable military support for keeping intact portions of ACAN for strategic purposes. The US "still enjoyed the prestige and affection" of many of the world's people, went the argument—perhaps, then, foreign powers would acquiesce to "the continued maintenance and operation in certain areas" of ACAN. Navy Secretary James Forrestal was among those who resurrected Owen Young's vision for a single, consolidated US international company. Such a combination, declared Forrestal, could challenge Britain's Cable & Wireless which, with 233 cables in addition to its short-wave facilities, controlled 51 percent of world submarine cable mileage. In March and April, 1945, the Navy and War Departments joined the Federal Communications Commission in a joint show of support for consolidation—first, directly to Franklin Roosevelt and, after his death, to incoming President Harry Truman. "If the United States is to be a major power in this field," FCC Chairman Paul Porter wrote to Truman, "action now is imperative." The longstanding US goal—"cheapening, speeding, and affording greater and more secure communications to American commercial interests, and making more secure and complete American diplomatic and military communications," as a legislative report of 1946 put it—seemed within reach.[32]

ACAN, however, depended on ad hoc arrangements. US troops, hundreds of thousands of whom were stationed overseas, were not slow to demand an immediate demobilization; and tens of thousands of these soldiers also demonstrated publicly against US military attempts to help suppress revolutionary nationalism in Asia. Withdrawals of trained personnel and evacuations of some military bases as the Truman administration buckled under the soldiers' demands to come home, helped engender a rapid break-up of the ACAN system. Other factors, however, also contributed.[33]

ACAN's services rested on Allied countries' and territories' agreement to cooperate with US authorities "in knitting together such a world-wide communications service" to support their shared war mission. The "idyllic picture" of global harmony was quickly "modified" at war's end; indeed ACAN become a "major concern to the British government," according to historian Jill Hills, because it breached imperial territory. Now that the emergency had passed it was time to decommission it. Scant consensus existed, finally, among US government departments and US overseas carriers themselves as to the future structure of US international communications. As ACAN unraveled, Forrestal's plan for a combined company still found adherents; but it possessed too little support to be realized amid the vertiginous changes of the immediate postwar months. By early 1947, as the US carriers reverted to oligopolistic competition, a Senate committee conceded with dismay that "instead of seizing opportunities which appeared to have been available, it will be necessary, in most cases, to begin all over again, relying on our bargaining ability in international conferences" to spearhead subsequent initiatives.[34]

Withal, the US had made inroads; a financially drained Britain, asserted one news report, was "'freeing up' its former monopoly of Empire communications and giving the United States an increasing entrée"—and US radio and cable firms took over some commercially profitable segments of the existing global "belt line." The British Commonwealth's concessions in conferences to plan the postwar order indeed granted US carriers some direct links to previously inaccessible points within the British Empire. The US also seized the moment to reorient the International Telecommunication Union (ITU), the oldest interstate organization (established in 1865). This was a dramatic change in US posture for, beginning in the late nineteenth century, the United States had consistently denied the ITU's right to regulate its own carriers; and the US had refused even to join the agency, though it did send observers to meetings.[35]

The ITU's established functions were of great importance in enabling international electrical and electronic communications. They included technical standards-setting; radio frequency allocation; and arrangements to allow differently configured national and international networks to interconnect with one another. After World War II, the US at last determined that it would be advantageous to join this multilateral organization. The ITU's tone now was set at three conferences held in 1947, significantly, not in Europe but at Atlantic City in the US.[36]

At these meetings, the US moved to reinstitutionalize the ITU by altering its membership- and voting procedures. Though the US failed to resituate the

ITU's Swiss headquarters to the United States, it did replace the agency's lopsided voting scheme, which had accorded surplus weight to the big colonial powers: because Britain, Italy, Portugal and France each possessed six extra votes in light of their colonial possessions, they had exercised a commanding role in ITU policymaking. Instead, the ITU now adopted a one-nation-one-vote principle and, henceforward, its members also were required to be sovereign states (though colonial voting was not completely ended until 1973). Seemingly more democratic, the revised voting procedure actually transported the ITU into the forcefield of US power, in part owing to US informal influence over Latin American countries and their votes. One consequence was that, beginning in 1949, the just-established People's Republic of China was denied the opportunity to become an ITU member. For its part, the US declared that it would be bound by ITU regulations only selectively, as it might decide.[37]

Meanwhile, the US moved to bulk up its own policy-making for international telecommunications. After a high-level panel studied the issues, President Truman brought the FCC into a new Executive Branch committee, comprised of the State, Defense and Commerce Departments and the CIA, whose work was to "consist[] of drawing up detailed plans for the most efficient use of the nation's communications systems in the event of war."[38]

Larger structural forces were cascading into US telecommunications. To clarify their meaning, and the cycles of restructuring that they impelled, it is essential first to review how the United States expanded and reconfigured its own empire during and after World War II.

*

Britain and the United States cooperated in combat against the Axis, as they simultaneously grappled with one another over whether and how to reorganize the world political economy. Meanwhile, although the Roosevelt Administration had recognized the Union of Soviet Socialist Republics (USSR) in 1933, relations between the two states remained chronically distrustful. English elites' antagonism to the Soviets ran so deep that their leaders preferred the Nazis, with whom they negotiated as late as the eve of the Nazi-Soviet Pact of August 1939 (and even beyond). In turn this pact, which authorized the USSR to re-annex Latvia, Estonia, and Lithuania and to seize a part of Poland, both rendered official US and British hostility to the Soviets and deeply damaged popular support kindled during the United Front years. Hitler's invasion of the USSR in June 1941 then suddenly turned the tables, as the US, the Soviets and the British became allies. The US Administration made concerted efforts to propagandize this as a joint fight against fascism; and that the postwar world would be anchored in cooperation between the "Big Three": the United States, the Soviet Union, and Britain.[39]

The prosecution of the conflict itself meanwhile administered repeated shocks to the geopolitical economy. With fearsome speed, Japan expelled Britain from Southeast Asia (and threatened its Raj in India); though US naval victories in the Pacific halted Japan's offensive by 1943, the European colonial regimes in this vast region proved irretrievable. Britain was broke, continental Europe and Japan devastated. Apart from the United States, the productive capacity of leading capitalist countries was shattered and some of their societies verged on breakdown. But the changes went far beyond even this. Japan's occupation of large parts of China had been effectively resisted by Mao Zedong's Communists (though China's casualties rivaled the fearsome losses of the Soviet Union) and, with Japan's defeat, the civil war between China's Communists and Nationalists intensified. After the Soviet Red Army had turned back the Nazis, meanwhile, it marched through eastern Europe and into Germany. And rather than conciliating the US to gain support for its economic recovery, the USSR sharply opposed the bellicose character of US postwar policy. Contrary to US forecasts, meanwhile, Soviet output increased "remarkably quickly." Gathering sporadically since before World War I, finally, anticolonial struggles stood at the verge of breakthrough in parts of Asia and the Pacific, bringing with them the prospect of revolutionary social change. The prewar order had been blasted apart. If US leaders had arrived at a newfound conviction that geography no longer limited the exercise of American power, however, then their program for US global dominance would be far from unconstrained.[40]

A primary obstacle was domestic. Faced with opposition from a significant slice of the working class—which, we saw, began 1946 with an enormous, year-long strike wave, which remained attached to the economic policies of Roosevelt's New Deal, which distrusted the European imperialist powers, and which was open to cooperation with the Soviet Union through the United Nations, President Truman at first dissembled and vacillated. It required a couple of years of political effort to reorient the US polity and US public opinion.

Determined not to repeat the debacle that had followed World War I, ranking State Department officials had begun to outline plans and preferences for the peace in 1939—two years before the US entered World War II. During the months and years that followed, the shifting sands of domestic party politics; the changing balance between the US, Britain, and the USSR; and internecine friction between the State Department and US military agencies, repeatedly altered US preparations for the postwar world. Following the pivotal Soviet victory at Stalingrad in 1943, the foundational question became the US stance toward the USSR. US officials had projected that the Soviets would be so severely weakened by human and economic losses that they would be pliable to US foreign policy demands. Even before the war ended, this assumption was invalidated.[41]

Stalin showed scant interest in bending to US designs. Should the US try to cooperate with the USSR, as it had during the war? Agreeing that it should were New Dealers including Vice President Henry Wallace, Undersecretary of State Sumner Welles and a number of other ranking officials. Their stance was in keeping with President Roosevelt's hardheaded hopes for the postwar international settlement. His planners projected that the United States and the USSR, but also Britain and, more provocatively, Nationalist China would work together as "global policemen," to enforce world peace within the nascent United Nations system. Historians have found that US support for the UN went beyond officialdom. Weary of war and intent on finding jobs and resuming their lives, many GIs, especially those who had been CIO members, were committed to a "people's peace," based on international cooperation through the United Nations. So were numerous African American civil rights and labor activists who were committed to anti-imperialism and also supportive of working cooperatively with the Soviet Union.[42]

Before the end of World War II, and over protest by Iraq, Egypt, Guatemala, Argentina and (Nationalist) China, the US withdrew its doctrinal support for independence and self-determination by colonies that were administered by Europe's powers. Deeming many of the Pacific islands it had wrested from Japan essential to American security, the US Navy insisted on maintaining unrestricted US control: multilateral oversight, let alone sovereignty, was denied. As the African American historian Rayford Logan pointed out at the time, this move announced a "distinct retreat from the anticolonialism of Roosevelt" and seemed to signify that, henceforward, "American would forfeit its moral claim to oppose colonialism elsewhere in the world." Many of the newly independent states, as the US State Department later phrased it, "occupied strategic locations, others ... possessed significant natural resources." Their destinies were, in other words, too important to be left up to their inhabitants.[43]

In January 1946, President Harry Truman (who had been elevated at Roosevelt's death in April 1945) ordered a slowdown of the ongoing demobilization, in order to station a couple of million US troops as occupying forces at bases across the world—not only in defeated Germany and Japan but also in the Philippines, China, Guam, and other places. US soldiers participated in efforts to suppress revolutionary uprisings, by aiding the Chinese Nationalists and by attacking the Hukbalahaps, an anti-Japanese guerilla force which now was battling for radical agrarian reform in the Philippines. These counter-insurgency efforts, along with US military occupations to shore up imperialist interests in Korea and Indonesia, drew tens of thousands of GIs to protest; while, back in the US, through 1946 the CIO vocally opposed Truman's rapidly changing foreign policy. Conservative politicians, military officials and business leaders were determined to arrest and coopt the thumping anticolonialism espoused by some New Dealers, including (albeit selectively) President Roosevelt and, as mentioned, by many US workers and soldiers alongside a dominant fraction of African American civil rights- and labor activists, journalists, and intellectuals. Near its crest in 1945, this internationalist anticolonialism was expressed eloquently by W. E. B. Dubois: "The present war has made it clear that we can no longer regard Western Europe and North America as the world for which civilization exists." Altering US policies would soon collide with his hopeful assessment.[44]

The Soviet power-zone reached from Eastern Europe thousands of miles eastward across Asia, to the northern Pacific coast. Committed to flanking it in the first instance by rebuilding capitalism in Western Europe and Japan, the Truman administration decided "that the main postwar conflict would not be between the remaining capitalist powers, but between the capitalist world, headed by the United States, and the Soviet Union." Already by April 1945, US War Department officials proclaimed a need to build a "West-European-American power system" as a "counterweight to Russia." Throughout the immediate postwar years, however, prewar empires faltered, revolutionary nationalism surged, Western Europe tottered—and the US itself began to convulse around anti-Communism. Meaningful domestic opposition to US foreign policy by an organized left was quelled, it turned out, for a generation. As this epoch-making shift occurred, during 1947–1948, the prospect of a return to the open-ended reformism of the prewar New Deal came to a screeching stop. For present purposes more important, domestic political backing for US Cold War empire-making was now unhampered.

The war had vaulted to dominance US leaders whose foremost priority was to erect a global framework for asserting—and sustaining—US interests. European (and to a much lesser extent, Japanese) reconstruction became tied in turn to a restoration of linkages to former and still-existing colonies. For this reason, revolutionary nationalism and accelerating decolonization presented explosively sensitive challenges. The US preferred that the colonial powers undertake "a speedy transfer of power to local elites." However, the stream of revolt was stronger and more rapid than US (not to speak of British, French, Belgian, and Dutch) officials anticipated, as peoples throughout Asia and, thereafter, Africa seized the political moment. Where they were not already, many nationalists now became convinced that formal independence needed to be coupled to social and economic changes: that it was imperative to build greater control over their resources, their labor, their land—their history. After the dislocations and upheavals of the war, however, emerging nations exhibited a more or less unsettled balance of social forces. Just how far might these transitional states be willing and able to go, to uproot dominative socioeconomic arrangements? In prospect were fluid and domestically contested agendas for transformation: mobilizing natural endowments, rewriting trade and economic ties, transforming domestic social relations, reconstructing national cultures.[45]

A concomitant aspect of the challenge presented by revolutionary nationalism in Asia and Africa began to unfold. As postcolonial states became numerous, many recognized that safeguarding their national interests depended on whether they could cooperate with one another, to alter the global political economy. Nascent "worldmaking" initiatives commenced, as sovereign nations, some of them new, joined together informally to demand that international economic arrangements be altered. Again, this was not a smooth or straight-line process: unbalanced domestic social relations and regional animosities made for disunity among the new nations, conflicts that were frequently exploited by imperialist nations old and new. During the early postwar decades, nevertheless, the global South's interrelated programs for national transformation and international redistribution strengthened.[46]

All this placed substantial, sometimes severe, constraints on US policymakers. The latter were determined to prize and hold open colonial markets, markets that Britain and the other powers had formerly foreclosed. During World War II, however, they recognized that British cooperation in particular was essential, not only in prosecuting the war but in the US's project of building a postwar order that accorded pride of place to capital—preeminently US capital. If it would give rules to the world, in short, then the US often *needed* the (other) imperialist countries. By the Spring of 1945 the US was expressing support for the European colonialist to check Soviet influence in Asia, Africa and the Middle East.

The global objectives of the sometimes strained alliances that the US forged with the colonial powers during the late 1940s and 1950s were four. First was to strengthen the US policy of "containment"—which, as Leffler characterizes it, was actually "a policy of calculated and gradual coercion." A second US goal was closely linked: where possible, to canalize and redirect the socialist policies adopted by many emerging postcolonial states, for whom the centralized planning, technological capabilities, and industrial achievements of the USSR seemed an encouraging model. Third was to undercut or, at least, to deflect the postcolonial states' early moves to adopt a redistributionist agenda, which nevertheless would advance toward their demand, during the 1970s, for a "New International Economic Order." The US still often asserted a rhetorical anticolonialism; but it was increasingly in thralldom to an inscribed policy of anti-Communism, as US leaders sought an overriding fourth aim, termed by Leffler "a preponderance of power." This meant to reserve for the US and, by the same token, to deny to the Soviet Union, "control of critical industrial infrastructure, skilled labor, raw materials, and forward bases."[47]

There was no mistaking that capitalism's directing force had shifted to Washington, DC and New York City. The process through which, even before the war ended, the US established the new axes of global finance—the International Monetary Fund and the International Bank for Reconstruction and Development (the World Bank)—was hegemonic rather than by fiat. The General Agreement on Tariffs and Trade, aimed at reducing barriers to global trade, followed in 1947. The United Nations system was erected at a 1945 meeting at San Francisco; headquartered in New York City, the parent organization also housed a group of vital specialized agencies, from the Food and Agriculture Organization and UNESCO to the International Telecommunication Union. In the UN system, until around 1970, the US exercised a commanding influence. Starting in 1947, the Marshall Plan—a huge US-financed economic aid program—sought to re-stabilize capitalism in Western Europe by shoring up the big colonial powers. It aimed to establish an economic and political bulwark against the Soviets while thwarting domestic Communist parties and unions; and to align the postwar European economy with that of the United States. (The Marshall Plan was sold to the US people, meanwhile, as a means of bolstering the US's own economy and of thereby preventing a relapse into economic depression, a credible prospect at the time.) Within the US Executive Branch, the National Security Act of 1947 elevated presidential power, creating a top-down decision-making mechanism for clarifying, coordinating, and attempting to enforce US military and foreign policy. The North Atlantic Treaty Organization (1949) militarized US hegemony over Europe; but US preponderance quickly globalized, as military bases and treaty agreements were concluded with Australia, Japan and the Republic of Korea, and from the Indian Ocean to the Middle East. Nor did Central and South America break free from orbiting their northern neighbor. The US military government impelled a conservative social restoration in the western sectors of Germany between 1945 and 1949, and moved into Cold War confrontation with the Soviet-occupied eastern sector. Direct US military intervention to put down a Communist uprising in Greece, and US financial and propaganda aid to defeat the Communists in the Italian general election of 1948 signaled wider geopolitical intentions. While making these intentions explicit, the 1947 announcement of the Truman Doctrine—a commitment to combat what the US decided were Communist insurgencies or Soviet threats anywhere around the world—was mostly intended to "scare hell" out of the American people. Beginning in 1950, the Korean War upped the US military budget three-fold, as the nation transformed into a permanent global war-maker.[48]

Again, though, US postwar power was neither mechanical nor unopposed. The US political establishment experienced repeated shocks as it encountered the radical potential of movements for national self-determination and international restructuring—notably, in China. US wartime planners had cast Nationalist China as a strategic linchpin, imagining that Chiang's China should aid a projected US paramountcy in East Asia while serving as a pliable counter to both the Soviet Union and Britain. The planners seemed ignorant of—or hubristically indifferent to—the depth of popular support for China's Communist revolution. By 1946, as China's civil war raged, the US press magnate Henry Luce called for a more "vigorous" US foreign policy in Asia, to prevent what he arrogantly called the "loss" of China. The Chinese Communists paid no heed to Luce as they routed the Nationalists and marched in victory into Beijing in 1949. As decolonization struggles coursed through Asia, Africa, and the Middle East, "the United States would be confronted with an unmanageable crisis in much of the former colonial world." Even in the international organizations that had been established largely at its behest, furthermore, the US could not simply issue diktats.[49]

At war's end the US possessed more than half of the world's manufacturing capacity and two-thirds of available world financial reserves. This granted to it a decisive head-start on a new round of capitalist expansion, and the US also rapidly set out an enlarged and interrelated imperialism—less reliant on formally administered colonies; not centered in a government department expressly committed to it, such as Britain's Colonial Office; and not legitimized by a loudly proclaimed official rhetoric of liberal imperialism. Often hidden from the American people, this US imperialism was underpinned at scores of sites, not only by the federal government, but also by private international banks; corporate-military technological primacy; interlocking multilateral organizations whose major policies were brought into loose conformity with US priorities; and agreements to lease hundreds of strategically situated "small points"—military and intelligence bases—around the globe.[50]

Sustaining this more informal US imperialism was a Cold War foreign policy backed by unprecedented military might, political-economic power, and communications mastery. Never formalized into a single directive (though NSC-68, establishing the National Security Council, approached), this was a multifarious program. Direct economic aid to Western Europe and the US decision to divide Germany, whose capitalist western half became the Federal Republic of Germany, both countered the Soviets and helped US agencies to work with European elites to combat domestic radicalism—a project in which "cultural cold war" initiatives also were enlisted. After nuking Hiroshima and Nagasaki, mostly as a warning to the Soviet Union, the US posted an army of occupation in Japan, creating what China's Communist leaders viewed as one of two island battleships off their coast (the other was Taiwan). Another bastion was set as the US brought Britain into a globe-spanning system of electronic signals intelligence-gathering; by the mid-1950s, Australia, New Zealand, and Canada had also joined this super-secret UKUSA, or "Five Eyes," consortium.[51]

Nuclear weapons were the most terrifying indicator of US primacy in science and technology. But they were not the only one. Before the war, Germany science had led the world and the US seized defeated Germany's R&D trove as spoils of war. Throughout the immediate postwar months, US officials plundered the records held by the German patent office and, assisted by US corporate engineers, they scoured the country's factories and laboratories and scooped up economically valuable plans, reports, blueprints, and drawings. Binding postwar European reconstruction to the United States through the Marshall Plan, the US then granted financial support to major high-tech research centers, notably, the Conseil Europeen pour la Recherche Nucleaire (CERN) established in 1952. These permitted the US to track and benefit from European scientific development. A rapid enlargement of the US's own national research infrastructure, meanwhile, drew tens of thousands of talented foreign students to study—and, again, intertwine with—US science and engineering. (The microprocessor, invented in 1971, was designed by a team of engineers, one Italian, two American, and one Japanese.) We have already seen how, at home, during these same years, AT&T's Bell Laboratories was repurposed—and digital microelectronics innovated—in thralldom to US military industry. The breakthrough period, stretching from the invention of the transistor in 1947 through the integrated circuit's arrival in 1959, coincided with the zenith of US global power; even as late as the 1970s the US spent more than five times what all of Western Europe expended on computer research and development. During its formative decades, the implementation of digital technology under the auspices of the US military continually outran major international competitors.[52]

All this technology development interpenetrated an ongoing expansion of US overseas business investment and trade. At the onset of World War I, the US had accounted for a mere 6 percent of global foreign direct investment (Britain, France, and Germany had made up nearly 90 percent); by the early 1970s, by contrast, US companies held 52 percent of the world's much greater total foreign direct investment, as a result of an unprecedented eight-fold expansion since 1945.[53]

Before the war, overseas investment had been largely concentrated in the extraction of oil, minerals, and other resources, and in the distribution or assembly of US commodities to just a few branch plants, mostly Western Europe. At this point, the typical US manufacturing subsidiary "was either a plant that merely assembled components sent from the home country or a more integrated duplicate of the parent company adapted to the host country's markets and standing pretty much on its own feet." After World War I, by contrast, US-headquartered multinationals "exploded in number and size"—two hundred of them possessed affiliates in twenty or more countries by the early 1970s—and altered their strategic orientation toward production and trade. Many executives were considering whether manufacturing operations might be broken up and reconstituted: Could a corporation improve its logistics to the point that it could decentralize production across multiple sites in different countries? Could it coordinate flows of parts and components, some produced inhouse by subsidiaries and others by contractors, so as to locate the final assembly of a given commodity in a maximally profitable location? Could it augment its profits even further, through intracorporate trade, that is, by re-exporting finished commodities back to the United States? Early in the 1960s, a mere 4.1 percent of the sales of US foreign manufacturing affiliates were sent to the United States—but this proportion was increasing fast.[54]

The advantages of reorienting strategy in this way were palpable; indeed, they were presaged by US companies that already were relocating investment to poor, nonunionized regions of the southeastern United States. If untapped reserves of cheap labor could be tapped and locational, transport, environmental, and tax advantages suitably leveraged, then business processes could be operationally dispersed but centrally coordinated so that they could pump commodity flows back into the home markets of the wealthy countries. The character of foreign direct investment in turn shifted, as giant US corporations began to redesign their manufacturing operations. Visions of internationally decentralized operations coupled with cross-border administrative control were coming into prospect.

This entire transition in the structure and orientation of productive investment rested on freedom of investment and trade. Communications companies took a special role in legitimizing free trade. The huge domestic political economy had long since spawned very large US media companies, and given them a launchpad from which to propel cultural commodities into the world market. After World War II this movement expanded. Through joint effort by corporate media and US government agencies, US publishers built an "inside track to the world's bookshelves." The Hollywood film industry followed a similar course, because the war "destroyed to a great extent the protective measures" that had been put in place by Germany, Britain and France (Europe's largest markets) during the 1920s and early 1930s. For their part, television equipment manufacturers, program networks, and above all, corporate advertisers, cooperated to expand the reach of broadcast services based on the US commercial model. In some countries, including Britain where broadcasting as a public service funded by a levy on receivers was already entrenched, advertisers lobbied Downing Street for permission to establish rival ad-based services. Where public broadcasting had not put down roots, notably in many postcolonial countries, US (and French) media interests worked hand-in-glove with government authorities, national capital and big advertisers to predicate broadcasting upon advertiser dependence.[55]

These changes heightened the importance of what the US had already been calling "freedom of communications" or, often, the "free flow of information." Contributing to a more expansive and complex international movement for human rights, the free flow concept was a formidable weapon for expanding

US commercial media—and inducing commercial advertiser-contoured models even when US media interests were not directly present. I will return to these issues later; for now, let me add only that the self-serving cynicism of the free flow principle was amply evident in the 1940s to a much-weakened Britain—which possessed its own century-old experience of the similarly opportunistic policy of "free trade." In 1944, the London-based *Economist* magazine pointed to the "peculiar moral glow" displayed by a US media executive, as he found "that his idea of freedom coincides with his commercial advantage."[56]

As an occupying power in western Germany and Japan, significantly, the United States chose to restore these countries' devastated telecommunications systems within reconstructed government ministries of Posts, Telephones and Telegraphs (PTTs)—instead of transforming them into private corporations on the US model. The presence of hundreds of thousands of Soviet Red Army troops in Europe, the victory of China's Communist Party, and the outbreak of the Korean War were critical factors. In devastated Germany and Japan, functioning telecommunications infrastructures were an urgent priority for the US-coordinated reconstruction. The US imperative in Germany and Japan thus was not to open investment to capital, as it was generally, but to kick-start operational services: both territories were crucial for the US program of containment. Elsewhere around the world, in addition, telecommunications infrastructures remained mostly in the hands of government PTTs. Though it exercised a powerful role both in the International Telecommunication Union and in bilateral relations with correspondent countries, the US therefore contented itself to work with state telecommunications ministries, two of which its own military authorities resurrected.

During and after World War II, the United States thereby built up a semiglobal informal empire. An open system of investment and trade not only "would allow American goods and capital to flow everywhere" but, alongside this, would sustain "a huge infusion of American influence." This expanded notably on the informal imperialism of free trade through which Britain had ensnared newly independent nations of Latin America after 1820. Its hallmark was not direct territorial possession, though this persisted in Puerto Rico and Guam and in hundreds of US bases and island points elsewhere. It was the raging florescence of US multinational corporate investment and trade, accompanied by US hegemony over multilateral organizations and specialized agencies and other institutions; and over high-technology, including telecommunications networks. At its apexes, this complex political economy was bound together by what have been called "elite networks." And, as this Cold War empire coalesced, another attempt to actualize an American system of cross-border networking also took form.[57]

The US and the International Telecommunications Satellite Consortium

During the early 1960s, the US again sought to architect an international communications system—this one of vaulting scope. Initiated during the Kennedy Administration, carried forward under Lyndon Johnson, and finalized under President Richard Nixon, the International Telecommunications Satellite Consortium (Intelsat) constituted the first relatively lasting "American system of communications."

It needs to be underlined that, during the 1960s, international telecommunications in general was a multilateral endeavor anchored by states. There was little likelihood of establishing a cross-border system without government participation; the historic transition from a world of colonies and empires to one of nation-states was reaching its culmination during these years. As the nation-state became "the natural unit of political order" Daniel J. Sargent explains, "it shaped the choices available to US policymakers." Private capital in telecommunications was mindful of this; in the US context, indeed, private capital worked closely with government authorities, to profitable advantage.[58]

After decades of indifferent and often insecure service via radio circuits, AT&T's installation of voice-grade submarine cables marked a milestone. In 1956, reflecting a prolonged period of technical innovation and buildouts along short routes (such as Key West to Havana), AT&T placed in service a Trans-Atlantic cable (TAT-1), boasting 36 circuits. A cable connecting San Francisco to Hawaii was laid the next year, and another followed in 1964: Trans Pacific 1 (Transpac), connecting Hawaii, now a state, to US island colonies—Midway, Wake Island, Guam—and from there to Japan. For help with cable construction, AT&T initially drew in Britain-based STC (a company AT&T had sold to ITT back in 1925). The US carrier established consortia to operate both of these costly and complex infrastructures; its partners were government PTT ministries such as the British Post Office. AT&T simultaneously threw itself into developing a second new telecommunications medium.[59]

After the Soviet Sputnik launch in 1957, United States military industry concentrated tremendous effort on satellites. In 1959 NASA contracted with AT&T to install eighteen large ground stations at locations across the world, to support its first attempt at manned space flight: Project Mercury. One of these was constructed in Zanzibar and, Lisa Parks shows, it was built against the will of Zanzibaris. Indeed political contestation between a rising anticolonialism and an insistent US Cold War imperialism colluding with a British empire in decline, constituted the formative historical context. Not only were local protests against the earth station both militant and large—10,000 people demonstrated against its installation in June 1960; prefiguring the movement for a New World

Information and Communication Order, it also was expansive. The next month, delegates attending a Pan African Union meeting in Cairo "demanded that all military and satellite tracking stations be eliminated from Africa due to concerns about militarization." With Zanzibar's revolution and political independence in 1964, one of the first acts of its new president was to order the closure of this earth station. From the beginning, then, the implementation of international satellite service was conflictual.[60]

As satellite technology improved and engineering issues were solved, US policy moved to the forefront. Who should provide international satellite service, government or corporate capital? Should an international satellite service be harmonized with ocean cables, so that satellites' cost advantages did not jeopardize the massive investments that underwrote submarine cables such at TAT-1 and Transpac-1? Or, should a satellite service be organized independently, to compete with the US and foreign submarine cable consortia? At the US end, should the existing international service providers (of telegraph and telex and, perhaps, also voice services) be allowed to offer (meaning, take over) satellite service as well? If so, ought they to be merged to create a monopoly supplier comparable with the PTTs with whom the new supplier would negotiate? Last, but not least, how might foreign countries be motivated to affiliate with a US international satellite organization? For that it would be US-led was not open to question. For US policymakers, a major advantage of satellites over submarine cables, was that multilateral cooperation would be arranged so as to elevate US rule-making power.[61]

At the outset, the pace of development was intense. Even before the type of satellite technology to be used by Intelsat was fully proven, even before the organizational questions were answered, in his 1961 State of the Union address President Kennedy invited the nations of the world to join the US satellite program. The US thereupon established a Communications Satellite Corporation in 1962. Endowed with a monopoly over US satellite service, Comsat was charged with organizing Intelsat. Interim Arrangements for Intelsat were agreed in 1964. Both Comsat and Intelsat were seen by US liberals as a carrier-driven boondoggle; by radicals as a strategic frontier of the military-industrial complex. The Interim Arrangements gave Comsat, a private company with a couple of presidential appointees on its board, equal status with Intelsat's other signatory members: seventeen nation-states represented through their PTTs. All, apart from Japan, Australia and Canada, were European states. The US thus succeeded in constituting Intelsat as a "single international global system at the earliest possible time." Both points were fundamental.[62]

Several European countries had already begun to pursue their own plans for satellite communications. A number of European aerospace companies formed Eurospace in 1961; an alliance of PTTs established a European Conference on Satellite Communications in 1962; and the European Space Research Organization as well as the European Space Vehicle Launcher Organization followed in 1964. Only through what it regarded as a nominal concession, that foreign countries might participate in the system's ownership and management, did the US manage in 1964 to bring forward Interim Arrangements for Intelsat.[63]

Even close US allies had pushed for alternative arrangements, or granted only grudging consent for Intelsat's institutionalization. According to Jill Hills, "Canadians originally favored executive control by either the United Nations or the ITU"; but this was too much multilateralism for the US. Hills also has unearthed a statement by the head of Britain's PTT in 1964 "that the only way of preventing an American monopoly in this sphere is to join a partnership with the United States and other countries and so secure the right to influence the course of events." France looked to establish its own satellite launch capability and a Francophone satellite consortium. Akin to other quickly recovering countries in Western Europe, the Federal Republic of Germany desired equipment contracts and technology transfer in exchange for cooperating with the US in Intelsat.[64]

Setting Intelsat in place preempted independent European satellite initiatives and generated first-mover advantages for the United States. An interlocking second proviso contributed to the same aim, as President Johnson's telecommunications advisor underlined a few years later: "The importance of the single global system . . . cannot be overemphasized." Intelsat's bylaws required that, before they could lawfully establish any other satellite system, country-signatories needed to gain formal approval from the consortium—meaning, as we will see, from Comsat. And Comsat remained uniformly indisposed. US management of Intelsat thus enabled it to suppress—or, as it turned out, at least to delay—rival satellite system buildouts and, by this means, to inhibit competition in key high-tech fields of rocketry, aerospace, and satellite equipment making. (The sole exception would be Inter-Sputnik, established somewhat later to serve the Soviet bloc and, thus, falling outside the scope of US influence.) Despite European pressure, Intelsat continued to award satellite equipment contracts overwhelmingly to US aerospace companies. Suppressing intercapitalist competition in a high-tech industry was an important feature of this American system of international communication.[65]

The version of multilateralism animated by Intelsat was organized much as it had been for the IMF and the World Bank. Voting rights were set as a function of ownership, and ownership was unequal. The United States—whose ownership share of Intelsat, set initially at 61 percent, was not permitted by the Interim Agreements to fall below 50.5 percent—commanded policymaking by virtue of its perpetual veto (In second place stood Britain, with 8.4 percent.) In addition, the Interim Agreements designated Comsat the manager of Intelsat, making Comsat's regular coordination with US military and intelligence agencies another fulcrum of US power. Coming in the same context with US export controls over high-technology parts and equipment, these arrangements for international satellites deepened European and Japanese disenchantment.[66]

The European signatories had been uncomfortable from the outset; this was one reason the US initially brought into Intelsat two Pacific allies, Australia and Japan—as counterweights. A US presidential advisor acknowledged a few years later that the tension had not abated: "Major continental European nations are critical of the 'excessively dominant' position of the United States in the decisions of the International Consortium. Actions to reduce U.S. dominance ... are expected during the 1969 negotiations to extend the existing Interim Agreement or consummate a more permanent one."[67]

Despite US efforts to suppress it, intercapitalist competition was intensifying. The European Space Research Organization as and the European Space Vehicle Launcher Organization were merged into the European Space Agency in 1973, around when Intelsat's Definitive Agreement—drafted after three years of negotiations—was finally accepted by two-thirds of its growing membership. Throughout this interval the Europeans, writes Heather Hudson, were "increasingly concerned about U.S. domination of Intelsat as they strove to protect their cable investments and win Intelsat procurement contracts."[68]

Though the US and Comsat unfailingly painted the consortium as a positive force for national development, Intelsat's unbalanced internal structure compounded its difficulties. By 1969, when Nixon became President, Intelsat possessed sixty-four national members. These countries were mostly represented in the International Telecommunication Union, the United Nations agency whose longtime function was to coordinate key elements of international telecommunications, notably spectrum allocation and, also essential for satellites, scarce orbital slots. Why not vest international satellite communications within the ITU—which, as mentioned, now operated on the principle of one-nation-one vote—rather than instituting permanent arrangements for the US-centric Intelsat? In 1967, France again proposed this. The US rejected the option out of hand.[69]

Because it was so saturated by US interests, Intelsat's cohesion remained fragile. As wealthy member-nations looked to create alternative systems, the centrifugal force increased. Often conducted in the shadows of international diplomacy, fierce infighting characterized Cold War economic policy, and satellites were no exception to this. Quite a number of nations pressed against US control of space, and planned (or hoped) to build or buy their own satellites: Japan, Egypt, Germany, India, France. As early as 1967, a US official declared a need to decide how to deal with "more limited national interests which seek to break up the global system concept and create a pattern of regional hegemonies." This push to introduce separate satellite systems, he feared—in a portent of an argument that would return in the context of the internet nearly fifty years later—could usher in a "general disorder" which might soon pose "increasingly serious threats to the future success and viability of both COMSAT and INTELSAT." Meanwhile, though the dominant US carrier had been substantially frozen out of satellite communications development, AT&T allied with leading PTT ministries to protect their massive existing investments in submarine coaxial cables. To try to ensure their future viability, AT&T also scrambled to develop much more capacious fiber optic cables.[70]

Other stress points reflected Intelsat's dual relation to the postcolonial states and to the project of global economic redistribution. On one hand, Intelsat offered postcolonial countries much-improved access to advanced electronic communications—which, for most of them, remained utterly inadequate. By the mid-1970s, to illustrate, Algeria was using an Intelsat transponder to operate a domestic telephone and television service for outlying communities in the Sahara. This was not exceptional: By 1983, Intelsat provided domestic service to 23 countries. Throughout the poor world, then, the general social need was great. On the other hand, big transnational companies were also among Intelsat's chief customers, because their "operations can be centrally integrated while exploiting resources and employing personnel in all parts of the world with complete flexibility." Intelsat's centrality to the expansion of transnational capital aided their exploitation of postcolonial peoples, and their transgressions on postcolonial states' sovereignty. This feature stirred early counter-movement: India, notably, initiated space research in 1962 and announced a domestic satellite program in 1975.[71]

Even as the Definitive Agreements were being negotiated, the longstanding contradiction that ran through Intelsat—attempting "to reconcile unilateral prerogative with multilateral legitimacy"—intensified. As the US pushed to institutionalize a permanent system under its aegis, competing capitalist powers and unhappy postcolonial states pushed back. The ten or fifteen years that followed Nixon's inauguration in 1969 were marked by increasingly serious geopolitical-economic conflict; and the first genuine "American system of international communications" was ultimately supplanted, as imperialism itself again altered.[72]

Global Rifts

Variably concerned over US commercial media encroachments on their national cultures, by the late 1960s and early 1970s rival capitalist countries became downright alarmed that network-based enterprises—collectively, a "sunrise" industry and a pole of high-profit growth—comprised an even greater US threat. France and Britain and Japan reacted assertively, proclaiming a need not to fall behind;

West Germany took a lower-profile approach. By this time the Third World political project was reaching its apogee. A small harbinger came when President Kwame Nkrumah appointed the radical Shirley Graham Du Bois to direct Ghana's new television service in 1965. Many Third World states apprehended that international telecommunication networks possessed a twofold importance: while they might be reconstructed to serve national development at some future time, in their present form they actively undercut sovereignty, let alone egalitarian redistribution. Submarine cables tied them to imperial metropoles but not to one another—unless indirectly and at extortionate rates; satellite service was at the beck and call of the United States. Members of both sets of countries now moved to confront the US paramountcy and the exploitation associated with it: During the 1970s, a widening set of issues pertaining to information, telecommunications, and culture became subject to international contestation.[73]

Numerous countries were determined to defend against—and, in the case of the advanced capitalist countries, to compete with—US technological modernization projects. Canada was first to launch a domestic satellite, Anik 1. We had best suspend the idea that such initiatives signified an invariable shared territorial identity between capital and the state: Canada's Anik satellite was supplied by an expansion-minded US aerospace company, Hughes. Western European countries, by contrast, organized independent European space-launch and satellite programs.

Competition over next-generation computing also increased. "In 1970," a US panel remembered in 1982, the US "was preeminent in all aspects of electronic, computer, and computational technology"; however, during the intervening twelve years, US leadership in supercomputers—especially vital for industry, the military, and academe—eroded. For the US to retain its lead would require augmented federal support, as "National thrusts in supercomputing are being pursued by the governments of Japan, West Germany, France, and Great Britain." The Japanese effort was especially formidable.[74]

The same tendency was evident in Intelsat. At the time that the Definitive Agreements for Intelsat were concluded in 1971, the US ownership share of 53 percent remained sufficient to guarantee that US policy objectives would be broadly met; however, after these negotiations, the distribution of ownership and control in Intelsat would change markedly. Not only did the US share drop to 38 percent in 1979, but Intelsat's governing structure was altered to reduce US power: Comsat was slated to lose its managing role. Overall, the first genuinely American system of international communication faced both internal erosion and external encroachment, with the development of alternative systems—both satellites and, in prospect, more capacious submarine cables built around optical fibers.[75]

Related contests also took a more directly political expression. During the 1930s and 1940s, Mexican policymakers had begun to clarify the connections between national impoverishment and a dominative international economic system—and, sometimes joined by other Latin American state officials, they called for redistributive measures. Throughout the 1950s and 1960s, many newly independent countries of Asia and Africa joined the Latin American countries to struggle against these exploitive arrangements. Their political energies were channeled through a burgeoning Non-Aligned Movement [NAM], growing out of an acclaimed conference held at Bandung Indonesia and formalized in 1961. The NAM pressed for redistributive changes to the overall structure of the international political economy: what began to be termed a New International Economic Order. The NAM soon targeted information, communications, and culture as a critical problem-area; and its proponents began to call for a New World Information and Communication Order [NWICO]—or, alternatively, a New International Information Order—in conjunction with their demand for New International Economic Order. Lending a sometimes sympathetic ear were several European states, anxious about US technological and market encroachments via direct broadcast satellites and cross-border computer networks.[76]

There were frictions, cross-currents, divergences. However, NAM spokespersons and sympathizers began to delineate how unequal relationships disfigured global communications. Many such inequities were documented. These included mass distribution for global audiences of distorted news about poor nations; the domination of the electromagnetic spectrum resource by US corporate and military agencies; copyright and patent restrictions benefiting US and Western European companies at the expense of less-developed countries; the lack of inclusive telecommunications infrastructures and media services; the undermining of indigenous audiovisual production through dumping of US television programs and films; and the use of corporate-commercial media to promote consumerism instead of national programs to improve access to education, food, and medical care. Demonstrating that the problem was not just a historical legacy but an actively extending process, finally, were actual and prospective violations of sovereignty by emerging supranational networks, advancing within the context of the informal imperialism that was now often called "neocolonialism." Principal among these were planned direct satellite broadcasting to homes and already-operational satellite remote sensing systems; and networked trans-border flows of computer data by and for multinational corporations. Without profound structural changes to international communications and information, in other words, NAM countries argued that both national self-determination and its concomitant New International Economic Order would be blocked. As this political struggle extended into computer networking services, what had once seemed remote issues quickly threatened to become major public controversies.

A 1976 inventory showed that the US possessed nearly 60,000 general-purpose computers; by contrast, Mexico possessed 550, and India 185. Recognition of this chasm, and of the importance of computation for oversight and planning, already had energized domestic technology initiatives by disparate poor states, including India, Chile, Brazil, and China. Attempting both to avoid technological dependency and to carve out space for independent development, these countries pursued home-grown computer development. National policymakers likewise turned attention to computer networks as these began to be innovated. A Brazilian diplomat declared that his country "does not allow the use of computers placed abroad, which through tele-informatics accomplish tasks whose solution can be obtained in the country." A 1982 survey estimated that more than sixty countries had established "informatics authorities." An established organization, the Intergovernmental Bureau for Informatics, seemed to be becoming a venue for discussion and coordinated action. Soviet information scientists studying the prospects for "an international data network" went one better than their French precursors had with respect to satellites, proposing in 1981 to place "all large information networks under the control of international organizations, such as UNESCO." Like France's, the Soviet suggestion went nowhere. US dominance over both existing and emerging modes of international communications nonetheless faced state-directed challenges.[77]

The NWICO is often associated with UNESCO, however, it may be better to see it as a social-political movement that barreled into the United Nations system; and again, some European countries shared Third World nations' concerns about US dominance. For about a decade beginning early in the 1970s, another UN affiliate—the ITU—also sponsored debates over unbalanced international power relations. By 1977, elite US opinion came to hold that the ITU was, as summed up by the State Department's William H. Read, "another U.N. forum passing out of Western control." Carrying forward from a 1975 UN General Assembly resolution equating Zionism with racism, at a Nairobi Plenipotentiary meeting of the ITU in 1982 a proposal to expel Israel from the conference was defeated by a thin margin (four votes)—even after what an official US document termed "a maximum effort by the U.S. Delegation in Nairobi, a worldwide diplomatic effort by the U.S. State Department, and the public pronouncement by the U.S. Secretary of State that if Israel were expelled from the ITU, then United States would leave the Plenipotentiary Conference, withhold further financial payments, and reassess its participation in the ITU." This government report pointedly underlined that "the tension caused during this debate spilled over and had ramifications in the substantive part of the Conference." Undersecretary of

State William Schneider told Abbott Washburn, who had led the US negotiating team for the Intelsat Definitive Agreements, "that we should be ready in advance for this sort of thing happening at some future Conference, and not have to make policy decisions of this magnitude in mid-Conference on the spot."[78]

What might happen to US dominance over international telecommunications—and to the profit projects that were pyramiding around computer networking in particular—were the NWICO movement to converge with rich nations' initiatives to develop their own satellite and computer-communications systems? This was a contest carrying very high stakes; and it drew correspondingly top-level political attention from the United States.[79]

The United States Regroups

Having been back-footed, the US began to regroup under President Ford (1974– 1976) and strengthened its responses under Presidents Carter (1976–1980) and Reagan (1980–1988). Throughout these years, the FCC continued to inject itself into "facilities planning" deliberations, which had dominated by foreign PTTs and US international carriers—intending to ensure that the satellite services demanded by many business users would not be sacrificed to the foreign and domestic carrier interests that clung to their submarine cable investments. The FCC also pressed to loosen restrictions prohibiting "voice-grade" circuits from being used to transmit data; and to widen the number of domestic US points at which interconnection could be arranged with international networks. However, the US counter-attack on state-led opposition to US international communications was stronger and more sweeping than this. It began by drawing up an inventory of the obstacles faced by US transnational business interests, tallied in light of an audacious program for regenerating the US informal empire.[80]

During the domestic networking policy struggles of the 1970s, President Carter offered emphatic support for liberalization; and US policymakers intensified their efforts to channel international conflicts in communications. "Looking ahead ten years," a report on the computer industry forecast at the moment of Carter's election in 1976, "the length of the American lead will depend on the ability of the U.S. firms to aggressively accelerate the process of innovation and introduce new products and applications concepts into the market." The obstacles were plentiful. In 1980, big business users and competitive network suppliers testified before Congress about the barriers and threats that inhibited "international data flow." Legislators responded with a call to "forg[e] a new framework" across a great span of international telecommunications and information policy issues. As late as 1983, the chairman of the US Senate Committee on Commerce, Science, and Transportation could declare with some justice that

"The United States faces a rising challenge to its technological telecommunications leadership."[81]

He elaborated that, "In the area of information services, there has been an increase in barriers to U.S. service offerings, limits on transmission facilities, problems of entry into foreign markets and restrictions on the flow of information across national boundaries." An accompanying Commerce Department report added that foreign companies "have made inroads in several key areas, including semiconductors, robotics, microcomputers, lasers, and satellite communications." As a result, "The long-held leadership position of the United States has been challenged by other countries . . . which also consider these sectors of vital national importance."[82]

The time for "complacency and indecision" was past. International telecommunications and information were "crucial for the United States . . . essential to our economic vitality." The US Government, the Senate leader underlined, "must establish a long-range strategy that will promote and protect U.S. long-range economic interests. The stakes are too high to do otherwise." "The information and telecommunications sectors are not only important as growth sectors in themselves," the Commerce Department explained in a crucial addition: "They also function as supporting factors in the growth of other industries—and constitute major contributors to restoring the strength and productivity of the U.S. economy." If the US faltered, it faced the likelihood of "catastrophic" impacts on its military, economic, and political strength.[83]

The Reagan Administration set the US on a forthright counter-course. On one hand, as a part of its "global antirevolutionary offensive" against the Third World political project, the US mounted a frontal attack on a multilateral institution that it had done much to shape, singling out what it called the "politicization" of the UN system. Synchronizing his action with British Prime Minister Margaret Thatcher, in 1984 Reagan withdrew the US from UNESCO. On the other hand, US administrations also devised damaging bilateral policies by which to extract leverage against (inevitably) smaller economies: trade measures against import-substitution policies for computerization, notably, by Brazil; diplomatic initiatives against European efforts to protect their domestic markets and to restrict corporate trans-border data flows; and threats against what the US deemed lax intellectual property laws throughout much of the world. Perhaps most important of all, the US targeted the world's state-operated telecommunications systems.[84]

The liberalization of market entry and network use within the world's largest national market exercised a boldly effective demonstration effect, as the Carter and Reagan administrations pressed insistently for comparable reforms by trading partners. This policy served two structural purposes. First, when profit opportunities in older industries were languishing, privatization opened a temptingly expansive field of investment—gigantic telecommunications infrastructures—directly to capital, often including US capital. Second, and perhaps even more important, as the state role in telecommunications was redrawn corporate capital gained a much-augmented ability to implement proprietary computer communications systems into its freshly expanding cross-border production networks—just as it had in the United States. The US Government thereupon reframed telecommunications as a trade issue, imposing jurisdiction by institutions whose rulemaking practices and substantive concerns excluded vital questions of social and economic policy. Within only a couple of decades, the political economy of global networking was up-ended. An early and paradoxical confirmation came, when US leaders determined that, to place cross-border network system development on these radically altered foundations, its own creation—Intelsat—had to be sacrificed.[85]

The United States Attacks Intelsat

US dominance over Intelsat had been developed, as we saw, at a remove from one-nation-one-vote multilateralism, but also in a context of state control of national system elements. Membership in the system was via national signatories—governmental ministries of posts, telephones, and telegraphs (PTTs). All over the world, governments coordinated and largely determined the nature of domestic access to the Intelsat space segment; the prices at which satellite service was made available to end users; the mix of satellite and submarine cable circuits; and the general terms on which satellite communications were integrated with their domestic terrestrial networks. If this was far from a comity, then Intelsat increasingly bespoke limited successes won by European and Third World countries within a context of multilateral cooperation.[86]

From its inception until the early 1980s, nevertheless, Intelsat had been trumpeted as "an unqualified success"—"a triumph of U.S. foreign policy" which "favorably compared to the Marshall Plan." In 1983, Intelsat's fifteen satellites and hundreds of locally owned earth stations carried two-thirds of all transoceanic communications and handled a reported $5 trillion in electronic funds transfers.[87]

However, as US leaders began to privilege the networking industry and its business customers more concertedly, Intelsat became a target: the system made too much room for (other states') sovereignty. Parallels and precedents were multiplying. One was the near-concurrent withdrawal from UNESCO. A more important precedent had come more than a decade earlier (1971), in the US's deliberate destruction of the Bretton Woods system of fixed currency exchange rates, a system that the US had done the most to shape. "For the first time since

1945, a historian relates, US leaders "looked more to their own bottom-line than to preserving and integrating the world economic system." The Reagan administration sharpened this turn to self-serving unilateralism.[88]

The US reversal with respect to Intelsat was precipitated by the arrival of brashly opportunistic private US-based satellite companies—start-ups that proposed to undercut Intelsat's integrated rate structure by charging lower rates on the high-volume North Atlantic and pan-American routes while placing improved earth station equipment—smaller, cheaper, and more specialized— directly on the premises of corporate users. Some of these fledglings planned to launch their own satellites. Under Intelsat's existing rules, these enterprises could proceed only after gaining the consortium's approval; and this, despite the reduced US ownership stake, was unlikely unless the US government decided to attack its own creation.

A bitter policy fight ensued within the high reaches of the Reagan administration; its outcome marked a turning-point. Political figures possessing both specialized expertise and impeccable Republican credentials—notably, Abbott Washburn—publicly opposed competitive entry. It took twenty-one months for the Executive Branch to complete its review. Soon after Reagan was reelected in 1984, he determined that "separate international communications satellite systems are required in the national interest." The President's directive signaled that the US had embarked upon a sweeping liberalization of international communications. Why was the US now willing to sacrifice Intelsat, its own instrument?[89]

Structural changes had intervened to alter the basis of US policy. These went beyond efforts by small US satellite companies to enter the market. As well, European and Japanese initiatives each had broken the US space monopoly. The Ariane rocket launched in 1979 by the European Space Agency (established in 1975); France's Projet Socrate (1969)—an unrealized attempt to bring educational television by satellite to 17 African countries; France's SPOT remote sensing program (1970s); the Franco-German Symphonie TV broadcasting satellite launched (1974); Eutelsat (1977): and Japan's commitment to a $10 billion space program were indicative. US aerospace and electronics companies, meanwhile, also were clamoring to expand the market for their satellites and related equipment. They underlay the US satellite company start-ups, which sought permission to provide service in competition with Intelsat. Submarine cable ventures, in addition, were instituting higher-capacity optical fiber networks which promised to out-perform satellite services much the way that satellites had out-done a prior generation of submarine cables. The ongoing break-up of AT&T was unleashing other new entrants and altering industry dynamics in US networking, adding further pressure to harmonize the state-centered order that prevailed elsewhere with the churning US market. After gaining operating advantages and cost-economies from US domestic satellites for a decade, finally, transnational business users were demanding to roll back national controls that limited their ability to reorganize operations and to capture efficiencies from trans-border satellite services. Taken together, these factors converged, pushing the Reagan administration to change course.[90]

The effects hit at more than industry structure. Soon after Nixon's 1972 visit, China had signed contracts with three US companies to build satellite ground stations; and in 1977, the PRC joined Intelsat. Like numerous other poor countries, China quickly built up significant dependence on Intelsat; and the PRC disapproved of the U-turn in US policy. The prospect that President Reagan would authorize private international satellite systems drew a strong response from Zhang Wenjin, its Ambassador Extraordinary. The Peoples Republic of China, Zhang stated by letter to William Schneider, the US Undersecretary of State for Security Assistance, Science and Technology, was concerned that these ventures "imperiled . . . the viability of the INTELSAT single global system"— which, ironically, had been one of Intelsat's strategic attractions for the United States. Zhang's worry was widely shared, but it did not deter the US from pursuing its liberalization program. Facing capacious optical fiber cables and tumultuous market conditions, Intelsat began to flounder. The consortium underwent privatization in 1999–2001; thereafter, its signatories hived off their shares to a private equity group. Intelsat became a play-thing for hedge funds, which in 2019 and 2020 piled in to acquire Intelsat stocks and bonds hoping to profit from government-mandated sell-offs of its assets as it entered bankruptcy. Still one of the world's largest fixed satellite service providers, Intelsat planned to emerge from bankruptcy in 2022 operating 52 satellites and still serving hundreds of business and government customers. But other approaches to the commercial exploitation of space satellites had long since overshadowed Intelsat.[91]

If Intelsat was engulfed by the liberalization trend that gripped network system development worldwide, then this liberalization process engendered a still more far-reaching result. Beginning in the late 1980s telecommunications capacity, above all long-haul and submarine cable capacity, was tremendously enlarged and continually extended. Especially notable was a proliferating fiber optic cable infrastructure.

The first transoceanic fiber-optic cable system, TAT-8, was built out by a consortium including AT&T, British Telecom, and France Telecom, and granted equipment supply contracts to companies from all three countries. Introduced in 1988, TAT-8 played a formative role in stimulating European acceptance of internet technology. Specifically, it supported a new high-speed circuit between Cornell University in upstate New York and CERN—the European Organization for Nuclear Research, located outside Geneva, Switzerland. In 1989, this highspeed capability helped induce network managers at CERN to decide to switch their facilities to the internet's TCP/IP protocols, and thus they opened their first external internet connections. By the next year, 1990, the number of internet sites in Europe had reached 30,000. That Tim Berners-Lee, who worked at CERN, chose to write software to enable the World Wide Web for the internet, instead of a different data networking standard (such as X.25), both attested and hugely amplified the internet's comparative importance.[92]

Multifaceted US computer communications buildouts were bound up in concurrent efforts to negotiate interstate jurisdictional issues. The process of liberalizing world telecommunications in particular rested on attempts both to overturn existing structures of control and to erect alternatives. Data networking in turn evolved not merely in light of the comparative superiority of specific technical standards, but also through a US campaign to dislodge and replace existing national and international telecommunications authorities. The principles and the policies that US policymakers hoped would anchor internet technology were preliminarily articulated even before this technology was fully innovated, during the early 1970s—as the global political economy also began to be reconfigured.

Data Networks and Intercapitalist Competition

During the early 1970s, the US computer industry and above all IBM dominated global computing. In part this was because the US companies possessed enormous first-mover advantages; in part because of unmatched state subsidies in the form of US military contracts; in part because their systems were strongly tied to the operations of hundreds of US transnational corporations. Confronted by IBM's amassment of a more than 70 percent share (by value) of worldwide computer system sales in 1971, rival capitalist states reacted with dismay. Not only did the "computerization of society," as the President of France soberly concluded in 1977, portend a massive transgression on his country's national sovereignty. In the context of capitalism's renewed stagnation—the deep recession of 1974–1975 was the turning-point—concerted state action was essential to make computing into a motor of economic rejuvenation.[93]

Ambitious plans for national computer industries were set out by competitors, Britain's Labour Government of the 1960s in the vanguard. An official US report observed that Germany, England, France and Japan, each of which watched as between one-half and four-fifths of its domestic computer market was ceded to US companies, became "committed to ensuring the survival of their national computer industries." Attempts to create and nurture national champions— to prevent US high-tech industry from permanently swamping their domestic markets—in turn worried US policymakers. Rival countries' attempts to advance national capital in and around computing seemed to be gathering strength.[94]

The stakes increased, the issues widened to include the networks needed to interoperate computers. The US had a big head-start here as well. Beginning in the 1950s, US military networks had pioneered the field of computer connectivity, not just domestically but also across international borders. Throughout the next two decades, as wave upon wave of online systems and services washed through the political economy, the US became the world's most data-dependent political-economy. The general public became familiar with online information retrieval in major part through visits to not-for-profit libraries; in 1965, however, remote access to databases actually was dominated by industrial applications including "hotel and airline reservations, stock market quotations, banking, insurance, timesharing services," and "of course military command and control systems."[95]

The US military continued to spearhead the US advance in data networking. Cocooned within pockets of military endeavor, engineers indulged spectacular fantasies: In 1968, when perhaps a total of 1000 people participated in US multiaccess networking, two of the US progenitors of internet technology imagined that networks might put a permanent end to unemployment, "as the entire population of the world is caught up in an infinite crescendo of on-line interactive de-bugging." Flights of fancy aside, rival states threw support to homegrown networking organizations and projects attempting to qualify or moderate US dominance. This competition converged around an emerging mode of data transport called packet switching.[96]

The tenet that packet-switching developed as a means of ensuring the "survivability" of computer-communications during a nuclear war is not unfounded. Nevertheless, within just a few years of when packet networks began to be implemented, their technical and economic advantages claimed primacy. During the 1960s, it was already apparent to a few computer scientists and engineers in England and the United States that packet switching might soon engender both nearly error-free transmission and steep reductions in cost for data communications.

Rather than reserving a scarce telecommunications circuit for the entire period of a communication exchange, as in the circuit-switched voice telephone network, a packet-switched system broke up an originating computer message and transmitted it as a series of packets along multiple pathways; packets carried address headers so that they could be reassembled in the proper order at their destination. Existing telephone circuits had been engineered for voice communication, and required modifications to transport data packets instead. In the initial stages, packet-switched networks were built around specially conditioned circuits leased from terrestrial and satellite carriers, after US Government officials authorized small commercial data services vendors they called "value-added carriers." One of the inventors of Internet technology, Robert Kahn, helped spin off Telenet in 1973, to commercialize the model pioneered by the military Arpanet in the domestic market; two other small companies, Tymnet and Graphnet, soon also offered "value-added" packet-switching services commercially.

The "much greater efficiency" of packet switching was heralded; Philip M. Walker of Telenet boasted in 1976 that, for interactive computer users, "an order of magnitude reduction" over circuit-switched service already had been achieved. This cost benefit could be extended to any communication, any form of expression, that could be reduced to digital form—although it took years, in some cases decades, before the ramifications became fully evident.[97]

Packet switching was, however, a generic term: it did not signify a unique technical standard. Computer makers set out varying schemes, some by trying to implement their time-tested strategy of locking in customers to proprietary standards so as to increase their sales of computers and networking gear. Piggybacking on IBM's primacy in the mainframe computer market, IBM's packet-switching product, Systems Network Architecture (SNA), which came to market in 1975, had been installed in no less than 20,000 networks by the end of 1985. Also formed in 1975 was Satellite Business Systems, a joint venture of IBM, Comsat, and Aetna Insurance to provide specialized data services to big businesses. Before its 1982 divestiture AT&T—still dependent on its enormous sunk investment in circuit-switched systems—belatedly pursued a different approach, deploying a data transport technology called Asynchronous Transfer Mode (ATM) early in the 1990s. An AT&T researcher acknowledged ruefully that this "was just as IP was beginning to pick up steam," meaning that, in the face of a now quickly ascending internet technology, AT&T's ATM proved unable to gain a sufficient user base to generate the network effects needed to become a general standard.[98]

Other industrialized countries, including Britain and France, began to devise and implement still another packet-switching approach. Indeed, early on—in the 1970s—European telecommunications operators found support from some US companies for developing a "reference model" for networking, dubbed "Open Systems Interconnection" (OSI). The technical standard that grew from OSI was called X.25. A sign of Western European countries' efforts to move beyond their strategy of backing "national champions," by expanding pan-European collaboration OSI became the basis for implementing "public data networks" within and among government PTT ministries. In part to make room for these X.25-based packet switched public networks, the European PTTs contemplated a variety of policies that US leaders quickly protested for being protectionist: restrictions on transborder corporate data flows; requirements for local data processing; and strengthened privacy protections. European proposals to limit, and even curtail, transnational companies' use of private line circuits were an anathema to the corporations, mostly US-based, which had built networks around these dedicated proprietary systems.

Computer communications, and packet-switching in particular, therefore made up a churning field of innovation. The technical standards needed to enable these fledgling systems to interoperate had not been fixed. And, because the environing political economy of data networking remained both fluid and contested, the direction that would be fixed for cross-border computer communications remained uncertain.

The issues were fundamental. How many data networks would there be? By whom would these networks be owned and controlled? Would they be built as adjuncts of more comprehensive voice telecommunications infrastructures operated by PTTs and, in the US, by AT&T—or as specialized, standalone systems provided by smaller "value-added carriers"? This touched immediately on other questions: how and to what extent would provision be made for interoperability across networks? Under which rules, and under whose auspices, would data networks interoperate across borders? Early in 1974, a University of Hawaii-based contractor to the US Advanced Research Projects Agency hosted a meeting of a Legal and Political Issues Committee of its International Network Working Group—which had been established by US, European, and a few other international researchers in October 1972. This small body held "frank and wide-ranging conversations" about matters including the types of interconnection arrangements that would be "easier politically"; "the restrictions and regulatory issues that PTT administrations might impose"; network accounting issues such as costs and tariffs; privacy and security considerations around databases and files: "and customs and licensing issues inherent in the communication of data across national boundaries." Technology development and policymaking proceeded, in other words, in loose concert. Ultimately, however, it was the needs of big business users of networks—multinational capital—and of military agencies that predominated in framing data networking initiatives.[99]

Archival evidence reveals that during the final year of the Nixon presidency, vital elements of a US strategy for reconstructing cross-border data networking were clarified. Hard-edged strategic objectives suffused this formative endeavor.

Data Networks and US Policy Change

The program of liberalization within the gigantic US domestic market inevitably generated repercussions beyond borders. The sheer weight of the US market within the global capitalist political economy, various planners understood, could be used to induce broader policy changes in international telecommunications. This can be stated differently, as I did in 1982; US market liberalization "can only be understood in light of an historically unfolding interaction between domestic and international policy . . . it signifies the hostaging of the domestic U.S. economy to transnational corporate interests." Throughout the 1970s, selective forays were undertaken at the FCC, in Congress, and in the Office of the Trade Representative; and organized groups of transnational corporate users began to wield lobbying power against what they deemed onerous restrictions imposed by PTTs, especially throughout Western Europe where the lion's share of US foreign investment then was concentrated. Within this wider context came an initiative specifically aimed at developing US cross-border computer communications as a battering ram against the existing control-structure.[100]

In 1974, a prominent MIT professor, Ithiel de Sola Pool, sent in a grant proposal to the Office of Telecommunications Policy—which, we saw, was acting as an Executive Branch force to privilege business users and deregulated suppliers. Pool's proposal referenced "the feasibility of a world wide packet switching network which would interconnect each country's domestic data network into a global system." Note that Pool used the singular: "domestic data network." This was still a period when country codes denoted unitary national telephone systems and, recall, when the primary multilateral cross-border network was Intelsat, an intergovernmental undertaking.[101]

A background paper by other analysts, which Pool attached to his proposal to OTP, served as a foil for Pool. In evaluating "the organizational form" that a "worldwide data communications system" might take, this paper suggested that "a logical extension" of Intelsat's "successful experiment in international telecommunications cooperation" "would be the establishment of an internationally owned packet data transmission network, connecting all participant countries' domestic networks and operated on principles similar to Intelsat." A presentation of this idea at an MIT seminar had specified that "The convergence of communications satellite technology and the ARPA-developed packet-switched data network could result in orders-of-magnitude reductions in the cost of international data communications."[102]

Pool appreciated these efficiencies, but he harbored deep reservations about the recommended approach. Were "a public or regulated organization" to be established, and "if Intelsat [were] to be taken as a model," he emphasized, "there could be major disagreements between nations over ownership and voting power re operation of the network." Pool voiced concern that such disagreements—which we have seen already bedeviled Intelsat—then might spread: "at issue would be the powers of the organization vis-à-vis the domestic networks and individual vendors/users over such issues as communications security, rights to information, economic subsidy of unprofitable links, economic liability for garbled information, and charging and accounting for services rendered."[103]

Pool much preferred a different option; and this became the anchor of his grant proposal. "It seems clear that, if current trends continue," he forecast—with an eye implicitly on Telenet and other fledgling US commercial packet-switched services vendors—"international data networks will emerge as privately owned competitive systems." How then might US policymakers evaluate "anticipated reactions to such a system of political leaders, existing international carriers, PTTs, and other interests"? Careful study of these issues was imperative, as they were already seen as explosive: the nascent US commercial data networks, Pool forthrightly allowed, "could make irrelevant the local PTT as currently constituted." The raison d'etre behind Pool's proposal thus was to help enable OTP to think systematically about how to advance a US program for multiple privately owned cross-border data networks—at the expense of other state authorities.[104]

Pool discerned that the issues he sought to probe also touched upon an adjacent industry. While US transnational companies needed networks for querying corporate databases, he acknowledged, there was also the US "information services industry, more accurately described as electronic data base publishing, [which] is in its infancy." "Although its trade association is only five years old, its sales have been estimated at $930 million with an expected growth rate of more than 20% per year. There is every reason to believe that electronic data base publishing will become a major industry in the next decade," Pool predicted, "and that U.S. enterprises have the capability to take world leadership in it." He emphasized that "a low cost international data communication network" exemplified by emerging packet-switched systems, "is necessary to allow the U.S. data base publishing industry to reach its full export potential." Emerging packet networks, that is, portended more direct and far-reaching linkages between telecommunications and information services. Pool apprehended that the prospective economic implications of these linkages were enormous. The US government should take due steps to accelerate cross-border data networking, he declared, because "the country that takes the lead in providing data communications is likely to have a long-term lead in providing technologies that others choose to borrow." Already looming large in US official discourse, the economic stakes attaching to networks stood to be become vastly greater.[105]

US priorities snapped into focus, as the Office of Telecommunications Policy assimilated Pool's grant proposal. In a memo reflecting his review of this submission, Abbott Washburn suggested that his colleague, John Eger—OTP's acting director—should query whether Pool saw the worldwide packet network "developing in a way that might jeopardize our traditional U.S. policy of keeping communications in the hands of the private sector?" On the other hand, Washburn suggested that Eger should also ask "Will not other countries react with suspicion that this is another example of the U.S. exploiting its technological advantages worldwide?" Washburn thought that a general summing-up also would be valuable: "How do you foresee a set of international 'rules-of the game' being agreed upon? Would it be a kind of international FCC? If so, how?" A manipulative intent showed through: "How can international cooperation and arrangements be made to avoid acerbating [sic] the issue of cultural imperialism and to assure that other countries will see the U.S. initiative as in their own interest?"[106]

Having digested Washburn's memo, Eger underlined in his response to Pool the significance of studying "the question of government involvement and/or the private, independent development of such a service." Eger stressed that "The study will have to come to grips with the question of the reaction of other countries to the United States' assumption of leadership in this venture." He apprehended the issues raised by international packet switched networks in terms that reflected a keen awareness of NAM's critique of the existing International Information Order: "Suspicions of two kinds can be expected: (a) fear of American 'cultural imperialism' via this most modern computer/satellite means of communication; and (b) suspicion that the whole thing is little more than another example of U.S. exploitation, worldwide, of its technological advantage over other countries."[107]

By 1974, therefore, US policymakers already were determined to dislodge the assumptions that cross-border packet-switched networking should proceed nation-to-nation, and that it should be overseen by an intergovernmental regulator. For the moment, the gap between principles and practice remained wide. Adaptability was the watchword: US policymakers had little choice but to acquiesce to the state-centered international networking projects that still predominated; but they also were working to expedite commercial 'value-added" networks and proprietary business networks. US policymakers thus had begun to settle on the essentials of a policy program for cross-border computer communications. Its basic aim was to heighten proprietary freedom for US capital, inclusive of both corporate network suppliers and corporate network users, to integrate data systems and services into emerging multinational production networks. The details remained sketchy: no full-fledged agenda for implementation could yet be framed. For the moment, the US was content with experiments and initiatives to upgrade and expand cross-border services. This was the context in which a fresh US-based approach to data networking materialized.

TCP/IP, the State, and Capital

As Richard Walker writes, the internet tends to be represented as an "immaculate innovation," a shimmering marvel of technology stripped of formative context and power relations. So abstracted, the internet then can appear to mark an overriding and generally positive break with existing practice and history. Swept away by the same token are the social and political forces that shaped this far-flung telecommunications system.[108]

A case for discontinuity can be based on the internet's architectural attributes. On one side engineers designed the Internet to support an indefinitely expanding series of services and applications, layered on top of its packet-switched data transport mechanism. On the other side, internet designers arranged it to accommodate a remarkable variety of transmission media, from satellites and packet radio to optical fibers, coaxial cables, and mobile phone masts. Together, the argument goes—and, though it assumes the rightful supremacy of market forces, it is a valid argument—these two features of internet data transport detonated explosive economic and cultural changes as the system matured.[109]

The digitization of the political economy indeed did mark an epic modernization of capitalism. Market forces had to be activated and sustained by the state, however, before they could grip the networking realm. This process took place, as we have seen, amid clashing social and political forces. The shift to internetworking, finally, occurred *within* the longer history of telecommunications. The internet's surpassing social feature was that in uniting networks and information services it climaxed an impressively long-lasting historical endeavor to erect a US-managed system of cross-border telecommunications. To fully understand the internet's significance requires that we place it on the sustained curve of American empire.

The moment of the internet's rise—the final quarter of the twentieth century—was framed by profound changes, nationally and internationally. Inside the United States, as we have seen, policymakers cut out data transport—designated an "enhanced service"—from the domain of regulated telecommunications. These decisions propelled computer communications in its different modes and formats to ascend outside and apart from the public utility model which had governed US telecommunications, in a zone where investment and profit strategies prevailed. By no means was this outcome haphazard. It resulted, as we saw, from a mobilization of the state by a coalition of business-friendly politicians, would-be suppliers of new generations of networking equipment and services and, above all, corporate users of networks. Eventually, as this process unfolded, computer networking within the world's largest national market tipped toward the data transport technology of the internet. "Enterprises"—companies based in every sector, alongside military agencies—were its primary beneficiaries. As rivals succumbed and proprietary vendor-centric models of data networking were eventually engulfed, the emerging internet also laid waste to foreign government-operated public data networks at national and international scales. It is arguable that this could not have been as sweeping a victory for the internet as it became, had it not occurred during a new and unprecedented moment of US global triumph. Data networking, and the internet above all, must be situated in this way to be understood as a historical outcome.

That, between 1986 and 1994, Internet data transport would overtake competing approaches to computer networking, could not have been predicted when the packet-switched Arpanet was put in service in 1969 as a tool of the "military-industrial-academic complex." Packet-switching's initial function was limited: to enable collaborative work between computer scientists and engineers working with incompatible computer systems, and situated both in Defense Department agencies and in the labs and offices of corporate- and university contractors. This system was called the Arpanet, after its Defense Department funder, the Advanced Research Projects Agency. Within only a few years, the engineers who devised it took up a related and more open-ended challenge: how to enable interoperation not just between incompatible computers, but between disparate military computer networks. As OTP was reviewing Pool's proposal in 1974, a breakthrough was occurring on this new front. It would take an additional fifteen or twenty years for contingency to diminish sufficiently for "the internet" to emerge as the outstanding victor in the competition over data networking standards—and as the most successful chosen instrument ever implemented to conduct US cross-border communications.[110]

There are numerous accounts of the development of internet technology. Many are simply celebratory. Often falling through the cracks are three fundamental and interrelated features. First, that the efforts to devise this distinct mode of data networking occurred within a formative context of intercapitalist competition. Second, befitting the fact that the issues were political-economic as well as technical, that both the state and capital played roles in organizing and shaping internet data transport. Third, that the eventual victory of TCP/IP over other approaches was folded into a reconfigured US capitalist imperialism, as a world sundered by the Cold War and revolutionary Third World nationalism gave way to a universal market.

During the early 1970s, several initiatives to enable communications between disparate computer networks were pursued by different groups of researchers in Europe and Japan; an International Network Working Group (INWG) was established in 1972, as an attempt to stimulate joint learning and to work toward an internationally accepted set of common protocols for interconnecting packet networks. Its first Chairman was Vinton Cerf, a recent computer science Ph.D. from UCLA; also involved was Robert Kahn, an electrical engineering Ph.D. who was well-seasoned in computer networking practice and theory from time spent working at AT&T. Separately, the two US researchers succeeded in producing a protocol for the US Advanced Research Projects Agency, to enable communications between disparate packet-switched networks. In 1975, Kahn and Cerf chose to stop collaborating with the INWG's attempt to implement an international common standard, as this would have required them to change direction in elaborating their already-minted protocol. Instead, they redoubled their independent effort, and soon devised the TCP/IP suite, which would enable what we know as the internet. Their decision to forgo international cooperation seems to have resulted from a mix of factors, including professional aspirations and personal ambitions, a conviction that the cumbersome European standards-making process might cause long delays and, at least on the part of Kahn, economic nationalism. A historian concludes that, whatever its impetus, the pair's unwillingness to continue working with INWG amounted to "a fateful strategic decision: to abandon the international standards process in order to build a network for their wealthy and powerful client, the American military." Meanwhile, the Americans' action, alongside in-fighting between fractious European research groups, ended INWG's preeminence.[111]

The effect was to cement divergences between US and European internetworking projects. Kahn and Cerf turned their attention to implementing their protocol for use across disparate packet networks and, in 1977, they succeeded—still within ARPA's ambit—in sending packet data across land lines, radio, and a satellite. In 1983, the ARPANET implemented TCP/IP, granting this US model of packet switching a significant institutional basis. This basis strengthened notably when the TCP/IP protocols were adopted for varied networking projects by the Energy Department, NASA, and the National Science Foundation.[112]

At the same time, attempts to devise and implement a common standard for public data networking gained momentum outside the United States. This prospectively centralized form of provision was anchored by government ministries—PTTs. By the end of the 1970s, Japan, Mexico, Brazil, and sixteen Western European telecommunications administrations planned to introduce x.25 public data networks "over the next few years." Nine countries concurrently hoped to implement a pan-European packet-switched network called Euronet. Euronet, within the wider context of ongoing European economic integration, aimed to provide subsidized distribution for European database companies—and a means by which to add other services later. (For this very reason it became a thorn in the side of expansion-minded US database providers, such as McGraw-Hill, which complained to the US Congress in 1980 that Euronet posed "an almost insuperable and wholly unjustified barrier to competition.")[113]

The momentum behind public data networks carried forward so that, as late as the early 1990s, they appeared to constitute a dynamic developmental axis. PTTs and telephone companies vowed to repurpose their existing networks so as to carry both voice and data: their model was called the Integrated Services Digital Network (ISDN). While Germany used its reunification a year after the fall of the Berlin Wall (1989) to call for a national data network, France actually implemented a highly successful system called Minitel, which equipped all home telephone subscribers with terminals for accessing varied information services. Still appearing to show bright economic prospects, Japan announced that it would invest fully $250 billion "to equip businesses and homes with a broadband Integrated Services Digital Network (ISDN) by the year 2015"—under the auspices of Nippon Telegraph and Telephone Corporation (NTT), its now-privatized but still dominant national network operator. In the United States itself, the Regional Bell Operating Companies which had been created through the AT&T divestiture in 1984 rolled out ISDN options.[114]

There were still other protagonists in this confusing contest over data networking. Throughout the 1980s, some of the most widely used computer networks were built out by end-users located in US universities and community groups. BITNET, Usenet, CSNET, and a growing array of "freenets" were of this type. Each possessed its own trajectory, of greater or lesser coherence; many evinced dynamism. BITNET began to run the Internet protocols (TCP/IP) during the mid-1980s and, in 1987, it merged with CSNET to form the Corporation for Research and Educational Networking. Half-detached—not entirely outside—the military-industrial-academic complex, many users of these networks nurtured democratic affinities and sought to make computerization a democratic practice.[115]

Commercial data networking ventures added to the complexity. Telenet—the commercial packet-switched service provider that Kahn had helped to establish, and that used private lines rented from AT&T and its affiliates—gained the scale and scope of a modest-sized national packet switched network within just a couple of years. Indeed a Telenet executive, Philip Walker, filed an application with the FCC to extend Telenet's domestic value-added service to Britain. Telenet's petition required FCC approval, and the agency duly noted an "increasing need for domestic users to access computers located overseas to retrieve or input information." Deciding in favor of extending its domestic liberalization program internationally, the FCC approved Telenet's application in 1977. In response, the European association of government ministries of Posts, Telephones and Telegraphs [CEPT] blocked the FCC's action, by prohibiting Europe's PTTs from dealing directly with these value-added US carriers. Economic rivalry over high-technology thus continued to extend. The PTTs, Telenet emphasized, exhibited "a wish to encourage the development of a strong local computer services industry, and, to the extent that terminals in such countries can efficiently and economically access the extensive computer and data base resources in the United States, the development of these resources in such countries might be discouraged." Europe's ministries reacted viscerally to the danger posed by the US commercial packet networks, and threatened to curtail international private line service—the preferred option among the largest corporate users of computers.[116]

Into the 1990s, outcomes remained inchoate while pressure to expand data networking intensified. Networked equipment had moved from mainframes and mini-computers to powerful small machines; competing manufacturers sprang to market incompatible desktops, personal computers and peripheral equipment: IBM as well as Apple in 1976, Compaq in 1982, Dell in 1984. Other devices into which computational capabilities were embedded also proliferated. Powerful but discrete modes of interoperation were devised nearly concurrently. Several hundred thousand local area networks (LANs) thus were operating across the world by 1987, principally inside corporations; and efforts were multiplying to interconnect these LANs themselves using long-haul or wide-area networks. Typically, though, the two chief LANs did not interoperate. Fragmentation in turn narrowed the scope of shared use. One analyst noted that "it was nearly impossible for subscribers on different electronic mail systems to communicate with each other." Variation, duplication, and incompatibility characterized not only the equipment being networked but also the protocols employed in different networks and, thus, the extent of these networks' interoperability. In some respects akin to the late nineteenth century US, network services and prices were bewildering. As Robert Kahn summed it up in 1987, "networks proliferate, and the cacophony grows."[117]

In this environment, a means of universalizing shared network use among companies, governments, and universities, and residential users still seemed remote. Indeed, even individual transnational companies found it challenging to establish and stabilize multifunctional cross-border data communications. Yet movement toward interoperable data transport systems was also undeniable. One expert, looking back in 1990, observed that "separate networks, originally developed to serve specific user communities, are becoming interlinked." An enumeration of "notable computer networks" published in 1986 perceived that, collectively, "research networks," "company networks," "cooperative networks," and "bulletin boards" were beginning to form a "worldwide metanetwork." By degrees, not only despite but, above all, because of this welter of approaches—Cerf referred to "the boiling ferment of modern telecommunications technology"—during the second half of the 1980s the internet approach to data networking gained a growing purchase in the United States. The chaos of rival and overlapping networks worked to the advantage of TCP/IP, which had been designed specifically to enable interoperability. More extensively and more immediately than any of its competitors, TCP/IP showcased how islands of connectivity, whether national, regional, or proprietary and corporate, might be supplanted by being, simply, spanned.[118]

How, though, was this potential to be actualized? At least some of the internet's operational competitors, notably France's Minitel, were brought forward as a result of well-publicized and highly coordinated state planning. The internet, by contrast, seemed to advance mysteriously across the land- and seascapes of global telecommunications. Though at first unanticipated and unlikely, the internet's ascent in cross-border data transport was not accidental. TCP/IP's versatility was, to be sure, advantageous; however, in itself, it incarnated no intrinsic capacity to compel adoption. Nor was the internet take-up powered by an invisible hand. Rather, the internet's growth arose through a series of ramifying actions by US state agencies, within the context of massing US corporate demand and a radically altering structure of network provision.

Political Economy of Internet Expansion

One precondition of the internet's eventual success stemmed from the AT&T divestiture of 1982–1984. The progress of this Justice Department prosecution was beset by contingency; nonetheless, its outcome set in stone a wider liberalization trend, whose ramifications carried beyond the United States.

Peter Huber apprehended soon after the breakup of the integrated AT&T into seven different local operating companies on one side, and a separate long distance carrier and equipment manufacturer on the other, that the foundationstone of US network system development had been shattered. The divestiture fractured a unit of corporate capital possessing what had been nearly unmatched political power, fragmenting the nation's telecommunications infrastructure: put differently, the world's largest national data networking market had been thrown open. The splintering of AT&T did not automatically favor TCP/IP, but it was propitious for the diverse data networking projects that spun across the US throughout the second half of the 1980s. No captive supplier any longer was bound to develop data networking to suit the needs of a national monopoly service operator—just as no unified national operator could dream of monopsonizing data services. Shane Greenstein underlines that the "lack of a dominant firm in . . . communications would be crucial for the Internet's growth." Network supply was itself becoming competitive and multifarious. Not only telecommunications equipment manufacturers but also microelectronics companies, computer- and other device makers and, of ever-escalating importance, software and services companies, collaborated and competed in network system development. This could be glimpsed at the moment of the Bell break-up with respect to military and intelligence activities. Because the divestiture summarily curtailed the prospect of "one-stop" shopping and coordination—with AT&T—the Reagan administration at once established a new National Security

Telecommunications Advisory Committee. Virtually ignored by scholars, NSTAC was a mechanism that enabled multiple carriers and equipment and software suppliers to participate in the counsels of military network planning.[119]

As the Justice Department severed AT&T's inhouse manufacturer Western Electric's exclusive tie to its erstwhile local exchange companies, furthermore, a crop of suppliers of specialized data networking gear sprang to market their wares to a widening number of buyers. Mostly unfamiliar names to residential consumers, some of these vendors specialized in internet technologies: Cisco (founded 1984), Apollo (1980), 3Com (1979), Sun Microsystems (1982), SynOptics (1985), Cabletron Systems (1983), Wellfleet Communications (1986). Sun in particular was vital to the eventual success of the internet's TCP/IP.

Sun built high-performance work-station computers which, from the outset of its corporate existence, included "hardware and software designed to be hooked up to the Internet." Sun's machines, moreover, came with a preinstalled version of AT&T's Unix operating system; developed by Bell Labs specifically for networking during the 1970s, UNIX was widely licensed to corporations— royalty-free—under the terms of the AT&T 1956 Consent Decree. This and subsequent refinements to UNIX made at UC Berkeley, came—fortunately, for the circulation of TCP/IP—before the AT&T divestiture of 1982–1984 tightened the legal basis for AT&T's licensing of new patents. Then, once more under a DARPA contract, during the late 1970s and early 1980s the Berkeley version of UNIX was supplemented so that TCP/IP came preinstalled on Sun workstations. Neither UC Berkeley nor Sun itself sought to profit directly from this groundbreaking software package. As a result of additional maneuvering by Sun after the ARPANET cut over to TCP/IP in 1983, buyers of its workstations found themselves "ready to plug into the Internet."[120]

An additional supportive factor was more general: the longstanding corporate reliance on private networks. Recall that businesses had long since instituted private line telecommunications. Since the late nineteenth century telegraph, US corporations had paid for so-called "dedicated circuits" from the carriers on a 24-hour, monthly, or yearly basis. These circuits were leased exclusively for each company's internal use: for example, to connect corporate headquarters to a specific manufacturing plant—or to link any two corporate locations requiring heavy and regular communications. During the late 1960s, US policy was loosened, to permit companies to connect their private lines with the public network and with networks operated by other corporations. This change now rapidly ramified. Within just the five years between 1981 and 1986, large corporate users of telecommunications doubled the size of their private networks within the United States (from 15 to 30 million stations). The economic efficiency of packet switching factored into this, as corporations implemented proprietary packet-switched networks to connect their high-traffic sites. A year or two before the AT&T breakup announcement, consultancies recommended that corporate users faced with monthly telecommunications expenses of at least $100,000— essentially, the 500 or so corporate members of the most important business user trade group, the International Communications Association—should install proprietary packet networks built around private line circuits. This trend was not bounded by US borders.[121]

In 1949, fewer than one million US telephone calls were made to and from overseas; three decade later (1979), when the Internet was a fledgling, there were nearly 182 million. In 1964, US and foreign billed telephone calling to and from the US totaled 32 million minutes; by 1996—its ascendancy apparent, but the internet not yet configured for voice over Internet applications—this figure had reached nearly 17.7 billion minutes, and annual growth of US outward calling averaged 20 percent. (Until it began to be supplanted, by fax machines in the mid-1980s and computer communications applications after that, telex traffic spiked comparably.) The internet emerged within an electronically networked capitalism that had long since operated transnationally.[122]

The pressure for corporate data networks in turn extended beyond the US domestic jurisdiction. An AT&T executive explained the reasoning behind this, shortly before the AT&T breakup: "there really is no longer a 'domestic market' separated from international dealings. Large customers increasingly expect to deal with their international telecommunications and data in a systematic, unified way. International systems solutions to communications needs are increasingly demanded." In Western Europe and Japan as well, corporate users clamored for private lines. By the early 1990s, in the Federal Republic of Germany there existed more than one million Private Branch Exchanges, and an astonishing 60 percent of total traffic volume reportedly either originated from or arrived at a PBX. To this extent, PTTs had to pursue their programs for public data networks in the face of growing counter-pressure from within their own countries. At the same time, US capital and the US Executive Branch organized a campaign to compel the International Telecommunication Union to retain the private line option for corporate networking.[123]

At a meeting of the ITU in 1988, they gained victory. The ITU gave new sanction to "special arrangements" whereby, "for the first time, private operators were explicitly allowed to use leased lines to provide services, including data services." This fundamental revision, Richard Hill observes, "facilitated the expansion of networks based on the TCP/IP protocol . . . by removing restrictions that could have impeded the expansion of such services." By the same token, it is true that the ITU's action also accommodated other modes of data communications. By 1990–1991, led by Britain, the European market for value-added networks totaled $4.7 billion; and the top providers were US-based—Telenet, IBM, General Electric Information Services, and Tymnet (taken over by British

Telecom in 1989). Archival evidence suggests that the Republican George H. W. Bush Administration (1988–1992) kept up the pressure in bilateral contexts, making the continued availability of private lines an express goal of US economic diplomacy both with the European Community and the Republic of Korea.[124]

However, this US effort to privilege expanded private line service as a building block for corporate networks does not begin to exhaust the liberalization drive that gathered force during the 1980s, as US capital, US state agencies, and US-centric multilateral organizations cooperated to induce structural changes to telecommunications worldwide. Japan had initiated telecommunications privatization in the early 1980s and, kick-started by Margaret Thatcher in Britain, most of Western Europe joined in during the ten or fifteen years that followed. Meanwhile, big business users and tech vendors were joined by the US Executive Branch, the World Bank, and the International Monetary Fund, to discredit state-operated telecommunications systems and to supplant them with private networks and liberalized terms of use. Throughout the 1970s, Latin American governments in particular had borrowed enormous sums to finance public investments, notably, in infrastructure, and to propel state-led industrial expansion. By the early 1980s there were some six hundred state enterprises in Brazil—nearly half of all big domestic companies; in Mexico, state companies had increased fivefold since the early 1970s, to number over one thousand. Seizing the opportunity presented by the grave international debt crisis that erupted after the US Federal Reserve Bank raised interest rates dramatically to curb inflation during the late 1970s and early 1980s ("the lost decade," the Latin Americans dubbed the ensuing years), the Reagan Administration insisted that the International Monetary Fund press radical restructuring programs—"structural adjustment," in the euphemism of that day—on numerous strapped countries. The transformation snowballed, as favored social classes in a variety of nations jumped on the bandwagon and, beginning late in the 1980s, telecommunications systems became a prime target. Between 1988, when Chile privatized its incumbent telecommunications operator, and 2005, eighty less-developed countries underwent network privatization. Corruption and nepotism flourished, as they also did in the United States. A highly capital-intensive industry of unmatched size and scale was thrown open to private—and especially foreign—investment: FDI flowing into the less developed countries' telecommunications systems increased tenfold during the decade after 1990. Not less important was to liberalize operating conditions, above all at the expense of telecommunications workers who opposed privatization in many countries. Concurrently, the bureaucratized planning common to the government PTT operators (their joint study groups at the ITU made decisions once every four years) was often bypassed and undercut by private market actors while, in addition to foreign investment rules, interconnection strictures and policies governing network use also were relaxed. A US Commerce Department report of 1990 crowed that "The market for private communications systems may prove to be the most open and competitive arena, both here and abroad." A free-for-all atmosphere prevailed, as capital found itself suddenly able to expand across a now-universal world market more or less at will.[125]

Just as Pool had foreseen, monopoly national telecommunications systems operated by government ministries were being supplanted—not necessarily replaced, but reorganized and even reconstituted. The center of gravity increasingly became giant transnational corporate systems, both those of network operators and of big business users conveying everything from research and engineering to production scheduling and inventory management as proprietary bitstreams. (By 2018, one of the two largest US carriers, AT&T, operated 19,500 "points of presence" in 149 countries for the exchange of internet traffic.) Amid greatly stepped-up investment and much rule-bending, physical networks were built out and overlaid with protocols and applications software to enable big companies to operate and manage their own facilities and to interoperate with the facilities of their suppliers. This supported an epic restructuring of multinational corporate investment, as production processes grew ever more far-flung and intricate.[126]

This consolidation of corporate private line networks in turn became the axis of internet development. At the moment that Tim Berners-Lee hit "send" to circulate his World Wide Web software in 1990, the Internet *was already* an international network of networks. Indeed, more. Corporate users' private line systems were enabling TCP/IP configured networks to act as another battering ram against public networks (as well as against proprietary protocols like SNA and DECNET). In Berners-Lee's recollection, the Web's success indeed was predicated significantly on these proprietary systems: "there were strong pockets of internal use" for early Web servers, he declared, that were "not available from the outside." He continued: "Years later, the media would suddenly 'discover' the 'rise' of these internal Web networks and invent the term intranet, with the notion that they were used largely for internal corporate communications. It seemed somewhat ironic to me, since this had been happening all along, and was a principle driving the need for the Web in the first place." It is still; late in 2019, to choose an example at random, the CEO of JP Morgan used his company's intranet to post messages to the huge bank's worldwide workforce. It is this capacious unity of communicative exchange and information production—publication—that most typifies today's internetworking technology.[127]

It cannot be sufficiently underscored that the keystone in the internet arch therefore was private corporate networks—both carriers' and users'. An influential early Internet engineer recollects that, "In the 1980s and into the 1990s there was much less confidence in the research community that the Internet architecture would prevail as a single, global solution." By the end of this period, however, as national configuration and control over data networks eroded to the point of collapse, corporate user networks (designated "autonomous systems" in Internet parlance) flocked to adopt TCP/IP. Giant carriers were relegated to supporting status—still crucial, but no longer the pivot of system development—as the terms of trade lurched in favor of business users and, amid surging investment in new fiber optic cables, the price of bandwidth plummeted. As between corporate users and carriers, both network topology and policymaking power were very nearly turned inside-out. Even in the mid-1980s, the author recollects, one of the largest multinational networks, owned by a major US bank holding company, rivaled the national network of a small country in size and exceeded it in reliability. Sharing out the costs of cables and the contracts for laying them on the sea-floor among operators based in several nations, the consortium model carried forward. However, beginning in 1997 submarine cables using optical fibers also began to be built out directly on behalf of large corporate users. Today this condominium approach is entrenched: giant content and cloud service providers, led by Google, Facebook, Amazon, and Microsoft, are now the primary sources of internet demand, accounting for two-thirds of global transmission capacity in use—and they own and operate on a proprietary basis some of the subsea cables they use.[128]

I have stressed that the successful push for data networking was broad and multifaceted—and that as such it did not automatically favor TCP/IP. Forceful US government action, both to ensure liberalization by breaking up AT&T and pressuring international organizations and foreign PTTs made for conditions conducive to private data networks. US government support for supercomputer access, however, injected momentum specifically into the take-up of the internet protocols. Supercomputers were being used for military and government purposes, as they also were integrated into the oil, automobile, aerospace, chemical, pharmaceutical, and electronics industries. In 1983, there were some sixty supercomputers in the United States and corporate demand for access to them was spiking (government and academic demand was also increasing, because at this time only three universities possessed one). As supercomputers became an urgent reference point for advocates of US economic "competitiveness," government agencies began to collaborate in a national effort.[129]

Originally subordinated to the Reagan administration's 1983 Strategic Computing Initiative, high-speed computer networking took on a life of its own. An important venue was the Federal Coordinating Council for Science, Engineering, and Technology (FCCSET, established by Congress in 1975 under auspices of the Office of Science and Technology Policy "to coordinate activities of the executive branch of government in technical realms"). An FCCSET Committee on High Performance Computing began to concentrate on networks in 1983, and a couple of years later it "called for the interconnection of existing federally supported telecommunications networks." TCP/IP became a preferred option for doing so, perhaps in part because a pivotal FCCSET panel was chaired by Robert Kahn—one of the creators of TCP/IP.[130]

Other federal initiatives converged. In 1981, the National Science Foundation had funded a "Computer Science Network" to offer internet services to computer science departments that had not been connected to the ARPANET; late in 1982, the Defense Communications Agency separated out a civilian ARPANET based on TCP/IP for military research contractors working in academic organizations, from its now-restricted "MILNET"—which used these internet protocols to interconnect exclusively military sites. Each widened the range of adoption of TCP/IP. The NSF added further momentum in 1985, when it determined to subsidize several universities to become hubs for interconnecting supercomputing facilities (which it also funded) using TCP/IP-structured networks. This NSFNET, as it was called, commenced in 1986 and contracted-out its operations to IBM, MCI and a regional interuniversity network in Michigan called MERIT. NSFNET became a progressively higher-capacity "backbone" network, providing expanded connectivity to supercomputer centers. This system quickly put down many roots: By 1989, the US possessed 400 supercomputers, some of which participated in NSFNET- and NSFNET also tied together regional data networks, which in turn interoperated with still smaller campus-wide and other networks (170 of them by 1988). Researchers based not only in computer science but in a growing host of other disciplines now were clamoring for email access, and demand for email service powered additional network expansion. Within only a few years, numerous academic, corporate, and governmental organizations were clustered around NSFNET, which continued to enjoy what Vinton Cerf would call "strong support" from the US government. The government mandated in 1986 that, to bid for federal contracts, manufacturers of computing equipment would be required to support UNIX—which, as we saw, came bundled with TCP/IP. NSFNET's initial reliance on corporate contractors was augmented when, in 1989, two government-supported regional networks connecting to NSFNET were privatized. Stephen Wolff, NSF's division director for Networking and Communications Research and Infrastructure, quietly commenced planning to privatize NSFNET itself.[131]

Support of TCP/IP by different branches of the federal government signified that the early take-up of internet technology in fact was not a "bottom-up" innovation. The Congress (notably, Tennessee Senator Albert Gore, Jr.) got into the act in 1986–1987 while, early in 1987, the Executive Branch's Office of Science and Technology Policy [OSTP] published "A Research and Development Strategy for High Performance Computing": A historian labels this report "a call to arms," and it pulsed with a rhetoric of economic nationalism. "We envision a nationwide computer communications capability," a group convened by the National Research Council proclaimed in 1988, "that would enable any computer in the United States to communicate with any other computer easily, reliably, and over a broad range of speeds commensurate with individual application needs." This proposal was disingenuous twice over. First, it was implicit that adopting TCP/IP was the best way to meet this objective. Second, it was purported that the US networking project was merely domestic, and this was palpably incorrect: Like its precursor, Arpanet—but much more so—NSFNET was an international construction.[132]

Following an upgrade to its backbone, networks attaching to the NSFNET mushroomed, from around 300 to around 2500 between July 1988 and January 1991 (traffic on NSFNET grew twenty-five fold during the two years to September 1991)—and foreign networks accounted for no less than one-third of this total. Urged on by equipment suppliers and business users, the US government accelerated the cross-border take-up of this nascent internet by deciding, after the fall of Soviet socialism in 1991, to abandon the export controls that had limited foreign sales of computing equipment and, specifically, of packet-switching systems. By mid-1991, just as World Wide Web software was beginning to circulate, the internet already operated in 26 countries and supported "several million users on more than 300,000 computers in several thousand organizations." With a parallel to Intelsat twenty years earlier, countries from Mexico to Japan, from Great Britain to India, were using the NSFNET backbone for *domestic* data communications. Crucially, however—and this in stark contrast to Intelsat—foreign governments possessed *no* formal standing in policymaking for NSFNET.[133]

The rapidly growing internet was imbued with a profoundly skewed decision-making structure, even as the matrix of organizations contributing to internet management and system development expanded. Originally known by other names, an Internet Architecture Board [IAB] was formalized in 1983, under the chairmanship of Vinton Cerf. An Internet Engineering Task Force [IETF] began to hold public meetings in 1986, to discuss the increasing scale and complexity of interoperating TCP/IP networks. Having departed direct government service, Robert Kahn formed a (too-little-studied) Corporation for National Research Initiatives (CNRI) in 1986, to foster R&D for a "National Information Infrastructure"—and CNRI channeled its shadowy funds into engineering for TCP/IP. These agencies joined an already existing body endowed with a critical operational function: the Internet Assigned Numbers Authority (IANA). Early on, a Defense Communications Agency contractor (SRI, or Stanford Research International) had assigned Internet addresses (unique identifiers), including to both non-US organizations and commercial entities. In 1988, however, IANA gained both its name and its institutional home at the University of Southern California. These nonstate actors, at this point still conducting business relatively informally, took over the Internet's engineering, its management, and its network and web-host address assignments. Though "blurring the boundary between the public and the private sector," all of the three were based within US jurisdiction. After 1991, when "High Performance Computing" was elevated into an express concern of Congress and President George H. W. Bush, another organization—the nonprofit Internet Society—was established (1992) as a legal home for IAB and IETF; at its first convocation, its board of trustees was made up (mostly) of Americans but included a few engineers and computer scientists based in allied countries in Western Europe, Australia, and Japan. IANA remained under the jurisdiction of the US Executive Branch. With the huge popularization of Web software, finally, in 1994 a World Wide Web Consortium (W3C) conformed to the trend as it constituted itself as a US-based nonprofit organization.[134]

The cohesion that these nonstate actors demonstrated must not be overstated: they did not share a single-minded purpose beyond their shared commitment to TCP/IP in its contests with rival standards. In addition, during the watershed years of the late 1980s and early 1990s, the administration of President George H. W. Bush (1988–1992) granted only lackluster support and a belated sanction for TCP/IP. As NSFNET expanded during these years, however, these institutions and, behind them, representatives of US universities, corporations, and military agencies, coalesced, maneuvering both domestically and internationally to propel the internet project. A tipping-point arrived as it became evident that the overriding US policy precepts for computer-communications—private ownership and control; liberalized use—were notably well-served by TCP/IP. TCP/IP's supple design architecture specifically enabled data transport between the border gateways that separated incompatible corporate networks; and this feature was uniquely well-adapted to a liberalizing telecommunications environment, in which these disparate corporate networks, or autonomous systems, were multiplying. By implementing the TCP/IP protocols, networks could enable relatively easy interoperability. In concert with the US-based agencies that coordinated and managed internet development and—prospectively—to help enable surging multinational corporate supply chains, in the early 1990s this feature granted to the internet an insuperable advantage.[135]

There was one big obstacle: the NSFNET lacked a comprehensive corporate and commercial orientation. Though it had never been vigilant in enforcing the restriction, the federal government had forbidden commercial use while TCP/IP had remained in the custody of a government agency as NSFNET. Following a bitterly controversial policy fight, however, the internet—now predicated increasingly on corporate users—now was expressly opened to commercial use under President Clinton. The early internet's extensive base of foreign users and the lack of foreign government voice in internet management meant that this shift at once ramified beyond borders: the US was resetting policy for the world. As the dotcom designation rapidly outpaced the take-up of other top-level domains, the Clinton Administration proceeded to set out a framework for *global* electronic commerce. Unblinkingly subjugating individuals' privacy rights to corporate profit-hunger, as Matthew Crain shows, this initiative simultaneously signaled that an "American system" of global communications was being powerfully renewed around the internet.[136]

The George H. W. Bush Administration had transferred the internet's name- and numbering functions to a civilian corporation called Network Solutions, Inc. While many countries merely looked on, some nations did protest—in vain—as the United States continued to structure a worldwide internet. Eschewing due process and democratic procedural safeguards, meanwhile, when a key insider in the internet's technical community threatened Executive Branch stewardship over a crucial technical function, a top advisor to President Clinton responded by summarily arrogating to the Commerce Department the management of this function. In 1998, again under Clinton, the whole array of internet management functions were specified and differentiated formally through legal contracts between the US Commerce Department, a new nonprofit California corporation, ICANN, and Network Solutions (acquired two years later by the Internet security company Verisign, for a stunning $21 billion). Now an unprecedentedly versatile and far-reaching global system, the internet had been re-consecrated to commercial functions without gaining approval from other governments. Behind a screen of what was labeled "multi-stakeholderism," US corporations and US state agencies likewise preempted multilateral regulation.[137]

Several additional factors converged to elevate the internet model of data networking above other contenders. The free circulation of software to enable a cheap and wondrously effective multimedia publishing and an intertwined retrieval system—the World Wide Web—was fundamental. The emergence of internet service providers catering for residential markets, and their rapid growth and consolidation, might have allowed old-timers to recall 1960s' visions of an "information utility." The release of browser and server software made interacting with Web services into child's play. Broadband access, wi-fi, and the availability of smartphones after 2007 effectively inserted a more capacious internet into a 24/7 quotidian. Extraordinary new applications—search engines, e-commerce sites and social networks—thereafter vastly expanded the internet's usefulness and desirability. Dozens of fiber optic submarine cables extended the system further across the world. All the while the internet came to underpin a greater share of business operations.[138]

As the hugely complex and variegated network system began to flower, during the second half of the 1990s, "access" in turn became a political issue. In 1995, the US Commerce Department began to publicize a "digital divide" in documenting the lag in "dial-up" internet coverage as between rural- and inner-city poor households and more well-off residents. As dial-up gave way to broadband service, delivered via cable television system modems and digital subscriber line telephone circuits and, going forward again, by smartphones, this reconfigured "digital divide" continued to reference—still tacitly—the twentieth century norm of universal telephone service. Not exhumed, though, was the public utility framework of social responsibility within which the norm of universal service had flourished.[139]

During the 1990s, disparate networking vendors and corporate users, alongside ICANN, Verisign, and the US Executive Branch, pushed ever outwards. They did so, however, in an atmosphere of celebration, even of triumph. Accusations of imperialism had been displaced—just as Pool and Washburn and Eger had hoped a quarter of a century before. Just the same, in actuality the internet's spectacular global growth merged into a final reconfiguration of US empire.

Internet and Empire

The winnowing of rival approaches to data networking produced an outcome as a historical epoch drew to an end. During the 1980s, the Reagan Administration launched "a major US offensive against the Left" throughout Asia, Africa, and Latin America, and deployed US influence in the IMF and the World Bank as a strong-arm tactic against the prevailing models of state-led economic development. Also aggravating conflicts among and within its member countries, these measures combined to defeat the Third World political project. The collapse of Communist regimes in eastern Europe followed as the decade ended; in 1991, the Soviet Union itself disintegrated (President George H. W. Bush worried that the collapse happened so fast that it would leave a dangerous power void). Western Europe was preoccupied with its own endeavor to institutionalize its long-time project of economic integration. All this, finally, was accompanied by China's decision to reinsert itself into the US-led world capitalist order. "The global transformations at the end of the Cold War," a historian relates, "seemed to privilege the United States in ways that former US leaders could hardly believe was achievable." The bulwarks breached, capital was freed to move pretty much where it desired and this was, essentially, everywhere. The overall political-economic consequences were profound, and these encompassed networks. Already existing was a capacity for cross-border communicative exchange via voice and telex and, between wealthy regions and enclaves, computer data. During the 1990s and 2000s a compounding ability to produce and circulate information in different modes and media gravitated toward the global internet.[140]

Decades before, perceptive analysts were already beginning to glimpse how new communications technology and multinational capital might co-evolve.

Richard Barnet and Ronald Mueller noted in 1974 that "revolutionary" changes in communications were complementing international capitalist production: "widely dispersed productive facilities can, thanks to such innovations as containerized shipping and satellite communications, be integrated into what is, conceptually, a global factory." Looking to the past rather than to the future, Harry Magdoff explained how new communications technologies had repeatedly enabled the world market to attain new heights "in integration." However, the internet's capacity to bond networking to variegated information services arrived concurrently with a secular boom in US foreign direct investment, including in telecommunications.[141]

The domain over which capitalist imperatives held sway widened spectacularly, as the formerly socialist countries were reintegrated and as, throughout the Global South, peasants were expropriated and transformed into landless workers. In a matter of decades—a historical instant—hundreds of millions of people entered the circuits of wage labor: between 1980 and 2007, the global labor force grew by 63 percent, from 1.9 billion to 3.1 billion people. Foreign direct investment accelerated to take advantage of this wage labor force, rising from 7 percent of world gross domestic product in 1980 to about 30 percent in 2009; and, for the first time, in a fundamental interrelated change, by 2012 less-developed countries absorbed more FDI than developed countries. The location of the global industrial labor force changed in concert. Whereas, in 1950, perhaps one-third of the world's industrial workers lived in "less developed regions," by 2010, four-fifths of them—upwards of half a billion industrial laborers—resided in the Global South. A titanic reorganization of the wage relationship was underway. It included the scale and location of foreign direct investment and of the industrial labor force, as well as the sequencing, spatial arrangement, structure, coordination, and management of production networks. All of these entered a period of ferment and reorganization, in part as a function of the availability and pricing of data communications—increasingly, internet—services.[142]

Both within foreign-owned manufacturing facilities and in the arms-length contractors that sprang up to contract with foreign multinationals without any equity investment, wage workers were subjected to newly "systematic rationalization," that is, profit-maximization, cost-minimization, and labor control. As I wrote in 2014, this reshaping of industrial organization and of the labor process was enabled, in part, by digital networks: "The sourcing of thousands of intermediate product inputs across many plants in multiple countries, the scheduling and tracking of complex and dispersed production processes, the distribution and marketing of final products: all of these needed to be brought into unison. Ever-expanding network functionality and liberalized terms of network use were essential correlates, because 'every step is accompanied by a body of information required to do the work.'" This was not a one-off outcome. Experiment, discovery, and innovation were ever-present, pushed ahead over years and decades. The result was an ' "increasing fragmentation of production into different activities and tasks along global commodity chains" by both direct and indirect means, namely, by foreign direct investment or outsourcing practices by lead firms and by the purchase of production inputs from a domestic supplier.' "[143]

At the core of this churning change was, however, a reconfiguring imperialism. Alterations to the system of production were based both on the new availability of a global wage labor pool and—concurrently—on what has been termed labor arbitrage: the gaping wage differentials that existed between wealthy and poor countries. Workers in low-wage countries were no longer conquered subjects, as they had been under colonialism: neither enslaved nor free. Nor, however, were they the equals of wage-earners in the wealthy countries; for they were paid a fraction of the earnings of their counterparts in the US, Western Europe, Japan and a few other rich nations (even as, in contrast with the past, sometimes they were set to work on the most modern production technologies). This engraved wage disparity, as John Smith shows, constituted the taproot of capital's ability to appropriate additional increments of value from workers—now typically manufacturing workers—in poor-pay countries. Multinational corporate production systems linked, coordinated, and controlled by cross-border data networks—above all, beginning in the mid-to-late 1990s, the internet—were a function of what was now truly an "empire of capital": an empire based on a historically unprecedented enlargement of disparately reimbursed wage labor. This is not to say that existing imperial arrangements were not carried over. Quite the contrary. The Global South's natural resources and primary commodities typically remained locked into economically disadvantageous relations with multinational capital. However, imperialism's emergent center of gravity was a globally generalized wage relationship, patterned unequally to confer super-profits on multinational capital.[144]

This transformation was masked, in the Northern countries and beyond, by a triumphalist discourse of "globalization" and "human rights." During the 1990s, "globalization" was presented as a movement of common uplift, in which human rights and data communications were advancing together. Ascribed links between telecommunications and democracy possess a tangled history.

Networks and Human Rights

After it broke through into the center of world politics after World War II, a polyvalent and sometimes cynical discourse of human rights saw arguments ricochet back and forth among contending actors. Historical scholarship demonstrates that the Universal Declaration of Human Rights (UDHR), acclaimed by the

United Nations in 1948, betokened not global adherence to common norms of human well-being, but a rolling contest over fundamentals. The conception espoused in the UDHR was famously "indivisible," in that it encompassed *both* civil and political rights *and* economic and social rights. This rich conception drew in part on the themes of economic citizenship that had arisen during the 1930s and 1940s, in the US most commandingly by President Roosevelt's "Four Freedoms" 1944 inaugural address. Though Roosevelt's "freedom from want" and "freedom from fear" both flowed into the Declaration, the UDHR did not arrive as a US gift to the world. From Asia, Africa, and the Middle East—territories long subjected to colonialism—economic and social rights as well as civil rights constituted homegrown demands, as, indeed, they were also demanded by African Americans within the United States. The 1948 Declaration artfully affirmed these. As historian Robin Blackburn sums it up, "The Declaration had far-reaching significance because it defined the meaning of the defeat of fascism and, by incorporating significant social and economic rights," it acknowledged that a momentarily untrammeled conception of human rights—one that backed an adequate standard of living as well as voting rights—"commanded real regard for much of humankind."[145]

By the late 1940s, however, changing US foreign policy priorities made even a rhetorical embrace of such a conception of human rights problematic. Often supported by the US, colonialism continued to make a mockery of the UN's Declaration, while US-backed coups and military as well as political and propaganda measures were becoming hallmarks of its attempt to secure a preponderance of global power. Domestically, meanwhile, economic and social rights were far from equally distributed across a multiply divided US class society. Minorities experienced second-rate opportunities for jobs, housing, schools, and health care, and African Americans faced a denial of voting rights throughout the South, within an encompassing system of segregation based on racist violence. In the face of demands by revolutionary nationalists in the decolonizing countries and by African American freedom activists in the United States, a full-throated US endorsement of human rights would necessarily be equivocal; more important for US diplomats and policymakers, it could be painted as sheer hypocrisy. Right-wing US legislators, meanwhile, were quick to label human rights in general, and economic and social rights in particular, as Communist subversion. Early in the 1950s, US leaders entombed the indivisible conception and withdrew human rights themselves from the agenda of US foreign policy—with but a single exception.[146]

This exception revolved around a carefully crafted doctrine of freedom of information. Under various names, freedom of information was retained as a totem of US foreign policy: US leaders expressly insisted on it from the interwar period onward. The highly placed Republican corporate lawyer and diplomat John

Foster Dulles exclaimed that "if I were to be granted one point of foreign policy and no other, I would make it the free flow of information." In a 1946 broadcast, Assistant Secretary of State William Benton specified the practical content of this catchphrase: "The State Department plans to do everything within its power along political or diplomatic lines to help break down the artificial barriers to the expansion of private American news agencies, magazines, motion pictures, and other media of communications throughout the world." While it repeatedly trumpeted the virtues of borderless information flows, US officials were obdurate in rejecting measures to enable multidirectional communications, brushing aside proposals to redistribute scarce communication resources such as newsprint, electromagnetic spectrum, and satellite slots.[147]

Contending during the later 1940s with repression and cooptation and beset by internecine conflicts, the African American freedom struggle relinquished the indivisible conception of human rights. As some of its leaders embraced the US's anti-Communist foreign policy, the mainstream civil rights movement made notable gains in civil rights; however, economic and social rights—equal treatment with respect to jobs, housing, medical care, and schooling—remained vastly underserved. The nearly universal achievement of decolonization between the 1940s and the mid-1970s, meanwhile, brought political independence but fell dismally short of actualizing economic redistribution and social equality. The Third World political project of a New International Economic Order was defeated. These developments enabled US leaders to recalibrate the policy of disregard toward human rights that had stood service since the early 1950s (apart from their self-serving insistence on the free flow of information). During the 1970s, US Ambassador to the United Nations Daniel Moynihan, alongside Democratic Senator Henry Jackson, led the implementation of a freshly assertive US human rights platform. It emphasized civil and political rights—and remained silent about economic and social rights. Through a complex call-and-response with non-state actors, this truncated conception became a touchstone of US foreign policy. It proved effective in discrediting regimes that US leaders feared and disliked, preeminently but far from exclusively the Soviet Union.[148]

The about-face was performed by the Carter Administration; the changed US stance became entrenched by the administration that followed. Without compunction, President Reagan rebranded some of the functions performed by a flagrant violator of democratic norms, the CIA, as "democracy promotion." The National Endowment for Democracy, another misnomer, was created to channel government funds to private organizations—labor unions, news media, nongovernmental organizations and other nonstate actors—based in countries that drew Executive Branch condemnation. Economic and social rights remained buried; all that US leaders would proffer in response to continued demands in these realms was a parallel discourse of "development." "Development" possessed its own, also complex history: the US rearticulated poor states' early redistributive demands during and after World War II, and showcased its programs during the Kennedy administration's "Development Decade." These US programs granted a pivotal place to communications in development.[149]

Thus a ready-made rhetoric—already distilled, to purge concerns about economic redistribution and social equality—was available when, during the late Bush–Clinton years, the internet was supplied with institutional foundations. This rhetoric was fully activated, and indeed gained unprecedented status, as the collapse of socialism between 1989 and 1992 opened space for capital to operate in a genuinely universal market. However unlikely it may seem, networks took pride of place in the exaltation of the US democratic triumph over its historic Communist adversary.

The same 1990 *New York Times* front page that carried a photo of Soviet president Mikhail Gorbachev and smiling East German leaders agreeing to put "an end to the notion of the West as 'ideological enemy,'" also showcased a report that the National Science Foundation had enlisted some of the biggest US communications and computer companies in "the first comprehensive attempt in the United States to advance the critical technological area of computer networks." By that time, the Berlin Wall had fallen and Eastern Europe's productive facilities were being annexed to West German capital. As existing European socialism crumbled, a swelling chorus sang that computer networks—above all, the internet—incarnated the policies being pursued by the USSR's final leader, Mikhail Gorbachev: decentralization (perestroika) and—above all—openness (glasnost). In 1991, the Soviet Union disintegrated while the Web-enabled internet ascended. Propagated was the bizarre contention that corporate-commercial expansion of a cross-border "information infrastructure" constituted a mighty force of democratization.[150]

Two formative elements of the US's attenuated human rights discourse fitted it for this role. First, human rights ostensibly elevated individuals above state sovereigns. This concorded with the era's "tidal wave of talk about 'civil society,' i.e., the ensemble of voluntary citizens' organizations or private activities, taking the place of authoritarian states"; and with its enveloping discourse of "globalization" which stressed the positive value of transgressing (other) jurisdictions. Second, again, the US conception abstracted away from the indivisible conception of human rights: valorizing political and civil rights, as Samuel Moyn emphasizes, US officials continued to offload economic and social rights from their human rights agenda. The economic side of human rights had already been referred to a different category, "development," which the World Bank in particular had been connecting specifically to telecommunications for decades. Its recommendations recurrently emphasized that the "less-developed countries" should adopt private ownership and competition in telecommunications.[151]

Dozens of poor countries had joined or were about to join Europe and Japan in privatizing their telecommunications systems, as we saw—transforming at a stroke what had often been a nation's largest unionized employer into its most heavily traded stock. In these countries workers often acted collectively to stave off or, at least, to moderate and qualify privatization. We lack a global history of these national struggles, which typically pitted workers simultaneously against multinational capital, their own country's domestic middle class, and their home state. The unions in particular were often pivots of opposition. From Britain and Canada in the early 1980s, to Argentina and Chile and France between the late 1980s and the mid-1990s, to India and South Korea and Pakistan in the late 1990s and 2000s, telecommunications unions led resistance to liberalization and privatization and—when they transpired anyway—the unions helped shape the terms of an altered settlement. These struggles were neither automatic nor one-dimensional: different national contexts saw distinct responses. As far as I know, they did not target the internet per se as an imperialist projection. The success of these variously contested national privatizations nevertheless formed a predicate for the internet's rapid growth, which came soon after or even amid the defeat of the antiprivatization campaigns.[152]

That workers did not halt or even fully identify the significance of the shift to an internet-denominated infrastructure overseen by the US is hardly surprising. The internet was built out during a historic reassertion of US capital's power, nationally and globally. This triumph was not only over Communist adversaries. Decisively, it came amid an accelerating reorganization of the international political economy by and among capitalist classes—strongest in the US, strong in Western Europe and Japan, rising throughout some of the large countries of the Global South—and united in their hope of subduing working class and peasant power and participating together, in varying measure, in multinational production networks enabled in part by data networks.

Francis Fukuyama, who crowed that the US victory in the cold war signified nothing less than "the end of history," concurrently—to his credit—questioned whether "global information technology and instant communications have promoted democratic ideals." While his "end of history" thesis garnered copious admiring publicity, his skepticism about information technology was buried in a deluge of contrary discourse. Networks, a large majority of US intellectuals, business leaders and politicians declared, formed the center of an ostensibly beneficent and democratic globalization. Democratic Senator Al Gore led the charge, conceiving that information networks and human rights comprised an integral unity. "Capitalism and representative democracy rely on the freedom of the individual," Gore intoned in 1991, three months before the Soviet Union dissolved, "so these systems operate in a manner similar to the principle behind massively parallel computers. These computers process data not in one central unit but rather in tiny, less powerful units." By contrast, he imagined, "Communism . . . attempted to bring all the information to a large and powerful central processor, which collapsed when it was overwhelmed by ever more complex information." Throughout the three years that followed Gore drew repeatedly on this idealist fantasy. Strengthening a purported link between computer communications and democracy, he insisted that only by effecting radical policy alterations to the still-existing structure of nationally anchored telecommunications might a better world be brought forward. A 1994 meeting of the International Telecommunications Union in Buenos Aires offered now-Vice President Gore a high-profile opportunity to elaborate.[153]

The speech was initially temperate: "I have come here, 8,000 kilometers from my home, to ask you to help create a Global Information Infrastructure," Gore began. "The development of the GII must be a cooperative effort among governments and peoples. It cannot be dictated or built by a single country. It must be a democratic effort . . . And the distributed intelligence of the GII will spread participatory democracy." The US vice president then arced back to his often-stated but insecure thesis: "the GII will be a metaphor for democracy itself. Representative democracy does not work with an all-powerful central government, arrogating all decisions to itself. That is why communism collapsed. . . . The GII will not only be a metaphor for a functioning democracy, it will in fact promote the functioning of democracy by greatly enhancing the participation of citizens in decision-making. And it will greatly promote the ability of nations to cooperate with each other. I see a new Athenian Age of democracy forged in the fora the GII will create."[154]

Gore's rhetoric of networked democracy made substantial room in which to get down to business. He did so with enthusiasm, citing "five principles" on which the US buildout of its new "information highways" was proceeding. First and foremost was "private investment." Instituting "competition" was tightly bonded; and Gore proposed "that private investment and competition be the foundation for the development of the GII." Establishing a "flexible regulatory framework" was third. Fourth was to open network access to all information providers by ensuring that telephone and video network owners charged nondiscriminatory prices for access to their networks. Bringing up the rear was an entreaty to work toward universal service. Gore urged the ITU to incorporate these principles into its Buenos Aires Declaration, still to be drafted at the meeting. Once completed, this document would serve as a touchstone for the next four years of world telecommunications development.[155]

"I assure you," Gore took care to point out, "that the U.S. will be discussing in many fora, inside and outside the ITU, whether these principles might be usefully adopted by all countries." "All agencies of the U.S. government are potential sources of information and knowledge that can be shared with partners across the globe." He singled out, predictably, the World Bank, USAID and US businesses as sources of finance and training for the new networks.[156]

The VP closed on a familiar note. "To promote ... to protect ... to preserve freedom and democracy, we must make telecommunications development an integral part of every nation's development. Each link we create strengthens the bonds of liberty and democracy around the world. By opening markets to stimulate the development of the global information infrastructure, we open lines of communication ... By opening lines of communication, we open minds."[157]

This discourse of openness veiled a system whose origins were actually, according to one internet historian, "autocratic." In the unipolar moment that followed the collapse of Communism, a system devised by Cold War engineers and expanded under the sign of capitalist empire was transmuted into an icon of democratic self-realization. A thousand pundits chimed in; for example, Thomas Friedman sanctified the middle-class sensibility which, he assured his readers, a benevolent internet was quickly making global. In the early 2000s, the ITU's World Summit on the Information Society exalted the notion that communication constitutes a human right; and, as this right to communicate circulated throughout NGO-, philanthropic foundation-, and academic discourse, a more targeted "right to internet access" cohered. A few years further on, Secretary of State Hillary Clinton elevated "Internet freedom"—"freedom to connect"—into a hallmark of US foreign policy. A special rapporteur of the United Nations reported in 2011 that the right to freedom of opinion and expression articulated by the Universal Declaration on Human Rights in 1948—the right to seek, receive, and impart information across borders and using all kinds of media—now demanded that all people be enabled to access the internet. (Vinton Cerf demurred from the argument that internet access itself should be classed as a human right.)[158]

The power relations that saturated the internet were simply evacuated from such talk. And, even after these power relations began to be revealed (notably, by the Edward Snowden exposures of 2012), the internet continued to be positioned within a wider US human rights discourse—which itself was tethered, in Blackburn's phrase, "to the liberal-imperial masthead." Neither US business leaders nor state officials wished to hint that this great American system of communications was animated by principles other than benevolence and democratic uplift.[159]

A US Digital Capitalism

Adam Segal writes that "For almost five decades the United States has guided the growth of the Internet. From its origins as a small Pentagon program to its status as a global platform that connects more than half of the world's population and tens of billions of devices, the Internet has long been an American project." Presented to the world as a beacon of democracy, the internet reinflated a US hegemony that had been losing air. It constituted the fountainhead of investment and profitable new industries (though these profits often owed as much to financial legerdemain as to market demand): a pole of economic growth. It helped underpin the multinational production systems that often relied upon labor arbitrage. Standing at the head of a century of schemes to install US-managed cross-border telecommunications, the internet supported a full-fledged US digital capitalism.[160]

Fashioning the internet as an American system involved both military and political-economic elements. During its first weeks in office, the Reagan administration demonstrated one potential of the nascent internet. Executive Order 12333 granted authority to the US National Security Agency to eavesdrop on communications which originate and terminate in foreign countries but which transit US territory. This directive was tailor-made for the emerging system, most of whose international traffic then was routed through the United States. Though this was decreasingly so as the internet was built out globally, disclosures based on classified documents showed that, around 2010, AT&T operated at least eight US facilities where NSA operatives tapped and monitored much of the traffic that transits from across the world through these hubs, even if it did not originate on AT&T's own network. What else would one expect when, as one of the internet's architects acknowledged, "much of our early advice about security came from the intelligence community, and their particular view biased our thinking." In the prison-house of internet operations, a related purpose, disrupting the communications of adversaries, remained in the shadows—unless one became a target. Cyber-weapons were a focus of intense developmental effort; by the Obama years US offensive operations—attacks—against foreign networks reputedly took place on a daily basis. The internet's endlessly vaunted private satisfactions and commercial pleasures, and its genuine capacities for aiding oppositional politics, were crisscrossed by circuits of violence.[161]

State surveillance and cyber-war interlaced with the political-economic changes that I have sketched (and fully discussed elsewhere): the extension and reworking of capitalist imperatives. Here, US corporations enjoyed a precocious lead: "U.S. companies developed the routers and servers that carry the world's data, the phones and personal computers that people use to communicate, and the software that serves as a gateway to the Internet." In turn, the US became the early launchpad for a vast multinational industry. Cisco supplied routers. IBM and Compaq and Dell and Apple provided personal computers, while Apple also went on to pioneer highly profitable designer mobile devices. Intel manufactured microelectronic processors; Microsoft provided operating system- and applications software, and a browser. Google and Facebook created applications that scooped up most users outside China—as well as the lion's share of the online advertising that hounded them. Again outside China, Amazon presided over worldwide electronic commerce. US tech companies did not remain uniformly dominant; nevertheless between 2006 and 2021 the US tech sector's contribution to total corporate dividends paid to investors by S&P 500 companies increased from 5.6 percent to 17 percent—the most of any industry sector.[162]

This swelling market encompassed more than consumer delights. Amid a network investment boom like the world had never seen (interrupted, it should be noted, by an impressive crash in 2001–2002), wired broadband internet access was built out for about 1.3 billion households by 2021, alongside mobile infrastructure sufficient to support over 6.2 billion smartphone subscriptions. Nonetheless, big business users of networks remained—as they always had been—the fulcrum. Near the end of the twenty-first century's first decade, consumer spending on information and communications technologies amounted to less than one-third of the total (29 percent); business and government users accounted for 71 percent. The capital expenditures needed to deploy networks and related technologies by the largest individual US banks, manufacturers, retailers, energy companies and other corporate users lagged behind those of the leading network suppliers, such as Verizon and AT&T, and tech companies such as Alphabet—but not by much. The suppliers of course were vital, not only in that some of them were the largest and most profitable companies of all, but also because they pioneered in redesigning and reorganizing the political economy *in general*. An upward trend in US capital investment in information processing equipment and software had been ongoing for decades; as the internet took hold, ICT outlays shot up further, from 38 to 55 percent of *all* corporate US equipment spending between 1990 and 2001. This upswing persisted, with only a momentary lull after the financial collapse of 2008–2009. A large and growing share of the world's business system was equipped with internet systems, and with the services and applications that piggybacked on this capacious data transport mechanism. An official summed it up before the European Parliament in 2019: "there are only two types of business: those that are already digital and those that soon will be."[163]

*

In 2019, an anonymous "early Google executive" reflected frankly on the search company's success at avoiding government oversight ever since its founding in 1998: "We thought we had 10 years—it turned out we had 20." Though movements to impose government oversight on the giant internet suppliers were accelerating, it remained unclear just how far-reaching or effective any ensuing accountability measures might be. Characteristically, the multinational data networks operated by giant corporate users remained less well-scrutinized. For those who had erected this system—the tech developers and industry executives, financiers and investors, spy-masters and warriors—it was still the best of times.[164]

Nevertheless, twenty-first-century digital capitalism and its correlative empire of capital will be remembered principally for engendering disorder and multifaceted crisis: financial, economic, environmental, and political. Half a century ago, the last great anti-imperialist movements—above all the NWICO—already discerned an urgent need to restructure unbalanced international communications. In a global political economy that has since been rendered still more reliant on dominative US networks, can anyone doubt that the next anti-imperialist surge—whenever it comes—will do likewise?

Conclusion

Liberalization was sealed in stone by the government-mandated break-up of the Bell System in 1982–1984. Until then, within market boundaries and regulatory limits set by government and in light of constraints imposed by its big business customers, a giant integrated carrier had managed the world's largest telecommunications system as a peak corporate power-unit. The divestiture blasted away this firmament. It invited growing historical contingency into telecommunications development, as demanded by business users and independent suppliers of data networking equipment.

Carved out of AT&T under the modified consent decree that set the terms of the break-up were seven regional Bell companies (RBCs), which provided monopoly local service to much of the country. Now stripped of these local exchange units, a rump AT&T still remained by far the largest long-distance carrier; and it also held on to most of its huge equipment manufacturing subsidiary, Western Electric, and to Bell Laboratories. Beyond this, a couple of large independent local carriers and thousands of smaller operators continued to interconnect with long-distance companies to provide a full complement of service to US subscribers: for the politically induced liberalization process had engendered two substantial independent long-distance companies: MCI and Sprint. During the decade or so after 1984, when the fracture occurred, innovations in network technologies and service offerings, and oversight of the settlement by a single strong-willed judge, became factors prompting the RBCs to become intensely dissatisfied with the legal regime—and restrictions—established by the 1982 consent decree. In 1996, with strong bipartisan support—and much lobbying by the industry—a new Telecommunications Act swept away this regime.[1]

Where before there had been careful (critics said arbitrary) restrictions placed on the RBCs' businesses, now the entire telecommunications industry was thrown open to competition—and indeed, new competitors appeared in both local- and long-distance service markets. At once, however, a concurrent process of industrial consolidation also commenced. Indeed, this acquisitions and investment binge proved overwhelming, as network operators pursued both consolidation and diversification. The account that follows sketches only some of the leading elements in this epic reorganization.

The regional Bell companies both merged with one another and (after federal authorities reversed a stricture in the divestiture which had banned this) acquired long-distance companies. Bell Atlantic purchased NYNEX in 1997 and went on to rename itself Verizon, following a merger the next year with the largest independent, GTE—which itself possessed a long-distance unit and subsidiaries in or affiliates in Canada, the Dominican Republic, Puerto Rico, and Venezuela. In 2006, after the collapse of a rival bid, Verizon then acquired MCI, the second-largest US long-distance carrier. Southwestern Bell, or SBC, announced a takeover of Pacific Telesis two months after the Telecommunications Act was passed in 1996; it went on to purchase the largest long-distance carrier, and its former parent company, AT&T, in 2005. Renaming itself AT&T, in 2006, it bought out a sixth RBC, Bell South. The seventh RBC, US West (whose disproportionately dispersed and rural subscriber base made it a less-enticing target), merged in 2000 with Qwest, a recently established provider of long-distance services for businesses; this combination was then ingested by CenturyLink in 2010. CenturyLink (which renamed itself Lumen in 2020) became a more formidable rival when it acquired Level 3, another vendor of business network services, which developed a focus on "hybrid networking, cloud connectivity, and security solutions" for multinational corporations in sixty countries. Verizon and AT&T likewise invested heavily in network facilities to support their business customers across scores of countries. Optical fiber cables in particular were needed, to carry swelling internet message streams, to extend high-capacity circuits to corporate users, and to support back-haul carriage of the carriers' ever-increasing wireless communications.[2]

Wireless service underwent a veritable explosion in use, and this industry segment also rapidly concentrated. At first mostly to safeguard their tremendous legacy investments in wireline networks, AT&T and Verizon began to acquire (and for a period, in Verizon's case, to be acquired by) mobile phone companies and to make hugely costly purchases of spectrum—a public resource that was turned into a marketed commodity during the 1980s and 1990s by the federal government. T-Mobile was established by the German operator Deutsche Telekom in 2001 through its purchase of VoiceStream, a digital wireless carrier serving the western United States. Initially a secondary force, T-Mobile became one of the top three operators after it gained regulatory approval to take over Sprint, which had been owned (since 2012) mostly by the Japanese company Softbank. Wireless became the carriers' bread-and-butter consumer service after smartphones became a preferred device for accessing the internet as well as the dominant channel for voice calls.[3]

Carriers in turn found themselves negotiating a simultaneous transition not only into successive generations of wireless service both also into internet service provision. Mergers and acquisitions multiplied here as well. Thousands of what had often been not-for-profit local internet service providers were taken over by telecom companies. As the big carriers became internet service providers they now found themselves competing against cable TV multiple system operators, companies which had likewise entered the market for broadband internet delivery to households. The cable conglomerates were concurrently making investments in "content": television programming, film, and cable network assets. The largest cable operator, Comcast, acquired full control over NBC Universal in 2013. AT&T decided to join the party. It had already purchased what was then the largest US cable company, Tele-Communications, in 1999 (for about $44 billion) and, in a spectacular display of bravado, between 2015 and 2021 AT&T spent about $170 billion to buy satellite service provider DirecTV and content provider Time-Warner (including new debt). Verizon also invested in content assets, but on a less improvident scale.[4]

As if this dizzyingly costly diversification were not enough, telecom carriers also indulged in still other strategic experiments. Amid much fanfare, in 1991 AT&T bought a big computer company, NCR—only to spin it off five years later. AT&T's subsidiary Western Electric—which, for many decades before the divestiture had been a near-monopoly supplier to the US national telecommunications market—became something of a hot potato after the break-up. Renamed Lucent in 1996 in the biggest corporate spin-off in US history, the now-independent manufacturer faced growing competition from both domestic and foreign suppliers. Its core market was quickly eroding as purveyors of internet gear seized growing chunks of the US networking market; while other manufacturers catered successfully for wireless systems. A once politically unthinkable outcome transpired when, in 2006, Lucent merged with the French telecom equipment manufacturer Alcatel—and the company's headquarters remained in Paris.[5]

These reorganizations necessitated financing on a titanic scale. This in turn resulted in stupendous debt-loads, heightened strategic risks and, in one especially high-profile instance, felonious practices. In a harbinger of the more encompassing financial crisis that struck a few years later, in 2000–2002—for the first time since it had been stabilized by New Deal regulators, and despite forewarnings by skeptics—major bankruptcies hit the industry. WorldCom, a market entrant viewed as a paragon throughout the 1990s for completing seventy deals, perpetrated what was later revealed as an $11 billion accounting fraud which led to the largest corporate bankruptcy in US history in 2002. WorldCom's CEO was convicted and sent to prison; but its bondholders profited, while employees in their thousands got the boot. And, once the industry regained its footing, mergers and acquisitions resumed.[6]

At the end of 2021, Verizon carried $147.5 billion in long-term debt—about equal to the Gross Domestic Product of Qatar. AT&T shouldered $152.8 billion in debt, just a bit less than the GDP of Hungary. Annual investments in network system development, notably 5G wireless and fiber optic cables, were unrelenting: AT&T planned capital expenditures of $24 billion in 2022 (the most of any US company); and Verizon $21.5 billion. When coupled with high indebtedness and high capital expenditures, their relatively slow growth and languishing share prices spelled trouble. AT&T performed a sharp U-turn in 2022, when its newly appointed CEO determined that the huge outlays needed to support its media businesses could not be sustained; he announced that AT&T would divest its just-acquired media assets. Basic connectivity—built around 5G and fiber—became the new mantra.[7]

There was no denying the impressive scale of the carriers. With 171 million "connections" across devices (phones, but also watches, tablets and others) for its wireless services in 2020, in the years 2016–2021, AT&T garnered annual revenues of between $160 and $182 billion and net income between $13 billion and $29 billion—apart from a $5.4 billion loss in 2020. With about 125 million consumer wireless subscribers and 25 million business wireless subscribers in 2021, Verizon's revenues hovered at around $133 billion and its net income seesawed between $13 and $30 billion; its global network served business customers across 180 countries. T-Mobile boasted revenues of over $58 billion and served 109 million customers for 2021.[8]

Despite their reach the carriers were dwarfed by their extraordinary recent rivals, the internet platforms. With $118 billion in revenue in 2021, Meta's net income was $39 billion; its Facebook unit reported 1.93 billion daily active users. Google's parent Alphabet claimed revenue of $258 billion in 2021, with net income of $76 billion. Early in 2022, in the US alone, Google sites were ranked first among most-visited web sites, with 270 million unique visitors—but of course, Google is a global company. Its search engine commanded a 91 percent share of the worldwide desktop search market; its YouTube video site reached upward of two billion users; and its Android operating system possessed a 72 percent share of the global mobile market. Microsoft 2021 revenue was $168 billion, with net income of $61 billion; its Office 365 occupied about 48 percent of the global market for what is called "office productivity software," while its LinkedIn subsidiary reached 775 million people worldwide. Amazon took in $470 billion in 2021, with net income of $33 billion. Increasingly ubiquitous across both economy and culture, Amazon Prime serviced more than 200 million subscribers. With 1.8 billion active devices worldwide in early 2022, finally, Apple enjoyed revenues of $366 billion and net income of $95 billion. Neither Verizon nor T-Mobile nor a born-again AT&T could muster the concentrated national political power that had been exercised by their progenitor, or the reach of the internet platforms. Nor could the carriers approach the financial might of their new rivals, whose collective market capitalization in April 2022 approached $9 trillion.[9]

Nor was this all. No longer was policy set within a tightly bounded FCC-PUC-AT&T nexus. The carriers that provided connectivity were now members of a more variegated group of companies, government agencies and nonprofit corporations which, through both conflict and cooperation, together established the terms of system development. Within this context, corporate users had been elevated, and these now notably included the giant internet platform companies. For, though we may not be accustomed to thinking of them in this way, the platforms had indeed become unrivaled consumers of connectivity, which they bundled into their devices, apps and services.[10]

The carriers continued to exercise near-monopoly power with respect to tens of millions of individuals and household subscribers. Scholars and "net neutrality" activists cited this power, with justification, when holding that nondiscrimination should apply as an overarching policy principle—including in internet service provision. With respect to large corporate customers, nevertheless, the carriers exhibited mounting structural weakness.[11]

Throughout this book we have seen how US business users recurrently strengthened themselves as a policymaking force. With the ascent of data networking—above all, around the internet—network topology itself altered, both as an expression and a further source of users' political-economic ascendancy. There were new participants and intermediaries: Giant proprietary data centers owned by tech companies and cloud service suppliers, and stuffed with racks containing tens of thousands of servers; internet service providers (ISPs) like Cogent and Lumen and Hurricane Electric as well as AT&T and Verizon; internet colocation hubs run by intermediaries with unfamiliar names like Equinix, NTT, and Cyxtera, for "peering" between big internet service providers and users; and, finally, corporate internets (or "intranets"), assigned "autonomous system numbers" for purposes of interconnection. These autonomous systems were an internet-denominated successor of the private wires leased by businesses a century earlier from Western Union and AT&T. A more specialized but still comparable updating came during the early 2020s, as corporate users deployed private 5G wireless networks. Within this radically liberalized environment, big business users were often able to swing the terms of trade with the carriers further in their own favor.[12]

A special subset of these users actually turned the telecom carriers' foundational voice market inside-out. On one side, Google and Facebook and Microsoft and Amazon, now dubbed "content delivery networks" (CDNs), or simply "content providers," were among the multinational users that migrated partly off the carriers' networks by constructing their own purpose-built transoceanic and nationwide systems. Cooperating at the downstream end with other ISPs to target both computers and wireless smartphone users—there were an estimated 6.2 billion smartphones in service in 2021, meaning that a goodly share of the world's people, perhaps as many as half, possessed one—on the other side, content providers rolled out "over the top" (OTT) voice and video calling applications. Microsoft's Skype was succeeded by Facebook Messenger and WhatsApp—each of which claimed 1.3 billion users by 2020; Apple FaceTime, Viber, KakaoTalk, QQ, and WeChat (Weixin). These apps stimulated unprecedented data traffic, an increasing fraction of which passed over the content providers' own networks. By 2017, along both Atlantic and Pacific routes, CDNs made up over half of *total* demand for connectivity, and by 2019 the four giants (Facebook, Google, Amazon and Microsoft) accounted for nearly two-thirds of all international capacity in use. They overtook the carriers in international voice calling specifically in 2016. By 2021, OTT apps reportedly accounted for more than four times the international voice traffic of the carriers (1.4 trillion minutes versus 375 billion minutes). As demand for global internet bandwidth surged, and as submarine cable investment increased correspondingly, the carriers' tally of international voice minutes declined—for the first time since the Great Depression. Unlike in the 1930s, however, this lapse looked to be permanent.[13]

This swing attested a radically different market dynamic in a second respect: social calling among individuals supplanted business communications as the major driver of international long-distance usage. As recently as 1990, businesses contributed two-thirds of international voice revenue, but during the following three decades individual calls grew ever more important. Ever-increased (though territorially uneven) network investment and cheapening access to networks via mobile services translated into spikes in consumer demand. Over-the-top apps brought this trend to fruition. If the consumer was now paramount in the international market, then this was because voice communication was now delivered through apps that were layered over the carriers' networks by content delivery networks. These specialized business users were preempting the carriers' onetime basic function: to provide voice communication.[14]

In this regime telecommunications workers fared indifferently at best. Its 268,000 employees in 2018 made AT&T the largest employer in US telecommunications; but the indebted company then cut 65,000 workers to show a total of only 202,600 in 2021. Verizon's 144,500 workers in 2018 were down to 118.400 in 2021; T-Mobile, 75,000; and (2020) Lumen, 39,000. Two points need to be made about this workforce. First, it had shrunk in half since the break-up of the Bell System, the nation's largest private employer at the time (1982) with over a million workers. Second, again in marked contrast with the old AT&T, telecommunications had become a mostly nonunion field of employment. Unions represented 46 percent of AT&T's workforce in 2017, but just 37 percent in 2021—and perhaps 27 percent of Verizon's in 2020; collective bargaining agreements covered a very small fraction of employees at Lumen, and unions were a negligible force at T-Mobile. This meant that wages, benefits, working conditions, and jobs themselves came under sustained attack from employers: the networking labor force that operated digital capitalism was far less well-defended than its precursor. It also meant that labor's political voice had been muted. Especially telling here is the historical contrast between the small American Communications Association which, backed by a militant CIO, staved off for years a merger between Postal Telegraph and Western Union, and contemporary unions' inability to curtail the scores of mergers that followed the 1996 Communications Act.[15]

The Postal Service experienced sharper confrontation even as the USPS was placed under relentless strain. The USPS Board of Governors and its corporate-style managers pushed ceaselessly against the postal network's reach and service responsibilities, and against its workers—disproportionately African American—in a climate of legislative and, sometimes, presidential antagonism. Postal workers and residential users had to contend specifically with Congress's calculated imposition of an utterly gratuitous pension burden on the USPS—to prefund employees' future retirement health benefits. Residential users continued, by contrast, and by a wide margin, to view the USPS as the most popular federal agency. The number of postal employees shrank, and more of these workers found themselves handling packages rather than first-class letters, the volume of which declined in the face of electronic billpaying, email and instant messaging. Postal workers were swept into the circuits of e-commerce, above all, those of Amazon—the single largest postal system user. Amazon was in turn granted special status by the agency. Threats to service continued, including attempts to reduce deliveries to five days a week. Initiatives to curtail the postal unions' legal right to engage in collective bargaining over wages and to privatize the system—both stoutly resisted by the postal unions—signaled that the Trump administration hoped to complete the transformation of what had long been an icon of US democracy into merely another outlet for finance capital.[16]

It did not succeed. Despite the dire condition of the Postal Service, the widely sung heroism of postal employees in ensuring the carriage of medicines and other necessities throughout the Covid crisis resulted in passage of the Postal Service Reform Act of 2022 as this book was completed. This legislation eliminated the retirement benefits prefunding mandate that had so unduly burdened the Postal Service; and it guaranteed six-day delivery going forward. Whether a universal Postal Service and full-time union postal jobs were secure was another matter.[17]

The networking industry of the 2020s bore striking similarities to its forbear a century earlier. On one side there were weak providers, suffering from ruinous competition; hawking mature services; extracting unjust concessions from their employees; and, where they could, relying on debt-finance to carry on. On the other side were icons of the new capitalism, exploiting their colossal corporate power to purvey shiny new gadgets and services at the expense of both workers and the environment. At both ends—as had also been true a century earlier—the cardinal problem was how to impose public accountability.

During the early decades of the republic, the US Post Office was the major institutional incarnation of central-state power. It acted simultaneously as a spearhead of territorial imperialism, an irreplaceable foundation of capital's market expansion within this "nation without borders," and an overwhelmingly popular agency of inter-communication. Implemented as a profitmaking capitalist industry soon after it emerged, the corporate telegraph shared only the first two of these purposes—for it was built out as a specialized business service and most Americans enjoyed no regular access to it. In addition, the telegraph was an exemplar of the financial machinations and corruptions that saturated its era, the so-called Gilded Age. Both systems were vital to an ongoing restructuring of the US political economy and were caught up in conflicts over its direction.[18]

While a spectrum of reformers assailed the corporate telegraph for fifty years, by contrast they looked to the Post Office as a positive model—despite its entanglement in party politics and despite its exploitation of its workforce. This was because the Post Office, again in part owing to social and political pressure, was implementing policies that actually made the agency both an inclusive service and an efficient one. During the post–Civil War era, the leading template for political-economic reorganization was formed around antimonopoly doctrines; and a surging sociopolitical movement arose in hopes of checking the prerogatives of big capital. This struggle to abridge and discipline corporate power foregrounded the goal of universalizing access to efficient telecommunications services and—above all for the postal and telegraph workers who helped lead it—of improving the working conditions of those who provided telecommunications to the public. By the late nineteenth century antimonopolists were targeting not only Western Union but also AT&T, whose upgraded network was engulfing its precursor.

Though they did not refer to it this way, the network imaginary that fired the hopes of many antimonopolists may be seen in terms of decommodification: They wished to lift telecommunications out of what they saw as the corrupt, inefficient, and exploitative web of practice that was being spun by big capital and its political allies. They campaigned for far-reaching structural change: the postalization of the telegraph and the telephone and, perhaps, also other services. Some groups in the antimonopoly alliance began to peel away from it, however, in favor of a separate peace with AT&T—which proffered ameliorative measures to both business users and, more selectively, smaller independent telephone companies. Workers, by contrast, still cherished a hope that the state would act in behalf of the laboring population. This hope, however, was proved chimerical during and after World War I, as a result of the one-year operation of the wireline services by a singularly repressive federal administrator. Workers' experience of postalization finally broke the back of an already-unraveling movement. However, antimonopoly reform left a deep impress.

Growing out of the antimonopoly struggle, a reconfigured project of reform coalesced during the interwar years. Rooted in the administrative commissions established around the turn of the twentieth century, the state public utility commissions systematized norms and practices but also narrowed the scope of the impulse to accountability. They accorded standing not to workers and consumers but merely to those who possessed a property interest in telecommunications: business users and independent network operators. The results, predictably, were neglect of labor conditions and, to a substantial extent, of the need of American households for telephone service. Immediately after World War I, nevertheless, a scattering of PUC commissioners began to respond to the power of the great monopoly which everywhere repulsed their efforts at exercising effective jurisdiction: AT&T. Unexpectedly, the onset of the Great Depression opened fresh political opportunities to them. The public utility conception was re-energized, and rapidly endowed with potentially radical possibilities, above all, through passage in 1934 of legislation establishing a Federal Communications Commission. Regulators striving to strengthen their oversight were now allied, sometimes uncomfortably, with telecommunications workers—who began to press anew a struggle for corporate accountability and economic justice. The newly established CIO affiliate, the American Communications Association, was the chief propellant of this reactivated reform push. Its goals were to elevate organized labor not only industrially but politically. The ACA and the early CIO sought improved pay and working conditions, to be sure; but they also demanded that the telegraph industry not be made a Western Union monopoly. Further, they embedded these telecommunications struggles within a more encompassing drive to represent the working class public while pushing for far-reaching alterations to the US political economy.

World War II and its aftermath brought a ramifying counter-attack against labor—the CIO's radical social unionism in particular—by big business and political conservatives. As domestic political reaction and imperial foreign policy also saw ferocious infighting within the labor movement, the pattern of US telecommunications was altered. With backing from the top CIO leadership, the Communications Workers of America, a cautious and anti-Communist industrial union, preempted the left-led ACA's CIO jurisdiction over telecommunications. CWA did strive for economic improvement and accountability, but its leaders accepted US Cold War foreign policy and its militarized public utility framework. Meanwhile the FCC and the PUCs built on New Deal precepts and policy innovations to bring telephone service, at last, to most US households.

Although public utility principles certainly were freshly hedged, by no means had they collapsed: doctrines of public responsibility, despite the cavils of some liberals and radicals, were not something that AT&T's corporate managers could manipulate at will. Rather, a truly inclusive system of telecommunications provision was belatedly established, a system that operated an effective nationwide service by telephone utilities literally strung together and stewarded by AT&T, and one that operated through increasingly well-defined social welfare principles. While domestic household access increased year upon year, long-distance services dominated by business were freighted with much of the cost of providing this expanded access. Meaningful service standards were codified. Patent monopoly gave way to easy licensing. Telephone employees had achieved union recognition and they belatedly gained a recognized right to engage in national bargaining with AT&T. Greater job security, enhanced benefits and better wages were the fruits of their successful struggle. Concurrently, in their different ways both the CWA and AT&T took places in the firmament of postwar US imperialism, the former by affiliating with an anti-Communist international labor federation and the latter by profitably germinating military network innovations. AT&T's forward role in a permanent war economy was ratified by an antitrust case brought by the Justice Department which, despite restricting AT&T's monopoly to regulated services, did not break up the company. For many liberals and radicals, this was a travesty. Now mostly isolated from the union movement, and carrying memories of the FCC's capitulation to AT&T less than twenty years before, for them the judgment confirmed that the public utility framework was a sham—an institutionalization of corporate power masquerading as accountability to the commonweal.

The casement of public utility doctrine began to shiver and convulse as it was beset by pressures from two sides. First, during the later 1960s and early 1970s social and political movements organized by Blacks, Latina/os, and women assailed the employment discrimination that pervaded electronic telecommunications—and breathed new life into the formal conception that governed it. Expressly citing the telephone industry's legal status as a public utility, activists belatedly gained standing for those lacking a property interest. This was not a predictable result. It reflected support not only from the recently created Equal Employment Opportunity Commission and a maverick FCC Commissioner but also, in an unlikely twist, from the Supreme Court. Through a precedent-setting consent decree signed by AT&T, one that carried antidiscriminatory ramifications for the entire US corporate economy, occupational structures in the telephone industry began to be equalized for minorities and women.

At the same time, however, an opaque but contrary impetus was strengthening. Even as Blacks, Latina/os and women pressed to open jobs in regulated telecommunications, and as many existing telecom workers expressed dissatisfaction with bureaucratic union structures and arbitrary corporate power, business users and would-be suppliers of specialized data networking gear mobilized into a formidable pressure group. Their key demand was that the Nixon administration should grant them special privileges within the changing system of provision. It was characteristic that this furtive administration did not forthrightly state that this demand signified a far-reaching departure from existing policy.

The theaters of policy action included both major telecommunications systems. Under cover of so-called "deregulation" and "competition," an FCC that was now closely coordinating its actions with high Executive Branch officials took repeated steps to liberalize electronic telecommunications. These measures successively elevated corporate network users and suppliers of enhanced technology, while they concurrently restricted and displaced the very public utility framework to which women and minorities had—it seemed—successfully appealed.

The Post Office, by contrast, underwent a dramatic one-off transformation. Nixon exploited an unprecedented wildcat strike by straitened Post Office workers seeking pay increases, to turn a long-standing cabinet department into a government corporation: the US Postal Service. Democrats as well as Republicans backed this change, as did big business users of the mails; many, perhaps most, unionized postal workers opposed it. As a condition of the changeover to the USPS, however, Nixon was compelled to concede to the postal unions additional collective bargaining rights beyond those permitted to other federal workers. While some postal unions thereupon combined, postal management succeeded in expanding the use of computerized equipment in mail processing in support of what it called efficiency. Networking across its range began to undergo a historic transformation, as computer-networked systems elevated and privileged the largest corporate customers of both electronic telecommunications and the mails.

When they did not condemn it outright for being intrinsically flawed—a transgression on marketplace efficiency—like many Republicans, Democrats had wearied of the public utility conception, viewing it as hopelessly broken in practice. This overlap meant that opposition to jettisoning the public utility framework no longer possessed a meaningful legislative or executive base. Virtually no well-informed, carefully reasoned and electorate-wide public deliberation took place, therefore, as the momentous politically induced trend to market liberalization gathered momentum. Already by the late 1970s it was evident that the public utility framework was being dislodged, and that this came directly at the expense of a growing fraction of US workers. Indeed, for employers this attribute became (where it had not been evident already) liberalization's leading attraction.

Intensifying pressures hit at pay and benefits and working conditions, in short, at the security of the US working class. On one side, encouraged by the antilabor Reagan administration, the big carriers went on an offensive to reduce the costs imposed by their organized workforce. By no means were they uniformly successful; however, their campaigns placed the habitually cautious telecommunications unions further on the defensive—and kept them there. Still more important, on the other side, was large corporate users' heightened ability under the liberalized regime to place networks into service within their programs to relocate investment and jobs. These programs deterred an increasingly fearful industrial workforce from mounting militant challenges. Indeed, during the three decades that followed labor's most potent collective action—the strike—all but vanished. Even had CWA succeeded in the early 1970s in establishing "one big union" to represent workers in both postal-dom and electronic telecommunications, it is unlikely that this would have constituted a sufficient defense.[19]

Between the 1980s and the 2000s the telecommunications industry underwent a near-simultaneous reorganization around wireless systems and data networks; however, this sectoral transformation may be understood only by placing it within the more encompassing reconstruction of the political economy to which it contributed. This larger metamorphosis bore little resemblance to the rosy forecasts offered by pundits. First, as networks were woven into the quotidian, carriers paradoxically lost what had been their singular capacity to set the terms of system development. Second—and more important—the social relations that structure divided societies moved extensively onto networks: the new telecommunications, we might say, helped to modernize the contradictions of capitalism.

For let there be no mistake: the technological transformation of telecommunications betokened a further phase-change *within* capitalism. Both continuities and discontinuities were noteworthy. The form and location of production processes, the composition of capital investment, the commodities that generated the highest profits, the valued and devalued categories of labor, the profile of commercial consumption, the respective roles of capital, labor and the state, the balance of social class forces, and the character of the geopolitical economy: since the 1970s each of these constituted a realm of wrenching, sharp-edged change. Substantially propelling these shifts were engraved capitalist imperatives of profit-maximization, cost efficiency, and labor control. Not only were these long-established priorities carried forward, they were extended and enlarged—both socially and territorially. As it conformed to the same old compulsions, digital capitalism refashioned the world.

Neither domestically nor internationally was this a recipe for conflict-free development. This fact impressed itself with renewed force after the crash of 2008–2009. It seemed that a sliding US hegemony had been arrested during the 1990s and early 2000s. Thereafter, however, one US diminishment followed another. The multilateral institutions that had helped anchor the US's informal imperialism in and after World War II became newly contingent battle-zones. With a record of experience at China's former Ministry of Posts and Telecommunications and, thereafter, as a senior staff member in the International Telecommunication Union, Houlin Zhao was elected Secretary-General of this key organization in

2014—and reelected in 2018. In 2020, the ITU was one of four specialized UN agencies (of fifteen making up the UN system) headed by a Chinese national. US policymakers reacted with dismay and lobbied allies; yet the trend persisted and their steadfast allies diminished. China had long sought to wrest global internet governance from the multistakeholder model that held it principally within the power-orbit of just one state: the US. Despite its being caricatured as a despotic aim, this hope in fact was more widely shared. If only out of self-interest, numerous nations sought greater parity with the United States in setting the terms of internet development—just as they had with respect to Intelsat many decades earlier. Reinstating jurisdiction over the internet within a multilateral body such as the ITU, where each state possessed one vote, was by no means an anathema within the community of nations.[20] Thus, the US exulted when it succeeded in getting its preferred candidate elected as Secretary General of the ITU, as this book was going to press.[21]

Rival capitalist countries concurrently pursued regional and national political measures to gain maneuvering room within and, in some instances, against a US-centric digital capitalism. The European Union's General Data Protection Regulation came into force in 2018, to expressions of anger and dismay by US internet companies and their political allies (though its actual impact on the reach and profitability of Google and Facebook was initially hard to discern). The next year, cognizant that mighty German companies were falling behind in the face of Silicon Valley's continuing incursions, then-Chancellor Angela Merkel called for measures to engender Europe's "data sovereignty."[22]

Additional measures ensued. Fines levied early in the 2020s against the big US internet companies for violating antitrust strictures were substantial; and a sweeping Digital Markets Act, to block powerful US tech platforms from anticompetitive practices, was being finalized as this book neared completion. Yet, while its auto industry stumbled and its banks faltered, the EU's program for digital regeneration remained more reactive than assertive. Conspicuously absent was what one journalist called an "ecosystem of support from military and intelligence services" such as those that continued to power digital development in the US and China.[23]

The People's Republic of China established a direct internet connection to the US telecommunications company Sprint in 1994. Soon after this, China's Party-state was promoting nationwide internet adoption, while reserving portions of China's swelling domestic market for digital equipment and services for national capital. With passage of another decade, China's national market was overtaking those of most other big countries and select Chinese suppliers were heading overseas and claiming international significance. Its profitable industry of multinational internet equipment supply was led by Huawei, which boasted an extensive product line, low prices, 80,000 patents and a $15 billion R&D budget, and which seized the largest share of the world market for internet gear during the 2010s. Stepping into the gap left by the traditional US and West European vendors—once-preeminent but now faltering—and competing handily against higher-priced providers of internet equipment suppliers, Huawei also took a commanding lead over 5G wireless technology development.[24]

As Europe dithered and Japan deferred, China now posed a formidable rival to the United States in the digital heartland of capitalist growth. The Obama administration responded with moves to contain China's expansion, not only setting up roadblocks against Huawei within the US market but also announcing a more general policy "pivot" to East Asia—looking to surround China within a perimeter-ring of allies (Japan, South Korea, India). The Trump administration escalated this into a trade war. "National security" operated as a pretext for a rolling campaign against Chinese rivals. Strictures against Huawei, whose attempts to enter the US internet market had been repeatedly stymied by US state agencies, were escalated and formalized. There were two reasons to target this specific company.[25]

We have seen how AT&T and its erstwhile equipment manufacturing unit, Western Electric, worked closely with the US military from World War I onward; it was not unreasonable to assume that Huawei likewise would cooperate with China's military. As a major internet equipment supplier, Huawei might obstruct, or subvert, the continued monitoring of networks and signals intelligence by the spy agencies of the United States and its allies—though this was not said in public. Huawei thus became a target of intense US diplomacy, with high US officials warning other countries against contracting with Huawei. Trump also introduced wider sanctions, "to cut Chinese companies out of US supply chains, denting the telecoms group Huawei, China's supercomputer groups and eight of the country's leading artificial intelligence surveillance companies." His administration policed US corporations' exports to Chinese competitors and stepped up oversight of Chinese companies' market behavior in the US, via both the Executive Branch's Committee on Foreign Investment in the United States and the Commerce Department. Carried over and expanded by the Biden administration, US moves to obstruct and slow China's tech industry exacted a growing toll on China's tech industry—but they only strengthened the resolve of China's Party-state to build autonomy for Chinese capital in the digital political economy. A complex process of independent reconstruction was underway.[26]

This rivalry edged toward the erection of digital trade blocs. An interlocking US digital capitalism faced domestic challenges as well.

Historically, US telecommunications workers had often put themselves at the forefront of movements to restructure networks: as the actual builders and operators of telecommunications systems, they had their own ideas about how and for whom these systems might best function. However, led by bureaucratic unionists and facing the brunt of a liberalization that enabled capital and the state to administer repeated shocks, beginning in the late 1970s workers fell back. Had they been rendered devoid of substantial social and political agency? Were workers no longer a forward factor in the evolution of networking?

A leading historian of the US working class distilled a lifetime of scholarship this way: "No historical resolution of the conflict between wage labor and capital . . . has enjoyed a permanent lease on life." Across US industry as a whole, during 2018 and 2019 the number of workers involved in a major work stoppage marked a thirty-five-year high, and analysts observed that workers remained restive throughout the early 2020s. This resurgence encompassed the networking industry.[27]

In 2016, 39,000 Verizon workers struck for forty-five days, winning wage increases, a reversal of Verizon's demands for concessions on job security and flexibility, as well as 1300 additional union jobs and a first contract at seven Verizon Wireless stores. Two years later, Verizon prudently extended this contract to 2023, to avert a prospective new confrontation with CWA and the Electrical Workers (IBEW). After the pandemic struck, meanwhile, CWA members working at General Electric's Lynn, Massachusetts plant called on their employer to commit to a wider public purpose, by reorganizing its facilities there to build much-needed ventilators. In 2019, AT&T workers walked out for four days across the Southeast, putting paid to the company's attempt to raise their health care costs and winning wage increases and pension enhancements. It was the largest private sector strike in the South for a decade, involving 20,000 workers. For their part, long-unionized postal workers explicitly revived their attempt to represent the general public. Led by activist president Mark Dimondstein, the American Postal Workers Union in particular emphasized "the unity between the demands of postal workers for a good contract and the demands of the American people for an expanded, vibrant, public Postal Service."[28]

The internet segment of the industry was led by billionaires who were tooth-and-nails hostile to unions, certainly as much so as their forebears at Western Union and AT&T had been early in the twentieth century. Just the same, stirrings of collective self-organization were again apparent among their employees. Between 2017 and 2019, cleaners, couriers, cafeteria workers, contractors, and security guards stood up to several tech-company employers. Evident was rising anger at low-paid jobs; onerous, sometimes shocking, working conditions; and gaping economic inequality. In 2020, unorganized Amazon workers in Sacramento and Chicago banded together to compel the e-commerce leviathan to pay them when a warehouse shut down during a heat wave; they also gained improved health and safety provisions and a reinstatement of fired workers. Warehouse employees again protested unsafe working conditions when Amazon did not provide adequate protective equipment following the onset of the coronavirus. In 2022, Amazon warehouse workers in Staten Island, New York, gained a historic labor victory when they mounted a successful unionization campaign—the first in the company's history. With 65,000 retail employees, meanwhile, Apple found itself contending with organizing drives at four US locations in 2022. The Alphabet Workers Union, formally aligned with the Communications Workers of America and still representing a tiny sliver of Alphabet's 260,000 workers, was established in 2021. Silicon Valley sexism, militarism, racism, and environmental despoliation became related protest-points among significant numbers of tech workers.[29]

A season of discontent had arrived, though how it might develop remained unknown. But the contest to define and determine the uses of telecommunications continued to carry forward.

*

Why do the people who I have placed at the center of this book matter?—workers and consumers and political radicals—all lumped in the margins in most accounts of telecommunications? It is not only that they merit mention as actors, alongside the engineers and system-builders, the managers and politicians who are usually showcased. It is that their actions were consequential, indeed, sometimes vital.

Lakota, Cheyenne and other Native American warriors tore down telegraph lines in the 1860s, slowing US occupation of their territories and making plain their resistance to conquest. At the turn of the twentieth century, a broad coalition of antimonopolists agitated for "US Tels and Tels," setting out a program to make the Post Office a hub for societal improvement and imparting a reform impulse that would carry forward for decades. In Chicago and Los Angeles, workers and municipal reformers of the 1910s campaigned for "penny" phone service, powering norms of inclusive local provision. New England's women telephone operators staged a historic strike for collective bargaining rights and wage increases against the Post Office in 1919—and, in victory, helped precipitate denationalization of the wires and the discrediting of postalization as an alternative to corporate control. Maverick government officials and trade unionists succeeded in imposing substantial public utility responsibilities on telecommunications carriers between the 1920s and the 1940s, including an obligation to provide universal service. Radical industrial unionists staved off a corporate telegraph merger for the better part of a decade, between the 1930s and the middle of World War II, arguing that a "mass-layoff" would be both an inevitable and unacceptable consequence of such a government-sanctioned combination. Through a grinding campaign in the 1940s, independent unionists and CIO members beat the odds and organized AT&T—the country's largest private employer and its most intractable antiunion company. During the 1960s and 1970s, social movement activists and individual Black, Latina/o and women telephone workers allied to rejuvenate the public utility conception around equal rights at work. They succeeded in compelling not just AT&T but corporate America at large to institute affirmative action programs. Through varied, often intense struggles, these people placed limits on what corporate carriers, business users, and state authorities preferred to do—and actually did do. Their interventions called forth responses, from employers, state authorities and, sometimes decisively, from other groups of workers—and the course of events changed. Continually, they imagined and tried to actualize a different telecommunications for a different world. *Crossed Wires* is *their* story.

Notes

Introduction

1. U.S. Department of Labor, Bureau of Labor Statistics, *Analysis of Work Stoppages, 1968, Bulletin 1646* (Washington, DC: Government Printing Office, 1970), 1, 5, 10–11; "Daley Denies City Will Lose Convention Because of Strike," *Chicago Tribune*, July 4, 1968, 2; "Phone Strikers Make Peace Bid," *New York Times*, July 15, 1968, 19.
2. James Strong, "Chicago Retains Dem Convention thru Union Pact," *Chicago Tribune*, July 24, 1968, 1, 2; James Strong, "Convention Phone Work Begins Today," *Chicago Tribune*, July 25, 1968, 1, 2.
3. "Accuse Cops in Beating of Newsmen," *Chicago Tribune*, August 27, 1968, 5; David Farber, *Chicago '68* (Chicago: University of Chicago Press, 1994), 165–207.
4. David Farber, *Chicago '68*, 158; R. Sam Garrett, "Lights, Camera, Chaos? The Evolution of Convention 'Crises,'" in Costas Panagopoulos, ed., *Rewiring Politics: Presidential Nominating Conventions in the Media Age* (Baton Rouge: Louisiana State University Press, 2007), 118–119.
5. Robert Davis, "A 36-Month Contract Is OK'd by Union," *Chicago Tribune*, September 22, 1968, 1, 4.
6. Paul Kennedy, *Victory at Sea: Naval Power and the Transformation of the Global Order in World War II* (New Haven, CT: Yale University Press, 2022), 73–76.

Chapter 1

1. Richard R. John, *Spreading the News: The American Postal System from Franklin to Morse* (Cambridge, MA: Harvard University Press, 1995), 3. In 1865, more than half of the federal government's 53,000 civil servants labored in postaldom. Ari Hoogenboom, *Outlawing the Spoils: A History of the Civil Service Reform Movement 1865-1883* (Urbana, IL: University of Illinois Press, 1961), 1; Richard White, *The Republic for Which It Stands: The United States during Reconstruction and the Gilded Age, 1865-1896* (New York: Oxford University Press, 2017), 356; U.S. Census, "Government Employment—Federal Government Employment 1816 to 1945," Series P62–68, *Historical Statistics of the United States 1789 to 1945* (Washington, DC: U.S. Department of Commerce, 1949), 294.
2. Steven Hahn, *A Nation without Borders: The United States and Its World in an Age of Civil Wars, 1830-1910* (New York: Viking, 2016), 122 ("ocean-bound"); Peter S. Onuf, "Imperialism and Nationalism in the Early American Republic," in Ian Tyrrell

and Jay Sexton, *Empire's Twin: U.S. Anti-Imperialism from the Founding Era to the Age of Terrorism* (Ithaca, NY: Cornell University Press, 2015), 25 ("unleashing").
3. Joshua D. Wolff, *Western Union and the Creation of the American Corporate Order, 1845-1893*. Cambridge: Cambridge University Press, 2013.
4. Wayne E. Fuller, *The American Mail: Enlarger of the Common Life* (Chicago: University of Chicago Press, 1972), 190 ("necessity"); Daniel Immerwahr, *How to Hide an Empire: A History of the Greater United States* (New York: Farrar, Straus and Giroux, 2019), 27 ("polities").
5. Gordon S. Wood, *Empire of Liberty: A History of the Early Republic, 1789-1815* (New York: Oxford University Press, 2009), 358, 2 ("plans"); Hahn, *A Nation without Borders*, 117 ("power"); Immerwahr, *How to Hide an Empire*, 29-32; Onuf, "Imperialism and Nationalism," 35 ("empire"); Wood, *Empire of Liberty*, 357-399, esp. 376, 377 ("scientific"), 2, 398; Hahn, *A Nation without Borders*, 88 ("opening"); Wood, *Empire of Liberty*, 361; Immerwahr, *How to Hide an Empire*, 35 ("violently").
6. John, *Spreading the News*, 45; Alan R. Pred, *Urban Growth and the Circulation of Information: The United States System of Cities 1790-1840* (Cambridge, MA: Harvard University Press, 1973); Alan R. Pred, *Urban Growth and City Systems in the United States, 1840-1860* (Cambridge, MA: Harvard University Press, 1980); John, *Spreading the News*, 207. I take the term "market intensification" from Hahn, *A Nation without Borders*, 83-89; Pred, *Urban Growth and the Circulation of Information*, 81; John, *Spreading the News*, 54; Clyde Kelly, *United States Postal Policy* (New York: D. Appleton and Company, 1931), 143. Mail robbery declined after the Railway Mail Service was instituted; Kelly, *United States Postal Policy*, 70-71.
7. George L. Priest, "The History of the Postal Monopoly in the United States," *Journal of Law & Economics* 18, no. 1 (April 1975): 54; for the burgeoning importance of commercial contracting, Cameron Blevins, *Paper Trails: The U.S. Post and the Making of the American West* (New York: Oxford University Press, 2021); Kelly B. Olds, "The Challenge to the U.S. Postal Monopoly, 1839-1851," *Cato Journal* 15, no. 1 (Spring/Summer 1995): 8.
8. Priest, "Postal Monopoly," 53; John, *Spreading the News*, 31, 46-53; Blevins, *Paper Trails*, 33.
9. John, *Spreading the News*, 4, 5, 52; Daniel P. Carpenter, *The Forging of Bureaucratic Autonomy: Reputations, Networks, and Policy Innovation in Executive Agencies, 1862-1928* (Princeton, NJ: Princeton University Press, 2001), 68; U.S. Bureau of the Census, *Historical Statistics of the United States, Colonial Times to 1970*, bicentennial ed., Part 2 (Washington, DC, 1975), 805, 1114-1115, 1103.
10. In England during the 1830s and 1840s, workers often relied on free franking of newspapers to transmit private—often coded—messages. Derek Gregory, "The Friction of Distance? Information Circulation and the Mails in Early Nineteenth-Century England," *Journal of Historical Geography* 13, no. 2 (1987): 130-154; Pred, *Urban Growth and the Circulation of Information*, 81; Pred, *Urban Growth and City Systems*, 144, 148; Olds, "The Challenge to the U.S. Postal Monopoly," 2; Pred, *Urban Growth and the Circulation of Information*, 81-82; *History of the Railway Mail: A Chapter in the History of Postal Affairs in the United States* (Washington,

DC: Government Printing Office, 1885), 49; *Report of the Postmaster General*, December 2, 1843, 28th Cong., 1st Sess., Senate Documents 1843–1844, President's Message to Congress with Supporting Documents, 597; U.S. Congress, Senate, 28th Cong. 1st Sess., Senate Documents 137, Report to Accompany Bill S. 51, February 22, 1844: 2–4.

11. John, *Spreading the News*: 37, 39; *History of the Railway Mail*, 49; *Report of the Postmaster General*, 28th Cong., 1st Sess., Senate Documents 1843–1844 (Washington, DC, December 2, 1843); *President's Message to Congress with Supporting Documents*, 593–633 at 597; 28th Cong. 1st Sess., Senate Documents 137, *Report to Accompany Bill S. 51*, February 22, 1844: 2–4; John, *Spreading the News*: 57; Robert W. McChesney and John Nichols, *The Death and Life of American Journalism* (New York: Nation Books, 2010), 121–125.

12. Richard B. Kielbowicz, "News Gathering by Mail in the Age of the Telegraph: Adapting to a New Technology," *Technology and Culture* 28, no. 1 (January 1987): 30, 38; John, *Spreading the News*, 31–42, 49. Books—less easily adapted to the search for competitive advantage among politicians and businesspersons—were not so well treated. Richard B. Kielbowicz, "Mere Merchandise or Vessels of Culture?: Books in the Mail, 1792–1942," *Papers of the Bibliographical Society of America* 82, no. 2 (June 1988): 169–200; Dan Schiller, *Objectivity and the News: The Public and the Rise of Commercial Journalism* (Philadelphia: University of Pennsylvania Press, 1981); Meredith L. McGill, *American Literature and the Culture of Reprinting, 1834–1853* (Philadelphia: University of Pennsylvania Press, 2002)("culture"); John, *Spreading the News*, 37 ("every"); *Report of the Postmaster General*, December 1, 1845, 857 ("one-nineth"); Richard B. Kielbowicz, *News in the Mail: The Press, Post Office, and Public Information, 1700–1860s* (New York: Greenwood Press, 1989); McChesney and Nichols, *The Death and Life of American Journalism*; Paul Starr, *The Creation of the Media: Political Origins of Modern Communications* (New York: Basic Books, 2004); Culver H. Smith, *Press, Politics, and Patronage* (Athens: University of Georgia Press, 1977).

13. *Report of the Postmaster*, December 2, 1843, 597–599; Fuller, *The American Mail*, 173; John, *Spreading the News*, 83–84; Richard R. John, Jr., "Private Mail Delivery in the United States during the Nineteenth Century: A Sketch," *Business and Economic History* 15, 2nd series (1986): 135–147. On the special case of newspapers, see Richard B. Kielbowicz, "Speeding the News by Postal Express, 1825–1861: The Public Policy of Privileges for the Press," *The Social Science Journal* 22, no. 1 (January 1985: 49–64); Pred, *Urban Growth and City Systems*, 149.

14. Alvin F. Harlow, *Old Waybills: The Romance of the Express Companies* (New York: D. Appleton-Century, 1934), 73; John, *Spreading the News*, 153, 48 ("heyday").

15. Eli Bowen, *The United States Post-Office Guide* (New York: D. Appleton, 1851), 27 ("greatest"); *Report to Accompany Bill. S. 51*, 28th Cong., 1st Sess., Senate Documents #137, February 22, 1844, 5 ("not"). Olds asserts that the private carriers may have taken between one- and two-fifths of the market measured by revenue. Olds, "Challenges to the U.S. Postal Monopoly," 17.

16. Harlow reports that the expresses handled few newspapers "save those addressed to editors, and these they carried free" in hopes of securing favorable publicity. Harlow,

Old Waybills, 39; *Report of the Postmaster General*, December 2, 1843, 598 ("between"); *Report of the Postmaster General*, November 25, 1844, 672 ("will"); *History of the Railway Mail*, 42; Harlow, *Old Waybills*, 85–86; John, *Spreading the News*, 49.

17. Kelly, *United States Postal Policy*, 44–45, 49 ("withdrawing").
18. Kelly B. Olds, "The Challenge to the U.S. Postal Monopoly, 1839–1851," *Cato Journal* 15, no. 1 (Spring/Summer 1995): 2; John, *Spreading the News*, 88–100; Fuller, *American Mail*: 159–162.
19. Sean Wilentz, *Chants Democratic: New York City and the Rise of the American Working Class, 1788–1850* (New York: Oxford University Press, 1984); Schiller, *Objectivity and the News*, 12–46; Kielbowicz, "Speeding the News," 51 ("stop"), 53 ("whole"); John, *Spreading the News*, 85–86.
20. Kielbowicz, "Speeding the News," 53 ("advantage"); Richard B. Kielbowicz, "Newsgathering by Printers' Exchanges before the Telegraph," *Journalism History* 9, no. 2 (Summer 1982): 42–48; Kielbowicz, "Speeding the News," 54.
21. Richard R. John, "Recasting the Information Infrastructure for the Industrial Age," in Alfred D. Chandler, Jr., and James W. Cortada, ed., *A Nation Transformed by Information* (New York: Oxford University Press, 2000), 69–70. Even after major postal reforms, the issue continued to simmer; a formal resolution to repeal "all laws that restrain individuals or corporations from carrying mails" was tabled—and rejected—in the House Committee on the Post Office in 1859. *Post Office Department—Proposed Abolishment Of*, 35th Cong., 2d Sess., Report No. 135, January 21, 1859; Kelly, *United States Postal Policy*, 47, 64–65.
22. John, "Private Mail," 143 (Lieber); John, *Spreading the News*, 252–254, 135; Harlow, *Old Waybills*: 41; *Report of the Postmaster General*, December 2, 1843, 597 ("odious").
23. Richard R. John, "Private Enterprise, Public Good? Communications Deregulation as a National Political Issue, 1839–1851," in Jeffrey L. Pasley, Andrew W. Robertson, and David Waldstreicher, ed., *Beyond the Founders: New Approaches to the Political History of the Early American Republic* (Chapel Hill, NC: University of North Carolina Press, 2004), 338.
24. *U.S. Statutes at Large*, 28th Cong., 2d Sess., Ch. 43, Statute II, March 3, 1845, 732–740; Blevins, *Paper Trails*, 77 ("universal"). The postmaster also erroneously forecast that "a reduction of postage would be followed by an increase of mail matter, producing an amount sufficient to sustain the department." *Report of the Postmaster General*, November 25, 1844, 670; Olds, "Challenge to the U.S. Postal Monopoly," 16; Kelly, *United States Postal Policy*, 62–63; John, "History of Universal Service and the Postal Monopoly," 76–78 ("service first"); John, "History of Universal Service and the Postal Monopoly," 77 ("presumption").
25. Thomas Ewing, *Report into the Conditions and Proceedings of the Post Office Department*, 23rd Cong., 2nd Sess., 1835, S. Rpt 86 (Serial 268), 113–114.
26. Arthur P. Dudden, "Anti-monopolism, 1865–1890: The Historical Background and Intellectual Origins of the Antitrust Movement in the United States" (Ph.D. diss., University of Michigan, 1950); Richard R. John, *Network Nation: Inventing American Telecommunications* (Cambridge, MA: Belknap Press of Harvard University Press, 2010), 65–113.

27. Bowen, *United States Post-office Guide*, 27 ("pioneer"); *Report of the Postmaster General*, November 1844, 673 ("reduction"), 670 ("respectable"); Peter A. Shulman, *Coal and Empire: The Birth of Energy Security in Industrial America* (Baltimore: Johns Hopkins University Press, 2015), 16–24, 14 ("global").
28. *Report of the Postmaster General*, December 1, 1845, 857 ("reduction"); Charles M. Ellis, "The Postal System Exclusive," *Massachusetts Quarterly Review* 10 (March 1850): 271–274, quote in John, "Private Enterprise, Public Good?," 339 ("footing"); *Report of the Postmaster General*, December 6, 1847, 1316 ("Postage"); *Annual Report of the Postmaster General*, December 2, 1848, 1246 ("well digested").
29. William H. Goetzmann, *Exploration and Empire: The Explorer and the Scientist in the Winning of the American West* (New York: W. W. Norton, 1978), 231 ("explicit"); Thomas R. Hietala, *Manifest Design: Anxious Aggrandizement in Late Jacksonian America* (Ithaca: Cornell University Press, 1985); David Vine, *The United States of War: A Global History of America's Endless Conflicts, from Columbus to the Islamic State* (Berkeley: University of California Press, 2020), 43–91. The leading study of how expulsion became systematic federal policy during the 1830s is Claudio Saunt, *Unworthy Republic: The Dispossession of Native Americans and the Road to Indian Territory* (New York: W. W. Norton, 2020). For the longer history, see Roxanne Dunbar-Ortiz, *An Indigenous People's History of the United States* (Boston: Beacon Press: 2014); Vine, *United States of War*, 78.
30. Kelly, *United States Postal Policy*, 54–55 ("vital"). See, for comparison, Robert M. Pike, "National Interest and Imperial Yearnings: Empire Communications and Canada's Role in Establishing the Imperial Penny Post," *Journal of Imperial and Commonwealth History* 26, no. 1 (January 1998): 26. A definitive history of the post office in the West after the Civil War is unequivocal: "the US Post helped accelerate the seizure of Native territory and its transformation into a colonized landscape of settlements, mining claims, and post offices." Blevins, *Paper Trails*, 35; Hahn, *A Nation without Borders*, 155 ("cherish").
31. Le Roy R. Hafen, *The Overland Mail 1849–1869: Promoter of Settlement Precursor of Railroads*, reprint ed. (1926; repr., New York: AMS Press, 1969), 37 ("afforded"); Fuller, *American Mail*, 83; *Message from the President of the United States*, 29th Cong., 1st Sess, Senate Executive Documents, vol. 470, December 2, 3, 1845, 28 ("extension"); Robert R. Russel, *Improvement of Communication with the Pacific Coast as an Issue in American Politics, 1783–1864* (Cedar Rapids, IA: Torch Press, 1948), 18, 57–59, 200–201, 222–226, 237–238, 279–282, 291–293.
32. Kelly, *United States Postal Policy*, 129–130; Heather Cox Richardson, *The Greatest Nation of the Earth: Republican Economic Policies during the Civil War* (Cambridge, MA: Harvard University Press, 1997), 172–173; Matthew Karp, *This Vast Southern Empire: Slaveholders at the Helm of American Foreign Policy* (Cambridge, MA: Harvard University Press, 2016); Kevin Waite, *West of Slavery: The Southern Dream of a Transcontinental Empire* (Chapel Hill, NC: University of North Carolina Press, 2021); Alice L. Baumgartner, *South to Freedom: Runaway Slaves to Mexico and the Road to the Civil War* (New York: Basic Books, 2020). Since the Spanish conquest, much of the West had depended on unfree Indian labor: Andres Resendez, *The Other

Slavery: The Uncovered Story of Indian Enslavement in America (Boston: Houghton Mifflin Harcourt, 2016) 218–314.

33. Waite, *West of Slavery*, 83 ("southern-oriented"), 84 ("manned"), 81 ("western").
34. Fuller, *American Mail*, 231 ("drawing"). Two decades later, the post office contracted for a trans-Pacific mail service between San Francisco and ports in China and Japan in what a historian calls an "imperial commercial project." Blevins, *Paper Trails*, 90; Hafen, *Overland Mail*, 86 ("believe"); John, *Spreading the News*, 133 ("military"); Robert G. Angevine, *The Railroad and the State: War, Politics, and Technology in Nineteenth-century America* (Stanford, CA: Stanford University Press, 2004), 5–6; John, *Spreading the News*, 134; Hafen, *Overland Mail*, 54; see also 38–39, 136; *Annual Report of the Postmaster General*, December 6, 1847, 1324; *Annual Report of the Postmaster General*, December 2, 1848, 1241. On the difficulties of integrating coal into an expanding US network of steam-powered postal communications, Shulman, *Coal and Empire*, 14–38; Daniel Headrick, *The Tools of Empire: Technology and European Imperialism in the Nineteenth Century* (New York: Oxford University Press, 1981); Shulman, *Coal and Empire*: 248, n90 ("private").
35. Hafen, *Overland Mail*, 40, 134–135; Shulman, *Coal and Empire*, 27, 33–38; John, *Spreading the News*, 90; *Report of the Postmaster General*, 32 Cong. 1st Sess., Senate Documents 1851–1852, vol. 612, document 417, 417, 421. In 1835, the number of people employed in stagecoach mail transport was nearly twice that of postmasters. Carpenter, *Forging of Bureaucratic Autonomy*, 69, 72, 73, 66; Blevins, *Paper Trails*, 76–93.
36. Hafen, *Overland Mail*, 133; Blevins, *Paper Trails*, 97; Paul H. Bergeron, *The Presidency of James K. Polk* (Lawrence, KS: University Press of Kansas, 1987), 149; Carpenter, *Forging of Bureaucratic Autonomy*, 68 ("six-decade"); Dorothy Ganfield Fowler, *The Cabinet Politician: The Postmasters General 1829–1909* (New York: Columbia University Press, 1943); White, *The Republic for which It Stands*, 356 ("patronage army"); Blevins, *Paper Trails*, 98 ("campaign office"); John, "Private Mail," 144 ("marginal").
37. Olds, "Challenge to the U.S. Postal Monopoly," 14; *Report of the Postmaster General*, November 30, 1839, 617 ("radical").
38. *Report of the Postmaster General*, December 2, 1848, 1247 ("well digested"); 1247–1248 ("tax").
39. Clement Eaton, *Freedom of Thought in the Old South* (Durham, NC: Duke University Press, 1940), 316 (*"cordon sanitaire"*); Richard John, *Spreading the News*, 264, adopts this term; Elizabeth Hewitt, *Correspondence and American Literature, 1770–1865* (Cambridge: Cambridge University Press, 2004),: 115; Hewitt, *Correspondence and American Literature*, 1770–1865, 115; Hewitt, *Correspondence and American Literature*, 116.
40. George Fitzhugh, "Uniform Postage, Railroads, Telegraphs, Fashions, Etc.," *Debows Review* 5, no. 26: 658–659, 662. On the other hand, some Southerners objected to the disparity between the North's extensive postal network and the South's undeveloped system. Conrad Kalmbacher, *Secession and the U.S. Mail: The Postal Service, The South, and Sectional Controversy* (Bloomington, IN: AuthorHouse, 2013), 18.

41. Hahn, *A Nation without Borders*, 2, 268–318, Richard Franklin Bentsel, *Yankee Leviathan: The Origins of Central State Authority, 1859–1877* (New York: Cambridge University Press, 1990), 3–4; Kelly, *United States Postal Policy*, 175.
42. James Gamett and Stanley W. Paher, *Nevada Post Offices: An Illustrated History* (Las Vegas: Nevada Publications, 1983), 11, 17; John, "Private Mail," 139; Lucius Beebe and Charles Clegg, *U.S. West: The Saga of Wells Fargo* (New York: E. P. Dutton, 1949), 9–27; Edward Hungerford, *Wells Fargo: Advancing the American Frontier* (New York: Random House, 1949), 3–20; Alden Hatch, *American Express: A Century of Service* (Garden City: Doubleday, 1950); W. Turrentine Jackson, *Wells Fargo in Colorado Territory*, Monograph Series Number 1 (Denver: Colorado Historical Society, 1982); Peter Z. Grossman, *American Express* (New York: Crown, 1987); David J. Lewis, *Postal Express*, 62d Cong., 2d Sess., document No. 379, March 5, 1912 (Washington, DC: Government Printing Office, 1912), 66.
43. Daniel J. Czitrom, *Media and the American Mind: From Morse to McLuhan* (Chapel Hill, NC: University of North Carolina Press, 1983); Recent scholarship on the telegraph in the United States includes David Hochfelder, *The Telegraph in America, 1832–1920* (Baltimore: Johns Hopkins University Press, 2012); Richard R. John, *Network Nation: Inventing American Telecommunications* (Cambridge, MA: Belknap Press of Harvard University Press, 2010); Joshua D. Wolff, *Western Union and the Creation of the American Corporate Order, 1845–1893* (New York: Cambridge, 2013); and James Schwoch, *Wired into Nature: The Telegraph and the North American Frontier* (Urbana, IL: University of Illinois Press, 2018).
44. Robert Luther Thompson, *Wiring a Continent: The History of the Telegraph Industry in the United States 1832–1866* (Princeton, NJ: Princeton University Press, 1947), 30; Thompson, *Wiring a Continent*, 31; Richard A. Schwarzlose, *The Nation's Newsbrokers, Vol. 1: The Formative Years, from Pretelegraph to 1865* (Evanston, IL: Northwestern University Press, 1989), 41; Hochfelder, *Telegraph in America*, 83; Wolff, *Western Union*, 282; Schiller, *Objectivity and the News*, 45 ("hands"); *Report of the Postmaster General*, 29th Cong. 1st Sess., Senate Executive Documents 1845–1846, vol. 470, December 1, 1845, 861; John, *Spreading the News*, 88.
45. A. Hunter Dupree, *Science in the Federal Government: A History of Policies and Activities* (Baltimore: Johns Hopkins University Press, 1986 (1957), 48; *History of the Railway Mails*, 57; John, *Spreading the News*, 88.
46. Richard White, *Railroaded: The Transcontinentals and the Making of Modern America* (New York: W. W. Norton, 2011); Hahn, *A Nation without Borders*, 155 ("Indian"); Schwoch, *Wired into Nature*, 41, 44; Schwoch, *Wired into Nature*, 118–125; Lloyd Gardner, "Foreword," in William Appleman Williams, *The Tragedy of American Diplomacy*, 50th anniversary ed. (New York: W. W. Norton, 2009), xvi.
47. Jeffrey Ostler, "Native Americans against Empire and Colonial Rule," in Tyrrell and Sexton, ed., *Empire's Twin*, 52; Schwoch, *Wired into Nature*, 71; Schwoch, *Wired into Nature*, 66–74. The war and the Treaty of Fort Laramie in which it culminated are well illuminated in Pekka Hamalainen, *Lakota America: A New History of Indigenous Power* (New Haven, CT: Yale University Press, 2019), 248–293.

48. "An 1849 convention of railroad and telegraph promoters embraced the indefatigable telegraph promoter and builder Henry O'Rielly as their 'standard bearer.'" Cohen, *Western Union*, 51; Alfred M. Lee, *The Daily Newspaper in America: The Evolution of a Social Instrument* (New York: The Macmillan Company, 1937), 490; Cohen, *Western Union*, 51; "Methodless enthusiasm" was the description chosen by the industry's leading early historian. Thompson, *Wiring a Continent*, 95; Edwin Gabler, *The American Telegrapher: A Social History* (New Brunswick, NJ: Rutgers University Press, 1988), 38. The process is well explicated by Thompson, *Wiring a Continent*; Cohen, *Western Union*; White, *Railroaded*.

49. John Nathan Anderson, "Money or Nothing: Confederate Postal System Collapse during the Civil War," *American Journalism* 30, no. 1 (2013): 65 ("conjunction"); Cohen, *Western Union*, 82; John, *Network Nation*, 101; By 1860, following a decade of extraordinary growth in the South, the two adversaries possessed roughly equal railroad track mileage: 10,013 miles in the Northeast versus 9,535 miles in the South. The Confederacy's management of railroads, however, was qualitatively less effective than that of the Union. Angevine, *Railroad and the State*, 113, 130–164; Benjamin Sidney Michael Schwantes, "Fallible Guardian: The Social Construction of Railroad Telegraphy in 19th-century America" (Ph.D. diss., University of Delaware, 2008), 12, 111–152.

50. Cohen, *Western Union*, 66; Cohen, *Western Union*, 66, 68; Cohen, *Western Union*, 64; also John, *Network Nation*, 101–102.

51. Hochfelder, *Telegraph in America*, 11.

52. A share of Western Union valued at $100 in 1860 was worth nearly $1,500 in May of 1864. Cohen, *Western Union*, 73; John, *Network Nation*, 98–99; Hochfelder, *Telegraph in America*, 24–28; Cohen, *Western Union*, 61–83; Wolff, *Western Union*, 82–83.

53. In an account strongly tinged by economism, Gerald R. Brock discusses this point in *The Telecommunications Industry: The Dynamics of Market Structure* (Cambridge, MA: Harvard University Press, 1981), 73–87.

54. Eric Foner, *Reconstruction America's Unfinished Revolution 1863–1877* (New York: Harper & Row, 1988), 465–488; John, *Network Nation*, 116–124.

55. Hahn, *Nation without Borders*, 4; This is a fundamental argument running through Hahn, *A Nation without Borders*. Also see Megan Black, *The Global Interior: Mineral Frontiers and American Power* (Cambridge, MA: Harvard University Press, 2018); and Foner, *Reconstruction*, 460–463.

56. Foner, *Reconstruction*, 512; Hahn, *Nation without Borders*, 324; Another recent historian states that telegraph reform "showed remarkable continuity over its fifty-year life" between the end of the Civil War and the end of World War I. Hochfelder, *The Telegraph in America*, 71.

57. Cohen, *Western Union*, 228, 231; for the speculative impulse in railroads themselves, White, *Railroaded* is unmatched; Cohen, *Western Union*, 264, Hochfelder, *Telegraph in America*, 101–137; John, *Network Nation*, 156–199; Montgomery Cohen, *Western Union*, 151–231; White, *Republic for which It Stand*s, 246.

58. Paul Israel, *From Machine Shop to Industrial Laboratory: Telegraphy and the Changing Context of American Invention, 1830-1920* (Baltimore: Johns Hopkins University Press, 1992), 121-151; Wolff, *Western Union*, 214-217.
59. Gabler, *American Telegrapher*, 41, 44; Brock, *Telecommunications Industry*, 85.
60. Frank Parsons, *The Telegraph Monopoly* (Philadelphia: C. F. Taylor, 1899); Cohen, *Western Union*, 119-120; Schwantes, *Fallible Guardian*, 184.
61. Daniel R. Headrick, *The Invisible Weapon: Telecommunications and International Politics, 1851-1945* (New York: Oxford University Press, 1991), 32, 46, 60, 101-102; Robert M. Pike and Dwayne Winseck, "Monopoly's First Moment in Global Electronic Communication: From Private Monopoly to Global Media Reform, Circa 1860-1920," *Journal of the Canadian Historical Association* 10, no. 1 (1999): 152-153.
62. Pike and Winseck, "Monopoly's First Moment," 154; George A. Schreiner, *Cables and Wireless and Their Role in the Foreign Relations of the United States* (Boston: Stratford Company, 1924), 87; Schreiner, *Cables and Wireless*, 76-107.
63. Menahem Blondheim, *News over the Wires: The Telegraph and the Flow of Public Information in America, 1844-1897* (Cambridge, MA: Harvard University Press, 1994), 48-52.
64. Hochfelder, *Telegraph in America*, 103-116; Blondheim, *News over the Wires*, 194; Blondheim, *News over the Wires*, 161.
65. James Smart, "Information Control, Thought Control: Whitelaw Reid and the Nation's News Services," *Public Historian* 3, no. 2 (1981): 37-38; Blondheim, *News over the Wires*, 162; Blondheim, *News over the Wires*, 177, 180-187; Blondheim, *News over the Wires*, 181; Cohen, *Western Union*, 266; Blondheim, *News over the Wires*, 177-182.
66. White, *The Republic for which It Stands*, 582-583, Hochfelder, *Telegraph in America*, 102, Alexander James Field, "The Magnetic Telegraph, Price and Quantity Data and the New Management of Capital," *Journal of Economic History* 52, no. 2 (June 1992): 401-413.
67. Richard B. Du Boff, "Business Demand and the Development of the Telegraph in the United States, 1844-1860," *Business History Review* 54, no. 4 (Winter 1980): 459-479; Kenneth D. Garbade and Robert A. Kavesh, "Technology, Communication and the Performance of Financial Markets: 1840-1975," *Journal of Finance* 33, no. 3 (June 1978): 819-832; Ann Moyal, "The History of Telecommunication in Australia: Aspects of the Technological Experience, 1854-1930," in Nathan Reingold and Marc Rothenberg, ed., *Scientific Colonialism: A Cross-cultural Comparison* (Washington, DC: Smithsonian Institution Press, 1987), 35-54, 40; Du Boff, "Business Demand and the Development of the Telegraph in the United States," 459-479, 467; Headrick, *Invisible Weapon*, 109; for European comparisons, Eric Hobsbawm, *The Age of Capital* (New York: Charles Scribner's Sons, 1975), 48-68; Gene Fowler, *A Solo in Tom-toms* (New York: The Viking Press, 1946), 83. Years after Fowler's book was published, telegrams continued to bear sorrowful tidings. Emily Neville, *It's Like This, Cat* (New York: Harper & Row, 1963), 147-148. Military reliance on the telegraph to notify families of soldiers' deaths contributed to the longevity of this perception. Hochfelder, *Telegraph in America*, 77.

68. David, *Beyond Equality: Labor and the Radical Republicans, 1862–1872* (New York: Vintage, 1967), 29–30; Massachusetts Bureau of Statistics of Labor, *Fourth Annual Report* (Boston: 1873), 440, in Amy Dru Stanley, *From Bondage to Contract: Wage Labor, Marriage, and the Market in the Age of Slave Emancipation* (New York: Cambridge University Press, 1998), 62; Sven Beckert, *The Monied Metropolis: New York City and the Consolidation of the American Bourgeoisie, 1850–1896* (New York: Cambridge University Press, 2001); White, *The Republic for which It Stands*, 13. As railroad and telegraph enabled firms in a growing number of product markets to compete across greater distances, "wage cuts in one place put pressure on wages in another." White, *The Republic for which It Stands*, 243. Wages, however, did not trace the same leveling pattern as agricultural commodities because, as Hahn emphasizes, local labor markets were shaped by numerous factors, particularly scarcities of skilled workers and the greater or lesser prevalence of workers' shopfloor control. Hahn, *Nation without Borders*, 341.
69. Gary Fields, *Territories of Profit: Communications, Capitalist Development, and the Innovative Enterprises of G.F. Swift and Dell Computer* (Stanford, CA: Stanford Business Books, 2004); JoAnne Yates, *Control through Communication: The Rise of System in American Management* (Baltimore: Johns Hopkins, 1989); Gabler, *American Telegrapher*, 43; Thomas C. Jepsen, *My Sisters Telegraphic: Women in the Telegraph Office, 1846–1950* (Athens: Ohio University Press), 2000.
70. Arthur P. Dudden, "Antimonopolism"; Hahn, *Nation without Borders*, 402–412; White, *The Republic for which It Stands*, 898 ("significant"); Macdougall, *The People's Network*, 10; Richard R. John, "Robber Barons Redux: Antimonopoly Reconsidered," *Enterprise and Society* 6; White, *The Republic for which It Stands*, 849–854; White, *The Republic for which It Stands*, 275; Alexander Saxton, *The Indispensable Enemy: Labor and the Anti-Chinese Movement in California* (Berkeley, CA: University of California Press, 1995); Liping Zhu, *The Road to Chinese Exclusion: The Denver Riot, 1880 Election, and the Rise of the West* (Lawrence, KS: University Press of Kansas, 2013).
71. Charles Craypo, "The Impact of Changing Corporate Structure and Technology on Telegraph Labor, 1870–1978," *Labor Studies Journal* 3, no. 3 (Winter 1979): 285; John, *Network Nation*, 116–122; Cohen, *Western Union*, 108–112; Nancy Cohen, *The Reconstruction of American Liberalism 1865–1914* (Chapel Hill, NC: University of North Carolina Press, 2002).
72. U.S. Bureau of the Census, *Historical Statistics*, 1102, 804–805. The most comprehensive study of network development in the West throughout this period is Blevins, *Paper Trails*.
73. John, "Recasting the Information Infrastructure for the Information Age," 71–72; Carpenter, *Forging of Bureaucratic Autonomy*, 78; Carpenter, *Forging of Bureaucratic Autonomy*, 82, 91; Gregg Cantrell, *The People's Revolt: Texas Populists and the Roots of American Liberalism* (New Haven, CT: Yale University Press, 2020), 126.
74. Samuel Kernell and Michael P. McDonald, "Congress and America's Political Development: The Transformation of the Post Office from Patronage to Service," *American Journal of Political Science* 43, no. 3 (July 1999): 797; Wayne E. Fuller, *RFD: The Changing Face of Rural America* (Bloomington, IN: Indiana University

Press, 1964); Fuller, *RFD*, 58; U.S. Bureau of the Census, *Historical Statistics*, 807; *History of the Railway Mail*, 57; Carl H. Scheele, *A Short History of the Mail Service* (Washington, DC: Smithsonian Institution Press, 1970), 97.

75. *Government Ownership of Electrical Means of Communication*, 63d Cong. 2d Sess., Senate Document No. 399 (Washington, DC: Government Printing Office, 1914), 28, 25; Richard R. John, "History of Universal Service and the Postal Monopoly," appendix D, "Study on Universal Postal Service and the Postal Monopoly," George Mason University School of Public Policy, November 2008, 25; Carpenter, *Forging of Bureaucratic Autonomy*, 92; Carpenter, *Forging of Bureaucratic Autonomy*, 146.

76. Richard B. Kielbowicz, "Postal Subsidies for the Press and the Business of Mass Culture, 1880–1920," *Business History Review* 64 (Autumn 1990), 458 ("tantalized"); generally, Richard Ohmann, *Selling Culture: Magazines, Markets, and Class at the Turn of the Century* (New York: Verso, 1996); Susan Strasser, *Satisfaction Guaranteed: The Making of the American Mass Market* (New York: Pantheon 1989).

77. Louise V. Stendhal, *The Telegraph: Lucien Leuwen Book 2* (New York: New Directions, 1950); Brock, *The Telecommunications Industry*, 126–147; Eli Noam, *Telecommunications in Europe* (New York: Oxford University Press, 1992), 134, 18, 240, 69; Patricia L. Maclachlan, *The People's Post Office: The History and Politics of the Japanese Postal System, 1871–2010* (Cambridge, MA: Harvard University Asia Center, 2011), 35, 31.

78. Daqing Yang, *Technology of Empire: Telecommunications and Japanese Expansion in Asia, 1883–1945* (Cambridge, MA: Harvard University Press, 2010).

79. Dallas Smythe, *The Structure and Policy of Electronic Communications* (Urbana, IL: University of Illinois Press, 1959), 16–17; Ithiel de Sola Pool, *Technologies of Freedom: On Free Speech in an Electronic Age* (Cambridge, MA: Belknap Press of Harvard University Press, 1983), 94; Although not necessarily to favor London, say, over Delhi or Johannesburg. Daniel Headrick, *Tentacles of Progress* (New York: Oxford University Press, 1988), 97–144; P. M. Kennedy, "Imperial Cable Communications and Strategy 1870–1914," *English Historical Review* 96 (October 1971), 728–753; Dwayne Winseck and Robert Pike, "Monopoly's First Moment," *Empire of Communications* (Durham, NC: Duke University Press, 2007); Maclachlan, *People's Post Office*, 38; Noam, *Telecommunications in Europe*, 134 ("Governments"). The silk-workers of Lyon had erupted in the so-called "Canut Revolts" of 1831, 1834, and 1848.

80. Karl Rodabaugh, "Congressman Henry D. Clayton and the Dothan Post Office Fight: Patronage and Politics in the Progressive Era," *The Alabama Review* 33, no. 2 (April 1980): 125–149; United States Senate Committee on Education and Labor, *Report of the Committee of the Senate upon the Relations between Labor and Capital* (Washington, DC: Government Printing Office, 1885), vol. 1, 345 (P. J. Maguire, General Secretary of the Brotherhood of Carpenters and Joiners); Blevins, *Paper Trails*, 81–88; Susan G. Davis, "Gershon Legman Confronts the Post Office," *CounterPunch* 9, no. 18–19, 15 (October–November 15, 2002): 5 (quotes); Wayne E. Fuller, *Morality and the Mail in Nineteenth-century America* (Urbana, IL: University of Illinois Press, 2003, 104–121; Carpenter, *Forging of Bureaucratic Autonomy*, 83–88,

103–106; Carpenter, *Forging of Bureaucratic Autonomy*, 104–106, 144–145; Notably in mining company towns. In one contemporary account, a congenial attitude toward the powers-that-be only underscores the point: "The company is thus responsible for the welfare of the town. It is the sanitary officer with all his usual functions. It takes care of the roads, provides the lighting, determines the variety of amusements, and sometimes supplies the police protection. It can exercise supervision over persons coming into the town and events there. It can keep undesirable people out. It can, if it wants to, even censor the mail, since the Post Office is usually located in its general store and one of its employees is Postmaster." Winthrop D. Lane, *Civil War in West Virginia: A Story of the Industrial Conflict in the Coal Mines* (New York: B. W. Huebsch, 1921), 22. Company control, a historian sums up, extended to "all facets of non-working life," often including the post office. Michael Goldfield, *The Southern Key: Class, Race, and Radicalism in the 1930s and 1940s* (New York: Oxford University Press, 2020), 53, 54. With official approval, the mail of Mexican and Mexican-American revolutionaries in the United States was intercepted and surveilled during the 1900s. Kelly Lytle Hernandez. *Bad Mexicans: Race, Empire, and Revolution in the Borderlands* (New York: W.W. Norton, 2022), 176–190. Control of the post office also meant that, "During a 1931–32 Harlan County coal miners' strike, owners cut off the delivery of 'the miners' favorite newspaper, the *Knoxville News-Sentinel*, because it was critical of local operators." John W. Hevener, *Which Side Are You On? The Harlan County Coal Miners, 1931–39* (Urbana, IL: University of Illinois Press, 1978), 20.
81. Kelly, *United States Postal Policy*, 77; Wayne E. Fuller, *The American Mail: Enlarger of the Common Life* (Chicago: University of Chicago Press, 1972); Shelton Stromquist, *Reinventing "The People": The Progressive Movement, the Class Problem, and the Origins of Modern Liberalism* (Urbana, IL: University of Illinois Press, 2006), 4, 7.
82. Christopher Hill, *The World Turned upside Down* (Middlesex: Penguin, 1975), 137–138.
83. Richard B. Kielbowicz, "Origins of the Second-Class Mail Category and the Business of Policymaking, 1863–1879," *Journalism Monographs* 96 (1986); Fuller, "Populists and the Post Office," 1–16; White, *The Republic for which It Stands*, 642; Quoted in Stromquist, *Reinventing "The People,"* 73; Stromquist, *Reinventing "The People,"* 14; Eugene V. Debs, "'Better to Buy Books than Beer': Speech at Music Hall, Buffalo, New York," January 15, 1896, in Tim Davenport and David Walters, ed., *The Selected Works of Eugene V. Debs, Vol. 2, The Rise and Fall of the American Railway Union, 1892–1896* (Chicago: Haymarket Books, 2020), 547.
84. Fowler, *Cabinet Politician*, 192; Richard White states that the Pendleton Act "created a nonpartisan gloss on a persistent partisan system." White, *The Republic for Which It Stands*, 465, 466; Fowler, *Cabinet Politician*, 215; The department "represented the bastion of the patronage system well into the New Deal." Carpenter, *Forging of Bureaucratic Autonomy*, 176.
85. Laurence Gronlund, *The Cooperative Commonwealth*, Stow Persons, ed. (Cambridge, MA: Belknap Press of Harvard University Press, 1965), 109, 132, 153.
86. Stromquist, *Reinventing "The People,"* 14–15, 20; Edward Bellamy, "'Looking Backward' Again," *North American Review* (March 1890), in John L. Thomas,

Alternative America: Henry George, Edward Bellamy, Henry Demarest Lloyd and the Adversary Tradition (Cambridge, MA: Harvard University Press, 1983), 273; cf. the Bellamyite journal which, in 1892, declared, "It is the post office, not the militia service, the civil service and not the military service, in which the prototype of nationalism is to be found, and not even there by any means completely until civil service reform shall have had its perfect work." In "Nationalism Considered in the Light of a Very Odd Objection," *New Nation* 2, no. 42 (October 15, 1892); Arthur Lipow, *Authoritarian Socialism in America: Edward Bellamy and the Nationalist Movement* (Berkeley, CA: University of California Press, 1982), 269; Edward T. O'Donnell, *Henry George and the Crisis of Inequality* (New York: Columbia University Press, 2015), 23; Rosanne Currarino, *The Labor Question in America: Economic Democracy in the Gilded Age* (Urbana, IL: University of Illinois Press, 2011), 156 n17; O'Donnell, *Henry George*; on the wider tradition, Thomas, *Alternative America*; Gronlund, *Cooperative Commonwealth*, 111; *Government Ownership of Electrical Means of Communication*.
87. Daniel T. Rogers, *Atlantic Crossings: Social Politics in a Progressive Age* (Cambridge, MA: Harvard University Press, 1998). To the chagrin of private insurance companies, early in his tenure as US President, Franklin D. Roosevelt asserted to his brain-trusters that the post office might be deployed to administer a comprehensive risk insurance for Americans in case of unemployment, ill health, and disability, including an old-age annuity. Rogers, *Atlantic Crossings*, 438, 444; Karl Marx and Frederick Engels, *Manifesto of the Communist Party, February 1848. Marx/Engels Selected Works Vol. 1* (Moscow: Progress Publishers, 1969), 26, https://www.marxists.org/archive/marx/works/download/pdf/Manifesto.pdf
88. Robert Blatchford, *Merrie England* (London: 1894), 124; Noel Thompson, *Political Economy and the Labour Party: The Economics of Democratic Socialism, 1884–1995* (London: UCL Press, 1996), 12; Blatchford, "Britain for the British," in Thompson, *Political Economy and the Labour Party* (London: Clarion, 1906), 143, 13.
89. Karl Marx, "The Paris Commune," in *The Civil War in France*, https://www.marxists.org/archive/marx/works/1871/civil-war-france/ch05.htm; Marx and Engels, "Preface," *The Communist Manifesto*, German ed. (1872), https://www.marxists.org/archive/marx/works/1848/communist-manifesto/preface.htm; for discussion, see Francis Mulhern, "Afterlives of the Commune," *New Left Review* 96 (November/December 2015), 134; Karl Kautsky, *The Class Struggle*, trans. William E. Bohn (New York: W. W. Norton, 1971), 109–110.
90. Emile Vandervelde, *Socialism Versus Statism* (Chicago: Charles H. Kerr, 1919), 13, 15, 51, 52.
91. Kautsky, *Class Struggle*, 109; V. I. Lenin, *The State and Revolution* (Peking: Foreign Languages Press, 1970), 59–60. Cf. John, *Spreading the News*, 289, n39.
92. James Connolly, "State Monopoly Versus Socialism," *Workers Republic* 10 (June 1899), https://www.marxists.org/archive/connolly/1901/evangel/stmonsoc.htm.
93. Marion Butler, quoted in Wayne E. Fuller, "The Populists and the Post Office," *Agricultural History* 65, no. 1 (Winter 1991): 11; Jane Addams, "A New Impulse to an Old Gospel," *Forum* (November 1892), 346, quoted in Currarino, *Labor Question in America*, 8.

94. White, *The Republic for Which It Stands*, 865; Donald Bruce Jackson, comp., *National Party Platforms*, rev. ed., vol. 1, 1840–1956 (Urbana, IL: University of Illinois Press, 1978), 65.

95. Gretchen Ritter, *Goldbugs and Greenbacks: The Antimonopoly Tradition and the Politics of Finance in America* (New York: Cambridge University Press, 1997), 47; Jean Reith Schroedel and Bruce Snyder, "People's Banking: The Promise Betrayed?," *Studies in American Political Development* 8 (Spring 1994), 177.

96. Edwin W. Kemmerer, *Postal Savings: An Historical and Critical Study of the Postal Savings Bank System of the United States* (Princeton, NJ: Princeton University Press, 1917), 2; Robert A. Brady, *Crisis in Britain: Plans and Achievements of the Labour Government* (Berkeley: University of California Press, 1950), 286–287; National Monetary Commission, *Notes on the Postal Savings-Bank Systems of the Leading Countries*, 61st Cong, 3d Sess., doc. 658 (Washington, DC: Government Printing Office, 1910); Noam, *Telecommunications in Europe*, 81; a giant insurance fund also contributed to the size and financial significance of the Japanese post office. Phred Dvorak, "Japan's Postal Behemoth Digs in on Deregulation," *Wall Street Journal*, January 6, 2000, A14. For a historical account, Maclachlan, *People's Post Office*; There were only 18,000 members. Directorate General of Posts, Ministry of Communications, China, *Report on the Working of the Chinese Post-Office Savings Bank* (Shanghai: Directorate General of Posts, 1922); Schroedel and Snyder, "People's Banking," 174.

97. Blevins, *Paper Trails*, 131; Blevins, *Paper Trails*, 119, 129.

98. Kelly, *United States Postal Policy*, 177. Actually, a postal savings bill passed and was signed into law only after more than one hundred attempts during the thirty-eight previous years. Schroedel and Snyder, "People's Banking," 179; Schroedel and Snyder, "People's Banking," 186; Maureen O'Hara and David Easley, "The Postal Savings System in the Depression," *Journal of Economic History* 93, no. 3 (September 1979): 742; Kemmerer, *Postal Savings*, 12; Kemmerer, *Postal Savings*, 61.

99. O'Hara and Easley, "Postal Savings System," 743–744; Schroedel and Snyder, "People's Banking," 187–193; Kemmerer, *Postal Savings*, 33, 34; Kemmerer, *Postal Savings*, 108.

100. Carpenter, *Forging of Bureaucratic Autonomy*, 163; Yet the important argument about the "Atlantic crossings" of many reform proposals also needs to be augmented by considering "Pacific crossings" as well. Rogers, *Atlantic Crossings*; Ministry of Communications, *Report on the Working of the Chinese Post-Office Savings Bank*; Kemmerer, *Postal Savings*, 53–54, 98, 104, 57–58, 62, 74, 78; Carpenter, *Forging of Bureaucratic Autonomy*, 153. Carpenter concludes that "European and Asian immigrants, not western and southern agrarians, were the most important" (162); Irving Bernstein, *The Lean Years: A History of the American Worker, 1920–1933* (Chicago: Haymarket Books, 2010), 103; *Discontinuance of the Postal Savings System*, Hearings before the Committee on Post Office and Civil Service on S. 1995 and H.R. 8030, January 27 and February 3, 1966, 89th Cong, 2d Session, 15, 6, 9–10. It is worth noting that the US Post Office, in the 1920s, also became a precocious institutional backer of the fledgling credit union movement. J. Carroll Moody and

Gilbert C. Fite, *The Credit Union Movement: Origins and Development, 1850-1970* (Lincoln, NE: University of Nebraska Press, 1971), 113.
101. Fuller, *RFD*, 202; Thomas Donald Masterson, "David J. Lewis of Maryland: Formative and Progressive Years, 1869-1917" (Ph.D. diss., Georgetown University, 1976), 269; Fuller, *RFD*, 202-203; Nathan B. Williams, *The American Post Office, A Discussion of Its History, Development, and Present-Day Relation to Express Companies*, 61st Cong. 2d Sess., Committee on Post Offices and Post Roads, doc. 542 (Washington, DC: Government Printing Office, May 11, 1910), 29; Masterson, "David J. Lewis," 289; Richard B. Kielbowicz, "Government Goes into Business: Parcel Post in the Nation's Political Economy, 1880-1915," *Studies in American Political Development* 8 (Spring 1994), 150-172.
102. Blevins, *Paper Trails*, 140; Fuller, *RFD*, 26, 34; Blevins, *Paper Trails*, 142; Kelly, *United States Postal Policy*, 111.
103. Blevins, *Paper Trails*, 142 144, 146; Carpenter, *Forging of Bureaucratic Autonomy*, 123-135; Carpenter, *Forging of Bureaucratic Autonomy*, 124; Fuller, *RFD*, 53, 81; Carpenter, *Forging of Bureaucratic Autonomy*, 135-137; Blevins, *Paper Trails*, 147; Carpenter, *Forging of Bureaucratic Autonomy*, 140; Carpenter, *Forging of Bureaucratic Autonomy*, 142.
104. *Parcels Post*, Hearings Before Subcommittee No. 4 of the Committee on the Post Office and Post Roads, 62d Cong. 1st Sess., June 1911 (Washington, DC: Government Printing Office, 1911), especially at 166, 168, and 117; Scheele, *A Short History*, 143-146; Fuller, *RFD*, 219-220; Kelly, *United States Postal Policy*, 182; Kielbowicz, "Government Goes into Business," 150; Daniel C. Roper, "Fundamental Principles of Parcel-Post Administration," *Journal of Political Economy* 22 (June 1914): 535; Masterson, "David J. Lewis," 374-377, 425 (quote at 377); Masterson, "David J. Lewis," 375.
105. Leonard Laborie, "Global Commerce in Small Boxes: Parcel Post, 1878-1913," *Journal of Global History*, 10 (2015): 257; Chester Lloyd Jones, "The Parcel Post in Foreign Countries," *Journal of Political Economy* 22, no. 6 (June 1914): 509; Laborie, "Global Commerce in Small Boxes," 257; "With such an outside stimulus, the United States Post Office Department found itself involved with parcel post in connection with foreign mails long before a reasonable domestic service had been developed." Scheele, *A Short History*, 143, 144.
106. Keith Clark, *International Communications: The American Attitude* (New York: AMS Press, 1968 (1931)), 120-121; Czitrom, *Media and the American Mind*, 25-29; Lester G. Lindley, *The Constitution Faces Technology: The Relationship of the National Government to the Telegraph, 1866-1884. Dissertations in American Economic History* (New York: Arno Press, 1975); Charles Greenhalgh of Denver, representing AFL Core Makers' Union 6355, in Stuart B. Kaufman and Peter J. Albert, ed., *The Samuel Gompers Papers, Vol. 3 Unrest and Depression 1891-94* (Urbana, IL: University of Illinois Press, 1989), 632; Delegate McCraith in the AFL's discussion on "A Political Programme at the Denver Convention of the American Federation of Labor," in Kaufman and Albert, *The Samuel Gompers Papers*, 629. Twenty years after civil service reform was instituted that prohibited covered government employees

from political activities, then-President Theodore Roosevelt reacted to the letter carriers' endorsement of William Randolph Hearst's presidential candidacy by confidentially ordering his Postmaster General Henry Clay Payne, "Any man who has had any share in introducing resolutions endorsing Mr. Hearst . . . should be removed at once from the service." David Nasaw, *The Chief: The Life of William Randolph Hearst* (New York: Houghton Mifflin, 2000), 170.

107. H. W. Orr, *Report on Relations between Labor and Capital, Volume 1*, 178–179; McClelland, in *Report on Relations between Labor and Capital*, Volume 1, 148.

108. Craypo, "Impact of Changing Corporate Structure," 289–291.

109. *Report on Relations between Labor and Capital*, vol. 1, 213, 147. During the contemporaneous strike against Western Union, McClelland, a member of the Brotherhood of Telegraphers and Secretary of the Knights of Labor, "deserted his own union near the end . . . and charged that the strike was unwise in its inception." Vidkunn Ulriksson, *The Telegraphers: Their Craft and their Unions* (Washington, DC: Public Affairs Press, 1953), 48. For an explanation of his action, see Terence V. Powderly, *The Path I Trod* (New York: Columbia University Press, 1940), 106–113; Gideon Tucker, probably a journalist, in *Report on Relations Between Labor and Capital*, vol. 2, 906.

110. Hochfelder, *Telegraph in America*, 71; One historian enumerates Presidents Ulysses Grant, Chester Arthur, and Woodrow Wilson. Hochfelder, *Telegraph in America*, 67–68, 70; Parsons, *Telegraph Monopoly*, 10–12; For example, see David A. Wells, *The Relation of the Government to the Telegraph* (New York: 1873); Parsons, *Telegraph Monopoly*; Richard T. Ely, "Why the Government Should Own the Telegraph," *Arena* 15 (December 1895): 49–54; *Report of the Postmaster-General. Executive Document 1, Part 4* (Washington, DC: Government Printing Office, 1890), 113. See also Ulriksson, *The Telegraphers*, 56–57. After citing comparable evidence, Hochfelder states that—apart from a few years after Jay Gould's takeover of Western Union— "the telegraph's major customers, the press and business, were mainly satisfied with private ownership." *Telegraph in America*, 65, 70; H. H. Goldin, "Governmental Policy and the Domestic Telegraph Industry," *Journal of Economic History* 7, no. 1 (May 1947): 57; *Report of the Postmaster-General, Being Part of the Message and Documents Communicated to the Two Houses of Congress at the Beginning of the Second Session of the Fifty-first Congress* (Washington, DC: Government Printing Office, 1890), 8.

111. Wells, *Relation of the Government to the Telegraph*, 32; Parsons, *Telegraph Monopoly*; David J. Lewis, *Postal Express as a Solution of the Parcels Post and High Cost of Living Problems*, 62d Cong., 2d Sess., document No. 379 (Washington, DC: Government Printing Office, 1912), 29–30; Kemmerer, *Postal Savings*, 10–11.

112. Parsons, *Telegraph Monopoly*, 13–15; A signal instance is William Z. Foster, who moved from syndicalism to the leadership ranks of the young Communist Party. James R. Barrett, *William Z. Foster and the Tragedy of American Radicalism* (Urbana, IL: University of Illinois Press, 1999), 33; William Z. Foster, *From Bryan to Stalin* (New York: International Publishers, 1937), 29; Hochfelder, *Telegraph in America*, 71.

113. David Montgomery, *Beyond Equality: Labor and the Radical Republicans, 1862–1872* (New York: Vintage Books, 1967), 311–323.
114. Sterling Denhard Spero, *Labor Movement in a Government Industry* (New York: George H. Doran, 1924), 64; Spero, *Labor Movement*, 65–67. Only in 1912, however, did Congress add a provision that "eight hours' service shall not extend over a period longer than ten consecutive hours." Kelly, *United States Postal Policy*, 199–200.
115. Spero, *Labor Movement*, 9; Bernstein, *Lean Years*, 93; Georg Leidenberger, *Chicago's Progressive Alliance: Labor and the Bid for Public Streetcars* (Dekalb, IL: Northern Illinois University Press, 2006), 15–16.
116. Spero, *Labor Movement*, 62–95; Carpenter, *Forging of Bureaucratic Autonomy*, 79–81 (quote at 81). Railroad work was hazardous; a Senate committee found in 1890 that, out of every 105 men directly engaged in the handling of trains, one was killed, while one out of twelve was injured. Employee mortality reached a national high in 1907, when 4,534 were killed. Hoogenboom, *A History of the ICC*, 35, 41; in 1893, of about 180,000 employed trainmen, one out of every nine was injured, and one out of every 115 was killed. Forty-four percent of casualties resulted from coupling cars. U.S. Interstate Commerce Commission, Interstate Commerce Commission Activities, 1887–1937 (Washington, DC: Government Printing Office, 1937), 117.
117. Carpenter, *Forging of Bureaucratic Autonomy*, 86–87, 107, 168–176; Spero, *Labor Movement*, 97–180; Margaret C. Rung, *Servants of the State: Managing Diversity and Democracy in the Federal Workforce, 1933–1953* (Athens: University of Georgia Press, 2002), 35–36; Kelly, *United States Postal Policy*, 208, 207.
118. White, *The Republic for which It Stands*, 784 (both quotes, including Olney's); Gerald S. Eggert, *Railroad Labor Disputes: The Beginnings of Federal Strike Policy* (Ann Arbor, MI: University of Michigan, 1967), 233. For a meticulous tracing of the evolution of this device, see Eggert, *Railroad Labor Disputes*, esp. 41–44; 90–98; 147–151; 171; Cleveland, quoted in Eggert, *Railroad Labor Disputes*, 171; for populist senators, 184, and for the unfolding federal role, 152–191. I also draw on White, *Railroaded*, 441; Ray Ginger, *Altgeld's America: The Lincoln Ideal Versus Changing Realities* (New York: Markus Wiener, 1986), 157–163; Painter, *Standing at Armageddon*, 123; Nick Salvatore, *Eugene V. Debs Citizen and Socialist* (Urbana, IL: University of Illinois Press, 1982), 128–137.

Chapter 2

1. The telephone, we should remember, remained a far from neutral feature of the landscape. Eula Biss, "Time and Distance Overcome," in Eula Biss, *Notes from No Man's Land* (Minneapolis: Gray Wolf Press, 2009), 3–11; Robert MacDougall, *The People's Network: The Political Economy of the Telephone in the Gilded Age* (Philadelphia: University of Pennsylvania Press, 2014), 59.
2. MacDougall, *The People's Network*, 9.

3. Although the structural and managerial relationships of individual Bell operating companies with the parent holding company—"American Bell" between 1880 and 1900, and thereafter, "American Telephone and Telegraph"—stabilized only during the 1910s, I will use "Bell" and "AT&T" as synonyms throughout the era.
4. MacDougall, *The People's Network*, 101–109; also, Christopher Beauchamp, "Who Invented the Telephone? Lawyers, Patents, and the Judgments of History," *Technology and Culture* 51, no. 4 (October 2010): 854–878; Robert MacDougall, *The People's Network*, 92; MacDougall is more emphatic in denying that a natural monopoly was present than John, who asserts that "in the telephone business, competition was always contrived." Richard R. John, "Robber Barons Redux: Antimonopoly Reconsidered," *Enterprise and Society* 13, no. 1 (March 2012): 31.
5. Richard R. John, *Network Nation: Inventing American Telecommunications* (Cambridge, MA: Belknap Press of Harvard University Press, 2010), 352–353, 368; MacDougall, *The People's Network*, 91; MacDougall, *The People's Network*, 225.
6. Shelton Stromquist, *Reinventing "The People": The Progressive Movement, The Class Problem, and the Origins of Modern Liberalism* (Urbana, IL: University of Illinois Press, 2006); Joshua D. Wolff, *Western Union and the Creation of the American Corporate Order, 1945–1893* (Cambridge: Cambridge University Press, 2013), 287.
7. Arthur P. Dudden, "Anti-monopolism, 1865–1890: The Historical Background and Intellectual Origins of the Antitrust Movement in the United States" (Ph.D. diss., University of Michigan, 1950), 271; Senate Committee on Education and Labor, *Report of the Committee of the Senate upon the Relations between Labor and Capital*, vol. 1 (Washington: Government Printing Office, 1885), 793; Charles Postel, *The Populist Vision* (New York: Oxford University Press, 2007), 144; MacDougall, *The People's Network*, 108; *Alliance-Independent* (Lincoln), March 2, 1893, in Norman Pollack, *The Just Polity: Populism, Law, and Human Welfare* (Urbana, IL: University of Illinois Press, 1987), 186–187; also Gregg Cantrell, *The People's Revolt: Texas Populism and the Roots of American Liberalism* (New Haven, CT: Yale University Press, 2020), 125–128; Stromquist, *Reinventing 'The People,'* 73–74; Julie Greene, *Pure and Simple Politics: The American Federation of Labor and Political Activism, 1881–1917* (Cambridge: Cambridge University Press, 1998), 61–63. Claiming that 15,000 petitions had been circulated to member unions across the country for signatures to present to Congress, the president of the labor grouping was forced to concede "that the petitions have either not been signed to a very great extent, or if signed, comparatively few have been returned to our headquarters." The Committee on the President's Report was moved to "deplore" this "apathy" and recommended that "when similar requests are made hereafter, the names of delinquent organizations be reported to the next succeeding convention of this Federation." *Report of Proceedings of the Thirteenth Annual Convention of the American Federation of Labor*, Chicago, December 11–19, 1893 (American Federation of Labor, 1893), 13, 41.
8. Only in 1994 did AT&T shorten its name from "American Telephone and Telegraph" to "AT&T"; MacDougall, *The People's Network*, 76–77; J. Warren Stehman, *The Financial History of the American Telephone and Telegraph Company*, repr. ed. (1925; repr., New York: Augustus M. Kelley, 1967), 17; Stehman, *Financial History of the*

American Telephone and Telegraph Company, 147; Kenneth Lipartito, *The Bell System and Regional Business: The Telephone in the South, 1877-1920* (Baltimore: The Johns Hopkins University Press, 1989), 51-52, 67-68; H. H. Goldin, "Government Policy and the Domestic Telegraph Industry," *Journal of Economic History* 7, no. 1 (May 1947): 61.

9. "Telephone Trust Easy to Dissolve," *New York Times*, December 22, 1913.
10. Edward Reynolds, Vice President Postal-Telegraph Cable Co. to Thomas W. Gregory, Attorney General, July 21, 1915, in National Archives and Records Administration (hereafter NARA) RG 60, Department of Justice Central Files—Classified Subject Files—Correspondence, Box 39, 60-1-1; The Telegraphers of New York Jewish Boys to President Woodrow Wilson, March 21, 1915, NARA RG 60, Department of Justice Central Files—Classified Subject Files—Correspondence, Box 39, 60-1-1; A Telegrapher of New York to Mr. Todd (84 Walker St., New York City), NARA RG 60, 60-1-0, Section 6, Box 38. During 1918, another illicit telegram made the same point, this time to the postmaster general: "Vail is Prest of the W UTel Co Give us govt ownership of the telegraph," NARA RG 28, Box 39, received April 24, 1918.
11. "Address of Mr. F. B. MacKinnon, President of the U.S. Independent Telephone Association, in NARUC," *Proceedings of the 34th Annual Convention Held at Detroit, Michigan November 14-17, 1922* (New York: State Law Reporting Company, 1923), 139; MacDougall, *The People's Network*, 93. The Midwestern locus was well-known. Paul Latzke, *A Fight with an Octopus* (Chicago: Telephony Publishing Co, 1906), 15; Federal Communications Commission (FCC), *Investigation of the Telephone Industry in the United States*, 76th Congress, 1st Sess., House Document No. 340 (Washington: Government Printing Office, 1939, 125-130), 248; Gerald R Brock, *The U.S. Telecommunications Industry: The Dynamics of Market Structure* (Cambridge, MA: Harvard University Press, 1981), 103-104; MacDougall, *The People's Network*, 101-108; MacDougall, *The People's Network*, 96; Statement to Honorable George W. Wickersham, Attorney General of the United States, by John H. Wright, Jamestown, NY, September 10, 1912, NARA RG 60, Department of Justice Central Files, Classified Subject Files, Enclosures, Box 129, 60-10, 3.
12. FCC, *Investigation of the Telephone Industry*, 126; Robert Bornholz and David S. Evans, "The Early History of Competition in the Telephone Industry," in David. S Evans, ed., *Breaking up Bell: Essays on Industrial Organization and Regulation* (New York: 1983), 25 ("46%"). For local profits, see Ralph L. Mahon, *The Telephone in Chicago 1877-1940* (Chicago: Illinois Bell Telephone Co. Interdepartmental Historical Committee, May 22, 1962), 8, 15. For national earnings, see, FCC, *Investigation of the Telephone Industry*, 491-568. David Gabel, in a study of the profit rate of Bell's Wisconsin Telephone, reports that during the period of patent monopoly, "the firm's rate-of-return was up to five times higher than that available from alternative investments." David Gabel, "Evolution of a Market," 66. AT&T's very high profit rate paled by comparison with the awesome profits achieved by Western Union; an investment of $1,000 in Western Union in 1858, stated Postmaster General Wanamker, would have brought in more than $50,000 in stock dividends and $100,000 in cash dividends over the next thirty years, for a total of

500 percent annually. Vidkunn Ulriksson, *The Telegraphers: Their Craft and their Unions* (Washington, DC: Public Affairs Press, 1953), 13; FCC, *Investigation of the Telephone Industry*, 41 ("gradual"); Claude S. Fischer, *America Calling: A Social History of the Telephone to 1940* (Berkeley, CA: University of California Press, 1992), 49; U.S. Census, *Historical Statistics of the United States, from Colonial Times to 1970*, Series R1–12 (Washington, DC: Government Printing Office, 1975), 784; Milton Mueller, "The Telephone War: Competition, Interconnection and Monopoly in the Making of Universal Service" (Ph.D. diss., University of Pennsylvania, 1989), 161, 165; Fischer, *America Calling*, 41, 50; Ithiel de Sola Pool, *Forecasting the Telephone: A Retrospective Technology Assessment* (Norwood: Ablex, 1983), 22; Mahon, *The Telephone in Chicago*, 30; Meighan Maguire, "The Local Dynamics of Telephone System Development: The San Francisco Exchange, 1893–1919" (Ph.D. diss., University of California San Diego, 2000).

13. Paul J. Miranti, Jr., "Probability Theory and the Challenge of Sustaining Innovation: Traffic Management at the Bell System, 1900–1929," in Sally H. Clarke, Naomi R. Lamoreaux, and Steven W. Usselman, ed., *The Challenge of Remaining Innovative: Insights from Twentieth-century American Business* (Stanford: Stanford Business Books, 2009), 119–120; Arthur B. Smith and William L. Campbell, *Automatic Telephony* (New York: McGraw-Hill, 1915), 379, in de Sola Pool, *Forecasting the Telephone*, 46. Deliberating on telephone service provision to the city of Ottawa in 1902, executives at Bell Canada—then interlocked with the New York–based AT&T—went on record that "of the 60,000 people in the city not more than 1200 have or require telephones." Robert M. Pike, "Kingston Adopts the Telephone: The Social Diffusion and Use of the Telephone in Urban Central Canada, 1876 to 1914," *Urban History Review/Revue d'histoire urbaine* 28, no. 1 (June 1989): 44. Bell Canada was even more contemptuous of the access needs of French-speaking Canadians in Montreal. MacDougall, *The People's Network*, 87–88; Mueller, "The Telephone War," 261; Mahon, *The Telephone in Chicago*, 16.

14. Roy Alden Atwood, "Telephony and Its Cultural Meanings in Southeastern Iowa, 1900–1917" (Ph.D. diss., University of Iowa, 1984), 92.

15. Mahon, *The Telephone in Chicago*, 16; David Gabel, "Competition in a Network Industry: The Telephone Industry, 1894–1910," *Journal of Economic History* 54, no. 3 (September 1994): 546; In Atwood, "Telephony and Its Cultural Meanings," 106–107; Gabel, "Evolution of a Market," 237–240; Alan Stone, *Public Service Liberalism: Telecommunications and Transitions in Public Policy* (Princeton, NJ: Princeton University Press, 1991), 138; Harry B. MacMeal, *The Story of Independent Telephony* (Chicago: Independent Pioneer Telephone Association, 1934), 132.

16. Claude S. Fischer "The Revolution in Rural Telephony, 1900–1920," *Journal of Social History* 21, no. 1 (Fall 1987): 13; Fischer, "Revolution in Rural Telephony," 8. Transcontinental long-distance service was not offered until 1915. On the independents, see MacMeal, *The Story of Independent Telephony*; Donald C. Power, *"General Telephone": The Function of the Modern Independent Telephone Company* (New York: The Newcomen Society in North America, 1956); W. D. Torrance, "Great

Independent: The Lincoln Telephone Company, 1903–1908," *Business History Review* 33 (1959): 359–382; and Helen B. Gardner and Quenton T. Bowler, "The People's Progressive Telephone Company, 1912–1917: The Dream and the Reality," *Utah Historical Quarterly* 61, no. 1 (Winter 1993): 79–94. The most comprehensive early study of rural independents is Atwood, "Telephony and Its Cultural Meanings"; the most authoritative is MacDougall, *The People's Network*.

17. Bureau of the Census, *Quinquennial Censuses of the Telephone and Telegraph Industry, 1902–1937*, Bulletin No. 17, Special Reports: Telephones and Telegraphs, 190S; Special Reports: Telephones, 1907; Telephones and Telegraphs and Municipal Electric Fire-alarm and Police-patrol Signaling Systems, lilt; *Census of Electrical Industries: 1917*, Telegraphs and Municipal Electric Fire-alarm and Police-patrol Signaling Systems; *Census of Electrical Industries: Telephones*—1917, 1922, and 1927; Fischer, *America Calling*, 93; Florence E. Parker, "Cooperative Telephone Associations," *Monthly Labor Review* 46, no. 2 (February 1936): 399, 400; MacDougall, *The People's Network*, 29–30, 164–167.

18. MacDougall, *The People's Network*, 64; Latzke, *A Fight with an Octopus*, 15; Joseph Patrick Sullivan, "From Municipal Ownership to Regulation: Municipal Utility Reform in New York City, 1880–1907" (Ph.D. diss., Rutgers University, 1995), 73. Among the eight leading gas companies in the city in 1885 were the Municipal, Mutual, and Citizens; Political agitation by independents crested between 1908 and 1913, when a national reform coalition, within which agrarian Democrats were preponderant, dominated Congress and found strong, if selective support, from the Wilson White House. See Elizabeth Sanders, *Roots of Reform: Farmers, Workers, and the American State 1877–1917* (Chicago: University of Chicago Press, 1999), 175.

19. In Gabel, "Evolution of a Market," 50; E. R. Harding, Vice President of Holtzer-Cabot Electric Company, to Attorney General McReynolds, December 20, 1913, NARA RG 60, Box 38, 60-1-0, Section 6; F. D. Houck to T. Roosevelt, October 5, 1908, NARA RG 60, Box 37, 60-1-0, Section 1; Gabel, "Evolution of a Market," 78, 89, and chapter 10. A biographer relates that La Follette, who "liked to live the good life," "invested [in] a horse ranch, an apartment building, a mine, and a telephone company in the hope that one would yield riches." David P. Thelen, *Robert M. La Follette and the Insurgent Spirit* (Madison, WI: University of Wisconsin Press, 1985), 17–18. For an insightful study situating LaFollette's antimonopolism in the context of his burgeoning opposition to US imperialism, see Richard Drake, *The Education of an Anti-Imperialist: Robert LaFollette and U.S. Expansion* (Madison, WI: University of Wisconsin Press, 2013).

20. Atwood, "Telephony and Its Cultural Meanings," 176; MacMeal, *The Story of Independent Telephony*: 195–196; As David Gabel shows, rate restrictions and other franchise stipulations sometimes ironically acted to retard the success of independent telephone companies, which were thereby encumbered with obligations Bell affiliates did not face. The latter avoided franchise obligations as one of numerous "first mover" advantages; city authorities were not inclined during the late 1870s and 1880s to view the telephone as more than an unproven experiment and thus did not impose obligations. Bell in turn exploited this comparative advantage to the full. David Gabel, "Competition in a Network Industry: The Telephone Industry, 1894–1910,"

Journal of Economic History 54, no. 3 (September 1994): 560–564; as in Chicago—to be discussed below—and Milwaukee. Gabel, "Evolution of a Market," 236.

21. Mueller, "The Telephone War," 218; Milton Mueller, "The Switchboard Problem: Scale, Signaling, and Organization in Manual Telephone Switching, 1877–1897," *Technology and Culture* 30, no. 3 (July 1989): 534–560; "The Dial Telephone and Unemployment," *Monthly Labor Review* 34, no. 2 (February 1932): 236; Stanley Swihart, "Independents Show Bell the Way to Big-city Dial Service, and Their Sudden Purchase by Bell," *Telecom History*, no. 2 (Spring 1995): 82–83; Venus Green, *Race on the Line: Gender, Labor, and Technology in the Bell System, 1880–1980* (Durham, NC: Duke University Press, 2001); Paul J. Miranti, Jr., "Probability Theory and the Challenge of Sustaining Innovation: Traffic Management at the Bell System, 1900–1929," in Sally H. Clarke, Naomi R. Lamoreaux, and Steven W. Usselman, ed., *The Challenge of Remaining Innovative: Insights from Twentieth-century American Business* (Stanford, CA: Stanford University Press, 2009), 125.

22. Pool, *Forecasting the Telephone*, 35. During the next decade, the rate of growth decelerated, leaving the nation with 20,202,000 telephones in 1930; As in John, *Network Nation*, 295–298; MacDougall, *The People's Network*, 52–53; Leon Trotsky, *My Life* (New York: Pathfinder, 1970), 271; Swihart, "Independents Show Bell the Way to Big-city Dial Service," 96; Mueller, "Universal Service," 358.

23. Michelle Martin, "'Rulers of the Wires'? Women's Contribution to the Structure of Means of Communication," *Journal of Communication Inquiry* 12, no. 2 (1988): 89–103; Lana F. Rakow, "Women and the Telephone: The Gendering of a Communications Technology," in Cheris Kramarae, ed., *Technology and Women's Voices* (New York: Routledge and Kegan Paul, 1988), 207–228; Claude S. Fischer, "'Touch Someone': The Telephone Industry Discovers Sociability," *Technology and Culture* 29, no. 1 (January 1988): 51; Fischer, "The Revolution in Rural Telephony," 15. A continuing historical significance of gender to the telephone was noted, in an Australian context, by Ann Moyal, who underscored the existence of "a deeply entrenched... feminine culture of the telephone... which underpins family, community, and national development." "This largely invisible information flow... conducted in 20–28 individual, personal telephone calls a week lasting 10–45 minutes, filled a vital need for women, and was as important to the country's 'social good' as the business, commercial and technological information flow was to the nation's 'economic good.'" Ann Moyal, "Women and the Telephone," *CIRCIT Newsletter*, South Melbourne, Australia, September 1989, 1; Ann Moyal, "The Gendered Use of the Telephone: An Australian Case Study," *Media Culture & Society* 14 (1992): 51–72; The 5,000-odd Iowa telephone systems reporting an income of less than $5,000 in 1917 employed almost twice as many women as men: 794 women to 408 men. Many of these systems did not, of course, actually employ anyone, but existed on donated labor. Atwood, "Telephony and Its Cultural Meanings," 116; Fischer, "Touch Someone," 48; Fischer, "Revolution," 13–14; MacDougall, *The People's Network*: 149 (quote), 146–153.

24. Mahon, *The Telephone in Chicago*, 26; Mueller, "The Telephone War," 255–260; *AT&T Annual Report 1907* (Boston: Alfred Mudge, 1908), 17.

25. Enrique Bonus and Corynne McSherry provided research assistance that was essential in carrying out this comparison; Among Home Telephone Company subscribers were accountants (4), attorneys (8), bankers (5), real estate brokers (4), physicians (9), and even one bishop. Bell's affiliate likewise included attorneys (3), real estate brokers (6), and physicians (8).
26. Also claimed by Mueller, "The Telephone War," 261; American Telephone and Telegraph Company, *Annual Report* (Boston: George H. Ellis, 1910), 23.
27. U.S. Census Bureau, *Historical Statistics of the United States*, Series R 1-12; As they were in Wisconsin during this period. Gabel, "Evolution of a Market," 167. True transcontinental service was not furnished until 1915; Malcolm M. Willey and Stuart A. Rice, *Communication Agencies and Social Life* (New York: McGraw-Hill, 1933), cited in Fischer, *America Calling*, 25.
28. David F. Weiman, "Reaching out to America: Building Telephone and Urban Networks in the Bell System," paper presented to the 52d Annual Meeting of the Economic History Association, Boston, September 1992, 8, 13; Mueller, "The Telephone War," 262; Mueller, "The Telephone War," 262.
29. Mueller, "The Telephone War," 156; Mueller, "Universal Service," 356. See also, Robert W. Garnet, *The Telephone Enterprise: The Evolution of the Bell System's Horizontal Structure, 1876-1909* (Baltimore: The Johns Hopkins University Press, 1985), 67-69; Stone, *Public Service Liberalism*, 94, 113-114; Gabel, "Evolution of a Market," 53; Frederick Leland Rhodes, *Beginnings of Telephony* (New York: Harper & Brothers, 1929), 197; Erik Barnouw, *A Tower in Babel* (New York: Oxford University Press, 1966), 44; MacDougall, *The People's Network*, 85; American Telephone and Telegraph Company, *Annual Report* (New York: 1910), 25.
30. Mueller, "The Telephone War,"160; "The Bell system was founded on the broad lines of 'One System,' 'One Policy,' 'Universal Service,' on the idea that no aggregation of isolated independent systems, not under common control, however well built or equipped, could give the public the service that the interdependent, intercommunicating, universal system could give." American Telephone and Telegraph Company, *Annual Report 1909*, 18. Mueller, "Universal Service," 356.
31. George Wickersham to Charles A. Prouty, January 7, 1913, 6 Section 4, Box 36, Record Group 60, NARA. For another instance, Jeffrey E. Cohen, "The Telephone Problem and the Road to Telephone Regulation in the United States, 1876-1917," *Journal of Policy History* 3, no. 1 (January 1991): 53-54; Pacific Tel. & Tel. Co., 15 Cal. R.C.R. 993, 994 (1918) in Stone, *Public Service Liberalism*, 189; Albert Sidney Burleson to Woodrow Wilson, May 7, 1919 (cable), in Arthur S. Link, ed., *The Papers of Woodrow Wilson, Vol. 58, April 23-May 9, 1919* (Princeton, NJ: Princeton University Press, 1988), 533.
32. AT&T *Annual Report 1909*, 33; AT&T *Annual Report 1911* (New York: 1912), 40-43;AT&T *Annual Report 1912* (New York: 1913), 30 (emphasis in the original).
33. Theodore N. Vail, untitled memo dated 12/8, in letter to A. S. Burleson, January 13, 1919, in NARA RG 28, Records of the Post Office Department, Box 38, 3; Vail, untitled memo in letter to A.S. Burleson.

34. "The understanding of what is meant by 'universal service,'" writes one researcher of present-day trends in telecommunications, "is by no means uniform." Jill Hills, "Universal Service: Liberalization and Privatization of Telecommunications," *Telecommunications Policy* 13, no. 2 (June 1989): 129–144 at 130. Distinct versions of "universal service" might provide an instance of how, as Stuart Hall et al. once suggested, there may exist "[t]wo different class realities . . . expressed inside [an] apparently single stream of thought." Stuart Hall, Chas Critcher, Tony Jefferson, John Clarke, and Brian Roberts, *Policing the Crisis: Mugging, the State, and Law and Order* (London: Macmillan, 1978), 165; "Never in their wildest dreams," Milton Mueller concludes, "did the early Bell managers think that telephone service could be demanded by, and profitably extended to, as many people and places as turned out to be possible." Mueller, "The Telephone War," 240; MacDougall, *The People's Network*, 83, 119; 63d Cong. 2d Sess., Senate Document No. 399, *Government Ownership of Electrical Means of Communication* (Washington, DC: Government Printing Office, 1914), 10–11 (emphasis added); In NARA RG 60, Box 38, 60-1-0, Section 9 (emphasis in original); American Telephone and Telegraph, *Annual Report 1910*, 23.
35. U.S. Bureau of the Census, *Historical Statistics*, Series R1–12, 783; Susan Porter Benson, *Household Accounts: Working-class Family Economies in the Interwar United States* (Ithaca: Cornell University Press, 2007), 132–133; and David Montgomery, "Class, Gender, and Reciprocity," in Benson, *Household Accounts*, 171–175; Fischer, "Touch Someone," 52–53, 57; Pike 35; Carolyn Marvin, *When Old Technologies Were New* (New York: Oxford, 1987) details the sexism, racism, and class prejudice that suffused early telephonic social interaction; Miranti, Jr., "Probability Theory," 120.
36. Los Angeles The Citizen August 4, 1911, v. 5 #12, No. 364, "One Telephone System." Presumably this writer placed quotes around "his" to refer to workers who rented their living quarters. The McNamara brothers, who were iron workers, admitted four days before the mayoral election that they had dynamited the open-shop *Los Angeles Times*, which came as a hard blow to trade unions and radicals who had turned the "framing" of the MacNamaras into a signature issue nationwide. D. J. Waldie, "Red Flags over Los Angeles," KCET, *Lost LA*, April 26, 2016, https://www.kcet.org/shows/lost-la/red-flags-over-los-angeles-part-2-bombs-betrayal-and-the-election-of-1911; Los Angeles The Citizen, May 26, 1916, "Who Opposes a Municipal Telephone System?" IX #50.
37. NARA RG 28, Box 102, Sam Gompers to Honorable Albert Sidney Burleson, Postmaster General, March 16, 1918. In promoting "social" long-distance telephone service at Chicago's Century of Progress Exposition in 1933, AT&T sought to monitor and analyze the elements of what one of its researchers called the "emotional thrill" attaching to such calls. Robert W. Rydell, *World of Fairs: The Century-of-progress Expositions* (Chicago: University of Chicago Press, 1993), 126; J. Rarusfelder [?] to Honorable Governor [sic] Wilson, July 23, 1913, in NARA RG 60, Department of Justice Central Files, Correspondence, 60-1-0, Section 5, Box 38.
38. In "Wiremen Favor U.S. Ownership," *Washington Herald*, May 5, 1919; *53d Annual Convention of the American Federation of Labor Report of Proceedings*, Resolution No. 51, 177.

39. Carl Shapiro and Hal R. Varian, *Information Rules: A Strategic Guide to the Network Economy* (Cambridge, MA: Harvard Business Review Press, 1998); Mueller, "Universal Service," 19–25; "as the value of telephone service was considered to be in part a function of the number of people connected to the network, the rationale and incentive for long-distance operations developed." Cohen, "The Telephone Problem," 48; Joseph Straubhaar and Robert La Rose, *Communications Media in the Information Society* (Belmont, CA: Wadsworth Publishing, 1996), 57; Michael Schrage, "This Road Will Be Tough One to Pave," *Los Angeles Times*, January 13, 1994, D5.

40. Mueller, "The Telephone War"; Milton Mueller, "Universal Service in Telephone History: A Reconstruction," *Telecommunications Policy* 17, no. 5 (1993): 352–369; John, *Network Nation*, 340–369; MacDougall, *The People's Network*, 160, 242–255.

41. "A historian has shown that Gompers actually pursued political as well as strictly union-based action. Greene, *Pure and Simple Politics*; Shelton Stromquist, "The Crucible of Class: Cleveland Politics and the Origins of Municipal Reform in the Progressive Era," *Journal of Urban History* 23, no. 2 (January 1997): 194.

42. In 1909, Bell's average residential rate, at just under $2 per month, comprised around 4 percent of the average manufacturing employee's monthly wages. Fischer "'Touch Someone,'" 36. In 1910, perhaps a seventh of working-class households in Kingston, Ontario, could afford a phone; John, *Network Nation*, 291–301. John grants too much, perhaps, when he declares that a rising generation of "telephone managers...invented telephone sociability." John, *Network Nation*, 304.

43. For one treatment, framed within the context of Progressive expertise, see David Nord, "The Experts versus the Experts: Conflicting Philosophies of Municipal Utility Regulation in the Progressive Era," *Wisconsin Magazine of History* 58, no. 3 (Spring 1975): 219–236. Contrary to Garnet's assertion, adherents were not confined to the Western states. Garnet, *Telephone Enterprise*, 150; Charles E. Sumner, who in 1915 was directing the San Diego Home Telephone Company, merits notice, according to MacMeal, "for it was he who, to force the granting of Independent franchises in Portland, Spokane, Tacoma and other cities, invoked the first initiative and referendum elections ever held in the United States—and won." MacMeal, *The Story of Independent Telephony*, 215; Daniel T. Rodgers, *Atlantic Crossings: Social Politics in a Progressive Age* (Cambridge, MA: Belknap Press of Harvard University Press, 1998), 112–159; Richard Allen Swanson, "Municipal Utilities Reform in the United States, 1885–1907: The Theory and Technique of Urban Collectivism" (master's thesis, University of Illinois, 1961); Rodgers, *Atlantic Crossings*, 101–111; 112–159 passim; John, *Network Nation*, 264.

44. John reduces the Chicago struggle to a case of "only the occasional gadfly." John, *Network Nation*, 297.

45. For an overview, see, Clyde Lyndon King, ed., *The Regulation of Municipal Utilities* (New York: D. Appleton, 1914), 37–51. On electrical utilities, see, Patrick McGuire, "Instrumental Class Power and the Origin of Class-based State Regulation in the U.S. Electric Utility Industry," *Critical Sociology* 16, no. 2-3 (Summer-Fall 1989): 181–203; David Morris, *Seeing the Light: Regaining Control of Our Electricity System* (Minneapolis: Institute for Local Self-Reliance, 2001), 12; Scott E. Masten, "Public

Utility Ownership in 19th-century America: The 'Aberrant' Case of Water," Journal of Law, Economics and Organization 27, no. 3 (October 2011): 605; A. R. Bennett, *The Telephone Systems of the Continent of Europe* (London: Longmans, Green, 1895), 4; Rodgers, *Atlantic Crossings*, 122; Pete Bell, "To Hull and Back: KCOM Creates UK's First Fiber City," December 12, 2019; "History of the Hull Telephone Department," https://strowger-net.telefoniemuseum.nl/tel_hist_hull.html; Rodgers, *Atlantic Crossings*, 152.

46. Herbert H. Rosenthal, "William Randolph Hearst and Municipal Ownership," *Tamkang Journal of American Studies* 1, no. 1 (1984): 7–8, 14–15; Edward W. Bemis, *Municipal Monopolies: A Collection of Papers by American Economists and Specialists*, rev. ed. (New York: Thomas Y. Crowell, 1899); Frank Parsons, The City for the People, or the Municipalization of the City Government and of Local Franchises (Philadelphia, 1901).

47. Chester McArthur Destler, *American Radicalism 1865–1901* (Chicago: Quadrangle, 1966), 105, 124; Destler, *American Radicalism*, 120, 114, 115, 117–118; In Philip S. Foner, *The AFL in the Progressive Era, 1910–1915*, vol. 5, *History of Labor Movement in the United States* (New York: International Publishers, 1979), quoting the Columbus Dispatch, May 15, 1899, 64; Foner, *The AFL in the Progressive Era*, 66–73.

48. Rosenthal, "William Randolph Hearst and Municipal Ownership," 9; Rosenthal, "William Randolph Hearst and Municipal Ownership," 11; Foner, *The AFL in the Progressive Era*, 79; Rosenthal, "William Randolph Hearst and Municipal Ownership," 14–22; Foner, *The AFL in the Progressive Era*, 80; Roy Everett Littlefield, III, *William Randolph Hearst: His Role in American Progressivism* (Lanham, MD: University Press of America, 1980), 88, 102, 245.

49. Littlefield, *William Randolph Hearst*, 183–184, 230, 210; David Nasaw, *The Chief: The Life of William Randolph Hearst* (Boston: Houghton Mifflin, 2000), 186–201; Littlefield, *William Randolph Hearst*, 147–236; AT&T managers bemoaned press articles and editorials in favor of government ownership of the telephone and arranged for an interview at the Ritz Hotel in New York between Hearst and then-AT&T president Walter S. Gifford. AT&T Archives and History Center, Warren, New Jersey, Box 55, Government Ownership vs. Private Ownership—1925.

50. C. F. Taylor, "Prefatory Note," in Parsons, *The City for the People*; Stromquist, *Reinventing 'The People,'* 77; William John Dickson, "Labor in Municipal Politics: A Study of Labor's Political Policies and Activities in Seattle" (master's thesis, University of Washington, 1928), 111. Studying related initiatives in succeeding years is Dana Frank, *Purchasing Power: Consumer Organizing, Gender, and the Seattle Labor Movement, 1919–1929* (New York: Cambridge University Press, 1994); Foner, *The AFL in the Progressive Era*, 56.

51. Foner, *The AFL in the Progressive Era*, 83; Swihart, "Independents Show Bell the Way to Big-city Dial Service," 87–89.

52. An important contribution to this discussion is Maguire, *Telephone in San Francisco*.

53. Greene, *Pure and Simple Politics*, 219; Foner, *The AFL in the Progressive Era*, 75. An organizing flyer from 1918 put the number of Chicago telephone and telegraph workers in both manufacturing and operating departments at 50,000, out of 300,000

US wireline workers overall. See "Chicago Telephone Workers' Bulletin," appended to H. F. Hill, Vice-President, Chicago Telephone Company, to N.C. Kingsbury, AT&T, November 13, 1913, NARA RG 28, Records of the Post Office Department, Special Reports, Box 223.

54. John, *Network Nation*, 324, 326 (quote).
55. John, *Network Nation*, 324; John, *Network Nation*, 336.John, *Network Nation*, 332; John, *Network Nation*, 332.
56. John, *Network Nation*, 338.
57. Ray Ginger, *Altgeld's America: The Lincoln Ideal versus Changing Realities Chicago from 1892-1905* (New York: Markus Wiener Publishing, 1986), 168–188; James R. Barrett, *Work and Community in the Jungle: Chicago's Packinghouse Workers 1894–1922* (Urbana, IL: University of Illinois Press, 1987); George Leidenberger, *Chicago's Progressive Alliance: Labor and the Bid for Public Streetcars* (DeKalb, IL: Northern Illinois University Press, 2006) 85.
58. Leidenberger, *Chicago's Progressive Alliance*, 89; Leidenberger, *Chicago's Progressive Alliance*, 124.
59. Leidenberger, *Chicago's Progressive Alliance*, 101; Perry R. Duis, *Challenging Chicago: Coping with Everyday Life, 1837–1920* (Urbana, IL: University of Illinois Press, 1998), 34; One reformer charged, in a letter to the US Department of Justice in 1913, that collusion between the Tunnel Company and Bell might date as far back as 1899. The Tunnel Company, he declared, was created to give the Bell affiliate in Chicago "a dummy competitor that would keep real competition out of the field, and to give the Tunnel Company an excuse for building a freight tunnel system by using the telephone tunnels as a pretext." Harold D. Stroud, Secretary, Telephone Users' Association, to Attorney General James C. McReynolds, October 4, 1913, NARA RG 60, Box 45, 60-1-89; Leidenberger, *Chicago's Progressive Alliance*, 172 n9, 124.
60. Leidenberger, *Chicago's Progressive Alliance*, 99–123; Truman Cicero Bingham, "The Chicago Federation of Labor" (Ph.D. diss., University of Chicago, 1925), 107, 100, 101; Leidenberger, *Chicago's Progressive Alliance*, 123–127; Leidenberger, *Chicago's Progressive Alliance*, 151.
61. John, *Network Nation*, 324, 326; In April 1913, AT&T sought unsuccessfully to break a militant strike by Boston telephone operators by staging "one of the most massive and expensive importations of strikebreakers in the history of the United States." Stephen H. Norwood, *Labor's Flaming Youth: Telephone Operators and Worker Militancy 1878–1923* (Urbana, IL: University of Illinois Press, 1990), 120–121.
62. Tetzlaff, "The Electrical Workers and Bell Mergers," 485–486. Some time before this, a "Telephone Users' Association" had been formed in Chicago. Its secretary, Harold D. Stroud ("expert and engineer") had contacted the Attorney General to complain of Bell's collusion with the Tunnel Company in fall 1913. See Harold D. Stroud to Honorable James C. McReynolds, October 4, 1913, in NARA RG 60, 60-1-89, Box 45.
63. Such tactics were, as we will see, far from unique. In Buffalo in the summer of 1916, similar concerns about collusion prompted the "Central Council of Businessmen's, Taxpayers' and Residents' Associations" to launch a petition drive, first, to prevent a telephone merger between the local independent company and the Bell affiliate

and, second, to pave the way for a vote in favor of a municipal takeover. The Central Council opposed any telephone merger on the grounds that such a consolidation would cause the waiver of a forfeiture clause in the independent company's franchise, by which its property would revert to the city, thereby making municipalization. A municipal telephone system, the group asserted, would "be enabled to carry out the purposes" for which the independent firm's franchise had been issued, "namely: low rates and adequate unlimited service." NARA RG 60, Enclosures, Box 134, 60-1-85, "Central Council of Businessmen's, Taxpayers' and Residents' Associations of Buffalo," September 1, 1916. "We regard the seeming active competition . . . is real," wrote a Minnesota Independent Telephone Association leader concerning conditions in his state in 1911, "but in many specific instances unfair and not resulting in the good of the general public and the smaller telephone companies." Lucius Clark for Minnesota Independent Telephone Association to ICC, December 7, 1911, NARA RG 60, Box 37, 60-1-0, Section 2; John, *Network Nation*, 326; Mahon, *The Telephone in Chicago*, 65–66. Nevertheless, the purchase price for Illinois Telephone and Telegraph was considered excessive by an expert. John, *Network Nation*, 326.

64. Ben. A. Tetzlaff, "The Electrical Workers and Bell Mergers," *The Journal of Electrical Workers and Operators* 14, no. 4 (October 1914): 486; Bigham, "The Chicago Federation of Labor," 109, 132–133.

65. Lawrence Glickman, *A Living Wage: American Workers and the Making of Consumer Society* (Ithaca, NY: Cornell, 1997); Glickman, *A Living Wage*, 105; see also, Roy Rosenzweig, *Eight Hours for What We Will: Workers and Leisure in an Industrial City, 1870–1920* (New York: Cambridge University Press, 1985); Frank, *Purchasing Power*.

66. Maureen A. Flanagan, "Gender and Urban Political Reform: The City Club and the Woman's City Club of Chicago in the Progressive Era," *American Historical Review* 95, no. 4 (October 1990): 1032; see also, Daphne Spain, *How Women Saved the City* (Minneapolis: University of Minnesota Press, 2001), 205–235; NARA RG 60, Box 38, 60-1-0, Section 7, pamphlet titled "Penny Phone League vs. Bell Telephone Trust," December 1913; James Weinstein, *The Decline of Socialism in America, 1912–1925* (New Brunswick, NJ: Rutgers University Press, 1984), 157.

67. For an argument that "with proper management and organization, we could have telephone service at a penny a call or at 2 cents at the most," see Los Angeles The Citizen, December 25, 1914, Vol VIII #24 "Public Telephones."; Edward N. Nockels, Secretary, Chicago Federation of Labor, "To the Honorable the Mayor and the City Council of the City of Chicago," November 4, 1907, 2. Thanks to Richard John for this reference; NARA RG 60, Box 38, 60-1-0, Section 7, Morton L. Johnson, President Penny Phone League to Honorable T. W. Gregory, Attorney General, November 21, 1914, 1, 14; "Penny Phone League vs. Bell Telephone Trust."; By 1907, the Chicago Federation of Labor was once again pressing Chicago's mayor to investigate the Bell affiliate. "The Chicago Federation of Labor, on behalf of the employees and the public urges and demands that an investigation be made into the conditions of the employees of the Chicago Telephone Co. as to the conditions of labor including wages, hours of labor, height of switch boards, speed-rate, right to organize, and other conditions, and to determine whether the health and safety of these employees, most of whom

are women are properly safeguarded and their power to render efficient service preserved." Nockels, "To the Honorable the Mayor," 2–3.
68. David F. Weiman and Richard C. Levin, "Preying for Monopoly? The Case of Southern Bell Telephone Company, 1894–1912," *Journal of Political Economy* 102, no. 11 (1994): 103, 122.
69. MacDougall, *The People's Network*, 196; MacDougall, *The People's Network*, 196–197; Stone, *Public Service Liberalism*, 160–164; E. H. Outerbridge, "Lower Telephone Rates for New York City," in Emory Johnson, ed., "State Regulation of Public Utilities," *The Annals of the American Academy of Political and Social Science* 53 (May 1914): 66–70; Mahon, *The Telephone in Chicago*, 37; MacDougall, *The People's Network*, 197; American Telephone and Telegraph Company, *Annual Report 1910*, 21; Weiman and Levin, "Preying for Monopoly?," 31; see also, Stone, *Public Service Liberalism*, 161–163. The Milwaukee Merchants' and Manufacturers' Association threatened to support competition against Bell in 1895 if Wisconsin Telephone did not lower its rates. Gabel, "Evolution of a Market," 99–109. By the 1910s, even some leaders of the independent telephone movement had grown defensive on the question. One wrote to the attorney general in 1913 that "I am not one of those willing to admit that a single service in a considerable city is more desirable than two"—but then conceded that "That question might be debated at some length." E. B. Fisher, Secretary, Citizens Telephone Company and President, Michigan Independent Telephone Association, to J. C. McReynolds, NARA RG 60, Box 45, 60-1-89, October 8, 1913, 3.
70. Mueller, "The Telephone War" and Mueller, "Universal Service" contain perceptive comments on these strategies; MacDougall, *The People's Network*, 195.
71. MacMeal, *Independent Telephony*; N. B. Danielian, *AT&T: The Story of Industrial Conquest* (New York: Vanguard, 1939); MacDougall, *The People's Network*, 201–203; Gabel, "Competition in a Network Industry," 553–555; L. D. Kellogg to Honorable William Howard Taft, December 9, 1911, in NARA RG 60, Department of Justice Subject Classified Files Correspondence, 60-1-0, Section 2, Box 37; "Memorandum for the Attorney General in re: The Telephone Trust," July 24, 1912, 9–11; "Memorandum for the Attorney General with reference to the Telephone Situation," April 28, 1913, NARA RG 60, 60-1-0, Section 5, Box 38, 5–7. According to MacMeal, a leader of the independent telephone movement, Vail's proposals for mergers included "a capitalization of losses 'which were caused by the public's demand for competition. Let 'em pay,' he is quoted as saying." MacMeal, *The Story of Independent Telephony*, 186; MacDougall, *The People's Network*, 203–205; MacDougall, *The People's Network* is the definitive interpretation. Also see the desultory discussion of relations between Bell and independents in MacMeal, *The Story of Independent Telephony*, 178, 183–185, 187–188, 191, 195.
72. Rodgers, *Atlantic Crossings*, 150; MacDougall, *The People's Network*, 195. The originating federal case is *Munn v. Illinois*, 94 U.S. 113 [1876]. By 1900—seven years before Theodore Vail assumed AT&T's presidency—twenty-four states had passed legislation allowing the regulation of telephone companies as public utilities. *U.S.A. v. AT&T*, in the U.S. District Court for the District of Columbia, Civil Action

No. 74-1698, Defendants' Third Statement of Contentions and Proof, March 10, 1980, vol. 1, 137, 149-150, 157; vol. 2, 1927-1928.

73. After 1920, "the evolving common law was one of the strongest weapons in the regulatory arsenal, equaling and often superseding 'commission law.'" Charles M. Haar and Daniel Wm. Fessler, *Fairness and Justice: Law in the Service of Equality* (New York: Simon & Schuster, 1986), 142. For an able exposition of the emergent regulatory regime in telecommunications, see Stone, *Public Service Liberalism*, 212-237. For the relationship between the Interstate Commerce Commission and the courts, although with somewhat later emphasis and a focus on railroads rather than telecommunications, Carl McFarland, *Judicial Control of the Federal Trade Commission and the Interstate Commerce Commission 1920-1930* (Cambridge, MA: Harvard University Press, 1933), 100-169; Stone, *Public Service Liberalism*, 44, 45, 48-50; Sanders, *Roots of Reform*, 179-216; Alan Stone, *Wrong Number: The Breakup of AT&T* (New York: Basic Books, 1989), 33; Haar and Fessler, 109-140, 145-151.

74. John, *Network Nation*, 338.

75. Horace M. Gray, "The Passing of the Public Utility Concept," *Journal of Land and Public Utility Economics* 16, no. 1 (February 1940): 8-20; Robert B. Horwitz, *The Irony of Telecommunications Regulatory Reform* (New York: Oxford, 1989), 34, 37, 38, 43.

76. Ari and Olive Hoogenboom, *A History of the ICC: From Panacea to Palliative* (New York: Norton, 1976), 8; Cantrell, *The People's Revolt*, 112, 87; Parsons, *City for the People*, 105. "We have seen that regulation cannot cure the evils of private monopoly, because it does not destroy the antagonism of interest that is the root of those evils. Regulation is a wrestling match—the people may get the monopolist down sometimes, but he will be forever on the squirm, ready to flop his antagonist at the earliest opportunity." Parsons, *The Telegraph Monopoly*, 116.

77. Nord, "The Experts versus the Experts."; N. G. Warth to President Woodrow Wilson, October 6, 1913, NARA RG 60, Box 38, 60-1-0, Section 6; Daniel W. Hoan, *Regulation a Failure and a Fraud, Especially in Wisconsin* (Chicago: Socialist Party of the United States, 1914); Daniel W. Hoan, "The Failure of Regulation" (Chicago: Socialist Party of the United States, 1914), 3; Delos F. Wilcox, "Effects of State Regulation upon the Municipal Ownership Movement," *The Annals of the Academy of Political and Social Science* 53 (May 1914): 75; see also, J. Allen Smith, "Effect of State Regulation of Public Utilities upon Municipal Home Rule," *The Annals* 3 (May 1914): 85-91; In James W. Sichter, *Separations Procedures in the Telephone Industry: The Historical Origins of a Public Policy* (Cambridge, MA: Harvard Program on Information Resources Policy, 1977), 14.

78. NARA RG 60, Box 38, 60-1-0, Section 7, Morton L. Johnson, President Penny Phone League to Honorable T. W. Gregory, Attorney General, November 21, 1914, 2; Morton L. Johnson, "Bell Telephone Monopoly," *The Journal of Electrical Workers and Operators* 14, no. 6 (December 1914): 615-622; Johnson, "Bell Telephone Monopoly," 615-616; also, MacMeal, *The Story of Independent Telephony*, 177-202.

79. In Mansel Griffiths Blackford, "Businessmen and the Regulation of Railroads and Public Utilities in California During the Progressive Era," *Business History Review*

14, no. 3 (Autumn 1970): 315; Nord, "The Experts versus the Experts," 236; Sichter, *Separations Procedures*, 14.
80. Clyde Lyndon King, ed., *The Regulation of Municipal Utilities* (New York: D. Appleton, 1914), 23; Nathaniel T. Guernsey, "The Regulation of Municipal Utilities," *The Annals of the American Academy of Political and Social Science* 57, no. 1 (January 1915): 20, 27.
81. "It was," Robert Garnet states, "regulation of the municipal variety that Vail hoped to outflank by accepting the authority of the state utility agencies. The proponents of municipal ownership embodied a movement that seemed to be of a more radical bent." Garnet, *Telephone Enterprise*, 130–131. Delos Wilcox, writing in 1914, carefully analyzed the political composition of the movement for state regulation. The public service corporations themselves, Wilcox contended—along with a small number of "uncompromising municipal ownership men" and a group of "corrupt . . . political leaders"—were at first opposed to state regulation because they "were naturally hostile to a movement promising more minute and more rigid public control of their activities, and which, much as they disliked the interference of local governments and state legislatures, had by long practice learned how to meet these interferences and, therefore, preferred to keep on fighting in the old way rather than to face a new enemy and have to learn new tactics." Wilcox, "Effects of State Regulation," 72; Richard B. Kielbowicz, "AT&T's Antigovernment Lesson-drawing in the Political Economy of Networks, 1905–1920," *History of Political Economy* 41, no. 4 (2009): 673–708; Wilcox, "Effects of State Regulation," 80; American Telephone and Telegraph Company, *Annual Repot 1908* (Boston: George H. Ellis, 1909), 24; For an expose of AT&T press-agentry even before the advent of its embrace of state regulation, see Latzke, "Fight with an Octopus," 87–90; John, *Network Nation*, 332; to take just one example, regulatory agencies in the Midwest and Mid-Atlantic states put "intense" pressure on AT&T to reconfigure its local operating companies to conform to state political boundaries between 1909 and 1921. Garnet, *Telephone Enterprise*, 149.

Chapter 3

1. U.S. Senate Committee on Interstate Commerce, *Hearing on S. 4395, Interstate Telegraph and Telephone Business* (Washington, DC: Government Printing Office, 1908); U.S. House of Representatives, *45th Congressional Record* (1910), 5533–5537; 5577–5578; 8455; U.S. Senate, *45th Congressional Record* (1910), 7264–7266; 8391; Charles M. Haar and Daniel W. Fessler, *Fairness and Justice: Law in the Service of Equality* (New York: Simon & Schuster, 1987), 138–139, 157; Mann-Elkins Act 36 Stat. 539. I. L. Sharfman, *The Interstate Commerce Commission: A Study in Administrative Law and Procedure*, part 1 (New York: The Commonwealth Fund, 1931), 52–70; Ari and Olive Hoogenboom, *A History of the ICC: From Panacea to Palliative* (New York: W. W. Norton, 1976), 52, 60–61.

2. *Report of Proceedings of the 26th Annual Convention of the AFL, held at Minneapolis, 12–24 November 1906* (Washington, DC: Graphic Arts Printing, 1906), 152, 235–236. As often occurred, state law pointed the way. Just as the telegraph was already classed as a common carrier of news, in 1885, the Supreme Court of Nebraska had ruled that the telephone—"to all intents and purposes part of the telegraphic system of the country"—was a common carrier. *State ex. rel. Webster v. Nebraska Telephone Co.*, 17 Neb 126, 134 (1885) in Haar and Fessler, *Fairness and Justice*, 148.

3. Robert MacDougall, *The People's Network: The Political Economy of the Telephone in the Gilded Age* (Philadelphia: University of Pennsylvania Press, 2014), 205–211; Alan Stone, *Public Service Liberalism: Telecommunications and Transitions in Public Policy* (Princeton, NJ: Princeton University Press, 1991), 179, 186–195; "Ohio Declares against Monopoly," *Telephony* 18, no. 26 (December 25, 1909): 709; "Five States Battle with Telephone Trust," *Telephony* 59, no. 2 (July 9, 1910): 29–33; "Government Now Investigating Bell Telephone Company," *Telephony* 62, no. 2 (January 13, 1912): 41; For example, George W. Wickersham, Attorney General to Honorable Charles D. Hilles, Secretary to the President, November 14, 1911, for evidence of the Attorney General's unsuccessful attempt to insert an interconnection clause in the act conferring rate regulatory jurisdiction over telegraph and telephone companies to the Interstate Commerce Commission; National Archives and Records Administration (hereafter NARA), RG 60, Box 37, 60-1-0, Section 2; N. G. Warth to President Woodrow Wilson, October 6, 1913, NARA RG 60, Box 38, 60-1-0, Section 6; James A. Fowler, Assistant to the Attorney General, to H. B. McGraw, January 25, 1913, NARA RG 60, Box 44, 60-1-68, Section 1.

4. Memorandum for the Attorney General in regard to Telephone Situation on the Pacific Coast, J. A. Fowler, March 17, 1913, NARA RG 60, Box 39, 60-1-3 Section 1; G. Carroll Todd, Assistant to the Attorney General to Clarence L. Reames, U.S. Attorney, Portland, March 14, 1914, NARA RG 60, Box 39, Section 2; Docket N. 5462 Telephone and Telegraph Investigation, NARA RG 60, Box 39, 60-1-1; Interstate Commerce Commission—Investigation Docket 5462—1913, N. C. Kingsbury to T. N. Vail, August 14, 1913, AT&T Archives and History Center, Warren, New Jersey (hereafter AT&T-NJ), Box 47. The attorney general's letter to the ICC, referring the telephone question to that agency, was made public on January 20, 1913, just before the transition from the Taft to the Wilson presidency. The *Postal Telegraph*, a monthly journal published by the Mackay company of the same name, which was Western Union's main competitor, editorialized in February 1913 that the move to turn over to the ICC "the question of what to do about the numerous charges of illegality on the part of the American Telephone and Telegraph Company" constituted an "extraordinary" and "unprecedented step" by an outgoing attorney general and suggested that AT&T President Vail had foreknowledge that this move would occur. "The Latest," *Postal Telegraph* (February 1913): 1–2; the Library of Congress prepared a bibliography on government ownership of wireline systems in 1912. The list was supplemented the following year, but, as Assistant Postmaster General Daniel Roper was advised when he requested the bibliographies in June 1913, the supply of copies of the supplement had been temporarily exhausted. Library of Congress, Division of

Bibliography, "Select List of References on Government Ownership of the Telegraph and the Telephone," March 4, 1912 and June 13, 1913, NARA RG 28, Records of the Post Office Department, General Correspondence, Box 38.

5. C. G. DuBois to Theodore N. Vail, November 11, 1913, AT&T-NJ, Box 47, Government Administration of Telephone Business—Plan for—1913. As early as 1907, Vail had declared that the movement for independent telephony had "encouraged attempts at regulation of rates and business on lines that if obligatory or persisted in would be ruinous." *AT&T 1907 Annual Report* (Boston: Alfred Mudge: 1908), 15.
6. "Western Union Exposed; Brooks Denial Challenged," *The Commercial Telegraphers Journal* 12, no. 1 (January 1914): 3; Saltzman [?] to Daniel C. Roper, December 9, 1913, NARA RG 28, Box 38.
7. "Telephone Stock Breaks Sharply," *New York Times*, December 16, 1913, 14; "Usual Tel. & Tel. Dividend," *New York Times*, December 17, 1913, 13; "Won't Push Federal Ownership of Wires," *New York Times*, December 18, 1913, 14.
8. The resolution (H.R. 355) was forwarded to the Committee on the Post Office and Post Roads on December 20. 63d Cong., 2d Sess., *Congressional Record* 5 (December 20, 1913): 1324. Lewis gave his speech on the subject two days later. 63d Cong., 2d Sess., *Congressional Record* 5 (December 22, 1913): 1377–1412. "Lewis Opens Fight for U.S. Telephones," *New York Times*, December 23, 1913, 5; "Telephone Trust to Dissolve, Giving up Western Union Control," *New York Times*, December 20, 1913, 1. "Federal Ownership Halts," *New York Times*, December 21, 1913, 2.
9. Arthur S. Link, *Wilson: The New Freedom* (Princeton, NJ: Princeton University Press, 1956), 117 and n83; MacDougall, *The People's Network*, 214; See "More Trusts Plan to Meet the Law," *New York Times*, December 20, 1913, 1–2; A. Bower Sageser, *Joseph L. Bristow: Kansas Progressive* (Lawrence: University Press of Kansas, 1968), 27–52; "More Trusts Plan to Meet the Law."
10. E. R. Harding to Attorney General McReynolds, December 20, 1913, in NARA RG 60, 60-1-0 Section 6, Box 38.
11. "Western Union Exposed," *The Transmitter*, January 1914, 19, 18, 17. Also A. Smith, ed., Transmitter, to President Woodrow Wilson, January 4, 1913, NARA RG 60, 60-1-0, Section 6 Box 38; Harry B. MacMeal, *The Story of Independent Telephony* (Independent Pioneer Telephone Association, 1934), 203–209; Link, *Wilson: The New Freedom*, 421.
12. Eighty years later, for example, when a carrier called MCI announced a multibillion-dollar effort to enter the local telephone service market, its attempt depended on the rights-of-way MCI had purchased from Western Union. Edmund L. Andrews, "MCI Plans to Enter Local Markets," *New York Times*, January 5, 1994, C1. Throughout the intervening decades, the continued existence of Western Union played a pivotal role in the twists and turns of system development.
13. Stone, *Public Service Liberalism*, 175, 176; Roy Alden Atwood, "Telephony and Its Cultural Meanings in Southeastern Iowa, 1900–1917" (PhD diss., University of Iowa, 1984), 108, 181–182.
14. Reprinted in *AT&T Annual Report 1913* (New York: 1914), 27.

15. Roger Shales, "Memorandum RE AT&T Company's Commitment" November 12, 1919, NARA RG 60 Box 40, 60-1-4, 14.
16. Station gains calculated from FCC, *Proposed Report Telephone Investigation (Pursuant to Public Resolution No. 8 78th Congress)* (Washington, DC: Government Printing Office, 1938), 156, Table 35.
17. Milton Mueller, "The Telephone War: Competition, Interconnection and Monopoly in the Making of Universal Service" (PhD diss., University of Pennsylvania, 1989), 328–344; Shales, "Memorandum RE AT&T," 11, 13; Martin J. Sklar, *The Corporate Reconstruction of American Capitalism, 1890–1916* (Cambridge: Cambridge University Press, 1988), 26.
18. Steven H. Norwood, *Labor's Flaming Youth: Telephone Operators and Worker Militancy 1878–1923* (Urbana, IL: University of Illinois Press, 1990), 167. Then-Postmaster General Albert S. Burleson expressly pursued a policy of coordination and consolidation of competing telephone and telegraph systems. FCC, *Proposed Report Telephone Investigation*, 157; MacDougall, *The People's Network*, 219.
19. MacMeal, *The Story of Independent Telephony*, 269, 274–275; By 1985, the top ten independents served about 85 percent of independent customers, with 1,300-odd smaller companies furnishing local connections to 15 percent of subscribers. Charles A. Pleasance, *The Spirit of Independent Telephony* (Johnson City, TN: Independent Telephone Books, 1989), 169, 286–287; 73d Cong. 2d Sess., *Report on Communication Companies*, House Report No. 1273, part 2, no. 1, submitted by Mr. Rayburn Pursuant to House Resolution 59, 72d Congress and House Joint Resolution 572, 72d Congress, June 4, 1934 (Washington, DC: Government Printing Office, 1935), 901, 843; Joseph Goulden, *Monopoly* (New York: G. P. Putnam's Sons, 1968), 77.
20. AT&T's emergent role as de facto network manager did not mean that every commercial independent shed its antagonism to AT&T or automatically lined up with the Bell interests in policymaking. During the mid-1940s, for example, the Gary telephone group diverged from AT&T over the then-important issue of building out network access via government support for rural telephony. See C. J. Durr, [FCC] Commissioner, "Memorandum to Senator [Lister] Hill November 23, 1944, in Clifford Durr Papers, Alabama Department of Archives and History, Montgomery, Alabama. Thanks to Victor Pickard for this reference.
21. In 1875, according to John Junior Thornborrow, "A National Policy for Electrical Communications for the United States (with Special Reference to Competition and Monopoly)" (Ph.D. diss., University of Illinois, 1935), 44–45; Interstate Commerce Commission (ICC), "Private Wire Contracts," Report No. 5421, 50 ICC, 731–766 (Washington, DC: Government Printing Office, 1918). Decided August 3, 1918.
22. 60th Cong., 2d Sess., Document No. 725, Committee on Interstate Commerce, *Investigation of Western Union and Postal Telegraph-Cable Companies* (Washington, DC: Government Printing Office, 1909), 22; "Railroads West Said to Be Unable to Get All the Telegraphers Needed," *Wall Street Journal*, August 31, 1909, 6. Thanks to Richard John for this reference; Gary Fields, *Territories of Profit: Communications, Capitalist Development, and the Innovative Enterprises of G.F. Swift and Dell Computer* (Stanford University Press, 2004), 115, 127; 50 ICC, 738; 50 ICC, 738.

23. Richard B. DuBoff, "The Telegraph and the Structure of Markets in the United States, 1845–1890," *Research in Economic History* 8 (1983): 268; 50 ICC, 734, 735; "Telegraph Business West," *Wall Street Journal*, December 30, 1909, 6. Thanks to Richard John for this reference; "Railroads West Said to Be Unable to Get All the Telegraphers Needed," 6; 60th Cong., 2d Sess., Committee on Interstate Commerce, "Investigation of Western Union and Postal Telegraph-Cable Companies," Document No. 725, 22. See DuBoff, "Telegraph and the Structure of Markets," 268; Interstate Commerce Commission Reports, *Decisions of the Interstate Commerce Commission of the United States May 1918 to August 1918*, vol. 50 (Washington, DC: Government Printing Office, 1918), 734–735, 738–739; 50 ICC, 736, 738. It bears emphasizing that AT&T had only just demonstrated that its long-distance technology could enable voice calls from New York to San Francisco.
24. National Recovery Administration, *Hearings on the Telegraph Communication Industry*, vol. 1 (Washington, DC: Jesse L. Ward), 59; David Hochfelder, "Constructing an Industrial Divide: Western Union, AT&T, and the Federal Government, 1876–1971," *Business History Review* 76, no. 4 (2002): 724; Harvey Hoshour and F.R. Elsasser, "Brief of the American Telephone and Telegraph Company," in NRA, *Hearings on Telegraph Communications*, 124–125; 50 ICC, 735.
25. 50 ICC, 732; 50 ICC, 732–733; 50 ICC, 759.
26. 50 ICC, 756; 50 ICC, 732.
27. 50 ICC, 735–736.
28. 50 ICC, 733; Francis R. Starke, General Solicitor, "Memorandum Brief for the Western Union Telegraph Company on Certain Questions of Law," in NRA, Hearings on Telegraph Communications: 138.
29. 50 ICC, 731; 50 ICC, 731, 732; 50 ICC, 766; "Brief Filed by Postal Telegraph and Cable Corporation," NRA, *Hearings on Telegraph Communications*, 207.
30. 50 ICC, 766; see also, NRA, *Hearings on Telegraph Communications*, 258.
31. *Report of Proceedings of the 27th Annual Convention of the AFL*, 337–338; August E. Gans to A. Burleson, Postmaster General, February 2, 1914, "Telephone and Telegraph Ack. 1-2-14 to 2-12-14," NARA RG 28, Box 39; see also, "Proceedings of the Fourteenth Regular Session of the General Assembly [of the Knights of Labor] Held at Denver, Colorado, November 1890," *Report of November 11, 1890 of the National Legislative Committee*, 2–3; "Committee on Postal Telegraph and Telephone Service," *Reports of Officers to the 64th Session of the International Typographical Union, Scranton, Pennsylvania, 12–17 August 1918, The Typographical Journal*, Supplement (August 1918): 273.
32. *AT&T Annual Report 1913* (New York: 1914), 28–62. Discussions of government ownership recurred in later years. See, for example, *AT&T Annual Report 1916* (New York: 1917), 49–51; C. I. Barnard, Commercial Engineer to N. C. Kingsbury, Vice President, AT&T, March 6, 1917, "Review of the Government Ownership Situation during 1916," 9–10, AT&T-NJ, Box 23, *Government Ownership—Report On—1914–1917*. Municipal ownership was written about favorably in 1910 in the organ of one of the unions seeking to represent telephone and telegraph workers—the International Brotherhood of Electrical Workers. Edward P. E. Troy, "The Advantages

of Municipal Ownership," *The Electrical Worker* 11, no. 1 (July–August 1910), 48–50. For *The Appeal to Reason*, see, Elliott Shore, *Talkin' Socialism: J. A. Wayland and the Role of the Press in American Radicalism, 1890–1912* (Lawrence, KS: University Press of Kansas, 1988).

33. Beginning with the Greenback National and Anti-Monopoly Parties in 1884 and continuing through the People's, Prohibition, and Socialist Labor Parties in 1892 and the Independence, People's, and Socialist Parties of 1908 to the Farmer-Labor and Socialist Parties in 1920. See Donald Bruce Johnson, Comp., *National Party Platforms*, rev. ed., vol. 1, 1840–1956 (Urbana, IL: University of Illinois Press, 1978); Barnard to Kingsbury.

34. Thomas Donald Masterson, "David J. Lewis of Maryland: Formative and Progressive Years, 1869–1917" (PhD diss., Georgetown University, 1976), 22–29; 352, 384, 392–394, 428–429, 471, 587–588; Masterson, "David J. Lewis of Maryland," 510–511.

35. *Congressional Record—House*, 63d Cong., 2d Sess., 1913, V. 51, December 22, 1913: 1385; Lewis repeated the charge twice in 1915. 63d Cong., 3d. Sess., *Hearing Before the Committee on the Post Office and Post Roads "The Postalization of the Telephone,"* H.R. 20471 (Washington, 1915); and "The Postalization of the Telephone: Extension of Remarks of Hon. David J. Lewis," March 4, 1915, *Congressional Record*, 63d Cong., 3d Sess. vol. 52, Pt. 6, Appendix, March 4, 1915, 847; Warth to President Woodrow Wilson.

36. John M. Blum, *Joe Tumulty and the Wilson Era* (Boston: Houghton Mifflin, 1951), 31, 58; Christopher N. May, *In the Name of War: Judicial Review and the War Powers since 1918* (Cambridge, MA: Harvard University Press, 1989), 31; U.S. Commission on Industrial Relations, *Final Report* (Washington, DC: Barnard & Miller Print, 1915), 104–108; May, *In the Name of War*, 31. MacDougall comments, "Wilson himself had privately told Burleson he supported the postalization of the telegraph, without specifically mentioning the telephone one way or the other." MacDougall, *The People's Network*, 218; John, *Network Nation*, 371–372.

37. Dan Lacy, *From Grunts to Gigabytes: Communications and Society* (Urbana, IL: University of Illinois Press, 1996), 87; Parsons, in Edward W. Bemis, *Municipal Monopolies: A Collection of Papers by American Economists and Specialists* (New York: Thomas Y. Crowell, 1899); and Arthur N. Holcombe, *Public Ownership of Telephones on the Continent of Europe* (Boston: Houghton Mifflin, 1911); Eli Noam, *Telecommunications in Europe* (New York: Oxford University Press, 1992), 70, 136–137, 103; Christopher Armstrong and H. V. Nelles, *Monopoly's Moment. The Organization and Regulation of Canadian Utilities, 1830–1930* (Philadelphia: Temple University Press, 1986), 175–185; Albert Sidney Burleson, "Why We Should Keep the Wires," *Forum* 61, no. 2 (February 1919): 153; Joseph A. McCartin, *Labor's Great War: The Struggle for Industrial Democracy and the Origins of Modern American Labor Relations, 1912–1921* (Chapel Hill, NC: University of North Carolina Press, 1997), 37.

38. Theodore N. Vail to P. L. Spalding, President, New England Telephone and Telegraph Company, February 18, 1914; and "Government Administration of Telephone Business—Plan For—1913," C. G. Dubois to Theodore N. Vail, November 11, 1913,

AT&T-NJ, Box 47, Government Ownership—1912-1918; AT&T-NJ, "Government Ownership—1912-1913."; Walter S. Allen to Vice President N. C. Kingsbury, September 19, 1912, AT&T-NJ, Box 20, "Public Relations Bureau Establishment—1912."; "Report from Commercial Engineer C. F. Barnard to Vice Presidents N. C. Kingsbury and H. B. Thayer," October 20, 1914, AT&T-NJ, Box 23, "Government Ownership—Report On—1914-1917."

39. Postmaster General to Honorable Thomas R. Marshall, Senate of the United States, March 4, 1918, in Albert Sidney Burleson Papers, Library of Congress, Washington, D.C., 7. Thanks to Richard John for this reference; Postmaster General to Marshall, 8-9,10; *Report of Proceedings of the 35th Annual Convention of the AFL. San Francisco, 2-22 November 1915* (Washington, DC: The Law Reporter Printing Co., 1915), 308. Owing to "the tremendous amount of legislative matter" referred by the San Francisco Convention, the AFL found itself "unable to press for attention several subjects, among them ... Resolution No. 72, declarative of public ownership of public utilities for the transmission of intelligence, better known as the Lewis bill 355, providing for government ownership of telegraph and telephone." *Report of Proceedings of the 36th Annual Convention of the AFL. Baltimore 13-25 November 1916* (Washington: Law Reporter Printing Co., 1916), 107-108.

40. Barnard to Kingsbury; Morton L. Johnson, "Bell Telephone Monopoly," *The Journal of Electrical Workers and Operators* 14, no. 6 (December 1914): 622. Soon after the wireline systems were in fact taken over by the post office, John Fitzpatrick, president of the Chicago Federation of Labor, cautioned in a union organizing flyer that government representatives "will be glad to meet you, their employees, to adjust any grievances or wage demands that you may make, but you should have a good, strong Union to present your side of the case." "Hello Girls," appended to N. C. Kingsbury to J. C. Coons, First Assistant Postmaster General, October 15, 1918, NARA RG 28, Records of the Post Office Department, Special Reports Box 223; Johnson, "Bell Telephone Monopoly," 622; Edward N. Nockels, Secretary, Chicago Federation of Labor, to Honorable A. S. Burleson, February 1, 1917, NARA RG 28, Records of the Post Office Department, General Correspondence Box 39; NARA RG 28, Box 39, letters of February 1917; Box 102, February 1917. In hearings on the bill, Oliver Wilson, master of the National Grange representing one million members in thirty-three states, declared he was in favor of the bill as a means of establishing a better system than Bell's "or any other." 64th Cong., 2d Sess., *Hearings before the Committee on the District of Columbia on "Government Monopoly of Telephone Communication in the District of Columbia"* (Washington, DC: Government Printing Office: 1917), 12-13.

41. John Walsh and Garth Mangum, *Labor Struggle in the Post Office: From Selective Lobbying to Collective Bargaining* (Armonk, NJ: M. E. Sharpe, 1992), 80; Sterling Denhard Spero, *Labor Movement in a Government Industry: A Study of Employee Organization in the Postal Service* (New York: George H. Doran, 1924), 208-28; Spero, *Labor Movement in a Government Industry*, 62-243; Postmaster General Burleson gave a foretaste of the policies he would seek to implement in the telephone industry in his unrelenting attacks on postal employee organizations. Wayne E. Fuller, *RFD: The Changing Face of Rural America* (Bloomington, IN: Indiana University

Press, 1964), 162–163. In assenting to the proposal for government ownership, Vice President Perlham suggested that the telegraph systems in recent years had regularly "distorted and delayed . . . labor news." His sentiments were amplified by the socialist S. M. Hayes of the Typographical Union, who insisted that the convention should not adopt the resolution "in a perfunctory sort of way," expecting the Executive Council "to secure action on the part of Congress." Rather, he urged the convention to "instruct the delegates and the officials of national and international unions, state and city central bodies, to use their influence with Congressmen and Senators from their districts by writing them letters and sending telegrams demanding that the telegraphic monopoly be taken over by the government at the earliest possible date." *Report of Proceedings of the 38th Annual Convention of the AFL. Saint Paul, 10–20 June, 1918* (Washington, DC: The Law Reporter Printing Company, 1918), 201–202.

42. Berger in William English Walling, *Progressivism—and After* (New York: Macmillan, 1914), 171; Morris Hillquit, *Socialism Summed Up* (New York: H. K. Fly, 1913), 30; Hillquit, *Socialism Summed Up*, 73–74.

43. Alan Clinton, *Post Office Workers: A Trade Union and Social History* (London: George Allen & Unwin, 1984), 243–244, 388–391; Spero, *Labor Movement in a Government Industry*, 289–290; Judith Wishnia, *The Proletarianizing of the Fonctionnaires* (Baton Rouge, LA: Louisiana State University, 1990), 176–222; Andreas Kunz, *Civil Servants and the Politics of Inflation in Germany 1914–1924* (Berlin: Walter de Gruyter, 1986), 136–137; Daniel Orlovsky, "The Lower Middle Strata in Revolutionary Russia," in Edith W. Clowes, *Between Tsar and People: Educated Society and the Quest for a Public* (Princeton, NJ: Princeton University Press, 1991), 257–263. For a couple of years following the October Revolution, it has been argued that the Soviet state was not an agency of a "vanguard" Communist Party, but rather a workable alliance between Bolsheviks and Social Revolutionaries—an alliance that betokened wider representation for Russia's workers and peasants. Lara Douds, *Inside Lenin's Government: Ideology, Power and Practice in the Early Soviet State* (London: Bloomsbury, 2019), 28, 29–30; Stephen Ferguson, *GPO Staff in 1916: Business as Usual* (Cork: Mercier Press, 2012), 96, 98, 36, 17 (quote). Ferguson relates that "the vast majority of Post Office staff played no part in the Rising," 82.

44. Daniel T. Rodgers, *Atlantic Crossings: Social Politics in a Progressive Age* (Cambridge, MA: Harvard University Press, 1998); May, *In the Name of War*, 33–34.

45. This term is from Sklar, *Corporate Reconstruction*, 17; In May, *In Time of War*, 28; Edith C. Simpson, "Trade Union Organization among the Telephone Operators in the United States," *The Union Telephone Operator* 1, no. 9 (October 1921): 16. This lesson endured into the 1920s. Responding to a conference held by the Public Ownership League of America in 1922, the operators' journal, *The Union Telephone Operator*, underscored the same point that the Socialist Hillquit had made nearly a decade before: "No program of public ownership can secure any measure of consideration or co-operation from the labor movement unless it stresses the necessity of democratic control as a necessary corollary to public ownership." "Editorial The New Philosophy in Public Ownership," *The Union Telephone Operator* 2, no. 1 (January 1922): 4.

46. Kendrick A. Clements, *The Presidency of Woodrow Wilson* (Lawrence, KS: University Press of Kansas, 1992), 73–91; Milton Derber, "The Idea of Industrial Democracy in America 1898–1915," *Labor History* 7, no. 3 (Fall 1966): 259–286; Milton Derber, "The Idea of Industrial Democracy in America: 1915–1935," *Labor History* 8, no. 1 (Winter 1967): 3–29; Jacob Kramer, *The New Freedom and the Radicals: Woodrow Wilson, Progressive Views of Radicalism, and the Origins of Repressive Tolerance* (Philadelphia: Temple University Press, 2015), 42–43; McCartin, *Labor's Great War*; McCartin, *Labor's Great War*, 8.
47. Harry W. Laidler, *Public Ownership Here and Abroad*, 2nd ed. (New York: League for Industrial Democracy, 1924), 15; Spero, *Labor Movement in a Government Industry*, 289–292.
48. Maurine Weiner Greenwald, *Women, War, and Work: The Impact of World War I on Women Workers in the United States* (Ithaca, NY: Cornell University Press, 1990); McCartin, *Labor's Great War*, 48–49, 111–114; Norwood, *Labor's Flaming Youth*; Venus Green, *Race on the Line* (Durham, NC: Duke University Press, 2001); Kramer, *The New Freedom and the Radicals*, 45–46 (quote); Philip F. Rubio, *There's Always Work at the Post Office: African American Postal Workers and the Fight for Jobs, Justice, and Equality* (Durham, NC: Duke University Press, 2010), 29.
49. *Seattle Times*, November 1, 1917, in Cal Winslow, *Radical Seattle: The General Strike of 1919* (New York: Monthly Review Press, 2020), 113.
50. Andrew Plecher to Postmaster General, November 13, 1915, NARA RG 28, Box 39; Plecher to Postmaster General; *Report of the Proceedings of the Thirty Eighth Annual Convention of the American Federation of Labor Held at Saint Paul, Minnesota, June 10 to 20, Inclusive, 1918* (Washington, DC: The Last Reporter Printing Company, 1918), 202.
51. Ronald W. Schatz, *The Electrical Workers: A History of Labor at General Electric and Westinghouse, 1923–60* (Urbana, IL: University of Illinois Press, 1983), 17; John N. Schacht, *The Making of Telephone Unionism 1920–1947* (New Brunswick, NJ: Rutgers University Press, 1985), 3; William Brown to the Attorney General, August 12, 1914; William Brown to the Department of Justice, August 27, 1914; Carroll Todd to William Brown, September 1, 1914, NARA RG 60, Box 39, 60-1-1.
52. The more rational economy of a projected cooperative commonwealth, wrote the socialist Laurence Gronlund in 1884, would require that the nation "shut up those gambling shops: the stock and produce-exchanges." Laurence Gronlund, *The Cooperative Commonwealth*, Stow Persons, ed. (Cambridge, MA: Belknap Press of Harvard University Press, 1965), 97. The Prohibitionist Party Platform for 1916, which also came out for government ownership of "natural monopolies," inveighed against "gambling in grain or trading in 'options' or 'futures' or 'shortselling,' or any other form of so-called speculation wherein products are not received or delivered, but wherein so-called contracts are settled by the payment of 'margins' or 'differences' through clearing houses or otherwise." Donald Bruce Johnson, comp., *National Party Platforms, Vol. 1, 1840–1956* (Urbana, IL: University of Illinois Press, 1978), 203.
53. David Hochfelder, *The Telegraph in America, 1832–1920* (Baltimore: Johns Hopkins University Press, 2016), 121–34; Archie E. Rainey to Postmaster General Burleson,

May 7, 1918, NARA RG 28n, Box 39. "The operators are driven to the wall and working like tigers but they are doing it for the govt . . . they are the poorest paid men today in the country A first class salary for a telegraph opr under this telephone regime is 18 dollars per week." NARA RG 28, Box 39, received April 24, 1918.
54. L. L. Lauundine (?) to PMG, April 12, 1918, 9–10, NARA RG 28, Box 102. For a highly literate and almost equally extensive critique, also by a woman telegraph operator from New Jersey that also hinted at harassment, see Martha Van Ausdall to Honorable Secretary of Labor, January 6, 1917, and Martha Ausdall to President Woodrow Wilson, March 16, 1918 (telegram), *General Reports of the Department of Labor 1907–1942*, Chief Clerk's Files, Box No. 66, 20/113, "Western Union Telegraph Company 1913–19," NARA RG 174.
55. McCartin, *Labor's Great War*, 63.
56. Barnard to Kingsbury.
57. May, *In Time of War*, 27; N. B. Danielian, *A.T.&T: Story of Industrial Conquest* (New York: Vanguard, 1939), 244.
58. May, *In Time of War*, 94–97.
59. Laidler, *Public Ownership Here and Abroad*, 27; Valerie Jean Conner, *The National War Labor Board: Stability, Social Justice, and the Voluntary State in World War I* (Chapel Hill, NC: University of North Carolina Press, 1983), xiii; This plight persisted: telegraphers' relative real earnings in 1926 were a mere 2 percent above what they had been in 1902. Paul H. Douglas, *Real Wages in the United States 1890–1926* (Boston: Houghton Mifflin, 1930), 341–342; Douglas, *Real Wages in the United States*, 341–342; Douglas, *Real Wages in the United States*, 193–194, 379.
60. Union membership grew tenfold between 1900 and 1919. May, *In Time of War*, 98. During the first six months of US participation in the war, the number of strikes exceeded those in the same months of 1916, 2,314 versus 2,296. Conner, *National War Labor Board*, 24; In Conner, *National War Labor Board*, 44; McCartin, *Labor's Great War*, 92–93; Conner, *National War Labor Board*, 44; Vidkunn Ulriksson, *The Telegraphers: Their Craft and Their Unions* (Washington, DC: Public Affairs Press, 1953), 106–117. Gregory J. Downey, *Telegraph Messenger Boys* (New York: Routledge, 2002), 178–179. The progress of this deadly serious game of bluff and counterbluff can be followed in "Goes West to Call Telegraph Strike," *New York Times*, June 5, 1918, 17; "President May Avert Telegraphers Strike," *New York Times*, June 11, 1918, 22; "Labor Policy Told by Western Union," *New York Times*, June 17, 1918, 8; "President Hopes to Avert Seizure of Telegraphs," *New York Times*, June 19, 1918, 1, 9; "Threat to Quit Soon by Telegraph Union," *New York Times*, June 27, 1918, 11; "Telegraph Strike Called for July 8; President May Act," *New York Time*, July 1, 1918, 1, 6; "President Asks Power to Control All Wire Systems," *New York Times*, July 2, 1918, 1, 6; "Fight Begins to Limit Wires Control to War," *New York Times*, July 3, 1918, 1, 11; "Quotes Burleson as Opposing Union," *New York Times*, July 5, 1918, 15; "House Votes Wire Control; Senate Waits," *New York Times*, July 6, 1918, 1; "Rejects Report on Wire Control," *New York Times*, July 9, 1918, 1, 11; "Washington Plea Prevents Strike on Western Union," *New York Times*, July 8, 1918, 1, 6; "Congress Recess Held up by Fight on Wire Control," *New York Times*, July 7, 1918, 1, 10; "Votes 7 to 3 for Wire Control,"

New York Times, July 10, 1918, 1; "Wire Control Bill Passed by Senate," *New York Times*, July 14, 1918, 1, 8; "Taft Peace Offer Is Rejected by Western Union—Company Refuses to Compromise on Question of Employees Joining Union," *New York Times*, June 3, 1918, 1; "Consults Gompers on Wire Strike," *New York Times*, June 4, 1918, 14.

61. *Congressional Record*, 65th Cong., 2d Sess., 8719, in Arthur S. Link, *The Papers of Woodrow Wilson, Vol. 48, May 13–July 17, 1918* (Princeton, NJ: Princeton University Press, 1985), 458; May, *In Time of War*, 29; A leading Progressive and a newspaper publisher from North Carolina, Daniels was a committed white supremacist. For this, and for his tenure as Navy Secretary, see Lee A. Craig, *Josephus Daniels: His Life & Times* (Chapel Hill: University of North Carolina Press, 2013); 65th Cong., 2d Sess., Committee on Interstate and Foreign Commerce, Hearings on H.J. Res. 309, Federal Control of Systems of Communication (Washington: Government Printing Office, 1918), 27, 29, 34–36, 38; May, *In Time of War*, 43; May, *In Time of War*, 35, 37; The strike failed in July 1917. "The union's efforts succeeded not," one historian avers, because its threat to shut down service "was taken seriously but because its plea for federal operation fell on sympathetic ears." May, *In Time of War*, 30. The Wilson administration nevertheless judged the threat of disruption real enough. The issue was not only the strike itself, however, but also the attendant upending of its machinery for stabilizing more widely contested labor relations, the NWLB. The best-documented account of this episode is Conner, *National War Labor Board*, 35–49; 163–167. Relying on Conner is McCartin, *Labor's Great War*, 92–93.

62. Compare David Montgomery, *The Fall of the House of Labor* (New York: Cambridge University Press, 1987), 328.

63. By the President of the United States of America. A Proclamation, July 22, 1918, 65th Cong., *The Statutes at Large of the United States of America, from April 1917, to March 1919*, pt. 2 (Washington, DC: Government Printing Office, 1919), 1807–1808.

64. In Danielian, *AT&T: Story of Industrial Conquest*, 251-2.

65. Link, *Wilson: The New Freedom*, 135; Link, *Wilson: The New Frontier*, 159; Blum, *Joe Tumulty and the Wilson Era*, 69.

66. Spero, *Labor Movement in a Government Industry*, 186-7; Norwood, *Labor's Flaming Youth*, 164.

67. E. N. Nockels to Honorable A. S. Burleson, July 8, 1918, in NARA RG 28, General Correspondence, Box 39.

68. Julia S. O'Connor, "History of the Organized Telephone Operators' Movement, Part IV," *The Union Telephone Operator* 1, no. 4 (May 1921): 15; In Simpson, "Trade Union Organization among the Telephone Operators in the United States," 16; Norwood, *Labor's Flaming Youth*; O'Connor, "History of the Organized Telephone Operators' Movement, Part IV," 15.

69. Norwood, *Labor's Flaming Youth*, 162–163; Archibald M. McIsaac, *The Order of Railroad Telegraphers* (Princeton, NJ: Princeton University Press, 1933), 34, 47; Downey, *Telegraph Messenger Boys*, 178–180.

70. The Postmaster General's close and continuing ties to Theodore Vail, his "industrial advisor," receive careful treatment in Grace Palladino, *Dreams of Dignity, Workers of Vision: A History of the International Brotherhood of Electrical Workers* (Washington,

DC: International Brotherhood of Electrical Workers, 1991), 109–115; "David J. Lewis Resigns from Wire Control Board," *Telephony*, March 13, 1919, 17; Palladino, *Dreams of Dignity*, 112; K. Austin Kerr, *American Railroad Politics 1914-1920: Rates, Wages, and Efficiency* (Pittsburgh: University of Pittsburgh Press, 1968); Norwood, *Labor's Flaming Youth*, 181; *News* (Providence, RI) to Joseph Patrick Tumulty, April 16, 1919, in Arthur S. Link, ed., *The Papers of Woodrow Wilson, Vol. 57, April 5-22, 1919* (Princeton, NJ: Princeton University Press, 1967), 425; "Intervene to End Telephone Strike," *New York Times*, April 19, 1919, 6.

71. Norwood, *Labor's Flaming Youth*, 193.

72. "Fears Censorship in Wire Control," *New York Times*, July 12, 1918, 1, 8; "Strive to Allay Censorship Fear," *New York Times*, July 13, 1918: 1, 5; James R. Mock, *Censorship 1917* (Princeton, NJ: Princeton University Press, 1941), 73–93. A masterful recent study focusing on propaganda but including significant material on censorship is John Maxwell Hamilton, *Manipulating the Masses: Woodrow Wilson and the Birth of American Propaganda* (Baton Rouge, LA: Louisiana State University Press, 2020) (for press criticism of Burleson's censorship, 342–345). See also, Donald Johnson, "Wilson, Burleson, and Censorship in the First World War," *Journal of Southern History* 28, no. 1 (February 1962): 46–58; John Sayer, "Art and Politics, Dissent and Repression: *The Masses* Magazine versus The Government, 1917-1918," *American Journal of Legal History* 32, no. 1 (January 1988): 42–78; and May, *In Time of War*, 162–190; Samuel Gompers to Woodrow Wilson, April 23, 1919, in Arthur S. Link, *The Papers of Woodrow Wilson, Vol. 58, April 23–May 9, 1919* (Princeton, NJ: Princeton University Press, 1988), 48–53. See also, "Bans Propaganda by Wire Workers," *New York Times*, April 23, 1919, 19; "New Charges by Burleson," *New York Times*, April 25, 1919, 17; "Asserts Burleson Resorts to Trick," *New York Times*, April 26, 1919, 13; "Burleson Gives the Lie," *New York Times*, April 26, 1919, 13; May, *In the Name of War*, 50–51.

73. May, *In the Name of War*, 45, 52; Danielian, *AT&T*, 243–265.

74. "Court Continues Bar on 'Phone Rate Rise," *New York Times*, April 3, 1919, 18; "Rules Burleson Cannot Fix Rates within a State," *New York Times*, April 27, 1919, 1; Joseph Patrick Tumulty to Woodrow Wilson, May 8, 1919, in Link, *Papers of Woodrow Wilson, Vol. 58*, 561; "Must Now Raise Telephone Rates," *New York Times*, April 22, 1919, 24; "On all personal telephone bills that are being sent throughout the country there is a notice attached that increases are made necessary by reason of the action of the Postmaster General." Joseph Patrick Tumulty to Woodrow Wilson, May 5, 1919, in Link, *Papers of Woodrow Wilson, Vol. 58*, 460.

75. "Mackay Assails Higher Wire Rates," *New York Times*, April 2, 1919, 20; "Postal Says Higher Rates Are Illegal," *New York Times*, April 28, 1919, 6; Joseph Patrick Tumulty to Woodrow Wilson, May 9, 1919, in Link, *Papers of Woodrow Wilson, Vol. 58*, 602.

76. Blum, *Joe Tumulty*, 158–159, 186; "Denies Employing Convicts," *New York Times*, April 27, 1919, 1, 3; Gompers to Wilson in Link, *Papers of Woodrow Wilson, Vol. 58*, 51; "Burleson Charges Zone Law Intrigue," *New York Times*, April 24, 1919, 1, 3.

77. "Telegraphers Get Sanction for Strike," *New York Times*, April 20, 1919, 5. The ensuing strike by CTUA failed early in July. Conner, *National War Labor Board*, 166–167.

78. Blum, *Joe Tumulty*, 169–199; In May, *In the Name of War*, 99; This big business group included AT&T, Western Union, and the rest of the telecommunications industry. NARA RG 28, Records of the Post Office Department, Office of the Solicitor, Records Relating to Operation of Telephone, Telegraph and Cable Companies by the Postmaster General, 1918–1921, General Correspondence Box 38, War Service Executive Committee of American Industries,, Joseph H. Defrees, Chairman, to Albert S. Burleson, December 31, 1918, reporting results of the Reconstruction Congress of American Industries, Atlantic City, December 3–6, 1918, resolved that "We are opposed to government ownership and operation of telegraphs, telephones, and cables."
79. Gompers to Wilson in Link, *Papers of Woodrow Wilson, Vol. 58*, 50.
80. A second cable on April 27 supplied a text of the statement Burleson hoped to release to this effect. Albert Sidney Burleson to Woodrow Wilson, April 24, 1919, in Link, *Papers of Woodrow Wilson, Vol. 58*, 106; Albert Sidney Burleson to Woodrow Wilson, April 27, 1919, in Link, *Papers of Woodrow Wilson, Vol. 58*, 176; Blum, *Joe Tumulty*, 196; Joseph Patrick Tumulty to Woodrow Wilson, April 25, 1919, in Link, *Papers of Woodrow Wilson, Vol. 58*, 145; Joseph Patrick Tumulty to Woodrow Wilson, April 25, 1919, in Link, *Papers of Woodrow Wilson, Vol. 58*, 145–146; Woodrow Wilson to Albert Sidney Burleson, April 28, 1919, in Link, *Papers of Woodrow Wilson, Vol. 58*, 215; "Burleson Advises Return of Cables and Wire Systems," *New York Times*, April 29, 1919, 1, 6; "Directs Return of Ocean Cables to Owners Friday," *New York Times*, April 30, 1919, 1, 5.
81. Albert Sidney Burleson to Woodrow Wilson, May 2, 1919, in Link, *Papers of Woodrow Wilson, Vol. 58*, 365.
82. Norwood, *Labor's Flaming Youth*, 183; The Merchants' Association of New York, "I: Opposing Government Ownership and Operation of Public Utilities; II: Advocating Exclusive Regulation of All Railroads by the Federal Government," November 1916, 5; See "Mr. Burleson Returns the Wires," *Literary Digest*, June 21, 1919, 17; and "Doubtful Future of the Wires," *Literary Digest*, August 23, 1919, 14. Thanks to James Katz for these references; "Government Operation," *New York Times*, April 20, 1919, Section 3, 1; "Government Operation," *New York Times*, April 20, 1919, Section 3, 1; "Mr. Burleson's Adventure," *New York Times*, April 30, 1919, 10.
83. "Illinois Laborites' Radical Platform," *New York Times*, April 13, 1919, Section 2, 1; "Georgians Want Burleson Ousted," *New York Times*, April 18, 1919, 6; "Telegraphers Get Sanction for Strike," *New York Times*, April 20, 1919, 5; "Burleson Must Go, Gompers Declares," *New York Times*, April 27, 1919, 3; For example, according to S. J. Small, former president of the CTUA, "an insistent campaign throughout the country in favor of government ownership" of the telegraph would "be carried up and into the 1920 Presidential campaign." "Wiremen Favor U.S. Ownership," *Washington Herald*, May 5, 1919, NARA RG 28, Special Reports Box 223; James Weinstein, *The Decline of Socialism in America, 1912–1925* (New Brunswick: Rutgers University Press, 1984), 225, 229, 236; Julia S. O'Connor, "History of the Organized Telephone Operators' Movement," *The Union Telephone Operator* 1, no. 6 (July 1921): 18, 19;

Julia S. O'Connor, "The British Telephonist: Her Work, Her Wages and Her Union, Part II," *The Union Telephone Operator* 2, no. 1 (January 1922): 20.
84. John Brooks, *Telephone: The First Hundred Years* (New York: Harper & Row, 1976), 159.
85. "Confidential to the Directors," AT&T-NJ, Box 1, Government Control—Confidential Report to Directors—1919, 1; "Report of the U.S. Postmaster, 1919," 23, in Laidler, *Public Ownership*, 27; Norwood, *Labor's Flaming Youth*, 254–300; Schacht, *Making of Telephone Unionism*, 6–48; Richard Gillespie, *Manufacturing Knowledge: A History of the Hawthorne Experiments* (Cambridge: Cambridge University Press, 1991). In this, the American experience was not altogether exceptional. As the socialist Harry Laidler stated in 1924, it was not only the United States that had recently witnessed "the powerful pressure brought to bear by the big business interest to revert to private enterprise, and to restore their ancient privileges." Nor was it solely in the United States that this "swing to reaction" had weakened and impaired "the whole edifice of collective control." Laidler, *Public Ownership*, 29.
86. Spero, *Labor Movement in a Government Industry*, viii.

Chapter 4

1. *Munn v. Illinois*, 94 U.S. 113 (1876). For historical context, see also, Thomas K. McCraw, *Prophets of Regulation* (Cambridge, MA: Belknap Press of Harvard University Press, 1984); *Munn v. Illinois*, 113, 130; see also, Jonathan E. Nuechterlein and Philip J. Weiser, *Digital Crossroads: American Telecommunications Policy in the Internet Age* (Cambridge, MA: MIT Press, 2005), 537 n9; *Verizon Communications Inc. v. FCC*, 535 U.S. 467 (2002), in Nuechterlein and Weiser, *Digital Crossroads*, 47. Nuechterlein and Weiser state that public utilities were "commercial enterprises charged with providing an essential public service and subject to pervasive regulation to protect the public interest."
2. David J. Goldberg, *Discontented America: The United States in the 1920s* (Baltimore: Johns Hopkins University Press, 1999); Irving Bernstein, *The Lean Years: The American Worker, 1920–1933* (Chicago: Haymarket Books, 2010).
3. William J. Novak, "The Public Utility Idea and the Origins of Modern Business Regulation," in Naomi R. Lamoreaux and William J. Novak eds., *Corporations and American Democracy* (Cambridge, MA: Harvard University Press, 2017), 173, 175.
4. James William Spurlock, "The Bell Telephone Laboratories and the Military-Industrial Complex: The Jewett-Buckley Years, 1925–1951" (Ph.D. diss., George Washington University, 2007).
5. Albert Sidney Burleson to Woodrow Wilson, May 7, 1919, in Arthur S. Link, ed., *Papers of Woodrow Wilson, Volume 58* (Princeton, NJ: Princeton University Press, 1988), 532–533; Burleson to Wilson, May 7, 1919, in Link, *Papers of Woodrow Wilson, Volume 58*, 532–533.

6. A. S. Burleson, Postmaster General, to Honorable John A. Moon, House of Representatives, May 22, 1919, in US FCC, Special Investigation, Docket No. 1, *Report on Control of Telephone Communications*, "Appendix A," "Data Relating to Federal Control of the Bell Telephone System, August 1, 1918 to July 31, 1919," June 15, 1937, 134–135, National Archives and Records Administration (hereafter NARA), RG 173, Box 67, Exhibit 2096B.
7. 36 Stat. 539. See also, I. L. Sharfman, *The Interstate Commerce Commission: A Study in Administrative Law and Procedure, Part One* (New York: The Commonwealth Fund, 1931), 52–70; Ari Hoogenboom and Olive Hoogenboom, *A History of the ICC: From Panacea to Palliative* (New York: W.W. Norton, 1976), 30; *Houston, East and West Texas Railway Company v. United States. Texas and Pacific Railway Company v. United States*, 234 U.S. 1913 342, 350, in William R. Childs, "State Regulators and Pragmatic Federalism in the United States, 1889-1945," *Business History Review* 25, no. 4 (Winter 2001): 715; Henk Brands and Evan T. Leo, *The Law and Regulation of Telecommunication Carriers* (Boston: Artech House, 1999), 41–48; Childs, "State Regulators and Pragmatic Federalism," 719; James Schwoch, *The American Radio Industry and Its Latin American Activities, 1900–1939* (Urbana, IL: University of Illinois Press, 1990); Dwayne Winseck and Robert Pike, *Empire and Communications* (Durham, NC: Duke University Press, 2007); Jill Hills, *The Struggle for Control of International Telecommunications* (Urbana, IL: University of Illinois Press, 2002); Jonathan Reed Winkler, *Nexus: Strategic Communications and American Security in World War I* (Cambridge, MA: Harvard University Press, 2008).
8. T. N. Vail to Honorable A. S. Burleson, November 23, 1918, in FCC, Special Investigation, NARA RG 173, Box 67, Exhibit 2096B, 84; A. S. Burleson to Union N. Bethell, Chairman, U.S. Telegraph and Telephone Operating Board, March 19, 1918, in US FCC, Special Investigation, *Report on Control of Telephone Communications*, "Appendix A," "Data Relating to Federal Control of the Bell Telephone System, August 1, 1918 to July 31, 1919," June 15, 1937, NARA RG 173, Box 67, Exhibit 2096B, 84; In N. R. Danielian, *A.T.&T.: The Story of Industrial Conquest* (New York: The Vanguard Press, 1939), 264.
9. T. N. Vail to W. T. Gentry, October 22, 1918, in FCC, Special Investigation, NARA RG 173, Box 67, Exhibit 2096B, Exhibit 2096B: 82; Danielian, *A.T.&T.*, 254–260; Theodore N. Vail, February 17, 1919, in FCC, *Telephone Investigation, Report on Control of Telephone Communications*, "Appendix A," "Data Relating to Federal Control of the Bell Telephone System, August 1, 1918 to July 31, 1919, 15 June 1937," NARA RG 173, Box 67 Exhibit 2096B, 130; FCC, *Telephone Investigation, Report on Control of Telephone Communications*, "Appendix A," "Data Relating to Federal Control of the Bell Telephone System, August 1, 1918 to July 31, 1919," June 15, 1937, NARA RG 173, Box 67 Exhibit 2096B, Section 5, 63–130; see especially, Theodore N. Vail, February 17, 1919, 130; Theodore N. Vail, memorandum dated "12/8," to Honorable A. S. Burleson, January 13, 1919, in NARA RG 28 Records of the Post Office Department, Box 38 Correspondence; T. N. Vail to Charles Frances Adams, Esq., May 3, 1919, in FCC Special Investigation, NARA RG 173, Box 67, Exhibit 2096B, 131. On Adams, see McCraw, *Prophets of Regulation*, 1–56.

10. Office of the Postmaster General, Letter to Honorable Thomas R. Marshall, Senate of the United States of America, March 4, 1918, 9, in Albert Sidney Burleson Papers, Library of Congress, Washington, DC. Thanks to Richard John for this reference; Danielian, a tough-minded critic, still conceded that Burleson's "disappointment . . . must have been deep and painful" as his hope faded that he would gain sufficient time to demonstrate the efficiency of a postalized system. Danielian, *A.T.&T.*, 269; *First Report of the Telephone Committee on Telephone Rate Standardization*, December 12, 1918, 3, in U.S. District Court for the District of Columbia Civil Action No., 74-1698, *United States of America, Plaintiff, v. American Telephone and Telegraph Company; Western Electric Company, Inc.; and Bell Telephone Laboratories, Inc., Defendants*, March 10, 1980, Defendants' Third Statement of Contentions and Proof, vol. 1, 235; *Report of the Postmaster General on Administration of the Telephone Systems, First Report*, October 31, 1919, 11, in Defendants' Third Statement of Contentions and Proof, vol. 1, 236; *A Report of the Telephone Toll Rate Subcommittee of National Association of Railroad and Utility Commissioners and Federal Communications Commission FCC-NARUC, Message Toll Telephone Rates and Disparities* (Washington, DC, July 1951), 101.
11. Hunt Chipley to Mr. Guernsey, August 4, 1918, in FCC, *Telephone Investigation, Report on Control of Telephone Communications*, Appendix A, Data Relating to Federal Control of the Bell Telephone System, August 1, 1918 to July 31, 1919, June 15, 1937, NARA RG 173, Box 67 Exhibit 2096B, 76; Childs, "State Regulators and Pragmatic Federalism," 701-738.
12. Danielian, *A.T.&T.*, 269; "He Will Apologize for Introducing Wire Control Law," *New York World*, April 7, 1919.
13. N. T. Guernsey to Honorable W. H. Lamar, March 14, 1919, in FCC Special Investigation, NARA RG 173, Box 67, Exhibit 2096B, 101; N. T. Guernsey, Memorandum for U.N. Bethell, Esq., March 31, 1919, in FCC Special Investigation, NARA RG 173, Box 67, Exhibit 2096B, 104; Hunt Chipley to N. T. Guernsey, April 23, 1919, in FCC Special Investigation, NARA RG 173, Box 67, Exhibit 2096B, 112-113; National Association of Railway and Utilities Commissioners (NARUC), *Proceedings of Thirty-First Annual Convention, Held at Indianapolis, Indiana, October 14-17, 1919* (New York: Law Reporting Company, 1920), 70; NARUC, *Convention*, 70.
14. Danielian, *A.T.&T.*, 261; 25 U.S. 163 (1919). See also, Christopher N. May, *In the Name of War: Judicial Review and the War Powers since 1918* (Cambridge, MA: Harvard University Press, 1989), 54-59; 25 U.S. 163 (1919). The quotes are from the ruling in Report on Control of Telephone Communications, Appendix A, Data Relating to Federal Control of the Bell Telephone System, August 1, 1918 to July 31, 1919, June 15, 1937, FCC, Special Investigation, NARA RG 173, Box 67, Exhibit 2096B, 123, 120; Danielian, *A.T.&T.*, 264.
15. Danielian, *A.T.&T.*, 269; Danielian, *A.T.&T.*, 268.
16. Eugene S. Wilson to N. T. Guernsey, June 5, 1919 (telegram) in FCC Special Investigation, NARA RG 173, Box 67, Exhibit 2096B, 147; H. J. Pettengill to H. B. Thayer (telegram), June 10, 1919, FCC Special Investigation, NARA RG 173, Box 67, Exhibit 2096B, 156; E. S. Bloom to N. C. Kingsbury (telegram), June 10, 1919, in FCC Special Investigation, NARA RG 173, Box 67, Exhibit 2096B, 157; Ben S. Read

to N. C. Kingsbury (telegram) June 9, 1919, in FCC Special Investigation, NARA RG 173, Box 67, Exhibit 2096B, 157–158; Ben S. Red to Kingsbury, June 9, 1919, FCC Special Investigation, NARA RG 173, Box 67, Exhibit 2096B, 158–159; Charles B. Hill (letter), June 4, 1919, in FCC Special Investigation, NARA RG 173, Box 67, Exhibit 2096B, 162–163; NARUC, *Convention*, 227–228. "In some states," charged President Elmquist, "98 percent is local." NARUC, *Convention*, 229.

17. I. L. Sharfman, *The Interstate Commerce Commission: A Study in Administrative Law and Procedure, Part Two* (New York: The Commonwealth Fund, 1931), 108; Dill in 69th Cong., 1st Sess., Committee on Interstate Commerce, Hearings on S. 1 and S. 1754, "Radio Control, January 8–9, 1926" (Washington, DC: Government Printing Office, 1926), 215. A tally of the ICC's actions throughout its tenure on telephone and telegraph matters is given in 71st Cong., 2d Sess., "Commission on Communication," *Hearings before the Committee on Interstate Commerce on S.6, A Bill to Provide for the Regulation of the Transmission of Intelligence by Wire or Wireless, Part 10, December 4–17, 1929* (Washington, DC: Government Printing Office, 1930), 1572–1581; Sharfman, Interstate Commerce Commission Part Two, 278–287. A postal telegraph executive testified before the National Recovery Administration in 1934 that, "In 1914, at the instigation of the Postal Telegraph, the Interstate Commerce Commission started an investigation of leased [telegraph] lines and finally, in 1918, the Commission published its findings." The study can be consulted, but the documentation on which it was based and records detailing the ICC's deliberative process have been lost, according to NARA. U.S. National Recovery Administration, *Hearing on the Telegraph Communication Industry, May 2, 1934, vol. 1* (Washington, DC: Jesse L. Ward, Official Reporter), 54.

18. See, for example, 71st Cong., 2d Sess., Commission on Communications, *Hearings before the Committee on Interstate Commerce On S.6, Part 15, January 29–31 and February 1–8, 1930* (Washington, DC: Government Printing Office, 1930), 2121. The quote is from Childs, *State Regulators and Pragmatic Federalism*, 735; F. B. MacKinnon in Commission on Communications, *Hearings before the Committee on Interstate Commerce On S.6*, 2121.

19. Alan Dawley, *Struggles for Justice: Social Responsibility and the Liberal State* (Cambridge, MA: Belknap Press of Harvard University Press, 1991); James T. Patterson, *The New Deal and the States: Federalism in Transition* (Princeton, NJ: Princeton University Press, 1969).

20. Alan Stone, *Public Service Liberalism: Telecommunications and Transitions in Public Policy* (Princeton, NJ: Princeton University Press, 1991), 218; Ellsworth Nichols, *Public Utility Service and Discrimination* (Rochester, NY: Public Utilities Reports, Inc., 1928); NARUC v. FCC, 525 F.2d 630 (D.C. Cir.), cert. denied, 425 US 992 (1976); and discussion in Henk Brands and Evan T. Leo, *The Law and Regulation of Telecommunications Carriers* (Boston: Artech House, 1999), 122–133.

21. Bancroft Gherardi and F. B. Jewett, "Telephone Communication System of the United States," *Bell System Technical Journal* 9 (January 1930): 63; Gherardi and Jewett, "Telephone Communication System," 43; David Weintraub, "Unemployment and Increasing Productivity," in *National Resources Committee, Technological Trends*

and *National Policy* (Washington, DC: 1937), 77, cited in Bernstein, *Lean Years*, 54; Gherardi and Jewett, "Telephone Communication System," 40.

22. Danielian, *A.T.&T.*, 318; Roland Marchand, *Creating the Corporate Soul: The Rise of Public Relations and Corporate Imagery in American Big Business* (Berkeley, CA: University of California Press, 1998), 48–87; C. M. Bracelen Memorandum for Mr. H. B. Thayer, October 6, 1922, in FCC, Special Investigation, NARA RG 173, Box 13, Exhibits 139–155, Part 1.

23. Stone, *Public Service Liberalism*, 236–237.

24. Robert Britt Horwitz, *The Irony of Regulatory Reform: The Deregulation of American Telecommunications* (New York: Oxford University Press, 1989), 104.

25. James G. Bonbright and Gardiner C. Means, *The Holding Company: Its Public Significance and Its Regulation* (New York: McGraw-Hill, 1932), 141–143; William Dunton Kerr, "Meeting Federal Regulation Half Way," *Telephony* 59, no. 12 (September 17, 1910): 323–324; *1910 Annual Report of the Directors of American Telephone & Telegraph Company to the Stockholders for the Year Ending December 31st, 1910* (New York: American Telephone & Telegraph Company, 1911); *1911 Annual Report of the Directors of American Telephone & Telegraph Company to the Stockholders for the Year Ending December 31st, 1911* (New York: American Telephone & Telegraph Company, 1912); *1912 Annual Report of the Directors of American Telephone & Telegraph Company to the Stockholders for the Year Ending December 31st, 1912* (New York: American Telephone & Telegraph Company, 1913); *1914 Annual Report of the Directors of American Telephone & Telegraph Company to the Stockholders for the Year Ending December 31st, 1913* (New York: American Telephone & Telegraph Company, 1914); *1915 Annual Report of the Directors of American Telephone & Telegraph Company to the Stockholders for the Year Ending December 31st, 1915*(New York: American Telephone & Telegraph Company, 1916); *1916 Annual Report of the Directors of American Telephone & Telegraph Company to the Stockholders for the Year Ending December 31st, 1916* (New York: American Telephone & Telegraph Company, 1917); Stuart Ewen, *PR!: A Social History of Spin* (New York: Basic Books, 1996); Marchand, *Creating the Corporate Soul*, 48–87. AT&T's precocious and enveloping public relations strategies were documented by the Federal Communications Commission. FCC, Special Investigation, NARA RG 173, Boxes 18-22 and Boxes 35-6; *AT&T Annual Report, 1915* (New York: 1916), 38; Noel L. Griese, *Arthur W. Page: Publisher, Public Relations Pioneer, Patriot* (Atlanta: Anvil Publishers, 2001); U.S. Federal Communications Commission, *Proposed Report Telephone Investigation (Pursuant to Public Resolution No. 8 74th Congress)* (Washington, DC: Government Printing Office, 1938).

26. U.S. FCC Accounting Department, Telephone Investigation, Special Investigation Docket No. 1, Exhibit No. 2104, *Report on Comparison of Bell System and Commission Resources, Pursuant to Public Resolution No. 8*, 74th Congress, June 15, 1937, 11. The documentary record compiled by the commission testifies powerfully to AT&T's success during the 1920s and early 1930s in checking state regulation through the courts. See C. M. Bracelen, General Solicitor, "Memorandum for Mr. H. B. Thayer, President," October 6, 1922, "Exhibits Introduced in Hearings before the FCC,"

no. 1. vol. 8, Exhibits 139-155, NARA RG 173, Box 3; and Arthur W. Page, "To All Publicity Managers," June 15, 1933.

27. James W. Sichter, *Separations Procedures in the Telephone Industry: The Historical Origins of a Public Policy*, Publication P-77-2 (Cambridge, MA: Harvard Program on Information Resources Policy, 1981), 43; Federal Communications Commission, Special Investigation, Exhibit 2089A, *Report on American Telephone and Telegraph Company Depreciation Accounting and Engineering Methods. Pursuant to Public Resolution No. 8*, 74th Congress, vol. 1, *Depreciation Accounting Methods: Objectives of Depreciation Accounting, May 25, 1937*, 16-26, 35. NARA RG 173, Box 3. In the three years following denationalization, NARUC's anxiety over the ICC's incarnation of a "paternalistic . . . centralizing tendency" that came "at the expense of the state" was sharply expressed. See "Address of President Carl D. Jackon," in NARUC, *Proceedings of Thirty-fourth Annual Convention Held at Detroit, Michigan, November 14-17, 1922* (New York: State Law Reporting Co., 1923), 7-11; Plaintiff's Third Statement of Contentions and Proof, Part Six, 1960-1964, paras. 1-16.

28. Robert Garnet, *The Telephone Enterprise* (Baltimore: Johns Hopkins, 1985), 150; During this era, opposing pressures sometimes became intense as reformers sought to recast telephone company boundaries along state lines to accommodate more effective oversight of the capital base upon which rates were determined. In the East and the Midwest, the force of this pressure sometimes compelled AT&T to abandon plans to combine its local operating companies into interstate supergroups. In the West, by contrast, AT&T won critical battles as multistate operating companies were forged and state regulators sometimes consigned to a "passive" status. Garnet, *Telephone Enterprise*, 146-152, 150; George B. Leverett to President Frederick P. Fish, October 17, 1901, in U.S. Federal Communications Commission, *A Report of the Federal Communications Commission on the Investigation of the Telephone Industry in the United States [Pursuant to Public Res. No. 8, 74th Cong.]* (Washington, DC: Government Printing Office, 1939), 352; MacDowell, *People's Network*, 227-258; J. Warren Stehman, *A Financial History of the American Telephone and Telegraph Company* (Boston: Houghton Mifflin, 1925), 197-198. One-quarter of AT&T's increase in stock and bond holdings of its operating companies occurred during the three years 1917-1919. Stehman, *Financial History*, 184.

29. FCC, *Report on the Telephone Investigation*, 176; Stehman, *Financial History*, 265, 118; Thayer in *NARUC Convention 1922*, 129-31, quotes at 129; Stehman, *Financial History*, 266; NARUC and FCC, *Message Toll Telephone Rates and Disparities: A Report* (Washington, DC, 1951), 15; Bonbright and Means, *The Holding Company*, 142-143; Bonbright and Means, *The Holding Company*, 200.

30. FCC, *Report on the Telephone Investigation*, 155-156; Mary O. Furner, "Knowing Capitalism: Public Investigation and the Labor Question in the Long Progressive Era," in Mary O. Furner and Barry Supple eds., *The State and Economic Knowledge: The American and British Experiences* (Cambridge: Woodrow Wilson International Center and Cambridge University Press, 1990), 276; Thayer in *NARUC Convention 1922*, Detroit, 133.

31. John V. Langdale, "The Growth of Long-Distance Telephony in the Bell System, 1875–1907," *Journal of Historical Geography* 4, no. 2 (1978): 145–159; 77th Cong., 1st Sess. Pursuant to S. Res. 95.—76th Congress, *Hearings Before a Subcommittee of the Committee on Interstate Commerce, Study of the Telegraph Industry, Part 1, May 9–29, 1941* (Washington, DC: Government Printing Office, 1941), 10–11; M. D. Fagen, ed., *A History of Engineering & Science in the Bell System, The Early Years (1875–1925)* (Bell Telephone Laboratories, Inc., 1975); Arthur F. Rose, "Twenty Years of Carrier Telephony," *Bell Telephone Quarterly* 17, no. 4 (October 1938): 245–263. As a result, regulators observed in 1951, while Bell operating company investment per circuit mile in and around local exchanges had declined only a little, rapid technological innovation in carrier systems and coaxial cable within AT&T Long Lines' network had reduced its investment per circuit mile from about $109 in 1943 to less than $60 in 1950. Continued development of microwave radio relays and improvements in coaxial cable techniques allowed regulators to project that "further line haul economies" were in store. FCC-NARUC, *Message Toll Telephone Rates and Disparities*, 282.

32. Milton L. Mueller, Jr., *Universal Service: Competition, Interconnection, and Monopoly in the Making of the American Telephone System* (Washington, DC: MIT Press and the AEI Press, 1997), 41; FCC-NARUC, *Message Toll Telephone Rates and Disparities*, 54.

33. FCC-NARUC, *Message Toll Telephone Rates and Disparities*, 90; FCC-NARUC, *Message Toll Telephone Rates and Disparities*, 63.

34. Fagen, *History of Engineering & Science*, 1004, Figure P-1, "United States Telephone Statistics."

35. Horwitz, *Irony of Telecommunications Reform*, 133.

36. FCC, *Report on the Telephone Investigation*, 360–361; Walter Gifford in 71st Cong., 2d. Sess., Commission on Communications, *Hearings Before the Committee on Interstate Commerce on S.6, Part 14, January 17–31, 1930* (Washington, DC: Government Printing Office, 1930), 1990. Slightly more than two-thirds of all toll revenues came from intrastate long-distance calls, and most intrastate toll calls were to points within a radius of 50 miles of the initiating local exchange. Joseph B. Eastman, Commissioner, Interstate Commerce Commission, in 71st Cong., 2d Sess., Commission on Communications, *Hearings Before the Committee on Interstate Commerce On S.6, Part 12, January 9–11, 1930* (Washington, DC: Government Printing Office, 1930), 1586; F. B. MacKinnon, in U.S. Congress, Senate, 71st Cong., 2d Sess., Commission on Communications, *Hearings Before the Committee on Interstate Commerce On S.6, Part 15, January 29–31 and February 1–8, 1930* (Washington, DC: Government Printing Office, 1930), 2121.

37. U.S. Federal Communications Commission, *Proposed Report Telephone Investigation (Pursuant to Public Resolution No. 8 74th Congress)* (Washington, DC: Government Printing Office, 1938), 685; FCC, *Report on the Telephone Investigation*, 352.

38. FCC, *Proposed Report on the Telephone Investigation*, 656; Carl I. Wheat, "The Regulation of Interstate Telephone Rates," *Harvard Law Review* 51 (March 1938), reprinted in 75th Cong., 3d Sess., Document No. 176, "The Regulation of Interstate Telephone Rates," presented by Mr. Bone, April 20, 1938 (Washington, DC: Government Printing Office, 1938), 18, 20; FCC, *Proposed Report on the*

Telephone Investigation, 682; FCC, *Proposed Report on the Telephone Investigation*, 660–661.

39. Wheat, "The Regulation of Interstate Telephone Rates," 2. For a fullblown critique of public utility regulation, see the well-known article by Horace M. Gray, "The Passing of the Public Utility Concept," *Journal of Land and Public Utility Economics* 16 (February 1940): 8–20; *Public Service Commission v. Chesapeake and Potomac Tel. Co.*, P.U.R. 1925B, 545, 566 (Md. Pub. Serv. Comm'n 1924), in Plaintiff's Third Statement of Contentions and Proof, Part 6, 1952, para. 64; Stehman, *Financial History of the Telephone Industry*, 256; Sichter, *Separations Procedures in the Telephone Industry*, 92.

40. Memorandum for Mr. J. H. Ray, General Solicitor, New York, April 3, 1929, in NARA RG 173, Box 10, Summary of Action on State Legislation, Part 2; FCC, *Proposed Report on the Telephone Investigation*, x–xi; Frederick D Drake and Lynn R. Nelson, "Introduction," *States' Rights and American Federalism: A Documentary History* (Westport: Greenwood Press, 1999), xx. For NARUC, see especially NARUC, *Convention 1922*, 119–151; and NARUC, *Proceedings of 37th Annual Convention Held at Washington, DC, October 13–16, 1925* (New York: NARUC, 1926), 41–75.

41. Walter S. Gifford in 71st Cong., 2d Sess., Commission on Communications, *Hearings before the Committee on Interstate Commerce, S.6, Part 14, January 17–31, 1930* (Washington, DC: Government Printing Office, 1930), 1989–2059; Eastman, in U.S. Cong., Senate. 71st Cong., 2d Sess., Commission on Communications, *Hearings before the Committee on Interstate Commerce, S.6, Part 12, 9–11 January 1930* (Washington, DC: Government Printing Office, 1930), 1565–1597; 73d Cong., 2d Sess., H.R. Report No. 1273, "Preliminary Report on Communications Companies," submitted April 18, 1934, pursuant to H.R. Res. 59, 72d Cong., 1st Sess. (1932), and H.J. Res. 572, 72d Cong., 2d Sess. (1933), xvi.

42. Plaintiff's Third Statement of Contentions and Proof, Part 6, 1965, para. 17; FCC, *Proposed Report on the Telephone Investigation*, x; Wheat, "Regulation of Interstate Telephone Rates," 2.

43. Honorable Clyde M. Reed, Chairman, Public Utility Commission of Kansas, "The Viewpoint and Interest of the Public," in NARUC, *Convention 1922*, 144, 145, 150, 151.

44. H. B. Thayer, President of AT&T, Address, in NARUC, *Convention 1922*, 128; Federal Communications Commission, Telephone Rate and Research Department, Telephone Investigation, "The Problem of the 'Rate of Return' in Public Utility Regulation with Special Reference to the Long Lines Department of the American Telephone and Telegraph Company" (Washington, DC: FCC, 1938), 1, NARA, RG 173, Box 3.

45. Gifford in *Senate Interstate Commerce Committee Hearings on S. 6, January 1930*, quotes at 2016, 2010, and 2004, respectively.

46. FCC, *Proposed Report on the Telephone Investigation*, 495–497; *53d Annual Convention of the American Federation of Labor, Washington, D.C., October 6–10, 1933, Report of Proceedings, Resolution No. 51* (Washington, DC: American Federation of Labor, 1933), 177.

47. Meighan Maguire, "The Local Dynamics of Telephone System Development: The San Francisco Exchange, 1893–1919" (Ph.D. diss., University of California San Diego, 2000), 265; Maguire, "The Local Dynamics of Telephone System Development," 276, 283 (quote), 279. Rate increases were forthcoming, but mostly to small, non-Bell carriers.

48. 71st Cong., 2d Sess., Committee on Interstate Commerce, *On S. 6 A Bill to Provide for the Regulation of the Transmission of Intelligence by Wire or Wireless*, vol. 2 (Washington, DC: Government Printing Office, 1930; *Annual Report of Railroad Commission of the State of California, July 1 1924, to June 30, 1925*, 128. Five years later, CEO Walter Gifford sought to justify his company's massive capital outlays by linking them to this network industry's intrinsic character: "the telephone business is a strange business in that the more business we do the more the cost per unit to do it." Gifford in *Senate Interstate Commerce Committee Hearings on S. 6, January 1930*, 2030. This point was reestablished for scholars by Milton L. Mueller, "The Switchboard Problem: Scale, Signaling, and Organization in Manual Telephone Switching, 1877–1897," *Technology & Culture* 30, no. 3 (July 1989): 534–560.

49. In 71st Cong., 2d Sess., *Hearings before the Committee on Interstate Commerce on S.6, Commission on Communications, January 17–31, 1930* (Washington, DC: Government Printing Office, 1930), 1940 ff.

50. New York Public Service Commission, *Annual Report for the Year 1930, Volume 1* (Albany: J. B. Lyon Co., 1931), 217–218. This extended rate case may also be followed by consulting, at the Franklin D. Roosevelt Presidential Library (hereafter FDR Library), the Leland Olds Papers, Box 18 Folder, "New York Telephone Co. Rates (1930)."

51. "Starts Phone Rate Fight," *New York Times*, November 13, 1919, 17; "Expect Hard Fight on Phone Rate Rise," *New York Times*, August 27, 1920, 26; "Hylan Calls Phone Rate Rise Gouging," *New York Times*, September 20, 1920, 27; "Orders State-Wide Cut in Phone Rates; Five Per Cent. Here," *New York Times*, March 4, 1922, 1, 4.

52. "City and Labor Join Fight on Phone Rise," *New York Times*, December 29, 1925, 25; "Cities Join Fight on Phone Rates," *New York Times*, May 14, 1926, 21.

53. "Cities Join to Fight Higher Phone Rates," *New York Times*, September 4, 1926, 1; Public Utility Rate League to Honorable Franklin D. Roosevelt, February 5, 1930, FDR Library, Franklin Delano Roosevelt, New York State Office of the Governor 1929–1932 Papers, Record Group 18-1, Roll 117; State of New York Executive Chamber, Albany, "For Immediate Release, Guernsey T. Cross, Secretary to the Governor, 'Governor Roosevelt Today Issued the Following Statement,' January 31, 1930," FDR Library, Franklin Delano Roosevelt, New York State Office of the Governor 1929–1932 Papers, Record Group 18-1, Roll 117.

54. "Phone Rate Inquiry Fills 31,000 Pages," *New York Times*, January 22, 1928, 44.

55. Daniel R. Fusfeld, *The Economic Thought of Franklin D. Roosevelt and the Origins of the New Deal* (New York: Columbia University Press, 1954), 145, quoting letter from Roosevelt to Frederic A. Delano, November 22, 1929; Frank Friedel, *Franklin D. Roosevelt: A Rendezvous with Destiny* (New York: Little, Brown, 1990), 57–58. For Roosevelt's own portrayal of his gubernatorial engagement with utilities, see

Samuel I. Rosenman, *The Public Papers and Addresses of Franklin D. Roosevelt, Volume One, The Genesis of the New Deal 1928-1932* (New York Random House: 1938), chapters 4 and 7; Ernest Gruening, *The Public Pays: A Study of Power Propaganda* (New York: Vanguard Press, 1931); Thomas K. McCraw, *TVA and the Power Fight 1933-1939* (Philadelphia: J. B. Lippincott, 1971); Danielian, *A.T.&T.*, 291-333; AT&T-NJ, Box 1066, Ellsworth—James D.—Biography—1928, and Memoranda—1929-1931.

56. W. A. Warn, "Utility Board Seeks Some Way to Block Higher Phone Rates," *New York Times*, January 30, 1930, 1, 2; W. A. Warn, "Roosevelt Hunting Aggressive Chief for Utility Board," *New York Times*, February 6, 1930, 1.

57. Rosenman, *The Public Papers and Addresses of Franklin D. Roosevelt, Volume 1*, 731; "Heeds Roosevelt in Phone Rate Move," *New York Times*, February 8, 1930, 1; "Phone Rates Cut 20 Per Cent by Utility Board's Order, Making a $3,000,000 Slash," *New York Times*, February 1, 1930, 1; "Utility Board Asks Extension of Power," *New York Times*, February 16, 1930, 12; Bernard Bellush, *Franklin D. Roosevelt as Governor of New York* (New York: Columbia University Press, 1955), 261; Franklin D. Roosevelt, "State of New York Executive Chamber, Albany, for Immediate Release, Guernsey T. Cross, Secretary to the Governor, Governor Roosevelt Today Issued the Following Statement," January 31, 1930, in Franklin Delano Roosevelt, New York State Office of the Governor 1929-1932 Papers, Record Group 18-1, Roll 117; Franklin D. Roosevelt, "State of New York Executive Chamber, Albany, For Immediate Release Guernsey T. Cross, Secretary to the Governor, January 27, 1930, to the Legislature," in Franklin Delano Roosevelt, New York State Office of the Governor 1929-1932 Papers, Record Group 18-1, Roll 117; Roosevelt, "Governor Roosevelt Today Issued the Following Statement."; Roosevelt, "Governor Roosevelt Today Issued the Following Statement." I have altered the word sequence and changed "abrogated" to "abrogate." See S. H. Rifkind Secretary to Samuel Roseman [sic] Counsel to Governor, January 25, 1930 (telegram); and F. H. Laguradia [sic] to Honorable Franklin Roosevelt, January 30, 1930 (telegram), S. 3085, 71st Cong., 2d Sess., January 6, 1930, in Roosevelt, "Governor Roosevelt Today Issued the Following Statement." Commonweal suggested that, "Granted the temper of public opinion, he is sure to win his point later, if not now." *The Commonweal*, February 12, 1930, in Roosevelt, "Governor Roosevelt Today Issued the Following Statement."; Governor Franklin D. Roosevelt, Hunts Point Palace, Bronx, New York, October 27, 1930. 9:30 p.m., 4, in FDR Library, Louis Howe Papers, Box 23, Folder "FDR Speeches—Hotel Biltmore 10-27-30 Hunts Point Palace 10-27-30 Advertising Club 10-28-30."

58. In Bellush, *Roosevelt as Governor*, 259.

59. Charles Francis Adams inaugurated the "sunshine commission," as a historian calls the strategy of using regulation to expose the operations of a regulated industry to public view, in Massachusetts in 1869. Thomas K. McCraw, *Prophets of Regulation* (Cambridge, MA: Belknap Press, 1984), 1-56; *Annual Report of the New York Public Service Commission for the Year 1930* (Albany: J.B. Lyon, 1931), 256-257.

60. Albert Lepawsky, *Home Rule for Metropolitan Chicago* (Chicago: University of Chicago Press, 1935) carries the story forward and breaks it down by economic sector.

"The cities of Illinois," wrote one analyst in 1927, "have waged . . . [a] determined and consistent fight . . . for local control of their public utilities." Charles Mayard Kneier, "State Regulation of Public Utilities in Illinois" (Ph.D. diss., University of Illinois at Urbana-Champaign, 1927), *University of Illinois Studies in the Social Sciences* 14, no. 1: 174; J. C. Slippy, *Telephone Appraisal Practice* (Pittsburgh: J. C. Slippy, 1915), 88.

61. Edward W. Bemis, "Report on the Investigation of the Chicago Telephone Company Submitted to the Committee on Gas, Oil, and Electric Light of the City Council, Chicago, Ill.," October 25, 1912, 8.

62. Bemis, *Report on the Investigation*, 9; Bemis, *Report on the Investigation*, 15–16. Bemis's tally of telephones includes most of the suburban lines; Bemis, *Report on the Investigation*, 16.

63. Illinois hosted the public utility commissions of nineteen states when they attempted to challenge Postmaster Burleson's power to set intrastate rates. "Utility Bodies Unite to Oppose Phone Toll Rate," *Chicago Daily Tribune*, January 14, 1919, 9; William Hale Thompson, "Mayor Cites His Record in Plea to Be Returned," *Chicago Daily Tribune*, February 20, 1919, 11; Ralph L. Mahon, "The Telephone in Chicago 1877–1940," Illinois Bell Telephone Management, 1962, 93–94, AT&T-NJ.

64. "'Nickel A Day' and Flat Rate Phones to Go," *Chicago Daily Tribune*, June 7, 1919, 17; "City Prepares to Fight Raise in Phone Rates," *Chicago Daily Tribune*, June 8, 1919, B9; "Council Today Launches Fight on Phone Rates," *Chicago Daily Tribune*, June 9, 1919, 17; "Raised Phone Rates without City Hearing," *Chicago Daily Tribune*, July 24, 1919, 9.

65. State of Illinois, Illinois Commerce Commission, *Illinois Commerce Commission vs. Chicago Telephone Company, Now, Illinois Bell Telephone Company, Relative to Rates*, No. 11894, "Citation," September 13, 1921; Illinois Commerce Commission, Springfield, Illinois, inquiry at the ICC office in Springfield revealed that the official transcript of evidence and arguments (which ran to 4,500 pages by 1923) has been lost; Mahon, "Telephone in Chicago," 93; Oscar Hewett, "Supreme Court Upholds Ban on Phone Rate Cut," *Chicago Daily Tribune*, October 20, 1925, 6; Richard R. John, *Network Nation: Inventing American Telecommunications* (Cambridge, MA: Belknap Press, 2010), 295–299; Illinois Bell Telephone Company, "Rates for Service," *Annual Report 1923* (Chicago: 1924), n.p.; Hewett, "Supreme Court Upholds Ban on Phone Rate Cut," 6.

66. *Smith v. Illinois Bell Telephone Company*, 282 U.S. 133 (1930); *Smith v. Illinois Bell Telephone Company*, 282 U.S. 133 (1930); Brands and Leo, *The Law and Regulation of Telecommunications Carriers*, 48–55.

67. *Lindheimer v. Illinois Bell Telephone Co.*, 292 U.S. 151 (1934).

68. Illinois Bell Telephone Company, *Annual Report 1934* (Chicago: 1935), 8; Illinois Bell Telephone Company, *Report of the Board of Directors 1937* (Chicago: Illinois Bell, 1938), 9; "High Court Will Hear Phone Rate Case Next Week," *Chicago Daily Tribune*, October 9, 1925, 6.

69. Lepawsky, *Home Rule*, 86; "Thompson Asks $513,464 More for Fare Fight," *Chicago Daily Tribune*, June 23, 1920, 1; "Public Service Board May Say, Go to Courts," *Chicago Daily Tribune*, July 2, 1920, 5; "Fare and Phone Fight Costs Us $745,843 In

Year," *Chicago Daily Tribune*, February 2, 1921, 17. Nearly a decade later, the city council awarded $150,000 to corporation counsel to press the litigation for a telephone rate reduction. Oscar Hewitt, "$150,000 Phone Fund Provides Juicy Job List," *Chicago Daily Tribune*, May 23, 1929, 8.

70. *Illinois Commerce Commission vs. Chicago Telephone Company*, 11894, "Interlocutory Order," December 22, 1921, 2; "Resume Fight to Cut Rates of Phone Service," *Chicago Daily Tribune*, June 27, 1923, 9; "Phone Rate Cut Looms; Clash Ends Hearings," *Chicago Daily Tribune*, August 1, 1923, 1; "City Demands Share of Phone Royalties for Subsidiaries," *Chicago Daily Tribune*, May 21, 1932, 5; "Phone Rate Case Ruling Expected Next December," *Chicago Daily Tribune*, October 22, 1930, 30.

71. Mahon, "The Telephone in Chicago," 109.

72. "Suburbs Seek Reduction in Phone Rates," *Chicago Daily Tribune*, March 11, 1927, 31; "Hotels Silence Pay Phones in Rate Deadlock," *Chicago Daily Tribune*, January 3, 1929, 1.

73. Mahon, "The Telephone in Chicago," 125; Illinois Bell Telephone Company, *Annual Report 1930*, 3; Illinois Bell Telephone Company, *Annual Report 1931*, 3; Illinois Bell Telephone Company, *Annual Report 1932*, 5; Illinois Bell Telephone Company, *Annual Report 1933*, 5; Illinois Bell Telephone Company, *Annual Report 1934*, 6; Mahon, "The Telephone in Chicago," 109–110 (quote).

74. In 1933, for example, an AT&T tally of ongoing telephone rate investigations stated, "The Boston Central Labor Union started agitation for reduced rates in December, 1930," and detailed the status of this ongoing proceeding, which was deemed "relatively unimportant" by the carrier's legal department. AT&T, "Telephone Rate Investigations," June 12, 1933, in FCC, Telephone Investigation, NARA RG 173, Box 13; "American Telephone and Telegraph Company," *Fifty-third Annual Convention of the American Federation of Labor 1933, Resolution No. 51*, 177; Edward N. Nockels, in 73d Cong 2d Sess., *Hearings before the Committee on Interstate Commerce on S. 2910, 9–15 March 1934* (Washington, DC: Government Printing Office, 1934), 197–199. On Nockels, see also, Nathan Godfried, *WCFL: Chicago's Voice of Labor, 1926–1978* (Urbana, IL: University of Illinois Press, 1997).

75. Before the Public Service Commission of Wisconsin, "In the Matter of the State-Wide Investigation on the Commission's Own Motion of the Rates, Rules, Services, Practices and Activities of the Wisconsin Telephone Company," Docket 2-U-35, Opinion and Order, decided July 5, 1933, 104–105; "Wisconsin Reduces Phone Rates 12%," *New York Times*, July 6, 1932, 34.

76. Public Service Commission of Wisconsin, "Opinion and Order," 90 (quote), 93.

77. Mahon, *The Telephone in Chicago*, 123.

78. McCraw, *TVA and the Power Fight*, 44. In 1946, Lilienthal was appointed chair of the Atomic Energy Commission; McGraw, *TVA and the Power Fight*, 45 (italics in the original).

79. Wayne Lintton McMillen, "The Effects of the Current Depression upon the Telephone Business, with Special Reference to the Bell System" (master's thesis, University of Illinois, 1933), 16–17; McMillen, "The Effects of the Current Depression upon the Telephone Business," 20–21.

80. Willard Bliss, Executive Vice President, American Communications Association, in 75th Cong., 3d Sess., "Investigation of Conditions in the Wire Communications Industry," *Hearing before a Subcommittee on the Committee on Interstate Commerce on S. Res. 247, June 6, 1938* (Washington, DC: Government Printing Office, 1938), 15; Hyman H. Goldin, "Governmental Policy and the Domestic Telegraph Industry," *Journal of Economic History* 7, no. 1 (May 1947): 61; John Junior Thornborrow, "A National Policy for Electrical Communications for the United States (with Special Reference to Competition and Monopoly)" (Ph.D. diss., University of Illinois, Urbana, Illinois, 1935), 63.

81. Gregory J. Downey, *Telegraph Messenger Boys: Labor, Technology, and Geography, 1850-1950* (New York: Routledge, 2002), 142; Goldin, "Governmental Policy," 62.

82. Hyman Howard Goldin, "The Domestic Telegraph Industry and the Public Interest: A Study in Public Utility Regulation" (Ph.D. diss., Harvard University, 1950), 24.

83. Bancroft Gherardi and F. B. Jewett, "Telephone System of the United States," *Bell System Technical Journal* 9 (January 1930): 69-71; Griswold in *NRA Hearings on Telegraph Communications*, 59, 58; Griswold in *NRA Hearings on Telegraph Communications*, 59.

84. Downey, *Telegraph Messenger Boys*, 142, quoting T. A. Wise, "Western Union, by Grace of FCC and AT&T," *Fortune*, March 1959, 116; Goldin, "The Domestic Telegraph Industry," 250.

85. Harvey Hoshour and F.R. Elsasser, "Brief of the American Telephone and Telegraph Company," *NRA Hearings on Telegraph Communications*, 118; Thornborrow, "A National Policy for Electrical Communications," 65.

86. James Lawrence Fly, Chairman, FCC, in 77th Cong., 1st Sess., "Study of the Telegraph Industry," *Hearings before a Subcommittee of the Committee on Interstate Commerce Pursuant to S. Res. 95-76th Congress (Extended by S. Res. 268-76th Congress), Part 1, May 19-29, 1941* (Washington, DC: Government Printing Office, 1941), 9; Fly, "Study of the Telegraph Industry," 9.

87. Griswold in *NRA Hearings on Telegraph Communications*, 73; Clair Wilcox, *Competition and Monopoly in American Industry, Monograph No. 21, 76th Cong., 3d Sess., Senate Committee Print, Temporary National Economic Committee, Investigation of Concentration of Economic Power* (Washington, DC: Government Printing Office, 1940), 99; E. O. Sykes, Chairman, Federal Communications Commission, *Letter Transmitting Recommendations of Three Proposed Amendments to the Communications Act of 1934, 74th Cong., 1st Sess., House of Representatives, Document No. 83, January 21, 1935* (Washington, DC: Government Printing Office, 1935), 10-12; Goldin, "Domestic Telegraph Industry," 83-84; 45; 85.

88. Goldin, "Domestic Telegraph Industry," 78, 67.

89. Goldin, "Domestic Telegraph Industry," 32; "Along the Highways of Finance," *New York Times* May 8, 1931, 45; "Western Union Plan To Join Postal Seen," *New York Times*, April 14, 1932, 1, 15.

90. "Drafted At Washington," *New York Times*, December 14, 1933, 1, 2; "Approve Rail Bill, Drop Wire Merger," *New York Times*, June 9, 1933, 8; "Telegraph Merger Unlikely for Year," *New York Times*, June 11, 1933, 5, 7; Goldin, "Domestic Telegraph Industry," 43.

91. James C. Bonbright and Gardiner C. Means, *The Holding Company: Its Public Significance and Its Regulation* (New York: McGraw-Hill, 1932), 149; In its first years, the ICC had tried to negotiate both railroad monopolies and rate wars. Ari and Olive Hoogenboom, *History of the ICC*, 29; Joseph Gaer, *The First Round: The Story of the CIO Political Action Committee* (New York: Duell, Sloan and Pearce, 1944), 199.
92. Ellis W. Hawley, *The New Deal and the Problem of Monopoly: A Study in Economic Ambivalence* (1966; repr., New York: Fordham University Press, 1995), vii–viii.
93. William J. Novak, "The Public Utility Idea and the Origins of Modern Business Regulation," in Naomi R. Lamoreaux and William J. Novak eds., *Corporations and American Democracy* (Cambridge, MA: Harvard University Press, 2017), 139–140.
94. For instances, see, FCC, Telephone Investigation, NARA RG 173, Box 36, Exhibits 1091 and 1101; "50% Phone Rate Cut Asked in Minnesota," *Wall Street Journal*, March 14, 1933, 4; F.M. Hoag, Southwestern Bell Telephone Co., "Plan for Meeting Rate Situation Texas," undated but probably 1931, in NARA, RG 173, Records of the FCC, Office of the Secretary, Docket Section, Special Investigation, Case File No. 1, NARA RG 73, Box 36, Exhibit 1095; McMillen, "The Effect of the Current Depression," 78–79.
95. McMillen, "The Effect of the Current Depression," 79, 81; "California: Attack Is Made on Los Angeles Telephone Rates," *Public Utilities Fortnightly* 10 (July 7, 1932): 46; Samuel Crowther, "Lessons of the Depression," *Public Utilities Fortnightly* 5 (January 1933): 3. "The power trust," writes a leading historian, "was a special demon . . . one that was actively hated by large numbers of people." Hawley, *The New Deal and the Problem of Monopoly*, 486; "The Fortune Survey," *Fortune* 19, no. 6 (June 1939): 112; Fred W. Henck and Bernard Strassburg, *A Slippery Slope: The Long Road to the Breakup of AT&T* (New York: Greenwood Press, 1988), 7.
96. McMillen, "The Effects of the Current Depression," 81.
97. McMillen, "The Effects of the Current Depression," 37; McMillen, "The Effects of the Current Depression," 38, 40; Herbert Hoover Presidential Library, President's Personal File, "Gifford, Walter S. 1931–32," "Memorandum for Mr. Richey," October 6, 1931. An unidentified writer told the president's secretary about a telephone conversation with Mr. Gifford's assistant, Mr. O'Connor, who "told him that I had received a tip from what seemed to be a reliable source that the United Press and the Scripps-Howard Service were coordinating in the preparation of a serious attack upon Mr. Gifford, and his relief responsibilities, on the contention that while dividends were being maintained by the A.T.&T. wages and personnel were being reduced—probably on an indirect basis. . . . I thought, however, it would be best to let Mr. Gifford know so that he could prepare a convincing counter attack to be used immediately if the critical news story appears."
98. Venus Green, *Race on the Line: Gender, Labor, and Technology in the Bell System, 1880–1980* (Durham: Duke University Press, 2001), 161–165; Amy Sue Bix, *Inventing Ourselves out of Jobs? America's Debate over Technological Unemployment 1929–1981* (Baltimore: Johns Hopkins University Press, 2000); Green, *Race on the Line*, 162–163; Gabel, *Separations Principles in the Telephone Industry*, 31; New York Public Service Commission, *1930 Annual Report*, 251.

99. James M. Herring and Gerald C. Gross, *Telecommunications; Economics and Regulation* (New York: McGraw-Hill, 1936), 129; McMillen, "The Effects of the Current Depression," 38.
100. *Smith v. Illinois Bell Telephone Company*, 282 U.S. 133 (1930); Carol L. Weinhaus and Anthony G. Oettinger, *Behind the Telephone Debates* (Norwood: Ablex, 1988), 53, 61 (quote).
101. Hawley, *The New Deal and the Problem of Monopoly*, 327; H.R. Rep. No. 1273, 73d Cong., 2d Sess., 1934, Pt. I, xxxi, xxix–xxxi, in Plaintiff's Third Statement of Contentions and Proof, Part Six, 1966, 1967, quote at para. 22; H.R. Rep. No. 1273, Splawn Report, xxi, in Plaintiff's Third Statement, 1967 at para. 23.
102. Dallas Smythe to Dan Schiller, June 29, 1982 (letter in author's possession); S. Comm. Print, 73d Cong., 2d Sess., January 23, 1934, 5–8, in Plaintiff's Third Statement of Contentions and Proof, 1968, paras. 25–28.
103. Nockels, in 73d Cong., 2d Sess., *Hearings Before the Committee on Interstate Commerce on S. 2910*, 199; Nockels, in 73d Cong., 2d Sess., *Hearings Before the Committee on Interstate Commerce on S. 2910*, 199.
104. Edward N. Nockels, in 71st Cong. 2d Sess., *Hearings Before the Committee on Interstate Commerce on S.6 Commission on Communications, Part 14* (Washington, DC: Government Printing Office, 1930), 2079.
105. Carl Sandburg, "Nockels," Carl Sandburg Collection, Connemara Purchase, Manuscripts, Box 21, Folder 16, Item 1. Thanks to Dennis Sears for this reference. On Carl Sandburg's deep involvement in left-wing politics throughout the first two decades of his career, see, Philip R. Yannella, *The Other Carl Sandburg* (Jackson, MS: University Press of Mississippi, 1996); Nathan Godfried, *WCFL: Chicago's Voice of Labor, 1926–78* (Urbana, IL: University of Illinois Press, 1997).
106. S. Doc. No. 144, 73d Cong., 2d Sess., 1934, in Plaintiff's Third Statement of Contentions and Proof: 1969, para. 30; *Congressional Record Senate, Vol. 78, Part 8, 73d Cong., 2nd Sess.*, May 15, 1934, 8823.
107. NARUC, *Proceedings of Forty-Sixth Annual Convention, Held at Washington, D.C., November 12–15, 1934* (Rochester: E. R. Andrews, 1935), 386; FDR Presidential Library, Official File 1059 FCC Box 1933, "Telegram to Honorable Franklin D Roosevelt from Kit F. Clardy, Chairman Legislative Committee (NARUC) and Chairman Michigan Public Utilities Commission 16 December 1933": "Recent Press Dispatches Indicate Possibility of your pressing for enactment of bill establishing communications commission Stop Every member of every state regulatory commission is vitally interested in such proposal STOP With proper safeguards assuring states of proper protection of their powers to regulate intrastate rates the National Association of Railroad and Utilities Commissioners Will be glad to Render Assistance Stop Its Views were generally presented in conferences with Senator Couzens following hearing on senate bill six introduced at seventy first congress Stop The Association desires that my committee be accorded privilege of consulting with those preparing bill in order that conflict and opposition after introduction may be avoided." Also OF 1059 FCC 1933, Telegram 12/16/33, Kit F. Clardy, Michigan Public Utility Commission, and NARUC to President Franklin Delano Roosevelt,

with enclosed card of Paul A. Walker, Chairman, Corporation Commission of Oklahoma, Reply from M. H. McIntyre to Kit F. Clardy, 12/28/33: "Telegram received Suggest conference with Sec. Roper best way to accomplish results you desire. Incidentally Mr. Paul Walker, Chairman Corporation Commission for Oklahoma here now. Would you want me arrange appointment for him with Roper Regards M H McIntyre."

108. Walter S. Gifford, in 73d Cong., *2d Sess., Hearings Before the Committee on Interstate Commerce on S. 2910, Federal Communications Commission, March 9, 10, 13, 15, 1934* (Washington, DC: Government Printing Office, 1934), 76, 77; Communications Act of 1934, Section 215 (a). For Gifford, see *Hearings on S. 2910*, 78–84; *Hearings on H.R. 8301*, 176–184; Clarence Dill in *Congressional Record, Senate, Vol. 78, Part 8, 73d Cong., 2d Sess. May 15, 1934*, 8824.

109. Rupert Maclaurin, *Invention and Innovation in the Radio Industry* (New York: Macmillan, 1949), 227; Robert W. McChesney, *Telecommunications, Mass Media and Democracy* (New York: Oxford University Press, 1993); Erik Barnouw, *A History of Broadcasting in the United States, Volume 2 1933 to 1953 The Golden Web* (New York: Oxford University Press, 1968), 22–36.

110. Morton Keller, *Regulating a New Economy: Public Policy, and Economic Change in America, 1900–1933* (Cambridge, MA: Harvard University Press, 1990), 79; Kimberly A. Zarkin and Michael J. Zarkin, *The Federal Communications Commission: Front Line in the Culture and Regulation Wars* (Westport, CT: Greenwood Press, 2006), 6; Glen O. Robinson, "The Federal Communications Act: An Essay on Origins and Regulatory Purpose," in Max D. Paglin, ed., *A Legislative History of the Communications Act of 1934* (New York: Oxford University Press, 1989), 3; Horwitz, *Irony of Regulatory Reform*, 126, 127. "When Congress determined that telecommunications should be regulated in 1934, the industry took on the structure that would be maintained for the next 50 years. . . . The period from 1934 to 1956 brought relative stability to the structure of the telecommunications industry." Susan E. McMaster, *The Telecommunications Industry* (Westport, CT: Greenwood Press, 2002), 66, 87.

111. As the U.S. Department of Justice would recognize fifty years later. Plaintiff's Third Statement of Contentions and Proof, 1971-71, para. 38; FDR Presidential Library, PPF, "FCC Telephone Industry," copy of FCC typescript, "Current Regulatory Problems Summary and Findings and Conclusions and Recommendations," *Report on Telephone Investigation, Part II*, 813; Plaintiff's Third Statement of Contentions and Proof, Part Six, 1972; *U.S. District Court for the District of Columbia Civil Action No. 74-1698, United States of America, Plaintiff, v. American Telephone and Telegraph Company; Western Electric Company, Inc.; and Bell Telephone Laboratories, Inc., Defendants*, Defendants' Third Statement of Contentions and Proof (Washington, DC: Bryan S. Adams, 1979), 217; Quoted in Alan Brinkley, *The End of Reform: New Deal Liberalism in Recession and War* (New York: Knopf, 1995), 153.

112. Biographical data drawn from *Who Was Who In America 1897–1942*, vol. 1 (Chicago: A. N. Marquis, 1942) (Brown and McNinch), n.p.; *Current Biography Yearbook 1940* (Hackensack, NJ: H. W. Wilson, 1940), n.p. (Fly); *Current Biography*

Yearbook 1952 (Hackensack, NJ: H. W. Wilson, 1952), n.p. (Walker); see, also, McCraw, *TVA and the Power Fight*; Lawrence W. Lichty, "Members of the Federal Radio Commission and Federal Communications Commission 1927–1961," *Journal of Broadcasting* 6, no. 1 (Winter 1961–1962): 23–34; Lichty, "The Impact of FRC and FCC Commissioners' Backgrounds on the Regulation of Broadcasting," *Journal of Broadcasting* 6, no. 2 (Spring 1962): 97–110; Henck and Strassburg, *A Slippery Slope*, 9–11.

113. Paul A. Walker, "How Cooperation Works in Communications Regulation," *Public Utilities Fortnightly* 23, no. 5 (September 2, 1943): 267; Paul A. Walker, "Co-Operation between Federal and State Commissions," *Public Utilities Reports Fortnightly* 1928D, no. 5 (October 4): 19; Public Service Commission of Wisconsin to Mr. Marvin McIntyre, Secretary to the President, January 22, 1934, with attachment by Public Service Commission of Wisconsin, "Memorandum to the Secretary of Commerce State and Federal Regulation of Telephone Communication," "Telegraph, Radio, Cable Cos 1933–45," FDR Presidential Library, FDR Official File, Box 859; Paul A. Walker, Chairman, Oklahoma Corporation Commission to Honorable Marvin H. McIntyre, Secretary to the President, March 14, 1934 (letter to Senator Dill attached), "Telegraph, Radio, Cable Cos 1933–45," FDR Presidential Library, FDR Official File, Box 859; 73d Cong., 2d Sess., *Hearings before the Committee on Interstate and Foreign Commerce on H.R. 8301, Federal Communications Commission, 10 April 1934* (Washington, DC: Government Printing Office, 1934); Statement of Paul Walker, Chairman of the Corporation Commission of the State of Oklahoma, 69–70.

114. Section 212, Communications Act of 1934; 2 FCC 741,745–746, "In the Matter of Interlocking Directorates," decided July 3, 1935; In its original form, the Public Utility Holding Company Act of 1935 sought to authorize the Securities and Exchange Commission "to dissolve within five years any utility holding company that could not prove its usefulness." Known as the "death sentence" clause, this provision was passed by the Senate but was rejected by the House. Somewhat watered down when it was signed into law in August 1935, the act still was "very stringent," according to historian Thomas K. McCraw, and "it represented a victory over one of the richest war chests ever collected to fight a single piece of legislation." Also called the Wheeler-Rayburn Act, it charged the SEC with eliminating "holding companies more than twice removed from their operating companies, and those whose systems were incapable of physical interconnection." McCraw, *TVA and the Power Fight*, 82, 84.

115. Brinkley, *Age of Reform*, 133–134.

116. 1 FCC 54 (1934); *Congressional Record, Senate, 74th Cong., 1st Sess., Vol. 79 Part 2, February 12, 1935*, 1841, vol. 79 Part 3, March 4, 1935, 2908-13; 74th Cong., Final Session, Vol. 79 Part 4, March 19, 1935, 3934; "A.T.&T. Inquiry underway 'Full Blast with 60 Experts Gathering Data for FCC,'" *New York Times*, June 22, 1935, 21.

117. Robert Griffith, "Forging America's Postwar Order: Domestic Politics and Political Economy in the Age of Truman," in Michael J. Lacey, ed., *The Truman Presidency* (Cambridge: Cambridge University Press, 1989), 58; Joseph C. O'Mahoney, "Regulation of Business Competition," in Joseph C. O'Mahoney papers, Accession

NOTES 671

No. 275-53-06-00, Box 127, "Speeches 1938 #6," American Heritage Center, University of Wyoming, Laramie; Freidel, *Franklin D. Roosevelt: A Rendezvous with Destiny*, 202; S. Doc. 173, 75th Cong., 3d Sess., in David Lynch, *The Concentration of Economic Power* (New York: Columbia University Press, 1946), 1; Meg Jacobs, *Pocketbook Politics* (Princeton, NJ: Princeton University Press, 2005), 130, 164, 167–168.

118. FDR Presidential Library, Leland Olds Papers, Box 25 Folder, "Article Yale Review 1935," April 10, 1935, W. Cross, Editor, *The Yale Review*, to Leland Olds, Esq., Secretary, New York Power Authority.

119. "Roosevelt Orders Telephone Investigation," *New York Times*, March 16, 1935, 21; AT&T charged the FCC with both procedural violations of due process and innumerable factual misstatements. "Brief of Bell System Companies on Commissioner Walker's Proposed Report on the Telephone Investigation," December 5, 1938, in NARA RG 173, Box 8; FCC staffers produced eighty separate reports between March 1936 and June 1937. NARA, RG 173, Box 8, "List of Reports in Special Investigation Docket No. 1." One glaring gap existed in the FCC's otherwise encompassing research: the status of telephone industry labor and employment.

120. "Roosevelt to Decide A.T.&T. Inquiry's Fate," *New York Times*, April 3, 1936, 23; "Becker Quits Post In A.T.&T. Inquiry," *New York Times*, February 21, 1937, 25.

121. FCC, *Proposed Report on the Telephone Investigation*, 686–687.

122. FCC, *Proposed Report on the Telephone Investigation*, 698.

123. Wheat, "Regulation of Interstate Telephone Rates," 3–4; 76th Cong 3d Sess., Temporary National Economic Committee Investigation of Concentration of Economic Power, Clair Wilcox, *Competition and Monopoly in American Industry, Monograph No. 21* (Washington, DC: Government Printing Office, 1940), 15.

124. "25% Cut In Phone Rates Feasible, The FCC Is Told; Three-Year Inquiry Ended," *New York Times*, April 2, 1938, 1; John H. Bickley, "That Two-Year Phone Probe," *Public Utilities Fortnightly* 21, no. 13 (June 23, 1938); FCC, *Final Report on the Telephone Investigation*, 600–601.

125. FCC, FCC, *Proposed Report on the Telephone Investigation*, 707, 710.

126. Plaintiff's Third Statement of Contentions and Proof, Part Six, 1973–1979, paras. 39–52, quote at para. 52 (from Report of the Antitrust Subcommittee of the House Committee on the Judiciary, Pursuant to H. Res. 27, on Consent Decree Program of the Department of Justice, 82–83.); Plaintiff's Third Statement of Contentions and Proof, Part Six, 1981, para. 55.

127. "Economic Power of the Federal Government," 42, in Joseph C. O'Mahoney Papers, Accession No. 275-53-06-00, Box 45, "TNEC," American Heritage Center, University of Wyoming, Laramie.

Chapter 5

1. Steve Fraser, "The New Deal in the American Political Imagination," *Jacobin*, June 2019, www.jacobinmag.com/2019/06/new-deal-great-depression; Meg Jacobs,

Pocketbook Politics: Economic Citizenship in Twentieth-Century America (Princeton, NJ: Princeton University Press, 2005), 91; Irving Bernstein, "Workers in Depression and War," U.S. Department of Labor, https://www.dol.gov/general/aboutdol/history/chapter5; Randi Storch, *Red Chicago: American Communism at Its Grassroots, 1928–1935* (Urbana, IL: University of Illinois Press, 2007), 33; Perhaps the leading US labor historian of his generation framed this with customary clarity: "Instead of listening for the 'voice of the working class' . . . we must be attuned to many different voices, sometimes in harmony, but often in conflict with one another. Nevertheless, it remains not only possible but imperative to analyze the American experience of the late nineteenth and early twentieth centuries in terms of conflicting social classes." David Montgomery, *The Fall of the House of Labor* (New York: Cambridge University Press, 1987), 1.

2. John Newsinger, *Fighting Back: The American Working Class in the 1930s* (London: Bookmarks Publications, 2012), 85; Bruce Nelson, *Divided We Stand: American Workers and the Struggle for Black Equality* (Princeton, NJ: Princeton University Press, 2001), xxxii. Twenty-six of the AFL's one hundred member unions excluded blacks in the 1940s, and many others allowed segregation in Jim Crow local affiliates. Philip F. Rubio, *There's Always Work at the Post Office* (Durham, NC: University of North Carolina Press, 2010), 362 n31. See also, Michael Goldfield, *The Southern Key; Class, Race, & Radicalism in the 1930s and 1940s* (New York: Oxford University Press, 2020); By 1945, it had doubled again, to 14.3 million. Gerald Mayer, "Union Membership Trends in the U.S.," *CRS Report for Congress* (Washington: Congressional Research Service, 2004), 23.

3. James R. Barrett, *William Z. Foster and the Tragedy of American Radicalism* (Urbana, IL: University of Illinois Press, 1999), 198–200; Roger Keeran, *The Communist Party and the Auto Workers Unions* (Bloomington, IN: Indiana University Press, 1980), 170–171; Goldfield, *Southern Key*, 356; Joe William Trotter, Jr., *Workers on Arrival: Black Labor in the Making of America* (Oakland, CA: University of California Press, 2019), 111. Goldfield argues that despite its successful organizing drive explicitly covering both Black and white workers, the CIO-affiliated steelworkers union abandoned "any pretenses" that it "stood firmly for racial equality" by the early 1940s.: *Southern Key*, 324–329, 162; Robert H. Zieger, *For Jobs and Freedom: Race and Labor in America Since 1865* (Lexington, KY: University Press of Kentucky, 2007), 106; Fraser, "The New Deal in the American Political Imagination," 9; Robert S. McElvaine, *The Great Depression: America, 1929–1941* (New York: Three Rivers Press, 1993), 291; Goldfield, *Southern Key*, 220.

4. Michael Denning, *The Cultural Front: The Laboring of American Culture in the Twentieth Century* (London: Verso, 1996); Alan Dawley, *Struggles for Justice: Social Responsibility and the Liberal State* (Cambridge, MA: Belknap Press of Harvard University Press, 1991), 377, 376; Elizabeth Borgwardt, *A New Deal for the World: America's Vision for Human Rights* (Cambridge, MA: Belknap Press of Harvard University Press, 2005), 27, 45, 52, 136, 137–138, 153–154; Samuel Moyn, *Not Enough: Human Rights in an Unequal World* (Cambridge, MA: Harvard University Press, 2018), 68–88; Caroline Ware, in Temporary National Economic

Committee, Investigation of Concentration of Economic Power, Hearings Part 30, Technology and Concentration of Economic Power, 76th Cong., 3d Sess., April 8–26, 1940, 17205, in Jacobs, *Pocketbook Politics*, 174.

5. John E. Edgerton, in Jerold S. Auerbach, *Labor and Liberty: The La Follette Committee and The New Deal* (Indianapolis: Bobbs-Merrill, 1966), 141; Ahmed White, *The Last Great Strike: Little Steel, the CIO, and the Struggle for Labor Rights in New Deal America* (Berkeley, CA: University of California Press, 2016), 76, 75 (quote); also Wendy L. Wall, *Inventing the 'American Way': The Politics of Consensus from the New Deal to the Civil Rights Movement* (New York: Oxford University Press, 2008), 40–48; Jacobs, *Pocketbook Politics*, 82.

6. Irving Bernstein, *The Turbulent Years: A History of the American Worker, 1933-1940* (Chicago: Haymarket Books, 2010), 469; Mary Earhart Dillon, *Wendell Willkie, 1892-1944* (Philadelphia: J.B. Lippincott, 1952), 217. See also, David Levering Lewis, *The Improbable Wendell Wilkie* (New York: Liveright, 2018); Bernstein, *Turbulent Years*, 719; and Robert W. McChesney and John Nichols, *People Get Ready: The Fight against a Jobless Economy and a Citizenless Democracy* (New York: Nation Books, 2016), 30, 174, 178–179; Fraser, "The New Deal in the American Political Imagination," 4.

7. Frances Fox Piven, " Introduction," in Irving Bernstein, *The Lean Years: A History of the American Worker 1920-1933* (Chicago: Haymarket Books, 2010), xvii; Bernstein, *Turbulent Years*, 39–40.

8. Gary Gerstle, *Liberty and Coercion: The Paradox of American Government* (Princeton, NJ: Princeton University Press, 2015), 228; I follow Gerstle, *Liberty and Coercion*, 227–243; Kathryn S. Olmsted, *Right out of California: The 1930s and the Big Business Roots of Modern Conservatism* (New York: New Press, 2015), 3; Christopher Tomlins, *The State and the Unions Labor Relations, Law, and the Organized Labor Movement in America, 1880-1960* (Cambridge: Cambridge University Press, 1985), 132–140, 162–184; Ahmed, *The Last Great Strike*, makes extensive use of the La Follette Committee's findings. Jerold S. Auerbach, "The La Follette Committee and the CIO," *Wisconsin Magazine of History* 48, no. 1 (Autumn 1964): 3–20.

9. Stanley Vittoz, *New Deal Labor Policy and the American Industrial Economy* (Chapel Hill, NC: University of North Carolina Press, 1987), 7; Vittoz, *New Deal Labor Policy*, 10; Tomlins, *The State and the Unions*, 95; Nelson Lichtenstein, "Taft-Hartley: A Slave Labor Law?," *Catholic University Law Review* 47, no. 3 (Spring 1998): 765.

10. Gilbert J. Gall, *Pursuing Justice: Lee Pressman, the New Deal, and the CIO* (Albany: State University of New York Press, 1999), 84; Steve Fraser, *Labor Will Rule: Sidney Hillman and the Rise of American Labor* (Ithaca: Cornell University Press, 1993), 335; Fraser, *Labor Will Rule*, 373 (quote), 349; Lichtenstein, "Taft-Hartley," 778.

11. Grace Palladino, *Dreams of Dignity, Workers of Vision: A History of the International Brotherhood of Electrical Workers* (Washington, DC: International Brotherhood of *The Electrical Workers*, 1991), 142; Zieger, *The CIO*, 35; Venus Green, *Race on the Line: Gender, Labor, and Technology in the Bell System, 1880-1980* (Durham, NC: Duke University Press, 2001), 171–173. A minority of radicals opposed NLRA for granting government an ability effectively to license trade unions, which the state would indeed later use, to potent effect.

12. Montgomery, *Fall of the House of Labor*, 464; Statement of Mr. Howard L. Kern, Vice President, Postal Telegraph and Cable Corporation, National Recovery Administration Hearings on the Telegraph Communication Industry, Volume 1, May 2, 1934 (Washington, DC: Jesse L. Ward, 1934), 32.

13. Statement of Colonel A.H. Griswold, Executive Vice President, Postal Telegraph and Cable Corporation, NRA Hearings on the Telegraph Communication Industry, 92; Kern, NRA Hearings on the Telegraph Communication Industry, 13, 9, 10; Kern, NRA Hearings on the Telegraph Communication Industry, 9; Kern, NRA Hearings on the Telegraph Communication Industry, 10, 12.

14. Brief Filed by Postal Telegraph and Cable Corporation, NRA Hearings on the Telegraph Communication Industry, 209; Brief Filed by Postal Telegraph, NRA Hearings on the Telegraph Communication Industry, 209–211; Brief Filed by Postal Telegraph, NRA Hearings on the Telegraph Communication Industry, 208: "It would, therefore, seem that if the leased line question were reviewed today by the Interstate Commerce Commission, they must, to be consistent, find that leased line telegraph service is discriminatory for the same reasons that they found leased line telephone service discriminatory in 1918."

15. Griswold, NRA Hearings on the Telegraph Communication Industry, 55, 58; Griswold, NRA Hearings on the Telegraph Communication Industry, 20; Griswold, NRA Hearings on the Telegraph Communication Industry, 33.

16. "Code for Four," *Time*, May 28, 1934, https://content.time.com/time/subscriber/article/0,33009,754168,00.html.

17. "Roosevelt Issues Wire Code Demand," *New York Times*, December 21, 1934, 37. The reference must be to the recently established National Industrial Recovery Board, which was not created until 1935. Thanks to James Barrett for finding this error.

18. The CTUA asserted that Western Union suffered from overcapacity of one hundred percent. Vidkunn Ulrikkson, *The Telegraphers, Their Craft and Their Unions* (Washington, DC: Public Affairs Press, 1953), 131; "Study of Communications by an Inter-Departmental Committee," to the President from the Secretary of Commerce, Washington, DC, January 23, 1934, 11, 1; NRA, Hearing on the Telegraph Communication Industry; John Junior Thornborrow, "A National Policy for Electrical Communications for the United States (with Special Reference to Competition and Monopoly)" (Ph.D. diss., University of Illinois, Urbana, Illinois, 1935), 185, 188; Section 215(b) of the Communications Act of 1934 47 U.S.C. 151 mandated that the new FCC "investigate the methods by which and the extent to which wire telephone companies are furnishing wire telegraph service . . . report its findings to Congress, together with its recommendations as to whether additional legislation on this subject is desirable."; 10 FCC Reports 162. N.B. the phrase "adequate regulation" in regard to a monopoly provider. "From the beginning it [FCC-ds] took the position that as a first step in the rehabilitation of the industry Western Union and Postal should be permitted to merge." Hyman H. Goldin, "Governmental Policy and the Domestic Telegraph Industry," *Journal of Economic History* 7, no. 1 (May 1947): 62.

19. Hy Kravif, "Telephone and Telegraph Workers," *International Pamphlets*, no. 44: 30; "CTU Opposes Telegraph Merger," *Commercial Telegraphers Journal* (December 1934); "ruinous competition" from "How to Restore the Telegraph Industry," *Commercial Telegraphers Journal* (February 1935): 16; all cited in Ellen Knutson, "Labor and Legislation: A 10-Year Chronicle of the Western Union and Postal Telegraph Merger," unpublished paper, December 12, 2001, 4, 5. Author's collection.
20. Henry Miller, *Tropic of Capricorn* (New York: Grove Press, 1961), 16, 17, 21, 19–20, 28. I was alerted to Miller's work for Western Union by his appearances in Gregory J. Downey, *Telegraph Messenger Boys: Labor, Technology, and Geography, 1850–1950* (New York: Routledge, 2002). For discussion of Miller, Mary V. Dearborn, *The Happiest Man Alive: A Biography of Henry Miller* (New York: Simon & Schuster, 1991), 66–67.
21. Archibald M. McIsaac, *The Order of Railroad Telegraphers* (Princeton, NJ: Princeton University Press, 1933), 51, 62.
22. Sanford M. Jacoby, *Modern Manors: Welfare Capitalism since the New Deal* (Princeton, NJ: Princeton University Press, 1997); Ulrikkson, *The Telegraphers*, 122; Ulrikkson, *The Telegraphers*, 125.
23. The Depression of 1893–1894 spawned both a significant drop-off in telegrams transmitted by Western Union and a decline in the carrier's revenues; the Panic of 1907 had an even sharper effect. *Annual Report of the President of The Western Union Telegraph Company (Incorporated) to the Stockholders, Made at their Meeting, October 12, 1910* (The James Kempster Printing Company); Thornborrow, "A National Policy for Electrical Communications," 63; 10 FCC Reports 148–198, "In the Matter of the Application for Merger of the Western Union Telegraph Company and Postal Telegraph, Inc.," Docket No. 6517, Decided September 27, 1943; Goldin, "Governmental Policy," 62; Thomas P. Swift, "Western Union-Postal Merger, Long Urged, Approaches Actuality," *New York Times*, August 2, 1942, 1–2.
24. Ulrikkson, *The Telegraphers*, 129; Thornborrow, "A National Policy for Electrical Communications," 65–66.
25. Ulrikkson, *The Telegraphers*, 131–132; The NRA named Edward N. Nockels of the Chicago Federation of Labor and WCFL as labor advisor to its Radio Broadcasting Code Authority. Dennis William Mazzocco, "Democracy, Power, And Equal Rights: The AFL vs. CIO Battle to Unionize U.S. Broadcast Technicians, 1926–1940" (Ph.D. diss., University of California, San Diego), 59, 69, 71. But its enabling legislation also enabled a great expansion of company unions, which gained 2.5 additional members during 1933–1934. Mazzocco, "Democracy, Power, and Equal Rights," 118; Ulrikkson, *The Telegraphers*, 131. "Western Union has been very profitable to investors. In the seven years 1928–1934, after paying out $28 millions in interest to bondholders, its *net income* after all charges totaled nearly $52 million." Kravif, *Telephone and Telegraph Workers*, 5.
26. Statement of Mr. Frank B. Powers, International President, Commercial Telegraphers Union, NRA Hearing on the Telegraph Communication Industry, 290–291; Powers, NRA Hearing on the Telegraph Communication Industry, 291–292.

27. "Reply Brief Submitted by Postal Telegraph and Cable Corporation," NRA Hearing on the Telegraph Communication Industry, 253–254; Statement of Mr. K. M. Whitten, General Organizer, Commercial Telegraphers Union, NRA Hearing on the Telegraph Communication Industry, 313, 316.
28. An RCA executive testified that "I.T.&T."—Postal's owner—"is hiding behind labor, in the effort to secure competitive advantages, and to use N.R.A. as a catspaw for its own ends." Statement of Mr. Frank W. Wozencraft on behalf of R.C.A. Communications, NRA Hearing on the Telegraph Communication Industry, 356; Statement of Mr. W. J. Shinnick, General Chairman, Commercial Telegraphers Union in NRA Hearing on the Telegraph Communication Industry, 307–310; Whitten, NRA Hearing on the Telegraph Communication Industry, 315; "U.T.A. Takes up Grievances with Postal Officials," The United Telegraphers of America (Independent) Bulletin. Room 304 World Bldg 63 Park Row, N.Y.C., September 1934, 1. Author's collection; Statement of Mr. Harold L. Bates, Vice-President of the United Telegraphers of America, NRA Hearing on the Telegraph Communication Industry, 384; Bates, NRA Hearing on the Telegraph Communication Industry, 368–371; Bates, NRA Hearing on the Telegraph Communication Industry, 364; Bates, NRA Hearing on the Telegraph Communication Industry, 372, 373, 364–366; Bates, NRA Hearing on the Telegraph Communication Industry, 384.
29. Downey, *Telegraph Messenger Boys*, 158–167; Downey, *Telegraph Messenger Boys*, 373–380, quote at 380; Statement of James Lawrence Fly, Chairman, FCC, in 77th Cong., 1st Sess., Senate, *Study of the Telegraph Industry, Hearings Before a Subcommittee of the Committee on Interstate Commerce, Part 1, May 19–29, 1941* (Washington, DC: Government Printing Office, 1941), 33.
30. Kravif, *Telephone and Telegraph Workers*; Increasingly dissatisfied with the service that resulted, members of the general public then turned—to the extent that they could—to alternatives like airmail and long-distance telephone service. As discussed, this only increased the tempo of telegraph industry decline. 75th Cong., 3d Sess., *Hearing before a Subcommittee of the Committee on Interstate Commerce On S. Res. 247, Investigation of Conditions in the Wire Communications Industry*.
31. "TMU, ARTA, UTA, Meet in Joint Council," *Telegraph Messengers Voice*, no. 7 (September 10, 1934) (New York, NY: Telegrapher Messengers Union), 3. Author's collection.
32. Robert George Huck, "Radio and the American Communications Association" (master's thesis, Stanford University, 1947), 3, 10; Joseph P. Goldberg, *The Maritime Story: A Study in Labor-management Relations* (Cambridge, MA: Harvard University Press, 1958), 255. Informative but often distorted glimpses of the ACA's early history are found in "Statement of Karl Baarslag," 82 Cong., 1st Sess., U.S. Senate, Committee on the Judiciary, Subcommittee to Investigate the Administration of the Internal Security Act, *Hearings on Subversive Infiltration In the Telegraph Industry, May 14–June 14, 1951*, 1–26; and Karl Baarslag, "Communists in Communications or Sovietizing American Communications or (any other suitable title)," Hoover Institution Archive and Library, Stanford University, Baarslag Accession 85040-8.38, Box 2 Folder 4, "Writing: Communists in Communications" 1940. There is

no biography of Baarslag, but see Rubio, *There's Always Work at the Post Office*, 343 n31. ACA's efforts to organize radio broadcast technicians are the focus of Mazzocco, "Democracy, Power, and Equal Rights." ACA's representation of messengers is foregrounded in Downey, *Telegraph Messenger Boys*. For a contemporary study, see, Huck, "Radio and the American Communications Association."; Bruce Nelson, *Workers on the Waterfront: Seamen, Longshoremen, and Unionism in the 1930s* (Urbana, IL: University of Illinois Press, 1990), 235–236, 238; This complex history is traced in Bernstein, *Turbulent Years*, 574–589; Goldberg, *The Maritime Story*, 144–150; Goldberg, *The Maritime Story*, 173, 248.

33. Roy A. Pyle, Secretary, Local Number 3, ARTA, to James B. Carey, President, United Electrical & Radio Workers, March 5, 1937, in American Communications Association Additions (hereafter ACA Records), Records, 1934–1966, State Historical Society of Wisconsin, Mss. 734, Box 3, Folder 5.

34. For accounts of the early organizational efforts of the radio manufacturing workers, Bernstein, *Turbulent Years*, 103–104, 383–384, 603–607; and Ronald W. Schatz, *The Electrical Workers: A History of Labor at General Electric and Westinghouse, 1923–1960* (Urbana, IL: University of Illinois Press, 1982), 63–64; For Carey, see Schatz, *The Electrical Workers*, 96–99; Pyle to Carey, ACA Records; Pyle to Carey, ACA Records.

35. John L. Lewis, no title, *Communications Journal* 1, no. 10 (June 1937): 1; Agreement signed by James B. Carey, Mervyn R. Rathborne, and John Brophy, April 5, 1937, in ACA Records, 1934–1966, Mss. 734, Box 3, Folder 5.

36. John Brophy, Director, CIO to Mervyn Rathborne, President, ARTA, May 20, 1937, in ACA Records, Mss. 734, Box 3, Folder 5; Mervyn Rathborne, President, ARTA, to John Brophy, Committee for Industrial Organization, May 25, 1937, in ACA Records, Mss. 734, Box 3, Folder 5; Ulrikkson, *The Telegraphers*, 144; Catherine McKercher, *Newsworkers Unite: Labor, Convergence, and North American Newspapers* (Lanham, MD: Rowman & Littlefield, 2002); Vincent Mosco and Catherine McKercher, *The Laboring of Communication: Will Knowledge Workers of the World Unite?* (Lanham, MD: Lexington Books, 2008, 81–149). The longtime president of the Communications Workers of America, which, as we will see, was built by telephone industry employees, recalled that in late 1939, he had "sat down" with Jim Carey, the president of the United Electrical Workers because "we had an understandable jurisdiction that would fit into theirs. He tried more than once to persuade me to take the position of going into the UE." Joseph A. Beirne Oral History by John N. Schacht, August 30, 1971, University of Iowa Library Special Collections, 34; Downey, *Telegraph Messenger Boys*, 169–190; Mazzocco, "Democracy, Power, and Equal Rights," 107, 112, 145.

37. Steven Kalgaard Ashby, "Shattered Dreams: The American Working Class and the Origins of the Cold War, 1945–1949" (Ph.D. diss., University of Chicago, 1993), 13 n14; Ellen Schrecker, *Many Are the Crimes: McCarthyism in America* (Boston: Little, Brown and Company, 1998), 90–97; Goldfield, *Southern Key*, 220–221, 353–362.

38. Statement of Joseph P. Selly in 82d Cong., 1st Sess., U.S. Senate, Committee on the Judiciary, Subcommittee to Investigate the Administration of the Internal Security Act, *Hearings on "Subversive Infiltration in the Telegraph Industry,"* May 14–June 14,

1951, 145–148; All these organizations and many others had been cited as "subversive" by the attorney general, meaning that Selly potentially risked going to prison for admitting an affiliation. His interrogators affixed to him and other union officers the stigma now attached to each such organization: once classed as a "Communist Front," each was reduced to a reflex of a supposed overarching Soviet conspiracy by the U.S.' corporate commercial media apparatus; Denning, *The Cultural Front*.

39. Set up in 1919 by the new Soviet Union, the Comintern helped establish and finance affiliated Communist parties in numerous other countries. While the Comintern granted to itself "the right to dictate" to these member parties, the latter did not always conform to its edicts. Jonathan Haslam, *The Spectre of War: International Communism and the Origins of World War II* (Princeton, NJ: Princeton University Press, 2021), 23 (quote); Silvio Pons, *The Global Revolution, A History of International Communism 1917–1991* (New York: Oxford University Press, 2014), 30, 34; Haslam, *The Spectre of War*, 328. Haslam superbly documents and analyzes how the hatred and fear borne by most of England's top leadership for the Soviet Union, especially after the rise of Popular Front governments in France and Spain in 1936, led England to try to work with Hitler until 1940; Victor Rabinowitz, *Unrepentant Leftist: A Lawyer's Memoir* (Urbana, IL: University of Illinois Press, 1996), 52; 82d Cong., 1st Sess., U.S. Senate, Committee on the Judiciary, Subcommittee to Investigate the Administration of the Internal Security Act, *Hearings on "Subversive Infiltration In The Telegraph Industry,"* May 14–June 14, 1951.

40. Joseph P. Selly to the Honorable Franklin D. Roosevelt, September 27, 1941, in Box 1, Folder 11, Records of the Congress of Industrial Organizations, Special Collections of the University Libraries of the Catholic University of America, Washington, DC (hereafter CIO Papers); Allan S. Haywood to Joseph P. Selly, September 30, 1941, in Box 1, Folder 11, CIO Papers. One of the unions that backed ACA in its stand-off against RCA, in an interesting portent, was the United Telephone Organizations, representing New York City's "telephone plant men." Letter to the Honorable Franklin D. Roosevelt, September 26, 1941, in Box 1, Folder 11, CIO Papers.

41. After the U.S. Congress passed legislation in 1941, mandating that political organizations under foreign control register with the Justice Department, the U.S. Communist Party withdrew from the Comintern, which was dissolved in 1943. Fridrikh Igorevich Firsov, Harvey Klehr, and John Earl Haynes, *Secret Cables of the Comintern 1933–1943* (New Haven, CT: Yale University Press, 2014), 238–244; Goldfield, *Southern Key*, 333, 331 (quote); Randi Storch, *Red Chicago: American Communism at Its Grassroots, 1928–35* (Urbana, IL: University of Illinois Press, 2007). For St. Louis, Rosemary Feurer, *Radical Unionism in the Midwest, 1900–1950* (Urbana, IL: University of Illinois Press, 2006); Denning, *The Cultural Front*; Michael E. Brown, Randy Martin, Frank Rosengarten, and George Snedeker, eds., *New Studies in the Politics and Culture of U.S. Communism* (New York: Monthly Review, 1993); James R. Barrett, *William Z. Foster and the Tragedy of American Radicalism* (Urbana, IL: University of Illinois Press, 1999), 208; Rosswurm, ed., *The CIO's Left-Led Unions* (New Brunswick, NJ: Rutgers University Press, 1992); and Judith Stepan-Norris and Maurice Zeitlin, *Left Out: Reds and America's Industrial Unions* (New York: Cambridge University Press, 2003); Lichtenstein, "Taft-Hartley," 785; also Zieger, *The CIO*, 255–256.

42. Rabinowitz, *Unrepentant Leftist*, 78; *Constitution of The Commercial Telegraphers of America, Revised and Amended at the 13th Regular and 10th Biennial Convention, Chicago, Illinois, September 14th to 18th, 1925* (Chicago: Frank J. Kain and Son, 1925), 5, Article III; Abram L. Harris, *Race, Radicalism, and Reform: Selected Papers* (New Brunswick, NJ: Transaction Publishers, 1989), 195; Louis R. Harlan and Raymond W. Smock, eds., *The Booker T. Washington Papers, Volume 12, 1912–1914* (Urbana, IL: University of Illinois Press, 1982), 210. After Whites voted to segregate the union of railway mail clerks in 1912, Blacks responded by forming their own union, the National Association of Postal Employees. Rubio, *There's Always Work at the Post Office*, 30–31; Joe William Trotter, Jr., *Workers on Arrival: Black Labor in the Making of America* (Oakland, CA: University of California Press, 2019), 90; Schrecker, *Many Are the Crimes*, 42–45; Testimony of Karl Baarslag, Research Specialist, The American Legion, in 82d Cong., 1st Sess., U.S. Senate, Committee on the Judiciary, Subcommittee to Investigate the Administration of the Internal Security Act, *Hearings on "Subversive Infiltration in the Telegraph Industry," May 14–June 14, 1951*, 9–10. From an AFL base, Baarslag leveled public charges against Communists in the post office in 1945; see Karl Baarslag, *History of the National Federation of Post Office Clerks* (Washington, DC: National Federation of Post Office Clerks, 1945), 183–186, 189. Also, "Karl Baarslag, Author and Ex-Congress Aide," *New York Times*, January 14, 1984; The ACA *News* joined in attacking the frame-up of Willie Magee, a Black man found guilty by a Mississippi jury of raping a white woman with whom he had had an extended consensual relationship. In spite of Bella Abzug's courageous antiracist defense, Magee was executed in 1951. That "this was a savage injustice, that the man was being tried for a crime which, what we knew about the case, indicated he did not commit, and that he was being tried, convicted, and executed because he was a Negro"—the view expressed in articles published about Magee by ACA *News*, according to the journal's editor in his Senate Internal Security Committee testimony— became fodder for the claim that the union was controlled by Communist Party outsiders. Statement of Charles Silberman, editor, ACA *News*, in 82d Cong., 1st Sess., U.S. Senate, Committee on the Judiciary, Subcommittee to Investigate the Administration of the Internal Security Act, *Hearings on "Subversive Infiltration in the Telegraph Industry," May 14–June 14, 1951*, 244; Trotter, *Workers on Arrival*, 131.
43. Keeran, *The Communist Party and the Auto Workers Unions*, 207.
44. Rathborne to Brophy, May 25, 1937, ACA Records, Mss. 734, Box 3, Folder 5.
    Ulrikkson, *The Telegraphers*, 144.
45. Huck, "Radio and the ACA," 12; Zieger, *The CIO*, 96; Mervyn Rathborne to Kehoe, Selly, Driesen, September 7, 1939, ACA Records, Box 24, Folder 1. Rathborne was to testify as a government witness against his erstwhile friend and fellow labor leader, Harry Bridges, president of the International Longshoremen's and Warehousemen's Union, CIO, in hearings on whether Bridges had perjured himself when he denied being a Communist. Lawrence K. Davies, "Bridges Ex-friend Charges Pressure," *New York Times*, March 3, 1950, 8; Lawrence K. Davies, "Lied to Congress, U.S. Witness Says," *New York Times*, March 1, 1950, 4. Dallas Smythe, who worked on telegraph labor issues at Central Statistical Board and thereafter at the FCC before

becoming one of the foremost political economists of communications, met Driesen and Kehoe in 1938. Smythe characterized them as "supremely intelligent, sensitive, and Marxist. Besides, they loved life and people. We . . . had a very close relationship from 1938 on. I learned much from them both." Dallas Smythe, *Counterclockwise*, Thomas Guback, ed. (Boulder, CO: Westview, 1994), 17; Something of the tenor of these early initiatives may be gotten from the memoranda, telegrams, and letter correspondence in Box 1, Folder 11, CIO Papers; Mervyn Rathborne to Ralph Hetzel, Jr., August 23, 1938, in Box 1, Folder 10, CIO Papers; Mervyn Rathborne to Frank McNinch, August 24, 1938; Mervyn Rathborne to Ralph Hetzel, August 24, 1938; Ralph Hetzel, Jr., to Mervyn Rathborne, August 25, 1938; Mervyn Rathborne to Colonel Somerville, August 25, 1938, all in Box 1, Folder 10, CIO Papers; "ACA Convention Maps Plans for Union Drive," *CIO News* 1, no. 34 (July 30, 1938): 4.

46. Its agreement with RCA, covering 1,300 workers, was notable, in the words of a 1947 historian, for its "strong clause protecting the workers in the event of increased mechanization." ACA insisted that any profit attained through the introduction of new technologies be shared with workers in the form of shorter hours, higher pay, and job security. An ACA leader expressed the union's policy commitment to "controlled mechanization": "unions are not opposed to technological development but are opposed to technological displacement." Huck, "Radio and ACA," 18–19 (quote); Mazzocco, "Democracy, Power, and Equal Rights," 148.

47. Daniel Driesen, "Memorandum to R. Bailey-Stortz," May 25, 1939, ACA Records, Mss. 298, Box 24, Folder 1.

48. "To: All Telegraph Locals From: National Office Subject—Status of Merger," 3/14/38, ACA Records, Mss 298, Box 24, Folder 1. In December 1939, the chief of staff of the Senate Committee on Interstate Commerce wrote ACA to complain that "during the past week the subcommittee has been deluged with form letters, form post cards and form telegrams urging the committee to hold hearings. . . . Under the circumstances it is almost impossible for our slightly-staffed subcommittee to attempt to answer three or four thousand petitions." Edward Cooper, Chief of Staff, to Mr. Mervyn Rathborne, December 12, 1939, in Mss 298, Box 24, Folder 1, ACA Records. The next month, ACA informed its locals that "our campaign was unprecedented for a single union. Senator Wheeler received over 34,000 communications." "To: All Locals and Chairmen of Legislative Committees From: ACA Merger Investigating Committee," January 3, 1940, Box 24, Folder 2, ACA Records; Lee Pressman, General Counsel, CIO to Honorable Harry L. Hopkins, Secretary, U.S. Department of Commerce, February 7, 1939, in Mss 298, Box 24, Folder 1, ACA Records; Burton K. Wheeler to Mr. Mervyn Rathborne, President, American Communications Association, March 3, 1938, Mss 298, Box 24, Folder 1, ACA Records; Mervyn Rathborne to Honorable Burton K. Wheeler, November 6, 1939, in Mss 298, Box 24, Folder 1, ACA Records; Joseph P. Selly to James Lawrence Fly, Chairman, FCC, November 28, 1939, in Mss 298, Box 24, Folder 1, ACA Records. During November and December of 1939, ACA suggested to FCC Chairman Fly "that the FCC establish a Labor Division," the purposes of which would be "to gather and collate statisics relative to the wages, hours and working conditions of workers in the communications industry; advise

the Commission concerning the effect on labor of rules and regulations which the Commission might promulgate, and act as a liaison between the Commission and the labor organizations in the communications industry." Mervyn Rathborne to Mr. James L. Fly, Chairman, FCC, December 4, 1939, in Mss 298, Box 24, Folder 1, ACA Records. See also, "C.I.O. Leader Hits FCC on Wire Plan," *New York Times*, December 9, 1939; "To: Mervyn Rathborne From: Daniel Driesen Subject: Wheeler-F.C.C. and Merger Legislation," November 4, 1939; Mervyn Rathborne to Thurman Arnold, December 14, 1939; Thurman Arnold to Mervyn Rathborne, December 27, 1939, all Mss 298, Box 24, Folder 1, ACA Records; "Supplementary Memorandum Regarding the Present Condition of the Telegraph Industry in the United States," September 27, 1939, in Mss 298, Box 24, Folder 1; "Report By Analysis Committee," May 21, 1941 in Box 24, Folder 4, 4, ACA Records.

49. William Burke, "ACA Michigan Head Asks CIO Fight Telegraph Merger," *CIO News* (Michigan edition), March 19, 1940, 10; From: C. Silberman, ACA, "CIO Hits FCC On Telegraph Merger Plan," For Release Thursday Evening Papers, January 4, Mss. 298, Box 24, Folder 2, ACA Records; "To: All Telegraph and Point-To-Point Locals From: Merger Investigating Committee," May 9, 1940, Mss 298, Box 24, Folder 1, ACA Records; "President Roosevelt Joins Monopolists," April 18, 1940, Mss 298, Box 24, Folder 2, ACA Records.

50. Statement of James Lawrence Fly, Chairman, FCC, in 77th Cong., 1st Sess., Senate, *Study of the Telegraph Industry, Hearings before a Subcommittee of the Committee on Interstate Commerce, Part 1, May 19–29, 1941* (Washington, DC: Government Printing Office, 1941), 33; Statement of Joseph P. Selly, 77th Cong., 1st Sess., Senate, *Study of the Telegraph Industry, Hearings Before a Subcommittee of the Committee on Interstate Commerce, Part 1, May 19–29, 1941* (Washington, DC: Government Printing Office, 1941), 128, 130–131.

51. Smythe, *Counterclockwise*, 21, 26, 17; Selly, *Hearings before a Subcommittee of the Committee on Interstate Commerce*, 128, 133–134.

52. Jerold S. Auerbach, *Labor and Liberty: The La Follette Committee & the New Deal* (Indianapolis: Bobbs-Merrill, 1966), 52–53; National Labor Relations Act, 29 U.S.C. 151–169; Auerbach, *Labor and Liberty*, 217; Auerbach, *Labor and Liberty*, 78; Auerbach, *Labor and Liberty*, 211.

53. 301 US 1 (1937). According to the La Follette Committee's pivotal staff member, secretary Robert Wohlforth, in 1937 at the height of its influence, the committee was drawing 48,000 words out of Washington on the Associated Press every night. Auerbach, *Labor and Liberty*, 83; J. Warren Madden, National Labor Relations Board chairman, in hearings on Senate Resolution 266, April 10, 1936 (authorizing the Civil Liberties Committee), in Auerbach, *Labor and Liberty*, 65.

54. Tomlins, *The State and the Unions*, 57, for Samuel Gompers' expression of this belief in 1899. See also, Montgomery, *The Fall of the House of Labor*; Gall, *Pursuing Justice*, 166; also White, *The Last Great Strike*; Wall, *Inventing the American Way*; Dale Benjamin Scott, "Labor's New Deal For Journalism: The Newspaper Guild in the 1930s" (Ph.D. diss., University of Illinois at Urbana-Champaign, 2009); Auerbach, *Labor and Liberty*, 78.

55. Frank Freidel, *Franklin D. Roosevelt: A Rendezvous with Destiny* (Boston: Back Bay Books, 1990), 142. For an account emphasizing bottom-up demands in St. Louis, Feurer, *Radical Unionism in the Midwest*, 31–34; Clarence Dill in *Congressional Record Senate, Vol. 78, Part 8, 73d Cong., 2nd Sess., May 15, 1934*, 8824.

56. E. O. Sykes, Chairman, Federal Communications Commission, *Letter Transmitting Recommendations of Three Proposed Amendments to The Communications Act of 1934, 74th Cong., 1st Sess., House of Representatives, Document No. 83, January 21, 1935* (Washington, DC: Government Printing Office, 1935), 4; *Recommendations of Three Proposed Amendments to the Communications Act of 1934*, 2 (quote), 2–3.

57. *Recommendations of Three Proposed Amendments to the Communications Act of 1934*, 3; *Recommendations of Three Proposed Amendments to the Communications Act of 1934*, 4–5.

58. "August 18, 1937 Delegation Consists of the Following," Mss 734, Box 3, Folder 5, ACA Records; *AT&T Annual Report 1915* (New York: 1916), 39–44.

59. United States of America before the National Labor Relations Board, Case No. C-344, In the Matter of The Western Union Telegraph Company, and American Communications Association, "Brief in Support of the Allegations in the Complaint," August 11, 1938, in Box 1, Folder 9, CIO Papers; Ulrikkson, *The Telegraphers*, 194; Mervyn Rathborne, "Memorandum To: John L. Lewis and Allan Haywood," April 24, 1940, 3–4, in Box 1, Folder 11, CIO Papers; Rathborne, "Memorandum To: John L. Lewis and Allan Haywood," CIO Papers; "Memorandum To: Phillip [sic] Murray From Joseph Selly Re Organization of Western Union Telegraph Company," January 6, 1941, 1–2, Box 1, Folder 12, CIO Papers.

60. Rathborne, "Memorandum To: John L. Lewis and Allan Haywood," CIO Papers; "Memorandum To: Phillip [sic] Murray From Joseph Selly, 1–2, Box 1, Folder 12, CIO Papers.

61. "Resolution Opposing the Creation of an Unregulated Monopoly in the Telegraph Industry," 1939, Mss 298, Box 24, Folder 1, ACA Records.

62. U.S. Cong., Senate. 75th Cong 3d Sess., *Hearing Before a Subcommittee of the Committee on Interstate Commerce On S. Res. 247, Investigation of Conditions in the Wire Communications Industry. 6 June 1938* (Washington, DC: Government Printing Office, 1938), 15; also, 20, 26–27.

63. "CTU President Cites ACA Communists Want to Control Western Union," *Telecommunications Reports* 6, no. 17 (November 29, 1939): 7–8; Statement of W. L. Allen, Secretary-Treasurer, CTU, Chicago, in 77th Cong., 1st Sess., Senate, *Study of the Telegraph Industry, Hearings Before a Subcommittee of the Committee on Interstate Commerce, Part 1, May 19–29, 1941* (Washington, DC: Government Printing Office, 1941), 182. AFL leaders and some affiliate unions had been stalwart anti-Communists since the Russian Revolution, sometimes barring Communists from union office. Bernstein, *The Lean Years*, 94, 141; "ARTA Mass Meeting, February 3, 1938, P.S. 95, New York City," Mss 298, Box 24, Folder 1, 2–3, ACA Records.

64. Danny Driesen, "ARTA Mass Meeting, February 3, 1938, P.S. 95, New York City," Mss 298, Box 24, Folder 1, 4–5, ACA Records; W. V. Wheaton to Hon. Carl Hatch, Albuquerque N.M., February 6, 1938, Mss 298, Box 24, Folder 1, ACA Records.

65. "ACA Position on Merger," Mss 298, Box 24, Folder 3, ACA Records; A long San Francisco strike against Western Union by operators, managers, clerks, and "the entire messenger force of 172" had by December "seriously crippled" the provision of telegraph service there. At RCA, too, things were heating up. Mervyn Rathborne to Thurman Arnold, December 14, 1939, Mss 298, Box 24, Folder 1, ACA Records; "President Roosevelt Joins Monopolists," April 18, 1940, Mss 298, Box 24, Folder 2, ACA Records.

66. "To: Mervyn Rathborne From: Daniel Driesen Subject: Wheeler-F.C.C. and Merger Legislation," November 4, 1939, Mss 298, Box 24, Folder 1, ACA Records; Attached to Joseph P. Selly to Burton K. Wheeler, December 2, 1941, Box 24, Folder 4, ACA Records.

67. "Confidential Memorandum To Joseph Selly From Daniel Driesen," November 28, 1939, Mss 298, Box 24, Folder 1, ACA Records; "ACA Position on Merger."

68. Zieger, *The CIO*, 145–146; Zeiger, *The CIO*, 147; Nelson Lichtenstein, *Labor's War at Home: The CIO in World War II* (New York: Cambridge, 1982); Andrew E. Kersten, *Labor's Home Front: The American Federation of Labor during World War II* (New York: NYU Press, 2006), 22–23; Brian Waddell, *The War against the New Deal: World War II and American Democracy* (Dekalb, IL: Northern Illinois University Press, 2001); Paul A.C. Koistinen, *Arsenal of World War II: The Political Economy of American Warfare 1940–1945* (Lawrence, KS: University Press of Kansas, 2004), 416–418; Joseph P. Selly to Phillip Murray, March 19, 1941, Mss 298, Box 24, Folder 3, ACA Records; Joseph P. Selly to Charles Silberman, Editor, ACA *News*, March 27, 1941, Mss 298, Box 24, Folder 3, ACA Records; also Huck, "Radio and the ACA," 37–38; Natalie Brennecke to Joseph P. Selly, April 11, 1941, Box 24, Folder 3, ACA Records; Marie Michalski to Joe Selly, April 11, 1941, Box 24, Folder 3, ACA Records.

69. Huck, "Radio and ACA," 34; Koistinen, *Arsenal of World War II*, 370. For the labor-management context, see, Lichtenstein, *The CIO's War at Home*; "Board of War Communications," No. 63359, September 17, 1942; Koistinen, Arsenal of World War II, 402, 370 (quote).

70. Joseph P. Selly, Dominick Panza, Daniel Driesen to All Locals, April 25, 1942, Box 24, Folder 4, ACA Records; Huck, "Radio and the ACA," 40; "Memorandum," February 6, 1942, Box 24, Folder 4, ACA Records; "Memorandum," February 6, 1942, Box 24, Folder 4, ACA Records.

71. "Report by Analysis Committee," May 21, 1941, Box 24 Folder 4, ACA Records.

72. Statement of James Lawrence Fly, Chairman, FCC, in 77th Cong., 1st Sess., Senate, *Study of the Telegraph Industry, Hearings Before a Subcommittee of the Committee on Interstate Commerce, Part 1, May 19–29, 1941* (Washington, DC: Government Printing Office, 1941), 6; Statement of James Lawrence Fly, Chairman, FCC, in 77th Cong., 1st Sess., *Hearings Before a Subcommittee of the Committee on Interstate Commerce*, 43; David F. Noble, "Present-Tense Technology," *democracy: A Journal of Political Renewal and Radical Change* 3, no. 2 (1983): 8–24.

73. "ACA Emergency Merger Defense Conference," May 21, 1941, Box 24, Folder 4, ACA Records; "To: All Locals From: Joseph P. Selly," July 28, 1942, Box 24, Folder 5, ACA

Records; "To: All Locals From: Daniel Driesen," December 17, 1942, Box 24, Folder 6, ACA Records; Illegible to Hon. Franklin D. Roosevelt, February 15, 1943, Box 24, Folder 6, ACA Records; Ulrikkson, *The Telegraphers*, 164.

74. "Subject: Wages for Victory vs. Merger for Profit," January 22, 1943, Box 24, Folder 6, ACA Records; Huck, "Radio and ACA," 33–34.

75. Ulrikkson, *The Telegraphers*, 164. These figures are probably not reliable; American Communications Association, CIO, "Organizing Guide for Field Organizers and Volunteer Organizers Western Union Organizing Campaign," [no date, but 1944], n.p., but fourth page. Author's collection; American Communications Association, CIO, "Organizing Guide for Field Organizers."; American Communications Association, CIO, "Organizing Guide for Field Organizers," first page; American Communications Association, CIO, "Organizing Guide for Field Organizers," fifth page; Ulrikkson, *The Telegraphers*, 165.

76. Ulrikkson, *The Telegraphers*, 166; Ulrikkson, *The Telegraphers*, 178; Statement of J. L. Wilcox, Vice President, Employee Relations, Western Union Telegraph Co., 82d Cong., 1st Sess., U.S. Senate, Committee on the Judiciary, Subcommittee to Investigate the Administration of the Internal Security Act, *Hearings on "Subversive Infiltration in the Telegraph Industry," May 14–June 14, 1951*, 86; Joseph P. Selly to Philip Murray, September 14, 1945, Box 1, Folder 13, CIO Papers; Dennis Mazzocco, in a study of ACA's role in radio broadcasting, states that the union "focused its resistance on the expected employer introduction of advanced electronic technology and forced mechanization. It agreed with the CIO that automation would eventually eradicate the strong craft demarcations that the AFL sought to maintain. Instead, it argued for an industrial broadcasting union which would eventually grow to include all U.S. communications workers." Mazzocco, "Democracy, Power, and Equal Rights," 159, 164; Huck, "Radio and the ACA," 4.

Chapter 6

1. W. A. Bastian, "The Story of the CWA Third Annual Convention," June 1949, 2, Box 12 Folder 12, Records of the Congress of Industrial Organizations, Special Collections of the University Libraries of the Catholic University of America, Washington, DC (hereafter CIO Papers); John N. Schacht, *The Making of Telephone Unionism, 1920–1947* (New Brunswick, NJ: Rutgers University Press, 1985), 19–20.

2. Schacht, *The Making of Telephone Unionism*, 20; Joseph A. Beirne Oral History by John N. Schacht, August 30, 1971, CWA-University of Iowa Oral History Project, University of Iowa Library Special Collections, 14; Beirne Oral History, 28 (hereafter Beirne Oral History); Venus Green, *Race on the Line: Gender, Labor, and Technology in the Bell System, 1880–1980* (Durham, NC: Duke University Press, 2001), 199; Schacht, *The Making of Telephone Unionism*, 23; Green, *Race on the Line*.

3. Green, *Race on the Line*, 137–158, sums up the toll taken by employee representation plans—company unions—on the self-understanding of Bell system employees. Also, Steven Peter Vallas, *Power in the Workplace: The Politics of Production at AT&T*

(Albany, NY: State University of New York Press, 1993), 35–81. A contemporary analyst wrote, "Employees are recruited carefully, and those that remain employed are treated fairly well, as modern business standards go. Of course, employees could gain greater advantages if they were organized. But the system has cultivated the 'white collar' psychology among its workers; and with employee welfare and benefit schemes, it has taken the edge off the psychology of self-help. . . . The company participates in the Special Conference Committee with eleven other 'blue ribbon' companies . . . devoted to the creation of 'harmonious relations' with employees, and to the promotion of company unions." N. B. Danielian, *AT&T: The Story of Industrial Conquest* (New York: Vanguard, 1939), 402; Schacht, *The Making of Telephone Unionism*, 6, 71; Green, *Race on the Line*, 96.

4. Danielian, *AT&T*, 280, 200, 206; Danielian, *AT&T*, 200–222; Schacht, *The Making of Telephone Unionism*, 37–38; Schacht, *The Making of Telephone Unionism*, 36; Danielian, *AT&T*, 280, 200, 206; Danielian, *AT&T*, 200–222; Schacht, *The Making of Telephone Unionism*, 37–38; Schacht, *The Making of Telephone Unionism*, 36; Schacht, *The Making of Telephone Unionism*, 66; Statement of Charles H. Parsons, General President of the United Telephone Organizations of New York, in 77th Cong., 1st Sess., Senate, Study of the Telegraph Industry, *Hearings Before a Subcommittee of the Committee on Interstate Commerce, Part 1, May 19–29, 1941* (Washington, DC: Government Printing Office, 1941), 200. See also, Beirne Oral History, 16.

5. Green, *Race on the Line*, 183.

6. Mary Heaton Vorse, *Labor's New Millions* (New York: Modern Age Books, 1938), 13; Danielian, *AT&T*, 402–403.

7. Schacht, *The Making of Telephone Unionism*, 52–53; June McDonald, who went on to be a top organizer for NFTW and a district representative for CWA, in 1939 started working as a Bell operator at age 18, in Waukegan, Illinois. At a meeting of the company union, she was elected a steward. "Strangely enough," she recalled, "we started working into a real union." June McDonald interview by John N. Schach, February 12, 1969, in CWA-University of Iowa Oral History Project, University of Iowa Library Special Collections, 5. This movement from company unionism to a genuinely independent union of telephone workers found a historical parallel in the CIO's strategy to organize the steel industry by encouraging its employee representation plans and ultimately incorporating them into a CIO umbrella organization called the Steel Workers Organizing Committee. Michael Goldfield, *The Southern Key: Class, Race, and Radicalism in the 1930s and 1940s* (New York: Oxford University Press, 2020), 136, 155–158; Jack Barbash, *Unions and Telephones: The Story of the Communications Workers of America* (New York: Harper and Brothers, 1952), 26, 80; Quote in Thomas R. Brooks, *Communications Workers of America: The Story of a Union* (New York: Mason/Charter, 1977), 100.

8. Brooks, *Communications Workers of America*, 85; Beirne Oral History, 14; Schacht, *The Making of Telephone Unionism*, 59; Green, *Race on the Line*, 173; Barbash, *Unions and Telephones*, 50; Schacht, *The Making of Telephone Unionism*, 58; CWA, "Affiliation: Stewards and Officers Fact Sheet," 2, Box 2, Folder 11, CIO Papers; J. A. Beirne, President, Communications Workers of America, "CIO Affiliation," March 21, 1949, Box 2, Folder 11, CIO Papers.

9. Judith Stepan-Norris and Maurice Zeitlin, *Left Out: Reds and America's Industrial Unions* (Cambridge: Cambridge University Press, 2003), 317–319, 172–182, 202–206; TWNS, "A.F.L.-C.I.O. Independent," *The Telephone Worker* 2, no. 5 (November 1943): 13; TWNS, "A.F.L.-C.I.O. Independent," *The Telephone Worker* 2, no. 5 (November 1943): 13; Henry L. Mayer, "The Tormented Telephone Worker Open Season Again," *The Telephone Worker* 2, no. 6 (December 1943): 10–11.

10. Brooks, *Communications Workers of America*, 83; Given that, as Goldfield shows, Philip Murray had previously expressly targeted company unions as ripe for organization by the CIO, this disparagement may have harbored a sexist element, as the telephone workforce contained a large fraction of women. Goldfield, *Southern Key*, 136, 148–158; Ruth Wiencek interview by John N. Schacht, April 30, 1970, in CWA-University of Iowa Oral History Project, University of Iowa Library Special Collections, 4, 17.

11. See "Jurisdictional Disputes with I.B.E.W. Continue in Ohio," *The Telephone Worker* 2, no. 8 (February 1944): 11; "IBEW Still Trying to Grab Telephone Work," *The Telephone Worker* 2, no. 8 (February 1944): 14; "More IBEW Raiding Attempts," *The Telephone Worker* 2, no. 8 (February 1944): 15. See also, "President Beirne Addresses San Francisco Radio Audience," *The Telephone Worker* 5, no. 7 (January 1945): 4; McDonald interview, 10; June McDonald interview, 11; "ACA Lies Again," *The Telephone Worker*, May 1944, 14.

12. Wiencek interview, 13, 1; "Telephone Workers on Trial!," *Long Lines Federation Voice* 5, no. 9 (October 1945): 8; "Henry Mayer's Monthly Report," *Long Lines Federation Voice* 5, no. 1 (January 1945): 16. Mayer followed up later in 1945 with updates. "Mayer's Monthly Report," *Long Lines Federation Voice* 5, no. 7 (July 1945), 16–17; Schacht, *The Making of Telephone Unionism*, 70, 106; Schacht, *The Making of Telephone Unionism*, 136–142.

13. It helped that erstwhile ACA President Mervyn Rathborne had ties to Harry Bridges, the head of the longshoremen and state CIO director. "Telephone Department Report to the 20th Meeting of the International Executive Board," September 24, 1946, 1, Mss 734, Box 2, Folder 16, American Communications Association Additions, 1934–1966, State Historical Society of Wisconsin (hereafter ACA Records); Joseph P. Selly to Philip Murray, President, Congress of Industrial Organizations, April 18, 1942, Box 1, Folder 13, CIO Papers; Paul Schnur to Allen S. Haywood, Director of Organization, September 24, 1942, Box,1 Folder 13, CIO Papers; Joseph P. Selly to R. J. Nugent, March 2, 1943; and Claire Brown to Allan Haywood, March 15, 1943, both Box 1, Folder 13, CIO Papers; Schacht, *The Making of Telephone Unionism*, 174, 108, 235, n31.

14. "High Labor Turnover in Phone Industry," *The Telephone Worker* 2, no. 8 (February 1944): 15; Schacht, *The Making of Telephone Unionism*, 104–105. Schacht cites a contemporary survey of fifty-five industries that revealed that "telephone's relative wage ranking declined further than that of any other industry" (104); J.A. Beirne, "A 'Phone Girl's Expenses," *The Telephone Worker* 2, no. 5 (November 1943): 7; McDonald interview, 5.

15. Barbash, *Unions and Telephones*, 41–42; Schacht, *The Making of Telephone Unionism*, 110, 136–140; Pearce Davis and Henry J. Meyer, eds., *Labor Dispute Settlements in the Telephone Industry 1942–1945* (Washington, DC: Bureau of National Affairs, 1946); McDonald interview, 8; Wiencek interview, 10.
16. "Report of ACA Local 101 to the I.E.B. (Telephone)," February 7, 1945, Mss 734, Box 2, Folder 14, ACA Records.
17. "Report of Local 103 to 16th Meeting of the I.E.B.," 1945, Mss 734, Box 2, Folder 14, ACA Records; William Burke to Allan S. Haywood, August 12, 1946, Box 1, Folder 13, CIO Papers; Schacht, *The Making of Telephone Unionism*, 108; "Telephone Department Report to the 20th Meeting of the International Executive Board."; Schacht, *The Making of Telephone Unionism*, 159.
18. Roger Keeran, *The Communist Party and the Auto Workers Unions* (Bloomington, IN: Indiana University Press, 1980), 236; Ronald L. Fillipelli and Mark D. McColloch, *Cold War in the Working Class: The Rise and Decline of the United Electrical Workers* (Albany, NY: SUNY Press, 1994), 86; George Lipsitz, *Rainbow at Midnight: Labor and Culture in the 1940s* (Urbana, IL: University of Illinois Press, 1994). Zieger claims 3 percent of available working time was lost. Robert H. Zieger, *The CIO 1933–1955* (Chapel Hill, NC: University of North Carolina Press, 1995), 223; Steven Kalgaard Ashby, "Shattered Dreams: The American Working Class and the Origins of the Cold War, 1945–1949" (Ph.D. diss. University of Chicago, 1993), 125–172, 167 (quote).
19. McDonald interview, 7; Henry Mayer to Honorable John Steelman, December 3, 1945, Harry S. Truman Presidential Library and Museum, Independence, Missouri (Hereafter Truman Presidential Library), Official File Box 1929, Folder 407-B; Schacht, *The Making of Telephone Unionism*, 147–150; John W. Gibson to J. J. Moran, President, American Union of Telephone Workers, January 19, 1948, Papers of John W. Gibson, Assistant Secretary of Labor, Labor Disputes File Box 22, "Telephone Strike, 1947," Truman Presidential Library.
20. Twentieth Century Fund, "Facts and Issues in the Telephone Dispute," Washington, DC, April 5, 1947, 2, Official File Box 1229, Folder 407-B, Truman Presidential Library; Schacht, *The Making of Telephone Unionism*, 150–153.
21. Wiencek interview, 10; Wiencek interview, 25.
22. Schacht, *The Making of Telephone Unionism*, 165–166; Ashby, "Shattered Dreams," 242–303.
23. Joseph A. Beirne, *Challenge to Labor: New Roles for American Trade Unions* (Englewood Cliffs, NJ: Prentice-Hall, 1969), 20, 12, 24, 25, 29–30, 27.
24. Schacht, *The Making of Telephone Unionism*, 162–172. Retail prices rose 30 percent between June 1946 and August 1948. Christopher Tomlins, *The State and the Unions Labor Relations, Law, and the Organized Labor Movement in America, 1880–1960* (Cambridge: Cambridge University Press, 1985), 255; Brooks, *Communications Workers of America*, 119; Schacht, *The Making of Telephone Unionism*, 162.
25. Twentieth Century Fund, "Facts and Issues in the Telephone Dispute," Washington, DC, April 5, 1947, 2, Official File Box 1229, Folder 407-B, Truman Presidential Library; McDonald interview, 8, 12; Helen W. Berthelot interview by John Schacht,

May 6, 1969, 12, in CWA-University of Iowa Oral History Project, University of Iowa Library Special Collections.
26. Schacht, *The Making of Telephone Unionism*, 166; Berthelot interview, 11, 10; Berthelot interview, 12.
27. Alfred P. Sloan, in Nelson Lichtenstein, *State of the Union: A Century of American Labor*, 2nd ed. (Princeton, NJ: Princeton University Press, 2013), 107.
28. *93d Congressional Record, Volume 93, Part 3, House of Representatives*, April 16, 1947, 3524; *Congressional Record—House*, April 3, 1947, 3123; *Congressional Record—House*, April 3, 1947, 3124.
29. Archibald Cox, "Seizure in Emergency Disputes," in Irving Bernstein, Harold L. Enarson, and R. W. Fleming, *Emergency Disputes and National Policy* (New York: Harper & Brothers, 1955), 227.
30. Labor-Management Relations Act 1947, 29 U.S.C. Sec. Sec. 141–197, Sections 206–209. See William S. White, "Injunction to Bar Phone Halt Asked in Emergency Bill," *New York Times*, April 1, 1947, 1; Harry A. Millis and Emily Clark Brown, *From the Wagner Act to Taft-Hartley: A Study of National Labor Policy and Labor Relations* (Chicago: University of Chicago Press, 1950), 271–392; Gilbert J. Gall, *Pursuing Justice: Lee Pressman, the New Deal, and the CIO* (Albany, NY: State University of New York Press, 1999), 206–215; Bernstein, Enarson, and Fleming, *Emergency Disputes and National Policy*; Nelson Lichtenstein, "Taft-Hartley: A Slave Labor Law?," *Catholic University Law Review* 47, no. 3 (Spring 1998): 779–789; A. H. Raskin, "New Jersey Ready for Phone Seizure," *New York Times*, April 4, 1947, 4; Brooks, *Communications Workers of America*, 120; Arthur Krock, "Virginia Shows Way," *New York Times*, April 9, 1947, 19; Millis and Brown, *From the Wagner Act to Taft-Hartley*, 331; William S. White, "Enjoining of Great Strikes Favored by Senate Group," *New York Times*, April 8, 1947, 1, 18.
31. Louis Stark, "Phone Seizure Is Weighed; Truman Doubts Legality," *New York Times*, April 4, 1947, 1; Louis Stark, "Opinion Assailed," *New York Times*, April 5, 1947, 1; "Memorandum For: Clark Clifford From: Charles Denny," April 5, 1947, President's Secretary's Files Box 119, Folder "Strikes: Telephone," Truman Presidential Library; Caplan, "Hello, CIO Speaking," *CIO News* 10, no. 31 (August 4, 1947): 7.
32. Memorandum To: Clark Clifford From: Charles R. Denny, April 10, 1947, Memorandum To: Clark Clifford From: Charles R. Denny, April 21, 1947, and Memo For: Clark Clifford From: Charles Denny, FCC, April 8, 1947 Official File Box 1229 Folder 407-B, Truman Presidential Library; Memo For: Clark Clifford From: Charles Denny, FCC, April 8, 1947, Official File Box 1229, Folder 407-B, Truman Presidential Library; "Flood of Business at Western Union," *New York Times*, April 8, 1947, 16.
33. Statement of J. L. Wilcox, vice president employee relations, Western Union Telegraph Co., New York, 82d Cong., 1st Sess., U.S. Senate, Committee on the Judiciary, Subcommittee to Investigate the Administration of the Internal Security Act, *Hearings on "Subversive Infiltration In The Telegraph Industry," May 14–June 14, 1951* (Washington, DC: Government Printing Office, 1951), 80.
34. "Western Electric Phony Union Exposed by UE Members," *UE News* 7, no. 2 (January 13, 1945): 12; "UE Trounces Company Union in 2nd Western Electric Plant," *UE News*

7, no. 29 (July 21, 1945), 12; Schacht, *The Making of Telephone Unionism*, 169; United Brotherhood of Telephone Workers, Telegram to Phillip Murray, April 10, 1947, Phillip Murray Papers, #64, CIO Series Unions Subseries CWA, Box 97, Folder 5, CIO Papers.

35. Green, *Race on the Line*, 165; Vivian E. Pierson to Harry Truman, April 16, 1947, Official File Box 1229, Folder P, Truman Presidential Library and Museum, Independence, Missouri. Mary V. Marstellar, president of this union, attacked Secretary Schwellenbach's radio broadcast equally forthrightly. Mary V. Marstellar to President Truman, telegram to President from Los Angeles, April 16, 1947, Official File Box 1229, Folder M, Truman Presidential Library; Charles H. Loeb, *The Future Is Yours: The History of the Future Outlook League 1935–1946* (Cleveland: Future Outlook League, 1947), 75, 76, 84, 86; Brooks, *Communications Workers of America*, 90; Wiencek interview, 20.

36. "U.S. Department of Labor Report on the Telephone Strike by Secretary L. B. Schwellenbach on American Broadcasting System 9:30 p.m., April 15, 1947," Official File, Box 1229, Folder 407-B, 1, 3, 6, 7, 8, Harry S. Truman Presidential Library.

37. Quoted in Schatz, *Electrical Workers*, 170; Wilson quoted in Schatz, *Electrical Workers*, 170; "Labor-Management Relations in Bell System," *CWA News* 10, no. 2 (February 1951): 9; Quoted in Brooks, *Communications Workers of America*, 137; Richter wrote to President Truman, "I know some of your advisors believe that the only people who count in this country are those with big money. Perhaps it is easy for them to forget that labor cannot be separated from 'the public.'" Quoted in Ashby, "Shattered Dreams," 401.

38. George Gallup, Director, American Institute of Public Opinion, "The Gallup Poll Public Sympathy With Worker In National Telephone Strike," clipping, no source indicated (perhaps *Washington Post*), dateline Princeton, New Jersey, April 28, papers of John W. Gibson, Assistant Secretary of Labor, Labor Disputes File Box 22, "Telephone Strike, 1947," Truman Presidential Library.

39. James Boylan, *The New Deal Coalition and the Election of 1946* (New York: Garland, 1981); Schacht, *The Making of Telephone Unionism*, 80; Schacht, *The Making of Telephone Unionism*, 170; In Lipsitz, *Rainbow at Midnight*, 336–337; Margaret Millar, *Beast in View* (1955; repr. ed., New York: Syndicate Books, 2018), 21. Still, in 1955, occupational statistics reveal that Millar's "white" face reflected the fact that the operator workforce was overwhelmingly white. Green, *Race on the Line*, 183.

40. Telephone Department Report to the 20th Meeting of the International Executive Board."; Telephone Department Report to the 20th Meeting of the International Executive Board."; Schacht, *The Making of Telephone Unionism*, 108.

41. Barbash, *Unions and Telephones*, 180; "TWOC Failures," *The CWA News* 7, no. 2 (February 1948): 4; CWA, "Questions and Answers on Affiliation," March 3, 1949, in Box 2 Folder 11, CIO Papers; CIO, "Leaders Hail Affiliation of Communication Workers to CIO," May 9, 1949, 2, Box 1, Folder 17, CIO Papers; Philip Murray to Howard Jones, March 17, 1949, Box 1, Folder 15, CIO Papers.

42. "TWOC Pressure," *The CWA News* 6, no. 4 (October 1947): 4; Barbash, *Unions and Telephones*, 95; "CIO Should Drop TWOC," *The CWA News* 6, no. 3 (September 1947): 6.

43. Stanley Ruttenberg and Leslie Fishman, *Economic Data about the Telephone Industry, For Use of Negotiators of the Various Unions Affiliated with the Telephone Workers Organizing Committee, C.I.O., April 15, 1948* (Washington, DC: Telephone Workers Organizing Committee, C.I.O., 1948), Section Six, 2; National Federation of Telephone Workers, "A Brief Resume of the Telephone Strike which Began April 7, 1947" (Washington, DC, 1947), 4, Philip Murray Papers, Files for "Telephone Workers Organizing Committee," The American Catholic History Research Center and University Archives, Catholic University of America.
44. For the AFL offer to CW, and the response by the CWA Executive, Box 2, Folder 11, CIO Papers; International Brotherhood of Electrical Workers, February 11, 1949, 2, Box 2, Folder 11, CIO Papers; Ruth Wiencek recalled that "the telephone workers I met and worked with who were pro-CWA were a nucleus of older women, in their fifties, who had been part of the IBEW and had participated in the 1925 strike that was so disastrous." Wiencek interview with John N. Schacht, 23.
45. Schacht, *The Making of Telephone Unionism*, 174–175; Wiencek interview, 12; Interview with Joseph Selly by John N. Schacht, 1972, in Schacht, *The Making of Telephone Unionism*, 234 n29.
46. CIO, "Leaders Hail Affiliation of Communication Workers to CIO," May 9, 1949, 2, Box 1, Folder 17, CIO Papers.
47. Ronald L. Filipelli and Mark D. McColloch, *Cold War in the Working Class: The Rise and Decline of the United Electrical Workers* (Albany, NY: SUNY Press, 1994); Steve Fraser, *Labor Will Rule: Sidney Hillman and the Rise of American Labor* (Ithaca, NY: Cornell University Press, 1993), 517; Lichtenstein, "Taft-Hartley," 771; Ashby, "Shattered Dreams," 5.
48. Ashby, "Shattered Dreams," 409–458. For a vivid account of life in postwar Germany, see Harald Jahner, *Aftermath: Life in the Fallout of the Third Reich 1945–1955* (London: W. H. Allen, 2021).
49. Gall, *Pursuing Justice*, 192–211, esp. 198; Keeran, *The Communist Party and the Auto Workers*, 256, 258, 262; Landon R. Y. Storrs, *The Second Red Scare and the Unmaking of the New Deal Left* (Princeton, NJ: Princeton University Press, 2013); Carey was a longtime FBI collaborator. Sigmund Diamond, "Labor History vs. Labor Historiography: The FBI, James B. Carey, and the Association of Catholic Trade Unionists," in *Religion Ideology and Nationalism in Europe and America: Essays Presented in Honor of Yehoshua Arieli* (Jerusalem: The Historical Society of Israel and the Zalman Shazar Center for Jewish History, 1986), 299–328. Zieger, *The CIO*, 257–277; I am generally indebted to Ashby, "Shattered Dreams."
50. Steve Rosswurm, "The Catholic Church and the Left-Led Unions: Labor Priests, Labor Schools, and the ACTU," in Steve Rosswurm, ed., *The CIO's Left-led Unions* (New Brunswick: Rutgers University Press, 1992), 119–137; Douglas P. Seaton, *Catholics and Radicals: The Association of Catholic Trade Unionists and the American Labor Movement, from Depression to Cold War* (Lewisburg: Bucknell University Press, 1981), 173, 61; James B. Coogan, President, New York Local, National Association of National Association of Telephone Equipment Workers, to J. A. Beirne, January 13, 1948; and J. A. Beirne to James B. Coogan, January 14, 1948, both in WAG 124, CWA

Papers, Box 69, Folder 13, Tamiment Library, Robert F. Wagner Labor Archives, New York University.

51. Ellen W. Schrecker, "McCarthyism and the Labor Movement: The Role of the State," in Rosswurm, *The CIO's Left-led Unions*, 139; Andrew E. Kersten, *Labor's Home Front: The American Federation of Labor during World War II* (New York: New York University Press, 2006), 42; Tomlins, *The State and the Unions*; Filipelli and McColloch, *Cold War in the Working Class*, 105. For the years-long run-up to Taft-Hartley, see also, James C. Foster, *The Union Politic: The CIO Political Action Committee* (Columbia, MO: University of Missouri Press, 1975), 1–107; Millis and Brown, *From the Wagner Act to Taft-Hartley*, 271–392; Zieger, *The CIO*, 241–252; For clarification, Lichtenstein, "Taft-Hartley."; Statements of Walter John Jacobsen, James P. Ryan, and Louis Wallis in 82d Cong., 2d Sess., Senate, *Subversive Infiltration in the Telegraph Industry, Supplemental Hearing before the Subcommittee to Investigate the Administration of the Internal Security Act and Other Internal Security Laws of the Committee on the Judiciary, January 22, 1952* (Washington, DC: Government Printing Office, 1952), 273–289, 293; Ashby, "Shattered Dreams," 326, 327, 335; Michael Denning, *The Cultural Front: The Laboring of American Culture in the Twentieth Century* (London: Verso, 1996).

52. Labor Management Relations Act, 29 U.S.C. Sec. Sec. 141–197 [Title 29, Chapter 7, United States Code] Section 1B; Gary Gerstle, *Liberty and Coercion: The Paradox of American Government from the Founding to the Present* (Princeton, NJ: Princeton University Press, 2015), 243; Tomlins, *The State and the Unions*, 280; Howell John Harris, *The Right to Manage: Industrial Relations Policies of American Business in the 1940s* (Madison, WI: University of Wisconsin Press, 1982), 127; Lichtenstein, "Taft-Hartley," 765, 763.

53. Zieger, *The CIO*, 261–266.

54. Letter from Paul E Griffith, President NFTW, May 22, 1942, and handwritten note from "M. W.," both in OF 168 Folder Telephones 1941–1942, Franklin D. Roosevelt Presidential Library and Museum, Hyde Park, New York (hereafter Roosevelt Presidential Library); Lawrence Kammet, "ACA Parley Backs Steel Demands, Urges Fourth Term," *CIO News* 7, no. 15 (April 10, 1944): 2; President's Personal File 8687-8753 PPF 8701, "American Communications Association, C.I.O." Later in 1944, the NFTW, now seemingly accredited as an independent organization, secured a somewhat warmer greeting from FDR himself as it convened in Denver. President Franklin D. Roosevelt to Joseph A. Beirne, June 7, 1944, President's Personal File 8754-8828, Folder "National Federation of Telephone Workers," Roosevelt Presidential Library; *CWA News, Convention Issue* 7, no. 7 (July 1947): front cover.

55. "The CIO Should Clean House," *The Telephone Worker* 4, no. 3 (September 1945): 11; "Who's Who in the CIO," *The Telephone Worker* 4, no. 5 (November 1945): 3; "A Communist TWOC?," *The CWA News* 7, no. 2 (February 1948): 4. See also, CWA, "Questions and Answers on Affiliation," March 3, 1949, Box 2, Folder 11, CIO Papers.

56. Zieger, *The CIO*, 97–102; "TWOC, a Step-Child," *The CWA News* 6, no. 6 (December 1947): 4.

57. Schacht, *The Making of Telephone Unionism*, 175; Barbash, *Unions and Telephones*, 89; Joseph P. Selly to Allan S. Haywood, September 2, 1947, Box 1, Folder 14, CIO Papers.
58. "Agreement regarding Telephone Workers Organizations in California, now Local Unions of the American Communications Association, between Allan S. Haywood, Chairman, Telephone Workers Organizing Committee, C.I.O., and Joseph P. Selly, President, American Communications Association," January 8, 1948, Box 1, Folder 14, CIO Papers.
59. Wiencek interview, 12; "To: All I.E.B. Members; From: Joseph P. Selly, President; Subject: Telephone Jurisdiction," January 20, 1948, Box 1, Folder 14, CIO Papers; Philip Murray to Joseph Selly, January 8, 1948, Box 1, Folder 14, CIO Papers; "To: All I.E.B. Members; From: Joseph P. Selly, President; Subject: Telephone Jurisdiction," January 20, 1948, Box 1, Folder 14, CIO Papers.
60. W. R. Steinberg to R. J. Thomas, April 6, 1949, 3, Box 1, Folder 16, CIO Papers; "To All CIO Union Members," March 2, 1949; Philip D. Boothroyd to Philip Murray, March 5, 1949; Frank A. Lenahan to Phillip [sic] Murray, March 7, 1949; Joseph P. Selly to R. J. Thomas, March 23, 1949, all Box 1, Folder 15, CIO Papers; R. J. Thomas to Joseph P. Selly, October 6, 1949, Box 2, Folder 13, CIO Papers.
61. Joseph P. Selly to Philip Murray, April 12, 1949, 1, Box 1, Folder 16, CIO Papers. On Goldberg, see David L. Stebenne, *Arthur J. Goldberg: New Deal Liberal* (New York: Oxford University Press, 1996).
62. Selly to Murray, April 12, 1949, 2, in Box 1, Folder 16, CIO Papers.
63. R. J. Thomas to William Steinberg, April 21, 1949, Box 1, Folder 16, CIO Papers. A parallel may be found in the CIO's acquiescence to raids against the UE by some of its most powerful unions, notably the UAW. Filipelli and McCulloch, *Cold War in the Working Class*, 118–121; Morton Bahr, *From the Telegraph to the Internet* (Washington, DC: National Press Books, 1998), 42–43, 46.
64. CWA Northwestern Division #45, "Division Board Bulletin—Volume 2—Number 6," March 8, 1949, 3, Box 2, Folder 11, CIO Papers; CWA Northwestern Division #45, "Division Board Bulletin—Volume 2—Number 3," March 3, 1949, and CWA, "Questions and Answers on Affiliation," March 3, 1949, 6, both Box 2, Folder 11, CIO Papers; J. A. Beirne, President, CWA, to D. W. Tracy, International President, IBEW, February 23, 1949, 3, Box 2, Folder 11, CIO Papers; Brooks, *Communications Workers of America*, 140.
65. Allan S. Haywood to Edward V. Piel, February 4, 1949; Philip Murray to Joseph A. Beirne, February 6, 1949; and Allan S. Haywood to Joseph Beirne, February 14, 1949, Box 1, Folder 15, CIO Papers; "Report and Recommendations of the Joint Committee for Uniting CWA-CIO and TWOC-CIO," Box 10, Folder 21, CIO Papers; Joseph A. Beirne Oral History, 38; Brooks, *Communications Workers of America*, 159–162.
66. "Leaders Hail Affiliation of Communication Workers to CIO," May 9, 1949, Box 1, Folder 17, CIO Papers; Philip Murray to C. W. Werkau, July 8, 1949, Box 2, Folder 13, CIO Papers; "Big CWA Drive Launched," *CWA Beacon* 1, no. 1 (August 12, 1949): 1.
67. In W. A. Bastian, "The Story of the CWA Third Annual Convention," June 1949, 3, Box 2, Folder 12, CIO Papers.

68. Zieger, *The CIO, 1933–1955*, 277–293; "Resolution Expelling the American Communications Association," Box 1, Folder 17, CIO Papers.
69. Alessandro Brogi, "The AFL and CIO between 'Crusade' and Pluralism in Italy, 1944–1963," in eds. Robert Anthony Waters, Jr., and Geert Van Goethem, *American Labor's Global Ambassadors: The International History of the AFL-CIO during the Cold War* (New York: Palgrave-Macmillan, 2013), 66; C.W. Werkau, quoted in Brooks, *Communications Workers of America*, 149; "Can We Afford the Status Quo?," *The Telephone Worker* 3, no. 10 (April 1945): n.p.; "A Program Needed," *CWA News* 7 (March 3, 1948), 4; "Greed for Profits," *CWA News* 7 (December 12, 1948): 4; "Beirne Asks Congress to Pass Equal-pay Legislation to End Exploitation of Women Workers," *CWA News* 7 (March 3, 1948): 3; "CWA Calls for Progressive Democratic Platform; Party Gives Approval to Program," *CWA News* 7 (August 8, 1948): 1 (quote); "Beirne Raps AT&T for 'Excessive' Phone Rates," *CWA News* 8 (January 1, 1949): 7. This reform program was carried forward to CWA's 1949 Convention. W. A. Bastian, "The Story of the CWA Third Annual Convention," June 1949, 12–13, Box 2, Folder 12, CIO Papers; Green, *Race on the Line*: 207, 324 n66.

Chapter 7

1. Sinclair Lewis, *Babbit* (Harmondsworth: Penguin, 1961); Robert S. Lynd and Helen Merrell Lynd, *Middletown: A Study in Modern American Culture* (New York: Harcourt, Brace & World, 1929); Robert S. Lynd, with the assistance of Alice C. Hanson, "The People as Consumers," in *Report of the President's Research Committee on Social Trends, Recent Social Trends in the United States* (New York: McGraw-Hill, 1933), 857–911.
2. Roy Rosenzweig, *Eight Hours for What We Will: Workers and Leisure in an Industrial City* (New York: Cambridge University Press, 1983); David R. Roediger and Philip S. Foner, *Our Own Time: A History of Labor and the Working Day* (New York: Verso, 1989); Stuart Ewen, *Captains of Consciousness* (New York: McGraw-Hill, 1976); William Leach, *Land of Desire: Merchants, Power, and the Rise of a New American Culture* (New York: Vintage, 1994); Lizabeth Cohen, *A Consumers' Republic: The Politics of Mass Consumption in Postwar America* (New York: Vintage, 2003); Thomas A. Stapleford, "Defining a 'Living Wage' in America: Transformations in Union Wage Theories, 1870–1930," *Labor History* 49, no. 1 (February 2008): 1–22; Stephen Meyer, III, *The Five Dollar Day: Labor Management and Social Control in the Ford Motor Company, 1908–1921* (Albany, NY: SUNY Press, 1981); Lawrence B. Glickman, *A Living Wage: American Workers and the Making of Consumer Society* (Chapel Hill, NC: University of North Carolina Press, 1997); Into the 1920s, "working-class consumption habits remained largely . . . security conscious, and tied to communal functions. Relatively small sums were spent on recreation, movies, household help, and vehicles. While the technology of mass culture—radio, phonograph, movies, the automobile—were [sic] certainly becoming commonplaces in the material

culture of working-class immigrants, they were embedded within the intertwined networks of family, church, ethnicity, and even trade union." Steven Fraser, *Labor Will Rule: Sidney Hillman and the Rise of American Labor* (Ithaca, NY: Cornell University Press, 1991), 226; see also, Elizabeth Ewen, *Immigrant Women in the Land of Dollars: Life and Culture on the Lower East Side* (New York: Monthly Review, 1985); Kathy Peiss, *Cheap Amusements: Working Women and Leisure in Turn-of-the-century New York* (Philadelphia: Temple University Press, 1986); David Nasaw, *Going Out: The Rise and Fall of Public Amusements* (Cambridge, MA: Harvard University Press, 1999); Ewen, *Immigrant Women in the Land of Dollars*; Richard Ohmann, *Selling Culture: Magazines, Markets and Class at the Turn of the Century* (New York: Verso, 1996). The transition encompassed sporadic cooperatives and other kinds of nonprofit and collective consumption. Dana Frank, *Purchasing Power: Consumer Organizing, Gender, and the Seattle Labor Movement, 1919–1929* (Cambridge: Cambridge University Press, 1994); James Gilbert, *A Cycle of Outrage: America's Reaction to the Juvenile Delinquent in the 1950s* (New York: Oxford University Press, 1988); Michael Denning, *The Cultural Front: The Laboring of American Culture in the Twentieth Century* (New York: Verso, 1996).

3. Rosanne Currarino, *The Labor Question in America: Economic Democracy in the Gilded Age* (Urbana, IL: University of Illinois Press, 2011), 86–113, esp. 95.

4. Edward A. Filene, *The Way Out: A Forecast of Coming Changes in American Business and Industry* (New York: Doubleday, Page & Company, 1925), 71–72, 96, 176; Irving Bernstein, *The Lean Years: A History of the American Worker 1920–1933* (Chicago: Haymarket Books, 2010), 250; Mark Hendrickson, *American Labor and Economic Citizenship: New Capitalism from World War I to the Great Depression* (Cambridge: Cambridge University Press, 2013).

5. Bernstein, *The Lean Years*, 179–180; Hendrickson, *American Labor and Economic Citizenship*, 35–77, 299; Stapleford, "Defining a 'Living Wage' in America," 11; Quoted in Robert H. Zieger, *The CIO, 1935–1955* (Chapel Hill, NC: University of North Carolina Press, 1995), 15; see also, Fraser, *Labor Will Rule*: 208, 215; Stapleford, "Defining a 'living wage'": 11–14; Hendrickson, *American Labor and Economic Citizenship*, 14, 124–139, 301.

6. Steve Fraser, "The New Deal in the American Political Imagination," *Jacobin* (July 2019): 3, 4, https://jacobin.com/2019/06/new-deal-great-depression.

7. Christopher L. Tomlins, *The State and the Unions* (Cambridge: Cambridge University Press, 1985), 195, 99 (quote); Bernstein, *The Lean Years*, 476; Lawrence B. Glickman, *A Living Wage: American Workers and the Making of Consumer Society* (Chapel Hill, NC: University of North Carolina Press, 1997), 132; Robert F. Wagner, "Address at the Institute of Social Order," May 7, 1947, quoted in Tomlins, *State and the Unions*, 282. See also, Meg Jacobs, *Pocketbook Politics: Economic Citizenship in Twentieth-century America* (Princeton, NJ: Princeton University Press, 2007); Communications Workers of America Northwestern Division No. 45, *Division Board Bulletin* 2, no. 6 (March 8, 1949): 3, in Box 2, Folder 11, Papers of the Congress of Industrial Organizations, The Catholic University of America Research Center, Washington, D.C. (hereafter CIO Papers).

8. Ellis Hawley, *The New Deal and the Problem of Monopoly: A Study in Economic Ambivalence*, rev. ed. (New York: Fordham University Press, 1995); David Harvey, *The Condition of Postmodernity* (Oxford: Basil Blackwell, 1989), 125–126, 128 (quote).

9. Stanley Vittoz, *New Deal Labor Policy and the American Industrial Economy* (Chapel Hill, NC: University of North Carolina Press, 1987), 81; A portent arrived when, responding to "rank-and-file pressure" induced by rampant and chronic joblessness, in 1931. the leaders of the American Federation of Labor broke with their own earlier voluntarism and called to institute federally supported unemployment insurance. Bernstein, *The Lean Years*, 351, 353; Filene, *The Way Out*, 95, 99.

10. Denning, *The Cultural Front*, 6–8, 21–38.

11. Caroline F. Ware and Gardiner C. Means, *The Modern Economy in Action* (New York: Harcourt, Brace and Company, 1936), 75–78, 181–195; 76th Cong., 3d Session, Pursuant to Public Resolution No. 113, *Hearings before the Temporary National Economic Committee, Investigation of Concentration of Economic Power, Part 30: Technology and Concentration of Economic Power, April, 1940, Testimony of Caroline F. Ware* (Washington, DC: Government Printing Office, 1940), 17204–17219; Currarino, *Labor Question*, 4–5, 87, 112–113, 148; Jacobs, *Pocketbook Politics*, 174. On Ware, see, Eleanor Capper, "Caroline Ware and the Office of Price Administration: A Case Study of Consumer Politics during the Second World War," in Daniel Scroop, ed., *Consuming Visions: New Essays on the Politics of Consumption in Modern America* (Newcastle: Cambridge Scholars Publishing, 2007), 43–69; Anne Firor Scott, Pauli Murray, and Caroline Ware, eds.,. *Forty Years of Letters in Black & White* (Chapel Hill, NC: University of North Carolina Press, 2006); Elizabeth Borgwardt, *A New Deal for the World: America's Vision for Human Rights* (Cambridge, MA: Belknap Press of Harvard University Press, 2005), 27, 45, 52, 136, 137–138, 153–154; Samuel Moyn, *Not Enough: Human Rights in an Unequal World* (Cambridge, MA: Harvard University Press, 2018), 68–88.

12. William J. Novak, "The Public Utility Idea and the Origins of Modern Business Regulation," in eds. Naomi R. Lamoreaux and William J. Novak, *Corporations and American Democracy* (Cambridge, MA: Harvard University Press, 2017), 144. Public utilities overlap with what economists call public goods—"which all enjoy in common in the sense that each individual's consumption of such a good leads to no subtraction from any other individual's consumption." Paul A. Samuelson, "The Pure Theory of Public Expenditure," *The Review of Economics and Statistics* 36, no. 4 (November 1954): 387; Victor Pickard, *America's Battle for Media Democracy* (Cambridge: Cambridge University Press, 2014), 152–189.

13. David E. Kyvig, *Daily Life in the United States, 1920–1940* (Chicago: Ivan R. Dee, 2004), 57, 68; U.S. Census Bureau, Historical Census of Housing, Plumbing Facilities, https://www.census.gov/data/tables/time-series/dec/coh-plumbing.html.

14. 10 FCC 148. Federal Communications Commission, Merger of Western Union Telegraph Company and Postal Telegraph Company, September 27, 1943; see also, John A. Salmond, *The Conscience of a Lawyer: Clifford J. Durr and American Civil Liberties, 1899–1975* (Tuscaloosa, AL: University of Alabama Press, 1990), 76–77; Hyman Howard Goldin, "The Domestic Telegraph Industry and the Public Interest: A

Study in Public Utility Regulation" (Ph.D. diss., Harvard University, December 1950), 262; Gregory J. Downey, *Telegraph Messenger Boys: Labor, Technology, and Geography, 1850–1950* (New York: Routledge, 2002), 131; Downey, *Telegraph Messenger Boys*, 131, quoting 77th Cong., 1st Sess. U.S. Senate, Study of the Telegraph Industry, report of the Committee on Interstate Commerce. Washington: Government Printing Office, 1941: 23; "Consolidations and Mergers of Telegraph Operations," 77th Cong, 2s Sess., Hearings on S. 2598, July 21–23 1942, 128–129, Statement of W. L. Allen, International President, Commercial Telegraphers Union, quoting Western Union President A. N. Williams; Goldin, "Governmental Policy," 184 n1.

15. H. H. Goldin, "Governmental Policy and the Domestic Telegraph Industry," *The Journal of Economic History* 7, no. 1 (May 1947): 116; Goldin, "Governmental Policy," 67–68; Goldin, "Governmental Policy," 67–68; Goldin, "Governmental Policy," 68; Goldin, "Governmental Policy," 68.

16. T. A. Wise, "Western Union, by Grace of FCC and A.T.&T.," *Fortune*, March 1959, 114–116, 217–218, 222; Goldin, "Governmental Policy," 257, 248, 254; David S. Rotenstein, "Towers for Telegrams: The Western Union Telegraph Company and the Emergence of Microwave Telecommunications Infrastructure," *Industrial Archeology* 32, no. 2 (2006): 5–22; Wise, "Western Union, by Grace of FCC and A.T.&T.," 114–116, 217–218, 222.

17. Goldin, "Governmental Policy," 239; Goldin, "Governmental Policy," 242; Vidkunn Ulrikkson, *The Telegraphers Their Craft and Their Unions* (Washington, DC: Public Affairs Press, 1953), 191.

18. Wise, "Western Union," 115; Kevin Boyle, *The Shattering: America in the 1960s* (New York: W. W. Norton, 2021), 322; Shelly Freierman, "Telegram Falls Silent Stop Era Ends Stop," *New York Times*, February 6, 2006, C7.

19. Sterling Denhard Spero, *The Labor Movement in a Government Industry* (New York: George H. Doran Company, 1924), viii; Wayne Fuller, *The American Mail: Enlarger of the Common Life* (Chicago: 1972).

20. Clyde Kelly, *United States Postal Policy* (New York: D. Appleton, 1931), 136; Karl Baarslag, *History of the National Federation of Post Office Clerks* (Washington, DC: National Federation of Post Office Clerks, 1945), 175, 57; Goldin, "Governmental Policy," 70.

21. "The years 1923-29 were mainly one long, bitter struggle against the frigid, parsimonious little Vermonter in the White House." Baarslag, *History of the National Federation of Post Office Clerks*, 148. "Post Office Here Will Be Model for Whole U.S.," *Chicago Daily Tribune*, August 16, 1927, 3; "Biggest Post Office to Be Built in Chicago," *Popular Science* 5, no. 119 (August 1931): 29; Christopher W. Shaw, *First Class: The U.S. Postal Service, Democracy, and the Corporate Threat* (San Francisco: City Lights, 2021), 77–78; Marlene Park and Gerald E. Markowitz, *Democratic Vistas: Post Offices and Public Art in the New Deal* (Philadelphia: Temple University Press, 1984); James A. Farley, *Behind the Ballots: The Personal History of a Politician* (New York: Harcourt, Brace, 1938), 253. For Farley, see, Daniel Scroop, *Mr. Democrat: Jim Farley, The New Deal, and the Making of Modern American Politics* (Ann Arbor: University of Michigan Press, 2006); Farley, *Behind the Ballots*, 253–254; Ralph Nader, "Preface,"

in Kathleen Conkey, *The Postal Precipice: Can The U.S. Postal Service Be Saved?* (Washington, DC: Center for Study of Responsive Law, 1983), ix.
22. Richard Wright, *Lawd Today!* (Boston: Northeastern University Press, 1993). Not only Wright, but also other Black radicals found work at the post office during the first four decades of the century, notably Hubert Harrison in 1907. A biographer had this to say of Harrison's experience there: "the oppressive work conditions accelerated his development of a deeper class consciousness." Jeffrey B. Perry, *Hubert Harrison: The Voice of Harlem Radicalism, 1883–1918* (New York: Columbia University Press, 2011), 83. Black Communist Party leader Harry Haywood labored at the Chicago Post Office, where, by one account, "he met other young blacks who were also questioning American society's racism." Randi Storch, *Red Chicago: American Communism at Its Grassroots, 1928–1935* (Urbana, IL: University of Illinois Press, 2008), 50; Scroop, *Mr. Democrat*, 116. Roosevelt, however, rejected collective bargaining by federal employees and linked it to strikes which, he held, would be "unthinkable and intolerable." Joseph A. McCartin, *Collision: Course: Ronald Reagan, the Air Traffic Controllers, and the Strike that Changed America* (New York: Oxford University Press, 2011), 31.
23. Kelly, *United States Postal Policy*, 88–89.
24. Vern Baxter, "The Reorganization of the Post Office in Historical Perspective," *Insurgent Sociologist* 8, no. 4 (Winter 1979): 20.
25. U.S. Census Bureau, U.S. Statistical Abstract 1957, No. 631, Post Office Employees, By Type: 1930 to 1956, 510; U.S. Census Bureau, U.S. Statistical Abstract 1964, No. 698, Post Office Employees, By Type: 1950 to 1963, 512; U.S. Census Bureau, U.S. Statistical Abstract 1972, No. 789, Post Office Employees, By Type: 1950 to 1971, 490; "U.S. Post Office: Bedeviled by Deficits . . . Snail-Mail Service and Inexperienced Help," *Newsweek*, April 7, 1952, 39; U.S. Census Bureau, U.S. Statistical Abstract 1957, No. 631, Post Office Employees, By Type: 1930 to 1956, 510; U.S. Census Bureau, U.S. Statistical Abstract 1964, No. 698, Post Office Employees, By Type: 1950 to 1963, 512; U.S. Census Bureau, U.S. Statistical Abstract 1972, No. 789, Post Office Employees, By Type: 1950 to 1971, 490.
26. Baxter, "Reorganization of the Post Office," 21. See also, Vern K. Baxter, *Labor and Politics in the U.S. Postal Service* (New York: Plenum Press, 1994), 55–78; John T. Tierney, *The U.S. Postal Service: Status and Prospects of a Public Enterprise* (Dover, MA: Auburn House Publishing, 1988), 15. During the early postwar years, postal unions were notably successful in deploying an obscure strategy, known as the discharge petition, to thwart administration attempts to bottle up pay-raise legislation in the House of Representatives. Wilson R. Hart, *Collective Bargaining in the Federal Civil Service* (New York: Harper & Brothers, 1961), 250; Arthur D. Little, Inc., "The U.S. Post Office and Organizational Options for Its Improvement," Report of the General Contractor to the President's Commission on Postal Organization (Kappel Commission), Annex Contractors' Reports, vol. 1, June 1968, 10, 17, in Nicole Woolsey Biggart, "The Creative-Destructive Process of Organizational Change: The Case of the Post Office," *Administrative Science Quarterly* 22, no. 3 (September 1977): 412; House of Representatives, 94th Cong., 2d Sess., Committee on Post Office and Civil Service,

Report of the President's Commission on Postal Organization—Entitled "Toward Postal Excellence" (1968) (Washington, DC: Government Printing Office, 1976), 156.

27. Maurice H. Stans, "Financial Reorganization in the U.S. Post Office," *Journal of Accountancy*, June 1957, 55, 54; Charles B. Coates and Robert LL McCormick, "An Analytical View of Post Office Business or Public Service," *Nation's Business* 42, no. 1 (January 1954): 46.

28. *New York Times*, March 8, 1949, 37; "Truman Signs Bill Lifting Mail Rates $117,000,000 Yearly," *New York Times*, October 31, 1951, 1, 20; Lawrence F. O'Brien Interview 15 with Michael L. Gillette, November 20, 1986, 9, LBJ Presidential Library, Austin, Texas.

29. "Loss by Post Office on Papers Denied," *New York Times*, March 21, 1951, 39; Magazine Publishers Association, Inc., "Postal Policy and Rates—A Statement of Position by the Magazine Publishers Association, Inc." (New York: MPA, Inc., 1956), 2; Magazine Publishers Association, Inc., "Postal Policy and Rates," 10, 8–9, 12; Magazine Publishers Association, Inc., "Postal Policy and Rates," 11; Magazine Publishers Association, Inc., "Postal Policy and Rates," 15.

30. Peter Bart, "Advertising: Name-dropping Is Profitable," *New York Times*, September 10, 1961, F12; "Watch Those Mail-order Catalogs," *Kiplinger Magazine: The Changing Times* 3, no. 4 (April 1949): 32–34; Laurence A. Armour, "The Printed Word," *Barron's National Business and Financial Weekly* 28 (November 1960): 3.

31. Magazine Publishers Association, Inc., "Postal Policy and Rates," 4.

32. There are portents that the original Hoover Commission—the Commission on Organization of the Executive Branch of the Government—which reported in 1949, was already spearheading a movement toward greater management flexibility and business-type budgeting. "Summary of Reports of the Hoover Commission," *Public Administration Review* 9, no. 2 (Spring 1949): 84. But the first Hoover Commission still accepted that certain postal rates should be fixed, not primarily to generate income, but as an element of public policy in the dissemination of information; "Post Office Methods Hit," *New York Times*, January 22, 1950, 50; Quoted in William R. Divine, "The Second Hoover Commission Reports: An Analysis," *Public Administration Review* 15, no. 4 (Autumn 1955), 264; Stans, "Financial Reorganization," 53; Coates and McCormick, "An Analytical View," 46–47; David L. Babson & Co., Inc., "Post Office vs. Ma Bell," *Barron's National Business and Financial Weekly* 54, no. 14 (April 8, 1974): 7; Joseph A. Loftus, "Postal Chief Hits at Carrier Group," *New York Times*, May 13, 1950, 18; W. H. Lawrence, "One Mail Delivery a Day in Homes Set in Postal Economy," *New York Times*, April 19, 1950, 1, 24; "Postcards to Cost 2 Cents after 12:01 A.M. January 1," *New York Times*, December 30, 1951, 17. The Hoover Commission, which originated the suggestion to double the price of postcards, estimated that about 85 percent of the 3.3 billion postcards sent in 1947 were used for business purposes. A. Freeman Holmer, "To the Editor," *New York Times*, March 17, 1949, 24. Meanwhile, railroads were awarded a 32 percent increase in rates for carrying the mail. "Railroads Receive 32% Mail Pay Rise," *New York Times*, November 17, 1951, 6; Leonard Sloane, "Companies Glad to Pay for Own Postal Service," *New York Times*, July 21, 1968, F18.

33. Stanley E. Cohen, "What Ails the Post Office?" *Nation*, November 30, 1963, 365. For working conditions, "U.S. Post Office: Bedeviled by Deficits . . . Snail-Mail Service and Inexperienced Help," Newsweek, April 7, 1952, 39.
34. U.S. Census Bureau, U.S. Statistical Abstract 1964, Table No. 694, "Pieces of Mail Received Per Capita: 1945 to 1963," 510; The rate remained stable for a quarter-century between 1933 and 1958. Christopher H. Lovelock and Charles W. Weinberg, "The Role of Marketing in Improving Postal Service Effectiveness," in Joel L. Fleishman, ed., *The Future of the Postal Service* (New York: Praeger, 1983), 140–141; Shaw, *First Class*, 52.
35. Goldin, "Governmental Policy," 258; U.S. Census Bureau, Historical Census of Housing, Historical Census of Housing, Telephones, https://www.census.gov/data/tables/time-series/dec/coh-phone.html.
36. Ronald C. Tobey, *Technology as Freedom: The New Deal and the Electrical Modernization of the American Home* (Berkeley: University of California Press, 1996); Eric Foner, *The Story of American Freedom* (New York: W.W. Norton, 1998), 210.
37. Michael A. Bernstein, "Why the Great Depression Was Great: Toward a New Understanding of the Interwar Economic Crisis in the United States," in eds. Steve Fraser and Gary Gerstle, *The Rise and Fall of the New Deal Order 1930-1980* (Princeton, NJ: Princeton University Press, 1989), 12–54; Michael A. Bernstein, *The Great Depression: Delayed Recovery and Economic Change in America, 1929-1939* (Cambridge: Cambridge University Press, 1987).
38. Thomas K. McCraw, *TVA and the Power Fight 1933–1939* (Philadelphia: J. B. Lippincott, 1971), 74.
39. Tobey, *Technology as Freedom*, 165, 91 (Table 3.6); 93d Cong., 1st Sess., House Document 93-78; U.S. Department of Commerce, Bureau of the Census, Historical Statistics of the United States, Part Two: Series R1-12, 783; Richard R. John, *Network Nation: Inventing American Telecommunications* (Cambridge, MA: Belknap Press of Harvard University Press, 2010), 293–301.
40. Honorable Clyde M. Reed, Chairman PUC of Kansas, "The Viewpoint and Interest of the Public," in NARUC, *Proceedings of Thirty-fourth Annual Convention Held at Detroit, Michigan, November 14–17*, 1922 (New York: State Law Reporting Co., 1923), 150; Claude S. Fischer, *America Calling: A Social History of the Telephone to 1940* (Berkeley, CA: University of California Press, 1992), 107–108, 115, 117, 112–113, quote on 149.
41. Louisiana Public Service Commission v. Southern Bell Telephone Co., 8 P.U.R. (NS 1, 25) LA 1935; AT&T, *Report of a Toll Market Study Conducted in Peoria, Illinois* (New York: AT&T, 1930), 107.
42. Norman Perelman, *What Price Telephones?* (New York: League for Industrial Democracy, 1941), 36; *A Report of the Telephone Toll Rate Subcommittee of National Association of Railroad and Utility Commissioners and Federal Communications Commission* (hereafter FCC-NARUC), "Message Toll Telephone Rates and Disparities" (Washington, DC: (n.p.), July 1951), 292.
43. Federal Communications Communication (FCC), *Third Annual Report for the Year Ended June 30, 1937* (Washington, DC: Government Printing Office, 1937), 87.

44. Carl I. Wheat, "The Regulation of Interstate Telephone Rates," *Harvard Law Review* 51 (March 1938), reprinted in 75th Cong., 3d Sess., *Document No. 176, "The Regulation of Interstate Telephone Rates," presented by Mr. Bone, April 20, 1938* (Washington, DC: Government Printing Office, 1938), 16–17.
45. FCC, *Third Annual Report*, 87; Ira Katznelson, *When Affirmative Action Was White* (New York: W. W. Norton, 2005).
46. FCC, *Third Annual Report*, 104, 103. Also see FCC, *Fifth Annual Report for the Year Ended 30 June 1939* (Washington, DC: Government Printing Office, 1939), 19; 8 FCC 342, 343, "Department of Public Service of Washington v. Pacific Telephone & Telegraph," Decided February 3, 1941; Paul A. Walker, "How Cooperation Works in Communications Regulation," *Public Utilities Fortnightly* 43, no. 5 (September 2, 1943): 268; FCC, *Third Annual Report*, 89.
47. *United States of America, Plaintiff, v. American Telephone and Telegraph Company; Western Electric Company, Inc.; and Bell Telephone Laboratories, Inc., Defendants, Plaintiff's Third Statement of Contentions and Proof. Civil Action No. 74-1698. In the U.S. District Court for the District of Columbia, January 10, 1980*: 1991–1999 (hereafter "Plaintiff's Third Statement"); *United States of America, Plaintiff, v. American Telephone and Telegraph Company; Western Electric Company, Inc.; and Bell Telephone Laboratories, In., Defendants, Defendants' Third Statement of Contentions and Proof. Civil Action No. 74-1698. In the U.S. District Court for the District of Columbia, March 10, 1980*: 246 (hereafter Defendants' Third Statement"); Walker, "How Cooperation Works," 267; Walker, "How Cooperation Works," 269; Walker also had advised on this legislation. This approach was further validated during World War II, when AT&T faced pressure to forestall rate increases from the Office of Price Administration. John N. Schacht, *The Making of Telephone Unionism* (New Brunswick, NJ: Rutgers University Press, 1985), 107.
48. U.S. Federal Communications Commission, *Proposed Report Telephone Investigation (Pursuant to Public Resolution No. 8 74th Congress)* (hereafter, FCC, *Proposed Report Telephone Investigation*) (Washington, DC: Government Printing Office, 1938), 685, 712; FCC, *Proposed Report Telephone Investigation*, 689.
49. *Second Annual Report of the Federal Radio Commission to the Congress of the United States* (Washington, DC: Government Printing Office, 1928), 26; *By-Products Coal Co. v. Federal Radio Commission, No. 4984*, in *U.S. Federal Radio Commission, Third Annual Report 1929* (Washington, DC: Government Printing Office, 1929), 37; *Intercity Radio Telegraph Co., appellant, v. Federal Radio Commission, No. 4987, etc.*, in *FRC, Third Annual Report*, 40.
50. End-to-end responsibility by telephone companies for quality, safety, and effectiveness of each and every network component was, asserts Alan Stone, "the single most important service obligation of public service companies." Alan Stone, *Public Service Liberalism: Telecommunications and Transitions in Public Policy* (Princeton, NJ: Princeton University Press, 1991), 221, 223 (quote).
51. U.S. Federal Communications Commission, *Eleventh Annual Report for Fiscal Year Ended 30th June 1945* (Washington, DC: Government Printing Office, 1945), 32.
52. FCC, *Proposed Report Telephone Investigation*, 453, 452.

53. *Plaintiff's Third Statement*, 1992.
54. James M. Herring and Gerald C. Gross, *Telecommunications; Economics and Regulation* (New York: McGraw-Hill, 1936), 135; Richard Gabel, *Development of Separations Principles in the Telephone Industry* (East Lansing, MI: Institute of Public Utilities, Michigan State University, 1967), vii, 154; Carol L. Weinhaus and Anthony G. Oettinger, *Behind the Telephone Debates* (Norwood, NJ: Ablex, 1988), 51; *Defendants' Third Statement*, 254.
55. Weinhaus and Oettinger, *Behind the Telephone Debates*, 55; U.S. Federal Communications Commission, *A Report of the Federal Communications Commission on the Investigation of the Telephone Industry in the United States [Pursuant to Public Res. No. 8, 74th Cong.]* (hereafter FCC, *Report on the Telephone Industry*) (Washington, DC: Government Printing Office, 1939), 364; FCC, *Report on the Telephone Industry*, 371.
56. Reed, "The Viewpoint and Interest of the Public," 151.
57. Commissioner John O'Hara, Michigan Public Service Commission, in *National Association of Regulatory Utility Commissioners, Proceedings of 52d Annual Convention, 10–12 December 1940, Miami* (Washington, DC: NARUC, 1941), 367; *Comparisons of Telephone Rates, National Association of Regulatory Utility Commissioners, Proceedings of 53d Convention, St. Paul Minnesota, 26–29 August 1941* (Washington, DC: NARUC, 1942), 394–408; Commissioner Richard J. Beamish of the Pennsylvania Public Utility Commission, *National Association of Regulatory Utilities Commissioners Proceedings 54th Convention, St. Louis, 10–12 November 1942* (Washington, DC: NARUC, 1943), 179.
58. A later review of some of these is provided by Beverly C. Moore, Jr., "AT&T: The Phony Monopoly," in Mark J. Green, ed., *The Monopoly Makers: Ralph Nader's Study Group Report on Regulation and Competition* (New York: Grossman Publishers, 1973), 74–79; During the 1920s, AT&T itself had provided evidence for this line of reasoning: its huge toll network investment program had been accompanied by modest long-distance rate reductions, probably in an effort to reduce pressure from state regulators and to harvest what goodwill might be garnered from leading business customers as much as to enlarge calling volume.
59. FCC, *Proposed Report Telephone Investigation*, 421, Table 62; By way of comparison, these reductions were roughly double the size of those that AT&T had instituted as a private matter during the late 1920s. FCC, *Proposed Report Telephone Investigation*, 756; FCC-NARUC, "Message Toll Telephone Rates and Disparities," 98–99; FCC-NARUC, "Message Toll Telephone Rates and Disparities," 135–136; FCC-NARUC, "Message Toll Telephone Rates and Disparities," 25.
60. "Cooperation between State Commissions and the Federal Communications Commission," *National Association of Regulatory Utilities Commissioners Proceedings 1943 War Conference, 55th Annual Meeting, Chicago, 14–16 September 1943, edited by Ben Smart* (Washington, DC: NARUC, 1944), 320; The figure of $50 million representing "the exchange revenues necessary to support the toll business in addition to the revenues from the quoted toll rates if the rates were established on a nationwide board-to-board basis." "Report of the Special Committee Cooperating

with the Federal Communications Commission in Studies of Telephone Regulatory Problems," *NARUC Proceedings 14–16 September 1943*, 376.

61. "Report of the Special Committee Cooperating with the Federal Communications Commission in Studies of Telephone Regulatory Problems," *NARUC Proceedings 14–16 September 1943*, 383.

62. "Report of the Special Committee Cooperating with the Federal Communications Commission in Studies of Telephone Regulatory Problems," *NARUC Proceedings 14–16 Sept 1943*, 389; Gabel, *Development of Separations Principles*, 47; FCC-NARUC, *"Message Telephone Toll Rates and Disparities,"* 118, 301; "Where important points, such as St. Louis, Mo., and East St. Louis, Ill., Portland, Ore., and Vancouver, Wash., or Kansas City, Kans., and Kansas City, Mo., are concerned the differences in state and interstate rates for messages to and from such points gave rise to frequent customer comment," stated an investigatory committee in 1951. FCC-NARUC, *"Message Toll Telephone Rates and Disparities,"* 117–118; Gabel claims that formal separations procedures acted merely "as a device to maneuver price and revenue requirements," the timing and substance oof which were largely at the disposal not of regulators but of AT&T. Gabel, *Development of Separations Principles*, 31.

63. James W. Sichter, *Separations Procedures in the Telephone Industry: The Historical Origins of a Public Policy*, Publication P-77-2 (Cambridge, MA: Harvard Program on Information Resources Policy, 1981), 128; Sichter, *Separations Procedures in the Telephone Industry*, 128–129.

64. U.S. Census Bureau, Historical Statistics of the United States, Series R 1-12; David F. Weiman, "Reaching out to America: Building Telephone and Urban Networks in the Bell System," paper presented to the 52d Annual Meeting of the Economic History Association, Boston, September, 1992; Gabel, *Development of Separations Principles*, 10; AT&T, *Report of Toll Market Study Conducted in Peoria, Illinois* * (New York: AT&T, 1930), 101.

65. *Plaintiff's Third Statement*, 1997; *Defendants' Third Statement*, 247–248; Robert A. Nixon, Commissioner, Public Service Commission of Wisconsin, "The Public Interest in Uniformity of Interstate and Intrastate Toll Rates," *National Association of Regulatory Utility Commissioners, Proceedings of 52d Annual Convention, 10–12 December 1940, Miami* (Washington, DC: NARUC, 1941), 360; *Defendants' Third Statement*, 248, 249; *Defendants' Third Statement*, 250; *Plaintiff's Third Statement*, 1997; Robert Britt Horwitz, *The Irony of Regulatory Reform: The Deregulation of American Telecommunications* (New York: Oxford University Press, 1989), 135. Also *Defendants' Third Statement*, 251. The FCC claimed in 1967 that the revisions had generated a shift from intrastate to interstate of about $500 million in revenue requirements, "based on 1965 volume of business." AT&T, Charges for Interstate and Foreign Communication Service, 9 F.C.C.2d 30, 111 (1967), in *Defendants' Third Statement*, 258; Weinhaus and Oettinger, *Behind the Telephone Debates*, 63; *Defendants' Third Statement*, 260; Cf. Fraser and Gerstle, *Rise and Fall of the New Deal Order, 1930–1980*.

66. William H. Melody, "Telecommunications in Nova Scotia: A Cost of Service Study for Maritime Telegraph & Telephone Company, Limited," Part 1, Final Report, March

1983, prepared for The Board of Commissioners of Public Utilities, Province of Nova Scotia.
67. Speech of Governor Franklin D. Roosevelt delivered at the Democratic Luncheon, in Chicago, Illinois, Tuesday, December 10, 5, Lewis M. Howe Papers, Box 22, Folder "New York State Campaign of 1930 Speeches and Speech Material," Franklin D. Roosevelt Presidential Library and Museum, Hyde Park, New York.
68. *Plaintiff's Third Statement*, 1983; see also 1984–1985; *Plaintiff's Third Statement*, 1983; see also 1984–1985; Pacific Telephone & Telegraph Co., P.U.R. 1919D 345, 370–371 (1919), in *Defendants' Third Statement*, 225–226, 227.
69. *Spriggs v. Bell Telephone Co. of Pennsylvania*, 3 P.U.R. (n.s.) 42, 45 (Pa. Pub. Serv. Comm'n 1934), quoting Uniform Telephone Rates (1917), 2 Pa. P.S.C. 1019, 1020, in *Defendants' Third Statement*, 233; Carl I. Wheat, Telephone Rate Counsel, FCC, before the Public Utility Section of the American Bar Association, 28 September 1937, in *Defendants' Third Statement*, 237; *Plaintiff's Third Statement*, 1990; *Plaintiff's Third Statement*, 1990; Wheat, "Regulation of Interstate Telephone Rates," 21. AT&T self-servingly echoed Wheat, asserting that rate averaging had been intended "to permit residents of areas that are most costly to serve to obtain telephone service at the same rates as users in areas in which the same service can be provided at lower costs." *Defendants' Third Statement*, 230–231; Federal Communications Commission, *Eighteenth Annual Report, Fiscal Year Ended June 30, 1952* (Washington, DC: Government Printing Office, 1953), 43–44, in *Defendants' Third Statement*, 241–242.
70. Norman Perelman, *What Price Telephones?* (New York: League for Industrial Democracy, 1941), 36; *Plaintiff's Third Statement*, 1939–1940. Also, 81st Cong., 1st Sess., *Hearings before a Subcommittee of the Committee on Agriculture, Rural Telephones, 14–16 February, 1949* (Washington, DC: Government Printing Office, 1949).
71. *Plaintiff's Third Statement*, 1938; 81st Cong., 1st Sess., *Report No. 246, Committee on Agriculture, Rural Telephone Service, March 9, 1949* (Washington, DC: Government Printing Office, 1949), 4, 3, 7, 11.
72. *Branch v. Southwestern Bell Tel. Co.*, 11 Mo. P.S.C. 675, 678 (1912), quoted in *Defendants' Third Statement*, 220–221; also, 155–156; Clifford Durr, Memorandum to Senator Lister Hill, 23 November 1944, Clifford Durr Papers, Alabama Department of Archives and History, Montgomery Alabama, Box 30, Folder 2. Thanks to Victor Pickard for this reference.
73. House Committee on Agriculture, *Report No. 246, Rural Telephone Service*, 8; House Committee on Agriculture, *Report No. 246, Rural Telephone Service*, 8; U.S. Federal Communications Commission, *Thirteenth Annual Report for the Year Ended 1947* (Washington, DC: Government Printing Office, 1948), 56; U.S. Federal Communications Commission, *Fourteenth Annual Report for the Year Ended 1948* (Washington, DC: Government Printing Office, 1949), 3; U.S. Federal Communications Commission, *Fifteenth Annual Report for the Year Ended 1949* (Washington, DC: Government Printing Office 1950), 96; House Committee on Agriculture, *Report No. 246, Rural Telephone Service*, 4–5; *Plaintiff's Third Statement*,

1942; Statement of A. Harold Peterson, in 91st Cong., 1st Sess., Rural Telephone Supplemental Financing, *Hearings before the Committee on Agriculture on H.R. 7, H.R. 81, H.R. 4020, H.R. 4192, and H.R. 7872, 19–21 February and 13 March 1969* (Washington, DC: Government Printing Office, 1969), 11.

74. Daniel J. Clark, *Disruption in Detroit: Autoworkers and the Elusive Postwar Boom* (Urbana, IL: University of Illinois Press, 2018); 81st Cong., 1st Session, Joint Committee on the Economic Report, Factors Affecting Volume and Stability of Investments, in FCC-NARUC, "Message Toll Telephone Rates and Disparities," 21; Don Wharton, "So You'd Like to Have a Phone," *Nation's Business* 36, no. 6 (June 1948): 50–51; Jack Barbash, *Unions and Telephones: The Story of The Communications Workers of America* (New York: Harper & Brothers, 1952), 154; FCC-NARUC, "Message Toll Telephone Rates and Disparities," 21–22.

75. Ben W. Lewis, "State Regulation in Depression and War," *American Economic Review* 36, no. 2, Papers and Proceedings of the 58th Annual Meeting of the American Economic Association (May 1946): 401; *Defendants' Third Statement*, 340; *Defendants' Third Statement*, 341–342; *Defendants' Third Statement*, 342.

76. M. Karydes, "The Real Cost of Basic Telephone Service to the Average Worker in Fifteen Developed Countries," OT Report 73-17, Table 2, 1973, in *Defendants' Third Statement*, 342–343; U.S. Department of Commerce, National Telecommunications and Information Administration, *NTIA Telecom 2000 Charting the Course for a New Century*, NTIA Special Publication 88-21 (Washington, DC: Government Printing Office, October 1988), 209; U.S. FCC, *Statistics of the Communications Industry in the United States for 1956* (Washington, DC: Government Printing Office, 1958), 24.

77. *Defendants' Third Statement*, 209–211; U.S. FCC, 14 AR 1948, 78; *Defendants' Third Statement of Contentions and Proof*, I:, 215.

78. Federal Communications Commission, *Fourteenth Annual Report, Fiscal Year Ended June 30, 1948* (Washington, DC: Government Printing Office, 1948), 3; FCC, *Statistics of the Communications Industry for 1956*, 12; President's Task Force on Communications Policy, *Final Report* (Washington, DC: Government Printing Office, 1968), 5.

79. Calculated from data in the annual reports of the Federal Communications Commission for these years.

80. Illinois Bell Telephone Company, *Planning for Home Telephone Conveniences* (American Telephone & Telegraph Co., 1928), 7. See also, Fischer, *America Calling*; Illinois Bell, *Planning for Home Telephone Conveniences*, 13.

81. Sally Clarke, "What's Efficient? Who's Abnormal?: Consumer Demand and Bell Labs' French Phone," paper presented at Princeton University Davis Center Seminar, Princeton, New Jersey, April 28, 1995; Prescott C. Mabon, *Mission Communications: The Story of Bell Laboratories* (Murray Hill, NJ: Bell Telephone Laboratories, 1975), 123.

82. "To meet the trend toward styling by color, the Bell System has been offering telephones in dark gold, old brass, oxidized silver, statuary bronze, dark blue, gray-green, ivory, old rose or Pekin red," stated an article in the business press in 1940. But these colors were not part of a mass marketing campaign, and their very appellations

continued to connote a "class" segmented market. "On the Business Horizon," *Barron's* 20, no. 48 (November 25, 1940): 5.
83. Russell Flinchum, *Henry Dreyfuss Industrial Designer: The Man in the Brown Suit* (New York: Cooper-Hewitt, National Design Museum, Smithsonian Institution and Rizzoli, 1997), 104; Michael Sorkin, "Just a Phone Call Away," *Industrial Design* 30, no. 2 (March/April 1983): 25.
84. "Telephones, Inc., Plans to Eliminate Extra Fee for Its Color Phones," *Wall Street Journal* October 20, 1964: 6; Venture Development Corporation, *Retail Telephone Markets 1979-1984. Study Team: Raymond L. Boggs, Lewis I. Solomon* (Wellesley, MA: Venture Development Corporation, July 1979), 3, 175.
85. "New Telephone," *Life* 5, no. 27 (1949): 67.
86. Willis Park Rokes, "Consumer Be Damned! The Ma Bell Rental Agency," *The Nation*, June 30, 1969, 820–821.
87. "New York Telephone Is Seeking to Charge for Information Calls," *Wall Street Journal*, July 19, 1972, 4; Norma Walter, "Despite a New Name, Information Operators Get Same Old Queries," *Wall Street Journal*, July 1, 1969, 1; This seems also to have been true of long-distance operators. "Locating the person called for, is the forte of the long distance operator. . . . Many stories are told of the ingenuity and persistence of long distance operators in 'getting their man.' There is one about an operator who was asked to locate a man driving to Florida; his mother had become suddenly ill and he was wanted at home. The operator asked if he made a habit of always using one kind of gasoline. 'Yes, he has a credit card for Standard,' she was told. The next time he stopped to fill his tank, the man received the message about his mother. 'Long Distance' had asked more than fifty service stations to look out for him." Marion May Dilts, *The Telephone in a Changing World* (New York: Longman's, Green, 1941), 124–125; Walter, "Despite a New Name," 1; Walter, "Despite a New Name," 1; Green, *Race on the Line*, 224–225.
88. "An End to Free Phone Information," *Business Week*, June 22, 1974, 57; Ellen Stern Harris, "Information, Please—for a Fee," *Los Angeles Times*, February 15, 1976, F4; Associated Press, "Directory Assistance to Start Charging Jan. 1," *New York Times*, October 30, 1988, CN16.
89. As late as 1954, a human-interest story reported that a housewife who prodded the telephone company had not prompted a new marketing effort but had been issued "a head-set such as invalids sometimes wear in bed with a long coil extension" to permit her to talk while "sweeping, dusting, baking, washing, ironing." "Now She's Done It!," *American Mercury* 5, no. 158 (July 1954): 48; Mabon, *Mission Communications*, 124–125; "Telephones, Inc., Plans to Eliminate Extra Fee for Its Color Phones," *Wall Street Journal*, October 20, 1964, 6.
90. "See Your Local Ford Dealer Conveniently Listed in the Yellow Pages of the Telephone Directory," *Wall Street Journal*, August 8, 1950, 16; Robert Alden, "One Office Can Now Link Nation's 4000 Classified Telephone Directories," *New York Times*, May 17, 1960, 59; "Business Bulletin," *Wall Street Journal*, October 5, 1967, 1.
91. "Pacific Telephone Asks $181 Million Annual Rate Rise," *Wall Street Journal*, February 13, 1967, 8; Leonard Sloane, "Yellow Pages Proving Lucrative," *New York Times*,

August 14, 1975, 51; Dan Schiller, *Telematics and Government* (Norwood, NJ: Ablex, 1982), 92; Christopher H. Sterling and Timothy R. Haight, "Total Advertiser-expenditures on U.S. Media, by Medium and Types of Advertising, 1935–1976," Table 303-B, *The Mass Media: Aspen Institute Guide to Communication Industry Trends* (New York: Praeger, 1978), 129.

92. James C. Hyatt, "Those '800' Phone Lines Deal with Many Things, Like Making Sure Your Grasshoppers are Welcome," *Wall Street Journal*, June 20, 1972, 40; Technically distinct, another nationally standardized telephone number was announced in 1968: the 911 Emergency service. Efforts to install 911 Emergency were boosted, then-FCC Chair Rosel H. Hyde and Democratic Commissioner Lee Loevinger agreed, "as a result of last summer's widespread civil disorders in major cities." "AT&T Units Plan '911' Emergency Number Nationwide; Cost Will Exceed $50 Million," *Wall Street Journal*, January 15, 1968, 4.

93. Listfax Will Conduct Army Recruiting Drive," *New York Times*, February 22, 1971, 45. See also, "Debugging Campaign for Subaru," *New York Times*, January 28, 1971, 56; Hyatt, "Those '800' Phone Lines Deal with Many Things," 40; Federal Communications Commission, *Statistics of the Communications Common Carriers for 1995–96* (Washington, DC: Government Printing Office, 1997), Table 6.3, Toll Service Revenues, 1950–1995; AT&T, *Annual Report 1980* (New York: AT&T, 1980), 30; see also, Schiller, *Telematics and Government*, 15; "What's News," *Wall Street Journal*, June 20, 1972, 1.

Chapter 8

1. "Since patents are privileges restrictive of a free economy," Supreme Court Justice William O. Douglas declared in 1942, the rights of patent holders "must be strictly construed." Masonite Corp., 316 U.S. 265 (1942) at 280, in C. Paul Rogers, III, "The Antitrust Legacy of Justice William O. Douglas," 56 *Cleveland State Law Review* 895 (2008): 936; Doron S. Ben-Atar, *Trade Secrets: Intellectual Piracy and the Origins of American Industrial Power* (New Haven, CT: Yale University Press, 2004).

2. Larry Owens, "Patents, the 'Frontiers' of American Invention, and the Monopoly Committee of 1939: Anatomy of a Discourse," *Technology and Culture* 32, no. 4 (October 1991): 1092, 1077; Jon Gertner, *The Idea Factory: Bell Labs and the Great Age of American Innovation* (New York: Penguin, 2012).

3. Michael Perelman, *Steal This Idea: Intellectual Property Rights and the Corporate Confiscation of Creativity* (New York: Palgrave, 2002); Alex Roland, *Model Research: The National Advisory Committee for Aeronautics 1915–1958* (Washington, DC: NASA, 1985), vol. 1, 41, quote at 37 (quoting a consulting engineer to the War Department prior to the cross-licensing agreement). On the subsequent growth of the aviation industry following additional aggressive federal efforts to support it, see David D. Lee, "Herbert Hoover and the Development of Commercial Aviation,

1921–1926," in eds. Carl E. Krog and William R. Tanner, *Herbert Hoover and the Republican Era: A Reconsideration* (Lanham, MD: University Press of America, 1984), 36–65.
4. 74th Cong., House of Representatives, 1st Sess., Committee on Patents, Pooling of Patents, *Hearings on H.R. 4523, February 11–March 7, 1935* (Washington, DC: Government Printing Office, 1935), 299.
5. Hugh G. J. Aitken, *The Continuous Wave: Technology and American Radio, 1900–1932* (Princeton, NC: Princeton University Press, 1985), 501.
6. Gertner, *The Idea Factor*, 31; James William Spurlock, "The Bell Telephone Laboratories and the Military-Industrial Complex: The Jewett-Buckley Years, 1925–1951" (Ph.D. diss., George Washington University, 2007); Kenneth Lipartito, "Rethinking the Invention Factory: Bell Laboratories in Perspective," in eds. Sally H. Clarke, Naomi R. Lamoreaux, and Steven W. Usselman, *The Challenge of Remaining Innovative: Insights from 20th Century American Business* (Stanford, CA: Stanford University Press, 2009), 132–159.
7. Federal Trade Commission, *Report on the Radio Industry, In Response to House Resolution 548, 67th Cong., 4th Session, 1 December 1923* (Washington, DC: Government Printing Office, 1924), 24; L. S. Howeth, *History of Communications-Electronics in the United States Navy* (Washington, DC: Government Printing Office, 1963), 34; David M. Hart, *Forged Consensus: Science, Technology, and Economic Policy in the United States, 1921–1953* (Princeton, NJ: Princeton University Press, 1998), 52–53, 74.
8. Leonard S. Reich, *The Making of American Industrial Research: Science and Business at GE and Bell, 1876–1926* (Cambridge: Cambridge University Press, 1985), 221; Owen D. Young, in Senate, 71st Cong. 2d Sess., *Hearings before the Committee on Interstate Commerce On S. 6 "Commission on Communications," Part 10, 9 December 1929* (Washington, DC: Government Printing Office, 1930), 1116; FTC, *Report on the Radio Industry*, 3 (2,000 patents); W. Rupert Maclaurin, *Invention and Innovation in the Radio Industry* (New York: Macmillan, 1949), 107; Aitken, *Continuous Wave*, 498; AT&T executives claimed afterward that they had preferred nonexclusive licensing terms, but that they had acquiesced to the exclusivity provisions demanded by GE. Aitken, *Continuous Wave*, 440, 506–507.
9. This story is foundational in many historical accounts of the emergence of US broadcasting. See, among others, Erik Barnouw, *A Tower in Babel* (New York: Oxford University Press, 1966) 57–61, 114–124; Maclaurin, *Invention and Innovation*, 99–131.
10. Oswald F. Schuette, "Analysis of the Arrangements by which the American Telephone & Telegraph Co., the Radio Corporation of America, the General Electric Co., the Westinghouse Electric & Manufacturing Co., and the United Fruit Co. Created the Radio Trust," in 71st Cong., Senate, 1st Sess., Committee on Interstate Commerce, *Hearings on S.6, Commission on Communications. Part 9, 24 May–7 June 1929* (Washington, DC: Government Printing Office, 1929), 898; FTC, *Report on the Radio Industry*, 50–68. Especially early on, the RCA group sought to cast its endeavor in explicitly nationalistic terms. In a letter reprinted by the FTC, Owen D. Young of

GE and RCA, noted that arrangements concluded between representatives of RCA, British Marconi, CGT from France, and GD from Germany with respect to South American markets were "carrying the principle of the Monroe Doctrine into the field of communications in the Western Hemisphere and giving the American effective leadership." Owen D. Young to James R. Sheffield, December 7, 1921, in FTC, *Report on the Radio Industry*, 61. However, international cooperation and market sharing rather than bellicose nationalism soon took primacy in RCA's corporate strategy; Aitken, *Continuous Wave*, 490; Maclaurin, *Invention and Innovation*, 107, quoting Exhibit DD, Traffic Agreement, RCA and Marconi Wireless Telegraph Co., in FTC, *Report on the Radio Industry*, 239; Aitken, *Continuous Wave*, 486–494; Howeth, *The History of Communications-Electronics*, 365, 378.

11. Oswald F. Schuette, in Senate, 70th Cong., 1st Sess., Committee on Patents, *Hearings on S. 2783, Forfeiture of Patent Rights on Conviction under Laws Prohibiting Monopoly, January* [sic: should be February] *8 and 9, 1928* (Washington, DC: Government Printing Office, 1928, 4. Schuette was executive secretary of the Radio Protective Association, a group of smaller manufacturers opposed to the cartel; FTC *Report on the Radio Industry*, 131–132; Schuette in 71st Cong., Senate, 1st Sess., Committee on Interstate Commerce, *Hearings on S.6, Commission on Communications, Part 9, 24 May–7 June 1929* (Washington, DC: Government Printing Office, 1929), 900–901. This covenant was successively modified by AT&T and GER to bring in other companies and in an ultimately unsuccessful attempt to obviate the disruptive impact of radio broadcasting as it emerged in the early 1920s. Exhibit 5, "Modification of License Agreement Dated July 1, 1920," dated July 1, 1926, reprinted in 74th Cong., House of Representatives, Committee on Patents, *Appendixes to Hearings on H.R. 4523, Pooling of Patents, February–December 1935, Part 2* (Washington, DC: Government Printing Office, 1936), 1219–1222; *Report of the Federal Trade Commission on the Radio Industry, in Response to House Resolution 548, 67th Cong., 4th Sess., 1 December 1923* (Washington, DC: Government Printing Office, 1924); Aitken, *Continuous Wave*, 500; Maclaurin, *Invention and Innovation*, 133, 140.

12. In "Hoover Condemns Private Monopoly of Broadcasting," *New York Times*, March 11, 1924, 1, 4; Maclaurin, *Invention and Innovation*, 114.

13. In "Hoover Condemns Private Monopoly of Broadcasting," *New York Times*, March 11, 1924, 1, 4; Maclaurin, *Invention and Innovation*, 114; Reich, *The Making of American Industrial Research*, 231; Maclaurin, *Invention and Innovation*, 118, 124–126; Howeth, *The History of Communications-Electronics*, 378.

14. House Resolution No. 568, March 3, 1923; see also, "Monopoly in Radio by Eight Concerns Charged in Action," *New York Times*, January 28, 1924, 1. The FTC had already responded to complaints by independent manufacturers by moving to investigate the radio industry on its own account in 1921–1922. Aitken, *Continuous Wave*, 428; Schuette in 71st Cong., Senate, 1st Sess., Committee on Interstate Commerce, *Hearings on S.6, Commission on Communications, Part 9, 24 May–7 June 1929* (Washington, DC: Government Printing Office, 1929), 909; Member companies of the Radio Protective Association are listed in 71st Cong., 1st Sess., Committee on Interstate Commerce, *Hearings on S.6, Commission on Communications, Part 9, 27*

May 1929 (Washington, DC: Government Printing Office, 1929), 894. Quote from "Radio Patents and Copyright Questions," 328; Leonard S. Reich, *The Making of American Industrial Research*, 229; Hoover quoted in Gleason L. Archer, *Big Business and Radio* (New York: American Historical Company, 1939), 136.

15. Ernest Reichmann in 70th Cong., Senate, 1st Sess., Committee on Patents, *Hearings on S. 2783, Forfeiture of Patent Rights on Conviction under Laws Prohibiting Monopoly, January* [sic: should be February] *8 and 9, 1928* (Washington, DC: Government Printing Office, 1928), 13.

16. *U.S. v. Motion Picture Patents Company*, 225 Fed. 800 (E.D. Pa. 1915) at 811, quoted in Cassady, "Monopoly in Motion Picture Production and Distribution," 388; *Motion Picture Patents Co. v. Universal Film Mfg. Co.*, 243, U.S. 502, 518 (1917), in Cassady, "Monopoly in Motion Picture Production and Distribution," 389; see also, Clayton Act, Section 3, 38 Stat. 730, 731 (1914); Swagar Sherley, Esq., of Sherley, Faust & Wilson, Attorneys-at-law, Washington, D.C., appearing as attorney for the Radio Corporation of America, in 70th Cong., Senate, 1st Sess., Committee on Patents, *Hearings on S. 2783, Forfeiture of Patent Rights on Conviction Under Laws Prohibiting Monopoly, Part 2, February 20–21, 1928* (Washington, DC: Government Printing Office, 1928), 134; Dane Yorke, "The Radio Octopus," *The American Mercury* 23, no. 92 (August 1931): 385–400. Also, Reich, *The Making of American Industrial Research*, 218–238; Because it embraced more than merely radio technology, AT&T continued to function as a member of the cartel, albeit on a reduced basis. This charge surfaced explicitly in congressional testimony, for example, that of Oswald F. Schuette in 71st Cong., Senate, 1st Sess., Committee on Interstate Commerce, *Hearings on S.6, Commission on Communications, Part 9, 24 May–7 June 1929* (Washington, DC: Government Printing Office, 1929), 905–906; Maclaurin, *Invention and Innovation*, 133.

17. Public Law No. 632, 69th Cong., February 23, 1927, "An Act for the regulation of radio communication, and for other purposes," in Barnouw, *Tower in Babel*, 300–315. Barnouw's discussion of these provisions is on 198.

18. "Radio Patents and Copyright Questions," *Journal of the Patent office Society* 12, no. 7 (July 1930): 327; 54 A.B.A. Report 480 (1929) in John C. Cooper, Jr., Chair Legislative Committee of the American Academy of Air Law, "Radio and the Anti-Trust Laws," National Conference on the Relation of Law and Business, First Session with Specific Emphasis on the Anti-Trust Laws, New York University, 1931, 152–153, Presidential Papers Subject File, "Anti-Trust Laws 1931," Herbert Hoover Presidential Library and Museum, West Branch, Iowa (hereafter Hoover Presidential Library).

19. 54 A.B.A. Report 480 (1929), 152–153.

20. The key patent was for amplification of tuned radio frequency. See Statement of J. I. McMullen, Judge Advocate General's office, War Department, in 71st Cong., 1st Sess., Committee on Interstate Commerce, *Hearings on S.6, Commission on Communications, Part 9, 24 May 1929* (Washington, DC: Government Printing Office, 1929), 867; Harold Dodd, Lieutenant Commander, U.S. Navy, officer in Charge of the Patent Section of the office of the Judge Advocate General of the Navy, in 71st Cong., 1st Sess., Committee on Interstate Commerce, *Hearings on S.6, Commission*

on *Communications, Part 9, 24 May 1929* (Washington, DC: Government Printing Office, 1929), 945.

21. 71st Cong., 1st Sess., Committee on Interstate Commerce, *Hearings on S.6, Commission on Communications, Part 7, 18–22 May 1929* (Washington, DC: Government Printing Office, 1929), 314; *FADA Radio Limited v. Canadian General Electric Company Limited, on Appeal from the Exchequer Court of Canada*, Supreme Court of Canada 1927, 520–524. Also, Maclaurin, *Invention and Innovation*, 127–129; "Radio Patent and Copyright Questions," *Journal of the Patent office Society* 12, no. 7 (July 1930): 327, reprinted from section 11 of the Report of the Standing Committee on Radio Law Presented at the 52d Annual Meeting of the American Bar Association held at Memphis, Tennessee, October 23–25, 1929; McMullen in 71st Cong., 1st Sess., Committee on Interstate Commerce, *Hearings on S.6, Commission on Communications, Part 7, 18–22 May 1929* (Washington, DC: Government Printing Office, 1929), 312–314; 85, 86.

22. Hooper in 71st Cong., 1st Sess., Committee on Interstate Commerce, *Hearings on S.6, Commission on Communications, Part 7, 18–22 May 1929* (Washington, DC: Government Printing Office, 1929), 312–314; McMullen, 867–874; Dodd, *Hearings on S.6, Commission on Communications*, 944–957; 71st Cong., 1st Sess., Committee on Interstate Commerce, *Hearings on S.6, Commission on Communications, Part 7, 18–22 May 1929* (Washington, DC: Government Printing Office, 1929), 317.

23. Peter H. Irons, *The New Deal Lawyers* (Princeton: Princeton University Press, 1982), 18; A descriptive chronology of this case appears in Archer, *Big Business and Radio*, 349, 352–359, 364–386; U.S. Department of Justice, "Progress in Radio Anti-trust Suit," July 1, 1931, Presidential Papers Subject File, "Radio Corporation of America 1929–1932 and Undated," Hoover Presidential Library; William D. Mitchell, Attorney General to Honorable Lawrence Richey, Secretary to the President, June 14, 1932, Presidential Papers Subject File, "Radio Corporation of America 1929–1932 and Undated," Hoover Presidential Library; District Court of the United States District of Delaware in Equity No. 793, *U.S. v. Radio Corporation of America, et al.*, November 21, 1932, in Presidential Papers Subject File, "Radio Corporation of America 1929–1932 and Undated," Hoover Presidential Library.

24. Aitken, *Continuous Wave*, 505–507.

25. Aitken, *Continuous Wave*, 506; District Court of the United States, District of Delaware in Equity No. 793, *United States of America, Petitioner, against Radio Corporation of America, et. al., Defendants*, Consent Decree, November 21, 1932, IV, V, 6–8; Reich, *The Making of American Industrial Research*, 234; "Anti-trust Decree to End Radio Group," *New York Times*, November 22, 1932, 1; "Decree Dissolving Radio Group under Anti-trust Law," *New York Times*, November 22, 1932, 17; "The RCA Consent Decree," *George Washington Law Review* 1 (1933): 513–516; Maclaurin, *Invention and Innovation*, 147; Aitken, *Continuous Wave*, 508.

26. Owen D. Young to the Honorable William D. Mitchell, October 1, 1931; J. G. Harbord, President, RCA to the Honorable Herbert Hoover, October 13, 1931; Owen D. Young to Mr. Charles Neave, October 23, 1931; Owen D. Young to the Honorable Herbert

Hoover, May 11, 1932; William D. Mitchell, Attorney General to the Honorable Lawrence Richey, Secretary to the President, June 14, 1932, all in Presidential Papers Subject File, "Radio Corporation of America 1929–1932 and Undated," Hoover Presidential Library; Aitken, *Continuous Wave*, 500–508; "R.C.A. Seen Stronger Following Split-up," *New York Times*, November 22, 1932, 1, 5; Reich, *The Making of American Industrial Research*, 234–235.

27. Maclaurin, *Invention and Innovation*, 139–152.

28. Christopher Beauchamp, *The Telephone Patents: Intellectual Property, Business, and the Law in the United States and Britain, 1876–1900* (New York: Oxford University Press on behalf of the Business History Conference, 2008), 591–601; David F. Noble, *America by Design: Science, Technology, and the Rise of Corporate Capitalism* (New York: Knopf, 1977); Dan Schiller, *Theorizing Communication: A History* (New York: Oxford University Press, 1996), 15–17; Reich, *The Making of American Industrial Research*, 137–138; N. B. Danielian, *AT&T: The Story of Industrial Conquest* (New York: Vanguard, 1939), 94; In Reich, *The Making of American Industrial Research*, 137.

29. Paul J. Miranti, Jr., "Probability Theory and the Challenge of Sustaining Innovation: Traffic Management at the Bell System, 1900–1929," in eds. Sally H. Clarke, Naomi R. Lamoreaux, and Steven W. Usselman, *The Challenge of Remaining Innovative: Insights from Twentieth-Century American Business* (Stanford: Stanford University Press, 2009), 125; FCC, *Proposed Report on the Telephone Investigation* (Washington, DC: 1938), 196.

Civil Action No. 17–49, in the District Court of the United States for the District of New Jersey, *USA v. Western Electric Company, Incorporated, and American Telephone & Telegraph Company*, Complaint, Filed January 14, 1949, 54, 68–71.

30. FTC, *Report on the Radio Industry*, 132; 74th Cong., House of Representatives, Committee on Patents, *Appendixes to Hearings on H.R. 4523, Pooling of Patents, February–December 1935, Part 2* (Washington, DC: Government Printing Office, 1936), 901.

31. Edward M. Nockels, in 70th Cong., Senate, 1st Sess., Committee on Patents, *Hearings on S. 2783, Forfeiture of Patent Rights on Conviction under Laws Prohibiting Monopoly, January* [sic: should be February] *8 and 9, 1928* (Washington, DC: Government Printing Office, 1928), 47–48; John L. Lewis, *The Miners' Fight for American Standards* (Indianapolis: Bell, 1925), 70, in Irving Bernstein, *The Lean Years: A History of the American Worker, 1920–1933* (Chicago: Haymarket Books, 2010), 125; Nockels quoted in Bernstein, *The Lean Years*, 46, 48.

32. House of Representatives, 74th Cong., Committee on Patents, *Hearings on H.R. 4523, Pooling of Patents, February 11–December 12, 1935, Part 1* (Washington, DC: Government Printing Office, 1936), 711, 273 (quote); Mortimer Feuer, "Patent Monopoly and the Anti-trust Laws," *Columbia Law Review* 38, no. 7 (November 1938): 1146.

33. 75th Cong., 3d Sess., on H.R. 9259, H.R., 9815, H.R. 1666, *Hearings before the Committee on Patents, Subcommittee on Compulsory Licensing, "Compulsory Licensing of Patents," March 21–31, 1938* (Washington, DC: Government Printing Office, 1938),

121 (quote from Harold E. Stonebraker); Nockels in Senate, 70th Cong., 1st Sess., Committee on Patents, *Hearings on S. 2783, Part 1, January 8 and 9, 1928,* 48.

34. John C. Merriam, "The Relation of Science to Technological Trends," *Report of the Subcommittee on Technology, National Resources Committee, Technological Trends and National Policy, Document No. 360,* 75th Cong., House of Representatives, 1st Sess. (Washington, DC: Government Printing Office, 1937), 92; Honorable William I. Sirovich, in 75th Cong., 3d Sess., on H.R. 9259, H.R., 9815, H.R. 1666, *Hearings before the Committee on Patents, Subcommittee on Compulsory Licensing, "Compulsory Licensing of Patents,."* March 21–31, 1938 (Washington, DC: Government Printing Office, 1938), 46.

35. 75th Cong., 3d Sess., on H.R. 9259, H.R., 9815, H.R. 1666, *Hearings before the Committee on Patents, Subcommittee on Compulsory Licensing, "Compulsory Licensing of Patents,"* March 21–31, 1938 (Washington, DC: Government Printing Office, 1938), 164 (John E. Elliott, President, Elliott Core Drilling Co.), 157 (Allison J. Thompson, Thompson Electric Co.).

36. 75th Cong., 3d Sess., On H.R. 9259, H.R., 9815, H.R. 1666, *Hearings before the Committee on Patents, Subcommittee on Compulsory Licensing, "Compulsory Licensing of Patents,"* March 21–31, 1938 (Washington, DC: Government Printing Office, 1938), 169 (William L. Finger).

37. FCC, *Proposed Report on the Telephone Investigation,* 243; FCC, *Proposed Report on the Telephone Investigation,* 664; FCC, *Patent Study of Bell Telephone System, Special Docket No. 1* (Washington, DC: 1937), quoted in Bernhard J. Stern, "Resistances to the Adoption of Technological Innovations," in *Report of the Subcommittee on Technology, National Resources Committee, Technological Trends and National Policy,* 75th Cong., House of Representatives, 1st Sess., Document No. 360 (Washington, DC: Government Printing Office, 1937), 50.

38. Danielian, *AT&T,* 165.

39. FCC, *Proposed Report on the Telephone Investigation,* 712.

40. In Spencer Weber Waller, *Thurman Arnold: A Biography* (New York: NYU Press, 2005), 88. President Roosevelt, in calling for the establishment of the Temporary National Economic Committee, declared "Generally speaking, future patents might be made available for use *by anyone* upon payment of appropriate royalties" (emphasis in the original) in "Patent System Probe First on Monopoly Inquiry's List," *Newsweek,* December 5, 1938, 34. William O. Douglas affirmed, "It is the public interest which is dominant in the patent system . . . The patent is a privilege." In Hart, *Forged Consensus,* 94.

41. In fact, as the debate was intensifying during the mid-1930s, AT&T executives interceded to suppress the company's world-class research and development work in the field of recording devices to attach to the telephone network. Mark Clark, "Suppressing Innovation: Bell Laboratories and Magnetic Recording," *Technology & Culture* 34, no. 3 (July 1993), 516–538; AT&T's public relations programs were legendary. During the 1930s, Southern Bell alone made financial contributions to the Boy Scouts, Community Chest, the Police Relief Association, YMCA, Jewish Women's Association, Bethesda Orphanage, American Red Cross, Salvation Army, Country

Clubs, Chambers of Commerce, Rotary Club, Kiwanis, and other groups. National Archives and Records Administration (hereafter NARA), RG 173, Box 21, Exhibit 228-B-25. For a more general contemporary survey, see Danielian, *AT&T*, 291–325; Ellis W. Hawley, *The Problem of Monopoly: A Study in Economic Ambivalence* (New York: Fordham University Press, 1995), 368–370, 462; Hart, *Forged Consensus*, 62–116; Danielian, *AT&T*, 408–421.

42. FCC, *Proposed Report on the Telephone Investigation*, 264–5; On TNEC, Ellis Hawley, *New Deal and the Problem of Monopoly*, 404–419. For compulsory patent licensing, 77th Cong., House of Representatives, 1st Sess., Temporary National Economic Committee, *Verbatim Record of the Proceedings of the Temporary National Economic Committee, vol. 14, January–April 1941* (Washington, DC: Bureau of National Affairs, 1941).

43. Waller, *Thurman Arnold*, 91; Waller, *Thurman Arnold*, 90; "Patent System Probe First on Monopoly Inquiry's List," *Newsweek*, December 5, 1938, 34; 77th Cong., Senate, 1st Sess., Document No. 35, *Investigation of Concentration of Economic Power, Final Report and Recommendations of the Temporary National Economic Committee* (Washington, DC Government Printing Office, 1941), 36; 77th Cong., House of Representatives, 1st Sess., *Final Report of the Executive Secretary to the Temporary National Economic Committee* (Washington, DC: Government Printing Office, 1941), 20; Testimony of Frank B. Jewett, President, Bell Telephone Laboratories, Inc., 75th Cong., House of Representatives, 2d Sess., *Verbatim Record of the Proceedings of the Temporary National Economic Committee, vol. 1, no. 16, January 18, 1939* (Washington, DC: Bureau of National Affairs, 1939), 476–488; David Lynch, *The Concentration of Economic Power* (New York: Columbia University Press, 1946), 162; Labor Research Association, *Monopoly in the United States* (New York: International Publishers, 1942), 25.

44. Hawley, *New Deal and the Problem of Monopoly*, 442; Mark R. Wilson, *Destructive Creation: American Business and the Winning of World War II* (Philadelphia: University of Pennsylvania Press, 2016), 114; Alan Brinkley, *The End of Reform: New Deal Liberalism in Recession and War* (New York: Alfred A. Knopf, 1995), 106–122; Wyatt Wells, *Antitrust and the Formation of the Postwar World* (New York: Columbia University Press, 2002), 43–89. In 1940, the *New York Times* editorialized in regard to international patent licenses that "they are in effect private treaties which have worldwide economic effects." *New York Times*, August 10, 1940, 12, quoted in Wells, *Antitrust*, 66; Executive Order No. 8977, Establishing the National Patent Planning Commission, F.R. Doc. 41-9471, filed December 16, 1941; 78th Cong., House of Representatives, 1st Sess. House Document No. 239, "The American Patent System," *Message from the President of the United States Transmitting the Report of the National Patent Planning Commission, 18 June 1943* (Washington, DC: Government Printing Office, 1943), 3. Quote from Wells, *Antitrust*, 87; for the war period, 43–89.

45. U.S. Department of Justice, *Investigation of Government Patent Practices and Policies, Report and Recommendations of the Attorney General to the President* (Washington, DC: Government Printing Office, n.d., but probably 1946 or 1947); Hart, *Forged Consensus*, 95. These cases constituted what Hart terms "a hidden legacy of

reform liberals in the postwar period, the legal shaping of corporate R&D policy" (91); Carroll W. Pursell, Jr., "The Administration of Science in the Department of Agriculture, 1933–1940," *Agricultural History* 42 (1968): 231–240. During 1935, some 6,700 different research projects were being carried out in the department. Pursell, "The Administration of Science," 238; Hart, *Forged Consensus*, 70–71, 210; Hart, *Forged Consensus*, 121. For the role played by secrecy in military-sponsored fire control projects from World War I forward, see David A. Mindell, *Between Human and Machine* (Baltimore: Johns Hopkins University Press, 2002), 41, 179–180. Ultimately, the nation's research and technology infrastructure was both hugely enlarged and re-engineered along the conservative lines preferred by war-time science and technology policy leaders such as Vannevar Bush and his friends, Bell Laboratories President Frank Jewett, MIT President Karl Compton, and Harvard President James Conant. However, it took years to accomplish this. Hart, *Forged Consensus*, 122.

46. Michael Riordan and Lillian Hoddeson, *Crystal Fire: The Invention of the Transistor and the Birth of the Information Age* (New York: W. W. Norton, 1998), 102–103. The authors are characterizing those who worked on crystal detectors, but the point holds more generally as, for example, in the field of radar. David Kite Allison, "New Eye for the Navy: The Origin of Radar at the Naval Research Laboratory," *NRL Report 8466* (Washington, DC: Naval Research Laboratory, 1981), 124, 148; Maclaurin, *Invention and Innovation*, 149.

47. Daniel J. Kevles, "The National Science Foundation and the Debate over Postwar Research Policy, 1942–1945: A Political Interpretation of Science—The Endless Frontier," *Isis* 68, no. 1 (March 1977): 4–26; Robert F. Maddox, "The Politics of World War II Science: Senator Harley M. Kilgore and the Legislative Origins of the National Science Foundation," *West Virginia History* 41 (1979); Hart, *Forged Consensus*, 96–116, 137–143; Statement of Leo T. Crowley, Alien Property Custodian, before the Committee on Patents of the Senate of the United States (Bone Committee), Washington, DC, April 27, 1942, in O'Mahoney Papers, Accession Number 275, Box 290, "Legislation Patents 1943," 1, American Heritage Center, University of Wyoming, Laramie (hereafter American Heritage Center).

48. Hart, *Forged Consensus*, 90–96. By the end of fiscal 1939, the Justice Department had 1,375 complaints pending in 213 cases involving forty industries with 185 continuing investigations—"the most extensive program of civil and criminal enforcement in the history of antitrust." Waller, *Thurman Arnold*, 96, 87; Brinkley, *The End of Reform*, 122; Waller, *Thurman Arnold*, 109, 108; Waller, *Thurman Arnold*, 87, 109; Wendell Berge, *Cartels: Challenge to a Free World* (Washington, DC: Public Affairs Press, 1944), 45, quoted in Wells, *Antitrust*, 86.

49. Wells, *Antitrust*, 70; Wells, *Antitrust*, 87; Testimony, 3/30/43, Thurman W. Arnold Collection, Accession 0627, Box 4, "Addresses, Speeches, Statements 1943," American Heritage Center.

50. At this point, according to two knowledgeable contemporaries, "AT&T management had reason to eye Washington nervously. The company was served with 'sweeping' interrogatories . . . making it appear that the Justice Department was preparing for trial. As they began the massive job of complying, company officials

felt they were facing one of the biggest antitrust trials in history." Fred W. Henck and Bernard Strassburg, *A Slippery Slope: The Long Road to the Breakup of AT&T* (New York: Greenwood Press, 1988), 59.
51. Military departments had intervened in the proceeding nearly from its outset. For the view that the case was a boondoggle, see Joseph C. Goulden, *Monopoly* (New York: G.P. Putnam's Sons, 1968), 86–103; Goulden, *Monopoly*, 96.
52. Henck and Strassburg, *Slippery Slope*, 57–58; Goulden, *Monopoly*, 87. Mention of the state PUCs' role in triggering Justice Department action is in Robert B. Horwitz, *The Irony of Regulatory Reform: The Deregulation of American Telecommunications* (New York: Oxford University Press, 1988), 141; For instance, this prosecution "came about not because of pressures or complaints from customers or competitors but because of the dispositions of autonomous officials." Alan Stone, *Wrong Number: The Break-up of AT&T* (New York: Basic Books, 1989), 71; Hart, *Forged Consensus*, 146.
53. According to research director Oliver E. Buckley, quoted in Spurlock, "The Bell Telephone Laboratories," 213; L. G. Woodford, AT&T Assistant Vice President to Bell System Operating Vice Presidents, March 20, 1941, in Spurlock, "The Bell Telephone Laboratories," 281; Buckley, quoted in Spurlock, "The Bell Telephone Laboratories," 244; Wilson, *Destructive Creation*, 66, Table 3; Spurlock, "The Bell Telephone Laboratories," 232–329.
54. Public Law 603 Section 12, 77th Cong., 2d Sess., June 11, 1942.
55. John S. James, "Memorandum for Mr. Herbert A. Berman Re: Electrical Investigation," September 17, 1943, 3, in response to Dan Schiller, June 4, 1999, Freedom of Information Act Request No. ATFY99-175, Department of Justice file number 60-9-96-7 (hereafter FOIA Request No. ATFY99-175). In reply to this FOIA request, these documents were said to have been sent to the NARA, accessible under file accession number 57A50. Ann Lea Harding to Dan Schiller, October 20, 2000, author's collection.
56. Sigmund Timberg to Holmes Baldridge re: Western Electric Case—Patent Story, May 1945, 9, in response to FOIA Request No. ATFY99-175; Former AT&T President Theodore Vail had used this phrase as early as 1879. Danielian, *AT&T*, 95.
57. Timberg to Baldridge.
58. Sigmund Timberg to Houston Harsha re: Proposed Lease of Fairchild's North Carolina Plant to Western Electric, March 6, 1946, in response to FOIA Request No. ATFY99-175; Goulden, *Monopoly*, 87; John F. Baecher, "Memorandum for the Attorney General," June 3, 1948. A handwritten memo dated "6/48" on stationery marked "Office of the Attorney General" stated, "I suggest we take this up with F.C.C. and see if this would be of any help to them in securing lower rates." Another memo of 6/3/48 from "HAB" (Holmes A. Baldridge) relayed, "I have taken this up with Comm. Walker of F.C.C.—he is their telephone man—and he is heartily in favor of our going ahead. He says they can't reach this problem themselves although they are acutely aware of it. He offered us whatever assistance we may need. The complaint has been recast in the way I originally suggested. I think this a good law suit and recommend that we file it soon." All this was in response to FOIA Request No. ATFY99-175.

59. Charles Zerner, "U.S. Sues to Force A.T.&T. To Drop Western Electric Co.," *New York Times*, January 15, 1949, 1; Zerner, "U.S. Sues," 1.
60. Holmes Baldridge, Memo for Assistant Attorney General Bergson, "Press Release—A.T.&T.-Western Electric Complaint," December 15, 1948, File: 60-9-96-7, Papers of Holmes Baldridge, Box 2, Justice Department Chronological File 1948-52, Harry S. Truman Presidential Library and Museum, Independence, Missouri; Baldridge, Memo for Assistant Attorney General Bergson. Baldridge reiterated this foundational theory publicly ten years later in congressional hearings on the outcome of the case. See testimony of Homes Baldridge, May 7, 1958, 85th Cong., House of Representatives, 2d Sess., *Hearings before the Antitrust Subcommittee of the Committee on the Judiciary, "Consent Decree Program of the Department of Justice," Serial No. 9, Part 2, Vol. 3* (Washington, DC: Government Printing Office, 1959), 3603–3643.
61. Garry Wills, *Bomb Power: The Modern Presidency and the National Security State* (New York: Penguin Press, 2010), 15; Margaret B.W. Graham, *The Business of Research: RCA and the Video Disc* (Cambridge: Cambridge University Press, 1986), 68–69; Henry E. Guerlac, *Radar in World War II*, Sections D-E, Volume 8 in *The History of Modern Physics 1800–1950* (College Park, MD: American Institute of Physics, 1987), 691; By 2010, according to two *Washington Post* reporters, 1,271 government organizations and 1,931 private companies occupying sites at 10,000 locations and supporting 854,000 people with top-secret security clearances made up a veritable "alternative geography of the United States." Dana Priest and William M. Arkin, "A World Too Big and Too Secret?," *Santa Fe New Mexican*, July 19, 2010, A1, A7.
62. Hart, *Forged Consensus*, 127–143; American Telephone and Telegraph Company, *Annual Report 1945* (New York: AT&T, 1945), 13–14; Ralph Brown, "Inventing and Patenting at Bell Laboratories," *Bell Laboratories Record* 32, no. 1 (January 1954), 5; Keith S. McHugh, Vice President, AT&T, "Bell System Patents and Patent Licensing," *Bell Telephone Magazine* 27, no. 2 (January 1949): 48–49.
63. Arthur A. Bright, Jr., and John Exter, "War, Radar, and the Radio Industry," *Harvard Business Review* 25, no. 2 (Winter 1947): 272; Maclaurin, *Invention and Innovation*, 256.
64. Robert A. Lovett, Secretary of Defense, "Memorandum on Western Electric Antitrust Case," December 23, 1952, 85th Cong., House of Representatives, 2d Sess., *Hearings before the Antitrust Subcommittee, Committee on the Judiciary, "Consent Decree Program of the Department of Justice," Part II–Volume 1, American Telephone & Telegraph Co., Serial Number 9* (Washington, DC: Government Printing Office, 1958), 1940–1941; for the complicated story of this memo, 1932–1946, 2016–2017; C. E. Wilson to Honorable Herbert Brownell, Jr., July 10, 1953, 85th Cong., House of Representatives, 2d Sess., *Hearings before the Antitrust Subcommittee, Committee on the Judiciary, "Consent Decree Program of the Department of Justice," Part II–Volume 1, American Telephone & Telegraph Co. Serial Number 9* (Washington, DC: Government Printing Office, 1958), 2024–2038; 85th Cong., House of Representatives, 2d Sess., *Hearings before the Antitrust Subcommittee, Committee on the Judiciary, "Consent Decree Program of the Department of Justice," Part II–Volume 1, American Telephone*

& *Telegraph Co. Serial Number 9* (Washington, DC: Government Printing Office, 1958), 1953.
65. 85th Cong., House of Representatives, 2d Sess., *Hearings before the Antitrust Subcommittee, Committee on the Judiciary,* "Consent Decree Program of the Department of Justice," *Part II–Volume 1, American Telephone & Telegraph Co. Serial Number 9* (Washington, DC: Government Printing Office, 1958), 2381–2392; 85th Cong., House of Representatives, 2d Sess., *Hearings before the Antitrust Subcommittee, Committee on the Judiciary,* "Consent Decree Program of the Department of Justice," *Part II–Volume III, American Telephone & Telegraph Co. Serial Number 9* (Washington, DC: Government Printing Office, 1958), 3669–3677; 85th Cong., House of Representatives, 2d Sess., *Hearings before the Antitrust Subcommittee, Committee on the Judiciary,* "Consent Decree Program of the Department of Justice," *Part II–Volume III, American Telephone & Telegraph Co. Serial Number 9* (Washington, DC: Government Printing Office, 1958), 3428–3453; 85th Cong., House of Representatives, 2d Sess., *Hearings before the Antitrust Subcommittee, Committee on the Judiciary,* "Consent Decree Program of the Department of Justice," *Part II–Volume 1, American Telephone & Telegraph Co., Serial Number 9* (Washington, DC: Government Printing Office, 1958),1674–1675; vol. 3, 3698.
66. "Antitrusters Score Patent Victory in AT&T Case, Settle with IBM," *Business Week,* January 28, 1956, 160.
67. *United States v. Western Electric Co.*, 1956 Trade Cas. 68246, D.N.J., January 24, 1956, in Defendants' Third Statement, vol. 1, 189.
68. "Outline of Bell System Patent Licensing Policy," House of Representatives, 85th Cong., 2d Sess., Consent Decree Program of the Department of Justice, *Hearings before the Antitrust Subcommittee of the Committee on the Judiciary, March–May 1958, Serial No. 9 Part II Volume II* (Washington, DC: Government Printing Office, 1958), 2502; Horace P. Moulton, Vice President and General Counsel, AT&T in House of Representatives, 85th Cong., 2d Sess., Consent Decree Program of the Department of Justice, *Hearings before the Antitrust Subcommittee of the Committee on the Judiciary, March–May 1958, Serial No. 9 Part II Volume II* (Washington, DC: Government Printing Office, 1958), 2568; *American Telephone and Telegraph Company Annual Report 1951* (New York: AT&T, 1951), 20; 86th Cong., Senate, 2d Sess., Committee on the Judiciary, *Staff Report of the Subcommittee on Patents, Trademarks, and Copyrights, Pursuant to S. Res. 240, "Compulsory Patent Licensing Under Antitrust Judgments"* (Washington, DC: Government Printing Office, 1960), 46; "The Impact of Two Historic Antitrust Decrees," *Business Week,* February 4, 1956, 27–28.
69. AT&T, Memorandum for the Attorney General, April 1953, 28, U.S. Congress, House of Representatives, 85th Cong., 2d Sess., *Hearings before the Antitrust Subcommittee, Committee on the Judiciary,* "Consent Decree Program of The Department of Justice," *Part II–Volume 1, American Telephone & Telegraph Co. Serial Number 9* (Washington, DC: Government Printing Office, 1958), 1985; No less than 55 percent of AT&T's hundreds of predecree patent licensing agreements already contained "grant-back" provisions, most of which involved no royalty payments. 85th Cong., House of Representatives, 2d Sess., Consent Decree Program of the Department of Justice.

Hearings before the Antitrust Subcommittee of the Committee on the Judiciary, March–May 1958, Serial No. 9 Part II Volume II (Washington, DC: Government Printing Office, 1958), 2664–2665. *Business Week* observed that the settlement actually formalized this benefit for AT&T: "In an industry where many a small electronics company has been launched on the strength of a single development, broad application of the reciprocity clause could make it difficult for any company to keep exclusive control of inventions in any way related to communications." "The Impact of Two Historic Antitrust Decrees," 28.

70. Victor R. Hansen, Assistant Attorney General Antitrust Division, House of Representatives, 85th Cong., 2d Sess., Consent Decree Program of the Department of Justice, *Hearings before the Antitrust Subcommittee of the Committee on the Judiciary, March–May 1958, Serial No. 9 Part II Volume III* (Washington, DC: Government Printing Office, 1958), 3726.

71. Not only did the wartime Justice Department initially formulate what became the AT&T suit within a wider framework of investigatory concern, but the Zenith Radio Corporation also filed suit against RCA, General Electric, Westinghouse, and AT&T's Western Electric unit in 1946, charging them with conspiring to keep Zenith out of the world market. "Zenith to Get $10 Million From RCA, 2 Others in Antitrust Suit Settlement," *Wall Street Journal*, September 16, 1957, 6; "RCA to Open up 10,000 Radio, TV Patents as It Settles Antitrust Suit," *Wall Street Journal*, October 29, 1958, 3; "IBM Trust Suit Ended by Decree; Machines Freed," *New York Times*, hary 26, 1956, 1. For IBM, which was just beginning to transition from punched-card machines to electronic computing, the case "cast a long shadow over . . . US operations for years." James W. Cortada, *IBM: The Rise and Fall and Reinvention of a Global Icon* (Cambridge, MA: MIT Press, 2019), 186, 185 (quote).

72. House of Representatives, 85th Cong., 2d Sess., *Consent Decree Program of the Department of Justice. Hearings before the Antitrust Subcommittee of the Committee on the Judiciary, March–May 1958, Serial No. 9 Part II Volume III* (Washington, DC: Government Printing Office, 1958), 3692; 86th Cong. 2d Sess., Senate, Committee on the Judiciary, *Staff Report of the Subcommittee on Patents, Trademarks, and Copyrights, Pursuant to S. Res. 240, "Compulsory Patent Licensing Under Antitrust Judgments"* (Washington, DC: Government Printing Office, 1960), 42–46.

73. Victor Hansen testimony, House of Representatives, 85th Cong., 2d Sess., Consent Decree Program of the Department of Justice, *Hearings before the Antitrust Subcommittee of the Committee on the Judiciary, March–May 1958, Serial No. 9 Part II Volume III* (Washington, DC: Government Printing Office, 1958), 3694–3695.

74. Mervin J. Kelly, President, Bell Telephone Laboratories, Inc., House of Representatives, 85th Cong., 2d Sess., *Hearings before the Antitrust Subcommittee, Committee on the Judiciary, "Consent Decree Program of the Department of Justice," Part II–Volume 1, American Telephone & Telegraph Co. Serial Number 9* (Washington, DC: Government Printing Office, 1958), 2068; *American Telephone and Telegraph Company, Annual Report 1950* (New York: AT&T, 1950), 15; *American Telephone and Telegraph Company, Annual Report 1956* (New York: AT&T, 1956), 18; Fortune 500 1956, http://archive.fortune.com/magazines/fortune/fortune500_archive/full/

1956/; House of Representatives, 85th Cong., 2d Sess., *Consent Decree Program of the Department of Justice. Hearings before the Antitrust Subcommittee of the Committee on the Judiciary, March–May 1958, Serial No. 9 Part II* (Washington, DC: Government Printing Office, 1958), vol. 3, 3690–3692; vol. 1, 2198–2201.
75. Spurlock, "The Bell Telephone Laboratories," 358.
76. Spurlock, "The Bell Telephone Laboratories," 373–374; Spurlock, "The Bell Telephone Laboratories," 383; Wilson also decided that to protect AT&T, its operation of Sandia Labs should not be conducted for profit, but operated on a cost-basis, with no management fee. M. D. Fagen, ed., *A History of Engineering and Science in the Bell System: National Service in War and Peace (1925–1975)* (Bell Telephone Laboratories, Incorporated, 1978), 650–655, quote at 653–654; L. A. Wilson, Memo for File, August 15, 1949, 4:50 p.m., in Spurlock, "The Bell Telephone Laboratories," 386; Charles A. Coolidge, "Memorandum for the Secretary," February 29, 1952, in House of Representatives, 85th Cong., 2d Sess., *Hearings before the Antitrust Subcommittee, Committee on the Judiciary, "Consent Decree Program of The Department of Justice," Part II–Volume 1, American Telephone & Telegraph Co. Serial Number 9* (Washington, DC: Government Printing Office, 1958), 1691.
77. Spurlock, "The Bell Telephone Laboratories," 388–389.
78. Herbert S. Matthews, "A Salem Yankee at King George's Court," *New York Times*, October 8, 1950, SM7; Gertner, *Idea Factory*, 245–246; 94th Cong., 1st Sess., House of Representatives, Committee on the Judiciary, Subcommittee on Courts, Civil Liberties, and the Administration of Justice, *Hearings on the Matter of Wiretapping, Electronic Eavesdropping, and Other Surveillance, February 6, 18, March 4, 18, 21, May 22, June 26, July 25, September 8, 1975, Serial No. 26, two volumes* (Washington, DC: Government Printing Office, 1976), 31–32.
79. Notably, Fagen, *A History of Engineering and Science in the Bell System*; Gertner, *Idea Factory*, 159–161, 271; Dr. M. J. Kelly, Bell Telephone Laboratories Incorporated, "Bell System Contributions to the National Defense During the Past 15 Years," June 11, 1953, 1. Timothy K. Nenninger to Dan Schiller, September 15, 2007 in response to FOIA Request No. ATFY99-175; Kelly, "Bell System Contributions," 2.
80. Kelly, "Bell System Contributions," 3–4; Kelly, "Bell System Contributions," 5; Kelly, "Bell System Contributions," 6–7.
81. Kelly, "Bell System Contributions," 8–20, Lovett quote at 20; Kelly, "Bell System Contributions," 22; Melvyn P. Leffler, *A Preponderance of Power: National Security, the Truman Administration, and The Cold War* (Stanford: Stanford University Press, 1992), 11.
82. Kenneth Flamm, *Creating the Computer: Government, Industry, and High Technology* (Washington, DC: Brookings Institution), 1988.
83. Flamm, *Creating the Computer*, 29–30; Riordan and Hoddeson, *Crystal Fire*, 181; Waller, *Thurman Arnold*, 98–99.
84. Riordan and Hoddeson, *Crystal Fire*, 82, 108–109; Riordan and Hoddeson, *Crystal Fire*, 158.
85. AT&T, "Report Regarding Equipment Manufactured by Western for the Bell System," in House of Representatives, 85th Cong., 2d Sess., Consent Decree Program of the

Department of Justice, *Hearings before the Antitrust Subcommittee of the Committee on the Judiciary, March–May 1958, Serial No. 9, Part II, Volume III* (Washington, DC: Government Printing Office, 1958), 3895; Mervin J. Kelly, "The First Five Years of the Transistor," *Bell Telephone Magazine* 32 (Summer 1953): 77; House of Representatives, 84th Cong., 2d Sess., Distribution Problems, *Hearing before Subcommittee No. 5 of the Select Committee on Small Business, Pursuant to H. Res. 114. 29 March 1956, Part V, Antitrust Consent Decrees A Case Study—The A.T.&T Consent Decree* (Washington, DC: Government Printing Office, 1956), 10.

86. Riordan and Hoddeson, *Crystal Fire*, 197; Riordan and Hoddeson, *Crystal Fire*, 204; Misa, "Military Needs," 272, 268.
87. Leslie Berlin, *The Man behind the Microchip: Robert Noyce and the Invention of Silicon Valley* (New York: Oxford University Press, 2005), 135, 171; Flamm, *Creating the Computer*, 17; Berlin, *The Man behind the Microchip*, 135, 171; Misa: "Military Needs," 281, 286.
88. "Outline of Bell System Patent Licensing Policy," in House of Representatives, 85th Cong., 2d Sess., Consent Decree Program of the Department of Justice, *Hearings before the Antitrust Subcommittee of the Committee on the Judiciary, March–May 1958, Serial No. 9, Part II, Volume II* (Washington, DC: Government Printing Office, 1958), 2502.
89. Ithiel de Sola Pool, *Technologies of Freedom* (Cambridge: Belknap Press, 1983); Peter W. Huber, *The Geodesic Network: 1987 Report on Competition in the Telephone Industry* (Washington, DC: U.S. Department of Justice, Antitrust Division, 1987), 1, 35.

Chapter 9

1. Kevin Boyle, *The Shattering: America in the 1960s* (New York: W.W. Norton, 2021).
2. Aaron Brenner, "Rank-and-File Rebellion, 1966–1975" (Ph.D. diss., Columbia University, 1996); eds. Aaron Brenner, Robert Brenner, and Cal Winslow, *Rebel Rank and File: Labor Militancy and Revolt from below during the Long 1970s* (London: Verso, 2010).
3. Dorothy Sue Cobble, *The Other Women's Movement: Workplace Justice and Social Rights in Modern America* (Princeton, NJ: Princeton University Press, 2004); Nancy MacLean, *Freedom Is Not Enough: The Opening of the American Workplace* (Cambridge, MA: Harvard University Press, 2006).
4. Murray B. Nesbitt, *Labor Relations in the Federal Government Service* (Washington, DC: Bureau of National Affairs, 1976), 46–47; John Walsh and Garth L. Mangum, *Labor Struggle in the Post Office: From Selective Lobbying to Collective Bargaining* (Armonk: M. E. Sharpe, 1992), 62–69; Robert H. Zieger, *For Jobs and Freedom: Race and Labor in America since 1865* (Lexington: University Press of Kentucky, 2007), 86; Martha Biondi, *To Stand and Fight: The Struggle for Civil Rights in Postwar New York City* (Cambridge, MA: Harvard University Press, 2003), 140–141. The loyalty boards established during the Truman presidency often imposed racially discriminatory

tests "that were strongly biased against civil rights activists, especially in departments like the Post Office, which had large numbers of black employees." The Post Office, she relates, was subjected to the highest proportion of discharges of any federal department for supposed suspected disloyalty. Ellen Schrecker, *Many Are the Crimes: McCarthyism In America* (Boston: Little, Brown, 1998), 282, 285; Philip F. Rubio, *There's Always Work at the Post Office: African American Postal Workers and the Fight for Jobs, Justice, and Equality* (Chapel Hill, NC: University of North Carolina Press, 2010), 192; Rubio, *There's Always Work at the Post Office*, 211; Rubio, *There's Always Work at the Post Office*, 185; Rubio, *There's Always Work at the Post Office*, 176; President Kennedy issued Executive Order 10988 in January 1962, which permitted limited collective bargaining rights (although neither the right to strike nor to bargain on economic issues) for federal worker unions that did not practice racial discrimination. Kennedy's Executive Order 10925, issued in March 1961, mandated that federal agencies undertake studies and recommendations for equal employment opportunity. The Civil Service and the Post Office established affirmative action EEO committees. Philip F. Rubio, *Undelivered: From the Great Postal Strike of 1970 to the Manufactured Crisis of the U.S. Postal Service* (Chapel Hill, NC: University of North Carolina Press, 2020), 25, 31, 225 n6; Rubio, *There's Always Work at the Post Office*, 149–151. The National Association of Letter Carriers, led by a Nixon partisan, did not allow African Americans to join in some areas until the 1970s. Richard Rothstein, *The Color of Law: A Forgotten History of How Our Government Segregated America* (New York: Liveright Publishing, 2017), 161; Rubio, *There's Always Work at the Post Office*, 371 n1. For general background, Mary L. Dudziak, *Cold War Civil Rights: Race and the Image of Modern Democracy* (Princeton, NJ: Princeton University Press, 2011).

5. John Darnton, "Postman's Pay a Little Too High for Welfare," *New York Times*, March 25, 1970, A31; Rubio, *There's Always Work at the Post Office*, 207, quoting mail handler Richard Thomas of the Manhattan General Post Office in 1968; Kennedy's EO 10988 permitted collective bargaining over some noneconomic issues; Rubio, *Undelivered*, 28; Rubio, *Undelivered*, 47 ("three-quarters"); Christian G. Appy, *Working-Class War: American Combat Soldiers and Vietnam* (Chapel Hill, NC: University of North Carolina Press, 1993), 244–247.

6. Rubio, *There's Always Work at the Post Office*, 213; Rubio, *There's Always Work at the Post Office*, 145; Cobble, *The Other Women's Movement*, 146; Rubio, *Undelivered*, 38; Rubio, *Undelivered*, 29–30, 35–37, 40–46; Kappel linked this "disquiet" to "antiquated personnel policies, poor working conditions, limited career opportunities and training"—the very conditions that he pushed to address through more extensive mechanization and management control, first as head of the Task Force on the Post Office and eventually as the head of the new USPS Board of Governors. "The Enduring Mail Mess," *Time*, March 30, 1970, 14.

7. Donald Janson, "Chicago Postal Officials Back O'Brien's Plan to Replace the Department with a Nonprofit Corporation," *New York Times*, April 9, 1966, 76; "Negro Sworn as Head of Chicago Post Office," *New York Times*, September 27, 1966, 34. An African American NAACP member was chosen to head Manhattan's Post Office

two months later. "Negro Appointed Postmaster Here," *New York Times*, November 3, 1966, 41; "Chicago Rights Activist Robert Lucas," *New York Times*, September 5, 1966, 8; Zieger, *For Jobs and Freedom*, 54, 86; Joe William Trotter, Jr., *Workers on Arrival: Black Labor in the Making of America* (Berkeley, CA: University of California Press, 2019), 133; Rubio, *There's Always Work at the Post Office*; McGee, "The Negro in the Chicago Post Office."; "A Logjam of Mail Broken in Chicago," *New York Times*, October 19, 1966, 30.

8. "Backlog of Mail Jams Post Office in Chicago," *New York Times*, October 10, 1966, 43; "Mail Distribution Tied up in Chicago," *New York Times*, October 14, 1966, 22; "Post Office Retains Its Christmas Help in 'Junk Mail' Rush," *New York Times*, December 29, 1966, 33; Interview with Lawrence F. O'Brien by Michael L. Gillette, 15, 11/20/86, 34, Lyndon Baynes Johnson Presidential Library, Austin, Texas (hereafter Johnson Presidential Library), http://www.lbjlibrary.net/assets/documents/archives/oral_hi stories/obrien_l/OBRIEN15.PDF.

9. Janson, "Chicago Postal Officials Back O'Brien's Plan."; Janson, "Chicago Postal Officials Back O'Brien's Plan."

10. Janson, "Chicago Postal Officials Back O'Brien's Plan."; O'Brien interview; Janson, "Chicago Postal Officials Back O'Brien's Plan."

11. "O'Brien Says Post Office Faces a 'Catastrophe,'" *New York Times* March 20, 1967, 18; Lawrence F. O'Brien, "A New Design for the Postal Service: A Private Corporation," *Vital Speeches of the Day* 33, no. 14 (May 1, 1967): 418; O'Brien stated, "We had the Chicago crisis, which was mammoth, at the Christmas period. We got to that period while I had attention directed to postal reorganization." O'Brien interview, 15. Rubio writes that O'Brien formulated a plan for corporatization two months prior to the Chicago breakdown. Rubio, *Breakdown*, 35.

12. Murray Schumach, "City's Postal System Is Snagged by Traffic and Skyscrapers," *New York Times*, April 9, 1967, 1, 77; "Post Office Retains Its Christmas Help in 'Junk Mail' Rush."

13. Marjorie Hunter, "O'Brien Proposes Corporation Run Postal Service," *New York Times*, April 4, 1967, 1, 18; Hunter, "O'Brien Proposes Corporation."; "O'Brien Prices Modern Postal Service at $5-Billion," *New York Times*, April 16, 1967. 1, 66; "O'Brien Prices Modern Postal Service at $5-Billion," 66; "O'Brien to Go to Senate Group to Ask for More Postal Funds," *New York Times*, April 5, 1967, 29.

14. "Text of Johnson Message on Pay and Mail Rates," *New York Times*, April 6, 1967, 33; Johnson in John D. Morris, "Commission Is Directed to Submit a Report within One Year," *New York Times*, April 9, 1967, 1.

15. In Marjorie Hunter, "O'Brien Proposes Corporation Run Postal Service," 18; "Avoiding Postal Catastrophe," *New York Times*, April 6, 1967, 38.

16. Janson, "Chicago Postal Officials Back O'Brien's Plan."; "Realism on Postal Rates," *New York Times*, May 15, 1967, 42; Janson, "Chicago Postal Officials Back O'Brien's Plan."

17. The Report of The President's Commission on Postal Organization, *Towards Postal Excellence* (Washington, DC: Government Printing Office, 1968); Richard R. John, "History of Universal Service and the Postal Monopoly," George Mason School of

Public Policy, Study on Universal Postal Service and the Postal Monopoly, Appendix D, November 2008: 33–36, file:///Users/dschille/Desktop/History_of_Universal_Service_and_the_Po-1.pdf.
18. David R. Jones, "Mail Study Asks a Nonprofit Unit," *New York Times*, June 30, 1968, 30; In John, "History of Universal Service and the Postal Monopoly," 33.
19. "Newark Mail Diverted to Philadelphia in Riot," *New York Times*, July 16, 1967, 54; "Mail Service in Australia Paralyzed as Strike Grows," *New York Times*, January 19, 1968, 21; "South Vietnam Mail Delayed," *New York Times*, February 7, 1968, 44; "House Bars an End to Saturday Mail," April 10, 1968, 73; "Hope for the Mails," *New York Times*, May 28, 1969, 46.
20. Russell Baker, "Observer: Stay, Courier, from Your Appointed Rounds," *New York Times*, April 27, 1969, E16.
21. Robert Sherrill, "Bring Back the Pony Express," *New York Times Magazine*, November 3, 1968, 282.
22. Joseph P. Fried, "$100 Million General Post Office to Be Built Here," *New York Times*, June 26, 1968, 1, 35; "Post Office Sets a 'Command Post,'" *New York Times*, November 30, 1968, 79; "Automation to Speed Christmas Mail to Vietnam," *New York Times*, October 19, 1967, 3.
23. Rubio, *Undelivered*, 39; Rubio, *There's Always Work at the Post Office*, 260; Rubio, *Undelivered*, 60; Murray B. Nesbitt, *Labor Relations in the Federal Government Service* (Washington, DC: Bureau of National Affairs, 1976), 386; Prior studies of the strike include Brenner, "Rank-and-File Rebellion, 1966–1975"; Vern K. Baxter, *Labor and Politics in the U.S. Postal Service* (New York: Plenum Press, 1994); Rubio, *There's Always Work at the Post Office*, 207–261; and Rubio, *Undelivered*, 60–118.
24. H. R. Haldeman, H. Notes, January–March 1970 Pt. II, HRH Box 41, Haldeman Collection, Nixon Presidential Materials Project, in Brenner, "Rank-and-File Rebellion," 134–135; Rubio, *There's Always Work at the Post Office*, 254; Rubio, *There's Always Work at the Post Office*, 254.
25. "As you know," Colson related to the President's Chief of Staff, "several hundred thousand letters have been written to the President regarding postal pay." White House Special Files, Staff Member Office Files, Charles W. Colson Meetings Files, December 5, 1969, "For H. R. Haldeman From C. W. Colson, Subject: Answer To Postal Employees' Letter, Administratively Confidential," Richard Nixon Presidential Library and Museum, Yorba Linda, California (hereafter Nixon Presidential Library); "For John Rose from Chuck Colson," February 11, 1970, White House Special Files, Staff Member Office Files, Charles W. Colson Meetings Files, Box 82, Nixon Presidential Library. Nixon himself had met with NALC president Rademacher twice in December 1969. Rubio, *Undelivered*, 48–49; Charles W. Colson, March 6, 1970 To: Murray Chotiner Subject: Political Problems of the Post Office," White House Special Files Staff Member Office Files (SMOF), Charles W. Colson Subject Files, Box 51 Folder "Contacts with Rademacher—Conversations, Memos, Telephone [2 of 2], Nixon Presidential Library; See also, Rubio, *Undelivered*, 48; "Telephone Call James Rademacher, President NALC, Recommended by Chuck Colson and Henry Cashen,"

March 12, 1970. Box WH Special Files Staff Member Office Files (SMOF), Charles W. Colson Meetings Files, Box 82, Nixon Presidential Library.
26. Rubio, *There's Always Work at the Post Office*, 263.
27. Box WH Special Files Staff Member Office Files Charles W. Colson Subject Files Box 49, Folders "Concerning Postal Strike and Reform," Nixon Presidential Library; Homer Bigart, "Tie-up Is Spreading—L.I., Connecticut and Jersey Are Affected," *New York Times*, March 19, 1970, A1; "The Strike That Stunned the Country," *Time*, March 30, 1970, 11–16; Robert J. Cole, "City's Economy Worsens in 2d Day of Postal Strike," *New York Times*, March 20, 1970, A1.
28. "Congress to Act Soon on Pay Rise," *New York Times*, February 26, 1970, A14; Robert Semple, Jr., "President Says Issue Is Survival of Rule Based upon Law," *New York Times*, March 24, 1970, A1, A34; Richard L. Madden, "Mailmen Invited to Bargain Today," *New York Times*, March 25,1970, A1, A30; Eileen Shanahan, "Mailmen Offered 12% Rise in Wages," *New York Times*, April 1, 1970, A1; Eileen Shanahan, "7 Postal Unions Win 14% Pay Rise Tied to Reform," *New York Times*, April 3, 1970, A1. "Excerpts from the President's Message to Congress Proposing Postal Reform and Increases in Pay," *New York Times*, April 17, 1970, 19; Rubio, *There's Always Work at the Post Office*, 268; Haldeman Diaries, January 1, 1970–January 1, 1971, Vol. 2, Entries for March 20–24, April 1–4, and April 7, Nixon Presidential Library.
29. H. R. Haldeman, H. Notes January–March 1970 Part I to H Notes April–June 1970 Part II Box 41, Folder H Notes Jan–March 1970, February 21–March 31, 1970, March 23. NPMS, WH Special Files Staff Member and Office Files, Nixon Presidential Library. NB: Mention of "7" postal unions is significant in that it excludes the two Black-led organizations, the NPU and the NAPE.
30. Box WH Special Files Staff Member Office Files (SMOF) Charles W. Colson Subject Files Box 51 Folder "Contacts with Rademacher—Conversations, Memos, Telephone [1 of 2]," Nixon Presidential Library.
31. "Colson Memorandum for John Erlichman March 25, 1970 Subject: Rademacher/Postal Strike," Nixon Presidential Library; Alfred E. Clark, "Postal Workers Put Off a Strike," *New York Times*, June 12, 1970, A12.
32. Rubio, *There's Always Work at the Post Office*, 268, 15, 262–265; Eileen Shanahan, "Postal Unions Win 14% Raise," *New York Times*, April 3, 1970, A20; U.S. Cong., House of Representatives, 91st Cong., 2d Sess., *Hearing before the Committee on Post Office and Civil Service. Hearings on Postal Reform. Serial 91-22, April 22, 23, 27, 1970* (Washington, DC: Government Printing Office, 1970), 114, 118.
33. "It was an organized effort and it was funded by mail-users who were persuaded that this was the right way to go, all of them sharing a common concern about postal service." O'Brien interview, 22–23; Rubio, *Undelivered*, 36; Marjorie Hunter, "Postal Pay Rise and Reform Plan Passed by House," *New York Times*, June 19, 1970, A31.
34. Rubio, *There's Always Work at the Post Office*, 265; John, "History of Universal Service and the Postal Monopoly," 80; Rick Geddes, *Saving the Mail: How to Solve the Problems of the U.S. Postal Service* (Washington, DC: AEI Press, 2003), 98.
35. Rubio, *There's Always Work at the Post Office*, 264; Rubio, *Undelivered*, 119–168; Rubio, *There's Always Work at the Post Office*, 263, 268; Christopher W. Shaw, *First Class: The*

U.S. Postal Service Democracy, and the Corporate Threat (San Francisco: City Lights Books, 2021), 123–140.

36. O'Brien interview, 9; John T. Tierney, *Postal Reorganization: Managing the Public's Business* (Boston: Auburn House, 1981), 21–22; Rubio, *Undelivered*, 127–128, 140–141.

37. Walsh and Mangum, *Labor Struggle in the Post Office*, 100–102; Rubio, *Undelivered*, 149–152; Rubio, *There's Always Work at the Post Office*, 265.

38. United Federation of Postal Clerks, "Three Merger Pacts Set; Top Negotiator Hired," *The Union Postal Clerk* 67, no. 1 (1971): 5; The remaining postal unions included the National Rural Letter Carriers' Association, the National Alliance of Postal and Federal Employees, and the National Postal Mail Handlers Union. United Federation of Postal Clerks. "Vote Yes!," *The Union Postal Clerk* 67, no. 4 (1971): 10; United Federation of Postal Clerks, "It's Go on NPU Merger!," *The Union Postal Clerk* 67, no. 3. (1971): 3; David Silvergleid, "Practical Labor-Management Relations," *The American Postal Worker* 1, no. 2 (1971): 13; David Silvergleid, "NALC Merger Terms," *The American Postal Worker* 2, no. 1 (1972): 23; Silvergleid, "NALC Merger Terms," 23.

39. American Postal Workers Union, "Board Wrestles Giant Agenda," *The American Postal Worker* 2, no. 5 (1972): 37; John N. Schacht, *The Making of Telephone Unionism, 1920–1947* (New Brunswick, NJ: Rutgers University Press, 1985), 182; Jack Barbash, *Unions and Telephones: The Story of the Communications Workers of America* (New York: Harper & Brothers, 1952), 131, 129; Sylvia B. Gottlieb, "The Telephone Worker's Wage Case," Labor-Management Relations in The Bell Telephone System, 81st Cong., 2d Sess., Senate, *Hearings before the Subcommittee on Labor-Management Relations of the Committee on Labor and Public Welfare, August 10–September 12, 1950, Appendix 10* (Washington, DC: Government Printing Office, 1950), 842. See also, Barbash, *Unions and Telephones*, 171–175; Her "biggest problem," she recalled, was the Federal Communications Commission. Interview with Helen W. Berthelot by John Schacht, May 6, 1969, in CWA-University of Iowa Oral History Project, University of Iowa Library Special Collections, Iowa City, Iowa, 12, 18, 21; Joseph A. Beirne, *Challenge to Labor: New Roles for American Trade Unions* (Englewood Cliffs, NJ: Prentice-Hall, 1969), 52.

40. Schacht, *The Making of Telephone Unionism*, 182; Joseph A. Beirne Oral History, CWA-University of Iowa Oral History Project, University of Iowa Library, Special Collections, 46, 49; Admiral Ben Moreell, "To Communism . . . Via Majority Vote," Address to the Marketing Division of the American Petroleum Institute, Chicago Illinois, November 10, 1952; National Labor Relations Board, v. 98, no. 168, "Chesapeake & Potomac Telephone Company of West Virginia and Lois Patty," Case No. 6-CA-307, April 9, 1952, https://www.casemine.com/judgement/us/591490c3a dd7b0493457c439.

41. "Senate Labor Committee Urges National Bargaining with Bell; Approves Labor Relations Report," *CWA News* 10, no. 3 (March 1951): 1, 6; "CWA Wins Major Victory," *CWA News* 11, no. 5 (May 1952): 1; "Quarter Million Telephone Workers out during Strike," *CWA News* 11, no. 5 (May 1952): 1, 16; "CWA Observes Independent's

Picket Lines in Jersey Strike," *CWA News* 11, no. 4 (April 1952): 3; Thomas R. Brooks, *Communications Workers of America, The Story of a Union* (New York: Mason/Charter, 1977), 172–190, quote at 190; see also, http://www.cwa6300.org/history.asp.

42. Cobble, *The Other Women's Movement*, 21; President Beirne wrote to twenty-three independent unions representing 175,000 workers scattered across New England, the Mid-Atlantic, Chicago and Southern California, "inviting them to join in the drive for 'one industry—one union.'" John L. Crull, "Thoughts on Organizing," *CWA News* 8, no. 1 (January 1949): 7; "Independent Unions Invited into CWA," *CWA News* 9, no. 8 (August 1949): 6; "[W]e might have had a decertification election a year after the strike, and we might have lost it," recollected one Southern Bell CWA leader, George E. Gill. In Brooks, *Communications Workers of America*, 190; "CWA Membership up for Second Month in a Row, Hackney Hopes Gain Continues," *CWA News* 19, no. 8 (August 1960): 5; June McDonald interview by John Schacht, February 12, 1969, 10, CWA-University of Iowa Oral History Project, University of Iowa Library Special Collections, Iowa City, Iowa, 25.

43. Schacht, *The Making of Telephone Unionism*, 183; Brooks, *Communications Workers of America*, 210; Brooks, *Communications Workers of America*, 226; Bernard E. Anderson, *The Negro in the Public Utility Industries*, Report No. 10, Industrial Research Unit, Wharton School of Finance (Philadelphia: University of Pennsylvania Press, 1970), 63.

44. Aaron Brenner, "Rank-and-File Struggles at the Telephone Company," in eds. Aaron Brenner, Robert Brenner and Cal Winslow, *Rebel Rank and File: Labor Militancy and Revolt from Below during the Long 1970s* (London: Verso, 2010), 255; Brenner, "Rank-and-File Struggles at the Telephone Company," 255; Venus Green, *Race on the Line: Gender, Labor, and Technology in the Bell System, 1880–1980* (Durham, NC: Duke University Press, 2001), 210–211.

45. J. A. Beirne, "Big Job Now Is to Bring Industrial Democracy to Communications Industry," *CWA News* 18, no. 5 (March 1959): 4; Brooks, *Communications Workers of America*, 229.

46. Brooks, *Communications Workers of America*, 234.

47. Beirne, *Challenge to Labor*, 159; Beirne *Challenge to Labor*, 160; Beirne, *Challenge to Labor*, 167–168, 169 (quote); Beirne, *Challenge to Labor*, 206.

48. Beirne, *Challenge to Labor*, 135; Beirne, *Challenge to Labor*, 28–29, 204; Beirne, *Challenge to Labor*, 213; Beirne, *Challenge to Labor*, 181; Beirne, *Challenge to Labor*, 134.

49. CPI Inflation Calculator, Bureau of Labor Statistics, U.S. Department of Labor, http://www.bls.gov/data/inflation_calculator.htm; Joseph A. Beirne interview by Thomas A. Baker, March 4, 1969, Johnson Presidential Library Oral History Collection, 7, 27, Johnson Presidential Library, Austin, Texas, https://www.discoverlbj.org/item/oh-beirnej-19690304-1-74-170.

50. "Strike Report," *United Action*, February 8, 1971, 1; Brenner, "Rank-and-File Struggles at the Telephone Company," 273.

51. "Major Emphasis Placed on Organizing by Convention," *CWA News* 19, no. 7 (July 1960): 6.

52. Brooks, *Communications Workers of America*, 228; Brenner, "Rank-and-File Struggles at the Telephone Company," 255–256; Brenner, "Rank-and-File Struggles at the Telephone Company," 267; Brenner, "Rank-and-File Struggles at the Telephone Company," 252, 260; Joseph A. Beirne Oral History, 45–47.
53. "Strike Report," *United Action*, February 8, 1971, 1; "Operators: It's Your Strike Too," quote excerpted in Brenner, "Rank-and-File Struggles at the Telephone Company," 268; The Militant Rank & File, "Strike Is Still On," New York City, January–February 1971.
54. "Company Upheld in Phone Dispute," *New York Times*, February 1, 1971, 28; "Judge Orders End to Phone Strike," *New York Times*, January 12, 1971, 12; "Phone Union Head in Private Talks," *New York Times*, January 24, 1971, 32; Brenner, "Rank-and-File Struggle at the Telephone Company," 269.
55. Brenner, "Rank-and-File Struggles at the Telephone Company," 270; U.S. Acts to Avert Rail Strike Today," *New York Times*, July 17, 1971, A1, A62; "No Turning Back!," *United Action* no. 7 (June 21, 1971): 1–2.
56. "Twenty-Five Per Cent Isn't Enough," *United Action*, no. 3 (April 12, 1971): 1; "Show the Company We Are United: All out for the Local Meeting!," *United Action*, no. 6 (June 7, 1971): 1, 4; "Show the Company We Are United: All out for the Local Meeting!," 1, 4. See also, "No Turning Back!," *United Action*, no. 7 (June 21, 1971): 1–2; Brenner, "Rank-and-File Struggles at the Telephone Company," 271.
57. Frank C. Porter, "Phone Workers Set to Walk Out; Strikes May Idle 2 Million Soon," *Washington Post*, July 14, 1971, A1, A9; "Phone-y," *Berkeley Tribe* 5, no. 24 (July 16–22, 1971): 8; "Union Wins Biggest Pact in History of the Industry," *CWA News* (August 1971): 2; Philip Shabecoff, "Accords Reached in Phone Strike and Postal Talks," *New York Times*, July 20, 1971, A1, A20; Byron E. Calame, "Female Telephone Workers Hit Labor Pact, Say Men Still Get the Best Jobs, More Pay," *Wall Street Journal*, July 26, 1971, 22.
58. "Up to 90,000 Telephone Workers Still out, But New Jersey Bell, IBEW Near Accord," *Wall Street Journal*, July 22, 1971, 2; "Reject the Sellout," *United Action*, no. 8 (July 26, 1971): 1–2; "Leaders of Phone Locals in the State Turn down Nationwide Settlement," *New York Times*, July 20, 1971, 20; "Phone Company Seeks Mediation," *New York Times*, December 31, 1971, 17; "No Turning Back!," 1; Brenner, "Rank-and-File Struggles at the Telephone Company," 277; "Rebuild the Strike!" *United Action*, no. 8 (July 26, 1971): 3.
59. Incoming call to R. N. from H. I. Romnes 1:25 pm, "Chm of Amer Telephone + Telegraph" with notation checkmark and "Bull" signifying that the call was taken by Staff Assistant Stephen B. Bull, President's Office Files President's Telephone Calls July 1971–October 1971, Box 108 Folder President's Phone Calls (July 1971—August 1971 [1 of 2] Telephone Log 7/14, Nixon Presidential Library.
60. Telephone Log 7/21 Outgoing call 2:43–2:47 pm "Mr. Hy Romnes NYC AT&T" President's Office Files President's Telephone Calls July 1971–October 1971, Box 108 Folder President's Phone Calls (July 1971–August 1971 [1 of 2], Nixon Presidential Library.

61. "Twenty-Five Per Cent Isn't Enough," 4; United Action, "Vote CWA One Union One Contract"; United Action, "Traffic, Commercial, Accounting It's Our Strike, Too!" United Action, "Reject the Sellout Win the Strike!," All February 1972, Local 1101, Communication Workers of America, Local 1101, New York University, Tamiment Library-Robert F. Wagner Labor Archives (hereafter Tamiment-Wagner); United Action, "Take the Dollar and Shove It up Their Ass!," February 1972, Communication Workers of America, Local 1101, New York University, Tamiment-Wagner.

62. United Action, Bell Workers Action Committee, "Tell Joe Bierne No Sellout!! Rally," Communication Workers of America, Local 1101, Tamiment-Wagner; "Reject the Sellout," United Action Number 8, Monday July 26, 1971, 1–2, Communication Workers of America, Local 1101, Tamiment-Wagner; United Action, "Stop the Sellout!," and "1101 Members—Come to the Membership Meeting and Fight for These Resolutions!!!" In a different broadside, the Absence Control Plan was identified as giving "the company an ever ready weapon of control over us." United Action, "To the Women of Traffic & Commercial," Communication Workers of America, Local 1101, Tamiment-Wagner; United Action, "Take the Initiative!" September 23, 1971, 2, Communication Workers of America, Local 1101, Tamiment-Wagner.

63. United Action, "Take the Initiative!," September 23, 1971, 1, Communication Workers of America, Local 1101, Tamiment-Wagner; United Action, "Win the Strike!!! Demonstrate against the Freeze," October 1971; "President Nixon's wage controls were used against us and other unions but the Miners have shown that they cannot and will not be enforced," United Action, "Out of Town Scabs Must Go!!!," December 6, 1971; see also, United Action, 9, December 9, 1971; United Action, no. 10, January 3, 1972, Communication Workers of America, Local 1101, Tamiment-Wagner.

64. United Action, "Operators—Join CWA, 1101!," New York University, TL-RFWLA; United Action, "March for Peace Join the Telephone Workers Contingent"; United Action, "Labor Can End the War—And We Are Labor," Communication Workers of America, Local 1101, Tamiment-Wagner; "Telephone Workers and the War," United Action, no. 3, Monday April 12, 1971, 3, Communication Workers of America, Local 1101, Tamiment-Wagner. For background on contemporary opposition to imperialism, Max Elbaum, *Revolution in the Air: Sixties Radicals Turn to Lenin, Mao and Che* (London: Verso, 2006).

65. "Co. Makes Killing from War," *Operating Underground*, Operators Defense Committee, Oakland, California, no date but late June 1971, 1. Self-identified Communist organizations, including Progressive Labor and Revolutionary Union, were among the groups fielding activists in the telephone workforce in the Bay area and elsewhere. "Ma Bell Has Fleas," *Red Papers*, 3 (1970): 32–40; "Strike to Win," flyer produced by the San Francisco Progressive Labor Party, July 13, 1971; Brenda and Peggy, Boston YAWF Women, "Dial 'O' for—Oppression," *Battle Acts* 1, no. 4 (March 1971). See also, Elbaum, *Revolution in the Air*, 93–180.

66. Public Law 89-368, Tax Adjustment Act of 1966, Paragraph 66, March 15, 1966; Karl Meyer, "Hang up on War," *WIN Peace and Freedom through Nonviolent Action* 2, no. 17 (1966): 3, 14 (quote); "Tax Resistance," *War Tax Monthly* 1, no. 1 (January 15, 1973): 1, 2. Also, "Disconnect the War," flyer, April 24 1971, Marin, San Francisco,

Santa Clara; "Our Telephone Taxes Pay for War!," booklet, East Patchogue, New York, National War Tax Resistance Coordinating Committee, n.d.
67. United Action, Communication Workers of America, Local 1101, Tamiment-Wagner; United Action, "1101 Delegates Must Represent the Members," Communication Workers of America, Local 1101, Tamiment-Wagner; "Elect Joe Nabach Convention Delegate," flyer, spring 1972.
68. New York Telephone, "The Strike of New York Telephone Craftsmen Is Now in Its Ninth Week," *New York Times*, March 29, 1971, A26; "Unions Reject No-strike Appeal," *New York Times*, August 19, 1971, 1; "Phone Men Still on the Line," *New York Times*, January 1, 1972, 21; "Backlog Is Huge in Phone Strike," *New York Times*, September 19, 1971, 34; Beirne, *Challenge to Labor*, 48.
69. "Strike to Win," *The Bell Wringer* (Cerritos, CA: 1972), 1–2; "Strike '74?," *The Bell Wringer-Yellow Pages* 2, no. 1 (April 17, 1973): 1, 5, 6. Two years earlier, a mimeographed, twelve-page pamphlet published anonymously by workers at the same Pacific Telephone & Telegraph facility in Oakland indicated that these workers had distanced themselves from postalization adherents of the Progressive era, while preserving their progenitors' concerns to limit excess costs: "if Western *workers* instead of AT&T or the government ran this show, it wouldn't be hard to cut off the fat and give quality" (emphasis in the original). Red Baron, "Meet Ma Bell," *The Laymen's Press*, no. 2 (March 31, 1970): 4; "Meet Ma Bell," eight-page pamphlet, n.d. Internal evidence shows that it was probably produced by the same person(s) who published *The Laymen's Press* in 1970, around the same time, and that it was directed at members of CWA Local 9490 in Oakland and Richmond, California.
70. "Vote for out of state Picketing," and "Support the N.Y. Plant Strike," *United Action* (January 1972); "Strike Report," *United Action* (February 8, 1971): 2, 5–6.
71. "What to Do," *United Action* (February 8, 1971): 1, 6; "We Need a Union Meeting Now!," *United Action*, no. 5 (May 10, 1971): 1; "Rebuild the CWA," *United Action*, no. 2 (March 8, 1971): 5, 6.
72. *The Bell Buster*, September 1980: 1–2.
73. U.S. Department of Labor, Manpower Administration, "Technology and Manpower in the Telephone Industry 1965–1975," *Manpower Research Bulletin*, no. 13 (November 1966): 16, Table 1; During World War II, women made up 72 percent of all telephone workers. Cobble, *The Other Women's Movement*, 21. Twenty years later, their share had dropped to around 55 percent. U.S. Department of Labor, Manpower Administration, "Technology and Manpower in the Telephone Industry 1965–1975," 42, Table 4; In 1960, less than three percent of female telephone workers were black, almost all of them concentrated in big Northern and Western cities. Cobble, *The Other Women's Movement*, 83; Rubio, *There's Always Work at the Post Office*, 402 n26.
74. Schacht, *The Making of Telephone Unionism*, 140; Cobble, *The Other Women's Movement*, 22; During the formative period between 1939–1946, the traffic department of NFTW in which women operators were based was able to claim only one or two of nine NFTW executive board positions. Schacht, *The Making of Telephone Unionism*, 84. Green, *Race on the Line*, 242–250, offers the most compelling account.

75. Green, *Race on the Line*, 196, 199; Green, *Race on the Line*, 200; Jacqueline Patterson, "Why Public Utilities/Service Commissions Are Important to the NAACP," February 2015, 26, www.naacp.org; "The PSC: An Introduction to Your Georgia Public Service Commission," www.psc.ga.gov.
76. Cornelius L. Bynum, *A. Philip Randolph and the Struggle for Civil Rights* (Urbana: University of Illinois Press, 2010), 92; Green, *Race on the Line*, 201; Green, *Race on the Line*, 196, 201–202; Horace R. Cayton and George S. Mitchel, *Black Workers and the New Unions* (Chapel Hill, NC: University of North Carolina Press, 1939), 418; Biondi, *To Stand and Fight*, 105.
77. Trotter, *Workers on Arrival*, 134–140, 150; Bynum, *A. Philip Randolph and the Struggle for Civil Rights*, 157–184; Thomas J. Sugrue, *Sweet Land of Liberty: The Forgotten Struggle for Civil Rights in the North* (New York: Random House, 2008), 32 (quote).
78. Charles H. Loeb, *The Future Is Yours: The History of the Future Outlook League 1935–1946* (Cleveland: Future Outlook League, 1947), 75, 76, 84, 86; Loeb, *The Future Is Yours*, 86; Willard S. Townsend, "One American Problem and a Possible Solution," in Rayford W. Logan, ed., *What the Negro Wants* (Notre Dame, IN: University of Notre Dame Press, 2001), 185. Historian Kenneth Janken states that Townsend was a political "centrist" rather than a "radical." Janken, "Introduction," in Logan, *What the Negro Wants*, xi n7.
79. Biondi, *To Stand and Fight*, 267; "Plant Seizures—Reports File—Western Electric Company, Inc.—Point Breeze Plant of," Papers of John H. Ohly, War Department File Box 45. Box 49 contains five bulky files on "Plant Seizure-Western Electric Company—Policy Planning," Harry S. Truman Presidential Library and Museum, Independence, Missouri; see also, Schacht, *The Making of Telephone Unionism*, 114. There were numerous government plant seizures throughout the war, but only two military takeovers in response to white supremacist workers, the other of the Philadelphia transit system in August 1944. Mark R. Wilson, *Destructive Creation: American Business and the Winning of World War II* (Philadelphia: University of Pennsylvania Press, 2016), 217. On hate strikes generally, see George Lipsitz, *Rainbow at Midnight: Labor and Culture in the 1940s* (Urbana, IL: University of Illinois Press, 1994), 69–95.
80. Green, *Race on the Line*, 207; Ruth Wincek interview by John N. Schacht, April 30, 1970, in CWA-University of Iowa Oral History Project, University of Iowa Library Special Collections, Iowa City, Iowa, 20; Green, *Race on the Line*, 324 n66; Robert H. Zieger, *The CIO 1935–1955* (Chapel Hill, NC: University of North Carolina Press, 1995), 227–241; Brooks, *Communications Workers of America*, 173.
81. Anderson, *The Negro in the Public Utility Industries*, Table 21, 76–77, 73 (statistics), 101, 107; Harry Fleischman and James Rorty, *We Open the Gates: Labor's Fight for Equality* (New York: National Labor Service, 1958), 39; Fleischman and Rorty, *We Open the Gates*, 40; Beirne interview, 7, 27.
82. Cobble, *The Other Women's Movement*; Green, *Race on the Line*, 195.
83. Fleischman and Rorty, *We Open the Gates*, 40; John D'Emilio, *Sexual Politics, Sexual Communities: The Making of a Homosexual Minority in the United States, 1940–1970*, 2nd ed. (Chicago: University of Chicago Press, 1998), 197, 208, 211, 213. Further demonstrations were scheduled for April 20, 1973 and weekly thereafter. "Gays to

Zap Ma Bell," *Bay Area Reporter* 3, no. 7 (April 4, 1973): 1; "Gaypeoples, female and male are participating in this landmark event," the first in a fifty-two–week "offensive against discrimination." "Zap Ma Bell" (flyer), no publisher, place, or date, but 1973; Green, *Race on the Line*, 205, 244; Petition for Intervention, before the FCC, Washington, D.C. Docket No. 19129, *Equal Employment Opportunity Commission v. American Telephone and Telegraph Company*, December 10, 1970, 12, footnote 18.

84. MacLean, *Freedom Is Not Enough*, 70; EEOC, Petition for Intervention.
85. "A Landmark Settlement," *Equal Employment Opportunity Commission 8th Annual Report (1973)* (Washington: EEOC, 1974), 25; EEOC, Petition for Intervention, 27; Phyllis A. Wallace and Jack E. Nelson, "Legal Processes and Strategies of Intervention," in Phyllis A. Wallace, ed., *Equal Employment Opportunity and the AT&T Case* (Cambridge, MA: MIT Press, 1976), 244.
86. For a kindred comparison, *Robert Samuel Smith, Race Labor & Civil Rights:* Griggs versus Duke Power *and the Struggle for Equal Employment Opportunity* (Baton Rouge, LA: Louisiana State University Press, 2008); MacLean, *Freedom Is Not Enough*, 133.
87. Phyllis A. Wallace, "Introduction," in Wallace, ed., *Equal Employment Opportunity and the AT&T Case*, 1–2.
88. Herbert R. Northrup and John A. Larson, *The Impact of the AT&T-EEO Consent Decree* (Philadelphia: University of Pennsylvania Press, 1979); MacLean, *Freedom Is Not Enough*, 131–133; Marjorie A. Stockford, *The Bellwomen: The Story of the Landmark AT&T Sex Discrimination Case* (New Brunswick, NJ: Rutgers University Press, 2004); Karen D. Frazer, "EEOC Testimonies in the AT&T Employment Discrimination Case," unpublished paper, University of California, San Diego, 1993; Christy Lynn Odell, honors thesis, University of California, San Diego, 2000; Oral Testimony of Lorena Weeks, in EEOC field hearing included in FCC Docket 19143, 1972, Volume 3, Box 156, AN 173-76-12, RG 173, NARA Suitland, Maryland, 1057–1074. I am grateful to Karen D. Frazer, who photocopied the FCC's Docket 19143 EEOC-AT&T records at NARA Suitland MD for an paper she wrote under my supervision in 1993 at the University of California, San Diego; *Weeks v. Southern Bell Telephone and Telegraph Co.*, 408 F.2d 228, 236 (15th Cir. 1969).
89. Oral Testimony of Helen J. Roig, in EEOC field hearing included in FCC Docket 19143, 1972, Volume 3, Box 156, AN 173-76-12, RG 173, NARA Suitland, Maryland, 1075–1085 and 890–980; *Roig v. Southern Bell Telephone & Telegraph Co.* (E.D. La., Civil Action No. 67-574).
90. EEOC, *Intervenor, v. American Telephone and Telegraph Company*, Respondent, before the FCC, Washington, D.C. Memorandum in Support of EEOC Petition to Intervene, BOX 154, RG 173 Records of the FCC, FCC Docket 19143, 3; citing FCC, Report and Order 35 Fed. Reg. 12892, 12893 (August 14, 1970); Anderson, *The Negro in the Public Utilities Industry*, 219.
91. EEOC, Memorandum in Support of EEOC Petition to Intervene, 28; EEOC, Memorandum in Support of EEOC Petition to Intervene, 29.
92. EEOC, Memorandum in Support of EEOC Petition to Intervene, 35; "public trustee" quoted by EEOC from *Office of Communications of the United Church of Christ v. Federal Communications Commission* (I), 359 F.2d 994, 1003 (D.C. Cir.).

93. Robert B. Horwitz, "Broadcast Reform Revisited: Reverend Everett C. Parker and the 'Standing' Case (*Office of Communications of the United Church of Christ v. Federal Communications Commission*)," *The Communication Review* 2, no. 3 (1997): 311–348; Horwitz, "Broadcast Reform Revisited," 315; Under the Administrative Procedure Act, 79-404, 60 Stat. 237 June 11, 1946. For discussion, Paul Sabin, *Public Citizens: The Attack on Big Government and the Remaking of American Liberalism* (New York: W. W. Norton, 2021), 7–9; Horwitz, "Broadcast Reform Revisited," 313, 317.

94. Sabin, *Public Citizens*, 94–96; Horwitz, "Broadcast Reform Revisited," 333, second quote from *Office of Communications of the United Church of Christ v. FCC*, 1966, 1003–1005; Horwitz, "Broadcast Reform Revisited," 333.

95. The two dissenters, who wrote a lengthy opinion, were Democratic Commissioners Nicholas Johnson and Kenneth Cox. Horwitz, "Broadcast Reform Revisited," 334–341; Horwitz, "Broadcast Reform Revisited," 342.

96. EEOC, *Memorandum in Support of EEOC Petition to Intervene*, 35.

97. EEOC, *Memorandum in Support of EEOC Petition to Intervene*, 44; EEOC, *Memorandum in Support of EEOC Petition to Intervene*, 48.

98. In the United States District Court for the Eastern District of Pennsylvania, *Equal Employment Opportunity Commission, James D. Hodgson, Secretary of Labor, United States Department of Labor and United States of America vs. American Telephone and Telegraph Company et al.* (Civil Action No. 73-149, January 18, 1973), "A Landmark Settlement," 25.

99. MacLean, *Freedom Is Not Enough*, 133; "A Landmark Settlement," 26.

100. Green, *Race on the Line*, Vallas, Power in the Workplace; MacLean, *Freedom Is Not Enough*, 57, 58; Green, *Race on the Line*, 195–196; Brenner, "Rank-and-File," 262.

101. Rustin quoted in John D'Emilio, *Lost Prophet: The Life and Times of Bayard Rustin* (Chicago: University of Chicago Press, 2003), 328; MacLean, *Freedom Is Not Enough*, 4.

102. Like other wage-earners selected by EEOC to testify, Jimenez was an activist, not only within the union but, at the time of her testimony, also as regional director of the Mexican American Political Association in the Los Angeles area. Paula V. Jimenez, *Federal Communications Commission, EEOC et al. v. AT&T et al., FCC* (1973), 3001–30027, Volume 7, Docket No. 19143, Box 156, AN 173-76-12, RG 173, NARA Suitland, Maryland; All quotes from Oral Testimony of Paula V. Jimenez, *Federal Communications Commission, EEOC et al. v. AT&T et al., FCC* (1973).

103. Odell, "*Equal Employment Opportunity Commission and 1960s' Civil Rights Organizations vs. AT&T*: Creating Equality in the Telecommunications Industry," 53; FCC, *EEOC et al. v. AT&T et al., FCC* (1973), CRLA Exhibit 10, pp. 1–19, Vol. 52, Box 167, AN 173-76-12, RG 173, NARA, Suitland, Maryland; Odell, "Equal Employment Opportunity Commission," 54; All quotes from Oral Testimony of Paula V. Jimenez, Federal Communications Commission, EEOC et al. v. AT&T et al., FCC (1973).

104. David R. Cashdan, Counsel for CRLA and MALDF, Motion to Chief Examiner Requesting the Holding of a Field Hearing, in the Matter of Petitions Filed by the EEOC, et al., before Hearing Examiner Frederick W. Denniston, FCC Docket

No. 19143, February 18, 1971, 2; also David R. Cashdan, Counsel for CRLA and MALDF, Petition for Rate Suspension, Hearing Intervention, and Declaration of Unlawfulness, in the Matter of American Telephone & Telegraph Co., Revision of Tariff FCC No. 263, FCC Docket 19143, January 18, 1971; David R. Cashdan, Counsel for CRLA and MALDF, Motion to Chief Examiner Requesting the Holding of a Field Hearing, 4; Anthony Giorgianni, "Services Vary Widely for Hispanic Consumers," *Hartford Courant*, January 30, 1995.
105. Quoted in D. C. and R. S., "Ma Bell Gets Yellow Suit!!!," *Vector* 4, no. 10 (October 1968): 29; also, Elizabeth A. Armstrong, *Forging Gay Identities: Organizing Sexuality in San Francisco, 1950–1994* (Chicago: University of Chicago Press, 2002), 39–41; D'Emilio, *Sexual Politics, Sexual Communities*, 203–204. Pacific Bell did permit individual homosexual organizations to list separately; its denial was for a collective listing.
106. "Tell-A-Woman" 4, no. 3 (March 1975); People's Yellow Pages Collective, "People's Yellow Pages." New York: Emmaus House, March 1972; Donna Goddard, Shirley Lustig, Diane Sampson, Sandy Taylor, and Jan Zobel, *People's Yellow Pages*, 2nd. 3d. (San Francisco: The People's Yellow Pages Collective, 1972).
107. EEOC, *Memorandum in Support of EEOC Petition to Intervene*, 42; quote on the values used to determine the public interest from *Association of Data Processing Service Organizations v. Camp*, 397 U.S. 150, 154, 90 S. Ct. 827, 830 (1970); EEOC, *Memorandum in Support of EEOC Petition to Intervene*, 42.
108. This thesis is systematically elaborated in Robert W. McChesney, *Communication Revolution: Critical Junctures and the Future of Media* (New York: New Press, 2007); *Red Lion Broadcasting Co., Inc. v. FCC* 395 U.S. 367 (1969). Also, McChesney, *Communication Revolution*, 33, 75, 123; Sabin, *Public Citizens*, 35–108. In communications, one little-remembered group, which performed and published valuable research as well as testifying before Congress and producing radio documentaries was the Network Project, based at Columbia University during the early-mid 1970s.
109. The labor movement "is considered by many to be part of the 'Establishment,'" but, he purported, "it was not." His active involvement in Cold War foreign policy makes it necessary to qualify Beirne's judgment, although perhaps not to reject it completely. Beirne, *Challenge to Labor*, 12; Rubio, *There's Always Work at the Post Office*, 253.
110. Trotter, *Workers on Arrival*, 161.

Chapter 10

1. Nelson Lichtenstein, *The Most Dangerous Man in Detroit: Walter Reuther and the Fate of American Labor* (New York: Basic Books, 1995), 220–222; James T. Sparrow, *Warfare State: World War II Americans and the Age of Big Government* (New York: Oxford University Press, 2011), 248; Walter P. Reuther, "Reuther Challenges 'Our Fear of Abundance,'" *New York Times Sunday Magazine*, September

16, 1945, SM5; Walter P. Reuther, "Let's Use The War Plants," *Antioch Review* 5, no. 3 (Autumn 1945): 351–358; Mark R. Wilson, *Destructive Creation: American Business and the Winning of World War II* (Philadelphia: University of Pennsylvania Press, 2016), 250, 242; Hoover was selected to lead two different reviews of the organization of the federal government in the decade after the war, the second of which (coordinating with the Eisenhower administration) proved especially influential in its call for privatization; Sparrow, *Warfare State*, 249; Wilson, *Destructive Creation*, 271–276; Sparrow, *Warfare State*, 249.

2. David A. Mindell, *Between Human and Machine: Feedback, Control, and Computing before Cybernetics* (Baltimore: Johns Hopkins University Press, 2002); Colin Burke, *Information and Secrecy: Vannevar Bush, Ultra, and the Other Memex* (Lanham, MD: Scarecrow Press, 1994).

3. Max Hastings, *The Secret War: Spies, Cyphers, and Guerillas 1939–1945* (New York: Harper, 2016), 385; Peter J. Hugill, *Global Communications since 1844: Geopolitics and Technology* (Baltimore: Johns Hopkins University Press, 1999), 159–221; Robert Buderi, *The Invention that Changed the World* (New York: Simon & Schuster, 1996).

4. Arnold Thackray, David C. Brock, and Rachel Jones, *Moore's Law: The Life of Gordon Moore, Silicon Valley's Quiet Revolutionary* (New York: Basic Books, 2015), 92–93; Thackray, Brock, and Jones, *Moore's Law*, 141; For an indication, Jonathan E. Lewis, *Spy Capitalism: Itek and the CIA* (New Haven: Yale University Press, 2002).

5. See http://www.afcea.org/site/?q=History; Thackray, Brock, and Jones, *Moore's Law*, 163; Christophe Lecuyer, *Making Silicon Valley: Innovation and the Growth of High Tech, 1930–1970* (Cambridge: MIT Press, 2006), 166–167. Strong institutional growth of venture capital, however, awaited the Nixon presidency. Thirty venture capital companies were formed on the San Francisco Peninsula between 1968 and 1975 as the country's traditional financial centers of New York and Boston were displaced. Lecuyer, *Making Silicon Valley*, 258.

6. Lecuyer, *Making Silicon Valley*, 118–119, 141; Lecuyer, *Making Silicon Valley*, 236; Herbert I. Schiller, *Mass Communications and American Empire* (New York: Augustus M. Kelley, 1969), 51, 59; Lecuyer, *Making Silicon Valley*, 253; Seymour Melman, *The Permanent War Economy* (New York: Simon & Schuster, 1974).

7. "Economics for Consumers: AT&T and Your Phone Bill," *Consumer Reports* 14, no. 3 (March 1949): 134–135; "The Transistor AT&T versus the Vacuum Tube RCA," *Consumer Reports* 14, no. 9 (September 1949): 415; Fred W. Henck and Bernard Strassburg, *A Slippery Slope: The Long Road to the Breakup of AT&T* (New York: Praeger, 1988), 62; Leslie Berlin, *The Man behind the Microchip: Robert Noyce and the Invention of Silicon Valley* (New York: Oxford University Press, 2005), 83, 125; Gerald W. Brock, *The Second Information Revolution* (Cambridge: Harvard University Press, 2003), 96.

8. Kenneth Flamm, *Creating the Computer: Government, Industry, and High Technology* (Washington, DC: Brookings Institution, 1988), 81; Paul E. Ceruzzi, *A History of Modern Computing* (Cambridge: MIT Press, 1998), 65; Martin Campbell-Kelly and William Aspray, *Computer: A History of the Information Machine* (New York: Basic

Books, 1996), 130, 105; James W. Cortada, *The Digital Hand, Volume 1: How Computers Changed the Work of American Manufacturing, Transportation, and Retail Industries* (New York: Oxford University Press, 2004), 10; Cortada, *The Digital Hand*, 11; Nathan Ensmenger, *The Computer Boys Take Over: Computers, Programmers, and the Politics of Technical Expertise* (Cambridge: MIT Press, 2010), 28; Martin Campbell-Kelly, *From Airline Reservations to Sonic the Hedgehog: A History of the Software Industry* (Cambridge: MIT Press, 2004), 13, 26, and 18–19, Table 1.2. These amounts radically understate the importance of software, a great portion of which was written in-house by corporations and thus is not captured in revenue figures. It also needs to be recalled that IBM's decision to stop bundling software with its computers, in response to antitrust pressure in 1970–1971, legitimized and stimulated the growth of an independent software industry.

9. 98th Congress, 1st Sess., Senate Committee Print 98-22, Committee on Commerce, Science, and Transportation. "Long-Range Goals in International Telecommunications and Information: An Outline for U.S. Policy," March 11, 1983 (Washington, DC: Government Printing Office, 1983), 217; Lisa Endlich, *Optical Illusions: Lucent and the Crash of Telecom* (New York: Simon and Schuster, 2004), 11; Christopher Rhoads, "AT&T Inventions Fueled Tech Boom, and Its Own Fall," *Wall Street Journal*, February 2, 2005, A1: "AT&T's monopoly status meant that it rarely exploited its own inventions . . . executives felt little need to seize on the lab achievements since AT&T already enjoyed steady profits from its lock on the phone business."; Michael Denning, *Noise Uprising: The Audiopolitics of a World Musical Revolution* (New York: Verso, 2015), 70. For the concept of electrical acoustics, Steve J. Wurtzler, *Electric Sounds: Technological Change and the Rise of Corporate Mass Media* (New York: Columbia University Press, 2007).

10. Flamm, *Creating the Computer*, 87–90. SAGE also generated contracts for other high-tech companies as well as for MIT; Arthur L. Norberg and Judy E. O'Neill, *Transforming Computer Technology: Information Processing at the Pentagon, 1962–1986* (Baltimore: Johns Hopkins University Press, 1996), 22; Emerson W. Pugh and William Aspray, "Creating the Computer Industry," *IEEE Annals of the History of Computing* 18, no. 2 (1996): 7–17; Judy E. O'Neill, "'Prestige Luster' and 'Snow-Balling Effects': IBM's Development of Computer Time-sharing," *IEEE Annals of the History of Computing* 17, no. 2 (1995): 50–54; Daniel S. Diamond and Lee L. Selwyn, "Considerations for Computer Utility Pricing Policies," *Proceedings of the 1968 23d ACM National Conference, August 27–29, 1968* (New York: Association for Computing Machinery, 1968), 189–200; Norberg with O'Neill, *Transforming Computer Technology*, 68–118; T.A. Wise, "Western Union, by Grace of FCC and A.T.&T.," *Fortune*, March 1959, 222.

11. Wise, "Western Union, by Grace of FCC and A.T.&T.," 218, 220; Wise, "Western Union, by Grace of FCC and A.T.&T.," 222.

12. "The Future Role of Western Union as a Nationwide Information Utility, Company Strategic Plans, March 30 1965," Section 1, 1, Smithsonian National Museum of American History, Lemuelson Center for the Study of Invention & Innovation, Western Union Telegraph Company Records 1820–1995, http://invention.smit

hsonian.org/resources/fa_wu_index.aspx. Thanks to Bob McChesney for this reference; "The Future Role of Western Union," Section 1, 1; "The Future Role of Western Union," Section 1, 7, 8; Section 2, 1–2; "The Future Role of Western Union," Section 1, 2; "The Future Role of Western Union," Section 1, 7.

13. Vincent Mosco, *To the Cloud: Big Data in a Turbulent World* (Boulder: Paradigm, 2014), 6, 18–21.
14. Martin Greenberger, "The Computers of Tomorrow," *The Atlantic*, May 1964, https://www.theatlantic.com/past/docs/unbound/flashbks/computer/greenbf.htm; Greenberger, "The Computers of Tomorrow."
15. William Shelton Mackenzie, "The Legal and Competitive Aspects of the 'Computer Utility'" (master's thesis, Wharton School, University of Pennsylvania, 1968); Greenberger, "The Computers of Tomorrow."; Greenberger, "The Computers of Tomorrow."; Kevin Robins and Frank Webster, "Cybernetic Capitalism: Information, Technology, Everyday Life," in eds. Vincent Mosco and Janet Wasko, *The Political Economy of Information* (Madison: University of Wisconsin Press, 1988), 45–75; see also, Kevin Robins and Frank Webster, "Information Is a Social Relation," *InterMedia* 8, no. 4 (1980): 30–35; Greenberger, "The Computers of Tomorrow."
16. American Management Association, *The Future of the Computer Utility* (New York: 1967), 16; D. F. Parkhill, *The Challenge of the Computer Utility* (Reading, MA: Addison-Wesley, 1966), 52; Manley R. Irwin, "Federal Regulation and Monopoly," in Fred Gruenberger, ed., *Computers and Communications—Toward a Computer Utility* (Englewood Cliffs, NJ: Prentice-Hall, 1968), 203; see also, Paul Armer, "Social Implications of the Computer Utility" (Santa Monica, CA: Rand Corporation, 1967).
17. Manley R. Irwin, "The Computer Utility: Competition or Regulation?," *The Yale Law Journal* 76 (June 1967): 1299; Irwin, "Computer Utility," 1320.
18. Alfred D. Chandler, Jr., *Inventing the American Century* (Cambridge: Harvard University Press, 2005), 81; Manley R. Irwin, "Some Implications of Time-shared Computer Systems," *Quarterly Review of Economics and Business* 7, no. 1 (Spring 1967) 26, 25.
19. Dan Schiller, *How to Think about Information* (Urbana: University of Illinois Press, 2007), 61–79; Murray Edelman, *The Licensing of Radio Services in the United States, 1927 to 1947; A Study in Administrative Formulation of Policy* (Urbana: University of Illinois Press, 1950); Randy Johnson, "Herbert Hoover and the Aeronautical Telecommunications System: His Influence on Its Development and Deployment, as Secretary of Commerce, 1921–1927" (Ph.D. diss., Ohio University, 2000); Ulrike Gretzel, "Economic and Political Conditions in the 1920s and 1930s that Shaped Commercial Aviation and Paved the Way for the Establishment and Growth of Aeronautical Radio, Inc." (graduate paper, University of Illinois, 2001), author's collection.
20. National Telecommunications and Information Administration, U.S. Department of Commerce, "Current and Future Spectrum Use by the Energy, Water, and Railroad Industries," NTIA Special Publication 01-49, Report Authors Marshall W. Ross and Jeng F. Mao, January 2002, 2–3; Dan Schiller, *Telematics and Government*

(Norwood: Ablex, 1982), 13; Charles Stanley Rhoads, *Telegraphy and Telephony with Railroad Applications* (New York: Simmons-Boardman Publishing, 1924); Schiller, *How to Think about Information*, 61–79; James W. Cortada, "Economic Preconditions that Made Possible Application of Commercial Computing in the United States," *IEEE Annals of the History of Computing* 19, no. 3 (1997): 28; Walter Wriston, CEO of Citicorp, proclaimed that a so-called "information standard" had replaced a superannuated gold standard, and the cover of the company's 1981 *Annual Report*, graced with a depiction of a satellite, pictured digital communications as central to any great contemporary "financial intermediary." *Citicorp Reports 1981* (New York: Citicorp, 1981).

21. Schiller, *Telematics and Government*, 1–96; Dan Schiller, *Digital Capitalism: Networking the Global Market System* (Cambridge: MIT Press, 1999), 2–7; James W. Cortada, "Commercial Applications of the Digital Computer in American Corporations, 1945–1995," *IEEE Annals of the History of Computing* 18, no. 2 (1996): 18–28; see also, Cortada, *The Digital Hand*, 1–3; Gary Fields, *Territories of Profit: Communications, Capitalist Development, and the Innovative Enterprises of G. F. Swift and Dell Computer* (Stanford, CA: Stanford Business Books, 2003); David L. Stebenne, "Thomas J. Watson and the Business Government Relationship, 1933–1956," *Enterprise & Society* 6, no. 1 (March 2005): 45–75.

22. *Annual Report 1950 American Telephone & Telegraph Company* (New York: American Telephone and Telegraph Company, n.d.), 3; *AT&T Annual Report 1959* (New York: American Telephone & Telegraph Company, n.d.), 9; *American Telephone & Telegraph Company Annual Report 1957* (New York: American Telephone and Telegraph Company, n.d.), 10; U.S. Department of Labor, Manpower Administration, "Technology and Manpower in the Telephone Industry, 1965–1975," *Manpower Research Bulletin No. 13* (November 1966): 13; Edgar C. Gentle, Jr., *Data Communications in Business: An Introduction* (New York: American Telephone & Telegraph Company, 1965), 6.

23. The following paragraphs draw on material published in Dan Schiller, "Business Users and the Telecommunications Network," *Journal of Communication* 32, no. 4: 84–96; and Schiller, Telematics and Government, 8–22.

24. Business users generated 58 percent of domestic long-distance revenues in 1976, and the largest 3.9 percent of their number accounted for over three-fifths of this total. 97th Cong., 1st Sess. House of Representatives, Committee on Energy and Commerce, Subcommittee on Telecommunications, Consumer Protection, and Finance, Committee Print, A Report by the Majority Staff, "Telecommunications in Transition: The Status of Competition in the Telecommunications Industry" (Washington, DC Government Printing Office, 1981), 87–89; *United States of America, Plaintiff, v. American Telephone and Telegraph Company; Western Electric Company, Inc.; and Bell Telephone Laboratories, In., Defendants*, Defendants' Third Statement of Contentions and Proof. Civil Action No. 74-1698, In the U.S. District Court for the District of Columbia, March 10, 1980, 273, n18, n19; U.S. Federal Communications Commission, "In the Matter of Allocation of Frequencies in the Bands Above 890 Mc.," Docket 11866, Comment of the Automobile Manufacturers

Association, March 15, 1957, 849–850, 850, 851. National Archives and Records Administration (hereafter NARA), Suitland, MD.

25. A critic of Celler agrees on the ideological importance of these hearings in reestablishing political criticism of AT&T. Alan Stone, *How America Got On-line: Politics, Markets, and the Revolution in Telecommunication* (New York: Routledge, 1997), 47–48; 85th Cong., 2d Sess., House of Representatives, Committee of the Judiciary, Antitrust Subcommittee, Consent Decree Program of the Department of Justice (Washington, DC: Government Printing Office, 1958), 3585, 3467, 3684, 3549; 85th Cong., 2d Sess., U.S. House of Representatives, Committee of the Judiciary, Antitrust Subcommittee, Consent Decree Program of the Department of Justice, 1958, 2231. Thanks to Peter Nicholai for his help with these findings. McConnaughey's successor as FCC Chair, Wisconsin's John C. Doerfer, presided over payola and quiz show scandals and was ultimately forced to step down as chair.

26. Harvey Averch and Leland L. Johnson, "Behavior of the Firm under Regulatory Constraint," *American Economic Review* 52, no. 5 (December 1962): 1052–1069.

27. See Chapter 2; see also, William J. Novak, "A Revisionist History of Regulatory Capture," in eds. Daniel Carpenter and David A. Moss., *Preventing Regulatory Capture: Special Interest Influence and How to Limit It.* (New York: Cambridge University Press, 2014), 25–48; Gilbert J. Gall, *Pursuing Justice: Lee Pressman, the New Deal, and the CIO* (Albany: State University of New York Press, 1999), 34. John Strachey, *The Coming Struggle for Power* (New York: Modern Library, 1935), 398, 402; Horace M. Gray, "The Failure of the Public Utility Concept," *The Journal of Land & Public Utility Economics* 16, no. 1 (February 1940): 8–20; For references, see, Vincent Mosco, *Reforming Regulation: The FCC and Innovations in the Broadcasting Market*, Harvard University Program on Information Technologies and Public Policy, Publication P-76-2 (Cambridge: Harvard University, 1976), 28; James M. Landis, *Report on Regulatory Agencies to the President-Elect* (Washington, DC: Government Printing Office, 1960).

28. Generally, Paul Sabin, *Public Citizens: The Attack on Big Government and the Remaking of American Liberalism* (New York: W.W. Norton, 2021); Richard Gabel, *Development of Separations Principles in the Telephone Industry* (Lansing: Michigan State University, 1967), 164; "Negroes in Alabama Town Upset because They Can't Get Phones," *New York Times*, January 5, 1968, 32.

29. A historian writes of capture theory that, "though the attack from the right and economics is most well-known, blood was drawn first on the left." Novak, "A Revisionist History of Capture Theory," 30. A more sweeping argument has recently been made, although without referencing telecommunications, in Sabin, *Public Citizens*, 10–12, 15–32; Reviewing *Quinn Slobodian's Globalists: The End of Empire and the Birth of Neoliberalism*, Alexander Zevin stresses that this current of thought actually returns to the interwar period. Alexander Zevin, "Every Penny A Vote," *London Review of Books* 41, no. 16 (August 15, 2019), https://www.lrb.co.uk/v41/n16/alexander-zevin/every-penny-a-vote; Carried forward into our own time in Jane Mayer, *Dark Money: The Hidden History of the Billionaires Behind the Rise of the Radical Right*

(New York: Doubleday, 2016); and Nancy MacLean, *Democracy in Chains: The Deep History of the Radical Right's Stealth Plan for America* (New York: Viking, 2017); Milton Friedman, *Capitalism and Freedom*, 2nd ed. (Chicago: University of Chicago Press, 2020), 34–36, 43–44, 155.

30. I thank Nicholas Johnson for permitting me to consult his extensive papers at the University of Iowa Library Special Collections. A major study is waiting to be done here.

31. Sabin, *Public Citizens*; Beverly C. Moore, Jr., "AT&T: The Phony Monopoly," in Mark J. Green, ed., *The Monopoly Makers: Ralph Nader's Study Group Report on Regulation and Competition* (New York: Grossman Publishers, 1973), 96; Walter Adams, "The Antitrust Alternative," in eds. Ralph Nader and Mark J. Green, *Corporate Power in America*, 2nd ed. (Harmondsworth: Penguin, 1977), 133; Andrew Hacker, "Citizen Counteraction?" in Nader and Green, *Corporate Power in America*; see also, Martha Derthick and Paul J. Quirk, *The Politics of Deregulation* (Washington, DC: Brookings Institution, 1985), 42; Sabin, *Public Citizens*.

32. Roger G. Noll, *Reforming Regulation: An Evaluation of the Ash Council Proposals* (Washington, DC: Brookings Institution, 1971), 110; Harry Trebing, "Realism and Relevance in Public Utility Regulation," *Journal of Economic Issues* 8, no. 2 (June 1974): 209; Robert D. Hershey, Jr., "Alfred E. Kahn, 93, Dies; Led Airline Deregulation," *New York Times*, December 29, 2010, A19; Lloyd Cutler, quoted in Vincent Mosco, *Pushbutton Fantasies: Critical Perspectives on Videotex and Information Technology* (Norwood: Ablex, 1982), 23.

33. "Telephone Calls Set Record Here during Blackout," *New York Times*, November 11, 1965, 40; Randi Weiss, "Revered to Reviled: New York Telephone Service in 1965 and 1969" (undergraduate paper, University of California, San Diego), author's collection.

34. John Brooks, *Telephone: The First Hundred Years* (New York: Harper & Row, 1976), 288, 289–290; "Nickerson Appeals for Action by State over Phone Service," *New York Times*, July 19, 1969, 27; "Sorry, Wrong Tactic," *New York Times*, January 15, 1971, 42; Alvin von Auw, *Heritage and Destiny: Reflections on the Bell System in Transition* (New York: Praeger, 1983), 10–11.

35. Brooks, *Telephone*, 290; Brooks, *Telephone*, 294; William McWhirter, "Great Telephone Snarl," *Life* 67 (1969): 86; "Hello? Hello? Hello?" *Newsweek*, July 7, 1969, 75–76; Gene Smith, "Phone Users Dial Frustration, Too," *New York Times*, July 6, 1969, 2; Weiss, "Revered to Reviled"; von Auw, *Heritage and Destiny*, 38–39; Smith, "Phone Users Dial Frustration," 2.

36. David Bird, "Phone Rates Are Linked to Monopoly Protection," *New York Times*, August 26, 1969, 35; Peter Millones, "City Panel Finds Phone Inequities," *New York Times*, October 11, 1969, 22; W. Stewart Pinkerton, Jr., "Out of Order," *Wall Street Journal*, September 18, 1969, 1; Sylvan Fox, "Phone Aides See No Relief in Sight," *New York Times*, July 29, 1969, 43; Gene Smith, "'Ma Bell' and Children Pressing Rate Rises," *New York Times*, April 13, 1969, F1; "AT&T Seeks a Return of 8.5 to 9% on Investment," *New York Times*, September 9, 1969, 71; "FCC on AT&T Data," *Wall Street Journal*, September 18, 1969, 4; David Bird, "City Aide Would Cut Bill if

a Phone Fails," *New York Times*, August 19, 1969, 1; McWhirter, "Great Telephone Snarl."; W. Stewart Pinkerton, Jr., "Out of Order," *Wall Street Journal*, September 18, 1969, 1; Fox, "Phone Aides See No Relief, " 46; "Bell System Sending in Workers to Help New York Cope with Service Crisis," *Wall Street Journal*, July 28, 1969; "Why You Hear a Busy Signal at AT&T," *Business Week*, December 27, 1969, 44; Wyatt Wells, "Certificates and Computers: The Remaking of Wall Street, 1967 to 1971," *Business History Review* 74 (Summer 2000): 207, 209; Brooks, *Telephone*, 289; In Joseph C. Goulden, "Indiscretions of Ma Bell," *The Nation*, October 6, 1969, 346–349.

37. Donna Goddard, Shirley Lustig, Diane Sampson, Sandy Taylor, and Jan Zobel, *The San Francisco and Bay Area People's Yellow Pages No. 2* (San Francisco: 1972), n.p.

38. In what might have been a riposte, one Pacific Bell operator wrote around the turn of 1970, "Some days I want to scream, 'Yes, I'm an operator, but I'm also alive, aware, emotional and intelligent. I feel' "; "I'm aware of the people—'our customers'—that I come in contact with. Real live people who are attempting to relate to me, the operator—machine. But I am instructed to remain aloof, impersonal. 'Do not become involved.' How can I, a human being, be impersonal when a lonely, frightened soldier, leaving for the war games the next day, just wants someone to rap with? How can I justify 'unplugging' him because rapping would not be profitable for the Bell System?" Anonymous, "Operators and Installers," *The Laymen's Press* 1 (1969–1970): 1, 2.

39. U.S. Federal Communications Commission, "In the Matter of Allocation of Frequencies in the Bands above 890 Mc," Docket No. 11866 (Preliminary Notice of Hearing Released November 9, 1956). 2. F.C.C. 359 (1959); Under these FCC regulations, corporate users were prohibited from joining together to form cooperative networks, and private microwave networks were barred from interconnecting with the public network; This paragraph borrows from Manley R. Irwin, "The Communication Industry and the Policy of Competition," *Buffalo Law Review* 14 (1964–1965): 265–269. TELPAK rates marked a reduction of as much as 80 percent of former AT&T charges for private line offerings. Irwin, "The Communication Industry," 269. Also, Schiller, *Telematics and Government*, 13–15; Irwin, "The Communications Industry," 256.

40. Thirty-five congressmen were unhappy enough with the proposal for a privately owned system that they wrote to President Kennedy to oppose it. 87th Cong., House of Representatives, 2d Sess., Committee on Aeronautical and Space Science, Staff Report, February 25, 1962 (Washington, DC: Government Printing Office, 1962), 160; *Congressional Record*, vol. 108, A5845; Herbert I. Schiller, *Mass Communications and American Empire* (New York: Augustus M. Kelley, 1969), 71–76, 130–133.

41. von Auw, *Heritage and Destiny*, 8; David J. Whalen, *The Rise and Fall of Comsat: Technology, Business, and Government in Satellite Communication* (New York: Palgrave-Macmillan, 2014), 31–36; "The Future Role of Western Union," Section 1, 6; Ralph Lee Smith, "The Wired Nation," *The Nation*, May 18, 1970, 599–600; Mosco, "Reforming Regulation," 22, citing FCC, First Report and Order (on

Cable Television), 38 FCC 683, April 22, 1965, at 700; and FCC, Cable Television Report and Order, 36 FCC 2d 143 (1972), para. 70.

42. David Martin Miller, "Governing Practices of Cable Television and Its Relationship to the Telephone Companies" (Ph.D. diss., Ohio State University, 1976), 324; Miller, "Governing Practices," 226, 241; Miller, "Governing Practices," 245; Sol Taishoff, "CATV's Big Issue: Pole Lines," *Broadcasting*, July 12, 1965, 54–55.

43. The story is well told by Miller, "Governing Practices," 217–299. For contemporary treatment, see, Smith, "The Wired Nation," 587; Ralph Lee Smith, *The Wired Nation: Cable TV: The Electronic Communications Highway* (New York: Harper & Row, 1972); and Mosco, "Reforming Regulation," 20–25.

44. FCC Memorandum Opinion and Order, Charges for Interstate and Foreign Communication Service, Docket 16258, October 27, 1965; Regulatory and Policy Problems Presented by the Interdependence of Computer and Communications Services and Facilities, 28 FCC 2d 267 (1971); Carterphone 13 FCC 2d 606 (1968). Quotes from Bernard Strassburg, "The Computer Utility—Some Regulatory Implications, An Address to the American Management Association, Inc.," March 10, 1967, *Jurimetrics Journal* 9 (September 1968): 19, 21. The First Computer Inquiry was not resolved until 1971; the Carterphone proceeding was decided by the commission in June 1968, but remained enmired in litigation for years to come. See also, Schiller, *Telematics and Government*, 15–41; and Richard H. K. Vietor, *Contrived Competition: Regulation and Deregulation in America* (Cambridge: Belknap Press of Harvard University Press, 1994), 193.

45. "Memorandum for the President from the Chairman of the President's Task Force on Communications Policy," December 1968, 3. National Security File, Subject File, Communications Policy—Task Force On, Lyndon Baines Johnson Presidential Library, Austin, Texas (hereafter Johnson Presidential Library).

46. Lyndon Baines Johnson, "Special Message to the Congress on Communication Policy," August 14, 1967, The American Presidency Project, University of California, Santa Barbara, https://www.presidency.ucsb.edu/documents/special-message-the-congress-communications-policy; "Aerospace Outlook: LBJ Will Seek Greater Communications Role for the Executive," *New York Times*, August 27, 1967. See also, "Task Force to Study Development of New National Communications Policy Established by President Johnson," *Telecommunications Reports* 33, no. 36 (August 21, 1967): 1.

47. "One of the major problems requiring a social decision in our time is whether we could achieve a wider dispersal of power and opportunity, and a broader base for the class structure of our society, by a more competitive organization of this and other industries, in smaller and more independent units," Rostow also wrote. Eugene V. Rostow, *A National Policy for the Oil Industry* (New Haven: Yale University Press, 1948), xii–xiii. Rostow also served as a member of the attorney general's National Committee for Study of the Antitrust Laws in 1954–1955. 89th Cong., Senate, 2d Sess., Committee on Foreign Relations, Nominations of Nicholas deB. Katzenbach, Eugene V. Rostow, and Roy D. Kohler, September 27 and October 4, 1966 (Washington, DC: Government Printing Office, 1966), 30; Alan

R. Novak oral history interview by Dan Schiller, September 19, 2014, author's collection; "Memorandum for the President by Eugene V. Rostow," December 7, 1968, National Security File, Subject File, Box 7, Communications Policy—Task Force On, Johnson Presidential Library; Presidential Task Force on Communications Policy, Minutes of the Fifth Meeting, January 19, 1968, 2, Alan R. Novak, Memorandum to All Task Force Staff Representatives, February 8, 1968, "Communications Task Force: Minutes and Agendas," Johnson Papers, University of Iowa Library Special Collections, Iowa City, Iowa.

48. The Executive Branch included three units that shared responsibility for various communications issues: the Office of Telecommunications Management, the Commerce Department, and the National Security Agency—still a "black" agency, with close ties to AT&T.

49. "Industry Views Re: the Role of the Federal Government in Telecommunications," 1. CTF General-II (Papers, etc.), Nicholas Johnson Papers, University of Iowa Library Special Collections, Iowa City, Iowa (hereafter Nicholas Johnson Papers); Rejecting the option of an industry advisory committee, the task force did interview some executives, notably AT&T's corporate adversary, MCI's William McGowan. Richard A. Posner, "The Decline and Fall of AT&T: A Personal Recollection," *Federal Communications Law Journal* 61, no. 1 (2008): 11–19; see also, Peter Temin with Louis Galambos, *The Fall of the Bell System* (New York: Cambridge University Press, 1987).

50. Alan R. Novak oral history interview; "Memorandum for the President by Eugene V. Rostow," December 7, 1968, National Security File, Subject File, Box 7, Communications Policy—Task Force On, Johnson Presidential Library; On whom, see, Becky Lentz and Bill Kirkpatrick, "Wanted: Public Interest Mavericks at the FCC," *International Journal of Communication* 8 (2014): 2503–2518; Letter from Nicholas Johnson to Professor Eugene Rostow, September 23, 1966, FCC Box 428, Subject File Folder CTF-OCJ Correspondence, Public Statements, Daily Records, Notes, Nicholas Johnson Papers; Letter from Nicholas Johnson to Eugene V. Rostow, August 28, 1967, FCC Box 428, Subject File Folder CTF-OCJ Correspondence, Public Statements, Daily Records, Notes, Nicholas Johnson Papers. Johnson indeed forwarded suggested topics, readings, and clippings to Task Force Executive Director Alan Novak. Novak reciprocated by sending Johnson drafts of staff papers and reports; Memorandum from Eugene V. Rostow, Chairman, for Members, Presidential Task Force on Communications Policy, October 12, 1967, "Work Statement for President's Task Force on Communications Policy," Communications Task Force—Minutes and Agendas," Nicholas Johnson Papers; Commissioner Johnson's involvement, interestingly, cannot be discerned by scrutinizing the official files housed at the Johnson Presidential Library, but only by examining Nicholas Johnson's own papers at the University of Iowa Library Special Collections in Iowa City, Iowa.

51. In opting to establish a presidential task force rather than an intragovernmental committee, LBJ placed the Federal Communications Commission in a defensive position. Because of the president's charge to the task force, the FCC needed

to be involved; however, because the agency was not located within the executive branch, it could not be a formal party without transgressing on the constitution's separation of powers requirement. Intra-Governmental Committee on International Telecommunications, *Report and Recommendations to Senate and House Commerce Committees* (Washington, DC: Executive Office of the President, Office of Telecommunications Management, 1966); U.S. Federal Communications Commission, Docket No. 16828, Memorandum Opinion and Order, December 21, 1966, Dissenting Opinion of Commissioner Nicholas Johnson; Order on Petition for Reconsideration of ITT-ABC Merger, February 1, 1967, Concurring Statement of Commissioner Nicholas Johnson; Opinion and Order on Petition for Reconsideration, Adopted June 22, 1967, Dissenting Opinion of Commissioners Robert T. Bartley, Kenneth A. Cox, and Nicholas Johnson; James Ridgeway, "Rosel H. Hyde: The Voice of ITT," *New Republic*, July 8, 1967, http://www.tnr.com/article/politics/90833/the-voice-itt; Robert B. Horwitz, "Broadcast Reform Revisited: Reverend Everett C. Parker and the 'Standing' Case (*Office of Communications of the United Church of Christ v. Federal Communications Commission*)," *The Communication Review* 2, no. 3 (1997): 311–312; FCC, "In re: Application of Lamar Life Broadcasting Company, 1968, Dissenting Opinion of Commissioners Kenneth A. Cox and Nicholas Johnson," 14 F.C.C.2d 431 at 457–458; Nicholas Johnson, "The Public Interest and Public Broadcasting: Looking at Communications as a Whole," *Remarks Prepared for Delivery to the Resources for the Future and the Brookings Institution Conference on the Use and Regulation of the Radio Spectrum, Airlie House, Warrenton, Virginia, September 11, 1967* (Washington, DC Institute for Policy Studies Document, 1967), 1, 3; In Elizabeth Brenner Drew, "Is the FCC Dead?," *The Atlantic*, July 1967, 32–33.

52. Howard Junker, "The Greening of Nicholas Johnson," *Rolling Stone*, April 1, 1971, 32–39; For Johnson's place within the longstanding effort to attain media reform, Victor Pickard, *America's Battle for Media Democracy: The Triumph of Corporate Libertarianism and the Future of Media Reform* (New York: Cambridge University Press, 2015), 206; Radicals had long understood that capital's control of the media exercised potent antidemocratic effects. Robert W. McChesney and Ben Scott, eds., *Our Unfree Press: 100 Years of Radical Media Criticism* (New York: New Press, 2004); Presidential Task Force on Communications Policy, Minutes of the Fifth Meeting, January 19, 1968, 2, in Alan R. Novak, Memorandum to All Task Force Staff Representatives, February 8, 1968, Folder "Communications Task Force: Minutes and Agendas," Nicholas Johnson Papers.

53. For example, Johnson supported activists' efforts to gain standing before the FCC to try to compel AT&T, as a public utility, to end its flagrant job discrimination and to introduce equal employment opportunity programs. After protracted sociolegal struggle, as we saw, this victory was won. Letter from Nicholas Johnson, FCC, to Luther Holcomb, July 10, 1969; letter from Luther Holcomb, EEOC, to Nicholas Johnson, July 14, 1969, in Nicholas Johnson Papers, FCC Box 107, Correspondence.

54. Nicholas Johnson, "Communications Task Force General Discussions," August 28, 1967, appended to Letter from Nicholas Johnson to Eugene V. Rostow, August

28, 1967, FCC Box 428, Subject File Folder CTF-OCJ Correspondence, Public Statements, Daily Records, Notes, Nicholas Johnson Papers; In a September 1967 letter, Johnson asked Novak to "have your edited version of" a letter he, Johnson, had drafted "signed by Gene today, and send me a copy. (I have referred to it in a speech being publicly distributed.)" Nicholas Johnson to Alan R. Novak, September 8, 1967, FCC Box 61A, Correspondence, Novak, Alan R. Nicholas Johnson Papers; Nicholas Johnson to Alan R. Novak, January 10, 1968, FCC Box 61A, Correspondence, Novak, Alan R. Nicholas Johnson Papers.

55. Irving Bernstein, *Guns or Butter: The Presidency of Lyndon Johnson* (New York: Oxford University Press, 1996); Kevin Boyle, *The UAW and the Heyday of American Liberalism, 1945–1968* (Ithaca: Cornell University Press, 1998), 206–233, 228 (quote); Bernstein, *Guns or Butter*, 103; The administration's moves to actualize universal medical insurance, equal opportunity employment, and civil rights actually were patchy and incomplete—sometimes by design. Joshua B. Freeman, *American Empire: The Rise of a Global Power, The Democratic Revolution at Home 1945–2000* (New York: Viking, 2012), 200. See also, Rick Perlstein, *Nixonland: The Rise of a President and the Fracturing of America* (New York: Scribner, 2008), 7–8; and Boyle, *The UAW and the Heyday of American Liberalism*, 185–205; Ellen Schrecker, *The Lost Promise: American Universities in the 1960s* (Chicago: University of Chicago Press, 2021), 132–213; Boyle, *The UAW and the Heyday of American Liberalism*, 256; Bernstein, *Guns or Butter*, 471; Thomas F. Jackson, *From Civil Rights to Human Rights: Martin Luther King, Jr., and the Struggle for Economic Justice* (Philadelphia: University of Pennsylvania Press, 2007), 22; Boyle, *The UAW and the Heyday of American Liberalism*, 188; Freeman, *American Empire*, 204 (quote); Robert Zieger, *American Workers, American Unions, 1920–1985* (Baltimore: Johns Hopkins University Press, 1989), 187–190; Boyle: *The UAW and the Heyday of American Liberalism*, 254.

56. Boyle, *The UAW and the Heyday of American Liberalism*, 248; The speech is available at https://millercenter.org/the-presidency/presidential-speeches/march-31-1968-remarks-decision-not-seek-re-election. LBJ's chief of staff in 1968, James R. Jones, recollected that Johnson discussed not running for reelection in late 1967, and that the reason for this decision was not his health, but Vietnam. James R. Jones, "Behind L.B.J.'s Decision not to Run in '68," *New York Times*, April 16, 1988, http://www.nytimes.com/1988/04/16/opinion/behind-lbj-s-decision-not-to-run-in-68.html; Jackson, *From Civil Rights to Human Rights*, 22 (quote); see also, Bernstein, *Guns or Butter*, 471; Jackson, *From Civil Rights to Human Rights*, 22 (quote); see also, Boyle, *The UAW and the Heyday of American Liberalism*, 256.

57. Alan Novak wrote in a progress report to members of the task force that he "hoped" to have a draft of Posner's paper in time for task force staff members to consider at a meeting on July 25, 1968. Eugene Rostow, "Memorandum for Task Force Members and Staff Representatives," "Progress Report," July 9, 1968, CTF General-II (Papers, etc.), Nicholas Johnson Papers; Alan Novak oral history interview.

58. Memorandum For: The President from James Rowe, and "Reported Conclusions of Staff of President's Task Force on Communications Policy," June 21, 1968, in FG

600, Confidential File, Box 35, Johnson Presidential Library. See also, Memorandum for the President, from DeVier Pierson, June 27, 1968, in WHCF, Subject File, FG (Exec) 600, Box 362, Johnson Presidential Library. I have not confirmed that AT&T was a client of Rowe's law firm.
59. He argued "that Chapters 6 and 7 would 'poison the well,' by stirring up so much controversy as to imperil the possibility of gaining support for the rest of the program proposed in the Report." "Memorandum for the President by Eugene V. Rostow," December 7, 1968, in National Security File, Subject File, Box 7, Communications Policy—Task Force On, Johnson Presidential Library. As late as October 1968, Rostow recollected, "at a meeting of the members of the Task Force chiefly concerned with this controversy," he had been told by LBJ's legal counsel DeVier Pierson that he had "'a green, or at least an amber light' to proceed on the basis of the work program which the Task Force had approved, and to see how much of a consensus could be reached on the full Draft Report, including the two chapters in dispute." "Memorandum for the President by Eugene V. Rostow," December 7, 1968, in National Security File, Subject File, Box 7, Communications Policy—Task Force On, Johnson Presidential Library; Memorandum to Mr. Eugene V. Rostow from Dixon Donnelley, August 21, 1968, National Security File, Subject File, Box 7, [Communication Policy—Task Force On], and attached "Excerpt from the Noon Briefing, Friday, August 16, 1968," Johnson Presidential Library; and "Making New Waves in Communications," *Business Week*, November 16, 1968, 34–35. Samuel Sharkey, Jr., "LBJ to Get Plan to Break up AT&T," *Newark Star-Ledger*, August 16, 1968, attached to Eugene V. Rostow to Joseph A. Beirne, August 16, 1968, Box 69 Folder 95, "Task Force on Communications," CWA Papers Beirne, Tamiment Library-Robert F. Wagner Labor Archives, Bobst Library, New York University (hereafter Tamiment-Wagner).
60. Statement by State Department on August 16, 1968," attached to Eugene V. Rostow, Undersecretary of State for Political Affairs to Joseph A. Beirne, President, CWA, August 16, 1968, Box 69 Folder 95, "Task Force on Communications," CWA Papers Beirne, Tamiment-Wagner; R. B. Porch to Joseph A. Beirne, August 23, 1968, Subject: President Johnson's Task Force on Communications Policy," Box 69 Folder 95, "Task Force on Communications," CWA Papers Beirne, Tamiment-Wagner.
61. Memorandum for the President from DeVier Pierson, December 9, 1968, WHCF, Subject File, FG (Exec) 600, Box 362, Johnson Presidential Library.
62. President's Task Force on Communications Policy, *Final Report* (Washington, DC: Government Printing Office, 1968), Chapter One, 8; President's Task Force on Communications Policy, *Final Report*, Chapter One, 6; President's Task Force on Communications Policy, *Final Report*, Chapter Six, 16–17; President's Task Force on Communications Policy, *Final Report*, Chapter Six, 1, 2; President's Task Force on Communications Policy, *Final Report*, Chapter One, 9. This long-range planning function had been flagged as far back as a Truman-era report on international telecommunications. *The President's Communication Policy Board, Telecommunications: A Program for Progress* (Washington, DC: Government Printing Office, 1951); President's Task Force on Communications Policy, *Final*

Report, Chapter One, 3; President's Task Force on Communications Policy, *Final Report*, Chapter One, 17, 20.

63. President's Task Force on Communications Policy, *Final Report*, Chapter One, 21; Chapter Six, 26–28, 29–36; Nicholas Johnson, "*Carterfone*: My Story," *Santa Clara Computer & High Tech Law Journal* 25 (2009): 690–691.

64. President's Task Force on Communications Policy, *Final Report*, Chapter One, 9; Chapter Six, 9–25; 18 FCC 2d 953 (August 13, 1969); Christopher Lyndon, "Small Company Wins Phone Line," *New York Times*, August 15, 1969, 47; "Efficiency: How Sharp Is AT&T?," *Time*, November 2, 1970, 89.

65. "Memorandum for the President from the Chairman of the President's Task Force on Communications Policy," December 2, 1968, 7, National Security File, Subject File, Communications Policy—Task Force On, Johnson Presidential Library; Alan Novak oral history interview.

66. Memorandum for the President, by Leonard Marks, Douglass Cater and DeVier Pierson, September 26, 1968, in WHCF Subject File, FG (Exec), Box 362, Johnson Presidential Library. Domestic issues "in the 'study' stage by the Task Force and/or its staff," wrote the Commerce Department's Fred Simpich disapprovingly to Commerce Secretary C. R. Smith in August, included permitting businesses "to lease lines from AT&T and sell unused capacity to others, without regulation as a carrier"; to "bring about a divestiture of Western Electric from AT&T, on the basis of the need for greater competition in supplying equipment to domestic carriers." Memorandum for the Secretary, Subject: International Communications," Fred Simpich to C. R. Smith, August 26, 1968 in WHCF, Subject File, FG (Exec), Box 362, Johnson Presidential Library; Letter from Eugene V. Rostow to "S—The Secretary," November 27, 1968, in National Security File, Subject File, Box 7, Communications Policy—Task Force On, Johnson Presidential Library. Another controversial issue pertained to US international communications. Rostow stated in December, "the battle is over the entity proposal." The "entity" signified the reorganized company in which the task force hoped to vest all of the US' international telecommunications facilities—cables and satellites together. It was therefore a primary site of infighting between AT&T, the "record" carriers RCA, ITT, and WUI, and COMSAT, the US satellite operator, signatory to Intelsat and likely choice as the preferred "entity." "For Mr. W.W. Rostow The White House," cover note on letter from Eugene V. Rostow to the President, December 7, 1968, in National Security File, Subject File, Box 7, Communications Policy—Task Force On, Johnson Presidential Library; Memorandum for the President from DeVier Pierson, December 9, 1968, WHCF, Subject File, FG (Exec) 600, Box 362, Johnson Presidential Library; Memorandum for the President from DeVier Pierson, December 9, 1968, WHCF, Subject File, FG (Exec) 600, Box 362, Johnson Presidential Library.

67. "Memorandum for the President by Eugene V. Rostow," December 7, 1968, National Security File, Subject File, Box 7, Communications Policy—Task Force On, Johnson Presidential Library.

68. Citation No. 13808, WH 6812.02 Program 1, December 16, 1968, 9.32 a.m., Johnson Presidential Library.

69. "Memorandum for the President by Eugene V. Rostow," December 7, 1968, in National Security File, Subject File, Box 7, Communications Policy—Task Force On, Johnson Presidential Library; "The President's Task Force on Communications Policy," Eugene V. Rostow to the President, January 7, 1969, in National Security File, Subject File, Box 7, Communication Policy—Task Force On. Apparently, Eugene Rostow still hoped to publish the report: on this memo there is a handwritten note from "G"—Gene Rostow—that reads: "Walt: Now is the time to *charge*. Let's do it. This is cleared with DeVier" (emphasis in the original).
70. "Making New Waves in Communications," *Business Week*.
71. M. Kent Sidel and Vincent Mosco, "U.S. Communications Policy Making: The Results of Executive Branch Reorganization," *Telecommunications Policy* 2, no. 3 (September 1978): 211–217.
72. Massachusetts Representative Torbert H. Macdonald asked FCC Chairman Rosel Hyde about the status of the Task Force Report in March 1969: "we would be interested in learning if you can tell us when we can expect to have the task force report." 91st Cong., House of Representatives, 1st Sess., Hearing before the Subcommittee on Communications and Power, Committee on Interstate and Foreign Commerce, Serial No. 91-1, "Review of Federal Communications Commission Activities—1969," March 6, 1969, 1; Douglas Martin, "Peter M. Flanigan, Banker and Nixon Aide, Dies at 90," *New York Times*, August 1, 2013, A20 (Nader quote); note on Flanigan records by Richard Nixon Presidential Library and Museum, Yorba Linda, California, https://www.nixonlibrary.gov/finding-aids/peter-m-flanigan-white-house-special-files-staff-member-and-office-files. Flanigan was instrumental in the Justice Department's decision not to pursue an antitrust case against IT&T as an illegal conglomerate. See also, James Reichley, *Conservatives in an Age of Change: The Nixon and Ford Administrations* (Washington, DC: Brookings Institution, 1981), 73.
73. Peter G. Peterson, *The United States in the Changing World Economy*, vol. 1, *A Foreign Economic Perspective* (Washington, DC: Government Printing Office, 1971), 34, 35; Peterson, *The United States in the Changing World Economy*, 31.
74. "Dale Grubb Memorandum for John Erlichman, January 30, 1969, Subject Task Force on Communications Policy"; "RN: Burns; Memorandum for Honorable Lee A. DuBridge, Science Advisor to the President"; Robert Ellsworth, Assistant to the President, Memorandum for Honorable Lee A. DuBridge, Honorable Henry A. Kissinger, Honorable Robert Mayo Honorable Paul McCracken Subject Telecommunications Policy, February 7, 1969, UT Utilities Gen UT 3/21/74–3/31/74 through EX UT 1 9/18/69 Box 13, Folder WHCF Subject Files UT 1 Communications-Telecommunications Begin—6/30/69, White House Central Files Subject Files, Richard Nixon Presidential Library and Museum, Yorba Linda, California (hereafter Nixon Presidential Library); "RN Memorandum for Honorable Maurice H. Stans, Secretary of Commerce, February 17, 1969," Subject Files UT Utilities Gen UT 3/21/74–3/31/74 through EX UT 1 9/18/69 Box 13, Folder WHCF Subject Files UT 1 Communications-Telecommunications Begin—6/30/69, White House Central Files, Nixon Presidential Library.

75. Nicholas Johnson wrote to congratulate Alan Novak upon publication in June 1969, Nicholas Johnson to Alan R. Novak, June 9, 1969, Box 61A, Correspondence, Alan R. Novak, Nicholas Johnson Papers; "Clay T. Whitehead Memorandum for Mr. Higby, May 22, 1969," Subject Files UT Utilities Gen UT 3/21/74–3/31/74 through EX UT 1 9/18/69 Box 13, Folder WHCF Subject Files UT 1 Communications-Telecommunications Begin—6/30/69, White House Central Files, Nixon Presidential Library; Alan Novak oral history interview; Facing Democratic majorities in Congress and trying to win over to the Republicans some traditionally Democratic constituencies, Nixon "supported the core New Deal economic and social programs from which they benefited." Freeman, *American Empire*, 267; Memorandum from Clay T. Whitehead Staff Assistant for Mr. Rosel Hyde, Chairman, FCC, May 7, 1969; Memorandum from Clay T. Whitehead Staff Assistant for General O'Connell May 13, 1969. [EX] FG FCC Beginning 1/23/69–12/1/69 to [GEN] FG 118 FCC 69-70 Box 1, Folder—WHCF Subject Categories EX FG 118 FCC Beginning 1-23-69–12/31/69, White House Central Files Subject Files FG 118, Nixon Presidential Library.

76. "Clay T. Whitehead Memo to Mr. Flanigan 6/4/69," [EX] FG FCC Beginning 1/23/69–12/1/69 to [GEN] FG 118 FCC 69-70 Box 1, Folder—WHCF Subject Categories EX FG 118 FCC Beginning 1-23-69–12/31/69, White House Central Files Subject Files FG 118, Nixon Presidential Library.

77. Dwight L. Chapin Memorandum for Mr. H. R. Haldeman, May 14, 1969. UT EX UT 1-2 Telegraph-Cables through GEN UT 1-3 Telephone 1/1/73, Box 19, Nixon Presidential Library.

78. Roger G. Noll, *Reforming Regulation: An Evaluation of the Ash Council Proposals*, Studies in the Regulation of Economic Activity (Washington, DC: Brookings Institution, 1971), 13. The Ash Commission proposed that the FCC be streamlined by reducing the number of its commissioners from seven to five. Noll, *Reforming Regulation*, 10. This change was made in 1983; Noll, *Reforming Regulation*, 3, 110, 2.

79. "Memorandum for Mr. Rosel Hyde, Chairman, FCC from Peter M. Flanigan, Assistant to the President, 1 July 1969," Subject Files FG 118, [EX] FG FCC Beginning 1/23/69–12/1/69 to [GEN] FG 118 FCC 69-70 Box 1, Folder—WHCF Subject Categories EX FG 118 FCC Beginning 1-23-69–12/31/69, White House Central Files Subject Files, Nixon Presidential Library; "Memorandum from Clay T. Whitehead for Jon Rose July 3, 1969," [EX] FG FCC Beginning 1/23/69–12/1/69 to [GEN] FG 118 FCC 69-70 Box 1, Folder—WHCF Subject Categories EX FG 118 FCC Beginning 1-23-69–12/31/69, White House Central Files Subject Files, Nixon Presidential Library; "Clay T. Whitehead Memorandum for Dr. Lee A. DuBridge, Dr. Paul McCracken, Mr. Robert Mayo, General James O'Connell, Chairman Rosel Hyde, Mr. Richard LcLaren, and Dr. Thomas O. Paine, August 5, 1969," [EX] FG FCC Beginning 1/23/69–12/1/69 to [GEN] FG 118 FCC 69-70 Box 1, Folder—WHCF Subject Categories EX FG 118 FCC Beginning 1-23-69–12/31/69, White House Central Files Subject Files, Nixon Presidential Library.

80. "Clay T. Whitehead Memo for Mr. Flanigan, July 1, 1969," UT Utilities Gen UT 3/21/74–3/31/74 through EX UT 1 9/18/69 Box 13, WHCF Subject Files, EX UT1 7/

1/69–9/17/69 folder, Subject Files, White House Central Files, Nixon Presidential Library; "Clay T. Whitehead Memorandum for Mr. Peter Flanigan, Dr. Lee A DuBridge, Mr. Paul McCracken, General George A. Lincoln, December 18, 1969, copy to Dean Burch," UT Utilities Gen UT 3/21/74–3/31/74 through EX UT 1 9/18/69 Box 13 Folder EX UT 1 9/18/69, Subject Files, White House Central Files, Nixon Presidential Library; "Peter Flanigan Assistant to the President Memorandum for Mr. Erlichman, January 22, 1970," FG 118, [EX] FG FCC Beginning 1/23/69–12/1/69 to [GEN] FG 118 FCC 69-70 Box 1, Folder, "WHCF: Subject Categories EX FG 118 1/1/70–5/4-70f Subject Files, White House Central Files, Nixon Presidential Library.

81. "Ken Cole Memorandum for John Erlichman, January 22, 1970," FG 118, [EX] FG FCC Beginning 1/23/69–12/1/69 to [GEN] FG 118 FCC 69-70 Box 1, Folder, "WHCF: Subject Categories EX FG 118 1/1/70–5/4-70, White House Central Files Subject Files, Nixon Presidential Library.

82. Whalen, *The Rise and Fall of Comsat*, 145, 252; Christopher Lydon, "White House Asks Open FCC Policy," *New York Times*, January 23, 1970, 1; "Peter M. Flanigan Memorandum for the President, February 2, 1970," FG 118, [EX] FG FCC Beginning 1/23/69–12/1/69 to [GEN] FG 118 FCC 69-70 Box 1, Folder, WHCF: Subject Categories EX FG 118 1/1/70–5/4-70, White House Central Files Subject Files, Nixon Presidential Library.

83. "Peter Flanigan Memorandum for John Erlichman, December 6, 1969," FG 6-14, EXEC FG 6-14 Office of Telecommunications BEGIN 4/30/70 To GEN FG 6-14/A Box 1, Folder OTP Begin—4/30/70 Box 1 (1), White House Central Files Subject Files, Nixon Presidential Library; "Peter Flanigan Memorandum for John Erlichman, December 6, 1969," Attached Document 1, "Executive Branch Organization for Telecommunications."; "Peter Flanigan Memorandum for John Erlichman, December 6, 1969," Attached Document 1, "Executive Branch Organization for Telecommunications."

84. "Peter Flanigan Memorandum for John Erlichman December 6, 1969," Attached Document 2, "Responsibilities of the Office of Telecommunications Policy," FG 6-14, EXEC FG 6-14 Office of Telecommunications BEGIN 4/30/70 To GEN FG 6-14/A Box 1, Folder OTP Begin—4/30/70 Box 1 (1), White House Central Files Subject Files. Nixon Presidential Library; "Peter M. Flanigan Memorandum for the President June 22, 1970," FG 6-14, EXEC FG 6-14 Office of Telecommunications BEGIN 4/30/70 To GEN FG 6-14/A Box 1 Folder OTP Begin—4/30/70 Box 1 (1), White House Central Files Subject Files, Nixon Presidential Library.

85. "A Hot New Breath down FCC's Neck," *Broadcasting*, September 28, 1970, 24; Clay T. Whitehead Tribute by Thomas W. Hazlett, Telecommunications Policy Research Conference, George Mason University School of Law, Arlington, Virginia, September 26, 2009, 1, In re: Establishment of Domestic Communications-Satellite Facilities by Non-governmental Entities, Docket No. 16495, 38 F.C.C. 2d 665 (Dec. 22, 1972).

86. "Clay T. Whitehead Memorandum for Don Baker, Chief of Evaluation Section, Antitrust Division, Department of Justice August 17, 1970," FG 17 (The Department of Justice), EX FG 17-13/ST/A U.S. Marshalls/States and Territories/Appointments to EX FG 17/18A Drug Enforcement Administration/Appointments Box 11 Folder

EX FG 17-14 Antitrust Division Box 11 #3, White House Central Files Subject Files, Nixon Presidential Library; Office of Telecommunications Policy, Executive Office of the President, *The Telephone Industry and Antitrust: A Report on Anticompetitive Practices of the Bell System* (Washington, DC: OTP, 1973).

87. "Clay T. Whitehead Memorandum for Mr. John Erlichman, February 2, 1971," FG 118, [EX] FG FCC Beginning 1/23/69–12/1/69 to [GEN] FG 118 FCC 69-70 Box 1, Folder WHCF: Subject Categories EX FG 118 FCC 1/1/71–[1972], White House Central Files Subject Files, Nixon Presidential Library.

88. "Dorothy Andrews Elston, Treasurer of the United States, to President Nixon, August 1, 1969," FG 118, [EX] FG FCC Beginning 1/23/69–12/1/69 to [GEN] FG 118 FCC 69-70 Box 1, Folder—WHCF Subject Categories EX FG 118 FCC Beginning 1-23-69–12/31/69, White House Central Files Subject Files, Nixon Presidential Library.

89. "A Hot New Breath down FCC's Neck," *Broadcasting*, September 24, 1970, 23–24; "Clear Sailing for White House Plan," *Broadcasting*, March 16, 1970, 38; FM MSS (1971–1973), 142, Box 42, Folders 3–6, Dean Burch Papers, Arizona State University Libraries, Department of Archives & Special Collections (hereafter Burch Papers).

90. The Network Project, "Office of Telecommunications Policy (The White House Role in Domestic Communication)," Notebook Number Four, April 1973 (New York: The Network Project, 1973), 1.

91. "Richard E. Wiley, General Counsel, FCC, December 7, 1971, to Mr. Charles W. Colson, Special Counsel to the President, 'Personal and Confidential,'" Charles W. Colson Subject Files Box 61, Folders Federal Communications Commission Box 1, White House Special Files Staff Member Office Files, Nixon Presidential Library; "Wiley Brings His Own Approach to a Key FCC Post," *Broadcasting Magazine*, May 3, 1971, 67.

92. "Appointment of Successor to Robert Wells as FCC Member," Dean Burch Memorandum for Honorable Peter M. Flanigan, Honorable Charles W. Colson, Honorable Frederic V. Malek, no date but probably early fall 1971, FM MSS (1971) 142 Burch Papers, Box 42, Folders 3–6.

93. President's Task Force Report on Communications Policy, *Final Report*, Introduction, 27; Bruce M. Owen, "A Novel Conference: The Origins of TPRC," in Sandra Braman, ed., *Communication Researchers and Policy-making* (Cambridge: MIT Press, 2003), 347–355.

94. Eugene V. Rostow, "The Case for Congressional Action to Safeguard the Telephone Network as a Universal and Optimized System," in 94th Congress, House of Representatives, 1st Sess., on H.R. 7047, Domestic Common Carrier Regulation, *Hearings before the Subcommittee on Communications, Committee on Interstate and Foreign Commerce, Nov. 10–11, 13, 17–18, 1975, Serial 94–100* (Government Printing Office, 1976), 255–284 at 248. Rostow's forecast of the consequences bears interest less for its acuity than for its embeddedness in New Deal assumptions: "In reliance on these deviant FCC rulings, large business firms are seriously planning to enter some of the most profitable parts of the industry. A Gold Rush is in the

making. The effect of this process cannot be confined to one or two sectors of the industry. Unless it is promptly checked, the real costs of telephone service will increase, through the duplication of expensive communications facilities; the rate of improvement of the network will slow down; the historic rate pattern will change; and telephone rates will increase, in the first instance for household subscribers."

95. Tim Wu, *The Curse of Bigness: Antitrust in the New Gilded Age* (New York: Columbia Global Reports, 2018), 94; see also, Temin with Galambos, *The Fall of the Bell System*, 99–112; Kirkpatrick Sale, *Power Shift: The Rise of the Southern Rim and Its Challenge to the Eastern Establishment* (New York: Vintage, 1976). The South and the Southwest were also home to low-wage, labor-intensive industries and to a "low-tax, anti-union, pro-business environment." Freeman, *American Empire*, 307; Dennis Hevesi, "Clay T. Whitehead, Guide of Policy that Helped Cable TV, Is Dead at 69," *New York Times*, July 31, 2008, http://www.nytimes.com/2008/07/31/washington/31whitehead.html?ref=obituaries&_r=0.

96. Gerald Mayer, *Union Membership Trends in the United States* (Washington, DC: Congressional Research Service, 2004), CRS-22, Table A-1 Union Membership in the United States, 1930–2003, https://sgp.fas.org/crs/misc/RL32553.pdf; Rubio, *There's Always Work at the Post Office*, 145; Brooks, *Communications Workers of America*, 226; Bernard E. Anderson, *The Negro in the Public Utility Industries*, Report No. 10, Industrial Research Unit, Wharton School of Finance (Philadelphia: University of Pennsylvania Press, 1970), 63.

97. Brenner, "The Political Economy of the Rank-and-File Rebellion," and Kim Moody, "Understanding the Rank-and-File Rebellion in the Long 1970s," in eds. Aaron Brenner, Robert Brenner, and Cal Winslow, *Rebel Rank and File: Labor Militancy and Revolt from below during the Long 1970s* (London: Verso, 2010), 37–74, 105–146; Aaron Brenner, "Rank-and-file Rebellion, 1966–1975" (Ph.D. diss., Columbia University, 1996); Brenner, Brenner, and Winslow, *Rebel Rank and File*; Dorothy Sue Cobble, *The Other Women's Movement: Workplace Justice and Social Rights in Modern America* (Princeton: Princeton University Press, 2004); Nancy MacLean, *Freedom Is Not Enough: The Opening of the American Workplace* (Cambridge: Harvard University Press, 2006); Cal Winslow, "Overview: The Rebellion from Below, 1965–81," in Brenner, Brenner, and Winslow, *Rebel Rank and File*, 1–35.

98. Joseph A. Beirne, *New Horizons for American Labor* (Washington, DC: Public Affairs Press, 1962); Joseph A. Beirne, *Challenge to Labor: New Roles for American Trade Unions* (New York: Prentice-Hall, 1969).

99. Which is where, indeed, it remains to this day. For a current instance, James Patrick Jordan, "What Is the AFL-CIO's Solidarity Center Doing in Venezuela? We Have a Right to Know!," *Alliance for Global Justice*, February 7, 2019, https://afgj.org/what-is-the-afl-cios-solidarity-center-doing-in-venezuela-we-have-a-right-to-know. I have drawn on formulations by Boyle, *The UAW and the Heyday of American Liberalism*, 36; Joseph A. Beirne, President of the Communications Workers of America, CIO, "Communism is a Criminal Conspiracy," 83d Congress, Senate, Committee on the Judiciary, Subcommittee on Internal Security, *Statement to the Task Force of the Senate Subcommittee on Internal Security Regarding S. 1606*, March

5, 1954; Angela Vergara, "Chilean Workers and the U.S. Labor Movement: From Solidarity to Intervention, 1950s–1970s," in eds. Robert Anthony Waters, Jr., and Geert van Goethem, *American Labor's Global Ambassadors: The International History of the AFL-CIO During the Cold War* (New York: Palgrave-Macmillan, 2013), 210; Beirne, *Challenge to Labor*, 114, 118–119; George Morris, *CIA and American Labor: The Subversion of the AFL-CIO's Foreign Policy* (New York: International Publishers, 1967), 154–158; Drew Pearson, "CIA Biggest Subsidizer of Unions," *Madera Daily Tribune*, February 24, 1967, 16; Tim Shorrock, "Labor's Cold War," *The Nation*, May 1, 2003, https://www.thenation.com/article/archive/labors-cold-war/; Beth Sims, *Workers of the World Undermined* (Boston: South End Press, 1992), Appendix B, 104–107; Peter B. Levy, *The New Left and Labor in the 1960s* (Urbana: University of Illinois Press, 1994), 62; "Beirne Supports U.S. Views," *CWA News* 25, no. 1 (January 1966): 3; "CWA Backs LBJ in Commie Battle," *CWA News* 25, no. 7 (July 1966): 2; "Beirne Is Viet War Panelist," *CWA News* 26, no. 11 (November 1967): 1, 4; Levy, *The New Left and Labor*, 181.

100. Michael Palm, *Technologies of Consumer Labor: A History of Self-Service* (New York: Routledge, 2017); Green, *Race on the Line*, 245; "Bell Admits Mechanization Causes Job Loss," *CWA News* 8, no. 12 (December 1949): 5. See also, "The Robot Takes Over," *CWA News* 10, no. 12 (December 1951): 9; "Mechanization Saves Industry Big Money," *CWA News* 11, no. 5 (May 1952): 11; "Beirne Urges Broad Attack on Problem of Automation," *CWA News* 20, no. 4 (April 1961): 3; "10 Million 'Automation' Job Loss in Next Five Years," *CWA News* 20, no. 5 (April 1961): 8. On the historical contours of the trend to automation in telephony, see Green, *Race on the Line*, 115–136, 159–169, 178–191, 214–218, 250–254; and Brenner, "Rank-and-file Struggles at the Telephone Company," in Brenner, Brenner, and Winslow, *Rebel Rank and File*, 277–279.

101. For contrasting views, Amy Sue Bix, *Inventing Ourselves out of a Job* (Baltimore: Johns Hopkins University Press, 2000); Jason Resnikoff, *Labor's End: How the Promise of Automation Degraded Work* (Urbana: University of Illinois Press, 2021); Statement of Joseph A. Beirne, 84th Congress, 1st Sess., *Hearings on Automation and Technological Change, Joint Committee on the Economic Report, Subcommittee on Economic Stabilization, October 25, 1955* (Washington, DC: Government Printing Office, 1955), 335–364; Joseph A. Beirne, 86th Cong., 2d Sess., *New Views on Automation, Joint Economic Committee* (Washington, DC: Government Printing Office, 1960), 491–496; Beirne, *New Horizons for American Labor*, 43–57; Communications Workers of America, "CWA Study Reveals Impact of Automation," *CWA News* 25, no. 5 (1965): 1. For the "ideology" of automation, Resnikoff, *Labor's End*, 1–13.

102. Joseph A. Beirne, *Challenge to Labor*, 172; Green, *Race on the Line*, 245; In Brenner, "Rank-and-file Rebellion, 1966–1975," 166; President's Task Force on Communications Policy, *Final Report*, Introduction, 26; Beirne, *Challenge to Labor*, 198, 173.

103. Beirne, quoted in James M. Naughton, "A Forward-looking Union Leader," *New York Times*, July 15, 1971, A21; Beirne, *Strategy for Labor*, 154.

104. David M. Gordon, Richard Edwards, and Michael Reich, *Segmented Work, Divided Workers: The Historical Transformation of Labor in the United States* (New York: Cambridge University Press, 1982); Brenner, "The Political Economy of the Rank-and-file Rebellion," 72; Lane Windham, *Knocking on Labor's Door: Union Organizing in the 1970s and the Roots of a New Economic Divide* (Chapel Hill: University of North Carolina Press, 2017), 76.
105. D. Guttmann and B. Willner, *The Shadow Government: The Government's Multibillion-dollar Giveaway of Its Decision-making Powers to Private Management Consultants, "Experts," and Think Tanks* (New York: Pantheon Books, 1976); Beirne, *Challenge to Labor*, 137–138.
106. Joseph Beirne, "A Report on Merger," *CWA News*, 31, no. 12 (1972): 3; Communications Workers of America, "Union," *CWA News* 31, no. 7 (1972): 5; Communications Workers of America, "Postal Union Gives Nod to Merger," *CWA News* 31, no. 8 (1972): 5; Communications Workers of America, "CWA Marches toward Its Growth Goal," *CWA News* 31, no. 9 (1972): 2; Communications Workers of America, "CWA Growth Activities," *CWA News* 32, no. 4 (1973): 9; Communications Workers of America, "Growing Bigger Every Day," *CWA News* 32, no. 5 (1973): 2; Joseph A. Beirne, "Report on Growth," *CWA News* 32, no. 5 (May 1973): 3; Beirne, "A Look at the Year Ahead," *CWA News* 32, no. 1 (1973): 3; Communications Workers of America, "Delegates Approve Merger Resolution," *CWA News* 31, no. 6 (1972): 2.
107. Communications Workers of America, 'Delegates Approve Merger Resolution."
108. PTTI eventually became the UNI Global Union. See www.uniglobalunion.org; At this point, Britain's postal union remained a separate organization, even though postal workers and telephone and telegraph workers labored in different departments of the government postal ministry. Later, British postal and telephone unions merged. Joe Jacobs, *Sorting out the Postal Strike* (London: Solidarity, 1971), https://libcom.org/history/sorting-out-postal-strike-1971-joe-jacobs.
109. "Beirne Urges Fast Action in Setting up Privately Owned Space Communications System," *CWA News* 21, no. 5 (March 1962): 2; Reuther in 1945, quoted in Boyle, *The UAW and the Heyday of American Liberalism*, 23; Joseph A. McCartin, *Collision Course: Ronald Reagan, the Air Traffic Controllers, and the Strike that Changed America* (New York: Oxford University Press, 2011), 9–10, 32, 42–43, 53.
110. Their compensation rose by 94 percent between 1970 and 1977—when the consumer price index rose by 65 percent while federal workers apart from the Postal Service experienced a decline in the purchasing power of their pay. Federal workers' compensation overall rose during these years by 47 percent. McCartin, *Collision Course*, 238, citing U.S. General Accounting Office, *Comparative Growth in Compensation for Postal and Other Federal Employees since 1970: Report to the Congress by the Comptroller General of the United States* (Washington, DC: U.S. General Accounting Office), 1979; Rubio, *There's Always Work at the Post Office*, 264; Rubio, *There's Always Work at the Post Office*, 263, 268; John Walsh and Garth Mangum, *Labor Struggle in the Post Office: From Selective Lobbying to Collective Bargaining* (Armonk: M.E. Sharpe, 1992), 37–39; In addition to the National Association of Letter Carriers, the remaining postal unions included the National Rural Letter Carriers' Association,

the National Alliance of Postal and Federal Employees, and the National Postal Mail Handlers Union.

111. United Federation of Postal Clerks, "Three Merger Pacts Set; Top Negotiator Hired," *The Union Postal Clerk* 67, no. 1 (1971): 5; United Federation of Postal Clerks, "152,460 Postal Workers Say Yes to One Big Union," *The Union Postal Clerk* 67, no. 6 (1971): 2–3; United Federation of Postal Clerks, "It's Go on NPU Merger!," *The Union Postal Clerk* 67, no. 3 (1971): 3; David Silvergleid, "Practical Labor-management Relations," *The American Postal Worker* 1, no. 2 (1972): 1. NALC stipulated in November that, among other conditions, a merged APWU would have to be a "federation of Postal Service labor organizations" and that "each division shall operate under its own Constitution and By-Laws" David Silvergleid, "NALC Merger Terms," *The American Postal Worker* 2, no. 1: 23; American Postal Workers Union, "Board Wrestles Giant Agenda," *The American Postal Worker* 2, no. 5 (1972): 36–37; Gene R. Hailey, "Giant Postal Union Chief Francis (Stu) Filbey Dies," *Washington Post*, May 19, 1977, https://www.washingtonpost.com/archive/local/1977/05/19/giant-postal-union-chief-francis-stu-filbey-dies/5262a7da-067a-46e2-ac3c-7f442a1b644b/?utm_term=.6fdbcace7609.

112. American Postal Workers Union, "Merger Again?," *The American Postal Worker* 2, no. 8 (1972): 6–7; Cathy McKercher and Vincent Mosco, *The Laboring of Communication: Will Knowledge Workers of the World Unite?* (Lanham, MD: Lexington Books, 2008).

113. Communications Workers of America, "CWA-APWU Merger Resolution," *CWA News* 31, no. 6 (1972): 6; Janet Abbate, *Inventing the Internet* (Cambridge, MA: MIT Press, 1999), 106–111; John Carey and Martin C. J. Elton, *When Media Are New: Understanding the Dynamics of Media Adoption and Use* (Ann Arbor: University of Michigan Press, 2010), 222–223.

114. American Postal Workers Union, "Merger Again?," 6–7; American Postal Workers Union, "Foes' Tactics Boomerang: Filbey Given Broad Power to Seek Merger with CWA," *The American Postal Worker* 2, no. 10 (1972): 6–7; Communications Workers of America, "NALC Adopts Resolution on Trade Union Merger," *CWA News* 31, no. 7 (1972): 2; National Association of Letter Carriers, "Merger Recommendations," *Postal Record* 85, no. 8 (1972): 66; National Association of Letter Carriers, "Three Unions in Merger Talks," *Postal Record* 85, no. 12 (1972): 7.

115. [George Meany], "Speaking at the Testimonial Dinner for President Stu Filbey of APWU on November 18," *The American Postal Worker* 2, no. 12 (1972): 6.

116. Communications Workers of America, "CWA Takes Another Step towards Merger," *CWA News* 31, no. 11 (1972): 4; Joseph A. Beirne, "Off My Mind: A Report on Merger," *CWA News* 31, no. 12 (1972): 3; Beirne, "Off My Mind."

117. Francis Filbey, "Merger," *The American Postal Worker* 3, no. 3 (1973): 9; Beirne, "Off My Mind," 3.

118. "Proposed Constitution, American Communications Union," January 8, 1973, 1, 46; CWA Papers Box 79, Folder 46, Tamiment-Wagner.

119. "Communications Workers of America—American Postal Workers Union Proposal for Merger," 5/10/72, 5/22/72, 5/31,72, attached to G. C. Cramer to Joseph A. Beirne and Glenn E. Watts, "Statement for Merger," May 31, 1972, CWA Papers, Box 79 Folder 48l, Tamiment-Wagner.

120. American Postal Workers Union, "Question and Answer," *The American Postal Worker* 1, no. 2 (1971): 29; M. Cullen, "NALC Violation," *The American Postal Worker* 10, no. 10 (1971): 30; J. Strong, "Letter Carriers Weigh Merger with Teamsters," *The Chicago Tribune*, January 29, 1973, 2. The NALC ultimately also rejected the Teamsters' plan.
121. National Association of Letter Carriers, "Merger Committee, Council Says 'No' to Proposed Merger Constitution," *Postal Record* 86, no. 4 (1973): 11; National Association of Letter Carriers, "Merger Committee, Council Says 'No.'"; American Postal Workers Union, "Merger Talks to Continue," *The American Postal Worker* 3, no. 3 (1973): 20.
122. The American Postal Workers Union and the Communications Workers of America resuscitated merger talks at least three times: in the late 1970s, the mid-1980s, and the late 1990s. Mike Causey, "Two Mail Unions Talking Merger," *The Washington Post*, November 12, 1979, C2; Morton Bahr, *From the Telegraph to the Internet* (Washington, DC: National Press Books 1998).
123. Windham, *Knocking on Labor's Door*; Kim Moody, *An Injury to All: The Decline of American Unionism* (London: Verso, 1988); Kim Moody, *U.S. Labor in Trouble and Transition: The Failure of Reform from Above, the Promise of Revival from Below* (New York: Verso, 2007); Judith Stein, *Pivotal Decade: How the United States Traded Factories for Finance in the Seventies* (New Haven: Yale University Press, 2010); Kate Bronfenbrenner, quoted in Timothy J. Minchin, *Labor Under Fire: A History of the AFL-CIO since 1979* (Chapel Hill: UNC Press, 2017), 127; Barry Bluestone and Bennett Harrison, *The Deindustrialization of America: Plant Closings, Community Abandonment, and the Dismantling of Basic Industry* (New York: Basic Books, 1982); Dan Schiller, *Digital Capitalism: Networking the Global Market System* (Cambridge, MA: MIT Press, 1999), 37–46; Dan Schiller, *Digital Depression: Information Technology and Economic Crisis* (Urbana, IL: University of Illinois Press, 2014), 27–42; Minchin, *Labor Under Fire*, 12.
124. CWA intervened in only one of the FCC's liberalizing decisions, in 1978. Its opposition to the agency's proposed authorization of a data carrier (Graphnet) into domestic US delivery of international data service messages seems idiosyncratic; certainly, it was a belated intervention. U.S. FCC, In the Matter of Graphnet Systems Inc. Application to participate in hinterland delivery of International communication Messages, CC Docket No. 78-95, 78-96, Comments of Communications Workers of America, June 1, 1978, in CWA Papers Watts, Box 81, Folder 9, Tamiment-Wagner; During the controversy over ownership and control of the Comsat satellite system in 1962, and over Richard Posner's 1968 recommendation to Rostow's Task Force that AT&T divest Western Electric; CWA Executive Board, "Telecommunications Policy Statement," Thursday March 26, 1976, attached to Glenn E. Watts, President, Communications Workers of America, April 12, 1976, Box 8, Folder "Communications—Meeting with Charlie Walker, William Ellinghaus, and Paul Hensen, June 9, 1976 (1)," James M. Cannon Files, Gerald R. Ford Presidential Library, Ann Arbor, Michigan. Between 1976 and 1981, AT&T executive Alvin von Auw recounted in 1983, nine different bills to reorganize US telecommunications were introduced into the two houses of

Congress. Originating as an attempt to reverse the FCC's liberalizing policies and to restore the primacy of the regulated telecommunications industry, the legislative momentum soon reversed—so that its objective became to strengthen the liberalization trend. The trajectory of these bills thus amounted to another defeat for AT&T—refuting, as von Auw observed, "the legend that AT&T operates as an irresistible political steamroller"—even though, as he ruefully added, "the Bell System employs more voters than any other institution outside the government itself." It has been asserted that CWA's role in this debacle was simply to "clear" AT&T's plan and to "climb on board" in backing the early antiliberalizing legislation, but this is incorrect: the CWA was an ally rather than a parrot. Auw, *Heritage and Destiny*, 100–101; Temin with Galambos, *The Fall of the Bell System*, 118. See also, for further discussion, Schiller, *Telematics and Government*, 56–61, 66; Temin with Galambos, *The Fall of the Bell System*, 113–131; and Alan Stone, *Wrong Number: The Break-up of AT&T* (New York: Basic Books, 1989), 297–298. For primary reference materials, see CWA Papers, Glenn E. Watts, President, Boxes 76, 78, 80 and 81, Tamiment-Wagner; and 94th Congress, House of Representatives, 2d Sess., Subcommittee on Communications of the Committee on Interstate and Foreign Commerce, *Hearings on Competition in the Telecommunications Industry*, Serial 94-129, September 28, 29, 30, 1976 (Washington, DC: Government Printing Office, 1976), 1167–1206.
125. Stuart E. Eizenstat, *President Carter: The White House Years* (New York: St. Martin's Press, 2018), 297–300, 382 (quote), 384; Ronald Frank, "Carter against Bell Bill (Maybe)," *Computerworld* 10, no. 34 (August 23, 1976): 1, 4; Stein, *Pivotal Decade*, 155–167, 176–204.
126. Nelson Lichtenstein, "From Corporatism to Collective Bargaining: Organized Labor and the Eclipse of Social Democracy in the Postwar Era," in eds. Steve Fraser and Gary Gerstle, *The Rise and Fall of the New Deal Order* (Princeton: Princeton University Press, 1989), 245; Sam Gindin, "The Power of Deep Organizing," *Jacobin*, https://www.jacobinmag.com/2016/12/jane-mcalevey-unions-organizing-workers-socialism.
127. Frank, "Carter against Bell Bill (Maybe)."
128. John Boyko and Dan Schiller, "Labor Relations in the Information Society: The Impact of the 1983 Telephone Strike" (unpublished paper, 1984), author's collection; First quote from Steve Early and Rand Wilson, "How a Telephone Workers' Strike Thirty Years Ago Aided the Fight for Single Payer," *Jacobin*, https://jacobinmag.com/2019/07/telephone-workers-strike-single-payer; second quote from Verizon technician and CWA shop steward Pam Galpern; see also, Daniel DiMaggio, "Victory at Verizon: The Anatomy of a Strike," *New Labor Forum* 26, no. 1 (2017): 28–35.
129. Louis Harris and Associates, Inc., "Public Attitudes toward Competition in the Telecommunications Industry," Study No. 782254, prepared for AT&T, July 1979, Tables 17 and 24, cited in von Auw, *Heritage and Destiny*, 27; von Auw, *Heritage and Destiny*, 27; Calvin Sims, "On 5th Anniversary, Customers Still Fault Bell System Breakup," *New York Times*, December 22, 1988, A1, C8.

130. Moreover, "we never envisioned such a radical break-up of the Bell monopoly as eventually unfolded." Bahr, *From the Telegraph to the Internet*, 71, 19; Bahr, *From the Telegraph to the Internet*, 65; Bahr, *From the Telegraph to the Internet*, 19. According to historian Venus Green, only in the 1980s did top union leaders "even contemplate strikes or other more militant actions against the introduction of new technologies." Green, *Race on the Line*, 260.
131. Carey and Elton, *When Media Are New*, 222–223; Schiller, *Telematics and Government*, 213; Ryan N. Ellis, "The Premature Death of Electronic Mail: The United States Postal Service's E-COM Program, 1978–1985," *IJOC* 7 (2013): 1954.
132. Fred Block, "No Mandate for Market Fundamentalism," Longview Institute, http://192.119.65.12/research/block/nomandate/; Horwitz, "Broadcast Reform Revisited," 344; Jonathan E. Neuchterlein and Philip J. Weiser, *Digital Crossroads: Telecommunications Law and Policy in the Internet Age*, 2nd ed. (Cambridge: MIT Press, 2013), 21; Another analyst terms it the "atrophy of the public service principles." Stone, *Wrong Number*, 338.
133. Julia Beckhusen, *Occupations in Information Technology* (Washington, DC: Census Bureau, 2016), Report ACS-35, 1–2; David Landes, *The Unbound Prometheus: Technological Change and Industrial Development in Western Europe from 1750 to the Present* (Cambridge: Cambridge University Press, 1969); Daniel DiMaggio, "Victory at Verizon: The Anatomy of a Strike," *New Labor Forum* 26, no. 1 (2017): 33; U.S. Commerce Department, Bureau of Labor Statistics, "Union Members 2016," news release, January 26, 2017, 2; Joe Davidson, "Federal Unions, except Postal Groups, Grow as Other Labor Organizations Decline," *Washington Post*, January 28, 2013, https://www.washingtonpost.com/national/federal-uni ons-except-postal-groups-grow-as-other-labor-organizations-decline/2013/01/28/ 292747cc-698a-11e2-95b3-272d604a10a3_story.html; USPS, "Postal Facts," https:// facts.usps.com/total-career-employees/.

Chapter 11

1. Acknowledging Herbert I. Schiller, *Mass Communications and American Empire* (New York: Augustus M. Kelley, 1969); Stuart Hall, "The Great Moving Right Show," *Marxism Today* 23, no. 1 (January 1979): 14–20.
2. Harry Magdoff, *Imperialism From the Colonial Age to the Present* (New York: Monthly Review Press, 1978), 135 (first quote), 3 (second quote), 97; see also, Gabriel Paquette, *The European Seaborne Empires: From the Thirty Years' War to the Age of Revolutions* (New Haven, CT: Yale University Press, 2019), 177; and Intan Suwandi, *Value Chains: The New Economic Imperialism* (New York: Monthly Review Press, 2019), 152; In the case of Africa, as late as the 1870s, European powers controlled areas "at the northern and southern extremities," trading centers along coasts and major rivers, and two small settler colonies for freed slaves—all told, less than 10 percent of the continent. Robert Harms, *Land of Tears: The Exploration and Exploitation of Equatorial Africa* (New York: Basic Books, 2019), 113.

3. Paquette, *The European Seaborne Empires*, 53–54; 77 (quote); Eric Hobsbawm, *Industry and Empire: The Birth of the Industrial Revolution*, rev. ed. (New York: New Press, 1999); David Onnekink and Gijs Rommelse, *The Dutch in the Early Modern World: A History of a Global Power* (Cambridge: Cambridge University Press, 2019), 1–32; Paquette, *The European Seaborne Empires*, 207 (first quote); Magdoff, *Imperialism*, 100 (second quote); Paquette, *The European Seaborne Empires*, 77.

4. Steven Hahn, *A Nation without Borders: The United States and Its World in an Age of Civil Wars, 1830–1910* (New York: Viking, 2016); Peter S. Onuf, "Imperialism and Nationalism in the Early American Republic," in eds. Ian Tyrrell and Jay Sexton, *Empire's Twin: U.S. Anti-imperialism from the Founding to the War on Terror* (Ithaca, NY: Cornell University Press, 2015), 21; James Schwoch, *Wired into Nature: The Telegraph and the North American Frontier* (Urbana, IL: University of Illinois Press, 2018), 118–125; Katharine Bjork, *"Prairie Imperialists": The Indian Country Origins of American Empire* (Philadelphia: University of Pennsylvania Press, 2018). For a "continental imperialism," see Peter J. Hugill, *Global Communications Since 1844: Geopolitics and Technology* (Baltimore: Johns Hopkins University Press, 1999), 38; John Mason Hart, *Empire and Revolution: The Americans in Mexico since the Civil War* (Berkeley, CA: University of California Press, 2002), 126; see also, Cynthia Baur, "Incommunicado: The Arrested Development of Telecommunications Systems in Latin America" (Ph.D. diss., University of California, San Diego, 1995).

5. The Western Union adventure helped pave the way for the US purchase of Alaska in 1867. Robert Luther Thompson, *Wiring a Continent: The History of the Telegraph Industry in the United States 1832–1866* (Princeton, NJ: Princeton University Press, 1947), 427–439; Quoted in Dwayne R. Winseck and Robert M. Pike, *Communication and Empire* (Durham, NC: Duke University Press, 2007), 46; Quoted in Leslie Bennett Tribolet, *The International Aspects of Electrical Communications in the Pacific Area* (Baltimore: Johns Hopkins University Press, 1929), 158.

6. Michael Patrick Cullinane, *Liberty and American Anti-imperialism 1898–1909* (New York: Palgrave Macmillan, 2012). South Dakota Republican Senator Richard F. Pettigrew led the anti-imperialist fight; beginning in the 1910s, Wisconsin Progressive Party Senator Robert La Follette became prominent. Richard F. Pettigrew, *Imperial Washington* (Chicago: Charles H. Kerr, 1922), 120; Richard Drake, *The Education of an Anti-imperialist: Robert La Follette and U.S. Expansion* (Madison, WI: University of Wisconsin Press, 2013). Anti-imperialism in this period was often marred by racism. Tyrrell and Sexton, *Empire's Twin*, 1–3; *U.S. Congressional Record*, Senate, 55th Cong., 3d Sess., "Pacific Cable System," February 10, 1899, 1686, https://www.govinfo.gov/content/pkg/GPO-CRECB-1899-pt2-v32/pdf/GPO-CRECB-1899-pt2-v32-14-1.pdf; L. S. Howeth, *History of Communications-Electronics in the United States Navy* (Washington, DC: Government Printing Office, 1963).

7. P. M. Kennedy, "Imperial Cable Communications and Strategy, 1870–1914," *English Historical Review* 341 (October 1971): 739, 741; Daniel R. Headrick, *The Invisible Weapon: Telecommunications and International Politics 1851–1945* (New York: Oxford University Press, 1991), 39.

8. Hugill, *Global Communications*, 45; Ludwell Denny, *America Conquers Britain: A Record of Economic War* (New York: Knopf, 1930), 369.
9. Godfrey Isaacs, quoted in Hugill, *Global Communications*, 99.
10. Daqing Yang, *Technology of Empire: Telecommunications and Japanese Expansion in Asia, 1883–1945* (Cambridge, MA: Harvard University Press, 2011); Headrick, *The Invisible Weapon*, 53–55; 64–65; 102–105; Headrick, *The Invisible Weapon*, 105–110.
11. Jonathan Reed Winkler, *Nexus: Strategic Communications and American Security in World War One* (Cambridge, MA: Harvard University Press, 2008), 278. The next several paragraphs draw on Dan Schiller, "Geopolitical-Economic Conflict and Network Infrastructures," *Chinese Journal of Communication* 4, no. 1 (March 2011): 90–107.
12. Hugh G. J. Aitken, *The Continuous Wave: Technology and American Radio, 1900–1932* (Princeton, NJ: Princeton University Press, 1985), 432; *Annual Report of the Directors of Radio Corporation of America to the Stockholders for the Year Ended December 31, 1923* (New York: 1924), 3; Hugill, *Global Communications*, 100; *RCA Annual Report 1923*, 3; *RCA Annual Report 1923*, 4; Hugh G. J. Aitken, *The Continuous Wave: Technology and American Radio, 1900–1932* (Princeton, NJ: Princeton University Press, 1985), 481.
13. *Radio Corporation of America Annual Report for the Year 1930* (New York: 1931), 14–17.
14. Aitken, *Continuous Wave*, 465.
15. Susan J. Douglas, *Inventing American Broadcasting 1899–1922* (Baltimore: Johns Hopkins University Press, 1987), 292–322; James G. Harboard, "Is the Radio Corporation's Patent Control against Public Interest? Con," *The Congressional Digest*, 118–119; Winkler, Nexus: 260, 265; Aitken, *Continuous Wave*, 486–513.
16. Hugill, *Global Communications*, 125. For Latin America, see James Schwoch, *The American Radio Industry and Its Latin American Activities, 1900–1939* (Urbana, IL: University of Illinois Press, 1990); Hugill, *Global Communications*, 107.
17. *Annual Report of the Directors to the Stockholders 1922, International Telephone and Telegraph Corporation* (New York: 1923), 5–6.
18. *Annual Report of the Directors to the Stockholders 1922, International Telephone and Telegraph Corporation*, 5; *Annual Report of the Directors to the Stockholders 1924, International Telephone and Telegraph Corporation* (New York: 1925), 5. ITT then relied on US government authorities to forestall Spain's attempts to expropriate its telephone concession there. Douglas J. Little, "Twenty Years of Turmoil: ITT, the State Department, and Spain, 1924–1944," *Business History Review* 53 (Winter 1979): 449–472.
19. *Annual Report of the Directors to the Stockholders 1925, International Telephone and Telegraph Corporation* (New York: 1926), 9; "Buys Plants to Aid World Phone Plan," *New York Times*, August 15, 1925, 14; *Annual Report of the Directors to the Stockholders 1928, International Telephone and Telegraph Corporation* (New York: 1929), 5; *Annual Report of the Directors to the Stockholders 1929, International Telephone and Telegraph Corporation* (New York: 1930), 9–11.
20. "The Foreign Business of the Western Electric Company," Western Electric Company—Foreign Business—Charles G. DuBois—August 1923, Box 50, AT&T

Archives and History Center, Warren, New Jersey (hereafter AT&T-NJ); "The Foreign Business of the Western Electric Company," Western Electric Company—Foreign Business—Charles G. DuBois—August 1923, 7, Box 50, ATT-NJ; "The Foreign Business of the Western Electric Company," Western Electric Company—Foreign Business—Charles G. DuBois—August 1923, 10–11, Box 50, ATT-NJ.

21. Nominal because the figure did not reflect the appreciation of its International Western Electric properties. Accounting for this appreciation reduced AT&T's profit to a still considerable $10 million. Letter of July 8, 1925, from Walter S. Gifford, President of AT&T, to H. B. Thayer, past President of AT&T, Sale of International Western Electric Company—1925, Box 50, ATT-NJ.

22. Letter of W. S. Gifford to A. E. Berry, President, Chesapeake and Potomac Telephone Company, August 19, 1925, Sale of International Western Electric Company—1925, Box 50, ATT-NJ.

23. "The Foreign Business of the Western Electric Company," Western Electric Company—Foreign Business—Charles G. DuBois—August 1923, ATT-NJ Box 50, 2. Between 1921 and 1925, AT&T had published for its own use studies of five South American telephone and telegraph industries: Argentina, Colombia, Brazil, Chile, and Uruguay. Baur, "Incommunicado"; "The Foreign Business of the Western Electric Company," Western Electric Company—Foreign Business—Charles G. DuBois—August 1923, 4, Box 50, ATT-NJ; "The Foreign Business of the Western Electric Company," Western Electric Company—Foreign Business—Charles G. DuBois—August 1923, 4–5, Box 50, ATT-NJ.

24. H. B. Thayer to W. S. Gifford, July 10, 1925, Sale of International Western Electric Company—1925, Box 50, ATT-NJ.

25. H. B. Thayer to W. S. Gifford, July 10, 1925, Sale of International Western Electric Company—1925. Box 50, ATT-NJ.

26. In Hugill, *Global Communications*, 132; G. Stanley Shoup, "The Control of International Cable and Radio Communications," *The Congressional Digest* 9, no. 4 (April 1930): 108.

27. Quoted in Ludwell Denny, *America Conquers Britain: A Record of Economic War* (New York: Alfred A. Knopf, 1930), 401–402; Owen D. Young, "Should Communications Services Be Permitted to Consolidate? Pro," *Congressional Digest* 9, no. 4 (April 1930): 114; "Radio Merger Held Forbidden by Law," *New York Times*, April 10, 1929, 22; Young, "Should Communications Services Be Permitted to Consolidate? Pro," 114.

28. Testimony of Sosthenes Behn, Chairman of ITT, in 71st Cong., Senate, 2d Sess. *Hearings before the Committee on Interstate Commerce, On S.6 A Bill to Provide for the Regulation of the Transmission of Intelligence by Wire or Wireless, Commission on Communications, 2 Volumes, Volume 1, Part 9, 7 June 1929 and Volume 2, 26 February 1930* (Washington, DC: Government Printing Office, 1929), 1930; Hugill, *Global Communications*, 49.

29. Elizabeth Borgwardt, *A New Deal for the World: American's Vision for Human Rights* (Cambridge, MA: The Belknap Press of Harvard University Press, 2005), 14–45. The

Atlantic Charter of August 1941 was a major instance. Borgwardt, *New Deal for the World*, 29–30.
30. Mark R. Wilson, *Destructive Creation: American Business and the Winning of World War II* (Philadelphia: University of Pennsylvania Press, 2016), 48–189; Daniel Immerwahr, *How to Hide an Empire: A History of the Greater United States* (New York: Farrar, Straus, Giroux, 2019), 219, 216. In general, see also, Alfred W. McCoy, *In the Shadows of the American Century* (Chicago: Haymarket Books, 2017).
31. 80th Cong., Senate, 1st Sess., January 3–December 19, 1947, *Miscellaneous Reports V. 1, Report No. 19, Investigation of International Communications by Wire and Radio, 7 February 1947* (Washington, DC: Government Printing Office, 1947), 4; 79th Cong., Senate, 2d Sess., *Miscellaneous Reports Volume 4, 14 January–2 August 1946, Report No. 1907, Investigation of International Communications by Wire and Radio, 31 July 1946* (Washington, DC: Government Printing Office, 1946), 2.
32. 79th Cong, Senate, 2d Sess., January 14–August 2, 1946, *Miscellaneous Reports, Report No. 1907, Investigation of International Communications by Wire and Radio, 31 July 1946* (Washington, DC: Government Printing Office, 1946), 3–4; 80th Cong., Senate, 1st Sess., January 3–December 19, 1947, *Miscellaneous Reports Volume 1, Report No. 19, 7 February 1947, Investigation of International Communications by Wire and Radio* (Washington, DC: Government Printing Office, 1947), 6; 79th Cong., Senate, 1st Sess., Committee on Interstate Commerce, *Hearings Pursuant to S. Resolution 187, 78th Cong., Extended by S. Resolution 24, 79th Cong., Directing Study of International Communications by Wire and Radio, 19 March–3 April 1945, Study of International Communications*, 3, 492–512; George Raynor Thompson and Dixie R. Harris, *The Signals Corps: The Outcome* (Washington, DC: Government Printing Office, 1991), 622; Paul A. Porter, Chairman, FCC, "Memorandum to the President, Subject: International Communications Merger," April 19, 1945, in WHCF, Confidential File Box 17, Harry S. Truman Presidential Library and Museum, Independence, Missouri (hereafter Truman Presidential Library); 79th Cong., Senate, 2d Sess., *Miscellaneous Reports Volume 4, 14 January–2 August 1946, Report No. 1907, Investigation of International Communications by Wire and Radio, 31 July 1946* (Washington, DC: Government Printing Office, 1946), 4.
33. Immerwahr, *How to Hide an Empire*, 230–234; 80th Cong., Senate, 1st Sess., January 3–December 19, 1947, *Miscellaneous Reports V. 1, Report No. 19, Investigation of International Communications by Wire and Radio, 7 February 1947* (Washington, DC: Government Printing Office, 1947), 5; Wilson, *Destructive Creation*, 241–285.
34. 79th Cong., Senate, 2d Sess., *Miscellaneous Reports, Volume 4, 14 January–2 August 1946, Report No. 1907, Investigation of International Communications by Wire and Radio, 31 July 1946* (Washington, DC: Government Printing Office, 1946), 2; Jill Hills, *Telecommunications and Empire: Power Relations within the Global Telecommunications Empire* (Urbana, IL: University of Illinois Press, 2007), 35; It was rejected by the President's Communication Policy Board, a group Truman convened that reported early in 1951. *Telecommunications—A Program for Progress, A Report by the President's Communications Policy Board* (Washington, DC: Government Printing Office, February 1951), 22; 80th Cong., Senate, 1st

Sess., January 3–December 19, 1947, *Miscellaneous Reports, V. 1, Report No. 19, Investigation of International Communications by Wire and Radio, 7 February 1947* (Washington, DC: Government Printing Office, 1947), 5, 6. Also, Thompson and Harris, *The Signals Corps*, 623.

35. William H. Stringer, "From Nation to Nation," *Christian Science Monitor*, March 16, 1946, 2; Treaties and Other International Acts Series 1518, Telecommunications Agreement between the Government of the United States of America and Certain Governments of the British Commonwealth, Signed at Bermuda December 4, 1945, https://www.google.com/books/edition/The_Department_of_State_Bulletin/wh3FmeNtHJ8C?hl=en&gbpv=1&dq=Treaties+and+Other+International+Acts+Series+1518,+Telecommunications+Agreement+Between+the+Government+of+the+United+States+of+America+and+Certain+Governments+of+the+British+Commonwealth,+Signed+at+Bermuda+December+4,+1945&pg=PA1194&printsec=frontcover.
36. Hills, *Telecommunications and Empire*, 29–63.
37. George A. Codding, Jr., *The International Telecommunication Union* (Leiden: E. J. Brill, 1952), 362–363, 417–419; George A. Codding, Jr., and Anthony M. Rutkowski, *The International Telecommunication Union in a Changing World* (Dedham, MA: Artech House, 1982), 11, 22, 39, 62.
38. Telecommunications—A Program for Progress, A Report by the President's Communications Policy Board, February 1951; Haraden Pratt, Telecommunications Advisor to the President, Memo "Immediate Release," August 28, 1952, File 2651-C, Official File Box 1708, Truman Presidential Library (quote).
39. Jonathan Haslam, *The Spectre of War: International Communism and the Origins of World War II* (Princeton, NJ: Princeton University Press, 2021), 258–325; 336–352; Ashby, "Shattered Dreams," 28–63.
40. Christopher Bayly and Tim Harper, *Forgotten Armies: The Fall of British Asia, 1941–1945* (Cambridge, MA: Belknap Press, 2005); Sugata Bose, *His Majesty's Opponent: Subhas Chandra Bose and India's Struggle against Empire* (Cambridge, MA: Belknap Press, 2011); Craig L. Symonds, *World War II at Sea: A Global History* (New York: Oxford University Press, 2018), 267–399. With undiminished hauteur, Britain, France, and the Netherlands maneuvered savagely after the war to reestablish their prewar colonial possessions, but revolutionary nationalism overcame them. Christopher Bayly and Tim Harper, *Forgotten Wars: Freedom and Revolution in Southeast Asia* (Cambridge, MA: Belknap Press, 2007); Odd Arne Westad, *The Cold War: A World History* (New York: Basic Books, 2017), 126–127. China's casualties were nearly on a par with those of the Soviets, but these losses stemmed not only from Japanese military aggression, but also from China's civil war. Rana Mitter, *Forgotten Ally: China's World War II, 1937–1945* (New York: Houghton Mifflin Harcourt, 2013); Michael Sherry, *Preparing for the Next War* (New Haven, CT: Yale University Press, 1977), 198–205.
41. Christopher D. O'Sullivan, *Sumner Welles, Postwar Planning, and the Quest for a New World Order, 1937–1943* (New York: Columbia University Press, 2007); William Roger Louis, *Imperialism at Bay: The United States and the Decolonization*

of the British Empire 1941–1945 (New York: Oxford University Press, 1978); Sherry, *Preparing for the Next War.*

42. Ashby, "Shattered Dreams," 28–63, especially, 125–172; Penny M. von Eschen, *Race against Empire: Black Americans and Anticolonialism, 1937–1957* (Ithaca, NY: Cornell University Press, 1997), 96–107.
43. Borgwardt, *A New Deal for the World*, quotes on 186, 187 (Rayford Logan); see also, von Eschen, *Race against Empire*, 69–95; U.S. State Department Office of the Historian, "Decolonization of Asia and Africa, 1945–1960," www.history.state.gov.
44. Ashby, "Shattered Dreams," 28–63, 125–172; Undersecretary of State Sumner Welles used an address at Arlington National Cemetery in May 1942 to characterize World War II as a struggle against imperialism—a "people's war" for liberation throughout the colonial world. This address was broadcast in English and other languages over All India Radio and transcribed in more than 500 newspapers throughout the Raj. O'Sullivan, *Sumner Welles*, 142–143; and, for the general picture, 137–179. President Roosevelt himself carefully framed his approach "as anticolonial rather than in the broader language of anti-imperialism." Tyrrell and Sexton, *Empire's Twin*, 12. But Roosevelt would brook no grant of independence to Puerto Rico; Ashby, "Shattered Dreams," 125–172; von Eschen, *Race against Empire*, 22–68; W. E. B. Dubois, *Color and Democracy: Colonies and Peace* (New York: Harcourt, Brace and Company, 1945), v.
45. Westad, *The Cold War*, 96–97; Quoted in Sherry, *Preparing for the Next War*, 181; Westad, *The Cold War*, 132.
46. Adom Getachew, *Worldmaking after Empire: The Rise and Fall of Self-Determination* (Princeton, NJ: Princeton University Press, 2019), especially 142–175; see also, Vijay Prashad, *The Darker Nations: The Third World* (New York: New Press, 2006).
47. Melvyn P. Leffler, *A Preponderance of Power: National Security, the Truman Administration, and the Cold War* (Stanford, CA: Stanford University Press, 1992), 357; Laura A. Belmonte, "Promoting American Anti-imperialism in the Early Cold War, in Tyrrell and Sexton, *Empire's Twin*, 187–201; Leffler, *A Preponderance of Power*, 11 (quote).
48. Leo Panitch and Sam Gindin, *The Making of Global Capitalism: The Political Economy of American Empire* (London: Verso, 2012), 67–87; Eric Helleiner, *Forgotten Foundations of Bretton Woods: International Development and the Making of the Postwar Order* (Ithaca, NY: Cornell University Press, 2014), 1–28, especially 12; Christy Thornton, *Revolution in Development: Mexico and the Governance of the Global Economy* (Berkeley, CA: University of California Press, 2021), 39–98; Panitch and Gindin, *The Making of Global Capitalism*, 93–94; Victor Bulmer-Thomas, *Empire in Retreat: The Past, Present, and Future of the United States* (New Haven, CT: Yale University Press, 2018), 141–145; Panitch and Gindin, *The Making of Global Capitalism*, 89–101; Leffler, *A Preponderance of Power*, 157–165, 182–219; Douglas T. Stuart, *Creating the National Security State: A History of the Law that Transformed America* (Princeton, NJ: Princeton University Press, 2008); Leffler, *A Preponderance of Power*, 175–179; Leffler, *A Preponderance of Power*, 208–218; Carolyn Eisenberg, "U.S. Policy in Post-War Germany: The Conservative Restoration," *Science and*

Society 45, no. 1 (Spring 1982): 24–38; Magdoff, *Imperialism*, 179; von Eschen, *Race against Empire*, 107 (quoting Senator Arthur Vandenberg).

49. Robert E. Herzstein, *Henry R. Luce, Time, and the American Crusade in Asia* (Cambridge, UK: Cambridge University Press, 2005), 74, 79–111, 120; O'Sullivan, *Sumner Welles*, 141, 166 (quote).

50. Caroline Elkins, *Legacy of Violence: A History of the British Empire* (New York: Alfred A. Knopf, 2022), 12–18; Magdoff, *Imperialism*, 117–147; Westad, *The Cold War*, 57; Immerwahr, *How to Hide an Empire*, 216, 355–371 ("small points"); Borgwardt, *A New Deal for the World*, 120. Britain had also tended to favor "informal mechanisms," but it was repeatedly willing to annex territories and establish formal political control. Elkins, *Legacy of Violence*, 9.

51. Borgwardt, *A New Deal for the World*, 119. Frances Stonor Saunders, *The Cultural Cold War: The CIA and the World of Arts and Letters* (New York: New Press, 2001); Justin Hart, *Empire of Ideas: The Origins of Public Diplomacy and the Transformation of U.S. Foreign Policy* (New York: Oxford University Press, 2013); Tsuyoshi Hasegawa, *Racing the Enemy: Stalin, Truman, and the Surrender of Japan* (Cambridge, MA: Belknap Press, 2006); Matthew M. Aid, *The Secret Sentry: The Untold History of the National Security Agency* (New York: Bloomsbury Press, 2009); Jeffrey T. Richelson and Desmond Ball, *The Ties that Bind: Intelligence Cooperation between the UKUSA Countries* (Boston: Allen & Unwin, 1985).

52. John Gimbel, *Science, Technology and Reparations: Exploitation and Plunder in Postwar Germany* (Stanford: Stanford University Press, 1999). For the US and British seizure of the archive of the German Foreign Ministry, Astrid M. Eckert, *The Struggle for the Files: The Western Allies and the Return of German Archives after the Second World War* (Cambridge: Cambridge University Press, 2012), 13–98; John Krige, *American Hegemony and the Postwar Reconstruction of Science in Europe* (Cambridge, MA: MIT Press, 2006), 15–56, 57–73; Simon Reid-Henry, *Empire of Democracy: The Remaking of the West since the Cold War* (New York: Simon & Schuster, 2019), 72.

53. Magdoff, *Imperialism*, 170.

54. Bulmer-Thomas, *Empire in Retreat*, 9; Magdoff, *Imperialism*, 176; Magdoff, *Imperialism*, 133–134.

55. John B. Hench, *Books as Weapons: Propaganda, Publishing, and the Battle for Global Markets in the Era of World War II* (Ithaca, NY: Cornell University Press, 2010), 257; Thomas H. Guback, *The International Film Industry* (Bloomington, IN: Indiana University Press, 1969), 16.

56. Herbert I. Schiller, *Communications and Cultural Domination* (White Plains, NY: International Arts & Sciences Press, 1976), 24–45; Diana Lemberg, *Barriers Down: How American Power and Free-Flow Policies Shaped Global Media* (New York: Columbia University Press, 2021), 20–79; Quoted in Morris L. Ernst, *The First Freedom* (New York: The Macmillan Company, 1946), 87.

57. Sherry, *Preparing for the Next War*, 181; Paquette, *The European Seaborne Empires*, 209–213; Inderjeet Parmar, *Foundations of the American Century: The Ford, Carnegie, and Rockefeller Foundations in the Rise of American Power* (New York: Columbia University Press, 2015).

58. Daniel J. Sargent, *A Superpower Transformed: The Remaking of American Foreign Relations in the 1970s* (New York: Oxford University Press, 2015), 33, 23.
59. Hugill, *Global Communications*, 228–230.
60. Lisa Parks, "Global Networking and the Contrapuntal Mode: The Project Mercury Earth Station in Zanzibar, 1959–64," *ZMK* 11 (2020): 46, 47 (quote).
61. David J. Whalen, The Rise and Fall of Comsat (New York: Palgrave Macmillan, 2014), 75–77.
62. Whalen, *The Rise and Fall of Comsat*, 20. Kennedy said, "I now invite all nations—including the Soviet Union—to join with us in developing a weather prediction program, in a new communications satellite program and in preparation for probing the distant planets of Mars and Venus, probes which may someday unlock the deepest secrets of the universe." John F. Kennedy, Annual Message to the Congress on the State of the Union, January 30, 1961, http://www.presidency.ucsb.edu/ws/?pid=8045; Michael E. Kinsley, *Outer Space and Inner Sanctums: Government, Business and Satellite Communication* (New York: Wiley, 1976); Herbert I. Schiller, *Mass Communications and American Empire* (New York: Augustus M. Kelly, 1969); Schiller, *Mass Communications and American Empire*, 135.
63. Hills, *Telecommunications and Empire*, 75, 69.
64. Hills, *Telecommunications and Empire*, 68; Quoted in Hills, *Telecommunications and Empire*, 70; Hills, *Telecommunications and Empire*, 70, 73; Hills, *Telecommunications and Empire*, 72.
65. Foreign Relations of the United States [FRUS], 1964–1968, vol. 34, Energy Diplomacy and Global Issues, Document 93, Memorandum from the President's Special Assistant for Telecommunications (James O'Connell) to President Johnson, February 17, 1967, 174, National Security File, Subject File, Communications (National Communications System, COMSAT, etc.), vol. 3 (2 of 3), Box 6, Confidential, Lyndon Baines Johnson Presidential Library and Museum, Austin, Texas (hereafter Johnson Presidential Library).
66. Hills, *Telecommunications and Empire*, 71; Schiller, *Mass Communications and American Empire*, 70–73, 127–146.
67. Whalen, *The Rise and Fall of Comsat*, 86; FRUS, 1964–1968, vol. 34, Energy Diplomacy and Global Issues, Document 93, Memorandum from the President's Special Assistant for Telecommunications (James O'Connell) to President Johnson, February 17, 1967, 173–174, National Security File, Subject File, Communications (National Communications System, COMSAT, etc.), vol. 3 [2 of 3], Box 6, Confidential, Johnson Presidential Library.
68. Whalen, *The Rise and Fall of Comsat*, 82; Heather E. Hudson, *Communication Satellites: Their Development and Impact* (New York: Free Press, 1990), 32.
69. Schiller, *Mass Communications and American Empire*, 135. By 1983, Intelsat claimed 109 member nations. 98th Cong, Senate, 1st Sess., Committee on Foreign Relations. S. Prt. 98–94, *International Telecommunications and Information Policy: Selected Issues for the 1980s, A Report Prepared by the Congressional Research Service, Library of Congress, by Jane Bortnick* (Washington, DC: Government Printing Office, 1983),

9; Katherine Johnsen, "France Backs UN Intelsat Control," *Aviation Week & Space Technology*, February 13, 1967, 26–27.
70. Frank Cain, *Economic Statecraft during the Cold War: European Responses to the U.S. Trade Embargo* (London: Routledge: 2007); 90th Cong., House of Representatives, 1st Sess., Committee on Appropriations, Statement of Honorable James D. O'Connell, Office of Telecommunications Management, Executive Office of the President, March 7, 1967, 16; FRUS, 1964–1968, vol. 34, Energy Diplomacy and Global Issues, Document 93, Memorandum from the President's Special Assistant for Telecommunications (James O'Connell) to President Johnson, February 17, 1967, 174, National Security File, Subject File, Communications (National Communications System, COMSAT, etc.), vol. 3 [2 of 3], Box 6. Confidential, Johnson Presidential Library; Foreign Relations of the United States, 1964–1968, vol. 34, Energy Diplomacy and Global Issues, Document 94, Letter from the President's Special Assistant for Telecommunications (James O'Connell) to Secretary of State Rusk, Washington, February 21, 1967, 176, National Archives and Records Administration, RG 59, Records of the Department of State, Central Files, 1967–1969, TEL 6, Confidential; Jeff Hecht, *City of Light: The Story of Fiber Optics* (New York: Oxford University Press, 1999), 204.
71. Pike, "Space is Big Business." Between the early 1970s and the late 1980s, satellites also carried most of the world's cross-border telephone communications. Hugill, *Global Communications*, 237; Hudson, *Communication Satellites*, 202–205.
72. Christy Thornton, *Revolution in Development: Mexico and the Governance of the Global Economy* (Berkeley, CA: University of California Press, 2021), 24.
73. Acknowledging L. S. Stavrianos, *Global Rift: The Third World Comes of Age* (New York: William Morrow, 1981); Victoria de Grazia, *Irresistible Empire: America's Advance through 20th-century Europe* (Cambridge, MA: Belknap Press, 2005); "Ghana Opens TV Service," *New York Times*, August 2, 1965, https://www.nytimes.com/1965/08/01/archives/ghana-opens-tv-service.html.
74. Report of the Panel on Large Scale Computing in Science and Engineering, Peter D. Lax, Chairman, under the Sponsorship of Department of Defense and National Science Foundation, December 26, 1982, 2, 3; The competition to develop the world's fastest and most powerful supercomputer continues. In 2017, China possessed 202 of the world's 500 fastest computers, the U.S., 143—its lowest number in twenty-five years. Richard Waters, "IBM Builds World's Most Powerful Supercomputer to Crack AI," *Financial Times*, June 8, 2018. In 2021, China had 173, the U.S., 149. "Top 500 List Statistics," https://www.top500.org/statistics/list/.
75. Whalen, *The Rise and Fall of Comsat*, 76–79, 86; Schiller, *Mass Communications and American Empire*, 133–140.
76. Thornton, *Revolution in Development*, 18; A. W. Singham and Tran Van Dinh, eds., *From Bandung to Columbo: Conferences of the Non-aligned Countries, 1955–75* (New York: Third Press Review Books, 1976); The NWICO was formalized in 1975–1976. UNESCO, *A Documentary History of a New World Information and Communication Order Seen as an Evolving and Continuous Process 1975–1986*, Documents in Communication and Society 19 (Paris: Unesco, 1986), x. Kaarle

Nordenstreng with Lauri Hannikainen trace the diplomatic history and professional ramifications of one key conflict in *The Mass Media Declaration of UNESCO* (Norwood, NJ: Ablex, 1984). A genuine social history of the movement for a New World information and communication order has not yet been written. Two suggestive entry-points are Lisa Parks, "Global Networking and the Contrapuntal Mode: The Project Mercury Earth Station in Zanzibar, 1959-64," *ZMK* 11 (2020): 41–57; and Lemberg, *Barriers Down*, 52–63; For direct broadcast satellites, Kaarle Nordenstreng and Herbert I. Schiller, eds., *National Sovereignty and International Communication: A Reader* (Norwood, NJ: Ablex, 1979), 115–165; and Lemberg, *Barriers Down*, 130–151; for computer networks, Herbert I. Schiller, *Who Knows: Information in the Age of the Fortune 500* (Norwood, NJ: Ablex, 1981), 40–42, 99–114, 135–152.

77. International Data Group, "Computer Census," in W. V. Thomas, "America's Information Boom," *CQ Researcher* (1978): 6; Quoted in 96th Cong., House of Representatives, 2d Sess., Committee on Government Operations, House Report No. 96-15345, *International Information Flow: Forging A New Framework, December 11, 1980* (Washington, DC: Government Printing Office), 31; 98th Cong., Senate, 1st Sess., Committee on Foreign Relations, S. Print 98-94, *International Telecommunications and Information Policy: Selected Issues for the 1980s, A Report Prepared by the Congressional Research Service, Library of Congress, by Jane Bortnick* (Washington, DC: Government Printing Office, 1983), 30; Eileen Mahoney, "The Intergovernmental Bureau for Informatics: An International Organization within the Changing World Political Economy," in eds. Vincent Mosco and Janet Wasko, *The Political Economy of Information* (Madison, WI: University of Wisconsin Press, 1988), 297–315; V. A. Vinogradov, L. S. Kiouzadjan, T. V. Andrianova, S. K. Vilenskaya, G. B. Kossov, A. M. Kul'kin, R. R. Mdivani, A. I. Rakitov, V. R. Khisamutdinov, and L. V. Shemberko, "Toward an International Data Network," in eds. George Gerbner and Marsha Siefert, *World Communications: A Handbook* (New York: Longman, 1984), 224.

78. William H. Read, "Communications Policy: An Agenda," in 95th Cong., Senate, 1st Sess., Senate Committee on Foreign Relations, Subcommittee on International Operations, *Hearings on International Communications and Information, June 8, 9, 10, 1977* (Washington, DC: Government Printing Office, 1977), 43; United Nations General Assembly, Thirtieth Session, Resolution 3379, "Elimination of All Forms of Racial Discrimination," November 10, 1975, https://www.un.org/unispal/document/auto-insert-181963/; Lemberg, *Barriers Down*, 189; National Telecommunications and Information Administration, "Long-range Goals in International Telecommunications and Information: An Outline for U.S. Policy," 98th Cong, Senate, 1st Sess., Print 98-22, March 11, 1983, 39; Abbott Washburn, "Discussion on Orion-type Systems and on U.S/I.T.U. Relationship—Undersecretary Schneider and Abbott Washburn, 8/10/83, State Department." Washburn Papers, Box 215, Folder "Orion Challenge (1983) (3)," 2, *Dwight David* Eisenhower Presidential Library, Museum, and Boyhood Home, Abilene, Kansas (hereafter Eisenhower Presidential Library).

79. Eileen Marie Mahoney, "Negotiating New Information Technology and National Development: The Role of the Intergovernmental Bureau for Informatics" (Ph.D. diss., Temple University, 1987).
80. Dan Schiller, *Telematics and Government* (Norwood, NJ: Ablex, 1982), 105–149.
81. U.S. Department of Commerce, Office of Business Research and Analysis, *The American Computer Industry in its International Competitive Environment* (Washington, DC: Government Printing Office, 1976), 4; 96th Cong., House of Representatives, 2d Sess., Subcommittee of the Committee on Government Operations, *Hearings on International Data Flow, March 10, 13, 27 and April 21, 1980* (Washington, DC: Government Printing Office, 1980); National Telecommunications and Information Administration, "Long-range Goals," III.
82. National Telecommunications and Information Administration, "Long-range Goals," III; National Telecommunications and Information Administration, "Long-range Goals," 6; National Telecommunications and Information Administration, "Long-range Goals," XI, 5.
83. National Telecommunications and Information Administration, "Long-range Goals," XV, III, 6, XII.
84. Westad, *The Cold War*, 554; Herbert I. Schiller, "Is There a U.S. Information Policy?" in eds. William Preston, Jr., Edward S. Herman, and Herbert I. Schiller, *Hope and Folly: The United States and UNESCO 1945-1985* (Minneapolis: University of Minnesota Press, 1989), 303–308; Sara Schoonmaker, *High-tech Trade Wars: U.S.-Brazilian Conflicts in the Global Economy* (Pittsburgh: University of Pittsburgh Press, 2002), 122–157; Schiller, *Telematics and Government*, 123–135; Schiller, *Who Knows*, 154–164; Dan Schiller, *How to Think about Information* (Urbana, IL: University of Illinois Press, 2007), 45–48; For early assessments, Schiller, *Telematics and Government*, 99–188; National Telecommunications and Information Administration, "Long-range Goals," 5–33, 131–174.
85. Schoonmaker, *High-tech Trade Wars*, 67. Early in 1997, this culminated in the Basic Telecommunications Agreement of the WTO. Schiller, *Digital Capitalism*, 47–49.
86. I draw here on my article, "Intelsat—Latest Object of US Unilateralism?," *Le Monde diplomatique*, February 1985, 14–15.
87. National Telecommunications and Information Administration, "Long-range Goals," 114; Abbott Washburn, "Transocean Systems Separate from Intelsat?," *Satellite Communications*, April 1984; Reginald Stuart, "Intelsat: Time of Uncertainty," *New York Times*, November 10, 1984, D1, D24; James T. Broyhill and Timothy E. Wirth, Letter to President Reagan, April 9, 1984, in U.S. National Committee of the International Institute of Communications, Document Service III (8), April 1984; Gregory C. Staple, "The Assault on Intelsat," *The Nation* December 22, 1984, 665, 679–682.
88. Westad, *The Cold War*, 396.
89. Reginald Stuart, "Reagan Endorses Limited Intelsat Competition," *New York Times*, November 29, 1984, at http://www.nytimes.com/1984/11/29/business/reagan-endorses-limited-intelsat-competition.html.

90. "The USA was the only Western nation to possess launch vehicles, but the conditions they set for launching European satellites were totally unacceptable," said Charles Hanin, then the Belgian minister for science. "They wanted our satellites to be functional exclusively over the European zone, which of course would have prevented Europe from extending its political and cultural influence around the world and from competing with them on the global marketplace." "History of Europe in Space," http://www.esa.int/About_Us/Welcome_to_ESA/ESA_history/The_origins_of_Ariane; "Japan Plans New Launcher, 78 Satellites," *Aviation Week & Space Technology*, August 22, 1983; The Soviet Union also possessed advanced satellites and rockets capable of launching them.

91. Marquis Childs, "Mainland China joins Intelsat," *United Features*, October 1, 1977, https://news.google.com/newspapers?nid=1955&dat=19771001&id=59shAAAAIBAJ&sjid=yaAFAAAAIBAJ&pg=4068,34168&hl=en; Zhang Wenjin, Embassy of the People's Republic of China to Honorable Dr. William J. Schneider, Jr., Undersecretary of State, June 25, 1984, Abbott Washburn Papers Box 218, Folder "Separate Systems 1987 (1)," Eisenhower Presidential Library; Whalen, *The Rise and Fall of Comsat*, 223. The private equity firms were Apollo Management, Madison Dearborne Partners, Apax Partners and Permira Partners. Yuki Noguchi, "Intelsat Agrees to Merger Deal with Panamsat," *Washington Post*, August 29, 2005, http://www.washingtonpost.com/wp-dyn/content/article/2005/08/28/AR2005082801185.html. For a recap of how the private equity investors milked Intelsat, see Steven Pearlstein, "Sweet Deals Buried Intelsat in Debt," *Washington Post*, August 18, 2006, http://www.washingtonpost.com/wp-dyn/content/article/2006/08/17/AR2006081701578.html; Ortenca Aliaj, "David Tepper Joins Throng of Hedge Fund Managers in Intelsat," *Financial Times*, February 18, 2020, https://www.ft.com/content/6815eb5c-527e-11ea-8841-482eed0038b1; www.intelsat.com; Peggy Hollinger, "Intelsat Chief Set for $4m 'Golden Goodbye' after Chapter 11 Recovery," *Financial Times*, January 17, 2022, https://on.ft.com/3GIYDyT.

92. Brian Carpenter, *Network Geeks: How They Built the Internet* (London: Copernicus, 2013), 90; James Gillies and Robert Cailliau, *How the Web Was Born: The Story of the World Wide Web* (New York: Oxford University Press, 2000), 90, 87.

93. James W. Cortada, *IBM: The Rise and Fall and Reinvention of a Global Icon* (Cambridge, MA: MIT Press, 2019), 283–324; Marie Hicks, *Programmed Inequality: How Britain Discarded Women Technologists and Lost Its Edge in Computing* (Cambridge, MA: MIT Press, 2017), 195; Simon Nora and Alain Minc, *The Computerization of Society*, repr. ed. (1978; Cambridge, MA: MIT Press, 1980).

94. U.S. Commerce Department, *The American Computer Industry in Its International Competitive Environment* (Washington, DC: Government Printing Office, 1976), 2.

95. Schiller, *Who Knows*; Herbert I. Schiller and Anita R. Schiller, "Libraries, Public Access to Information, and Commerce," in eds. Vincent Mosco and Janet Wasko, *The Political Economy of Information* (Madison, WI: University of Wisconsin Press, 1988), 146–166; Richard H. Veith, *Multinational Computer Nets* (Lexington, MA: Lexington Books, 1981), 15.

96. J. R. Licklider and Robert W. Taylor, "The Computer as a Communications Device," *Science and Technology*, April 1968, 40, in Robert W. Taylor, "In Memoriam: J. C. R. Licklider 1915–1990," http://memex.org/licklider.pdf.
97. 94th Cong., House of Representatives, 2d Sess., Subcommittee on Communications of the Committee on Interstate and Foreign Commerce, Hearings on Competition in the Telecommunications Industry, Serial 94–129, September 28, 29, 30, 1976, Testimony of Philip M. Walker, Telenet Communications, 493–531 at 493, 503. Also, Ronald A. Frank, "Independents Warn Bell Bill Threatens Their Existence," *ComputerWorld*, October 11, 1976, 26.
98. Richard Thomas DeLamarter, *Big Blue: IBM's Use and Abuse of Power* (New York: Dodd, Mead, 1986), 282–283; Robert E. Jacobson, "Satellite Business Systems and the Concept of the Dispersed Enterprise: An End to National Sovereignty?," *Media, Culture & Society*, July 1, 1979, 235–353; Charles Kalmanak, "A Retrospective View of ATM," *ACM SIGCOMM Computer Communications Review* 32, no. 5 (November 2002): 16.
99. Andrew L. Russell, *Open Standards and the Digital Age: History, Ideology, and Networks* (Cambridge: Cambridge University Press, 2014), 175.
100. Schiller, *Telematics and Government*, 103.
101. "Prospects for an International Packet-switched Data Network," presented by Arthur Corte (MIT), Joseph Markowitz (MIT) and Craig Fields (Harvard), November 14, 1974, abstract in MIT Research Program in Communication Policy: First Annual Report, December 1974, 21, http://files.eric.ed.gov/fulltext/ED109 991.pdf, 6. It is worth recalling that, well into the 1980s, the precursor of the Internet interconnected a small number of networks.
102. Corte, Markowitz, and Fields, "Prospects," 9; Corte, Markowitz, and Fields, "Prospects," 21.
103. Ithiel de Sola Pool, "A Study of a Worldwide Packet-switched Data Communication and Information Retrieval System." Proposal to Office of Telecommunications Policy, 1974, Washburn Papers, Box 124, Folder "Ithiel Pool (2)," Eisenhower Presidential Library.
104. Pool, "A Study of a Worldwide Packet-switched Data Communication and Information Retrieval System."
105. "Memorandum on Various U.S. Government Interests in a Worldwide Data Communication System," Washburn Papers, Box 124, Folder "Ithiel Pool (2)," Eisenhower Presidential Library. In 1966, the US possessed a mere handful of computerized databases, and a mere 20,000 individual listings could be retrieved remotely; by 1976, there were 360 databases with 71 million stored listings; and by 1987, there were 3,369 databases containing over 1.7 billion records, available through 528 online services, which had increased from two million in 1974 to 18 million in 1985. W. V. Thomas, "America's Information Boom," *CQ Researcher*, November 3, 1978, 1; U.S. Department of Commerce, National Telecommunications and Information Administration, *NTIA Telecom 2000: Charting the Course for a New Century*, NTIA Special Publication 88-21 (Washington, DC: Government Printing Office, October 1988), 411, 420; "Memorandum on Various U.S. Government

Interests in a Worldwide Data Communication System," Washburn Papers, Box 124, Folder "Ithiel Pool (2)," Eisenhower Presidential Library.
106. Abbott Washburn, OTP, to John Eger, OTP, "Questions for Dr. Ithiel Pool," April 9, 1974, in Box 124, "Ithiel Pool (1)," Eisenhower Presidential Library.
107. John Eger, OTP, Executive Office of the President, to Ithiel de Sola Pool, May 15, 1974, 2–3, Washburn Papers Box 124, Folder "Ithiel Pool (1)," Eisenhower Presidential Library.
108. Although a denatured process of market commercialization and/or a reified process of democratization may be invoked. Richard A Walker, *Pictures of a Gone City: Tech and the Dark Side of Prosperity in the San Francisco Bay Area* (Oakland, CA: PM Press, 2018), 13; "Internet advocates, popular writers, and the general public have a poor understanding of the Internet's history." Russell, *Open Standards and the Digital Age*, 263. This, despite some variably piercing scholarly accounts, including Janet Abbate, *Inventing the Internet* (Cambridge, MA: MIT Press, 1999); Robert W. McChesney, *Digital Disconnect: How Capitalism Is Turning the Internet against Democracy* (New York: New Press, 2013); Nathan Newman, *Net Loss: Internet Prophets, Private Profits, and the Costs to Community* (University Park, PA: Pennsylvania State University Press, 2002); Jack Goldsmith and Tim Wu, *Who Controls the Internet? Illusions of a Borderless World* (New York: Oxford University Press, 2006); Milton L. Mueller, *Ruling the Root: Internet Governance and the Taming of Cyberspace* (Cambridge, MA: MIT Press), 2002; Laura DeNardis, *The Global War for Internet Governance* (New Haven, CT: Yale University Press, 2014); Sandra Braman, *The Emergent Global Information Policy Regime* (Basingstoke: Palgrave Macmillan, 2004); Shawn M. Powers and Michael Jablonski, *The Real Cyber War: The Political Economy of Internet Freedom* (Urbana, IL: University of Illinois Press, 2015); Shane Greenstein, *How the Internet Became Commercial: Innovation, Privatization, and the Birth of a New Network* (Princeton, NJ: Princeton University Press, 2015).
109. For this characterization, David Clark, *Designing an Internet* (Cambridge, MA: MIT Press, 2018).
110. Schiller, *Digital Capitalism*; Schiller, *Digital Depression*; W. Stuart Leslie, *The Cold War and American Science: The Military-Industrial-Academic Complex at Stanford and MIT* (New York: Columbia University Press, 1992).
111. "Cerf and Kahn simply were unwilling to require all ARPA contractors to abandon their work on TCP and instead introduce the end-to-end protocol defined in [the International Network Working Group] INWG . . . into the Arpanet." Russell, *Open Standards and the Digital Age*, 187; A historian suggests that Kahn in 1975 "had already abandoned hope that a consensus within the INWG would generate meaningful results." Russell, *Open Standards and the Digital Age*, 187; and for the longer history of INWG, 171–193; Russell, *Open Standards and Digital Networks*, 188. In the 1980s, Robert Kahn stated, "The nation that dominates this information processing field will possess the keys to world leadership in the twenty-first century." Kahn's view of computer technology during the 1970s and 1980s was that "the country that stayed out in front of this wave would reap enormous economic and

military benefits. To fall behind would threaten the very health and safety of the nation." Alex Roland with Philip Shiman, *Strategic Computing: DARPA and the Quest for Machine Intelligence, 1983-1993* (Cambridge, MA: MIT Press, 2002), 13 (Kahn quote), 33. However, later in the book, Kahn's conviction that Japan might surpass the US in computers is questioned. Roland with Shiman, *Strategic Computing*, 91-93; Russell, *Open Standards and Digital Networks*, 190.

112. "Cerf's departure for ARPA, combined with Kahn's evident opposition to a consensus international protocol, meant that Cerf would be free to focus all his energies on Arpanet experiments for the military and the development of the TCP protocol that could facilitate communication between three different packet-switched networks being developed by ARPA." Russell, *Open Standards and Digital Networks*, 188-189; Intelpost (a trademark of USPS) was initiated in 1978 to transmit electronic messages internationally between post offices via Comsat, using a modified version of TCP; participants also included Canada, UK, France, West Germany, Argentina, Switzerland, and the Netherlands. B. I. Edelson, H. Raag, and R. Smith, "Intelpost—An Experimental International Electronic Message System, Computer Communications: Increasing Benefits for Society," Jack Salz, ed., *Proceedings of the Fifth International Conference on Computer Communication, Atlanta, Georgia, 27-30 October 1980* (Kingsport, TN: North-Holland Publishing, 1980), 251-256.

113. D. Lewin and T. Johnson, "The Impact of Public Data Networks in Western Europe in the 1980's," Jack Salz, ed., *Computer Communications: Increasing Benefits for Society, Proceedings of the Fifth International Conference on Computer Communication, Atlanta, Georgia, 27-30 October 1980* (Kingsport, TN: North-Holland Publishing, 1980), 23-28; Schiller, *Telematics and Government*, 183; Organization for Economic Cooperation and Development, *The Usage of International Data Networks in Europe* (Paris: OECD, 1979), 224-247; 96th Congress, House of Representatives, 2d Sess., Committee on Government Operations, House Report No. 96-15345, *International Information Flow: Forging A New Framework, December 11, 1980* (Washington, DC: Government Printing Office), 33; 96th Cong., House of Representatives, 2d Sess., Subcommittee of the Committee on Government Operations, *Hearings on International Data Flow. March 10, 13, 27 and April 21, 1980* (Washington, DC: Government Printing Office, 1980), 671-673.

114. U.S. General Accounting Office, *High-performance Computing*, GAO/IMTEC-91-69 (Washington, DC: GAO, 1991), 7; George A. Keyworth, II, "Goodbye, Central: Telecommunications and Computing in the 1990s," *Vital Speeches of the Day* 56, no. 12 (April 1, 1990): 358-361.

115. Gillies and Cailliau, *How the Web Was Born*, 78.

116. Schiller, *Telematics and Government*, 180-181.

117. Robert E. Kahn, "Networks for Advanced Computing," *Scientific American* 257, no. 4 (October 1987): 138; Clifford A. Lynch, "The Growth of Computer Networks: A Status Report," *Bulletin of the American Society for Information Science* 16, no. 5 (June/July 1990): 10; Some of these issues remained alive through the 1990s, as the Internet ascended. Eli Noam and Aine Nishuilleabhain, eds., *Private*

Networks, Public Objectives (Amsterdam: Elsevier, 1996); Kahn, "Networks for Advanced Computing," 141.

118. John S. Quarterman, *The Matrix: Computer Networks and Conferencing Systems Worldwide* (Burlington, MA: Digital Equipment Corporation, 1990); Lynch, "The Growth of Computer Networks," 10; John S. Quarterman and Josiah C. Hoskins, "Notable Computer Networks," *Communications of the ACM* 29, no. 1 (October 1986): 932; Vinton G. Cerf, "Networks," *Scientific American* 265, no. 3 (September 1991): 79.

119. Greenstein, *How the Internet Became Commercial*, 38; Peter W. Huber, *The Geodesic Network: 1987 Report on Competition in the Telephone Industry* (Washington, DC: Government Printing Office, 1987); Schiller, *Digital Depression*, 62.

120. Newman, *Net Loss*, 105; Newman, *Net Loss*, 105–111; Gillies and Cailiau, *How the Web Was Born*, 43 and 82 (quote).

121. U.S. General Accounting Office, "High-Performance Computing," 7–8; Huber, *The Geodesic Network*, 2.6; Schiller, *Telematics and Government*, 54.

122. Schiller, *Telematics and Government*, 101–102; Linda Blake and Jim Lande, *Trends in the U.S. International Telecommunications Industry* (Washington, DC: FCC, 1998), 3; Blake and Lande, *Trends in the U.S. International Telecommunications Industry*, Figure 6.

123. Schiller, *Telematics and Government*, 104; Eli Noam, *Telecommunications in Europe* (New York: Oxford University Press, 1992), 85.

124. Richard Hill, *The New International Telecommunications Regulations and the Internet: A Commentary and Legislative History* (Geneva: Schulthess, 2014), 8; see also, Peter Cowhey and Jonathan D. Aronson, "The ITU in Transition," *Telecommunications Policy* 15, no. 4 (August 1991): 298–310; Noam, *Telecommunications in Europe*, 372–373; Bush Presidential Records, WHORM, Subject File PRO12, 246478 to Cabinet Affairs—Casse, Daniel, Files—Document Number 115134CU and "Telecommunications Report: Continuation of Talks with the European Community and Korea," George Bush, n.d. (but March 9, 1990), WHORM TA 119588 Trade, George H. W. Bush Presidential Library and Museum, College Station, Texas (hereafter George H.W. Bush Presidential Library).

125. Westad, *The Cold War*, 571–572; World Bank, *Information and Communications for Development: Global Trends and Policies* (Washington, DC: World Bank, 2006), 7; For the Mexican case, Diego Osorno, *Carlos Slim: The Power, Money, and Morality of One of the World's Richest Men* (London: Verso, 2019), 35–55, 196–207; World Bank, *Information and Communications for Development*, 7, 17; Verizon, "Global Free Flow of Information on the Internet: Hearing before the Department of Commerce," NTIA Docket No. 100921457–0457–01, Washington, D.C., December 6, 2009, 8; see also, World Bank, Private Participation in Infrastructure Database, https://ppi.worldbank.org/en/ppi; Richard Hill, *The New International Telecommunication Regulations and the Internet* (Geneva: Schulthess, 2013), 8; U.S. Commerce Department, "U.S. Telecommunications in a Global Economy: Competitiveness at a Crossroads: A Report from the Secretary of Commerce to the Congress and the President of the United States as Mandated by the Section 1381 of the Omnibus

Trade and Competitiveness Act of 1988," Washington, D.C., August 1990, 2; Schiller, *Digital Capitalism*, 40–66.
126. Ryan Gallagher and Brian Moltke, "The Wire-tap Rooms: The NSA's Hidden Spy Hubs in Eight U.S. Cities," *The Intercept*, June 25, 2018 https://theintercept.com/2018/06/25/att-internet-nsa-spy-hubs/.
127. Tim Berners-Lee with Mark Fischetti, *Weaving the Web* (New York: HarperCollins, 1999), 57; Laura Noonan, "JP Morgan's Dimon Issues Racism Warning to Staff," *Financial Times*, December 13, 2019, https://www.ft.com/content/af41881c-1df7-11ea-97df-cc63de1d73f4?shareType=nongift.
128. David D. Clark, *Designing an Internet* (Cambridge, MA: MIT Press, 2018), 106; Shinjoung Yeo, *Behind the Search Box: Google and the Global Internet Industry* (Urbana: University of Illinois Press, forthcoming); TeleGeography, *The State of the Network* (Washington, DC: TeleGeography, 2022).
129. Report of the Panel on Large Scale Computing in Science and Engineering, Peter D. Lax, Chairman, under the Sponsorship of the Department of Defense and the National Science Foundation, December 26, 1982, Executive Summary.
130. Vincent Mosco, "Star Wars Is Already Working," *Science as Culture* 1, Supplement 1 (1987): 12–34; Alex Roland with Philip Shiman, *Strategic Computing: DARPA and the Quest for Machine Intelligence, 1983-1993* (Cambridge, MA: MIT Press, 2002), 288, 290 (quote); Roland, *Strategic Computing*, 293; This group was attended by representatives of the Energy Department, NASA, NSF, the Commerce Department, the National Security Agency and the CIA. Roland, *Strategic Computing*, 290.
131. Richard Mandelbaum and Paulette A. Mandelbaum, "The Strategic Future of the Mid-level Networks," in Brian Kahin, ed., *Building Information Infrastructure* (New York: McGraw-Hill, 1992), 59–118; and Larry L. Smarr and Charles E. Catlett, "Life after Internet: Making Room for New Applications," in Kahin, *Building Information Infrastructure*, 144–173; Roland, *Strategic Computing*, 294–299; Cerf, "Networks," 80; Newman, *Net Loss*, 108; Richard Mandelbaum and Paulette A. Mandelbaum, "The Strategic Future of the Mid-level Networks," in Brian Kahin, ed., *Building Information Infrastructure* (New York: McGraw-Hill, 1992), 59–118; and Larry L. Smarr and Charles E. Catlett, "Life after Internet: Making Room for New Applications," in Kahin, *Building Information Infrastructure*, 144–173; Roland, *Strategic Computing*, 294–299; Cerf, "Networks," 80; Newman, *Net Loss*, 108; Greenstein, *How the Internet Became Commercial*, 23, 38, 73, 79–80; Jay P. Kesan and Rajiv C. Shah, "Fool Us Once, Shame on You—Fool Us Twice, Shame on Us: What We Can Learn from the Privatizations of the Internet Backbone Network and the Domain Name System," *Washington University Law Quarterly* 79 (2001): 89–220.
132. Roland, *Strategic Computing*, 295, 314 (quote); The report's very first summary finding was that "A strong domestic high performance computer industry is essential for maintaining U.S. leadership in critical national security areas and in broad sectors of the civilian economy." Executive Office of the President, Office of Science and Technology Policy, "A Research and Development Strategy for High Performance Computing," November 20, 1987, 1; National Research Council, Computer Science and Technology Board, *The National Challenge in Computer*

Science and Technology (Washington, DC: National Academy Press, 1988), 14; Franklin F. Kuo, "Political and Economic Issues for Internetwork Connections," *Computer Communication Review* 5, no. 1 (1975): 32–34.

133. Bilal Chinoy and Hans-Werner Braun, "The National Science Foundation Network," San Diego Supercomputer Center, 1992, Figure 6: 8; see also, Janet Abbate, "Privatizing the Internet: Competing Visions and Chaotic Events, 1987–1995," *IEEE Annals of the History of Computing*, January–March 2010, 14; U.S. General Accounting Office, "High-Performance Computing," *GAO/IMTEC-91-69* (Washington, DC: GAO, 1991), 4; This probably does not include subnetworks, since just between the beginning of 1986 and the end of 1987, these grew from 2,000 to 30,000. "Internet History of the 1980s," http://www.computerhistory.org/internethistory/1980s/; In 1992, the American Electronics Association told an official in the first Bush Administration, "AEA welcomes the Administration's willingness to open foreign telecommunications markets to U.S. suppliers and urges that it attend to the same competitive needs of the computer industry." It specified that, "just as packet-by-packet switching in telecommunications was decontrolled" at a recent high level meeting between the US and its Coordinating Committee for Multilateral Export Controls (COCOM) allies, "so too should packet-by-packet switching for computers be decontrolled. This should take effect in the same timeframe as the decontrol for telecommunications." Fax, Greg Garcia to Rich Barth, n.d., with copy of letter from William K. Krist, Senior VP for International Trade Affairs, American Electronics Assn Joan McEntee, Acting Under Secretary for Export Administration, Bureau of Export Administration, U.S. Department of Commerce, June 19, 1992, George H. W. Bush Presidential Library. For Cocom, see Frank Cain, *Economic Statecraft During the Cold War: European Responses to the U.S. Trade Embargo* (New York: Routledge: 2006); Cerf, "Networks," 80; Kimberly C. Claffy, George C. Polyzos, and Hans Werner Braun, *Tracking Long-term Growth of the NSFNET* (San Diego: San Diego Supercomputer Center, 1993), Figure 12, 13.

134. Milton L. Mueller, *Ruling the Root: Internet Governance and the Taming of Cyberspace* (Cambridge, MA: MIT Press, 2002), 90–91; Mueller, *Ruling the Root*, 92; Mueller, *Ruling the Root*, 76, 93; Mueller, *Ruling the Root*, 99; Mueller, *Ruling the Root*, 94–95; Internet Society, Board Meeting No. 1—Minutes, June 15, 1992, Kobe Japan, http://www.internetsociety.org/who-we-are/board-trustees/meetings/1/minutes.

135. I draw here on Mueller, *Ruling the Root*, 90–95.

136. Kesan and Shah, "Fool Us Once, Shame on You," 91–217; Schiller, *Digital Capitalism*, 70, 87–88; Matthew Crain, *Profit Over Privacy: How Surveillance Advertising Conquered the Internet* (Minneapolis: University of Minnesota Press, 2021), especially 41–73 and 93–134.

137. Meghan Grosse, "Governing the Commercial Internet: Multistakeholder Influences on Clinton Era Governance of the Global Internet" (Ph.D. diss., University of Illinois at Urbana-Champaign, 2018), 144–192; Jack Goldsmith and Tim Wu, *Who Controls the Internet? Illusions of a Borderless World* (New York: Oxford University Press, 2006), 40–46.

138. Chris Forman, "The Corporate Digital Divide: Determinants of Internet Adoption," *Management Science* 51, no. 4 (April 2005): 641–654.
139. U.S. Department of Commerce, National Telecommunications and Information Administration, "Falling through the Net: A Survey of the 'Have Nots' in Rural and Urban America," July 1995, https://www.ntia.doc.gov/ntiahome/fallingthru.html; U.S. Commerce Department NTIA, "Falling through the Net: Defining the Digital Divide," July 8, 1999, https://www.ntia.doc.gov/report/1999/falling-through-net-defining-digital-divide.
140. Westad. *The Cold War*, 532; Eric Hobsbawm, *The Age of Extremes: A History of the World, 1914–1991* (New York: Pantheon, 1995); Simon Reid-Henry, *Empire of Democracy: The Remaking of the West since the Cold War* (New York: Simon & Schuster, 2019), 237–284; Westad, *The Cold War*, 556.
141. Richard J. Barnet and Ronald E. Muller, *Global Reach: The Power of the Multinational Corporations* (New York: Simon & Schuster, 1974), 27–28; Magdoff, *Imperialism*,168, also 118, 174. Hobsbawm attended to submarine telegraphs in his 1976 account of the establishment of a more cohesive international market during the mid-nineteenth century. Eric Hobsbawm, *The Age of Capital* (New York: Charles Scribners, 1976), 58–60; One historian observes that "businesses began using telecommunications networks long before the wide availability of the Internet," implementing systems "worth trillions of dollars in prior investments." James W. Cortada, "New Wine in Old and New Bottles: Patterns and Effects of the Internet on Companies," in eds. William Aspray and Paul E. Ceruzzi, *The Internet and American Business* (Cambridge, MA: MIT Press, 2008), 415, 417.
142. John Bellamy Foster, Robert W. McChesney, and Jamil Jonna, "The Global Reserve Army of Labor and the New *Imperialism*," *Monthly Review* 63, no. 6 (November 2011): 21; Schiller, *Digital Depression*, 35; Suwandi, *Value Chains* 21, citing United Nations Commission on Trade and Development, *World Investment Report: Non-Equity Modes of International Production and Development* (Geneva: United Nations, 2011), 131; Schiller, *Digital Depression*, 30; Suwandi, *Value Chains*, 23; Smith, *Imperialism*, 101; John Bellamy Foster, Robert W. McChesney, and R. Jamil Jonna, "The Global Reserve Army of Labor and the New *Imperialism*," *Monthly Review* 63, no. 6 (2011): 1–31, https://doi.org/10.14452/MR-063-06-2011-10_1. The International Labor Organization estimated that between 1980 and 2007, the global labor force expanded from 1.9 to 3.1 billion, a 63 percent increase, with nearly three-quarters of the 2007 total located in the developing countries. Ajit K. Ghose, Nomaan Majid, and Christoph Ernst, *The Global Employment Challenge* (Geneva: International Labor Organization, 2008), 9–10, in John Bellamy Foster and Robert W. McChesney, *The Endless Crisis* (New York: Monthly Review Press, 2012), 127. For a lucid historical exposition, Ellen Meiksins Wood, *Empire of Capital* (London: Verso, 2003); Schiller, *Digital Depression*, 27–42.
143. Schiller, *Digital Depression*, 33, quote from Cortada, *Information and the Modern Corporation*, 36; Suwandi, *Value Chains*, 22, quoting International Labor Organization, *World Employment Social Outlook: The Changing Nature of Jobs* (Geneva: ILO, 2015), 131.

144. Foster, McChesney, and Jonna, "The Global Reserve Army of Labor and the New Imperialism."; Elkins, *Legacy of Violence*, 10; There are other considerations such as transport costs and proximity to markets. John Smith, *Imperialism in the Twenty-first Century: Globalization, Super-exploitation, and Capitalism's Final Crisis* (New York: Monthly Review Press, 2016); Wood, *Empire of Capital*.
145. As did rhetoric in the Atlantic Charter of 1941, signed by Roosevelt and British Prime Minister Winston Churchill. Daniel J. Whelan, *Indivisible Human Rights: A History* (Philadelphia: University of Pennsylvania Press, 2010), 11–58; Elizabeth Borgwardt, *A New Deal for the World: America's Vision for Human Rights* (Cambridge, MA: Belknap Press of Harvard University Press, 2005), 14–86, 250–284; Robin Blackburn, "Reclaiming Human Rights," *New Left Review*, no. 69 (2011): 134, 137; see also, Eric Hobsbawm, "Labour and Human Rights," in Eric Hobsbawm, *Workers: Worlds of Labor* (New York: Pantheon, 1984), 297–316.
146. Leffler, *Preponderance of Power*, 141–181. For the 1950s, Blanche Wiesen Cooke, *The Declassified Eisenhower: A Divided Legacy of Peace and Political Warfare* (New York: Doubleday, 1981); Steven L. B. Jensen, *The Making of International Human Rights: The 1960s, Decolonization, and the Reconstruction of Global Values* (Cambridge: Cambridge University Press, 2016); von Eschen, *Race against Empire*, 78–85.
147. Lemberg, *Barriers Down*, 20–47; Herbert I. Schiller, *Communication and Cultural Domination* (White Plains, NY: International Arts & Sciences Press, 1976), 24 (Dulles quote); 29 (Benton quote). For a historical reckoning, Lemberg, *Barriers Down*; For a provocative argument that, years before the Bandung Conference, shared opposition to this US policy became a binding element in Third World solidarity. See Kenneth Cmiel, "Human Rights, Freedom of Information, and the Origins of Third-World Solidarity," in Mark Philip Bradley and Patrice Petro, *Truth Claims: Representation and Human Rights* (New Brunswick: Rutgers University Press, 2002), 107–130.
148. Von Eschen, *Race against Empire*, 96–121, 145–166; Mary L. Dudziak, *Cold War Civil Rights: Race and the Image of American Democracy* (Princeton: Princeton University Press, 2000). Dr. Martin Luther King, Jr., consistently viewed economic justice as a necessity alongside civil rights and, near the end of his life, returned this imperative to the forefront of struggle. Thomas F. Jackson, *From Civil Rights to Human Rights: Martin Luther King, Jr., and the Struggle for Economic Justice* (Philadelphia: University of Pennsylvania Press, 2007); Burke, *Decolonization and the Evolution of International Human Rights*, 10; Jensen, *The Making of International Human Rights*, 256–258; Focusing on the US abridgement of the indivisible conception during and after the 1970s is Samuel Moyn, *Not Enough: Human Rights in an Unequal World* (Cambridge, MA: Belknap Press of Harvard University Press, 2018).
149. Beth Sims, *Workers of the World Undermined: American Labor's Role in U.S. Foreign Policy* (Boston: South End Press, 1992); Robert Parry, "Key Neocon Calls on US to Oust Putin," *Consortium News*, October 7, 2016, https://consortiumnews.com/2016/10/07/key-neocon-calls-on-us-to-oust-putin/; Helleiner, *Forgotten Foundations of Bretton Woods*, 9–22; Michael E. Latham, *Modernization as Ideology: American*

Social Science and "Nation Building" in the Kennedy Era (Chapel Hill, NC: University of North Carolina Press, 2000), 21–68, especially 35–36; Herbert I. Schiller, "Waiting for Orders: Mass Communications Research in the United States," *Gazette* 20, no. 1 (1974): 11–21.

150. Frances X. Clines, "Warsaw Pact Pronounces the End of Ideological Conflict with West," *New York Times*, June 8, 1990, A1, A4; John Markoff, "Computer Project Would Speed Data," *New York Times*, June 8, 1990, A1, C6; Mandy D. Tröger, "On Unregulated Markets and the Freedom of Media: The Transition of the East German Press after 1989" (Ph.D. diss., University of Illinois at Urbana-Champaign, 2018).

151. Hobsbawm, *Age of Extremes*, 490. Over half the NGOs in Europe were founded in the 1990s, according to Sue Curry Jansen, *Stealth Communications* (Cambridge, UK: Polity Press, 2017), 143–144; World Bank, *Accelerated Development in Sub-Saharan Africa: An Agenda for Action* (Washington, DC: The World Bank, 1981), 108; Robert J. Saunders, Jeremy J. Warford, and Bjorn Wellenius, *Telecommunications and Economic Development* (Baltimore, MD: Johns Hopkins University Press, 1983); World Bank, *World Development Report "Knowledge for Development"* (New York: Oxford University Press, 1999), 56–70.

152. J. Howlett CBE, *"Report of the National Committee on Computer Networks," presented to the Secretary of State for Industry* (London: Department of Industry, 1978); British Telecommunications Union Committee, "The American Experience: A Report on the dilemma of Telecommunications in the U.S.A.," October 1983; Dan Schiller, "Telecommunications Workers Union Testimony before Canadian Television-Radio and Telecommunications Commission," Ottawa, 1983; Sybil Rhodes, *Social Movements and Free-Market Capitalism in Latin America: Telecommunications Privatization and the Rise of Consumer Protest* (Albany: State University of New York Press, 2006), 72–74 (Argentina), 116 (Brazil); Andreas Evagora, "France Telecom Unions Organize to Protest Utility Privatization," *Wall Street Journal*, June 4, 1996, https://www.wsj.com/articles/SB833835276356785000; J. P. Singh, *Leapfrogging Development? The Political Economy of Telecommunications Restructuring* (Albany, NY: State University of New York Press, 1999), 172–173; Don Kirk, "Korea Telecom in Last Leg of 15-Year Push to Privatize," *New York Times*, May 8, 2002, https://www.nytimes.com/2002/05/08/business/korea-telecom-in-last-leg-of-15-year-push-to-privatize.html; Anti-Privatization Alliance, eds., *The Great PTCL Strike 2005 against Privatization* (Lahore: Shanakht Press, 2005); Steve Dubb, *Logics of Resistance: Globalization and Telephone Unionism in Mexico and British Columbia* (New York: Garland Publishing, 1999); see also, Harry C. Katz, ed., *Telecommunications Restructuring Work and Employment Relations Worldwide* (Ithaca: ILR Press, 1997).

153. Francis Fukuyama, *The End of History and the Last Man* (New York: Free Press, 1992), 7. This book is an enlargement of Fukuyama's earlier article, first presented at the University of Chicago's Olin Center and thereafter published as Francis Fukuyama, "The End of History?," *The National Interest*, no. 16 (Summer 1989): 3–18; Al Gore, "Infrastructure for the Global Village," *Scientific American* 265, no. 3 (September 1991): 150.

NOTES 779

154. "Remarks prepared for delivery by Vice President Al Gore," International Telecommunications Union, March 21, 1994, 1, 2, https://seclists.org/interesting-people/1994/Mar/112.
155. "Remarks prepared for delivery by Vice President Al Gore," 3, 4, 5.
156. "Remarks prepared for delivery by Vice President Al Gore," 6.
157. "Remarks prepared for delivery by Vice President Al Gore," 7.
158. A leading historian argues that the internet's origins were "autocratic, not democratic." Russell, *Open Standards and the Digital Age*, 263; Thomas L. Friedman, *The Lexus and the Olive Tree: Understanding Globalization* (New York: Farrar, Straus and Giroux, 1999); World Summit on the Information Society, "Declaration of Principles," *WSIS-03-GENEVA/Doc/4-E* (Geneva: World Summit on the Information Society, December 2003; Elizabeth Dickinson, "Internet Freedom," *Foreign Policy*, January 21, 2010, https://foreignpolicy.com/2010/01/21/internet-freedom/; Frank La Rue, "Report of the Special Rapporteur on the Promotion and Protection of the Right to Freedom of Opinion and Expression," Seventeenth Session, Agenda Item 3, United Nations General Assembly, May 16, 2011; Schiller, *Digital Depression*, 161–169; William J. McIver, Jr., William F. Birdsall, and Merrilee Rasmussen, "The Internet and the Right to Communicate," *First Monday* 8, no. 12 (December 2003); Vinton Cerf, "Internet Access Is Not a Human Right," *New York Times*, January 5, 2012.
159. Blackburn, "Reclaiming Human Rights," 137. On Snowden and the internet, Dan Schiller, "Geopolitique de l'espionnage," *Le Monde diplomatique*, November 2014, 1, 10.
160. Adam Segal, "When China Rulesthe Web," *Foreign Affairs*, September/October 2018, https://www.foreignaffairs.com/articles/china/2018-08-13/when-china-rules-web; Min Tang, "Not Yet the End of Transnational Digital Capitalism: A Communication Perspective of the U.S.-China Decoupling Rhetoric," *International Journal of Communication* 16 (2022): 1506–1531, https://ijoc.org/index.php/ijoc/article/download/17624/3715.
161. Office of the Director of National intelligence, Ref Book EO 12333 United States Intelligence Activities, *Federal Register* 40, no. 235 (December 8, 1981), amended by EO 13284 (2003), EO 13355 (2004), and EO 13470 (2008); see also, Gallagher and Moltke, "The Wire-tap Rooms." The US had been monitoring foreign governmental messages transiting its networks since at least 1945. Schiller, *Who Knows*, 108; Gallagher and Moltke, "The Wire-tap Rooms."; Clark, *Designing an Internet*, 192; David Sanger, "U.S. Easing Reins on CyberAttacks," *New York Times*, June 18, 2018, A1, A13; see also, Schiller, *Digital Depression*, 211–228.
162. Segal, "When China Rules the Web."; Corrie Driebusch and Daniel Huang, "Dividends Boost Tech-stock Alliance," *Wall Street Journal*, August 1, 2016, A1–A2; Dave Baxter, "Tech Begins to Raise Its Dividend Game," *Financial Times*, February 21, 2022, https://www.ft.com/content/bc019351-524d-461e-8a18-c1de9360f6e5.
163. S. O'Dea, "Number of Fixed Broadband Internet Subscriptions Worldwide 2005–2021," *Statista*, December 9, 2021,t https://www.statista.com/statistics/268673/number-of-broadband-internet-subscriptions/; S. O'Dea, "Smartphone

Subscriptions Worldwide 2016–2027," *Statista*, February 23, 2022, https://www.statista.com/statistics/330695/number-of-smartphone-users-worldwide/; James W. Cortada, *Information and the Modern Corporation* (Cambridge, MA: MIT Press, 2011), 80; Schiller, *How to Think about Information*, 12; Cortada, *Digital Hand*, vol. 1, 376; In 2007, US capital expenditures on information processing equipment and software totaled $264 billion; in 2013, they came to $331 billion. For comparison, it is worth noting that only thirty-five countries possessed GDPs larger than this. U.S. Bureau of the Census, Information and Communication Technology Surveys, 2007 and 2013, Tables 1A and Table 2A, https://www.census.gov/data/tables/2007/econ/icts/2007-icts.html and https://www.census.gov/data/tables/2013/econ/icts/2013-icts.html. Total nonresidential fixed investment in 2013 was about $2 trillion. Council of Economic Advisors, Economic Report of the President 2015, Appendix B, Table B2, Gross Domestic Product, 2000 to 2014, 386, https://obamawhitehouse.archives.gov/sites/default/files/docs/cea_2015_erp.pdf. This was a 25 percent increase during an interval in which inflation increased by around 15 percent; Yasha Levine, "All EFF-d Up: Silicon Valley's Astroturf Privacy Shakedown," *The Baffler*, no. 40; Margrethe Vestager, in Valentina Romei, "Europe First: The EU's Digital Industrialisation Challenge," *Financial Times*, December 15, 2019, https://www.ft.com/content/73213036-1dd8-11ea-97df-cc63de1d73f4.

164. In Richard Waters and Hannah Murphy, "Facebook's Reckoning? The Global Battle to Regulate Social Media," *Financial Times*, April 12, 2019, https://www.ft.com/content/5a84179e-5d05-11e9-939a-341f5ada9d40.

Conclusion

1. Joseph D. Kearney, "From the Fall of the Bell System to the Telecommunications Act: Regulation of Telecommunications Under Judge Greene," *Hastings Law Journal* 50, no. 6 (1999): 1395–1472; Patricia Aufderheide, *Communications Policy and the Public Interest: The Telecommunications Act of 1996* (New York: The Guilford Press, 1999).
2. CenturyLink, "Company History," https://news.centurylink.com/company-history; Nicholas Rossolillo, "Where Will CenturyLink Be in 5 Years?," *MotleyFool*, April 14, 2019, https://www.fool.com/investing/2019/03/19/where-will-centurylink-be-in-5-years.aspx; "Lumen Technologies," Wikipedia, https://en.wikipedia.org/wiki/Lumen_Technologies.
3. Kadhim Shubber and Ortenca Aliaj, "U.S. Judge Clears T-Mobile's $59bn Sprint Takeover without Conditions," *Financial Times*, February 11, 2020, https://www.ft.com/content/b67503a2-4cd2-11ea-95a0-43d18ec715f5.
4. Nic Fildes and James Fontanella-Khan, "AT&T: Back to Basics after Four Decades of Botched Dealmaking," *Financial Times*, June 16, 2021, https://www.ft.com/content/0712c618-0a08-49a9-8f62-5d77c51f9e5e.

5. Edmund Andrews, "AT&T Acquisition, Soon to Be Spun off, Regains NCR Name," *New York Times*, January 11, 1996, https://www.nytimes.com/1996/01/11/business/att-acquisition-soon-to-be-spun-off-regains-ncr-name.html; Vikas Bajaj, "Alcatel and Lucent Agree to Merge in $13.4 Billion Deal," *New York Times*, April 2, 2006, https://www.nytimes.com/2006/04/02/business/alcatel-and-lucent-agree-to-merge-in-134-billion-deal.html. For an analysis arguing that U.S. government policy should have forsaken antitrust concerns with competition and instead accorded industrial policy support to Western Electric and its successor, Lucent, see Robert D. Atkinson, "Who Lost Lucent?: The Decline of America's Telecom Equipment Industry," *American Affairs* 4, no. 3 (Fall 2020), https://americanaffairsjournal.org/2020/08/who-lost-lucent-the-decline-of-americas-telecom-equipment-industry/.

6. Joshua Chaffin and Nic Fildes, "Former WorldCom Chief Bernard Ebbers Dies Aged 78," *Financial Times*, February 2, 2020, https://www.ft.com/content/d96ac2f6-4643-11ea-aeb3-955839e06441; Dan Schiller, *Bad Deal of the Century: The Worrisome Implications of the WorldCom-MCI Merger* (Washington, DC: Economic Policy Institute, 1998); Dan Schiller, "The Telecom Crisis," *Dissent* (Winter 2003): 66–70.

7. Verizon, "Schedule of Outstanding Debt," https://www.verizon.com/about/investors/schedule-outstanding-debt; AT&T, Inc., "Subsidiary Debt Detail," https://www.macrotrends.net/stocks/charts/T/at-t/long-term-debt#:~:text=AT%26T%20long%20term%20debt%20for%202021%20was%20%24152.82B%2C%20a,a%208.99%25%20decline%20from%202018; List of Countries by GDP (nominal), Wikipedia, https://en.wikipedia.org/wiki/List_of_countries_by_GDP_(nominal); https://www.macrotrends.net/stocks/charts/T/at-t/total-assets; AT&T, "AT&T Lays out Long-term Growth Strategy, Financial Outlook," https://about.att.com/story/2022/analyst-and-investor-day.html; "Verizon Plans Capex of $21.5 Bn in 2022, Focusing on 5G," *TelecomLead*, January 25, 2022, https://www.telecomlead.com/5g/verizon-plans-capex-of-21-5-bn-this-year-focusing-on-5g-103183; Nic Fildes, "Is Breaking up All That's Left for Telecoms to Do?," *Financial Times*, December 16, 2021, https://www.ft.com/content/c6806242-8ff1-468d-9ef9-954ecafb2f1e; Todd Spangler, "AT&T Sets Plan to Spin off WarnerMedia in $43 Billion Deal," *Variety*, February 1, 2022, https://variety.com/2022/biz/news/att-spin-off-warnermedia-43-billion-deal-1235168480/.

8. "AT&T Net Income 2010–2021," *Macrotrends*, https://www.macrotrends.net/stocks/charts/T/at-t/net-income; AT&T, "AT&T Reports Fourth-quarter and Full-year Results," January 26, 2022, https://about.att.com/story/2022/q4-2021-results.html; AT&T, "Q3 2019 AT&T Earnings Investor Briefing," October 28, 2019, https://investors.att.com/~/media/Files/A/ATT-IR/financial-reports/quarterly-earnings/2019/3q-2019/3Q19_Investor%20Briefing.pdf; S. O'Dea, "AT&T—Statistics & Facts," June 22, 2021, Statista, https://www.statista.com/topics/1252/atundt/#dossierContents__outerWrapper; "Verizon Net Income 2010-2021," *Macrotrends*, https://www.macrotrends.net/stocks/charts/VZ/verizon/net-income; "Verizon 2019 Revenues Reach USD 131.9bn," *TeleGeography*, January 31, 2020; Verizon Communications, Inc., Form 10-K for Fiscal Year Ended December 31, 2021, U.S. Securities and Exchange Commission (Washington, DC: SEC, 2022), 20, 29, https://www.verizon.com/about/sites/default/files/2021-Annual-Report-on-Form-10-K.pdf; U.S. Securities and

Exchange Commission, T-Mobile US Form 10-K, For the Year Ended December 31, 2018 (Washington, DC: SEC, 2019), 4–10, http://d18rn0p25nwr6d.cloudfront.net/CIK-0001283699/3bfba910-027f-4ec5-85a5-b8e91d073ba8.pdf; T-Mobile, "T-Mobile's Unique Formula Delivers Industry-leading Service Revenue and Cash Flow Growth and Exceeds 2021 Guidance," https://investor.t-mobile.com/news-and-events/t-mobile-us-press-releases/press-release-details/2022/T-Mobiles-Unique-Formula-Delivers-Industry-Leading-Service-Revenue-and-Cash-Flow-Growth-and-Exceeds-2021-Guidance/default.aspx.

9. "Meta Reports Fourth Quarter and Full Year 2021 Results," https://s21.q4cdn.com/399680738/files/doc_financials/2021/q4/FB-12.31.2021-Exhibit-99.1-Final.pdf; Alphabet, Inc., U.S. Securities and Exchange Commission, Form 10-K for the Fiscal Year Ended December 31, 2021, 50, https://abc.xyz/investor/static/pdf/20220202_alphabet_10K.pdf?cache=fc81690; ShinJoung Yeo, *Behind the Search Box: Google and the Global Internet* (Urbana, IL: University of Illinois Press, forthcoming); Joseph Johnson, "Global Market Share of Search Engines, 2010–2022," *Statista*, March 1, 2022, https://www.statista.com/statistics/216573/worldwide-market-share-of-search-engines/; GMI, "YouTube User Statistics 2022," https://www.globalmediainsight.com/blog/youtube-users-statistics/; "Mobile Operating System Market Share Worldwide," StatCounter Global Stats, https://gs.statcounter.com/os-market-share/mobile/worldwide; Microsoft, Inc., *Annual Report 2021*, n.p., https://www.microsoft.com/investor/reports/ar21/index.html; Lionel Sujay Vailshery, "Office Productivity Software Market Share Worldwide 2022," *Statista*, February 23, 2022, https://www.statista.com/statistics/983299/worldwide-market-share-of-office-productivity-software/; J. Degenhard, "LinkedIn Users in the World, 2017–2025," Statista, July 20, 2021, https://www.statista.com/forecasts/1147197/linkedin-users-in-the-world; "Amazon Reports 22% Increase in Full Year Net Sales for 2021," *Retail Insight Network*, February 4, 2022, https://www.retail-insight-network.com/news/amazon-results-2021/; Amazon Statistics 2022, https://www.businessofapps.com/data/amazon-statistics/; Julie Clover, "Apple Now Has More than 1.8 Billion Active Devices Worldwide," *MacRumors*, January 27, 2022, https://www.macrumors.com/2022/01/27/apple-1-8-billion-active-devices-worldwide/; Apple, Inc., U.S. Securities and Exchange Commission, Form 10-K for the Fiscal Year Ended December 31, 2021, 49, https://s2.q4cdn.com/470004039/files/doc_financials/2021/q4/_10-K-2021-(As-Filed).pdf.

10. Nic Fildes, "Why the Global Telecoms Dream Turned Sour," *Financial Times*, January 2, 2020, https://www.ft.com/content/874aa854-ff3c-11e9-b7bc-f3fa4e77dd47?shareType=nongift.

11. Victor Pickard and David Elliot Berman, *After Net Neutrality: A New Deal for the Digital Age* (New Haven: Yale University Press, 2019).

12. This paragraph offers a simplified description. For a fuller account, see Kristin Lee, "New State of the Network Report Examines Telecom in a Time of COVID-19," TeleGeography Blog, February 16, 2022, https://blog.telegeography.com/new-state-of-the-network-report-examines-telecom-in-a-time-of-covid-19; Nick Huber, "Industry Turns to Private 5G to Speed Digital Change," *Financial Times*, February 7, 2022, https://www.ft.com/content/d77add3f-2b7d-4b3d-b34d-de29c0419e3d.

13. "Number of Smartphone Subscriptions Worldwide from 2016 to 2027," *Statista*, https://www.statista.com/statistics/330695/number-of-smartphone-users-worldwide/; Jayne Miller, "New Year, New E-Book: The State of the Network 2019 Is Here, TeleGeography Blog, January 31, 2019, 16–17, https://blog.telegeography.com/the-state-of-the-network-2019-ebook; Paul Brodsky, "Let's Just Say Demand Is Thriving in the International Bandwidth Market," TeleGeography Blog, May 1, 2020, https://blog.telegeography.com/lets-just-say-demand-is-thriving-in-the-global-bandwidth-market; Lee, "New State of the Network Report Examines Telecom in a Time of COVID-19," 28; TeleGeography, The Covid-19 crisis interrupted this trend briefly, as the volume of voice calls unexpectedly spiked. Cecilia Kang, "The Humble Phone Call Has Made a Comeback," *New York Times*, April 9, 2020, https://www.nytimes.com/2020/04/09/technology/phone-calls-voice-virus.html.
14. Miller, "New Year, New E-Book," 16.
15. Matt Kapko, "AT&T Employees Pay Price for SDN," January 29, 2020, sdxcentral, https://www.sdxcentral.com/articles/news/att-employees-pay-price-for-sdn/2020/01/; "AT&T Issue Briefs Our Workforce," https://about.att.com/csr/home/reporting/issue-brief/workforce.html; S. O'Dea, "Number of Employees at Verizon from 2007 to 2021," *Statista*, March 22, 2022, https://www.statista.com/statistics/257304/number-of-employees-at-verizon/; "T-Mobile US: Number of Employees 2010–2021," TMUS, https://www.macrotrends.net/stocks/charts/TMUS/t-mobile-us/number-of-employees; "Lumen Technologies: Number of Employees 2010–2021," *Macrotrends*, https://www.macrotrends.net/stocks/charts/LUMN/lumen-technologies/number-of-employees; There were additional employers of workers in U.S. telecommunications, including big business users as well as many small carriers. Thousands of small carriers also existed in 1982. Perhaps as many as 15 percent of the total number of workers employed in 2020 were employed in other countries to support the big carriers' foreign operations. See also, Mike Dano, "Employee Headcount: The Rise and Fall of Job Numbers at Verizon, AT&T, T-Mobile, and Sprint," *FierceWireless*, June 14, 2017, https://www.fiercewireless.com/wireless/employee-headcount-rise-and-fall-job-numbers-at-verizon-at-t-t-mobile-and-sprint; Labor Notes, "Verizon Unions Win Model Paid Leave Policy for Coronavirus—Will Other Unions Demand the Same?," *Labor Notes*, March 18, 2020, https://labornotes.org/blogs/2020/03/verizon-union-wins-model-paid-leave-policy-coronavirus-will-other-unions-demand-same; Mark Gruenberg, "CWA: Labor Board Uses T-Mobile Case to OK Company Unions," *People's World*, October 9, 2019 https://www.peoplesworld.org/article/cwa-labor-board-uses-t-mobile-case-to-ok-company-unions/; Mike Dano, "Verizon, AT&T and T-Mobile Employees to Jointly Organize under CWA's 'Wireless Workers United' Group," *Fierce Wireless*, January 30, 2018, https://www.fiercewireless.com/wireless/verizon-at-t-t-mobile-employees-to-jointly-organize-under-cwa-s-wireless-workers-united.
16. Christopher W. Shaw, *First Class: The U.S. Postal Service, Democracy, and the Corporate Threat* (San Francisco: City Lights, 2021), 81–82; Dave Jamieson, "Donald Trump Is about to Put His Stamp on the U.S. Postal Service," *Huffpost*, January 11, 2020, https://www.huffpost.com/entry/donald-trump-us-postal-ervice_n_5

e18e358c5b6da971d15c76b?guccounter=1&guce_referrer=aHR0cHM6Ly93d3c uaHVmZnBvc3QuY29tLw&guce_referrer_sig=AQAAAJXHn3hzioefwTLkJJ5q fjJcoiDdBcUEeFV0K4BdH2MxFuhwtjQae0fw_UHHsLIhgLTJBEZjMQRRYh-WrgfZurqfng6Y56eg_9CanLSHCj_he307bP9Hb46eXQeD0d9g4UPT7kbWIcEk1 gwa_bVOkjwJu218QyG6mwzP5Ef2LUeX; Paul Prescod, "Defend the Post Office, Defend Black Workers," *Jacobin*, July 3, 2019, www.jacobinmag.com/2019/07/post-office-black-workers-bernie-sanders-usps?; Shaw, *First Class*, 79–100.

17. Jane Slaughter, "How Postal Workers Saved Us," *Labor Notes*, no. 501 (December 2020): 7; Alexandra Bradbury, "The Long Nightmare before Christmas," *Labor Notes*, no. 502 (January 2021): 1, 3–5; Jacob Bogage, "Senate Passes $101 Billion Overhaul of USPS, Lauding Mail Agency's Role in Pandemic Response," *Washington Post*, March 8, 2022; The White House, "Remarks by President Biden at Signing of H.R. 3076, the Postal Service Reform Act of 2022," April 6, 2022, https://www.whitehouse.gov/briefing-room/speeches-remarks/2022/04/06/remarks-by-president-biden-at-signing-of-h-r-3076-the-postal-service-reform-act-of-2022/; American Postal Workers Union, "The Postal Service Reform Act of 2022," https://apwu.org/postal-service-reform-act-2022.

18. Steven Hahn, *A Nation without Borders: The United States and Its World in an Age of Civil Wars, 1830–1910* (New York: Viking, 2016).

19. "The number of strikes has fallen from an average of over 5,000 a year in the 1970s to an annual average of fewer than 300 in the 2000s." Kim Moody, "Striking out in America: Is There an Alternative to the Strike?" in G. Gail ed., *New Forms and Expressions of Conflict at Work* (London: Palgrave Macmillan, 2013), 233.

20. Peter Navarro, "U.S.: Don't Give China Control of Intellectual Property Group," *Financial Times*, February 23, 2020, https://www.ft.com/content/91addb98-532b-11ea-a1ef-da1721a0541e. Through arm-twisting, the U.S. managed to avert the election of a Chinese national to the Director-Generalship of the World International Property Organization. IP Watchdog, "Singapore's Daren Tang to Succeed Gurry as Next WIPO Director General," *IPWatchdog*, March 4, 2020, https://www.ipwatchdog.com/2020/03/04/singapores-daren-tang-succeed-gurry-next-wipo-director-general/id=119582/; In 2020, to the alarm of the U.S., the ITU granted a hearing to Chinese proposals for a competing internet architecture. Anna Gross and Madhumita Murgia, "China and Huawei Propose Reinvention of the Internet," *Financial Times*, March 27, 2020, https://www.ft.com/content/c78be2cf-a1a1-40b1-8ab7-904d7095e0f2; Madhumita Murgia and Anna Gross, "Inside China's Controversial Mission to Reinvent the Internet," *Financial Times*, March 27, 2020, https://www.ft.com/content/ba94c2bc-6e27-11ea-9bca-bf503995cd6f.

21. Anthony J. Blinken, Secretary of State, "The Election of Doreen Bogdan-Martin as Secretary General of the International Telecommunication Union," Press Statement U.S. Department of State, September 29, 2022, https://urldefense.com/v3/__https://www.state.gov/the-election-of-doreen-bogdan-martin-as-secretary-general-of-the-international-telecommunication-union/__;!!DZ3fjg!6JX3Yvhr3IKPTOBe0TJY1s-3w1vu9eku7pI9XqGlGTvRQ_C9oJGx_6MawBS9t31vDzTsCcKZQuL3HS_XekTMmuw$.

22. "GDPR: Europe Takes Lead," *Financial Times*, https://www.ft.com/content/bd3eb 2ae-5ea0-11e8-9334-2218e7146b04; Guy Chazan, "Angela Merkel Urges EU to Seize Control of Data from U.S. Tech Titans," *Financial Times*, November 12, 2019, https://www.ft.com/content/956ccaa6-0537-11ea-9afa-d9e2401fa7ca; Guy Chazan, "Germany Acts to Stop Sale of Tech Companies to Non-EU Investors," *Financial Times*, November 29, 2019, https://www.ft.com/content/d0964cd0-12af-11ea-a7e6-62bf4f9e548a; Javier Espinoza and Sam Fleming, "Europe Urged to Use Industrial Data Trove to Steal March on Rivals," *Financial Times*, January 13, 2020, https://www.ft.com/content/8187a268-3494-11ea-a6d3-9a26f8c3cba4.

23. Adam Satariano, "Google Loses Appeal of $2.8 Billion Fine in E.U. Antitrust Case," *New York Times*, November 10, 2021, https://www.nytimes.com/2021/11/10/business/google-eu-appeal-antitrust.html; "The EU Tries to Loosen Big Tech's Grip," *Financial Times*, March 27, 2022, https://www.ft.com/content/def9de58-a9b7-4ed2-a05f-565c55814570; Patrick McGee and Guy Chazan, "The Apple Effect: Germany Fears Being Left behind by Big Tech," *Financial Times*, January 28, 2020 (quote), https://www.ft.com/content/6f69433a-40f0-11ea-a047-eae9bd51ceba.

24. Min Tang, *Tencent: The Political Economy of China's Surging Internet Giant* (New York: Routledge: 2020), 9; Yu Hong, *Networking China: The Digital Transformation of the Chinese Economy* (Urbana: University of Illinois Press, 2017); Hong Shen, "Across the Great (Fire)Wall: China and the Global Internet" (Ph.D. diss., University of Illinois at Urbana-Champaign, 2017); Hong Shen, *Alibaba: Infrastructuring Global China* (New York: Routledge: 2022); Tang, *Tencent*, 9–31; James Kynge and Nic Fildes, "Huawei: The Indispensable Telecoms Company," *Financial Times*, January 31, 2020; Sue-Lin Wong, "Huawei Sues Verizon for $1bn Intellectual Property Theft," *Financial Times*, February 6, 2020, https://www.ft.com/content/ba9f1cce-48c7-11ea-aeb3-955839e06 441; Yun Wen, *The Huawei Model: The Rise of China's Technology Giant* (Urbana: University of Illinois Press, 2020).

25. Schiller, *Digital Depression*, 230–239; A policy thinktank, the Information Technology & Innovation Foundation called the national security concerns cited by the U.S. administration in the Huawei case a "pretext" that would not aid U.S. national security and that would weaken the competitive position of U.S. tech companies. Robert D. Atkinson, "The Huawei Export Ban: Shooting U.S. Tech Exporters in the Foot," *Innovation Files*, January 24, 2020, https://itif.org/publications/2020/01/24/huawei-export-ban-shooting-us-technology-exporters-foot.

26. Simeon Gilding, the outgoing head of the Australian Signals Directorate's signals intelligence and offensive cyber missions unit (by no means a disinterested source), argues for this interpretation in "5G Choices: A Pivotal Moment in World Affairs," *Australian Strategic Policy Institute, The Strategist*, January 29, 2020, https://www.aspistrategist.org.au/5g-choices-a-pivotal-moment-in-world-affairs/; "Qui Surveille, La CIA ou Huawei? Le Monde Diplomatique," *Manie de Voir*, no. 170 (April–May 2020): 75–77; Yuan Yang, "U.S. Tech Backlash Forces China to Be More Self-reliant," *Financial Times*, January 14, 2020, https://www.ft.com/content/c6993 200-1ff3-11ea-b8a1-584213ee7b2b; Kiran Stacey, "U.S. Commerce Secretary to Vet Imports of Sensitive Technology," *Financial Times*, November 26, 2019, https://

www.ft.com/content/5ea156d8-1057-11ea-a7e6-62bf4f9e548a; Sean Kane, "Huawei Ban Timeline: Detained CFO Makes Deal with U.S. Justice Department," *C/Net*, September 30, 2021, https://www.cnet.com/news/privacy/huawei-ban-timeline-detained-cfo-makes-deal-with-us-justice-department/; Yang, "U.S. Tech Backlash Forces China to Be More Self-sufficient"; Kenji Kawase, "Chinese Telecom Groups Shift Focus to 'East-West' Data Project," *NikkeiAsia*, March 30, 2022, https://asia.nikkei.com/Business/Telecommunication/Chinese-telecom-groups-shift-focus-to-east-west-data-project.

27. David Montgomery, *The Fall of the House of Labor* (Cambridge: Cambridge University Press, 1987), 464; Heidi Shierholz and Margaret Poydock, "Continued Surge in Strike Activity Signals Worker Dissatisfaction with Wage Growth," *Economic Policy Institute*, February 11, 2020, https://www.epi.org/publication/continued-surge-in-strike-activity/; Josh Eidelson, "'Suicide Shifts,' 7-Day Weeks, Fuel Rare Flare-up in U.S. Strikes," *Bloomberg*, October 25, 2021, https://www.bloomberg.com/news/articles/2021-10-25/-suicide-shifts-7-day-weeks-fuel-rare-flare-up-in-u-s-strikes; Juliana Kaplan and Madison Hoff, "The Number of Major Strikes and Lockouts Doubled in 2021, Showing Workers Aren't Accepting the Old Status Quo," *Business Insider*, February 23, 2022, https://www.businessinsider.com/major-strikes-doubled-2021-great-resignation-labor-shortage-better-pay-2022-2; Liz Shuler and Jane McAlevey, "From Amazon to Starbucks, America Is Unionizing. Will Politics Catch Up?," *The Argument, New York Times*, April 20, 2022," https://www.nytimes.com/2022/04/20/opinion/amazon-starbucks-unions-the-argument.html.

28. Dan DiMaggio, "Verizon Strike Shows Corporate Giants Can Be Beat," *Labor Notes*, June 3, 2016, https://labornotes.org/2016/06/verizon-strikers-show-corporate-giants-can-be-beat; Aaron Pressman, "Exclusive: Verizon Extends Union Contract, Avoiding Possibly Tough Labor Talks Next Year," *Fortune*, July 19, 2018, https://fortune.com/2018/07/19/verizon-extends-union-contract-cwa/; Edward Ongweso, Jr., "General Electric Workers Launch Protest, Demand to Make Ventilators," March 30, 2020, *Vice.com*, https://www.vice.com/en_us/article/y3mjxg/general-electric-workers-walk-off-the-job-demand-to-make-ventilators; Heidi Shierholz and Margaret Poydock, "Continued Surge in Strike Activity Signals Worker Dissatisfaction with Wage Growth," *Economic Policy Institute*, February 11, 2020, https://www.epi.org/publication/continued-surge-in-strike-activity/; APWU, "Mark Dimondstein," (quote), www.APWU.org; Will Weissert, "Postal Workers Union with 200,000 members Endorses Sanders," January 30, 2020, https://abcnews.go.com/Politics/wireStory/postal-workers-union-200000-members-endorses-sanders-68641107.

29. Shierholz and Poydock, "Continued Surge in Strike Activity Signals Worker Dissatisfaction with Wage Growth."; Jordan House and Paul Christopher Gray, "Why Did Amazon Workers Win the Fight to Form a Union in Staten Island but Not in Alberta?," *The Conversation*, April 12, 2022, https://theconversation.com/why-did-amazon-workers-win-the-fight-to-form-a-union-in-staten-island-but-not-in-alberta-181042; Joe DeManuelle-Hall and Dan DiMaggio, "The Strike Is Back," *Labor Notes*, January 2020, 1–5, 3 (quote), 4 (Amazon); Bryce Covert, "Across Class Lines: Amazon Tech Workers Join Tech Workers in Protests," *The American Prospect*, May

1, 2020, https://prospect.org/labor/amazon-tech-workers-join-warehouse-worker-protests-coronavirus/; Eric Blanc, "Here's How We Beat Amazon," *Jacobin*, April 2, 2022, https://jacobinmag.com/2022/04/amazon-labor-union-alu-staten-island-organizing; Reed Albergotti, "Workers at Apple's Grand Central Store Move toward Unionizing," *Washington Post*, April 13, 2022, https://www.washingtonpost.com/technology/2022/04/16/apple-grand-central-station-retail-union-workers-united/; Jennifer Elias, "Google Workers Have Made Organizing Attempts in the Past. Here's Why This One Is More Significant," *CNBC*, January 5, 2021, https://www.cnbc.com/2021/01/05/google-workers-union-make-todays-announcement-significant.html; Ben Tarnoff and Moira Weigel, "Silicon Valley Workers Have Had Enough," *New York Times*, January 26, 2021, https://www.nytimes.com/2021/01/26/opinion/silicon-valley-tech-workers.html.

Index

For the benefit of digital users, indexed terms that span two pages (e.g., 52–53) may, on occasion, appear on only one of those pages.

Tables and figures are indicated by *t* and *f* following the page number

3Com, 573
5G wireless, 596–98, 606–7

Adams, Walter, 467–68
Adams Express, 29–30, 37, 62
Addams, Jane, 58–59
Admiral, 373
AEFG consortium, 348
Aeronautical Radio, Inc. (ARINC), 461
Aetna Insurance, 562
African Americans
  American Communications Association and, 240–41
  American Telephone and Telegraph Company and, 81, 264, 295, 337–38, 340–41, 410, 427–28, 430–31, 442
  anti-imperialism and, 539–40
  antimonopolism's targeting of, 47–48
  Black Power movement and, 467, 479–80
  Communication Workers of America and, 295, 425–26, 433–34
  Communist membership among and support for, 240
  Congress of Industrial Organizations and, 218, 240
  disenfranchisement of, 585
  Equal Employment Opportunity Commission and, 437–38
  mobilization against employment discrimination by, 10, 388–89, 408, 434, 438–39, 445, 446, 503, 506–7, 522, 603–4, 609–10
  Ohio Bell and, 280, 431–32
  as postal employees, 306–7, 389–90, 391–92, 430, 600
  Post Office segregation policies and, 52–53, 134–35
  public utility doctrine's equal employment opportunity provisions and, 193
air mail, 194, 303, 305

Aitken, Hugh, 345–46, 348, 354
Alaska, 38–39, 382–83, 524–25
Alcatel, 596
Algeria, 551
All America Cables, 261–63, 529
Allen, W. L., 252–53
Allende, Salvador, 504–5
Alphabet, 592, 597, 608–9. *See also* Google
Altgeld, John Peter, 70–71
Amazon
  annual profits at, 597
  as content delivery network, 598–99
  e-commerce and, 591–92
  labor organizing at, 608–9
  submarine cable network maintained by, 576–77
  US Postal Service and, 600
American Anti-Slavery Society, 35–36
American Bankers Association, 461–62
American Bar Association (ABA), 352
American Bell Telephone Company, 74–75, 78, 82, 89–90, 355–56. *See also* American Telephone and Telegraph Company (AT&T)
American Broadcast Company (ABC), 478
American Civil Liberties Union (ACLU), 425, 437
American Communications Association (ACA)
  African Americans' membership in and support from, 240–41
  American Radio Telegraphists Association as precursor of, 237
  Commercial Telegraphers Union of America and, 251–53, 255, 258
  Communication Workers of America and, 222, 290–92
  Communists' role in, 7–8, 238–39, 252–53, 267–68
  Congressional lobbying by, 243–44, 257

American Communications Association (ACA) (*cont.*)
  Congress of Industrial Organizations and, 6–8, 222, 237, 239, 240–41, 242–43, 251–52, 254–55, 260, 261*f*, 265–66, 267–68, 269–70, 271, 283, 289–94, 602
  Defense Communications Board and, 256
  election of 1940 and, 244
  election of 1948 and, 288–89
  establishment (1937) of, 237
  Federal Communications Commission and, 244–46, 254–55, 260
  Local 101 of, 271
  Local 103 of, 271
  Local 111 of, 271
  Local 120 of, 283
  National Federation of Telephone Workers and, 265–66, 268–70, 271–72, 279
  National Labor Relations Board and, 243, 249–51, 260
  Order of Repeatermen and Toll Testboardmen and, 269–70
  Pacific Telephone and Telegraph and, 271–72
  Postal Telegraph-Cable Company and, 6–7, 243, 251–52, 258
  Postal Telegraph-Western Union merger and, 243–44, 247–48, 249, 251–55, 257–60, 302–3, 599–600, 602
  Radio Corporation of America and, 239, 243, 261–63
  strikes (1939) and, 242
  strikes (1947) and, 275, 278–79, 290–91
  Taft-Hartley Act and, 287–88
  Telephone Traffic Employees Organization and, 271–72
  Western Union and, 249–51, 252–53, 254, 255, 260–63, 261*f*, 262*f*, 263*f*, 271
American Communications Union proposal, 12, 510–14, 515–16, 517, 519, 604–5
American Express, 37, 62
American Federation of Labor (AFL). *See also* American Federation of Labor-Congress of Industrial Organizations (AFL-CIO); Gompers, Samuel
  American Radio Telegraphists Association and, 234
  anti-Communism and, 260, 285–86
  call for telecommunications industry investigation (1934) by, 203
  Commercial Telegraphers Union of America and, 124–25, 128, 229, 235–36, 240–41, 255

  Communication Workers of America and, 284–85
  craft unionism and exclusionary practices at, 102–3, 217–18, 298
  federal regulation of telecommunications supported by, 111, 124–25
  government control of telephone and telegraph services advocated by, 77–78, 124–25, 128, 129, 142
  Great Depression and, 217–18
  International Brotherhood of Electrical Workers and, 111, 235–36, 260, 266–68, 284–85
  Lloyd-LaFollette Act and, 70
  long-distance phone service and, 179–80
  National Federation of Telephone Workers and, 267–68, 273, 279
  racism at, 217, 240–41, 298
  strikes (1947) and, 275
  United Electrical Workers (UE) and, 284–85
  War Labor Board and, 268–69
  World War I and, 142
  World War II and, 256
American Federation of Labor-Congress of Industrial Organizations (AFL-CIO)
  American Communications Union proposal and, 511
  Chile and, 504–5
  US Postal Service and, 308, 389–90, 401–2, 405–6, 426–27, 446–47
American GI Forum, 437
American Institute for Free Labor Development, 504–5
American Petroleum Institute (API), 461–62, 463
American Postal Workers Union (APWU)
  American Communications Union proposal and, 510–14, 515–16, 517, 519, 604–5
  establishment (1971) of, 406, 509–10
  National Association of Letter Carriers' potential merger with, 406–7
American Radio Association, 291–92
American Radio Telegraphists Association (ARTA), 233–37, 242. *See also* American Communications Association (ACA)
American Railway Union, 70–71
American Socialist Party. *See* Socialists
American Telegraph Company, 40–41
American Telephone and Telegraph Company (AT&T)
  5G wireless technology and, 596–97
  African Americans and, 81, 264, 295, 337–38, 340–41, 410, 427–28, 430–31, 442

annual profits at, 597
antimonopoly campaigns targeting, 4, 6, 76, 83–85, 99–100, 112, 113–14, 178, 601
antitrust case (1949–56) case against, 344, 366–87, 464–65, 602–3
anti-unionism of, 264
Asynchronous Transfer Mode of packet switching and, 562
breakup (1982–1984) of, 212, 518–20, 558–59, 572–73, 577, 594
cable television and, 473–74
Chicago Rate Case (1921) and, 188, 190
Communication Workers of America and, 10, 293–94, 408–9, 411, 509, 514, 515–16, 518–19
company unions at, 7, 222, 236, 237, 264–65, 266–67
Comsat and, 472
corporate structure of, 168–78, 375
data networking and, 451, 563
Dataphone service and, 462–63
dial technology and, 85, 152, 201, 264–65, 414–15
DirecTV and, 595–96
domestic network expansion during early twentieth century by, 165–66, 168–69, 171–72, 173–75, 179, 193–94, 195, 201
Federal Communications Commission and, 6, 207, 209–10, 212–13, 214–16, 321, 323–24, 325–27, 464–65, 602–3
fiber optic cables and, 550–51
founding (1885) of, 78, 173–74
government control of telecommunications during World War I and, 79, 141, 159, 161–63, 164
government investigation of telephone industry (1934–1938) and, 205–6, 210, 212–13, 214–16
Great Depression and, 5–6, 193–94, 201–2, 265
handset design and, 339–40
Hearst newspapers and, 97
International Brotherhood of Electrical Workers, 266, 268
Interstate Commerce Commission investigation (1917–1918) and, 111–13, 119–24, 166
ITT's purchase of international telephone manufacturing subsidiaries purchased (1925) of, 529–32
Justice Department consent decree (1914) with, 10, 111–13
Justice Department consent decree (1932) with, 354–55, 357

Justice Department consent decree (1956) with, 8–9, 212, 314, 367, 386, 451, 457–58, 461, 466, 473–75
long-distance service and, 74, 89–90, 105–6, 114–15, 173–75, 179–80, 189–90, 193, 278
merger spree during early twentieth century engineered by, 74, 105–6
monopoly power of, 73–75, 80–81, 90, 93–94, 104–6, 198, 213–14, 223–25, 231, 264, 329–30, 465
National Federation of Telephone Workers and, 257, 265–68
nationalization proposals fought by, 125, 127
National Recovery Administration and, 225
National Security Agency and, 591
New York City phone service breakdown (1969–1970) and, 469–70
number of employees at, 599–600
patents held by, 8–9, 73–75, 77–78, 80, 120, 177–78, 362–63, 602–3
Postal Telegraph Company's shares in, 78–79
President's Task Force on Communications Policy (Johnson Administration) and, 477, 481, 484–85
pricing strategies during 1920s at, 169–70, 174, 175, 179–80
private-wire contracts and, 119–21, 123, 195–96, 223–25
Public Relations Bureau of, 127, 361
public utility commissions and, 5–6, 74, 106, 107–8, 110, 112, 157–58, 161–62, 166–68, 170–71, 175–77, 178–80, 602–3
radio research and development at, 190, 349–50, 565
reprivatization of telecommunications infrastructure following World War I and, 147–48, 159–60, 164–65
residential and commercial phone use rates in early twentieth century and, 86–87
SAGE command and control system and, 456–57
Sandia National Laboratories and, 379–81, 385
strikes (1945–1947) at, 272–79, 280–81, 282–83
strikes (1971–1972) at, 413–29, 417f, 421f, 422f, 423f, 424f, 514
strikes (1983) at, 517–18
strikes (2019) at, 608
submarine cables and, 547, 550–51, 559–60
TELPAK private-line service and, 472
Telstar satellite and, 473
toll calling and, 89, 123

American Telephone and Telegraph Company (AT&T) (*cont.*)
  Traffic department of, 270–71
  TWX timed wire exchange service and, 196, 197–98, 224, 265, 303
  US space program and, 547–48
  Vail's universal wire system proposal and, 89–92, 105–6, 194–95, 319
  Western Electric as manufacturing subsidiary of, 175–76, 177–78, 182–83, 190, 319, 325, 360, 366
  Western Union controlling stake held (1909–1913) by, 41, 78–79, 90–91, 112, 120
  Western Union's cartel agreement (1879) with, 78
  Western Union's corporate synchronization (1910s) with, 79–80
  wireless services and, 595
  women employees at, 264–65, 270, 273
Anderson, Bernard E., 438–39
Android operating system, 597
Anik 1 satellite, 552
antimonopolism. *See also* antitrust enforcement; monopoly
  American Telephone and Telegraph and, 4, 6, 76, 83–85, 99–100, 112, 113–14, 178, 601
  Anti-Monopoly Party and, 59
  financial antimonopolism and, 59
  postalization model and, 48–68
  private-wire contracts and, 122–23
  public utility doctrine and, 157–58
  racism within movement for, 47–48
  Radio Act and, 351–52
  railroad strikes of 1877 and, 47–48
  Western Union and, 4, 42–43, 48, 66–68, 77–78, 601
antitrust enforcement
  American Telephone and Telegraph breakup (1982–1984) and, 212, 518–20, 558–59, 572–73, 577, 594
  American Telephone and Telegraph case (1949–1956) and, 344, 366–87, 464–65, 602–3
  Clayton Antitrust Act and, 153, 182–83
  Justice Department and, 8–9, 153, 365–66, 369–70, 377–78, 474, 495
  Sherman Antitrust Act and, 79–80, 153, 353–54, 365, 371
  Willis-Graham Act and, 118
Apollo, 573
Apple, 571, 591–92, 597, 598–99, 608–9
Arapaho Indians, 39

Ariane rocket (European Space Agency), 558–59
Armed Forces Communications and Electronics Association, 453
Army Command and Administrative Network (ACAN), 535–36
Arnold, Thurman W., 243–44, 361–62, 365–66, 369, 371, 468
Arpanet, 510–11, 561–62, 568–69, 573, 578–79
Arthur D. Little, Inc., 395, 507–8
Ashby, Steven, 238, 286, 287–88
Ash Commission, 490, 494–95
Associated Press (AP), 44–45, 55–56, 77–78, 119–20, 135
Association of American Railroads, 461–62
Association of Catholic Trade Unionists (ACTU), 241–42, 287–88, 295
Association of Data Processing Service Organizations, 454–55
Association of Western Union Employees, 227–29, 231, 236, 249–51, 252–53, 260
Aswell, James B., 140–41, 150
Atomic Energy Commission (AEC), 379–81
Auerbach, Jerold, 246–47
Australia
  Five Eyes intelligence consortium and, 543
  Intelsat and, 548, 550
  International Telephone and Telegraph and, 529
  mail strike (1968) in, 396
  Radio Corporation of America and, 527
  submarine cables and, 525–26
  US treaty agreements with, 541–42

Baarslag, Karl, 240–41
Bahr, Morton, 292, 415–16, 518–19
Baker, George, 490
Baker, Russell, 396
Baldridge, Holmes A., 370–72
Barbash, Jack, 284
Barnard, C. F., 127
Barnes, Stanley N., 378, 381–82, 384
Barnet, Richard, 582–83
Barnouw, Erik, 206–7
Barrett, James, 240
Bates, Harold L., 231, 233
Bauer, Cecil, 482
Baxter, Vern, 308
Baxter, William F., 477
Beamish, Richard J., 324–25
Becker, Samuel, 212
Behn, Sosthenes, 197–98, 531–34
Beirne, Joseph A.

American Communications Union proposal and, 12, 511–12
anti-Communism of, 504–5
Association of Catholic Trade Unionists and, 287
on AT&T's relationship with the National Federation of Telephone Workers, 267
automation in the telephone industry and, 414–15, 505–6
belief in importance of labor's proximity to policymakers of, 446, 516
biographical background of, 274–75
Communication Workers of America membership drive during 1960s and, 410, 507–8, 515
as Communication Workers of America's first president, 283
Congress of Industrial Organizations and, 285, 291
death of, 514, 515
democratic capitalism championed by, 274–75
Democratic Party and, 503–5, 507
economic citizenship approach promoted by, 411–12
efforts at consolidation of unions in telecommunications industry and, 292–93
on Eisenhower Administration's anti-unionism, 407–8
as National Federation of Telephone Workers president, 266–67
National Federation of Telephone Workers strike (1947) and, 275
New York Telephone strike (1971–1972) and, 415–16, 418–20, 426–27
photo of, 413f
on public opinion regarding trade unions, 281–82
on satellite industry and the private sector, 508–9
union jurisdictional questions and, 517
Western Electric and, 481–82
on women at AT&T, 264, 270
Bell, Alexander Graham, 73–74, 75–76, 78
Bell, John, 27
Bellamy, Edward, 55–56
Bell Atlantic, 594–95
Bell Laboratories
microelectronics research and, 543–44
military-oriented research at, 369, 375, 382, 543–44
Sandia National Labs and, 380–81
television research and, 358
transistor research at, 383–85, 456, 543–44
United Electrical Workers and, 236–37
UNIX operating system and, 456, 573
Bell South, 594–95
Bell Telephone. *See* American Telephone and Telegraph Company (AT&T)
Bell Workers Action Committee, 416–25
Bemis, Edward W., 96, 186–87
Bendix, 364, 373
Bennett, James Gordon, 37–38
Benton, William, 585–86
Bentsel, Richard, 36
Berge, Wendell, 365
Berger, Victor, 130
Berners-Lee, Tim, 559–60, 576
Berry, Chuck, 337
Berthelot, Helen W., 275–76, 407–8, 430
Bethell, U. N., 118
Biden, Joe, 607
BITNET, 570
Bittner, Van, 218
Blackburn, Robin, 584–85, 590
Black Power movement, 467, 479–80
Blatchford, Robert, 56
Blevins, Cameron, 22, 27–28, 60, 63
Bliss, Willard, 252
Blount, Winton "Red," 399–405
Blum, John, 148–49
Board of War Communications, 257, 282–83
Boston (Massachusetts), 80–81, 144–45
Brandeis, Louis, 134, 164
Brazil
domestic computer industry in, 554
International Telephone & Telegraph Corporation and, 529
public data networks in, 569
Radio Corporation of America and, 527
slavery in, 523
state-owned enterprises in, 575–76
US trade relations with, 556
Brennecke, Natalie, 256
Brenner, Aaron, 388, 399, 413–16
Brenner, Robert, 506–7
Bretton Woods fixed currency exchange system, 557–58
Bridges, Harry, 234
Brinkley, Alan, 210, 365
Bristow, Joseph L., 114–15
British Marconi, 348, 527
British Telecom, 559–60
broadband service, 581–82, 592, 595–96
Brock, Gerald, 454
Brooks, John, 152, 469–70

Brophy, John, 236–37
Brotherhood of Telegraphers, 65–66
Brown, Aaron V., 31–32
Brown, Thad, 208, 210
Brown, William, 135–36, 138
Brownell, Herbert, 375
Bryan, William Jennings, 525
"bucket shops," 136–37
Buckley, Oliver, 379–81, 452
Buenos Aires Declaration (1994), 588–90
Burch, Dean, 12, 437, 493–94, 497–99
Burger, Warren, 440–41
Burleson, Albert S.
  biographical background of, 141–42
  Committee on Telephone Rate Standardization and, 162–63
  government control of telecommunications services during World War I under, 140–41, 143, 145–48, 150, 151–52, 161–64, 179, 180, 187, 277–78, 317–18
  government ownership of telecommunications services supported by, 126–28, 150, 159–60
  Interstate Commerce Commission and, 160–61
  New England telephone operators strike (1919) and, 144–45, 150
  political patronage jobs and, 141–42
  postal savings banks reduced under, 61–62
  postal unions suppressed by, 129–30, 142
  reprivatization of telecommunications infrastructure following World War I and, 148–50, 151, 159–60, 164–65
  Vail's promise of a universal wire system and, 90
Busch, Adolphus, 99
Bush, George H. W., 574–75, 579–82
Bush, Vannevar, 363
business users
  communications unions and, 515–16, 517–18
  computer services development and, 454–55, 458–59, 463
  digital communications development and, 563, 576–77, 579, 592, 598–99
  Federal Radio Commission and, 320–21
  international business competition and, 555–56, 558–59, 575–76
  Nixon Administration telecommunications policy and, 497, 501–2
  postal service development and, 4, 29–30, 36, 53–54, 405, 604
  President's Task Force on Communications Policy and, 482–85
  private express companies and, 24–25
  private wire contracts and, 122–23, 224–25
  public utility commissions and, 5, 158
  social justice movements and, 522, 603–4
  submarine cable development and, 51–52
  telecommunications liberalization and, 12
  telegraph service development and, 8, 19–20, 51, 66–67, 196–97, 228–29, 231
  telephone service development and, 4, 74–76, 78–79, 87–88, 89, 104–6, 108, 119, 138–39, 144–45, 152–53, 173–74, 185–86, 318–19, 323–24, 325, 328, 337, 425–26
Butterfield Overland Mail, 31–32, 37

cable television
  American Telephone and Telegraph Company and, 473–74
  Federal Communications Commission and, 473, 496
  internet service provision and, 581–82, 595–96
  Office of Technology Policy and, 496
  public utility commissions and, 474
Cabletron Systems, 573
Cable & Wireless company, 165, 532, 535
California
  California Railroad Commission and, 109, 180
  California Rate Commission and, 180–81
  gold rush in, 37
  phone rate debates in, 180–82, 200
  postal services established in, 31–32
  Public Utilities Commission in, 98
California Rural Legal Assistance, 443–44
Cameron, Simon, 40
Campaign Against Utility Service Exploitation, 341–42
Canada
  American Telephone and Telegraph Company and, 168, 529–30
  Anik I satellite and, 552
  Five Eyes intelligence consortium and, 543
  Intelsat and, 548–49
  International Telephone and Telegraph and, 529
  postal savings banks in, 59–60
  private-wire contracts and, 119–20
  provincial governments' ownership of telephone services in, 126–27
  submarine cables and, 525–26
  union resistance to telecommunications privatization in, 588
  Verizon and, 594–95

Western Union expansion of telegraph service to, 524
Carey, James B., 235–38, 286–87
Carlton, Newcomb, 140–41
Carpenter, Daniel, 52–53, 63
Carson, Kit, 32–33
Carter, Jimmy, 12, 468, 516, 555–57, 586–87
Carterfone decision, 483–84
Celler, Emanuel, 464–65
Central Federation of Labor, 96–97
Central Intelligence Agency (CIA), 504–5, 537, 586–87
Central Labor Union, 96–97
Central Trades and Labor Council (New York City), 182
CenturyLink, 594–95
Cerf, Vinton, 568–69, 571, 578, 579–80, 590, 772n.112
Chavez, Dennis, 434
Chesapeake & Potomac Telephone Company, 129, 176–77, 408–9
Cheyenne Indians, 39, 609–10
Chicago (Illinois)
  American Telephone and Telegraph Company and, 99–100, 101–2, 103–5, 110
  City Council in, 99–102
  city-owned railway systems in, 96, 100
  Democratic Party convention (1968) in, 1–2
  independent telephone providers in, 82–83
  mayoral campaign of 1905 in, 100
  municipal phone system campaigns in, 98–104, 609–10
  municipal rate rights in, 5–6
  phone rate debates during 1920s in, 186–93
  Post Office breakdown (1966) in, 391–97
  Pullman strike (1894) and, 70–71
  Teamsters' Union strike (1905) in, 100–1
  telephone service in, 80–81
  trade unions' political power in, 94, 100–1, 104
Chicago Board of Trade, 99–100
Chicago Federation of Labor
  Chicago Rate Case and, 191–92
  government control of telephone and telegraph services supported by, 129, 142
  Illinois Bell strike (1968) and, 1
  municipal telephone system campaigns and, 101, 102–4, 638–39n.67
  street railway ownership debates and, 100
  Teamsters' Union strike (1905) and, 100–1
  World War I and, 142
Chicago Federation of Teachers, 99, 103
Chicago Hotel Men's Association, 191
Chicago Rate Case (1921), 186–87, 190–92, 318–19
Chicago's Women's City Club, 103
Chicago Telephone Company (CTC), 99–100, 101–2, 186–88
Chile, 504–5, 527, 529, 554, 575–76, 588
China
  civil war (1927–1949) in, 272, 539–40, 542–43, 546
  domestic computer industry in, 554
  Intelsat and, 559
  International Telecommunication Union and, 536–37, 605–6
  internet equipment supply industry in, 15, 606–7
  market capitalism reforms in, 14
  Open Door trade policy and, 524–25
  postal savings banks in, 59–60
  US relations with, 607
  World War II and, 538
Chinese Americans, 47–48, 52–53
Christian, Charlie, 305
Churchill, Winston, 534
Cincinnati Bell, 341–42
Cisco, 573, 591–92
Citizens Committee for Postal Reform, Inc, 404–5
Civic Council, 96–97
Civil Rights Act (1964), 430, 433–37
Civil War
  Confederate Post Office and, 40
  for-profit mail contractors and, 33
  telegraph services and, 38–39, 40–41
  trade union organization among urban postal workers during, 36
  Union Army and, 36, 60
  US imperialism and, 36
  US Post Office and, 36, 40, 49, 60
  wage labor economy and, 46–47
Clardy, Kit, 205–6, 668–69n.107
Clark, Tom C., 277–78, 371–72, 380–81
Clay, Henry, 37–38
Clayton Antitrust Act, 153, 182–83
Cleveland (Ohio)
  African Americans in, 389–90, 431–32
  city-owned power facilities in, 95
  independent telephone providers in, 82–83
  municipalization of service campaigns in, 96
  municipal phone system campaigns in, 98–99
Cleveland, Grover, 54–55, 70–71, 525
Clinton, Bill, 580–81
Clinton, Hillary, 590
Cobble, Dorothy Sue, 389, 430, 434, 438, 503

Coburn, James, 471
Cogent, 598
Cohen, Joshua, 39–40, 42–43
coin-box units, 188, 194–95
Cold War
  American Telephone and Telegraph antitrust case (1949–1956) and, 368
  Congress of Industrial Organizations and, 7–8, 539–40
  decolonization and, 541
  end of, 582, 587, 588–89, 590
  government's temporary takeover of industries during, 277
  Korean War and, 367, 375, 379, 382, 541–42, 546
  US imperialism and, 543, 546, 547–48
Cole, Kenneth, 493–94
Colson, Charles, 9–10, 399–401, 402–4, 498, 511
Columbia Broadcasting System (CBS), 236–37
Comcast, 595–96
Commerce Department, 159, 493–94, 495, 581–82, 607
Commercial Telegraphers Union of America (CTUA)
  American Communications Association and, 251–53, 255, 258
  American Federation of Labor and, 124–25, 128, 229, 235–36, 240–41, 255
  American Radio Telegraphists Association and, 234, 251
  anti-Communism emphasis at, 252–53
  federal control of telecommunications during World War I and, 144, 151
  federal regulation of telecommunications supported by, 111, 124–25, 128, 141
  founding (1903) of, 227–28
  Great Depression and, 222
  Kingsbury Commitment and, 115
  National Recovery Administration and, 229
  Postal Telegraph and, 227–31, 243, 258
  Postal Telegraph-Western Union merger and, 226–27, 251–52, 259, 302–3
  racist membership criterion at, 240–41
  strike (1919) authorized by, 147–48
  Western Union and, 140, 228–29, 252–53, 260–63
Commission On Industrial Relations, 126
common carriage principle, 106–7, 168
Commons, John R., 192
Communications Act of 1934
  broadcasting provisions of, 206–7
  cellular telephones and, 519–20
  Federal Communication Commission and, 205–6, 214–15
  public interest standard for granting radio licenses established by, 204
  Section 212 on interlocking directorates and, 209–10
  telecommunications industry investigation established by, 205–6
  telegraph company mergers prohibited in, 198
Communications Satellite Act of 1962, 472, 476, 489, 495
Communications Satellite Corporation, 473, 548
Communication Workers of America (CWA)
  African Americans and, 295, 425–26, 433–34
  Alphabet Workers Union and, 608–9
  American Communications Association and, 222, 290–92
  American Communications Union proposal and, 12, 510–14, 515–16, 517, 519, 604–5
  American Federation of Labor and, 284–85
  American Telephone and Telegraph Company and, 10, 293–94, 408–9, 411, 509, 514, 515–16, 518–19
  anti-Communism and, 602–3
  Arthur D. Little, Inc. and, 507–8
  automation in the telephone industry and, 505–6, 518–19
  collective bargaining gains by, 222
  Congress of Industrial Organizations and, 7–8, 265–66, 284, 285, 289–95, 408–9
  establishment (1947) of, 7, 265–66, 283, 407
  Federal Communications Commission and, 755–56n.124
  International Brotherhood of Electrical Workers and, 284–85, 292–93, 409–10
  jurisdictional questions regarding, 517
  Local 1101 and, 413–18, 419–20, 425–26, 428–29
  Local 9490 of, 427–28
  membership drive of 1960s and, 410, 507–8, 515
  National Federation of Telephone Workers as precursor of, 265–66
  New York Bell negotiations (1961) and, 410
  size of, 502
  social unionism and, 10
  strike (1952) by, 409
  strike (1971–1972) by, 413–29, 417f, 421f, 422f, 423f, 424f
  strike (1983) by, 517–18
  United Electrical Workers and, 222

Verizon and, 608
Vietnam War and, 420–25
Western Union and, 293
The Communist Manifesto (Marx and Engels), 56
Communists in the United States
  African Americans and, 240
  American Communications Association and, 7–8, 238–39, 252–53, 267–68
  Communist International (Comintern) and, 239–41
  Congress of Industrial Organization and, 218, 238–39, 241–42, 289, 294
  Dies Committee's targeting of, 238
  loyalty oaths targeting, 286
  McCarran Committee's targeting of, 238–39
  New Deal and, 238–39, 241–42
  Popular Front period of 1930s and, 240
  Postal Telegraph-Western Union merger and, 226–27
  Red Scare of 1950s and targeting of, 238–39, 241–42
  Soviet Union and, 239, 241
  Taft-Hartley Act's targeting of, 287–88, 291–92
  on telegraph industry monopoly, 233
  United Electrical Workers and, 238, 267–68
  World War II and, 239, 244
Compaq, 571, 591–92
Comsat
  American Telephone and Telegraph and, 472–73
  establishment (1962) of, 548
  Intelsat and, 13–14, 548, 549–50, 552
  private ownership of, 13–14
  Satellite Business Systems and, 562
Comstock Act (1873), 52–53
Confederate Post Office, 40
Confederation Generale du Travail (France), 131–32
Congress of Industrial Organizations (CIO). *See also* American Federation of Labor-Congress of Industrial Organizations (AFL-CIO)
  African Americans' membership in and support from, 218, 240
  American Communications Association and, 6–8, 222, 237, 239, 240–41, 242–43, 251–52, 254–55, 260, 261f, 265–66, 267–68, 269–70, 271, 283, 289–94, 602
  American Radio Telegraphists Association and, 234–36, 294
  anti-Communism and, 285–86
  Cold War foreign policy and, 7–8, 539–40
  Communication Workers of America and, 7–8, 265–66, 284, 285, 289–95, 408–9
  Communists' roles in, 218, 238–39, 241–42, 289, 294
  election of 1948 and, 288–89
  employer resistance against, 219, 221
  founding (1935) of, 217–18
  LaFollette Committee and, 247
  managerial and political elite allies of, 221–22
  Maritime Committee of, 234
  National Federation of Telephone Workers and, 267–68, 269–70, 273, 279, 283–84, 289
  New Deal and dramatic expansion of, 219–21
  strikes coordinated by, 221, 234–35, 242, 273, 275
  Telephone Workers Organizing Committee and, 283–85, 289–91, 292–94, 410
  United Electrical Workers and, 6–7, 235–36, 242, 267–68
  War Labor Board and, 268–69
  World War II and, 256
Congress of the United States
  eight-hour federal worker laws and, 69
  franking privileges and, 22, 33–34
  House Agriculture Committee and, 333–34
  House Antitrust Subcommittee and, 215
  Mail Classification Act of 1879 and, 50
  mail robbery laws and, 21–22
  postal road authorization issued (1825) by, 31
  postal savings banks and, 61
  Postal Telegraph-Western Union merger and, 259
  Post Office control of telecommunications services during World War I and, 140–41, 149–50, 164
  Post Office granted monopoly over first-class mail (1845) by, 27–30, 33–34
  private mail carriage regulations, 24–25
  proposals for government ownership of telephone services at, 177
  rural free delivery services and, 63
  telegraph services left in private hands by, 37–38
  telephone strikes (1947) and, 276
  US Postal Service's establishment (1970) and, 9–10
Connally, John B., 490
Connery, Lawrence J., 358
Connolly, James, 58, 130–31, 144
Conseil European pour la Recherche Nucleaire (CERN), 543–44, 559–60

Consumer Communication Reform Act, 515–16
Cooley, Thomas M., 160–61
Coolidge, Calvin, 145
Corporation for National Research Initiatives (CNRI), 579–80
Corporation for Research and Educational Networking, 570
Cortada, James, 462
Covid-19 pandemic (2020–2022), 520–21, 600, 608–9
Craig, Cleo, 273
Crain, Matthew, 580–81
Cramer, Gus, 414
Craven, T. A. M., 214–15
Cronkite, Walter, 2
Cross, Wilbur, 211–12
CSNET, 570
Cuba, 20–21, 32, 504–5, 524–25, 527–28
Currarino, Roseanne, 297

Daley, Richard, 1–2
Daniel, Franz, 218
Danielian, N. B., 161–62, 164, 169, 360
Daniels, Josephus, 126, 140–41, 352, 651n.61
data networking
 Euronet data network and, 569
 human rights and, 584–90
 IBM and, 563, 565, 569–71, 574
 Intelsat as potential model for, 564
 offshoring and, 583–84
 personal computers and, 571
 Pool's proposal international system for, 564–66, 576, 582
David, Archibald, 396
Dawley, Alan, 218–19
Day, J. Edward, 394–95
Dayton (Ohio) strikes (1944), 268–71
Debs, Eugene V., 54
deButts, John, 489–90
DeCaux, Len, 218
Defense Advanced Research Projects Agency (DARPA), 456–57
Defense Communications Board (DCB), 255–57
Defense Department. *See also* War Department
 American Telephone and Telegraph Antitrust Case (1949–1956) and, 377–78
 Arpanet and, 510–11, 561–62, 568–69, 573, 578–79
 Defense Communications Agency and, 578
 Information Processing Techniques Office at, 456–57
 microelectronics research and, 384–85
 transistors and, 454
Dell, 571, 591–92
Democratic National Convention (1968), 1–2
de Phillis, Dorothy, 340–41
Detroit (Michigan), 82–83, 95, 270–71, 273, 276, 280
Deutsche Telekom, 595
Diebold Group, 505
Dies, Martin, 238
digital divide, 581–82
Digital Equipment, 462
Digital Markets Act, 606
Dill, Clarence, 166, 203–4, 205–6, 248, 352–53
Dimondstein, Mark, 608
DirecTV, 595–96
Dixiecrats, 288–89
Dmytryk, Kay, 271
Dodd, Harold, 353
Donaldson, Jesse M., 309
Donnelly, Reuben H., 342
Douglas, Stephen, 19–20, 31, 38–39
Douglas, William, 361
Douglas Aircraft, 382–83
Doyle, Stephen, 496
Dreyfuss, Henry, 339
Driesen, Daniel, 242, 246, 253–54, 257, 259
DuBois, Charles, 530–31
Du Bois, Shirley Graham, 551–52
Dubois, W. E. B., 539–40
DuBridge, Lee A., 488
Dulles, John Foster, 585–86
Dunne, Edward, 100–1, 104–5
Durr, Clifford J., 333

Eastern and Associated Telegraph Company, 525–26
Eaton, Clement, 35–36
Edison, Thomas, 43
Eger, John, 565–66, 582
Eisenhower, Dwight D., 367–68, 375–76, 382–83, 407–8
Eliot, Charles W., 53
Ellinghaus, William, 515–16
Ellis, Ryan, 519
Ellsworth, Robert, 488–89
Elmquist, Charles E., 163–65
Elston, Dorothy Andrews, 497–98
Emerson, 349, 355
Endlich, Lisa, 455–56
Energy Department, 569
Engels, Friedrich, 56
England. *See also* Great Britain

imperialism and, 523
International Telephone and Telegraph and, 529
municipal telephone systems in, 95
parcel post services in, 64–65
postal worker unions in, 131–32
Post Office's seventeenth-century origins in, 53–54
Equal Employment Opportunity Commission (EEOC), 434–37, 438–39, 441–42, 443–44, 445
Equal Suffrage Association, 63–64
Erlichman, John, 402–3, 493–94, 498
Euronet data network, 569
European Conference on Satellite Communications, 548–49
European Space Agency, 550, 558–59
European Space Research Organization, 548–49, 550
European Space Vehicle Launcher Organization, 548–49
European Union, 606
Eurospace, 548–49
Eutelsat, 558–59
Executive Order 12333, 591

Facebook, 576–77, 591–92, 597–99, 606
Fairchild Semiconductor, 453
Fair Employment Practices Committee, 295, 431
Fair Labor Standards Act, 249
Farley, James, 306–7
Farmers' Alliance, 54
Farmers Educational and Co-operation Union, 125
Farmers Equity Society, 125
Farmers Union, 125
Federal Communications Commission (FCC)
 American Communications Association and, 244–46, 254–55, 260
 American Telephone and Telegraph Company and, 6, 207, 209–10, 212–13, 214–16, 321, 323–24, 325–27, 464–65, 602–3
 broadcast television and, 473–74
 cable television and, 473, 496
 Carterfone decision and, 483–84
 data networking and, 570–71
 Defense Communications Board and, 255, 256
 establishment of, 6, 185–86, 202–3, 205–6, 602
 jurisdictional cost separations and, 322–23
 jurisdictional limits of, 317
 microwave services regulation and, 461–62, 472, 474–75
 Postal Telegraph-Western Union merger and, 225–27, 244, 248–49, 258–59, 302–3
 public utility commissions and, 208–9, 318–19, 321, 326–28, 602
 racist content at commercial radio stations and, 478
 rate-averaging precepts and, 332
 Roosevelt and, 6, 185–86, 207–8, 212
 satellite technology and, 491–92, 493–94
 telephone industry investigation (1934–1938) by, 205–6, 210–16, 225–26, 244, 319
 telephone industry strikes (1947) and, 277–78
 universal residential service goals and, 316–18
Federal Coordinating Council for Science, Engineering, and Technology (FCCSET), 577–78
Federal Housing Administration, 314
Federal Radio Commission, 320–21, 351–52, 461
Federal Road, 32–33
Federal Trade Commission, 153, 350–51
Federation of Civil Servants (Germany), 131–32
Ferris, Charles D., 500–1, 516
fiber optic cables (optical fiber cables), 550–51, 558–59, 576–77, 581, 594–95, 596–97
Field, Cyrus, 42–43, 524–25
Filbey, Francis, 406, 510–13
Filene, Edward, 297–300
First Amendment, 70, 246–47
Fischer, Claude, 83, 86–87, 92, 315–16, 332–33
Fish, Frederick P., 171–72
Fish, Hamilton, 524–25
Fitzhugh, George, 36
Five Eyes intelligence consortium, 543
Flanagan, Maureen A., 103
Flanigan, Peter M., 11, 487–88, 491–92, 493–94, 495–96
Flicker, Theodore J., 471
Fly, James L. ("Larry")
 American Communications Association and, 254
 biographical background of, 208
 Defense Communications Board and, 256
 on Federal Communications Commission's lack of knowledge of working conditions, 244–46
 Postal Telegraph-Western Union merger and, 258–59
 on timed wire exchange service and, 196

Foner, Philip, 98
Ford, Gerald R., 515–16, 555
foreign direct investment (FDI), 575–76, 583
Forrestal, James, 535–36
Fowler, Gene, 46
France
  domestic computer market in, 560
  imperialism and, 20–21, 523, 540–41
  independent telephone providers in, 118
  International Telecommunication Union and, 536–37, 550
  International Telephone and Telegraph and, 529
  Louisiana Purchase and, 20–21, 30
  Minitel data network and, 569–70
  national computer industry in, 560
  nationalization of telephone industry in, 126–27
  packet-switching technology and, 562–63
  postal savings banks in, 59–60
  private mail carriage regulations in, 24–25
  radio industry in, 527–28
  satellite industry in, 549, 550–51, 558–59
  submarine cable network of, 526–27
  supercomputing capacity in, 552
  telegraph services under government ownership in, 50–51
  union resistance to telecommunications privatization in, 588
France Telecom, 559–60
Franchise Tax and Municipal Ownership League, 96–97
Frankfurter, Felix, 185
Fraser, Steve, 221–22, 285–86
freenets, 570
Friedman, Milton, 466–68
Friedman, Thomas, 590
Fukuyama, Francis, 588–89
Future Outlook League, 280, 431–32

Gabel, Richard, 466
Gallatin, Albert, 20–21
Galvin, 355
Gannett, Frank E., 288
Gardner, Lloyd, 38–39
Garland, Hamlin, 96–97
Gary Group, 118
gay rights movement, 10, 388, 434, 444–46, 471, 522
General Agreement on Tariffs and Trade, 13, 541–42
General Data Protection Regulation (European Union), 606

General Electric (GE)
  digital information processing technology and, 453
  electronics research by, 373
  General Electric Information Services and, 574–75
  labor unions and, 455, 608
  patents and, 345–46, 347, 374
  radar technology developed by, 373
  radio-based telephone service and, 531
  Radio Corporation of America's establishment and, 561
  radio industry and, 348, 349–50, 354–55
  transistors developed by, 384–85
  United Electrical Workers and, 235
General Motors, 274, 462
General Postal Union, 50–51
George, Henry, 55–56, 96–97
Germany. *See also* West Germany
  digital networks in, 569–70
  division (1949–1989) of, 543
  imperialism and, 523, 526–27
  independent telephone providers in, 118
  nationalization of telephone industry in, 126–27
  parcel post services in, 64–65
  postal savings banks in, 59–60
  Private Branch Exchanges in, 574
  reunification of, 587
  telegraph services under government ownership in, 50–51
  US military government (1945–1949) in, 541–42, 546
  World War I and, 525–26
  World War II and, 239, 244, 257, 534, 537–38, 543–44
Germer, Adolph, 218
Ghana, 551–52
Gibson, John, 272–73
Gifford, Walter S.
  as ambassador to England, 381
  on AT&T's network expansion in 1920s, 179
  call for telecommunications industry investigation by, 203–4
  Communications Act of 1934 and, 206–7
  Federal Communications Commission ruling on AT&T directorates and, 209–10
  President's Organization on Unemployment Relief and, 201
  Senate Interstate Commerce Committee hearings (1929–1930) and, 177–78
Glickman, Lawrence, 102–3

Global Information Infrastructure (GII), 589–90
Global South, 14, 541, 583–84, 588
Globe Radio, 243
Goldberg, Arthur, 292
Gompers, Samuel
  collective bargaining rights for postal workers and, 69
  Commercial Telegraphers Union of America's potential strike (1919) and, 148
  government control of telecommunications service during World War I and, 145–46
  government ownership of utilities rejected by, 69
  Hearst and, 96–97
  industrial democracy concept and, 134
  long-distance telephone service during World War I and, 92–93
  photo of, 143f
  on trade union-based remedies to social problems, 94, 297
Google, 458, 576–77, 591–93, 597, 598–99, 606, 608–9
Gorbachev, Mikhail, 587
Gore, Al, 516, 578–79, 588–90
Gottlieb, Sylvia B., 407–8
Gould, Jay, 42–43
Graham, Margaret, 372–73
Grain Dealers' National Association, 120–22
Granger movement, 50, 62–64, 84, 125
Graphnet, 519, 561–62
Gray, Horace M., 465–66
Great Britain
  domestic computer market in, 560
  Five Eyes intelligence consortium and, 543
  imperialism and, 20–21, 523, 540–41, 547–48
  independent telephone providers in, 118
  Intelsat and, 549–50
  International Telecommunication Union and, 536–37
  Latin America and, 546
  municipal telephone systems in, 95
  nationalization of telephone industry in, 126–27
  naval forces of, 13
  Oregon Treaty and, 30
  packet-switching technology and, 562–63
  postal savings banks in, 59–61
  postal strike (1971) in, 508
  Post Office in, 34, 51, 531, 547
  private mail carriage regulations in, 24–25
  privatization of telecommunications in, 575–76
  Soviet Union and, 537
  submarine cable network of, 13, 44, 91, 525–27
  supercomputing capacity in, 552
  telegraph services under government ownership in, 50–51
  union resistance to telecommunications privatization in, 588
  United Nations and, 539
  US postal treaty (1848) with, 29–30
  wireless radio technology and, 528
  World War II and, 534, 537–38
Great Depression
  American Telephone and Telegraph Company and, 5–6, 193–94, 201–2, 265
  phone rate debates during, 200–1
  phone subscription declines during, 191, 193–94, 313–14, 316
  postal savings banks and, 61–62
  strikes during, 217–18, 221, 234–35, 242
  telegraph industry and, 194, 196–97
  telephone industry unemployment during, 201–2, 265
Great War. *See* World War I
Greece, 286–87, 541–42
Green, Venus, 134–35, 201, 265–66, 267, 279–80, 340–41, 410, 430–31, 433
Greenbackers, 107, 125
Greenberger, Martin, 459–60
Greene, Julie, 99
Greenstein, Shane, 572–73
Griffith, Paul, 289
Griffith, Robert, 210–11
Griswold, A. H., 223–24
Gronlund, Laurence, 55–56, 136
Groves, Leslie, 372–73
GTE, 594–95
Guam, 525, 539–40, 546–47
Guernsey, Nathaniel, 109–10, 163–64

Hacker, Andrew, 467–68
Hahn, Steven, 20–21, 41–42, 524
Haldeman, H. R., 399, 401–3, 489–90, 498
Hale, James W., 29–30
Hand, Thomas Millet, 276
Harbord, J.G., 354–55, 532–33
Harding, Warren G., 153–54, 351–52
Harriman, Job, 92
Hart, Gary, 516
Hartley, Jr., Fred A., 277. *See also* Taft-Hartley Act
Haskins, Charles H., 84
Hatch, Carl, 254

Hawaii, 13, 32, 382–83, 524–27, 547
Hawley, Ellis, 199, 363
Hay, John, 524–25
Haywood, Allan S., 239, 269–70, 284, 290–91, 293–94
Hazeltine, 373
Hazlett, Thomas, 496
Headrick, Daniel, 32–33, 44
Hearst, William Randolph, 96–97, 100, 125
Henry, Aaron, 439–40
Hepburn Act of 1906, 111
Hettinger, Jr., A. J., 229–31
Hewitt, Elizabeth, 35–36
Hewlett-Packard, 453
Hill, Charles B., 165, 574–75
Hill, Lister, 333
Hillman, Sidney, 218, 298, 299–300
Hillquit, Morris, 130–31
Hills, Jill, 536, 549
Hisoka, Maejima, 50–51
Hitler, Adolf, 534, 537
Hoan, Daniel W., 107–8
Hochfelder, David, 66–67, 136–37
Hoddeson, Lillian, 364, 383–85
Hoffman, Clare, 276
Holcombe, Arthur, 126–27
Holm, Dion R., 181–82
Home Owners Loan Corporation, 314
Home Telephone Company, 83–84, 87–88, 87*t*, 98
Hooper, Stanford C., 353
Hoover, Herbert
  American Telephone and Telegraph Company and, 353–54
  Commerce Department (1921–1929) under, 159, 297–98, 350–51, 461
  Great Depression and, 217
  Hoover Commission (1949) and, 311–12, 698n.32
  potential Western Union-Postal Telegraph merger and, 198
  President's Organization on Unemployment Relief and, 201
  sale of World War II government factories and, 452
Hopkins, Harry, 243–44
Horwitz, Robert B., 175, 439–41
House, Edward, 141–42
Howell, Robert B., 353
Huawei, 606–7
Huber, Peter, 572–73
Hudson, Heather, 550
Hughes Aircraft, 454, 552
Hughes Semiconductor, 453
Hugill, Peter, 533–34

human rights movement, 545–46, 584–90
Huntington, Collis P., 42–43
Hurricane Electric, 598
Hyde, Rosel H., 478, 483–84, 489, 491, 497–98
Hylan, John F., 182

IBM (International Business Machines)
  American Telephone and Telegraph and, 531, 550–51
  anti-unionism at, 455, 506–7
  data networking and, 563, 565, 569–71, 574–75
  Eurospace and, 548–49
  Germany and, 546
  Intelsat and, 548–49, 557
  Japan and, 546
  Justice Department antitrust action (1952) against, 378
  market dominance before 1975 of, 560
  packet-switching technology and, 562–63
  personal computers and, 571, 591–92
  radio services and, 531–32
  SAGE command and control system and, 456–57
  Satellite Business Systems and, 562
  software development at, 454–55
  specialized data-processing systems made by, 460–61
  submarine cables and, 547, 550–51
  Systems Network Architecture (SNA), 562, 576
  Systems Network Architecture packet-switching product and, 562
ICANN, 581–82
Illinois
  Illinois Commerce Commission and, 187–89, 192–93
  phone rate debates in, 186–93, 200
  phone strikes during World War II in, 270–71
  public utility commission in, 165
  strikes (1945–1946) in, 272–73
Illinois Bell Telephone Company, 1–2, 187–93, 338–39
Illinois Manufacturers Association, 99
Illinois Telephone and Telegraph Company (Illinois T&T), 99–102
Immerwahr, Daniel, 534–35
imperialism (European)
  decolonization and, 14, 540–41, 542–43, 547–48, 551
  France and, 20–21, 523, 540–41
  Great Britain and, 20–21, 523, 540–41, 547–48
  parcel post services and, 64–65
  submarine cables and, 44

telegraph services and, 51, 525–27
World War II and, 534
imperialism (United States)
   Civil War and, 36
   Cold War and, 543, 546, 547–48
   internet and, 533–34, 582–84
   Native American populations displaced by, 19–21, 30–31, 32–33, 38–39
   postal services and, 4, 12–13, 19, 20–22, 25, 30, 31–32, 524, 601
   satellite technology and, 13, 547–55
   slavery and, 19–20, 31–32
   Spanish-American War and, 13
   telegraph services and, 4, 12–13, 19, 38–39, 523–25, 601
   transcontinental rail network and, 31–32, 38–39
independent telephone providers. *See also* municipal telephone systems
   antimonopolism and, 76, 82, 83–85, 108, 112, 116
   entrepreneurialism among, 82
   industry consolidation during 1920s among, 118
   innovation and, 85
   Kingsbury Commitment and, 114–16, 117, 118
   labor laws and, 84–85
   Mann-Elkins Act and, 111
   Midwestern states as a center of, 73–74, 80, 81–82
   municipal governments' franchising powers and, 80, 82–83
   patent lawsuits against, 80
   Populist movement and, 83–84
   rate schedules for, 85, 94
   residential and commercial phone use rates in early twentieth century and, 87–88, 87t
   rural America and, 83
India
   domestic computer industry in, 554
   market capitalism reforms in, 14
   NSFNET and, 579
   Obama Administration and, 607
   postal savings banks in, 59–60
   satellite technology and, 550–51
   submarine cables and, 525–26
   union resistance to telecommunications privatization in, 588
   World War II and, 538
Indiana, 73–74
Indochina war. *See* Vietnam War
Industrial Workers of the World, 134
"Information" telephone service, 340–42
Integrated Services Digital Network (ISDN), 569–70

Intel, 385, 455, 591–92
Intelsat (International Telecommunications Satellite)
   bankruptcy (2020) of, 559
   Comsat and, 13–14, 548, 549–50, 552
   International Telecommunication Union and, 550
   Johnson (Lyndon) and, 547
   Kennedy and, 547, 548
   national telecommunications ministries and, 13–14
   postcolonial states and, 551
   privatization (1999–2001) of, 559
   Reagan and, 558
   US aerospace companies' advantages in, 549
   US private satellite companies' undermining of, 558
   voting rules at, 549–50
Interdepartmental Committee on Communications, 202–3, 225–26
Intergovernmental Bureau for Informatics, 554
International Brotherhood of Electrical Workers (IBEW)
   American Federation of Labor and, 111, 235–36, 260, 266–68, 284–85
   American Radio Telegraphists Association and, 237
   American Telephone and Telegraph Company and, 266, 268, 517–18
   Chicago's phone system expansion and, 101–2
   Communication Workers of America and, 284–85, 292–93, 409–10
   establishment (1891) of, 266–67
   federal control of telecommunications during World War I and, 144
   government control of telephone and telegraph services supported by, 111, 128–29, 132–33
   Great Depression and, 222
   Illinois Bell strike (1968) and, 1–2
   municipal phone system campaigns and, 102–3
   National Federation of Telephone Workers and, 268
   racist membership standards at, 240–41
   strikes (1947) and, 275
   strikes (1989) and, 517–18
   Telephone Operators Department of, 132–33, 152, 284–85
   United Electrical Workers and, 236
   Verizon and, 608
   Western Union and, 260
   women telephone workers neglected by, 266–67, 284–85

International Brotherhood of Teamsters, 100–1, 276, 513
International Communications Association, 463, 573–74
International Longshoremen's and Warehouseman's Union (ILWU), 234
International Monetary Fund (IMF), 13, 541–42, 575–76, 582
International Network Working Group (INWG), 563, 568–69
International Telecommunication Union (ITU)
  Buenos Aires Declaration (1994) and, 588–90
  China and, 536–37, 605–6
  data networking and, 574–75
  institutional changes after World War II at, 536–37
  Intelsat and, 550
  Israel and, 554–55
  lobbying of Congress by, 135
  United States and, 546, 554–55
  World Summit on the Information Society and, 590
International Telephone and Telegraph Corporation (ITT)
  ABC takeover attempt by, 478
  AT&T's international telephone manufacturing subsidiaries purchased (1925) by, 529–32
  Communications Act of 1934's investigation of telephone industry and, 206
  founding (1919) of, 528
  Latin America and, 563
  Postal Telegraph-Cable Company and, 194, 231
  Radio Corporation of America and, 528, 532–33
International Typographical Union (ITU), 124–25, 135
internet
  AT&T's breakup and, 572–73, 577
  broadband service and, 581–82, 592, 595–96
  China's production of equipment for, 15, 606–7
  Conseil Europeen pour la Recherche Nucleaire and, 559–60
  digital divide and, 581–82
  Global Information Infrastructure and, 589–90
  human rights and, 14
  Internet Architecture Board (IAB) and, 579–80
  Internet Assigned Numbers Authority (IANA) and, 579–80

Internet Engineering Task Force (IETF) and, 579–80
internet service providers (ISPs) and, 595–96, 598–99
National Security Agency and, 591
net neutrality and, 598
packet switching and, 561–62, 567
political economy of expanding, 572–82
submarine cables and, 581
US imperialism and, 533–34, 582–84
US intelligence agencies' exploitation of, 15
utopian thinking regarding, 561, 566–67
World Wide Web software and, 340–41, 560, 576, 579–80, 581
Inter-Sputnik, 549
Interstate Commerce Commission (ICC)
  antimonopolism movement and, 153
  establishment (1887) of, 111
  Hepburn Act and, 111
  Mann-Elkins Act and, 74, 111, 160–61
  private-wire contracts and, 224
  public utility commissions and, 166, 171
  railroad regulation and, 160–61, 171
  Roper Report (1934) and, 202–3
  Shreveport Rate Cases and, 160–61, 166
  telecommunications industry inquiry on private-wire contracts (1917–1918) by, 111–13, 119–24, 166
  telecommunications regulation powers granted to, 74, 84, 107–8, 111–12, 159, 160–61, 171, 177–78, 206
  telegraph industry inquiry (1940s) by, 243–44
  Transportation Act of 1920 and, 198
  Uniform System of Accounts and, 171
  Willis-Graham Act and, 118
intranets, 576, 598
Inward WATS (wide area toll service), 342–43
Iowa Telephone Association, 73–74, 82
Ireland, 131–32
Irons, Peter, 353–54
Irwin, Manley R., 460
Israel, 554–55
Israel, Paul, 43
Italy, 50–51, 59–62, 529, 532–33, 536–37, 541–42

Jackson, Andrew, 22, 27, 30
Jackson, Henry, 586
Japan
  domestic computer market in, 560
  globalized corporate competition and, 503, 506–7, 588
  global telecommunications privatization initiatives and, 14

imperialism and, 51, 523, 526–27
Intelsat and, 548, 549–50
International Telephone and Telegraph and, 529
Meiji Restoration (1868) in, 50–51
NSFNET and, 579
postal savings banks in, 50–51, 59–61
post-World War II construction and, 540–41
private branch exchanges in, 574
privatization of telecommunications in, 575–76, 588
public data networks and, 569–70
Radio Corporation of America and, 527
satellite industry in, 558–59
supercomputing and, 552
US military government after World War II in, 543, 546
US treaties with, 541–42
World War II and, 257, 534, 538
Jefferson, Thomas, 20–21
Jewett, Frank B., 345, 357–58, 362–63
Jim Crow. *See* segregation
Jimenez, Paula V., 442–44
John, Richard R.
 on American Telephone and Telegraph's monopoly, 93–94
 on Bell System's gradual development, 74
 on Chicago's negotiations with AT&T in early twentieth century, 99–100, 102
 on coin box telephones, 188, 315
 on municipal telephone systems, 94–95
 on Postmaster Generals and military service, 32–33
 on the Post Office and frontier settlement, 24
 on Post Office privatization proposals, 27–28
 on private express companies, 24–25
 on societal notions of progress, 75–76
 on US Postal Service's establishment, 405
Johnson, Cave, 27–30, 34–35, 37–38
Johnson, Gus, 399
Johnson, Leland, 477
Johnson, Lester R., 472
Johnson, Lyndon B.
 Federal Communications Commission, 474–75, 742–43n.51
 Great Society programs and, 467
 Intelsat and, 547
 Kappel Commission for postal reform and, 394–95, 396–97, 401
 President's Task Force on Communications Policy and, 485–87
 Rostow Report (1968) and, 11
 Vietnam War and, 395, 467, 479–80
Johnson, Morton L., 102, 108, 128–29

Johnson, Nicholas, 467, 474–75, 477–80, 484, 489, 494, 519–20
Johnson, Tom, 96–97
Joint Council of Affiliated Postal Organizations, 389
Jones, Jesse, 302–3
Jones, Samuel M., 96

Kahn, Alfred, 468
Kahn, Robert, 561–62, 568–71, 577–80, 771–72n.111
KakaoTalk, 598–99
Kansas, 61, 178, 315–16
Kappel, Frederick, 391, 394, 490, 509–10
Kappel Commission, 394–95, 396–97, 401
Kautsky, Karl, 56–57
Keeran, Roger, 241
Kehoe, Joseph, 242, 246
Keller, Morton, 207
Kelly, Clyde, 60–61, 305, 307
Kelly, Mervin, 379, 384
Kendall, Amos, 34
Kennedy, John F., 389–90, 413*f*, 472, 508–9, 516, 547, 548, 586–87
Kennedy, Robert, 480
Kern, Howard L., 223–25
Keynesianism, 466–68
Kielbowicz, Richard, 63–64, 110
Kilgore, Harley, 364
King, Jr., Martin Luther, 479–80
Kingsbury Commitment
 AT&T's purchase of telephone stations in the years following, 117
 AT&T's sale of controlling stake in Western Union and, 114–16, 120, 194–95
 criticism of, 114–15
 independent phone service providers and, 114–16, 117, 118
 Justice Department's telephone regulatory power established by, 116–17
 nationalization of AT&T halted by, 114–15
 private-wire telegraph market and, 120
 Wilson and, 114–15, 116
Kissinger, Henry A., 419, 488
Knights of Labor, 47–48, 54, 69, 124–25
Koistinen, Paul, 257
Konenkamp, B. J., 140–41
Korea, Republic of, 541–42, 551, 607
Korean War, 367, 375, 379, 382, 541–42, 546

Laborie, Leonard, 64–65
La Follette, Robert, 84, 111, 247, 631n.19. *See also* Lloyd-LaFollette Act

Lakota Indians, 39, 609–10
Latin America. *See also specific countries*
  British undersea cable system and, 526
  debt-financed infrastructure expansion in, 575–76
  Great Britain and, 546
  imperialism in, 523
  International Telecommunication Union and, 536–37
  International Telephone and Telegraph Corporation and, 563
  Non-Aligned Movement and, 553
  Radio Corporation of America and, 527
  Reagan Administration and, 582
  trade unions in, 504–5
  US foreign parcel post services and, 64–65
  wireless radio technology and, 528
Latina/os
  mobilization against employment discrimination by, 10, 388–89, 408, 522, 603–4, 609–10
  as telephone industry workers, 430, 434
  telephone service to, 337–38, 443
  union membership and, 506–7
Laundine, L. L., 137–38
League of California Municipalities, 181–82
Lee, Alfred M., 39–40
Lee, H. Rex, 498
Leffler, Melvyn P., 286, 382–83, 541
Leggett, William, 27
Leiserson, William, 299
Lenin, Vladimir, 57, 130–32
letter express companies. *See* private express companies
Level 3, 594–95
Levin, Richard C., 104–5
Lewis, David J.
  biographical background of, 125–26
  government ownership of telecommunications services supported by, 113–14, 125–26, 127–28, 129
  municipal phone systems supported by, 103
  parcel post services and, 63–64, 125–26
  private express companies condemned by, 62
  US Senate campaign loss by, 126–27
  Vail and, 125–26
  Wire Control Board during World War I and, 141, 144–45, 146
Lewis, John L., 218, 236, 242, 357
LGBT people. *See* gay rights movement
Lichtenstein, Nelson, 240, 288, 516–17
Lieber, Francis, 27
Lilienthal, David, 192–93, 380–81

Lincoln, Abraham, 219
Lincoln, George A., 492–94
Link, Arthur S., 114–15, 141–42
LinkedIn, 597
Lloyd-LaFollette Act, 70, 129–30
local area networks (LANs), 571
Loevinger, Lee, 472, 474
Loew, Marcus, 349–50
Logan, Rayford, 539
Los Angeles (California)
  city-owned power facilities in, 95
  independent telephone providers in, 82–84, 98
  mayoral election (1911) in, 92
  Municipal Board of Public Utilities in, 98
  municipal phone system campaigns in, 98, 609–10
  Pacific Telephone and Telegraph in, 271
  phone rate debates during 1920s in, 181–82
  postal service established in, 31–32
  Public Utilities Commission of, 109
  residential and commercial phone use rates during early twentieth century in, 87–88, 87t
Louisiana Purchase, 20–21, 30
Lovett, Robert A., 375, 382–83
Lucas, Robert, 391–92
Luce, Henry, 542–43
Lucent, 596
Lumen, 594–95, 598–600

MacDougall, Robert, 73–75, 80, 83–84, 86–87, 91–92, 93–94, 105–6
MacFarland, Ernest W., 257
Mackay, Clarence H., 140, 146–47
Mackay, Claude, 78–79
Mackay, John, 66
Mackay Radio & Telegraph Company, 261–63, 291–92
Maclaurin, Rupert, 206–7, 349–50, 374
Maclean, John, 35
MacLean, Nancy, 437
MacMeal, Harry B., 115
Madison, James, 20–21
Magazine Publishers Association, 310–11
Magdoff, Harry, 582–83
Magee, Willie, 679n.42
Maguire, Meighan, 180–81
Mail Classification Act of 1879, 50
Mann-Elkins Act, 74, 111, 160–61
Mansur, George F., 496
Mao Zedong, 538
Marcantonio, Vito, 259
Marshall Plan, 286–87, 295, 541–42, 543–44

Marx, Karl, 56, 130–31, 408–9
Massachusetts, 157–58
Massachusetts Institute of Technology (MIT), 382–83, 456–57
Maverick, Maury, 364
May, Christopher, 132
May, Elaine, 471
Mayer, Henry, 272–73
Mayo, Robert, 488
McAdoo, William Gibbs, 144
McCarran, Pat, 238–39
McCarthy, Eugene, 480
McCartin, Joseph A., 134, 138
McChesney, Robert W., 206–7
McClelland, John C., 65–66, 626n.109
McConnaughey, George, 464–65
McCracken, Paul, 488
McDonald, June, 268, 275, 685n.7
McGee, Henry W., 391–92, 395, 400*f*
McGovern, George, 504–5
McGrath, J. Howard, 381
McGraw-Hill, 401, 569
MCI, 484, 506–7, 578, 594–95, 643n.12
McKinley, William, 69, 524–25
McLean, John, 21–22, 25–27
McMullen, Joseph I., 352–53
McNamara, James and John, 92, 634n.36
McNinch, Frank, 208, 242
McReynolds, James C., 114–15
Means, Gardiner C., 300–1
Meany, George, 394, 401–2, 404, 511
Melody, William, 329–30
Merchants' Association of New York, 104–5, 150
MERIT network, 578
Merkel, Angela, 606
Merriam, John C., 358–59
Meta, 597. *See also* Facebook
Metzen, Fred P., 400*f*
Mexican American Legal Defense and Education Fund, 437, 443–44
Mexico
 Mexican American War (1847–1848) and, 30, 38–40, 44–45
 Mexican Telephone and Telegraph Company and, 528–29
 Non-Aligned Movement and, 553
 North American empire of, 20–21
 NSFNET and, 579
 public data networks in, 569
 revolution (1910s) in, 147–48
 state-owned enterprises in, 575–76
Michalski, Marie, 256
Michigan, 268–69, 271–72, 409, 433–34, 578

Microsoft, 456, 576–77, 591–92, 597–99
microwave service, 2, 303–4, 461–62, 472, 474–75, 484
Miller, David, 473–74
Miller, Henry, 227, 233
MILNET, 578
Milwaukee (Wisconsin), 104–5, 129–30, 393
Mindell, David, 452
Minitel, 569–70, 572
Miranti, Jr, Paul, 85
Misa, Thomas J., 384–85
Mitchell, William, 353–54
monopoly. *See also* antimonopolism
 American Telephone and Telegraph Company, 73–75, 80–81, 90, 93–94, 104–6, 198, 213–14, 223–25, 231, 264, 329–30, 465
 "natural monopoly" theories and, 74–75, 93, 226
 patents and, 8–9, 73–75
 private express companies and, 26, 52, 62
 public interest arguments advocating, 214
 submarine cables and, 52
 telegraph services and, 4, 19–20, 38–40, 41, 42–43, 52, 223–26, 231, 233
 telephone services and, 52, 73–75, 104
Monopoly Committee. *See* Temporary National Economic Committee (TNEC)
Montana, 165
Montgomery, David, 223
Montgomery Ward, 50, 63–64, 310
Morgan, J. P., 42–43, 106
Morse, Samuel, 37–38
Motorola, 453–54
Moyal, Ann, 632n.23
Moyn, Samuel, 587
Moynihan, Daniel, 586
Mueller, Milton, 87, 89–90, 93–94, 117, 174
Mueller, Ronald, 582–83
Multi-Access Computing (Project MAC), 456–57
Municipal Ownership League, 96–97
municipal telephone systems
 anticorruption arguments regarding, 96, 103–4
 Chicago's effort to establish, 98–104, 609–10
 disappearance during World War I era of, 94–95
 European cities supporting, 95
 franchising processes for, 96
 Progressive Era "good government" reformers and, 94–95
 trade union support for, 94–95, 99

Murphy, Frank, 381
Murray, Philip
 American Communications Association and, 269–70
 on AT&T's anti-unionism, 264
 Communications Workers of America and, 291
 Defense Communications Board and, 256
 Democratic Party and, 218
 phone industry strikes (1947) and, 279

Nader, Ralph, 306, 467–68, 479, 487–88
Natchez Trace (road), 32–33
National Aeronautics and Space Administration (NASA), 547–48, 569
National Alliance of Postal Employees, 389–90, 391–92, 406
National American Woman's Suffrage Association, 63–64
National Association for the Advancement of Colored People, 437
National Association of Letter Carriers (NALC)
 AFL-CIO affiliation of, 389–90
 American Communications Union proposal and, 510–14, 515–16, 517, 519, 604–5
 American Postal Workers Union's potential merger with, 406–7
 heavily male membership of, 513
 International Brotherhood of Teamsters and, 513
 New York Local 36 of, 399
 size of, 391, 502
 wage negotiations and, 308
 wildcat postal strike (1970) and, 9–10, 399–400
National Association of Manufacturers, 274, 412
National Association of Railroad and Utilities Commissioners (NARUC)
 call for telecommunications industry investigation (1934) by, 205–6
 Committee on Cooperation between Federal and State Commissions and, 326
 cooperative federalism in telecommunications regulation and, 177
 government control of telecommunications services during World War I and, 163–64
 states' regulatory power as priority for, 165–66
National Association of Railway Mail Clerks, 240–41
National Board of Trade, 66–67

National Broadcasting Company (NBC), 236–37, 528
National Data Corporation, 342–43
National Endowment for Democracy, 586–87
National Federation of Postal Clerks, 69–70, 389–90
National Federation of Telephone Workers (NFTW)
 American Communications Association and, 265–66, 268–70, 271–72, 279
 American Federation of Labor and, 267–68, 273, 279
 AT&T company unions as predecessor of, 257, 265–67
 AT&T's relationship with, 267–68
 as Communications Workers of America precursor, 265–66
 company union practices carried over by, 267
 Congress of Industrial Organizations and, 267–68, 269–70, 273, 279, 283–84, 289
 establishment (1937) of, 266–67
 International Brotherhood of Electrical Workers and, 268
 mechanization of telephone industry and, 505
 Pacific Telephone and Telegraph and, 271–72
 strikes (1945–1947) and, 272–76, 277–78, 279, 280–81, 282–83
 Telephone Workers Industrial Union and, 271–72
 transformation into Communications Workers of America by, 222
 United Electrical Workers and, 268–69
 War Labor Board and, 268–69, 270–71
 Western Electric Employees Association and, 268–69
National Grange, 50, 62–64, 84, 125
National Guard, 1, 9–10, 399
National Industrial Recovery Act (NIRA), 219–21. See also National Recovery Administration (NRA)
National Labor Relations Act. See Wagner Act
National Labor Relations Board (NLRB). See also Wagner Act
 American Communications Association and, 243, 249–51, 260
 Congress of Industrial Organizations and, 292–93
 establishment (1935) of, 220–21
 LaFollette Committee and, 247
 Taft-Hartley Act and, 287–88, 291–92

United Electric-Western Electric case
  at, 268–69
  Western Union and, 260
National Labor Union, 77–78
National Maritime Union, 218, 234
National Postal Union, 389–90, 404, 406
National Public Ownership League, 128–29
National Recovery Administration (NRA).
  See also National Industrial Recovery
  Act (NIRA)
  employer-friendly corporatist model of, 223
  Supreme Court's invalidation of, 225
  telecommunications industry proposals
    at, 202–3
  telegraph industry and, 223–25, 227, 229–
    33, 248
National Science Foundation, 365–66, 578, 587
National Security Agency (NSA), 381, 454–
  55, 591
National Security Council (NSC), 377–78,
  382–83, 543
National Security Telecommunications
  Advisory Committee (NSTAC), 572–73
National Telegraph Act of 1866, 41
National War Tax Resistance Coordinating
  Committee, 426f
Native Americans
  Douglas on the removal of, 38–39
  Post Office services utilized by, 54
  telegraph equipment destroyed as retaliation
    by, 39, 609–10
  US imperialism and displacement of, 19–21,
    30–31, 32–33, 38–39
NBC Universal, 595–96
NCR, 454–55
Nebraska, 61, 200
Nesbitt, Murray B., 397–99
The Netherlands, 523, 540–41
net neutrality, 598
Network Solutions, Inc., 581
Nevada, 37, 318
New Deal. *See also specific agencies*
  Communists and, 238–39, 241–42
  consumer purchasing power and, 300–1, 326
  economic citizenship and, 218–19, 300
  patent policies and, 358–59
  post office construction and, 306
  public utility doctrine and, 6, 159, 176, 301
  residential electricity expansion
    during, 314–15
  telecommunications industry cartelization
    and, 199
  trade unions and, 219, 221

New England Telephone, 150
New International Economic Order, 541, 553–
  54, 586
New Jersey Bell Telephone Company, 277
New Jersey Telephone, 469–70
New Mexico, 165, 434
New World Information and Communication
  Order (NWICO), 553–55, 593
New York and New Jersey Telephone
  Company, 78
New York Bell, 410
New York City
  city-owned power and railway systems in, 96
  independent telephone providers in, 82–83
  mail pickups in financial district of, 50
  municipalization debates during mayoral
    campaigns in, 96–97
  municipally owned transit system in, 95
  phone rate debates during 1920s, 182
  residential telephone use during early
    twentieth century in, 86
  telephone service breakdown (1969–1970)
    in, 469–70
  telephone strike (1971–1972) and, 413–29,
    417f, 421f, 422f, 423f, 424f, 514
  wildcat postal strike (1970) and, 9–10,
    397–407
New York Federation of Labor, 182
New York Journal of Commerce, 28–29
New York Stock Exchange, 401, 470
New York Telephone Company
  AT&T affiliate status of, 104–5
  monopoly power of, 104–5
  phone rate debates during 1920s and, 182–84
  rates charged by, 104–5
  strike (1971–1972) at, 413–29, 417f, 421f,
    422f, 423f, 424f, 514
  Western Union's commercial stake in, 78
New York Women's Trade Union League, 97
New Zealand, 543
Nichols, Mike, 471
Nippon Telegraph and Telephone Corporation
  (NTT), 569–70, 598
Nixon, Richard M.
  Ash Commission and, 490
  election of 1968 and, 467
  global telecommunications privatization
    initiatives and, 14
  Office of Telecommunications Policy
    established by, 487, 494
  President's Task Force on Communications
    Policy and, 487–88
  resignation of, 515

Nixon, Richard M. (*cont.*)
  Rostow Report (1968) and, 11, 488
  satellite technology and, 491–94
  telecommunications liberalization and, 11–12, 489
  telephone strike (1971) and, 419
  US Postal Service's establishment (1970) and, 9–10, 604
  Vietnam War and, 304–5, 504–5
  wage-and-price controls issued by, 420, 427–28
  Watergate scandal and, 487–88
  wildcat postal strike (1970) and, 9–10, 397–407
Nkrumah, Kwame, 551–52
Noble, David, 258–59
Nockels, Edward N.
  call for telecommunications industry investigation (1934) by, 203–4
  Chicago Rate Case and, 191–92
  death of, 204–5
  patents and, 8–9, 356–57, 358, 361
  photo of, 143*f*
Noll, Roger, 490
Non-Aligned Movement (NAM), 553–54, 566
Nord, David, 109
North Atlantic Treaty Organization, 541–42
Norwood, Steven, 144–45, 150
Novak, Alan R., 477–79, 480–82, 489
Novak, William J., 158, 199, 301
Noyce, Robert, 385
NSFNET, 578–81
NYNEX, 594–95

Oakland (California), 181–82, 271, 427–28
Obama, Barack, 607
O'Brien, Lawrence F., 309, 392–95, 401, 404–5
O'Connell, James D., 477
O'Connor, Julia, 132–33, 133*f*, 143–45, 151–52
Office of Price Administration, 272
Office of Science and Technology Policy (OSTP), 495, 577–79
Office of Telecommunications Management, 477
Office of Telecommunications Policy (OTP)
  Ash Commission and, 495
  deregulation emphasis at, 496, 564
  Federal Coordinating Council for Science, Engineering, and Technology and, 577–78
  international data networking and, 563–66
  Nixon's establishment of, 487, 494
  Whitehead's directorship of, 495–97
Office of the Trade Representative, 563–64

O'Hara, John, 324–25
Ohio, 96, 165, 268–71
Ohio Bell Telephone Company, 280, 431–32
Ohio Supreme Court, 107–8
Oklahoma, 61, 83, 165, 208–9
Olds, Leland, 211–12
Olney, Richard, 70–71
O'Mahoney, Joseph C., 210–11
Onis-Adams Treaty of 1819, 30
Open Systems Interconnection (OSI), 562–63
Oppenheimer, J. Robert, 372–73
optical fiber cables (fiber optic cables), 550–51, 558–59, 576–77, 581, 594–95, 596–97
Order of Railway Telegraphers (ORT), 227–28, 235–36, 240–41
Order of Repeatermen and Toll Testboardmen, 269–70
Order of the Patrons of Husbandry. *See* National Grange
Oregon, 30, 32–33, 318, 330–31
Oregon Trail, 39
Orlovsky, Daniel, 131–32
Orr, H. W., 65–66
Orton, William, 43
Outward WATS, 343, 463
over the top (OTT) voice and video calling applications, 598–99
Owen, Bruce, 497, 500

Pacific Mail Steamship Company, 33
Pacific Telegraph Act (1860), 41
Pacific Telephone and Telegraph Company (PT&T)
  American Communications Association and, 271–72
  California Railroad Commission's regulation of, 180
  National Federation of Telephone Workers and, 271–72
  residential and commercial phone use rates in early twentieth century and, 87–88, 87*t*
  strikes (1971) at, 427–28, 434
Pacific Telesis, 594–95
packet switching, 456, 561–62, 564, 569, 573–74
Paget, Richard M., 490
Paiute Indians, 54
Pakistan, 588
Pan African Union, 547–48
Panic of 1873, 42
Panic of 1893, 42
Panic of 1907, 61
Paris Commune, 56
Parker, Everett C., 439–41

Parks, Lisa, 547–48
Parsons, Frank, 66–68, 96, 107, 126–27
patents
   American Telephone and Telegraph antitrust case (1949–1956) and, 344, 366–87, 602–3
   American Telephone and Telegraph Company and, 8–9, 73–75, 77–78, 80, 120, 177–78, 362–63, 602–3
   compulsory licensing and, 358–59, 361–63, 377–78
   cross-licensing and, 345–46, 349–50, 352–53, 357–58, 361–63, 377, 527–28
   German radio patents and, 352
   independent telephone providers as target of lawsuits regarding, 80
   monopoly and, 8–9, 73–75
   nineteenth century system of, 345–55
   Radio Group alliance and, 350–51, 353, 360, 531
   US Constitution and, 344, 351, 356–57
   Western Union and, 43, 78, 120
Pendleton Act, 54–55
Pennsylvania Federation of Labor, 63–64
Pennsylvania Public Service Commission, 331
Penny Phone League (PPL), 101–4
People's Yellow Pages, 444–45, 471
Peterson, Peter G., 487–88
Pettis, Charles, 466
Philco, 349, 355, 373, 453, 454–55
The Philippines, 13, 272, 524–25, 527, 539–40
Pierson, Vivian E., 279–80
Pierson, W. DeVier, 482, 485–86
Plecher, Andrew, 135
Point Breeze Employees Association, 432–33
Polk, James K., 31–34
Pony Express, 37
Pool, Ithiel de Sola, 564–66, 576, 582
Populists
   deposit guarantee laws and, 61
   independent telephone providers and, 83–84
   journals published by, 54
   Omaha Platform (1892) of, 54
   postalization reform model and, 54, 77–78
   proposals for government ownership of rail and communications industries by, 70–71, 77–78, 125
   public utility commissions criticized by, 107
Porch, Robert Ben, 482
Porter, Paul, 535
Posner, Richard, 477, 480–81, 484–85, 491
Post, Clarence J., 147
Post, Louis F., 96–97
Postal Policy Act of 1958, 396
Postal Reorganization Act (1970), 404–5, 509–10
Postal Telegraph-Cable Company
   American Communications Association and, 6–7, 243, 251–52, 258
   American Telephone and Telegraph Company shares held by, 78–79
   Great Depression financial troubles of, 193–94, 196–97, 225–26, 228–29
   International Telephone and Telegraph as parent company of, 194, 231
   National Recovery Administration and, 223–25
   post-World War II layoffs at, 304
   private-wire contracts and, 120–22, 195–96, 223–25, 229–30
   reprivatization of telecommunications infrastructure following World War I and, 146–47, 159–60
   Western Union's merger with, 6–7, 8, 197–98, 225–27, 231, 233, 243–44, 247–49, 251–55, 257–60, 599–600, 602
   World War I and, 140, 144
Postmaster General's Office
   censorship powers of, 35–36, 52–53
   mail rates and, 26
   political patronage and, 33–34, 54–55, 141–42
   postal road authority granted by Congress (1825) to, 31
   private express companies and, 28–29
Post Office. See also US Postal Service
   agency model of, 22–23
   air mail and, 194, 303, 305
   ban on labor strikes at, 222
   cabinet level status and, 19
   capital circulation and, 21–22
   Chicago Post Office breakdown (1966) and, 391–97
   Civil War and, 36, 40, 49, 60
   Enabling Act of 1792 and, 22
   federal eight-hour day law for urban letter-carriers (1888) and, 69
   first-class mail and, 27–28, 310, 312–13, 405, 600
   for-profit mail contractors and, 33, 52–53
   labor laws governing work at, 69–70
   as largest US federal agency, 19, 22–23, 54–55
   library rate and, 312–13
   mail rates and, 23–24, 25–26, 27–28, 29–30, 34–35, 36, 49
   as model for public service provision, 4
   money order services and, 60, 307

Post Office (*cont.*)
  monopoly over first-class mail granted by Congress (1845) to, 27–30, 33–34
  newspapers distributed by, 23–24, 27
  parcel post services and, 63–65
  Pendleton Act and, 54–55
  political patronage jobs and, 22, 27, 33–34, 52–53, 54–55, 141–42
  postal savings banks and, 59–62
  private express companies as competitors to, 24–26, 63–64
  privatization proposals regarding, 27–28
  Railway Mail Service and, 49–50, 68–69
  rural free delivery services (RFD) and, 49, 56, 59, 62–63
  salary schedules at, 55, 58
  second-class mail rate debates during 1960s at, 309–11, 393–94
  segregation practiced by, 52–53, 134–35
  "service first" mandate (1851) and, 27–28, 35–36
  slavery and, 35–36
  transcontinental rail network and, 31, 49–50
  US imperialism and, 4, 12–13, 19, 20–22, 25, 30, 31–32, 524, 601
  wildcat strike (1970) at, 9–10, 397–407
  working conditions at, 68–72, 132, 306–7
  World War I and control of nation's telecommunications services by, 5, 77, 111–12, 118, 124, 140–41, 142–48, 150–52, 161–64, 179, 180, 187, 249–51, 277–78, 317–18, 601
Post Office Engineering Union, 131–32
Potter, David D., 524–25
Powers, Frank B., 229–30, 234–35, 255
Prall, Anning, 210
President's Advisory Council on Executive Organization. *See* Ash Commission
The President's Analyst (film), 471
President's Commission on Postal Organization, 309
President's Task Force on Communications Policy (Johnson Administration)
  American Telephone and Telegraph Company and, 477, 481, 484–85
  on automation's impact on employment, 506
  call for interdisciplinary research on telecommunications policy in, 500
  Defense Department and, 477
  election of 1968 and, 486–87
  foreign attachment rules and, 483–84
  Johnson (Lyndon) and, 485–87
  membership of, 477
  microwave services and, 484
  Nixon and, 487–88
  Office of Telecommunications Management and, 477
  Post Office excluded from, 477
  Rostow Report and, 482–85
  telecommunications liberalization and, 476, 477, 480–81, 482–84, 486
  Western Electric and, 481–82, 491
Pressman, Lee, 218, 254–55, 465–66
private branch exchanges (PBXs), 92, 414, 574
private express companies
  monopolistic practices and, 26, 52, 62
  perishables carried by, 62
  as Post Office competitors, 24–26, 63–64
  railroad companies and, 62
  rates charged by, 29–30, 62
  US imperialism and, 37
Progress and Poverty (George), 55–56
Project Mercury (US manned space flight program), 547–48
Projet Socrate satellite, 558–59
Public Service Commission of New Jersey, 469–70
Public Utilities Consumers' League of New Jersey, 200
public utility commissions (PUCs)
  American Telephone and Telegraph Company and, 5–6, 74, 106, 107–8, 110, 112, 157–58, 161–62, 166–68, 170–71, 175–77, 178–80, 602–3
  cable television and, 474
  commissioners as political appointees at, 107
  common carriage principle and, 106–7
  duty to serve principle and, 106–7
  expansion following World War I of, 106, 157–58
  Federal Communications Commission and, 208–9, 318–19, 321, 326–28, 602
  federal courts and, 171, 185
  funding and staffing challenges at, 170–71
  government control of telecommunications services during World War I and, 163–64
  Interstate Commerce Commission and, 166, 171
  jurisdictional limits of, 175–77
  municipalities' ability to constrain powers of, 109
  New Deal and, 176
  phone rate debates during 1920s and, 180–93
  Populists' criticism of, 107

INDEX   813

regulatory capture and, 107–8
reprivatization of telecommunications infrastructure following World War I and, 165
service standards and, 168
telegraph services and, 197–98
Vail and, 74, 110, 162, 171–72
Western Electric and, 175–76
Willis-Graham Act and, 118
Public Utility Holding Company Act of 1935, 209–10
Public Utility Rate League, 182–83
Publishers Advisory Board, 147
Puerto Rico, 13, 525, 527–28, 546, 594–95
Pugh, Mrs. Willie I., 466
Pullman, George, 70–71
Pullman strike (1894), 70–71, 277
Pyle, Roy A, 235–36

QQ messaging app, 598–99
Qwest, 594–95

Rademacher, James
   American Communications Union proposal and, 510–12, 513
   Nixon campaign (1968) and, 9–10
   potential postal unions merger and, 406–7
   wildcat postal strike (1970) and, 399–400, 402–4, 446
Radio Act of 1927, 206–7, 351–52, 354–55, 357, 533
Radio Corporation of America (RCA)
   American Communications Association and, 239, 243, 261–63
   American Marconi and, 348
   commercial radio broadcasting and, 528
   Communications Act of 1934's investigation of telephone industry and, 206
   digital information processing technology and, 453
   establishment of, 346–47
   General Electric and, 527
   global reach of the 1920s radio network of, 527
   International Telephone and Telegraph Corporation and, 528, 532–33
   National Recovery Administration and, 225
   radiotelegraph carriers and, 194
   strike (1941) at, 239
   television-facsimile transmission and, 303–4
   United Electrical Workers and, 235
   vacuum tube technology and, 350–51

Radio Group, 350–51, 353, 360, 531
Radio Protective Association, 350–51
Railroad Administration, 144–45, 160–61
Railroad Relief Bill of 1933, 198
railroad strikes of 1877, 47–48, 70–71, 277
Railway Mail Service, 49–50, 68–69
Rainey, Archie E., 136–38
Randall, Alexander, 21–22
Randolph, A. Philip, 431
Rathborne, Mervyn, 234, 237, 242, 244, 251, 253
Raytheon, 355, 373, 384–85, 453
Read, William H., 554–55
Reagan, Ronald
   air traffic controllers fired (1981) by, 514–15
   anti-Communism and, 582
   Federal Communications Commission and, 555
   Intelsat and, 558
   International Monetary Fund and, 575–76
   market fundamentalism and, 519–20
   National Security Agency and, 591
   National Security Telecommunications Advisory Committee and, 572–73
   Strategic Computing Initiative and, 577–78
   telecommunications deregulation and, 12
   UNESCO withdrawal by, 556, 557–58
Reconstruction, 45
Reconstruction Finance Corporation, 228–29
Red Lion decision, 445–46
Reed, Clyde M., 178–79
Regional Bell companies (RBCs), 569–70, 594–95
Reich, Leonard, 350–51
Reuther, Walter, 286–87, 452, 504–5, 508–9
Ribicoff, Abraham, 2
Richter, Irving, 281–82
Riordan, Michael, 364, 383–85
Robinson, Glen O., 207
Rochester (New York), 80, 129
Rodgers, Daniel, 56, 95, 106
Roig, Helen J., 438
Romness, H. I., 419, 489–90
Roosevelt, Franklin D. *See also* New Deal
   antimonopolism and, 198–99
   death of, 7–8, 539–40
   deficit spending and, 299–300
   election of 1932 and, 158, 217
   election of 1934 and, 220–21, 248
   election of 1936 and, 221, 361
   election of 1940 and, 244
   Fair Employment Practices Commission and, 431

Roosevelt, Franklin D. (*cont.*)
  Federal Communications Commission and, 6, 185–86, 207–8, 212
  "Four Freedoms" and, 584–85
  patents and, 363, 364
  phone rate debates in New York State during 1920s and, 182–84, 185–86
  public utility commissions and, 184–85, 330
  Public Utility Holding Company Act of 1935 and, 209–10
  Rural Electrification Act and, 183–84
  as Secretary of the Navy, 346
  Soviet Union and, 537
  telegraph industry and, 225, 231, 302–3
  Temporary National Economic Committee and, 210–11
  Tennessee Valley Authority and, 183–84
  trade unions and, 218–19, 220–21
  United Nations and, 539
  Western Union-Postal Telegraph merger and, 198
  World War II and, 534
Roosevelt, Theodore, 70
Roper, Daniel C., 202–3, 208–9
Rostow, Eugene V., 11, 476–79, 481–87, 500
Rowe, Jr., James H., 480–82, 486
Rubio, Philip, 389–90, 405
Rural Electrification Act, 332–33
Rural Electrification Administration, 183–84
rural free delivery services (RFD), 49, 56, 59, 62–63
Rural Telephone Act, 333–35
Russia. *See also* Soviet Union
  AT&T operations in, 563
  Bolshevik Revolution in, 147–48
  imperialism and, 20–21
  postal savings accounts in, 59–60
  postal savings banks in, 59–62
  postal service in, 57
  Post and Telegraph Ministry employees in, 131–32
  Western Union operations in, 524–25
Rustin, Bayard, 442

SAGE command and control system, 456–57
Sandburg, Carl, 73, 204–5
Sand Creek massacre (1864), 39
Sandia National Laboratories, 379–81, 385
San Francisco (California)
  general strike (1934) in, 217–18
  independent telephone providers in, 82–84
  municipally owned transit system in, 95
  municipal phone system campaigns in, 98–99
  phone rate debates during 1920s in, 180–82
  postal service established in, 31–32
  submarine cables and, 547
  trade unions in, 94
Santulli Mail Service, 311–12
Sargent, Daniel J., 547
Sarnoff, David, 354–55
Satellite Business Systems, 562
satellite technology. *See also* Comsat; Intelsat
  Communications Satellite Act of 1962 and, 472, 476, 489, 495
  Federal Communications Commission and, 491–92, 493–94
  Nixon Administration and, 491–94
  Non-Aligned Movement and, 553–54
  postcolonial states and, 551–52
  Sputnik space launch and, 547–48
  Telstar satellite and, 473
  US imperialism and, 13, 547–55
Saxbe, William B., 501
Schacht, John N., 264, 275–76, 408–10
Schneider, William, 554–55
Schrecker, Ellen, 287–88
Schuette, Oswald F., 348–49, 353
Schwellenbach, Lewis B., 280–82, 286
Schwoch, James, 38–39
Sears, Roebuck, 50, 63–64, 310, 462
Seattle (Washington), 82–83, 95, 98–99, 147–48, 181–82
Segal, Adam, 590–91
segregation
  Civil Rights Movement's confronting of, 585
  Post Office's engagement in, 52–53, 134–35
  Reconstruction's end (1876) and, 45
  War Labor Board and, 432–33
  Wilson's federal government workforce and, 134–35
Selly, Joseph P.
  anti-Communist attacks against, 260
  Defense Communications Board and, 256
  on Federal Communications Commission's lack of knowledge of working conditions, 244–46
  McCarran Committee testimony (1951) by, 238–39
  Order of Repeatermen and Toll Testboardmen and, 269–70
  photo of, 245*f*
  Postal Telegraph-Western Union merger and, 257–58
  Radio Corporation of America strike (1941) and, 239
  Taft-Hartley Act and, 292

Shales, Roger, 117
Sherman, Carl, 182
Sherman Antitrust Act, 79–80, 153, 353–54, 365, 371
Sherrill, Robert, 396–97
Shinnick, W. J., 230–31
short-wave radio, 528, 532, 535
Shreveport Rate Cases, 160–61, 166
Shulman, Peter A., 29–30
Shultz, George, 402, 403, 446, 487–88
Sichter, James W., 109, 327
Silicon Valley companies, 454, 606, 608–9. *See also specific companies*
Silvergleid, David, 406
Singer Sewing Machine Store, 88
Sirovich, William I., 357–58
Sklar, Martin, 117
Skype, 598–99
slavery
   abolitionist movement and, 35–36, 52–53
   Civil War's abolition of, 41–42
   imperial expansion and, 19–20, 31–32
   Post Office expansion and, 35–36
   transcontinental rail network and, 31–32
Small, S. J., 93
smartphones, 581–82, 592, 595, 598–99
Smith, Charles L., 181–82
Smith, C.R., 481–82, 486, 746n.66
Smith, F. O. J., 38
Smith, John, 584
Smith, Ralph Lee, 473
Smith, Robert L.T., 439–40
Smith v. Illinois, 189–90, 192, 318–19, 355
Smythe, Dallas, 246, 270
Snowden, Edward, 590
Socialists
   cooperative worker control model and, 58, 131
   election of 1912 and, 130
   government ownership of telecommunications services advocated by, 130–31
   ideological divisions among, 56, 131
   industrial democracy concept and, 134
   Los Angeles mayoral campaign (1911) and, 92
   municipal phone system campaigns, 102–3
   postalization reform model and, 54, 56–58, 68
   state ownership model and, 56–57, 58, 130–31
Softbank, 595
Sorkin, Michael, 339

South Dakota, 61
Southern Bell Telephone Company, 78, 104, 409–11, 430–31, 437–38, 466
Southern California Telephone Company, 181–82, 200
South Korea, 541–42, 551, 607
Southwestern Bell (SBC), 91–92, 200, 594–95
Soviet Union. *See also* Cold War
   collapse of, 14, 579, 582, 587
   international data network proposed by, 554
   Sputnik satellite launch (1957) and, 547–48
   United Nations and, 539
   World War II and, 13, 239, 257, 534, 537–38
Spain, 13, 20–21, 30, 523, 524–25
Spero, Sterling, 69, 142
Sperry, 364, 373, 379, 454–55
Spievack, Edwin B., 498
Splawn, Walter, 202–3
Sprint, 594–95
Spurlock, James W., 369, 380–81
Sputnik satellite launch (1957), 547–48
Stager, Anson, 40
Stalin, Josef, 534, 539
Standard Oil, 84, 96, 114–15, 119–20, 178, 354
Stanford Research International (SRI), 500, 579–80
Stans, Maurice, 309, 311–12, 488
Stanton, Edwin M., 40
Steelman, John, 272–73
Stehman, J. Warren, 177
Stone, Alan, 106–7, 115–16, 169
Strachey, John, 465–66
Strategic Computing Initiative, 577–78
Stromquist, Sheldon, 54, 94
submarine cables
   American Telephone and Telegraph and, 547, 550–51, 559–60
   businesses as main users of, 46
   cartelized markets for, 44
   corporate developers and users of, 576–77
   European imperialism and, 44
   fiber optic cable and, 558–59, 576–77
   first US submarine cable (1866) and, 524–25
   Great Britain and, 13, 44, 91, 525–27
   internet and, 581
   monopoly practices and, 52
   postcolonial states and, 551–52
   TAT-1 transatlantic cable and, 547–48
   Transpac transpacific cable and, 547–48
   US reprivatization following World War I of, 148–50, 152
   Western Union and, 44, 91
   World War I and, 525–26

Sullivan, Joseph, 96–97
Sun Microsystems, 456, 573
supercomputers, 552, 577–78, 607
Swain, William, 37–38
Sweden, 59–60
Swift meat-packing company, 119–20, 122–23
Sylvania, 355, 384–85, 453, 457
Symphonie TV, 558–59
SynOptics, 573

Taft, Robert A., 277. *See also* Taft-Hartley Act
Taft, William H., 61, 70, 112, 140
Taft-Hartley Act, 277, 279–80, 287–89, 291–92
TAT-1 transatlantic cable, 547–48
TAT-8 transoceanic fiberoptic cable, 559–60
Tatzlaff, Ben A., 101–2
Taylor, Myron C., 219
TCP/IP internet protocols
  Arpanet and, 569, 578
  AT&T's breakup (1982–1984) and, 572–73, 577
  Conseil Europeen pour la Recherche Nucleaire, 559–60
  freenets and, 570
  interoperability of, 571–72
  NSFNET and, 578–81
  Office of Science and Technology Policy and, 578–79
  Sun Microsystems and, 573
  US capitalist imperialism and, 568–69
Teamsters Union, 100–1, 276, 513
Telecommunications Act of 1996, 594, 599–600
Telecommunications Coordinating Committee, 277–78
Telegraph Act of 1866, 41
Telegraph Messengers Union, 232*f*, 233–34
Telenet, 561–62, 565, 570–71, 574–75
Telephone Investigation League of America, 181–82
Telephone Traffic Employees Organization, 271–72, 283
Telephone Workers Industrial Union (TWIU), 271–72
Teletype Corporation, 78–79
Telstar satellite, 473
Temporary National Economic Committee (TNEC), 210–11, 362–63, 370, 712n.40
Tennessee Valley Authority, 183–84, 192–93, 314, 363–64
Texas, 30, 61, 82–83
Texas Instruments, 453
Thatcher, Margaret, 556, 575–76
Thayer, H.B., 127, 161–62, 172–73, 178, 531

Thayer, Walter N., 490
Thompson, Carl D., 128–29
Thompson, William, 187–88
Thurmond, Strom, 288–89
Tierney, John T., 308
Tilden, Samuel, 54–55
Timberg, Sigmund, 370–72
Time-Warner, 595–96
T-Mobile, 595, 597, 599–600
Tobey, Ronald, 314–15
Todd, G. Carroll, 135–36
Toledo (Ohio), 96
toll-free numbers, 342–43, 463
Tomlin, Lily, 471
Tomlins, Christopher, 221
Townsend, Willard S., 431–32
transcontinental rail network, 31–32, 38–39, 107
Transcontinental Telegraph, 38–39
transistors, 364, 383–85, 453–56, 543–44
Transpac transpacific cable, 547–48
Trebing, Harry, 468
Trotsky, Leon, 86
Trotter, Jr., Joe William, 240–41, 447
True Sun newspaper, 44–45
Truman, Harry S.
  ascension to presidency of, 7–8, 539–40
  China and, 272
  demobilization after World War II and, 535–36, 539–40
  election of 1948 and, 288–89
  Federal Communications Commission and, 537
  Sandia National Laboratories and, 379–81
  strikes (1945–1947) and, 272, 274, 277–78
  Taft-Hartley Act and, 287–88
  Truman Doctrine and, 286, 541–42
Trump, Donald, 600, 607
Tucker, Gideon, 66
Tumulty, Joseph P., 126, 146–49, 152
Twentieth Century Fund, 275
Tymnet, 561–62, 574–75

"Under a Telephone Pole" (Sandburg), 73
undersea cables. *See* submarine cables
Union Army, 36, 60
Union of Post Office Workers, 131–32
United Action, 416–26, 428–29
United Auto Workers (UAW), 273–74, 479–80
United Brotherhood of Telephone Workers, 279
United Electrical Workers (UE)
  American Federation of Labor and, 284–85

American Radio Telegraphists Association
and, 235–37
Bell Laboratories and, 236–37
Communication Workers of America and, 222
Communists' role in, 238, 267–68
Congress of Industrial Organizations and,
6–7, 218, 235–36, 242, 267–68, 455
General Electric and, 235
International Brotherhood of Electrical
Workers and, 236
National Federation of Telephone Workers
and, 268–69
Radio Corporation of America and, 235
Taft-Hartley Act and, 287–88
telephone industry and, 267–68
Western Electric and, 222, 236–37
Westinghouse and, 235, 455
United Federation of Postal Clerks, 308, 389–90
United Fruit, 347–48, 354
United Mine Workers, 77–78, 217–18
United Nations
establishment (1945) of, 541–42
New World Information and
Communication Order and, 554–55
UN Educational, Scientific and Cultural
Organization (UNESCO) and, 541–42,
554–55, 556, 557–58
Universal Declaration of Human Rights and,
584–85, 590
United Press, 135
United States Military Telegraph Corps
(USMT), 40
United Telecom Council, 461–62
United Telegraphers of America (UTA),
231, 233–34
Universal Declaration of Human Rights
(UDHR), 584–85, 590
Universal Postal Union, 50–51, 64–65
University of California-Berkeley, 573
UNIX operating system, 456, 573, 578
US Agency for International Development
(USAID), 504–5, 589–90
US Air Force, 454, 457
US Alien Property Custodian, 352
US Army
American Expeditionary Force in World
War I and, 159
Army Signal Corps and, 159
Democratic National Convention
(1968) and, 1
microelectronics research and, 384–85
postal roads built by, 32–33
Pullman strike (1894) and, 70–71

toll-free recruiting number during Vietnam
War and, 343
Usenet, 570
US Independent Telephone Association
(USITA), 117
US Navy, 32–33, 88, 159, 347, 352–53, 525,
527, 539
US Postal Service. *See also* Post Office
Amazon and, 600
American Federation of Labor-Congress
of Industrial Organizations (AFL-CIO)
and, 308, 389–90, 401–2, 405–6, 426–
27, 446–47
automation at, 519, 604
Board of Governors, 9, 394, 404–5, 509–
10, 600
collective bargaining rights at, 604
email service proposals at, 519
establishment (1970) of, 9–10, 404–5, 509–
10, 604
pension requirements at, 600
Postal Service Reform Act of 2022 and, 596–
97, 600
Trump Administration and, 600
workforce cuts (2006–2012) at, 520–21
US Steel, 219, 457
US Telephone and Telegraph
Administration, 144–45
US West, 594–95
Utility Consumer and Investor's League, 191

Vail, Theodore N.
American Telephone and Telegraph's
controlling interest in Western Union
(1909–1913) and, 112
American Telephone and Telegraph's merger
spree and, 74, 105–6, 112
on costs associated with regulation, 170
government control of telecommunications
during World War I and, 141, 161–62
Lewis and, 125–26
nationalization campaigns against AT&T
fought by, 127, 161–62
on potential nationalization of AT&T, 113–14
public utility commissions and, 74, 110,
162, 171–72
regulation-for-monopoly arrangement
negotiated by, 93
on residential and commercial phone use
patterns in early twentieth century, 87, 88
retirement of, 152
universal wire system promised by, 89–92,
105–6, 194–95, 319

value of service pricing concept, 330–31
Vandervelde, Emile, 57, 131
Varian Associates, 453
Venezuela, 527, 594–95
Vergara, Angela, 504–5
Verisign, 581–82
Verizon, 592, 594–600, 608
Veterans Administration, 314
Viber, 598–99
Vietnam War
  Cambodia invasion (1970) and, 504–5
  Communication Workers of America strike (1971–1972) and, 420–25
  inflation and, 390–91, 412–13, 429, 470
  Johnson Administration and, 395, 467, 479–80
  mail delivery related to, 396, 397
  Nixon Administration and, 304–5, 504–5
  protests against, 1, 9, 388, 389
  Tet Offensive (1968) and, 480
  toll-free recruiting telephone number during, 343
Vilas, William F., 53
Vittoz, Stanley, 221
VoiceStream, 595
Vorse, Mary Heaton, 266

Wagner, Robert, 185, 299
Wagner Act
  collective bargaining rights and, 222, 300
  company unions outlawed by, 249, 264–65
  right to organize trade unions established in, 220–21, 246–47
  Supreme Court's upholding (1937) of, 247, 249–51, 266–67
  Taft-Hartley Act and, 277, 287–88
Waite, Kevin, 31–32
Walker, Paul A., 205–6, 208–10, 212–13, 318
Walker, Philip M., 562, 570–71
Walker, Richard, 566–67
Wallace, George, 433–34, 467, 480
Wallace, Henry, 288–89, 361, 364, 368, 539
Walsh, Frank, 140
Wanamaker, John, 60, 63, 66–67
War Department, 32–33, 353, 432–33, 540. *See also* Defense Department
Ware, Caroline F., 300
War Labor Board (World War I), 132–33, 140
War Labor Board (World War II)
  American Communications Association and, 260
  American Federation of Labor and, 268–69
  Congress of Industrial Organizations and, 268–69
  equal employment for women and, 430
  membership maintenance agreements and, 256
  National Federation of Telephone Workers and, 268–69, 270–71
  National Telephone Commission of, 282–83
  National Telephone Panel at, 270–71
  segregation enforced by, 432–33
Warth, N. G., 112
Washburn, Abbott, 554–55, 558, 565–66, 582
Watson, W. Marvin, 397
Watts, Glenn, 429, 515–16
WeChat, 598–99
Weeks, Lorena, 437–38
Weiman, David F., 89, 104–5
Weller, John B., 32
Welles, Sumner, 539
Wellfleet Communications, 573
Wells, David, 67
Wells, Henry, 27
Wells, Robert, 499
Wells Fargo, 37, 62
Western Electric
  American Telephone and Telegraph's labor noncompete agreement with, 135–36
  as American Telephone and Telegraph's manufacturing subsidiary, 175–76, 177–78, 182–83, 190, 319, 325, 360, 366
  antitrust case against AT&T (1949–1956) regarding, 366–87, 602–3
  AT&T's breakup (1982–1984) and, 573, 594
  Chicago Rate Case and, 190
  Communication Workers of America and, 222
  corporate spinoff into Lucent (1996) of, 596
  Federal Communications Commission investigation of AT&T (1934) and, 213, 215
  manufacturing costs at, 175–76
  public utility commissions and, 175–76
  strikes (1952) at, 409
  telephone handset design and, 339
  United Electrical Workers and, 219, 222
  Western Electric Employees Association (WEEA) and, 268–69
Western Union
  American Communications Association and, 249–51, 252–53, 254, 255, 260–63, 261*f*, 262*f*, 263*f*, 271
  American Telephone and Telegraph Company's cartel agreement (1879) with, 78
  American Telephone and Telegraph Company's controlling stake (1909–1913) in, 41, 78–79, 90–91, 112, 120
  American Telephone and Telegraph Company's corporate synchronization (1910s) with, 79–80
  antimonopoly campaigns against, 4, 42–43, 48, 66–68, 77–78, 601

Associated Press and, 44–45, 55–56, 77–78, 119–20
Board of Directors of, 42–43
"bucket shops" and, 136–37
child labor and training schools at, 233
Civil War and, 40–41
Commercial Telegraphers Union of America and, 140, 228–29, 252–53, 260–63
Communications Act of 1934's investigation of telephone industry and, 206
Communication Workers of America and, 293
computer and information processing technology development at, 457–59
expansion during late nineteenth century of, 43
Federal Labor Unions and, 260
financial information and, 46
Great Depression financial troubles of, 193–94, 196–97, 225–26, 228–29
International Brotherhood of Electrical Workers and, 260
Interstate Commerce Commission investigation (1917–1918) and, 119
microwave service and, 303–4
money transfer services and, 304–5
monopoly power of, 20, 41, 42–43, 44, 47
National Recovery Administration and, 225
patents held by, 43, 78, 120
Postal Telegraph-Cable Company's merger with, 6–7, 8, 197–98, 225–27, 231, 233, 243–44, 247–49, 251–55, 257–60, 599–600, 602
post-World War II layoffs at, 304
potential RCA-ITT merger opposed by, 533–34
private-wire contracts and, 119–21, 195–96, 223–25
railroad companies and, 43–44, 119–20, 196–97, 225
reprivatization of telecommunications infrastructure following World War I and, 147–48, 159–60
research and development at, 43
speculative finance and, 42–43, 47
stakes in local telephone companies held by, 78
strikes at, 47, 65–66, 140, 261–63, 262f, 263f
submarine cables and, 44, 91
telephone industry strike (1947) and, 278–79
Transcontinental Telegraph developed (1861) by, 38–39
Western Union Employees Association as company union at, 217–29, 231, 236, 249–51, 252–53, 260
World War I and, 79, 140, 144
West Germany, 549, 550–51, 552, 560
West Indies, 64–65, 526–27, 528, 529
Westinghouse
  digital information systems and, 453
  electronics research by, 373
  Justice Department Consent Decree (1932) and, 354
  patents held by, 347, 350, 374
  Radio Act of 1927 and, 352
  radio technology and, 348–49, 354–55, 531
  radio telephone service and, 531
  research and development at, 345–46
  United Electrical Workers and, 235, 455
WhatsApp, 598–99
Wheat, Carl I., 213–14, 332
Wheaton, W. V., 254
Wheeler, Burton K., 243–44
Whig Party, 33–34
White, Richard, 47–48, 59
Whitehead, Clay T.
  Federal Communications Commission and, 489, 493
  Nixon telecommunication liberalization initiatives and, 11, 489
  as Office of Telecommunications Policy director, 495–97
  President's Task Force on Telecommunications and, 487–88
  Rostow Report and, 488–89, 491
  as satellite industry executive, 501
  satellite technology and, 492–93
Whitten, K. M., 229–31
Wickersham, George W., 90
Wiencek, Ruth, 268–69, 273, 280, 285
Wilcox, Clair, 196–97, 213–14
Wilcox, Delos, 107–8, 110, 641n.81
Wilcox, J.L, 278–79
wildcat postal strike (1970), 9–10, 397–407, 398f, 400f
Wiley, Richard E., 499
Wilkie, Wendell, 219
Willis-Graham Act, 118
Wills, Garry, 372–73
Wilson, Charles E., 281–82, 375
Wilson, Leroy, 380–81
Wilson, Mark R., 452
Wilson, William B., 125–26
Wilson, William L., 63
Wilson, Woodrow
  Democratic Party political patronage jobs and, 141–42
  federal takeover of railroads during World War I and, 139
  government ownership of telecommunications services supported by, 126

Wilson, Woodrow (cont.)
  Kingsbury Commitment and, 114–15, 116
  labor movement and, 126–27, 129–30
  long-distance telephone service during World War I and, 92–93
  Paris Peace Conference and, 147–48
  Post Office takeover of telecommunications services during World War I and, 124, 139, 141
  reprivatization of telecommunications infrastructure following World War I by, 5, 145–46, 147–50, 152, 157, 159–60
  segregation of federal workforce under, 134–35
  War Labor Board and, 132–33
  Western Union labor negotiations (1918) and, 140
Windham, Lane, 506–7
Winkler, Jonathan, 527
Winstanley, Gerrard, 53–54
Wire Control Board, 141, 144–45
Wire Operating Board, 118, 141
Wisconsin, 84, 187, 192–93
Wisconsin Telephone Company, 192–93
Wise, Anna Mae, 340–41
WLBT case, 439–41, 443–44
Wolff, Stephen, 578
Woman's Party, 103
women
  Chicago's municipal telephone campaign and, 103–4
  employment discrimination and, 134–35, 152, 264
  Great Depression job losses and, 265
  International Brotherhood of Electric Workers and, 266–67
  mobilization against employment discrimination by, 10, 389, 408, 434, 503, 603–4
  as postal workers, 389–90
  sexual harassment in the workplace and, 134–35, 138
  strike participation (1947) by, 275–76, 280
  telephone services employment among, 86–87, 134–35, 143–45, 151–52, 264–65, 270, 273, 279–80, 340–41, 410
  white supremacy and, 134–35
  World War I workforce and, 5
Women's Bureau (Labor Department), 434
Women's Civic League (Chicago), 103
Women's Party of Cook County, 103
Women's Trade Union League, 97, 103
Works Projects Administration (WPA), 242, 306

World Bank, 13, 541–42, 575–76, 582, 587, 589–90
WorldCom, 596
World War I
  federal takeover of railroads during, 139
  inflation during, 139, 161
  long-distance telephone service and, 92–93
  Post Office's operation of national telecommunications during, 5, 77, 111–12, 118, 124, 140–41, 142–48, 150–52, 161–64, 179, 180, 187, 249–51, 277–78, 317–18, 601
  potential telegraph strike during, 140–41, 142
  Railroad Administration (United States) and, 144–45
  War Labor Board and, 132–33, 140
World War II
  American Federation of Labor and, 256
  Board of War Communications and, 257, 282–83
  cable and radio circuit development during, 13
  Congress of Industrial Organizations and, 256
  Defense Communications Board and, 255–57
  demobilization after, 535–36, 539–40, 609–10
  inflation and, 272
  no strike pledges during, 256
  Postal Telegraph–Western Union merger and, 257–59
  trade union membership increases during, 257
World Wide Web, 340–41, 560, 576, 579–80, 581. See also internet
World Wide Web Consortium (W3C), 579–80
Worth, Tim, 516
Wovoka, 54
Wright, Richard, 306–7

X.25 networking standard, 559–60, 562–63, 569

Yellow Pages, 342–43, 444
Young, Owen D., 346–48, 354–55, 363, 532–33, 535
YouTube, 597

Zanzibar, 547–48
Zeiger, Robert, 272
Zenith, 349, 355, 373, 718n.71
Zhang Wenjin, 559
Zhao, Houlin, 605–6
Zhou Enlai, 419
Zych, Henry, 513